ALSO BY RICK PERLSTEIN

The Invisible Bridge

Nixonland

Before the Storm

REAGANLAND

AMERICA'S RIGHT TURN
1976–1980

RICK PERLSTEIN

SIMON & SCHUSTER
NEW YORK   LONDON   TORONTO   SYDNEY   NEW DELHI

Simon & Schuster
1230 Avenue of the Americas
New York, NY 10020

Copyright © 2020 by Eric S. Perlstein

First Simon & Schuster hardcover edition August 2020

SIMON & SCHUSTER and colophon are registered trademarks
of Simon & Schuster, Inc.

For information about special discounts for bulk purchases,
please contact Simon & Schuster Special Sales at 1-866-506-1949
or business@simonandschuster.com.

The Simon & Schuster Speakers Bureau can bring authors to your
live event. For more information or to book an event, contact the
Simon & Schuster Speakers Bureau at 1-866-248-3049
or visit our website at www.simonspeakers.com.

Manufactured in the United States of America

10 9 8 7 6 5 4 3 2 1

Library of Congress Control Number: 2020941283

ISBN 978-1-4767-9305-4
ISBN 978-1-4767-9307-8 (ebook)

To JHC

CONTENTS

BOOK THREE: 1978

BOOK FOUR: 1979

I met a Californian who would
Talk California—a state so blessed,
He said, in climate none had ever died there
A natural death.

— ROBERT FROST

BOOK ONE

1976

CHAPTER 1

"Nibbled to Death by Ducks"

RONALD REAGAN INSISTED THAT IT WASN'T HIS FAULT.

In July of 1976, Jimmy Carter emerged from the Democratic National Convention ahead in the polls against President Gerald Ford by a record thirty-three percentage points. By November, Ford had staged a monumental comeback. But it was not monumental enough. Jimmy Carter was elected President of the United States with 50.08 percent of the popular vote, and 55 percent of the electoral college.

What had stopped Ford just shy of the prize? In newspaper columns, radio commentaries, and interviews all through the rest of 1976 and into 1977, Reagan blamed factors like the Democrat-controlled Congress, for allegedly holding back matching funds owed to Ford's campaign. And *All the President's Men*, the hit Watergate movie from spring, which Warner Bros. had rebooked into six hundred theaters two weeks before the election, for reminding voters of the incumbent's unpopular act of pardoning Richard Nixon after Watergate. And even the United Auto Workers, for calling a strike that autumn against the Ford Motor Company—sabotaging the economy to boost Jimmy Carter, Reagan claimed.

Ronald Reagan blamed everyone and everything, that is, except the factor many commentators said was *most* responsible for the ticket's defeat: Ronald Reagan.

He had challenged Ford for the nomination all the way through the convention, something unprecedented in the history of the Republican Party. Then, critics charged, he sat on his hands rather than seriously campaign for the ticket in the fall. If Ford had pulled in but 64,510 more votes in Texas and 7,232 more in Mississippi, he would have won the electoral college; or 137,984 more in Kentucky and West Virginia plus 35,473 from Missouri; or if he had won Ohio, where he came but 5,559 short, while adding either Louisiana, Alabama, or Mississippi, which Ford lost by less than two points—all of these states where Reagan had droves of passionate fans. But according to one top Republican operative, "the only effective campaign work done by Reagan was for Carter, whose ads featured Reagan's primary attacks against Ford." "Former Gov. Ronald

Reagan has succeeded in running out the election campaign without being drawn into full, direct support for President Ford," the *New York Times* had concluded—in order, the cognoscenti whispered, to preserve his own chances for 1980 should Gerald Ford lose.

Reagan howled his defense: "No defeated candidate for the nomination has ever campaigned that hard for the nominee," but there had been "a curtain of silence around my activities." This was not true. They were covered widely—under headlines like "Reagan Shuns Role in Ford's Campaign."

Now they said his political career was over. The *Boston Globe*'s Washington columnist joked that Richard Nixon was a more likely presidential prospect in 1980. About Reagan, the *Times* said, "At 65, he is considered by some as too old to make another run for the presidency." Even rightwingers agreed—scouring the horizon, one columnist noted, "for a bright, tough young conservative whom Reagan might groom for the GOP nomination in 1980." The *Times* also said that "political professionals of both major parties" believed the GOP was "closer to extinction than ever before in its 122-year history": they controlled only twelve governorships, and according to Ford's pollster Robert Teeter, the loyalty of only 18 percent of Americans voters. Clearly, the Newspaper of Record concluded, "if the Republican Party is to rebuild it must entrust its future to younger men."

And less conservative ones. John Rhodes, the House minority leader, was a disciple of conservative hero Barry Goldwater. His tiny caucus of 143 would face a wall of 292 Democrats when the 95th Congress convened in January. After the election, he rued that "we give the impression of not caring, the worst possible image a political party can have." The American Conservative Union, chartered in 1964 to keep the faith after Goldwater's presidential loss that year as the Republican nominee, felt so unwelcome in the party that they met in Chicago the weekend after the election to consider chartering a new one. Reagan himself entertained the idea, until one of his biggest donors threatened to cut him off if he persisted—though Reagan did suggest that perhaps a name change for the Grand Old Party was in order. "You know, in the business I used to be in, we discovered that very often the title of a picture was very important as to whether people went to see it or not." Even so, he had no suggestion what that should be.

THE DEMOCRATS, ON THE OTHER HAND, APPEARED TO BE IN CLOVER. AFTER Watergate, America longed for redemption. They met Jimmy Carter, and fell in love.

One day that summer, the advertising man hired to make Gerald Ford's TV commercials turned on the radio. Jimmy Carter's mother, who'd joined the Peace Corps ten years earlier at the age of sixty-eight, whom an adoring nation called "Miz Lillian," dialed in to a sports talk show to gab about her favorite professional wrestlers. "I was spellbound," Malcolm MacDougall wrote. "One little phone call and 100,000 avid Boston sports fans had undoubtedly fallen in love with Jimmy Carter's mother."

He flipped on the TV. A Washington socialite was being interviewed by Johnny Carson. "She didn't want to talk about her new book. She wanted to talk about her trip to Plains, Georgia. In the beginning she wasn't a believer, she said. No, sir. She had been just as cynical as a lot of us liberals. But she'd talked with Jimmy Carter for hours. Just sat there on the porch, the two of them, talking about life and government and religion. And now she was a believer. Jimmy Carter was real, she said. . . . 'He is going to save our country. He is going to make us all better people.' "

MacDougall traveled to Boston's Logan Airport to fly to the Republican convention. At the newsstand, "Jimmy Carter's face was staring at me from dozens of magazines." And, from the covers of paperback books with titles like *The Miracle of Jimmy Carter*. He turned around: "a stack of T-shirts with peanuts on the front, and the words, 'THE GRIN WILL WIN.' This wasn't a clothing store."

Even so, 70 percent of the electorate told pollsters they had no intention of voting in November at all. One of them, a rabbi, wrote a *New York Times* op-ed. "I was one of the millions who rejected Barry Goldwater's foreign policy, voted for Lyndon Baines Johnson, and then got Mr. Goldwater's foreign policy anyway. I, too, voted for law and order and got Richard M. Nixon and Spiro T. Agnew. And now I think of the man who promised Congress that he would not interfere with the judicial process, and then pardoned Mr. Nixon as almost his first official act." So: no more voting. "If Pericles were alive today, he might be inclined to join me."

The epidemic of political apathy spread particularly thick among the young. During the insurgent 1960s, the notion of universities as a seedbed of idealism was accepted as a political truism for all time. No longer. A university provost explained that he was seeing "a new breed of student who is thinking more about jobs, money, and the future"—just not *society's* future. College business courses were oversubscribed. But politics? "Watergate taught them not to care," a high school civics teacher rued. A college professor gave a speech to his daughter's high school class, rhapsodizing about the excitement of the Kennedy years. "A few minutes into my talk I realized we weren't even on the same planet." He asked if they would protest if America began bombing Vietnam again. "Nothing. In desperation, I said: 'For God's sake, what *would* outrage you?' After a pause, a girl in a cheerleading uniform raised her hand and said tentatively, 'Well, I'd be pretty mad if they bombed this *school*.'"

JIMMY CARTER KICKED OFF HIS GENERAL ELECTION CAMPAIGN IN WARM Springs, Georgia, on the front porch of Franklin D. Roosevelt's "Winter White House." Democrats traditionally opened on Labor Day in Detroit's Cadillac Square. But Detroit was in the middle of a crime spree. Cadillac Square was only blocks from the Cobo Hall arena, where, the UPI reported, "gangs of black youth," taking advantage of the fact the cash-strapped city had been forced to lay off nearly a thousand cops, had recently set upon a rock concert, robbing, beating, and raping attendees.

So: Warm Springs it was.

Two of Roosevelt's sons were by Carter's side. A seventy-three-year-old black man, subject of a famous *Life* magazine picture showing him playing accordion in his Navy uniform as Roosevelt's funeral train trundled by, performed the New Deal anthem "Happy Days Are Here Again." The Roosevelt connection marked Carter as an heir to the Democrats' glorious liberal past. The Georgia setting invoked his Southern identity; if elected he would be the first president from the Deep South since Zachary Taylor in 1848. Featuring an African American spoke to his proud identity as a post-racist Southerner. Jimmy Carter would be the candidate for everyone. In his speech, he feinted left, comparing Ford to Herbert Hoover—another "decent and well-intentioned man who sincerely believed that government could not or should not with bold action attack the terrible and economic and social ills of our nation." He feinted right: "When there is a choice between government responsibility and private responsibility, we should always go with private responsibility. . ... When there is a choice between welfare and work, let's go to work." Then—and most importantly—he staked his claim as the candidate unconnected to the corrupt legacy of Richard Nixon:

"I owe the special interests nothing. I owe the people everything."

Ford opened at the White House, signing a series of bills before the cameras. What bills? It didn't matter. "We agreed," Mal MacDougall later explained, "there were no issues strong enough to decide the election." *Symbolism* mattered: a trustworthy man was now in charge.

"*Trust*," Gerald Ford said, jabbing at his opponent at his first campaign rally a week later, in the basketball arena of his alma mater, the University of Michigan, "is not cleverly shading words so that each separate audience can hear what it wants to hear, but saying *plainly* and *simply* what you mean."

He received an enthusiastic volley of applause.

"Not having to guess what a cand—"

A sound like a gunshot rang out. The president who had suffered two assassination attempts the previous September flinched—then, realizing that it was a firecracker, continued on as if nothing had happened. The applause swelled and swelled, until the entire crowd was up on its feet, as if in heartfelt gratitude at watching a political leader *not* being assassinated. The incident exemplified Ford's campaign theme: he had returned the United States to normalcy.

Americans no longer had a political leader who was lying to their face. They were no longer losing a morally corroding war. Arab oil sheiks were no longer holding the economy hostage. And maybe, just maybe, the awful everyday traumas of the 1960s and 1970s might finally be *over*. "*I'm feeling good about America!*" Ford's jingle bouncily intoned, in commercials that signposted his un-flashy ordinariness.

Jimmy Carter's commercials sounded the same notes. They told the story of a man who had learned self-sufficiency and the value of hard work farming the same Georgia soil his family had since the eighteenth century, soil he sifted earnestly, wearing jeans and a plain flannel work shirt. His wife, Rosalynn, said, "Jimmy is honest, unselfish, and truly concerned about the country. I think he'll be a great president." That presidential candidates were decent people had been "obvious until Watergate," a historian of campaign advertising observed. "Only in 1976 can a claim that a candidate is honest, unselfish, hard-working and concerned about the country warrant the conclusion that he will be a great president."

THIS, HOWEVER, PRODUCED A PARADOX: THE CAMPAIGNS' EAGERNESS TO prove their man the most sincere produced quantum leaps in artifice.

Carter's packagers were ahead in this game. In 1972, Atlanta adman Gerald Rafshoon suggested that a future Carter presidential campaign could capitalize on Carter's "Kennedy smile"; Carter, impressed, hired him. In 1974, Carter researchers learned audiences responded best to key words and phrases like "not from Washington," "competence," and "integrity"; those became Rafshoon's palette. The peanut emerged early as a key symbol; it projected humility—an advantage, a strategist explained, since "humility was not our long suit." On the trail in 1976, Carter carried his own garment bag onto the campaign plane, and posed for "candid" wire service photos washing his socks in a hotel sink. Carter's eight-year-old daughter was put up front for the cameras; by that summer, with what felt like half the country's political journalists camped out in Plains, population 632, there was hardly a United States citizen who didn't know that Amy charged ten cents a glass at her lemonade stand. (The couple's three adult children, less photogenic, barely appeared.)

A former news producer named Barry Jagoda was Carter's media wizard. He boasted that because he came from that world, not advertising, he was better at manipulating TV news—"the most critical battlefield in media politics." For instance, on the day of the crucial Wisconsin primary, while the rest of the candidates remained behind for victory or concession speeches, Jagoda flew Carter to New York so that he could react to the returns live on a network news set. "This kind of media politics is seamless," he explained. "It doesn't mimic the news or play off the news. It is the news." (The interview in which Jagoda said this was another novel feature of the 1976 campaign: image-makers publicly *explaining* how they made artifice look real.)

Marketing sincerity was the particular specialty of the advisor Carter admired most. Twenty-eight-year-old Patrick Caddell had been a mere seventeen when he first got into the business of political polling. He was an Irish-Catholic Massachusetts native whose family moved to Florida's Panhandle—Dixie, culturally speaking. In 1968, for a math project, the high school senior besotted with baseball statistics and the late President Kennedy went door to door in a working class Jacksonville neighborhood to poll residents about the upcoming presidential contest, and was struck by the insight that animated his career. He was shocked to hear, again and again: "Wallace or Kennedy, either one." Ideologically, that made little sense; during the Kennedy administration, the segregationist Governor George C. Wallace and the anti-segregationist Attorney General Robert F. Kennedy had been sworn enemies. When Caddell asked people to explain, they gave answers like "They're tough guys" and "You can believe them"; ideology seemed the last thing on their minds. While an undergraduate at Harvard University, Caddell opened a polling business out of his dorm room, and began devising innovative methods that built on this insight: tools for inquiring instead how the candidate made voters *feel*.

Americans' dominant feeling, he concluded, was *alienation*. He devised tools to measure it—"trust indices," "ladders of confidence"—and, from the results, language and symbols that his clients could deploy to convey to voters how they could *salve* that alienation. George McGovern hired Caddell as chief pollster for his presidential campaign in 1972 when Caddell was still at Harvard. McGovern lost soundly. But another Caddell client, twenty-nine-year-old Joseph Biden, won a senate seat after Caddell coached him not to criticize his incumbent opponent—that just made him another *politician*—but "Washington." That made him an *"anti*-politician"—the kind Caddell preferred: candidates who spoke to what he termed the electorate's "malaise," and what he began calling in 1974 America's "crisis of confidence."

Candidates, in other words, like Jimmy Carter. Caddell was instrumental in Carter's most important political breakthrough: trouncing George Wallace in the Florida Democratic primary. He first positioned Carter, Wallace-style, as alien to Washington; then Carter cemented the loyalty of Wallace fans by playing to Southerners' ancient longing to *really* stick it to the Yankees. George Wallace's longtime slogan was "Send them a message." Carter's was "This time, don't send them a message. Send them a president." "He is a generation ahead of most other technicians," a Ford campaign memo worried on the cusp of the general election. "No one has yet devised a system for protecting a GOP incumbent from the Caddell-style alienation attack."

FORD ADMAN MALCOLM MACDOUGALL WAS CALLED TO THE WHITE HOUSE for his first briefing for the fall campaign by a man they identified to him only as "Mr. Cheney," whose office, MacDougall observed, had a safe as big as a man "that had a big sign across it saying 'LOCKED.' "

Pollster Robert Teeter described his recent innovation, a polling instrument that measured how warmly voters felt at the mention of a candidate's name—a "feelings thermometer." Ford's temperature was forty-five: "Lukewarm." Carter's was twenty degrees higher. "*We* may fear that he's another Nixon—a cold, calculating son of a bitch without a nonpolitical friend in the world. But this"—he pointed to the chart—"is reality. *This* is the Carter we have to deal with."

Then he unveiled another innovation: the "perceptual map." He laid down a transparent acetate sheet with scattered dots printed thereupon; with a dramatic flourish, he layered another on top, then another, then another. Each point represented a surveyed voter; each sheet, a different voter bloc. "Thousands of little dots began to cluster around Jimmy Carter. Blue-collar workers started clinging to the Carter circle. Intellectuals gathered around him. Catholics and Jews . . . Blacks and Chicanos smothered him with their dots. People who cared about busing dropped at his feet. People who were for gun control sided with him as well. Conservative women kissed his feet. Liberal women hugged his head. Environmentalists swarmed around him. The rich touched him. The poor clung to him."

Their job, Teeter explained, was to wrench that geometry of pleasant associations from the opposing candidate to their own—by piling up proofs of their candidate's trustworthiness, even as Carter's side worked to turn Ford into the reanimated political corpse of Richard M. Nixon.

FBI director Clarence Kelley was revealed to have availed himself of $335 worth of home improvements from the FBI's carpentry shop, and Ford appeared to be doing nothing about it. Said Carter, "When people throughout the country, particularly young people, see Richard Nixon

cheating, lying, and leaving the highest office in disgrace, when they see
the previous attorney general violating the law and admitting it, when you
see the head of the FBI break a little law and stay there, it gives everybody
the sense that crime must be OK. 'If the big shots in Washington can get
away with it, well, so can I.' . . . The director of the FBI ought to be purer
than Caesar's wife." Bob Dole, Ford's hatchet-man running mate, gave the
campaign's response. He asked how Carter could claim to be for closing
tax loopholes and balancing the budget given his own "nice little savings"
of $41,702 on his 1975 taxes via a credit for equipment purchased for his
peanut warehouse. Then Dole was confronted with questions about a
$5,000 campaign contribution he had taken from the lobbyist in charge of
Gulf Oil's illegal slush fund.

   Peccadilloes were being elevated to blockbuster news status. After
Watergate, journalists were frantic to expose corruption. Of a TV commercial intended to convey Carter's untutored authenticity, the *New York
Times* reported, "The body attached to the hand, which is never visible
on the screen, belonged not to a newsman but to Gerald Rafshoon, the
Atlanta advertising man who designs Mr. Carter's ads." On the president's
strategy of campaigning via Rose Garden photo opportunities, they described aides placing a fiberglass mat on the White House lawn before
staging a "spontaneous" presidential stroll—then, "an hour later, the desk,
chair, and mat had been moved and the television cameras repositioned
so that Mr. and Mrs. Ford could be filmed striding into the garden from a
different door"; the photograph was captioned, "President Ford shaking
hands with his wife, Betty, in the Rose Garden . . . and doing it again for
photographers who asked for a better angle." This ceaseless questing after
transparency seemed to freeze the electorate in a state of confusion, and
by third week of September, one-third of voters told pollsters they had
no idea which candidate they would choose, with 40 percent saying they
would not vote at all.

PUNDITS HOPED THE TRIVIALITY WOULD ABATE ONCE AND FOR ALL AFTER
September 23, when the first televised presidential debate since Richard
Nixon and John F. Kennedy locked horns in 1960 took place.

   The first person ever to propose televised presidential debates was that
most high-minded of presidential aspirants, Adlai Stevenson, disgusted by
the development of electioneering via "the jingle, the spot announcement,
and the animated cartoon," and the prospect of yet one more year spent
reciting the same canned speech in town after town in 1956. His advisors
talked him out of the idea. He proposed it again for 1960 after his own political retirement: "Imagine discussion on the great issues of our time with
the whole country watching." It would "transform our circus-atmosphere

presidential campaigning into a great debate conducted in full view of all the people."

Federal statute, however, stood in the way: Section 315 of the 1934 Federal Communications Act mandated that broadcasters grant "equal time" for *every* announced presidential candidate, even if there were dozens. Kennedy and Nixon got around this in 1960 by having Congress vote a temporary suspension of Section 315. Subsequent incumbents, disinclined to grant their challengers equal TV billing, had their congressional allies block that option. Then keen legal minds devised a loophole: if an *independent entity*, like the League of Women Voters, staged debates, then the networks could cover them as "news events." So it was, for the first time in sixteen years, that the American public would at last be treated to a reprise of what Theodore White, in *The Making of the President 1960*, had called a "simultaneous gathering of all the tribes of America to ponder their choice between two chieftains in the largest political convocation in the history of man." The presidential election could finally become a contest of ideas.

Then two men set themselves down behind podia in a venerable Philadelphia theater—a TV stage set, actually: the panel of questioners sat in front of a wall that blocked the audience's view of the stage, and the audience was ordered not to make a sound. The producer boasted of creating a "completely controlled environment." Outside, police penned off an equally controlled area for demonstrators. The most cacophonous protested abortion. Carter had had his first run-in with the issue shortly after the convention, in a meeting with Catholic bishops in New York. The candidate pandered to them by disavowing a plank in his party's platform opposing a constitutional amendment overturning the *Roe v. Wade* decision legalizing abortion, promising he would not stand in the way of such an amendment. But the bishops were not satisfied; they demanded he *advocate* for such an amendment. "No one told him," the director of communications for the New York City archdiocese later remarked, "the bishops were talking of abortion as Auschwitz. Compromise was and is impossible for them." The next month, Carter was banned from speaking in a Catholic church. In Scranton, Pennsylvania, Secret Service officers had to hustle him away from an anti-abortion mob. But the issue went undiscussed at the debate; both candidates' positions were virtually identical: personally opposed; leave the question to the states.

Indeed, many of the most interesting issues went undiscussed. Questioning emphasized technical, bureaucratic concerns. The first exciting moments came when a producer broke a rule against showing reaction shots: Carter's face turned sour after Ford called him a hypocrite; Ford glowered when Carter accused him of public relations stunts. "Lousy television," the media guru Marshall McLuhan thought.

Until there arrived one of the most astonishing twenty-eight minutes in the history of TV.

Elizabeth Drew of the *New Yorker* asked the evening's final question, about Congress's eye-opening 1975 investigations of abuses by America's intelligence agencies, including assassinations of foreign leaders: "What do you think about trying to write in some new protections by getting new laws to govern these agencies?" The president, in his dullest Midwestern drone, insisted that his executive reorganizations and new wiretapping rules took care of the problem. "And I'm glad that we have a good director in George Bush, we *have* good executive orders, and the CIA, and the DIA, and NASA—I mean the NSA—are now doing a good job under proper supervision . . ."

He pursed his lips. He sounded nervous. This was a dodgy, almost Nixonian answer. Things were getting interesting. Carter had spoken frankly and harshly on the campaign trail about the abuses of intelligence agencies. Now, his Southern accent taking on intensity, he began lecturing: "One of the *very serious* things that has happened in our government in recent years, and has continued up until now, is a *breakdown* in the *trust* among our people in the—"

Silence. Even though his lips were moving.

A harsh electronic buzz.

The sonorous, authoritative voice of NBC anchorman David Brinkley: "The pool broadcasters in Philadelphia have lost the audio. It's not a con-spiracy against Governor Carter or President Ford . . . they will fix it as soon as possible."

For hadn't American know-how always fixed everything? Hadn't it beat Hitler, delivered the world its first mass middle class, rebuilt Europe, put a man on the moon, fought a war on poverty? It had, once upon a time. O upon a time, the voices of such authoritative gray-haired white men re-assured us, soothed us, guided us through the trauma of assassination and riot and Watergate and war, explained the inexplicable to us.

Not now.

The sound of a phone dialing. Carter gesticulating silently onscreen. David Brinkley breaking in, explaining nothing, again.

The scene shifted to backstage: "David, we don't know what is hap-pening, we're as surprised as you are, uh, they were talking and suddenly they quit"; the backstage correspondent then tried convincing the 53.6 percent of American households that were tuning in that the debate had been "very lively." He stuck microphones in the faces of campaign representatives, each dubiously claiming their men had scored knockout blows, that everything was going just smashingly (". . . but I think the real winner tonight was the American people . . ."). An interviewer pronounced with a hint of triumph in his voice, "And now back to David Brinkley!"

Who, not realizing he was on the air, said nothing, then cast a glance offstage, mumbling, "I gather the debate is over, is that right?"

Then to the camera, conclusively: "So the debate is over! That's it."

But neither man moved. So the cameras kept filming . . . nothing.

It took the length of a TV situation comedy before the gremlin was finally fixed. It was announced that Jimmy Carter would continue answering where he left off. He said, "There has been too much government secrecy and not enough respect for the privacy of American citizens," then grinned. The two men made closing statements. The ordeal ended. Eugene McCarthy, the former senator from Minnesota who was running a quixotic third-party bid but whose lawsuit to be included in the debate had failed, was asked what he thought about the interruption. He deadpanned, "I never noticed." F. Clifton White, the political organizer most responsible for Barry Goldwater's presidential nomination in 1964 and who was working unenthusiastically for Ford, was amazed at the sight of these "two men who were seeking to hold the most powerful office in the world . . . speechless at their podia like waxworks dummies, afraid to open their mouths and take charge," and observed that if one or the other had done so, they would have won the election right then and there.

But the candidates had been trained by their handlers—trained within an inch of their lives—that one could only *lose* a televised debate, so they should not try anything, anything at all, that risked a mistake, drilled not to sit down, or make any motion that might suggest weakness; indeed, it had required the intervention of a kindly stage manager just for the two men to wipe their sweaty brows during the interruption, because they would only do so when the cameras turned away. Some contest of ideas.

THE CONSERVATIVE WEEKLY *HUMAN EVENTS* BEGAN RUNNING ADS: "CONSERVATIVES You still have a choice, you can WRITE IN REAGAN." Reagan got letters from adoring fans asking him why they shouldn't. He always responded by pointing to the party platform—"written by people who support me . . . based on the positions I took during the campaign. . . . If Republican victory does occur based on our platform (and it is our conservative platform) then we can continue to build from there." He also said that if Ford should lose, it would be time to "reassess our party and lay plans to bring together the new majority of Republicans, Democrats, and Independents who are looking for a banner around which to rally."

The name he wished to see on that banner was clearly his own. Ronald Reagan had succeeded in turning his fight against a sitting president at the

Republican convention into a nail-biter—then, on the last night, delivered an apparently impromptu speech that received more acclaim than the nominee's, leaving many delegates in rapturous tears. Four days later he returned to the job he'd done after retiring from the California governor's office: a five-minute daily political broadcast syndicated on hundreds of radio stations. One of the commentaries he recorded that day blamed "machine politics" in states where he had lost primaries to Ford—suggesting Ford was a corrupt political boss. He was asked in a press conference on the sidewalk outside the studio where he recorded his broadcasts, on the corner of Hollywood and Vine, about the buzz to form a conservative third party. He answered, "The Republican Party, down to less than 20 percent of the voting public, has got to reassess"—hardly a ringing endorsement of Gerald Ford.

Ford phoned Reagan, asking him angrily if he even cared about beating Jimmy Carter. The *New York Times* said the Reagans declined an invitation to spend the night at the White House. Ford's running mate was asked if Reagan was snubbing them. "I don't see any problem with Governor Reagan," Bob Dole replied—but then Reagan's longtime press secretary Lyn Nofziger, who was working that fall for Dole's campaign, told the press, "It's hard for a lot of us to generate any enthusiasm."

What Reagan's fans *were* enthusiastic about, at party meetings convened to plot the general election attack, was punishing Ford loyalists from the primaries. The chairman of the California Republicans was a former Reagan protégé named Paul Haerle who had jumped ship. Conservatives wore "Hang Haerle" buttons, complete with nooses, to the state convention. Texas's "sounded like a convention of crickets": hundreds of "Reagan's Raiders" blew tiny whistles to sabotage proceedings to name a Ford man state chairman. Reagan's most loyal supporter in the Senate, Jesse Helms, endorsed the ticket—in a speech demanding that Ford's secretary of state Henry Kissinger embrace the party platform Reaganites had crafted or "resign immediately." That platform happened to include a plank, entitled "Morality in Foreign Policy," which excoriated the Nixon-Kissinger-Ford program of détente with the Soviet Union. Conservatives' price for supporting Ford, in other words, was Kissinger avowing loyalty to a platform that called them both immoral.

Reagan was finally persuaded to deliver a televised endorsement. The speech said virtually nothing about Gerald Ford, but a great deal about Reagan's ambitions.

It was a quintessential Reagan performance, in every way the opposite of the bland president he was affecting to support. The elaborately dressed office set recalled the image with which many Americans still primarily associated him: hosting *General Electric Theater* on Sunday nights in the

1950s and early 1960s. He opened with a twinkle in his eye, arguing that this election was *really* about the two parties' platforms. "There have been times in the past when party platforms were noted less for what they said than for what they avoided saying," he said. "But this year of our Bicentennial, we find the philosophies of our parties clearly stated and clearly visible for all to see."

("*Walk toward*," the teleprompter's stage directions read.)

"A party platform is an *actual guide* to the course a party will take if and when it comes to power."

("*Lean on chair.*")

"If that is true, then the 1976 platform of the Democrat Party charts the most dangerous course for a nation since the Egyptians tried a shortcut through the Red Sea."

("*Sit on desk.*")

He castigated the Democrats' endorsement of the bill cosponsored by Senator Hubert Humphrey and Congressman Augustus Hawkins, the African American representative of the Watts neighborhood of Los Angeles, to require the federal government to produce full employment, even if it had to create government jobs to do so—"so disastrous in its consequences to the national economy, that the Democratic leadership in the Congress dares not bring it up for a vote in this election year." Reagan claimed it cost as much as twenty-three stacks of $1,000 bills piled as high as a fifty-story building and would produce "complete and total control of the nation's economy from Washington."

("*Relax*," said the teleprompter. This was the sort of thing that tended to get Reagan's Irish up.)

He implied that Jimmy Carter had Hitlerian ambitions: "The great political temptation of our age is to believe that some charismatic leader, some party, some ideology or some improvement in technology can be substituted for an economy in which millions of individual human beings make their own decisions. . . . It only takes one man in power with the wrong ideas to ruin an economy, and a nation."

He flayed the Democrats' promise of universal health insurance, said their platform's energy plank would "economically cripple" the companies "that are the only hope we have for developing new sources and continuing to explore for oil," the education plank extracting "more money *from* you but less control *by* you"—while the Republican platform, which was "not handed down by party leadership" but "created out of a free and frank and open debate among rank-and-file members," understood "that *your* initiative and energy create jobs, our standard of living, and the underlying economic strength of the country," and that "no nation can spend its way into prosperity; a nation can only spend its way into bankruptcy."

Then he lit into the Democrats for proposing to cut $5 to $7 billion out of the defense budget: "There is simply no alternative to necessary spending on defense. We pay the necessary cost in terms of tax dollars now or in freedom and lives later on." He looked into the camera: "If you're with your children, take a look at them. They're very much involved in this decision. If the Democrats make a mistake in how much to spend for defense, *our children* will pay the ultimate price."

The next morning, the *New York Times* reported that, following failed negotiations between Reagan's advisor Michael Deaver and Dick Cheney, Reagan would not be speaking for Ford in the crucial states of Mississippi, South Carolina, Florida, Tennessee, and Kentucky, and that Cheney had received "a highly qualified answer" as to whether Reagan would cut commercials for Ford.

IN ANY EVENT, REAGAN WAS YESTERDAY'S NEWS. CAMPAIGN REPORTERS soon had something more entertaining to discuss.

That summer, Jimmy Carter had sat for several far-ranging interviews with a writer named Robert Scheer. He offered frank complaints about the numbness of campaign routine, and explained why he believed pardoning Vietnam draft evaders was civic duty; thoughtfully discussed why he refused to position himself simply in either the liberal or conservative camp despite media criticism that he was trying to be all things to all people; spoke candidly about his own moral failing in neglecting to speak against school desegregation until *Brown v. Board of Ed*, and in supporting the Vietnam War until 1971. He was blunt about America's failings, too, citing the CIA's abuses of power in particular; people had become inured to that sort of thing, he complained; some perhaps even "prefer lies to truth. But I don't think it's simplistic to say that our government hasn't measured up to the ethical and moral standards of the people in this country."

The subject turned to whether he'd ever discussed the possibility of assassination with his wife; Carter replied that he was not afraid to die, and that the reason was his religious faith; and whether liberal-minded Americans needed to fear the sort of judges a devout Southern Baptist president might appoint. This spurred a long, subtle theological discussion. There might never have been a document of a candidate's thinking quite this rich in the history of American electioneering. And if it had appeared in, say, a newsmagazine, that might have been how the interview was received. Instead, it appeared in the soft-core pornography magazine *Playboy*—and all anyone could think about was sex.

He was explaining why he wouldn't be "running around breaking down people's doors to see if they were fornicating." The answer, he said, lay within Christianity's conception of sin and redemption. "Christ said,

'I tell you that anyone who looks on a woman with lust has in his heart already committed adultery.' I've looked on a lot of women with lust. I've committed adultery in my heart many times. That is something that God recognizes I will do—and I have done it—and God forgives me for it. But that doesn't mean that I condemn someone who not only looks on a woman with lust but leaves his wife and shacks up with somebody out of wedlock."

"Fornicating," "adultery in my heart," "lust," "shacks up"—it was like he hadn't said anything else.

An advance text was circulated to journalists right around the time of the first debate. The Associated Press headed its dispatch with a warning: "You may find the material in this story offensive to the readers of family newspapers." Cartoonists naturally got in on the act: Carter, in a yokel's string tie, carrying binoculars, a Peeping Tom peeking from behind a pillar. South Carolina's Democratic senator Ernest "Fritz" Hollings said, "Let's hope that when he becomes president he quits talking about adultery." Georgia's Democratic chairman told reporters, "I've been everywhere today and the reaction is uniformly negative." Reverend Pat Robertson, the son of a senator, whose Johnny Carson–style Christian talk show *The 700 Club* reached 2.5 million viewers nationwide, said evangelicals were "making a serious reassessment of Carter."

After the complete *Playboy* issue came out—there was a spread on "Sex in Cinema 1976" featuring stills of carnal activity in no less than twenty-two films; the usual tasteless jokes and cartoons (guy leaving an orgy: "I don't know who to thank, but one or more of you gives great head!"); an editorial insisting heroin was not nearly so harmful as it was made out to be; a centerfold who described herself as "half liberal, half conservative" (not unlike the fellow whose interview Americans could finally read in full by flipping to page ninety-one, between a Scotch ad and an article praising Austin, Texas, as "the only wide-open dope-and-music resort available now that students were studying again")—and Ronald Reagan pronounced himself so disgusted leafing through it that he was too embarrassed to deposit it in a public garbage can.

A SECOND FRONT IN THE *PLAYBOY* CONTROVERSY OPENED IN TEXAS. FOR Carter had also said in the interview, "I don't think I would *ever* take on the same frame of mind that Nixon or Johnson did, lying, cheating, and distorting the truth." The insult to the honor of history's first Texan president portended a potential electoral college disaster.

Team Carter counted Southern states comprising 96 of the 270 electoral votes needed to win as in the bag, and that Democratic Massachusetts, Wisconsin, Minnesota, and the District of Columbia would bring their total to 125. Their most important swing states were Florida and Texas, both of which had begun a halting and uneven shift to the Republicans they hoped to arrest, but with Carter's LBJ gaffe, Republicans spied an opportunity to lock in Texas for good.

The Ford campaign assigned the task of turning the molehill into a Texas-sized mountain to John Connally, the state's larger-than-life former governor, a Lyndon Johnson protégé who had switched parties after serving as Richard Nixon's treasury secretary. A skilled student of his state's traditions of populist demagoguery, Democratic National Committee chairman Robert Strauss, an old college running buddy of Connally's, said giving him the job was like handing Jascha Heifetz a Stradivarius. Connally got to work; and soon, the Texas tide began turning.

Rosalynn Carter raced down to apologize to Lady Bird Johnson. Her husband made an emergency campaign trip. Hounded by reporters, he fudged that "after the interview, there was a *summary* made that unfortunately equated what I had said about President Johnson and President Nixon." ABC's pit bull Sam Donaldson then lectured him about the difference between a "summary" and a "transcription"; Carter backtracked, lamely; Press Secretary Jody Powell kicked up a distracting shouting match with the reporters; and Carter's numbers in Texas continued their slide. The Ford camp moved the state to its top-priority list—quickly cutting several commercials starring John Wayne.

This was a historic development. It had been a remarkable innovation when Barry Goldwater toured the Deep South for Richard Nixon in 1960—wearing "a Confederate uniform," Lyndon Johnson darkly joked—since no Republican had ever won electoral votes there. Then, in 1964, Goldwater won Mississippi, Alabama, Georgia, South Carolina, and North Carolina. When Richard Nixon attempted to repeat the accomplishment in 1968, intimating his sympathy for the region's desire to keep the federal government from forcing racial desegregation upon it, it was dubbed the "Southern strategy." When he swept the South along with almost all the rest of the nation in 1972, experts wondered whether the Party of Lincoln had flipped Dixie for good.

Then, however, the Democrats *nominated* a Southerner, and pundits began talking about the Republican Southern strategy as a thing of the past.

But now Carter was detouring to shore up his Southern flank. The *Playboy* interview rendered him a figure of mockery in this most pious of American regions—as when, at a rally in Nashville, someone held up a sign reading "SMILE IF YOU'RE HORNY." He also said, during the same event, "We've been deeply wounded in the last eight years. We have been hit by hammer blows in the Nixon-Ford administration"—an unforced tactical error: media referees called a foul on Carter for implicitly tying Ford too closely to Watergate, an unacceptably low blow.

He was foundering in big Northern cities, too, where his "anti-politician" ways drove leaders of urban political machines to distraction. Jules Witcover of the *Baltimore Sun* said the old clubhouse pols treated Carter "like a naturalized Martian rather than as a fellow soldier." He gave Democratic congressional leaders the cold shoulder, didn't pay respects to past Democratic presidential candidates, and was even said to hold his party's royal family, the Kennedys, in contempt; and who ever heard of a Democrat doing that? Boston's mayor called Carter "a very strange guy, and people out there sense it too."

Ford began gaining—until *his* campaign was rocked by a gaffe.

It turned on the issue of race. Richard Nixon had once been a friend to Martin Luther King Jr. and the civil rights movement, receiving 40 percent of the black vote in 1960. Then, however, the Republican Party changed directions on the issue for good: they nominated Barry Goldwater, who voted against the 1964 Civil Rights Act. He got only 6 percent of the black vote. In 1968, Nixon followed Goldwater's lead, aiming his appeal at white segregationists in the South, and white Northerners opposed to busing to desegregate public schools. In 1972, nonwhites were practically the only voters who *didn't* support Richard Nixon, giving him 13 percent. But for some Republicans this new reality had not yet sunk in. Mal MacDougall predicted Ford would receive "what a Republican presidential candidate can normally expect": 30 percent of the back vote.

Not likely now. Late in September a *Rolling Stone* dispatch related a conversation that took place aboard an airplane bearing pop star Sonny Bono, the squeaky-clean crooner Pat Boone, and a member of Ford's cabinet to California after the Republican convention.

"It seems to me that the Party of Abraham Lincoln could and should be able to attract more black people," Boone reflected. "Why can't this be done?"

The cabinet secretary smiled mischievously: "I'll tell you why you can't attract coloreds. Because the coloreds only want three things. You know what they want?"

Boone shook his head.

"It's three things: first a tight pussy; second, loose shoes; and third, a warm place to shit. That's all!"

Another magazine divined that the jokester was Secretary of Agriculture Earl Butz. He was an enormously consequential figure, the person most responsible for radically transforming American farming from a family-based to an industrial enterprise, but now the main thing he would be remembered for was a racist dirty joke. The press pounced—once their nervous editors figured out how to report it in a sufficiently family-friendly manner. (In San Diego, the biggest local paper offered readers a copy of the unexpurgated text only upon written request.) Senator Edward Brooke of Massachusetts, a Republican, the Senate's only African American, demanded Butz's resignation. Ford dithered for several days, then, on October 3, he convened a press conference at which an ashen-faced Butz announced he was quitting, then left the room; then, Ford warmly praised him.

A boost from Ronald Reagan sure would have helped about then. Dole traveled to Reagan's home to negotiate more campaign appearances. Reagan agreed to only one, in New Haven (where, he said, he was visiting his son for the Yale homecoming game), and refused a spot as honorary campaign chairman. In a driveway press conference, he once more praised the Republican platform; then, asked if Ford should campaign beyond the White House, mocked him. ("*Wellll* he's sure got the best-televised Rose Garden in America.") He had just published a column hymning the platform's "Morality in Foreign Policy" plank, "unique in party platform history in its implicit recognition of past foreign policy mistakes under the party's own leadership"—which meant Ford's leadership.

He finally agreed to tape some commercials. The scripts he submitted kept referring to the tainted word "Republican," which the campaign's strategy was to avoid at all costs. After Reagan refused to rewrite them, MacDougall concluded, "It was pretty clear to me that Reagan was either coming into this thing on his terms—and with his scripts—or not coming in at all."

THE REPUBLICANS DEBUTED A SLICK NEW SET OF COMMERCIALS WITH THE slogan "President Ford: He's Making Us Proud Again"; and an intentionally *non*-slick commercial starring the amiable black entertainer Pearl Bailey. ("I'm not reading this off any paper. . . . I like Gerald Ford. I don't know who you like. But mostly he has something I like very much in every human being—simplicity, and honesty." Then, with an authentic-sounding catch in her voice: "I don't know, please think about it!")

Carter spoke at the National Conference of Catholic Charities. He said that he believed the family was the "cornerstone of American life," regretted that "our government has no family policy, and that is the same as an anti-family policy," and promised a White House conference on the subject. This would prove an important development in years to come.

Ford signed a tax relief bill in the Oval Office. His handlers would have preferred the Rose Garden. But forecasts predicted rain.

Then it was off to prepare for the second televised debate, on foreign policy.

Ford scrimmaged with the help of another innovation of Bob Teeter's: demographically representative audiences pressed a button to register their reactions in real time. Carter was drilled to look at the camera and smile more—and to attack the Republican from the right. He answered the first question with steely eyes, sounding like Reagan: "Our country is not strong anymore; we're not respected anymore.... We talk about détente. The Soviet Union knows what they want in détente, and they've been winning. We have not known what we wanted, and we've been out-traded in almost every instance."

He looked into the camera and smiled—one of forty-two grins that night, according to researchers from the University of New York at Buffalo, compared to eight in the first: "This is one instance in which I agree with the Republican platform."

("That stiff, prissy man on the screen," the former Mrs. John F. Kennedy, Jacqueline Onassis, clucked to a friend.)

Max Frankel, a distinguished *New York Times* editor, in a follow-up question to Ford, *also* suggested détente had gone too far. "Our allies in France and Italy are now flirting with Communism. We've recognized a permanent Communist regime in East Germany; we virtually signed, in Helsinki, an agreement that the Russians have dominance in Eastern Europe, we bailed out Soviet agriculture with our huge grain sales, we've given them large loans, access to our best technology. Is that what you call a two-way street of traffic in Europe?"

"Helsinki" referred to a 1975 accord in which the Soviet Union acknowledged the importance of the principle of human rights in exchange for the U.S. affirming the territorial integrity of the Eastern European states within the Soviets' sphere of influence—which conservatives decried as a permanent surrender to Soviet control. Ford had worked very hard rehearsing an answer meant to deflect that impression. He was supposed to affirm "the independence, the sovereignty, and the autonomy of all Eastern European countries," while asserting "we do not recognize any sphere of influence by any power in Europe." He delivered the first part flawlessly, noting that among the Helsinki signatories was the Vatican, and that "I can't under any circumstances believe that His Holiness would agree, by signing that agreement, that the thirty-five nations have turned over to the Warsaw Pact nations the domination of Eastern Europe."

He miffed the second part. He said, "There is no Soviet domination of Eastern Europe, and there never will be under a Ford administration."

From the panelists' table in front of the stage, the moderator called for Carter's riposte—but Frankel broke in incredulously:

"I'm sorry, could I just follow—did I understand you to say, sir, that the Russians are not using Eastern Europe as their own sphere of influence and occupying most of the countries there and making sure with their troops that it's a Communist zone, whereas on our side of the line the Italians and the French are still flirting with the possibility of Communism?"

Ford dug in: "I don't believe, Mr. Frankel, that the Yugoslavians consider themselves dominated by the Soviet Union. I don't believe that the Romanians consider themselves dominated by the Soviet Union. I don't believe that the Poles consider themselves dominated by the Soviet Union . . ."—and when it came time for Carter to respond, he practically giggled: "I would like to see Mr. Ford convince the Polish Americans and the Czech Americans and the Hungarian Americans in this country that those countries don't live under the domination and supervision of the Soviet Union behind the Iron Curtain."

Ford's coaches had implored him: no matter what Jimmy Carter said, he need only underscore the words *peace* and *experience*. "He could have answered every conceivable question with just those two things," Ford's media advisor Doug Bailey sighed ruefully to a reporter later. Bailey paused for a long time, then shrugged. "I guess he froze."

Had he? At first, Ford's political people didn't think they had a crisis on their hands. Dick Cheney, keeping score backstage, thought his man had won nine questions to five; Ford's debate coach scored it fourteen to zero. And according to Bob Teeter's first poll, 11 percent more viewers thought Ford was the winner than named Carter. Henry Kissinger, however, thought differently. In his customarily obsequious manner, he told Ford he thought he'd done marvelously—then screamed to his protégé Brent Scowcroft that playing down Soviet domination of Eastern Europe was a political disaster. He was correct. Almost immediately, commentators began latching onto Ford's "no Soviet domination of Eastern Europe" formulation as a bubbleheaded misstatement, a "gaffe"—evidence that Ford was losing a step.

The facts were more complicated. Ford was speaking accurately about a complex reality on the ground. Conservatives described the nations occupied by the Soviet Union after World War II as an undifferentiated mass of "slave states." But Poland had resisted Russian control to a sufficient degree that Eisenhower granted it most favored nation trade status. (Joseph Stalin himself had supposedly observed that trying to impose his will on Poland was like trying to saddle a cow.) Kennedy said America should "seize the initiative when the opportunity arises" to reward Communist Bloc states for good behavior. Richard Nixon said Eastern Europe countries were "sovereign, not part of a monolith."

This was why Ford refused to apologize for what he saw, at worst, as an infelicity of expression. But reporters kept pestering him. Eastern European ethnic leaders—who had prevailed upon Congress in 1959 to establish a Captive Nations Week observance every July—piled on, too. "Our people do usually vote Democratic," said Aloysius Mazewski of the Polish American Congress, "but we were aware that many of them were not enthusiastic about Carter and were going to vote for President Ford. I think many of them will go back to the Democratic side now." Carter said Ford's words "disgraced our country."

That was the interpretation that stuck: "After twenty-four hours of being told it was a bad mistake," Ford's White House spokesman Ron Nessen lamented, "the public changed their minds." Teeter took another poll in which respondents gave the victory to *Carter* by a margin of 45 points. Ford had dared complexity where simplicity was supposed to reside. But with the joke circulating that people were hoarding "Poles for Ford" buttons as collectors' items, and Carter's running mate Walter "Fritz" Mondale joking that he could now drink for free in Polish bars, Ford surrendered. He called Mazewski with a groveling apology. They said this election was about forthrightness. But, plainly, not *too much*.

IT WAS AROUND THEN, HIS CAMPAIGN ROCKED ON ITS HEELS, THAT GERALD Ford's people began contemplating a new sort of Southern strategy—with religion, not race, at its center.

Back in August, at a strategy meeting, Bob Teeter had recited the findings of a Gallup poll: 39 percent of Americans said they'd had a life-changing experience of the presence of Jesus Christ at a time and place they could identify, 72 percent read the Bible regularly, and 71 percent thought political leaders should pray before making decisions. "We've got to have Billy Graham on the ticket," Doug Bailey replied. His partner John Deardourff nominated TV faith healer Oral Roberts. Someone suggested Ford could perform a small miracle at the Republican convention. Teeter warned them not to joke. "It could be the most powerful political force ever harvested. . . . They've got an underground communications network. And Jimmy Carter is plugged right into it."

Then the next month the Almighty bestowed upon Gerald Ford a miracle—that *Playboy* interview.

"Evangelicals Seen Cooling on Carter," read the *Washington Post* front page on September 27. It recalled an address the previous June at the annual meeting of America's largest Protestant denomination: Southern Baptist Convention president Reverend Bailey Smith, who pastored an Oklahoma church with ten thousand members, said the country needed a "born-again man in the White House." Some shuddered; Southern Baptists, the *Post* pointed out, "customarily prided themselves on their neutrality in political matters, on the non-hierarchical organization of their denomination." But others were thrilled—and gave him a standing

ovation when he roared next, "*And his initials are the same as our Lord's!*"
Now, however Smith said he wasn't even sure he'd vote for Jimmy Carter.

It had become apparent that Carter was an awkward fit with his core-
ligionists. He talked about legalizing marijuana. And appreciated liberal
theologians. And palled around with Bob Dylan and the Allman Brothers;
he was just not *one of us*. The SBC had been officially founded in 1845
after the national Baptists forbade slave owners from serving as missionaries. In 1918, an influential statement of the denomination's mission, *The
Call of the South*, argued that God had let the Confederacy lose the Civil
War in order to steel Southerners to rescue the rest of the nation from
the "new gospel of 'tolerance,'" the "false faiths" of "rationalism" and
"liberalism"—"Antichrist teachings under the guise of religion." Now
more and more Southern Baptists were returning to these reactionary
roots, making activism against feminism, homosexuality—and pornography in magazines like *Playboy*—part of their spiritual calling.

The bicentennial year was the watershed. Jerry Falwell, the Southern
Baptist televangelist, staged "I Love America" rallies in 141 cities, frequently on the steps of state capitol buildings, starring fresh-faced un-
dergrads from his own Liberty Baptist College, who sang patriotic songs
accompanied by what they called "stage movements." (Dancing was a sin.)
In 1965 he had published a widely distributed sermon aimed at Martin Luther King Jr., arguing, "Preachers are called to be soul-winners, not politicians." But now, at these rallies, his fiery sermon concluded with a line
from II Chronicles that joined civic and theological vocations seamlessly:
"If my people which are called by My name, shall humble themselves and
pray, and seek My face and turn from their wicked ways; then will I hear
from heaven and will forgive their sins, and will heal their land." Then, he
would duck inside the marble halls to lobby.

A Fairfax, Virginia, minister named Robert Thoburn, author of *How
to Establish and Operate a Successful Christian School*, whom conservatives admired because his own school was a for-profit business, ran unsuccessfully for Congress. So did the president of a fundamentalist college in
Hammond, Indiana, Reverend Robert Billings, author of *A Guide to the
Christian School*. A congressman from Arizona, John Conlan, together
with Bill Bright of the Campus Crusade for Christ, began Third Century Press, which published books like *One Nation Under God*, by Rus
Walton, which averred, "The Constitution was designed to perpetuate a
Christian order." Their organization, the Christian Freedom Foundation,
sent 120,000 ministers pitches to join "Intercessors for America," whose
membership benefits included Walton's book *The Five Duties of a Christian Citizen* and a manual about how to elect "real Christians" to office
by adopting a familiar Christian activity—home Bible study sessions—to

organize precincts. Explained Conlan, "The House of Representatives, which is composed of 435 members, is controlled by a simple majority of 218. At this time, there are at least 218 people in the House who follow in some degree the secular humanist philosophy which is so dangerous to our future."

Conlan ran for the Senate. His primary opponent was Jewish. One of his slogans was "A vote for Conlan is a vote for Christianity." Barry Goldwater, whose father was born Jewish, and Goldwater's best friend Harry Rosenzweig, the Jewish former chairman of the Arizona Republican Party, abandoned Conlan. He lost, left Congress, and threw himself into evangelical political organizing full-time. His ally Bright raised $25,000 each from twenty Christian businessmen, like Richard DeVos of the Amway Corporation, to purchase a Louis XIV–style mansion that had previously been inhabited by Washington D.C.'s Catholic archbishop, anointing it the "Christian Embassy."

Bright and Conlan insisted their efforts were nonpartisan and non-ideological: anyone was welcome to join. Then, the liberal evangelical magazine *Sojourners* published an exposé revealing that their organizing manual suggested screening candidates with the question "How do you feel about Nelson Rockefeller or Ronald Reagan as presidential candidates?" (A preference for the tribune of the Republican Party's liberal wing was disqualifying.) Bright insisted, "Campus Crusade is not political—in twenty-five years it has never been." But the article also quoted him as saying in Campus Crusade's magazine *Worldwide Challenge*, "There are 435 congressional districts, and I think Christians can capture many of them by next November," and Conlan's opinion of the Senate's two proudest evangelical Christians, Mark Hatfield and Harold Hughes—who were liberals—"These are not the kind people we want in government. We don't even want them to know what's going on." *Sojourners*' editor, Jim Wallis, complained that Bright and Conlan's project "gives an excuse for a lot of evangelicals who would like to find a reason not to vote for a Christian they perceive as a Democratic liberal."

The cascading damage from the *Playboy* interview suggested Wallis was right. A preacher from Pennsylvania said of Carter, "I do not feel he has been 'born again.' . . . He approves of social drinking." Jerry Falwell—whose *Old Time Gospel Hour* aired Sundays on 260 television stations, "sixty-five more than Lawrence Welk," the *Washington Post* noted—announced, "Like many, I am quite disillusioned. . . . Four months ago most of the people I knew were pro-Carter. Today, that has totally reversed."

The Carter campaign, busy reaching out to Democratic interest groups from feminists to homosexuals to union members—and *Playboy* readers—took the evangelical vote for granted. The crisis exposed a political Achilles' heel: Carter's success so far had been built on seeming to be all things to all constituencies—constituencies often at war with one another. Now, for the first time, a bill for this ideological profligacy came due—and the Ford campaign spied opportunity.

AT FIRST THE PRESIDENT, A STAID EPISCOPALIAN, WAS RELUCTANT TO TALK about faith; the campaign pressed the message via surrogates, like Ford's seminarian son Mike, who said, "Jimmy Carter wears his religion on his sleeve but Jerry Ford wears it in his heart," and released Ford's private letter to an evangelical film producer named Billy Zeoli: "Because I trusted Christ to be my savior, my life is His."

Then, Ford stuck his finger in the wind, and took the plunge himself.

Shortly after the foreign policy debate, Ford hosted thirty-four evangelical leaders—proprietors of telecasts like *Back to the Bible* and *The Hour of Freedom*, executives from Billy Graham's ministry and the Campus Crusade for Christ, Christian radio station owners, publishers, Bible college deans—for seventy minutes in the cabinet room. The star attendee was a preacher who'd first come to the nation's attention after *Brown v. Board of Education*, when he demanded, "Don't force me by law, by statute, by Supreme Court decision . . . to cross over in those intimate things where I don't want to go. Let me build my life. Let me have my church. Let me have my school. Let me have my friends. Let me have my home. Let me have my family. And what you give to me, give to every man in America and keep it like our glorious forefathers made—a land of the free and the home of the brave." He also said the movement for racial integration was "aching of idiocy and foolishness," that the "idea of the universal brotherhood of man and the fatherhood of God is a denial of everything in the Bible," and that civil rights activists were "a bunch of infidels, dying from the neck up." He claimed to have never seen a movie in his life and never intended to—until an actor named Ronald Reagan persuaded him that not *all of them* were sinful. ("I'm going to start going to some movies, and I'll tell my congregation that it's not a sin to see certain types of movies.") His name was Dr. W. A. "Wally" Criswell, and, Ford's campaign manager James Baker explained, "he's acknowledged as a leader not only among Southern Baptists but among evangelicals"—apparently unaware that "Southern Baptist" was a *subset* of evangelicals.

In 1960, when his First Baptist Church in Dallas had some fourteen thousand members, Criswell led a national day of prayer against the ascension of a Catholic to the White House—which would "spell the death of a free church in a free state and our hopes of continuance of full religious liberty in America." In 1968 he became the president of the Southern Baptist Convention. By 1972, he had come around on the question of segregation—but thundered so angrily against Richard Nixon's opening to Communist China that the president invited him to the White House to talk him down. In 1975, when Betty Ford praised legalized abortion on *60 Minutes* and took in stride the idea of her teenage daughter having a premarital affair, Reverend Criswell made national news again. "That's a gutter-type mentality," he said. "That's animal thinking." In the summer of 1976, he approvingly predicted a huge evangelical showing for Carter.

Then he and his colleagues met with the president in the cabinet room. Ford explained that his religion had "a tremendous subjective impact" on his decision-making, that he had "a deep concern about the rising tide of secularism," and that he and Betty read the Bible each and every night. Impressed, Criswell invited the president to pray in his church.

IT COINCIDED WITH A FINAL PIVOT IN FORD'S ELECTORAL CALCULATIONS. Carter held Texas only by a thread. Ford strategists had originally planned to concentrate on states like New York, New Jersey, Pennsylvania, and Illinois—the "big industrial states of the North," in the political reporters' cliché. Now they changed their mind. Which meant they were catching up with the electorate. For the "big industrial states" were no longer, comparatively, so big.

A 1969 book by Nixon aide Kevin Phillips, *The Emerging Republican Majority*, had been the first and most influential codification of the argument: the way forward for the Grand Old Party was exploiting conservative sentiment in the South and Southwest—the "Sun Belt." Demographic shifts informed the judgment. Changes in the number of votes states cast in the electoral college—calculated by adding up how many seats a state was apportioned in the 435-member House of Representatives plus each state's two senators—tell the story. In 1948, the year Ford was first elected to Congress, New York got forty-seven votes. Now they cast twenty-one. Pennsylvania went from thirty-five to twenty-seven, Illinois from twenty-eight to twenty-six. Meanwhile Florida's electoral votes doubled, Arizona's went up by half, and California replaced New York as the nation's most populous state. Reasons included the spread of air-conditioning, the Sun Belt's salubrious "business climate"—a term coined by General Electric executives in the 1950s to describe municipalities with low wages and weak unions—and the ballooning military-industrial complex, which appreciated a salubrious business climate, too: between 1950 and 1956, New York lost more than a third of its share of prime Defense Department contracts to the Sun Belt. Sun Belters were prickly about the Northeasterners who behaved as if the world still revolved around them—Texans most of all. So it was that, reviewing these facts in the context of Carter's LBJ gaffe, and Ford's success with the evangelicals, Ford's strategists scheduled a tour of the Lone Star State for the crucial second week in October, with Reverend Criswell's giant red-brick church as the first stop.

The interior was festooned with banners depicting Revolutionary War soldiers and Bicentennial thirteen-star flags. Criswell's hair was slicked back; he wore a cream-colored suit. He regaled his congregation with the story of his White House visit: "Mr. President," he recalled asking, "if *Playboy* magazine were to ask you for an interview, what would you do?" Ford replied, "I *was* asked by *Playboy* magazine for an interview, and I declined with an emphatic '*No*'!" Six thousand worshipers broke into a torrent of applause.

Then he berated Carter for saying in another interview that he was considering removing tax-exempt status from church businesses like radio stations, TV programs, colleges, and publishing companies. Criswell said reading that brought "dread and foreboding to my deepest soul. . . . To tax any of them is to tax the church . . . leading to the possibility of our destruction. . . . I hear Gerald Ford, our president, say boldly and coura-geously that he would interdict any such movement in America. May the Lord give him strength!"

The president, sitting beside what the pool reporter called "a full or-chestra larger than most Broadway pit orchestras," beamed. The choir broke into Handel's "Worthy Is the Lamb." Criswell, described in the pool report as "organ-lunged," remarked, "I think if Handel looked down from heaven, he would be proud of this choir and this orchestra. And Mr. President, that's why the White House ought to be in Dallas, Texas, instead of Washington." He described a speech President Ford gave to the Southern Baptist Convention as "one of the most moving and masterful addresses I have ever heard in my life." Theatrically dabbing a tear from his eye, he described Ford's seminarian son as "a sweet humble boy." Then he called his White House visit "one of the highest days of my life." The pair made their way down the aisle and out onto the church steps, where one of the waiting reporters asked if this meant the pastor was making a presidential endorsement. "Yes," he said, fearing not for his church's tax-exempt status. "I am for him. I am for him."

FORD STUMPED ACROSS THE LENGTH AND BREADTH OF CALIFORNIA, WHERE the undecided vote was an astronomical 23 percent—and he did so *sans* the Golden State's most prominent Republican, who cited a "prior com-mitment," exactly the reason Reagan had given for neglecting to call on the White House during a recent visit to Washington. The "prior commit-ment" was a meeting with his political supporters at his ranch near Santa Barbara, an article in the *Chicago Tribune* entitled "Reagan Snubs Ford Campaign in California" reported.

The final debate woke viewers up only when Carter offered an apology, of sorts: "Other people have done it and are notable—Governor Jerry Brown, Walter Cronkite, Albert Schweitzer, Mr. Ford's own Secretary of the Treasury, Mr. William Simon, William Buckley, many other people. But they aren't running for President, and in retrospect, from hindsight, I would not have given that interview had I to do it over again."

The lowest percentage of the voting-age population since 1948, 55.5 percent, turned out on Election Day. "The public has the feeling of being nibbled to death by ducks, not addressed by giants as should be the case," ABC's Howard K. Smith said when it was finally over.

Mal MacDougall said, "If Reagan had been willing to really speak out for President Ford, really work for Ford, I feel convinced that we would have carried Texas. The same goes, of course, for Mississippi." That would have covered fifty-two of the fifty-seven electoral college votes Ford required to win. Very few the of the issues that would actually end up convulsing the nation over the next years had been substantively discussed. Another thing that found no representation in the media: that, at the same time the nation chose a Democratic president, conservatives were mobilizing with a passion, creativity, and energy never seen before.

CHAPTER 2

"What Is an Orrin Hatch?"

SHORTLY AFTER ELECTION DAY, THE *NEW YORK TIMES* PUBLISHED A LITTLE humor piece relating the story of a young couple in suburban Long Island searching for a cocktail party theme. "A party celebrating Jimmy Carter's victory? Oh, everyone was doing that"—so, instead, they invited their friends to an evening of "drinks and debauchery" in honor of the possessor of a funny name they noticed in the newspaper. One guest "went to the library to see what an Orrin Hatch was. Another wrote 'Orrin Hatch' backward in the hope of discovering a code. Yet another held the invitation up to a mirror." They realized "there were some conservatives who probably might have liked Mr. Hatch if they had known who he was." But none did. Probably because they got their news from the *New York Times*. Orrin Hatch had just been elected to the Senate from Utah and would go on to exert more influence on the course of American politics than anyone else elected in 1976 except—possibly—Jimmy Carter. But in the pages of the Newspaper of Record, a column making fun of his name was the most in-depth treatment he got.

The election sent a bumper crop of conservatives to Washington from the Midwest and West. Wyoming elected Malcolm Wallop to the Senate, two years after he lost a run for governor as an environmentalist. (The *Times* made fun of his name once, too.) Indianapolis mayor Richard Lugar beat three-term liberal Democratic senator Vance Hartke. Mickey Edwards, national chairman of the American Conservative Union, won a congressional seat in Oklahoma. Dan Quayle, the handsome young scion of a Fort Wayne, Indiana, newspaper family, only two years out of law school, felled a Democratic incumbent that experts had thought unbeatable. Orange County sent up a TV talk show host, Bob Dornan, who had once burned Jane Fonda in effigy; Harrison "Jack" Schmitt, won New Mexico's Senate seat after promising to privatize Social Security. None received much coverage—not even the colorful linguist S. I. Hayakawa (a Japanese-American, he defended the wartime internment of Japanese citizens, and had become a right-wing hero fighting student antiwar activists in the 1960s as president of San Francisco State University), even though the new senator-elect would be representing the most populous state in the union after felling *another* supposedly unbeatable Democratic incumbent, and defeating three powerful establishment Republicans in the primary.

The *Boston Globe*, it is true, made note of the trend, in an editorial called "Last of the Mohicans." That they might be a political cutting edge, instead of representing the tattered remnants of a dying tribe, was the conclusion of precisely no one—nor was the expanding clout of Ronald Reagan, who, during the time he spent not campaigning for Gerald Ford, had been busy making all these victories possible.

UTAH'S NEW SENATOR-ELECT DEFEATED A DEMOCRAT NAMED FRANK MOSS— another incumbent previously considered unbeatable. Hatch was from a hardscrabble Pittsburgh family. He apprenticed at age sixteen as a lathe operator, then became the first in his family to attend college—which, since he came from a long line of Mormon elders, was Brigham Young in Salt Lake City. The brilliant student returned to Pittsburgh for law school on a full scholarship, housing his growing family in a former chicken coop while working the overnight shift as a dormitory desk attendant. Then, he moved to Utah to work as a general counsel in the oil and gas industry.

He had neither political experience nor connections, so when he began sending out feelers about challenging Senator Moss in 1976 he met only discouragement. According to Hatch's own account, he was still unde- cided only hours before the filing deadline. Then he had lunch with the chairman of the Utah Republican Party, who told him that he could win for the same reason Jimmy Carter could: "This is going to be an election year of anti-Washington sentiment."

Hatch visited the former president of Brigham Young, Ernest Wilkin- son, who was so conservative he had refused to accept federal funds lest the flagship Mormon university be subject to federal dictates, and refused to let economics professors teach Keynesianism—mainstream stuff most everywhere else, leftist heresy at BYU—even at the risk of the school los- ing its accreditation. Wilkinson liked the cut of this young man's jib and endorsed him.

A candidate became Utah's Republican senate nominee if he won 50 percent of the delegates to the state convention in August. If no one re- ceived an outright majority, the top two faced each other in a September runoff. One contender was a former four-term U.S. congressman. An- other had been White House assistant to Richard Nixon. The third was Dwight D. Eisenhower's budget director. Traveling the vast state in his family's green van, plying his six children with milkshakes to keep them behaved, the unknown Hatch proved utterly ineffectual at the county conventions, where he received two minutes to present the case for why he, and not these eminent worthies, should enjoy the attendees' support. His mien was stern and unsmiling; staffers thought his official campaign photo made him look like "Beelzebub."

Desperate, he booked a recording studio, and recorded an argument similar to the one Barry Goldwater used against *his* establishment opponents in 1964: that they were "me-too Republicans"—hardly different from Democrats. With $3,000 in borrowed money, Hatch sent out cassette tapes wrapped in Bicentennial red, white, and blue to the 2,512 state convention delegates. (The package also included a transcript, printed on ersatz 1776-style parchment, for Utahans who did not own tape recorders.) He approached a stalwart of Utah's far right, W. Cleon Skousen, whose book *The Naked Communist* printed what Skousen claimed was a leaked copy of the Communist Party's secret plan to take over the United States. (Its components included "Encourage promiscuity and easy divorce," "Gain control of all student newspapers," and "Eliminate all good sculpture from parks and buildings, substitute shapeless, awkward and meaningless forms.") Skousen also liked the cut of Hatch's jib, affording him access to Skousen's extensive mailing list.

Then Hatch scored another coup. At a gathering of Republicans north of Provo, a voter asked the aspirants whether they supported Gerald Ford or Ronald Reagan for president. The first two candidates hedged. The third endorsed Ford. All received polite applause. The outsider's turn came:

"I give my unqualified support to Ronald Reagan, and I believe that, if he is nominated, he will be our next president."

He got a frenzied ovation. He began repeating his endorsement everywhere he went—then finished in second at the state convention, qualifying for the runoff. He scrounged up enough money to retain the services of a high-end campaign consultant for a single day. The consultant advised him to call someone named Richard Viguerie, the godfather of a nascent political movement: the New Right. This proved his biggest bonaza yet.

THE TERM "NEW RIGHT" WAS COINED IN 1974 BY THE WRITER AND FORMER Nixon Justice Department official Kevin Phillips. One of the figures he was describing, a man named Paul Weyrich, was once asked to explain what made the New Right new. He answered that they weren't really conservatives. They were "radicals working to overturn the present power structure in this country."

The New Right's discontinuities from the old one would be exaggerated in the years to come—not least by its self-mythologizing leaders. But there were some important differences. For one thing, they believed Barry Goldwater, in whose presidential campaign many had cut their political teeth, was by then too much a member of the establishment to retain their respect. That made the outsider Orrin Hatch a natural recruit. "I'm a non-politician," he liked to say. "I've spent most of my professional life fighting the growing, oppressive federal bureaucracy, mostly for working people."

That notion—conservatism as an ideology for working people—was another New Right theme. Viguerie's father had been a construction worker; his mother toiled in a paper mill and sold milk from the family cow. Another movement principal was the son of a furnace stoker. Kevin Phillips grew up in the Bronx, and excoriated "conservatives whose game it is to quote English poetry and utter neo-Madisonian benedictions over the interests and institutions of establishment liberalism." He wished instead to build "a cultural siege-engine out of the populist steel of Idaho, Mississippi, and working-class Milwaukee, and then blast the Eastern liberal establishment to ideological-institutional smithereens." Another New Right pioneer said he was fighting "a guerrilla battle at the grassroots of a generation of lower-middle-class people who feel betrayed and exploited."

For the left, employers were the exploiters. The New Right replied that the true exploiters were federal bureaucrats grasping for tax dollars, and the media elites who shoved 1960s libertinism down Middle America's throats. New Rightists were obsessed with what were known as the "social issues"—crime, government intrusion into family life, sexual mores, the right to own a gun. Reagan's establishmentarian presidential campaign manager John Sears dismissed them as the "emotional issues." But the New Right *reveled* in emotion—particularly, the emotion of resentment.

The prototypical New Right crusade was a movement in 1974 of fundamentalist Christians in the union stronghold Kanawha County, West Virginia, against the "educrats" who issued textbooks they considered ungodly. The protests escalated to the point of dynamiting the school board building. The Heritage Foundation, the New Right's new think tank, sent a lawyer to represent the alleged bombers, and introduced the Kanawha organizers to fellow anti-textbook crusaders around the country. "We talk about issues that people care about," Weyrich said unapologetically: a voter brought into the conservative tent via an "alliance on family issues is bound to begin to look at the morality of other issues"—like "the unjust power that has been legislated for union bosses."

Jimmy Carter's pollster Pat Caddell understood how dangerous all this could prove to the Democratic coalition: blue-collar voters were vulnerable to conservative appeals because they were "no longer solely motivated by economic concerns—which have traditionally made them Democrats." Now that they feared "change in society" more than losing their place in the middle class, they were "one of the most vulnerable groups in the

Democratic coalition." The New Right social-issue strategy was rooted in just that—and not, at least at first, in the ideological convictions of its leaders. Those were more along the lines of the ones Barry Goldwater wrote about in *Conscience of a Conservative* in 1960: ending farm subsidies and the progressive income tax, facing down the Soviets even at the risk of nuclear war—the sort of notions that, when Goldwater ran for president, scared voters half to death. So the New Right searched for more tantalizing lures. As organizer Howard Phillips put it: "We organize discontent." Organizing discontent meant foraging for *whatever* issues roused an otherwise apathetic citizenry to conservative political action. Presently, social issues were it.

THE HEART OF THE NEW RIGHT WAS A VERY SMALL LEADERSHIP CADRE, whose political roots were in the lonely work of conservative organizing during the Kennedy years. Howard Phillips came from a Jewish New Deal family in working-class Boston. In the early 1960s, he helped found the conservative youth group Young Americans for Freedom—and proved himself a shrewd enough politician to win office as student body president at liberal Harvard. In 1971 he was appointed by President Nixon to head the Office of Economic Opportunity, which administered the federal war on poverty. Phillips loaded it up with so many young conservatives that veteran OEO bureaucrats started referring to Phillips' "YAFia." Then, however, in 1973, Phillips was let go after the press got wind of what Nixon had actually hired him to do at OEO: dismantle it. Phillips believed Nixon had given up without a fight. So he founded Conservatives for the Removal of the President to fight for his impeachment—not because of Watergate, but because, Phillips later explained, Nixon "was the most liberal president in American history, except Gerald Ford."

Shortly afterward, Senator Jesse Helms gave a speech to the American Conservative Union noting that only 38 percent of eligible voters had turned out for the congressional elections following Nixon's resignation. He argued that a plan targeting that nonvoting 62 percent—the "conservative majority," he called it—could set the political world on its ear. Young Phillips boldly approached Helms with just such a plan: a stealth grassroots organization with cells in all 435 congressional districts, to surface only once its infrastructure was in place, with the goal of taking over one or both of the political parties. ("It doesn't matter which party succeeds. Principles matter.") Helms conferred his blessing—then Phillips approached a political friend to help put the plan into action. That friend was Richard Viguerie. And once Phillips secured *his* participation, they were well on their way.

Viguerie's story would be told and retold many times in the decades to come, like right-wing holy writ. It began in 1961, when the twenty-eight-year-old was hired as a fundraiser by the right's P. T. Barnum, Marvin Liebman, the middle-age man who ran Young Americans for Freedom. The first thing Liebman told him was that YAF actually had two thousand paid members, but that he should always claim there were twenty-five thousand. That was another secret to the New Right's success: an eagerness to accept that their end—the survival of Western civilization—most decidedly justified nearly any means.

In 1965, Viguerie went into business for himself, renting a one-room office on Capitol Hill and marching a squad of temps into the office of the clerk of the House of Representatives, where, under the campaign finance laws then in effect, the identities of every citizen who had donated $50 or more to Barry Goldwater's presidential campaign were preserved. The hired secretaries scrawled as many names and addresses as they could before being chased from the premises by a nervous bureaucrat. Viguerie purchased fifty thousand more from a fundraiser for charities, then inherited more from his mentor Liebman, loaded on metal "Addressograph" plates that he packed into the trunk of his family car. A friend who operated Catholic Charities' mainframe computer moonlighted on the project after hours, transferring the data onto a reel of magnetic computer tape, so Viguerie could automate thousands of fundraising letters at a time. They were "my treasure trove, as good as the gold bricks deposited at Fort Knox." They became the foundation of an ideological empire.

Viguerie went to school on the august forebears who had mastered the arcane science of selling magazine subscriptions, encyclopedias, and charitable contributions by "direct mail"—what another mentor, Walter H. Weintz of *Reader's Digest*, called the "solid gold mailbox." "RAVCO" (for Richard A. Viguerie Company) began building a client base: the World Anti-Communist League, the National Right to Work Committee, the National Rifle Association, No Amnesty for Deserters, Citizens for Decent Literature—and George C. Wallace, for whose 1968 presidential campaign RAVCO raised some $6 million, an unheard-of 76 percent of the total. Each client—especially Wallace—helped Viguerie's mailing lists grow and grow and grow. So in November of 1974, Howard Phillips began recruiting for his new organization, which he named the Conservative Caucus, with a direct mail "piece" RAVCO sent to more than *two million* solid gold mailboxes:

Dear Friend:

Are you as sick and tired as I am of liberal politicians who: Force children to be bused; appoint judges who turn murderers and rapists

*loose on the public; force your children to study from school books
that are anti-God, anti-American, and filled with the most vulgar
curse words; give your tax money to communists, anarchist and
other radical organizations; do nothing about sex, adultery and
homosexuality and foul language on television?*

*Are you tired of feeling no power to change things? If so, why
don't you join the Conservative Caucus?*

It was signed by Governor Meldrim Thomson of New Hampshire, the
group's honorary chairman and a key figure in Reagan's 1976 presidential
campaign. It was likely written by Viguerie; crafting such hair-on-fire
prose was his favorite part of the job. Lurid invocations of sexual iniquity
were a constant—because, according to Weyrich, sex was "the Achilles
heel of the liberal Democrats." The pitch attracted half a million dollars
from 36,840 members in the next seven months. "There's no doubt about
it," Howard Phillips told an interviewer. "Viguerie really is the godfather."

Phillips began operating out of a warren of offices stuffed with other
conservative organizations above the Boston pizzeria of one of his board
members. A visiting journalist described him as a "great hulk of a man
who always looks as if he could use a trip to the cleaners." Naturally.
There was a civilization to win, and the hour was late. He wrote a leadership manual setting forth steps to organize a congressional district in
exactly 153 days. "By 1980," he said in 1976, "there will be conservative control of the House. The Senate will follow shortly thereafter." He
sounded like V. I. Lenin in 1913. No coincidence: studying radical organizers was one of his only hobbies.

In 1974, President Ford had tapped Henry Kissinger, co-architect of
détente with the Soviet Union, which some conservatives considered close
to treason, to be his secretary of state. Viguerie summoned a dozen outraged politicos to his Virginia headquarters to game-plan a strategy to tank
the nomination. What he saw horrified him: "The conservative leaders in
that room didn't know how to go from Point A to Point Z," he told one
of the many visiting journalists who came by his office to interview him
in the years to come. "I saw very dramatically that nobody knew how to
organize."

Paul Weyrich knew how to organize. He always claimed his awakening came while sitting in on a meeting of liberal activists trying to pass a
federal open housing bill—another of those legends that became right-
wing holy writ. A think tank officer was commissioned to write a research
report. A White House staffer was instructed to keep the president on
task. Senate aides were dispatched to ride herd on Capitol Hill. Civil
rights leaders agreed to flush protesters into the streets. *This* was how lib-

eralism had stolen Americans' conservative birthright, Weyrich reflected. "I saw how easily it could be done with planning and determination, and I decided to try it myself."

Weyrich was a former radio newsman from Wisconsin who turned his political hobby into a vocation after working for Barry Goldwater in 1964. In 1968, he converted to the Melkite Greek Catholic Church, having concluded that his natal Roman Catholics had fallen to liberalism. In 1971, Weyrich and a former senate staffer named Ed Feulner raised $250,000 from the beer magnate Joseph Coors and $900,000 from the petroleum heir Richard Mellon Scaife to found a more combative alternative to the American Enterprise Institute, a conservative think tank which, fearing for its IRS tax exemption and its reputation for scholarly probity, was loath to take sides in partisan disputes. For men like Weyrich, who drew their moral imagination from legends of the twilight struggle between lightness and dark as limned by former Communists like Whittaker Chambers, probity was counterrevolutionary. "We're not here to be some kind of Ph.D. committee giving equal time," the Heritage Foundation's first research director explained. Indeed Weyrich soon quit, finding Heritage not nearly aggressive enough. His next group, midwifed with the proceeds from a Viguerie letter signed by Senator Carl Curtis, was called the Committee for the Survival of a Free Congress. By Election Day 1974 it had distributed $412,248 in cash and services to seventy-one candidates. A reporter, noting that Weyrich's father was a German immigrant, said he retained "the precise orderliness of his Teutonic forebears, but none of their rollicking good humor. His mien is that of a formal, slightly constipated owl. He speaks in the clipped phrases of a man in a hurry."

Another piece of the New Right organizational puzzle involved campaign finance law. The legal vehicle known as the political action committee was not new; in 1943, after Congress prohibited campaign donations from labor unions, John Lewis and Sidney Hillman of the Congress of Industrial Organizations formed CIO-PAC to bundle individual contributions from members and route them to favored politicians. After the 1974 election, two veterans of the cutthroat world of conservative youth politics, Terry Dolan and Charlie Black, pointed Senator Helms to a loophole in the new post-Watergate laws intended to *limit* political fundraising: PACs could spend as much as they wanted on candidates, so long as they did not *coordinate* with the candidate. Helms helped them form the National Conservative Political Action Committee to provide candidates the things parties traditionally provided—press agentry, voter surveys, advertising consultants, campaign management, *cash*. But where the Republican National Committee was constitutionally bound to aid *all* Republicans, the National Conservative Political Action Committee need only nourish the ideologically correct. Dolan of NCPAC became the youngest figure in the New Right's central leadership cadre, with Viguerie, Phillips, and Weyrich.

NCPAC, CSFC, RAVCO, and more—this new Washington alphabet soup looked, and was reported as, a complex, variegated, and spontaneous grassroots revolt. Actually, the only thing complicated about it was the legal structure. One observer would soon write, "Any diagram of its organization looks like an octopus trying to shake hands with itself."

And, as Orrin Hatch's outreach from the Utah desert soon demonstrated, all it took was a single phone call to mobilize the entire beast.

HATCH CHECKED ALL THE NEW RIGHT'S BOXES. SOCIAL ISSUES: ONE OF HIS campaign promises was an anti-pornography law. ("We can define it as a law that would ban the sharing of human genitalia, for instance," he explained bashfully in a TV interview. "And the use of certain, uh, very vulgar, uh, words.") And social issues as a *wedge* to open up the possibility for undermining the reach of the liberal state—for instance, in another of his campaign proposals, organizing "a panel of the nation's top insurance actuaries" to work on privatizing Social Security. Paul Weyrich had met him at the Republican convention in Kansas City, and concluded Hatch might be presidential timber—though he was not yet even a Senate nominee, with no real prospect of becoming one.

Until, that is, a miracle arrived.

For months, his campaign had been frantically reaching out to Ronald Reagan. One influential Republican advised him to give up, for Reagan was said to follow an "Eleventh Commandment": never take sides in primaries. But Orrin Hatch was a very confident man. He became convinced that if they could only *talk* to Reagan, they could win him over. Aides pestered Reagan's man Michael Deaver by phone, until, worn down, Deaver told their pollster, Dick Wirthlin, a Mormon, about it—and Wirthlin said that his native state was trending so far right that this newcomer just might have a chance. The campaign was provided the phone number where Reagan was vacationing at the ranch of one of his rich friends. Hatch's novice twenty-five-year-old campaign manager dialed it and began fervently pleading his case. A faint voice interrupted:

"Tell Hatch I will be happy to endorse."

"Say that again, sir."

"Tell Hatch I'd be happy to endorse him!"

"Mr. Reagan, would you be so kind as to send us a telegram confirming our conversation for the press?"

"Well, yes, when do you need it?"

"The minute I hang up, sir!"

Full page ads ran the Sunday before the runoff election, prepared so hastily they contained a typo, "telegraph" instead of "telegram": "A TELEGRAPH FROM RONALD REAGAN TO ALL THE PEOPLE OF UTAH. 'To my many friends in Utah, I want to express my gratitude for the outstanding support I received from the people of Utah in my bid for the presidency. Now the time has come for me to do everything I can to endorse a man of quality, courage, discipline and integrity; a man of demonstrated ability, strength, and vision; a man who believes in individual freedom and self-reliance. With these qualities in mind, I enthusiastically endorse Orrin Hatch.'" On Monday, radio ads broadcast a recording of Reagan reiterating the endorsement. On Tuesday, Hatch beat the establishment's candidate in the runoff by a margin of two-to-one. The New Right had its first Senate nominee.

ORRIN HATCH'S OPPONENT, SENATOR FRANK MOSS, AUTHORED A LAND-mark 1974 law greatly expanding the power of the Federal Trade Commission to regulate industry. He published a slashing exposé of the nursing home business. He wrote the bills banning cigarette advertising on television and establishing federal standards for product warranties. He had been an outspoken opponent of the Vietnam War. He had also, the Mormon paper the *Deseret News* noted, earned "credibility among Utah voters as a hardworking senator who has kept his nose reasonably clean," with a "positive voting record where bread-and-butter issues are concerned"—which was traditionally how liberal Democrats had won over enough culturally conservative voters to win elections. And though he came off on TV as a bit of a smug liberal paternalist, he had recently received national publicity for going undercover to expose Medicaid fraud, and like Hatch supported a constitutional amendment banning abortion. He wasn't a Bolshevik. He was a Mormon.

He was also, however, a liberal Democrat in an increasingly conservative state, tacking to the right to save his hide: trumpeting support from mining executives, boasting of his filibuster of aggressive amendments to the Clean Air Act. Hatch replied that Moss supported legislation limiting strip mining and supported "federal land use planning"—which Skousen types considered a government conspiracy to Sovietize private land.

It worked. Moss began trailing. He started skipping debates. He sighed, "There's been a continued drift to the right."

He was correct.

In Moss's Utah, the Division of Health had announced its intention to add one part per million of fluoride to the state's drinking water to prevent tooth decay. Newspaper letters pages filled with outrage: "to require me to drink fluoridated water just because some 'experts' say it is not harmful is a violation of my rights"; "I resent others trying to force their will on me"; "Will a non-elected bureaucrat be able to force on us whatever he may wish?" Conservatives gathered enough signatures to get a proposition they called the Freedom from Compulsory Fluoridation and Medication Act on the November ballot, worded so vaguely that officials feared it might ban basic health measures like purifying drinking water with chlorine. The American Cancer Society complained that reports fluoride caused cancer were baseless; the anger did not abate. One citizen pointed out that most water went toward "washing, baths, watering the lawn, etc. Yet our wonderful bureaucrats want to spend millions of dollars, raise water rates, and [raise] taxes for a 97.5 percent waste. I am not opposed to fluoride but I am opposed to waste, and this is waste of the worst kind."

In Michigan, a University of Chicago economist and former advisor to Barry Goldwater's presidential campaign was neck deep in a campaign he believed was more important than electing Gerald Ford. "Proposition C" was an initiative modeled on a failed campaign Governor Reagan had sponsored in California in 1973 to cap taxes and limit state spending. On October 13, the professor was out electioneering for it when a long-distance phone call came from Stockholm announcing that he had won the Nobel Prize in Economics. His name was Milton Friedman.

Stockholm's choice signified an intellectual earthquake. Friedman was perhaps the most right-wing economist working at a top American university. His popular 1962 book *Capitalism and Freedom* argued, with breathtaking confidence, radical notions like that government should not regulate pharmaceuticals (unsafe drugs would be weeded out via the marketplace) and corporations must not make charitable contributions (their only legitimate function was making profit for shareholders). The next year, Friedman coauthored his academic magnum opus, *A Monetary History of the United States, 1867–1960,* which argued that government did not cure financial panics and depressions but caused them. Such ideas were so out of the mainstream that one economist compared him to a fencer attacking a battleship with a foil.

But "the bald little professor with the elfin face and the tart tongue," as a journalist described him, was also a relentless popularizer of those radical ideas. He had been writing a biweekly column in *Newsweek* magazine since 1966. For even longer, he spoke before just about any student audience that invited him—except at mandatory chapel services; those, he said, violated his ideal of liberty. His latest book, *There's No Such Thing as a Free Lunch*, was neatly summarized by Ronald Reagan in a radio commentary congratulating Friedman for his prize: "Business does not and cannot pay taxes. Only people pay taxes . . . the money they forward to internal revenue comes from the corporations' employees, customers, and stockholders. Politicians who advocate higher business taxes are really hiding the fact that they intend to raise the tax on all of us, as employees, consumers, and stockholders."

In Chicago, Friedman's wife and economist collaborator, Rose, told one inquiring reporter after another that since her husband considered Proposition C more important, he wouldn't be returning home for a press conference. She spoke on his behalf: "Milton is a conservative economist and the Swedish are quite left. . . . Your political leanings are as important for the prize as your achievement. Giving Milton the prize now is finally saying, 'He really isn't as bad as we thought he was.' "

As it happened, "the Swedes" chose not one but two American conservatives for Nobel Prizes that year. The other was Saul Bellow, whose novels cut the clichés of *bien-pensant* liberalism to ribbons, frequently in the voice of characters much like their creator—brooding, hyper-intellectual Jews who saw civilization collapsing around them as the unintended consequence of liberals' do-gooding schemes. He had also been a youthful Marxist. That made Bellow the pluperfect specimen of what had become known as "neoconservatism." A neoconservative, as their ex-Trotskyist godfather the *Wall Street Journal* columnist Irving Kristol defined it, was a "liberal mugged by reality." That perfectly described the protagonist of Bellow's 1970 masterpiece *Mr. Sammler's Planet.* "Mr. Sammler," Bellow wrote, "was testy with White Protestant America for not keeping better order. Cowardly surrender. Not a strong ruling class. Eager in a secret humiliating way, to come down and mingle with all the minority mobs, and scream against themselves."

And now Bellow and Friedman had won the prize Alfred Nobel had established to honor those "those who, during the preceding year, shall have conferred the greatest benefit to mankind"—quite the rebuke to those like the *Boston Globe* columnist who wrote, a few months later, that, given its domination by conservatives, the GOP was "not in the twentieth century yet."

On TV, five days after Milton Friedman's prize was announced, Norman Lear, the producer of *All in the Family*, debuted a situation comedy called *All's Fair* starring Richard Crenna as a conservative newspaper columnist and Bernadette Peters as his liberal girlfriend, with Irving Kristol as a consultant, and a young conservative named Ben Stein as a writer. ("Here's our resident fascist!" the warm-up comedian would introduce him at the live tapings.) The next week, in Utah, Ronald Reagan, on the same day Ford tried and failed to persuade him to campaign with him in California, began a two-day swing for Orrin Hatch before delirious crowds shouting for the sixty-five-year-old to run for president again.

Richard Viguerie made a rare appearance in the news. The National

Committee for an Effective Congress, a distinguished liberal D.C. institution cofounded by Eleanor Roosevelt, filed a complaint with the Federal Elections Commission against four New Right groups—two of which had little formal existence beyond incorporation papers filed by a Viguerie deputy. The four groups, the complaint charged, had funneled $7,500 to a conservative congressional candidate from Pittsburgh named Robert J. Casey—an illegal contribution from a corporation, the committee charged: the Richard A. Viguerie Company. Casey protested his innocence, credibly: he had used Viguerie to fundraise for his primary, then fired him—"frankly because his prices were too high." Viguerie protested his innocence, less convincingly. He termed the director of the National Committee for an Effective Congress "the godfather of the New Left," whining, "This is a two-way thing. They started it before we did." (The Federal Elections Commission made a preliminary finding that "a violation has occurred," then decided they didn't have the resources to commit to a prosecution.)

And in Utah, Viguerie's fundraising helped the underdog charge into the home stretch with a flurry of TV commercials branding his opponent a gun-grabbing, death-penalty-opposing "Eastern Seaboard liberal"; and Orrin Hatch won his senate seat with a comfortable margin—on the same ballot on which Utahans elected to protect state water supplies from adulteration by fluoride.

So did Daniel Patrick Moynihan. The merry Harvard policy intellectual had beaten three of New York's most prominent liberals for the Democratic nomination for United States Senate. The former Johnson and Nixon administration official was best known as the author of a 1965 Labor Department report attributing most of black America's woes not to racism but to its allegedly aberrant family structure. In Nixon's White House he recommended "benign neglect" of the nation's African Americans. Under Gerald Ford, as America's representative to the United Nations, he became known for his hawkish exhortations against the Soviet Union and the upstart Third World. And now he would be seated as the Senate's first neoconservative.

AFTER ELECTION DAY, NEOCONSERVATISM SCORED ITS MAJOR VICTORY BEhind the scenes.

The formerly Marxist immigrant Jews at the forefront of the movement had trained rigorously for political warfare in the hothouse ideological environment of the Depression, most famously in furious debates in the alcoves of the cafeteria of the City University of New York. They came of age in the passionate belief that Communism was the inevitable wave of the future. They still suspected this—only now they dedicated their lives to vanquishing it, for the survival of the West in the ongoing war for the world. Détente, they believed, was a fatal delusion. The ever-expanding cadres of quisling liberals within both parties, who refused to grasp that Communism was determined to conquer the world, were the Kremlin's objective allies.

They also still believed, as they had in their Marxist youth, that the most effective way to change history was to organize in subterranean cells, vanguardists guiding the hand of history by deploying the power of ideas. Thus did they burrow within the establishment to tutor Republican and Democratic politicians in these dire imperatives before it was too late.

Washington conventional wisdom had not been kind to them: it held that the world was "multipolar," and "interdependent," rivalry between the Communist and capitalist worlds no longer the central concern, that after the debacle in Vietnam the United States could no longer act as the world's policeman. David Rockefeller, president of Chase Manhattan Bank, established an organization called the Trilateral Commission in 1973 with the Polish-born strategic thinker Zbigniew Brzezinski to promote a new paradigm holding that such issues as terrorism, energy shortage, chaotic global financial flows, and environmental degradation were the problems of the future, that the Cold War framework of bipolar superpower rivalry no longer made much sense, and that North America, Western Europe, and Japan must devise institutions of cooperative—"trilateral"—responsibility to manage these new realities.

And when one of trilateralism's most dedicated converts, Jimmy Carter, won the presidency, and named Brzezinski as his national security advisor, the neocons girded their loins for war.

It began, naturally, underground. For years Gerald Ford's secretary of defense Donald Rumsfeld had argued that the arms agreements his rival Henry Kissinger had negotiated with the Soviet Union were not worth the paper on which they were printed: the Soviets simply built any weapons they pleased. Rumsfeld's neoconservative deputy Paul Wolfowitz had convinced him that the CIA's annual intelligence estimate of the Soviet's capabilities was biased toward détente. So Rumsfeld lobbied the president to generate a competing assessment of the Soviet threat.

CIA director William Colby was not amused by the bureaucratic insult. But in the fall of 1975, Rumsfeld engineered a bureaucratic coup that removed him. The following spring, at the height of the primaries against Reagan, President Ford took Rumsfeld's advice, authorizing a panel of sixteen "outside experts" to review the highly classified data by which the annual National Intelligence Estimate was produced, to write a counter-estimate of its own. The group became known as "Team B." (Team A was the CIA itself.) Team B concluded just what Rumsfeld wished it to: first, that the Soviet Union could wipe out virtually America's entire nuclear capability in a first strike if it wanted to; and second, that the USSR *did* want to.

Team B included Wolfowitz, a neoconservative Harvard professor of Russian history named Richard Pipes, and Paul Nitze, a hard-line defense intellectual who had served five presidents. Nitze had authored a similar report in 1957 whose leaked conclusions made their way into the 1960 presidential campaign when John F. Kennedy accused the Eisenhower administration of allowing a catastrophic "missile gap" with the Soviet Union. The report was based on inaccurate Air Force intelligence claiming the Soviet Union possessed as many as a thousand intercontinental ballistic missiles when in fact they only had four, a reality that proved that the Soviets were *not* in fact pursuing global dominations. The hard-liners remained unchastened by their mistake—as they would be again and again following many more bias-driven errors.

Team B focused on a class of evidence on Soviet intentions the CIA considered inherently unreliable: the writings of Soviet military leaders, like the officer who argued in a 1963 book that a nuclear war could be fought and won by the Soviet Union. They took this as open-and-shut evidence of official Kremlin policy, no matter that, during this period, Soviets had never even *tried* to build enough ICBMs to attempt it.

Team B also believed, based on speculative deductions, that the Soviets were increasing their commitment to civil defense. They thus concluded that the Soviets did not believe in the stabilizing doctrine upon which America's nuclear system was built: "mutually assured destruction," which held that because each understood that the other could obliterate them many times over, and that thus nobody could truly "win," the best way to prevent war was to negotiate a parity of firepower. Instead, Team B argued, the Russians were preparing to ride out a nuclear holocaust they intended to start.

Their analysis was concluded in time for Jimmy Carter's election. Then they leaked it to the press—in advance of the CIA's official National Intelligence Estimate, which would now look conspicuously weak. Well-placed, well-timed leaks were the most powerful weapon in the neoconservatives' arsenal. This one exploded with a political force in the megatons. In a season of supposed right-wing obsolescence, all Washington was atwitter with debates over whether détente hadn't been a naive, disastrous mistake, and whether America's weariness with its superpower status, which neoconservatives called "Vietnam Syndrome," was spurring unilateral disarmament.

"Vietnam Syndrome" was the coinage of neoconservative foreign policy's most prominent public face, Eugene Rostow, a law professor at Yale who had been an architect of the Vietnam War. In the fall of 1975, he had proposed forming a small bipartisan committee, with a membership so prominent it would be impossible to ignore, to warn the public that the Soviet peril was more dangerous than ever. Christened the Committee on the Present Danger, a tribute to a similar group formed in 1950 with that moniker, the committee was chartered in March of 1976; then, with the sedulousness of Dwight D. Eisenhower planning D-Day, Nitze took CPD underground, biding his time for a propitious moment to strike.

Nitze won a pre-inaugural meeting with the president-elect, lecturing him via a battery of charts and graphs about Team B's conclusions. Carter was unmoved. So the plotters publicly announced their new committee at an impassioned press conference. Cochairman Lane Kirkland of the AFL-CIO, said, "Our country is in a period of danger, and the danger is increasing. Unless decisive steps are taken to alert the nation, and to change the course of its policy, our economic and military capability will become inadequate to assure security." Others said the Soviet Union's "unparalleled military buildup" was "reminiscent of Nazi Germany's rearmament in the 1930s," and that Russia, which "does not subscribe to American notions of nuclear sufficiency and mutually assured destruction," was building forces "designed to enable the USSR to fight, survive, and win a nuclear war." Such language soon dominated security discussions in Washington.

"Carter to Inherit Intense Dispute on Soviet Intentions," the *Washington Post* front page trumpeted a little more than a fortnight before the inauguration, next to a picture of the incoming president looking meek in his plaid flannel shirt. A mainstream arms control expert protested that "there is a major effort underway to recreate the atmosphere of the 'missile gap' days of 1960." A liberal Democrat on the House Armed Services Committee called it "at least 75 percent bull." Senator Charles Percy, however, a bellwether centrist, said *he* was convinced: the Soviets were "seeking superiority."

The neocons' intention had been to establish a climate of opinion on the ground that would be very hard to reverse once a new president's team was in place. It was working. Jimmy Carter wasn't even inaugurated yet and his intention to work toward the elimination of nuclear weapons had already been on the rocks.

HOWARD PHILLIPS'S CONSERVATIVE CAUCUS MADE ITS PUBLIC DEBUT IN DEcember with a three-day convention in Chicago. The seven hundred delegates greeted Senator-elect Hatch as a conquering hero. A conservative Democratic congressman lamented that his party had been taken over by "out and out socialists." William Rusher said that Reagan "blew the chance" for a conservative victory in 1976 by sticking with the Republican Party.

Phillips promised "a guerrilla battle at the grass-roots level," suggested the creation of a national network of conservative newspapers, because "media is in the hand of the enemy," and announced the Conservative Caucus's intention to form a shadow cabinet. Congressman-elect Mickey Edwards noted the previous evening's episode *All in the Family*, in which the show's resident reactionary gleefully predicted that Ronald Reagan would be elected president in 1980: "Archie Bunker, a Democrat, is one of us!"

Much more media light was trained on the annual meeting of the Republican National Committee, picking a new party chairman. Bob Dole repeated the post-defeat conventional wisdom: Republicans could not win by "proudly clinging to a narrow notion of ideological purity." Reagan, conversely, appeared on *60 Minutes* and said that "the Republican Party is dead, unless it stands up and erects a set of principles around which people can rally and say, 'This is what we stand for,'" and that if he had been his party's nominee, Jimmy Carter would have lost.

Reagan's preferred candidate to lead the RNC—Utah party chair Dick Richardson, the person who had convinced Orrin Hatch to run—was defeated. The meeting crackled with right-wing energy all the same. Senator Hugh Scott, the guest of honor, railed against the "rednecks of Georgia," who "cannot long conceal their real views from the scrutiny of the media," and mis-called the opposition the "Democrat" Party, a baiting right-wing slur associated with Joseph McCarthy—and Hugh Scott was known as a *liberal* Republican.

Former Tennessee senator William E. Brock III, heir to a local candy company fortune, won. The media called him a compromise pick, but he was also plenty conservative: he was an original member of the committee that had drafted Barry Goldwater to run for president, and had won a senate seat in 1970 by savaging incumbent Al Gore Sr. for supporting school integration and opposing prayer in schools. Reagan blessed the pick, conditionally: "Recently he expressed to me his belief that the principles of the 1976 platform are those which can knit together a new majority. . . . He has my full support in his efforts to broaden the party in this way." In other words, Ronald Reagan supported Brock—so long as he acted like Ronald Reagan. The meeting also elected an Arizonan as Brock's cochair: a Sun Belt sweep.

Republican senators met to choose their leadership—elevating many conservatives, and booting several liberals. Orrin Hatch would head the Select Committee on Committees—an unprecedented honor for a new member. *Congressional Quarterly* labeled him "one of the most intriguing new figures in the Senate . . . Conservative interest groups are already counting on him as a spokesman in the 95th Congress, and some are even talking about him as a possible presidential candidate."

Word leaked that Jimmy Carter intended to pick JFK speechwriter Theodore Sorensen to head the CIA, with a mandate to reform the agency. Sorensen had been a conscientious objector during World War II. "What kind of insane asylum are we setting up here?" an unnamed intelligence official said to the press. Neoconservatives cunningly scotched the nomination, in part by intimating that Sorensen was complicit in Kennedy-era assassination plots against foreign leaders (even though neoconservatives *opposed* the reforms that banned such activities). Sorensen withdrew three days before the inauguration, saying "a substantial portion of the United States Senate and the intelligence community is not yet ready to accept . . . an outsider who believes as I believe." Carter praised the act as "characteristically generous and unselfish." Sorensen snapped back publicly: "Some say that Carter helped put the noose around my neck but that is not true. He helped kick the chair from underneath." It was a harbinger of bitterness to come.

The capital's foreign policy mood wrenched right. The *New York Times* reported that the CIA was revising their National Intelligence Estimate, to be placed on the new president's desk on his first day in office, in a more hawkish direction: "Team B (Hardline) Appears to Be More Influential Than Team A." Pollsters found Americans "significantly more sympathetic toward all military and defense spending": only 20 percent wanted the Pentagon's budget to be reduced, compared to 37 percent in 1972. A survey of listees in *Who's Who Among American High School Students* found 77 percent favored such an increase—and 39 percent wanted America to send troops if a Communist nation was involved in a Third World conflict.

Jimmy Carter was inaugurated on January 20. A black-tie-optional "Ball for the Unrepresented Conservative Majority" was held across the river in Arlington. Two days later, with Pennsylvania Avenue hardly swept clean from Jimmy Carter's inaugural parade, another stepped off: the annual "March for Life" mourning the Supreme Court's January 1973 *Roe v. Wade* decision legalizing abortion. In previous years hardly more than a handful participated. This time, police counted forty thousand, despite temperatures in the single digits. Newly sworn in congressman Bob Dornan—elected with the help of $65,000 raised by Richard Viguerie—said this was far more significant than Martin Luther King Jr.'s 1963 March on Washington: "The civil rights issue here is the difference between restricting the movement of free people and the slaughter of innocent people." Senator Hatch said federal subsidies for abortions made it "possible for genocidal programs as were practiced in Nazi Germany." *National Right to Life News* reported that when the march reached its terminus at the Capitol, "the crowd of chilled pro-lifers didn't want to

go home." So they carted their placards inside—"PICK ON SOME-
BODY YOUR OWN SIZE" (said a fetus in the womb, stern-faced, arms
crossed); "AUSCHWITZ, DACHAU, AND MARGARET SANGER";
"WE WANT LIFE NOT DEATH"—for impromptu citizen lobbying.

Thus did 1977 begin for the conservatives. Spiritual warriors; ex-
Trotskyist bureaucratic guerrillas; Nobel Prize–winning economists and
novelists; congressmen and senators armed with state-of-the art computers and a determination to make liberalism obsolete—objectively speaking, a promising emergent coalition. Even if, heading into Jimmy Carter's
first term, most people hardly knew it existed.

BOOK TWO
1977

multitudes. Then, over an open microphone, a child's voice rang out: *He is risen!*

That was just the kind of day it was—the kind of week. Monotonous

CHAPTER 3

"Hi, Jimmy!"

THE *WASHINGTON POST*'S PULITZER PRIZE–WINNING COMMENTATOR DAVID Broder offered a brooding reflection the morning of Jimmy Carter's inauguration: "Of the four presidents who have served since Dwight Eisenhower went peaceably into retirement, one was assassinated, one was rejected by his party, one was forced to resign and one was defeated for reelection."

He could have piled on further, non-presidential, traumas: a savage war that America lost; race riots; the assassinations of heroes like Martin Luther King Jr., Robert F. Kennedy, and Malcolm X; a polarizing youth rebellion that saw the generations lining each other up in their figurative sights as if preparing for an actual civil war—like the high school student who wrote, "The pigs' schools will be destroyed unless they serve the people," in an essay published in a widely read 1970 anthology, or, that same year, the popular movie *Joe*, in which a father shot his hippie daughter in the back.

1970 was also the year in which John Lennon and Yoko Ono had erected billboards around the country reading "WAR IS OVER IF YOU WANT IT." Subsequently, Richard Nixon worked to hound them out of the country as dangerous subversives. Now, however, here they were in Washington on Jimmy Carter's day—"looking," a reporter observed, for all the world "like a staid middle-aged married couple."

The civil war of the 1960s was over if you wanted it.

The day broke crisp and clear, after weeks of record blizzards—just as on John F. Kennedy's day. Other years, inaugural box seats had cost in the hundreds of dollars. This time they went for $25—and high officials had to pay for tickets, too.

Carter entered in an ordinary business suit he had bought off the rack, instead of the customary formal wear. Chief Justice Warren Burger administered the oath of office, then announced, "Ladies and gentlemen, the President of the United States." A roar issued forth from the assembled multitudes. Then, over an open microphone, a child's voice rang out: "*Hi, Jimmy!*"

That was just the kind of day it was—the kind of week. Monuments stayed open until midnight. Tourist buses drove past Amy Carter's new elementary school—an integrated public school. The "world's largest square dance" was held. An early morning People's Prayer Service for more than five thousand worshipers, was hosted by the Southern Baptists on the steps of the Lincoln Memorial, in twenty-five-degree cold. Nearly half the residents of Plains, Georgia, arrived in a chartered Amtrak train, in newly purchased thermal underwear. There was a special showing of *Yankee Doodle Dandy* starring James Cagney, and fireworks in Carter's campaign colors of green and white.

At the podium before the Capitol, Jimmy paused to etch the mood into history. Then he spoke:

"For myself, and for our nation, I want to thank my predecessor for all he has done to heal our land."

He reached down and shook Gerald Ford's hand: a healing act in itself.

The family Bible he had sworn his oath upon was opened to a verse from the prophet Micah: "What doth our Lord require of thee, but to do justly, and to love mercy, and to walk humbly with thy God." Humility was his theme. He spoke of our "recent mistakes," told Americans "your strength can compensate for my weakness," noted "that even our great nation has its recognized limits, and that we can neither answer all questions nor solve all problems. . . . We must simply do our best."

He asked for "fresh faith in an old dream." He nodded to Watergate, promising that "where there had been distrust" he would seek to restore "respect for the law and equal treatment under the law," so as to enable "our people to be proud of their own government again." This was met by an enthusiastic gust of applause. Another elephant in the room—Vietnam—was acknowledged with an avowal that America's strength would remain "so sufficient that it need not to be proven in combat: a quiet strength." This time he had to stop for a standing ovation.

It came as a surprise; that hadn't been written as an applause line. He got similar bursts when he said our "ultimate goal" was "the elimination of all nuclear weapons from this earth," for the three times when he promoted human rights as a foundation of America's foreign policy—and for his soaring concluding affirmation of "our belief in an undiminished, ever-expanding American dream."

It ended an unpretentious fifteen minutes after it began. The Carter family settled into a solar-heated reviewing stand in front of the White House—"symbolizing humility, closeness to the people, concern for the ecology," said the Georgia Tech engineer who designed it. The parade stepped off. Then, startlingly, the presidential limousine stopped moving. On TV you could hear loud cries from the crowd: *What emergency was this?*

They were cries of delight. The president, the first lady, and Amy stepped out and strode hand in hand down the middle of Pennsylvania Avenue. This was unprecedented. During the last inaugural parade, protesters had burned American flags and thrown wine jugs at Richard Nixon's armored limousine. A joyous chatter worked its way back through the rows of spectators, who started sprinting alongside, straining for a view, Jimmy and Rosalynn smiling and waving, nine-year-old Amy striking silly faces, as the first family walked the route of JFK's funeral cortege in reverse, as if unwinding the traumas of the 1960s altogether.

THE "PEOPLE'S INAUGURAL," THE PLANNERS DUBBED IT. *NEWSWEEK* CALLED it the "Denim Inaugural." The Washington establishment proved underwhelmed.

The night before, there had been a "New Spirit Inaugural Concert" at the Kennedy Center, featuring everyone from John Wayne to Johnny Cash to Aretha Franklin and the National Symphony. Dan Aykroyd of *Saturday Night Live* performed his Jimmy Carter impression ("*Ah* promise to be a *lusty* president"), which was when the guest of honor entered—laughing. He took his seat in the President's Box in the first balcony, shared a secret with Amy, who giggled (the picture made the front pages), led a standing ovation for Loretta Lynn, then for the poet James Dickey, who called Carter a "mythic hero." He received another "Hi, Jimmy!" when he stood up to leave after the performance. Carter replied by reaching down as if to touch that citizen's hand. Sally Quinn, the wife of *Washington Post* editor Ben Bradlee, daughter of one of Washington's most distinguished generals, all-but-uncrowned queen of Washington society, singled out that moment in her sour review in the *Post*: "There was no royal feeling."

Another citizen, stuck back in the fourth balcony, was even less pleased. That would be House speaker Tip O'Neill, an old-fashioned, back-slapping pol of the sort Carter reviled. He had requested a block of seats for his entourage. He called Carter's thirty-one-year-old campaign manager, soon to become his chief White House advisor, to demand to know why they were in the last row. Hamilton Jordan cockily volunteered to refund his money. Replied O'Neill, "I'll ream your ass, you sonofabitch!"

Both Senator Eugene McCarthy and columnist Robert Novak called the Carter team the "Snopes clan"; the *Boston Globe*, "the cast of *Gone with the Wind*"; Elizabeth Drew of the *New Yorker*, "a tight little group, suspicious of outsiders, protective of its power"; the word "yokels" was frequently heard. The nickname that stuck was "Georgia Mafia."

There was Ham Jordan, who wore work boots to the White House, and had hardly had any other job in his adult life except looking after

Jimmy Carter. His "disdain for members of Congress, as well as most politicians besides Jimmy Carter is well known," the *Wall Street Journal* said. Stuart Eizenstat, the skinny, bookish Atlanta lawyer in charge of policy, was compared to a cloistered monk. The mysterious "Mr. Kirbo"— Charles Kirbo, the quiet Atlanta lawyer and power broker, said to be Carter's most trusted advisor—was staying behind in Georgia. Carter's designated chief congressional liaison, Frank Moore of Dahlonega, Georgia, was described by a member of the Democratic leadership, in the *Washington Post*, as "one of those good 'ol boys," "not too bright." The only one not from Georgia, Midge Costanza, was the former vice mayor of Rochester, New York, a salty feminist whose only evident qualification for a West Wing office next to the president's was supporting Jimmy Carter before anyone else. Then there was budget director Bertram Lance, said to be Carter's best friend, who had loaned him the money that helped Carter beat one Washington insider after another for the presidential nomination. Identified in the press as a "country banker," he looked like one of those Southern courthouse bosses, the bad guys on TV news during the civil rights era. "What has been Mr. Lance's experience in the federal government?" asked Senator William Proxmire, whose banking committee was tasked with confirming him. "He has none—zero, zip, zilch, not one year, not even one week, not one day."

Thirty thousand invitations, in brown ink, on recycled paper, had gone out for the official inaugural "parties" (they used to call them balls), and one of them was reserved for eight hundred ordinary Americans in whose homes Jimmy Carter had stayed during the campaign. The *Post* reported— on the front page—that a Maryland man who had driven twenty-seven thousand miles in his own car campaigning for Carter since last February never received one. Though three Republicans in his town did, and a Louisiana man serving prison time, and the Reverend Jerry Falwel; but the staff volunteer in charge of rebutting Falwell's attacks on Carter had not, nor the president of the Norfolk and Western Railway—to a party he'd agreed to *host*.

How could this man run the federal government? He didn't even know whom not to snub.

WASHINGTON INSIDERS WERE LONELY IN THEIR COMPLAINTS. GALLUP found that 60 percent of Carter's countrymen, and 49 percent of those who had voted against him, thought more highly of him than they had on Election Day. The same percent believed he would reduce unemployment, 58 percent that he'd defeat inflation, 56 percent that he'd reduce the number of federal employees, more than three-quarters that he'd make the country more optimistic.

But the elites also had a point: you couldn't make Washington work only with outsiders. "The government is going to be run by people you have never heard of," Hamilton Jordan had boasted the previous summer, singling out two hoary fixtures of the defense establishment: "If, after the inauguration, you find a Cy Vance as secretary of state, and Zbigniew Brzezinski as head of national security, then I would say we failed. And I'd quit." Cy Vance was appointed secretary of state, Zbigniew Brzezinski national security advisor; Jordan did not quit—though even then the D.C. establishment criticized Carter for hiring "retreads." They criticized Carter for everything.

Came whispers that he might find a role in the administration for one of the most right-wing members of Gerald Ford's cabinet, William Simon, and name the anti-busing mayor of Pittsburgh to a Justice Department post. That enraged Washington liberals. Came news that he wanted the most liberal federal judge in the South, Frank Johnson, to head the FBI, and an antiwar activist, Sam Brown, to head the Peace Corps. That enraged Washington conservatives. Ralph Nader had first met Jimmy Carter in an Atlanta hotel room early in the primary season. He announced, back then: "Jimmy Carter is something special. . . . I've never met a politician quite like Carter, and I know a lot of them." Now he carped of his appointments, "There is not one who is not an old-line, money establishment corporate type." To Washington's permanent residents, their new neighbor couldn't win for losing.

THE DAY AFTER THE INAUGURAL, THE PRESIDENT'S REDNECK BROTHER Billy stepped out of a station wagon on F Street carrying a bottle of beer. Patrons poured out of the Old Ebbitt Grill for his autograph. He offered a review of the Kennedy Center concert: "I believe Amy and I could have written a better show."

America had voted for change, and here it was. But what, precisely, would it mean?

The new president had been an engineer. He had also been a Baptist missionary. The engineer believed that with the right information, perseverance, and his clear, clever mind, he could conquer any complexity. To reform the United States tax code, he began reading it—all one thousand pages. An old Washington hand compared him to his Navy mentor, the nuclear submariner admiral Hyman G. Rickover: "He has to know how every single engine or pump works. Carter is the same way. He looks upon government as machinery to be improved." The Baptist reached decisions in the manner of a biblical prophet wandering in the wilderness— then announced them with a confidence as if they were chiseled on tablets. Where the two modes of being, engineer and preacher, converged was in their passionate certitude, beyond compromise. An unusual base of mental operations for a president. Especially so in the 1970s, when governing was more than ever a profession of irresolvable conundrums.

The first issue to which Carter turned was healing a gaping wound from the 1960s: what to do with young men who had evaded service in the Vietnam War. Carter studied the problem from all angles. Surely, he prayed on it, too. Then he announced a hairsplitting conclusion, alien to both the dictionary and legal precedent, that while he opposed "amnesty" because it means "that what you did was right," he would "pardon" draft evaders, and would consider upgrading the discharges of approximately eight hundred thousand veterans from general to honorable, but would not review dishonorable or less-than-honorable discharges or penalties for desertion. An executive order to that effect was his first official act as president.

Barry Goldwater called it "the most disgraceful thing a president has ever done"; RNC chairman Bill Brock said it was "a slap in the face to all Americans and families who did their duty"; Governor Meldrim Thomson of New Hampshire ordered American flags in his state to fly at half-staff. The left was no less outraged. Vietnam Veterans Against the War pointed out that the deserters Carter's formula left in the cold were frequently from poor minorities, that the upgrading of general discharges stank of nepotism—for his own son had received a general discharge from the Navy for smoking marijuana. Congress passed a bipartisan amendment barring funds to implement the order. By summer, the Justice Department reported that hardly more than 10 percent of draft refugees had taken up the president's invitation to return to the United States.

The new president had managed to enrage potential allies from every point on the spectrum on his very first day.

HIS NEXT FOCUS WAS THE ECONOMY. CARTER INHERITED AN INFLATION rate of 5.8 percent, down from double digits a couple of years earlier. But the unemployment rate was an unacceptable 7.8 percent. On January 22, he proposed a stimulus package that would double public works spending and send a $50 rebate to every taxpayer. The rebate had been cooked up by the president-elect's technocrats as the quickest way to prime the economic pump. Carter sprung the unconventional notion on the Democratic congressional leadership only a few days before announcing it. The members most crucial to the fiscal success of the new administration—Russell Long of Louisiana, chairman of the Senate Finance Committee, said to know the tax code as thoroughly as the Pope knew the Lord's Prayer; Edmund Muskie, chair of the Senate Budget Committee; House Ways and Means chairman Al Ullman; Tip O'Neill—all thought it ridiculous. But, eager to accommodate the first member of their party to occupy the White House since 1969, they kept their beefs quiet.

Then there was energy. Until 1973, except during World War II, there really was no conception of energy as something susceptible to "shortages." The energy crisis that followed the embargo imposed that year on the U.S. by Arab members of the Organization of the Petroleum Exporting Countries to punish America's support of Israel in its war against Egypt had been a cataclysm while it lasted—but seemed to end almost as soon as it began. Subsequently, the price of petroleum in real dollars actually fell. Americans—including many senators—decided the crisis had been a temporary inconvenience staged by greedy oil companies. But when Jimmy Carter, following his election, donned his engineer's hat to study the problems he would inherit on January 20, he concluded that America *still* faced a dire energy crisis that required dramatic, immediate action.

That posed a political problem. As a ten-thousand-word "Initial Working Paper on Political Strategy" that Pat Caddell had sent Carter in December explained, trust in the government was at an all-time low. The White House "can promulgate energy regulations, can ask the people to conserve, but as long as the public refuses to believe that there is an energy crisis, they are unwilling to follow."

So the president endeavored to convince them that there was.

On February 2, he sat down in an austere wooden chair in the White House library, in a mustard-colored cardigan sweater. Behind the president, flames crackled: a fireside chat, just like Franklin Roosevelt used to do. Though FDR hadn't preempted *Charlie's Angels*.

"Good evening," Carter began. "Tomorrow will be two weeks since I became President. I have spent a lot of time deciding how I can be a good president. This talk, which the broadcast networks have agreed to bring to you, is one of several steps that I will take to keep in close touch with the people of our country, and to let you know informally about our plans for the coming months." The most urgent was "to develop a national energy policy."

He started with the energy problem the American people *did* know about: a shortage on home heating oil and natural gas in the Northeast during the record cold winter. "But the real problem—our failure to plan for the future or to take energy conservation seriously—started long before this winter, and it will take much longer to solve": it was, in fact, "permanent." Carter said that his special assistant for energy—Gerald Ford's defense secretary, James Schlesinger—was devising a complete national energy program that he would present to Congress on April 20, ninety days later, and that he soon would be asking Congress for a new cabinet-level Department of Energy "to bring order out of chaos."

(This was news to Congress.)

He promised "'town hall' meetings across the nation, where you can criticize, make suggestions, and ask questions," and radio call-in sessions "during which I can accept your phone calls and answer the questions that are on your mind."

And he ran through a laundry list of policy goals: laws to prevent strip mining and oil tanker spills; measures to fight inflation, unemployment, urban decay, and welfare fraud. He promised to start his plan to reorganize a "confused and wasteful" government "at the top—in the White House," with a one-third reduction in staff. He announced "a ceiling on the number of people employed by federal government agencies."

This was Carter the engineer.

Then came the Baptist minister, preaching from the Book of Caddell.

"If we all cooperate and make modest sacrifices"—he used that word, "sacrifice," six times—"if we learn to live thriftily and remember the importance of helping our neighbors then we can find ways to adjust and to make our society more efficient and our own lives more enjoyable and productive." He noted, "Because of the division in our country, many of us cannot remember a time when we really felt united. . . . During World War II we faced a terrible crisis—but the challenge of fighting Nazism drew us together. Those of us old enough to remember know that they were dark and frightening times—but many of our memories are of people ready to help each other for the common good. I believe that we are ready for that same spirit again."

Carter then implored Americans to lower their thermostats to 65 degrees during the day, 55 at night. He concluded, "If we are a united nation, then I can be a good president. But I will need your help to do it. I will do my best. I know you will do yours."

With the public, the address was a hit. But the legislators over whose heads the president was speaking lashed back. The next day, in a Senate Budget Committee hearing, Fritz Hollings lampooned Carter: "While he's asking us for sacrifice, his team is up here asking us to give everyone fifty bucks!"

Such stirrings from within a president's own party during the hundred-day honeymoon presidents traditionally enjoyed were unprecedented. They came at a time when Carter needed Democratic senators' help desperately. For, thanks to the neoconservatives, another key appointment was on the rocks.

PAUL WARNKE WAS A DISTINGUISHED AMERICAN DIPLOMAT AND DEFENSE intellectual who had served under presidents since Eisenhower. He was the highest-ranking Pentagon official to openly question the war in Vietnam, then served as chief foreign policy advisor in George McGovern's presidential campaign. In provocative articles in defense journals, he advocated bold moves by the U.S. to spur reciprocal actions from the Soviets to reduce nuclear arms.

Henry "Scoop" Jackson was the plodding, brilliant, and indefatigable fifth-term Democratic senator from Washington State. Jackson was quite liberal on some issues: running for president in 1972 he called for a federal jobs program; running in 1976 he called for breaking up big oil companies. But he was *very* conservative on defense. After Jimmy Carter named Warnke as chief negotiator for a new strategic arms limitation treaty with the Soviet Union, Jackson became determined to block his confirmation. Jackson was the Capitol Hill patron of the neoconservative defense intellectuals—bereft that, of the fifty-three names they had put forward for jobs in the new administration, only one was hired (as special negotiator for Micronesia). Paul Nitze was particularly perturbed; he had wanted Warnke's job for himself.

Roland Evans and Robert Novak's "Inside Report" was published in hundreds of newspapers and was perhaps Washington's most influential column. On the morning of Carter's fireside chat, Evans and Novak said, "Critics of Warnke see a distinct possibility that the Carter administration will experiment with unilateral reduction of the American nuclear deterrent," so his confirmation "could conceivably snowball into a major fight." Robert Novak, as it happened, was also a favorite conduit for neoconservative leaks. No Senate had ever rejected a cabinet-level appointment so early in a new presidency, let alone a Senate controlled by the president's party. Scoop's minions were determined to make history.

Nitze testified before the Senate Foreign Relations Committee that Warnke's ideas were "demonstrably unsound," "asinine," "a screwball, arbitrary, fictitious kind of viewpoint that is not going to help the security of the country."

Senator Thomas McIntyre of New Hampshire, a liberal Democrat, replied:

"Do you think you are a better American than he is?"

"I really do."

On February 7, Senator Robert Byrd of West Virginia, the majority leader, shocked everyone by announcing that he was keeping an "open mind" on Warnke, because "many senators think he is too soft to negotiate with the Soviet Union." Howard Baker of Tennessee, the minority leader and a Republican moderate, echoed Byrd. The two leaders' willingness to publicize such doubts meant the nomination was hanging by a thread.

At the president's first press conference reporters suspiciously well informed on the fine points of nuclear diplomacy peppered him with questions about Warnke's fitness. Evans and Novak's third column on the fight in as many weeks pointed up contradictions between Warnke's previous, liberal arguments and the more conservative things he was saying now. Then, before the Armed Services Committee, Warnke was grilled on writings like a 1975 article in which he described the nuclear arms race as a folie à deux that left both sides less secure. The U.S., he had written, could "be the first off the treadmill." The committee's hostile questions had been cued up from an anonymous memo composed by a Jackson protégé named Richard Perle that had artfully distorted Warnke's arguments. Warnke was rocked on his heels—and then, under questioning from Scoop Jackson, was knocked nearly flat on his back. Jackson ticked off thirteen separate weapons systems and upgrades, then demanded Warnke confirm under oath that he had opposed them. Warnke, to prove he was strong, replied that he had reversed many of those earlier views—which made him sound weak.

The New Right joined in: Paul Weyrich and Richard Viguerie engineered a deluge of sixty thousand anti-Warnke letters to senators. Warnke was confirmed as chief negotiator on March 9 by a shockingly slim margin of 58–40. "I don't think there were twenty-five votes against him three weeks ago," Scoop Jackson boasted.

Warnke's job would be negotiating treaties that required two-thirds of the Senate to pass. Fifty-eight was nine votes shy of that. The Soviets surely received that message about President Carter's weak negotiating position loud and clear.

CAPITOL HILL WAS EVEN ANGRIER WITH THE PRESIDENT ABOUT THEIR DAMS. In the middle of February word spread that the Engineer in Chief had got ahold of the Army Corps of Engineers' General Plan, studied it from cover to cover, then devised a "hit list" of dozens of federal water projects to eliminate. And if your interest was sensible stewardship of the nation's finite natural and financial resources, many of his decisions seemed sound. Wrote a historian of America's failed water policies, "One of the projects would return five cents in economic benefits for every taxpayer dollar invested; one offered irrigation farmers subsidies worth one million dollars each; another, a huge dam on a middling California river, would cost more than Hoover, Shasta, Glen Canyon, Bonneville, and Grand Coulee combined."

But what looked like an inexplicable boondoggle to an engineer often looked like a matter of life and death for the congressmen in whose districts those projects sat.

On February 18, the White House began informing Congress of eighty projects Carter intended to cancel. He hadn't consulted his interior secretary, who was humiliated to learn about that plan while stepping off a plane in Denver for a conference of Western governors—who were livid. Congressman Mo Udall of Arizona said that if Carter went ahead and canceled his dams, "Tucson and Phoenix are going to dry up and blow away." Enraged legislators threatened to hold Carter's priorities hostage. Carter's $50 tax rebate hemorrhaged votes, barely surviving a March 10 vote in the Senate Finance Committee.

Came the social event of the season, the annual Gridiron Club dinner when one-half of official Washington put on silly costumes to lampoon the other half. The curtain rose on a phalanx of Carterites, garment bags over their shoulders, singing, to the tune of "Marching Through Georgia," "*Repent, repent, you Yankees don't forget / We won, we won, you ain't seen nothing yet / We give all the orders now, and you'll like what you get.*" Scarlett O'Hara and Rhett Butler, dead broke, showed up at the White House, begging for a job; "Billy Carter" gave them a $50 tax rebate instead. A ragged remnant of Republicans nursed their battle wounds and plotted their comeback over golf in President Ford's new hometown, Palm Springs. A jokester playing Senator Ed Brooke, the only black Republican in Congress, reminded one playing Ronald Reagan that the GOP was doomed without black support. "I guess you're right," Reagan replied. "The party needs you, and I need you. Now gimme my driver, pick up my bag, and let's get on with it." From the podium, the real Howard Baker said the president had originally wanted to appoint his brother head of the CIA, but Billy hadn't wanted to be in charge of anything he couldn't spell.

All in good fun. Except, this year, the contempt was real. The biggest project on the hit list was a $900 million artificial waterway in the Red River basin in Louisiana, home of Russell Long—who promptly announced his willingness to take Carter's legislative priorities hostage. House majority leader Jim Wright of Texas wrote his colleagues to rally them to "help defend the Constitutional prerogatives of Congress." Robert Byrd, in whose home state of West Virginia a dam collapse had recently killed sixty people, roared: "A project is not 'pork barrel' to someone who . . . sees his home swept away." After meeting with the president on water projects in his state, Senator Paul Laxalt of Nevada told his close friend Ronald Reagan to leave his options open for 1980: "My gut tells me that I've just met with a one-termer."

Chastened, Carter pared the hit list to eighteen. Byrd was not appeased: on April 5 he said he'd kill the $50 rebate unless further compromise was forthcoming. Carter replied that the rebate was absolutely imperative, with his labor secretary insisting it would be impossible to get the unemployment rate below 7 percent that year without it.

Then, a week later, on the eighty-sixth day of his presidency, Carter began his fifth news conference with the announcement that since the economy had grown at nearly double the rate in January, February, and March as the previous quarter, he was canceling the rebate.

Senator Edmund Muskie had spent months twisting senators' arms and massaging the public for an idea he thought foolish. "What kind of fucking fiscal policy is this, Charlie?" he now raged to the chairman of Carter's Council of Economic Advisors, Charles Schultze. "Should we propose stimulus during the slowdown, oppose it when Christmas sales turn up, propose it again when the severe winter descends, and once again oppose it when spring raises the temperature and our spirits?"

You had to wonder: the next time Jimmy Carter asked congressional leaders to carry the ball on a controversial issue, how could they know he wouldn't leave them high and dry again?

HE STILL ENJOYED A HONEYMOON WITH THE PUBLIC, WHICH STILL MYSTI-fied the establishment. Columnist Mary McGrory compared his popularity to that of Detroit Tigers pitcher Mark "The Bird" Fidrych, who'd become a fan favorite for his charmingly oddball rituals on the mound: "He talks to the ball as lovingly and intimately as Jimmy Carter talks to the American people."

People loved the way Carter forced cabinet members to give up chauffeured limousines, and tried to sell Richard Nixon's beloved presidential yacht the *Sequoia* to save $800,000 in upkeep. How he and Rosalyn showed up unannounced three days after the inaugural to attend Sunday school at the First Baptist Church of Washington, and how he ordered that White House functions end at midnight to save staff overtime pay—with no hard liquor served. They loved his visit to the Department of Housing and Urban Development, where he lectured employees "who live in sin" to get married and "those of you who don't know your children's names, get to know them"; and Amy's White House tree house; and the sleepover party she hosted with her best pal from school, the daughter of a cook at the Chilean embassy; and her baptism by total immersion alongside the teenage daughter of an employee at the Liberian embassy.

And they loved *Ask President Carter*, during which, on Saturday afternoon, March 5, any American anywhere could ring him up to ask any question, live on the radio. Hosted by CBS News's beloved anchorman Walter Cronkite, Carter fielded forty-four calls from thirty-two states over two hours. Mike McGrath of Warsaw, Indiana, asked a question with four follow-ups about his taxes. ("If I can't find the answer before we go off the air, I will call Mike personally and give him the answer, if I can," the president promised.) A thirteen-year-old suggested shipping snow to the West to help with their drought. A Mrs. Phyllis Rogers of Albuquerque asked if it might "be possible to eliminate the word 'drug' from drug store advertising" to discourage drug abuse, which the president said he thought was a splendid idea. (*Saturday Night Live* did an affectionate lampoon. One frightened caller was suffering a bad LSD trip. The president calmly talked him down: "You did some Orange Sunshine, Peter. . . . Do you have any Allman Brothers? . . .")

He held his first town meeting, in Clinton, Massachusetts. And allowed four NBC camera crews to spend an entire day in the White House, with portable microphones clipped to his and his staffers' ties, affording NBC nearly carte blanche to choose clips for their *A Day with the President* documentary. One of the few moments the White House censored was a private meeting between Carter and Egyptian president Anwar Sadat, in town for a state dinner—but not the one right before, when Carter inquired whether Sadat might like to visit the restroom.

All were huge hits—and he even began breaking through, for the nonce, with the Washington insiders. Judged David Broder, "He has transformed himself from the very shaky winner of a campaign into a very popular president whose mastery of the mass media has given him real leverage with which to govern."

That was the idea. Garry Trudeau's *Doonesbury*, the first comic strip to win a Pulitzer Prize, featured an acerbic series of cartoons starring a suave blue-jean-clad operator named Duane Delacourt who ran the White House's "Office of Symbolism." ("Yeah, Jennifer, on the next fireside chat . . . I'd like to try a leisure suit on the boss.") The fictional Carter so appreciated his work he elevated Delacourt to cabinet status. ("Okay by me. I don't have to take a pay raise, do I?" "Heck, no! In fact, I'm sure you've got a cut coming to you.") Funny, but serious: symbols mattered. They determined, press secretary Jody Powell believed, "the single most crucial aspect for any president": the public's degree of trust in him. And it worked. "The percentage of those who have placed their trust in Jimmy Carter has streaked from the 51 percent who voted for him into the seventies and eighties," the *Post* announced. The respect even extended to Clark Clifford, a towering figure in the Washington establishment going back to Harry Truman's presidency—just the sort of person Carterites disdained. He hymned "a return of the confidence of the people in our government."

Now, the White House sought to spend some of that political capital to persuade the public that there was an energy crisis, and to propose bold action to fix it.

On April 18, Carter gave a televised speech from the Oval Office setting forth the massive bet upon which he intended to stake the success of his presidency: comprehensive energy legislation. A replica of Harry Truman's famous desk plate—"THE BUCK STOPS HERE"—sat in front of him as he intoned, "Tonight I want to have an unpleasant talk with you about a problem unprecedented in our history. With the exception of war, this is the biggest challenge our country will face during our lifetimes. The energy crisis has not yet overwhelmed us, but it will if we do not act quickly. . . . Our decision about energy will test the character of the American people and the ability of the president and the Congress to govern this nation. This difficult effort will be the moral equivalent of war, except that we will be uniting our efforts to build and not to destroy."

In-house, they called it the "sky is falling" speech. The purpose was to light a fire under an audience of 535—whom he addressed directly two nights later in his first speech to a joint session of Congress—the first time in his fifty-two years Jimmy Carter had set foot on the floor of that body. Engineer-like, he presented a complicated menu of proposals that he and James Schlesinger had devised, almost entirely in secret, without input even from White House staff. Two days after that came a televised press conference, his second in a week.

The president was on TV four out of six days, a veritable miniseries—way too much, the establishment now decided.

The *Boston Globe* lectured that this was "Jimmy Carter leading the television industry by the nose," called his popularity "abnormally high," and said TV had "all too readily acquiesced in the construction of that popularity." William Safire of the *New York Times* found NBC's documentary reminiscent of China's recent worshipful state funeral of Chairman Mao. Capitol Hill jokers coined the mocking acronym "MEOW" for Carter's "moral equivalent of war" formulation: as if tinkering with natural gas subsidies, researching synthetic fuels, and lowering thermostats somehow compared to the global crusade that defeated Tojo and Hitler.

Again, the public disagreed. His approval ratings ranged from 69 percent to 80 percent; Gallup had Congress at 36 percent. As for how many of the American people agreed with the president that the energy crisis was serious, that stood at 86 percent. "A rash of books about new presidents has become a well-established tradition" the Cox newspaper syndicate noted. "But publishing experts say that Jimmy Carter is inspiring a record glut"—like *A Cookbook of Carter Family Favorites*, starring hush puppies, fried fish, and grits.

BUT PUBLIC FASCINATION COULD CUT BOTH WAYS: LIVE BY THE SYMBOL, DIE by the symbol. His image-makers had managed to hoist him on a high pedestal indeed—a dangerous height from which to fall.

Some auguries:

On the ninety-ninth day of his term, the *New York Times* highlighted worrying quotes from unnamed aides that Carter was "brutal" and "intimidating" to his staff and refused to delegate, so immersing himself in detail that he had trouble making decisions.

Ham Jordan's reckless disdain for ordinary political alliances was becoming more and more troublesome, his Butch-Cassidy-and-the-Sundance-Kid pairing with Jody Powell progressively less charming. Like the time Powell was asked by a female reporter about rumors his friend didn't wear underwear. He replied that she would be the last to know. They were unrepentant: "stepping on toes and alienating groups of people" was just part of the job, Jordan said.

Another festering problem was Carter's radically impolitic ambassador to the United Nations. Andrew Young was a black former Georgia congressman and civil rights movement hero. He had recently said that England "almost invented racism," and that Cuban troops stationed in the African nation of Angola had brought "a certain stability and order." He apologized to the British ambassador—then stepped in it even worse on the subject of Cuban troops, averring that Americans should not "get all paranoid over a few Communists, or even a few thousand Communists." Carter, personally close to Young and grateful to him as one of his most prominent black surrogates during the campaign, got his old friend's back: "I do agree with it. It obviously stabilized the situation." Retorted a Republican congressman from North Carolina, "They stabilize you upside the head."

Here was a new discontent to organize. Richard Viguerie compiled an "'Andrew Young Must Go' Action Kit," distributed to the two hundred thousand addresses on the Conservative Caucus's national list. It included a vitriolic letter signed by Meldrim Thomson bearing the New Hampshire governor's official seal of office, a photograph of a child being burned to death, and a "handwritten" explanation composed to make it sound like this "wanton act of violence by black power terrorists," with whom "Andrew Young has long sided," had not taken place in Africa, but—well, just maybe in a town near you.

CHAPTER 4

Iceberg

THE WEEK OF JIMMY CARTER'S INAUGURATION, ABC AIRED AN EIGHT-PART television miniseries version of Alex Haley's best-selling slavery epic *Roots*. Executives had worried that sixteen hours of slavery would turn off viewers, so rather than waste a weekly prime-time spot for two months, they ran it on consecutive nights. It turned out their worries were misplaced. When the next week's Nielsen ratings were published, the top eight slots were occupied by *Roots*.

More than half of the American population watched all or part of it. A black professional from Nashville told a reporter that as his family sat before the TV, "We couldn't talk. We just cried." A journalist wrote, "This may be the first time millions of whites ever really identified with blacks as human beings."

There was, however, one public figure who disagreed. He would soon be the subject of front-page *Los Angeles Times* feature reporting that he had a "significant head start over anyone else in the drive for the Republican nomination." "Very frankly," Ronald Reagan said of *Roots*, "I thought the bias of all the good people being one color and all the bad people being another was rather destructive." He also couldn't imagine staying home eight nights in a row to watch it.

Reagan was doing a lot of dissenting from conventional wisdom. For instance, he alone found reason for optimism among Republicans in Gerald Ford's loss: "We're outnumbered two to one by the Democrats, or better, and yet we got almost half the votes. . . . If the polls are correct, if you take the label off our platform, a majority of people in this country subscribe to those beliefs." The only problem was that Republicans "haven't done a very good job of salesmanship."

For his part, Reagan got out and sold. A "New Year's Resolutions for Republicans" column argued that the GOP had a marvelous chance to attract black voters by providing them the same thing "most white citizens want: a chance at a decent job, a home, a good education for their kids, and streets free of crime"—rather than an accursed fate as "lifetime recipients of a dole." That was Reagan's political message on nearly every topic:

Republicans just needed to stop apologizing for what they knew to be true—which was conservatism. Five days before Carter's inauguration, he gave his first speech of 1977 to the Intercollegiate Studies Institute, an organization formed in 1953 to evangelize conservatism to college students. The timing coincided with the annual Washington meeting of the Republican National Committee. His words were a flare sent out to party leaders about what a Reagan-led GOP would look like.

The text had been drafted by former Nixon speechwriter William Gavin, who called himself a "street corner conservative"—a conception deeply influenced by the Catholic social philosopher Michael Novak, a passionate defender of Eastern European "white ethnics" against what both Novak and Gavin saw as the assaults to their traditional values from the nation's liberal elites. Gavin had explained how he intended to braid this perspective into Reagan's rhetoric in a memo to Michael Deaver: the speech would argue "conservatism is a majority belief, not a cult"; that Republicans "have to act and talk like a majority or we will lose support on the left *and* the right; blue collar and ethnic issues are very important"; that Republican rhetoric too often "sounds like a tape of a Rotarian banquet"; and that " 'family' is a key concept." From the podium before the ISI, that came out sounding like this: "I refuse to believe the Good Lord divided this world into Republicans, who defend basic values, and Democrats, who win elections. . . . The new GOP should have room for the man and woman in the factories, for the cop on the beat, and the millions of Americans who have never thought of joining our party before."

The argument closely resembled what George Wallace said on the presidential campaign trail in 1968 and '72. And, also, the strategizing of Chuck Colson in Richard Nixon's White House to craft a "new majority" by recruiting "hard hat" union members into the Republican Party. It recalled, too, the sentiments of Jesse Helms, in that 1975 speech arguing that the nonvoting 62 percent of the electorate who did not vote could become the foundation for a "conservative majority." And also the argument of a book that same year by *National Review* publisher William Rusher called *The Making of the New Majority Party*. In Reagan's words, the secret to reaching voters "usually associated with the blue-collar, ethnic, and religious groups, who are traditionally associated with the Democratic Party" was via "the so-called social issues—law and order, abortion, busing, quota systems." A Republicanism that could comfortably wear a blue collar, such thinking went, could put paid to the Democrats for good. Though for it to work, Reagan insisted, the party would have to erase the "country club big business image that, for reasons both fair and unfair, it is burdened with today." That he was able to convincingly argue that in the sumptuous ballroom of the Mayflower Hotel, only days before one of his wife's regular appearances in the *Los Angeles Times* society column (in one she wore "Adolfo's gray lace dress with the romantic high collar"), was a testament to his rhetorical skill.

IT ALSO HELPED THAT REAGAN WAS A LEADING ADVOCATE FOR ONE THE most potent social issues of all: restoring the death penalty. Lethal injection was best, he said in 1973: "Being a former farmer and horse raiser, I know what it's like to try to eliminate an injured horse by shooting him. Now you call the veterinarian and the vet gives it a shot and the horse goes to sleep—that's it."

Violent crime was skyrocketing: 4.6 murders per 100,000 Americans in 1950, 9.8 per 100,000 Americans in 1974. But America had not executed a criminal for almost a decade. A de facto national moratorium on executions had been formalized in 1972 when the Supreme Court, in *Furman v. Georgia*, decided 5–4 that the way death was administered violated the Constitution's ban on cruel and unusual punishment. That same year, in California, the state Supreme Court overturned a death penalty statute signed by then Governor Reagan. The death penalty sentences of the likes of Charles Manson were commuted to life imprisonment—and 70 percent of California voters voted to reinstate it in a referendum. In the summer of 1976, the U.S. Supreme Court spelled out in *Gregg v. Georgia* what guidelines for death penalty statutes were required to pass constitutional muster, and in quick succession thirty-seven states passed them. The first execution came in Utah, three days before Carter's inauguration. A murderer named Gary Gilmore had been glad when the jury sentenced him to death—and irritated that the American Civil Liberties Union was fighting to keep him alive. Then the ACLU exhausted their appeals, Gilmore faced the firing squad—and suddenly the issue was the hottest thing going.

In his next newspaper column, Reagan criticized opponents for relying on emotional arguments—forcing him to stoop to their level: "What about the murderer's victims? Their names aren't household words. One was a young man working in a gas station to earn his way through law school. The other was a hotel manager earning money to go back to school. Both were fathers of infant children." Though Reagan wasn't as gung-ho as John Connally, who said that if Gilmore's execution were televised it would serve as "an even more impressive deterrent," just as Arab countries discouraged robberies by cutting off thieves' hands in the public marketplace.

Civic bloodlust was a tributary in a roaring right-wing social-issue surge. A coalition of Miami conservatives called Save Our Children filed six times the required signatures to schedule a referendum to repeal Dade County's gay rights ordinance; and, on the same day, in a special election for an open congressional seat in Minnesota, a farmer named Arlan Stangeland won a shocking upset against an aide to Walter Mondale, stealthily outspending him with direct mail money raised by Richard Viguerie. He was the first Republican to capture the district in eleven years, and, the *Washington Post* explained, was "district leader of an activist 'New Right' group, the Conservative Caucus." The next week in Miami, many of the same activists who had circulated the anti-gay-rights petitions convinced the Dade County School Board to cancel a desegregation plan. "We don't want to lose control of our children," one activist explained, "and that is what happens when they are bused." Following their victory, Citizens in Favor of Neighborhood Schools reconstituted themselves as a lobby against an Equal Rights Amendment ratification bill pending in the state legislature.

And, also just then, a new biweekly newsletter made its way into the increasingly crowded mailboxes of conservatives. It promised to "print the news one seldom finds—but should—in the mass media." All conservative magazines said that, of course. What made this one different was that it promised an exclusive column by Ronald Reagan on the front page of every issue. It was the newsletter for Reagan's brand-new political action committee.

REAGAN'S PAC HAD BEEN CONCEIVED AT A STRATEGY MEETING WITHIN DAYS of his loss of the 1976 nomination. Under federal law, donations arriving too late to be spent were Reagan's to control as he wished. So his campaign organization, Citizens for Reagan, was reorganized as a "multi-candidate political action committee" called Citizens for the Republic. Reagan's longtime press aide Lyn Nofziger was hired to direct it, at a salary greater than that earned by the head of the Republican National Committee. He began his work with nearly $1 million in the bank and a mailing list of 183,000—which made it the largest conservative political action committee in the nation. The fundraising letters received by the lucky 183,000 began:

Dear Friend:

YOU CAN BET THAT SOMEWHERE IN THE VAST LABYRINTH OF THE FEDERAL BUREAUCRACY THERE'S A FILE ON YOU!

It may be a Social Security record, an FHA record, or an OSHA record.

It may be at HUD or the Department of Agriculture. Or it may be at the Federal Elections Commission.

BIG BROTHER GOVERNMENT WILL GO TO ANY LENGTH TO KEEP A TAB ON YOU.

By the end of 1976, CFR had raised $9 million, with more of that total coming from checks under $25 than from those over $1,000. Members got a newsletter subscription, a sturdy membership card with Reagan's drawing and signature and the legend "THE CAUSE WILL PREVAIL BECAUSE IT'S RIGHT" on it, magnetized for display on your refrigerator—and a place on the committee's direct mail list, rented out for additional revenue to allied conservative causes.

The PR office of Deaver and Hannaford continued its work for Reagan on the other side of town. Nofziger's niche was assembling a grassroots following, evaluating politicians requesting CFR cash, and publishing the newsletter. Deaver and Hannaford handled Reagan's business dealings, public relations, speeches, newspaper column, radio scripts, and media appearances—which were increasingly frequent. On March 1 he appeared on *Meet the Press*, thumping Carter's not-yet-announced energy program ("this isn't an energy program, it's a tax program"). The next morning Evans and Novak's "Inside Report" described Citizens for the Republic's "presidential-sized plans and budgets" and noted an unusual stop on Reagan's upcoming itinerary: a party fundraiser in "liberal, ethnic, heavily Democratic Rhode Island"—an invitation fellow 1980 prospects Howard Baker and John Connally had declined.

That day he also he taped his next batch of radio commentaries. They included the story of the railroad ticket-taker in London who refused to help foil a purse snatching because "there was nothing about helping a policewoman in his union rulebook," a paean to Campus Crusade for Christ's "Athletes in Action" program, a warning of dangers to Americans' liberty posed by the federally subsidized passenger rail company Amtrak, which reminded listeners that "Benito Mussolini began his career by making the trains run on time"—and Reagan's first introduction to his followers of a policy idea that would come to define him.

High taxes were a longtime Reagan obsession, one of the issues that had made him a conservative in the first place. Voters were not equally obsessed; the failure of Michigan's "Proposition C" tax limitation initiative in November by a vote of nearly two to one demonstrated that. On economics, in fact, public opinion leaned rather left—one of the reasons the New Right preferred recruiting with social issues. Ever since 1975, the Opinion Research Corporation, a Republican firm, had been asking citizens whether they favored keeping "taxes and services about where they are." A consistent 45 percent said that they did. America wanted to keep the government services they had, and they seemed willing to countenance the taxes they had to pay to keep them—or perhaps even pay more to *increase* them: seventy percent said the government should be responsible for providing a job for anyone who wanted one, and in a *New York Times*/CBS poll, a majority favored a government-provided minimum income.

But what about this *new* idea? "For four years a young New York congressman named Jack Kemp has been urging on his colleagues a tax plan based on common sense and backed by a record of success," Reagan announced breathlessly. "The pattern from his plan comes from the early 1960s and the late president John F. Kennedy. It calls for an across the board tax cut to provide incentives for long-term economic growth." Kennedy, Reagan claimed—not quite accurately—"cut the 91 percent bracket to 70 percent and the 20 percent bottom bracket down to 14. His Keynesian advisors swore that government would suffer a great loss of revenues. . . . Instead the stimulus to the economy was so immediate that actual tax revenues equaled a $54 billion increase in six years."

Jack Kemp was proposing a loaves-and-fishes policy miracle. Ronald Reagan was one of his first major converts. It was a development that would be central to his political story.

SO, HOWEVER, WOULD BE RIVALRIES WITHIN HIS POLITICAL ORGANIZATION— and they came to a head then, too.

The personnel involved would shift from year to year. The battle lines stayed the same: pragmatists versus ideologues. Presently, the latter category was represented by Deaver and Hannaford—buttoned-down businessmen far more interested in doing whatever it took to advance Reagan's political fortunes, even if it meant compromising their hero's ideological instincts. Nancy Reagan adored them, especially Deaver. The chief ideologue at this point in the story was Nofziger—a loudmouthed, pun-spouting, rumpled, cigar-smoking bon vivant who was never much for political discipline. Nancy *despised* him.

The tensions became impossible to ignore that March when Howard Phillips's Conservative Caucus approached Reagan to join, or at least endorse, its shadow cabinet. Reagan wanted to, but Deaver and Hannaford advised him that Phillips was recruiting extremists no serious presidential contender should have anything to do with. There was Congressman Ron Paul, the radical Texas libertarian who wanted to do away with the Federal Reserve. "Secretary of State" Meldrim Thomson wanted his New Hampshire National Guard units to be issued nuclear weapons. "Attorney General" Bill Rusher wanted to replace the GOP with a third party. Congressman Larry Patton McDonald of Georgia, as "Secretary of Defense," was in the John Birch Society and kept a photograph of Spain's fascist dictator Francisco Franco on his office wall. The "Secretary of Health, Education, and Welfare" was a Long Island high school principal who had barricaded himself in his office rather than accept a New York City Board of Education order to reinstate a troublemaker he had expelled without due process.

Nofziger disagreed—and slipped an article into the next *Citizens for the Republic Newsletter* lauding the shadow cabinet. Next, Deaver blocked Reagan's wish to campaign for Arlan Stangeland in the Minnesota special election—but Nofziger passed his campaign $1,000 in money from the Reagan political action committee, then ran a headline boasting "First CFR Candidate a Winner" in newsletter number three.

AND THEN ANOTHER SOCIAL ISSUE CAME TO THE FORE: THE FIFTY-YEAR-old debate over an Equal Rights Amendment to the Constitution—in the most striking possible dramatization of the conservative energies coursing just beneath the surface of Jimmy Carter's America.

Feminists first proposed the ERA in 1923, three years after the 19th Amendment guaranteed women the right to vote. Its first article was to read, simply: "Equality of rights under the law shall not be denied or abridged by the United States on Account of Sex." Its second gave Congress the power to enforce that with appropriate legislation. The Republican platform endorsed it in 1940. The Democrats endorsed it four years later, for it was more controversial for them: ERA's most vocal opponents were union leaders worried that it would strike down laws giving special protection to women factory workers. Versions that preserved such protective legislation passed the Senate in 1950 and 1953 but were unacceptable to feminists; progress stalled once more when John F. Kennedy appointed to head the Labor Department's Women's Bureau a feminist who preferred "specific bills for specific ills" instead of the ERA. But momentum exploded with the "second wave" feminist revival of the late 1960s, and in 1970 the House passed the ERA 352–15. In 1972 it passed the Senate 84–4. The first ratification by a state legislature, in Hawaii, followed thirty-two minutes later. Six more came, all unanimously, in the next seven days, twenty more in the next twelve months—often without debate. By 1974, thirty of the thirty-eight states needed to sear the amendment into the Constitution for good had signed on. First lady Pat Nixon wore a pro-ERA bracelet; and back then even Governor Reagan supported it. President Ford was an outright enthusiast, as was his successor.

In 1974, George Gallup reported that public support for passage was 79 percent. In 1976, *Time* replaced its customary "Man of the Year" selection with a dozen pioneering "Women of the Year," declaring that "the women's drive penetrated every layer of society, matured beyond ideology to a new status of general—and sometimes unconscious—acceptance."

Then, two days before Carter's inaugural, conservative Indiana ratified, pushed past the finish line via Rosalynn Carter's lobbying. Only three more state ratifications were left to go. Passage seemed inevitable.

Inevitable, that is, to those not noticing a parallel set of cultural developments.

The best-selling paperback of 1974, still on the *New York Times* paperback list for seven weeks in 1976, was a book from a fundamentalist press by a born-again Christian in Miami named Marabel Morgan. The media paid most attention to *The Total Woman*'s naughty advice to housewives about how to spice things up in the bedroom. A more typical passage, however, argued that if your husband was driving recklessly, you could pray for a policeman, but you mustn't complain; a wife's duty, Morgan wrote, was to "listen attentively to her husband, to admire his every trait, to pander to his every whim." As Scripture said, in Ephesians 5:22–23: "Wives, submit yourself to your husband, as unto the Lord. For the husband is the head of the wife, even as Christ is the head of the Church." "The total woman is not a slave," Morgan reassured readers. "She graciously chooses to adopt to her husband's way, even though at times she desperately may not want to." Because "it is only when a woman surrenders her life to her husband, reveres and worships him and is willing to serve him, that she becomes really beautiful to him."

A similar book sold two million copies. *Fascinating Womanhood: A Guide to a Happy Marriage* by the Mormon author Helen Andelin advised women to "visit a shop for little girls and study their clothes," because "childlikeness will make a man feel bigger, manlier, and more like the superior male." Eleven thousand trained instructors taught "Fascinating Womanhood" seminars around the country. *The Spirit-Controlled Woman*, by Beverly LaHaye, a pastor's wife from suburban San Diego, sold 500,000 copies. "The woman who is truly Spirit-filled will want to be totally submissive to her husband. This is a truly liberated woman," she explained. "As the woman humbles herself (dies to self) and submits to her husband (serves him), she begins to find herself within that relationship. A servant is one who gets excited about making somebody else successful. . . . You can live fully by dying to yourself and submitting to your husband." *The Secret Power of Femininity*, by Maurine and Elbert Startup, advised women to practice saying into the mirror, "I am just a helpless woman at the mercy of you big, strong men." And in *The Gift of Inner Healing*, the president's own sister Ruth Carter Stapleton counseled a woman desperately unhappy in her marriage, "Try to spend a little time each day visualizing Jesus coming in the door from work. Then see yourself walking up to him, embracing him. Say to Jesus, 'It's good to have you home, Nick.'"

A popular seminar program, "Eve Reborn," was taught by a woman named Susan Key, who grew up in Dr. W. A. Criswell's Dallas church, beneath a giant banner reading "A BURDEN OF GUILT" over an image of an apple. Women could be redeemed from Eve's sin of defiance, she told a *Texas Monthly* interviewer, by submitting to their husbands as Christ submitted to the cross—"since there is no authority that is not ordained of God."

The reporter sought clarification: "But you don't mean something like Hitler?"

Yes, she replied, even Hitler.

FOR WOMEN RESPONDING TO MESSAGES LIKE THESE, THE NOTION OF FEMI-nism penetrating every layer of society was an existential threat. By 1977, millions of them had signed on as soldiers in an anti-ERA guerrilla war to fight it. Their general was one of the most effective political organizers America had ever seen.

Phyllis Schlafly was born in 1924 to a devout Catholic family in St. Louis. Her father lost his job as a heavy-equipment salesman when she was six; her sister and mother went to live with relatives. Schlafly was sub-sequently raised in six different homes, all rented. Her mother worked in a department store—a humiliation, for she craved respectability. So did her daughter.

In the Girl Scouts, she piled up merit badges. At thirteen she single-handedly produced the school newspaper. At her Catholic high school, she graduated as valedictorian, with honors in classical languages and French. She wrote in her diary: "I've been very lucky in being in such a class at such a school, where the girls were not only gifted, and really nice, but who came from the good, long standing St. Louis families, whose homes I was always proud to visit." Her own family, meanwhile, could not afford store-bought dresses.

Her father found steady work in New Deal agencies. He despised that; he considered the New Deal to be a "war on the free-enterprise system." So did his hyper-political daughter. In 1946, when she was twenty-two, she called upon a St. Louis alderman running for Congress. He hired her on the spot as his campaign manager. "I had to keep looking at her to re-mind myself I was not talking to a fat old cigar-chomping ward heeler," he recalled. That same year her father hit it big with a patent he'd been tin-kering with. *So there*: in the fullness of time, conservatism and capitalism had provided—no government meddling necessary, thank you very much.

She graduated Phi Beta Kappa in three years from Washington Univer-sity in St. Louis while working the overnight shift testing guns at an ord-nance plant. She earned a master's degree at Radcliffe with straight A's. She won first prize in a national essay contest sponsored by the *Washington Daily News*, opposing a postwar version of affirmative action: "The cards are stacked against the enterprising and ambitious person," she wrote, "in favor of . . . the unqualified veteran." She took a job at Washington D.C.'s top conservative think tank, the American Enterprise Institute, where she refined her signature skill: crafting popular arguments for conservatism. She returned to St. Louis, hoping to teach at Washington University—but the dean said a woman could never "handle a bunch of tough-minded, battle-scarred GIs." She found a fortuitous substitute: publishing the newsletter of the St. Louis Union Trust Company, under the tutelage of a boss who mentored her in the arts of small-scale publishing. Then, she met the man of her dreams, John Schlafly, a thirty-nine-year-old lawyer, right-wing activist, and scion of a banking family in the small Mississippi River town of Alton, Illinois—and never held a paying job again. In 1952, she ran for Congress.

Press reports called her the "powderpuff candidate"—even as one newspaper described how she "offset the distracting influence of her femininity by . . . speaking with conviction as she exhibited various charts and maps," presenting her integrated military strategy for the Korean War while unspooling facts and figures such as the distance covered by China's mortar cannons, which she said outranged America's by a full mile. That, she suggested, might be the responsibility of Communists like Alger Hiss who had infiltrated the government. She won the primary. Newspapers ran pictures of her in an apron, standing at the stove. (Caption: "She doesn't allow politics to interfere with her wifely duties.")

This introduced what would become Schlafly's trademark: her insistence that the biblically ordained role of wifely subservience could be perfectly harmonious with a life of accomplishment. Later, she would begin her anti–Equal Rights Amendment speeches, "First of all, I want to thank my husband Fred, for letting me come—I always like to say that, because it makes the libs so mad!" Conservative ladies adored it. The example she set—squaring the circle of Christian duty and worldly ambition—was the greatest gift Phyllis Schlafly provided them.

She spied leftist conspiracies everywhere. Her husband had been a delegate for the conservative candidate Robert Taft at the 1952 Republican convention in Chicago. When Dwight D. Eisenhower won, conservatives called it "the steal of the century." Schlafly recorded how she believed that victory occurred: "The Madison Avenue public relations firms, the big national magazines, and four-fifths of the influential newspapers in the country turned themselves into propaganda organs to build the Eisenhower image. . . . All the vast publicity machine that always goes into concerted action for a liberal cause had gone to work." American elites ruled by pulling the wool over the eyes the American majority Schlafly believed to be ineluctably conservative.

She lost in the general election by nearly 30 points. An editorial memorialized her as "the best twister of facts who has appeared on the local political scene." Undaunted, she began organizing like-minded women into what she called the "pro-American underground"—work she compared to God's injunction to Abraham before He smote Sodom and Gomorrah: "Our republic can be saved from the fires of Communism which have already destroyed or enslaved many Christian cities if we can find ten patriotic women in each community." She churned out pamphlets, study guides, newsletters. Her husband produced the American Bar Association's "Report on Communist Tactics, Strategy, and Objectives." She hosted an anti-Communist radio show. In 1964, she self-published *A Choice, Not an Echo*, a 123-page paperback, with which she devoted herself to the election of Barry Goldwater, persuading rich angels to buy cartons of the book in bulk; with her anti-Communist underground as its distribution network, delegates to the Republican convention complained of receiving as many as fifty copies in the mail. By fall, there were 3.5 million in circulation. The book's argument was that "a few secret kingmakers based in New York selected every Republican presidential nominee from 1936 through 1960."

Yes, Phyllis Schlafly knew how these things worked. So she was well prepared when, in 1967, the kingmakers came for *her*.

She was by then the National Federation of Republican Women's vice chairman—who usually became chair at the next convention by acclamation—a crucial position, because female volunteers were the Republican Party's lifeblood. This time, however, the establishment put up an opponent to run against her; and, to better control the outcome, scheduled the convention, originally set for California in 1966, to take place in Washington, D.C., in 1967. Schlafly claimed she learned about the move in a phone call from "one of the extreme left-wing newspapers"—the *Washington Post*. She the word forth to her network: *the steal was on.*

At the convention, Schlafly's ladies wore eagle pins. (Isaiah 30:31: "They that wait upon the Lord . . . shall mount up with wings as eagles.") Schlafly deluged undecided delegates with expensive gifts. Her loyalists shouted "Rockefeller whores" at her rivals. (A seventy-two-year-old grandmother from Chicago said it reminded her of newsreels of Nazi Germany.) Her opponents spread rumors that Phyllis was a member of an armed underground right-wing militia, and that, raising six children while doing all that political organizing, she was guilty of "child neglect." The

New York Times described it as "one of the bitterest political fights now under way in the nation."

Schlafly lost. Her army of three thousand eagles crowded into a basement convention hall to decide what to do next. One had drafted a charter for a breakaway federation. An impassioned speech from Ronald Reagan's daughter Maureen dissuaded them. Instead, Schlafly collected names and addresses. That became the founding mailing list for the *Phyllis Schlafly Report*. Starting in 1968, then for another half a century, the newsletter went out monthly—originally to those three thousand names, eventually to tens of thousands more. And in February 1972, as the ERA passed Congress, the *Phyllis Schlafly Report* announced a new crusade.

THE HEADLINE ASKED, "WHAT'S WRONG WITH 'EQUAL RIGHTS' FOR Woman?" The article answered: just about everything.

It began with an axiom derived from Catholic doctrine: the family was "the basic unit of society." It then argued that "the laws and customs of our Judeo-Christian civilization" assured "the greatest single achievement in the history of women's rights": the right of a woman "to keep her own baby and be supported and protected in the enjoyment of watching her baby grow and develop." The "Christian tradition of chivalry" obliged men to support women. The American free enterprise system "stimulated the inventive geniuses" that rendered women's lives a paradise of labor-saving miracles. All these and more, Schlafly wrote, ERA would terminate "absolutely and positively." A crucial part of the argument was Schlafly's claim that that the 1963 Equal Pay Act and the 1972 Equal Employment Opportunity Act already provided women equal access to jobs, education, and fair compensation—that these were, yes, *desirable* things, and that if these remedies to secure them were not working, she would be glad to support new laws that did; but this was not what feminists were actually after. Since they "view the home as a prison, and the wife and mother as a slave," feminists believed that marriage and the family must be *destroyed*—but since they could never admit that in public, to mask "the deadly poison masquerading as 'women's lib,' " they doled out the "sweet syrup" of talk about equality.

She concluded as she always did: with a call to action. "Let's not permit these women's libbers to get away with pretending to speak for the rest of us. Let's not let this tiny minority degrade the role that most women prefer. Let's not let these women's libbers deprive wives and mothers of the rights we now possess. Tell your Senators NOW that you want them to vote NO on the Equal Rights Amendment. Tell your television and radio stations that you want equal time to present the case FOR marriage and motherhood."

And so they did.

Within days, one of Schlafly's loyalists from the National Federation of Republican Women, Ann Patterson of Oklahoma City, called her in a state of excitation. She said she had previously been an ERA supporter, until the essay changed her mind—passionately. She contacted a friend on the rules committee of the Oklahoma House who promised to delay consideration of an ERA ratification bill to give opponents more time to lobby. "So Phyllis," Patterson exclaimed, "I took your newsletter to the state legislature and they rejected ERA!"

That September, Schlafly gathered a hundred such supporters from thirty states and founded STOP ERA. The acronym stood for "Stop Taking Our Privileges." The logo was the familiar octagonal street sign. William F. Buckley, an old friend, put her on his PBS program, *Firing Line* to make her case. In January, "Equal Rights Amendment Slows Down" in the *Washington Post* quoted her: "The laws of all 50 states make it the primary obligation of the husband to support his family and his wife with a home. These would be invalidated by the ERA."

She developed a phalanx of regional leaders. In Oklahoma, it was a country singer, firefighter's wife, and Christian school founder named Beverly Findley. In North Carolina, it was Dot Slade, an unmarried John Birch Society activist who sold Tupperware to fund the crusade. In Tennessee in 1974, Tottie Ellis, who called ERA the "Extra Responsibility Amendment," had raised five hundred citizen lobbyists to win a legally questionable "rescission" of the state's ratification. A woman named Rosemary Thomson became Schlafly's key deputy in Illinois after studying biblical prophecy and arriving at a passage she believed commanded her to become a political activist. (Her nickname in the movement was "Isaiah.")

In Texas, it was a Bible teacher named Lottie Beth Hobbes, an author of books with titles like *Victory Over Trials: Encouragement from the Life of Job*. She called her organization Women Who Want to Be Women and created one of the movement's potent weapons at her kitchen table: a photocopied flyer that exhorted women to believe "God created you and gave you a beautiful and exalted place to fill. No women in history have ever enjoyed such privileges, luxuries, and freedom as American women." It set forth the ERA's alleged horrors—"The aim of NOW and other pro-ERA groups is to totally 'desexrigate' everything. . . . All women will register at age 18, subject to military duties including combat. . . . You can be forced to put your children in a daycare center. . . . *DO YOU WANT TO LOSE YOUR RIGHT NOT TO WORK?*" It was illustrated with clip art of two ladies chatting on the telephone. It became known as the "Pink Sheet." It was soon underneath windshield wipers, inside church bulletins, and stacked high on county fair literature tables nationwide. The STOP ERA coordinator in Georgia credited it with stopping the ERA's progress there in its tracks.

Women Who Want to Be Women; Mississippians for God, Family, and Country; Mississippi's FIG ("Factually Informed Gals"); Arizona's HOW ("Happiness of Women"); Utah's HOTDOG ("Humanitarians Opposed to Degrading Our Girls"); "Operation Wake-Up" in New York; Women for Responsible Legislation in Oklahoma; the Lotties and Totties and Dots—as with Richard Viguerie's New Right, it only looked chaotic. "Schlafly took scattered ad hoc organizations," wrote the most incisive scholar on the anti-ERA movement, sociologist Ruth Murray Brown, "folded them into a national one, coordinated their activities, facilitated communication among them, made sure that the members were provided with new suggestions, trained them in lobbying and speaking, and encouraged them to persevere."

They worked without pay, free of office expenses; their kitchen tables were their offices. Husbands were pressed into solidarity by pillow-talk pleas similar to the arguments made by the female nineteenth-century anti-suffrage movement this resembled: unfeminine activity in the cause of preserving femininity was licensed by exceptions to the normal rules. Fundamentalist preachers, reluctant to involve themselves in "worldly" politics, traditionally seen as inherently sinful, were persuaded by demonstrations of feminism's violation of God's "plan for the family" as revealed in the Bible. Church became the movement's arterial network. "People wonder how I got all this organized," Findley told a researcher. "It's really very simple. I just notified the people I worshiped with."

Schlafly ran annual Eagle Forum meetings in St. Louis like boot camps: workshops all day, with speakers in between, and also during meals; pastors and priests were brought for Sunday worship—"so you couldn't get away from her," one volunteer laughed. Rich underwriters funded training with organizers like Paul Weyrich. Debate drills were recorded with video cameras, attendees studying their progress mastering Schlaflyite rhetorical tactics—the most powerful being weaponizing liberals' arrogance against them: remain cool, calm, and reasonable-sounding, avoid arguments that were received as extremist—until invariably, the exasperated adversary lost her cool in response. Like the time Betty Friedan bellowed at Schlafly, "I'd like to burn you at the stake!" Schlafly coolly responded, "I'm glad you said that because it just shows the intemperate nature of proponents of ERA."

Then it was back home to disseminate their newly acquired skills through the countryside.

It was a little like how Lawrence of Arabia described his insurgent Arab army that captured great chunks of the Middle East during World War I—"a thing invulnerable, intangible, without front or back, drifting about like a gas"; or Von Clausewitz on guerrilla warfare, where "the element of resistance will exist everywhere and nowhere."

Schlafly's own contribution to counterinsurgency theory could be found in *A Choice, Not an Echo*: "The strategy of politics," she wrote, "like an iceberg, is eight-ninths under the surface." Just so with her own army: they were invisible—until, that is, a state legislature put the ERA on the docket. Then, her battalions would pounce: hand-delivering loaves of homemade bread to legislators and their staffs, wrapped in anti-ERA poetry; clogging state capitol switchboards and mailrooms; dispatching scores of bodies to crowd plazas like the one in front of the capitol in Springfield in Schlafly's home state of Illinois, the only Northern state that hadn't yet ratified—where legislative sessions became annual ERA circuses.

In the autumn of 1976, the year that *Time* magazine said the drive for women's rights had "matured beyond ideology to a new status of general—and sometimes unconscious—acceptance," the anti-ERA ranks suddenly swelled by millions when the Church of Jesus Christ of Latter-Day Saints, which taught its girls to sing "When I Grow Up I Want to Be a Mother" in Sunday school, declared the ERA a violation of "God-given feminine instincts" that would lead to "an increase in the practice of homosexual and lesbian activities." Then, shortly before the inauguration, the Georgia legislature turned back ratification. On February 11, heavily Mormon Nevada did the same. North Carolina was to decide the question on March 3; Jimmy and Rosalynn Carter personally called wavering legislators to plead for their vote. Howard Phillips's Conservative Caucus orchestrated thousands of anti-ERA postcards. What may have finally turned the tide for defeat by two votes in the state senate was a rumor spread by the John Birch Society that the ERA would require the abolishment of rape laws—though activists credited their "prayer chain," for which women signed on for hour shifts throughout the day. "We asked God that if this thing was not in His plan that he would see to it that it was defeated," said the Raleigh housewife who organized it.

Two days later, in Illinois, where the ERA had previously passed both houses—but never in the same session—senators decided that ratifying constitutional amendments would henceforth require a two-thirds vote. On March 15, as Jimmy Carter fought for his $50 rebate, Paul Warnke was sworn in to negotiate an arms control agreement with the Soviet Union, and the House voted to deprive the president of funds to carry out his draft-pardon plan, the ERA was defeated once more in Oklahoma after four last-minute defections. On the 16th, it went down in Missouri.

IT DIDN'T EXACTLY HELP THAT THE PRO-ERA SIDE RESEMBLED ONE OF THE lumbering regular armies that were flattened by T. E. Lawrence's guerrillas during World War I: the opposition kept blindsiding them. In fact, it had taken two such blindsiding defeats, in ERA endorsement referenda on the 1975 general election ballots in liberal New York and New Jersey, before a formal organization coordinating the ratification fight was even pulled together.

It was called ERAmerica, and it was a hyper-bureaucratic blunderbuss, a top-down federation of Washington- and New York-based nonprofits for whom the ERA was far down their list of organizational priorities—a structure that bogged down its decision-making to a standstill. It had Republican and Democrats cochairs. Liz Carpenter was an executive at the establishment public relations firm Hill & Knowlton and a former LBJ White House aide. The other cochair was former Michigan Republican Party chairman and Ford presidential campaign official Elly Peterson, known as the "mother of the moderate Republicans." They were, in other words, consummate Washington insiders—with few contacts in the state capitols where the fight was actually taking place. That couldn't be more different from Schlafly's everywhere-and-nowhere resistance. STOP ERA had been incorporated with the minimum bureaucracy required by law, with a single charismatic leader in control. Less than a year after it began, a consultant recommended ERAmerica be shut down as a "dismal failure."

One reason for their failure was the difficulty of articulating what the ERA would *do*. On the one hand, many legal experts predicted that the answer was: not much—which made it hard to insist it was a pressing necessity. On the other, no one could actually say for certain; that, ultimately, would be up to the federal judges charged with interpreting it. This provided the opening for Schlafly's side to deploy another classic tactic of guerrilla warfare: seeding *uncertainty*. National opinion polls showed the ERA to be very popular in the abstract—part of what lulled the establishment into such disastrous complacency. But then, in state after state, when ratification was called up for legislative consideration, Schlafly's forces would swoop in, armed with horror stories about what its passage would entail. And these were harrowingly specific.

They said judges would order women drafted into combat. (Probably not, but early on advocates made the disastrous decision not to fight this canard, reasoning that feminists should embrace the duties of full citizenship as well as the benefits.) They said it would place housewives' Social

Security benefits at risk. (More likely the opposite: married women did not directly earn Social Security from the government, and if a woman left her husband, she received none of his benefits. The ERA could conceivably fix this.) Perhaps, according to the John Birch Society, the "Marxist pressures and abuses inherent in the ERA" would lead to "co-sexual penal institutions" and "the legalization of rape." Or, an an Eagle Forum pamphlet distributed in the South suggested, "the sexes fully integrated like the races"—including ending separate men's and women's restrooms. That was almost certainly not so—but even just the suggestion of defilement of that most private of social spaces proved an exceptionally powerful weapon.

And, just maybe, ERA would even let men marry men and women marry women—a strange notion first raised in the 1972 Senate hearing by Senator Sam Ervin, who so despised the ERA that he lent Phyllis Schlafly his senatorial franking privileges. Schlafly amplified that concern with cheerful aplomb. "Why do homosexuals and lesbians support ERA?" one of her pamphlets asked, answering, "Because it will probably put their entire 'gay rights' agenda into the U.S. Constitution." Anti-ERA debaters loved to repeat the true story about how a liberal-minded county clerk in Colorado issued a marriage license to two men. A cowboy approached the same clerk to demand she let him marry his horse. (Thinking fast, she thought of an excuse to deny the license: Dolly was eight years old, and thus underage.)

Gay marriage seemed a slippery slope that, once breached, threatened the bounds of God's order itself. So did the ERA itself. It felt threatening to its opponents at the very core of their being. Ruth Murray Brown, the sociologist, asked Texas anti-ERA activists what their primary reason was for joining the movement. The most common answer, cited by 56 percent, was that the ERA was "against God's plan for the family." The second most common answer was that "it would encourage an un-biblical relationship between men and women." And for evangelicals, to call something un-biblical, or against God's plan, was no minor thing. It was not a matter of live and let live—you handle your family in your way, I'll handle my family in mine. The central evangelical tenet—the reason they *evangelized*—was the "Great Commission" in Matthew 28: "Therefore go and make disciples of all the nations." Fighting that which was "unbiblical" was more, even, than a matter of life and death. It was a matter of *eternal* life and death. Given that, it was hard for a Christian woman to complain about the burden of attending a couple of meetings a week, or making a few more phone calls, or baking a loaf of bread for a wavering state representative.

Brown made an even more crucial finding. This one came from North

Carolina, where the ERA had just been cut down at the last minute in the state senate by a mere two votes: her survey of Schlafly's activists there discovered that half had never before participated in politics in their lives. In politics, it is the rarest of gifts to be able to rouse an entire new population to throw themselves passionately into activism—especially so in a time of generalized political apathy.

Just like Howard Phillips—a crucial Schlafly ally—liked to say: *We organize discontent.* Tapping an existential discontent like this was the kind of development with the potential to birth revolutions. Florida's legislature was due to schedule a crucial ERA vote sometime in April; Phillips vowed to post 150,000 pieces of direct mail to rally the troops. Ronald Reagan joined the fight with one of his radio commentaries, merging Schlafly's favorite argument with his own: "It's just vague enough that it will almost certainly end up in the courts. The judges will then become legislators, designing its impact by their ruling from the bench. Bureaucrats would do the rest. Isn't it time we had a little less distortion of our federal system from the courts and the bureaucrats, rather than inviting more?"

SIMULTANEOUSLY, FLORIDA ACTIVISTS WERE GALVANIZED BY THE EMERgence of another tributary to merge into the social issue stream. The Dade County Commission passed an ordinance delivering civil rights protections to gays and lesbians. It wasn't that long ago that such a development would have been inconceivable. God's plan for the family was again being set on its ear.

In the 1950s, the federal government devoted more resources to purging gay men and lesbians than it did Communists. The state government in Tallahassee was especially proactive: in 1964, a legislative committee formerly infamous for hounding civil rights activists released the report *Homosexuality and Citizenship in Florida*, known as the "Purple Pamphlet" for its lurid violet cover featuring two men locked in passionate embrace, which concluded that "a great many homosexuals have an insatiable appetite for sexual activities and find special gratification in the recruitment to their ranks of youth. . . . If we don't act soon we will wake up some morning and find they are too big to fight." Handsome young men at Florida State University were thus paid $10 for the name of each homosexual who approached them, so that individual could be expeditiously expelled. Quite simply, before the 1970s, homosexuals had no rights which heterosexuals were bound to respect.

Having a sex life for gay men meant furtive encounters in restrooms or public parks, risking vigilante attack or arrest, or frequenting seedy bars run by the mafia that were often raided by police. Either way, arrest could mean losing your job or family—or commitment to a psychiatric ward, where you might find yourself strapped down and jolted with electricity as erotic images flashed on a screen. After a raid of a New York bar called the Snake Pit, a young man terrified of such exposure jumped from a window of the police station. He impaled himself on a fourteen-inch iron-spiked fence two stories below. But on June 28, 1969, the modern gay rights movement was born when police showed up to raid one of those bars, the Stonewall Inn in Greenwich Village—and, for the first time in history, gays violently fought back. In 1970, a gay rights bill nearly passed the New York City Council. In New York State, former Supreme Court justice and United Nations ambassador Arthur Goldberg came out for gay rights in his Senate campaign, and Bella Abzug campaigned for Congress at gay bathhouses. In 1971, a man named Frank Kameny, who had once been fired from his job at the U.S. Army's Map Service because he was gay, then bravely sued to get it back, ran to become the District of Columbia's nonvoting delegate to the U.S. Congress. He lost—but his effort earned a groundbreaking editorial from the *Washington Post*: "Persecution of homosexuals is as senseless as it is unjust. . . . Like anyone else, they have a right to privacy, a right to opportunity, and a right to serve their country."

In 1972 the Democrats' gay caucus won the right to hold a convention floor vote on a gay rights plank in the party platform. (The plank failed, in part because at an earlier meeting the caucus had voted 32–24 in to endorse abolition of "all laws governing the age of sexual consent.") In 1973 a state representative from Boston named Barney Frank drafted a bill to repeal Massachusetts's sodomy law and enshrine protections against anti-gay discrimination in employment, housing, and public accommodations. (He was gay, but didn't yet dare come of out the closet.) A similar bill became law in Minneapolis. In city after city, police harassment tapered down to practically nothing. Even down South in Atlanta, gay activists opened effective lines of communication with the mayor.

But progress was stutter-stepped. A former fundamentalist minister named Troy Perry opened gay churches in nine states. But in January of 1973, in Los Angeles, his first dedicated building burned down. So, that June, did the gay bar where the New Orleans branch of his Metropolitan Community Church met, killing thirty-two. Ashamed families refused to claim the bodies; churches refused to hold memorial services. Syndicated advice columnist Ann Landers answered a letter-writer agonizing over her gay brother's suicide by quoting a psychiatrist: "over and over again it is found that a homosexual male has had an intense relationship with the mother and a deficient relationship with the father." The advice columnist concluded, "Perhaps just knowing these facts will help some parents to rear their children to be sexually normal."

Then, however, activists won a change in the American Psychiatric Association professional bible, the *Diagnostic and Statistical Manual of Mental Disorders*: it would no longer classify homosexuality as a disease. After that, it felt like nothing but open-field running. In 1974, in Massachusetts, Elaine Noble became the nation's first openly gay state legislator. In 1975, San Francisco elected a pro-gay sheriff, Richard Hongisto, and a pro-gay mayor, George Moscone. By then, thirty-seven cities and counties had outlawed discrimination on the basis of "affectional or sexual preference" and eight states had repealed sodomy laws. The cover of the September 8, 1975, issue of *Time* pictured an Air Force officer named Leonard Matlovich. It read, "'I Am a Homosexual: The Gay Drive for Acceptance." In 1976, Jimmy Carter told the Reverend Troy Perry he would consider an executive order outlawing discrimination against gays in the military. He promised he would sign Abzug's gay rights bill. Then, on Tom Snyder's *Tomorrow Show*, he proclaimed, "I favor the end of harassment or abuse or discrimination about homosexuals." His White House head of public liaison, Midge Costanza, was a gay rights crusader. In the spring of 1977, Costanza began organizing a meeting of gay activists at the White House.

"The year of the gay," journalist Randy Shilts wrote in a book about the movement. "That was the way 1977 was supposed to turn out."

Then came Dade County, and the tide began to turn.

IN MIAMI, A GAY COMMUNITY THAT INCLUDED MANY RESPECTED BUSINESSmen organized themselves as a local political interest group: they mailed questionnaires to municipal candidates in the 1976 election, then provided the forty-nine whose answers they liked best with donations and volunteers. Forty-four won. One, a Dade County commissioner (who happened to be the wife of Anita Bryant's agent), introduced a bill outlawing discrimination against gays in employment, housing, and public accommodations. Which was exactly how America's pluralist democracy was supposed to work.

In December, the nine-member county commission voted unanimously to schedule a public hearing on gay rights for January 18—typically just a formality prior to a bill becoming law. But this hearing proved cantankerous. Local churches chartered buses full of congregants bearing signs reading things like "GOD SAYS NO, WHO ARE YOU TO SAY DIFFERENT?" and "PROTECT OUR CHILDREN, DON'T LEGISLATE IMMORALITY FOR DADE COUNTY." Among their number was a surprise witness.

Anita Bryant had been Miss Oklahoma 1959, and a runner-up for Miss America. She recorded a string of hit pop songs and became a regular at USO shows and Bob Hope's annual Christmas specials from Vietnam. In

1968 she belted out the National Anthem at the Republicans' convention in Miami and her trademark rendition of "The Battle Hymn of the Republic" at the Democrats' in Chicago. She also sang it at Lyndon Johnson's funeral in 1973. (Bryant was one of his favorite singers.) In the Bicentennial year she was so in demand she earned $700,000, even though she never performed in venues where alcohol was served. She became most famous for the commercials she starred in for the Florida Citrus Commission. They began with a chirpy "Hi! I'm Anita Bryant!" and closed with the tagline, "Breakfast without orange juice is like a day without sunshine." But "the best role I could possibly play," she insisted in her 1972 bestseller *Bless This House*, "is Anita Green, Bob's wife and our children's mother . . . People keep asking me what I think of women's lib. I tell them I was liberated when I received Christ as my personal Savior. That's the only liberation I would ever seek."

Now she testified to throaty cries of *Amen!*: "As an entertainer I have worked with homosexuals all my life, and my attitude has been live and let live. But now I believe it's time to recognize the rights of the overwhelming number of Dade County constituents." The bill passed 5–3 nonetheless. Miami was liberal. Miami was tolerant. Miami, the gay community pointed out, was also especially receptive to a message of human rights because it was a haven for Jewish retirees, a fifth of the Miami electorate, many of them refugees from Nazi Germany.

And now Miami was the first city in the South to enshrine gay rights in the books of law.

Bryant was quoted the next morning: "We are not going to take this sitting down. The ordinance condones immorality and discriminates against my children's rights to grow up in a healthy, decent community." But what could they do? The law was the law. To the ordinance's proud supporters, Bryant's argument sounded self-evidently absurd: how could granting homosexuals the right not to be fired or evicted or kicked off a seat at a lunch counter constitute "discrimination"?

A Catholic attorney named Robert Brake disagreed. He had decided, even before the ordinance had passed, that it would force his children's parochial schools to hire homosexual teachers. County law, he learned, authorized the scheduling of elections to repeal ordinances if ten thousand petition signatures were collected. After the Dade County Metropolitan Commission meeting, he walked up to the singer and asked if she would lead that crusade. Bryant responded according to a Christian wife's duty as she understood it: she asked her husband, Bob Green, and her pastor, William Chapman, for permission. This they immediately tendered. Chapman, for his part, had already avowed that he would burn his children's schools to the ground before he let homosexuals teach there.

The founding meeting of Save Our Children, Inc., was held in Bob Green and Anita Bryant's thirty-three-room oceanfront mansion, Villa Verde, complete with fountains, waterfall, a tropical garden, and a docking slip for the family yacht, the *Sea Sharp*—and a private altar. Attendees included leaders of Miami's Catholic, Baptist, Spanish Presbyterian, Orthodox Jewish, and Greek Orthodox communities, and, as their strategist, an advertising executive named Mike Thompson, who had run for lieutenant governor in 1974 on an anti-busing platform and was now a Republican national committeeman and chairman of the Florida Conservative Union. They got to work on a statement announcing their petition drive. Thompson interrupted their faltering attempt and asked if he could take a crack at it alone. He withdrew, returned, then handed the text to Anita Bryant. The pitchwoman for Coca-Cola, Kraft Foods, Holiday Inn, Tupperware—and Florida orange juice—delivered it with such aplomb that Thompson threw his arms around her. She gave him a smack on the cheek in return. He replied, "You kiss real good for a *girl!*"

Bryant froze. Thompson winked. A merry laugh was enjoyed by all. They were ready for war.

Their soldiers were already veterans. South Florida teemed with battles against busing, against abortion, against the ERA. They were all fought by the same people, as part of the same fight: protecting their families against the encroachment of the liberal state, and the heathen iniquities it intended to force down their throats.

They followed the news from Fort Lauderdale, where gays, according to the mayor, had so overrun the beaches that "straight businesses were losing regular customers by the droves." And they followed the news from New York, where in January, a psychiatrist who ran a rehabilitation center for teenage drug addicts, Dr. Judianne Densen-Gerber, held a press conference in Times Square to decry an epidemic of child pornography. A priest who operated shelters for runaways, Father Bruce Ritter, told reporters that Times Square pimps were prostituting boys as young as eleven on the "Minnesota Strip"—so called because so many of its victims were said to have been recruited from Minneapolis. Was *that* what was in store for Miami?

Bryant appeared before the press on January 24 underneath a banner reading "SAVE OUR CHILDREN FROM HOMOSEXUALITY" and surrounded by clerics: "The homosexual *recruiters* of Dade County already have begun their campaign! Homosexual acts are not only illegal, they are immoral. And through the power of the ballot box, I believe the parents and the straight-thinking normal majority will soundly reject the attempt to legitimize homosexuals and their recruitment plans for our children. We shall not let the nation down."

Less than four weeks later, her army had those 10,000 signatures, with 53,304 to spare.

Bryant received a telegram from a producer informing her a television pilot they were to work on was now canceled owing to "the extensive national publicity arising from the controversial political activities you have been engaged in Dade County." Developments like this rendered her opponents confident they were gathering the momentum they needed to win. What they did not understand was that this announcement helped energize Bryant's campaign by orders of magnitude. Evangelical culture is built upon narratives of martyrdom. Those Miamians organizing to preserve the ordinance called their organization the Coalition for the Humanistic Rights of Gays. That was naive, too. For years, evangelical leaders had been crusading against what they insisted was an actual, active conspiracy of "secular humanists," abetted by the federal government, to dethrone God from American life. So by using the word *humanistic* in their name, Bryant's adversaries placed themselves in the path of an evangelical buzz saw.

Bryant made a campaign trip to Virginia, raising $25,000 in donations via appearances on Pat Robertson's *700 Club* and Jim and Tammy Faye Bakker's *PTL Club*. On March 15, Dade County commissioners formally approved the ordinance. In doing so, they bucked Florida's popular Democratic governor, Reuben Askew—"Reuben the Good," as he was known, for opposing the use of tobacco and alcohol and embracing idealistic causes like the Equal Rights Amendment. At first, he had supported the ordinance. Then he changed his mind—because, he said, he would not want a "known homosexual teaching my children"—and also signed laws banning gay marriage, gay adoption, and men trying on women's clothing in retail stores.

THEN WORD LEAKED THAT FOR THE FIRST TIME IN HISTORY, THE WHITE House would host a delegation of gay and lesbian activists. For many of Jimmy Carter's wavering evangelical supporters, this was the last straw.

One was the Reverend Pat Robertson. After the election, he had pored through the "Plum Book," the fat volume that listed federal jobs, in order to prepare a memo recommending some thirty-five "good Christians" for specific appointments. He dispatched a private plane to the president's hometown in George to have it hand-delivered, along with his candidates' résumés, background-check information, and a cover letter reminding the president-elect that the American population of fifty million evangelicals had been "highly supportive" of his campaign, and pledging to "marshal this enormous reservoir of prayer and goodwill on your behalf" and to defend the president concerning "unpopular programs which are truly needed for the good of our country" but which his flock might otherwise oppose. Robertson did not get back so much as a thank-you note.

The Southern Baptist in Chief took this portion of his coalition for granted. Indeed, Stuart Eizenstat had drawn up a book of the campaign promises the president had made to dozens of groups, from miners to senior citizens, to keep track of which ones he fulfilled. It did not mention born-again Christians. Robertson began comparing Jimmy Carter unfavorably to Richard Nixon: "God wants stability. It's better to have a stable government under a crook than turmoil under an honest man."

Another strike against Carter was his refusal to back a constitutional amendment banning abortion. This had previously been a concern almost exclusively of Catholics. The record turnout at the March for Life in January, however, included a quantum leap in the number of Protestants. Many more were recruited to the cause beginning in the spring of that year by an unlikely activist: a theologian from Germantown, Pennsylvania, named Francis Schaeffer.

Schaeffer now lived with his family in a chalet in Switzerland that he had purchased in 1954 and turned it into a retreat center called *L'Abri*— "the refuge." Among those who found refuge there were rock musicians and hippies. Nearly uniquely among evangelical leaders, Schaeffer encouraged engagement with worldly art and culture. He was the evangelicals' missionary to the intellectuals—who treated him as just one more hip 1960s spiritual seer. Rank-and-file evangelicals venerated Dr. Schaeffer for his role in sanding away their community's anti-intellectual reputation. In 1972 the Christian filmmaker Billy Zeoli convinced him that with his reputation, eloquence—and dramatically long silver hair and puff of white beard—he would make a marvelous host for a Christian response to Sir Kenneth Clark's hit thirteen-part BBC and PBS series *Civilization*. That series had told the story of Western culture as an ascent from the superstition-soaked Dark Ages to the Enlightenment and beyond—a triumph of man's reason—a quintessentially "secular humanist" narrative: it sacrilegiously elevated humankind above God.

Schaeffer and Zeoli's response, *How Should We Then Live? The Rise and Decline of Western Thought and Culture*, inverted that story. The first eight episodes unfolded a leisurely Christ-inflected tour of European art, from Michelangelo's *David* (though they had to locate footage obscuring the genitals) to its degradation into abstract art and existentialist fiction that dethroned God, robbed humans of their dignity, and threatened liberty itself. "It was *Christianity*—the Reformation in Western Europe— which brought the forms of freedom that we have," Schaeffer said, his loose-fitting open-necked shirt flapping welcomingly in the breeze. It was the grinding advance of secular humanism, exemplified by Hitler, Stalin, and Mao, that portended the *real* dark age: not back in the Middle Ages, but *now*.

Then, episode nine took a striking turn.

It was the idea of Dr. Schaeffer's son Frankie, the film's director. Returning to Switzerland after a tour plying conservative billionaires like Bunker Hunt and Richard DeVos for donations, he argued that their series should depict legalization of abortion as the culmination of the diabolical forces they meant to explain. Schaeffer *père* was reluctant. He despised abortion, but considered it a Catholic issue—and a *political* issue. And preachers had no business in politics.

His son snapped back: "That's what you always say about the Lutherans in Germany! You say they're responsible for the Holocaust because they wouldn't speak up, and now you're doing the same thing." He won the argument.

The episode began with a screech of tuneless contemporary classical music, a Van Gogh self-portrait, an Ingmar Bergman film poster, covers of books by Sartre and Camus. Dr. Schaeffer explained how by the 1960s people were barraged by these artifacts' underlying message: "no fixed values whatsoever." They were promised in their place twin salves of personal freedom and affluence—"horrible, absolutely horrible values." Young people, searching for something deeper, tried drugs and political utopias, which failed: "They had tried to escape their parents' poor values and went around in a circle and ended up one inch lower." The screen filled with horrors—Woodstock, bombings, rioting in the streets, screaming hordes—as Shaeffer rushed via a headlong set of syllogisms to what he took to be the culminating horror: society's "Christian consensus" was abandoned, until "the Constitution of the United States can be made to say anything on the basis of sociological, variable law."

He had been delivering the lecture at a desk. The next shot found him pacing in front of the United States Supreme Court.

"I'd like to use an illustration. . . . Consider the human fetus—the unborn baby. In January of 1973, the United States Supreme Court passed the abortion law."

Next came gorgeous diaphanous images of fetuses that looked ready to leap forth fully formed from the womb. *Roe v. Wade* was "arbitrary legally and mentally"—yet American elites accepted that because "it was considered sociologically helpful. . . . And nobody knows where it will end."

He perched on a tree stump.

"The unborn child is considered not to be a person"—just like black slaves used to be. "The question has to be asked: in an age with no fixed values, why could not the aged, the incurably ill, the insane, and other classes of persons arbitrarily be declared to be non-persons on the basis of arbitrary law, if the court decided it was socially helpful?"

A final episode hammered home the conclusion: with legal abortion having institutionalized the heresy that "people are seen as no different from machines," society would descend into totalitarianism. Unless viewers did something about it.

The series was advertised as a "documentary spectacular two and a half years in the making." It debuted at Chicago's five-thousand-seat Arie Crown Theater. The format was a daylong seminar, with each half-hour episode interspersed with discussion sessions featuring Dr. Schaeffer and his wife, Edith. It toured fourteen more cities by April, including to audiences of 3,500 in Seattle, 3,800 in Atlanta, and 6,000 in Dallas, where Cowboys quarterback Roger Staubach emceed. Jerry Falwell made the book version required reading for all entering freshmen at his Liberty Baptist College.

It was a certified evangelical sensation. So were the lectures in megachurches around the country by a woman Maria Anne Hirschmann, author of a popular evangelical comic book narrating her escape from Hitler and her born again experience—who now began preaching, "Don't ever let anyone tell you that abortion does not lead to euthanasia, because that's exactly where it leads. I know—I saw it in my native land. . . ."

The non-Christian media didn't notice. What was it Phyllis Schlafly said about politics being like an iceberg, eight-ninths of it below the surface?

MIDGE COSTANZA WAS CAREFUL TO CONVENE THE FIRST WHITE HOUSE meeting for homosexuals on a Saturday, when the president wouldn't be around. Fourteen activists each made five-minute presentations on an aspect of gay persecution. The most moving came from Reverend Perry, narrating all the arson attacks against his Metropolitan Community Churches, and the story of the relatives who had been too embarrassed to claim the remains of victims in the 1973 fire in the tavern that hosted his church in New Orleans. A hush fell over the room. Costanza cried.

They emerged into a rainy day to find members of the White House press corps waiting in ambush. "I wish that the citizens of this nation could have joined me in that room to listen to the examples of the oppression I heard today," Costanza said in a snippet that ran on CBS News. "Perhaps the issue of homosexuality would be better understood and perhaps more widely accepted if they could hear what I heard." She said that she hoped this would be the first in a series of meetings between these activists and senior administration officials. A reporter asked Reverend Perry about Anita Bryant. He dismissed her as irrelevant. Jody Powell, the next morning on *Meet the Press*, said he wasn't sure whether Carter knew about the meeting. But did the president support the gay rights movement? Replied Powell, "Well, I don't want to speak to that."

Anita Bryant issued a statement lambasting the White House for "dignifying these activists for special privilege with a serious discussion of their alleged 'human rights'. . . . Behind the high-sounding appeal against discrimination in jobs and housing, which is not a problem to the 'closet' homosexual, they are really asking to be blessed in their abnormal lifestyle by the office the President of the United States." Then, she went to church, where she called homosexuality a "disguised attack on God," pledging "such a crusade to stop it as this country has not seen before."

Wyoming had just become the nineteenth state to decriminalize gay sex. A score more such bills were pending. Bella Abzug's federal bill kept adding sponsors. What was happening in Miami simply didn't feel threatening. After all, read a mailing to members of the National Gay Task Force, "Bryant is really the perfect opponent. Her national prominence . . . ensures national news coverage for developments in the Dade County struggle, while the feebleness of her arguments and the embarrassing backwardness of her stance make her attacks easier to counteract and tend to generate 'liberal' backlash in our favor."

On March 20, Save Our Children ads began running in the *Miami Herald* demanding "the civil rights of parents to save their children from homosexual influence." On March 22, a Latino gay was returning from appearing on a Spanish-language TV station to campaign against the recall of the gay rights ordinance when he found his car destroyed by a bomb. No liberal backlash in their favor ensued.

MIAMI GAYS GREW PESSIMISTIC. ONE OUTSIDER WHO SHARED THEIR PESSI-mism was David Goodstein, the publisher of the prominent Los Angeles–based gay newspaper the *Advocate*. He saw Anita Bryant's movement as akin to Hitler's successful advance on Czechoslovakia—a first step on the way to potential genocide. He sent two gay consultants with experience in presidential campaigns, Ethan Geto and Jim Foster, to help guide the defenders. The first thing they did was to commission a poll, which revealed a heartening result: a majority of Miamians supported the gay rights ordinance, and women favored it by a margin of two to one.

But Save Our Children had already discovered the same thing from their own polls. Explained their operative Mike Thompson, Miami's female voters "love their dogs and they love the people who love their dogs"; their hairdressers and florists, too. They saw the homosexuals they *knew* as charming and harmless. So the strategy would be convincing Miami women that the gay men they *didn't* know were absolutely terrifying.

Conditions were salubrious for the argument. Gays had few friends outside their community. At the annual Gridiron dinner, Senate Minority Leader Howard Baker, a Republican whom liberals respected, told homophobic jokes. The nation's most prominent liberal historian, the former Kennedy administration aide Arthur Schlesinger Jr., once wrote in the *New York Times*, " 'Gay' used to be one of the most agreeable words in the language. Its appropriation by a notably morose group is an act of piracy." A liberal columnist in the *Washington Post*, William Raspberry, now wrote that he had sat down to pen an "easy" column about Anita Bryant's "campaign of bigotry"—then he met her, found many of her arguments persuasive, and concluded that, since homosexuality was an "acquired taste," parents were perfectly within their rights not to "want their children placed in circumstances in which they might acquire it." Even the community's friends were not particularly friendly. "Homosexuals make me feel creepy inside," wrote another columnist in a piece otherwise excoriating Bryant. "The folly of publicly flaunting bedroom preferences disgusts me." And few in the liberal activist world, separated into an ever-proliferating number of interest-group silos, saw what was going on in Miami as their fight.

It was the opposite on the other side. Conservatives *increased* their operational unity each time some new discontent was stirred into the stew.

Look at what happened after President Carter, on March 22, sent a letter to Congress recommending a package of electoral reforms. The president was concerned that America ranked twenty-first in voter participation among the world's democracies. He argued that the problem was not voter apathy but that "millions of Americans are prevented or discouraged from voting in every election by antiquated and overly restrictive voter registration laws"—a fact proven by the record rates of participation in 1976 in states like Minnesota, Wisconsin, and North Dakota that let voters register on Election Day. So Carter recommended same-day registration be adopted universally—tempering concerns that such measures might increase opportunities for fraud by increasing penalties against it to five years in prison and a $10,000 fine. He asked for $25 million to help states comply, an expansion to congressional elections of the current system of federal matching funds for presidential campaigns, and closing a loophole in campaign finance law that advantaged rich contenders by allowing them to evade spending limits if they funded their own campaigns. He proposed revising the Hatch Act to allow federal employees "not in sensitive positions" the same rights of political participation as everyone else when not on the job. Most radically, he recommended a constitutional amendment to scrap the Electoral College, which, three times so far, had selected as president a candidate who had received fewer votes than his opponent.

It was among the most sweeping political reform proposals in U.S.

history—and soon afterward, legislators from both parties stood together at a news briefing to endorse all or most of it. The bill for universal registration, which RNC chairman Brock called "a Republican concept," was cosponsored by four Republicans. Senator Baker suggested going even further by making Election Day a national holiday, keeping polls open twenty-four hours, and instituting automatic registration. House minority leader John Rhodes, the conservative disciple of Barry Goldwater, predicted the proposal would pass "in substantially the same form with a lot of Republican support, including my own."

More democracy: who could object?

The answer was: the New Right, which took their lessons about "electoral reform" from legends of Kennedy beating Nixon via votes received from the cemeteries of Chicago.

The next issue of *Human Events* was bannered, "ELECTION 'REFORM' PACKAGE: EUTHANASIA FOR THE GOP." It argued that the current electoral system had never disenfranchised a single citizen—at least "no citizen who cares enough to make the minimal effort." So why was Carter proposing to change it? Because, Kevin Phillips insisted, it would "blow the Republican Party sky high." Phillips claimed that Carter had calculated that since he had won Wisconsin by a tiny margin, defying predictions, and since "most electoral analysts credited that upset to the 210,000 allowed to register on election day," he wanted to expand the scam to all fifty states. A Berkeley political scientist, *Human Events* noted, predicted national turnout would go up 20 percent under Carter's reforms—a bad thing, the editors said, because "the bulk of these extra votes will go to Carter's Democratic Party . . . with blacks and other traditionally Democratic voter groups accounting for most of the increase." The Heritage Foundation, meanwhile, got out one issue brief arguing that instant registration might allow the "eight million illegal aliens in the U.S." to vote, and another arguing that it was a mistake to "take for granted that it is desirable to increase the number of people who vote."

Ronald Reagan had been making similar arguments for years. "Look at the potential for cheating," he thundered in 1975 when Democrats proposed a system allowing citizens to register by mail. A voter "can be John Doe in Berkeley, and J. F. Doe in the next county, all by saying he intends to live in both places. . . . Yes, it takes a little work to be a voter; it takes some planning to get to the polls or send an absentee ballot . . . that's a small price to pay for freedom." He took up the same cudgel shortly after Carter's inauguration when California adopted easier procedures: "Why don't we try reverse psychology and make it *harder* to vote?" Now, following Carter's electoral reform message, Reagan wrote in his column that what this all was *really* about was boosting votes from "the bloc comprised of those who get a whole lot more from the federal government in various kinds of income distribution than they contribute to it.... Don't be surprised if an army of election workers—much of it supplied by labor organizations which have managed to exempt themselves from election law restrictions—sweep through metropolitan areas scooping up otherwise apathetic voters and rushing them to the polls to keep the benefit-dispensers in power."

He added, in a newsletter column on Hatch Act reform, "The intent of the bill seems to be to convert your friendly neighborhood bureaucrat into a machine politician. After all, he does have an interest in keeping government growing"—and if successful it would "render the Republican Party as dead as the dodo bird." He dedicated a radio broadcast to what he called the most terrifying idea of all: popular election of presidents. "The very basis for our freedom is that we are a federation of sovereign states. Our constitution recognizes that certain rights belong to the states and cannot be infringed upon by the national government." John C. Calhoun had pioneered that argument in South Carolina in the 1830s, as a way to cloak attempts to preserve slavery in noble constitutional raiment.

And the party establishment soon became convinced.

Republican National Committee Chairman Bill Brock met in Los Angeles with Reagan, who subsequently told supporters that the chairman had assured him "he is opposed to the election reform package," which "might better be called the Universal Voter Fraud Bill." Brock then penned an article in the RNC magazine *First Monday* on the "Democratic Power Grab"; when it had been proposed he called it a "Republican idea." The RNC passed a resolution claiming that same-day registration would "endanger the integrity of the franchise and open American elections to serious threat of fraud." Representative John Rhodes, after what the *Washington Post* called "unremitting opposition for his original stand"— including a cartoon in the Citizens for the Republic newsletter depicting a bleeding GOP elephant stabbed by a figure labeled "Rhodes" and "Universal Registration"—directed his House Republican Policy Committee to adopt a statement of formal opposition.

Several months later, thirty conservatives met in a private dining room at the Capitol Hill Club, the famous "home away from home" for GOP lawmakers, for a ceremony in which Nevada Senator Paul Laxalt, Reagan's 1976 campaign chairman, and Richard Viguerie received bronze plaques inscribed, "FOR LEADERSHIP IN PRESERVING FREE ELECTIONS," for their role in defeating same-day voter registration.

TO VETERAN WASHINGTON COLUMNIST MARY MCGRORY, THIS SWING TO THE right suggested a party committing suicide. She noted that six-term Ohio representative Charles Whalen was thinking of quitting the GOP because "the Republican Party of 1977 is not the party he joined in 1951." So was Senator Charles "Mac" Mathias, one of the most respected solons in either party. "Just why the Republican Party, with its enrollment of 18 percent, should be engaged in trying to saw off its left arm," McGrory concluded, "is beyond fathoming."

Bill Brock evidently did not agree—for presently, he hired New Right operative Charlie Black, a top staffer from Ronald Reagan's 1976 campaign, to head the RNC's political division, overseeing an ambitious, well-financed new effort to influence local elections. Black was also cofounder of the National Conservative Political Action Committee; and he hired two of his former NCPAC underlings as regional directors at the RNC. He was simultaneously managing the campaign of New Right operative Roger Stone to preside over the Republican Party's youth auxiliary. Stone had run the California branch of Reagan's 1976 presidential campaign. Black had been chosen for the RNC position, Evans and Novak reported, after "remorseless prodding by Lyn Nofziger." Richard Viguerie must have been especially pleased; Stone's wife Ann was his political director. Stone was promising, if he became Young Republican Federation president, to loosen its ties to the RNC and fund it independently—with, presumably, copious help from the offices Richard Viguerie. Howard Phillips soon wrote his Conservative Caucus activists, "Start thinking about what we should be doing when we take power."

Evans and Novak called it all an effort by Viguerie "to build a party within a party, with the child devouring the parent," and noted that Stone, "under the alias of Jason Rainer," had been "waist-deep in 1972 Nixon campaign dirty tricks." Now Stone was raising unprecedented amounts, tens of thousands of dollars, in his campaign to rule the Young Republicans. Where was the money coming from? It made the Republican establishment awfully nervous.

SHREWD DEMOCRATS ALSO BEGAN GETTING NERVOUS, WORRIED THAT Viguerie's octopus aimed to strangle them, too.

Representative Charlie Wilson of Texas began investigating, learning that little of what Viguerie raised for his clients reached its intended beneficiaries. A typical example, the Reverend Sun Myung Moon's Children's Relief Fund received only 6.3 percent of the $1,508,256 Viguerie brought in on its behalf. Sometimes clients actually *lost* money—like the organization that paid RAVCO $889,255 to solicit money to distribute Bibles in Asia but earned back only $802,028. On April 10, Wilson introduced a bill to force more transparency in the operation of direct mail companies. After Wilson won support from almost all national charities, the bill looked to be on the advance—until the New Right began manning the ramparts.

The Heritage Foundation distributed an issues bulletin arguing that the bill would subject "church leaders" to "vicious" accusations, would "increase the paperwork on every Christian organization," and might be "the first step to a legislative strategy to eliminate tax-exempt status for all non-profit organizations." John Conlan published an article explaining that even a mailing that "makes a small amount of money or breaks even" was extraordinarily valuable for promotional purposes—and that publishing the cost of fundraising campaigns as the bill demanded "would inhibit the effort to build a list of long-term friends and donors." The picture of Conlan that accompanied the piece bore the caption "DEFENDS CHARITIES AGAINST BIG GOVERNMENT." It was published in *Conservative Digest*. The publisher of *Conservative Digest* was . . . Richard A. Viguerie. Wilson's bill never made it out of committee.

As for Viguerie, he saw no reason to apologize. He saw himself like the biblical David, direct mail his slingshot, every terrifying Viguerie letter a voter received a stone denting Goliath's armor. "The left," he told a reporter, thinks of "direct mail as fundraising. They miss the whole boat if they think that. *It is a form of advertising.* It's not an evil conspiratorial thing. It is just a fact of life, which I haven't found anybody to deny, that the major media of this country has a left-of-center perspective. The conservatives can't get their message around the blockade, except through direct mail. . . . It's a way of mobilizing our people; it identifies our people; it marshals our people."

That fall, when congressmen complained to the attorney general that their names had appeared as endorsers in hair-on-fire fundraising letters they had never seen, for Viguerie-devised organizations like the Citizens Committee for the Right to Keep and Bear Arms, that group's chairman professed innocence, noting that the "names of members of Congress . . . are public information." Viguerie called it a clerical error and didn't change a thing.

THE GAY POLITICAL CONSULTANTS ETHAN GETO AND JIM FOSTER RETURNED to Miami after an absence on Sunday, April 10, with seven weeks to go. They discovered Anita Bryant's army in the lead. The next day, Florida's senate voted down ERA ratification. A month earlier, the *St. Petersburg Independent* had run the banner headline "Florida ERA Passage Assured." Spillover from the Bryant crusade, the *Miami Herald* explained, had shifted the balance: "fear of legal homosexual marriage" as a consequence of the ERA came to the debate.

Save Our Children, Inc., began running a TV commercial that opened with footage of floats and apple-cheeked majorettes leading marching bands. The announcer: "The Orange Bowl parade. Miami's gift to the nation. *Wholesome* entertainment." Then, a cut to men in leather and chains snapping whips, topless women on motorcycles, and drag queens—"But in San Francisco, when they take to the streets, it's a parade of homosexuals. Men hugging other men. Cavorting with little boys. Wearing dresses and makeup. The same people who turned San Francisco into a hotbed of homosexuality want to do the same thing in Florida."

Their direct mail reproduced a recommendation from the Democrats' gay rights caucus in 1972 calling for the abolition of age of consent laws. Their full-page newspaper ads boomed, "Many parents are confused, and don't know the real dangers posed by homosexuals—and perceive them as all being gentle, non-aggressive types. The other side of the homosexual coin is a hair-raising pattern of recruitment and outright seduction and molestation, a growing pattern that predictably will intensify if society approves laws granting legitimacy to the sexually perverted."

Anita Bryant raised funds nationwide, preaching to rapt audiences in church pews: "For several years I had been praying to revive America. When word came that there was an ordinance in Miami that would allow known homosexuals to teach my children, God help us as a nation to stand in these dark days."

It was a boon season for arguments concerning dark days. In Washington on March 9, Muslim extremists took more than one hundred hostages at Washington, D.C.'s, B'nai Brith headquarters and a rival mosque, killing a radio reporter and bringing the capital to a three-day, terror-filled standstill. The police commissioner in New York announced that a series of mysterious shootings of women had been committed by the same person with the same .44-caliber pistol; the streets of Queens and Brooklyn were soon deserted at dusk. A PBS documentary called *The Fire Next Door* reported that arson, the nation's fastest growing crime, was turning the New York neighborhood of the South Bronx, where there had been thirteen thousand fires in 1975 alone, into a pocked moonscape. A syndicated TV documentary predicting what America's next energy crisis would look was entitled *We Will Freeze in the Dark*. Isaac Asimov published a piece in *Time* imagining America twenty years in the future: "Work, sleep, and eating are the great trinity of 1997, and only the first two are guaranteed." A typical day of news that spring featured a security guard in Baltimore taking his wife, his eight children, and thirty-five others hostage with two guns and a machete; a Ford worker holding a nurse at knifepoint in Ypsilanti; and Puerto Rican separatists bombing a bank and an FBI office in New York. Dark days indeed.

And then, as President Carter began his second hundred days, another tributary for conservative organizing emerged.

The United Nations had declared 1975 "International Women's Year," and convened an epochal conference in Mexico City. Gerald Ford, sounding for all the world like an editor of *Ms.*—"Women's liberation is truly the liberation of all people"—endorsed plans for a similar conference in the U.S. Congress almost unanimously authorized a $5 million budget for a national commission to begin organizing it, with the goal of removing all "barriers to the full participation of women in our national life." The commission's first recommendation was ratification of the Equal Rights Amendment "at the earlier possible moment." They also announced that in the summer of 1977, conventions would be held in every state and U.S. territory to choose delegates for and draft resolutions to be debated at a national women's conference in November 1977 in Houston. The authorization also required that delegates "reflect the full diversity of the state's population," specifically including "groups which work to advance the rights of women; and members of the general public with special emphasis on the representation of low-income women, members of diverse racial, ethnic, and religious groups, and women of all ages."

What it did not require, conservatives would soon be pointing out, was *ideological* diversity.

President Carter fully embraced the idea, appointing Bella Abzug to run the project. Explained Congresswoman Patsy Mink of Hawaii, "The heart of all this is that we simply want for the first time in the history of this country an opportunity for women to meet." Who could possibly object?

CHAPTER 5

Human Rights

RONALD REAGAN ENJOYED A CROWDED AND PRODUCTIVE SPRING. CITIZENS for the Republic announced plans to stage a series of paid television broadcasts; the governor and his wife appeared on *The Merv Griffin Show* to some of the highest ratings in program history; on May 1, he was the hour's only guest on *Meet the Press*. And at Citizens for the Republic's offices in Santa Monica, Lyn Nofziger was engaged in a project crucial to wiring together a machine to drive a serious run for president, poring over volume upon volume of their own massive proprietary polling on legislative races nationwide, to decide which candidates Reagan's political action committee should fund.

This was serious business. The polling report on a special election in Washington State in May to replace President Carter's transportation secretary was 133 pages long; the one on a special election in California's 46th assembly district, for what could be the deciding vote to override Governor Brown's veto of a death penalty statute, 333 pages. "We're not in the business of creating a national political organization," Nofziger maintained to the *Los Angeles Times*. And if you believed that, he had a bridge to sell you.

Then, on May 17, Washington State senator Jack Cunningham upset a prominent environmental attorney after outspending the Democrat two to one, thanks to infusions from Citizens for the Republic, several other right-wing PACs, and Richard Viguerie's direct mail operation. Viguerie expeditiously called in the chit, recruiting the new conservative star to sign a fundraising letter against same-day registration: "The union bosses will have their troops out on the streets on election day, digging up derelicts, vagrants, and anyone else who will take a dollar to cast a vote.... We must stop these villains from seizing total and final control of our elections." Then the new congressman introduced his first piece of legislation: a "Native Americans Equal Opportunity Act," directing the president to abrogate all treaties between the United States and Indian tribes. The New Right was on its way.

On May 20, Reagan Reagan made his first East Coast swing of the year, to New York, New Jersey, and Rhode Island—states where Gerald Ford had received almost all of the delegates the previous year—speaking in cities where the electorate was almost exclusively Democratic. He also raised an estimated $25,000 in speaking fees. But he also harvested some skepticism about whether he was *actually* serious about running for president at all. For no serious candidate would have made the outlandish statement he made in Atlantic City that landed him in newspapers from coast to coast.

REAGAN'S ENDLESS ROUNDS OF SPEECHES TO MASSIVE HOTEL BALLROOMS filled with revelers enjoying professional conventions, Republican Party fundraisers, or annual galas for service organizations like the Rotary Club or the Elks—what he called the "mashed potato circuit"—were, along with his newspaper column and radio commentaries, now Ronald Reagan's profession. Deaver and Hannaford received some three hundred invitations for these services a month. For those they accepted, they developed an intricately choreographed routine, its every detail set down in a bulging advance manual.

First came an exclusive reception with the host organization's VIPs, or those willing to pay top dollar for the privilege. Then Reagan would make his entrance into the banquet hall—usually to the strains "California Here I Come"—harvesting the accompanying ovation, according to two columnists who had watched him do it dozens of times since his 1966 gubernatorial run described it, "with a look of pleased expectancy on his face, as if he could not imagine what delights lie ahead."

Then (his hosts having been informed the Reagans drank only decaf, and preferred their steaks well done), he would settle down to breakfast, lunch, or dinner. Most politicians skipped the meal, arriving only in time for their speech. Richard Nixon certainly did; he believed it made for a more dramatic entrance. Not Reagan. The meal was when he read the mood of the room, the better to calibrate his performance—even though, for the most part, he said the same words every time.

"He listens to the introductions," the columnists wrote, "or the Rotary Club business, with that same air of interest bordering on wonder. You would never know he has heard it all a thousand times in a thousand dining rooms." Finally, upon *his* introduction, he would stride dramatically via "a safe, uncluttered passageway" (per the advance manual) to a podium ("sturdy and if too short blocked up with bricks or 2X4s," free from "ashtrays, gavels, etc.") set to his six-foot-one height. He would plant himself at a mark taped down to ensure advantageous camera angles. He would pop out his right contact lens so he could simultaneously read the text in front of him with one eye and read the reaction at the first row of tables—

never more than eight feet away, so he would have faces to look directly into, to enhance the aura of sincerity—with the other. Lighting was carefully specified; once, but never again, Michael Deaver, who almost always traveled with him to such events, dimmed the houselights before he spoke. Reagan snapped at him: "Mike, don't ever let them turn down the house lights again. It causes me to lose my eye contact." On important occasions, his wife Nancy accompanied him—and "as she watches her husband give the speech she has heard countless times before," a reporter marveled, "her look of rapt, wide-eyed adoration never falters."

The same jokes, set down on the same stack of four-by-six index cards he'd been compiling since the 1960s, some of them yellowed with age. (A doctor had pronounced Reagan "sound as a dollar." He fainted straightaway. The reason the Little Old Lady Lived in a Shoe was because property taxes were so high. "The dollar's shrunk, the dime hasn't changed. You can still use it for a screwdriver." The government was like a baby, "an alimentary canal with an appetite on one end and no sense of responsibility on the other." "Our problem is a lack of movies that are rated E for Entertainment." . . . "Prices are so high you don't order a chuck roast anymore—you have to call it Charles.")

The same bromides about the government's tragically "hostile, adversarial relationship" with business, about how "profit, property rights, and freedom are inseparable, and you can't have the third without the other two"

The same horror stories. Did they know that "164 different federal agencies" regulated hospitals, adding $35 a day to the typical bill? That there were 151 taxes now in the price of a loaf of bread, more than half the cost of a loaf of bread" (though sometimes there were 131).

Then, finally, the same, glorious soaring perorations about America's ineluctable rendezvous with destiny as God's shining city on a hill, as the last best hope of man on earth—and then the same ecstatic, electric ovation, as if their Rotary club, Republican organization, or trade group had been touched by the hand of God.

There might be a question and answer period with the audience; attendees scribbled questions on index cards to be posed by the master of ceremony. (Once—again, only once—Deaver tried to show the boss the cards in advance. Reagan frowned and threw them in the garbage: "Mike, you can't hit a home run on a softball.") And, usually, beforehand or afterward, a fifteen-to-twenty minute "press availability"—for which the preparations were also rigorously prescribed: the room cooled to fifty-five degrees an hour prior to start time to counteract the TV lights' heat; backdrop light blue or beige ("ideal for TV cameras"), free from "fancy decorations that distract from the speaker"; a "reliable volunteer" posted outside with orders to admit "bona fide press," banning "well-wishers and friends" who might cause undue distraction.

It was Reagan's press availability in Atlantic City that caused the trouble.

A reporter asked his opinion on a subject on every political observer's mind: British talk show host David Frost's televised interviews with Richard Nixon. The first one had aired three weeks earlier, on May 4; that afternoon, Reagan had told an audience at the Hoover Institution that he would be "glued to the TV" (and also that while Reagan believed Nixon "was certainly guilty of political impropriety," he was not a crook, and "I don't think we've had a full report on Watergate"). Then forty-five million people, a record for a political interview, watched, riveted, as Nixon squirmed, sweated—then finally offered something like his first ever apology for Watergate: "I let down my friends, I let down my country, I let down our system of government." During the second interview, a week later, Frost elicited shocking jabs from Nixon at Henry Kissinger, whom the former president characterized as a pathologically jealous crybaby.

The third had been broadcast the previous night. Nixon complained that the antiwar movement created political divisions that hobbled his efforts to end the Vietnam War. Frost pointed out that Nixon had deliberately exacerbated those divisions for his own advantage, vilifying those in the antiwar movement as enemies of the United States. The former president, annoyed, replied that he had no choice: "Without having enough support at home, the enemy, in my opinion, would never have negotiated in Paris."

Frost's off-camera voice then introduced some context: that one of the ways Nixon sought to weaken the antiwar movement was by approving staffer Tom Charles Huston's plan to spy on and sabotage it, using tactics that they knew to be illegal.

He addressed Nixon directly:

"So, what in a sense, you're saying is that there are certain situations, and the Huston Plan or that part of it was one of them, where the president can decide that it's in the best interests of the nation or something, and do something illegal?"

Nixon: "Well, when the president does it that means that it is *not* illegal."

In Atlantic City, Reagan was asked about that astonishing claim. He replied that he could "understand" it: "When he was made commander-in-chief he was responsible for the national security." He then launched into an elaborate story, his go-to whenever he was called upon to defend the necessity of extraordinary measures in the interest of public safety. Radicals had threatened to kidnap his wife and send him her head if he would not release certain prisoners from jail. His criminal intelligence division had learned of the plot through underhanded means, and "the purpose of law and order, and civil rights and human rights, was served by someone being able to find that intelligence." In precisely the same way, "When the commander in chief of a nation finds it necessary to order employees of the government or agencies from the government to do things that would technically break the law, he has to be able to *declare* it legal for them to do that."

The comment rendered Reagan a laughingstock: "Has the governor taken leave of his senses?" one newspaper editorial cackled. "What if some administration were to declare Reagan illegal?" Reagan's former criminal intelligence chief in Sacramento, reached for comment, indignantly said his officers never had nor would break laws.

Reagan had certainly placed himself out on a political limb where public opinion was concerned. Of those who watched the Frost interviews, 72 percent responded that Nixon was a criminal, for which there could be no place in public life. But Reagan was hardly *alone*. More and more conservatives, in fact, were making similar arguments themselves, with the same sort of unapologetic brazenness with which Richard Viguerie tested campaign finance laws.

A Nixon speechwriter who was now a widely syndicated columnist, Patrick J. Buchanan, took the occasion of the Frost interviews to argue that "Watergate was the climactic battle in a political civil war that raged in this country for ten years"—in which "the Left, defeated and humiliated in November of 1972," cooked up a fake scandal for the simple reason that otherwise their mortal enemy "would enter the history books as a political genius who had read the nation better than they, who had ended honorably a war they had started, declared unwinnable, and from which they had deserted to places like Canada, Stockholm, Harvard, and the Ford Foundation." A book slated for June publication by the conservative journalist Victor Lasky, *It Didn't Start with Watergate*, claimed that Democrats going back to FDR were as lawless or even more so than Richard Nixon; another former Nixon speechwriter, William Safire, now a *New York Times* columnist, had argued that Watergate was "a secondary McCarthy Era, in which civil liberties were suspended in the name of civil liberty, and many of those who pointed the fingers of guilt were men with guilty hands."

Viva Nixon. To some on the right, he was beginning to sound like a role model.

THEN CAME GRIST FOR AN ARGUMENT THAT IN SOME RESPECTS JIMMY Carter was just as bad. Just as his second hundred days were beginning, the ten-thousand-word "Initial Working Paper on Political Strategy" that

Pat Caddell had presented him the month before the inauguration was leaked to the press and made the Man from Plains seem as shifty as Tricky Dick himself.

"Essentially," Caddell had written, "it is my thesis that governing with public approval requires a continuing political campaign.... Too many good people have been defeated because they tried to substitute substance for style." He then suggested a barrage of symbolic gestures—fireside chats, radio call-in shows, town meetings—that had once seemed some refreshing tokens of Carter's winsome genuineness, but were now revealed as cynical manipulations by hired guns. Carter was grilled mercilessly on the document in his press conference the next day. He lamely responded that, well, the idea of walking down Pennsylvania Avenue on Inauguration Day had been his and his alone.

Liberal Democrats had particular cause for dismay. Caddell wrote that with the Republican Party "bent on self-destruction," the White House could "adopt many of their issue positions," in order to "devise a context that is neither traditionally liberal nor traditionally conservative." He predicted that "more of the opposition to Carter programs will come from Democrats than Republicans," but that they should ignore "rumblings from the left of the Democratic Party"; the "liberal establishment" was "as antiquated and anachronistic a group as are the conservative Republicans." Caddell then proceeded to calumniate the congressional leadership, who could be expected to oppose his program merely because they resented "Carter's quick rise from relative obscurity to the White House," and labor and urban machine leaders, who would be "easiest to dominate" because all they cared about was patronage.

The *New York Times* had just published a big front-page feature, "All Quiet on the Potomac," on the complaints of the doyennes of Washington society concerning these Georgians and their bumptious, antisocial ways. There was "Mrs. Averell Harriman": "After Watergate and Vietnam, we are caught up in a syndrome where the emphasis is on work and doing good—it has overtaken frivolity." And "Mrs. Arthur Gardner of Washington and Watch Hill," widow of the ambassador to Cuba, who had once been well known for the lavish affairs she staged in dictator Fulgencio Batista's Havana. She clucked: "I don't know where they are, maybe they are too busy praying." They were busy working, replied the wife of Jody Powell—the man the *Times* noted had shocked *tout* Georgetown when at the White House Correspondents' Association dinner he "was found in mid-evening with black tie in hand, rather than at neck."

Meanwhile the Senate debated an ethics reform bill administration allies had drafted to follow up on a Carter campaign promise. One of its provisions would limit honoraria for speaking engagements—necessary, argued one liberal Democrat, Gaylord Nelson of Wisconsin, to keep fat cats from getting around contribution limitations. "You're throwing us to the wolves!" shot back Edmund Muskie. "The senator is putting a cap on my income, and he doesn't give a damn what the consequences are for my family."

The bill passed 86–9, a deceptive result: many senators, knowing they had no political choice, voted while figuratively holding their noses—banking yet more resentment for that stiff, prissy man breaking up the comfortable, cozy old ways of doing business. "I think we've gone completely ethics-happy around here," Senator John Glenn sighed. "We've gone crazy."

As if on cue, a festering scandal bubbled to the forefront. A South Korean businessman named Tongsun Park, who made a fortune as the sole agent for U.S. rice sales to his homeland and was famous for throwing the sort of lavish black-tie affairs considered so crucial by some to the capital's civic health, was revealed to have ties to Korean intelligence, buying influence to keep American troops stationed there. Dozens of congressmen who had enjoyed Park's hospitality were now in the crosshairs, whether they knew of his dodgy associations or not—including House speaker Tip O'Neill, who years earlier had appeared on the front page of the *Washington Post* Style section accepting a set of golf clubs from Park at a bash Park threw for the speaker's sixty-second birthday. William Safire dubbed it "Koreagate"—a clever gambit which insinuated with but four crisp strokes on his typewriter that questionable practices involving Democrats rose to Nixonian levels. Although, quite the opposite of Nixon's, this administration took the lead in calling for stepped up investigations. Carter and O'Neill, after all, as Evans and Novak observed in a column that appeared in the *Post* on May 21, maintained an "arm's length relationship"—unheard of between a speaker and president who shared the same party.

IT WAS THE 125TH DAY OF HIS PRESIDENCY. HE WAS SCHEDULED TO SPEAK later in the day at Notre Dame's commencement. The *New York Times* reported that he would be discoursing on strengthening America's Cold War alliances. They were wrong. The *Times* was working from a leaked draft produced by national security advisor Zbigniew Brzezinski. A young member of the White House speechwriting shop named Jerry Doolittle had argued that this text by the most traditional Cold Warrior on Carter's foreign policy team described antiquated goals that were indistinguishable from Carter's predecessors'. The foreign policy statements of Presidents Truman, Eisenhower, Kennedy, Nixon, and Ford, Doolittle argued, were "based on the implicit assumption that Communism is superior to Democracy," and "that if we give them an inch, they will take the globe. But the truth is that if we give them an inch, they are very likely to choke on it.... What is new about the Carter foreign policy is that it is not based on fear. Its basis is, instead, a calm confidence in the superiority of our own system." So he suggested Carter devote his first major foreign policy address to another proposition: "When you are confident of democracy's future, you are free of that inordinate fear of Communism which once led us to embrace any dictator who joined us in our fear."

And so, after praising his appreciative robed-and-mortarboarded audience for starting "a new trend which I don't deplore"—throwing peanuts on graduation day—he delivered a speech so radical that even White House staffers, the *Washington Post* related, were "wondering how literally to take the soaring rhetoric:

> *I have a quiet confidence in our own political system. Because we know that democracy works, we can reject the arguments of those rulers who deny human rights to their people.*
>
> *We are confident that the democratic methods are the most effective, and so we are not tempted to employ improper tactics here at home or abroad.*
>
> *We are confident of our own strength, so we can seek substantial mutual reductions in the nuclear arms race.*
>
> *And we are confident of the good sense of the American people, and so we let them share in the process of making foreign policy decisions. . . .*
>
> *Being confident of our own future, we are now free of that inordinate fear of Communism which once led us to embrace any dictator who joined us in that fear.*
>
> *It is a new world, but America should not fear it. It is a new world, and we should help to shape it. It is a new world that calls for a new American foreign policy—a policy based on constant decency in its values and on optimism in our historical vision.*

Ronald Reagan called it "just another Pat Caddell public relations stunt." Senator Moynihan said the president "must not be allowed to divert us from the reality of the military and ideological competition with the Soviet Union which continues, and, if anything, escalates." The *Wall Street Journal* said the speech's human rights commitments seemed "designed to hurt our allies more than our adversaries." William F. Buckley called it "so maladroit that one can draw reassurance only from the knowledge that he cannot possibly mean what he says."

But once more the citizens defied Carter's critics: in the next sounding, Carter's approval rating spiked to 66 percent; and the phrase "human rights" was now on everybody's lips.

It was, for example, the subject of Ronald Reagan's first major foreign policy address of Carter's presidency—held, the *Chicago Tribune* noted, in the same hotel, New York's Waldorf Astoria, and before the same group, the Foreign Policy Association, as Jimmy Carter's major foreign policy address in 1976.

Reagan said making human rights the "cornerstone of U.S. administration policy" was all well and good—but policy "must adhere to a single, not a double standard." Why was the administration negotiating with Panama for a treaty to turn over the Panama Canal, despite the human rights violations of its "tinhorn dictator"? Why, at the same time, did the president issue a "constant drumbeat of criticism toward South Africa and Rhodesia" despite the fact that the Soviet Union sought "the gradual encirclement of the West and the reduction of its strategic and economic influence" by conquering countries like these via "proxy mercenaries"? "Before rebuking them," he said of the two African nations ruled by white minorities, "we should keep in mind an American Indian maxim, whose origin is lost in time. It is this: 'Before I criticize a man, may I walk a mile in his moccasins.' "

He then flayed Carter for negotiating "with the conquerors of South Vietnam" and for reaching out to "Castro's Cuba, which Amnesty International estimates holds 80,000 citizens political prisoners. . . . That same Amnesty International, by the way, counts only 217 political prisoners in South Africa. And yet, partly because of past mistakes here at home and partly because of our basic belief in majority rule, we insist on applying our own political standards for South Africa" but not "the rest of the continent."

The Nobel Peace Prize–winning organization answered back: Reagan's figures were "completely incorrect." There were less than one-sixteenth of Reagan's claimed eighty thousand political prisoners in Cuba, an Amnesty International spokesman said, not 217 political prisoners in South Africa but 4,400 at a minimum—more than twenty times what Reagan claimed.

Be that as it may: the speech reaped a publicity bonanza. CBS News ran a large chunk of it. The *New York Times* moved Reagan further toward the front page than at any time since the 1976 convention. The *Chicago Tribune* sent a correspondent, who published a long profile. (It was not entirely flattering: "Camera lights flash and he lifts the chin a little higher to minimize the sagging flesh." He evaded questions about his presidential plans with a "dazzling, movie star smile." When "a reporter demanded, 'Governor, aren't you really a has-been?' Reagan looked stunned. His face dropped and he stared incredulously at the questioner. At last, he stammered, 'I don't feel like one.'")

That weekend, he spoke in Memphis before the Young Republicans convention—the same one that elected Roger Stone the group's president, after an extraordinary campaign that vindicated every one of the Republican establishment's fears. Stone's campaign manager, a twenty-eight-year-old named Paul Manafort, had brought along an organization that more closely resembled those at national party conventions: custom-installed telephone lines; thick "whip books" with intelligence on each of the eight hundred delegates; a rented Mississippi River paddleboat upon which delegates were plied with free booze; backroom horse-trading for votes in exchange for patronage. That night, Walter Cronkite frowned and reported sourly, "Delegates to the Young Republicans convention in Memphis have chosen as chairman a conservative with a Watergate past." They also, however, treated Ronald Reagan like a God. They welcomed him to the stage with an original song: "If Reagan Would Only Run." Then they interrupted him for applause a dozen times.

"HUMAN RIGHTS" WAS ALSO MUCH IN THE AIR IN MIAMI. GETO AND FOSTER noted a poll going into the home stretch before the June 6 vote indicating that 62 percent of Dade Countians favored the gay rights ordinance—but that only 15 percent of them were likely to turn out: "They are too removed from it." So they replaced their language about "gay rights" with a rhetoric of "human rights," campaigning heavily among Jews, with an argument that resembled the famous poem by Pastor Martin Niemöller reflecting on the Nazi concentration camps: "First, they came for the gays . . ."

But Mike Thompson again got there first. He recruited Miami's most prominent orthodox rabbi and put him out front, in full regalia, to call the other side's new rhetoric an anti-Semitic outrage: "Tell *us* about human rights? What right is there to corrupt our children?"

Arguments like the rabbi's won over a popular *Miami Herald* columnist, who wrote, "Gay rights spokesmen have got a lot of gall comparing their efforts to the civil rights struggles of blacks, or the human rights pronouncements of Jimmy Carter or the equality movement for women. As one black friend of mine put it: 'If I'm black, I can't hide in the closet.'" Meanwhile the *Herald* itself refused to run a pro-ordinance advertisement pointing voters to the Nazis' 1936 decree calling for extermination of "degenerates," including homosexuals; and another that pictured a 1950s automobile with a Confederate flag and banner on it reading "SAVE OUR CHILDREN FROM THE BLACK PLAGUE." They did not, however, object to one from the other side that invited readers to "SCAN THESE

HEADLINES FROM THE NATION'S NEWSPAPERS—THEN DE-
CIDE: ARE HOMOSEXUALS TRYING TO RECRUIT OUR CHIL-
DREN?" Those headlines included "Teachers Accused of Sex Acts with
Boy Students" and "Homosexuals Used Scout Troop."

In Washington, on the day of Carter's Notre Dame human rights
speech, the Department of Housing and Urban Development issued new
regulations opening public housing to anyone in a "stable family relationship," even if they were not blood relatives or legally married. The
HUD official who wrote the rules was asked if that included homosexual
couples. "Why exclude those persons?" she replied.

In Miami, a Save Our Children rally filled every nook and cranny
of the Miami Convention Center, capacity ten thousand. Women wore
dresses and men wore coats and ties. A retinue of "Cops for Christ" filed
onstage to a standing ovation, to sing a hymn. Jerry Falwell was introduced to another standing ovation. He assured the congregation he was
"not here for any political issue whatsoever"—"any time Sodom and
Gomorrah is to be considered political is the time when we've lost our
perspective."

He said that if the ordinance survived "it will cause a domino effect
that will cause city after city to fall." He remembered "back when this
kind of thing wasn't even talked about by reasonable and sensible and
decent people." He observed, "The Sermon on the Mount is the basis on
which our government found its roots . . . it's worked for 200 years! We
don't need a group of perverts, *moral* perverts—I don't call them gays. I
love—I love homosexuals, because Christ died for sinners, and all men
are sinners, whether homosexuals, or murderers, or liars and thieves, what
have you, all of us like sheep have been led astray—I love homosexuals!"
He reminded his listeners, holding up his Bible for emphasis, what happened to two other cities—one was called Sodom, the other Gomorrah—
that, like Miami, surrendered to the "vile affection," where a man had
become "*so low* and *so degraded* that he would offer his two daughters to
animals. Who no doubt would have raped them, and other unimaginable
things. Probably killed them . . ."

(A group of children clustered near the front looked a little bit afraid.)

He said, "I asked Anita to come tonight" (it was the other way
around). He summoned her onstage—"This little girl loves the Lord"—to
praise her courage in leading the movement against what he termed "a vile
and vicious and a vulgar *gang*. They'd kill you as quick as look at you.
And if you don't think that, you don't *know* the enemy." He directed her
to sing "My Eyes Have Seen the Glory." He concluded: "they" are "forcing our private and religious schools to accept them as teachers, forcing

property owners and employers to open their doors to homosexuals no matter how blatant their perverted lives may be."

"ANITA BRYANT VERSUS THE HOMOSEXUALS," READ *NEWSWEEK*'S COVER eight days before the election. (Inside, she called gays "human garbage.") The sheriff of San Francisco County, Richard Hongisto, arrived to campaign for the ordinance, explaining how gays had raised property values in San Francisco, refurbishing Victorian houses, opening new restaurants and retail establishments, and generally making San Francisco a more pleasant place to be. Mike Thompson countered that the City by the Bay had become a "cesspool of sexual perversion gone rampant."

The Sunday before the balloting, the *Miami Herald*, which had previously commended the county board for "mustering the courage to hold fast to the principles of non-discrimination," reserved itself, and endorsed Save Our Children. That same day, a gay political operative stopped at a red light. A car full of men pulled up beside him. One pointed a shotgun at his head and announced, "We're gonna blow your fuckin' brains out." The marauders then sped away.

And on Tuesday 50 percent of Dade County's eligible voters, a colossal showing for an odd-year municipal election, turned out to strike gay rights off the books by a margin of 69.3 percent to 30.7 percent.

In the Zodiac Room of the Collins Avenue Holiday Inn, Anita Bryant, resplendent in powder blue, pronounced, "Tonight the laws of God and the cultural values of man have been vindicated. I thank God for the strength He has given me and I thank my fellow citizens who joined me in what at first was a walk through the wilderness. The people of Dade County—*the normal majority*—have said, 'Enough! Enough! Enough!' " She promised, "We will now carry our fight against similar laws throughout the nation that attempt to legitimize a lifestyle that is both perverted and dangerous to the sanctity of the family, dangerous to our children, dangerous to our freedom of religion and freedom of choice, dangerous to our survival as a nation."

She performed a little jig. Her husband kissed her on the lips, then adopted a lisp: "This is what heterosexuals *doooo*, fellas!"

In a ballroom at the Fontainebleau, their opponents were funereal. Until they turned hopeful. Leonard Matlovich, the former Air Force officer whose appearance on the cover of *Time* had marked what now felt like a long-ago high tide, responded to Bryant's promise to travel from state to state to repeat her success, "When she gets there, she's going to find us waiting for her. We shall overcome." The congregation suddenly burst into song, adding a stanza to the old the civil rights anthem: "*Gays and straights together . . . we shall overcome . . .*" Three weeks later, at the Gay Freedom Day parade down Market Street in San Francisco, the line of march was led by men holding up placards depicting Hitler, Stalin, a Ku Klux Klan cross burning, the brutal Ugandan dictator Idi Amin—and a beaming Anita Bryant.

CHAPTER 6

"Little Hot Squat"

DURING MUGGY WASHINGTON SUMMERS, OFFICIAL BUSINESS SLOWS, CON-
gress goes into recess, and the thoughts of bored political reporters turn to
"thumbsuckers"—think pieces on the state of the nation and its politics.
This year the *Wall Street Journal*'s Washington bureau chief, Norman C.
Miller, heralded thumbsucker season in grand style with a piece atop the
editorial page called "Ailing GOP May Not Recover." "Even party professionals," Miller wrote, "no longer regard the death of the GOP as an
impossibility."

He quoted a young conservative congressman from Michigan, David
Stockman, who said, "Only a tidal movement in the electorate can allow
us to recover." The Ford presidential campaign's John Deardourff said
the party's future would "come down to a choice between a slow, painful
death and a mercy killing." Reagan's 1976 campaign manager John Sears
offered a species of optimism: "The Republican Party is like a fungus—it
may look dead, but you can never kill it." The RNC's former political director countered, "Anyone who says we are not potentially at the sunset
of the Republican Party is kidding himself."

In a letter to the editor, Representative Phil Crane of Illinois, a cerebral
former college professor who chaired the American Conservative Union,
offered a New Right–flavored response. He pointed to the upset victory
in Washington State eight days earlier, and Carter's slew of recent legislative setbacks—and that Gerald Ford had almost won—as evidence of "a
tangible resurgence of conservative ideas." He concluded, "What is in fact
occurring is a rebirth. The core of the Republican Party—conservatism—
is reasserting itself. This strong base, submerged during the unrealistic
groundswell attempt to gather every American into the GOP fold, is now
coming into its own."

His was a lonely counsel. The media looked at the stats—less than a
third of state legislators, control of both the statehouse and legislature in
only four states, so few governors that "two Checker cabs could carry"
them, party identification at under a fifth of the electorate—and piled on.

The *Boston Globe*'s David Nyhan said the "two party system is now down to one-and-a-half parties." That was because "the party of Abraham Lincoln forgot its heritage and started neglecting minorities." Nyhan's colleague Robert Healy interviewed Senator Edward Brooke, who manfully ticked down a list of strong Republican leaders, from Howard Baker to Ronald Reagan to Senator Dole ("don't forget he was the vice presidential candidate last time")—then lost heart, conceding there was "no real possibility of a 'whale' for the 1980 presidential contest against President Carter."

A particularly important straw in the wind, Nyhan noted, was that the "much-touted GOP opening in the South has been foreclosed by the Georgian." The *New York Times* reported that the table talk at the annual meeting of Southern Republicans was how the "survival of the party as a significant force in the South is believed to be at stake." The *Washington Post*, from the same meeting, reported that despite Ford's 45 percent of the Dixie vote in 1976, only two Republican candidates below the level of governor had been elected to any Southern statewide offices since 1973. "Gone is the dream of 'realignment,'" they concluded, the "unrealized expectation of mass defections of Democratic office-holders."

The thumbsuckers had the backing of one of the country's most distinguished experts on public opinion. Everett Carll Ladd's article "The Unmaking of the Republican Party" ran in *Fortune* in August. He said the GOP's intellectual narrowness made it more like a "church than a coalition," a mere "institution for conservative believers." The fiscal ordeals of the Nixon-Ford years had scotched the traditional notion that Republicans were better at managing the economy. "Signs of defection by big business are already evident," the "alienation of informed opinion and the intellectual community" from the party was at hand; all in all, Ladd concluded, "the GOP today is in a weaker position than any major party of the U.S. since the Civil War"—a mere "half-party." The next month *Fortune* ran his findings on the Democrats—"the established governing party to a degree unequaled by any other alliance since the Jeffersonians," ahead among every age, income, and educational group, even businessmen and executives, even self-identified conservatives, because of "the almost universal acceptance among Americans of the general policy approach of the New Deal."

THEY MISSED ALL THOSE RIGHT-WING ICEBERGS RESTING EIGHT-NINTHS below the surface, crashing into the light week by week by week.

On May 21, the National Rifle Association had held its annual convention, in Cincinnati. The organization was founded in 1871 to improve marksmanship for those who might be called on to serve their country in war, then branched out to serve the interests of sportsmen. During the mob-riddled Prohibition era, it led the movement for federal laws against machine guns. And as 1977 began, its leadership appeared perfectly content to work with the Bureau of Alcohol, Tobacco and Firearms to devise commonsense laws to limit firearms. They were even planning to move their headquarters from Washington, D.C., to Colorado Springs, to orient the NRA closer to its identity as an organization for sportsmen, and distance it from its constituency who preferred it as an advocacy organization for armed self-defense—who soon, however, raised their voices in alarm.

"It seems to me that the best way to deter murderers and thieves is to arm law-abiding folk and not to disarm them"—that was NRA cardholder Ronald Reagan, in a 1975 radio commentary responding to Gerald Ford's attorney general's proposal, welcomed by many NRA leaders, to ban the cheap handguns known as "Saturday Night Specials" because they were so frequently deployed in the commission of crimes of impulse. That same year, a California state senator and former John Birch Society recruiter named H. L. Richardson formed Gun Owners of America in alliance with Richard Viguerie. (The direct mail piece: "Radical . . . gun-grabbing . . . soft on crime . . . destroy our Constitution and unleash what could well be the most terrifying crime wave in history . . .") Within the NRA, a fundamentalist Christian gun-magazine publisher named Neal Knox, who opposed regulation even of machine guns, maneuvered to take over the organization's new lobbying arm, the Institute for Legislative Affairs, bringing in as its director the fearsome former architect of the 1950s federal illegal immigrant deportation program called "Operation Wetback," Harlon Bronson Carter, whose nickname was "Bullethead"—for his shaved head, and also his favorite medium of expression. (At the age of twenty he had been convicted of shooting to death a Mexican immigrant. The conviction was overturned because the judge had issued incorrect jury instructions.) In 1976 Carter chartered the NRA's first political action committee. They enjoyed excellent results on Election Day. Six days later—labeled "Bloody Monday" by its victims—Harlon Carter cleaned house at the NRA's Washington headquarters, firing eighty-four staffers; a secretary said she'd been ordered to perform sexual favors on one of their replacements from Carter's faction. Their new goal, Carter announced, was "No compromise. No gun legislation."

And when the opening gavel sounded May 21 in Cincinnati, Knox and Carter's faction, wearing blaze-orange hunting caps, began methodically disassembling the governing structure of the century-old organization piece by piece, via points of order, procedural votes, and credentials challenges, blindsiding the old guard, until, when the final gavel sounded at 3:30 a.m., they had taken it over, pledging the organization never to support gun control again. The next week, a columnist visited the NRA's

Washington headquarters. In the suite that had once belonged to the executive vice president (and now "had a bare look as if someone had cleaned out quickly"), Bullethead Carter told him "gun control has no relevancy to crime in this country"—except to exacerbate it. He cast his eye out toward the street; one of the reasons his predecessors had wanted to move to Colorado was all the crime in downtown Washington. He laughed, perhaps fingering a pistol beneath the desk: "We're staying."

American streets felt like harrowing places. A moral panic was afoot that spring concerning the drug PCP. The *Washington Post* said it could "turn a person into a rampaging semblance of a cornered wild animal," and blamed it for a nonexistent local schizophrenia epidemic. Actually, the drug delivered only a slightly more intense high than marijuana. Studies proved it usually had no more lasting harm. The stories about peaceful youth become feral beasts at their first taste of the stuff were myths. Which did nothing to abate all the breathless TV news segments about "angel dust" users plucking out their own eyes and bashing in car windows.

Another moral panic concerned an alleged epidemic of children being seduced from Midwestern streets and turned into Times Square sex slaves. On May 27, sensational hearings on the subject opened before the House Judiciary Committee's subcommittee on crime. "The horror stories," Father Bruce Ritter said of his experience ministering in Times Square, "were literally endless." Dr. Judianne Densen-Gerber claimed 120,000 children in the New York metropolitan area were ensnared in the trade. One witness claimed a guidebook to procuring boys for sex called *Where the Young Ones Are* had sold 70,000 copies at $5 each. Another told the tale of an eight-year-old hustler who plied his trade by inviting men to take him to the bathroom with the come on, "It's $10 and you have got ten minutes."

Representative Bob Dornan of Orange County berated all the "friends of child molesters" who "whimper" about the First Amendment. Cooler heads pointed out how dubious, even ridiculous, much of this testimony was. If *Where the Young Ones Are* was so readily available, one asked, why couldn't congressional investigators locate a copy? Another produced a nuanced piece by columnist Ellen Goodman that argued macabre tales like these let the statistically far more prevalent perpetrators of sexual abuse—parents and stepparents—off the hook. The cofounder of Los Angeles's Gay Community Services Center, the first such social service agency in the country, complained that the conservative members' "single-minded preoccupation with homosexuality" obscured the fact that 96 percent of sex crimes against children were committed by heterosexuals. (It arrived much later that one contributor to the remaining 4 percent was

Father Ritter himself, who used his Times Square ministry to lure young boys into sex.)

But when it came the subject of crime, as the spring of 1977 turned to summer, cooler heads held little sway.

Eight young women and two young men had been shot in parked cars in New York's outer boroughs since the previous summer. In March of 1977, Mayor Abraham Beame announced that the same .44-caliber pistol gun had been used in the shootings—and the local tabloids were suddenly filled with lurid daily headlines about the serial killer on the loose. On May 30, *Daily News* columnist Jimmy Breslin received a letter from a man claiming to be the killer—which police investigators, who were getting nowhere in the case, asked the tabloid to publish:

> *Hello from the gutters of N.Y.C. which are filled with dog manure, vomit, stale wine, and blood. Hello from the sewers of N.Y.C. which swallow up these delicacies when they are washed away by the sweeper trucks. Hello from the cracks in the sidewalk of N.Y.C. and from these ants that dwell in these cracks . . .*

It was signed, "Son of Sam." Breslin offered his services should the killer wish to turn himself in to authorities. (The story shared the front page with an image of burning cars captioned, "Two Dead in Chicago Riot.") The rival *New York Post*, recently purchased by the Australian yellow-journalism magnate Rupert Murdoch, ramped up the sensationalism to keep pace. You could read the terror at a distance, just walking down the street; an inordinate number of women cut their hair in Dorothy Hamill bobs. Son of Sam's victims all had long hair.

A week later, another alleged serial killer was on the loose—an interstate offender. Ted Bundy was a young, charismatic former law student with a face from out of a cologne ad, a Republican campaign volunteer who'd attended the 1968 convention as a Nelson Rockefeller delegate. In 1971, he began abducting, murdering, and sexually mutilating pretty young women around universities in Seattle. He moved to Utah, became a Mormon, then slaughtered some more. He was captured and went to jail in Colorado in January 1977—then, six months later, during a preliminary hearing, he jumped out a courthouse window and eluded his captors for almost a week.

THE NEWS WAS A BANQUET OF TERRORS. A LONGING FOR INNOCENCE, FOR good guys putting paid to bad guys, was one result. It showed up at the box office before it registered at the ballot box.

In the 1960s, after a long decline brought on by the rise of television and the waning of the old studio system, Hollywood began abandoning formulaic stories and a predictable stable of stars in favor of adventurous fare from filmmakers like Martin Scorsese, Arthur Penn, Dennis Hopper, and Robert Altman, who drew inspiration from the art cinema of Europe. Films began featuring moral ambiguity, dark moods, a suffusing skepticism toward establishments of every description—and the public flocked to them. Hits were movies like Bernardo Bertolucci's *Last Tango in Paris* (1972), a picture about a kinky random sexual encounter, a rape, and a murder, which made $96.3 million on a budget of $1.25 million. Francis Ford Coppola's 1972 and 1974 *Godfather* films, which treated mainstream and mafia success in the United States as nearly interchangeable, earned in the hundreds of millions. *Last Tango* and *The Godfather* starred Marlon Brando at a time when he was fat and nearly fifty years old. Leading men who were not conventionally attractive—short, awkward Dustin Hoffman and shaggy Elliott Gould, both visibly Jewish; Jack Nicholson, carrying himself with a cruel air of menace—was another sign of what critics celebrated as the country's newly maturing cinematic taste. At the Oscars in 1976 the deeply subversive anti-institutional parable *One Flew Over the Cuckoo's Nest*, starring Nicholson—another $100 million earner—took home all five of the major statues.

But at the ceremony on March 28, 1977, the Academy overlooked sophisticated New Hollywood fare like *All the President's Men*, the Watergate thriller; *Bound for Glory*, a visually luscious biopic of Woody Guthrie featuring depictions of American poverty as searing as any ever committed to the screen; and *Taxi Driver*, a sepulchral masterpiece of urban alienation, about a Vietnam veteran named Travis Bickle, driven insane by the "open sewer" that New York City had become, who tries to assassinate a presidential candidate to impress a child prostitute played by a thirteen-year-old. Instead, they celebrated a conventionally inspiring and vaguely reactionary picture in which the audience's every emotion was cued by a swelling musical score, a movie labeled "pure 1930s make-believe" by Vincent Canby of the *New York Times*. *Rocky* was the story of an Italian-American boxer who went the distance against a mouthy black champion modeled on Muhammad Ali. Its Academy Awards for Best Picture and Best Director felt to disappointed critics like a political statement: New Hollywood, with all its vaguely left-wing pretensions, was down for the count.

The knockout blow came in the summer of 1977.

George Lucas was one of the young directors who got his chance with the New Hollywood wave. His first film, a freakish dystopian sci-fi nightmare called *THX 1138*, was a commercial disaster. His next, *American Graffiti*, about high school kids hanging out in hot rod–crazed early-sixties California, was nostalgic, ebullient, and a hit. "I discovered that making a positive film is exhilarating," Lucas later reflected. "I thought, 'Maybe I should make a film like this for even younger kids. . . . Kids today don't have any fantasy life the way we had—they don't have Westerns, they don't have pirate movies." He decided to aim his next movie at eight- or nine-year-olds. "Everybody's forgetting to tell the kids, 'Hey, this is right and this is wrong.'" The action consisted of one Old Hollywood pastiche after another. *Star Wars* was a Ronald Reagan sort of film.

When Lucas was writing the script, in a room with a nostalgic Wurlitzer jukebox, he was sure it wouldn't go far. "I've made what I consider the most conventional kind of movie I can possibly make," Lucas explained, "a Disney movie. . . . All Disney movies make $16 million, so this picture is going to make $16 million." Instead, it grossed $100 million in three months.

Pauline Kael of the *New Yorker* wrote in dismay, "The excitement of those who call it the film of the year goes way past nostalgia to the feeling that now is the time to return to childhood." By November, *Star Wars* had become the highest grossing movie of all time. The public longed for escape. There was more than enough unpleasantness outside the theater already.

STAR WARS WAS NOT A JIMMY CARTER SORT OF FILM. THE NATION'S cardigan-wearing prophet of sacrifice drew little inspiration from morality tales. His favorite theologian was Reinhold Niebuhr, an anti-utopian who despised simple answers and cheap grace, let alone conservatives who believed that all the answers for living could be easily and painlessly extracted from the plain text of the Bible. Niebuhr believed that a too-simple division of the world into lightness and dark led to calamity. Carter's favorite quote from him was "The sad duty of politics is to establish justice in a sinful world"—not exactly a Disney sort of message. The president's taste for Niebuhrian moral complexity was one of the things that made him so ideologically ambiguous—not an easy thing to be in a culture clamoring more and more for easy solutions in confusing times.

You could see this in July after the *Washington Post* reported the existence of a secret strategy document, "Presidential Review Memorandum 10," that some claimed outlined a new, harder line against the Soviet menace—but which others, including one of Evans and Novak's anonymous neoconservative sources, argued was pushing greater *accommodation* with the Soviet Union. In fact, it did both, in different ways for different contexts. The world was a complex place—and that was not always an easy thing for a politician to explain.

In a democracy, ideological difference-splitting can be a dangerous game. Done well, it can suture together an expanded political coalition.

Done indelicately, it can convince every potential supporter that the politician is working for the other team. Which was what was happening now. Sometimes Carter did things that pleased conservatives and outraged liberals—like his pledges to reduce federal spending. Other times, he outraged conservatives and pleased liberals—like when he canceled development of a new B-1 strategic bomber. Which ended with everyone just being outraged. And the challenge was particularly vexing when it came to the social issues, which just became more and more polarizing as the summer advanced.

Anita Bryant's triumph spurred an angry counter-mobilization. In San Francisco, the night of the vote in Miami the cry echoed across the Castro district: "Out of the bars and into the streets!" Five hundred people marched spontaneously to Union Square, chanting all the way. In New York, the spontaneous throngs that massed in front of the Stonewall Inn before coursing through Greenwich Village streets numbered in the thousands. Though the response in Houston was perhaps the most impressive of all. Anita Bryant came to town to sing before a convention of the Texas State Bar Association. A crowd estimated at six thousand, including a considerable number of clergy, massed before the convention hotel to chant and sing their opposition to her presence—in a part of the country where declaring for gay rights could cost a career.

Another demonstration was less uplifting. Protesters gathered on Boston Common before a Chinese wok shooting forth flames like a witch's cauldron. An activist attired in doctoral robes he hoped would make him look like a warlock incinerated his Harvard diploma, a dollar bill, a letter from Boston College denying his request to teach a gay studies course, the Commonwealth's seventeenth-century sodomy statute—and then, to shocked cries of "*No! No! No!*"—a Bible.

Richard Viguerie made sure to feature that in the fundraising piece for a new organization, Anita Bryant Ministries, which aimed to take her crusade nationwide:

Dear Friend:

I don't hate the homosexual.

But as a mother, I must protect my children from their evil influence.

I am sure you have heard about my fight here in Dade County. . . . When the militant homosexuals lost the public vote in Dade County, their friends in New England burned the Holy Bible! . . .

Even five- and six-year-olds are being photographed and used for perverted sexual appetites.

The Gallup Organization now recorded that two-thirds of the voting public thought gays should have equal rights on the job—mostly; the same proportion also believed that gays should *not* be allowed to teach in public schools. In Orange County, California, a state senator and Oklahoma Pentecostal preacher's son named John Briggs hoped to ride that statistic to unseat Governor Jerry Brown in 1978.

Briggs had traveled to Miami to watch the Save Our Children campaign in action. On the day of the vote, he expressed his awe in an interview: "You got half the voters of Dade County at the polls just to vote for *this*." He compared that to the turnout on the Election Day that elected Governor Brown in 1974: also 50 percent. He returned home and promised to introduce what he called a "right-to-discriminate bill" banning the hiring of gay teachers in California schools; and, if that failed, to get enough signatures to put it on the ballot as an initiative for the November 1978 general election—"to make sure the normal majority gets its voice heard here in California." First, however, he introduced a senate resolution praising Bryant's "courageous stand to protect American children from exposure to blatant homosexuality." It was rejected 36–2. Then, on Tuesday, June 14, he set up a podium in the magnificent plaza in front of San Francisco's City Hall, a glorious domed structure that outshone many statehouses, called the place "the fountainhead of all homosexuality activity in the country," "in captured-nation status," and announced his candidacy for governor—on, as it were, Anita Bryant's coattails.

"Normal people have a right to be heard!" he cried.

"Stop the new Hitler now!" came the response from the scores of angry gays who came to heckle him. Briggs had to be escorted from the scene by policemen with drawn batons.

That day, the Sacramento legislature debated one bill outlawing employment discrimination against gays, and another outlawing gay marriage—even though it was already illegal. Four days later, Congress voted to strike down the new regulation opening public housing to unmarried couples, including homosexual couples. The *New York Times* asked the president to comment. He responded, "I don't see homosexuality as a threat to the family"—then split the difference: "I don't feel that it is a normal relationship." And that "highly publicized confrontations" over the subject were unfortunate—perhaps referring to another event that day in San Francisco in which Vice President Mondale appeared with Mayor George Moscone in Golden Gate Park and was drowned out by hecklers shouting, "Gay rights are human rights!"

The next day, the *New York Times* reported that preliminary plans to realize Jimmy Carter's campaign promise for a White House conference on the family were bogging down over "differences over homosexuality, feminism, and abortion" that might sink the project altogether.

And, two days after that, in San Francisco, a man named Robert Hillsborough was stabbed fifteen times in the face and chest by four men calling out the "faggot" and crying, "Here's one for Anita!" Mayor George Moscone said Briggs would "have to live with his conscience" for the murder.

POLARIZING SOCIAL ISSUES CRASHED IN ON ONE ANOTHER: HOMOSEXUALITY— then abortion.

Conservatives had been trying and failing to ban Medicaid, the free federal healthcare program for the poor, from paying for abortions since shortly after *Roe v. Wade*. Then, in the closing weeks before the 1976 election, a first-term congressman from suburban Chicago named Henry Hyde—"a 626-month-old fetus," as he liked to introduce himself at pro-life meetings, in a working-class Chicago accent that made him sound like he had just knocked off work at a construction site—decided hostage-taking might better accomplish the job. He attached a rider to the combined appropriation bill for the Departments of Labor and Health, Education, and Welfare—a bill that, if it did not pass, would force those departments to shut down. For the first of many, many times, overwhelmingly male legislators launched into an acrimonious debate over the "Hyde Amendment": "the right to life" versus "the right to choose"; "the health and safety of the mother" versus "the right to life of the unborn"; medical exceptions, rape exceptions, incest exceptions . . . until, one day, the chamber hit a gruesome new low with angry arguments ringing out for and against which *sorts* of rape victims should qualify.

Early in 1977, the House passed the Hyde Amendment but not the Senate, sending the appropriation to a conference committee, which deadlocked; then it was back to the respective chambers, and on June 17, the day before Jimmy Carter announced he didn't believe homosexuality was a threat to the family, and Congress banned gay couples from public housing, the House once more approved the Hyde Amendment in an even more resounding vote—a result coincidentally announced live to a deafening roar from the three thousand delegates to the National Right to Life Committee's convention in Chicago. "I've never seen such joy," one activist said.

They then reelected their president to a third term by acclamation. Dr. Mildred Jefferson was a beloved figure in the movement: the first black woman to graduate from Harvard Medical School, and one of the rare Protestants to have joined the pro-life movement before *Roe v. Wade*, after the American Medical Association considered ruling that it was ethical for its members to perform abortions, when she began conceptualizing abortion as a white plot to limit the black population. Now, in Chicago, Dr. Jefferson stepped up to the podium before her enraptured admirers and decried "the cruel use of poor people as pawns in the emotional game of those who demand abortion as a social expedient," and reiterated the NRLC's foundational goal: a "Human Life Amendment" to the Constitution outlawing all abortions, forever. She hailed the House vote as a welcome first step—and a useful political tool: "By this time Tuesday, every organization affiliated with us will know who voted for us and those who voted against us." Lyndon Johnson liked to call political moments of truth like that "getting down to the nut cutting."

NEXT UP WAS CAPITAL PUNISHMENT.

The California Supreme Court, in December, had struck down that state's death penalty statute for falling afoul of one of the tests established by *Gregg v. Georgia*: it mandated executions for certain sorts of murders without requiring juries to approve the sentence. In May, the state senate's criminal justice committee advanced a revised bill written by Republican George Deukmejian, even though a majority of that committee *opposed* capital punishment. The reason it advanced anyway was that the majority feared an even more draconian version might be put forward if this one was not. That became one of the signposts of the extremely emotional debate that would rock the state in the weeks to come: a fear of the lengths demagogic politicians might go to sate the public's bloodlust in a state where the homicide rate had quintupled since 1963.

Governor Brown, back when he was a Jesuit seminarian, begged his father, Governor Pat Brown—to no avail—to spare the life of kidnaper Caryl Chessman in 1960. He was adamant in his pledge to veto *any* death penalty bill, "as a matter of conscience." That meant proponents needed a two-thirds majority in both chambers to override him. They started out three votes shy in the eighty-member assembly, with twenty-eight Democrats for and nineteen against—and not a single Republican opposed. Eight members were reported to be on the fence. And so the ugly business began.

A "Law and Order Campaign Committee" headed by Senator H. L. Richardson of Gun Owners of America and Los Angeles county sheriff Ed Davis, an unannounced candidate for governor, ran an "open letter to the criminals of California" in newspapers across the state, orchestrated from Richard Viguerie's shop: "We, the law abiding and peaceful citizens of California, do hereby declare all-out war against you who have been literally getting away with murder. We are sick and tired of the soft-on-crime judges and bleeding heart 'reformers' who have time and time again set you free to make victims of our friends and families." Readers were invited to clip out a handy coupon to send to their representatives. It read, "I strongly urge you to vote FOR Senator Deukmejian's bill to restore the death penalty in Cali. Restoration of the death penalty is vital to the protection of Californians against the merciless killers who have little fear of being caught and NO fear of being fully punished for their vicious crimes."

"Getting away with murder": Jerry Brown became fond of that phrase as well. He deployed it in boasts that this was what was happening before *he* strengthened criminal penalties left over from the days of that old softy Governor Reagan. People saw society becoming "more lawless," he told TV's Phil Donahue in an interview before five hundred spectators outside the Sacramento Convention Center—which was why he had added new mandatory sentences for crimes like selling heroin and committing crimes using a gun, and increased those that already existed for repeat offenders.

But he would not back down when it came to restoring the gas chamber: "That's an absolute and I don't like absolutes."

His constituents did. Donahue asked the live audience to register whether they agreed with a show of applause; the governor lost overwhelmingly. The next day, he announced he would gladly give up give up his power to commute life sentences, but also reiterated that he would veto the death penalty bill even if it he knew it would be overridden, and issued no objection when the California Senate Judiciary Committee passed a "law and order" bill allowing prosecutors to obtain convictions with evidence that had been obtained illegally. The concessions were to no avail: consistently, polls showed two-thirds of Californians wanted those gas chambers back.

The two sides fought it out in the letters pages. A liberal said social science had demonstrated that the deterrent effect of capital punishment was a myth. An assemblyman from Glendale retorted, "The people of California have spoken, and they feel it is a deterrent to murder." A Mrs. A. Sullivan of Long Beach wrote, "I would like to say if Governor Brown vetoes the death penalty he is encouraging murder.... A few public executions would change the minds of some of these people." Her neighbor William Tuggle riposted that the ancient English practice of publicly hanging pickpockets hadn't prevented pickpockets from having a field day among the gawking spectators at the hangings.

They debated the effectiveness of incarceration:

"I am Todd Murray, a son of a policeman. I am thirteen years old, and I am for the death penalty. People go out and kill a person and then go to jail. . . . The taxpayers pay for the food and support for the criminals that have killed and then been paroled only to kill again. They are not worried about serving a few years in prison. They are supposed to serve time in jail and have a terrible time so they never think of killing again. They're not supposed to have a party in jail!" One response read, "Let me congratulate you on your intelligence. You have more brains that Governor Brown will ever have." Another ran, "Todd goes to my school and we are in the same social studies class. A few years ago I visited a local sheriff's station. To me it didn't look like life in jail was all fun 'n' games. Perhaps the sentence of life imprisonment without possibility of parole would make people think before they commit a crime."

("In the class discussion," the last letter writer added, "I was a minority of one.")

On May 14, Governor Pierre DuPont reversed his former intention to veto Delaware's death penalty bill. On May 16, the California assembly debated Deukmejian's. A conservative from Fullerton said, "Our role is clear—to reinstate a law that God gave at the beginning of time." A liberal from San Diego responded, "I hope God forgives you, but personally I don't."

The final dramatic "aye" pushing it past the tally required to override a veto was cast at the last possible minute by an anti–death penalty Democrat terrified that a more draconian initiative being drawn up by law enforcement interests might become law instead. Another last-minute supporter said he had reached "the most agonizing decision of my life" after visiting the death row at San Quentin and being "struck by the utter remorselessness of some of these people." (He possibly was also struck by a poll showing 84 percent of his constituents were pro–death penalty.) Already that day members had rejected amendments intended to assure the law's approval by the U.S. Supreme Court, which the bill's floor manager said liberal judges could use to "nullify every death penalty verdict in the state"—and, in a separate debate, passed a measure making it harder for convicted murderers to obtain parole.

The *Los Angeles Times* editorialized that capital punishment adds "to the pervasive savagery that defiles this age." Brown's veto message a few days later echoed that: "Statistics can be marshaled and arguments propounded. But at some point, each of us must decide for himself what sort of future he would want. For me, this would be a society where we do not attempt to use death as a punishment." And any hope the grinding acrimony might soon abate was dashed when Senator John Briggs, in a press conference recalling with relish his attendance at the state's *last* execution, in 1967, announced that he would *not* vote to override the governor's veto—for it would be much preferable to hang the issue around his neck seventeen months later, when the ballot for his election would be shared with a death penalty initiative Briggs promised would be "much tougher than the Deukmejian bill," which lamentably provided a role for "fuzzy-thinking, soft-hearted judges."

After Briggs recruited a supportive cadre of fellow Republicans, and one said, "It would be interesting to have Governor Brown go before every audience and explain why he's against the death penalty," a columnist predicted the 1978 governor's race would be a "campaign by death"; a cartoonist depicted California trussed up in a noose. The letters pages once more filled with vituperation. Briggs said he would pursue his initiative *even if* Deukmejian's bill succeeded: he would run for governor on Anita Bryant's coattails and Gary Gilmore's, both. The state's attorney general, Evelle Younger, who had the inside track to face Brown in 1978, first begged Briggs to withdraw it—then, failing, announced he might launch his *own* death penalty initiative campaign, floating the name of Ronald Reagan as chairman. Reagan, panicked at the prospect, begged "every California voter to write to his or her legislator today, asking them to override the veto."

Independence Day approached. Death talk was everywhere.

The Supreme Court struck down a Louisiana law mandating death for cop killers. ("Every day it becomes more apparent that the day will soon arrive when the American people will have to resort to force to overthrow the government in order to protect their own interests," responded a writer in the *Long Beach Independent*.) On June 22, the governor of Illinois signed capital punishment into law. The next day, the California senate overrode Brown's veto without a vote to spare—but the ordeal wasn't nearly over, because the assembly would not hold *its* override vote until after a July recess.

During debate, Senator H. L. Richardson wheeled a cart out onto the floor piled high with mail bags he claimed contained two hundred thousand signed coupons from his and Sheriff Ed Davis's open letter to the criminals of California. He made sure to note that computers could easily sort the signatories by assembly district.

Word was that Sheriff Davis would be running for governor, too. He was even more homophobic than Briggs. He called gays "lepers," and got a hooting and hollering standing ovation at the California Correctional Officer Association for griping, "I always felt the federal government was out to force me to hire four-foot-eleven-inch transvestite morons." Some officers stood on their chairs.

Crashing, crashing, crashing.

In New York, on June 26, the Son of Sam claimed his fifth corpse. The manhunt was the largest in city history; the task force dedicated to catching the killer began receiving as many as a thousand tips a day, to no avail.

In Washington, D.C., on June 27 the House voted 230–133 for an amendment written by Representative Larry McDonald banning funding for federal "legal assistance with respect to any proceeding or litigation arising out of disputes or controversies on the issue of homosexuality or so-called 'gay rights.'"

On June 29, the Senate approved a weakened version of the Hyde Amendment after the most caustic floor debate so far. Senator Birch Bayh of Indiana noted "a remarkable parallel" between abortion foes and those voting against housing and education bills, who "do not have the same degree of sensitivity for the quality of life *after* birth." Orrin Hatch replied that he discerned "remarkable similarity between those who believe in abortion and those who are spending us into bankruptcy." Many abortion supporters cast votes for the compromise because they expected a Supreme Court decision any day now that, given the relevant precedents concerning equal protection of the laws, would outlaw the Hyde Amendment altogether.

On Saturday, July 2, a community activist wrote a desperate appeal to the President of the United States about the rash of vandalism against businesses on San Francisco's Castro Street, including his own camera store: "It is now open season on gay people. . . . Please. I will come to Washington to meet you. The nation needs leadership." His name was Harvey Milk, and he was planning a new run for the city's board of supervisors. An Irish-Catholic former San Francisco cop and fireman was preparing to run, too. He composed an election pamphlet promising, "I am not going to be forced out of San Francisco by splinter groups of radicals, social deviates, and incorrigibles." His name was Dan White.

On the nation's 201st birthday, a car full of teenagers picked up a hitchhiker. A girl put a gun to his head: "If you breathe, we're gonna kill you, faggot." They drove to a dark street, where two boys took turns raping him, crying, "Anita is right! Anita is right!" When the victim told an emergency room doctor at the University of California Medical Center what had happened, the doctor replied, "Well, you are homosexual, aren't you?"

On July 5, the Shah of Iran received an honorary doctorate of humane letters from the University of Southern California—in recognition, its president intoned before an audience that included Ronald Reagan, Mayor Tom Bradley, and Pearl Bailey, for "your magnificent service to your country and man and womankind." He thanked the shah's wife the Empress Farah Diba Pahlavi for her gift of an endowed chair in petroleum engineering. Outside, a hundred police in riot gear stood on tactical alert, eying livid Iranian students burning the royal couple in effigy, calling the shah a "butcher" and "puppet," decrying his "honorary degree for fascism." They wore masks to hide their identity from agents of the shah's savage secret police force SAVAK. At the reception at Chasen's, guests including Clare Boothe Luce, Eva Gabor, Dinah Shore, the Gregory Pecks, the James Masons, and an Iranian security force of sixty-five. "There was beaucoup Dom Perignon, Pouilly-Fuissé, and an excellent Chateau Margaux '66," the *Los Angeles Times* society page reported. "The buzzing that went on all through the party came from the helicopter that circled over the restaurant protectively."

THE NEXT DAY JIMMY CARTER FACED A CONUNDRUM. LIBERALS CONSIDERED the ban on Medicaid funding abortions an outrageous injustice. Conservatives considered the Senate version of the ban, as Henry Hyde put it, "a Christmas tree of exemptions and loopholes" that "permits abortions for everything, including athlete's foot." A decisive Supreme Court ruling would absolve the president of the necessity of taking a side. Instead, the court sent the ruling back down to the U.S. district court of Judge John F. Dooling Jr. for further consideration. The Senate vote having fallen far short of the veto-override threshold meant the ball would soon be in the president's court: he could split differences no more.

"Mr. President," he was asked at a televised press conference on July 12, whether *he* thought the federal government should be "obligated to provide money for abortions for women who cannot afford to pay for them themselves." He responded, "As you know, there are many things in life that are not fair that wealthy people can afford and poor people cannot. But I don't believe that the Federal Government should take action to try to make these opportunities exactly equal, particularly when there is a moral factor involved." He had chosen Henry Hyde's side.

White House public liaison Midge Costanza's phone began ringing off the hook. She wrote Carter a blistering letter conveying the sense of betrayal of many administration staffers. She received an unsatisfying response: "My opinion was well-defined to the U.S. during the campaign. . . . My statement was more liberal than I feel personally." She gathered nearly all of the forty-two female presidential appointees at the Old Executive Office Building, where they drafted an outraged letter to the commander in chief: "Is it moral to force a 15-year-old girl on welfare to carry a pregnancy to term? Is it moral to ask a mother of five to have yet another child, to lose her job and forgo any possibility of ever getting off welfare? Above all, is it moral for this country to advocate human rights and liberty abroad, while depriving the weakest in our society of their moral and human rights?" Gloria Steinem, the editor of the feminist magazine *Ms.*, had once been a Carter enthusiast. No longer. The cover of the magazine's end-of-the-year wrap-up issue depicted him with a bulging, pregnant belly, and a cover line that doubled as a jab at his mounting political woes: "Carter Discovers 'Life Is Unfair.'"

Liberals thought they knew him. They thought *he was one of them*. Now many were beginning to despise him. Such were the wages of election by making everyone think you were on their side. Jules Witcover and Jack Germond, joint authors of a widely syndicated column, encapsulated Carter's political problems at the six-month mark by quoting a Republican voter: "The party told me last year he was a liberal, but now everybody says he's a conservative, and then he does something like cave in on that bomber. I don't know what the hell he is."

Crashing, crashing, crashing.

The day after Jimmy Carter's "life isn't fair" press conference, at 9:27 p.m., the five boroughs of Travis Bickle's open sewer suddenly went dark, and the mad vortex of the fictional *Taxi Driver* became real.

New York had suffered a blackout in 1965. During its thirteen hours, the crime rate declined. Indeed, once New Yorkers became convinced that Russian missiles weren't on the way, the wary anonymity of the city had transformed itself into a contagion of joy. They even made a movie about it, *Where Were You When the Lights Went Out?*, a frothy Doris Day romp that ended with a blessed event precisely nine months later. The posters advertised, "Oh, the liberties that were taken the night New York City flipped its fuse . . ."

In 1977, different sorts of liberties were taken: 1965-inverted, formerly alienated, atomized Gothamites once more united in carnivalesque communion, this time to strip the city bare.

Police arriving at one of the first Manhattan stores to be looted, at 99th and Broadway—not a slum—were met with a hail of bottles. In depressed neighborhoods like Bushwick in Brooklyn, marauders pried open stores' steel shutters with crowbars, or jimmied hooks beneath them to pull them free with automobiles. People punched through display windows, their fists wrapped in towels to keep blood off the clothes they ripped from the mannequins. Sporting goods stores were relieved of guns and ammo. A *Daily News* reporter witnessed fifty Pontiacs driven off a new car lot in the Bronx "in a motorcade with horns blaring and pretty girls waving from the windows."

Since New York's near bankruptcy in 1975, 3,400 police and 1,000 firemen had been laid off. Those remaining had had their wages frozen. The year 1976 was the worst for crime in New York's history. In the 83rd Precinct in Bedford-Stuyvesant, rookies were given three simple rules: "Don't walk close to the buildings (someone might drop a brick on you). Don't let neighborhood kids wear your hat (lice). Always check the earpiece on call boxes before using it (dog shit)." And that was under *normal* circumstances.

Every officer was ordered to report to duty immediately; 40 percent didn't bother. Others arrived in street clothes, unarmed. (Helpfully, looters had left behind the baseball bats at a big sporting goods store in Brooklyn; and in any event, cops were under orders to keep their guns holstered.) So many support staff had been laid off that it took at least ten hours to process each arrest. City buses filled with men in chains stopped at jail after jail, searching for empty cells. A riot broke out at the Bronx House of Detention. Prisoners escaped from Rikers Island. The gay magazine *Michael's Thing* reported an orgy on Weehawken Street in the West Village. ("Nudity was the rule; many guys were pushed against cars and performed upon with the full consent of everyone there.") In Times Square, entrepreneurs with flashlights sold secure passage for $2. "Considering the dubious occupations of some of those characters," the BBC's Alistair Cooke ventured, "I think I would have chosen to stagger alone."

Political conclusions were drawn. Herbert Gutman, a respected left-wing professor of labor history, said the boundary decent folks insisted on drawing between the supposed "vultures" and "jackals" infesting the city and their own, more upright immigrant forebears was specious, that in 1902, Yiddish-speaking Jewish housewives rioted over the price of kosher meat and were called "animals" and "beasts," too. Midge Decter responded in her husband's neoconservative magazine *Commentary* that that the looters *were* in fact "urban insect life," that it was like "having been given a sudden glimpse into the foundations of one's house and seen, with horror, that it was utterly infested and rotting away," and that the real problem was that "liberal racists" refused to hold minorities to the same moral standards they demanded of themselves.

It just so happened that, the day before the blackout, New York's governor Hugh Carey had vetoed a death penalty bill: "It lowers all of us who abide by the law and the Judeo-Christian tradition of preserving and perfecting the dignity of all life." As in California, he defied public opinion. And also, as it also happened, New York City was in the middle of a mayoral campaign.

THE DEMOCRATIC PRIMARY'S FIRST ROUND WAS SEPTEMBER 6. ONE CANDI-date, Manhattan borough president Percy Sutton, all but suspended his campaign. It didn't matter that he had been running commercials proclaiming himself the tough-on-crime candidate. He was African American. After the riots, that meant he no longer stood a chance. For a similar reason—he was Puerto Rican—Congressman Herman Badillo was way back in last place.

The second-place contender was the incumbent, Abraham Beame, a dull, plodding product of the Democratic clubhouses, doing the best he could to manage the awful hand he'd been dealt. The city had lost 340,000 jobs since 1973. (About the only business thriving was pornography: a new huge storefront named "Show World" had just opened up at 42nd Street and 8th Avenue, featuring live sex acts behind plexiglass. It hosted some four thousand customers a day.) The *Daily News* ran an editorial in spring, then the *Times* a couple of days later, arguing that the sorry state of New York under his mayoralty suggested Beame shouldn't even be running.

In fourth place, with 6 percent, was Congressman Edward Koch. He had been a brash fixture in the city since 1961, when he defended beatniks arrested for performing in Washington Square Park without a permit. He was known as a liberal, had cosponsored the federal gay rights bill—the one introduced by Bella Abzug, who was running in first place in the mayoral race. Her flamboyant hats, abrasive manner, and uncompromising liberalism had made her a national celebrity, her candidacy heralded on *Saturday Night Live*, when Gilda Radner's hard-of-hearing character Emily Litella asked if Abzug would throw her "cat into the ring." Running on a promise to give every out-of-work civil servant his or her job back, she began the race ahead by a comfortable thirty-six points.

Third place belonged to a wild card named Mario Cuomo. The son of an Italian grocery store owner, after graduating at the top of his class at St. John's School of Law in Queens, he turned his resentment at being denied job after job in Manhattan's white-shoe law firms into a righteous rage for justice—tempered, unlike many liberals', with a profound empathy for the white ethnic world of his childhood, confused and displaced by the tumult of the 1960s. When the city made plans to bulldoze sixty-nine lower-middle-class homes in the neighborhood of Flushing-Corona in Queens, Cuomo became a tabloid hero by successfully representing the homeowners. When he lost a run for lieutenant governor in 1974, Governor Carey made him secretary of state. Carey persuaded Cuomo to run for mayor to block Abzug. Jackie Onassis said, "He reminds me of my husband." He better resembled RFK. He quoted Augustine, read deeply in the classics, and wrote in his diary every day. He opposed the death penalty on religious grounds. But the "Italian Hamlet" had driven his aides crazy by refusing to decide until May. The *New York Times* endorsed him: "Mr. Cuomo, to End the Tribalism." The *Village Voice* called him "New York's Great Smart Hope." For Cuomo, it appeared the sky was the limit.

Until, that is, blackout rioting in a city already teetering on the brink of madness threw it all into confusion.

Abzug fearlessly ventured into the riot zone with a blackout-inspired slogan—"Vote Bella: She's the greatest energy source in America"—imploring New Yorkers to stop paying bills to Consolidated Edison, "this rapacious monopoly," arguing that the city should take it over. One day, before a pocket of whites in a crime-ridden outer-borough neighborhood, her polka-dotted sundress swaying in the breeze, she argued her most unpopular position: granting police the right to strike.

"But what would you have done if the police had been on strike during the blackout?"

"Mobilize the community organizations and get them into the streets."

"The community *was* mobilized. They were all out looting."

On July 31, the Son of Sam produced his sixth corpse. On August 3, a terrorist's bomb exploded in the Manhattan office of the Defense Department. Minutes later, a caller to a TV newsroom announced that others had been placed in a nearby skyscraper housing several Latin American consulates, the World Trade Center, and office towers housing American Brands and Mobil Oil. Thirty-five thousand officer workers were evacuated from the twin towers. Two hundred more bomb threats poured into switchboards across the city. Soon, some one hundred thousand evacuated office workers stood idle on the streets.

"What do they want, anyway?" one asked another.

"I think they want freedom for Puerto Rico."

"Puerto Rico isn't free?"

The metropolis was a waking nightmare—and suddenly the defining issue in the mayoral race became which candidates would "bring back little hot squat," which was what the *Daily News* called the electric chair. Even though mayors had no jurisdiction over the question.

"Battling Bella," naturally, was opposed. She had been a radical since at least the age of thirteen, when she defied her family's Orthodox rabbi and said Kaddish every morning—even though she was a girl—after her mother died in 1933. Elected student body president at Hunter College, the *New York Post* called her a "known campus pink." When she defended alleged Communists, Joseph McCarthy called her "one of the most subversive lawyers in the country." On her first day in Congress in 1971, a year and a half before the Watergate break-in, she introduced a resolution to impeach Richard Nixon. She cosponsored one bill for a national childcare system, and another forbidding the federal government from using titles indicating marital status. And yet her radicalism had not prevented her from coming within a single point of defeating Daniel Patrick Moynihan in the 1976 Democratic senate primary.

But suddenly, in New York's summer of rage, it was an open question whether she would make the runoff.

Cuomo, when asked why he opposed capital punishment, responded, "The death penalty cannot provide jobs for the poor. The electric chair cannot balance the budget. The electric chair cannot educate our children.

The electric chair cannot give us a sound economy or save us from bankruptcy or even save my seventy-seven-year-old mother." One time when he said it, an old lady in Brooklyn spat in his face. Another, someone stood up and cried, "Kill them!"

Ed Koch hardly disagreed—and he made sure everyone knew it. Graceless, impolitic, and gnomish-looking, his own media advisor, the savvy David Garth, originally gave him a forty-to-one shot. He worked to improve the odds by framing his client as a street-smart neoconservative—a "liberal with sanity." Koch would pull up in his campaign Winnebago, the speaker blaring his theme song from the hit musical *Annie*: "*N! Y! C! What is it about youuuu? You're big! You're loud! You're tough!*" His lumpy six-foot-two frame leaning in, he'd blare lustily into the battery-powered loudspeaker about how he was sick of all the "poverty pimps" and "poverticians" holding a broke city hostage, demand the abolition of the Board of Education (a "lard barrel of waste"), denounce welfare fraud, decry "the nuts on the left who dump on middle class values"—and, defying all received New York political wisdom, sock it to the city's supposedly all-powerful municipal unions, even the Patrolman's Benevolent Association. (Why should cops get free vacation days for donating blood? "All I get is a Lorna Doone and a cup of coffee.") And, as for the death penalty, Koch not only said he was for it, but that he had *always* been for it.

His liberal former friends, remembering the man who spent the summer of 1964 in Mississippi doing civil rights legal work for free, were beside themselves. He delighted in baiting them. "The Jews of Forest Hills have to pay their dues!" one yelled during a heated exchange over whether they should have accepted a low-income housing project in their neighborhood instead of protesting it. Shot back Koch, "On the day your kids were born, you registered them in private school . . . they're willing to pay *their* dues. They are not willing to pay *yours*." The slogan Garth devised for him made a virtue of his contrast to Beame and his glamorous but failed predecessor John Lindsay: "After eight years of charisma and four years of the clubhouse, why not try competence?" In the *Voice*, Denis Hamill countered, "After eight years of charisma and four years of the clubhouse, why not try the chair?"

But even high-minded Mario Cuomo was now asking why cops had been so restrained the night of the blackout. Evans and Novak, noting the "naked fear here that the looters may reassert their impunity some ordinary evening at sunset without waiting for a power blackout," reported that Abzug's lead was disappearing. Beame asked for Son of Sam to be declared a "terrorist" so he would be eligible for the death penalty. "For those who have lived through this mad week in New York," the *Times* editorialized, "there is a shared sense of outrage and impotence. Why can't

300 policemen find 'Son of Sam'? How many more innocent people will be killed by madmen with guns or bombs? Is New York City, after all, a failed ultra-urban experiment in which people eventually crack, social order eventually collapses, and reason ultimately leads to despair?" The editorial called all death-penalty lust "The Added Danger of a Savage Week"—"as great as that posed by mad gunmen or fanatic bombers: that their barbarism will provoke ours, that their contempt for the social order will be mirrored in ours."

That familiar argument: *We could succumb to capital punishment. But aren't we better than that?* It was countered by the likes of William F. Buckley, who argued that *thoughtful* liberals—like Ed Koch—now understood that "a failure to terminate a murderer's life isn't a celebration of life but the opposite . . . a society irresolute about its commitment to human life flirts with barbarism."

The California assembly debated the matter again on August 11. A Democrat cried, "We kill and then we say we will not tolerate killings or violence. . . . This kind of rationalization allowed the killing of witches in Salem, the starving of prisoners at Andersonville, the killing of Indians at Wounded Knee, the lynching of blacks in the Deep South, and the extermination of Jews in Germany." A Republican answered that he would feel differently if he returned home and found his wife and children murdered. The veto was overridden. California would now once again put criminals to death. Four days later, a painting by Andy Warhol of poor unfortunate Bella Abzug was bumped from the cover of *Rolling Stone* by the death of Elvis Presley. By then, Ed Koch had shot from 6 percent to 14 percent in the polls—and with a third of Gotham's voters undecided, he had plenty of room to grow. And if liberalism was losing its appeal in America's most cosmopolitan city, what chance did it have anywhere else?

AS NEW YORK CITY SEETHED AND *Star Wars* STILL PACKED THEATERS, RONald Reagan enjoyed a long summer break, spending his happiest moments working on the nineteenth-century adobe house at his ranch, repairing the fence he and the property's caretaker, a retired California Highway Patrolman, had constructed themselves, or paddling Nancy around on the ranch's reservoir—"Lake Lucky"—in a canoe he'd bought her for their silver anniversary and christened *Tru Luv*.

Nancy stepped up their entertaining in Pacific Palisades, hosting elaborate dinner parties for the clutch of wealthy socialites the who called themselves "the Group," lovingly recording the details in an elaborate "party book" she had learned to maintain from her best friends Betsy Bloomingdale, of the department store Bloomingdales, and Marion Jorgenson, whose husband was in steel. ("We had crudités, salmon mousse with sauce *verte*, chicken parmesan, corn sauté, vegetable platter, raspberries and blueberries with Kirsch and whipped cream, brownies, and Mouton Rothschild '52," she wrote of one evening spent hosting the Jorgensens, the Tuttles, the Bloomingdales, and Buff Chandler, owner of the *Los Angeles Times*.) Ronnie always gave an appropriate toast. How far he was from being taken entirely seriously by the nation's gatekeeping elites was suggested that July when Viking published Jules Witcover's massive best-selling chronicle *Marathon: The Pursuit of the Presidency, 1972–1976*. The cover featured a collage of Carter, Ford, and the eleven other serious aspirants for the White House from the previous year—with Reagan squeezed onto the very end, nearly falling off the side.

In Washington, conservatives chipped away at the remnants of the president's electoral reform package. Two New Right congressmen did so by ordering seven fake IDs from an ad in an underground newspaper, taken out in the names of seven Democrats on the House Committee of Jurisdiction. Fanning the fake driver's licenses before him at a press conference, Bob Dornan said their stunt showed "how easy it would be to register and vote under an assumed name."

The stunt was timed to coincide with a Senate filibuster against the same-day registration bill, directed by Senator James Allen. A product of George Wallace's Alabama political machine, Allen was the Senate's acknowledged master of the South's hundred-year tradition of minority sabotage. Filibustering demanded extraordinary preparation, a second-by-second command of the ebb and flow of Senate action, and an encyclopedic understanding of its rules. Some even said Allen had *memorized* those rules. In 1975, he had kept a filibuster alive almost single-handedly for seven weeks, pouring out florid, densely legalistic sentences for hours at a time, sucking on cherry-flavored glucose syrup from a tube for sustenance. The bill he fought would have made it harder to filibuster. In the tradition of Dixie reaction Allen upheld, nothing was worse than majority rule. And on July 27, 1976, he made short work of the same-day registration measure despite a rare bout of arm-twisting of senators from the president. Any chance enough Republicans would break ranks was stanched by grassroots pressure orchestrated by Richard Viguerie.

Public financing of congressional elections was defeated on August 21. "We put together a massive public relations effort," Viguerie said, "and we're going to do the same for the Panama Canal." He was already well on his way when a White House scandal threatened to knock the nation's moralist in chief off his pedestal at last.

CHAPTER 7

Lancegate

IN THE BEGINNING, THOMAS BERTRAM "BERT" LANCE WAS THE CARTER AD-ministration's breakout star. "'Aw-Shucks' Banker for Jimmy," *Time*'s glowing profile of the new director of the Office of Management and Budget called him. Said another, "There were snickers when he lumbered into Washington to take over as budget director. But it soon became clear that he's bound to make a big mark in town." A third called him "smart, affable, and noble."

Bert Lance was not just Jimmy Carter's best friend. He was one of his only close friends. The big, ebullient, high-living man had been a major investor in the Carter family's peanut operation, then in his presidential operation. His loans to Carter had helped him leapfrog the competition in the spring of 1976 when Congress dilly-dallied on paying out Federation Election Commission matching funds. Lance's was the first appointment the president-elect announced.

The Senate Government Affairs Committee's confirmation hearing had flushed out some disquieting facts, for example, that Lance's First Georgia Bank in Atlanta let his relatives overdraw their accounts, and that Lance had illicitly loaned his own failed 1974 gubernatorial campaign $250,000 via an overdraft. But this proved hardly enough for senators to delay his work getting America's fiscal house in order. Republicans were pleased to have a conservative banker in the job—especially one the U.S. comptroller of the currency reported "enjoys a very good reputation in the banking community."

In May, a report emerged that Lance was "hip deep in debt"—not a good look for the man charged with balancing the nation's books. Lance warned Carter that the article might herald further inquiry, and that his bank in Atlanta was in financial trouble, which meant that when he honored his promise to the Senate committee to divest himself of its stock—his principle asset—he would do so at a loss. He offered to resign. Jimmy Carter wasn't having it. He asked the Senate for an extension of Lance's deadline to sell the stock. They agreed. The man the magazine the *Nation's Business* now described as the "unofficial assistant president" stayed put.

It was a former Nixon administration official who moved the matter into scandal territory. William Safire was a New York native who had dropped out of college to take a job as a legman for columnist Tex McCrary of the *New York Herald-Tribune*, a celebrity journalist who also hosted his own TV show with his wife. In violation of the most basic canons of journalistic ethics, McCrary was also a public relations agent—a denizen of the twilight realm immortalized in the 1957 film *Sweet Smell of Success*, where gossip columnists and publicists conspired to titillate the masses and aggrandize themselves. His young protégé watched and learned.

In 1959, Safire cleverly maneuvered the two most powerful men in the world into the "typical American home" set up at the American National Exhibition in Moscow's Sokolniki Park by a McCrary PR client. There, Richard Nixon and Nikita Khrushchev semi-spontaneously engaged in a legendary "kitchen debate" over the relative merits of the communism and capitalism. As Safire told the story in his 1963 book, *The Relations Explosion*, a manual on how to manipulate public perception, Khrushchev's security forces attempted to block a *New York Times* reporter from the enclosure. Safire claimed the man was there to demonstrate the refrigerator—then that a *Life* magazine photographer was with the manufacturer of the washing machine. The media coup that resulted helped catapult Richard Nixon to the 1960 Republican presidential nomination.

Nixon hired Safire as a presidential speechwriter. Upon leaving the White House in 1973, he joined the *New York Times* as a Washington columnist, enjoying the fruit of one of Richard Nixon's most successful PR coups: intimidating the Eastern establishment media into hiring conservatives. Sneaking the norms, standards, and techniques from the world of *Sweet Smell of Success* into the Newspaper of Record, he became one of Washington's most effectual pundits. One thing every gossip columnist knew how to do was destroy a reputation. Indeed, his 1963 book offered a step-by-step how-to. In 1977, he set out to destroy Jimmy Carter's.

He began sending up trial balloons. A January 24, 1977, column punned that Carter's inaugural was "pedestrian." But Safire was about the only one who thought so. So on February 3 he tried another angle of attack, tying a Carter State Department official, Warren Christopher, to "the infamous 'Doar Plan' . . . the then-secret but now-notorious inter-division information unit of the LBJ Justice Department to war on dissenters."

Not so infamous, apparently: no other journalist bit. Safire moved on.

On February 28 he insinuated that House Speaker Tip O'Neill was conspiring with the head of the Justice Department's criminal division, Benjamin Civiletti, to bury the Korean influence-peddling scandal. The column included a favorite Safire technique, listing objective-sounding, but actually insinuating, questions—raising an aura of guilt without the burden of facts: "Will Mr. Civiletti inform the Senate in writing every 30 days about the status of this chimerical investigation of House members?" "Will he agree to resign if given an arbitrary time limit?" In March he said Civiletti's service as treasurer of a Democratic Senate campaign was an abuse of power "that would have made John Mitchell blush." The only pickup these charges got, however, was a letter to the editor from Senator Joseph Tydings, who said that comparing Jimmy Carter's Justice Department to Richard Nixon's was like "equating *Hustler* magazine with the *New York Times*." (As it happened, one Safire column praised a *Hustler* magazine article—unjustly neglected, he sniffed—which argued that Watergate was a Democratic coup.)

In April he teed off on Paul Warnke for "ideological bias" in his hiring practices; in May, he went after two State Department officials with a supposedly corrupt business connection to a TV station; in June, the target was Vice President Mondale, for supposedly installing a "gang of four" of pro-administration prosecutors in the Justice Department; none of these seeds took root with other investigators. Then, after the revelation of Pat Caddell's ten-thousand-word political strategy memo, Safire lamented that the Carter administration believed "the way to stay in the corridors of power is to turn them into halls of mirrors." Which, coming from the architect of the Kitchen Debate, was pretty rich.

He hoped to exploit as a point of leverage Carter's self-anointment as something better than a politician: easier, after all, to knock a man down when he's perched on a pedestal. He hoped to prick journalists into going after Jimmy Carter in the same way they'd supposedly sabotaged Nixon or else be dismissed as Democratic hacks. So Watergate and Nixon references studded nearly every Safire column: a document he alone found incriminating was a "smoking gun"; President Carter rejecting a two-cent import duty on sugar suggested supposed suspicious ties to Atlanta-based Coca-Cola just liked Nixon's actual ones to Pepsi-Cola back in the day; "If this is an open administration, let's get some answers." It seemed a promising rhetorical strategy, precisely because during Watergate, almost every vague suspicion about Nixon's malfeasance turned out to be *true*. But it wasn't working. Safire was the only one finding anything scandalous in the Carter administration: the columnist who kept crying wolf. Going into August, a Harris Poll pegged Jimmy Carter's favorability rating at 59 percent, with 67 percent admiring "the way he has taken over the leadership of the country."

And even after Safire finally discovered a promising club with which to knock Jimmy Carter off that damned pedestal, it took a while to begin landing blows.

His first attempt came July 21. "Carter's Broken Lance" was an unconvincing mess. Safire said Lance had directed Jimmy Carter to meet an officer of the Manufacturers Hanover Trust in New York, charging this was quid pro quo for a loan. But the meeting had been in June of 1975, when Jimmy Carter was a lowly ex-governor nobody imagined might someday be president.

Safire then wondered why the corrupt Teamsters Central States Pension Fund had deposited $18 million into Lance's bank in early 1976, "as Mr. Carter's star began to rise." Here Safire, a literary popinjay who loved to load his columns with puns, dictionary-busters, and neologisms, coined the word "banktician" to characterize Lance as an influence peddler who saw "no impropriety in a Cabinet designee helping to line up some future business with the fund that the Labor Department says corruptly bankrolls Las Vegas mobsters." Which was odd, because in fact, Carter's Justice Department had gone after the Teamsters mercilessly.

He then brought up the refinancing of Lance's Manufacturers Hanover loan with "another Democratic banktician, J Robert Aboud, the go-go boss of First National Bank of Chicago, who has replaced his mentor, the late Mayor Daley, as the city's most powerful man. . . . Why? Mr. Lance (give him credit, he answers his phone) says 'First Chicago is moving aggressively in the Chicago area.' I see a more sinister motive": it was a "sweetheart loan," "Mr. Aboud's chance to gain life-and-death financial control over the man closest to the President."

Teamsters, gangsters, financiers with suspiciously Arab-sounding names, "the Chicago loan"—it certainly sounded bad. Senator Abe Ribicoff, chairman of government affairs, and Senator Charles Percy, the ranking minority member, called Lance back for further questioning—but couldn't find anything improper. "You have been smeared from one end of the country to the other, in my opinion unjustly," Ribicoff apologized. "We can just imagine what this has done to you and your family." The senator blamed the post-Watergate, scandal-obsessed press: "The name of the game today is 'get everybody.'"

New York Times executive editor A. M. Rosenthal finally called Safire in to ask what law, exactly, he imagined Lance might be in violation of. "18 U.S. Code 656," Safire snapped back: "misapplication of bank funds. Abe—the President's best friend could be going to jail." Perhaps to humor his token Republican, Rosenthal put reporters on the case.

AS HE DID, THE PRESIDENT HAD TWO HEAVY POLITICAL LIFTS AHEAD OF him: his energy package and finalizing two treaties, more than a decade in the making, to turn over the Panama Canal to its host country. Negotiations had been ongoing since shortly deadly riots broke out over the flying of the American flag over Panamanian territory on January 9, 1964—later memorialized as a Panamanian national holiday, "Martyr Day." Though the issue had received no attention in the presidential campaign, back in Plains, Jimmy Carter had applied his engineer and evangelist's mind to the problem, then decided to jump into the issue with both feet, as a corner-stone of his foreign policy.

The case seemed to him unanswerable—as it had for presidents John-son, Nixon, and Ford. Morally, the chicanery that loosed the 553-square-mile Canal Zone from the native inhabitants had been one of the ugliest chapters in the near-continuous history of interventions by the United States into Latin American sovereignty going back to America's inva-sion of Puerto Rico in 1809. "What nation," Panamanian president Omar Efrain Torrijos Herrera asked plaintively, "can withstand the humiliation of a foreign flag piercing its own heart?" Strategically, the Joint Chiefs of Staff advised President Carter that Panama's resentments were spiraling out of control, and might soon lead to an insurgency that would require a hundred thousand American troops to defeat. The canal wasn't worth it economically, since the state-of-the-art "super-tankers" were too large to navigate its locks. Militarily, the Navy's aircraft carriers were too big to pass through the canal, making it useless during a war.

Carter hoped to have texts of the two treaties, one to establish the ca-nal's neutrality and providing for its joint defense by the two countries, the other to relinquish its operations in the year 2000, ready for senators, whose two-thirds approval was required for ratification, by summer. Three years earlier, when Strom Thurmond, the far-right South Carolina senator, had learned about the negotiations, he succeeded in getting thirty-four senators to vote for a resolution of disapproval—the same number of senators required to block ratification. Thirty-one of those senators were still in office. Now, however, things were looking reasonably favorable. As his negotiators, who had also been Gerald Ford's negotiators, closed in on a final agreement, they began briefing senators about their provisions. Ma-jority Leader Byrd pronounced himself in favor; Minority Leader Baker had an open mind; even Senator Goldwater seemed to be leaning yes. Senator S. I. Hayakawa, who had said on the campaign trail that America should keep the Panama Canal because we "stole it fair and square," now said he had only been joking. On August 7, the president contacted sena-tors to ask them to avoid committing one way or another until they'd had a chance to read the text, which would be soon. Most agreed, he wrote in his diary—"except a few nuts like Strom Thurmond and Jesse Helms." It was true that the majority of voters still opposed giving up the Panama Canal. But on August 26, President Carter told a gathering of editors and broadcasters that he was confident an upcoming televised fireside chat would turn public opinion his way—because, he said, he was confident of the intelligence of the American people.

Though there *was* that old saying attributed to H. L. Mencken: no one ever went broke underestimating the intelligence of the American people.

When Ronald Reagan was running for the Republican presidential nomination in 1976, he coined a resounding slogan to signify his belief that the Canal Zone was sovereign American territory: "We built it, we paid for it, it's ours." Which was not quite true: the 1907 treaty granted America the right, "in perpetuity" to *operate* the Canal Zone "as if" it were sovereign. But Reagan's claim had enough persuasive power to bring his presidential campaign back from the dead. Americans had always thrilled to the epic tale of engineering's conquest of the Panamanian jungle at the cost of the lives of some 20,000 workers—and were thrilling to it anew, thanks to the release of David McCullough's new seven-hundred-page bestseller *The Path Between the Seas: The Creation of the Panama Canal, 1870–1914.* It was "greater than the Tower of Babel or the Pyramids," TR declared. Its chief engineer loved showing it off to American visitors—"because they all say it makes them better Americans." Opinions had hardly changed in the seventy-four years since.

One constituent confronted his congressman in a town meeting in Upstate New York: "We spent billions of dollars to build it and maintain it, and now we're going to *pay them* to take it?" In California, a citizen importuned his senator, "It was bought with people's lives, and why should we *give* it away?" An Illinoisan confronted Representative John Anderson: "If they want a canal, let *them* build one." A *Washington Post* columnist, who like virtually the entirety of the media and foreign policy establishment supported the treaties being negotiated, cited a recent letter to a newspaper saying that yielding the canal "would represent a first step toward the dismemberment of our nation." After all, it was only two years since America's humiliating retreat from Vietnam. "The very thought," he observed, "seems to raise psychological problems, problems of national identity: What is a country if its territory is not ideologically as well as physically secure?"

But the political momentum finally seemed to be flowing the other way. A conservative senator told Paul Weyrich that Carter's Panama negotiators—Ellsworth Bunker, an exceptionally distinguished retired general and diplomat, and Sol Linowitz, a founder of Xerox—had just about convinced him. Senator Joseph Biden, a centrist bellwether, called the Canal Zone "the last vestige of U.S. imperialism." Gerald Ford accepted Jimmy Carter's invitation for an overnight White House visit to plot strategy—a cheering example of the high ideal that politics stops at the water's edge.

Nonetheless, New Right activists believed that Carter had handed them a precious political gift. "It's an issue we can't lose on," Richard Viguerie said. "If we lose the vote in the Senate, we will have had the issue for eight or nine months. We will have rallied many new people to our cause. We will have given our supporters an issue, a cause to work for." Howard Phillips said, "I can't think of any other issue that better unites grassroots conservatives than the Canal."

NEW RIGHT LEADERS WERE ALREADY HARD AT WORK PREPARING FOR THE 1978 congressional elections, sifting through the 0-to-100 ratings bestowed on members of Congress by organizations like the American Conservative Union, the American Security Council, and Americans for Constitutional Action, to decide whom to support or oppose. Paul Weyrich's Committee for the Survival of a Free Congress even inaugurated its own index, the "Conservative Register," the sternest of them all: it branded anyone scoring less than fifty-six—meaning two-thirds of Congress—as "Left-Wing." Armed with this intelligence, a former ACU official revealed, the New Right leaders "sit around with their pocket calculators and go around the table, discussing different candidates; and one will say: 'We can give $5,000,' and another will say: 'We can give $15,000.'"

The day after Carter's briefing of the editors at the White House on Panama, Robert Livingston of Louisiana became the third New Right candidate in a row to win a special election, replacing a corrupt Democrat who resigned and becoming the first Republican to represent Baton Rouge since 1874—in a district with only 10 percent Republican registration. Weyrich bragged that he had won commitments from thirty-two of the necessary thirty-four senators necessary to block Carter's Panama Canal treaties. "I have been making speeches around the country in the last few months, and Panama is a real grassroots issue," he said. "Nothing gets more of an emotional reaction than saying, 'At no time are we going to surrender the Panama Canal.'" The ACU began running newspaper ads: "There is NO Panama Canal! There is an AMERICAN Canal in Panama. Don't let President Carter give it away." They claimed $15,000 in donations a day.

A key target was Howard Baker. The Senate minority leader had presidential ambitions, which demanded displays of foreign policy gravitas. But it also demanded getting reelected in 1978, in conservative Tennessee, where the treaties were anathema. On September 4, three days before General Omar Torrijos was to travel to Washington for a signing ceremony and state dinner, an ACU ad in the *Nashville Tennessean* directed, "If you are concerned about the giveaway of the Panama Canal (and you should be), then don't delay making your opinion known to Senator Howard Baker." Baker received 3,600 such messages in the next three days. At an ACU meeting, Jesse Helms was proud to be able to report that Baker was "squirming like a worm on a hot brick."

WHAT RONALD REAGAN'S ROLE WOULD BE IN THE PANAMA FIGHT WAS A subject of some confusion. "Reagan Leads Drive to Halt Canal Pact," headlined the *Boston Globe* on August 12. "Reagan Less Adamant in Anti–Canal Treaty Stand," said the *Los Angeles Times* on the same day. Both, like the parable of the blind man and the elephant, were reporting on the same statement.

Reagan had released it after meeting for a second time with Bunker and Linowitz. The statement said that while he hadn't yet made up his mind, "I have found nothing that would lead me to alter my belief that we should maintain control of the canal." Which, however, was considerably more measured than the red meat he'd thrown out the previous year on the campaign trail—that the Canal Zone was "every bit the same as Alaska and all the states that were carved from the Louisiana Purchase."

The ambivalence betokened another behind-the-scenes battle between the pragmatists and the ideologues in the Reagan camp. In July, a far-right intriguer from Jesse Helm's staff named James Carbaugh presented a top-secret plan to Peter Hannaford to deploy Reagan in the anti-treaty campaign, capped off with dramatic testimony by Reagan in hearings on Capitol Hill. Hannaford responded with alarm in a frank note to his partner Mike Deaver—apparently typing it himself, clumsily, as if to keep it even from a secretary's prying eyes. "My recommendation: don't do it," it began.

"Not only because prior commitment (the alibi), but also because I am very worried about the natl press ending up blaming RR for torpedoing a treaty. I have a strong hunch that the Congress will turn down Carter's new treaty. Torrijos, to rationalize his hold in Panama, will let loose the goons and the PC will be sabotaged or the US will otherwise be engaged in a confrontation. Carter will no doubt temporize or—in some other fashion—cave in—There will be a lot of loose guilt-and-blame talk flying around in that event and, if RR is out front with his 'American Canal, in Panama' talk, I worry that he will catch some of the flak. There are already disturbing signs in the press that he is thought of as being jingoistic on this issue. I hate to see that, since he has carefully nurtured the idea that he is a thoughtful critic of Ford and Carter foreign policy. It could be thrown to the winds over this issue. . . . I think it is most unwise for RR to be lumped in with Jesse and Strom on this issue, as he would undoubtably be if he becomes a media cat's paw at the hearings they are engineering." He recommended only written testimony—"almost invisible, but demonstrates to our anti-treaty friends that RR has done his part."

The memo was a window into deeply etched divisions in Reagan's organization: on one side, the tender, protective instincts of Hannaford and Deaver, eager to save him from himself; on the other, conservatives eager to set loose Reagan's unmatched instincts for tapping into and channeling grassroots discontent—what Hannaford and Deaver's rival Lyn Nofziger called "letting Reagan be Reagan." The subterranean battle showed as ripples on the surface of newspaper articles. One report said that Nofziger's Citizens for the Republic had sent a memo to 250 key supporters asking them to pressure Senator Hayakawa—"a likely tip off to Reagan's own ultimate intentions." Another the next day, however, had a "spokesman for former Governor Ronald Reagan" insisting that the governor had nothing to do with that memo.

Such dramas would play themselves out scores of times in the years to come. This one the pragmatists lost. Evans and Novak reported that when anti-treaty senators asked Reagan to testify at subcommittee hearings, aides "embarrassed last year by his dramatic use of the canal in primary elections against Gerald Ford" told them, "Sorry, the governor is busy that day." (That would be the "alibi" referred to in Hannaford's memo—suggesting that Deaver or Hannaford had leaked that intelligence to Evans and Novak.) But it turned out Reagan *would* be coming to D.C. to testify, the column reported. (That suggested a leak from Jesse Helms's aide Carbaugh, double-crossing the establishmentarians.) Which turned out to work to Reagan's great benefit—for suddenly he was at the center of the action.

On August 13 the president called Reagan personally to ask for his support. That weekend, Reagan traveled to the East Coast for his third briefing from Bunker and Linowitz. He also spoke to the national convention of Young Americans for Freedom, railing that the treaties would not "prevent a Panamanian regime from simply nationalizing the Canal and demanding our immediate withdrawal," claiming the Soviet Union was already scouting development opportunities in Panama, and calling Carter's lobbying "a medicine show, a wave of propaganda." Planting this flag received him so much press notice that his syndicate arrayed the headlines in a collage for a promotional piece—including a column from the *New York Times'* legendary James Reston, who praised the treaties as a "a signal to the world that Washington is ready to move away from the policies of domination that have led to two world wars and endless massacres in this century." He noted the Joint Chiefs' estimate that it would likely take a hundred thousand soldiers to defend the canal from sabotage if the treaties failed—then seemed to scowl when he added, "so far as is known, the former governor didn't ask the Young Americans for volunteers."

Which was pretty scalding. But if you were Ronald Reagan, seeking to mobilize his base for a potential presidential run, it was useful stuff indeed. Soon, a political cartoon showed Reagan being baptized by full immersion between the Pacific and Atlantic Oceans. It read, "Ronald Reagan . . . born again in the waters of the Panama Canal."

JIMMY CARTER, MEANWHILE, WAS STARTING TO DROWN.

The comptroller of the currency, the federal regulator in charge of banks, began investigating whether damning information about Bert Lance's First Bank of Georgia had been suppressed during his security check. William Safire promptly took up the cudgel: "By not asking the president a single question about this first scandal at his press conference last week, the White House press corps completed its transformation from attack dog to lap dog." He then helpfully suggested what questions they might ask to atone.

On August 11, Safire anointed the scandal "Lancegate"—once more implying Nixon-level perfidy on the part of Democrats, baiting the rest of the press to follow his lead lest they show themselves in the pocket of the liberals. On August 12, as if rising to the call, the *Washington Post* presented evidence that in 1971 Lance had ignored warnings that a vice president at his first bank had embezzled nearly $1 million. The next day came the first call for Lance's resignation, from John Anderson of Illinois, chairman of the House Republican Conference. Then, the Associated Press reported Lance had illicitly used the same stock as collateral for two different loans.

That bankers cut each other favorable deals had never much exercised Washington before. But that was before Watergate—and also before the Georgia Mafia came to town. The White House became more and more convinced: the media onslaught of inquiries into Lance was little more than the establishment seeking to confirm their prejudice that Jimmy Carter surrounded himself with bumpkins. So they circled the wagons. They did so according to a narrative framed by Bert Lance himself.

He had dropped out of college to work at the bank in his hometown of Calhoun, Georgia, population 3,231; after marrying the founder's grand-daughter, he took the bank over. Even after making it big in Atlanta—and buying himself a forty-room mansion—he described himself as no more than a small-town banker, steeped in small-town banker ways. He liked to tell a story about why those ways were, in fact, *superior* to how they did things in the big city. It went like this. One of his Calhoun neighbors borrowed money from his bank to buy a new milk cow. She got behind in her payments, then presented herself at the bank one morning:

"Mr. Lance, I brung you your cow."

"Susie, you did what?"

"I brung you your cow. You've got the mortgage on her, and I can't pay it, so I've got my cow tied up outside."

"Well, Susie, this is a serious situation. Let's just think about this for a minute. First of all, you need that cow badly so you'll have milk for your family. Second, we don't have a thing in the world to do with that cow. We don't have any place to put it, and I don't know how to milk it. So I'm going to make a suggestion to you: We'll extend your loan until such time as you think you can take care of it. You take that cow home with you now and look after it so it will continue to provide milk for you and your family."

The lesson, as he explained it, was "one that you might not have the opportunity to learn as easily in a big-city bank: collateral in hand is a poor substitute for paying a loan."

Friendship, handshakes, *trust*: that, Lance insisted, was the soul of sound banking. That, because he himself was trustworthy, none need worry about his myriad rounds of refinancing with so many banks, leveraging his collateral to the breaking point. "Each time a new allegation was raised against me and my practices as a country banker," he complained, "the media didn't go to a country banker as a source"—who would have told them that extending the privilege of overdrafts to citizens of good character was a sound and honorable practice. Instead, they asked "big-city bankers . . . like asking a football scout to evaluate a baseball prospect. It's just not logical."

"Country bank," however, hardly described the First National Bank of Georgia—or First Chicago, where FNB maintained a non-interest-bearing "correspondence account" that looked suspiciously to critics like a kickback for refinancing a Lance debt on particularly generous terms. Maybe these were sweetheart deals, or maybe they were not; and, indeed, in the end, Lance was acquitted of the criminal charges he eventually faced. For himself, Lance was convinced that if the United States budget director had come from the white-shoe world of Wall Street instead of Calhoun, Georgia, no one would have thought to consider anything amiss in the first place.

And lo, his best friend agreed.

Hamilton Jordan sent the president a confidential memo: "This unfortunate incident—which involves Georgians and close personal friends—could do great damage to your presidency if not handled properly. . . . You pledged that you would not tolerate wrongdoing or even the appearance of wrongdoing. . . . We cannot allow this or any other incident to erode the moral authority of your presidency." After all, hadn't Carter said on the campaign trail, when President Ford's FBI director availed himself of $335 worth of home improvements from the FBI's carpentry shop, that a government official "ought to be purer than Caesar's wife"?

The comptroller of the currency released a 394-page report that simultaneously cleared Lance of legal jeopardy in the charges so far, and added several new lines of suspicion. The president latched onto the positive, ignored the negative—and helicoptered in from a Camp David vacation for a dramatic press conference. "My faith in the character and competence of Bert Lance has been reconfirmed," he said with Lance by his side on August 18. "I see no other conclusion that can be drawn from an objective analysis of these findings. . . . Bert enjoys my complete confidence and support. I am proud to have him as part of my administration." He turned to his best friend: "Bert, I'm proud of you."

That made it Jimmy Carter's scandal, too.

The *New York Times* ran eleven Lance stories the next day, including one reporting that Carter might have broken federal election law by flying on First Bank of Georgia airplanes for free. James Reston's next column was an imaginary dialogue with Caesar's wife. ("If you had borrowed money on the old man's power and reputation, what would Julius have done?" "He would have thrown me to the lions.") The *Los Angeles Times* called for Lance's resignation. At a presidential news conference four days later, a reporter asked: "Do you think the American taxpayer has reason to question the competence of a man in charge of the federal budget who, after he has taken that job, wrote seven overdrafts on his own account?" Carter parried with a joke: "Well, obviously it's better not to write overdrafts." When the laughter died down, he continued, "I can't deny that I have written overdrafts on my own bank accounts on occasion and so has my wife, not deliberately, but because of an error or because of higher priorities that were assigned to other responsibilities that I had at the time."

He had stepped in it again.

Angry letters to the editors gushed forth: "President Carter's embrace of Mr. Lance's honesty and integrity do nothing to reassure me of Mr. Lance's honesty and integrity. However, they do lead me to question Mr. Carter's standards." And: "I would like to quote from a notice I have just received from my bank when I overdrew my account by $1.13: 'Please call at once, so that the error, if any, may be corrected as it is against banking laws to pay overdrafts.'" The editorial cartoonist Oliphant drew Carter saying, "Stonewall it. . . . They're out to get us." The *Washington Post*'s legendary Nixon-hating cartoonist Herblock gave Carter a "Checkers Award." *Doonesbury*'s secretary of symbolism rang up Hamilton Jordan: "I'd like to recommend a staff memo encouraging *all* White House personnel to overdraw their checking accounts. . . . I'd start with the secretaries. Just send them all shopping or something." On the sitcom *Good Times*, a character defended kiting a check with a joke about Lance.

And after twice exonerating him, the Senate Governmental Affairs Committee scheduled new hearings for September 7, the day Carter and

Torrijos were to sign the Panama Canal treaties. A *Newsweek* poll found
that 67 percent thought Lance should resign. More than half of the respondents said Carter protected him "too much." In the Harris poll, the
president's approval rating sank to 44 percent. David Broder connected
dots: "What is unsettled in the public mind is whether the renunciation
of America privilege in Panama is an act of cowardice, part of the retreat
of American power, or an act of generosity and historical wisdom, which
vindicates America's devotion to principle. . . . And that moral authority is
what is in jeopardy as the White House fights its dogged defense of Lance
against the cascading charges of improprieties." The president responded
in his diary: "The *Washington Post* is conducting a vendetta against Bert
and has apparently ordered two front-page stories about him each day."

Fueled by paranoia, seeing enemies everywhere: he *did* sound a lot like
Richard Nixon—just as William Safire had hoped.

On September 7, hundreds of outraged conservatives rallied on the
Capitol Steps to hear Representative Larry McDonald call the Panama
Canal treaties "bipartisan treason," Representative Sonny Montgomery
accuse Carter of "giving away the 51st state," Representative Mickey
Edwards say he was playing "Russian roulette with the future security of
every American," and Representative Bob Dornan accused General Torrijos of "skimming money from whorehouses." Presidents Carter and
Torrijos affixed their signatures to the documents inside the Pan American
Union Building, backed by the flags of all the North and South American nations, as, outside, 150 more conservatives held up umbrellas to tie
Carter symbolically to Neville Chamberlain, the British prime minister
who insisted in 1938 that if Hitler were only given Sudetenland, he would
not seek to conquer anything more.

Carter proclaimed, "We have shown the world a spirit which recognizes and respects the rights of others and seeks to help all people to fulfill
their legitimate aspirations with confidence and dignity." Torrijos called
Carter "a man of great morality fully dedicated to the cause of the weak."
It made for impressive pictures on the front pages—though the president
would not want to save that day's *Washington Post* for his scrapbook.
Nine articles were on Lance, including speculation that he would resign;
reports of Senators Percy and Ribicoff's regret at confirming him in the
first place; and columnist Joseph Kraft's observation that the nation's "first
view of Jimmy Carter under pressure" had revealed "a lonely man surrounded by an inexperienced staff, who is not exempt from moral blindness and poor judgment."

IT WAS THE DAY AFTER PRIMARY DAY IN NEW YORK CITY. IN THE WEEKS
leading up to it, polls had Bella Abzug and Mayor Beame battling for the

two spots in the runoff. Then, events broke the back of the incumbent. The Securities and Exchange Commission released an eight-hundred-page study of why New York had almost defaulted on its loans in 1975. It concluded that Mayor Beame engaged in "deceptive practices masking the city's true and disastrous financial condition," like issuing bonds based on future tax revenues.

His predecessors had done that, too—but Beame was the one left holding the bag. Governor Carey said the report revealed Beame as a "weakling." Rupert Murdoch's *New York Post* headlined, "BEAME CONNED THE CITY." They had already endorsed Ed Koch and run so much fawning coverage of him on the news pages that fifty of Murdoch's editors and reporters signed a petition of complaint. Murdoch invited them to resign. A dozen took him up on the offer—a remarkable act in the midst of the city's near depression.

Son of Sam was caught. The next day's *Post* sold twice the usual number of copies. When the young suspect, David Berkowitz, was arraigned, mobs surrounded the courthouse chanting, "Kill! Kill! Kill!"

Edward Koch had cosponsored the federal gay rights bill, and jokingly dubbed his platform for his first state assembly race in 1962 "SAD," for "sodomy, abortion, and divorce" (he advocated laws liberalizing all three). Now he ran away from that record—in part because he was rumored to be gay. At the urging of David Garth, he began appearing everywhere with Bess Myerson, the first Jewish Miss America, on his arm.

Koch also made sure voters knew he was the most enthusiastic booster of that red-hot issue over which an New York City mayor had no jurisdiction: the death penalty. A liberal former friend, Nat Hentoff, wrote in the *Village Voice*, "This once and former man of plain decency has become an advocate of mindless barbarism."

Mario Cuomo was the candidate for voices like these. His slogan was "Put your anger to work. Make New York what it can be again." When the SEC report came out, boxing in poor Mayor Beame, Cuomo asked what good it would do to "jump up and down on this man's head." The *Daily News's* liberal columnist Pete Hamill praised Cuomo as "tough on the side of reason," someone who "won't churn up still more irrationality in this disturbed city. . . . He could have presented himself these last few months as the big tough Italian who was going to club and electrocute people into lawfulness. He didn't do that."

Cuomo's surrogates churned up the irrationality instead. Signs began showing up in the outer boroughs reading "VOTE FOR CUOMO NOT THE HOMO"—an anti-Koch smear campaign. Governor Carey announced he might reconsider his opposition to the death penalty—*if* Mario Cuomo was elected. Cuomo also accepted the endorsement of

Congressman Mario Biaggio, a former cop who promised he would work to turn his friend around on the subject of capital punishment.

Two days before the primary, at the U.S. Open tennis tournament, in a new location abutting a public park in Queens—in a neighborhood that was "95 percent Negro," a member of the board of its previous home courts at a leafy country club complained—a spectator was shot in the leg during a match, possibly from a nearby apartment tower, or perhaps by a man described as "a male Hispanic wearing a red shirt and dark pants" who people claimed to have seen fleeing the stadium. Just perhaps, he was fleeing because these days, in feral New York, a dark-skinned man surrounded by white people after a shooting placed his safety in danger by sticking around.

Bella Abzug shed support day by day. Her cool, too. At a meeting of Hasidic men, she was asked how she could support perverts. "You want to talk about perverts?" she asked. "Look at all these men wearing fur hats and ear curls." At a beach club in Canarsie, a cardplayer called her a "bigot." She yelled back: "Hitler spread the big lie, too." She got in another screaming match with someone who said cops should have shot looters, then with an old lady who said she didn't care about people like her. "Then go vote for that schmuck we have now," Abzug screeched.

They voted for neither. Beame finished in last place; Abzug came in third. Cuomo and Koch made the runoff with 19 and 20 percent respectively.

Which gave Bella Abzug plenty of time to focus on her other job: organizing the November 18 national women's conference in Houston. Which was *not*, she insisted, a front for advancing the fortunes of the Equal Rights Amendment, as Phyllis Schlafly claimed—just a gathering where "women from all walks of life will come together in public meetings financed with federal money to air their frustrations about the inequities that greet them everywhere they go and to devise means of ending sex discrimination in this country." Surely those both "for and those against the ERA" could agree on that. Then, however, in an interview with *Ms.*, she said, "I'd like to see Phyllis Schlafly stay home where she belongs, and while she's at it, I'd like to see her take Anita Bryant with her."

The National Commission for the Observance of International Women's Year began sending out its organizational handbook, with a logo featuring the biological symbol for female nested inside a dove of peace. Its title, *A More Perfect Union*, was not meant to be ironic.

CHAPTER 8

"The Moral Womanly Woman Is Alive and Well in Mississippi"

IT WAS HARD TO BE A WOMAN IN THE 1970S. JUST LISTEN TO THE TESTI-mony.

"I made the decision to stay home with my children because I wanted to provide them with an enriched, stimulating environment," an anonymous letter-writer wrote to a women's magazine. "Every day is taken up with caring for their needs and those of the household in general; time for myself is pure fantasy. Sure, I love them and they're adorable, and they're turning out fine. But I never knew that I'd have to give up myself in the bargain."

A stay-at-home mother wrote in a book, "When my baby was born, I wanted to be a good mother, but I felt even more trapped . . . then three more babies were born in rapid succession and each one, so beautiful, terrified me." After her fourth, she tried to commit suicide by jumping out of a moving car.

A third described "the smoldering resentment caused from the endless little tasks that had to be repeated over and over again and seemed so futile": picking up the dirty socks, hanging up wet towels, "creating a path through the clutter of toys. These jobs seemed so unproductive, and they were performed with drudgery. . . . Resentment mounted and in turn produced depression."

In 1975, Ann Landers asked her readers who were mothers whether having children had been worth it. The flood of letters she received in response—70 percent of them voting *no*—recorded the same sort of agonies. But women who chose careers instead weren't necessarily any more satisfied. "I work in an office," wrote another correspondent to the same women's magazine. "I feel bored, abused, and angry. I go home and snap and cry at everything and feel useless and empty."

The complaints were similar. The complainers were distinctly different. The first and fourth testimony were printed in the feminist magazine *Ms.* The second and third came from evangelical Christian authors. The difference between the Christians and the feminists was the route they found to redemption.

The Christians recited their Job-like trials for the express purpose of narrating the relief they found once they accepted the Scriptural injunction to submit more fully to the Lord above in heaven, and the lord of the family at home. Feminists' redemption came from a moment of awakening that was named after a classic article in the first issue of *Ms.* in 1972 by Jane O'Reilly called "Click: The Housewife's Moment of Truth." *Clicks* came when women realized a crisis they had believed to be merely personal was actually part of a *structure* of oppression—and that they could work together with other women and *change* that structure: *the personal is political,* ran the slogan. "Your magazine has become a bible of my faith in my own voice," one grateful woman wrote to *Ms.* "The Women's Movement affirms my growing self-trust, and I rejoice from the hell and heaven of my soul."

The lesson was affirmed in millions of living-room "consciousness raising sessions," where women in pain discovered they were legion. Conservative women held consciousness raising sessions, too, though they did not call them that. They were meetings to organize against gay rights, the ERA, federally mandated busing orders, or abortion on demand. A leader might shamefacedly read aloud a passage from some appalling book, like *Our Bodies, Ourselves,* which had been published by the Boston Women's Health Book Collective to help feminists navigate a hostile, patronizing, male-dominated healthcare system. It advised, "Touch yourself, smell yourself, even taste your own secretions. After all, you are your body and you are not obscene." Another favorite example was a European sex education book for children, *Show Me.* The most offending passage: "My older sister told me that sometimes she rubs inside her VULVA on her CLITORIS and thinks about nice things, and then she gets excited and she has an ORGASM. That's BEAUTIFUL." Phyllis Schlafly's Illinois deputy Rosemary Thomson cited that in her own book *The Price of LIBerty* as evidence that feminism was literally satanic.

Volumes anti-feminists found satanic were sacred for feminists. Like the 1977 novel *The Women's Room* by Marilyn French, which traced the fortunes of a group of women who in the 1950s had pursued the supposedly happiness-guaranteeing path of home and family; it drove them to misery instead. French's narrator observed, "I know that lots of Chinese women, given in marriage to men they abhorred and lives they despised, killed themselves by throwing themselves down the family well." In America, "there are so much easier ways to destroy a woman. You don't have to rape or kill her; you don't even have to beat her. You can just marry her." *The Women's Room* spent forty-four weeks on the *New York Times* bestseller list.

THE BACKGROUND TO THIS IDEOLOGICAL CLASH WAS A SOCIETY WHOSE presumptions about gender and the family were turning upside down—objectively so. It wasn't just the cultural convulsions of the 1960s. It was economic. Between the end of World War II and the oil shocks of 1973, the real income of ordinary American working families approximately doubled—then, it flatlined or even declined. The change came so suddenly, and felt so foreign to Americans' received way of knowing the world, that it could hardly be perceived whole. It registered, instead, as millions of uncoordinated individual family decisions, in response to millions of individual family struggles keeping up with mortgage payments, car payments, tuition, grocery bills, and the rising price of everything: so Mom began working outside the home. At the height of World War II, only 26 percent of married women worked. By 1977, about half did—including half of women with children under eighteen.

Another aspect of the ordeal was built into American public policy. Whereas other industrialized nations built robust state institutions to protect citizens in times of economic stress, in laissez-faire America the task of care was mostly allotted to individual families—which is to say, wives and mothers. A housewife did not directly earn Social Security from the government, or health insurance from an employer. So if she left her husband, or if he left her, she lost both. Thus, a foundational feminist argument was that society must afford women security as a right, not as a reward for winning and keeping a husband: married *women* should have *individual* Social Security accounts into which half the husband's contributions would be placed, money she would keep whether she stayed married or not. Or, in a more radical proposal, the government would pay housewives wages for housework. But conservatives who saw the federal government as a diabolical, devouring Leviathan reacted to these ideas by deciding that liberals were plotting to *replace* the family with the state. That was what anti-feminists meant when they snarled out the charge—so baffling to feminists who cherished their spouses and children, too—that feminists were out to "destroy" the family. Feminism, in this view, threatened their deepest sense of themselves and their value in the world.

Evangelical culture had already co-opted in acceptably biblical form many of the best things feminism had to offer married women. Protestant fundamentalism's traditional deficiencies—its insular inability to compete with the blandishments of liberal, modern therapeutic culture—were long past by the closing years of the 1970s. Quietly, beneath the notice of the mainstream, the evangelical culture that Anita Bryant exemplified had adapted to meet every imaginable need.

The annual convention of the Christian Booksellers Association drew more than five thousand attendees. The retailers sold greeting cards, T-shirts, placemats; they were one-stop centers for what was called "Christian living"—and if you wanted to know where to find one of them, you could consult the newly published *Christian Yellow Pages*. Explained its publisher, "It is out of harmony with Kingdom principles for a Christian to give his business to those who are part of the anti-Christ system simply because he can get a 'better deal.' . . . If you need an electric drill you should buy it from a Christian hardware store. . . . Wouldn't you as a Christian rather see this go to help support another Christian who has the blood of Jesus Christ flowing through his veins?"

For child-rearing help, turn to Dr. James Dobson, a psychotherapist whose Christian-inflected self-help books, such as *Dare to Discipline* (1970) and *What Wives Wish Their Husbands Knew About Women* (1972), and "Focus on the Family" seminars and videos distributed on 16-millimeter film or videotape, were so popular by 1977 that Dobson quit his therapy practice and incorporated a nonprofit to produce a fast-growing radio advice show. (Dobson was particularly revered for his guidance on how to "cure" homosexuality.) Or, in extremis, you could call the Reverend Pat Robertson's crisis counseling service, staffed by six thousand friendly folks who worked around the clock fielding one and a quarter million calls in the first half of 1976 alone. Most "concern potential suicides, alcoholics, unwed mothers, drug abuses, and marital problems," the *Los Angeles Times* reported.

Then there were the books and lectures of the president's sister Ruth Carter Stapleton—dismissed as a witch doctor–like "faith healer" in the mainstream media, even though her message actually joined fundamentalism to fashionable therapeutic notions familiar to readers of *New York* magazine or *Jonathan Livingston Seagull*. Stapleton trained supplicants to communicate with their "inner child," reasoning, "Psychiatrists and psychologists have for years held the theory that an unborn child can pick up negative emotions from his environment." Though naturally, she advised that, ultimately, "there is no other way to reach them except through the grace of Jesus." Stapleton drew her following, *Newsweek* reported, "from those middle-class evangelicals who have discovered that personal happiness does not automatically follow from being born again or baptized in the Holy Spirit."

Interested in pop music? There was Pat Boone, of course, who'd become a superstar in the 1950s with bowdlerized versions of hits by black singers like Fats Domino and Little Richard, and whose Christian witness included a refusal to appear in a sexy film with Marilyn Monroe. But now there was his daughter Debby, too, whose saccharine anthem "You Light Up My Life" (Jesus, she meant) was one of the biggest hits in twenty years, bested only by the Beatles, Elvis—and Pat Boone. Dad and daughter toured together, performing gospel favorites from albums like *The Boone Family* and *The Family Who Prays*, released by the Boone family's own label, Lion & Lamb Records.

A night out with the wife? Try one of the proliferating Christian nightclubs. Problems in the bedroom? Turn to Pastor Tim and Mrs. Beverly LaHaye's *The Act of Marriage: The Beauty of Sexual Love*, which insisted, "Modern research has made it abundantly clear that all married women are capable of orgasmic ecstasy. No Christian woman should settle for less." (Then, in one of the most curious biblical exegeses in the history of Christendom, the LaHayes revealed a Scriptural instruction for manual clitoral stimulation: "The wife lying on her back with her knees bent and feet pulled up to her hips and her husband lying on her right side"—just like the Song of Solomon said: "Let his left hand be under my head and his right hand embrace me.")

The Act of Marriage also observed that "a woman thinks about economics occasionally, but usually with limited, short, duration"—even though in their own family, Mrs. LaHaye oversaw economic matters, including the couple's considerable San Diego–area real estate holdings, and the $1 million budget and forty-member staff at Family Life Seminars, which delivered instruction on subjects like "Overcoming Human Weakness" and "Spirit-Controlled Living."

And she did this all without feminism. Why couldn't you?

ANTIFEMINISTS ALSO HAD POWERFUL SECULAR ARGUMENTS. ONE WAS THAT the feminism, by stripping social sanctions against extramarital sex, turned women into disposable toys, freeing men to cast them economically adrift. Another involved social class. According to one study of the pro-choice movement, 94 percent of its activists worked, almost 40 percent had gone to graduate school, and one in four had an MD, a PhD, or a law degree. Feminist leaders tended to be lawyers, professors, and foundation executives. No wonder they viewed working outside the home as fulfilling. The same survey found that most antifeminist activists who worked were unmarried, had menial, deadening jobs, and 90 percent had no college degree. In the world as these women experienced it, marriage was what *rescued* you from work. Feminists wanted to force you back.

Anti-ERA rhetoric crackled with vaguely Marxist descriptions of the alienating realities of capitalist America. "I call the Equal Rights Amendment the liftin' and totin' bill," explained the anti-ERA executive secretary of Negro Women of America. "If the Amendment becomes law, we will be the ones liftin' and totin'." A mimeographed anti-ERA plaint sent to legislatures observed, "These women lawyers, women legislators, and women executives promoting ERA have plenty of education and talent to get what they want in the business, political, and academic world. . . .We, the wives and working women, need you, dear Senators and Representatives, to protect us."

The same rhetoric reverberated across the heartfelt letters they sent to representatives begging them to vote against the ERA: "I want to remain on a pedestal." "I want to remain a homemaker." "I want to remain a *woman*." Just like Tammy Wynette sang in "Don't Liberate Me (Love Me)": "*Today a group of women came to see me / To convince me women don't have equal rights / And they left me when I told them I feel equal to an angel / When my man holds me at night.*" One reason such arguments were so effective was that they caught feminists off-guard. Dr. Joyce Brothers, the celebrity psychotherapist, appeared on *The Merv Griffin Show* with Phyllis Schlafly. Dr. Brothers exclaimed, "The idea that a woman can go sit home and be supported by her husband, that has long ago died out!" Came back Schlafly, calm as ever: "Forty million women are being supported by their husbands today." The retort stunned Dr. Brothers into a glum silence.

These were the women, aliens to one another, who were to gather together at the National Women's Conference in Houston on November 18. An observer noted the feminists projected "a harmonious conference in the belief that all women faced the same problems and needed similar solutions." They had no idea.

MORE THAN 130,000 WOMEN TOOK PART IN THE STATE MEETINGS THAT summer to elect delegates and choose resolutions to debate in Houston. They were organized by appointees to Bella Abzug's National Commission on the Observance of International Women's Year, chosen from groups like the League of Women Voters, the American Association of University Women, and labor unions. They made extraordinary efforts at diversity—as they understood it: they reached out African American women, bilingual women, Native American women, elderly women, welfare women, handicapped women, even formerly incarcerated women. They did not reach out to conservative women. Which was how the trouble began.

The first gathering came in February, in Vermont, billed as a "Women's Town Meeting." It featured free bus service to Montpelier, complimentary all-day childcare, no admission fee or formal banquet—just bring a brown-bag lunch. Half the attendees represented no organization;

45 percent had never attended a meeting concerning women's issues in their lives.

Nellie Gray, founder of the March for Life, attended as an observer. "Parliamentary procedures were ignored," Gray reported back to her comrades. "Rules fluctuated at the whim of the committee . . . the election process was unfair." In what actually had more to do with inexperience and informality, Gray spied conspiracy—a scheme by the federal government to force abortion, the ERA, and lesbianism onto the Houston agenda. At Gray's instigation, Schlafly's Eagles started researching, and discovered a list of "core recommendations" distributed to state coordinating committees by Abzug's national commission that included discussing just these matters. Schlafly delegated Thomson to organize to make sure these recommendations did not get voted through in Houston as the *official* desires of American women. The name they chose for the group—the International Women's Year Citizens' Review Committee—was significant: their adversaries were *not* citizens. They were agents of a malign federal government.

One evening, Thomson received a call from a woman named Dianne Edmondson, volunteering to serve as IWYCRC chair for Oklahoma. Thomson sent her the necessary materials, and received by return post a cassette tape recorded by Edmondson: "They want your child taught that there is no right or wrong, nor normal or ideal circumstances for sexual intercourse, such as, you might be teaching your child the ideal place for sex is within marriage. . . . I can't even share with you some of the language in some of the books they recommend." The tape became the committee's most powerful recruiting tool. Copies were duplicated and distributed forth in the thousands. The phone trees were activated. The church bulletins were deployed. One recipient wrote the president: "It has come to my attention that you have added more people to the National Commission on the Observance of International Women's Year. . . . None represented the average Judeo-Christian woman." The writer suggested that Phyllis Schlafly would make an excellent member.

THE SECOND STATE CONFERENCE WAS MOTHER'S DAY WEEKEND IN GEORGIA. Two of Thomson's activists reported back on a workshop in which there was "a roomful of lesbians who were patting each other's bodies and calling out dirty names," and that there had been no minister's invocation, no pledge to the flag, indeed no American flag in sight—though, to their horror, there *had been* a prayer from a female minister that began, "Our Creator who nurtures us like a mother." Conservatives won only three of twenty-nine delegate slots. They lost a vote on a resolution that public school textbooks "reflect the moral and religious values of parents." One walked out, shaken, sobbing: "The IWY has just used our own tax money to cast a vote against God."

At the next dozen state meetings, conservatives made little headway; then their momentum began to increase. In Texas, a conservative Democratic county chairwoman was so appalled by all the lesbians "with Levis on and hair on their legs" that she corralled a group of friends to reserve airplane tickets and hotel rooms for the national conference. In Michigan conservatives almost defeated an establishment group led by the Republican governor's wife. The next was Oklahoma—where, the conservative columnist James J. Kilpatrick wrote in language calculated to offend liberals, "the troops of Bella Abzug got scalped." The antifeminists had secured a ruling from the IWY national office allowing for same-day registration. "Came the dawn. From as far away as Guymon, Boise City, and Texhoma, out in the Panhandle, from as far south as Altus and Lawton, Durant, and Broken Boy, the buses began to roll"—until, by 7 a.m., "500 good Christian ladies were waiting quietly in line at the Student Union Building of Oklahoma State University." They passed a resolution calling homemaking the "most vital and rewarding career for women. . . . Language was heard more suited to stevedores and to hockey players than to gentle ladies. In the end, the 200 libbers rumped off to the theater within the Student Union. The thousand anti-libbers took over the ballroom. . . . Christians, 1,000, Lions 200!"

Conservatives began repeating the trick. In Missouri, four hundred feminists were outnumbered by five hundred conservative same-day registrants—who then sped off in their buses in time for Sunday morning church. In Washington State, where the meeting coincided with the deadline for signature gathering for an ERA referendum, the organizing was carried out through Mormon Relief Society meetings, the women's auxiliary gatherings held after Mormon church services. Two days before the conference, with all the available housing booked and the programs and ballots printed, the final planning meeting was coming to an end when a Mormon housewife and county Republican vice chairman knocked on the door, entered, and stunned the assemblage by announcing that she represented about two thousand Christian women who would soon arrive and pay the $5 surcharge for late registration. The next days were pandemonium for the organizers: Where in the hell do you find two thousand pencils in forty-eight hours?

On Saturday morning four thousand women waited in a line that snaked to the horizon, wrapped in sleeping bags against a blustery wind, eying one another like enemies, uniformed in tribal raiment: on one side, jeans and T-shirts and suspiciously short hair; on the other, floor-length frocks, neat coifs that wilted in the hot July sun, and blue and white ribbons—colors representing the Virgin Mary. The parking lot displayed endless rows of cars and campers, many with Utah license plates. At a session on gay parenting, the convener grew so exasperated with all the tirades ("all homosexuals should wear H's"; "we hope you women are discovered by a nice man and settle down") that she walked out; a Mormon woman gladly took over in her stead. A childcare discussion became a shouting match between radicals demanding free twenty-four-hour federal daycare and conservatives who called government daycare centers the equivalent of toddler concentration camps. During the plenary session, Mormon men suddenly appeared—to signal "their" women how to vote.

But then, five conservative women had broken ranks, standing up *in favor* of the Equal Rights Amendment. Chaos ensued. Perhaps they had been convinced by the hot-pink stickers in the ladies' room stalls: "Washington has had an Equal Rights Amendment for five years. Do you see any men in your bathroom?"

The balloting lasted until 1 a.m.; in a state with a Mormon population of 2 percent, Mormons cast almost half the votes. Feminists pulled out a victory by stealing the other side's march—rushing the pay phones and begging friends to come with $5, cast votes, and leave. The antifeminists filed suit for fraud. A more perfect union indeed. Feminists had thought they were organizing friendly gatherings of allies. They found themselves accused of proving, in Rosemary Thomson's words, that Satan was "alive and well on planet earth." Conservatives exchanged stories of the "25 lesbian-type workshops" in Minnesota; California's resolution to decriminalize prostitution was backed by a group called COYOTE, which stood for "Call Off Your Tired Old Ethics." In Utah, so many Mormon women packed the meeting that the final count of attendees was fourteen thousand—3 percent of the female population of the state; planners had prepared for two thousand. "Organizers said they had hopes of opening a 'dialogue' with the Mormons that might begin to reverse the polarization that has existed in Utah between churchwomen and feminists for some time," the *New York Times* reported. Not hardly. "It was like a war," said a woman the *Times* reported was believed to be the only radical feminist in the entire state, "only they had atomic weapons and we had words"— and conservatives said the same thing about the liberals.

MISSISSIPPI'S MEETING ON JULY 8 AND 9 WAS THE UGLIEST OF ALL. IT WAS also the most historically significant.

This was the state where, hardly more than a decade earlier, the governor had refused to investigate Klansmen who lynched civil rights workers and burned black churches. This was the summer when 69 percent of Miamians voted against giving gay men and lesbians equal access to employment, the death penalty was passing in state after state, gun-rights militants had taken over the NRA, and the ERA was going down in flames. And, against that backdrop, the Magnolia State chose as their keynote speaker: the director of the U.S. section of the Women's International League for Peace and Freedom, who had been one of two Americans invited by the Communists to represent the peace movement at the signing ceremony ending the Vietnam War. She had just recently returned from Cuba. Conservatives lost their minds. Planners were shocked: "It never occurred to us that there would be an organized right wing."

The conservative leader was a self-described "farm wife" from Pelahatchie named Eddie Myrtle Moore. She explained that, after she heard about the upcoming meeting from Phyllis Schlafly, "we just got on the telephone and called friends." No one knew to which religious denomination anyone else belonged. "The question wasn't even asked," Eddie Moore recalled. "We were just all concerned about the basic assault on the American principle of the family." By not asking, they were making history. A decade earlier, that would have been inconceivable.

In 1960, Reverend W. A. Criswell had said that a Catholic president would "spell the death of a free church in a free state and our hopes of continuance of full religious liberty in America"—attitudes held over from 1920s Ku Klux Klan conspiracy theories that the Catholic Church sought to infiltrate and overthrow the American government. This had, originally, proven an enormous impediment to recruitment of Protestant evangelicals to the predominantly Catholic anti-abortion movement. Protestants, who had spent centuries splitting hairs over the doctrinal errors of ministers the next church over, had—until only recently—hardly been eager to share a dais with them. "I turned on my television the other night and there were Rex Hubbard, Kathryn Kuhlman, Pat Boone, Oral Roberts, and a hodgepodge of charismatics bringing disgrace to the cause of Jesus Christ," the Southern Baptist Jerry Falwell thundered on his *Old Time Gospel Hour* in 1976, before adding that Catholics and Mormons "struck out before they ever got to first base."

Then came the imperative of fighting the liberals on every front—and political necessity begat theological flexibility.

Baptists might consider Pentecostals heretics. But the Pentecostals Pat Robertson and Oral Roberts were two of the most-watched conservative TV preachers—allies not worth offending for reasons of theological nicety. Catholics, *Christianity Today* advised in a 1975 editorial imploring evangelicals to join the anti-abortion movement, should "no longer be dismissed as a group of cold-hearted Catholics simply taking orders from the pope." Gerald Ford might be, of all things, an Episcopalian—but that didn't stop Wallie Criswell from holding him to his bosom in the

1976 campaign against his fellow Baptist Jimmy Carter. At the record-shattering March for Life in January in Washington, Protestants who had typically identified the Holy See as the Whore of Babylon in the Book of Revelation had marched side by side with priests. As a Catholic bishop described fighting alongside Protestants for the Hyde Amendment: "We are movingly encountering each other as brothers and sisters in Christ."

And after fourteen thousand conservatives packed the IWY meeting in Utah, who could deny the nation's 4.7 million Mormons a place at the table? Or even Jews—for hadn't it been the intervention of Rabbi Phineas Weberman in Miami that had turned the tide against gay rights in Miami in June?

The word for this new way of organizing on the traditionalist right, without concern for religious doctrine, was "cobelligerency." Its preeminent theorist was Dr. Francis Schaeffer, host of the film series *How Should We Then Live? The Rise and Decline of Western Thought and Culture*. He explained it with a parable: "If I live in a suburb and suddenly the sewer system begins to back up into the water system and all my neighbors are atheist, it does not mean we cannot sign a petition together. . . . I do not have to wait for them to become Christians to do that. It is the same for the issues we are discussing. We should be glad for every co-belligerent." When Jerry Falwell had at first proved reluctant, Dr. Schaeffer reminded him that it was Cyrus the Great of Persia, after all, who had ended Israel's exile and ordered the Temple rebuilt. "God used pagans to do his work in the Old Testament, so why don't you use pagans to do your work now?"

Jackson, Mississippi, on July 8, 1977, provided proof of concept of what that could accomplish at the grassroots.

Three hundred fifty women, mostly ERA supporters, had registered in advance—before 1,119 conservatives arrived for same-day admission; more than a tenth of that boarding party were men, who circulated, with walkie-talkies, under the command of a Jackson white supremacist leader named Richard Barrett, who had chaired Democrats for Reagan in Mississippi in 1976. Many of the conservative women carried their children into battle. Free daycare was provided. Conservatives refused it on principle. Eddie Moore explained that the International Women's Year program was part of "a plan started back in 1972 in the United Nations to bring about the destruction of the American family and home as we know it." The only resolutions both sides agreed to were for equal pay for equal work and better public education (once the resolution was amended to omit an endorsement for kindergarten in all public schools). Resolutions supporting affirmative action, gender equality in schools and the military, and international cooperation to promote world peace were shouted down. Another passed affirming that "the IWY extends our moral support to our allies and friends of the Free World." (South Africa was specifically named as one of those friends.) Another declared the meeting "opposed to sin and injustice in all its forms. . . . BE IT RESOLVED that sin and injustice be defined as that which is condemned in the Holy Bible." The delegates elected for Houston included the wife of the grand dragon of the Mississippi Knights of the Ku Klux Klan—who was *not*, she insisted, herself a Klan member. She only attended its rallies, as "a concerned citizen."

Afterward, Barrett said, "When you talk about legalizing perversion you're touching on the soul of America. It's undisputed and undoubted that we have sent a mandate to the nation that the ERA is dead, and that the moral womanly woman is alive and well in Mississippi, and that she will win this battle." The grand dragon's wife, for her part, said Russia had tried and failed for years to take over the country using "the blacks," so now they were trying again with feminists. "My husband's been telling me about socialism and Communism for years. But I didn't really know until I saw it for myself in Jackson during the IWY state conference."

A pro–civil rights columnist for the *Jackson Clarion-Ledger* noted the familiar faces from his reporting on White Citizens Council meetings back in the 1950s and '60s. Only one thing was different: "Their enemy now is not the black man but 'liberalism,' in any form, as they see it."

CHAPTER 9

"God Made Adam and Eve, Not Adam and Steve"

THE NATIONAL WOMEN'S POLITICAL CAUCUS, A BIPARTISAN GROUP FORMED in 1971 to increase female representation at the national party conventions, was terrified: they feared the National Women's Conference in Houston would devolve into some sort of red, white, and blue Nuremberg Rally. So they strategized to thwart right-wing takeovers of the remaining state organizing meetings. Senator Jesse Helms got ahold of their meeting notes, introduced them into the Congressional Record, and claimed they proved a plot against "all women who believe in the social and moral values of womanhood" via "rigged sessions, hand-picked committees, stacked pre-registration, and little or no publicity to women at large." They actually were not nearly so cunning as all that, as the next weekend's state meeting in Indiana proved.

Members of Phyllis Schlafly's Citizens Review Committee poured out of their church buses and badly outmaneuvered the feminists on the convention floor, voting according to instructions flashed in code by men lurking on the perimeter. At one point, the conservatives' leader, State Senator Joan Gubbins, tumbled floorward and claimed assault—"an example of how feminists and fellow travelers . . . force their militant extremes on us all," she told a reporter. "Being a lady, I didn't retaliate." Outside, two ministers from Terre Haute brayed about all the "whores, prostitutes, and lesbians" inside and the "yellow-bellied men without backbones" who were abetting them, then began sprinting up the down escalator and down the up escalator, screaming about "women who wear men's clothes," in a parable of a world turned upside down. The conference chairwoman, a college affirmative action officer, asked security personnel at the convention center to eject the disruptors rendering the escalators impassable , but they rebuffed her; they agreed with the ministers. The conservatives won a majority of the delegates. A right-winger called it the "Pearl Harbor to the feminist movement." A feminist likened it to a Fellini movie.

Two months out from the national conference, Senator Helms convened hearings to get it canceled. One conservative testified about "hundreds of purple arm-banded lesbians . . . with gestures of clenched-fist defiance" holding "workshops on revolution and sex, including one on oral sodomy." Another bemoaned an alleged workshop in Pennsylvania on necrophilia. ("Do you know what that is? Making love with a corpse!") Henry Hyde said that "if even 10 percent of the allegations are true, the conference organizers could teach Brezhnev a thing or two." Bob Dornan said, "Only in the violent days of Communism did we see some of the suppression of speech we have seen under the guise of this conference." The wife of a California state senator named John Schmitz described displays of "masturbating wands, vibrators, and speculums for self-examination. One pregnant woman looking at abortion devices was offered instruction on how to perform an abortion on herself." Rosemary Thomson claimed this was "shocking" to "even the press."

THE PRESS WAS SURELY INDIFFERENT. THEY WERE FAR MORE INTERESTED IN matters like Bert Lance, Jimmy Carter's stalled energy bill, Senate hearings on the Panama Canal treaties—and a galvanizing Supreme Court case stirring a new subject into the social issue stew: "affirmative action."

Oral arguments were set for October 12 in the case brought by a thirty-three-year-old NASA research engineer named Allan Bakke, who sued the University of California in 1973 after twice being denied admission to the medical school at UC Davis. He blamed his misfortune on the school's policy of reserving sixteen slots for "educationally and economically disadvantaged minorities." In September of 1976 the California Supreme Court sided with him. The university appealed to the high court—which now had received more friend-of-the-court briefs from both sides than on any case in the previous twenty years.

Supporters of affirmative action argued that, far from being foreign to the American constitutional order, racial quotas were an implicit component of much Reconstruction-era legislation. Others said that UC Davis's program honored the spirit of President Johnson's famous commencement address in 1965 at Howard University: "You do not take a person who, for years, has been hobbled by chains and liberate him, bring him up to the starting line of a race and then say, 'You are free to compete with all the others,' and still justly believe that you have been completely fair." They also pointed to Howard itself, created as a black university by Congress in 1865; and to the "Philadelphia Plan," more than a century later, which gave contractors three years to bring minority employment up to 20 percent on federal construction, a policy affirmed in federal appeals court. And they pointed out the ways whites had specifically benefitted from federal policies—for example those subsidizing construction of, and transportation to, the suburbs—from which minorities had been explicitly excluded by Federal Housing Administration guidelines.

Bakke's supporters included groups like the Sons of Italy and the Polish-American Affairs Council, whose briefs turned a certain sort of barroom argument into legalese: "My ancestors had been serfs. They made it without special privileges. Why can't blacks?" This was a discourse mirrored in popular culture, which was saturated with sentimental reminiscences of ethnic hardship and resilience like Irving Howe's breakout bestseller on immigrant Jews, *World of Our Fathers*. Antique-looking signs bearing inscriptions like "No Dogs or Irish" found their way into basement rec rooms. "Everyone wants a ghetto to look back to," a writer observed.

Jews, themselves victims of religious quotas a generation earlier, also joined Bakke's side—setting traditionally liberal Jewish organizations at odds with the civil rights groups they had proudly fought beside in the time of Martin Luther King Jr. Another left-leaning group supporting Bakke was the American Federation of Teachers, a union historically led by Jewish socialists, but which was still stinging from savage battles in the late 1960s in Brooklyn, when blacks and the liberal foundations that supported them demanded "local"—i.e., black—control of schools, whatever the consequences for union protections for mostly Jewish teachers.

Right-wing organizations borrowed language from the black civil rights struggle, dubbing affirmative action "reverse racism" or "Crow Jim": the same bigotry, only now with whites as the target—*Affirmative Discrimination*, as a book by the neoconservative scholar Nathan Glazer put it. Indeed, at the height of the *Bakke* debate, Glazer's neoconservative confrere, Senator Daniel Patrick Moynihan, railed on the floor of the Senate against a memorandum of understanding from the federal Office for Civil Rights calling for schools with minority students to hire minority teachers. "This wretched contract," he bellowed, resembled "the sorting out of human beings for the death camps of Hitler's Germany."

Martin Luther King Jr. himself had warned a decade earlier about this sort of "white ethnic" resistance to the federal amelioration of the conditions of blacks. He argued that "the situation of other immigrant groups a hundred years ago and the situation of the Negro today cannot be usefully compared. Negroes were brought here in chains long before the Irish decided *voluntarily* to leave Ireland or the Italians thought of leaving Italy. Some Jews may have left their homes in Europe involuntary, but they were not in chains when they arrived on these shores. Other immigrant groups came to America with language and economic handicaps, but not with the stigma of color. Above all, no other ethnic group has been a slave on American soil, and no other group has had its family structure deliberately torn apart." This was why the appearance of *Roots* on TV the month of Jimmy Carter's inauguration was greeted so ecstatically by African

Americans: *now* the rest of America would finally get it. But that was not what happened. Instead, a historian wrote, Americans "from all backgrounds embraced *Roots* as a generic romance of ancestry lost and found . . . quickly appropriated as a movable template for considering *anyone's* familiar origins in *any* distant village." In March of 1977 *Time* reported, "So many Jews today seek memories of *shtetl* forebears that East Europeans call them 'roots people.'" Governor Michael Dukakis of Massachusetts raised his political profile with an "odyssey of discovery" in Greece. Then came the Academy Award for *Rocky*—a cinematic version of the argument about white ethnics oppressed by blacks. It was based on a true story: in 1975, boxing promoter Don King had announced that Muhammad Ali, as an "equal opportunity employer," was seeking out a Caucasian for a shot at his title. The palooka that emerged, a thirty-five-year-old liquor salesman from New Jersey named Chuck Wepner, went the distance. The delirious cheers he received from an all-white audience in a closed-circuit showing in Philadelphia inspired Sylvester Stallone to write a script that turned Wepner into an Italian-American, battling a black man who had received all the breaks.

One source for the anger over affirmative action was economic. The doctrine of compensatory employment quotas was invented back when the economic pie was growing. Now it seemed to be shrinking—especially for blue-collar workers. In September, Youngstown Sheet and Tube in Ohio shut down its largest plant with hardly a warning, idling five thousand workers, the largest civilian layoff in U.S. history. Twenty thousand steel mill jobs disappeared in 1977. Recession fears were widespread. White people were not in a sharing mood. Eighty-three percent of Americans opposed preferential treatment on the basis of race. Which left Jimmy Carter in a political pickle. Reported the *Washington Post* in its article on the amicus arguments in *Bakke*, "What potentially is the most influential brief has yet to be filed by the Justice Department, which has been struggling with the language of its arguments under intense pressure from civil rights leaders and the administrators of affirmative action plans in a number of federal departments." Affirmative action was the perfect issue to keep the Democratic Party divided—which was why Richard Nixon had advocated expanding the Johnson administration's Philadelphia Plan.

On Monday, September 19, the Justice Department released its seventy-four-page *Bakke* brief. It was another hedging Carter administration performance. It endorsed the principle of "reasonable goals or targets," but rejected "rigid exclusionary quotas"—without which, civil rights groups protested, the principle of affirmative action was moot. The argument was considerably to the left of an earlier, leaked draft. The administration insisted the shift had nothing to do with the flood of calls that had tied up the White House switchboard for hours after a DJ on a black radio station mistakenly announced the administration was conducting a public poll on the issue. "People who call in don't make much of an impact on influencing administration policy," an assistant press secretary told the black magazine *Jet*. That certainly was a switch from the White House line back when Carter was answering questions from random citizens on the radio.

THE WHITE HOUSE WAS IN A PERIOD OF DISARRAY. CARTER'S ENERGY PACKage was going nowhere in Congress. Getting the public to grasp their common interest in solving the problem was turning out to be impossible. Because when it came to energy, there was no common interest.

The Northeast and Midwest were net energy consumers. The states of the South and West were energy producers. A key component of the plan was a "standby" tax on gasoline that would kick in if Americans failed to meet lower consumption targets, a tax that would be rebated to taxpayers at the end of the year—so gas companies, not consumers, would be punished. This was resented by voters in states like Texas or Oklahoma, who owed their livelihoods to those companies. There, responding to calls to lower the skyrocketing price of the oil Northeasterners used to heat their homes, drivers sported bumper stickers reading "LET THEM FREEZE IN THE DARK."

Another vexing problem was whether to lift long-standing government-mandated prices on natural gas, a policy known as "decontrol." Carter favored keeping controls because removing them would give windfall profits to producers without significantly increasing supply. But that didn't solve the political problem. The producing states were more conservative and, because they were smaller in population, overrepresented in the Senate. The more liberal consuming states, desperate for cheaper prices, controlled the House.

And decontrol and the standby tax were but two of no less than 113 interlocking provisions that made up the proposed program. Moving it through Congress was a nightmare of political horse-trading—just the sort of work the president found most distasteful. Early results were discouraging. On a single day in June the House Commerce Committee voted down both Carter's proposals for a rebate to consumers who bought small cars and the standby gas tax, and the House Ways and Means Committee crossed the president by approving an amendment Carter didn't like to decontrol natural gas.

House Speaker Tip O'Neill put aside past slights and rode to the rescue with a clever strategy: convening a series of temporary party task forces instead of standing committees to draft the bill, shrewdly parceling out leadership roles to more than a hundred young up-and-comers with a stake in showing their constituents they could get things done. That broke the logjam. An energy bill passed the full House in the first week of August. Jimmy called Tip from Air Force One and thanked him so effusively he brought tears to the old Irishman's eyes.

The Senate would not prove so propitious. The only Democrat available for Tip O'Neill's role were Energy Committee chairman Scoop Jackson, Carter's sworn political enemy—and far to Carter's left on economic policy—and Louisiana's Russell Long, emperor of the tax-writing Senate Finance Committee, who controlled considerable energy leases himself that his father, the legendary Governor Huey Long, had helped himself to, and whom Carter had alienated by killing his pet water project. He had less interest in helping Carter out than Jackson did. And on September 26, two liberal Democrats, Senator James Abourezk of South Dakota and Senator Howard Metzenbaum of Ohio, shattered a possible breakthrough on natural gas with a filibuster to preserve price controls.

Back in spring, Carter had called passing comprehensive energy reform the moral equivalent of war. Now, a White House staffer said, it felt like the moral equivalent of the *Vietnam* War. Arthur Schlesinger wrote in his diary that he smelled the welcome possibility of Carter being denied re-nomination.

ON SEPTEMBER 29, THE PRESIDENT ENDEAVORED TO UNSTICK THINGS IN HIS now patented way: by going directly to the people. "With every passing day, our energy problems become more severe," he said to open a televised press conference. "There is no easy way to establish a comprehensive energy policy. No interest group can be totally satisfied with every part of our plan. . . . We are now at a turning point. . . . The House of Representatives has acted. . . . I sincerely hope that the Senate will not let the American people be disappointed."

Then he opened things up to the press—who hammered him: Why wasn't he working with Republicans? How naive was he to believe he could get a tax on oil wells around Senator Long? Then: "You told us twice that you'd learned on December 1, which was just two days before you appointed Mr. Lance, that aspects of the Lance case had been referred to the Justice Department. Jody Powell had told us that you didn't know at the time, you didn't learn until much later. Who is right? Is Jody right, or are you?"

"I don't recall," the president began—a Nixonian response.

On October 5, Carter jetted to New York, where Ed Koch had handily won the mayoral runoff, placing him on a glide path to election in November. Before addressing the United Nations on human rights, the president made a surprise stop in the South Bronx on a burned-out block where not a single building stood. He promised federal assistance to aid the borough's reconstruction. The *New York Daily News* said he should have visited Bushwick, where "the few working, middle-class families left in the dying neighborhood"—the word "white" was left implicit—"can give Carter the kind of first-hand knowledge of what's killing the nation's cities."

The association of Carter with the failing South Bronx felt appropriate. The *Daily News* had greeted him with a prediction he would be a one-term president. *Newsweek*—under the headline "Can Carter Cope?"—asked what it called "the Eptitude Question—the suspicion abroad in Washington's power factories that Carter and his Georgia irregulars have not yet fully mastered their jobs." William Safire thrusted that "if the klut-zification process proceeds at the current rate, and the economy is down in 1979, Carter could be the second president in succession to be challenged for his party's nomination."

Washington was a fashion-conscious town. Carter was now out of fashion.

He set off on a six-state tour to promote his energy package sans mediation from Washington elites. He insisted on doing so without prepared speeches. Halfway through the tour, reviews proved so poor that his twenty-eight-year-old speechwriter James Fallows lectured him via memo: "As you know, I share your belief that you should speak extemporaneously whenever you can. But the results of last weekend's trip suggest to me that sometimes we must choose a different approach."

On October 31, by a vote of 52 to 35, the Senate passed an energy tax bill so different from the House's that it felt more like a step backward. The White House announced a televised speech for November 8 to rally the nation. The speechwriting shop brought in a ringer: Richard Goodwin, the scribe behind some of JFK's and LBJ's most stirring words. The president inspected their draft, pronounced it a failure, and wrote his own. *Time*'s Hugh Sidey ranked it among the worst speeches ever given. The *Boston Globe* called it "the moral equivalent of Sominex"—the over-the-counter sleep aid. The review by *Washington Post*'s Nicholas von Hoffman stung deepest: "Either the people who hand Carter these texts should send away to the Great Writers' School, or, heaven forfend, the president is writing his own stuff."

SENATORS STREAMED SOUTH TO PANAMA ON FACT-FINDING EXPEDITIONS ahead of the February 8 opening of Senate debate. They found their host, General Torrijos, far from the tinhorn dictator of Ronald Reagan's imaginings. Like Castro, yes, he smoked cigars. But he also boasted a far better human rights record, respected international law, lived in a modest house, and lavished the rural peasantry with land, schools, housing, and infrastructure. Even Reagan's best friend in Washington, Senator Paul Laxalt, was impressed at the way Torrijos, walking in public sans bodyguards, was "hailed like a conquering hero." A senator described peppering the general with "one of the toughest interrogations that could have been made of any man": when he planned to hold elections, why he had sent citizens into exile, whether he would ever step down; Torrijos held his own. Another was so impressed by his "honesty and frankness" that "I would not have any difficulty in confirming that I would vote for the ratification of the treaties."

But senators also had constituents to contend with. Or, as Hamilton Jordan put it, "Some of these bastards don't have the spine not to vote their mail. If you can change their mail you can change their minds." So the White House dispatched officials to chambers of commerce and Jaycees meetings around the nation and brought in delegations of businessmen, editors, and labor leaders from key states to receive marathon White House briefings—where they might hear a White House assistant call right-wing direct mail "terror tactics," a military officer lecture about the Canal's strategic irrelevancy, brief remarks from Vice President Mondale and Secretary of State Cyrus Vance, and a lecture as long as forty-five minutes from the president himself, standing dramatically beneath the White House State Dining Room's life-sized portrait of Abraham Lincoln, repeating estimates that civil unrest in Panama would require he commit a hundred thousand American troops to quell it. At the talk the *New York Times* looked in on, Carter got a standing ovation.

The American Conservative Union began airing a half-hour program in three hundred TV markets called *There Is No Panama Canal . . . There Is an American Canal in Panama.* It yielded a $245,000 profit and fifty-eight thousand new addresses for the ACU's mailing list. The mail-order right was on track to raise nearly a million dollars to defeat the treaties. Richard Viguerie told a reporter, "We're going to look *very* carefully at the votes when all this is over and do an *awful* lot of punishing next election." Hamilton Jordan insisted the danger to senators up for reelection was "greatly exaggerated," that public opinion was "reversible—if we can just get the facts disseminated to a lot of people." Public opinion, however, was now tending the other way.

DEMOCRATS COMFORTED THEMSELVES WITH THE RELEASE OF A SURVEY REvealing that the Republican Party was suffering its lowest approval rating ever, below 20 percent—and with how divided the Republicans were over *why* they were unpopular. Syndicated columnist Clayton Fritchey quoted

Nancy Reagan saying that the mission of her husband was "to revive the Republican Party." Party liberal John Anderson replied that Reaganism would "bury it." Another public opinion result complicated matters: reported *Time* magazine, "All surveys show that a growing majority of the American people consider themselves to be conservative."

Conservative opinion and organizing now was everywhere. A formerly liberal magazine, *Harper's*, was becoming a veritable neoconservative organ. A typical contribution, by Norman Podhoretz, on Jimmy Carter's foreign policy, argued, "The parallels with England in 1937 are here, and this revival of the culture of appeasement ought to be troubling our sleep." (Cultures of appeasement arose, he concluded, when "the best people looked to other men for sex.") The Republican National Committee officially endorsed a bill filed by Congressman Jack Kemp of New York and Senator William Roth of Delaware. "Kemp-Roth" would lower income tax rates by 30 percent across the board over three years. Sheriff Ed Davis did a star turn at the California state Republican convention, insisting he hadn't been joking when he said the best way to deal with the epidemic of airline hijackers was to "hang 'em at the airport"; Witcover and Germond reported a consensus among experts that he he would win the gubernatorial nomination. His opponent, John Briggs, had bought Anita Bryant's mailing list to solicit petition signatures for his initiative to ban "open and notorious" homosexuals from teaching in schools, flooding California mailboxes with pamphlets featuring pictures of Briggs and Bryant staring purposefully into each other's eyes, Briggs snuggled up with a little blond girl ("Homosexuals are raising millions to defeat us. Normal decent Californians MUST ACT or THEY will win")—and pictures of a portly topless woman beside a protest banner reading "GAY LIBERATION THROUGH SOCIALIST REVOLUTION." His activists importuned passers-by in shopping malls—"Do you want to protect your children against molesters?"—then displayed pictures of a bludgeoned teenager lying in a pool of his own blood, and a collage of headlines like "R.I. Sex Club Lured Juveniles with Gifts" and "Former Scoutmaster Convicted of Homosexual Acts with Boys." He was having no trouble getting his signatures.

Conservatives were also busy taking on the ABC situation comedy *Soap*, the first network show to feature a gay character. "Opposition to the program has brought together some unusual coalitions," *Christianity Today* reported, "including Protestant, Catholic, and Jewish leaders." The director of Family and Special Moral Concerns of the Southern Baptist Convention called for a boycott of the show's advertisers, then boasted that the network had lost $1 million in revenue from their actions. Nielson confirmed that the show had posted a 3 percent decline in viewership since the protest began. CBS's standards and practices chief said he'd never seen anything like it: "This is coming right out of the grassroots of this country. The network is deluged with mail."

This was not precisely accurate. "The concept of a 'grass-roots movement' as a nebulous mass that will somehow exert a mystical influence for change on the Congress or local legislative bodies," as Dr. Mildred Jefferson of the National Right to Life Committee instructed her activist cadre, was "romantic noise." Things were much more top-down, with conservative organizers aggressively taking advantage of a transformed legal terrain. An unintended consequence of the liberally intended Tax Reform Act of 1976 allowed organizations that were mainly "educational" to use 20 percent of their budgets for direct lobbying without losing their tax-exempt status. The loophole was instrumental in a successful campaign in Pennsylvania to pass a state a "Human Life Amendment" identical to the one introduced in Congress in 1975 by Jesse Helms—"From the moment of fertilization every human being . . . shall be deemed to be a person and entitled to the right to life"—that would instantly render all abortion illegal should the Supreme Court overturn *Roe v. Wade*.

The loophole also let groups raise much more money, which they deployed to bulk up their mailing lists. Christians for Life bought the membership lists of the nation's thirty-five thousand Southern Baptist congregations, encompassing a quarter of the residents of Alabama and a sixth of those in Texas. The National Right to Life Committee claimed eleven million "active supporters" in three thousand chapters— twenty-two new ones in September in Mississippi alone. The National Rifle Association was on a path to tripling its membership, and strengthening its radical leadership cadre's grip. Analysts complained that these were "single-issue groups." This was an unfortunate misperception. The pro-life movement, for instance, had formed working alliances, the *New York Times* noted, "with groups that range from those fighting to 'Stop the Equal Rights Amendment!' to 'Stop the Panama Canal Giveaway!'"

This was how the right worked: each discontent reinforced the others. All of which became glaringly evident as the November 18 opening of the National Women's Conference in Houston approached.

THE NATION'S FIRST NATIONAL WOMEN'S CONFERENCE HAD HAPPENED IN 1848 in Seneca Falls, New York, where pioneering feminists like Susan B. Anthony and Elizabeth Cady Stanton resolved in a famous Declaration of Sentiments that "all men and women are created equal." Now, in Seneca Falls, on September 28, President Carter's daughter-in-law unfurled a great hand-lettered scroll and read a revised Declaration of Sentiments composed by the poet Maya Angelou. A majestic bronze torch was set ablaze in a candlelit ceremony. It flickered through the night; then, the next morning, a direct descendent of an original Seneca Falls attendee handed it to the first of over two thousand runners who would bear it 2,600 miles to Houston, where it would be presented at the nation's *second* national women's conference.

In November, it crossed the Mason-Dixon Line. "That's when the trouble started," a relay official said.

Truckers tried to run torchbearers off the side of the road. The Birmingham Road Runners Club, recruited to supply participants, canceled after a pressure campaign orchestrated by Phyllis Schlafly. A panicked phone call produced a nineteen-year-old marathoner from Houston who saved the day by covering sixteen miles along the most symbolically powerful leg—the stretch of Highway 80 where Martin Luther King Jr. and his pilgrims had marched to Montgomery for voting rights in 1965. A woman in the tiny town of Prattville watched her pass: "Now why would a woman want to get involved in something like that for? There's no law against it. But it takes her femininity away." Another called it "so much nonsense. . . . Look, I want men to open doors for me and pull out chairs and tell me I'm pretty. Why should I want to run halfway around this country with some old torch? I don't want to be a man."

The torch was borne the last mile by a triumvirate: an African American, a Hispanic—and Peggy Kokernot, the ringer who had heroically plugged the sixteen-mile hole in Alabama. Hundreds fell in behind them down Allen Parkway at noon, portly Bella Abzug leading the way in hat and high heels. The cheers as the flame crossed the threshold of the Sam Houston Coliseum drowned out a fundamentalist preacher's bullhorn: "Men are designed to lead! The women are designed as a help to the man!"

Conservative delegates, who comprised 20 percent of the total, and called themselves the "Pro-Family Caucus," held their own ceremony. Phyllis Schlafly presided, singling out the movement to provide government-funded shelters for battered women for opprobrium: "It is beyond me how giving a wife who has been beaten an R&R rest tour or vacation at the taxpayers' expense is going to solve our problems. I would think that the husband would be more inclined to beat her more if he thinks she will just get a taxpayers' paid rest cure." Martha Griffin, the former U.S. representative from Michigan who'd shepherded the Equal Rights Amendment through Congress, exploded to a reporter: "They are anti-family. I have sat on legislative bodies for twenty-five years, and I've never seen one of these people testifying on anything for the family."

At the Hyatt and Sheraton, a booking snafu rendered the lobbies chaotic makeshift cattle pens. Rumor had it conservatives were responsible. "I saw this very right-wing-looking woman pasting some sort of secret code up in our elevators at the Hyatt," an IWY commissioner confided to one of the local organizers. "You'll be relieved to know I went around behind her taking them down." And, also, that liberals were responsible: for hadn't they been witnessed tearing down pro-family posters in the elevator?

Schlafly held court for women reporters in her suite. One asked what her problem was with wives having their own Social Security accounts—which Ronald Reagan had endorsed in 1976. She answered: "I think that is putting a tremendous penalty to your right to have a wife in the house."

The newspapers carried condescending previews of what was to come. The *New York Post* headline was "It's a Big Day for the Ladies." The *Washington Post* worried it might descend into a polarizing brawl that would confirm the "public's most harmful stereotypes of women." In the *New York Times*, coverage ran on the Family/Style page. An editorial in the *Houston Post* warned readers not to think all the attendees were lesbians, noting the presence of Rosalyn Carter, Betty Ford, and Lady Byrd Johnson. But in the same edition an ad displayed a darling little girl holding a bouquet of flowers and asking, "Mommy, when I grow up, can I be a lesbian?" The copy continued, "If you think this idea is shocking, read what the IWY is proposing for your children." It listed gay marriage, abortion, compulsory daycare, and the "destruction of the American way of life" as among the conference's goals.

The line for the delegate credentials was so long an Arizona delegate went into labor. She named her new daughter Era. Dallas Higgins arrived with her Klan-leader husband in tow. She expressed worry that the organizers would force them to room with black lesbians. In the parking lot, attendees rushed past a minister from Oklahoma braying to them not to succumb to the evils of lesbianism. An imposing radical lesbian writer in overalls named Andrea Dworkin engaged him in conversation. She found him kind and warm—until she pointed out that some of the women filing past him *were* lesbians. He startled, she noted, "as frightened girls do to mice or bugs or spiders. . . . He seemed visibly sick from the recognition."

Inside, a battle of banners unfurled: "WE'RE LADIES, NOT LIBER-ALS" and "SIN IS STILL SIN, EVEN IF IT'S LEGAL" and "FOLLOW JESUS CHRIST AND YOUR HUSBAND AND YOUR PASTOR . . . REPENT" from one side; "JESUS WAS A FEMINIST" and "WAGES FOR HOUSEWORK" and "I OWN MY OWN BODY BUT I SHARE" from the other. A thirty-foot-long banner up in the rafters read "VIVA LA MUJER." One in the Wisconsin section announced, "WOMEN'S RIGHTS ARE AS AMERICAN AS APPLE PIE." Feminist Nebraskans said "WE DIDN'T BURN OURS"—and swung brassieres over their heads to prove it.

Women from Guam and Hawaii wore tropical muumuus. Delegates from Puerto Rico wore "*jibaro*" hats in solidarity with sugarcane workers. District of Columbia delegates wore "Free D.C." tricorns, a plea for statehood; Wisconsin women wore red cowboy hats; New Yorkers waved big apples. "Pro-family" delegates wore yellow ribbons that read "MAJORITY." Gay rights advocates wore ones in lavender. Seventy-three-year-old Betty Hamburger of the Grey Panthers senior citizens' rights group wore a hard hat reading "Pro-God, Pro-Family, Pro-ERA." A Mississippi conservative demurely knit a pair of baby booties; a feminist Republican from Arizona clicked away at a scarf.

There were two thousand delegates in all, plus several hundred "at large" delegates representing groups like Hadassah and the National Organization of Negro Women, and three thousand volunteers, fifteen hundred reporters, two thousand invited guests, and thousands of spectators up in the bleachers. One was an autoworker from Peoria who had asked her union to send her to Houston after STOP ERA overran the state IWY meeting in Illinois. The union declined. So she emptied her savings account and flew there on her own dime, returning in time to punch in at the plant on Monday morning.

A lawyer from Milwaukee named Mandy Stellman wore gargantuan round black eyeglasses and a whistle around her neck, her trademark: in 1973, as a volunteer for Milwaukee's women's crisis line, she had been called to a police station to assist an eighteen-year-old rape victim. She was refused admission to the room where the victim was being interrogated like a criminal (though a criminal at least would have been allowed to have a lawyer present). She subsequently became a crusader for the reformation of sexual assault laws, ordering up thousands of whistles with the crisis line's phone number printed on them and distributing them everywhere. In Houston she blew hers whenever something met with her approval. Which would have singled her out as a shrill feminist indeed—had not Senator Joan Gubbins of Indiana, the pro-family delegates' floor leader, resplendent in a flamboyant gold-feathered Beau Brummel hat, not worn a whistle around her neck, too, and blown it even more.

ON THE DAIS, BEFORE A COLOSSAL WHITE CURTAIN READING "WOMAN," the national president of the Girl Scouts held up a gavel last used in 1896 by Susan B. Anthony—whose grandniece, also named Susan B. Anthony, was granted the floor and pronounced the most famous words of America's greatest warrior for women's suffrage: "Failure is impossible!" The gavel was handed to Bella Abzug, who called the raucous assemblage to order. A minister invited a moment of silence to reflect "the commitment of the conference to ask for guidance in her or his own way." The torch parted the convention floor, accompanied by an all-female drum and bugle corps, and chants of "Hey, Hey, what do you say? Ratify the ERA!" (the flame nearly went out; a tampon was patched onto the wick to save the day). Billie Jean King bounded up to the platform and handed off the torch to the three first ladies. Rosalynn Carter said, "Jimmy asked me to be his personal emissary today." Betty Ford said, "We have both found a great deal of respect and appreciation in knowing that each of us can speak our own minds as we felt necessary." (She added a conspiratorial wink.) Lady Bird Johnson said, "I once thought that the women's movement belonged more to my daughters than to me. But I have come to know that it belongs to women of all ages." Then they added their signatures to Maya Angelou's scroll.

Barbara Jordan, the black congresswoman who had become a national hero for a great speech at the impeachment hearings for Richard Nixon, delivered a stirring keynote address: "Human rights apply equally to Soviet dissidents, Chilean peasants, and *American* women," she said. And those who predicted "chaos and failure" over the next three days? "Tell them they lie—and move on."

Debate began on the twenty-six resolutions to be presented to the president and Congress as the will of American womanhood, and it immediately became clear how different this would be from the political conventions Americans were used to seeing on TV: these women were daring democracy, with all its attendant messiness. Delegates lined up at the microphones to speak as they wished. Volunteers held up giant yellow cards when someone requested a point of order. A black public official from Pennsylvania, a kerchief stretched over her head, offered a formal objection to the seating of an all-white Mississippi delegation. She was ruled out of order, to hisses and boos. But liberals were determined to be fair—and her objection hadn't followed proper parliamentary procedure.

The resolutions came in alphabetical order. An "Arts and Humanities" plank demanding more equal representation in grants and cultural institutions sailed through—but the next concerned "Battered Women," and feminists braced themselves for combat.

It had only recently become illegal in many places for a husband to beat a wife. In 1962, New York State made the penalty for assaulting a spouse lower than for assaulting a stranger. In 1966 battery became grounds for divorce in New York State for the first time—but only if the plaintiff established that a "sufficient" number of beatings had taken place. In 1968 the Harris Poll found that 20 percent of Americans of both sexes approved of slapping one's spouse on "appropriate occasions." In Chicago, women who left their husbands were denied welfare benefits if their husband had too much income—whether they received any of it or not. In 1972 *Ms.* reprinted an ad for a bowling alley in Michigan. It read, "Have some fun. Beat your wife tonight. Then celebrate with some good food and drink with your friends." That year, Detroit's police commissioner reported that of 4,900 battered women's cases, 300 went to trial. In 1974 the FBI established that of the 132 police officers killed in the nation, 29 had died answering domestic disturbance calls. It was still legal for a husband to force sex on his wife. The nation's first trial for spousal rape didn't happen until 1978. The husband was acquitted.

The draft resolution was read from the podium. It called for Congress to establish a national informational clearinghouse and "technical and financial assistance to locally controlled public and private nonprofit organizations providing emergency shelter and other support services for battered women and their children." This was what Schlafly had been referring to when she spoke of a "taxpayer-paid rest cure." Had that been a signal for a floor fight? Mandy Stellman, after all, had said that fundamentalist Christian women with bruises all over their bodies consistently denied that their husbands ever beat them, in the belief that "God will punish her if she complains." Was *that* the attitude "pro-family" forces wanted to visit upon on the rest of the nation?

The vote was called. Feminists eyed the women with the "MAJORITY" ribbons nervously. But the battered women plank sailed through, too.

The draft on child abuse was read. It called for government-provided counseling and twenty-four-hour protective services. A woman in a "MAJORITY" ribbon introduced a substitute plank calling for the federal government to stay out of private family business. "Did you know," she testified, that "spanking is now called 'child abuse'?" It was defeated without a fight. Another conservative demanded the plank "include those one million pre-born children killed by abortion last year." That was ruled out of order. The draft passed as written.

The childcare plank called for a federally funded national childcare system like that vetoed by Nixon in 1971. Over an objection that "the similarity between Hitler's camps and these youth camps might produce the same consequences," this resolution sailed through, also. Planks on Credit and Disabled Women passed unanimously.

The strategists on the feminist side began to worry. This was too easy.

WITH AN 80–20 DELEGATE SPLIT IN THEIR FAVOR, FEMINISTS' CONCERN HAD never been a right-wing amendment or two, but floods of amendments—that right-wingers would exploit parliamentary procedure to sabotage the meeting by bogging it down. Organizers had also expended considerable energy to persuade feminist militants from gumming up the works with well-meaning but impractical amendments—and wondered if that would hold, too.

Then the evening session began with easy passage of the education plank calling for "nonsexist and non-racist counseling at every level," women's history curricula, and nonsexist language in textbooks. Then, during debate on the plank calling for affirmative action for officeholders, women at the back began raising signs, as if on a signal: "ABORTION EXPLOITS WOMEN." "RESCIND ERA." "ONLY A RAT WOULD RATIFY." "ERA: SIT ON IT!" (That was a catchphrase from *Happy Days,* the sitcom celebrating 1950s domestic bliss.)

Delegate-at-large Dr. Mildred Jefferson made a surprise stroll down the center aisle of the floor. The minority who called themselves "MA-JORITY" raised a great cheer. The chair banged down Susan B. Anthony's gavel:

"Visitors! . . . Refrain from walking in the center aisles!"

Dr. Jefferson duly exited.

The general secretary of the National Council of Churches took the podium and said seven words: "The Equal Rights Amendment should be ratified." The hall reverberated with roars. Hundreds of small black "ERA YES!" placards were raised as one. But the foreboding also reached a peak.

Bella Abzug had tabbed a charismatic newcomer from Texas, a county commissioner named Ann Richards, to give the first pro-ERA speech. Then Dianne Edmondson, Schlafly's Oklahoma lieutenant, gave one, introducing an amendment opposing efforts to extend the deadline for ratification of the constitutional amendment in the states from the original date in 1979 until 1982. Next came Susan B. Anthony's niece—who concluded, to pandemonium, "Failure is impossible!"

"Impossible! Impossible!"

"Three more states! Three more states!"

The next speaker was Jean Westwood of the Democratic National Committee. She began, "I am a Mormon woman speaking in favor of the ERA!" That got even greater cheers—and eyes turned to Utah's demure delegates in matching black floor-length dresses, sent by the men in their stakes to "vote for correct principles."

But the ERA passed by more than *five* to one—which meant some "pro-family" delegates had crossed sides to vote for it, too. The snake-dancing and singing and waving of apples and scarves and brassieres and floral leis and *jibaro* hats and tricorns was so boisterous that the chair didn't dare try to restore order. It took Bella Abzug to finally do that, dismissing the assemblage with the gentle words, "Good night, my loves."

And the organizers wondered if the antifeminist onslaught would ever come.

IN FACT, IT ALREADY HAD.

Once it became evident, that summer, that conservatives would only comprise a fifth of the delegates, Lottie Beth Hobbs of Women Who Want to Be Women, now vice president of the Eagle Forum, proposed not to fight on the convention floor. Instead, she suggested a massive counter-rally, a pageant for the TV cameras to display who *truly* represented the will of American womanhood. Hobbs proposed booking the eight-thousand-seat Astro Arena across town. Terrified of the optics of a half-empty hall—or a full one with half the attendees feminists bent on sabotage—her comrades wondered whether a nice big church might not be more appropriate. Phyllis Schlafly vetoed that straight off. She had devoted her annual conference in St. Louis to organizing the counter-rally, which she decided must be massive. Another cassette tape was produced by Dianne Edmondson to recruit attendees. ("At the Virginia IWY conference, there was a workshop on witchcraft, conducted by witches . . .") Copy after copy of a formal petition to Congress was sent forth to every church and organization they could think of to fill with signatures to display for the cameras, too.

At a meeting the night before the event, Senator Gubbins read the story from the Book of Judges of the prophet Gideon, who with God's help defeated the mighty Midianite army of 135,000 with a force of but 300—just like their pro-family delegates. Then, the leaders stood before the yawning expanse of empty seats in the Astro Arena, and, nervously, waited.

Verily, there arrived a biblical flood.

Twenty-five busloads came from Fort Worth, fifty-six from Tennessee—two hundred fifty buses in all. Six hundred vehicles had California license plates. A bus from Sacramento took twenty-eight hours to arrive. A mother of nine who drove seven friends down from Bismarck, North Dakota—a mere twenty-two hours away—said, "We felt we had the Lord knocking on the top of the van all the way down." *Their* people, organizers were pleased to inform the press, *had to* drive all night: they were working people who couldn't afford airplanes or hotels, couldn't afford to take Friday off from work, had paid their own way—unlike all those rich feminists downtown who got their airfare and a $50 per diem out of $5 million drawn from the United States Treasury.

At the entrance, a platoon from something called the Freedom Heritage Society—they said their black uniforms stood for America's sinful society, their gold braid the return of Jesus Christ—stood sentry. By the time the fire marshal closed the doors, fifteen thousand pilgrims had filed past them and five thousand were turned away to listen over loudspeakers in the parking lot.

A woman from Massachusetts with an infant in a backpack and a toddler by her side carried a sign reading, "IF YOU LIKED JUDGE GARRITY, YOU'LL LOVE THE ERA," referring to the federal judge administering the desegregation of the schools in South Boston. "For a lot of these ERA people giving the feds control over the school doesn't matter because they're not having families," she explained to a reporter. "They're having abortions." A young woman pushing a baby stroller said, "I want to keep my children at home and I don't want to be drafted." A thirty-two-year-old man, his wife and six-year-old child in tow, cited Bible verses, and said this was first political rally they had ever attended. "And I doubt very seriously that it will be the last."

Placards read:

"WOMEN'S LIP."
"THE GRASSROOTS WON'T BE STEPPED ON ANYMORE."
"ABORT LIBBERS NOT BABIES."
"PARENTS RIGHTS BEFORE GAY RIGHTS"
"DRAFT FEMINISTS—NOT LADIES"
"IWY—INTERNATIONAL WITCHES YEAR"
"SIN IS STILL SIN, EVEN IF IT'S LEGAL."

And one slogan people found so clever it took on a life of its own: "GOD MADE ADAM AND EVE, NOT ADAM AND STEVE."

Lottie Beth Hobbs stepped up to the podium to explain what those file boxes stacked six feet high around the platform were: 300,000 signatures' worth of anti-ERA petitions addressed to Congress. Elisabeth Elliot, a mainstay on the evangelical circuit who had returned to the same isolated Ecuadoran jungle to minister to a tribe of Indians even after they had murdered her husband, preached, "For the Christian woman, submission is not weakness, femininity is not frivolity. . . . Egalitarianism to me is not a goal to be desired. It is a dehumanizing distortion. *Let me be a woman!*" Another speaker called himself a "reformed homosexual." Nellie Gray of the March for Life spoke with a red rose in her hand, representing the un-born. Phyllis Schlafly took the stage, to delirium.

It had been an even busier autumn for Schlafly than usual. She had matriculated at Washington University's Law School. She was working on a possible 1978 primary challenge to Illinois's liberal Republican sena-tor Charles Percy. She had published a bestselling book, *The Power of the Positive Woman*, which was a rhetorical masterpiece; with nary a conspiratorial word, it framed the battle over ERA according to a dichotomy: a woman could choose a bitter, shrunken identity as "just another faceless victim of society's oppression"; or she could be the kind of woman whose "positive mental attitude has built her an inner security that the other people can never fracture," with "a capability for creativity that men can never have."

In Houston, she snapped forth her customary opening line: "First of all, I want to thank my husband Fred, for letting me come. I always like to say that opener. It makes the libs so mad!" The crowd went wild. She announced that she was "staying in a Ramada Inn suite protected by an armed guard!" They went wild again, with boos.

She referred to "the little people—people such as you and I—we can sew up the moral fabric of this country." ("Phyllis is one of the little people like Prince Grace of Monaco is one of the little people," grumbled an Illinois ERA leader watching her on TV.)

"The libs want ERA to give an equal right for women not to be pregnant, just like men. . . . If you don't like the fact that women are the ones who have babies and nurse them, you will just have to take that up with God."

"If we had the $5 million Congress spent on the women's conference, we'd have buried ERA five years ago!" Instead, that money went to "a charade, to go through the motions of these phony state conferences and national conferences, in order to pass resolutions that were pre-written and pre-packaged a year and a half ago. . . . By coming here today, you have shown that that is *not* what American women want. American women do not want abortion. They do not want lesbian privileges. And they do not want universal childcare in the hands of the government. . . . We have Somebody on our side who is more powerful than the president of the United States!"

Bibles waved. Cardboard buckets were passed, and filled to overflowing with bills. Anita Bryant spoke via video. Perhaps she was concerned for her security. A month earlier, in Des Moines, to receive a key to the city and promote her new book, *The Anita Bryant Story: The Survival of Our Nation's Families and the Threat of Militant Homosexuality*, she was smacked in the face by a protester's pie. She got off a good one-liner— "Well, at least it's a fruit pie"—then broke down in tears. (Her husband allegedly had pinched her to remind her to produce them.) Then, she was scheduled to do a live interview in New York on the *Today* show. The network received so many threats that they had her tape it surreptitiously, spiriting her in and out a side entrance.

Representative Bob Dornan came very much in person. Ramrod straight, he scowled and in his newscaster's voice said that "the greatest tragedy of all" was that three first ladies could sit primly alongside Bella Abzug, "approving of the sexual perversion and murder of young people in their mothers' wombs. What a disgrace!" The response from the crowd was frenetic. (Gloria Steinem yelled at her TV: "If we're all lesbians, where are we getting all these unborn babies to kill?")

The last word belonged to a black state legislator from Texas named Clay Smothers, a 1972 George Wallace delegate at the Democratic National Convention who had recently introduced a bill to ban homosexuals from his state's public colleges and universities. He began calmly—until the audience's enthusiastic interruptions overwhelmed him: "I am overcome! I feel like I'm in a black Baptist church!"

"Some of my black friends ask me why I am working with this movement, when most of the blacks are on the other side of town. I have enough civil rights to choke a hungry goat. I ask for *public* rights. . . . Let's do something about these misfits and perverts over in the Sam Houston Coliseum. I want to segregate my family from them!" He cried, "I'm sick and tired of the president's wives flimflamming with these libbers!" The audience leapt to its feet.

The meeting was called to a close after three electric hours and several rousing choruses of "God Bless America." Some drove straight home overnight—to make it to Sunday morning church. In the Sam Houston Coliseum, they were 20 percent. The show of force at the Astro Arena guaranteed that henceforth, they got at least half of the coverage, or more.

THE NEXT DAY, THE GREATEST TENSION CAME FROM THE FEMINISTS WHO had organized as the "Susan B. Anthony Caucus" in order to oppose the gay rights plank they considered a distraction from passing the ERA. National Organization for Women founder Betty Friedan was especially averse to gays. She once called them the "lavender menace."

Andrea Dworkin obtained a convention floor pass. She rushed to the Mississippi section. The women wouldn't make eye contact with her, so she approached one of the men, who looked at the letters *Ms.* dangling from her neck, laughed, and whispered into the ear of the woman next to him. They passed the message down the row, telephone style; some giggling, others gasping. Dworkin asked the man why he had come. He said he hoped to protect women's right to procreate. She asked if he was a member of the KKK. He replied that he was a high official. She asked him another question. He stared—"You're a Jew, ain't ya?" he said—then turned away. The women turned away, too.

Before the debate over gay rights, delegates took up the minority affairs plank. Three weeks before the conference, California's entire Chicana caucus had walked out of a planning meeting to protest their marginalization. Others protested that the minority affairs plank included only ten lines. Women from Washington, D.C., meanwhile, had brought a "Black Woman's Agenda" they hoped to force into the final document. Then, in Houston, in a minor miracle of democratic deliberation, under extraordinary time pressure, with Gloria Steinem ("our token Caucasian") moderating, a consensus statement was produced noting the "double discrimination" suffered by—a novel coinage that proved durable—"women of color."

This plank was the only one read from the floor: the first section by a black assemblywoman from California named Maxine Waters; the second by a Native American activist, then a Japanese-American, then a Mexican-American, a Cuban-American, a Puerto Rican—and, finally, by Coretta Scott King, who wiped a tear from her eye: "When we are divided, we can be conquered; when we are united, we can achieve. With this kind of unity, we cannot lose."

When the vote came, even Utahns rose up from their seats to cast their *ayes*. Then, in a mighty wave, delegates stood, joined hands—even some of the Mississippi women—and swayed like waves of grain for the singing of "We Shall Overcome." What could possibly break unity like this?

Maybe what came next: the reproductive freedom debate.

In Washington, a House-Senate conference committee was entering its sixth month of deliberation on the Hyde Amendment. The proceedings alternated between horror stories about fetuses with incurable genetic diseases and "backroom butchers" performing abortions for those who could not afford clinics and talk about legalized genocide—all of it uttered by men. During one session, a male staffer queried a female colleague: "Is ovulation the same as orgasm?" During another, during debate over whether the definition of rape should include statutory rape, a congressman cracked, "It's not a question of consent. The question is whether she enjoyed it." A female Capitol staffer who logged debates began arranging for someone to replace her during the abortion discussion. She couldn't take it anymore.

In Houston a commissioner read the draft of the reproductive freedom plank, directing "all branches of federal, state, and local governments to give highest priority" to complying with *Roe v. Wade*, demanding abortion receive the same government subsidies as other forms of healthcare, and that "all schools, including elementary schools" teach sex education, that "all levels of government" provide "confidential family planning services," and that involuntary sterilization—the "Mississippi appendectomy," as it was known in the South, where it was still allegedly sometimes carried out on black women in clinics funded by the U.S. Department of Health, Education, and Welfare—be banned.

Conservatives began ferrying massive banners across the floor with grisly color photographs of fetuses. Feminists held aloft signs bearing coat hangers.

Came the vote: 80 percent to 20 percent, no crossovers. Now it was dismayed conservatives' turn to sway and sing—"*All we are saying / Is give life a chance . . .*"—as feminists ripped down a massive "GIVE LIFE A CHANCE" banner, replacing it with "IF MEN COULD GET PREGNANT, ABORTION WOULD BE SACRED."

FINALLY IT WAS TIME FOR THE DEBATE ON SEXUAL PREFERENCE. AS THE draft was being read. Andrea Dworkin saw a group of Utahns in their matching black dresses in the highest balcony "slowly, grimly exiting." She raced to interview them. One told her, "If you had a child and he was playing out in the street and a car was coming you would move him out of the way, wouldn't you? Well, that's all we're trying to do—get homosexuality away from our children." Another said, "You're a Jew. And probably a homosexual too."

(Down below, a woman read a statement at the microphone that said gay rights "compels the sympathy of all concerned people. But it has always been an albatross on the neck of the feminist movement." She was booed. The chair cried, "Stay of order!" The woman: "The political reality is that passage of this resolution is an extra burden we do not need. I urge you to defeat this resolution!")

Dworkin remembered, "I found myself slowly being pushed farther and farther back against the balcony railing. I kept trying to turn myself around as we talked, to pretend that my position in relation to the railing and the fall of several hundred feet was not precarious. . . . They kept advancing, pushing me closer and closer to the railing until my back was arched over it. They kept talking about homosexuals and Jews. . . . I kept trying to make myself human to them, they kept transforming me into the direct cause of their frustration and anger, they kept saying there was no middle ground and sin had to be wiped out."

(Betty Friedan received recognition from the chair. Lesbians—perhaps 10 percent of the delegates, though Rosemary Thomson said they were half—tensed themselves for a speech about the lavender menace. But Friedan surprised them. She began speaking about her recent divorce: "As someone who has loved too well, I have had trouble with this issue. Now my priority is passing the ERA. And because there is nothing in it that will give any protection to homosexuals, I believe we must help the women who are lesbians." The vote was called—and rights for lesbians were now inscribed as the official will of American womanhood. But with a 60-40 vote, not an 80-20 one. Hundreds of pink and yellow balloons were released to the rafters, reading, "WE ARE EVERYWHERE." The delegates from Mississippi, their feminist solidarity exhausted, turned their backs, lowered their heads in prayer, and held up "KEEP THEM IN THE CLOSET" signs.)

Dworkin felt herself further pushed toward the railing. Brilliant, difficult, and fearless, she had a particular gift for describing what she saw as the psychological traumas that lay behind anti-feminist commitment. "Women fight for meaning just as women fight for survival," she wrote, "by attaching themselves to men and the values honored by men. . . . The right promises to put enforceable restraints on male aggression, thus simplifying survival for women. . . . The promise is that if a woman is obedient, harm will not befall her." Conservative Christianity, meanwhile, "offers women the love of Jesus, beautiful brother, tender lover, compassionate friend, perfect healer of sadness and *ressentiment*, the one male to whom she can submit absolutely . . . without being sexually violated or psychologically abused." She was particularly cutting in her analysis of women like Anita Bryant, who "has spent a good part of her life on her knees begging Jesus to forgive her for the sin of existing." She concluded of women like these, "Subservient to male will, women believe that subservience itself is the meaning of female life."

No wonder she now was now terrified she might be thrown off a balcony.

At last she spotted two women out of the corner of her eye. She drew the Mormons' attention to the fact they were no longer alone. Then, trembling, she retreated. "You shouldn't have been alone with them," her rescuers said.

THE CONVENTION'S LAST SESSION WAS A MESSY ANTICLIMAX. "THE DELegates were ready to go home, and parliamentary procedure lost out," a female newscaster reported. "So did the resolution to set up a cabinet level Department of Women." It was the only resolution to fail.

Each side accused the other of slow-walking; pro-family delegates, singing "We Shall Overcome," staged a walkout. So did some minority delegates. The meeting adjourned with the most important agenda item undiscussed: a plan to pass the platform into law.

The press had already lost interest. In an extraordinary geopolitical development, President Anwar Sadat of Egypt announced to the Egyptian People's Assembly, "I am ready to travel to the ends of the earth if this will in any way protect an Egyptian boy, soldier, or office from being killed or wounded. . . . Israel will be surprised to hear me say that I am willing to go to their parliament, the Knesset itself, and debate with them."

"Surprised" was an understatement. A landslide upset in May by Israel's conservative Likud Party had brought a hawkish right-wing prime minister to power. The conservative magazine *Human Events* welcomed Menachem Begin as "Israel's Ronald Reagan." But Begin accepted Sadat's overture. So little time elapsed between Sadat's shocking announcement and his arrival, so unlikely was the prospect of a visit from a leader of a country with which Israel was still technically at war, that the military band was unable to find music to play the Egyptian national anthem on the tarmac for Sadat. They had to play it by ear. The distrust between the two nations was so suffusing that snipers were posted on the roof—in case a Trojan jetliner disgorged not Anwar Sadat but a company of Egyptian commandos, guns blazing.

The real risk, however, was Sadat's. Within hours of the announcement of his travel plans, a bomb wracked the Egyptian embassy in Damascus. Leaders in Syria, Iraq, and Libya openly called for his assassination; touring the Arab quarter of Jerusalem, he was jeered. Sadat persevered. He laid a wreath at an Israeli military cemetery, and received a yarmulke from Begin before touring the Yad Vashem Holocaust memorial. ("It's a *Kippah*," Begin said. "It's our custom to cover our heads during prayers or when entering a house of prayer.") Sadat wrote in the guestbook, "May God guide our steps toward peace. Let us put an end to the suffering for mankind." He prayed at al-Aqsa Mosque on the Dome of the Rock, where the bullet holes were still visible from a 1951 assassination attempt against King Abdullah I of Jordan, the last Arab leader to inaugurate negotiations with the Israelis. Sadat's speech to the Knesset was heralded by bugle calls. The media was spellbound. *Time* described the visit "as if a messenger from Allah had descended to the Promised Land." The *Today* show devoted its entire Monday program to it; and on that evening's newscasts, Sadat received seven times more coverage than the convention intended to reveal the political will of half the American citizenry.

MEANWHILE, IN HOUSTON, THERE WAS SOMETHING THE MEDIA MISSED.

The coliseum had featured an exhibit hall with displays from government agencies, occupational associations, states and territories, and religious denominations. There were makeshift art galleries and booths for businesses hawking their wares, for the YWCA, for a feminist group opposing pornography, one sponsored by NASA where women could have their picture taken sticking their head through an astronaut-suit standee.

And also a few Marxist sects, some gay advocacy groups, and lesbian businesses hawking certain . . . wares. Which was why a sign outside read, "Some displays may not be suitable for all ages." Said a cop standing sentry outside, "Wait 'til I tell my wife what I'm protecting. Ordinarily, I'd be raiding a place like this."

Eagles from Oklahoma rescued box upon box of this offensive material from the dumpsters. They pasted what they claimed to have found—though a feminist was certain they'd supplemented the haul from visits to adult bookstores—onto sixty sheets of poster board. They displayed the material a few weekends later at a Farm Bureau convention. An organizer related that as many as eight hundred stunned people visited the display. ("There was a chair down there at the end and sometimes they just had to sit down and catch their breath.") Phyllis Schlafly learned about it, and had the display shipped to an anti-feminist meeting in Atlanta, where it again was a hit. She put forth word of its availability in her next *Eagle Forum Newsletter*, fudging the truth: "It will shock you to know that this kind of material is financed with $5 million of YOUR money." (In fact, exhibitors had paid a vendors' fee.) "You should be informed about the radical and lesbian forces that are waging war on the American family." The display then toured at least thirty states.

Thousands of feminists had left Houston exultant, airborne, having proven, wrote Megan Rosenfeld of the *Washington Post*, that the women's movement was not some "small group of intellectuals" but "a force considered socially acceptable by president's wives and housewives from South Dakota, by the middle aged and the older women as well as the young." Gloria Steinem called it the "Constitutional Convention for women," the "sort of milestone that divides our sense of time."

Schlafly left warning, "The Women's Lib movement sealed its own doom by deliberately hanging around its neck the albatross of abortion, lesbianism, pornography, and federal control." A preacher from Calcasieu Parish, Louisiana, wrote back to his congregants, "Moral rottenness filled the hall with the stench of death." Tottie Ellis returned home to Nashville to stage an anti-ERA rally for ten thousand people. The governor of Missouri, a Democrat, announced that "after they went down to Houston and got all tangled up with all those lesbians, I can tell you, Missouri will never ratify the ERA," and Schlafly's chief deputy in Oklahoma, Bunny Chambers, said all it took to turn any gathering against ratification was twenty minutes spent reading aloud the twenty-six Houston resolutions. She called them "the best recruiting tool I ever had."

CHAPTER 10

Boardroom Jacobins

ACCORDING TO THE THEORIES OF KARL MARX, REVOLUTIONS HAPPEN WHEN a group of people in a similar position in the economic structure become a "class for itself": when they become conscious of their collective grievances, stop fighting one another, and organize to fight their common oppressor instead. That was what was happening in America now. Only the class in question wasn't the proletariat. It was the corporate executives.

Their revolt was a belated one. The early twentieth-century Progressive Movement, then the New Deal, engendered plenty of anger from America's monied classes. But their political resistance was scattershot. The United States Chamber of Commerce, chartered in 1912 at the request of President William Howard Taft as a bulwark against organized labor, accomplished surprisingly little in its first two decades; organized business's callous response to the Great Depression helped ensure it would subsequently accomplish even less. The prosperous decades that followed the end of the Depression and World War II were marked by a continued growth of the American state: federal spending doubled as a share of economic output between 1948 and 1968; unions became more powerful; regulations increased. Corporations that thrived were generally the ones that best accommodated this new state of affairs. In 1950 the marriage between Big Business and Big Labor was solemnized by the "Treaty of Detroit," a historic contract between General Motors and the United Automobile Workers that guaranteed annual "cost of living" adjustments and free healthcare. It became the pattern for thousands of contracts around the country. So did the next GM contract, signed five year's later, which provided unemployment compensation during layoffs at 65 percent of wages. Ordinary blue-collar workers now had just about more economic security than they had ever known in history, anywhere.

Some resisted these developments. In 1947 the Advertising Council spent $100 million on a promotional campaign preaching that the free market was "the most democratic institution ever devised by man." General Electric distributed millions of copies of a cartoon version of the laissez-faire economist Friedrich Hayek's best-selling 1944 polemic *The Road to Serfdom*, which argued that when government told businesses what to do, the inevitable result was slavery for everyone. (One drawing depicted a government commissar breaking a golf club over his knee as workers performed soul-killing calisthenics—"It is no coincidence that sports and amusements have been carefully 'planned' in all regimented nations." The last panel depicted a firing squad: "What used to be an *error* has now become a *crime* against the state. *Thus ends the road to serfdom!*") By 1954, companies including International Harvester and Coca-Cola and trade groups like the American Petroleum Institute were spending $50 million a year on pro-laissez-faire curriculum materials—half of what was spent nationally on regular textbooks.

Return on their investment was paltry. A Republican president expanded Social Security, increased the minimum wage by a third, chartered a new cabinet department of Health, Education, and Welfare, and installed a New Dealer as his labor secretary. In 1955, a young conservative intellectual named William F. Buckley tried to interest America's tycoons in funding a new conservative magazine, *National Review*, whose prospectus said the only legitimate role for government was "to protect its citizens' lives, liberty, and property. All other activities of government tend to diminish freedom and hamper progress," and complained, "The public has been taught to assume—almost instinctively—that conflicts between labor and management are generally traceable to greed and intransigence on the part of management." His pitch yielded practically no donations. Older businessmen had lost hope the New Deal could ever be unhorsed. Younger ones didn't find anything to complain about: that year, after all, America's gross domestic product grew 7.1 percent. Conservatives might call this the road to serfdom. But to both ordinary and elite Americans, this kind of economic liberalism had come to seem part of the national DNA.

In 1960, a conservative polling firm surveyed thousands of high school students. The majority agreed with Karl Marx: "The fairest economic system is one that 'takes from each according to his ability' and 'gives to each according to his needs.'" Conservative views on economics were seen as the province of the sort of irrelevant cranks who voted for Barry Goldwater—who lost in a historic 1964 landslide defeat against a liberal president who got more support from corporate executives than any Democrat in the twentieth century: in a speech that year before the U.S. Chamber of Commerce, Lyndon Johnson was interrupted for applause some sixty times.

The *New Republic* called it "The New Partnership: Big Government and Big Business," led by a "new breed of corporate executive . . . professionally trained and more oriented to the science of management than to the perpetuation of an ideology which looks upon government as intrinsically evil. The modern company officer accepts government (much like he accepts the labor union) and works actively with it." A 1966 poll found that 85 percent of Americans agreed that "government and business are learning to work together for the well-being of the country."

It helped that almost two-thirds of Americans also agreed that the U.S. would "always" have the world's highest standard of living. The business-labor-liberalism accord, *Fortune* magazine said, was granting America a prosperity that canceled previous laws of ideological gravity: "As the range of conscious choice widens, it is possible to think of vast increases of federal government power that do not encroach upon or diminish any other power." Experts began calling this the "American consensus."

AT THE SAME TIME, HOWEVER, A SEPARATE ANTI-LIBERAL BACKLASH WAS taking root. It was spurred by summer after summer of race riots, and its political base was not business but middle-class homeowners, who blamed civil rights and the War on Poverty for a civilization-threatening break-down in law and order. Business was largely on the liberal side of this issue—like the author of a 1966 article in the *Harvard Business Review* predicting "riots and arson and spreading slums" if "the businessman does not accept his rightful role as leader in the push for the goals of the 'Great Society' (or whatever tag he wants to give it)."

No, business's backlash, its emergence as a *klasse an sich*, came a little bit later, in response to a new, and different, sort of liberalism—one whose buzzwords were "environmentalism" and "consumerism," and which, un-like Lyndon Johnson's War on Poverty, placed corporate power squarely in its sights.

Date its origin to the summer of 1967. Around the same time Congress was responding to middle-class constituent anger over black riots by vot-ing down a modest bill funding rodent control in the slums, a remarkable hearing was held by the Senate Committee on Commerce, Science, and Transportation, chaired by Senator Warren Magnuson of Washington State. Magnuson had been approached by a Seattle physician who de-scribed a "chronic, unrelenting procession of burned and scarred children" in his work at Seattle Children's Hospital, caused by the sort of flammable fabrics that had supposedly been outlawed by the Flammable Fabrics Act of 1953. That law, however, had been written by industry lobbyists. Back then, Commerce Committee members were classed by what industry they served: "textile senators," "trucking senators," "railroad senators," "tobacco senators" (the leading tobacco senator was the former president of the Tobacco Institute). They sponsored protectionist laws written by their benefactors—like the Wool Products Labeling Act, which banned manufacturers from selling a product as wool if it contained a single strand of recycled or synthetic fiber; or bills fixing prices for legacy companies. The process was so corrupt that when Chairman Magnuson hired a young lawyer in 1964 named Michael Pertschuk to run the committee's portfolio of consumer products legislation, the fellow he replaced congratulated him on all the price-fixed products, from audio equipment to toasters, that he soon would be getting for free.

This all would soon be a thing of the past.

Magnuson had been a fisheries senator and an aviation senator. After almost losing his seat in 1962, however, he reinvented himself aggressively as a new kind of liberal legislative entrepreneur: a *consumerist* senator. He put Pertschuk to work toughening up the limp Flammable Fabrics Act. A textile industry lobbyist replied "blood would run in the halls of Congress" before his industry let it pass. But the hearings Pertschuk staged in July of 1967 were a masterpiece of legislative melodrama. The Seattle doctor testified: "In all honesty, I must say I do not consider it a triumph when the life of a severely burned child is saved. . . . Death may be more merciful." A beloved CBS News commentator told the story of his eleven-year-old daughter, burned nearly to death when a cotton blouse that met federal safety standards combusted when a match was dropped on it. A representative of the Cotton Textile Council boasted of the "admirable" results produced by its standards committee. The square-jawed and stentorian Magnuson replied:

"How often does your standards committee meet?"

"Regularly, Senator."

How often, Magnuson followed up, *before* they'd received his recent letter warning them of impending congressional action?

"Ten years," the lobbyist admitted.

The amendments passed the committee unanimously, then both houses, virtually unchanged. President Johnson signed the bill with Magnuson by his side. The following day he signed the first update to meat inspection law since the 1906 Pure Food and Drug Act, with Upton Sinclair, the novelist whose 1905 exposé *The Jungle* had inspired it, standing next to him. A landmark "truth in lending" bill went to conference six weeks later. The former senator Paul Douglas, a New Deal economist who had lost his seat in 1966 largely because white Chicago factory workers turned their back on him because of his advocacy for a failed bill outlawing housing discrimination, had been pressing for it since the 1950s, but was defeated in the Finance Committee session after session. Now, however, it passed the committee unanimously.

The floodgates opened: to laws fighting deceptive practices by door-to-door salesmen and moving companies, outlawing hazardous radiation from electronics equipment, closing gaps in poultry and fish inspection, demanding accuracy in product warranties, regulating cigarettes. "Consumer Interests: Legislative Derby Has Begun," one Midwestern newspaper reported early in 1968. That headline appeared just as Congress voted to outlaw housing discrimination in a desperate response to the riots following the April 4, 1968, assassination of Martin Luther King Jr. The version that passed, however, weaker than one killed in 1966, added near-police-state provisions limiting militant blacks' freedom to travel. Riots had burned down Lyndon Johnson's War on Poverty. "Consumerism" sprung forth phoenix-like from the ashes.

Politicians discovered that scourging industry greed was the smart political play. It certainly was for Magnuson, who glided to reelection in 1970 with ads that bragged, "There's a law that forced Detroit to make cars safer—Senator Magnuson's law. There's a law that keeps the gas pipelines under your house from blowing up—Senator Magnuson's law. There's a law that makes food labels tell the truth—Senator Magnuson's law. Keep the big boys honest; let's keep Maggie in the Senate."

It heralded a remarkable shift in public opinion. In 1966, 55 percent of Americans had a "great deal of confidence in the leaders of major companies." Five years later, the percentage was 27 percent. Between 1968 and 1970, the portion believing "business tries to strike a fair balance between profits and the interest of the public" fell from 70 percent to 33 percent. Wrote pollster Lou Harris, "People have come to be skeptical about American 'know-how,' worried that it might pollute, contaminate, poison, or even kill them."

WHAT HAD HAPPENED TO CAUSE IT?

The collapse of American economic dominance was one factor: 1971 was the first year since 1893 when the U.S. ran a trade deficit with the rest of the world. By the mid-1970s, with inflation and unemployment both reaching 10 percent, few had faith that their nation would always have the world's highest standard of living, and it was hard to see the economic masters of the universe in as beneficent a light.

Corporate America's aloofness didn't help. A manufacturer of cribs, informed by a regulator that his product was contributing to infants' deaths, responded, "So what?" Frederick Donner of General Motors, which together with its suppliers comprised some 10 percent of America's gross domestic product, had once been called to testify in auto safety hearings convened by Senator Abraham Ribicoff of Connecticut. Donner boasted that GM had earmarked $1 million for safety research in 1964.

Senator Robert. F Kennedy then archly pointed out that that was but one-twentieth of 1 percent GM's profits for the year.

You might also attribute it, simply, to "the sixties"—which is to say, the rise of radicalized post–World War II youth raised amid apparently limitless prosperity, doted on by the media as moral lights unto the nation, who decided that a decent society was more important than material comfort and institutional stability. The same pollsters who found the public affirming the public-spiritedness of business in 1966 would have gotten a different result if they had asked just college seniors, only 12 percent of whom, in a *Newsweek* survey that year, said business was their first career choice, with 74 percent describing it as a "dog eat dog" world that "cares too little about the individual."

Another major factor, however, was the emergence of a single determined individual.

Ralph Nader was born in 1934 to Lebanese-American parents who ran a restaurant in industrial Winsted, Connecticut. They were Antiochian Greek Orthodox Christian—but the true family faith was American citizenship. The restaurant they owned was a New England town hall meeting that never stopped. One frequent topic was the chemicals that workers were exposed to in local factories.

Ralph received a scholarship to Princeton. His dad insisted the money go to needier students. So Ralph worked his way through college with jobs like managing a bowling alley. He also, while simultaneously excelling in his classes, indulged his bottomless intellectual curiosity in extracurricular studies, and posted rarely published letters to the Princeton newspaper on subjects like the dangers to the bird population posed by the pesticides sprayed on university lawns.

Nader's next stop, Harvard Law, was not so salubrious. At the opening convocation a dean invited students to look to their right and left, then announced with pride that one of those classmates would not make it through to graduation. *Dog eat dog*: Nader found it appalling. If this was the way the elite ran society, it was an elite he wished no part in. He began disappearing for weeks at a time, hitchhiking around the country, carrying out independent study on matters like Native American treaty rights, the condition of migrant workers, the legal status of Puerto Rico, and the then esoteric subject of auto safety, inspired by all the crashes he'd witnessed on the road. He was brilliant enough to attain a masterly grasp of the law nonetheless.

He fulfilled his military requirement in the Army reserve, where he learned to love combat boots—sturdy, practical, unpretentious. (They were what he wore for special occasions, like testifying. Before Congress.

All his other shoes came from the same pool of a dozen pairs he bought at a clearance sale in 1959.) He ground out freelance articles at a mind-blowing pace, for magazines like the *New Republic* and the *Nation,* including one in 1959 called "The Safe Car You Can't Buy." He practiced law in Connecticut, while indulging an unremunerated passion for lobbying the state legislatures for sensible governmental reforms like ones he admired in Scandinavia.

In 1963, he settled in Washington, D.C., consulting for an ambitious assistant secretary of labor, Daniel Patrick Moynihan, who shared Nader's passion for auto safety. Nader buttonholed state troopers, truck drivers, and parking-lot attendants (who frequently injured themselves on the knife-edged fins of cars), imploring them to tell him everything they knew about the dangers of automobiles. He ducked underneath Chevrolet's sporty new Corvair model, studying its "innovative" rear-engine design and suspension—which rendered the rear wheels prone to tucking under the car sideways, flipping it upside down. Because the 236-page report on auto safety he produced was so thorough and groundbreaking, Moynihan hardly minded that his strange young charge was rarely in the office.

He won a $3,000 advance for a book on auto safety. One day he reported on its progress to Mike Pertschuk, now chief of staff of Senator Magnuson's new consumer subcommittee. "With barely contained fury," Pertschuk remembered, "he delineated for me the industries that have evolved with an economic stake in the continued high level of automobile accidents . . . the auto repair shops, the personal injury lawyers, the wreckers and salvage yards; even the surgeons and the emergency rooms. But, above all, the auto companies. With their extremely profitable market for crash parts, the automobile industry, he maintained, had no economic incentive to improve the crashworthiness of new cars—and would not do so until compelled by federal legislation." Pertschuk was sympathetic— but smugly lectured this strange young man why the sort of reforms he had in mind were politically impossible.

Unsafe at Any Speed: The Designed-in Dangers of the American Automobile came out in November 1965. The *New York Times* acknowledged it in a short item on page 68. Eight months later, *Times Book Review* included it last in a wrap-up of eight other new automotive books that better reflected how Americans thought of their cars—titles like *The Gallery of the American Automobile* and *The Motor Car Lover's Companion. Unsafe at Any Speed* sold respectably, and the modest, quiet community of auto safety advocates welcomed Nader into their ranks. This was far less than the author had in mind. "The American auto industry," a historian observed, "was at the absolute height of its power, so rich and mighty that

its arrogance, its certainty that it *was* America, was almost unconscious."
That was about to change.

NADER HAD TAKEN AN UNPAID POSITION WITH SENATOR ABRAHAM RIBI-
coff, who was advocating for an automobile safety law so aggressively that
Americans began ranking the issue as one the nation's six or seven most
pressing concerns. It had not even shown up in surveys before.

Nader testified at a Ribicoff hearing. Eloquently, he proved that GM's
engineers knew the Corvair was unsafe but had no institutional power to
make changes; documented how cost and styling concerns trumped safety
in automotive design; explained how a bought-and-paid-for automotive press reported on the Corvair's handling irregularities as a charming
sports-car quirk; and how Detroit sold necessary safety features as costly
options, and GM buried the life-and-death fact information that the Corvair's rear tires should be inflated at approximately twice the pressure as
the front ones (if owners didn't want the car to flip over) deep inside the
owner's manual, like instructions on how to open the trunk. He scourged
industry safety propaganda that focused obsessively on driver error—"It's
the nut behind the wheel" was a slogan of the industry-captured National
Safety Council—even though most injuries, Nader rivetingly explained,
were caused by what *Unsafe at Any Speed* called the "second collision":
knobs that protruded like daggers, steering wheels that shot forward like
projectiles, dashboard edges so sharp they might as well be shards of glass.

Government was complicit. The President's Committee for Traffic
Safety, Nader said, was an agency staffed by civil servants but funded by
the auto and insurance industries. Laws were "written almost exclusively
in terms of driver fault," with "the role of automobiles in *causing* accidents
and injuries going virtually unchallenged."

And above all, Nader said in tones of controlled anger, it was a question of *corporate power*. "Death on the highway produces income and
profit for hundreds of thousands." The vaunted competitive marketplace
"centers around exaggerated touting of trivial differences garnished by
throbbing adjectives and beckoning young women," ritualistic annual
model changes "aimed not at the reason of men but their ids and hypogas-
tria." A "civilized society should want to protect even the nut behind the
wheel from paying the ultimate penalty for a moment's carelessness, not
to mention protecting the innocent people who might get in his way." He
concluded by demanding of the solons before him, as if he were their superior, that they never again pass another "no-law law"—one pretending
to address problems, but actually shielding industry from blame.

Selah.

Senator Carl Curtis, a conservative Republican from Nebraska, attempted to debunk Nader's claims, and was humiliated by Nader's factual command in return. He then complained that Nader was "using this forum to sell his book." Robert F. Kennedy replied that "the person who sold the most books today for Mr. Nader was the Senator from Nebraska."

THE BUMPTIOUS GENTLEMAN FROM NEBRASKA WAS NOT, IT SOON ARRIVED, Ralph Nader's only harasser. While he was working on *Unsafe at Any Speed*, Nader had complained to friends that strange men were following him. That an attractive woman approached him, seeking his company. That, the night before his congressional testimony, at the $80-a-month boardinghouse where he rented a room, he got several harassing phone calls.

Ralph Nader had always been an odd duck. Now his friends wondered whether he might actually be insane.

Then, a journalist discovered that General Motors had hired a detective agency to spy on him. GM denied involvement—before admitting they had merely "initiated a routine investigation . . . to determine whether Ralph Nader was acting on behalf of litigants or their attorneys in Corvair design cases pending against General Motors." That Nader might be acting on principle had apparently never occurred to them.

Senator Ribicoff, livid, reminded GM that the criminal codes prescribed a $55,000 fine, five years imprisonment, or both for threatening or intimidating a witness in a congressional inquiry. He called Nader back to Capitol Hill a month after his first testimony—and also GM president James Roche. It proved a committee room showdown as dramatic as any since the Army-McCarthy Hearings of 1954. Visibly shaken, Roche read an apology drafted by a GM lawyer. He testified that, yes, General Motors had undertaken an investigation, entirely legal, "to ascertain necessary facts preparatory to litigation." He claimed to have learned about it only two weeks earlier, and that to the best of his knowledge it "did not employ girls as sex lures" or surveillance. He claimed to be "just as shocked and outraged" as Abraham Ribicoff. And that, again, he was so very, very sorry. Ribicoff, however, read into the record the instructions of the detective GM had retained, Vincent Gillen, to his underlings: "Our job is to check his life, and current activities, to determine 'what makes him tick,' such as his real interest in safety, his supporters, if any, his politics, his marital status, his friends, his women, boys, etc., drinking, dope, jobs—in fact all facets of his life. This may entail surveillance." Gillen himself explained under oath that he had been instructed "to get something, somewhere, on this guy to get him out of their hair and to shut him up."

When Robert Kennedy asked Nader why he got involved in this work in the first place, Nader said that no one would ask him such a thing if his passion was cruelty to animals. "But because I happen to have a scale of priorities which leads me to engage in the prevention of cruelty to humans, my motives are consistently inquired into. Is it wrong to talk about defective cars, diseased meats, corporate cheating? Is it really distasteful that a person cares enough about issues like these to dedicate his life to changing them?"

Then, shoulders hunched, thick Mediterranean eyebrows arching for emphasis, he brought the blasé Capitol Hill habitués in the standing-room-only crowd to stunned silence:

"*I* am responsible for my actions, but who is responsible for those of GM? An individual's capital and soul is basically his integrity. He can lose only once. A corporation can lose many times and not be affected."

The six-hour proceeding received live TV coverage, then led every newscast. The *New York Times* profiled Nader. A *Washington Post* editorial accused GM of traducing "one of the bedrocks of a free society." It headlined a follow-up, "GM's Goliath Bows to David; Individual Conscience Scores." A star was born—and with it a legislative juggernaut. The next week a bill introduced by Senator Magnuson providing for the first mandatory product grading system in the nation's history (for tires) passed the Senate 79–0. *Unsafe at Any Speed* began a fourteen-week run on the *New York Times* bestseller list. The National Highway Traffic and Motor Vehicle Safety Act passed the Senate and the House unanimously. ("When they started looking in Ralph Nader's bedroom, we all figured that they must be really nervous," a senator explained. "We began to believe that Nader must be right.") Lyndon Johnson signed the bill in September 1966, then turned and shook Nader's hand—just, as it happened, as his new civil rights bill was being filibustered into dust.

The National Highway Traffic and Motor Vehicle Safety Act was anything but a no-law law. Indeed, in a reversal of regulatory precedent, it was strengthened during each step in the legislative process. The same thing happened with the flammable fabrics and meat inspection laws—which Nader had been instrumental in, too. He embarked on a ten-state tour, and armed with a $425,000 legal settlement from GM as seed money, set out to change the world. It had once been said that what was good for General Motors was good for the U.S. That was the attitude Ralph Nader laid to rest—for approximately a decade, that is, until business started getting class conscious.

IDEALISTIC YOUNG LAWYERS FLOCKED TO THE ORGANIZATIONS NADER began forming. The first product of these "Nader's Raiders" was a 185-page report on the Federal Trade Commission, a notoriously toothless regulatory body that took, on average, four years to investigate every complaint, punishing the guilty with unenforceable orders to cease and desist. The monograph was couriered to 150 key journalists out of the back of a Raider's Volkswagen. It called the FTC a "self-parody of bureaucracy, fat with cronyism, torpid through inbreeding unusual even for Washington, manipulated by the agents of commercial predators, impervious to government or citizen monitoring," ridden with "alcoholism, spectacular lassitude, and office absenteeism."

By then the president was Richard Nixon, who had to accede to the new anti-corporate mood just to maintain political credibility. He ordered up his own FTC investigation. It arrived at similar conclusions. So Nixon replaced the FTC director with the shrewdest bureaucrat in his administration, Caspar "Cap the Knife" Weinberger, who roared out of the starting gate with actions against dubious advertising claims of such blue-chip products as Hi-C, Listerine, Wonder Bread, and McDonald's.

Nixon then signed a landmark mine safety law and the National Environmental Policy Act, establishing the first new independent federal regulatory agency since 1938, then added another with a law authorizing the Occupational Safety and Health Administration. That project was inherited from the Johnson administration, and at first, Nixon's version was so mild that the U.S. Chamber of Commerce endorsed it. But the "creature that ultimately stomped out of Congress," a historian recounted, was a "Frankenstein of Chamber members' nightmares." Federal agents had never had the authority to inspect individual businesses for health and safety violations. OSHA gave them the power to do it without warrants, then levy hefty fines with no avenue for appeal. Richard Nixon didn't dare veto it.

Nor did he veto tough amendments to the Clean Air Act of 1963 that included something nearly unprecedented in previous environmental legislation: specific deadlines for compliance. It also enjoined the new EPA from considering costs in establishing ambient air standards—inspiring Robert Griffin, a Republican automotive senator from Michigan, to snarl that the 1975 deadline for limiting auto exhaust pollutants "holds a gun to the head of the American automobile industry in a very dangerous game of roulette." The technology to implement the standards, he complained, did not exist. Democrat Edmund Muskie of Maine, the leader of senate environmentalists, responded, "This deadline is based not, I repeat, not, on economic and technological feasibility, but on considerations of public health. . . . Detroit has told the nation that Americans cannot live without the automobile. This legislation would tell Detroit that if this is the case, then they must make an automobile with which the American people can live." The version that passed the Senate 73–2 was stronger than what had been debated in any hearing. A cowed GM lobbyist told the *National Journal* that "the atmosphere was such that offering amendments seemed pointless," and that "I wouldn't think of asking anybody to vote against the bill."

The Senate Commerce Committee, that former redoubt of trucking senators, railroad senators, textile senators, and tobacco senators, became a regulator's paradise. At confirmation hearings for a new FTC head, Frank Moss congratulated the agency for having "stretched its powers to provide a credible countervailing public force to the enormous economic and political power of huge corporate conglomerates which today dominate American enterprise. That is as it should be." Then one of Moss's conservative colleagues, Senator Ted Stevens, Republican of Alaska, asked the nominee to "become a real zealot in terms of consumer affairs," tough enough that "these big businesspeople will complain."

In 1971, Webster's added the word *consumerism* to its *Third New International Dictionary*. A book called *America, Inc.: Who Owns and Operates the United States?* coauthored by the *Washington Post Post*'s consumer reporter and original Nader champion Morton Mintz rode the bestseller list for months. Children begged at bedtime to hear Dr. Seuss's new book *The Lorax*, in which a pitiless capitalist "biggers" his business by harvesting every last Truffula tree, crying triumphantly, "Business is business and business must grow!" and leaving behind a barren hellscape. Gore Vidal published a cover article in *Esquire* touting Nader for president, and 78 percent of columnist Mike Royko's readers who sent back a questionnaire he published said they wanted him as the Democrats' presidential nominee. Another new independent regulatory agency, the National Highway Traffic Safety Administration, was born. Congress passed bills requiring childproof packaging for poisonous substances, killing federal subsidies for a supersonic transport plane, restricting lead in house paint, and establishing safety standards for recreational boats. Nixon signed them—not because he was a closet liberal, but because, as his aide Bryce Harlow, a former lobbyist for Procter & Gamble, delicately explained to the American Advertising Federation, though "President Nixon profoundly respects the critical contribution made by industry to the vitality and strength of the American economy, if this respect were to over-influence his actions, I am certain that the fall of 1972 would bring a new and hostile team to the White House."

Nader had by then established a permanent presence in the capital, based in a decrepit mansion which had been slated for demolition in the down-market Dupont Circle neighborhood, where, amid a shambles of borrowed third-hand furniture and wooden fruit crates stuffed with books and files, staggeringly devoted young Ivy League–trained Nader's Raiders institutionalized their hero's agenda. The neighborhood was pocked with similar offices. Common Cause, Friends of the Earth, the Natural Resources Defense Council, Nader's own Public Citizen, Environmental Action, the Center for Law and Social Policy, and the Consumer Federation of America were all established in 1969 or 1970. Nader started six new organizations in 1971 alone, including Public Citizen, a membership group that raised more than $1 million from sixty-two thousand donors in its first year.

That was another new pattern. Throughout the seventies, pundits cast their eye on declining election turnout and agonized over voter apathy. But apathy at the polls did not extend to joining consumer and environmental organizations, whose memberships exploded, thanks in part to the same computer-based direct mail technology that Richard Viguerie employed. Nearly one hundred thousand households contributed at least $70 to not one, not two, but *three* progressive membership groups. Major foundations pitched in, too. Thanks to the shower of cash—and because most new consumer and environmental laws awarded attorneys' fees to plaintiffs who sued to enforce them—lawsuits against corporations increased exponentially.

George McGovern considered Nader as his running mate. (He replied, "I'm an advocate for justice and that doesn't mix with the needs of politics.") Nixon vetoed the 1972 Clean Water Act, for its "staggering, budget-wrecking" $24 billion cost—but his veto was overridden with considerable Republican votes. In October, he signed a law establishing the Consumer Product Safety Commission, the third new regulatory agency in three years.

Then, however, following his landslide reelection, he proposed a radical right-wing budget that *Newsweek* described as "one of the most significant American political documents since the dawning of the New Deal," intended to "pull the government back from the proliferating social concerns of the years from Franklin Roosevelt to Lyndon Johnson." Thanks to Watergate, he never got the chance. Senator Sam Ervin's televised hearings had reverberated with accounts of briefcases full of corporate cash laundered through the Mexican subsidiaries of blue-chip firms like American Airlines, Goodyear, and 3M. In the midst of it came the first energy crisis, which a majority of Americans—and some senators—believed the big energy companies had cooked up to line their pockets. Pollster Daniel Yankelovich found that 70 percent of Americans believed big business controlled government through illegal bribes. And that was *before* spectacular revelations, following Nixon's resignation, that the same slush funds companies maintained to bribe Nixon were also used to pay off foreign officials. The Securities and Exchange Commission's chief of enforcement was gobsmacked. "Until two or three years ago," he said, "I genuinely thought the conduct of business. . . was generally rising. But what can you say about the revelations of the last couple or three years?"

Under President Ford, government checks on corporate power expanded yet further. One of the first laws he signed was the Employment Retirement Income Security Act, or ERISA, which strictly enforced the pension promises companies made to their employees, placing thousands of company's books under federal scrutiny for the first time. In 1975 he signed the Energy Policy and Conservation Act, a landmark law demanding that every American car manufacturer achieve a "Corporate Average Fuel Economy," or CAFE, of eighteen miles per gallon by the 1978 model year. That meant every manufacturer had to redesign every car on the drawing boards. An automotive think tank estimated that it would cost manufacturers $60 billion to $80 billion, virtually their entire store of capital assets, and made the companies fear for their very survival. A group of automotive lobbyists approached the chief of staff of Edmund Muskie's environmental subcommittee, Leon Billings, with a memo suggesting some ideas on the bill. Billings fashioned a paper airplane out of the document and sailed it straight over their heads.

BUSINESS FELT HELPLESS TO FIGHT BACK. DURING THE FAT YEARS, THEY HAD let their lobbying operations on Washington's K Street become decrepit. A 1964 study of 166 large corporations found that only thirty-seven had had any communications with Congress in the previous two years. Business lobbying was practiced as a political zero-sum game: Pratt & Whitney fighting Lockheed for the contract to make the engine for a new Air Force jet; spinners of natural wool vs. manufacturers of synthetics; car dealers against car manufacturers; insurance companies against banks. In 1966, when the highway safety debate began, it had never occurred to GM to recruit thousands of dealers, suppliers, or auto-parts retailers into the fight, and lobbying over the 1970 Clean Air Act amendments was little more than a tussle between factions hoping to lessen the burden of pollution abatement that would fall upon *them*. "We don't have a business community," one executive complained. "Just a fragmented bunch of self-interested people." Another rued that if American corporations sold their products as ineptly as they lobbied, "America's gross national product would be less than Iceland's codfish catch."

Compare that to the opposition. In 1976, Senator Abraham Ribicoff marveled at how "you have had practically every committee in Congress according 'equal time' to public interest people" at hearings. The fifth-term liberal Democrat Abner Mikva called the fact that the kind of people you used to see "handing out leaflets on a street corner" were now respected witnesses at Capitol hearings "the biggest change in Congress since I first came here."

There were now eighty-six public interest law firms in the capital, half founded since 1968. The Massachusetts attorney general placed Ralph Nader's name on the 1976 Democratic presidential primary ballot and said he wouldn't remove it unless Nader said he would not serve as president. Polls suggest that if Nader ran, he might win. Advisors to one 1976 presidential candidate, Senator Birch Bayh, suggested that he announce he would clear all cabinet appointments with Nader.

Then came Jimmy Carter's victory. Consumerists were thrilled: when Carter had met Nader early in 1976, Carter had been positively deferential. Following the election, Nader's two suggestions for appointees—Mike Pertschuk to run the Federal Trade Commission and original Nader's Raider Joan Claybrook to head the National Transportation Safety Board, the seven-hundred-person agency *Unsafe at Any Speed* had virtually conjured into existence—were both confirmed to those jobs. Five days before Jimmy Carter's inauguration, Nader hosted *Saturday Night Live*, whose hip young cast mobbed him like he was a rock star when he arrived for rehearsals.

1977 looked to be the best year for consumerists yet. Crowed one, "We can raise the ante—push for new policy initiatives that have been blocked off in recent years."

THE CENTERPIECE WAS A PROJECT NADER HAD BEEN LABORING MIGHTILY on since 1969—"the most important piece of consumer legislation ever to come before Congress," he called it. It would be a capstone of the consumer revolution, stitching the movement permanently into the very fabric of the American state, and its passage now seemed assured.

The idea for a federal consumer agency was born in 1959, when Democratic Senators Estes Kefauver and Hubert Humphrey, frustrated that most witnesses at Senate regulatory hearings represented industry, introduced a bill to establish a cabinet-level Department of Consumer Affairs. It went nowhere. When Ralph Nader revised it a decade later he proposed a striking innovation: an agency funded at a mere $15 million per year— compared, say, to the $203 million budget of the Environmental Protection Agency, or OSHA's $136 million—that would not *write* regulations, or enforce them, but serve as a sort of federal public interest law firm, ombudsman office, and informational clearinghouse all rolled into one to ensure the smooth functioning of regulations that already existed. Its lawyers, scientists, and economists would testify before congress in regulatory hearings; they would also help businesses comply with federal regulation, protecting them from potential costly legal action down the road.

It seemed modest, but it actually was far *more* radical than yet another typical bureaucracy. Those bureaucracies quickly became cozy with the industries they regulated; dealing constantly with the same industry, staffers came by turns to *think* like representatives of that industry. Or they acted against the public interest outright, in the hopes of landing a lucrative job in the future. Meanwhile, industries regulated by a single, identifiable, office found its staff an easy target to intimidate, seduce, or even bribe. Scholars called this "regulatory capture," and it was such an endemic problem that one prominent public interest lawyer complained that "regulation of industry would have to be regarded as one of the least successful enterprises ever undertaken by American democracy." Nader's idea, he hoped, would repair this broken dynamic — and legislators in both parties agreed. A 1969 bill passed the Senate 74–4. The House Government Operations Committee endorsed it 31–4.

Then representatives from various industries lunched one day at an expense account restaurant — a rare example of business lobbyists recognizing they shared interests in common. Together they decided to test out their own novel idea: an ad hoc organization to lobby against a common foe. They called it the Consumer Issues Working Group, and its lobbying was able to limit the bill to only seven votes in the fourteen-member House Rules Committee in 1970, blocking it from further consideration in the 92nd Congress.

Then, in 1972, after the bill passed by a resounding 344–14 in the House, the Working Group realized for the first time that they had a cavalry at their disposal: ordinary businessmen. The National Association of Manufacturers (NAM) sent a mass mailing warning that the Senate was about to pass a law that "permanently federalizes and subsidizes the consumer movement as conceived by Ralph Nader." The Grocery Manufacturers of America sent out "Businessmen's Responsiveness Kits" on the "Nader Enabling Act" with form letters to send to Capitol Hill railing against "the most serious threat to free enterprise and orderly government ever to be proposed in Congress." This flush of letters from terrified factory owners helped steel senators to successfully filibuster the bill.

Those early efforts were relatively ham-handed compared to what was to come. Senator Percy's office easily figured out that this supposedly spontaneous outburst of concern had been drummed up by the trade groups spreading false information. And in the next Congress, impaneled in 1973, Ralph Nader was able to fight back by assembling ninety-five major firms, like Levi-Strauss and Gulf & Western, to lobby for his side.

He was taking advantage of a fissure within American capitalism. His allies were transnational and "consumer-facing" companies, mostly headquartered in Manhattan, that traded on the stock market and had national brands to protect—the kind of companies who had come to dominate the global economy during the golden decades following World War II and had gladly accommodated themselves to the growth of the liberal state: blue-chip firms, safe, stable, and perennially profitable, impervious to economic downturns. The companies that made up NAM and the Grocery Manufacturers were smaller, family-held, concentrated in midsized cities that ordinary citizens rarely dealt with, who didn't care what the *New York Times* said about them: the most reactionary segment of the business world. A prototypical such firm was Allen-Bradley, the Milwaukee-based manufacturer of industrial controls, which in 1957 had devoted a portion of its corporate treasury to distributing a poster headed, "Will You Be Free to Celebrate Christmas in the Future?" It republished testimony to the House Committee on Un-American Activities alleging that the Soviet Union conquered nations by using mind-control techniques borrowed from the science of animal husbandry. These companies tended to operate with less secure profit margins compared to blue-chip firms, and felt far more vulnerable to federal regulation. They saw liberalism-supporting companies like Levi-Strauss and Gulf & Western as liberal quislings—who, in turn, saw the Allen-Bradleys of the world as retrograde embarrassments.

Exploiting this division was one of the ways environmentalists and consumerists had been able to score so many successes—and how, in 1973, Nader's coalition was able to bring the consumer agency bill a tantalizing three votes away from final passage. Two years later, it came even closer—until a new president, genial Jerry Ford, who supported the measure when he'd been a congressman but had now been effectively lobbied by the Consumer Issues Working Group, shocked Washington by threatening a veto, which killed the idea again.

Polls showed the public supported it by a ratio of two to one. All it needed now was a friendly president. Who, on January 20,1977, finally arrived. Jimmy Carter had promised to support a consumer agency as one of his first priorities. The bill was reintroduced in April. "With Congress and the administration working together, this should finally be the year for enactment," House sponsor Jack Brooks of Texas pronounced. One hundred fifty labor, senior citizen, and citizens groups joined together to form a coalition to lobby for it.

By then, the Consumer Issues Working Group had grown to four hundred members. A new, juggernaut style of business lobbying was about to come of age.

Conservative think tanks like the Heritage Foundation had been perfecting intellectual ammunition—like the argument that there *was* no singular "consumer interest," and that any attempt to oppose one from the top down would invariably help some people while hurting others. (Some car-buyers might want airbags. Others might prefer cheaper cars.) Ronald Reagan spread their ideas: the very first batch of radio commentaries he recorded in 1975 included one introducing the proverbial housewife whom arrogant far-off bureaucrats presumed "too dumb to buy a box of corn flakes without being cheated," who resented being bossed around by "the professional consumerists in Washington," who "are really *elitists* who think they know better than you what's good for you." He called it the "biggest threat to our free economy as anything that's been proposed," the "big new federal government bureau that would have the power to supersede all other government agencies." Another time, he said the consumer agency would be like something out of George Orwell's *1984*. Its bureaucrats "will equate their own opinions with those of all consumers." His voice darkened: Did members of congress even understand that "*the people* are tired of having their hard-earned money thrown away at yet more bureaucrats who interfere with [their] daily lives?" When Reagan's right-hand man Peter Hannaford wrote to the editor of the *National Enquirer* that same year pitching Reagan as a columnist for the weekly scandal sheet, of the sample pieces he sent them one was a jeremiad against the consumer bill—"which really should be called the Friends of Ralph Nader Act."

The consumerists were hardly concerned. The other side had a washed-up, extremist former governor. They had the guest host of *Saturday Night Live*. Consumerism, a commentator reflected, was joining "the ranks of apple pie and motherhood." Dupont Circle, not K Street, ruled Washington now.

But K Street was finally getting its act together.

"HENRY GONZÁLEZ OF SAN ANTONIO . . . SHOULD WE USE SEARS? . . . OK, let's use González with Sears . . ."

The setting was a suite in the bowels of an office building a few blocks from the White House. The conversation was between two staffers of the Business Roundtable, an organization formed in 1972 whose membership consisted of approximately two hundred corporate chief executive officers, mostly from *Fortune* 500 firms like United States Steel, Campbell's Soup, Sears, and General Electric. They were portioning out lobbying assignments to those members to crush the consumer agency bill. They were confident enough of success to let a *Fortune* reporter sit in.

Representative James Delaney of Long Island, chairman of the crucial House Rules Committee, could be approached by the CEO of Bristol-Myers, to whom he was close; Al Gore Jr., a new congressman from Tennessee, was on the fence, but might be moved by Lloyd Hand of the

TRW Corporation, a former aide to Lyndon B. Johnson, a friend of his father's, Senator Albert Gore Sr. Joseph Gaydos came from a district that included many aluminum mines, so he could be approached by the CEO of Alcoa—the days when corporate America lobbied diffidently and incompetently were now past. In part because, on some days, it *did* feel like America's GDP might someday sink to less than Iceland's codfish catch.

In 1950, America's share of the world economy was 40 percent. Now it was 11 percent. America's first trade deficit, in 1971, was $1.3 billion; now it approached $27 billion. The seventeen-month recession following the Arab oil shock in the fall of 1973, the longest and deepest since the 1930s, was a wakeup call. So was rising inflation, which now approached 7 percent annually; in the 1960s, it had often dipped below 1 percent. Corporate profits declined by a third since their postwar peak. In 1966, a dollar of capital invested earned an average 9 percent return. In 1977, it earned 4 percent. And suddenly the palpitating fear of an Allen-Bradley that the regulatory maw would somehow devour them sounded far less extremist to a General Motors, now that blue-chip firms felt economically vulnerable, too.

They decided regulation was mostly to blame. "If the state's environmental laws were fully enforced," a New Jersey industrialist claimed to the *New York Times*, its economy "would grind to a halt." Liberals insisted this was nonsense, that, in fact, by 1975 fewer than a hundred factories anywhere had closed down due to environmental regulation—even as a million new jobs were created in fields those regulations spurred, like water treatment, waste management, and mass transit—and that a major reason for the declining profit of U.S. corporations was that fewer and fewer people wanted to buy their products: so much easier to blame Ralph Nader than their failure to build a better widget.

Be that as it may: after a decade of pummeling by liberals, the denizens of America's better boardrooms, who had once comported themselves with such ideological gentility, began behaving like the legendary Jacobins of the French Revolution. They declared war without compromise. The first big battle was Nader's beloved consumer agency bill.

Late in April, it sailed through the Senate Governmental Affairs Committee 10–2, the first step in what was presumed to be an easy path to President Carter's signature. That was when the word went forth to boardrooms of every description: *aux armes, citoyens!*

THE ARMY WAS LEAN AND MEAN, PURPOSE-BUILT FOR GUERRILLA WARFARE: the Consumer Issue Working Group had no independent budget or bureaucracy, just a twenty-five-member steering committee divided evenly between company lobbyists and trade organization representatives to handle strategy and parcel out tasks to subcommittees whose work was paid for out of corporate and trade organizations' own treasuries, and executed by their own staffs. This became the model for many more armies that would fight business battles in the future.

Thirty-four lobbyists worked the issue full-time—"living, eating, sleeping CPA," one of them recalled. Another front was handled by the National Federation of Independent Businesses, an organization for the sort of small business that had absorbed the passage of the Occupational Health and Safety Act as blunt force trauma; the NFIB's staff, six hundred at headquarters and four hundred in the field, worked to produce a flood of letters, calls, and visits from its four hundred thousand member companies to congressional offices, spreading talking points like viruses: "unbridled power," "absolute power," "enormous power"; "self-appointed consumerists," "self-appointed police," "self-appointed vigilantes," "more OSHA-like regulation." (OSHA had a $136 million annual budget, a full staff of regulation-writers, platoons of enforcement officers with the power to inspect without a warrant and fine without appeal; the "massive new superagency" would have a $15 million budget and none of these powers.)

Watergate heroes were recruited for cunning raids into liberal territory. Sam Ervin recorded a video distributed free to more than a hundred cable television systems claiming in his famous orotund voice that "the bill would give such vast power to the administrator of the Consumer Agency that there is only one Being in this entire universe who can exercise those powers with wisdom, and that it the Lord God almighty." Leon Jaworksi, the special prosecutor who had earned his reputation for constitutional probity by putting most of Richard Nixon's closest advisors in jail, was paid $5,000 to write a letter to the House Committee on Government Operations worrying that the proposed agency "would be vested with authority so broad that it could easily be turned to the political advantage of those who control it." On May 6, an excerpt of that letter appeared as an op-ed under Jaworski's byline in the *Washington Star*, with no indication that corporations had paid for it. The next week the bill survived in the Government Operations Committee by only a single vote in a weakened version, with a provision to "sunset" the agency in 1982.

The U.S. Chamber of Commerce circulated materials claiming that "over 400" newspapers had "spoken out against the new consumer agency." In fact, at least a quarter of those "over 400" newspaper editorials were the *same* editorial—written by Business Roundtable staffers. They produced cartoons that ran in more than two thousand papers. One showed a citizen groaning under the weight of a sack marked $203 million—the amount it had cost to set up the EPA in 1977.

Then, when they were home for Memorial Day recess in 1977, a surprisingly large number of well-informed small business constituents lectured their representatives using identical words: "superagency" "needless added layer of bureaucracy"; "another OSHA"—language from the "Congressional Alerts" the U.S. Chamber of Commerce had sent to members. The Chamber full-page ads said that "81 percent of Americans are opposed to a new consumer agency"—a finding a Congressional Research Service of the Library of Congress report concluded was the product of a poll question "slanted to produce a particular conclusion." The latest Harris Poll had found 52 percent still supporting the agency. But the Library of Congress, unlike the United States Chamber of Commerce, commanded no public relations brigades.

President Carter's special assistant for consumer affairs, Esther Peterson, a beloved figure in the consumer movement since the 1950s, began holding town hall events to drum up support. She was tailed by corporate ringers armed with questions written by lobbyists. She began meeting with the eighty-three congressmen reported to be on the fence. One told her he would be glad to support the bill—if they could match the $100,000 in campaign contributions promised by its opponents. In June, after Nader's organization Public Citizen invited their members in those eighty-three districts to send their congressmen nickels to represent the five cents the agency cost for every man, woman, and child in America, a congressional conservative seriously proposed they be investigated for bribery.

As the consumer side grew increasingly dispirited, long-submerged complaints about Ralph Nader began surfacing: his arrogance, his insistence on making perfection the enemy of the good, his eagerness to cast his critics into the outer darkness: "Ralph just won't let us be reasonable," one longtime friend complained. Though by autumn, the situation had grown so dire that even Nader was willing to cut a deal: the bill was stripped of a requirement that corporations answer written questions submitted by the agency under oath.

Compromise didn't work. Tip O'Neill had scheduled the bill for consideration by the full House by the first Wednesday in November. Now he removed it from the legislative calendar to muster support for another try in 1978.

BOOK THREE
1978

CHAPTER 11

"Hang Sen. Dick Clark on a Telephone Pole"

THE PRESIDENT BEGAN THE YEAR IN TEHRAN AS A HOUSEGUEST OF MOHAM-mad Reza Pahlavi, the Shah of Iran, part of a seven-nation, eighteen-thousand-mile globe-spanning tour. The shah was returning the president's hospitality from a state visit to Washington seven weeks earlier, when the monarch presented the president with a portrait of George Washington rendered in tapestry, 160 knots per square inch, that had taken two years to weave. Carter presented the king with an elaborate reception on the White House South Lawn at which Sarah Vaughan, Earl "Fatha" Hines, and Dizzy Gillespie entertained. The president sat in on vocals for Gillespie's signature tune, "Salt Peanuts," and said it was a high point of his life when the *New York Times* complimented his singing.

In their meeting afterward, Carter challenged the shah on his record of human rights violations. The shah defended himself by observing he had recently allowed those arrested for being Communists to be represented by attorneys; the president pronounced himself satisfied. Then, the shah agreed to buy U.S. nuclear reactors for civilian power production. All in all, a successful visit—except that during the arrival ceremony Iranian students across the street from the White House protesting the shah as a torturer and murderer attacked the police, who fought back with tear gas volleys which misted across the South Lawn. The audience had to dab their eyes with handkerchiefs. Carter, stung too, confided to his diary, "I didn't want to admit it was hurting me so bad."

This time, with the president in Tehran, Iranian students in front of the White House protected their faces against tear gas—and the prying eyes of SAVAK agents—by wearing masks. Their leaflets read, "Jimmy Carter, the peanut baron, will have much to say about 'human rights.' The 'rights' talk is empty propaganda. It is no secret that the primary reason for his visit is to negotiate sale of additional U.S. arms to Iran to assure the continued suppression of the Iranian people and defend the interests of imperialism."

Their pleas were little noticed. There was nothing particularly controversial for an American to pay court at the Peacock Throne; two weeks earlier, Ronald Reagan, on a visit to D.C., had stayed at the Iranian embassy. Though Carter claimed human rights as the cornerstone of foreign policy, when it came to the country that allowed the U.S. to place listening posts along the two-thousand-mile border it shared with the Soviet Union, and controlled the two main sea routes through which petroleum flowed to the West, and had rescued the American economy in 1974 by keeping the oil flowing during the OPEC boycott, he was willing to make allowances.

The president was also counting on the shah to help broker his dearest diplomatic priority: peace talks between Israel and Egypt. Building international support for those talks was his main goal on this trip. The project was delicate and complex. Carter felt warm toward Sadat but distrusted Begin, who consistently went back on his pledges to limit Israel's illegal settlement in the occupied West Bank of the Jordan River. Sadat needed to win the support, or at least the noninterference, of Arab leaders still stinging from the humiliation of Israel's 1973 military victory; Begin would have to answer to an Israeli electorate outraged at the idea of talking to a country that was officially pledged to push Israel into the sea. Egypt's prime minister, Anwar Sadat, was eager to begin. Israel's new right-wing prime minister, Menachem Begin, was not.

To bolster international support, Carter came bearing concessions, from increased American troops for NATO forces in Europe to nuclear technology for India. In Jordan, Carter pled with King Hussein to soften the heart of King Khalid of Saudi Arabia—but in Riyadh, the king proposed a price for that support: speedy consummation of Gerald Ford's promise to allow his kingdom to purchase sixty F-15 fighter jets, the mightiest in the American arsenal. This would be the first time the U.S. had sold such advanced weaponry to an Arab nation. And in Tehran, Carter requested the shah to travel to Saudi Arabia and Egypt to advocate for Carter's plans—and, since Iran was one of Israel's biggest suppliers of oil, to lean on Menachem Begin, too. To the president's relief, the shah proved willing—then, having thus earned Carter's gratitude, he complained about the United States not granting him enough latitude to deal with those demonstrating against his regime.

Shortly thereafter, four thousand Islamic scholars in the holy city of Qom, which consisted almost entirely of mosques and seminaries, protested the death of the son of their exiled spiritual leader the Ayatollah Khomeini, at what they presumed was the hands of SAVAK. Police shot into the crowd, killing as many as seventy-two. The United States did not protest. That was followed, in the city of Tabriz, during protests marking the traditional Islamic forty-day period of mourning, by the pillaging of hotels, cinemas, liquor stores, and all the town's government buildings. Security forces responded with another massacre, killing either nine people, according to SAVAK, or one hundred, according to the insurgents.

BACK HOME, JIMMY CARTER'S APPROVAL RATING WAS HOVERING AT 50 PERcent. He had to navigate a minefield to keep it that high. He had announced in October that Americans should measure the "success or failure of my first year in office" on "what happens in energy." His first year in office drew to a close; and nothing had happened in energy.

The new year brought the thirtieth day of a violent coal strike in Appalachia. The possibility of a coal shortage weakened Carter's bargaining hand for his stalemated energy bill. Subsequently, the *Washington Post* reported that he had quietly offered Western Democratic governors "unconditional surrender" on his former plans to cancel their states' water projects.

Senate debate on the first Panama Canal treaty was set to begin February 8. Richard Viguerie predicted it would unite the right in the same way the Vietnam War had galvanized the left. The *Wall Street Journal* reported that he was planning "a blizzard of anti-treaty mail, broadcasting of a half-hour television program in at least eighteen states this month, and a publicity-oriented tour of major cities by anti-treaty lawmakers riding a private jet."

Senator Howard Baker was in Panama, having "decided not to decide until I know what I'm talking about." His pollster had informed him that only 23 percent of his constituents were in favor of giving up the canal—but that when the question was reworded to ask whether they would support a treaty that "guaranteed" American ships the right to jump the line to pass through the canal first during military emergencies, support grew to 58 percent. His pollster also advised him that if he wished to run for president, the "careful political course" was outright opposition, since conservatives "would be very resentful and have long memories"; but that, on the other hand, "for you to lead the fight for 'guarantees' will tend to increase the perception of Baker as a leader with courage, knowledge about foreign policy and defense, and the kind of competence now lacking in the White House."

Carter would soon offer his first formal address on the state of the union—which was not great. The plummeting value of the dollar had spurred emergency measures not taken since 1968. The Dow Jones Industrial Average hit a two-year low. Cities north and south were wracked by acrimonious battles over busing to achieve school integration. A twenty-five-part *Chicago Sun-Times* series demonstrated that Al Capone's city's system of building inspections was actually just a system of bribes. Investigators at the Department of Health, Education, and Welfare, revealed that in the first half of 1977 $440 million of welfare funds had gone to recipients who did not qualify for welfare, or in amounts greater than what the law allowed. Vietnam invaded Cambodia; twenty-two thousand Cuban troops, half of their army, were stationed in various hot spots in Africa, fighting against America's side in the Cold War. The serial killer Ted Bundy escaped again—made his way to Tallahassee, Florida, and bludgeoned four sorority sisters with an oak log, two of them to death; then, three weeks later, abducted a twelve-year-old girl from her junior high. Her half-mummified remains were found in a pig farrowing shed in Utah.

Capitol Hill was in mourning. Hubert Humphrey had died on January 13 at the age of sixty-seven, after a long fight with cancer. Carter called him "a hero"—and worked to cut to ribbons the measure Humphrey had hoped to leave behind as his greatest legacy. As introduced in 1974, the Humphrey-Hawkins Full Employment Act would have required the federal government to lower the unemployment rate of 3 percent within eighteen months, first trying via labor-friendly monetary policy from the Federal Reserve, then, should that fail, by hiring people for government jobs at locally prevailing wages on projects decided upon by local planning boards; and to create wage and price controls; and to provide federal aid to states where employment lagged; and to give citizens the power to sue the federal government for failing to provide them with a job—which would be thus enshrined as a right.

This was a degree of direct intervention in the economy unknown since World War II. But its prospects for congressional passage had looked good in 1975—when the unemployment rate was 9 percent, and Democrats welcomed the prospect of making President Ford look like a grinch going into an election year if he vetoed it. Then, however, in the spring of 1976, with unemployment trending downward, what *Business Week* called a "*Who's Who* of liberal economists" called the plan a recipe for inflation. Joe Biden complained that Humphrey wasn't "cognizant of the limited, finite ability government has to deal with people's problems." A watered-down version emerged, which Carter held his nose at and endorsed on the campaign trail as the price for liberal support. But presently, with unemployment down to 6.4 percent, even that looked like a solution in search of the problem—or, rather, the wrong problem: the public was now far more worried about inflation, which had risen to 6.8 percent. Relations with the Congressional Black Caucus (*they* still cared about jobs; the black unemployment rate was 20 percent) grew frosty because Carter refused to advocate restoring the jobs guarantee in the further-weakened bill the House was considering—with speculation

Carter might veto even that, his fulsome eulogy for its namesake not-withstanding.

Richard Nixon made his first visit to Washington since his resignation for Humphrey's memorial. At a reception in Howard Baker's office, an observer noted that no one noticed him off in a corner. He advanced toward President Ford, who smiled stiffly and made awkward small talk. Jimmy Carter made his way across the room to greet his predecessors—and someone said he looked more awkwardly out of place, in his own capital, than Nixon did.

He certainly felt alienated from his party's liberals: "I feel more at home with the conservative Democratic and Republican members of Congress," he wrote in his diary the day of his State of the Union address. In a meeting with corporate executives, he pledged to decrease the percentage of GDP spent by the federal government from 23 percent to 21 percent. In his State of the Union address, he praised Hubert Humphrey as a tribune for "the weak and the hungry and the victims of discrimination and poverty"—then intoned: "Government cannot solve our problems, it can't set our goals, it cannot define our vision. Government cannot eliminate poverty or provide a bountiful economy or reduce inflation or save our cities or cure illiteracy or provide energy."

And liberals were not pleased.

THE NEXT DAY, THE ANNIVERSARY OF HIS INAUGURATION, CARTER UN-veiled his long-awaited tax plan. In just about every campaign speech he had called America's tax code a "disgrace to the human race." Planning its reform had set his engineer's heart to racing. On one side of the ledger, he wanted to reduce business deductions for entertainment and increase taxes on foreign subsidiaries; on the other, he wanted to offset the bite by reducing the corporate tax rate and making Gerald Ford's temporary investment tax credit permanent. For individuals, he wanted to reduce the top income tax rate from 70 percent to 50 percent, reduce taxes for Americans making less than $10,000, end double-taxation of dividends, and end the half-century-old practice of taxing "capital gains"—income from selling investments like stocks or real estate—at a rate lower than ordinary income. He intended the plan to be "revenue neutral," with the amount of new revenue leveed from the top half of the income distribution precisely matched by the relief afforded to the bottom.

The elegance, on paper, was well-nigh Euclidian. But Euclid never wrote a tax code. That was a job for grubby politicians—and Jimmy Carter was anything but. He had already begged Congress's leave to pass a payroll tax increase to shore up Social Security—and, out of anger at that, both labor unions and the African American interest group the

Urban League came out in opposition to the package before it was officially introduced. Then, the chairman of Carter's Board of Economic Advisors warned that forecasts portended a slowing economy and even weaker dollar in 1978, and prevailed upon the president to adjust his package to give back $5 billion more than it took in order to produce an economic stimulus.

Prospects for reform were dire in any event. Ways and Means chairman Al Ullman was exhausted from carrying the president's water on his politically compromising energy package and the previous year's goofy $50 tax rebate and offended at not having been consulted on this package in advance; he let it be known he had no interest in spending political capital fighting for it. Another potential broker for reform, Republican Senator Robert Packwood, was so frustrated that Carter didn't "understand the power structure of the Congress or the interrelationship of economic issues" that he expressed a disinclination to help with his caucus. The president had been warned about tax reform's weakening political mandate for some time. He ignored that. By his lights, he had campaigned on a promise to simplify the code, he had won—and that was all the mandate he needed.

But there was no natural constituency for "tax simplification." There was, however, a very powerful constituency for tax *complexity*. They were already hard at work. For instance, the hotel and restaurant lobbies went to ground to fight Carter's proposal to rein in abuses of the tax code's allowance for "ordinary and necessary business expenses"—what the press dubbed his war against the "three-martini lunch." Carter responded, "I don't care how many martinis anyone has with lunch. But I do care who picks up the check. I don't think a relatively small minority has some sort of divine rights to have expensive meals, free theater tickets, country club dues, sporting events tickets, paid for by heavier taxes by everybody else." The populist promise appeared to cut little ice with the voters. On January 23, George Gallup announced the president's new approval rating: down four points to 51 percent.

Carter then announced *another* politically draining fight: he would seek the required congressional approval to sell Saudi Arabia sixty F-15s, along with a lesser number of planes. Israel promised to "mobilize all our friends" to block that. The American Jewish Committee said the announcement represented the end of America's "special relationship with Israel."

Negotiators worked around the clock to settle the crippling coal strike. Steel producers said they only had a seventy-five-day supply of the fuel left before they would have to shut *their* factories. The president threatened to invoke his power to outlaw the work stoppage as a threat to national security. The United Mine Workers' president replied, "If you think the members of the UMW are soft and weak and are going to roll over and play dead, you're crazy as hell," and hinted that if miners were ordered back to work they would not mine, all but daring Carter to call out federal troops.

Hard times for the president—then, on January 31, a key senate ally, young Joseph Biden of Delaware, visited him bearing three pieces of news. The first was that Jewish leaders whom Carter hoped to persuade to stand down in the fight over selling jets to Saudi Arabia distrusted him because he was a Southern Baptist—a denomination actively working to convert Jews to Christianity, including in Israel, where efforts had become so aggressive that the Knesset was debating a law outlawing financial inducements to convert. The second was that the arrogance of Hamilton Jordan toward Capitol Hill was pushing Democratic congressional leaders to the breaking point. The third was that one of those liberals enraged by Carter's rightward-tilting State of the Union address—Senator Edward M. Kennedy of Massachusetts—appeared to be lining up support to run against Carter for the 1980 Democratic presidential nomination.

IN THE FIRST WEEK IN FEBRUARY THE NORTHEAST WAS STRUCK BY A CATA-strophic blizzard. The ordeal was compounded in New York City by the fact that 40 percent of the cash-starved city's snow removal equipment was nonfunctional. Treasury Secretary Michael Blumenthal was working out terms with Congress for a financial bailout for the city. The rest of the nation was unsympathetic. "Hey Washington?" a hobo in a political cartoon from the *Washington Star*'s Oliphant said into a pay phone, surrounded by a pile of garbage as he placed a collect call. "This here's New York! I'm broke again and if you don't send me a big, fat relief check at once, I'm gonna hang myself."

This daunting congeries of political challenges also included the consumer agency bill, which was scheduled for a vote in the House on February 8—the challenge the president now appeared the *least* interested in fighting for. Ralph Nader visited the White House with a list of twenty-four undecided congressmen. Carter rang up six of them, got six hard *no*'s, and gave up. The Consumer Issues Working Group had gotten there first—in what one member said was the most comprehensive onslaught he had witnessed in his twelve terms in Congress.

Companies pressured employees, and begged stockholders, to write their congressmen. CEOs combed the congressional corridors like lowly vice presidents. Small businessmen arrived in droves, importuning their hometown representatives from a devastatingly effective script provided them by the U.S. Chamber of Commerce: "I've always supported you and

I've never asked you for anything before. I'm asking you to vote against this bill." This was a novel technique. So was one deployed by the professional lobbyists, who descended on the same offices in teams of three or four bearing rolls compiled by Chamber computers of the representatives' anti-bill small businessmen constituents. "You give a Congressman a list of people in his district, he invariably looks down on it to see whom he knows," a Democrat from Wisconsin explained. "He can't ignore them. Any time you give him an expression of how they feel, he's going to think twice."

Ralph Nader's hubris helped the anti-Nader cause. Democratic Representatives Pat Schroeder of Colorado and Mark Foley of Massachusetts had voted for the consumer agency in 1974 and 1975, but were now wobbling—so Nader published an op-ed labeling the pair "deceptive" "mushy liberals" with "a lack of political courage." Then he flew to Schroeder's district for a press conference accusing her of selling out to corporate contributors. He called an Indiana representative a "reactionary," the California liberal Republican Pete McCloskey "disgustingly repulsive and a double-crosser."

On the day before the vote it looked to be close. But the opposition received a startling gift that morning. The *Washington Post* had been a bulwark of support for the consumer revolution ever since 1962, when its reporter Morton Mintz, inventor of the newspaper "consumer beat," broke the story of thalidomide, a drug that had come within a hair's breadth of being approved for sale in the U.S. even though it caused monstrous birth defects. His scoops were trumpeted on the editorial page, which had been thundering against attempts to weaken consumer bills for more than a decade. Now, however, the paper was changing its tune. Publisher Katharine Graham had recently asked her editorial page editor Philip Geyelin to resign because his page was too hard on business. Geyelin begged for another chance, received it, and assigned one of Graham's closest associates on his staff the task of trashing the consumer bill. The resulting diatribe was full of self-refuting points, tautologies, and unsupported assertions. It concluded that the paper could no longer support the idea because "the legislation and the conditions have changed"—even though the *way* the bill had changed made it weaker.

The editorial completed the job. The bill was crushed 227–189. One hundred and one Democrats voted against it. One of the ones who voted *aye* rued that "if we had voted today on a bill to abolish the U.S. government, it probably would have passed."

Explanations from formerly supportive congressmen echoed business propaganda: "I just don't think we need another agency"; "enough is enough"; "faceless bureaucratic intrusion." Many cited "grassroots opposition." One even said that, philosophically, he supported the bill but that he didn't have the patience to "explain five hundred times back home why this isn't just more big government." Another, more bluntly, offered, "I'm afraid that the Chamber will run a candidate against me in the primary." A corporate lobbyist gloated that from now on one wouldn't "have to feel ashamed as a member of Congress to vote against something Ralph Nader wanted." The media described it as a spontaneous anti-government uprising: "Representatives were listening to their constituencies, and what they were hearing signaled some real changes in their mood," the *New York Times* said. "National sympathy has apparently swung against further government growth and specifically against further regulation." The *Chicago Tribune* editorialized that "everybody wanted a consumer agency except the consumers."

The boardroom Jacobins had successfully hidden their hand. And since their subterranean efforts had gone undetected, they were able revive them for the next battle—and the one after that, and after that, and after that.

RONALD REAGAN CELEBRATED THE DEFEAT OF THE CONSUMER BILL WITH A victory column. Consumerism, he wrote, was "swimming upstream." Ralph Nader would "no doubt come back thundering on one issue or another, but will anybody listen?"

Reagan himself was doing quite a bit better. His newspaper syndication contract was extended for two years. The Gallup Poll reported that he was the first choice of Republicans as their 1980 presidential nominee. His name recognition with the public was 90 percent. So, shortly before Christmas, Reagan's top political associates gathered for dinner at the mansion his former employer General Electric had built for him in Pacific Palisades for him to show off all their latest electrical gadgets on TV. The agenda was a presidential campaign: to be or not to be?

Attendees included his 1976 campaign manager, John Sears; that campaign's press secretary, Jim Lake; its chief organizer in the South, David Keene; his political action committee chief, Lyn Nofziger; his publicist Peter Hannaford; his policy advisor Martin Anderson; his gubernatorial chief of staff, Edwin Meese; and a representative of Reagan's "kitchen cabinet" of rich California friends. The attendees counseling in favor prevailed. Evans and Novak's column of January 16 quoted one of the skeptics: "I wouldn't have thought it possible, but believe me, this guy is running." That, the columnists reported, "reverses the conventional wisdom of the past year, shattering preconceptions of 1980 presidential politics. If Reagan runs other conservative aspirants can abandon hope . . . even though he would be the oldest presidential nominee in history, unless his candidacy caused Gerald Ford to renew their 1976 death struggle."

Although they also reported a fly in the ointment: Ford had privately pledged he would do anything to keep Ronald Reagan from the Oval Office.

Then Reagan suffered a political setback at the Republican National Committee's annual winter meeting in Washington. His preferred candidate for the RNC vice-chair position, reserved for a woman, was a conservative housing policy expert named Dr. Gloria Toote. She lost in a landslide to the incumbent, Mary Crisp, a leading Republican feminist.

The defeat got more press than it might have otherwise because Dr. Toote was one of Ronald Reagan's few African American supporters. RNC chairman Bill Brock had budgeted two-thirds of a million dollars in 1977 toward recruiting black Republicans. He reasoned that if the party could add five percentage points to the ten Ford won among blacks in 1976, that could tip the next presidential election. So the keynote speaker at the RNC meeting was Jesse Jackson. "We must pursue a strategy that prohibits one party from taking us for granted and another party from writing us off," he said. "The only protection we have against political genocide is to remain necessary." He also said that the Republicans would have a decent shot at black support if they ceased the "ill-informed or ill-intentioned" practice of opposing government intervention that helped poor blacks, but taking government intervention for granted when it benefitted whites. He got a standing ovation.

"I wish we had Republicans who could talk like that," Chairman Brock said when he was finally able to quiet the crowd. He forecast the day when Republicans could hope for 40 percent of the black vote.

Then, the RNC voted 118–37 against Dr. Toote.

REAGAN CONTINUED DELIVERING THE CONSERVATIVE CATECHISM WITHOUT apology in his columns and radio commentaries. He shared his delight at a poll of the youngsters listed in *Who's Who Among High School Students*— "more conservative in their outlook on both politics and morality than their counterparts only a few years back." (He was particularly delighted to relate that 70 percent had not had sex, 56 percent of that number because they were morally opposed, not because of lack of opportunity.) He flayed pedagogical recommendations from the National Education Association to downgrade mere "retention of facts" in favor of "processes of inquiry, comparison, interpretation, and synthesis." He lashed out at meddling state judges and legislators who insisted on equalizing funding of school districts by paying for them through state general funds instead of local property taxes (what really motivated them was that "control of funding would also mean control of education"). And in a particularly impassioned commentary, he maintained that the argument for Jesus

Christ's divinity was indisputable. How else could it be that "this uneducated, propertyless young man who preached on street corners for only
three years, who left not a written word, has for two thousand years had a
greater effect on the entire world than all the rulers, kings, and emperors,
all the conquerors, the generals, and admirals, all the scholars, scientists,
and scientists who ever lived, all put together . . . unless He really was
what He said He was?"

On some days, the fare was heartwarming tales of determined, philanthropic individuals beating government at its own game. On others, it
was outrageously lenient sentences for criminals; or the folly of pursuing
diplomatic relations with Vietnam when there were "some 2,500 of our men
listed as missing in action"; or the fraudulence of Jimmy Carter's pieties
about "human rights" when Communists got away with literal murder. He
complimented the public spiritedness of the oil companies, who had raised
the price of a gasoline only 88 percent since 1958, during the same period
in which the cost of mailing a letter had gone up 333 percent, and claimed
that the Soviets were developing "killer satellites," "orbital bombardment
vehicles," and "laser weapons." He rued that the federal government spent
"$57 million an hour round the clock every day (including Sundays and
holidays)," at a rate growing "250 times as fast as population."

One day he expressed his exasperation at conservationists (who
"should be ashamed of themselves") seeking to expand Redwood National Park, even though "virtually all of the great superlative redwoods
are already preserved in a number of state parks." On another day it was
the environmental "special interest groups" fighting the Disney Corporation's development of a ski resort called Mineral King in Sequoia National
Park: "Is public land really for the public or for an elite who want to keep
it for their own use?" He, for one, would side with the public who wanted
their ski resort, not the selfish elite campers who wanted to keep that land
pristine.

ANOTHER MAJOR CATEGORY OF COLUMNS AND COMMENTARIES CONCERNED
the absurdity of conventional, "liberal," wisdom about race.

Consider a situation in southern Africa that he returned to again and
again. Jimmy Carter had reversed Richard Nixon to sign the U.S. onto
a United Nations ban on importing the strategically crucial commodity of chromium from Rhodesia, which was ruled by its tiny minority
of whites. That spurred Prime Minister Ian Smith to engage in talks to
step down. Reagan excoriated these negotiations. "African nationalism,
as such" he claimed, "does not exist." Neither did white imperialism in
Rhodesia, except the kind threatened from Moscow: "The 'African problem' is a Russian weapon, aimed at us." He pooh-poohed claims that black

Rhodesians were oppressed; after all, "50 percent of Rhodesia's senate is black." (Which was not so impressive if you knew Rhodesia was 95 percent black, and that blacks controlled virtually none of the nation's land or capital.) He also said South Africa, because it had more than one political party, was one of only five admirable post-independence African states — instructing readers, "Whatever we may think of South Africa's internal policies, control of its mineral riches and its strategic position are the Soviet Union's ultimate goal in Africa."

Another favorite Reagan subject was a conference on energy policy held by the NAACP. It had approved a task force that resolved to withdraw support from President Carter's energy program, and endorse deregulation of oil and natural gas prices instead, because "We cannot accept the notion that our people are best served by a policy based on the inevitability of energy shortage and the need for government to allocate an ever-shrinking supply among competing interests." Reagan lauded what he called the NAACP's rejection of "the pessimistic belief of those who today control the Democratic Party that we must lower our expectations," and saw in this development a matchless opportunity to attract blacks into the Republican Party: "In American politics, the party of optimism has taken the high ground. The Republicans had it from just after the Civil War for most of the years till the late 1920s. The Democrats seized it in the Depression, but the roles are showing signs of reversing again. . . . If the Republicans can persuade black voters that they are the party of optimism on the energy issue and the Democrats are the party of pessimism, they may have the beginnings of the resurgence they have been looking for."

One reason this political judgment was so dubious was the *way* the nation's venerable civil rights organization had ended up aping petroleum industry propaganda. As two radical journalists discovered, the NAACP had originally convened *two* energy task forces. One, chaired by a consumer activist and made up of civil rights figures, concentrated on energy demand, and made liberal recommendations. The other, on energy supply, was chaired by a lobbyist for Mobil Oil, and was stuffed with energy executives. The full NAACP energy conference voted to endorse the liberal group's recommendation. Then, the board of directors overruled them, propounding the *other* task force's preference for energy deregulation as the all-but-official will of black America. The NAACP's chairman, Margaret Bush Wilson, also a board member of the agribusiness giant Monsanto, had stacked the board with people like a retired natural gas executive and the first black member of the Federal Reserve Board of Governors, who opposed the minimum wage. Following her successful coup, she released a statement averring that the Carter energy policy had been "put together by a lily-white coterie of White House advisors who subscribe to a limits-to-growth philosophy." Replied Representative John Conyers of the Congressional Black Caucus in frustration, "How on earth could deregulation be in the interests of black people?"

But Reagan loved it—and turned it into a Republican talking point. "I like what Mrs. Margaret Bush Wilson, the head of the NAACP, the National Association of Colored People said," he told Bill Moyers of PBS. "She said a no-growth policy's fine for a twenty-eight-year-old, $50,000 a year White House advisor. It's not so good for a fella down there trying to get his foot on the bottom rung of the ladder." Rich liberal environmentalists and greedy White House staffers: they "can have that monastic life that they want to live and say to all of us that the better days are over. No, they're not. We live in the future in America, always have. And the better days are yet to come." It was a magnificent specimen of what made Reagan such a valuable figure on the right: his ability to effortlessly package the quest for corporate profit into an uplifting vision of a righteous citizens' crusade.

BUT IF THE RHETORICAL MAESTRO WAS TO BECOME A SERIOUS PRESIDENtial candidate, stupefying organizational tasks lay ahead. His janissaries were already hard at work.

Citizens for the Republic's pollster Dick Wirthlin was gathering data from a scientific sample of fifteen hundred voters in forty-four key congressional districts in thirty-four states to divine which parts of Reagan's message sold best and where. ("Some people think there should be an absolute limit to the percentage of national income the government can take in taxes to control the growth of government spending. . . . Others think the government should be allowed to tax and spend as much as it decides is needed. Where would you place yourself?") The findings would eventually comprise seventeen bound volumes.

CFR signed a deal with direct mail guru Bruce Eberle, a disciple of Richard Viguerie, to manage their burgeoning mailing list—inexpensively, in exchange for the right to rent it to his other clients. They refined their newsletter into a sharp fortnightly roundup of useful and amusing news to keep the conservative troops inspired (how the federal government was subsidizing the coal strike via food stamps; how visitors to the Madame Tussauds wax museum in London voted Jimmy Carter the fourth most "hated and feared" of all the figures on display, tied with Count Dracula). The "Ronald Reagan Speaks Out" column evolved a special function: testing out ideas that might or might not be ready for prime time. (For instance, "Nuclear 'Wastes' Have Valuable Uses": "radioactive waste worries could become a thing of the past if we would turn from a preoccupation with disposing of wastes to the 'recycling' of their byproducts,

according to Milton Copulos, energy analyst for the Heritage Foundation.
. . . The anti–nuclear power people may actually enjoy their naysaying. As
for the rest of us, it sounds as if there is a new frontier out there—right in
those piles of nuclear 'wastes.' ") The publication also retained a full-time
political cartoonist.

Each column also listed Reagan's speaking schedule—the execution
of which was a massive enterprise in itself. It was run out of the offices of
Deaver & Hannaford by an Austrian émigré named Helene von Damm.
(She used to travel with him, too, until Nancy Reagan grew jealous and
forbade it.) She first encountered Reagan in 1964 when her employer, the
American Medical Association's political action committee, booked him
as a speaker for their fundraising banquet for Barry Goldwater. He "went
into a long and passionate description of totalitarianism," she wrote in
her memoir. "I was rapt. He was describing things I had lived and seen
with my eyes. . . . I resolved then and there that I was going to work for
that man and help him, should he ever seek political office." Two years
later she drove from Chicago to San Francisco to present herself on the
doorstep of his gubernatorial campaign and proved herself so useful that
Reagan invited her to be his executive assistant in Sacramento. She replied
that her Austrian accent might prove an embarrassment. Reagan reassured
her: "You know, you symbolize the American dream, Helene. So don't try
to lose that accent. It's just fine with me."

For the 1976 presidential season, she edited *Sincerely, Ronald Reagan*,
a tender biographical portrait drawn from letters he had sent and received
as governor. An entire chapter—"The Ogre in Sacramento"—was devoted to Reagan's acts of kindness toward strangers, like the nine-year-
old who wrote that his mother's welfare check went missing just before
Christmas (after clearing up the administrative error, Reagan arranged for
a yuletide visit to the family from his friend Frank Sinatra); the mentally
retarded man whose dearest wish was a rocking chair (the governor sent
his own); and the gentleman who needed a suit for his upcoming nuptials
and wondered if the governor could loan him one, since they were about
the same size. (In a thank-you note, "the constituent disclosed his age.
He was 80.")

Now, however, a big part of von Damm's job was disappointing people. She filed 333 letters in her "Turndown" drawer in 1978: supplicants
like the Utah State Dental Association, the Washington State Republican
Assembly, and the National Welfare Fraud Association. She wrote excuses
like, "This is just to let you know that it is much too early to know what
the Governor's schedule will be next August." (It wasn't; Reagan was
booked through April 1979.) When she had to turn down a public official

or potential major donor, she wrote letters for the governor to sign, sorted them into two piles, one with a blank for his signature above a printed "Ronald Reagan," the other, for particularly important personages, with space for him to scrawl an intimate "Ron."

The attention to detail was meticulous. (Clomping the giant "BLACK TIE" stamp onto the wrong schedule page could make for quite the sartorial embarrassment.) She had to make sure the correct speech text traveled with Reagan in his luggage, for, though for the most part the speeches were largely identical—had been since the early 1960s—sometimes, sections were torqued to fold in recent events ("Having seen so many legal barriers against blacks and other minorities removed in recent years, the NAACP has shifted its focus to the economy front. . . .") or to curry favor. In one speech, for example, Reagan endorsed a technical change in capital gains assessment favored by brewer Joseph Coors. For remarks to the National Association of Broadcasters in Las Vegas, he included language drafted by a communications lawyer named Mark Fowler decrying the Federal Communication Commission's enforcement of a certain burdensome regulation. (Fowler later became FCC commissioner.) Another time, construction executives requested he decry "the practice engaged in by many California governmental units of using employees for construction work which should properly be going out to bid." A flack for the California Thoroughbred Breeders Association suggested his audience would be "far more receptive" if Reagan mentioned "government interference in . . . breeding or horse racing."

The standard fee was $5,000, marked down to $1,000 for Republican functions. That January, he gave twelve speeches in seven states. Each required a detailed preparatory in-person visit by an advance person to handle tasks like installing extra phone lines in the hotel room so it could serve as a traveling business office; an inspection of the banquet hall to make sure the lighting, sound, and layout met the maestro's exacting specifications; a briefing with organizers about whether and how a question-and-answer session would take place. Often sessions with a key donor, candidate, or politician had to be choreographed. Sometimes, Reagan was provided a script for the occasion. ("Larry Lennon will be present at the Orlando Finance meeting the morning of 9/19/79. Larry is the nephew of Fred Lennon, Ohio Finance Chairman. Fred tells me that Harry is actively and effectively raising money for us in Florida. Fred suggests, if you have the opportunity, that you chide Harry by saying, 'I hear that you are spending more time playing golf than working.'")

Los Angeles, Las Vegas, Kansas, Idaho, Los Angeles. Plane trip, news conference, reception, speech, handshaking, autographs, rest. Get on the airplane again; repeat, repeat, repeat. The sixty-seven-year-old did this some two hundred times in 1978 alone.

JANUARY 13, 1978, BROKE THE ROUTINE. REAGAN TRAVELED TO SOUTH Carolina for a live debate on the Panama Canal with William F. Buckley, on his television program *Firing Line.*

They had become friends after Reagan signed up as a charter subscriber to *National Review.* They had recently been exchanging letters debating the treaties. Buckley had traveled to the isthmus in 1976, finding in the man Reagan called a "tinhorn dictator" someone the U.S. could do business with, coming to agree with the elite bipartisan consensus: America, he columnized, should "get out—while the initiative, still, is clearly our own. That is the way great nations should act."

Some conservatives agreed. John Wayne, who had been married to a Panamanian woman, sent letters to every senator supporting the treaties. Reagan had signed a direct mail letter for the Republican National Committee begging funds to support "an all-out grass roots 'Campaign to Defeat the Treaty'" that raised over $1 million. Reagan was subsequently enraged that the money was funneled into the RNC's general fund instead. John Wayne was outraged by the arguments in the letter. "I hope they weren't your views," he wrote his old friend. "This is more the style of a liberal punk who doesn't have to answer for his words. . . . I'll show you point by God damn point in the Treaty where you are misinforming the people. This is not my point of view against your point of view. These are facts."

Reagan and Buckley argued those facts on a special two-hour broadcast live from the University of South Carolina. Senate debate began in twenty-eight days. Sam Ervin moderated. Buckley spoke first. He said the canal had no military value: wars were now nuclear wars, and in a nuclear war shipping lanes did not matter. ("The Pan-*ahh-mahh* can-*ahhl* will re*vaht to a* land*mahhhsss,* and the *fahst* survivor who makes his way across the *Issssthmus* will relive a historic experience like stout Cortez when with eagle *ahhhye* he stared a*crahhhs* the Pacific," he said. Then he quoted Keats.) He imputed racism for predictions of disaster when the Panamanians took over, insisted Panama's national pride was a legitimate concern, and quoted President William Howard Taft: "We do not want to own anything in Panama. What we want is a canal that goes through Panama"—just what these treaties guaranteed. He mocked concerns over the expense of the handover by noting that it would cost about one-three-thousandth of the $1.29 billion America sent in foreign aid to Spain. ("I do hope and pray that Mr. Reagan, whose propensity to fru-*gah*-lity with the public purse is one of his most endearing characteristics, will not devote an ex-*stray*-vagant amount of our time tonight to telling us how ignomini-ous it is, under *thah* circumstances, to cede forty or fifty million dollars a year—out of revenues—to the Republic of Panama.")

Then, finally, eighteen minutes in, as he lurched into an unfunny joke, Sam Ervin broke in, apologizing—"as one who loves to filibuster"—and said his time was nearly up. Buckley promised he needed only a minute and took four—ending with a rousing salute to America's belief in human rights and sovereignty even "for little countries, whose natural resources, where and when necessary, we are entitled to use, but not to abuse?"

The applause was merely respectful. When Governor Reagan rose, the room felt lighter. The gales of laughter from his first of many jokes made Buckley look like an amateur. And his opening salvo incinerated the un-derlying logic of Buckley's entire presentation: "Mr. Buckley, if you don't mind, I feel compassion for all those other peoples in the world that we've been hearing about here tonight, but let's get back to the canal." Ronald Reagan knew how to debate.

He sketched out a harrowing scenario: that though the first treaty stipulated that Panama would gain control in the year 2000, on the day the treaties were signed, under international law, "there would be nothing to prevent the government of Panama from expropriating our property and nationalizing the Canal"—nothing America could do to stop it, in other words, short of going to war.

This was a cutting claim. America had just lost her first war in history. She had no appetite for another. The most effective pro-treaty argument was American generals' claim it would take a hundred thousand troops to defend the Canal against attack. Reagan was flipping that logic on its head: these treaties *tempted* war.

And even assuming the transfer occurred peacefully and on schedule, he claimed, the second, "neutrality" treaty guaranteeing the Canal's op-eration as an international waterway in perpetuity, and America's right to jointly defend it with Panama, was "so ambiguous in its wording as to be virtually meaningless." This, too, was a sharp attack. Back in October, a leaked cable from Panama's chief negotiator suggested that Panama dis-agreed that the treaties granted America sweeping power to defend the canal. A week later, Senator Baker visited Panama. He told Torrijos that he had received 21,500 letters the previous month on the subject, with only 500 supporting the turnover. He threatened that the Senate would not ratify anything until that sticking point was clarified. Torrijos hastened to Washington for several hours of emergency negotiations with Carter and agreed on a "statement of understanding" affirming America's interpreta-tion. In the weeks to come, the nagging question of the precise legal status of this "understanding" was the gossamer thread upon which this epochal debate came to hang. Reagan lectured, like a litigator, that an "understanding" was not a "guarantee," that the only guarantor for that understanding was Torrijos—a corrupt tin-pot dictator, Reagan insisted. He mocked the treaties' provision for "joint defense": "*'Joint defense!'* Now, that brings to mind a picture of friendly allies going forward, shoulder to shoulder, in friendly camaraderie, the Americans voicing, probably, their customary marching chants, such as the well-known 'Sound off. One, two.' The Panamanian *Guardia Nacional* will be chanting the words they use in their present training. They march to these words: *'¡Muerta al gringo! ¡Gringo abajo! ¡Graindo al parad_on!'* Translation: 'Death to the gringo! Down with the gringo! Gringo to the wall!' "

He closed by offering, "with all due respect," that "our negotiators did the best they could, given their assignment—which was to concede as little as possible while still pacifying a thug. Therefore, it was time to tear up treaties which had taken fourteen years to negotiate and start all over again—this time without a gun to America's head. "We would become a laughingstock by surrendering to unreasonable demands," he concluded. We "cloak weakness in the suit of virtue. I think the world would see it as, once again, Uncle Sam putting his tail between his legs and creeping away rather than face trouble."

And there could be no question about it: on TV, Reagan won that debate.

Then, however, Buckley, devoted a newspaper column to fact-checking him. "We're being asked to turn over a $10 billion investment," Reagan had said; the actual amount was $1.02 billion. He said we were bailing out "a Panamanian government that has accumulated the highest per capita debt... of any nation in the world"; actually, U.S. debt was 4.5 times greater. Reagan said Panama got a quarter of its gross domestic product from the Canal; it was 12 percent. Reagan had also spun out terrifying visions of the Canal as a superhighway for enemy warships—but Buckley devastatingly countered that "during the past two world wars, no enemy ship used the Panama Canal," and that if they ever tried, "our Navy or our Air Force will sink them—just like that!"

Re-score it on points for William F. Buckley. If only newspaper columns had as much impact as TV shows that had run many weeks earlier, facts had as much power as stories.

IN THE DEBATE, REAGAN HAD NARRATED WHAT ONE OF THE EXPERTS ON Buckley's side dismissed, to audience laughter, as an "*imaginative* history of the Canal." It began with a desperate, plucky little nation trying "more than fifty times to free itself from Colombia," until America rode to the rescue, buying out the stalled canal project from the bankrupt French company Colombia had contracted to build it. He claimed that Colombia stalled to get better terms, and, during that delay, "Panama saw its chance for freedom," and approached the U.S. "We not only bought the Zone from Panama; we did something I believe was unique in the history of great nations in their dealings with smaller countries. We went into the Zone and we bought, in fee simple, all the privately owned land from the owners, including even homestead claims and squatters' rights. I've seen the figure of those purchases set at $163 million." (That was one of the facts Buckley corrected in his column: it was actually $4 million.)

Reagan continued, thrillingly, "We built a sanitation system for their cities. We built bridges and highways and a water and power system. . . . We took a country which was a disease-infested, swampy jungle and gave it a death rate that was actually lower than the one we have in the United States. . . . The new nation began free of debt. . . . They had no fear of aggressive neighbors or of retaliation from Colombia because, at their request, the United States guaranteed their independence." Which was why, Reagan claimed, Panama's provisional Congress approved the 1907 treaty unanimously. "Then," he had pronounced triumphantly, "we proceeded to build the eighth wonder of the world!" We operated it "for more than sixty years on a non-profit basis, open to all the world's shipping." And we midwifed a nation that now "has the highest per capita income of any country in Central America!"

When he recited this, Buckley had looked up from his notes, an expression of awe on his face at the brazenness of the words.

You could get more accurate history in funny papers. *Doonesbury* did a series in which the strip's resident stoner-philosopher, Zonker Harris, educated his teammates in a football huddle about the story of the conspiracy cooked up in a single meeting at the Waldorf Astoria Hotel in New York City that ended with the French director of the bankrupt company that had begun and abandoned the project signing the treaty creating the nation of Panama absent the intervention of a single Panamanian, which the United States Senate ratified while the rest of the Panamanian delegation was still en route to the U.S., and the USS *Nashville* steamed to the isthmus to protect America's imperial claim. Secretary of State Elihu Root had joked to Theodore Roosevelt, "You have been accused of seduction, and you have unquestionably been proved guilty of rape." Attorney General Philander Knox joked, also approvingly, "Mr. President, do not let so great an achievement suffer from any taint of legality." This was the stain on American innocence Reagan had deployed all his rhetorical charm to blot out.

He claimed that "inference" of "some kind of skullduggery on our part" was "pure unadulterated nonsense." That Americans were not bullies, but angels. That the canal had been America's *gift*. Guilt-ridden liberals were insisting that because America had supposedly once been cruel, it must now be weak. But America was the kindest and most generous nation on earth. So what did we have to prove to some tin-pot dictator?

It was the epitome of Reagan's rhetorical gifts, that capacity to cleanse any hint of doubt regarding American innocence. That was the soul of his political appeal: his liturgy of absolution. And a key aspect of his value to the conservative cause—for other exemplars of the movement were revealing themselves as increasingly nasty and foul.

CONGRESS STRUCK A COMPROMISE TO RENEW THE HYDE AMENDMENT FOR the next fiscal year: Medicaid could pay for abortions for victims of rape or incest, or "where severe and long-lasting health damage to the mother would result if the pregnancy were carried to term when so determined by two physicians." Then, in Columbus, Ohio, arsonists attempted to burn an abortion clinic to the ground. In Akron, an ordinance was introduced that would require women seeking an abortion to wait twenty-four hours after being lectured by a doctor with "a general description of the fetus at that stage of pregnancy."

On Panama, a mailgram sent to every congressman by something called the "Committee of the Silent Majority" complained that "the executive branch of our government is now totally controlled by the Tri-Lateral Commission," who "have negotiated, drafted, signed and are about to have the Panama Canal treaties ratified. Through interlocking directorships and bureaucratic control, they have been able to silence the media." Phyllis Schlafly, in her own *Firing Line* debate, said much the same thing, noting darkly, "There are seven members of the Commission in the Carter administration at the cabinet level." A letter to Senator Mark Hatfield of Oregon made a similar point less decorously: "Don't bail out the Rockefellers and the kike bankers. I'm tired of my senator representing the Jew interests."

Governor Meldrim Thomson of New Hampshire said that when Panamanian students rioted in 1964 over the American flag, "spineless" officials should have issued "an order similar to the one given by John Dix, the New Hampshire–born customs official at the outbreak of our Civil War. . . . 'If anyone attempts to haul down the American flag, shoot him on the spot.'" Then he left for South Africa in his capacity as "secretary of state" in the Conservative Caucus's shadow cabinet. Upon his arrival, he said Prime Minister John Vorster was moving "his nation toward greater opportunities for all of its 25 million inhabitants" and was "one of the great world statesmen of today." He added, "I was greatly impressed by the constructive manner in which he and his administration are resolving the internal problems of their country with calmness, compassion, and courage," and praised South Africa's "free elections"—a story "not being told in the world press." In fact, the government had recently massacred at least 176 and as many as 700 student demonstrators, protesting, among other things, the fact that the country's black majority could not vote.

At the conclusion of his visit, the proprietor of the *Manchester Union Leader,* William Loeb, a political and personal friend of Governor Thomson, published Thomson's statement lavishly praising the "low-cost housing" in the townships of Soweto and Sebokeng (under the country's governing Group Areas Act, blacks were forced to live in such townships, often at great distance from their places of work, and could only travel outside them by presenting "pass books"). President Carter, on a visit to Nashua, observed that Governor Thomson was "the only American leader that I know who has endorsed, in effect, apartheid, or condoned or approved the attitude of the South African government." Thomson demanded an apology, insisting he had never endorsed apartheid. William Loeb published a front-page editorial in support of his friend, explaining, "Most of the blacks in South Africa are from right out of the jungle."

WHAT WILLIAM LOEB SAID MATTERED. THE *UNION LEADER* WAS NEW HAMPshire's only statewide newspaper. His scouring editorials against Edmund Muskie in 1971, George Romney in 1967, and Nelson Rockefeller in 1963 had helped scotch these men's presidential ambitions by sabotaging their chances in the nation's first-in-the-nation primary. More proximately, New Hampshire's liberal third-term senator Thomas McIntyre was up for reelection, and Loeb dearly wished to replace him. If McIntyre voted for the Panama Canal treaties, that would provide the perfect cudgel with which to do it.

McIntyre was a high-minded and deliberative legislator. He gave a speech on the Senate floor carefully weighting the deal's pros and cons, ending up on the fence. The New Hampshire Conservative Caucus responded by publishing a "resolution of censure" that summoned him, Torquemada-like, before a meeting to answer for his sins. Nonappearance, the resolution explained, would constitute prima facie evidence of his intent to vote for ratification—and the Conservative Caucus's commitment to his political execution. McIntyre chose to ignore the summons.

One of McIntyre's announced opponents supported the treaties. Another opposed them in a lukewarm way. Then, a third candidate emerged. He was a thirty-seven-year-old airline pilot named Gordon Humphrey, who had joined the Conservative Caucus in the middle of 1977, proved his mettle as an organizer, and then become the group's New Hampshire state director, growing the chapter to an impressive fifteen hundred members.

At an anti-treaty rally Humphrey had organized in the state capital, Howard Phillips told him that McIntyre was a "political sitting duck" because of his agnostic position on Panama, and that Humphrey should run for Senate with the treaties as his defining issue. Humphrey predicted that the Cuban military would seize the Panama Canal and turn the isthmus into "the People's Democratic Republic of Panama." At a "Save the Canal" rally at the statehouse that he organized, "GIVE AWAY CARTER, KEEP THE CANAL" bumper stickers were distributed. Humphrey also pledged to fight to limit how much "piggish government" could take in from income tax revenue, and to solve the energy crisis by removing the "dead hand of government."

He was so obscure, however, that he campaigned wearing a badge that read, "Hello, my name is Gordon Humphrey."

Unknown New Right candidates like that were popping up everywhere. In New Jersey, one of the Senate's most liberal Republicans, Clifford Case, was being challenged by a conservative activist who had been one year old in 1943, when Case entered Congress, and twelve when Case had had his last competitive race. Jeffrey Bell was a pure product of the Goldwater revolution. As a researcher for Richard Nixon's 1968 presidential campaign, he penned a memo complaining that every time Nixon ventured a right-wing position "the initial flurry of protests from the liberal press . . . caused it to be modified—if not dropped." In 1971 he joined a group of activists who refused to support Nixon's reelection because of his "excessive taxation and inordinate welfarism," "overture to Red China," and alleged responsibility for "a deteriorated American military position." In 1977, Bell had argued in *Human Events* that the only way conservatism could prosper was if its candidates pressed "issue militancy"—making their opposition to liberalism their calling card. Then he moved to Trenton to put his theory to the test by running for Senate. Political experts remembered him as the man who ruined Reagan's chances in the 1976 New Hampshire primary by convincing Reagan to pledge a $90 billion cut in the federal budget, which allowed Gerald Ford to argue in tax-allergic New Hampshire that Reagan would force state taxes to skyrocket. Bell's ideological purity remained undisturbed. He often sounded like some sort of right-wing Chairman Mao: "Our central task as a party must be to lead government away from its recent obsession of income redistribution, toward a new era of income and growth," was one of his recent *pronunciamentos*. The *New York Times* covered him frequently, with the fascination of a gawker at a train wreck.

Another underdog, Colorado Representative Bill Armstrong, was an evangelical brought to Jesus by Bill Bright of the Campus Crusade for Christ. He hoped to win the nomination to take down the Democratic senator Floyd Haskell. Before being elected to Congress, Armstrong committed a week each year to travel to Washington to evangelize to public officials. In the House, he led the conservative Republican Study Group, and his signature issue was outlawing ceilings on campaign contributions, which he called a "limit to the right of voters to speak out." He also owned two Colorado radio stations. Even with the head start that offered him, he was not favored to win over his primary opponent, Jack Swigert, the hero-astronaut who had defied death in 1970 leading Apollo 13's aborted moon mission.

In suburban Atlanta the unknown was an eccentric history professor who headed Georgians Against the Proposed Panama Canal Treaties. Dr. Newton Leroy Gingrich had had just been denied tenure at West Georgia College for spending too much time on politics. (To cushion the blow, wealthy backers paid him $13,000, structured for them as a tax shelter, to write a novel about World War III. His friend the futurist author Alvin Toffler wrote back after reading a fragment, "You are obviously better at shaking hands than writing fiction." He never finished the book.) In a speech to a convention of Georgia Young Republicans, Gingrich said, "One of the great problems we have in the Republican Party is that we don't encourage you to be nasty. We encourage you to be neat, obedient, and loyal, and faithful, and all those Boy Scout words, which would be great around the campfire but are lousy in politics . . . . You're fighting a war. A war for power. . . . What we really need are people who are willing to stand up in a slug-fest." Ever since he was a teenager, Gingrich had been conceptualizing himself as a "transformational figure" who would save America from its enemies. He was running for a congressional seat he had already lost twice.

In Massachusetts, there were two: Edward King, the head of Massachusetts for Limited Taxation, trying to take away the Democratic nomination from whiz-kid Governor Michael Dukakis, and a conservative talk radio host named Avi Nelson, "whose political experience," David Broder observed, "consists of losing a race for the House of Representatives."

In Southeastern Illinois, there was dentist Dan Crane. In suburban Indianapolis, there was Dan Crane's brother David, a lawyer and psychologist. Their father, a physician, was a minor national celebrity for his folksy, conservative advice column, "The Worry Clinic," syndicated in small-town newspapers since the 1940s. ("Women are just naturally frigid creatures," was one of Dr. Crane's oft-repeated morsels.) They hoped to join their other brother, Representative Phil Crane, in the Capitol to become the first sibling trio to serve in the United States Congress. In North Central Illinois, it was a local TV preacher named Don Lyon, who said the federal government should get out of the education business and that

unemployment insurance had bred "a society of parasites." He was challenging the House's third-ranking Republican, John Anderson.

And in the Hawkeye State, Roger Jepsen, a twinkly-eyed two-time
lieutenant governor who billed himself as "The Right Republican," was
running in a primary to face incumbent Senator Dick Clark, a former college professor who had won his seat in an upset in 1972 by walking across
the entire state. Clark's hair was longish, his positions far to the left of the
typical Iowan: he favored school busing, supported the Panama Canal
treaties, and his signature issue was championing majority-black rule in
southern Africa. Conservative Iowans were so eager to be rid of him they
didn't care much care *who* opposed him. As a farmer wrote to accompany
his $25 check by return mail to Paul Weyrich's Committee for the Survival
of a Free Congress, "Please make Good use of the proceeds. As soon as we
hear that a good Republican, a Lawyer I hope, has announced his candidacy for the U.S. Senate, we Republicans will try to Hang Sen. Dick Clark
on a telephone pole!"

FIVE DAYS AFTER REAGAN'S DEBATE WITH WILLIAM F. BUCKLEY, HE BOARDED
a DC-9 chartered by the American Conservative Union, joined by senators and representatives, Howard Phillips, the executive director of
the Veterans of Foreign Wars, and three distinguished retired military
officers—a "Panama Truth Squad," which embarked upon a five-city
campaign-style tour. At the first stop, Miami, one of the truth-tellers said
the treaties would "let Cuba and Moscow proceed with their master plan
for takeover of the Caribbean." Paul Laxalt barked, "The basic gut issue is
this: Do we or do we not give away the Panama Canal?" In St. Louis, Senator Bob Dole begged his colleagues to, "for once, put our country first."

Reagan and Laxalt had asked for $50,000 to fund the tour from the $1
million raised from Reagan's Panama Canal letter for the RNC. But the
RNC chair had no intention of embarrassing President Ford, or Howard
Baker, who had just made the difficult decision to support them, by committing party money to the anti-treaty fight. So Richard Viguerie raised
$110,000 for the crusade in only two weeks. The ACU had already spent
$600,000. Conservatives decided they didn't need the party's support in
any event. They were doing fine building para-party institutions of their
own.

For instance, after Reagan spoke to a Truth Squad rally in Atlanta, he
appeared at a Citizens for the Republic training seminar for grassroots
activists, dropping in on sessions like "Making News for Your Candidate"
and "Campaign Management"; the *Los Angeles Times* reported that CFR's
intention was raising up challengers to "regular party candidates." Similar
campaign schools were operated by the National Conservative Political

Action Committee, Young Americans for Freedom, and Paul Weyrich's Committee for the Survival of a Free Congress.

Weyrich's was the most elaborate. Candidates could enter a new training class once every six weeks, either in Milwaukee or Washington. There, they imbibed a heretical theory. The conventional wisdom on the best use of a campaign's limited resources was to identify supporters most likely to get to the polls on Election Day by canvassing only the most promising precincts. "We're opposed to that kind of thinking," Weyrich said. "We think no area, black, labor, etc. should be ignored."

The New Right believed right wing–friendly discontent could break out anywhere, even where you least expected it. Even, say, in the trade union mecca of Youngstown, Ohio—which is where Panama Truth Squad members Phil Crane, Paul Weyrich, Mickey Edwards, and Howard Phillips alighted next, for a meeting with union leaders to discuss whether they might be able to do business together. "Our paramount motive for the meeting was to learn from them," Representative Crane explained to reporters afterward, "to determine what they saw as the major factors behind the recent closing of the Youngstown Sheet and Tube plant with the consequent loss of 4,000 jobs. We also wanted to explore the possibility that we might have more in common with labor than we realize—especially on economic issues."

They found that they shared quite a lot. According to the American Conservative Union's magazine *Battle Line*, the unionists "spoke of the injury to investment climate because of our nation's tax laws; of the inability to absorb mounting production costs imposed by government regulations; of the unfair trading practices of some of our nation's foreign competitors; of the lack of a coherent energy policy designed to provide abundant resources; and of inflation dictated by uncontrolled deficit spending. In short they articulated the very concerns shared and articulated by conservatives in Congress." Said Weyrich, "It nearly blew my mind. I've never heard anyone in the New Right movement talk as harshly about environmental laws as these guys."

BIG FEATURE STORIES ON THE NEW RIGHT RAN THAT WINTER IN THE *Wall Street Journal*, the *New York Times*, the *Washington Star*, and the *National Journal*. Richard Viguerie was quoted claiming possession of the names and addresses of five million "right-of-center people," and "as many as 20 million others who might respond to a variety of conservative appeals." He insisted his movement was poised to set America's political order of battle on its ear. *National Journal*, however, described them "an anomaly on the political scene . . . that both the press corps and the politicians in Washington are watching—if not yet taking too seriously."

But that might be about to change. What Paul Weyrich called the Achilles' heel of the liberal Democrats—*sex*—was moving to the political forefront.

On January 17 in St. Paul, Minnesota, a thirty-three-year-old Baptist preacher named Richard Angwin announced that 150 volunteers from his group Citizens Alert for Morality, going door to door in subzero weather, had collected more than seven thousand signatures to force an April referendum to repeal the city's three-year-old gay rights ordinance. He explained, "I don't want to live in a community that gives respect to homosexuals." A similar petition succeeded in Wichita, Kansas, after the city council approved a gay rights ordinance by a vote of 3–2. The deciding vote was cast by a councilman who insisted that as a Christian he had no choice. The next day, a Southern transplant pastor named Reverend Ron Adrian announced a petition drive to get a repeal vote on the city's May 9 ballot: "If God spared not Sodom and Gomorrah, what makes us think God will spare our country when it is reaching its nadir of moral degeneracy?" Forty percent of Wichita registered voters signed the petitions. And in Eugene, Oregon, a liberal college town with a strong and visible lesbian community, a coalition of Mormons, Protestant fundamentalists, and blue-collar lumbermen needed only a week to get ten thousand signatures to qualify a vote on the primary ballot on May 23 for repeal of a gay rights ordinance that had been on the books since 1973.

But liberals in these cities were confident. Anita Bryant was becoming a pariah. The Florida Citrus Commission was considering terminating her contract. In a survey of eight hundred teenagers in *Ladies' Home Journal* Anita Bryant won laurels as the woman who had "done the most damage to the world." (The male winner was Adolf Hitler.) Bookings for the anti-gay movement's Joan of Arc fell 70 percent, and even her natural constituency seemed now to find her embarrassing: when she headlined a "rally for decency" in support of a campaign to restore sodomy as a felony in the state of Indiana, the hall was only half-full—but 650 marched against her outside. The Twin Cities' archbishop put out a bold statement of support for St. Paul's gay rights ordinance that went about as far as, or perhaps even further than, Catholic doctrine allowed. "The attitude of the community is much better up here," a confident local gay rights leader explained. "They wouldn't dare take our rights away."

ALTHOUGH, IF THIS CRUSADE FADED, THERE WAS ALWAYS ANOTHER DISCON-tent for right-wingers to organize over the next hill. Ronald Reagan had an idea what it should be. "Talk of property tax revolt continues to simmer just about anywhere that inflation-swollen assessments are the rule—and that's just about everywhere," he wrote in a column released January 24.

"But, California is the place where the revolt is coming to a boil. It should reach that temperature June 6, the date of the Golden State's primary election."

California's post–World War II economic boom had increased home values astronomically. In Los Angeles, Reagan pointed out, "bungalows that were built for about $20,000 three and four decades ago are being snapped up at a quarter-of-a-million dollars today." Property taxes, consequently, were increasing five times faster than inflation. Again and again, legislators in Sacramento had tried to devise fixes, always coming up short. Several times, a tax-obsessed seventy-four-year-old eccentric named Howard Jarvis circulated petitions to try to get a referendum on the statewide ballot for a constitutional amendment to cap property taxes at 1 percent of a home's assessed value, ban reassessments until a property changed hands, and require a two-thirds vote of the people for any future state or municipal tax. He called it "The People's Initiative to Limit Property Taxation"—and this time, it hadn't just qualified for the ballot, it had shattered the state's petition-signature record with 1.2 million. "If the Jarvis proposals pass in California," Reagan promised, "watch the prairie fire sweep to all points on the compass."

Experienced hands had reason to dismiss that prediction. It wasn't hard to buy an initiative onto the ballot in California with paid signature gatherers. In 1973, Governor Reagan had sponsored a tax limitation initiative which failed spectacularly. And in 1976, five tax-limitation initiatives had failed nationwide, including the Michigan one championed by Milton Friedman. Then there was the matter of this crotchety old coot Howard Jarvis himself.

One journalist described the former farmer, miner, semiprofessional boxer, baseball player, Herbert Hoover press agent, newspaper publisher, real estate developer, and gadget manufacturer as "something from a page of Horatio Alger with an assist from Mel Brooks' Two-Thousand-Year-Old Man." Add in Don Quixote, and that about covered the waterfront. Jarvis's failed anti-tax crusades—like one to repeal the "un-American and illegal" income tax—dated to 1962, when he ran for Senate on the ticket of his own self-devised Conservative Party. He received 0.2 percent of the vote. When he subsequently began filing futile lawsuits to ban Communist Party members from running for office, a civil liberties activist said in a memo, "Nobody here takes Jarvis seriously. . . . He hasn't even succeeded in getting acceptance among the right-wing organizations."

In 1966 he tried a countywide tax strike; in 1967, an initiative to ban property taxes (it received a fifth of the required signatures); in 1968 and 1972, initiatives restricting property tax revenue to merely paying for police and fire protection. All failed. He had joined the National Tax Limi-

tation Committee's recent efforts to enshrine a top tax rate of 25 percent
into the U.S. Constitution. That was going nowhere fast, too. In 1977, he
ran in the Los Angeles Republican mayoral primary on a platform that included the elimination of garbage pickup. He came in a distant third. Jarvis
was undeterred. "I'm going to stay in this tax thing," he said, "until I win
or I die."

He was more successful as a political grifter. First in 1964 "for" Barry
Goldwater, then in 1976 "for" S. I. Hayakawa, he set up unauthorized
fund-raising committees but pocketed the cash himself—which hardly inspired trust from his fellow activists. He was also a near-permanent fixture
at meetings of the Los Angeles Board of Supervisors, whom he harangued
so vociferously they took to cutting off his microphone. (He would just
keep on bellowing.) One journalist likened him to an "angry Muppet."
Another said his face looked like a "California mudslide." Not the sort of
rock upon which sturdy political churches were built.

Now, however, finally, he had gotten something onto the statewide ballot for the June primary. It would be listed as Proposition 13. But in a January poll, only 30 percent of Californians said they planned to vote for it.

ON FEBRUARY 1, THE WHITE HOUSE FIREPLACE WAS LIT FOR A TELEVISED
chat on the Panama Canal treaties, which the public now favored, barely,
45 percent to 42 percent—a margin that swelled to 57–39 among citizens
who were well informed about them. So, calmly and with a palpable seriousness of purpose—in a suit this time, not a cardigan sweater—Jimmy
Carter partook to inform the rest.

He said the opposing arguments were "based on misunderstanding and
misinformation." He promised passage would transform Panama "from
a passive and sometimes deeply resentful bystander into an active and interested partner whose vital interests would be served by a well-operated
canal," causing anti-American sentiment to abate. He said the treaties'
rejection "would strengthen our competitors and adversaries in this hemisphere"—and might inspire sabotage of the Panama Canal that would
require "a large number of American troops" to stop. (He, added, sternly,
that if that became the case, "I would not hesitate to deploy whatever
armed forces are necessary.") He concluded by claiming that Theodore
Roosevelt would have joined Americans "in our pride for being a great
and generous people, with the national strength and wisdom to do what is
right for us and what is fair to others."

His hope was that a bestirred citizenry would flood their senators with
pro-treaty communications. They did not. "I don't think he had much
impact outside of Washington, and probably none in Washington." Barry
Goldwater, once a faint hope as a supporter, scowled. "I've heard many

fireside chats by many presidents, and I have never listened to one so completely filled with misinterpretations, lack of honesty, and lack of candor as the one I listened to tonight." Senator Ted Kennedy was even harsher: "I don't know why President Carter can't level with the American people and tell them the truth about the defense of the Panama Canal and how many taxpayers' dollars these treaties would cost them." Paul Laxalt said ratification was "up for grabs." Which meant, perhaps, that the success of Jimmy Carter's presidency was up for grabs, too. Win, and he banked momentum for future, grander, initiatives, like a Mideast peace deal. Lose, and his cupboard of political capital would be bare.

Three days of Senate debate opened on February 8—broadcast live on National Public Radio, which was unprecedented. Cameras would not be allowed in Congress for another year. The word on the street was that Carter had forty-eight sure votes out of the sixty-seven he needed. Or fifty-eight. Or thirty-one—with every nose-counter claiming a different collection of senators for, against, and undecided.

Debate opened with an objection from James Allen of Alabama, the master obstructionist, to the presiding officer's call to expedite debate on the Panama Canal treaty via voice vote. He thus successfully forced every vote on every amendment—of which Senator Allen promised "dozens"—to be recorded. It was the first time a treaty had been debated in this laborious way in fifty years—and would produce a useful record for right-wingers seeking to end pro-treaty senators' careers via direct mail to home-state voters.

Minority Leader Baker had appeared on TV across Tennessee the previous evening, promising he would not vote for the pacts unless they were amended to codify America's right to defend the canal, and for its warships to go to the head of the line in any military conflict. He repeated that stipulation in his opening statement, which was made, uncharacteristically, from the back of the room: Baker had swapped his desk in the front of the chamber with that of Laxalt, the floor manager for the anti-treaties side, to "calm tempers and passions a bit."

It didn't work.

Laxalt proved so aggressive that Senator Frank Church of Idaho, managing the debate for the Carter side, was forced to interrupt one of his interruptions: "I *do* have the floor." Senator Laxalt interrupted him again.

Church's Nevadan colleague first ascribed the treaties' defects to Communist chicanery, then to the bankers on Wall Street; then back and forth between the two several times. Which was it, Church demanded, the bankers or the Communists?

"I believe it is both."

"How can it be both? The two interests conflict!"

America's ambassador to Panama William Jorden called the right-wing senators' speeches an "unremitting trickle of poison." Senator Church said they had him feeling he was living inside *Alice's Adventures in Wonderland*. General Torrijos was listening to the debates on a radio. Until he smashed it to the ground.

RONALD REAGAN WAS GRANTED TIME THAT NIGHT ON CBS TO DELIVER A half-hour response to Carter's fireside chat, on behalf of anti-treaty forces. He repeated his well-practiced arguments to his biggest audience yet, with a conclusion that was particularly stirring: "Greatness can be measured in many ways. Carrying out our responsibilities as a nation is one of them. ... We have shown in recent years that we can get weary of shouldering our burdens. But if not us, then who? The Panama Canal is vital to the free world, and that world depends on us!" He borrowed his favorite line from a famous speech by Franklin Delano Roosevelt—"it's part of our rendezvous with destiny"—and added a melodramatic fillip: "We must not shrink from it, for the ultimate price we pay may one day be our own freedom."

The next morning Senator Byrd of West Virginia acknowledged there was no political upside in voting for the treaties; "I know what my constituents are saying. But I have a responsibility not only to follow them but to inform them and lead them"—otherwise senators could just be replaced by a set of scales, weighing constituent mail. "I owe them not only my industry but my judgement. That's why they send me here." He began a historical exegesis of the original 1903 treaty, pointing out that it was not signed by any Panamanian citizen—

Laxalt interrupted: "The treaty was ratified by the people and federal government!"

"As if it were with a pistol at its temple!" the majority leader shot back.

By the third day, Senator Church had grown so disgusted with Laxalt that he implored him to imagine what *he* would do if "there was a strip of land ten miles wide and forty miles long in Nevada, occupied by a foreign power, controlled by foreign military forces, and any Nevadan who went in there was subject to the jurisdiction of that foreign power, could be arrested, could be tried, could be jailed? What would happen in Nevada?"

The gentleman from Nevada responded with a joke: "The people of my state feel that that is their condition now, since 87 percent of the land is in the federal government, which *we* consider to be a foreign power."

It made for gripping listening on National Public Radio. But as usual in legislative debates, the partisans were not where the action was. The real power belonged to the fence-sitters. The fence-sitter who seized *this* moment was a freshman Democrat from Arizona who had barely snuck into the Senate following the vicious 1976 primary in which John Conlan opposed his Jewish opponent with the slogan "A vote for Conlan is a vote for Christianity." After his Arizona colleague Barry Goldwater decided against the treaties, Dennis DeConcini was denied any political cover for voting with his president—and in conservative Arizona, moderation in pursuit of diplomatic virtue was a political vice.

So it was that DeConcini stood up and moved for a "reservation" stipulating that, should the canal be closed or its operations interfered with, "the United States of America and the Republic of Panama shall each independently have the right to take such steps as each deems necessary, in accordance with its constitutional processes, including the use of military force in the Republic of Panama."

These words—which would give the United States the right to *invade* Panama—became the drama's time bomb. The success of Jimmy Carter's first term might depend on whether it could be defused.

CHAPTER 12

In Which the President of the United States Is Said to Have Nearly Killed an Indian

ACCORDING TO AN ASSOCIATED PRESS REPORT PUBLISHED ON FEBRUARY 10, a certain Chief Redbird, age seventy-eight, rendered voiceless by cancer of the larynx, had sent Jimmy Carter an elaborate Cherokee headdress in honor of his election. The White House, citing Carter's policy of not accepting gifts, returned it. The dejected man's son-in-law complained, "This bonnet isn't a gift. . . . It's a symbolic headdress to the nation's chosen leader." Chief Redbird bestowed them upon presidents-elect going back to Woodrow Wilson. "Thinking about presenting the bonnet to the president is keeping him alive. . . . It's his will to live."

The bad publicity inaugurated a season of bad luck for the White House. On February 12, the mine workers rejected a tentative agreement in the coal strike. West Virginia ordered a 10 percent reduction in power supplies to industry; Indiana's governor called out the National Guard to protect coal convoys; factories started laying workers off for lack of fuel. Tongsun Park, the principal in the Koreagate scandal, testified to House and Senate investigators about the nearly $1 million he had funneled to congressmen, mostly Democratic, on behalf of the Korean Central Intelligence Agency. Republican legislators had pressed him, so far unsuccessfully, for information that might implicate the White House. The president dipped down to 47 percent in Gallup's next approval soundings.

Reporters peppered him aggressively at his next press conference: on his failure to take command of the coal situation; on the wisdom on his proposed sale of F-15s to Saudi Arabia, which one journalist described as selling "sophisticated weapons of war with the argument that they would help bring about peace"—and, in a new development, whether he would fire a certain Republican United States attorney.

Newsmen were following the post-Watergate principal: where there was smoke, look for fire. The smoke was the removal of a United States attorney in Philadelphia, David Marston, for unexplained reasons, but after it emerged that Marston was investigating two Democratic congressmen. Allegedly one of those congressmen had called the White House to demand Marston's ouster, and Carter had encouraged Attorney General Griffin Bell to "hurry up" and replace him. Though not technically illegal, a commitment to "appoint and retain attorneys solely on merit" had been part of the 1976 Democratic platform. Attempting to explain, Carter caught himself up in a swirl of contradictions. Safire pounced; *Doonesbury* mocked; Ronald Reagan suggested it was Jimmy Carter's Watergate: "If there was a 'smoking gun' in the David Marston affair, the Carter administration seems to be hoping no one will find it."

A *Washington Post* gossip columnist reported that Hamilton Jordan, recently divorced, had been rebuffed by a woman at a singles bar and allegedly spat a great gob of cocktail down her dress—an amaretto sour, to be precise. Two months earlier, Jordan had made the papers for allegedly groping the buxom wife of the Egyptian ambassador while saying, "I always wanted to see the pyramids."

The White House at first refused comment on the drink-spitting report. Then it released not just a comment but an entire elaborate dossier, reconstructing the evidence down to the minute, in an attempt to debunk it. William Safire responded, "When a woman, who refuses to be identified, claims a White House aide spewed a drink down her back at a swinging bar—that's not news. But when the White House press secretary, whose office did not return a reporter's call for comment before the gossip item appeared, issued an 8,000-word, 33-page collection of documents to refute the charge—that's news." Amateur hour, agreed Reagan: "At a time when the Senate was in debate over the Panama Canal treaties, the Cuban foreign legion was galloping across Ethiopia, the Russians were trying to best us in SALT negotiations, and Congress was wrestling with another budget-busting deficit, we were treated to the spectacle of a White House lawyer taking down a 24-page statement from the bartender."

Reagan twisted the knife: True or not, "the story raised the question of whether Jordan's effectiveness in his job had been compromised. When they said that about Bert Lance it was the beginning of the end."

THE ABORTION ISSUE GREW NASTIER. IN CLEVELAND, A CLINIC EMPLOYEE opened the door to a visitor, who rushed in, blinded a technician by throwing an agent of chemical warfare into his face, then set the place on fire. Fifteen people barely escaped with their lives. Nine days later, there was another attack, in Akron; shortly thereafter, board members of a clinic in St. Paul received threats that their children would be kidnapped and that the director would be killed. It was the seventh clinic in twenty months shut down or moved because of terrorist attacks.

An ABC News segment opened with the camera zooming in on a

listing in the Cincinnati phone book reading, "Abortion, Birth Control & Pregnancy Testing Clinic." The private home of the pro-life activist where that phone number rang was shown next. A woman who had called it said that her parents and parish priest were subsequently informed she was seeking an abortion. Another woman, her identity obscured, said that after reaching out to the "clinic," she received a call from a stranger informing her that abortion caused nervous breakdowns.

The National Organization for Women invited pro-life activists to a "peaceful dialogue." "Although we know our respective positions on abortion itself will not change," NOW's president Eleanor Smeal said, "We believe it is time for both sides to seek ways to lessen the need for abortion, to reduce the incidence of unwanted and troubled pregnancies, and to end the increasing polarization and violence that surround the issue." The March for Life's leader Nellie Gray, whose motto was "no exceptions, no compromises," refused in a blistering five-page letter: "I view this as fiddling while the babies are being killed, and, of course, I shall not participate in such fiddling." No meeting took place.

The White House just wished this polarizing issue would go away. When Carter's secretary of health, education, and welfare, Joseph Califano, met with the Senate Appropriations Committee to review his department's budget, all the committee wanted to talk about was abortion. Califano, a pro-life Catholic, was "visibly nervous," the *New York Times* reported, "like a man walking on eggshells."

THE BOARDROOM JACOBINS GREW MORE RUTHLESS. PRESENTLY, THEIR TARget was the chairman of Carter's Federal Trade Commission, Mike Pertschuk. They had watched nervously as the onetime backwater sparked to life under President Nixon, then grew much stronger with "Magnuson-Moss"—the 1975 law introduced by Senator Magnuson, when he was Pertschuk's boss, and Senator Moss of Utah, whom Jesse Helms subsequently defeated, authorizing the agency to issue wide-ranging regulations covering entire industries, instead of, as was previously the case, rulings covering only one company. Each "rule-making" process under Magnuson-Moss was a monumental endeavor, requiring years of research and thousands of pages of testimony. By 1978 Ralph Nader's old friend and ally Pertschuk was riding herd on more than seventeen of them, with at least a dozen more in prospect.

One would require used car dealers to inspect vehicles for sale and paste the results on a car window, to serve as binding warranties once the cars were sold. Another would end the ban the professional association of optometrists enforced against members posting prices in advertisements, a price-fixing technique. Others sought to check shady vendors of hearing aids, door-to-door encyclopedia salesmen, appliance labeling, vocational schools, undertakers, life insurance grifts, and shifty gas station lotteries.

Pertschuk was politically shrewd, thanks to his years working within the bowels of Congress. He was also imaginative and aggressive; he wished to extend the agency's mandate even further. His staff was considering the problem of regulating advertising that deceived viewers through "sensory experience," not just words, in ads for products like alcohol or cigarettes that relied on emotional appeals—cowboys smoking in front of a campfire, looking hale, hearty, and healthy; silhouettes of naked women faintly outlined in the ice cube in a tumbler of Scotch. Pertschuk was also committed to fighting monopolies more stalwartly. As every Economics 101 student knows, a monopoly is when a single corporation abuses its market power to push out competitors. Since 1972, however, FTC lawyers had been developing an expansion of this principle: "shared monopoly," where several companies collectively maintained high prices without direct collusion. Under that novel doctrine, Pertschuk was pursuing a suit against Kellogg's, General Mills, and General Foods—the source of Ronald Reagan's favorite anti-regulation one-liner that liberals had gone so far off the rails they insisted "a housewife can't buy a box of breakfast cereal without being cheated unless there's a government agency there to protect her."

Then, in November of 1977, in a speech to the advocacy group Action for Children's Television, Pertschuk unveiled his farthest-reaching initiative, the most important one he hoped to stake his legacy on: a process for regulating advertising of unhealthy foods on children's television. "The commercial exploitation of children is repugnant to a civilized society," he said. "It may be that only a ban on advertising of these products on programs directed toward the young child can help remedy their inherent defect."

He had discussed the idea at his first hearing before the Senate Appropriations Committee following his confirmation—then received a letter from the senators avowing that the panel "shares the commission's growing concern about the effects of advertising on children," and hoped "sufficient funds can be made available from fiscal year 1977 resources to implement a viable program in this critical field." Privately, Senator Ernest "Fritz" Hollings of South Carolina assured Pertschuk they meant it. He had no reason to believe he didn't have a solid issue on his hands. The issue the media soon enshrined with the shorthand "kidvid" seemed a winner every which way.

Legally, protecting children from commercial exploitation had been a core jurisprudential principle going all the way back to the Code of Hammurabi. The public health research said tooth decay from sugared cereal was epidemic. Constitutionally, experts agreed that the First Amendment did not protect *deceptive* speech (which was why the FTC had been able to ban commercials starring men in white coats with stethoscopes around their necks unless they specified that the actors were not actually doctors). Behavioral science supported Pertschuk's initiative, too. Scholars had established that preschoolers, who watched on average twenty thousand commercial television ads a year, believed the figures they saw on TV—like the cartoon character who introduced himself, "Hi, I'm Tony the Tiger, and I love you. I'm your friend, and I want you to eat Sugar Frosted Flakes because I want you to grow up to be big and strong like me"—lived *inside* the set. Who could disagree that this was a deceptive commercial transaction?

And if Anita Bryant had proven anything in Miami the previous summer, it was that protecting children from predation was a *political* winner. Giant corporations exploiting children's demands for instant gratification, usurping parental authority to decide what their children should eat— what politician would go to bat against *that*?

Pertschuk boasted to Ralph Nader that he had discovered his Chevy Corvair. Nader strenuously disagreed. He said the issue would not galvanize the public—and that "if you take on the advertisers you'll end up with so many regulators with their bones bleached in the desert." Pertschuk pressed ahead.

PERTSCHUK HAD BEEN ENJOYING SWIFT, SMOOTH PROGRESS ON SEVERAL structural measures to strengthen the FTC's power to protect consumers. The first would allow class action suits for redress of violations of FTC rulings. The second provided for what lawyers called "equitable relief": the power to petition courts to put companies that the FTC had fined into receivership, so they could not intentionally "dissipate their assets" to avoid paying. No one had objected much in friendly appropriations hearings in both houses on the FTC's 1978 budget request. The full Senate advanced the appropriations bill with little debate.

In the full House, however, things got sticky. Equitable relief and class action powers were stripped out by overwhelming votes. Then a conservative Republican from North Carolina named James Broyhill, scion of a furniture manufacturing fortune, introduced an amendment to give the House of Representatives the right to review any FTC rule before it went into effect and veto it if they disapproved. This so-called "legislative veto" would have been unprecedented for any regulatory agency. A newspaper editorial compared it to "the small-town practice of clearing police investigations through the mayor's office."

The People's House, you might say, was just doing what the People's House was designed to do: responding to its most organized constituents. "Every little bitty town in America has a funeral director," a lobbyist explained. Also car dealers. And life insurance agents. And optometrists. Who began sending their congressmen letters. "When a Congressman gets a letter from his local optometrist that's John Q. Businessman. That's different. That's heartland stuff. And the Congressman knows when he gets a letter like that that means something. That guy almost never sits down to take pen to paper. But he must be awfully frustrated when he goes to that step."

Class action powers and equitable relief nonetheless survived a Senate-House conference committee. The legislative veto was removed after scrupulous members of the upper chamber insisted it was unconstitutional. The Senate approved the conference committee report by voice vote. The Chamber of Commerce endorsed the result. The House vote on the report was scheduled for the end of February 1978, and Pertschuk's legislative aide, Nancy Chasen, said that she was confident of success. Then on February 8, Congress killed the consumer bill—the vote that had a representative marveling that a proposal to abolish the U.S. government probably would have passed. The subsequent House FTC debate on whether to approve the conference report was a bloodbath—"just unbelievable," Chasen reported back to Pertschuk. "What you don't see in the Congressional Record is that the Republicans were stamping their feet and yelling and cheering. It was a circus."

A young first-term Democrat named Ted Risenhoover spoke first: "As I travel across my district in Oklahoma the cry most commonly heard is for Congress to bridle the bureaucracy. The most effective control would be to have review and veto over the rules and regulations which are imposed daily upon the people of this representative democracy by a bunch of faceless, nameless bureaucrats. And of all the agencies which are running amok the Federal Trade Commission is the worst example. The latest example is a 346-page report by the staff of the FTC concerning television advertising of certain products containing sugar. . . . TV already has enough troubles with the FCC—but now it is facing a new intrusion by these bureaucratic dictators. . . . I urge my colleagues to stand up strongly and state our feelings—and the views of a vast majority of Americans—on this key issue affecting one of the most dangerous agencies of government."

The second speaker, Elliott Levitas, was also a first-termer, elected to fill the Georgia seat vacated by United Nations ambassador Andrew Young. He wondered why commissioners "not elected by anybody" had the right to seize "from the American people this operation of government by the consent of the governed." He *also* singled out "new regulation coming forward which will prohibit advertising for certain foods. . . . Why should we deny the American people, who elect us to this body, the option to have some say about their lives?"

And so it went, one congressman after another, Democrat and Republican, vituperating the FTC with strikingly similar words—"overzealous staff people," "running amok" ("millions of them," a Republican claimed) in order to "to regulate virtually every aspect of America's commercial life"—with kidvid as their prime example. Elliott Levitas, meanwhile, always seemed to have his arm around somebody, whispering, as if coaching them. Then the conference report was voted down 255 votes to 146, an even greater defeat than the consumer agency vote three weeks earlier— "an extraordinary margin," an observer noted, "for a bill that you planned to win and the other side thinks he's going to lose."

The next morning's *Washington Post* ran an editorial flaying kidvid as "a preposterous intervention that would turn the agency into a great national nanny . . . designed to protect children from the weakness of their parents—and the parents from the wailing insistence of their children. That, traditionally, is one of the roles of a governess—if you could afford one. It is not the proper role of the government." In other words, it took what Pertschuk thought was the proposal's political *strength*—it upheld the prerogatives of parents *against* the power of corporations—and boomeranged it against him. That resonant phrase "national nanny" soon began appearing everywhere, describing not just the kidvid proceedings but everything the FTC was up to. Perplexed, Pertschuk started asking plugged-in Washington figures what the hell had happened. A public opinion expert said, "You hit the money nerve." A rainmaking lawyer agreed: "You woke the sleeping giant."

Pertschuk soon learned precisely what that meant. An anti-kidvid ad hoc campaign had been organized by a coalition of thirty-two trade associations and businesses, on the same model as the one against the consumer bill. It was coordinated by Washington super-lobbyist Tommy Boggs, son of the late House majority leader Hale Boggs, who commanded a war chest estimated from a low of $15 million to a high of $30 million. (The entire annual budget of the Federal Trade Commission for the year was only a little more than twice that.)

Elliott Levitas was Boggs's floor leader. He subsequently reaped nice rewards—like a check in the maximum amount allowed by law from the American Dental Political Action Committee. James Broyhill, who'd introduced the one-house veto, got the same donation from the same group. The dentists hoped to gut the FTC because it was going after their prohibition on member advertising—like the optometrists' rules against advertising prices. All told, they showered $614,526 on congressional candidates in the upcoming election cycle; previously, they had never donated a cent.

ON FEBRUARY 28, THE SENATE WAS ENGAGED IN YET ANOTHER DRONING SESsion debating the Panama Canal, the same pro and con arguments in endless loop, so numbing that Mark Hatfield of Oregon began dozing off—until he heard his colleague Thomas McIntyre of New Hampshire swelling to an angry crescendo—". . . the campaign waged against ratification in my state and across the nation has impugned the loyalty and the motives of too many honorable Americans to be ignored or suffered in silence a minute longer. . . ."

Hatfield perked up.

The Oregonian was a liberal Republican. Since 1964 he'd been haunted by the hisses and boos from Goldwaterites responding to a speech he gave keynoting that year's Republican National Convention, on a platform amendment he'd thought would be uncontroversial—a condemnation of extremism from all sides of the political spectrum. Subsequently, he led congressional opposition to the Vietnam War—and began noticing something disturbing: hate mail questioned whether he was really a Christian at all. In 1976, he had been blackballed from participating in Bill Bright and John Conlan's efforts to organize evangelicals in Washington because of his supposed ideological heresies. By 1977, the number of conservatives articulating a desire to "destroy anyone seen as the enemy" had begun to seem to him an epidemic. Now a colleague was finally decrying it, in terms far blunter than customary in the Senate. Hatfield was riveted.

Thundered McIntyre, "The techniques used to exploit the issue of the canal treaties are the most compelling evidence to date that an ominous change is taking place in the very character and direction of American politics. I see abundant evidence everywhere that dangerously passionate certainties are being cynically fomented, manipulated, and targeted in ways that threaten the amity, unity, and purposeful course of government in order to advance a radical ideology that is alien to the mainstream of political thought." Conservatives were indulging a "blind and obsessive" illusion: a belief that those disagreeing with them—even on matters that were plainly controversial—could only be explained by "something sinister in our motivation," that their own positions were "so unassailable they justify any means, however coarse and brutish, of imposing them on others."

McIntyre didn't mention his reelection opponent, the airline pilot Gordon Humphrey, who had announced his Senate campaign two days earlier. Instead he singled out the "loutish primitivism" and "politics of threat and vengeance" of William Loeb and Meldrim Thomson: the two most powerful political voices in his state, who together had the power to break him—but "my political fate is not my concern here today. My concern is the desperate need of people of conscience and good will to face down the bully boys of the radical right before the politics of intimidation does to *America*, what it has *tried* to do in New Hampshire."

It wasn't only the right that was the problem, McIntyre wished to emphasize: he had felt the same way about Vietnam War protesters lying down in the halls of the Senate. He longed, he said, for the glorious spirit of bipartisan consensus he had witnessed during the nation's Bicentennial celebrations, and at Hubert Humphrey's funeral. So he concluded with a challenge to his colleagues:

"If you want to see the reputations of decent people sullied, stand aside and be silent.

"If you want to see people of dignity, integrity, and self-respect refuse to seek public office for fear of what might be conjured or dredged up to attack them or their families, stand aside and be silent. . . .

"If you want to see dissent crushed and expression stifled, stand aside and be silent.

"If you want to see the fevered exploitation of a handful of highly emotional issues distract the nation from problems of great consequence, stand aside and be silent.

"If you want to see your government deadlocked by rigid intransigence, stand aside and be silent.

"If you want this nation held up to worldwide scorn and ridicule because of the outrageous statements and bizarre beliefs of its leaders, stand aside and be silent and let the Howard Phillipses, the Meldrim Thomsons, and the William Loebs speak for all of us."

Spontaneously, Senator Hatfield asked for recognition from the chair. "I have seldom received letters that spew forth such a venom of hatred as I have received from within this group now called the Radical Right who so violently oppose the Panama Canal treaties," he said. He read from them aloud: of his supposed affection for "kike bankers"; about his patriotism ("You are not an American"); on the state of his immortal soul ("I *thought* you were a born-again Christian"). Hatfield marveled, "They chose to make a judgment on my religious salvation on the basis of my position regarding the Panama Canal treaty!"

Newspapers in Boston, San Francisco, Hartford, St. Louis, and Chicago all reprinted large chunks of McIntyre's speech. The *Washington Post* ran it in full under the headline "A Profile in Granite." Even conservative colleagues praised it. (Though Orrin Hatch peevishly added, "I've seen a lot more one-philosophy rule from the old left, which I think is killing the country, than I've ever seen from the New Right," singling out the followers of Ralph Nader.) When an undecided Republican, John Danforth of Missouri, broke for the treaties in response to McIntyre's speech, political handicappers wondered whether it wasn't a straw in the wind—as if someone had finally said something many were thinking but feared to utter aloud.

Governor Thomson was unbowed. He gave a keynote address at a John Birch Society regional meeting in Los Angeles, wondering "why we Americans allow the foreign born," like Henry Kissinger and Zbigniew Brzezinski, to "draw us into the maelstrom of world communism," and cried, "Every senator up for reelection who fails to vote against the treaties must be swept from office as though he were a Benedict Arnold."

McIntyre's mailbox overflowed; supporters outnumbered detractors by a ratio of 3 to 2. Three years ago, he had given another heated speech against extremism, dismayed that George Wallace was contemplating a fourth run for the presidency. He noticed a telling difference between then and now, however: "In 1975, a great many letter writers did not sign their names; in 1978, nearly all did. Clearly, the intervening years had seen a rapid growth in the confidence and assertiveness of these people."

SENATOR MCINTYRE HAD THRUST THE NEW RIGHT BEFORE THE NATION'S attention just as the *New York Times*, the *Chicago Tribune*, AP, and UPI sent reporters to Rockford, Illinois, to report astonishing news: John Bayard Anderson, the chairman of the House Republican Conference running for his tenth term in Congress, known affectionately in his hometown as "John B.," was fighting for his political life.

John B.'s dilemma had begun the previous summer, during House debate over funding for the federally funded Legal Assistance Corporation. Larry McDonald, a John Birch Society stalwart, offered a surprise amendment barring funds for lawsuits concerning "homosexual or gay rights." It was rejected on a voice vote amid hearty cackles of laughter.

Then, however, McDonald demanded a roll call.

"Abruptly," the AP reported, "the mood turned sour. One rural Midwestern congressman who asked not to be identified later admitted he quietly ducked the roll call. 'In my district, I couldn't vote right and I certainly wasn't going to vote wrong, so I just took a walk.'"

Not so John B. His brave *nay*, and long record of similarly liberal apostasies, soon yielded the proud, cerebral, eloquent, and intensely principled Republican what the AP termed a "mail-order political nightmare." Constituents began receiving stinging letters about the supposedly Christian congressman who doled out food stamps to coal strikers, foreign aid to corrupt Third World potentates, and free legal help to "homosexual activists," when he wasn't rendering honest citizens prostrate before murderous thugs via gun control. The letters then introduced voters to his primary challenger: Don Lyon, a right-wing minister who ran a minor Illinois evangelical Christian empire.

John Anderson was an evangelical, too, and once had been quite pushy about it. Upon entering the House of Representatives in 1961, then in 1963 and 1965, he introduced a constitutional amendment to "recognize the law and authority of Jesus Christ." In 1966, he opposed the failed civil rights bill banning housing discrimination. Then, however, in 1968, after reading the report of the National Commission on Civil Disorders, with its searing warning that America was fast becoming "two societies, one black, one white—separate and unequal," he helped save a similar bill from oblivion. In 1970 he said the Vietnam War was "the most tragic error in diplomacy and military policy in our nation's history."

He had begun a long journey to the left. The question was whether his hometown cared to travel with him. In Rockford, it was said that you could tell how close it was to election time by the length of John B.'s hair: it got shorter and shorter. Not short enough this year, apparently. Just look at the extraordinary head of steam his opponent was building up. The Reverend Don Lyon's pews held two thousand congregants. For sixteen years he had hosted a Sunday evening TV broadcast called *Quest for Life*. He operated an FM station with eighty-five employees, a ten-story apartment building for senior citizens, a fleet of buses, a K–12 Christian school with 250 students, a daycare center, and a seminary. And now, he had an estimated $250,000 earned via Viguerie's solid gold mailboxes for his underdog campaign.

The *New York Times*' Adam Clymer watched the incumbent speak in Ronald Reagan's hometown of Dixon, Illinois. "Mr. Anderson sounded more like the preacher than his opponent," he wrote, "striving to convince a Rotary audience that foreign aid promotes international stability or that the Panama Canal treaties 'befit us as a great nation.'" Then at a small-town nursing home Clymer heard Reverend Lyon, who scowled and said that the Equal Rights Amendment only "helps the lesbian, the homosexual."

Anderson persuaded Jerry Ford and Henry Kissinger to come to town to campaign. That, however, played into Lyon's campaign strategy. The independent-minded, hardworking, and eloquent Anderson was always showing up in the national prints. So every time a Washington bigwig praised Anderson, Lyon could foreground how distant he had supposedly become from Winnebago County. That cleverly framed the erstwhile local hero as the cat's-paw of out-of-town elites. Though actually that description better described Reverend Lyon—for this strategy had been devised by the best minds of the New Right, who had picked *this* particular race for the shrewdest of reasons: it would be an earthquake if the New Right managed to fell a Washington media darling. What's more, reporters had been parachuting into Illinois's 16th Congressional District for decades, reading it as a Middle American bellwether for the rest of the nation. Finally, Illinois's congressional primary was early, on March 21. So even just singeing John Anderson would serve as an early warning for other Republicans: follow him to the left, and you might be sacrificed, too.

The New Rightists might be zealots. But they were far from stupid. By the middle of March, Washington buzzed with the talk of the preacher fighting the third-ranking House Republican nearly to a draw.

Washington buzzed, too, with news from across the Potomac, and across the party aisle: the Virginia *Democratic* Party was being thrown into disarray by the surprising surge of a Norfolk automobile dealer and city council member named G. Conoly Phillips after he announced that, after days of prayer and fasting, and despite his wish to remain a "private person," the Lord had called him to vie for the Senate, as he explained to the *Washington Post*, "as a ministry" to call "Christians to active political participation."

Conventional wisdom concerning the New Right began shifting. In the *Post*, a reporter named T. R. Reid had begun a monumental series of dispatches, "Running: A Political Serial," that ended up comprising twenty-four articles, most appearing on the front page, on the race to fill the U.S. House seat from Illinois's sprawling, rural 22nd District following the surprise retirement of a veteran Democratic congressman. Three early installments focused on the man Reid judged the Republicans' shoo-in, Gene Stunkel, a local magnate funding his own race who had a life story, Reid wrote, "like a Horatio Alger tale," sold to great effect via slick television commercials produced by Gerald Ford's 1976 media advisor John Deardourff and running in saturation rotation. Another candidate, a powerful state legislator named Roscoe Cunningham, ran on his deep party contacts and good old-fashioned ward-heeling. Reid reported that he was the favorite of the political professionals. The Republican running a distant third Reid at first barely mentioned at all.

Daniel Crane could "be called conservative," he wrote on February 6, "but that description cannot do justice to the breathtaking scope of governmental change that Dan Crane would like to see in the United States." Gently mocking his family's greatest claim to fame—his physician father's conservative advice column—Reid observed, "For nearly every societal ill, Crane has the same prescription: 'Get the government off of our backs.'" On February 26 he wrote, "Through the intercession of his brother, Rep.

Philip M. Crane, Dan Crane has also gained the support of two conserva-
tive congressmen, Steven Symms and Mickey Edwards," of Idaho and
Oklahoma—then deadpanned, "Neither claims a following of any size in
Southern Illinois."

Reid deployed two fashionable explanations for why a candidate like
Crane was irrelevant. The first, associated with Jimmy Carter's guru Pat
Caddell, was that voters didn't care about ideology. Reid depicted Stunkel
poring over a briefing from his pollster, responding with knowing sophistication, "Everybody in Washington is flapping his lip about the Panama
Canal, right? Big deal. We asked 300 people about national problems, and
you know how many mentioned the Panama Canal? Four of 'em. You
think I'm going to waste my breath on the Panama Canal?"

The second explanation, associated with House Speaker Tip O'Neill,
was that all politics was local. Here, Reid quoted the Democrats' front-
runner, a promising young state senator named Terry Bruce, explaining
confidently how the race would be decided on "how you shake the hand,"
and "whether you got them a deer permit."

Dan Crane was awful at shaking hands. ("Campaigning—that's a
drag," he told Reid.) Hardly the deer-permit type, he preferred flapping
his lip about Panama, for he was an unapologetic ideologue. "When our
forefathers came to this country 200 years ago they had a revolutionary
idea of creating a government of the people, but what's happened is the
government bureaucracy has become the master," he intoned—when he
wasn't repeating chestnuts from the right's store of tribal lore, like the one
about all the government money wasted on some study about bumble-
bees' sex lives.

But heading into the homestretch, the man from the *Post* suddenly
had to reconsider these fashionable nostrums when the ideologue pulled
ahead.

Reid's article two days before the primary described the reason why:
direct mail. "On his brother's behalf," he reported, "Phil Crane last month
sent out 70,000 letters nationwide to veterans of Ronald Reagan's 1976
presidential campaign. That solicitation brought thousands of dollars
back." He tracked down one of the donors, "Ellen Garwood, a cheerful
grandmother from Austin, Texas, who knew Phil Crane from the Reagan
drive. . . . She had never heard of the candidate before, and wasn't exactly
sure where the 22nd District was, but all that was secondary." She sent a
$250 check "the minute she received Phil Crane's letter." The next day,
Reid reported that Crane had deluged a carefully targeted group of voters
with more than a quarter million pieces of mail. He also noted a new factor emerging in the year's congressional contests, so novel it sat between
quotation marks: "By last week the Crane campaign boasted contribu-

tions from 'political action committees'" which had elevated Crane's campaign budget to $60,000—a considerable amount, if hardly a match for Stunkel's $100,000.

Two days later on Tuesday, March 21, 22nd District Republicans gave Dennis Stunkel only 18 percent of the vote. The party regular, Cunningham, got 36. That made Dan Crane, with 46 percent, the winner in a landslide. Further upstate, John Anderson squeaked by with 53 percent and had to raise $250,000 to do it. He had never spent more than $40,000 on a campaign before. The word in Washington was that the only reason he prevailed was that many Democrats and Independents registered as Republicans to keep him in office. The New Right had arrived. Heading into the home stretch of the Panama Canal debate, Washington took note.

CHAPTER 13

Capital Gains

THE FIRST PANAMA VOTE WAS ON THE AGREEMENT PROVIDING FOR THE CA-nal's neutrality and joint defense. If it received sixty-seven votes, debate on the second treaty, authorizing the actual transfer on January 1, 2000, would begin.

Pennies rained on Capitol Hill—after a Conservative Caucus mailing imploring recipients to send one-cent pieces to senators to remind them of the patriot's response to a 1797 demand to the U.S. government for protection money to stop plundering American ships: "Millions for defense, but not one cent for tribute." It included an oath to direct to their senators to sign and return: "I pledge allegiance to the United States of America. I pledge never to cast my vote for any elected official who supports the surrender of U.S. sovereign jurisdiction." Iowa's liberal senator John Culver received 4,958 anti-treaty messages in a single week. Phil Crane published a paperback called *Surrender in Panama* with an upside-down American flag on the cover and a preface by Ronald Reagan. The American Conservative Union distributed a hundred thousand copies. The American Legion recorded a cassette tape starring Senator Orrin Hatch, distributed by Richard Viguerie's magazine *Conservative Digest*. In New Hampshire, Governor Thomson declared an official "Keep Our Canal Day," directing his constituents to drive with their headlights on—Granite Staters as Diogenes, mourning the lack of honest men in Washington. When few followed, Thomson blamed environmentalists for obsessing people with energy conservation.

United Mine Workers members voted to reject a proposed strike settlement, despite a TV commercial blanketing coal country in which Johnny Paycheck, composer of the hit country song "Take This Job and Shove It," implored his "coal miner buddies" to accept the settlement. President Carter handed down a Taft-Hartley injunction to force them back to work, which the UMW ignored, without consequence. And senators on the fence over Panama took advantage of Carter's evident weakness. Even though White House legislative liaison Frank Moore counted only fifty-nine sure votes, he advised the president, "No overt offers to trade for a vote on Panama should be made. The press has been on the lookout for these 'deals.'" Carter chose not to listen. Henry Bellmon, Republican of Oklahoma, extorted a desalinization plant. Democrat Spark Matsunaga of Hawaii received favorable consideration on sugar legislation. S. I. Hayakawa got economic help for logging communities. The problem was that when one request was fulfilled, an aide lamented, "they'd come back with another." Then, senators ran to the press to brag about their success. The *New York Times* front page reported two days before the vote, "Last week, the White House reversed itself and supported a plan to have the government buy $250 million worth of copper for the nation's strategy stockpile." That was at the request of Senator Dennis DeConcini of Arizona, who promptly displayed his ingratitude: "I made it clear that if this had anything to do with the Panama Canal treaties, forget it. It doesn't move me at all."

Gerald Ford, Henry Kissinger, and the Joint Chiefs of Staff all made phone calls; Secretary of State Cyrus Vance spent entire days on Capitol Hill; the first lady contacted senatorial wives. The president implored Saudi Arabia to help cement Senator Abourezk, an Arab-American, Mormon elders to nail down Howard Cannon of Utah, and even read a book on semantics by Senator Hayakawa, a linguist, to flatter him into support. Progress was glancing, and, for a politician who hated logrolling, excruciating.

One day, he was forced to take time out to speak with a gentleman named Randy Coleman, best friend and business partner of his wastrel baby brother. Billy Carter made the gossip columns day after day doing things like hawking his own brand of "Billy Beer," guesting on the corn-pone syndicated TV show *Hee Haw*, feuding with sister Ruth and her friend the pornographer and born-again Christian Larry Flynt, doing belly flops for news cameras, and fleecing Plains, Georgia, tourists. Now the embarrassments grew more serious: congressmen asked the attorney general to name an independent prosecutor to investigate whether Billy had taken advantage of his brother's name to receive an "unwarranted and highly advantageous fuel allocation" for his two-pump gas station in Plains during the 1973 oil crisis. So it was that the Leader of the Free World squeezed in a call between meetings on Panama with Mr. Coleman for a briefing on what the *Chicago Tribune* had christened as "Billygate." "This has to be one of the worst days of my political life," he confided to his diary. The next day might have been worse.

At 9:10 a.m., he took a short meeting with Senator DeConcini, who delivered an ultimatum: he would support the neutrality treaty if the president would support his reservation allowing America to unilaterally use military force. America's ambassador to Panama advised Carter to refuse, that the DeConcini reservation would cause Torrijos to scotch the deal. Undersecretary of State Warren Christopher advised the opposite.

Panama's ambassador to the U.S. said the DeConcini reservation violated both the UN and Organization of American States charters. Senator Frank Church agreed with the Panamanians—"100 percent."

The president decided he had no choice but tactical retreat. He hoped, after granting DeConcini his tantrum, that he could convince him to abandon the reservation in time for the second treaty vote in April. The White House press room spun the decision with an elegant falsehood: "The president emphasized that in our view the reservations are in keeping with the principles and spirit of the treaties." The president did not, however, clear it with General Torrijos, who went ballistic.

Though this all would be academic if the next day's vote did not cross the threshold of sixty-seven senators.

THE MORNING THE WORLD WOULD DISCOVER WHETHER FIFTEEN YEARS OF negotiations and the lion's share of President Carter's political capital would be flushed down the drain, an airplane buzzed above Capitol Hill. It trailed an ACU banner informing an exclusive audience of one hundred that it was not too late to save America's honor. President Ford called President Carter to tell him he had won the votes of Republicans Ed Brooke, John Heinz, and Henry Bellmon, which gave him sixty—"if no one changes," Carter wrote in his diary. The anticipation in the packed Senate galleries was near to a roar; Senator Byrd had to bang his gavel again and again.

Then, the same tedious arguments—this time for an interminable thirty minutes per senator.

A team of four bright young men were billeted in a tiny room in Vice President Mondale's Senate suite, surrounded by research materials, listening to NPR's live broadcast, frantically ferrying counterarguments to pro-treaty forces. Senator Church said it was like "re-digging the canal with a teaspoon" for all the effect it had on long-debunked falsehoods.

A specter hung over the proceedings: Vietnam. Conservatives conjured the ghost every time they spoke of losing the canal as a national humiliation and the vote as a test of national virility. Liberals conjured the ghost every time they warned of the cost of defending the canal from the angry locals the Pentagon predicted would rise up if the turnover did not go through—and when they argued that the DeConcini reservation would repeat the moral soiling of the nation in the 1960s in Southeast Asia, and make America colonialists again. They argued to no avail. The DeConcini reservation passed with seventy-five votes. Handily, it provided fence-sitting Democrats cover: they could vote for the treaty, pleasing their president, but could hardly be blamed if the DeConcini reservation *sank* the treaty by spurring Torrijos to withdraw—for the president himself had endorsed the reservation.

Then came the vote on ratification. Paul Laxalt spied his Nevada colleague Howard Cannon, a member of the Democratic leadership, who he had assumed was on his side, given that Nevadans polled overwhelmingly against the treaties and Cannon was up for reelection. Cannon greeted Laxalt by asking, "How are you doing?"—and Laxalt knew that he had lost him. If he was with them, he would have asked, "How are *we* doing?"

Senator Byrd spoke last. He declaimed Shakespeare—"There is a tide in the affairs of men, which taken at the flood, leads on to fortune"—and pleaded that "nothing can be politically right if it is morally wrong." Vice President Mondale ordered the well of the Senate cleared for the vote, a rarely observed formality. The roll was called. Senators observed another rare formality, voting immediately when their names were called—mostly. For when it was time to hear from Jennings Randolph, Democrat of West Virginia, he sat silent, hands folded in his lap. He was up for reelection. He hoped he would not be forced to sabotage his chances by voting with his president. Then Gaylord Nelson of Wisconsin cast the sixty-seventh vote for passage. The clerk once more called on Randolph, whose vote was no longer needed, and he cried out a joyous, clarion "No!"

A half hour later Jimmy Carter took the podium in the White House press room, no less joyous, and said he was "confident the Senate will show the same courage and foresight" in a month. To his diary, he confided the truth: "The vote on the second treaty is going to be even more difficult."

A Gallup Poll came out. The president's approval rating was up four points to 51 percent, the first increase since December—though after the same amount of time in office John F. Kennedy's had been 78 percent, Lyndon Johnson's 68 percent, and Richard Nixon's 56 percent. And his good fortune did not last. Bert Lance was charged with crimes by the Securities and Exchange Commission for exploiting his relationship with the president to win a deal with a Saudi Arabian sheik. Menachem Begin traveled to Washington for a meeting with the president that turned sour: a faction of militants from the Palestinian Liberation Organization had attacked a town on the Israeli coast, killing thirty-six; four days later, Israel retaliated by obliterating the attackers' villages in Lebanon, killing one thousand and destroying the homes of tens of thousands more—and Carter was livid. The two men, after disagreeing on every point, emerged unsmiling for the cameras. "At this historic moment," Carter remarked coldly, "peace seems far away."

AT THE CONSERVATIVE POLITICAL ACTION CONFERENCE IN WASHINGTON the day of the vote, Senator Laxalt had told lurid tales of White House arm-twisting on Panama before heading up to Capitol Hill for the debate; then the delegates listened to the final roll call on NPR in the hotel ballroom, booing when Minority Leader Baker cast his aye. Ronald Reagan spoke following the vote. He said the treaties proved that Carter's human rights policy was a fraud: "They have ceaselessly scolded authoritarian governments of countries that are friendly and ignored authoritarian countries that are not." In his next newspaper column, he passed on the claim of a former Panamanian intelligence agent that Torrijo's Guardia Nacional constituted "a mob of racketeers involved in the drug trade, prostitution, gambling, and shakedowns that can only be compared with the Mafia." (The following year, the agent claimed this was a falsehood he had been paid $6,000 by Senator Paul Laxalt's brother John, who was the Washington director of Citizens for the Republic and an associate of Richard Viguerie, to spread. Both denied this.)

Given that several Republicans from the moderate wing, including Minority Leader Baker, had, by voting for the treaties, sided with the people the right wing smeared as Mafiosi, a reasonable observer might conclude that this was not a party at peace. In fact, when RNC Chairman Brock noted shortly before that vote, "We are more unified than I have seen the Republican Party in fifteen years," he was likely quite sincere. A reason for the miracle was taxes—specifically something called the "Steiger Amendment," which had moderates and conservatives joined at the hip.

Congressman William Steiger was a Republican from Oshkosh, Wisconsin, elected to the House in 1966 at twenty-eight years of age, when he looked so young, he was often mistaken for a page. He sponsored the legislation creating OSHA, was an avid environmentalist, and championed legal services for the poor. Pundits admired his eloquent idealism. So on March 22, 1978, when Steiger—not some reactionary, or money-grubbing corporate shill—introduced to the pending tax legislation an amendment to lower the tax rate on capital gains almost by half, Capitol Hill paid serious attention. Not least because another eloquent Republican idealist, John Anderson, was a cosponsor.

This was a surprising development. Capital gains had been taxed at a lower rate than ordinary income since the 1920s. The rationale was that this encouraged job-creating investments. Then, in 1969 a liberal Congress rejected that argument outright, raising the rate to 49 percent as part of the most liberal tax reform since the introduction of the federal income tax—which was blessed with President Nixon's signature. But any affluent person with a half-decent accountant could still easily get his or her capital gains burden down to 16 percent. Which was why, seven years later, Gerald Ford signed a law before the TV cameras just prior to Election Day to close still more loopholes (among them, as it happened, one involving phony losses on investments in cattle that Ronald Reagan had used to pay little or no federal income tax in 1970).

This was how the politics of taxation had worked since the days of Franklin Roosevelt: politicians sought favor with ordinary voters, especially right before elections, by soaking the rich. Yet here was a congressional liberal, a supporter of those 1969 and 1976 reforms, proposing to lower from 49 percent to 25 percent the rate for a tax paid almost exclusively by the rich—even as the share of the tax burden borne by corporations had fallen almost by half since 1960, from 23 to 14.1 percent. What was going on?

Steiger had heard a convincing macroeconomic argument. A former aide of his worked for an organization called the American Council for Capital Formation. On March 7, he dropped by his old boss's office, accompanied by a lobbyist for the American Electronics Association named Edward Zschau, who argued that the higher capital gains rate was decimating the burgeoning computer industry in Northern California's "Silicon Valley," and that radically lowering it would reverse the sclerosis not just in his industry but *all* industries. America's economic reversals since the 1974 recession, he argued, were largely caused by taxes eating up potential investment capital. Zschau even presented data suggesting that the federal treasury would not be starved by this tax cut but *enriched*—because the economic dynamism unleashed by ending the "capital shortage" would create so much more capital gains to be taxed.

The theory, if true, suggested a solution for an agonizing economic mystery. Labor productivity—average output per worker—had grown by an average of around 3 percent annually in the 1950s and 1960s, but since 1973, for reasons unknown, it had plunged to an average of 1.7 percent. When productivity increased, more goods could be purchased for lower prices, wages could be hiked without inflation, and more money became available for investment, whether for factories, roads, or the social safety net: a virtuous circle. When productivity stalled, economics became a nasty zero-sum game. Which looked a whole lot like America now. The prospect of reversing the calamity with a single small jigger in the tax code—almost like magic—tantalized Steiger.

It also tantalized Ronald Reagan. In a column released on March 23 he posed a riddle: "What creates jobs, increases U.S. exports, boasts tax revenues and expands technology all at the same time but is an endangered species?" The answer was venture capital, each $100 of which, he claimed, yielded an average of $70 in export sales, $33 in research and development, $15 in federal corporate income taxes, $15 in state and local taxes, and $15 in federal personal income taxes. And yet, he rued, this "golden goose" was being strangled in its crib by the U.S. Treasury, all out of a misplaced concern with "fairness."

Walter Wriston, the conservative chairman of Citibank, said this argument was based in a statistical illusion. He pointed out that interest rates were tracking inflation, which meant that the effective cost of borrowing money was close to zero, proving that there was no unmet demand for capital. Be that as it may, in April, a week and a half into the House Ways and Means Committee's markup on Carter's tax bill, Chairman Al Ullman was stunned to learn that nearly half of his committee supported the Steiger amendment—including several liberal Democrats.

Ullman complained that they had been "gotten to by several key industries in their districts." And indeed, the newly energized corporate coalition kept successfully throwing its weight around. Democratic members defied party leadership to kill the president's proposal for public funding for congressional campaigns. "The main reason for the vote," the *New York Times* explained bluntly, "was the strong feeling in the House that public financing could hurt some incumbent Democrats and some Republican challengers. In certain races, both groups can depend heavily on private campaign funds donated by special interests." Said Speaker O'Neill, "I worry about this Congress, if the PACs keep going crazy like this."

IN NEW HAMPSHIRE, GOVERNOR MELDRIM THOMSON ORDERED STATE FLAGS flown at half-mast on Good Friday in honor of the death of Jesus Christ— until a 5–4 United States Supreme Court decision hauled them back up. He lowered them again two weeks later to protest the possible loss of the Panama Canal. Which you could laugh at. Except, in the middle of it all, the *New York Times* reported that thanks to Thomson's unstinting opposition to taxes, experts predicted he would be reelected to a fourth term in November.

In Albany, the New York Assembly approved a death penalty bill 94–51, just shy of the two-thirds needed to override an expected veto from Governor Carey. And in Virginia, Conoly Phillips, the car dealer running for Senate at God's command, was piling up so many committed delegates for the June nominating convention that his establishment opponents— one the former chairman of a county board of supervisors, another the former state attorney general—were running scared.

The *Washington Post* reported that when Conoly announced his candidacy "there was, shall we say, some tittering. . . . They aren't laughing anymore." Most of his activists had never before been involved in politics; some had never voted. An Air Force major explained that he had resigned his commission "to join the campaign because the Lord called me to the ministry." A liberal Presbyterian minister responded by claiming Conoly's "superiority concept, that he has a 100 percent pure pipeline to God, has parallels to the rise of Nazism." He called him a "religious fanatic." Philips responded, "I'm not a religious fanatic. The Lord is very practical."

The Lord was also, that spring, proving industrious. Pat Robertson announced that by the fall of 1978 he would go on the air with a fourth national network, with forty hours of programming a week, a news division headed by a former *News York Times* editor, and a staff of two hundred — to fight back, he said, against "bias centered in the Washington/New York axis." The previous September, Robertson had begun beaming programming to sixty-nine U.S. television markets, with a special broadcast from five continents via a brand-new state-of-the-art satellite, culminating in a segment from the Mount of Olives in Jerusalem, the site of Jesus's expected second coming. He was now the largest syndicator of satellite-transmitted programming in the country. He also boasted four TV stations overseas. A $20 million Christian Broadcasting Network complex was under construction, which would also include a "CBN University" where a freshman class of two hundred would study in a 170,000-square-foot colonial-style building in the shape of a cross. "It's a big job," Robertson told *Christianity Today*. "It's like David taking on Goliath. But I think the time is now, and the project is economically viable."

The *Washington Post* reported that a new study found 28 percent of the public watched religious broadcasting, compared to 12 percent in 1963. "As the reach and power of religious broadcasting has become increasingly apparent, critics have charged that Robertson and colleagues such as Jim Bakker, host of TV's *PTL Club* (for 'Praise the Lord' and 'People that Love') too often overstep the FCC-drawn line between religion and politics." They reported that the April edition of the Virginian's monthly newsletter, *Pat Robertson's Perspectives*, called the president "honest and decent but unsuited for his task," and noted his work against gay rights, his suggestion that "the plight of blacks in Rhodesia may not be as bad as some have said," and his lobbying on behalf of Israel, "whose integrity he feels must be maintained if prophetic scriptures are to be fulfilled."

The *Jerusalem Post* reported that Menachem Begin's election had "triggered a distinct movement among American conservatives, away from the traditional backing of the Arabs to increasing support of Israel." Jerry Falwell traveled there as Begin's guest, on an itinerary that included an illegal West Bank settlement. Upon his return, he complained, "In recent years, there have been incidents at the very highest level that would indicate that America is wavering at this time in her position on the side of Israel. I believe that if we fail to protect Israel, we will cease to be important to God. For the Christian, political involvement on this issue is not only a right, but a responsibility. We can and must be involved in guiding America towards a biblical position regarding her stand on Israel." He submitted a report to President Carter, and felt wounded when it was paid no attention. The next year, Begin's government gave Falwell the gift of a Lear jet.

In Tulsa, Oral Roberts, a TV preacher who claimed an ability to heal physical ailments through faith, was on the verge of receiving state approval for a 294-bed hospital on the grounds of his own Oral Roberts University. Oklahoma's Health Systems Agency had twice rejected the application because it fell afoul of federal guidelines on duplication of services. Then, some four hundred thousand complaints from Roberts's viewers changed their minds. The preacher said that proved God's power "to move mountains."

In Minneapolis, the National Association of Evangelicals convention adopted a position paper, grounded in the same scriptural passage Jimmy Carter invoked at his inauguration ("do justice, love kindness, and walk humbly with thy God"), calling for a balanced federal budget and capping federal spending at a fixed percentage of the gross domestic product—citing as their scriptural authority Ford treasury secretary William Simon's scouring new jeremiad against the depredations of liberalism, *A Time for Truth*, with forwards by F. A. Hayek and Milton Friedman.

The NBC radio network refused to carry an episode of a program from the most conservative Lutheran synod because they judged its sermon opposing abortion too political. *Human Events* urged "every fair-minded citizen to inundate NBC radio (30 Rockefeller Plaza, New York, New York 10020) and the Federal Communications Commission (1919 M St., NW, Washington, D.C. 20554) with letters of protest, objecting to this flagrant example of elitist media censorship." CBS television, however, ran a hard-hitting special from Bill Moyers in which the former Baptist preacher proclaimed, "The opponents of abortion are asking—they're demanding—that a secular and pluralist society fix into law a certain moral opinion not shared by the community as a whole." He called the pro-life movement a fundamental threat to America's "two-hundred-year-old tradition of tolerance, which recognizes that in a society of conflicting religious convictions, the state, through its politicians, should not choose between them." Which was quite a contrast to what Dr. Mildred Jefferson said in a widely published interview with the UPI newspaper syndicate. She called abortion a "public health menace" that "should be treated as such by all responsible agencies," suggested that the spate of recent clinic bombs were the work of rival abortionists fighting for customers, and concluded, "We are going to push our crusade until we have won. We will not rest." Moyers called his special *The Issue That Will Not Go Away*. That was a pretty good bet.

NEITHER WOULD THE ERA DEBATE.

ACTION, the federal agency that included the Peace Corps, canceled a conference in Georgia because it hadn't ratified the ERA. Rosalynn

Carter hosted a White House reception for ERA supporters on Susan B. Anthony's birthday. The White House endorsed Bella Abzug's run to regain her House seat, and engineered a pro-ERA resolution at the National Governors Association convention. And in a heartwarming ceremony on March 22—one year before the deadline set in 1972 for ratification— Carter officially accepted *The Spirit of Houston*, the volume formalizing recommendations of the national women's conference, and announced both a National Advisory Committee for Women and an Interdepartmental Task Force for Women.

The National Organization for Women's Eleanor Smeal promised a new ERA campaign, including an economic boycott of non-ratifying states. In one of those states, Missouri, the young attorney general, John Ashcroft, filed suit against NOW for violating antitrust law. Nevada sued NOW as well.

The Illinois League of Women Voters held a pro-ERA lobbying day at the capitol in Springfield. The group's president was in the middle of her speech, braving heckles from Phyllis Schlafly's minions, when a STOP ERA reverend from Rockford began dancing in front of the podium in a gorilla suit waving a sign reading "Don't monkey with the Constitution." Then, at *their* podium, Schlafly announced that *Playboy* magazine had donated $5,000 to ERA organizing, the reverend in the gorilla suit presented her with a ceremonial banana, and Schlafly broke into song:

> *Here comes Playboy cottontail*
> *Hopping down the bunny trail*
> *Trying to buy the votes for ERA*
> *Telling every girl and boy*
> *You can only have your joy*
> *By becoming gender-free or gay.*

The cameras ate it up. Which was one reason, analyst William Schneider observed, that politicians had absorbed the mistaken impression that public opinion was swinging against the ERA. In fact, a large majority continued to favor it, with only 34 percent opposed.

AS THE SECOND PANAMA VOTE APPROACHED, TREATY SUPPORTERS GOT more and more letters like these: "Quisling Traitor Senator McIntyre: Conservative Republicans have added your despicable name to the list of TRAITORS in our stench-producing Senate dominated by those on the Radical Left and representing your ilk."

Fence-sitters got calls from the president, who took time out in between stops on a historic trip to South America and Africa—a symbol of America's renewed respect for the Third World, which he wished the Canal turnover to betoken. In Venezuela, he laid a wreath at Simon Bolívar's tomb and addressed the crowd on "the affection and respect due to the Liberator" and his "confidence in the success of our struggle for the dignity of man and the well-being of peoples in the Americas and through-out the world"—in Spanish, the first time a president had addressed a host country in a non-English native language. In Brazil, he spoke the words "human rights" sixteen times at his opening press conference—a sharp rebuke to a host government that habitually violated them. He became the first U.S. president to step foot in sub-Saharan Africa, where the images were gorgeous, inspiring: Amy Carter, now ten, bounding hand in hand with a little African girl down a busy Nigerian market street, sunshine in red-and-white gingham; Liberian and American flags waving side by side as representatives of both countries beamed; the president arm in arm with the seventy-ninth world leader he had met so far, a record, then being pre-sented a ceremonial bowl of cola nuts and rice by each of Liberia's tribal leaders—flashing that million-watt smile made so famous on the campaign trail. In his diary, he reflected on how in Caracas in 1959 Vice President Nixon had been set upon by a mob, and how Henry Kissinger had been banned from visiting Nigeria. "I hope the time of the 'Ugly American' is over, and from the reception we received, apparently this is true. I never saw a critical poster or banner or gesture among the hundreds of thou-sands of people along the highways and in the crowds during this entire trip."

Back home, citizens were less welcoming.

ON APRIL 6 HUNDREDS OF REPUBLICAN DONORS PAID FROM $500 TO $1,000 each to put on black tie for an annual GOP fundraising ritual: speak-ers from across the fruited plain were projected simultaneously on giant screens, one city's speakers relaying into the next. This year the bill of fare was filet mignon and Jimmy Carter.

Dwight D. Eisenhower's son David denounced "the most hopeless administration in history." The dinner chairman thanked Bert Lance for working for "the revitalization of the Republican Party." The first of six potential GOP presidential hopefuls, John Connally of Texas, speaking from Los Angeles, joked that at a reception Tongsun Park held for Demo-crats at the Korean embassy there'd been "an express line for anyone tak-ing $10,000 or less." Among those sharing hearty laughs was a resplendent Elizabeth Taylor, who accompanied her husband, John Warner, the former Navy secretary running for the Senate from Virginia.

Gerald Ford suggested he had no intention of retiring from politics: "The quality and experience of *any* Republican candidate"—he listed six, including himself—"surpasses unquestionably the leadership we currently have." Then, breaking Washington protocol, a former president laced into the patriotism of the current one, threatening "the safety of Western Europe and the preservation of Western culture" with his decision to spike development of the neutron bomb, a high-powered radiological weapon that killed people while still leaving infrastructure intact.

Howard Baker, speaking from Houston, said that Carter's decision meant the Soviets would eat Paul Warnke's lunch in strategic arms negotiations. Bob Dole said the same of Carter's decision to halt development of the B-1 bomber. From the Palmer House Hotel in downtown Chicago, George Herbert Walker Bush—an obscure enough figure that the *New York Times* had to identify him for readers as "the former Director of Central Intelligence"—held Carter responsible for "relentless inflation."

Though as usual Ronald Reagan said it better:

"Presidents, when in trouble, travel," he said, also from Chicago. "Someplace between a nightclub in Rio and the Ivory Coast, we who stayed home learned from the news wires that the dollar had nosedived again. Pretty soon it will be cheaper to eat money than to try and buy food with it."

He had written the speech himself, in longhand. It hammered Carter for presiding over the twenty-first month in a row of trade deficits, and for a tax package "taking from the productive to give to the unproductive"— that slur ignored a pending welfare reform proposal Carter had also advanced, which included a Reagan-type component requiring welfare recipients to seek work or lose benefits—"but not reducing the overall percentage of money government is taking from the private sector." He called Carter's Social Security reform the "second largest tax increase in history." He contrasted these to the "Republican-sponsored tax cut that is part of a program to stimulate investments, expand industry, and create jobs."

Republicans as the party of Hollywood glamor, Democrats as the party of scandal; Republicans bragging about their deep bench, mocking Democrats concerning their flailing figure in the Oval Office—this was promising terrain, especially since, twelve months earlier, Republicans had been supposed to be going the way of the Whigs.

And their conservative faction was supposed to have been their albatross. But now it was a *right-wing* idea—business tax cuts as the royal road to economic growth—that was winning over bipartisan converts.

Ronald Reagan had been prophesying for years that if Republicans would only raise "a banner of no pastels, but bold colors which make it unmistakably clear where we stand on all the issues troubling the people," Democrats and Independents would flock beneath it. It became easier now to entertain the idea he might be right, that it was Reagan, as the *Chicago Tribune* reported from the Palmer House—not the five other, more moderate aspirants—who was "now considered the head of the pack for the 1980 nomination."

He ended with the sort of starry-eyed peroration that was his trademark: The Democrats "would have us believe that the days of growth and expansion in our land are a thing of the past," and that "we must devote ourselves to a more equal sharing of what we have and accept a diminished standard of living. They preach a philosophy of resignation and despair; the sharing of scarcity instead of the creation of plenty. They have lost faith in the system handed to us by our fathers—they have lost faith in us.

"It is time for us to raise our voices; to proclaim to Democrats, Independents, and, yes, to fellow Republicans that we believe the future of America is as limitless as it was when our grandfathers and their fathers before them spread out across this land, plowing, planting, building cities and towns and a network of roads to connect them.

"If someone is going to tell newly arrived ethnic immigrants, our fellow Americans in the minority communities, and our own sons and daughters that America is now a place of no growth and limited opportunity—let it be the Democrat leadership. Republicans don't believe it nor do the American people."

Their president, however, was in a sour mood. A meeting between his HEW secretary, Senator Kennedy, and union leaders to plan the way forward for a Carter's long-delayed national health insurance proposals had turned contentious. He complained about a bill approaching passage giving him immediate power to appoint 150 new federal judges, a prospect "I certainly don't want. . . . In this four-year term I will have appointed more than half the total federal judges in the United States." The possibility of placing his stamp on the federal judiciary for generations to come would have made other presidents salivate. Carter considered it an ordeal. Then there was the tax package—an ordeal by anyone's lights.

The people wanted tax cuts. But according to the conventional wisdom since the days of John Maynard Keynes, tax cuts could cause inflation by overheating the economy. But now, all was confusion on the subject—because economists were no longer sure *what* a tax cut would do to the economy. A decade earlier, the confidence of experts about government's ability to control economic fluctuations had been staggering. "We have learned at last to manage a modern economy to ensure its continual growth," as Richard Nixon matter-of-factly proclaimed in his 1969 inauguration speech. Then, like Icarus flying too close to the sun, that confidence tumbled to earth: economists now seemed to have no idea about *what* caused what. Under the once-regnant theory, the fiscal formula had been easy: if prices started rising too fast, you slowed down the economy, for instance via an interest rate hike, and all would be peaches and cream. If growth looked to be cooling, you heated it up, with a tax cut or "countercyclical spending" or both. Inflation and economic growth were believed to be inversely proportional—definitionally so. Then, in 1974, inflation and unemployment *simultaneously* grew. Faced with what had been understood as an ontological impossibility—"stagflation," stagnant growth *and* inflation—economists found themselves bereft of conceptual tools to fight back. Now, in 1978, it was happening again: inflation was approaching 8 percent, and growth projections for 1979 were below 3 percent.

When Carter designed his original tax package, with the economy relatively stable, concerns about growth and inflation hadn't been salient. The package was "fiscally neutral"—taking in the same amount of new revenue via new levies and loophole-closing as it gave out in cuts. Then, with the specter of a slowing economy, the plan was rejiggered to offer $25 billion more in tax cuts to stimulate consumption, just as the old Keynesian formula demanded. But now Federal Reserve Chairman William Miller was warning Carter that greater budget deficits would accelerate inflation and advising him to delay until January the tax cuts he had wished to go into effect in October. However, Charles Schultze, chairman of the White House Council of Economic Advisors, counseled precisely the opposite. Business was divided, too: industrialists who needed free-spending customers wanted individual tax cuts, but bankers and bondholders did not.

Only 32 percent of Americans said they approved of Carter's economic policies. But what to do about it?

Reporters expected answers when Carter delivered a major address to hundreds of the nation's newspaper editors at their annual convention on April 11. He began with a laundry list of reforms to keep inflation in check: a freeze on the pay of executive branch appointees, renegotiation of federal procurement contracts, a promise to veto farm legislation if it looked to increase food prices. He asked Congress to pass his airline deregulation bill to lower the cost of plane tickets (it did so mainly by abolishing the board that sought to guarantee carriers covered all parts of the country, even the less profitable ones), to review the inflationary effect of all pending legislation, and pass a hospital cost containment bill. In a move that must have delighted boardroom Jacobins, he promised to "cut the inflationary costs which private industry bears as a result of government regulations." He also asked both labor unions and corporations, as a "sacrifice for the common good," to hold price and wage increases to less than the average of the increase over the previous two years.

Then came something curious: Carter blamed the *American people* for inflation—for not finding a way to "forget our differences and rally to the defense of the common good."

"I am asking American workers to follow the example of federal work-ers and accept a lower rate of wage increase."

Then he did something remarkable, he began *scolding* Americans. "We want something to be done about our problems—except when the solutions affect us. We want to conserve energy, but not change wasteful habits. We favor sacrifice, as long as others go first. We want to abolish tax loopholes—unless it is *our* loopholes. We denounce special interests, except our own." He quoted Walter Lippmann in 1940, "as the nation prepared for the challenge of war": "You took the good things for granted. Now you must earn them again. It is written: For every right you cherish, you have a duty which you must fulfill. For every hope that you entertain, you have a task that you must perform. For every good that you wish could happen . . . you will have to sacrifice your comfort and ease. There is nothing for nothing any longer."

Act like the nation was at war. *Sacrifice*—a word Americans certainly never heard from Carter on the campaign trail in 1976. With a Democratic president speaking this way, a fellow like Ronald Reagan insisting that the future of America was as limitless as when our grandfathers first spread out across the continent must have sounded pretty darned good.

BUT CARTER HAD ALSO RECENTLY GIVEN AMERICANS SOMETHING TO FEEL positive about: Presidential Directive 30, formally pronouncing, "It shall be a major objective of U.S. foreign policy to promote the observance of human rights around the world."

But this, for an oil-dependent global hegemon, was more easily said than done. For instance in Iran, which was locked in a forty-day cycle of mourning and massacre. On March 29, rioting militants inspired by a fiery speech from a radical cleric again attacked and burned symbols of the shah's power in broad daylight; that was followed by another SAVAK massacre which killed more than a hundred. It received no sanction from the State Department's new Bureau of Human Rights.

And in Romania. The night after Carter addressed the newspaper editors with his anti-inflation austerity plans, he hosted a state dinner for Nicolae Ceauşescu, one of the world's worst tyrants, whose secret police had just poisoned to death with radiation the leaders of a miners strike. But Romania, like Iran, was a major oil producer; and was also Carter's go-between to North Korean dictator Kim Il-Sung, who was seeking to improve relations with the United States and South Korea.

The world was a complicated, dangerous place. Only three weeks earlier, Aldo Moro, the prime minister of Italy, had been kidnapped by Marxist terrorists. His body was discovered in a trunk fifty-five days later. Israel attacked South Lebanon; Cuban forces were on the march in support of Marxist revolutionaries in Ethiopia and Angola and Zaire; Rhodesia's negotiations toward the end of white-minority rule were foundering; strategic arms limitations talks were hanging fire with the Soviets—*ad infinitum.* The most powerful nation in a fallen world needed cooperative partners to manage its interests in that world. That sometimes meant unpleasant compromises—and so, as a caveat in the first paragraph of PD-30 put it, human rights "shall be applied globally, but with due consideration to the cultural, political and historical characteristics of each nation, and to other fundamental U.S. interests with respect to the nation in question."

It was easier to hector from the sidelines—and Ronald Reagan took every opportunity to do so.

He columnized that Carter's policy was actually "the moral equivalent of imperialism": aid was being withheld from strong anti-Communist allies by State Department "ideologues" who "force their views on allies who don't conform to the American Civil Liberties Union's view of things." Carter's hat-in-hand tour of South America and Africa had made America the "laughingstock of the Western world." He complained of the "rich irony of Carter launching a verbal human rights assault on Southern Africa's white governments" while traveling in Nigeria, whose black government was a human rights abuser, too.

Then there was the cornerstone of Carter's human rights agenda, the treaties to turn over the Panama Canal—what the commander of U.S. forces in Latin America called "one of the most magnanimous acts in history by a great power." Reagan said that it was a surrender to mobs and racketeers. And that it "might be a better deal if we could throw in the State Department." The debate grew even *more* heated—when an amendment by Orrin Hatch was voted down that would have required, for the first time in the history of the United States, that the *House of Representatives* also ratify the treaty for it to go into effect.

Then, on April 18, the final showdown commenced on the Senate floor. But the politician besides Jimmy Carter whose future hinged the most on the outcome happened to be out of town.

REAGAN'S HANDLERS HAD BEEN PLANNING THIS ASIAN TOUR FOR OVER A year as a crucial step to establish him as a credible world leader. At a staff meeting eleven months out they worried over every detail: whether accepting the hospitality of the shah would be interpreted as approval of his human rights violations; whether going to Iran but skipping Saudi Arabia would be taken by Riyadh as an insult; whether bringing in Henry Kissinger would hurt them with conservatives; how to discreetly *seek* invitations from world leaders but make it look like the process had been initiated by the leaders; whether to accept free travel from foreign governments. (*No*, it was agreed unanimously.) The Bank of America's executive in charge of Asia provided an economic briefing. Shopping itineraries were worked out for Nancy Reagan. Reagan's scheduled was pared down to nearly nothing for a fortnight of preparation, another block of time following his return reserved to work on fulsome, personalized thank-you notes for every businessman, official, and journalist with whom he met. This was serious business.

Among those accompanying him was a new chief foreign policy advisor. Richard V. Allen had been foreign policy research coordinator in Richard Nixon's 1968 campaign. About to begin work under Henry Kissinger at the National Security Council, he had been subjected to a scathing Evans and Novak column reporting that in 1967 he had won a $25,000 essay contest on the "Role of Business in the Cold War," sponsored by the far-right Orange County owner of the Schick Safety Razor Company, with an entry "studded with praise for the Schick Safety Razor Company." Nineteen days later, Evans and Novak reported that the White House had decided to downgrade the duties of this "far-right pamphleteer": "The gap between Kissinger's sophisticated adult anticommunism and Allen's simplistic vision is a chasm.... Alone among the president-elect's high-level appointments Allen is a member of what more thoughtful conservatives regard as the 'sandbox right.'"

So Allen set up a literal sandbox in his NSC office, with literal engraved invitations for its "grand opening."

A month later, the *Washington Post* reported that he had not been awarded the PhD he claimed from the University of Munich. In 1971, Nixon considered assigning him the task of breaking into the Brookings Institution—then rejected him as not trustworthy enough. In 1975, he was investigated by the Senate for allegedly brokering a $1 million Nixon campaign contribution from the Grumman Corporation, which expected favorable consideration on an aircraft sale to Japan. He testified that "I was out of the loop," which was contradicted by a Grumman executive. The matter was dropped before it could be determined which one was lying. It was also Allen, in 1968, who came up with the idea of recruiting Republican intriguer Anna Chennault to work to sabotage peace talks to end the Vietnam War and increase Richard Nixon's chances of winning the White House.

And now, on April 14, 1978, he was winging his way to Asia in charge of foreign policy for the top prospect for the Republican presidential nomination.

In Taiwan, Reagan delivered a speech before representatives from ninety blue-chip corporations warning that the U.S. would pay a "serious price" if it granted formal diplomatic recognition to Communist China. In Iran, he met with the shah. In Japan he enjoyed audiences with both the prime minister and the leader of his parliamentary opposition, lunch with the chairman of Mitsubishi, and cocktails with the U.S. ambassador.

Then, on his way out of Tokyo, Reagan was besieged by reporters seeking comment on the dramatic news from home.

The Panama vote had gone down to the wire—thanks to the president's mismanagement of the DeConcini situation. Senator Church, Carter's floor manager, had begged his Arizona colleague to abandon it, arguing that Torrijos would tear up the second treaty if it allowed the military onto Panamanian territory whenever America wished. DeConcini answered, "It's not my problem what Panama thinks." As Church predicted, Torrijos labeled the DeConcini reservation "colonialist," and said it could not stand. That put Church in a terrible spot. Carter and DeConcini had put him there. Church was up for reelection in 1980—and he already was receiving hundreds of copies every day of a petition promising his defeat for his role in the "giveaway." Democratic senators had loyally stuck their neck out for their president on Panama—for instance Senator McIntyre, who told his wife the morning of the first vote, "Come on and watch me lose my seat." Then, they received messages like "Whenever you may again be a candidate for office, I will do all I can to defeat you." For senators like these, the president's acceptance of the DeConcini reservation, and Torrijo's apparent rejection of it, put them on record as supporting a treaty that was not only unpopular with their constituents but might *lose*.

Senator James Allen declared an early victory: he said that reassembling the coalition that voted for the first treaty would be "like trying to restore Humpty Dumpty. It can't be done." Then, on Sunday morning, April 16, an extraordinary conclave in Church's office endeavored to put Humpty together again. Two Panamanian diplomats, two State Department officials, and three Democratic senators—Paul Sarbanes of Maryland, Church, and Majority Leader Byrd—crowded around a low coffee table. Byrd plopped forth the treaty text, running a finger down its provisions: "We're in agreement down to *here*"—he looked to the ambassador—"and you want to change the rest?"

The ambassador nodded. Byrd sunk to his knees, scrawling, circling, slashing and un-slashing out words.

"Territorial integrity" had to be in there, the ambassador demanded; the senators insisted "sovereignty" should be enough—it subsumed the same meaning without raising red flags for DeConcini. This the ambassador refused—an impasse, a knife's edge, a teeter-totter, a hinge: history hanging in the balance.

Until someone had the wit to devise the formulation "*sovereign integrity.*"

There was a whispered conferral with a State Department lawyer, who assured them the words had no legal meaning. The seventy-one-old minority leader tried to rise from his crouch; his back kinked. Church massaged it until he could stand. Church made for his typewriter and hacked out the text Ambassador Lewis assured them General Torrijos would find acceptable.

Byrd then took it to DeConcini, who decided it was *not* acceptable, demanding "use of military force" be added.

Byrd locked his forty-year colleague in a stare that said his political future hung in the balance: "It has to be like this, Dennis. I will not accept any changes."

DeConcini surrendered.

But even then, they appeared to be two votes short.

On Monday night the president tried to enjoy a reception for the Country Music Association's twentieth anniversary; he kept getting interrupted for treaty matters—one outstanding concern being how to handle the violence they expected should the treaty vote fail. ABC preempted *Police Story* for a special ruminating on what the next day might reveal. The *New York Times* editorialized that the vote, "coverage notwithstanding, is not about Jimmy Carter's manhood." Among those who disagreed was something called the Committee of Tax-Weary and Concerned Americans, who bought a full page in the *Washington Post*: "President Carter says we have a moral obligation to give away the Canal. . . . Where does the Senate get the 'moral right' to ignore the wishes of the American people?"

Debate began. Senator DeConcini made a face-saving political feint: he pronounced himself "amazed," "puzzled," and "shocked" that his innocent reservation had caused so much consternation, claiming that endangering the treaty had never been his intention. Then, however, he carried out his pledge to Byrd, lending his name to an amendment solemnizing the language agreed to on the majority leader's coffee table.

Ratification passed by a single vote. In Idaho, a voter wrote his senator: "I've prayed night and morning now for many months that He 'the Lord' would strike you dead if you voted to give away our Canal in Panama. I now realize that it is his Wisdom that you should be allowed to live as a traitor and so be known to all men." In Tokyo, Ronald Reagan told reporters the outcome was "a very extreme case of ignoring the sentiment of the people of our country." Although, for his part Weyrich told the press that Reagan "did not overly exert himself after the fight was on," and that he was considering someone else for president.

CHAPTER 14

No One Shoots Santa Claus

THE DAY BEFORE THE FINAL PANAMA CANAL VOTE, AS THE HOUSE WAYS AND Means Committee began marking up Jimmy Carter's tax bill, a study was released from the economics analysis firm Chase Econometrics that some in the media began citing as if it were holy writ. It concerned Representative William Steiger's capital gains tax cut bill.

"Under such legislation, the rate of growth in constant dollar GNP for the period 1980–1985 would average 3.6 percent compared to 3.4 percent annual average growth rate otherwise," *Wall Street Journal*'s "Heard on the Street" column said, citing the study. "That would add 440,000 new jobs, boost spending on plants and equipment by a percentage point, lower corporate debt, decrease net tax revenues to the U.S. treasury only slightly, and lower the budget deficit by $16 billion by 1985." The *Journal* also claimed on Chase Econometrics authority that the stock market's declines in 1969–70 and 1976–77 were due almost exclusively to increases in the capital gains rate, and that its reduction to 25 percent by 1980 "could boost stock prices by 40 percent by 1982."

The *Journal*'s news pages did allow, in its Steiger Amendment assessment—fourteen paragraphs in—that the claim about stock prices, at least, was *controversial*. No such skepticism on the editorial page. Its lead piece on April 26 boasted, "The Carter tax package, already reeling from other setbacks, has been stopped in its tracks by the Steiger amendment," and was entitled "Stupendous Steiger." It was written by a fellow named Jude Wanniski, who went even farther than Chase Econometrics to argue that the dynamism the cut would unleash would actually *increase* tax revenue.

At least, one of that study's critics noted, they weren't claiming the Steiger Amendment would cure dandruff.

It did not concern the *Journal* that the U.S. Treasury said that this all was nonsense; "the Treasury," Wanniski wrote, "insists on using 'static analysis,' which calculates the effect of tax cuts by making the convenient but plainly silly assumption that nothing else in the economy changes as a result of different tax rates. Others work with 'dynamic analysis,' trying to calculate the feedback effects from the rate cuts themselves." He said these economists were "the cutting edge of an important intellectual and financial breakthrough."

Ronald Reagan said that, too—although, as usual when it came to conservative policy ideas, he said it better: that all those old-fashioned economists with their "static analysis" acted as if when "someone gets a tax cut he will bury the money in a tin can in the backyard. . . . The world doesn't work that way. . . . The tax savings pump through the economy, generating growth, new jobs, and thus new sources of revenue for the government."

No matter that respectable economists called "dynamic analysis" so much mumbo jumbo. Newspapers far beyond the ken of the *Wall Street Journal* commentators considered the furthest thing from ideologues, were suddenly filled with claims like these. Louis Rukeyser, a popular TV investment advisor, trumpeted a study commissioned by the Securities Industries Association—undertaken using "the world's largest computerized bank of economic information"—calculating that if *all* capital gains taxes were eliminated it would increase capital investment by $81 billion, boost gross national product by almost $20 billion, and raise $38 billion in new tax revenue. In the *Chicago Tribune*, Richard Nixon's former budget director Caspar Weinberger warned of a "alarming capital shortage" caused by too-high taxes. He complained that all measures to end it were "automatically opposed by the administration and the liberals whose lexicon is, 'If it does not redistribute income to equalize everyone, it is elitist and bad.'" You could read a *Washington Post* article, "Richer Half of U.S. Pays 94 Percent of Income Taxes: Upper-Income Brackets Shouldering Disproportionate Share of the Burden," or "Britain's High Taxes Seen as a Factor in Stagnation" in the *New York Times* on the very same day.

Capitol Hill echoed the message. Anxious talk of a "capital formation crisis" filled the congressional records. The House Ways and Means Committee whittled away at the actual reforms in the president's tax reform package one by one— some of the most active whittlers were Democrats—until it was little more than a bundle of tax cuts. Jimmy Carter fought back with stories like the one about the executive who claimed $10,000 worth of deductions for 338 so-called "business lunches"—"more than many American families make in all." It didn't work. House Ways and Means Committee chairman Al Ullman told Carter that ending the deductibility of business entertainment was dead in the water. A Ways and Mean Democrat told a reporter, "I've never seen the committee in the ten years I've been on it so anti-reform." By the last week in April, the Steiger Amendment had nineteen supporters on the thirty-seven-member committee. Tom Bradley, the black mayor of Los Angeles, testified that a capital gains cut would create a boatload of jobs in his city; the number of Steiger supporters grew to twenty-one, including nine Democrats. The president threatened to veto his own tax bill if the amendment passed. So Ullman postponed debate to approach pro-Steiger Democrats with side deals. He won no reversals. So he postponed the postponement.

The political oddity of all this was suggested by the title atop Caspar Weinberger's editorial. It read, "We Need Tax Policies to Aid Our Economy, Not Win Votes" This encapsulated the decades-old conventional wisdom that the *surest* way to win votes was demagogically raising taxes on rich people. That was certainly how things appeared the last time Congress undertook a major tax reform, in 1969: the Nixon Treasury Department received a record 1,930 letters from citizens, mostly urging the administration to soak the rich, and Ways and Means chairman Wilbur Mills said ignoring that popular tide would cause "complete breakdown in taxpayer morale." Now, however, a Harris Poll found that a majority of those who had an opinion said the taxes the rich paid on investments were too *high*.

And it all was mostly the fruit of a successful propaganda campaign from the nation's boardroom Jacobins, emboldened by their consumer agency victory to pursue yet more ambitious goals.

THE GROUP BEHIND IT WAS CALLED THE AMERICAN COUNCIL FOR CAPITAL Formation, and its staff had begun preparing the ground for some sort of campaign long before Carter's tax package was announced. Then they were shocked when the package turned out to be so much more friendly to business than they had even dared dream. "They were braced for an attack," a Capitol Hill insider observed. When that attack never materialized, he said, marveling at the brazenness, rather than retreat, "they decided to invade!"

The American Council for Capital Formation had commissioned that study from Chase Econometrics—a firm whose principal, *Time* magazine later reported, reached "far-out conclusions" because, his critics charge, he "sometimes cooks the books to come up with results favorable to his clients." It was ACCF that had recruited Mayor Bradley to testify about the wonders of capital gains cuts, Caspar Weinberger to write about the danger of a capital shortage. Then, they compiled press kits to persuade news producers and editors that opinions like these were the obvious expert consensus. It had even been ACCF's idea to recruit the idealistic young Kennedyesque liberal Republican Bill Steiger—rather than some stodgy old conservative—to introduce the capital gains cut.

The genius responsible was one of those behind-the-scenes figures who move history with few outside of Washington ever knowing their names. Charls—no "e"—Walker grew up a poor Texas boy who slept on the front porch because his mother was forced to rent out his room. He served with distinction as a bomber pilot in World War II, worked his way through the University of Texas, then earned a doctorate in economics at the University of Pennsylvania's Wharton School of Finance while simultaneously working at the Federal Reserve. He was hired as an assistant to Dwight D. Eisenhower's treasury secretary, Robert Anderson, a fellow Texan. When the Democrats took the Oval Office, he left public service to become chief lobbyist for the American Bankers Association; when the White House changed parties again, he became Richard's Nixon's deputy treasury secretary. It was only after deciding he would never achieve his dream of becoming treasury secretary *himself* that he spun through the revolving door one final time, forming a lobbyist firm serving the likes of General Motors, Gulf Oil, Alcoa, and several major airlines—"a few mom-and-pop clients," he liked to say.

Charls Walker was folksy like that. "I'm from Possum Kingdom," he liked to say to introduce himself—and that was where his Texas vacation home was, on the lake where he landed his amphibious plane. He was glad-handing and jovial, a master at bipartisan bonhomie, close friends with Capitol Hill's maestro of the tax code, Senator Russell Long, a Democrat, and godfather to the son of James Schlesinger, a Republican; they named a salad after him at the D.C. expense-account restaurant the Sans Souci. A phone seemed permanently glued to his ear; he even had one in his car. Still he somehow managed to radiate cornpone charm—precisely the sort of image Bert Lance had tried but failed to cultivate.

In 1975, the *Washington Post* called him a lobbying "wunderkind": he was pioneering that dark art's cutting edge. Walker excelled in explaining arcane fiscal issues in the vernacular (when he did so in op-ed columns, he made sure he was identified as a former treasury official, never as a lobbyist for the concern that commissioned the piece). He pioneered the labor-intensive trick, used to such great effect in the consumer bill fight, of shuttling constituent businessmen to congressional offices armed with statistics projecting the effects of a piece of legislation on their districts. He was shrewd at playing the long game, and making the compromises along the way it took to win it. He was cynical. (Once, when Gerald Ford introduced a tax cut, Walker replied, "Half my friends think it's too big, and half my friends think it's too small. And I never disagree with my friends.") He was a master at assembling coalitions. "There's a fiction around that you can't do anything with Congress, particularly if it's a Democratic Congress," he said after Carter's inauguration. "But that's not true. You can get things done up there if you know how to do it."

And above all, he was also a master at confounding his enemies. LBJ once called him "an S.O.B. with elbows." Returned Dr. Walker, "Where I come from, that's a term of endearment." His aim was to become a sort of Vladimir Ilyich Lenin of the new class-for-itself style of corporate lobbying. The 1978 tax reform fight was his main chance.

The strategy was an inside-outside pincer movement. For the outside game Walker hired a legendary publicist named Robert Keith Gray of the Hill & Knowlton lobbying shop, who recruited prominent liberals like Eugene McCarthy and Democratic establishment superstars like Clark Clifford to serve on the ACCF board—names that looked awfully good atop newspaper op-eds. For the inside game, he parceled assignments to lieutenants of what became known as the "Carlton Group"—so named because they held their secret meetings in the Ritz Carlton Hotel.

It worked. "The consensus is cohering on a different basis than the consensus Lyndon Johnson had," Walker soon exclaimed. "There's a crossover of party lines, an ignoring of party lines." Treasury Secretary Michael Blumenthal gave a speech to the annual convention of the Financial Analysts Federation demonstrating why a capital gains cut was the *worst* way to address the capital crisis, that a lower corporate income tax rate for small business did the job more cheaply without delivering 97 percent of its benefits to those making more than $200,000 a year. The secretary was spitting in the wind. Said Walker, "Within a relatively short period of time, capital formation has entered the lexicon of 'good' words—not quite equal to Home and Mother, but still a public policy goal few would disagree with."

POLICY ENTREPRENEURS LIKE STEIGER, WALKER—AND JACK KEMP— benefitted from good timing. Since the recession of 1974, the tools that had once seemed to hold the power to sculpt and smooth the economy like a lump of clay had proven useless; Keynesians, the young Michigan congressman David Stockman later reflected, "had been reduced to offering blathering and gibberish in lieu of analysis." Into the vacuum poured conservative economists, armed with panaceas.

Many mainstream economists had been convinced Keynesianism was exhausted ever since Milton Friedman, in his 1967 American Economic Association presidential address, took on the "Phillips Curve," the thesis positing an inverse relationship between inflation and unemployment. Faith in the Phillips Curve had meant that if unemployment threatened to rise to unacceptable levels, the Federal Reserve could simply act to speed up the economy by releasing more money into the system; and if inflation threatened to balloon, it could do the reverse, until the ideal mixture was obtained.

Friedman's proposed solution was to instead hold the growth rate of the money supply constant, and let the free market take care of the rest.

He called this "monetarism," and it bore the additional ideological advantage, for conservatives, of identifying government interference as the source of all macroeconomic woes. He believed the best way to remove the temptation toward such interference was "limiting the government's explicit tax revenue—just as a limited income is the only effective restraint on any individual's or family's spending."

Another conservative economic school of thought was "rational expectations," led by future Nobelist Robert Lucas, which demonstrated with sophisticated mathematics that business, in the aggregate, anticipates and adjusts for governmental actions before they happen, thus rendering government intervention futile. In his 1976 American Economic Association presidential address, Franco Modigliani of the Massachusetts Institute of Technology said the combination of Friedman's monetarism and Lucas's rational expectations model represented "the death blow to the already battered Keynesian position."

The "new public finance" camp, led by Harvard's Martin Feldstein, focused on "tax disincentives"—for instance, the way allegedly too-high capital rates discouraged productive investment. At the University of Virginia, the libertarian "public choice" theorists James Buchanan and Gordon Tullock argued against a foundational notion of the consumer movement, and, indeed, post–New Deal liberalism itself: that there existed an identifiable "public interest," on whose behalf politicians should legislate. There were only competing *interests*, including the interests of politicians and bureaucrats who aggrandized their power by *claiming* to act in the public interest—and the only institution that could fairly mediate between them was the unregulated marketplace. A similar approach was outlined in a summer 1978 issue of the neoconservative policy journal the *Public Interest* by an economist on Jack Kemp's staff named Paul Craig Roberts, who argued that Keynesianism was not merely wrong but corrupt, a "ramp for the expansion of the interests of government"—and also selfish economists grasping for recognition as "public-spirited social activists." Other argued that a power-hungry political class was in fact addicted to inflation because of the way it kicked taxpayers into higher brackets, which yielded more government revenue, which politicians cynically redistributed to the masses to buy them off, pretending they didn't know that this only created further inflation.

All these camps argued against one another vociferously; that was what intellectuals did. Their conclusions, however, were fundamentally in alignment—or closely enough for alert congressional staffers to easily brief their bosses that *experts agreed*: the problem with an economy heading further south every day was not the machinations of the far-off oil sheiks of OPEC, or the hangover from an underfunded Vietnam War, or underused industrial capacity, or the underfunding of public investment, or a lack of countervailing power to big business, or greedy corporations chasing higher profits—the liberals' explanations for America's economic woes. The problem was too much government.

Indeed, there was scant room in any of these paradigms for criticizing business at all. If companies were prospering, it was because they deserved to prosper—they were winners in the competitive marketplace. And if they were *not* prospering: that must be because regulation and high taxes had *distorted* the competitiveness of the marketplace. The devil, however, was still in the details. What should a tax bill that honored such premises look like? Milton Friedman was among those who insisted that any tax cut had to be accompanied by equivalent cuts in government spending. Paul Craig Roberts didn't think you necessarily had to cut spending at all.

Whose argument would prevail? To whom would the spoils of intellectual victory belong? Not the professor who could array his Greek-letter equations most convincingly to other professors, it turned out. This was Washington, after all; the battle went to the swift. Which in practice meant those willing to take intellectual shortcuts. And there, Paul Craig Roberts's school already had a considerable head start. Its name was supply-side economics.

ITS ARCHITECTS WERE A MOTLEY CREW. ONE WAS A THIRTY-YEAR-OLD JU-nior professor at the University of Chicago who joined Richard Nixon's Office of Management and Budget as chief economist. He offered an estimate of the 1971 gross national projection far more optimistic than any other in circulation. Nixon gladly seized on it in speeches. Embarassment followed, after actual GNP fell dramatically short of the young economist's predictions, which had relied on only four variables when most such forecasting models used hundreds. He left Washington a laughing-stock. His name was Arthur Laffer.

Another was something of an eccentric: as a professor at Columbia University, he had written a series of classic scholarly papers in the early 1960s on currency exchange rate dilemmas facing his native Canada that helped define a subfield. During the 1970s, however, he largely stopped writing in economics journals and presenting at mainstream conferences, instead convening his own at a villa in the Italian countryside. He grew his hair long, and began referring to the typical work product of his mainstream economist colleagues—including Milton Friedman—as "sheer quackery." His name was Robert A. Mundell.

A third figure was a journalist with no training in economics. At the age of thirty-three, in 1970, Robert Bartley took over the *Wall Street Journal*'s editorial page and "made clear," as a critic put it, "that the *Journal*

would henceforth be neither cautious nor even-handed on economic issues. Instead, it would campaign aggressively for what Bartley believed in.
And Bartley is a self-confident man, calmly sure that he is right even when
nearly everyone around him thinks he has lost his head."

Bartley's favorite editorial writer, like most of the New Right leaders
with whom he would become aligned, came from working-class roots:
he was son of an itinerant butcher from the Appalachian foothills. His
first job in journalism was at the *Las Vegas Review-Journal*, which was
where he claimed to have grasped the basics of economics—by pursuing
his hobby of counting cards to beat the house at blackjack. His name was
Jude Wanniski.

Together, these four men arguably became the most influential economic thinkers in the history of the United States, even though their theories turned out to be substantially wrong.

In 1973, Laffer tutored Bartley and Wanniski that what other economists believed about inflation—that its causes were complex and
obscure—was incorrect. Bartley, convinced, invited Laffer to compose a
series of articles in the *Journal*, in which he preached his heterodox theory
like it had been handed down on stone tablets.

The cadre began supping together at a tony Wall Street bistro called
Michael 1, where, with a passion befitting a religious sect, they confected
the doctrine that virtually all of America's economic problems had but
two causes: high taxes and the lack of a gold standard. In 1974 Wanniski
worked his excellent contacts in Washington to win an audience with
President Ford's chief of staff, Donald Rumsfeld, to whom he rhapsodized
about their convictions. So, following the 1974 congressional elections—a
disaster for Republicans—Rumsfeld sent his deputy, Richard B. Cheney,
to meet with this insistent Dr. Laffer.

They convened at the Two Continents restaurant across from the
Treasury Department. At the time, President Ford wanted to institute
a onetime tax rebate to stimulate the economy but was worried that the
resulting decline in federal revenues would increase the deficit. Aides who
shared that concern threatened to quit: fiscal rectitude, after all, had been
understood since time immemorial as the soul of sound conservative economic thinking. Deficits were a horror: when the Ford administration's
ballooning deficit projections were announced at the Conservative Political Action Conference banquet in 1975, snarked James Wolcott of the
Village Voice, "the shocked reaction suggested billions of charred babies."

Tax cuts were dessert: a treat dispensed to the public after forcing them
to eat the spinach of spending cuts. As the *Wall Street Journal* commanded
in 1953, "When we have a budget in balance tax reductions can follow
automatically. You can't unlock the door with any other key." Barry

Goldwater said much the same thing in *The Conscience of a Conservative* in 1960. What Laffer, Mundell, Wanniski, and Bartley claimed to have discovered, however, was that there *was* another key—and that it opened the door to political and policy miracles.

At Two Continents, Laffer struggled to explain to Cheney this truth that to him had become self-evident. He wasn't succeeding. So he took out a pen and cast his eye out for something to write on—

The napkins before them were starched linen.

He espied some paper cocktail napkins set out at the bar. He grabbed one, and sketched on it a graph. The vertical axis, he said, represented tax rates, from zero to one hundred percent; the horizontal represented the revenue realized at each rate. A zero percent tax rate, he explained, yielded the government no revenue. But so did a one hundred percent tax rate: if all the gains from economic activity were confiscated, no one would have an incentive to work or invest. He pointed to a theoretical sweet spot in the middle where taxes were low enough to maximize economic activity, and high enough to maximize revenue. He said the reason the economy was in its worst recession since the 1930s was because taxes were far too high to do either—axiomatically: just look at what a mess the economy was in.

His comrade Jude Wanniski described their solution in a massive *Wall Street Journal* essay that came out a few weeks later: "The correct prescription, says Professor Mundell, is a $30 billion tax cut and the temporary halting of open-market operations by the Federal Reserve to assure monetary restraint. . . . 'The national economy is being choked by taxes—asphyxiated.'" That created unemployment, and "unemployment has created vast segments of excess capacity greater than the size of the entire Belgian economy. If you could put that sub-economy to work, you would not only eliminate the social and economic costs of unemployment, you would increase aggregate supply sufficiently to reduce inflation."

What's more, "if taxes are not cut now, the size of the unemployed sub-economy will expand. Tax revenues of state, local and federal governments will decline. At the same time their outlays for unemployment relief and welfare will expand. Combined government deficits might even exceed the amount implied by a tax cut. But what's worse, the nation would be no closer to turning the economy around."

However, with "the announcement"—merely *the announcement*—"of a major tax cut," this economic desert would bloom: "the capital market would instantly"—*instantly*—"perceive that it is more profitable to do business in the United States than the rest of the world." Though the rest of the world would be healed of its woes as well: "The $30 billion tax cut is needed immediately to arrest the world slump, and if it is delayed even one month, the figure required will be higher."

(Indeed, it wasn't three months later before Laffer and Mundell followed up with an article insisting it was too late for $30 billion to do the trick, doubling the figure required.)

There was apparently no evidence behind these figures but intuition, no empirical research for what the sweet-spot tax rate should be; just Dr. Laffer's curve—which certainly looked, after all, like the sort that appeared in economics textbooks. Perhaps their faith was that this was all that was required.

Keynesians said the key to boosting an economy was to redistribute money downward, to consumers, to stimulate spending on the "demand side," to create the need for more jobs. The Michael 1 gang countered that you had to redistribute money directly to the "supply side," to the people who actually *created* the jobs—those who were already rich. Some of their conservative critics thus dubbed them the "supply-side fiscalists." The Michael 1 gang decided they liked the sound of that, and adopted "supply-siders" as their name.

"A FEW OF US AT MICHAEL I UNDERSTOOD WHAT WAS HAPPENING," BARTley wrote in his memoir. "But scarcely anyone else." So it was time the next year to evangelize everyone else. To do so, it was natural that they would go to the fifth key figure in the supply-side saga. His name was Irving Kristol.

Kristol was a textbook neoconservative. Born in a Brooklyn milieu of immigrant Jews, he graduated from the City University of New York, where tuition was free, following a college career, during the Depression, spent debating Marxist doctrine in the cafeteria alcoves. In the 1940s and '50s, as an increasingly powerful editor and essayist, he was a right-leaning liberal. By the late 1960s, however, he had become convinced the nation was careening toward collapse thanks to a liberal establishment that he had come to understand as nothing less than evil. For example he wrote in 1967 that intellectual critics of the Vietnam War weren't actually interested in peace at all but were instead "committed to the pursuit of temporal status, temporal influence, and temporal power with a single-minded passion that used to be found only in the high reaches of the Catholic church." This was Irving Kristol's central idea: that a "New Class" of liberal professionals, motivated by an unacknowledged will to power, was taking over American society under the guise of benevolence, and destroying it.

Ideas like these won him entrée to Richard Nixon's White House, where the two enjoyed discussing the parallels between America's insurgent youth and the children of the nineteenth-century Russian aristocracy who plotted the assassination of Czar Alexander II. In 1972, Kristol endorsed Nixon—and published a volume, *On the Democratic Idea in*

America, which argued that Americans' appetites had grown so profligate "that men take it as an insult when they are asked to be reasonable in their demands," and that American society was " vulgar, debased, and crassly materialistic."

Though he had also become convinced, in direct inverse to his youthful Marxism, that *business's* materialism, *its* demands, must be countenanced without bounds.

"The Founding Fathers *intended* this nation to be capitalist," he explained, "and regarded it as the *only* set of economic arrangements consistent with the liberal democracy that they had established." He would do whatever it took to ensure that the Founders' intentions as he understood them were honored. And if capitalists themselves hadn't the will or the wit to make it happen, he would show them how to do it himself. In 1972 he joined Robert Bartley's *Wall Street Journal's* board of editorial contributors. In one of his regular features there, written at the height of Ralph Nader's reign of terror, he offered a plan of action. "Some corporate executives seem to think that their corporate philanthropy is a form of charity," he lamented. "It is not." In so believing, they had become liberalism's useful idiots. They must stop donating to "those activities of the New Class which are inimical to corporate survival." Their money should be redirected instead to writers and intellectuals "who are interested in individual liberty and limited government. . . . You can only beat an idea with another idea, and the war of ideas and ideologies will be won or lost *within* the New Class, not against it."

A critic joked that in that op-ed Kristol "stopped short of giving his address and telephone number." He didn't have to. He sat on the board of five corporations, whom he had already begun showing the way.

He persuaded the foundation chartered in 1934 by the automotive titan Alfred P. Sloan, and also the one established in 1937 by the Lilly pharmaceutical family, to slather $12.5 million over five years for a Center for the Study of Government Regulation at the American Enterprise Institute, where he was a fellow. In 1976, it founded a magazine, *Regulation*, co-edited by an economist named Murray Weidenbaum and a legal scholar named Antonin Scalia. In 1978, Weidenbaum turned the number "$102.7 billion"—the amount, about 5 percent of America's annual GDP, that a Weidenbaum study claimed federal regulation cost the economy every year—into a veritable household phrase. Boardroom Jacobins received the study like an early Christmas present. Amway took out newspaper ads. So did the Chase Manhattan Bank and the National Cotton Council ("*Overregulation could cost your family a home of your own. . . .*")

Experts at the Congressional Service of the Library of Congress responded that Weidenbaum's study ignored ways regulations also *saved* money (say, by reducing the incidence of cancer), double-counted several inputs, and relied on a "multiplier" factor that he had pulled out of thin air. Let the critics carp. In the court of public opinion, Kristol was winning. In 1973, 60 percent of Americans had agreed "Government regulation is a good way of making business more responsive to people's needs." By 1979, only 49 percent did. Indeed one citizen was so impressed with Weidenbaum's conclusion that he appeared to take credit for it himself. "The cabinet discussed regulatory reform," Jimmy Carter wrote in his diary in the summer of 1978. "We estimate that government regulation cost $100 billion this year—about 5 percent of our GDP."

Carter had already ordered a major White House review of existing regulations. The Occupational Safety and Health Administration soon slashed about a thousand pages of them. Carter put on a show of this for the press, announcing the accomplishment next to piles of a thousand sheets of (blank) paper. Then, OSHA ceased introducing new health standards altogether.

Irving Kristol also edited a magazine of his own. He had cofounded the *Public Interest* in 1965 with the sociologist Daniel Bell, who left in 1969 in frustration with its rightward march. Much in its pages was respectable: statistics-laden studies, for example, claiming a failure of busing to achieve quality desegregated schooling, or the ways Washington-directed urban renewal was proving counterproductive in reversing blight. Work like this comprised the most important intellectual contribution of neoconservatism's domestic wing: the doctrine of "unintended consequences"—that the interventions of naive but well-intentioned reformers often left things worse than before. But even the most abstruse contributions to the *Public Interest* were not published according to normal academic routine: blind submission, followed by peer review by distinguished scholars in the submitter's field. Instead, articles just ran on the editor's say-so, just like in, say, *Better Homes & Gardens* or *Field & Stream*.

Which was a very good thing for Jude Wanniski. He believed that academic economics was a self-protecting racket. And if he couldn't get the truth out through them, he had no choice but to find another way. "After all," he wrote, "Columbus would have found it difficult to persuade Queen Isabella that sailing of the Indies was good policy if he had failed to convince her that the world was round not flat." In 1975, he asked Kristol if he was interested in an article explaining Arthur Laffer's magical curve. "Write it, and I'll run it," Kristol responded. Wanniski worked on it over four weekends. His piece, "The Mundell-Laffer Hypothesis—A New View of the World Economy," lacked most everything that made economic arguments convincing to other economists. There were only four footnotes, none citing any other scholars or texts. One of those footnotes admitted, "There is no joint Mundell-Laffer paper." Nor, apparently, any supporting data, for he cited none. Wanniski left those niceties to the hacks he dismissed as "academic theoreticians"—just about every school of which he managed to insult for missing "what some would call a 'Copernican revolution' in economic policy."

What was it these "economic doctors of Cambridge and Chicago" failed to understand? That stagflation could be easily fixed. Just combine tight money (ideally, via a "common simulated currency" pegged to the value of gold) and "fiscal ease"; in other words, radical tax cuts. Though Wanniski only called them "implied" tax cuts: for once the economy was "optimized by putting the unemployed resources to work," they weren't like tax cuts at all, because everyone would become richer. And unlike every other existing theory on fixing inflation, Mundell and Laffer's "would not involve a period of suffering by the world's population in order to achieve improvement."

Could it cure dandruff? Perhaps not. It could, however, cure the environmental crisis, because a global gold standard would limit the amount of money in circulation "to the limitations of the planet's resources (of which gold, of course, is one)."

Next up: Wanniski began arguing that these truths could even heal the Republican Party. Republicans who lost elections to Democrats who passed laws distributing goodies to the public, paid for from the federal purse, liked to complain, "Nobody shoots Santa Claus." Wanniski argued in a 1976 *Wall Street Journal* essay called "The Two Santa Claus Theory" that their complaint was "absolutely correct," and that the Republicans, with their continued insistence on lean budgets with tax increases to balance them if required, *had* been the Scrooges of American politics. Now, however, Democrats like Jimmy Carter and Jerry Brown were acting like Scrooges: *they* were the ones demanding that Americans do more with less. The supply-side revolution, Wanniski insisted, rendered that thinking obsolete—showed, in fact, that it had *always* been obsolete. "The only thing wrong with the U.S. economy is the failure of the Republican Party to play Santa Claus"—by not bestowing on every American the gift of a tax cut. Do so, and not only would Republicans deliver unprecedented economic dynamism; they would create a citizenry so flush with spare cash that they would gratefully rain down votes on them in return.

THE SUPPLY-SIDERS WON A YOUNG, CHARISMATIC CONGRESSIONAL CONvert. Jack Kemp was a native of Los Angeles whose mom was a Spanish teacher and social worker and whose dad raised the family out of the working class by building a trucking company. Jack grew up to become a star quarterback for the Buffalo Bills, adopting that brawling blue-collar town as his own—the opposite trajectory of the millions of Americans streaming out of the struggling cities of the Rust Belt for the Sun Belt. But Jack Kemp was very much his own man.

In the off-season he worked at the *San Diego Union*, edited by future Nixon White House communications director Herb Klein. He was a voracious reader who bragged of owning every selection of the Conservative Book Club. His favorite books included Barry Goldwater's *Conscience of a Conservative* and Ayn Rand's libertarian novels. Though he was also perhaps the world's only Ayn Rand fan to have helped found a union, serving five terms as president of the American Football League Players Association. In 1970 he won election to Congress. He considered the factory workers and poor blacks of Buffalo his core constituency. And, like Ronald Reagan, he was a bone-deep economic optimist, who believed in capitalism as a boundlessly dynamic cornucopia of opportunity—if only it were unshackled to work its powers.

"Football fans know," he said, "that there aren't a fixed number of touchdowns to go around. The only limits are time and the potential of each player." And like Reagan, Kemp insisted that what truly shackled citizens' potential was too-high taxes. In his third term he cosponsored a complicated set of business tax cuts called the Job Creation Act of 1975. In committee testimony, economist Leon Keyserling, a drafter of the Humphrey-Hawkins bill and a former John F. Kennedy advisor, barked that by "shifting a larger portion of the burden to those least able to pay," it was greedy "class legislation."

Arguments like Keyserling's kept Kemp awake at night: Why did it always have to be the Republicans who were the ones considered greedy? Kemp called himself a "bleeding heart conservative," and believed tax cuts for business was the opposite of "class legislation"—for wasn't it business that *made things*, and *making things* that created the jobs? But he needed a better way to make the argument. He found it by studying the late president whose initials he shared: John F. Kennedy.

It was Kennedy who had first advanced the counterintuitive notion that an across-the-board income tax cut would grow the economy so robustly it might *increase* revenue, in a speech Kemp and company never tired of quoting: "The final and best means of strengthening demand among consumers and business is to reduce the burden on private income and the deterrents to private initiative which are imposed by our present tax system. . . . There will be new interest in taking risks, in increasing productivity, in creating new jobs and new products for long-term economic growth." And, after Lyndon Johnson passed JFK's idea into law in 1964, that appeared, at least if you didn't look too closely, to indeed be the case: America proved fiscally healthy enough to pursue Johnson's "Great Society." Conservative Republicans could make society great, too, he decided—by offering tax cuts for *everyone* across the board.

Robert Bartley told Jude Wanniski, "You'd better get by and meet this guy Kemp. He's quite a piece of horseflesh." Kemp scheduled fifteen minutes with the *Wall Street Journal* writer. Instead they talked into the night. "I was exhausted and ecstatic," Wanniski remembered. "I had finally found an elected representative of the people who was as fanatical as I was." Richard Rahn, executive director of Charls Walker's American Council for Capital Formation, began ferrying Dr. Laffer from New York for overnight visits to Kemp's Bethesda home, which was where the economist told the handsome former football star he could *be* the next JFK. "Dressed in his bathrobe," Rahn dreamily recollected, Kemp "would cook breakfast for us while peppering Art with questions and challenging his assertions."

In 1977, Kemp directed his economic aid Bruce Bartlett to draft an income tax bill that would, like President Kennedy's, provide cuts by the same percentage points across every bracket. As cosponsor, he recruited Senator William Roth of Delaware, who had been inspired by his home state's success in attracting corporate headquarters by eliminating state income taxes altogether. The bill they introduced in July 1977 would lower every tax rate by 30 percent over a course of three years—from the top bracket, which was now 70 percent but would become 49, to the bottom one, which was now 14 percent but would become 9.8. It would also cut the corporate tax rate by a percentage point a year for three years.

THIS WAS NOT QUITE WHAT JOHN F. KENNEDY HAD DONE: HE'D PROPOSED cutting tax rates by an average 18 percentage points, and the cuts were not uniform across the board as with Kemp-Roth, but progressive, a 36 percent cut for the lowest bracket but only 6 percent for the highest; with the cuts Congress eventually authorized averaging 19 percent. As for "paying for itself," taxes captured from increased economic activity made up only a third of what the tax cut had cost in lost revenue.

But presently the political timing was opportune for something bolder. In 1977, ordinary Americans' tax bite was worse than at any time since the federal income tax was invented. Which explained why the latest hit from the singer of "Take This Job and Shove It," Johnny Paycheck, was called "Me and the IRS," and advised, "Take the 1040 forms and shove 'em / Put 'em where the sun don't shine."

Income taxes hadn't originally been intended to affect the middle class at all, and until recently this was still somewhat the case. By the time John F. Kennedy became president there were three marginal rates for the bottom

90 percent of the income distribution: zero for the bottom fifth, 20 percent for the half or so making between $2,700 and $7,000 a year, and 22 percent on the next $4,000 up to $11,000. A male factory worker, accountant, or even an attorney could keep getting raises—or his wife could go to work and effectively double the family's income—without his tax rate increasing. The number who paid the top marginal rate—70 percent after 1965—was miniscule. In the 1970s, the median family income grew modestly, but an increasingly large portion was eaten up by inflation—and now, if a factory hand was promoted to foreman and his wife got work as a secretary, the family might find their marginal tax rate shooting from 18 to 37 percent.

The name for this phenomenon of Americans paying a penalty for doing better was "bracket creep." Those victimized by it were beginning to inquire much more sharply what all this cash they were shoveling at the federal government was paying for. An increasing percentage—though still only a small portion of the federal budget—went for "means tested" programs for the poor like Medicaid, Aid to Families with Dependent Children, and food stamps; that meant less, relatively speaking, to members of the middle class (to whom, still, a much greater *amount* of government largesse went, in the form of things like Social Security and Medicare).

At the same time, the tax employees paid into the Social Security system—"the most unfair tax a worker pays," Ronald Reagan called it in one of his 1976 campaign commercials—had exploded 150 percent since Kennedy was elected. The cap for income above which employees no longer had to pay Social Security taxes increased far faster than inflation, too: from $4,500 in 1960 to $17,000 in 1977—and then, thanks to legislation Jimmy Carter championed and signed at the end of the year in order to guarantee the system's solvency for another seventy-five years, to $22,900. Carter could have cushioned taxpayers' pain by asking for the money out of general revenues; because he considered balancing the budget more important, he chose to increase payroll taxes. That meant that by 1979 the amount an experienced high school teacher or entry-level lawyer contributed to Social Security would increase *ninefold* compared to 1960. According to the economic researchers at the Conference Board, by 1977 the typical American family of four would have to have increased its pre-tax income by two-thirds just to maintain the same standard of living they had eight years earlier.

So whatever the *economic* merits of the Michael 1 theorists, the *politics* of putting more money into ordinary Americans' pockets with tax cuts was simple. It transformed Republicans from Scrooge into Santa Claus—whom no politician dared shoot.

In the fall of 1977, Kemp was the featured speaker at the Republican National Committee Meeting. He told them not to fret so much about balanced budgets anyway: "Republicans must not be bookkeepers for Democratic deficits." Then they voted to endorse Kemp-Roth as official party policy. The RNC magazine *First Monday* began publishing articles like "Union Members Would Get Work With Tax Cut," illustrated with beefy men in hard hats, and with a statistics-laden centerfold "suitable for use as a poster to spread the word that GOP congressmen and senators are pressing on Capitol Hill for a permanent tax cut to stimulate the economy and create jobs." In his newspaper column, Pat Buchanan called Kemp-Roth "the Republican response to Humphrey-Hawkins": a full employment bill that didn't create a single socialistic government job. And in the next issue of the *Public Interest* Wanniski published a head-spinningly ambitious defense of Kemp-Roth's foundational theory: "The idea behind the 'Laffer curve' is no doubt as old as civilization," he claimed, "but unfortunately politicians have always had trouble grasping it." He described instances throughout history when tax cuts were supposedly followed by economic booms, and tax hikes that brought forth economic Armageddon. Though his definition of "tax hikes" was a little bit loose. Nikita Khrushchev, for instance, supposedly sealed his "political downfall" by decreasing the size of private plots Soviet citizens were allowed to cultivate—thus serving to "increase the marginal tax rate of the *system.*"

Again there were no citations, no data, no formal model: just assertions ("By lowering the tax rate we find an increase to revenues") and arguments from authority ("The Caesars understood this . . . Hamilton, Madison, and Jay reveal an understanding of the notion"). There was also an inscrutable tale, as gnomic as a New Testament parable, involving three carpenters who, "if the tax rate on homebuilding is 49 percent, will work together," but who, if it "goes to 51 percent," will destroy their economic productivity by working alone. Wanniski even held up America's economic growth in the 1921–29 period as a "phenomenal" illustration of supply-side wisdom—as if it hadn't been followed by the Great Depression. Naturally he ignored the fact that the greatest economic boom in the history of civilization had come in the U.S. between 1946 and 1972, when that top marginal tax rate ranged up to 91 percent.

Wanniski's article was an excerpt from a newly completed book, *The Way the World Works: How Economies Fail, and Succeed,* written during nine months he spent as the American Enterprise Institute's first resident fellow, a sinecure arranged by Kristol with a single phone call to the Smith-Richardson Foundation, endowed by a cough drop fortune. The book was published by the prestigious Manhattan publishing house Basic Books. A typical review from a professional economist said the book "would be much less distressing if we were permitted to read it as satire rather than as scholarship."

Professors from across the ideological spectrum dismissed the supply-side enterprise as errant nonsense. Gardner Ackley, an architect of the Kennedy-Johnson tax, called Kemp-Roth "the most irresponsible policy proposal—seriously advanced by people who should know better—that I can recall during the nearly forty years I have been closely observing or participating in national economic policy making. I am ashamed of my profession for the fact that a handful of its members have suggested or endorsed this policy." Milton Friedman said the raging inflation it would produce made it merely "a proposal to change the form of taxes." Franco Modigliani said it would "do irreparable damage to the United States economy." Alan Greenspan, Gerald Ford's former chief economic advisor, said of Laffer, "I don't know anyone who seriously believes his argument." Another free-market economist, George Stigler, bound for a Nobel Prize four years later, labeled his former University of Chicago colleague "a propagandist." The economics editor of *Business Week* called supply-side "more a source of amusement than a basis for public policy." The conservative economist Herbert Stein called Laffer's curve "extreme to the point of bizarre," a "shoddy echo of silly self-serving businessmen's nostrums going back to time immemorial."

Stein then twisted the knife: "It may turn out that such a tax cut will raise revenue, just as it may turn out that there is human life on Mars. But I would not invest much in a McDonald's franchise on that planet."

Steiger's capital gains cut amendment came in for drubbings almost as severe. Herb Stein concluded that even "using the most favorable as-sumptions" it would take three decades "to regain the revenue level that would have been achieved without the tax cut," because investors would park much of their unearned windfall on luxuries like expensive art. And eventually, formal studies came forth confirming these preliminary takes. But the sort of studies commissioned by the American Council for Capital Formation and the Securities Industries Association came forth first— passed off in the media as "scientific fact," a critical journalist pointed out, to be debunked only after "the political war was over."

Indeed, among Republicans, there was no longer much debate. The an-nual Party retreat at the Tidewater Inn resort on Maryland's Eastern Shore the last weekend of April was attended by some fifty state and federal Re-publican officeholders, from liberal to conservative. Jack Kemp, hunching forward enthusiastically like he was working in his old job with the Bills, lectured them about the bad old days when Senator Robert Taft of Ohio begged Ike to reduce income taxes, which his flinty treasury secretary George Humphrey talked him out of. John Rhodes, the House's sixty-one-year-old minority leader, interjected, playing Old Man Scrooge: "But you were in high school!" Then, however, Rhodes conceded the debate. "He's tired of losing," an approving William Safire recounted. The gathering passed a resolution: "substantial permanent reductions in federal and capitals gains tax rates" would help "achieve a balanced budget." "The body of 'fiscal responsibility,' " Safire pronounced with satisfaction, "was gently interred."

IN 1977, DAVID BRODER, DEAN OF WASHINGTON PUNDITS, HAD WRITTEN OF the Democrats that "rarely has one political party enjoyed such a generous gift of power at all levels of American life." His dispatch from the Tidewater Inn enshrined a new conventional wisdom. He quoted Bill Brock: "There's an awful lot more that unifies people in this party than divides us." And Howard Baker: "There is a spirit of accommodation and a willingness to go forward together." Now that the Republicans had agreed on a way to become Santa Claus, it was the Democrats' turn to be yesterday's news—and Jimmy Carter's political position deteriorated further.

The previous year he had relieved a heavily decorated soldier's soldier, Major General John K. Singlaub, from duty as commander of U.S. troops on the Korean Peninsula after Singlaub criticized Carter's moves to remove those troops. Now, after Singlaub gave a speech scouring him for canceling the neutron bomb, Carter fired him; then reversed himself under a hail of criticism from the right—and Singlaub responded by noisily retiring, reinventing himself as a full-time Jimmy Carter scourge. He called the Panama Canal treaties "our first retreat on United States soil—because we buckled under the psychological warfare of our own State Department and the pressure from New York bankers." And he starred in a new half-hour documentary, *Soviet Might/American Myth: U.S. in Retreat*, produced by the American Conservative Union and syndicated on some 370 stations, which argued that the Soviet Union saw nuclear war as "both feasible and winnable"—but that Jimmy Carter didn't even care.

He was getting about as much abuse from the press. The *Washington Star*'s political gossip columnist reported that after finishing last in a school race, ten-year-old Amy Carter howled, "I want a trophy," so her Secret Service detail stole one to shut her up; the claim received wide media pickup. Promptly, Carter refused the White House Correspondents' Association's traditional invitation to the president to tell self-deprecating jokes at their annual gala dinner. Unprecedentedly, he turned them down, sending instead press secretary Jody Powell—who, the president recorded delightedly in his diary, "told them how we feel about them." So the correspondents let it be known how *they* were feeling about the White House. "Most of the people were embarrassed and looking at the floor," the *Post*'s Mary McGrory wrote. "There isn't any hatred toward this administration"—so she claimed—"but a feeling of disappointment."

The president then chose this delicate moment to launch a difficult political fight: a massive simultaneous arms sale to Saudi Arabia, Egypt, and Israel, intended to increase his chances of achieving a Middle East peace deal. Sales of the size he intended required a Senate resolution of approval. Senators said they would be much more likely to vote for these sales if they were called up individually. Carter stubbornly insisted on forcing their approval as a package: sixty F-15s to Saudi Arabia, twenty-five to Israel in addition to seventy-five F-16s, and fifty F-5E fighter-bombers, a sort of starter supersonic jet designed specifically for export to under-armed American allies, to Egypt. The American Israel Political Action Committee called this "a mortal threat to Israel"—a particularly potent political argument that spring. American Nazis were threatening to march through the Chicago suburb of Skokie, which had a large population of Holocaust survivors. NBC's four-part miniseries *Holocaust* was watched by half of American TV viewers. Impolitically, Carter also chose the week of the broadcast to plant a cedar from Lebanon on the White House lawn to recognize that country's suffering at the hands of Israel's invasion. The American Israel Public Affairs Committee, which had never lost a vote in Congress since its inception in 1953, took note of these facts on the ground, and prepared to turn up the heat. Gallup reported the president's approval rating at 39 percent. Only 26 percent of Democrats wanted Jimmy Carter as their 1980 nominee; 36 percent of them wanted Senator Edward "Ted" Kennedy. "Never before in the 43-year history of the Gallup Poll has an incumbent president eligible for reelection stood lower in his party's esteem," the *New York Times* said.

RONALD REAGAN WAS IN TROUBLE, TOO. "REAGAN WAS A BIT LONG IN THE tooth," one of the nation's most widely read conservative columnists, James J. Kilpatrick, observed. On the other hand, in "a nation of football nuts," forty-three-year-old Jack Kemp "might have great appeal."

The column ran May 6—"Tax Freedom Day," conservatives called it, when the average American was supposedly no longer toiling for Uncle Sam because it was 34.5 percent into the year, which was the bite conservatives claimed all taxes took out of the average American. "I will shortly move that the Senate be in recess for one minute to honor the struggling, downtrodden, exploited and neglected American taxpayer," Jesse Helms said on the Senate floor. Which was the kind of grandstanding a far-right figure like Jesse Helms might have performed in any year. Only now the message was mainstream. A Roper poll found voters supporting Kemp-

Roth by a ratio of two to one. If "the White House goes from a Jimmy to Jack," Kilpatrick concluded, "remember you heard it here first."

Evangelicals harvested good news. Debby Boone's "You Light Up My Life" won the Academy Award for best song in a motion picture; the Bee Gees had not even been nominated for their music from the smash hit *Saturday Night Fever*—a movie that the Boone family had walked out on as morally offensive fifteen minutes in, according to a *People* magazine article on "the nation's most relentlessly wholesome family west of the Osmonds." Twenty-one-year-old Debby, *People* readers learned, lived with her parents. "All dates in Debby's life must pass her possessive pop's scrutiny.... He boasts that Debby is a virgin, and that if she ever asked to move in with a fellow, 'I'd take her into a quiet part of the house and turn her over my knee.'"

Next came good news about anti–gay rights initiatives. In Minnesota, St. Paul Citizens for Human Rights had been overwhelmingly confident: they had Hubert Humphrey's widow, Senator Muriel Humphrey; the Urban League; five of seven city council members; the Democratic Farmer-Labor Party; all the big unions; and the American Lutherans, the United Methodists, the Episcopalians, the United Church of Christ, the Minnesota Rabbinical Association, and the Catholic archbishop on their side. The diocese newspaper, however, came out against "special protection for gays." Jerry Falwell gave a homestretch "Christians for God and Decency" rally at the civic center, where a hundred pastors and ten thousand activists cheered descriptions of homosexuality as a "murderous, horrendous, twisted act." On April 25, St. Paul voters struck gay rights protections from the books by a margin of two to one.

Since the murder of Robert Hillsborough the previous summer, San Francisco gays had begun carrying police whistles to protect themselves against attack. Now, as hundreds of them poured out onto Castro Street in a spontaneous rage, a twenty-three-year-old organizer named Cleve Jones demanded they blow them at the top of their lungs: "Tonight, we have been attacked."

Down the street the whistles shrieked, attracting hundreds more. Their now familiar five-mile protest route brought them past City Hall, by which time they were at least two thousand strong, then to Union Square, where they demonstrated past midnight with a new rallying cry—a pun: "*Gay riots now!*"

Awed by their own power, they worked to set up a new system to organize spontaneous demonstrations within hours the next time crisis should strike. Their chance came within the week. On May 1, State Senator John Briggs of Fullerton again stood at a podium at San Francisco City Hall, this time as the first stop on a daylong, three-county tour to celebrate the filing of five hundred thousand signatures to put on the November ballot his referendum to require school boards "to refuse to hire as an employee any person who has engaged in public homosexual activity or public homosexual conduct." That, in the measure's definition, included "advocating, soliciting, imposing, encouraging, or promoting private or public homosexual activity directed at, or likely to come to the attention of school children and or other employees."

Like, say, what hundreds of braying activists were doing to Senator Briggs now: chanting, "John Briggs, you can't hide! We charge you with genocide!" Briggs replied with relish that he had started his tour in San Francisco because it was "the moral garbage dump of homosexuality in this country."

Harvey Milk had in January been sworn in as the first gay member of San Francisco Board of Supervisors. Reporters swarmed him for a response to Briggs. He said, "Nobody likes garbage because it smells. Yet eight million tourists visited San Francisco last year. I wonder how many visited Fullerton."

Back in St. Paul, the shocked leader of the liberal United Methodist denomination groped for an explanation for their loss: "It appears that those who support human rights issues did not take seriously the possibility that the repeal vote would win and thus did not bother to vote."

Activists in Wichita, whose ordinance was up for public approval on May 9, responded by framing their campaign as a question of fundamental civil rights—and "thank *God* we're not voting on civil rights for blacks, for women, for Chicanos, for Indians, for handicapped people, for aged people," Mayor Connie Kennard said at a rally. "Because I'm not sure how that vote would come out if that were on the ballot next Tuesday either." The reverend leading the anti-gay campaign responded, "You're *not* talking about the color of a person's skin—you're talking about a type of behavior considered by society a deviant lifestyle." Wichita's gay rights ordinance was struck from the books by a shocking 83 percent of voters.

White House public liaison head Midge Costanza was paraphrased in a wire service story bemoaning "a growing movement in the nation, sponsored by the 'right wing' and supported by large amounts of money, whose aim was to strip minority groups of their human rights." She was identified as "assistant to President Carter on women's rights." For her forthrightness she was punished by losing her office next to the president's, consigned to a cubicle in the White House basement, her staff stripped to a single secretary, her duties limited to liaison with feminist groups.

PERHAPS THE PRESIDENT WAS SCARED OF THE MUSCLE ORGANIZED CHRIS- tians were starting to show. The week before the Wichita vote, Jerry Fal- well's *Old Time Gospel Hour* purchased an ad in the largest-subscription magazine in America, *TV Guide*, and newspapers across the country, inviting readers to send in to his Lynchburg, Virginia, headquarters answers (and their names and addresses, and a "fully tax-deductible" contribution) to survey questions like "Do you approve of PORNOGRAPHIC and obscene classroom textbooks being used under the guise of sexual education?" and "Do you approve of the present laws legalizing ABORTION-ON-DEMAND?" Three days after Wichita, regular pickets in front of the Sears Tower in downtown Chicago led the massive retailer that owned it to pull its advertising from ABC's racy offerings *Charlie's Angels* and *Three's Company*. The minister leading the campaign, Donald Wildmon, hardly satisfied, announced that he now would aim to convince a million customers to cancel their Sears charge cards if the company did not issue a statement committing itself only to "family-oriented television."

On a rainy Saturday in May, fifty-eight thousand people representing some sixty Christian denominations gathered at Giants Stadium in New York City for what was advertised as the largest ecumenical gathering in U.S. history. The featured speaker at "Jesus '78," Father John Bertolucci, was a leader in the flourishing movement of "charismatic Catholics"—worshipers who followed the ecstatic practices of Pentecostalism, such as speaking in tongues, and another charismatic Catholic priest provided a demonstration of just that practice. Another speaker, Mike Evans, was a leading "Messianic Jew"—he accepted Jesus Christ as his savior. Cardinal Terence Cooke blessed the gathering. The black gospel star Andraé Crouch sang, and Christian pop star Keith Green, who instructed the crowd to get on their knees and surrender their lives to Jesus. When audience members standing on the playing field hesitated—it was covered in four inches of mud—Green cried, "You can wash the dirt off your jeans, but if you don't get down on your knees, you'll never be able to wash the dirt from your heart." The assemblage duly splooshed down into the muck.

The gathering was officially nonpolitical. But the *reason* Catholics and Protestants were brushing aside formerly incommensurate theological differences was entirely political—a product of their common fight against abortion, the ERA, gay rights, and secularism. And Jimmy Carter surely took note; his sister Ruth was one of the speakers. At such a politically sensitive time, even fifty-eight thousand only *potentially* politically active religious diehards, glad to bury their knees in four inches of muck for the cause, was not easily dismissed. Keith Green's latest album, after all, was called *No Compromise*. Adversaries unwilling to compromise were the adversaries politicians feared the most.

THAT FRIDAY, THE DAY OF THE WEEK WHEN POLITICIANS ANNOUNCE NEWS they hope no one will notice, the White House announced that the $25 billion in tax cuts previously supposed to go into effect on October 1 would instead be $20 billion, and go into effect three months later. The stated reason was to avoid more inflation—but only seventeen days previously Carter had insisted that a $25 billion cut starting on October 1 would *not* cause more inflation. And in either related or unrelated news, a twenty-third, then twenty-fourth, then twenty-fifth Democratic senator joined the sixty cosponsors of the Senate version of the Steiger capital gains tax cut, which Carter still adamantly opposed.

You had to pity the president. In his first year he oversaw the biggest peacetime twelve-month employment gain in history. Then economic output declined in the first quarter of 1978 and the Consumer Price Index hit a 10.8 percent yearly rate of inflation—another peacetime record. Some of his economists said stimulus via a quick and hard tax would unleash more inflation, so he shouldn't do it; others said it would not, so he should. It was economics in Alice's Wonderland: none of it made sense. And this was the administration's second major change in tax policy in thirteen months—so the bottom line was that his announcement made an increasingly feckless-seeming president seem even more so.

Then on Monday the Senate took up Carter's arms sale to Israel, Saudi Arabia, and Egypt; two-thirds of the public was against it. With so many more apparently pressing fights on his hands—Panama, taxes, bailout aid to New York City—politicians and the press were baffled by the steel with which he pressed the matter.

They were unaware of the passion Carter was investing in seeking peace between Israel and Egypt; his diary suggested it was the subject he thought about most. National security advisor Zbigniew Brzezinski, about to shuttle to Asia for secret negotiations on diplomatic relations with China, saw facing down Begin's continued intransigence on illegal settlements and the massacre of Lebanese civilians as a crucial opportunity to demonstrate the administration's strength to other world leaders. The arms deal vote was a proxy for Carter's chances of winning Congress to this view. If he lost, Congress would have implicitly ratified Begin's snubs, and rebuffed the Arab nations Carter had praised for their moves toward moderation.

And so, directly after his near miss on Panama and in the thick of the tax debate, with his chits exhausted and with hardly a political friend in the world, Jimmy Carter took on Washington's mightiest lobby: the American Israel Public Affairs Committee, which declared all-out war against the administration.

One weapon was the *Holocaust* miniseries: AIPAC sent a copy of the novel version to every member of Congress and to leading members of the media with a letter avowing that "this chilling account of the extermination of six million Jews underscores Israel's concerns during the current negotiations for security without outside guarantees." Another weapon was Jewish groups nationwide, who tilted White House mail by a ratio of nine to one against the deal. They also enlisted the NAACP and interfaith religious groups, who pointed out that Saudi Arabia exercised a blanket economic embargo against Israel and banned American Jews who worked for U.S. companies doing business there. AIPAC also published a memo insisting that the F-15s Carter was selling "would enable Saudi Arabia to strike deep inside Israel," and might fall into "radical hands." Saudi Arabia's twenty-five registered lobbyists, meanwhile, reminded senators that the Kingdom supplied 23 percent of U.S. oil supplies, and argued that the jets were a bulwark against the neighboring Soviet client states Yemen and Ethiopia. Which might have been how their diplomat Prince Bandar bin Sultan personally convinced Ronald Reagan to join Henry Kissinger, Averell Harriman, and David Rockefeller in lobbying for the deal. As did the Fluor Corporation of Orange County, California—whose leadership was far-right, but which also built petroleum infrastructure. It organized its twenty thousand employees to flood the Senate with pro-deal letters. And for the second time in a month, citizen lobbyists flooded Senate offices—so many, a congressional aide remembered, that "you could not walk the halls because of people and groups clamoring for one side or the other on the F-15 thing."

It got ugly. The White House liaison to Jews said promoting the deal made him feel like a "political whore," and resigned. After the rabbi who led the organization of presidents of major American Jewish organizations called Carter a "question mark" in the eyes of Jews, Zbigniew Brzezinski complained of "intimidation" from Jewish groups whom he characterized as saying that "if you don't agree with us . . . we are going to stamp you as an anti-Semite." At AIPAC's annual policy conference Senator Lowell Weicker, an Episcopalian, cried, "We know from history that, time and time again, when national leaders ran into difficulties, they found it convenient to blame their problems on Jews. . . . If I were president, and I had a national security advisor who singled out American Jews as an impediment to my policies, I would have his resignation before sundown and his reputation for breakfast." White House counsel Robert Lipshutz, who was Jewish, promptly made an unscheduled trip to the podium to complain that Weicker was "preying on the emotions of the Jewish people," and was heckled.

On Friday, May 12, the Senate Foreign Relations Committee deadlocked on the arms sale. Frank Church cast a shocking *nay* vote—after he had tried to persuade other members to support the sale. "The lobbying pressure is the most intense that anyone had ever seen on the Hill," Carter wrote in his diary, listing all the Democratic senators up for reelection in

1978, like Thomas McIntyre, and 1980, like Frank Church—"all of whom agreed that the proposal should be approved, but can't stand up against the pressure."

The White House counted forty-three votes. Carter began furiously calling senators. On May 15, during ten hours of emotional Senate debate, Senator Thomas Eagleton of Missouri said he had agonized more over this than any decision he could recall, then voted *aye*—so Saudi Arabia could "defend against attacks on their vital resources" instead of American boys. Senator Jacob Javits of New York cried, "What do we want to do to the Israelis? Sap their vitality? Sap their morale? Cut their legs out from under them?" He voted *nay*.

Javits was Jewish. But so was Abraham Ribicoff of Connecticut. He voted *aye*—because "without a stable, predictable supply of oil from Saudi Arabia the West would face its worse depression of the industrial era." But Ribicoff was not up for reelection until 1980 like Javits was, and was considering retiring. Only two of the ten Democrats up for reelection in 1978 voted *aye*. Senator Mike Gravel of Alaska complained that voting against Israel's wishes "kisses away in the future all kinds of financial support that would insure a candidate for office."

Jimmy Carter won 54–44. It was AIPAC's first defeat in its twenty-eight-year history. Carter's personal lobbying surely made the difference. This added up to two striking come-from-behind foreign policy victories in a row. His critics were unimpressed. One *Washington Post* column was headlined, "Gang That Couldn't Shoot Straight Wins One." Another read, "Can Carter's Presidency Be Redeemed?" It ran beside a Jeff MacNelly syndicated cartoon that depicted Carter booming out FDR's old fireside chat salutation—"My friends . . ."—to a cavernous cathedral full of empty pews.

Congressional energy negotiations were stalemated. Cuban forces in Angola were reported to be training insurgents for an invasion of a copper-rich province of nearby Zaire, in defiance of White House protests. Frank Church, one of the Senate's most liberal members, came out for the Steiger amendment—"perhaps the strongest indication," the *Boston Globe* reported, that Carter might sign the first tax reform in history to make the tax code more regressive rather than less, rendering the president's attempt to achieve his marquee campaign promise a fiasco.

Desperate, Carter called in an old friend: Gerald Rafshoon, the adman who initially went to work him in 1966 when he was an obscure state senator running for the first time, unsuccessfully, for governor. Back then, Rafshoon remembered, Carter "didn't know which end of the camera to look in." In 1970 Carter credited Rafshoon's commercials for his upset gubernatorial victory. Six years later, just about everyone in Washington credited Rafshoon for Carter's astonishing primary and general election wins. Now Rafshoon's D.C.-based ad shop was flourishing, Carter's administration was floundering, and a desperate president appointed Rafshoon as a White House assistant to help set things right.

The hire was intended to help Carter look strong. But Washington interpreted it as more evidence that Carter was weak. Herblock drew the president looking glum, next to a "Communications Repairman" whose name tag read "Rafshoon": "It comes out fuzzy," Carter said of a televised image of himself. Another cartoonist depicted stern-faced White House aides deliberating over which color socks looked most presidential. Wits coined a new word, *Rafshoonery*—Washington's new shorthand for what used to be called "bullshit."

THE SUPREME COURT WENT INTO SESSION. ON MAY 15, THEY REJECTED without comment, for the second time, a request to review state laws banning what the North Carolina statute in question referred to as "crimes against nature." On May 23, Eugene, Oregon, like St. Paul a putatively liberal college town, voted on whether to keep gay rights protections in their human rights ordinance. Eugene had a large and visible lesbian population and a vibrant tradition of gay rights activism. A spokesman for Eugene Citizens for Human Rights predicted victory: "Wichita and St. Paul didn't target their voters, they did not undertake a massive get out the vote, which are two things we are doing."

But the college town of Burlington, Vermont, was supposed to be liberal, too—and an abortion clinic there had just been firebombed. The local paper was full of angry letters complaining that the editors had not made it sufficiently clear that pro-life activists abhorred violence—then it received one from a pro-lifer *recommending* terrorism to fight this "new, modern Holocaust."

And the 2.6 million-member United Presbyterian Church in the USA was supposed to be a liberal denomination. But at their 190th general assembly in San Diego, delegates debated a 150-page task force report, which had taken fifteen months to prepare, recommending that, since homosexuality was "a minor theme in Scripture," unmentioned by either Jesus or the prophets, and because the notion of homosexuality as a crime against nature was "conditioned by time and place," gays should allowed to enter the ministry. Six hundred out of 650 of the delegates, following a well-financed campaign led by a Pittsburgh minister against the "attempt of this militant minority to take over," voted against the recommendation. They resolved instead that gays could only be ordained if they remained celibate.

Jerry Falwell preached a nationally televised sermon on gay rights: "Like a spiritual cancer, homosexuality spread until the city of Sodom was destroyed. Can we believe that God will spare the United States if homo-sexuality continues to spread?" And Eugene voted against gay rights two to one. "The liberal voter is lazy," Citizens for Human Rights spokesman concluded, "whereas right-wingers do vote."

THE PREVIOUS EVENING, SAN FRANCISCO CITY SUPERVISOR HARVEY MILK had enjoyed a birthday party at a bar on Castro Street that used to be a pharmacy, in a neighborhood that used to be quiet, but now was Amer-ica's rollicking gay Mecca. Milk was Castro Street's de facto mayor. His camera store was up the street from that bar, the Elephant Walk, which Harvey Milk loved because it combined two qualities he considered very dear to the movement for gay liberation: it was a place where men who loved other men, and women other women, could feel safe and secure. And its patrons inside were *visible*—right there in the middle of a busy commercial thoroughfare, with big gaping picture windows to the outside. Milk remembered too well what it felt like to feel *un*-safe, and *in*-visible, back when he was an apparently comfortable investment researcher in the 1950s but had been reduced for romantic companionship to furtive assig-nations with the young men at Jacob Riis Park in Queens, or with the old men who congregated in the standing section in the back the Metropolitan Opera.

Milk had a stock speech he would delivery whenever and wherever he was asked. It began in mockery of Anita Bryant: "My name is Harvey Milk and I'm here to recruit you."

What he was recruiting them to was out, open, and unashamed politi-cal activism. He began ticking off the issues everyone was talking about in the news—the Panama Canal fight, the Steiger amendment and Kemp-Roth, the Hyde Amendment, nuclear arms negotiations with the Soviet Union, the failure of the consumer agency, Howard Jarvis. He summed up the media consensus on what they all added up to: a "move to the right." He then demanded attention be paid to another side of the story.

It included his own election as the first gay official in a major city in the U.S., and the decriminalization of marijuana in Mississippi, and the feminists' "convention of conventions" in Houston, and the growing movement to pressure the United States to take official action against South African apartheid. This, he argued, was why there was no excuse for gays not to have *hope*. In a version he gave in San Diego in March he repeated that word eighteen times in less than fifteen minutes:

"I remember the lack of *hope*," he said—the time back when homo-sexuals were "invisible . . . in limbo—a myth, a person with no parents, no brothers, no sisters, no friends who are straight, no important positions in employment." But he felt hope now: because Anita Bryant had blamed the state's awful drought the previous year on California's wicked sodomites, but that on the day after his election it had started to rain.

Because in 1977, when gay people were having their rights taken away from them in Miami, "the word 'homosexual' or 'gay' appeared in every single newspaper in this nation," and more people were discussing the issue than any time "probably in the history of mankind."

Because "once you have dialogue starting, you can break down prejudice."

Because now you could be "gay and proud of that fact and do not have to remain in the closet."

And he felt hope because he said people like him had no other choice—because "the young gay people in the Altoona, Pennsylvanias, and the Richmond, Minnesotas, who are coming out and hear Anita Bryant on television, and her story, the only thing they have to look forward to is hope. And you *have to* give them hope . . . if a gay person can be elected, it's a green light. And *you*, and *you*, and *you*—you have to give the people hope."

REPUBLICAN CONGRESSIONAL PRIMARY ELECTIONS CAME AND WENT. IN Texas's 19th District, the two conservative candidates left the moderates in the dust. The second-place finisher, Jim Reece, was a far-right former sports announcer who was sure he had finished off his rival by producing a copy of his birth certificate, proving that George Walker Bush, whom Reese referred to only as "Jr.," was a carpetbagging Yankee. "No, I was not born in Texas," the rakish son of the former CIA head George Herbert Walker Bush affably replied. "I wanted to be close to my mother that day." Bush was the primary's top vote-getter, but he didn't win 50 percent, so he would face Reece in a June runoff. He won the runoff, but Citizens for the Republic supported his opponent. His father developed a ferocious grudge against Reagan for the slight.

In Iowa, Roger Jepsen was hammered for weeks in the local media after one of his national fundraising letters was traced to the offices of Richard A. Viguerie. It had been signed by Meldrim Thomson, and noted Jepsen's endorsement by something called the National Alliance of Senior Citizens—another Richard Viguerie brainchild with a name seemingly intended to confuse voters into thinking it was the 3.5-million strong National *Council* of Senior Citizens. The *Des Moines Tribune* excoriated these "strange, outside forces" conspiring "to do great harm to our state." The *Des Moines Register* reported that the National Alliance of Senior Citizens based its endorsements not on issues actually having to do with the ordeal of aging, but on candidates' positions on things like whether striking workers should be eligible for food stamps or teenagers should be exempted from the minimum wage. The favorite in the three-way race called Jepsen a bought-and-paid for agent of "the Viguerie-announced effort to destroy the Republican Party and replace it with a coalition dedicated only to the promotion of its emotionally driven causes."'

In New Jersey, a May 18 poll showed the former Reagan aide Jeff Bell with 14 percent support against the incumbent liberal Republican Senator Cliff Case. *Chicago Tribune* columnist Jon Margolis took the occasion to declare the notion of a national move to the right a myth. "The New Right, conservatives proclaimed and liberals bewailed, was the coming thing," he wrote. "It was intense, cohesive, organized—and had a lot of money. The only thing it doesn't have a lot of, it seems, is votes. . . . Unless all the polls here are very wrong, an attractive young New Rightist is going to be positively swamped by just about the most liberal Republican in the Senate, if not the world."

Margolis also noted an unfortunate development for Bell: the decision of his "old boss, Reagan, who is trying to broaden his appeal for 1980, not to oppose Republican incumbents." That decision enraged conservatives close to Reagan. Justin Dart, a pharmaceutical magnate, hosted a dinner party for the Reagan social clique known "the Group" one evening, though Reagan himself was out of town. Guests included Arthur Laffer and William Simon, the former Ford treasury secretary and best-selling conservative author. The conversation turned to the New Jersey Senate race. Asked Laffer, "Hey, what's the boss doing? Is he supporting Jeff?"

"No he's not," Nancy Reagan, the family political enforcer, responded.

"*What?* He's not supporting Jeff?"

Nancy Reagan's face drew taut. Simon, who lived in New Jersey, and like Laffer was unfamiliar with the unspoken house rules, took up Laffer's cudgel: "Yeah, what *is* this?"

Nancy got up and walked around the table, placing herself right in the face of the former treasury secretary: "Don't you *ever* say anything nasty about my husband."

The stakes were too high to back losers. On May 14 Reagan was on CBS's *Face the Nation*; on the 16th he starred in a *Washington Post* column entitled "Reagan: More Serious Than Ever." Citizens for the Republic's Dick Wirthlin wrapped up his eighth volume of polling of key congressional districts, more than two dozen so far. CFR was on its way to taking in $3,114,514 over the 1977–78 congressional cycle, the most of any conservative or Republican political action committee. Reagan, under the influence of John Sears, was out to court Republican centers of power in the Northeast, not offend them. There would be no Jeff Bell endorsement.

But those tensions would not go away. After James J. Kilpatrick's column booming Jack Kemp for president, Peter Hannaford met with the congressman in D.C. to make sure he was not tempted to try. Jude Wanniski got wind of that, and told Jeff Bell—and suddenly Ronald Reagan was in the sights of the supply-side priesthood as a possible dangerous heretic. He was, after all, on the record—in a paperback produced for his 1976 presidential campaign, *Ronald Reagan's Call to Action*: "Several economists—hardheaded ones who aren't afraid to draw unpopular conclusions from logic and history—have said that higher unemployment is the necessary evil we must face if we are going to stop inflation." Maybe he was just another garden-variety Republican Scrooge. They persuaded Kemp to withdraw his loyalty to Reagan—who had, for now, just lost the loyalty of the *Wall Street Journal* editorial page. Pulling together a presidential coalition joining the Republican establishment and faith-drunk ideologues who searched out heretics like public-policy Torquemadas would be no easy thing.

The situation, however, was complicated. For there was one tax cut proposal for which Reagan was dizzy with enthusiasm that sounded too crazy even for the supply-siders. The *Journal* called Howard Jarvis's Proposition 13 "drastic" and "desperate," said it would "sow chaos" and "unpredictable damage"—though they allowed that, given the hash California had made of its property tax system, you could understand why it seemed "attractive to many eminently rational people." So attractive, it turned out, that it soon was setting *everything* on its ear.

CHAPTER 15

"The White, American Middle Class Plus Blacks Who Want the Same Thing"

THE WAY HOWARD JARVIS'S LEGIONS EARNED MANY OF THEIR 1.2 MILLION signatures to get Proposition 13 on California's June primary ballot was by setting up tables in shopping malls. The pitch was stone-simple: "Sign this—it will help lower your taxes." That did the trick. For in California, property taxes were out of control.

The prototypical California homeowner was the soldier in a foxhole depicted in a magazine ad during World War II: "Oh, boy, when I get out of this jungle, I'm going to build me a sweet little cottage in California, and stay there the rest of my natural life. It won't be big, but it'll have every convenience I can cram into it . . . a shower with hot and cold running water in every bathroom . . . a handy little kitchen . . . and a certain girl named Sally who knows how to make a juicy steak." He settled down in a suburb that used to be a citrus grove, where, because he was a veteran, he did not to have to make a down payment, and paid but $68 a month on the mortgage. Supply could not possibly keep pace with demand. The assessed value of homes went through the roof—and with that, their property taxes.

By the early 1960s, California was lousy with property tax protesters—by no means all of them right wing. When the Black Panther Party ran a slate of candidates in the 1973 Oakland municipal elections, property taxes were at the center of their campaign. The movement's preeminent voices were good-government liberals. They saw the issue as a technical problem. After San Francisco's crooked property tax assessor went to jail for a kickback scheme, it was their efforts that passed Assembly Bill 80 in 1966. The measure suggested the cool, scientific rationality of a NASA engineer. It mandated that all property be assessed at 25 percent of "actual market value," with those values being recalibrated annually, with the help of computers. However, it made the problem worse.

Under the former system, businesses (at least those who hadn't successfully bribed crooked assessors) paid higher rates than homeowners; under AB 80 those rates were equalized. Municipalities suffered, since they were over-reliant for revenue on property taxes, which paid for 50 percent of school budgets and 90 percent of fire budgets, but the new system eliminated their former flexibility in setting tax rates. So they increased special assessments and fees to make up for shortfalls. And the corrupt old system had the virtue of the human touch: an assessor might go easy on, say, a widow who couldn't afford to pay taxes twice as high as last year just because her once-sleepy neighborhood had suddenly become fashionable. Under the pitiless economics of AB 80, the computer crowned her as "rich," while actually making her annually more poor. "BRING BACK THE CROOKED ASSESSOR," a popular bumper sticker in San Francisco soon read.

The ratchet tightened further in the 1970s. Environmental concerns made it harder to develop new land. Pent-up demand from the 1974–75 recession led to a boom in the construction of tract houses, which were snapped up by speculators, who pushed up prices yet further. By 1976 the average value of a house in Southern California was rising by as much as 3 percent a month—in the rest of the country, it rose 3 percent a year—and Howard Jarvis began telling a story which reporters could never confirm: of the little old lady who earned $1,900 a year, opened a property tax bill demanding $1,800, and keeled over of a heart attack.

Once more, good-government liberals spied a technical problem, easily fixed. The state had a large budget surplus; tax formulae could be rejiggered to redistribute it to homeowners. The less-well-off could be helped by "circuit breakers" limiting property taxes to a certain percent of income. Or—in a reform Los Angeles county assessor Philip Watson tried several times to qualify for the ballot—tax increases could be limited to 1.5 percent of market value above $25,000. Watson consistently failed to get enough signatures. Perhaps because, as a responsible technocrat, his pitch was more complicated than "Sign this—it will lower your taxes."

There was nothing complicated about Jarvis's People's Initiative to Limit Property Taxation, which he began pushing in 1976. It would roll the assessed value of every property back to what it had been in 1975, and freeze it until the property changed hands—at which point it could not be increased by more than 2 percent, with the total tax capped at 1 percent of assessed value. That meant that the typical Los Angeles homeowner who previously paid $2,671 in property taxes on his $85,000 house would now pay $850. By one estimate this would starve the state of $7 billion in revenue—which Jarvis made no provision to replace. The opposite, in fact: a radical libertarian, he *wanted* the California treasury to implode, so the initiative also required a two-thirds legislative supermajority to hike any *other* tax.

On August 26, 1976, the Associated Press said the "outrage in normally placid middle-class bedroom communities" was "beginning to register on the political Richter scale." One retiree's tax bill had just gone from $861 to $1,450. "They said this place has a lot of potential. What am I going to do, go out and build an apartment house?" That year, Jarvis came a tantalizing 67,652 signatures short of the 557,000 required to qualify for the general election ballot.

In its 1977 session, California's majority-Democratic legislature assiduously applied themselves to fixing the problem. So did the governor, who was up for reelection in 1978. Jerry Brown was a strange man. He drove his own used Plymouth sedan, slept on a mattress on the floor in his bachelor apartment, and spent his spare time at the San Francisco Zen Center. When asked by a reporter if he was a Buddhist, he answered, "Those who know don't say, and those who say don't know." He was always saying gnomic things like that. When it came to policy, he could be extraordinarily flexible—critics said cynical and opportunistic. He was obsessed with quixotic pet projects (one was that California should build its own space program). But he also harbored a bedrock intellectual commitment: *limits.* "We have ecological limits, we even have human limits," he had said campaigning for the Democratic presidential nomination in 1976. "The human species is not going to make it unless we can figure out another way."

In practice, that meant things like this: The state's decrepit mental hospitals were suffering an awful epidemic of accidental deaths. Mental health officials blamed Ronald Reagan's budget cuts—but also Jerry Brown's. When CBS News confronted him with that charge, he replied, "Whether it be in schools, or highways, or mental hospitals, there is a limit. And I'm reluctant to invest enormous sums of money when ordinary citizens are finding it hard to meet their own bills. And it's my job to make those hard choices. . . . Every group wants a little more. And it's my job to give them a little less." He had inherited a budget surplus from Governor Reagan. Via austerity measures like these, he proceeded to out-Reagan Reagan, ballooning the surplus to $4 billion. The programs he slashed made his relationship with the Democratic legislature as frosty as Carter's with his. "Jerry Brown has screwed his friends more than I ever did my enemies," California's Democratic boss Jesse Unruh said.

On the one hand, that made it hard for him to get the necessary buy-in from members of his own party when he introduced a tax reform bill including property tax rebates for those making less than $36,000 a year. It failed by two votes. (The governor advised legislators to return home to "meditate.") On the other, Republicans recognized that if they could hand Brown a defeat on property tax reform, they could deflate his chances for reelection. So the next attempt to pass a reform bill failed, too.

After Watergate and the
Vietnam War, Americans
longed for redemption. They
met Jimmy Carter (above, in
the biographical film shown
at the 1976 Democratic
National Convention) and
fell in love—that is, those
not alienated from politics
altogether. One reader wrote
the *New York Times* that he
would no longer vote, and
"if Pericles were alive today,
he would join me."

Like Carter, Gerald Ford campaigned as an ordinary man, trustworthy and sincere—the president who had returned America to normalcy. Unlike Carter, his party was not united behind him. Ronald Reagan contested Ford for the nomination all the way through the convention (below), then built a political organization of his own (membership card, above right). He only campaigned reluctantly for the Republican ticket, and in a way that seemed calculated more to advance his own future than Ford's; his televised campaign speech (teleprompter script, right) focused on the contrast between the Democratic platform and the GOP's, which Reagan's loyalists had written: it was an advertisement for himself. Many blamed Reagan for Ford's loss; pundits judged his political career over.

YEAR...
RECENT RESEARCH
HAS REVEALED
THAT VERY
SIGNIFICANT
NUMBERS OF
PARTY PLEDGES
HAVE ACHIEVED
REALITY IN
LEGISLATION
AND PUBLIC
ADMINISTRATION
AND THAT
PROMISES MADE
FREQUENTLY ARE
CARRIED OUT -

THAT LAST
PART IS
SOMETHING I
ASK YOU TO
KEEP IN MIND.
A PARTY
PLATFORM IS AN
ACTUAL GUIDE
TO THE COURSE
A PARTY WILL
TAKE IF AND
WHEN IT COMES
TO POWER.

LEAN ON CHAIR

IF THAT IS
TRUE, THEN THE
1976 PLATFORM
OF THE DEMOCRAT
PARTY CHARTS
THE MOST
DANGEROUS
COURSE FOR A
NATION SINCE
THE EGYPTIANS
TRIED A
SHORT-CUT
THROUGH THE
RED SEA.

DESK-SIT

EACH PLATFOR

AFTER ITS

Citizens for the Republic

"THE CAUSE
WILL PREVAIL
BECAUSE
IT'S RIGHT."

Ronald Reagan
AUGUST 21, 1976

IS A SUPPORTER OF Citizens for the Republic

7

The Ford-Carter contest was full of strange and undignified incidents. During the first debate, the sound went out for twenty-eight minutes. Because the candidates had been drilled by their handlers to do nothing that might show "weakness"—like sit down—both just stood there, a political old hand reflected, "like waxworks dummies, afraid to open their mouths and take charge." NBC's anchorman David Brinkley babbled aimlessly, unable to explain anything, as, backstage, Carter and Ford handlers spun absurdly transparent distortions for the camera about their candidates' performance. It felt like an allegory of a nation that had lost its way. Outside, police kept protesters at bay in a designated pen. The most cacophonous protested an issue that hardly came up in the campaign: legal abortion. It was a harbinger of divisions to come.

8

WHY IS THIS MAN SMILING?

Instead of issues, a post-Watergate political media hankering for scandal—any scandal—turned peccadilloes into major stories. Carter gave a fascinating, searching interview to *Playboy* magazine, but his incidental mention of "lust" monopolized the coverage. Agriculture Secretary Earl Butz did more to transform American farming than any figure in history but was only remembered for telling a racist dirty joke. In a second televised debate, Ford restated American policy in Eastern Europe in an impolitic way and was hounded for days by reporters to apologize. At first, viewers said Ford had won the debate. After the media drilled it into them that Ford had made a major "gaffe," polling reversed.

Carter's highly informal "denim inaugural" featured an unprecedented surprise stroll down Pennsylvania Avenue. Americans thrilled to their new president and his colorful family (brother, Billy, above; daughter, Amy, below). But the Washington establishment was horrified. And that spelled trouble.

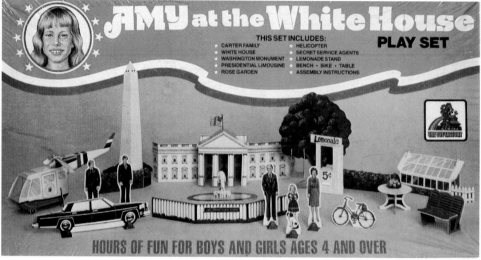

A telegraph from Ronald Reagan to all the people of Utah

ORRIN HATCH
Republican for U.S. Senate

ORRIN HATCH
U.S. SENATE / REPUBLICAN

Two days after Carter's inaugural, the issue hardly mentioned on the campaign trail became harder to ignore. A record 40,000 gathered in subfreezing temperatures for the annual "March for Life." It heralded the growing clout of conservatives. Orrin Hatch was the first senator to win with the help of a cadre of cutthroat operatives calling themselves the "New Right"—as well as with the help of Ronald Reagan's new organization. Conservative economist Milton Friedman (below, right) and neoconservative novelist Saul Bellow (below, left) won Nobel Prizes. "Neocons" were former radicals, largely Jewish. The movement's foreign policy wing had already drawn blood with a devastating stealth campaign against Jimmy Carter's foreign policy plans.

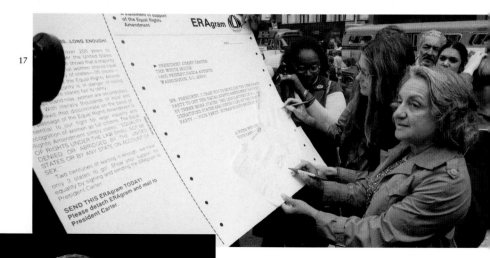

Liberal constituencies who hoped a Democrat in the White House would push long-pending projects over the finish line were mostly disappointed; Carter held his party's left wing in contempt. But feminists like Betty Friedan (above, right) and Gloria Steinem (above, left) found in him a dedicated advocate of the Equal Rights Amendment, which was on the verge of ratification by enough states to enter the Constitution. By spring, however, tireless and brilliant organizing by antifeminists led by Phyllis Schlafly (left), many involving themselves in politics for the first time, forced a series of shocking reversals.

20

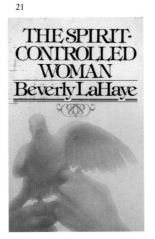

21

22

23

Time said feminism had "matured beyond ideology to a new status of general—and sometimes unconscious—acceptance." Not for the millions of women devouring therapeutic books instructing them that the path to happiness—and heaven—was surrender to their husband's authority. In one popular church seminar, "Eve Reborn," lecturer Susan Key (left) instructed wives that there was "no authority that is not ordained by God"—even Hitler's. For these women, Time's observation felt like an existential threat.

25

Activists for gay and lesbian rights also assumed their steady march to full civil rights would continue. In Miami, however, singer and former beauty queen Anita Bryant (right) led a "Save Our Children" referendum that repealed a county gay rights ordinance by an overwhelming vote. At the next gay pride parade in San Francisco, she joined a gallery of villains including Stalin, Hitler, and the KKK.

26

27

SIGN PETITION HERE
TO REPEAL METRO'S
'GAY' BLUNDER!

SIGN PE
TO REPE
'GAY' B

SAVE OUR
CHILD
FRO
HO
SEX

Death Penalty

... an open letter to the criminals of California

" We, the law-abiding and peaceful citizens of California, do hereby declare all out war against you who have been literally getting away with murder. We are sick and tired of the soft-on-crime judges and bleeding heart "reformers" who have time and time again set you free to make victims of our friends and families.

We demand restoration of the death penalty in California and intend to deliver that message to our State Legislators in no uncertain terms.

And that's a promise. "

Law & Order
CAMPAIGN COMMITTEE

... and the people of California

In a matter of days, the California State Assembly will vote Aye or Nay on Senator Deukmejian's Death Penalty Bill. Join us and help get that bill PASSED into law.

Here's what you can do:

1 Write or call your Assemblyman immediately and demand that he vote FOR restoration of the death penalty.

2 Complete and rush the petition below to the Law & Order Campaign Committee. Your petition, along with thousands of others, will be presented to the media and the California State Assembly.

3 Send your maximum contribution to LOCC to keep this campaign alive.

Petition To Restore the Death Penalty

To: The California State Assembly

By summer 1977, reaction was everywhere. After Gary Gilmore (above left) became the first American executed in a decade, citizens clamored for more. Debate over restoring the death penalty consumed California politics for months (above right: an ad campaign engineered by the New Right's Richard Viguerie). In New York City, a blackout brought widespread looting. Neoconservative Midge Decter blamed "urban insect life." With the "Son of Sam" serial killer on the loose, the death penalty became the defining issue of the New York mayoral campaign, even though mayors had no power over it. Meanwhile anti–gun control militants took over the National Rifle Association. One of their partisans was Ronald Reagan, who in his syndicated daily radio commentaries said "the best way to deter murderers and thieves is to arm law-abiding folk and not to disarm them." It all betokened the promise of the New Right's central political strategy: "organizing discontent."

30

31

32

America also turned right culturally. Audiences had previously flocked to dark, morally ambiguous films like 1975's *Taxi Driver* (above); now they embraced *Star Wars* (above right), whose director explained, "Everyone's forgetting to tell the kids, 'Hey this is right and this is wrong.'" A wholesome Christian family ubiquitous in the 1950s (right) became stars again in the late 1970s after Debby Boone's song sung to Jesus, "You Light Up My Life," became a huge hit. At the Oscars, it beat out music from *Saturday Night Fever*—a film which her father Pat Boone told *People* magazine his family walked out on. African Americans hoped that the hit miniseries *Roots* (below) would inspire a national reckoning with racism. Instead, it set off a boom in white ethnic nostalgia: "So many Jews today seek memories of shtetl forebears," *Time* reported, "that East Europeans call them 'roots people.'" Ronald Reagan said he couldn't imagine anyone staying home for eight nights to watch it: "I thought the bias of all the good people being one color and all the bad people being another was rather destructive."

33

34

Reagan spent August 1977 like he always spent his Augusts: relaxing on his ranch near Santa Barbara. Then he unexpectedly reemerged into the political spotlight leading conservatives fighting ratification of Jimmy Carter's treaties to relinquish the Panama Canal—not aggressively enough for New Right leaders, however, who said they might consider other prospects for 1980.

Left-right showdowns dominated ballots in 1978. In the spring, California shocked the nation with a landslide vote to slash property taxes in the face of warnings that "Prop 13" might decimate services. The professionals running the campaign intended to keep its architect, the uncouth extremist Howard Jarvis (above), out of the spotlight—until the public embraced him as a folk hero. "The politicians want to take everything we have—but now we're giving them an enema," he announced triumphantly on election night. The "tax revolt" went nationwide. In some Ohio cities, schools feared they wouldn't be able to open in the fall because citizens voted down so many bond issues. In Georgia, a former history professor named Newt Gingrich (below) ran for Congress on Prop 13's coattails, with a "fanaticism," his hometown *Atlanta Journal-Constitution* observed, "that only a starved dog can understand when it spots a foundling lamb."

FANCY THAT!

In an effort to protect consumer interests, the federal government has set up some 1,000 programs in 33 federal departments and agencies. Federal agencies designed to ride herd on businesses cost taxpayers about $4 billion a year.

Now Congress is considering bills to establish still another consumer agency to watch all the other watchdogs. To set up this super bureaucracy, taxpayers would have to come up with another $60 million for the first three years.

The federal government already employs nearly one percent of the U.S. population. The number of civil service workers in eight of the largest consumer service agencies is nearly 140,000.

Ralph Nader (above left) was a folk hero from the left. His unbroken train of victories constraining corporate power had people talking him up for president all through the first half of the decade. In 1977, Nader ally Michael Pertschuk (above right), chairman of the Federal Trade Commission, also emerged as a hero—"The Bureaucrat Who Makes Business Turn Blue," a *People* magazine profile called him. Business fought back with unprecedented aggressiveness and sophistication—as with the cartoon at left that helped defeat a widely popular proposal for a federal consumer agency. Others made war against taxes. Superlobbyist Charls Walker (below) ran a cunning PR campaign that had two-thirds of Americans supporting a capital gains tax cut that gave 97 percent of benefits to those making over $200,000 a year— almost $800,000 in 2020 dollars.

43

In September 1978, Carter called the chieftains of two warring tribes up to Camp David; Anwar Sadat of Egypt (left) and Menachem Begin of Israel (right) came down from the mountaintop bearing a miraculous accord. Carter's anemic approval rating shot up; his political aides celebrated. But almost immediately, it shot back down.

Jimmy Carter had won by appealing to everyone, left, right, center. Then the bills for this ideological profligacy came due. For instance, after he came out for a measure to end federal funding of abortions, with the comment, "As you know, there are many things in life that are not fair," the flagship magazine of the feminist movement mocked him in its year-end issue with a cover line that doubled as a jab at his mounting political woes.

Howard Jarvis took on a former rival in the tax-reform game, Paul Gann, as a partner. Gann had none of Jarvis's antic charisma, but he did have a massive mailing list of Northern California voters. In May, they began setting up their tables in the state's hundreds of shopping malls. That summer, the average property tax assessment increased by a third. By December, they were easily able to file many more signatures than required. Their critics suspected they had paid a political firm to gather signatures, which at going rates would have cost them half a million dollars. Actually, they did it themselves for $60,000.

In February 1978, Sacramento managed to pass a property tax reform package. It would provide a baseline 30 percent cut for homeowners, with special credits for renters and the elderly, and a higher rate for business properties. This "split rate" for homeowner and business, however, required a change in the state constitution, and that required approval from voters. An initiative to do so qualified to be listed on the ballot as Proposition 8. That staged an electoral showdown: Howard's Jarvis's "Prop 13" versus Jerry Brown's "Prop 8."

Jarvis relished the fight. He worked eighteen-hour days, journeying from one homeowners association meeting to another—to increasingly crowded rooms. He became a regular on the talk show of a popular radio personality who loved how this colorful crank boosted ratings among bored commuters stuck in L.A.'s endless traffic jams. "*You* are the people," Jarvis said, "and *you* will have to take control of the government again or else it is going to control you."

His movement soon had a slogan. It was from a hit movie that had come out late in 1976, an antic dystopian fantasy called *Network* in which a half-mad TV newscaster took to addressing the camera directly to decry a world gone mad. "I don't want you to riot," he cried. "I don't want you to write to your congressman because I wouldn't know what to tell you to write. I don't know what to do about the depression and the inflation and the Russians and the crime in the street. All I know is that first you've got to get mad. You've got to say, 'I'm a human being, Goddamn it! My life has value! So I want you to get up now. I want all of you to get up out of your chairs. I want you to get up right now and go the window. Open it, and stick your head out, and yell, '*I'm mad as hell and I'm not going to take this anymore.*'"

In the movie, his viewers ran to their windows and did exactly that. Metaphorically speaking, Californians were now doing it now.

FLUSHED WITH DONATIONS, JARVIS AND GANN HIRED A CUTTING-EDGE public relations firm, whose research revealed that people were blaming "politicians" for their problems. So the firm's director made an unexpected recommendation. The experts "thought Howard Jarvis was a goofy old gadfly who would hurt his own cause. We felt he was somebody ordinary taxpayers could identify with. So we said, 'Let's not diffuse this; let's make this one guy and his struggles the entire focus." He noted, "The other side thought that was great": the more the public saw Jarvis, the less they would respect Prop 13. He wore ill-fitting, unfashionable suits. He slouched. His voice was abrasive. He had no neck.

And, after all, the Prop 8 side had all the *sound* arguments. Prop 13 would starve local governments of almost a quarter of their revenue; the state's budget surplus would eventually evaporate; schools, firehouses, and parks would have to close. Prop 13 would deliver a windfall to wealthy businesses and landlords, where Proposition 8 would cut taxes only for homeowners. And Prop 8 enjoyed the support of just about every powerful institution in the state, even big business—who knew Jarvis's radical measure would save them boatloads of money in the short run, but feared it would ruin the state's investment climate and lead to higher corporate taxes in the long run. Even the California state Republican convention deadlocked over whether to endorse Proposition 13. Jarvis replied by calling Republicans "the stupidest people in the world except for businessmen."

It was the end of April when they lost the *Wall Street Journal* editorial page. The establishment coalition was slightly ahead, confident of victory, even if polls showed enormous numbers of undecideds; after all, Proposition C, the taxation initiative in Michigan that Milton Friedman had been campaigning for in 1976 when he learned he'd won the Nobel Prize, had been running ahead by more than two to one until the final weeks, then took a nosedive once fence-sitters wrapped their mind around the reality of the service cuts its passage would entail.

BUT THE ESTABLISHMENT'S EMBRACE WAS PROPOSITION 8'S ACHILLES' HEEL. For how could his critics accuse Howard Jarvis of being the handmaiden of the rich and powerful when all the rich and powerful institutions were on the other side?

Indeed, the Proposition 8 coalition was soon shocked to discover from all their expensive polling that middle-class homeowners didn't *care* that the rich would harvest the windfall—so long as they paid less money, too, and so long as Proposition 13 took a wrecking ball to the political class. Their anti–Proposition 13 TV commercials—"It may look good, but it costs too much"—excited no one. Jarvis's were killers. One pointed out that Proposition 8's "split rate" was well and good in theory, but the technicalities hadn't been written into the initiative text, left to the legislature to decide: "The people put Proposition 13 on the ballot. The politicians put Proposition 8 on the ballot. Now we know why." Their tagline was: "Give the politicians a budget instead of a blank check. Vote Yes."

The state school superintendent began saying that if Prop 13 passed it would force the layoff of thousands of teachers, require the average district to trim 38 percent from its budget, and cause classes with as many as sixty students—"nothing short of destroying education in California." Districts started sending out formal notices to teachers warning them to prepare to make other employment plans for fall—a "Chicken Little routine," Ronald Reagan called it. "If it passes, they will have to set spending priorities."

Los Angeles's ABC affiliate gave Jarvis a nightly spot to debate all comers; his appearances boosted ratings. Which only made the opposition more confident. They were sure his oafish gaffes would finish him. There was the time he demanded, after an L.A. Board of Supervisors press conference warning 80 percent of city libraries would close, "Why do we need books? The schools aren't teaching the kids to read anyway." Or the time he said, on live TV, "I'll die knowing I really put the hot rod up the butts of those damned stupid politicians!" He kept buffoonishly interrupting his opponents, calling them "liars." He spewed venom about illegal Mexican immigrants "who just come over here to get on the taxpayers' gravy train." He mocked a debate opponent's British accent. Taking on a representative from the League of Women Voters—"a bunch of nosy broads who front for the big spenders"—he pulled out an anti–Prop 13 editorial from Communist Party organ the *People's World*: "The Communist Party has an ally in the League of Women Voters!" A Jarvis-Gann consultant worried the Joe McCarthy imitation would cost them a hundred thousand votes.

Instead, they kept gaining. People loved this real-life Howard Beale. His status as a folk hero grew and grew.

JARVIS KEPT ON MAKING WHAT SEEMED LIKE INCREASINGLY PREPOSTEROUS predictions. One was insisting that Californians would open their mailboxes in July, after the election, to discover their property tax bills had doubled again, even though experts insisted this was inconceivable. Maybe *that* was what would finally slay him. Actually, it did the opposite—after Jarvis called the experts' bluff.

His organization began running a commercial in heavy rotation. It depicted a hand winding a jack-in-the-box, plinking out "Pop Goes the Weasel." A voice announced, "The politicians have a surprise for you. But they didn't want you to know it until after the election." The music stopped, and out popped a sign where the clown should, stating that assessments would double. This was the message they now hammered in every forum— "making it more and more outrageous" all the time, a Jarvis aide explained, "hoping that some assessor would crack": that is prove they were not party to a Nixonian cover-up by releasing before the June 6 balloting next year's assessments, which were supposed to be released in July.

Los Angeles had a new county assessor, Alexander Pope. Pope knew that Jarvis's jack-in-the-box estimate was, if anything, *conservative*: the average assessment would increase not by 100 but by *125* percent. Liberals on the County Board of Supervisors begged him not to yield to the pressure to release this information before the election. But Pope was a liberal, too—and a liberal is someone, as Robert Frost said, too broadminded to take his own side in a quarrel. Pope decided to prove he was a transparent public official. On Wednesday, May 17, he opened his eighteen offices in Los Angeles County to any property owner who wished to look their assessment up.

Lines snaked out the offices' doors for days—and news stories proliferated of homeowners ready to enact Jarvis's fable of the widow who keeled over from assessment-induced shock. "I don't know if I can walk to the car," one was quoted in the *Los Angeles Times* as saying upon learning her bill had soared from $2,000 to approximately $5,500.

Proposition 8, it was true, would have taken care of most of these disasters. It would not, however, allow them to thrust the hot rod up the butts of those damned stupid politicians.

The Proposition 13 campaign used computerized public records to send out a mailing a journalist called "barely legal." Official-looking envelopes read, "IMPORTANT ASSESSMENT INFORMATION INSIDE." They contained a letter from Howard Jarvis addressed to the recipient by name, beginning, "I was shocked to learn that your 1977 property tax was $_____," and predicting it would double. A fund-raising coupon was included. The take from the letter allowed Jarvis to buy more TV commercials. A month before Election Day, polls had Proposition 13 ahead by 3 percent, with 19 percent undecided. Soon after the opening of the Los Angeles assessment files, it was winning 42 percent to 30.

Almost a fifth of voters were still undecided—until, that is, the following week, when California's finance director gave voters *more* reason to distrust politicians: he announced California's budget surplus was not $4 billion but almost $5 billion. Pro–Prop 13 housewives marched down suburban streets bearing picket signs, Martin Luther King Jr.–style. Bumper stickers begged: "Save the American Dream. Vote Yes on Prop 13." A Palos Verdes life insurance executive was quoted offering a typical response from the state's middle class: "It's time to bring those cotton-picking legislators down to their knees."

AT THE END OF MAY IN THE CHICAGO SUBURB OF LINCOLNSHIRE, WITH THE vote in California a week way, two hundred activists met at a National Tax

Limitation Conference. An aide for one of sponsors, the American Legislative Exchange Council, an organization controlled by Paul Weyrich that wrote conservative "model legislation" for state legislators to introduce, described tax limitation as the perfect issue to build a broader conservative movement—to *organize discontent*: "It crosses all philosophies. Everybody is concerned with the increase in taxes."

Newsweek agreed: "Just as the New Deal of the 1930s launched Big Government, the Great Tax Revolt of 1978 may herald a conservative reaction." William Safire traveled to California and quoted a frightened politician: "The damn thing could pass." Safire concluded, "If the tax revolt succeeds here, in a fairly liberal state, there's no telling where it would lead."

People like Safire, the *Newsweek* writer, and the ALEC official attested to a fundamental political fact: movements become powerful enough to change history when they merge diverse tributaries: when people who would ordinarily blanch at sitting to dinner together—Howard Jarvis, the outsiders' outsider, say, and Charls Walker, the insiders' insider; a corporate executive in a tailored suit and a middle-class housewife spouting conspiracy theories about gender-neutral bathrooms—decide that their interests align. Around that Memorial Day weekend in 1978, such confluences were everywhere. Data-entry clerks laboring overtime to commit the millions of names and addresses harvested during the Panama Canal fight to the memory banks of mainframe computers; fundamentalist Christians celebrating their victories over gay rights in St. Paul and Wichita and Eugene who might just send a check to Howard Jarvis; New Right congressional candidates drafting general election literature referring to all these issues in anti-liberal laundry lists. All of them sharing a vague conviction that these various projects were, deep down, part of the same mighty river—to which, presently, *another* mighty tributary burbled up at fullest force. Potentially, the mightiest tributary of all, because it bore within it the potential to wash out a foundation of liberal political power.

IT CONCERNED AN APPARENTLY DRY SUBJECT: LABOR LAW.

In 1935, at the height of the Great Depression, the right of workers to organize into unions was enshrined as the law of the land by the National Labor Relations Act, known for its chief architect as the "Wagner Act." New York Senator Robert F. Wagner's law stipulated that if a majority of workers at a firm voted to affiliate with a union in an election overseen by the presidentially appointed National Labor Relations Board, that union was granted exclusive power to bargain for better wages and conditions in contracts covering all the workers at that firm. The law also made the formerly routine intimidation technique of firing workers for supporting a union a federal crime, punishable by costly fines and reinstatement of the worker with back pay. In the decades that followed, this principle was enshrined as civic holy writ.

"Labor unions are woven into the economic pattern of American life, and collective bargaining is part of the Democratic Process," the head of the Chamber of Commerce said in 1946. "I say recognize this fact not only with our lips but with our hearts." Dwight Eisenhower in 1952 said, "Only a handful of unreconstructed reactionaries harbor the ugly thought of breaking unions. Only a fool would try to deprive working men and women of the right to join the union of their choice." And why not? The Wagner Act was symbol and substance America's unique genius in solving one of world history's most persistent ongoing agonies: class conflict. Under it, American workers became wealthier than any proletariat in history—and capitalists reaped steadily increasing profits.

In 1977, America's accord between labor and capital seemed to reach an apotheosis. Carter followed the precedent of Presidents Nixon and Ford and convened a sixteen-member Labor-Management Group to advise him on economic issues, joining high labor officials with CEOs from companies like General Electric, Bechtel, Alcoa, GM, and Sears. Known as the "Dunlop Commission" after its chairman, the Harvard labor relation professor and Ford administration labor secretary John Dunlop, it functioned as a sort of economic shadow cabinet.

One of the Dunlop Commission's contributions was to help craft a bill closing loopholes that let companies get away with refusing to negotiate with unions even after workers won union representation elections. The poster child for such abuses was J. P. Stevens Textiles in North Carolina. Workers there voted to unionize in 1974. Ever since, the company dragged the union through a war of attrition rather than admit defeat—then, when they lost in the courts, they simply absorbed as a cost of doing business the negligible $1.3 million in fines and back pay assessed in fourteen separate NLRB rulings.

The bill introduced in May 1977 would make it harder to do that by increasing back pay for fired workers to 150 percent of lost wages. It would expand the National Labor Relations Board from five to seven members in order to hack away at its backlog of nineteen thousand union-recognition elections. It would also require companies that forced workers to attend company anti-union meetings to give equal time to union organizers, and deny federal contracts to companies violating labor law—like J. P. Stevens, which enjoyed $3.4 million in business from the Defense Logistics Agency.

Given the two-thirds Democratic majority in Congress and the first Democratic Oval Office occupant in eight years, labor could have asked for more—for instance, repeal of the provision in the 1947 Taft-Hartley Act allowing states to pass "right to work" laws. Instead, they settled for a bill that mostly only punished already illegal behavior more severely. Seven former labor secretaries, Republican and Democrat, endorsed it. But Jimmy Carter did not share their enthusiasm.

He worried about alienating business—even though Stuart Eizenstat argued that, while "the business community will certainly oppose the bill, they certainly view it as much more acceptable than earlier versions and will therefore be less vociferous in condemning the administration for its position." Carter worried, too, about siding too publicly with unions. Here Eisenstadt also pushed back: "It is difficult to overestimate the importance of this matter in terms of our future relationship with organized labor"—not least because, given "fiscal considerations, we will be unable to satisfy their desires in many areas requiring expenditure of federal funds." The president consulted with the Business Roundtable, who objected to a few of the bill's provisions, including one called "card check" that would radically speed up union elections. The White House convinced the AFL-CIO to agree to their removal, then endorsed the bill.

House subcommittee hearings began. Unions sent a parade of victims up to Capitol Hill, including a seventy-seven-year-old woman who had lost her job when the Deering Milliken textile company liquidated itself in 1956 rather than recognize a union. The new corporate entity that replaced it appealed the NLRB ruling against it all the way to the Supreme Court. In 1968, they were resoundingly defeated. The old woman testified that workers like her still had not yet received a single penny of the back pay the high court had mandated. Committee members traveled to J. P. Stevens's headquarters city in North Carolina, the state with the lowest wages and lowest union density in the nation, for nine days of hearings where laborers, activists, and clergymen described coordinated harassment from companies, politicians, and police that sounded little different from the stories that galvanized the nation during the civil rights revolution of the 1960s. The testimony established beyond a shadow of a doubt, a Republican economist said, that if you were a labor law violator, "crime pays." The House agreed. On October 7, they passed the bill in a 257–163 vote that included thirty-six Republicans. Opposition, a historian noted, was "limited to 'Cro-Magnon types.'" The system was working: extremists had been marginalized, compromise achieved. As 1978 began, labor law reform seemed assured.

Which was exactly what people had once said in a similar period in the process about the consumer agency bill.

CORPORATE IMPATIENCE WITH THE LABOR-MANAGEMENT ACCORD HAD been quietly building. The number of workers illegally fired for union activity rose from 3,779 in 1970 to 5,533 in 1978. Fines and mandatory back pay assessed by the NLRB rose from $2.7 million to $13.5 million. More and more companies were doing what J. P. Stevens did: absorbing those expenses as a cost of doing business, fighting organizing campaigns as if their corporate lives depended on it. In the first ten years of the Wagner Act, unions won 80 percent of representation elections. Nowadays, they won less than half, and union density was 20.1 of the private workforce, down from 34.5 percent in 1956.

Conservatives insisted that labor's wounds were self-inflicted—that workers voting against union representation were only reacting to, as Orrin Hatch put it in an op-ed that June, "pension fund embezzlements, extortions to obtain dues, union racketeering, misuse and unpopular political use of union dues, beatings and even deaths." He said labor leaders "earn kingly ransoms for a few hours work each day; travel the world in private, luxury jets; ride to work in chauffeured Cadillacs and Lincolns and enjoy French cuisine prepared by chefs at their offices." More and more, the public agreed. A 1977 Harris Poll revealed that by a margin of 64 to 13 percent, the public believed that union leaders were connected to criminal elements.

Some were, of course, but the data hardly bore out the prejudice. During the 1970–78 period, company complaints of union malfeasance deemed meritorious by the NLRB increased at precisely the rate of GDP growth—but meritorious complaints of lawbreaking by *companies* more than doubled. NLRB data also suggested *why* companies were becoming more willing to fight unions: the number of big strikes they called kept going up, during the same period in which corporate profits kept going down.

Business began fighting back in Washington. In 1975, a bill passed allowing construction unions to use a technique, previously outlawed by the Supreme Court, called "common situs": picketing an entire building site if a single contractor used non-union labor. In exchange, the bill made it easier for companies to end wildcat strikes. President Ford vetoed it after a deluge of seven hundred thousand telegrams and letters orchestrated by Richard Viguerie. When it was reintroduced, in the spring of 1977, conservatives scotched it before it could get to the president's desk. They key margin had come from Democrats deluged by lobbying from their small business constituents. At a gala for Ronald Reagan at the D.C. Hyatt Regency following that victory, emcee Efrem Zimbalist Jr., the dashing star of TV's *The FBI*, gloated: "I expect that a lot of people might have thought 'common situs' was a venereal disease. But the small business community did unite to defeat this bill. We demonstrated when the people are aroused, they will unite."

They had achieved it via an ad hoc coalition, the National Action Committee, led by the National Association of Manufacturers. In August of 1977, five months after the common situs defeat, at a meeting of the policy committee of the Business Roundtable, the CEO of Sears, Reginald Jones, took the floor and proposed that the Roundtable—NAM's blue-chip counterparts, the wheelhouse of the labor-management accord—*join* NAM's National Action Committee. This was a historic development.

Jones was a friend of President Carter and a member of the Dunlop Commission that had helped craft the labor reform bill. But he now saw the potential expansion of union power represented by its passage in apocalyptic terms—a step that "could push our country down the road to a labor- and government-controlled economy." He was also about to retire. Staving off that apocalypse was the legacy he wished to pass down to future generations. So he implored his colleagues to place themselves in harness with these conservative firms' planned fight against the bill in the Senate.

Jones was supported by the CEOs of Firestone and Goodyear—fierce competitors both based in Akron, Ohio, low down on the chain of manufacturing complexity, whose labor relations histories better resembled those of a NAM constituent. He was opposed by General Motors and General Electric, which both had in the 1930s recognized unions after what amounted to violent wars, and had little interest in upsetting the amicable relationship with labor that they had been building ever since. Sears's man argued that times had changed. A worldwide recession was putting downward pressure on profit margins. Aggressive labor settlements with cost of living adjustments built in were driving an inflation that threaten profit margins further. Ralph Nader's minions were still out there, demanding more and more costly regulation. Unions, given an inch, might decide it was time to start demanding a mile—perhaps extending unionization to classes of employees excluded from the National Labor Relations Act: managers, engineers, technicians.

He implored his fellow CEOs, in other words, to become *class conscious*, just like in the consumer agency fight—to remove their noses from their quarterly balance sheets, step back from their obsession with tomorrow's stock price, see the forest for the trees, and join the apocalyptic freedom fighters of the National Association of Manufacturers who held that capitalists must join, or die. *"Will You Be Free to Celebrate Christmas in the Future?"*

The position for a declaration of war against America's forty-year labor management accord prevailed 19 to 11. NAM's National Action Committee, which had fielded about one hundred trade organizations and firms for the common situs fight, grew to more than three hundred, including some of the biggest corporations in the world. History was turning on one of those narrow pivots.

A UNIQUELY AGGRESSIVE SENATOR BECAME THEIR LEGISLATIVE FIELD GENeral—a New Right senator: Orrin Hatch. Though later, in his memoir, Hatch was modest about how he ended up with the job: no one else, he wrote, "wanted to stand in front of a runaway train."

A more conventional first-termer might have accepted the assignment deferentially. Hatch set conditions: the coalition must present a united front—no side deals, no private understandings with the unions, no compromises. They agreed, and followed his ruthless command unconditionally. "When I first arrived, the business community was headed by a bunch of gutless wonders," he reflected the following year. That was changing now. On January 25, 1978, the labor law reform bill was recommended to the full Senate by the Labor Committee with an overwhelming vote of 16–2. On, February 8, the consumer bill was defeated. That provided the model, goad, and inspiration for the most aggressive fifteen-week lobbying drive in the history of the United States.

The public relations firm coordinating it reported on their progress in the middle of March: the distribution of 2,500 copies of a 704-page book of anti-labor-law newspapers editorials to legislators, editors, and opinion leaders (140 of those editorials were written by staffers of the Chamber of Commerce and the National Federation of Independent Businesses); 50,000 copies of a handbill claiming that trusting what labor said about the bill was like believing in Santa Claus, the Tooth Fairy, and the Easter Bunny; advertisements for local markets spelling out how many jobs the law would allegedly erase in each; for the Washington, D.C., market, a blockbuster ad starring Senator Sam Erving; also a memo to four hundred labor journalists annotating a National Labor Relations Board report boasting that the agency had closed a record number of cases—"proof from the government itself labor law 'reform' is not needed."

And, most ambitiously, the National Action Committee had commissioned a study from an economist with bipartisan credentials predicting with bracing confidence—directly contradicting the last forty years of economic history—that each 10 percent increase in union representation brought a 3 percent raise in the rate of inflation, a claim boosted in simultaneous press conferences in fourteen states in which spokesmen described the bill as "singularly inconsistent with the President's announced objective of reducing the current alarming high rate of inflation."

That study contained another crucial distortion. It claimed that the bill's "major economic burden" would be borne by businesses with fewer than 250 workers, comprising 66 percent of the workforce. In fact, four out of five American businesses were too small to be covered by the National Labor Relations Act, including most restaurants—which didn't keep the National Restaurant Association, whose members were mostly included in that 80 percent, from becoming one of the most active members of the coalition. Successfully recruiting small businesses was imperative to the drive's success—for there were many, many more small businesses than big ones, the better to barrage senators with greater volumes of lobbying and mail.

Senator Howard Metzenbaum, a liberal Democrat, soon became flabbergasted by all the small businessmen from Ohio flocking to his office. Each was armed, an aide complained, with "no more than the one-page briefing sheet somebody gave them." Metzenbaum began asking how much revenue their firms earned annually. He then found himself with the sad duty to report that they were too small to be covered by the law they insisted would ruin them. They would return to the ad hoc coalition's headquarters—where Hatch and his deputies would deliver rousing pep talks claiming that, though *this* bill did not cover them, the next one would be directed exclusively at them. Thus fortified, they gladly returned to the field of battle.

FLOOR DEBATE BEGAN MAY 16—BY WHICH TIME THE SENATE POST OFFICE was handling seven times the typical amount of mail, delivered to offices still backlogged with correspondence from the Panama Canal and consumer bill fights. "What will happen to you . . . your family's safety . . . our American way of life if the czars of organized labor have their way?" read the "ACTION communique" the United States Chamber of Commerce dispatched to get those letters flowing. The National Right to Work Committee distributed sixty million preprinted postcards to businesses to send to their representatives—buying out, reportedly, "nearly every postcard maker in the East." Labor did their part—though they could raise only $2.5 million for the fight, against business's $7 million. Arkansas Democrat Dale Bumpers, who was undecided, got one letter for every four people in his state; Senator Charles Percy of Illinois got more mail about labor law reform in the first half of 1978 than he had on the Vietnam War over six years.

Pundits worried this new, automated, "grassroots" politics might grind Washington to a halt. "It doesn't even matter that the majority of public opinion is on the other side," a commentator wrote: money talked—and its language was automated direct mail. When the Founders wrote the right to petition the government for redress of grievances into the Constitution, they never anticipated the mainframe computer, divining via algorithm which recipients were most likely to respond to entreaties to send a preprinted postcard to their congressman, and triggering a "personalized" form letter in response, with no human intermediation at all. "They go computer," a senator complained. "We go computer. We've reached the crazy point of *1984* already."

Another technological development sorely vexing senators was cheap air travel. Both sides "think nothing of putting a dozen people on a plane and sending them up here," a Senate aide from Kentucky marveled. "It was so well structured, so well organized," said a stunned assistant to fence-sitter Lawton Chiles of Florida of the business campaign. "I don't think they missed a single possible opponent of that bill in our state." The AFL-CIO set up near the Capitol a full-time "victims' vigil" comprised of illegally fired workers. "It's our macho versus their macho," a labor lobbyist said—though if macho was counted in dollars, business out-brawnyed labor by a factor of 2.9 to one.

GEORGE MEANY, THE AFL-CIO'S PRESIDENT, JUST COULDN'T WRAP HIS MIND around it. He published an anguished cri de coeur in the *Wall Street Journal*: "Why should law-abiding companies seek to continue a system that allows some employers to break the law with impunity?"

It was a good question. So was the one posted by a perplexed reader to a UPI columnist who answered citizen queries about the political process: "What are the real reasons there is such a big fight over a bill most of the general public doesn't seem to care about?" The answer was too complex for a single newspaper column. But it was very important. It helped explain the consumer agency fight, too, with all those conservative speeches and votes from congressmen who weren't necessarily all that conservative: it turned out that they just wanted to keep being congressmen.

There had always been lobbyists, of course. There had always been powerful interests big-footing legislators. Until the late 1970s, however, the most powerful force in Congress was committee chairmen, who struck backroom deals over cigars and bourbon on which bills would be allowed to reach the House and Senate floors, to be rubber-stamped by junior members, whose punishment for failing to defer to their elders was political banishment. Most of these power brokers were Southerners, and often quite conservative, but the Democratic Party nonetheless shepherded a remarkable series of populist reforms through Congress from the New Deal era on down. That was because old bulls decided their course via a myriad of factors—one of which being sticking their finger in the wind concerning what policies might win the most loyalty from constituents on Election Day.

Following Watergate a new cadre of idealistic reformers were swept into Congress and stripped the old bulls of their leadership positions.

They increased the number of committees and subcommittees and passed a rule that members could not chair more than one, increasing the number of "leaders." They opened most congressional committee meetings to the public and made it easier to successfully file Freedom of Information Act requests. They passed campaign finance reforms requiring public disclosure of all campaign donations, limiting individuals to $2,000 per candidate per election. All these changes were brought about with the intent of advancing liberalism as they understood it. But unintended consequences ensued.

The inexperienced new leaders proved easy prey for corporate lobbyists. And the new openness midwifed priceless opportunities for corporations who could afford to send lobbyists to hearing after hearing, keeping tabs on members to whom they had donated—or might donate. In 1971, only 175 businesses had federally registered lobbyists. Within a decade that had increased more than tenfold. Now a corporation getting what it wanted required so much more than wining and dining a single committee chairman: it required all those computer-driven postal assaults, op-ed-writing mercenaries, and platoons of outraged small businessmen invading congressional offices to win the votes of individual members, who now had so much more leeway to make decisions independently of their party's leadership. That was expensive. Which made it fortunate for them that an epic loophole freed up more money to flow into the political process than at any time since the Gilded Age.

The Federal Elections Campaign Act Amendments of 1974 made it easier to form political action committees—legal entities that pooled stakeholders' individual contributions. This reform was specifically requested by labor unions, who believed it could help them dominate political fundraising because they had the ability to coordinate donations from members. But the organizations that found it *easiest* to coordinate donations were corporations—whose employees had to please the boss or lose their jobs. Some corporations merely "invited" employees to deduct PAC contributions straight from their paycheck. Others leaned on them to send money themselves. ("This is your opportunity to voluntarily contribute to the benefit of United Technologies' employees and shareholders in signing a check," ran a typical letter from a senior vice president to his corporation's entire management upon the opening of the conglomerate's new PAC in 1977.) Stockholders were supplicated for PAC donations, too.

Under this money onslaught, the ideology of Democratic members of Congress shifted right—or rather, shifted *further* right. For the lion's share of new Democrats elected after Watergate, known as the "Watergate Babies," came from suburban districts previously represented by Republicans. They tended to be indifferent or even hostile to traditional Democratic constituencies like labor, and to populist economic legislation. They saw themselves not as loyal party members but as independents. So did the voters they viewed as their political base—educated professionals, who would never dream of letting themselves be told how to vote by some grubby ward heeler. Though that brought an irony: independent-minded voters tended to pick candidates like they would a consumer product. That made advertising much more important. And advertising, especially on television, was expensive. Which made attracting PAC money all the more imperative.

So arose a new breed of Democratic congressional entrepreneur, eager to make the ideological adjustments attracting corporate PAC cash required. For example, the congressman from suburban Atlanta, Elliott Levitas—who, back in February, had whipped his colleagues' near-identical harangues about the FTC's attempts to create a "nanny state." And Representatives Harold Ford Sr. of Tennessee, James Santini of Nevada, and Mike McCormack of Washington State, who all switched their votes from *aye* to *nay* on common situs picketing between 1976 and 1977, then saw their donations from businesses and trade associations go up far more than their donations from labor unions went down.

So, to answer that perplexed UPI reader: Why such a big fight over a bill most of the general public doesn't seem to care about? Follow the money. The *leaders* of both sides had labeled it a "holy war." The general public had little to do with it.

ORRIN HATCH ANNOUNCED HIS INTENT TO KILL LABOR LAW REFORM WITH an old-fashioned filibuster. Majority leader Robert Byrd announced he wouldn't attempt to break it until after the Memorial Day recess. By that time, Hatch and his pro-business friends had received two pieces of marvelous news from the United States Supreme Court. The first was a ruling, *First National Bank of Boston v. Bellotti*, which struck down a Massachusetts law banning corporations from funding advertisements to influence referenda—in this case, one to cut income taxes. *First National Bank of Boston* extended a 1976 Supreme Court ruling, *Buckley v. Valeo*, establishing the doctrine that money spent by a corporation was a form of free speech, guaranteed by the First Amendment.

The second was a gut-punch to one of Ralph Nader's favorite laws, the Occupational Safety and Health Act.

That case involved an air-conditioning company in Pocatello, Idaho, owned by one Ferrol G. "Bill" Barlow, a leader in the local John Birch Society. In 1975, an OSHA official showed up at his shop for an inspection. Barlow asked for a search warrant. The inspector responded that he did not require one. He nonetheless left the premises, returning three months later with an order admitting him, from a federal judge. Barlow turned him away again—and got in touch with the American Conservative Union's "Stop OSHA" project, which was looking for a plaintiff to challenge the Occupational Health and Safety Act's constitutionality.

In 1977, as Barlow's case ascended through the federal courts, Ronald Reagan celebrated him on the radio: "Here's a citizen who like the farmers at Concord Bridge took a stand, and thanks to him, freedom is a little more secure for all of us." The ACU sent letters to seventeen thousand "Victims of OSHA," drawn from a Freedom of Information Act request for a list of OSHA inspections, urging similar acts of "civil disobedience." A conservative Wisconsin congressman, Bob Kasten, claimed he received more complaints about OSHA and its "Hitler tactics" than those concerning any other agency. His liberal Wisconsin colleague David Obey tested Kasten's claim by sending out a mass mailing to businesses in his district asking if they personally had ever had any contact with OSHA, and if so whether they "thought the agency acted unfairly or capriciously." Only two out of four thousand could cite such an instance. But already, President Carter had responded to the raft of complaints about OSHA by directing it to write no further new regulations. That was how the new, PAC-driven political game worked: the squeaky wheel got the grease. Or, more accurately, got sand in the gears of its drive train.

The Supreme Court heard oral arguments in *Barlow* on January 9, 1978. Congress, meanwhile, was considering a law exempting employers with ten or fewer workers from OSHA regulations, and banning penalties for first-time infractions, and Labor Secretary Ray Marshall and President Carter approved revocation of eleven hundred OSHA regulations. In March, Carter signed Executive Order 12044 establishing a Regulatory Analysis Review Group and Regulatory Council in the White House to review the process of federal regulation altogether. And on May 23, the Supreme Court decided in a 5–3 ruling that warrantless searches by OSHA violated the Fourth Amendment, which "protects commercial buildings as well as private homes."

NEITHER THE *BARLOW* OR THE *MARQUETTE* DECISION RECEIVED MUCH NO-tice. The media obsession was Prop 13, to be decided eight days after Memorial Day. In California, undecided voters turned on their TVs, and were invited to choose from a banquet of terrors:

Vote *for* Proposition 13, a doctor said in a news report, and "literally thousands of handicapped children will go without care." Behind him, a line of children picketed with placards affixed to their wheelchairs. And leave your children without teachers: school districts had begun sending formal notices to employees that if the referendum passed, they might not have a job in fall.

Vote *against* Proposition 13, said Howard Jarvis, and Mexican immigrants will "just come over here to get on the taxpayers' gravy train."

He presented himself for a press conference, a shapeless mass in a sky-blue suit with garish stitching around the lapel, glasses sliding crookedly down his nose, greasy hair combed over his scalp, and introduced a new claim: under Proposition 8, property taxes would no longer be deductible on federal income tax returns. He claimed "someone at IRS" as his source.

"*Who?*" a journalist demanded.

"I can't tell you."

"*Why?*"

"Because he wouldn't tell me."

"Some anonymous person who claims to be at IRS?" the incredulous reporter returned.

"I have solid information he works at a high-ranking position at IRS! . . . It's clear to good lawyers. It's clear to the IRS. I can't see why there's any questions about it! This is the law! . . . This is Internal Revenue! . . . If you don't want to use them, it's your problem, not mine!" Then he predicted his side would gain a percentage point in the polls every day up until the election, winning with 65 percent.

Proposition 8 supporters accused Proposition 13 supporters of racism, of pulling up the drawbridge around their suburban paradise now that the government spending that had made that paradise possible was going toward minority-friendly policies like mass transit and integrated schools. Just about the only time Howard Jarvis got quiet was when he answered that charge. "The black and the brown are the biggest beneficiaries of 13," he would say, his voice turning gentle. "Because of course they make less money than other people."

Blacks disagreed: only 29 percent supported Prop 13. Though Jarvis had a (less gentle) answer for that one, too: too many blacks were *public employees*, and public employees were "moochers, and loafers, right up to their eyes." Just walk through the Los Angeles Municipal Building some time, he suggested: "You'll see more people asleep and reading *Playboy* than you do in a hotel." Ronald Reagan's next column mimicked that criticism: it labeled "the growing number of people whose self-interest is wrapped up in big government," the "New Reactionaries." William Safire, for his part, noting the newly announced inflation rate of 10.8 percent, called homeowners the "New Poor."

Governor Jerry Brown was up for reelection in six months. When Proposition 13 had first qualified for the ballot, he was cagey about where he stood. Then, after the legislature passed Proposition 8, Brown endorsed it, calling Proposition 13 "a consumer fraud" that was "unworkable and crazy." Then the other side took that "unworkable" criticism head-on, in what turned out to be their most effective campaign commercial. It starred Milton Friedman, who said, "Don't let politicians fool you. Proposition 13 will work. It will not force schools to close. It will not cause policemen or firemen to disappear. It will not require increases in other taxes." The words "NOBEL-PRIZE WINNING ECONOMIST" showed on the screen—and what could be more reassuring than that?

Then, Proposition 13 shifted into the lead—and Governor Brown decided he agreed with Milton Friedman: he promised to make a post–Prop 13 California work with a minimum of disruption. At that, support for Proposition 8 collapsed. If *some* sort of tax relief was going to pass anyway, mad-as-hell California seemed to have decided, why not vote with your middle finger?

The evening before Election Day David Brinkley led the *NBC Nightly News* in front of a hand-scrawled protest-sign reading "TAX on our HOME—UP 300% $6,700." "Good evening," he intoned in his distinctive, gravelly, stern-father voice. "Here in the California primary tomorrow people have the rare-and-no-doubt pleasing opportunity to vote their taxes down. And to tell the politicians they will pay *this much*, and no more. It is thought to be as much a vote against big, expensive wasteful government as it is against the property tax. And it seems that nobody loves government anymore. . . . It is possible this might be bringing something like a second Whiskey Rebellion. Going far beyond California, and perhaps eventually to Washington."

In New Jersey, where the primary was also June 6, Jeff Bell in his campaign against Senator Case now talked about taxes almost exclusively. An effective series of TV spots by a Philadelphia adman named Elliott Curson blamed the Garden State's epidemic of factory closings on them—and only three weeks after a poll showing Bell with only 14 percent support, Clifford Case was spooked enough to start sounding like a tax rebel himself.

And in Washington, the *Post* now observed that the notion that the "federal income tax took 'too much from the prosperous,' once the exclusive property of the more rigorous among the Republicans," now had "significant bipartisan support." What had started as a movement rooted in the technical problems of a single unfair tax in a single state was metastasizing into a revolt against taxes of every description, everywhere.

ON PRIMARY DAY RONALD REAGAN WAS SPEAKING AT THE COLORADO CONservative Political Action Convention in Denver. Joseph Coors, the beer baron who loved to deliver whopping checks to conservative causes, introduced him as the father of the tax revolt, "the man who should be in the White House, and will be after 1980." Middle-age Republicans leapt to their feet and cheered like college kids at the big game.

Jules Witcover buttonholed Reagan on the way out of the ballroom to ask about election returns coming out of his native state showing Proposition 13 way ahead. Reagan called them "the loudest message ever sent across the country that the people realize how much government costs, they want something done about it, and they're not going to wait."

They got in an elevator, and Reagan turned giddy: "I hope it's really big!"

It was: 65 percent—precisely as Jarvis had predicted. The total included a majority of public school teachers—despite the teacher's union's massive campaign against it. And 8 percent of public employees who didn't own homes—who stood to be directly harmed. It was a rout.

At the victory party, Howard Jarvis gloated: "Now we know how it felt when they dumped English tea in Boston Harbor! . . . We have a new revolution. We are telling the government, 'Screw you!' . . . People don't know the bastards we've been electing. They didn't know they elected people who were evil, 90 percent immoral. They want to take everything we have—but now we're giving them an enema."

Jeff Bell won in New Jersey. About the only person to predict it was New Right strategist Paul Weyrich, who had told CBS, "There are millions of voters out there who have demonstrated that under the right circumstances, they will vote for a Republican candidate if they are given a clear-cut liberal-conservative choice." Bell would now face the former professional basketball player Bill Bradley—who had won his nomination for much the same reason Bell had: he was an outsider who hammered his opponent, a former state treasurer, as the architect of a tax increase.

That same day in Ohio, the tax-revolt enema was delivered in the form of rejections of more than half of two hundred tax assessments and bond issues on local ballots. Columbus, Dayton, Cleveland, and Cincinnati officials said they were not sure schools would be able to open in autumn.

REPORTERS WHO SPENT A LONG NIGHT SCRIBBLING THINK PIECES ABOUT the tax revolt sweeping the nation little noticed, that same primary day, that the pro-life movement had scored victories almost as dramatic.

In Iowa, forty local chapters of a new Life Amendment Political Action Committee, formed in January, had conducted a methodical telephone survey to identify sixty thousand pro-life voters, who received mailers identifying every race in which a difference between candidates could be discerned on the issue. It read, "Your vote in the primary election Tuesday, June 6, will have the impact of ten votes or more since it is expected that less than 10 percent of the eligible voters will go to the polls. Don't pass up this unique chance you have to speak loud and clear for pro-life." The campaign had been carried out so quietly that some

Iowa political reporters learned about it from reading the *New York Times* after Election Day. It helped yield shocking upsets—including the defeat by New Right senate candidate Roger Jepsen of his less pro-life opponent. Jepsen himself had a hard time explaining the size of his victory, until Life Amendment PAC leader Marilyn Thompson pulled him aside at the victory party to explain what that they had done. "We're all Democrats," she added conspiratorially. "But we're crossing over this fall."

The new PAC also claimed victories in primaries in Virginia and South Dakota, and for contributing to Jeff Bell's margin in New Jersey. They celebrated the recent passage of a law in Tennessee mandating forty-eight-hour waiting periods for abortion-seekers, requiring physicians to instruct patients of the procedure's alleged "likely physical and mental consequences," and, in Phoenix, a recent ordinance granting the county board power to review medical files of women receiving abortions.

Meanwhile a New York City court was reviewing a law prohibiting abortions for minors without parental consent. And in Washington, on June 12, pro-life congressmen defeated a leadership amendment to make permanent the previous year's compromise language on the Hyde Amendment.

Also the next day, in Iowa City, the Emma Goldman Clinic for Women was firebombed.

Two weeks later, Life Amendment PAC's parent organization, the National Right to Life Committee, hosted two thousand delegates at their national convention in St. Louis. They attended thirty separate political seminars, where sanguinary rhetoric rang from the rafters. One doctor told a strategy seminar that "Jews may be statistically smarter than the average race, but they apparently were not smart enough to have learned from the Holocaust"—for if they were, they would be opposing the *new* Holocaust, *Roe v. Wade*.

TAX REBELS WERE MAD AS HELL. PRO-LIFERS WERE MAD AS HELL. OPPO-nents of gay rights were mad as hell. And so were the boardroom Jacobins fighting off labor law reform.

In the home stretch, Orrin Hatch sounded less like a freshman senator and more like General Patton—or, perhaps, a mafia don. He heard a rumor that a major company was considering leaving the coalition and supporting the bill. He called an emergency meeting at National Association of Manufacturers headquarters warning whatever corporation was thinking of changing sides, "Senator Long may be chairman now"—Russell Long of Louisiana, Democratic head of the Labor Committee—"but I'm going be here for thirty years or more, and whoever does that will be one sorry company."

In the White House, a pro-labor aide wrote President Carter in sorrow, "We are within one vote of defeating the most expensive and powerful lobby ever mounted against a bill in the nation's history," pleading that one last concerted push was not too much to ask to honor this "unusual opportunity to show our commitment to labor." But Carter's commitment to labor was never particularly strong in the first place. And 97 percent of White House mail now opposed the bill. He chose to sit on his hands.

The first cloture vote to break the filibuster was the day of the tax-revolt primary, Tuesday, June 7. It fell thirteen senators short; but many senators customarily voted *nay* on a first cloture vote, like a batter taking a first strike. Leading into the second, the next day, four senators were on the fence. Russell Long introduced a compromise amendment further limiting the impact on small businesses. Hatch declared it "cosmetic." Long was amazed at the freshman's audacity. For the New Right, the old rules of deference didn't apply.

Old public opinion patterns were changing as well. On June 11, the *Washington Post* reported "a fundamental shift in the national outlook over the past several years—the end of the share-the-wealth philosophy of the late 1960s and its willingness to enact new social programs that redistribute income, cut taxes for the poor, and close tax 'loopholes' that allow wealthy taxpayers to escape payments of taxes." Lou Harris's pollsters found that two-thirds of Americans favored a capital gains tax cut. House and Senate appropriators voted to curb the Federal Trade Commission's rule-making power as punishment for Mike Pertschuk's "kidvid" proposal, so the FTC would go into FY 1979 without any appropriation at all, funded at the 1978 level via a stopgap "continuing resolution." President Carter devoted an entire cabinet meeting to regulatory reform. RNC Chairman Brock filed a lawsuit to scuttle public financing of elections, arguing that limiting spending on campaigns violated contributors' First Amendment rights. The RNC also announced it was directing an unprecedented amount, $1.75 million, to be controlled by the former New Right and Reagan operative Charlie Black, to state legislative candidates, with the hope of taking over bodies that would control Congressional redistricting after the 1980 census.

The third cloture attempt got 54 of the required 60 votes. The fourth, then the fifth, both drew 58. Majority leader Byrd scheduled the final one for Thursday June 22—the showdown to determine whether America's forty-year labor-management accord would live or whether it would die.

Hatch strode across the Capitol parking lot carrying a briefcase containing a list of five hundred possible amendments, whose texts filled a

Capitol Hill storage room floor to ceiling—with, he claimed, twenty-five hundred more ready to go if required. Each would take about twenty minutes to dispose of. Hatch had been drilled in the dark arts of minoritarian legislative sabotage by Senator James Allen of Alabama—who would have led this filibuster had he not been on his deathbed that spring; then he passed away on June 1. Hatch was prepared to honor his mentor by sabotaging the Senate calendar for weeks or even months if it looked like the labor side had enough votes to end the filibuster.

Labor leaders crowded the gallery, casting threatening glares at the two senators, both Democrats, whose votes were still in doubt: Russell Long, a wily old man cagily hiding his intentions, and Edward Zorinsky, a callow first-term former Republican from Nebraska.

Hatch entered the chamber. Russell Long told him he would be voting to sustain the filibuster. The deciding vote thus belonged to the young Nebraskan. South Carolina's Senator Hollings buttonholed him:

"Ed, I really need your help on this one. This is a big issue back home, and if you can vote my way, then I'll be your man on something you need."

The freshman, vulnerable to the new system of punishment and reward via PAC, folded.

Senator Byrd tried one last stratagem, asking unanimous consent that the bill be sent back to committee to fold in more concessions. Fritz Hollings shouted an angry objection. An anti-labor senator accused Byrd of parliamentary tricks. A pro-labor one cried foul at the anti-labor senator's crying of foul; and soon, the Senate floor was all commotion: it was down to the nut cutting.

Until finally, the smoke cleared, a vote was called, and—cloture came seven votes shy of passage. Labor law reform was dead.

Orrin Hatch said, "I think it's just a tremendous thing that the small businessmen in this country are for once given some consideration in the United States Senate." A columnist said it was now time "to put 'Big Labor' up there with Santa Claus, the Easter Bunny, and the Tooth Fairy"—figures that just happened to have been featured prominently in the corporate coalition's propaganda.

And the president of the United Automobile Workers, Douglas Fraser, wrote an angry open letter resigning from the Dunlop Commission: "The leaders of industry, commerce and finance in the United States have broken and discarded the fragile, unwritten compact previously existing during a past period of growth and progress." They had colluded to enable a "certain group of rogue employers to keep workers from choosing democratically to be represented by unions." In this "one-sided class war . . . we have given stability and have been rewarded with hostility." Though labor secretary Ray Marshall put it more bluntly. "We have the only labor movement in the world that embraces capitalism." The business community was "trying to kill it."

THE *NEW YORK TIMES*'S TOM WICKER'S FIRST COLUMN AFTER THE CALIFORnia vote was headlined "Ronald Reagan's Magic" It anointed him the tax revolt's "prophet ahead of his time," reported that "some analysts" believed he would have beaten Carter in November 1976, and said that "Republicans all but unanimously ranked the Californian as the front-runner for the 1980 president nomination if he seeks it."

He made a crucial political trip to New York. It included a dinner with four of the most important neoconservatives, Irving Kristol, Midge Decter, Norman Podhoretz, and the Harvard University sociologist Nathan Glazer. He took a morning meeting with twenty-five CEOs, and a luncheon convened by a secretive group called Action Program for Business Leadership, hosted by the chairman of the pharmaceutical giant Pfizer, cosponsored by the National Association of Manufacturers, the United States Chamber of Commerce, the National Federation of Independent Businesses, and Dart Industries, the pharmaceutical powerhouse run by one of Reagan's best friends.

(Perhaps it was a coincidence, or perhaps it was not, that in one of his next radio commentaries Reagan flayed the "Kefauver Amendment," the breakthrough 1962 law requiring drug manufacturers to prove the safety and effectiveness of the drugs they sold and to disclose side effects. Reagan said this "seemingly innocuous" measure had actually proven a disaster, and hymned Congressman and Senate candidate Steve Symms of Idaho's effort to repeal it.)

Back in California, key advisors held a strategy session. It opened with bad news: a rumor that the American Enterprise Institute would establish a foreign policy project headed by one of Reagan's potential rivals for the Republican nomination, George H. W. Bush, backed by President Ford. That suggested that the marquee conservative think tank was leaning toward an "Eastern establishment" presidential candidate for 1980. Unfavorable poll results for the incumbent, revealing that 75 percent of Americans agreed "something was wrong with the world," featured a promising detail for Reagan—many blamed the weakening of conservative institutions like "church, family, social clubs"—followed with a punch to the gut: Reagan was doing terrible with lower-middle-class and middle-class voters because of his perceived "lack of compassion." "RR must show show care + understanding of hard-working people (middle America). Discontent, frustration + anger. Forget (avoid) standard Republican responses + doctrine," Michael Deaver scrawled in his notes.

Someone suggested a solution to square the circle: Reagan could deliver a "family speech" addressed to the "white, American middle class and blacks who want the same thing," focusing on tax cuts, with the message of "giving the working man his money back." The conservative writer Richard Whalen was sitting in, however, and poured cold water on the whole thing: the supply-side panacea was no panacea at all. The presumption that an across-the-board tax cut would pay for itself by spurring an economic boom whose benefits would be broadly shared, he pointed out, contained a fatal flaw. The precedent it relied on, the Kennedy-Johnson tax cut, had been accompanied by " 'Great Society' programs that vastly increased transfer payments"—and redistributed income downward. *That* was what had boosted economic growth—and a President Reagan certainly intended no such "demand-side" redistribution himself. What's more, 60 percent of Americans wanted a federal guaranteed health-care program, and Reagan certainly had no intention of proposing *that*. Someone chimed in that John Sears knew of an economist named Alain Enthoven who had a "free enterprise" plan, based on something he called "managed competition"; maybe Reagan could endorse something like that instead. "Reaganism" itself could never do the trick. With the middle-class masses they needed to succeed, it was a political non-starter.

It wasn't even working with the business leaders Reagan had just met with in New York: the head of the National Federation of Independent Businesses, Deaver related, said Reagan's presidential chances were "going downhill." Another attendee complained that his speeches were all "old hat." A third wondered "whether he is on top of the issues that will be important six months from now." In short, even Ronald Reagan's closest associates and natural allies did not share Reagan's defining faith—his exuberant professions in speech after speech that the only thing required to "bring about the great conservative majority party we know is waiting to be created" was "a Republican Party raising a banner of bold colors, no pale pastels, a banner instantly recognizable for certain values which will not be compromised."

Which, as congressional election season approached, was rather ironic—for the winds of history seemed suddenly to be blowing Reaganism's way.

In New York State, the commerce commissioner, who was close to Governor Carey, proposed constitutional amendments to slash the state payroll by seventy thousand workers and ape Prop 13's requirement for a two-thirds vote to approve any new tax. In Georgia, the brilliant and palpitatingly ambitious college professor Newt Gingrich began calling himself the candidate of "middle-class people who push a grocery cart," with tax cuts as the cornerstone of his appeal. One of his ads ran, "Newt will fight for 1,200,000 jobs. How? The same way President John F Kennedy did: by a drastic cut in taxes. Newt supports the Kemp-Roth tax cut bill, which would cut personal income taxes by 30 percent." He called the response to that message "nothing short of phenomenal." In California, Robert Novak met Arthur Laffer—"spouting ideas a mile a minute and sipping wine on the patio of his $225,000 home in Palos Verdes on a sun-drenched afternoon while a big green macaw perches on his shoulder." Laffer told him if he wished to fully appreciate the supply-side argument, he had to read Jude Wanniski's stupendous new book *How the World Works*. Novak described its life-changing effect on him as comparable to reading Whittaker Chambers's *Witness*, only better: "If Chambers pointed only to ultimate defeat at the hands of the Communists, Wanniski showed the way to prosperity and political success." The supply-siders had just recruited a new battering ram: the most widely read political columnist in the nation.

And in Washington, the United States House of Representatives, by a vote of 290 to 87, voted to slash a billion dollars from the budget of the Department of Health, Education, and Welfare. William Proxmire, the pinch-penny Democratic senator from Wisconsin, said it should have been $3.5 billion. An alarmed Ed Brooke responded, "We ought not come in here and panic under Proposition 13. It's not some magic word."

But maybe it was.

CHAPTER 16

"High and Dry"

IN *DOONESBURY*, THE FICTIONAL CONGRESSWOMAN LACEY DAVENPORT called in to her office for messages. She had received one, an aide told her, from "the people."

"The people sent me a message? What's it say, dear?"

"It says they're tired of big government bleeding them dry. They want across-the-board cutbacks in property taxes. They don't care if the chief beneficiaries of such a plan are big corporations. The people want instant relief. It's okay with them if you don't think the idea through."

"I see. Tell me, what was their mood, dear?"

"They seemed mad as heck... almost... almost as if they wouldn't take it anymore."

"I see. Any other messages?"

"Yes. The people again. They called back to see if you'd gotten the message."

Jerry Brown got the message. In a televised speech, he reinvented himself as a Prop 13 evangelist, laying out all the programs he would cut to accommodate the expected revenue shortfalls. "I swear he sounded like Howard Jarvis," said the Republican nominee for governor, Evelle Younger.

Howard Jarvis made the cover of *Time*, thrusting his fist as if delivering an uppercut to the reader. It read "Tax Revolt!" The exact same words were on that week's cover of *Newsweek*, complete with exclamation point. He visited Capitol Hill. Senator William Roth told Jarvis, "We're hoping you can give us some points on how it can be applied nationally." Robert Dole had already introduced a constitutional amendment to require a balanced federal budget, writing all fifty governors urging a constitutional convention to advance it. House Speaker Tip O'Neill at first told reporters, "I don't know any reason why I should talk with Mr. Jarvis." Then he talked for an hour with him. Perhaps, in between, Tip had read the polls: Harris said Americans wanted a Prop 13 in their own states by a margin of two to one.

In Michigan, three tax cut initiatives made the ballot. The leader of one of the campaigns announced that he was raising funds by recording an album of patriotic duets with Howard Jarvis. In Massachusetts, the legislature overwhelmingly voted to authorize a property tax referendum, and experts suddenly began wondering whether the quixotic challenge to Senator Edward Brooke by the conservative talk radio host Avi Nelson wasn't so quixotic after all. Delaware's Republican governor and Democratic lieutenant governor joined forces to propose a constitutional amendment requiring three-quarters legislative approval for tax increases. Hawaiians and Arizonans would vote on a cap on state spending growth. Prop 13 carbon copies advanced in Nevada, Indiana, and Utah. In Idaho, activists sought to scissor property taxes by 60 percent—in a state that was already in fiftieth place in per-pupil student spending.

Colorful tax revolt leaders emerged from every walk of life. One, a marijuana enthusiast from Portland named Jim Whittenburg, made Howard Jarvis look like the ambassador to the Court of St. James. At the height of his surging initiative campaign that summer, he was jailed for passing bad checks. His lawyer introduced a plea of innocence by reason of insanity. Then Whittenburg introduced another ballot proposition to decriminalize . . . passing bad checks. "We used to be the kooks," the American Conservative Union's director of tax issues said. "Now we're the moderates."

In the *Wall Street Journal*, Irving Kristol called it "a new kind of class war—the people as citizens versus the politicians and their clients in the public sector." *Fortune* said, "The property-owning class," which "now includes members of what used to be referred to as the working class," was "voting for capitalism." The *Chicago Tribune* inaugurated a thirteen-part tax revolt series. A letter writer to the *Los Angeles Herald-Examiner* called Proposition 13 the "Watts riot for the white middle class."

Liberals jumped on the bandwagon, too. Senator Alan Cranston, who had campaigned against Jarvis, served as his Capitol tour guide. "You certainly had a big victory!" he greeted Jarvis warmly. "You certainly got your ass kicked," Jarvis responded. They entered the Senate dining room. A covey of liberals including Charles Percy, Frank Church, John Glenn, and Mark Hatfield surrounded Jarvis to shake his hand. In New York, Governor Carey introduced legislation to authorize citizen initiatives for the very first time in state history.

Other liberals were bereft. The respected columnist Joseph Kraft said that behind it all lurked "a cloven hoof—self-indulgence by the relatively comfortable majority at the expense of the poor minorities." A *Los Angeles Times*/CBS poll provided evidence: more than two-thirds of Californians thought that any budget deficits Prop 13 might cause should be balanced by cuts in welfare. But welfare wasn't paid for by property taxes.

Fire services were—but only 1 percent wanted to cut *that*. Senator George McGovern, in his farewell address as president of the venerable progressive group Americans for Democratic Action, decried the vogue as "a kind of hysteria in the liberal community," and rued that politicians seemed to want "a mandate to govern against government itself." Jesse Jackson lectured delegates, "Make no mistake about it, it is an anti-black move." One of the liberal technocratic pioneers of the tax reform movement in California bemoaned, "Howard Jarvis is to the tax field what Joe McCarthy was to civil liberties."

The White House response, as so often, was jumbled. President Carter was in the midst of a crusade to beat back Bill Steiger's amendment to cut capital gains taxes, telling reporters he would not "tolerate a plan that provides huge tax windfalls for millionaires and two bits for the average American. That underestimates the intelligence of the American people." Treasury Secretary Michael Blumenthal labeled the Steiger Amendment the "millionaire's relief bill." But at the same time, a White House aide boasted to reporters, "Jimmy Carter was telling us long before Proposition 13 that the country was in a fiscally conservative mood."

SO IT CERTAINLY SEEMED. A NEW POLL REPORTED THAT 66 PERCENT OF Americans favored a corporate tax cut, with another 53 percent wishing to "encourage investment in business by reducing the tax on long-term capital gains." On July 14, as the Senate Finance Committee began hearings on the Kemp-Roth across-the-board income tax cut, the *New York Times* reported that there was "no stopping the momentum."

Two days later, a big spread in the *Times* provided some helpful context for understanding that momentum: though the Gray Lady was too polite to precisely state it outright, much of it had been purchased with cash on the barrelhead. A "growing number of companies," the *Times* reported, "concerned by the recent growth of government regulation and an apparent lack of public confidence in business," were funding "economics education": $500,000 from Goodyear Tire and Rubber granted to establish forty professorships devoted to the study of private enterprise; $800,000 from Phillips Petroleum to screen an "American Enterprise" film series in 80 percent of the public schools in New York State; the Advertising Council buying notices touting capitalism on buses and subways—"a lot of it," the liberal economist Lester Thurow complained, was "kind of pretending that the Depression didn't occur."

An accompanying article profiled William Simon, the "Billy Graham of capitalism," whose *A Time for Truth*, published by Reader's Digest Press, had become a surprise bestseller. It argued that "poverty may result from honest misfortune, but it also may result from sloth, incompetence, and dishonesty," that "FDR corrupted the philosophical concept of free-dom," and that liberal elites ruled over "a new despotism" and were "as stubborn and ruthless a ruling elite as any in history." These were familiar conservative bromides. The book's unique contribution, however, was this recommendation: "Funds generated by business . . . must rush by the multimillions to the aid of liberty" to "funnel desperately needed funds to scholars, social scientists, writers and journalists who understand the relationship between political and economic liberty"—a "counterintel-ligentsia" that would produce "a reservoir of antiauthoritarian scholarship on which to draw." Otherwise, conservatism was "destined to remain the Stupid Party and die."

The *Times* case study of the new counterintelligentsia was the Ameri-can Enterprise Institute. In 1970, it had employed twenty-four people on a budget of less than $1 million. It now employed more than five times that on a budget of $7 million. Distinguished fellows included Robert Bork, a former solicitor general of the United States, whose students at Yale Law School nicknamed his course on anti-trust law "Pro-Trust"; a former president of the American Political Science Association; and the most recent former president of . . . the United States. They published eight periodicals, produced "a ready-made set of editorials sent regularly to 105 newspapers and public affairs programs carried on more than 300 televi-sion stations, and centers for the display of AEI materials in some 300 college libraries." The institute was embarked upon a drive to raise a $60 million endowment, chaired by the CEOs of Citibank, General Electric, and General Motors.

BUT AEI'S AMBITION PALED NEXT TO THOSE OF THE UNITED STATES CHAM-ber of Commerce.

Its president, Dr. Richard Lesher, was the former executive director of the National Center on Solid Waste Disposal, a consortium of manu-facturers formed to oppose regulations on the disposal of packaging ma-terials. Lesher, a marketing genius, promptly changed that organization's name to the National Center for Resource Recovery, and concentrated its public relations on promoting recycling by consumers, captaining one of the most brilliantly deceptive marketing campaigns in media history. Like the "It's the nut behind the wheel" campaign of the auto industry's National Safety Council, it brilliantly reframed a crisis created by cor-porations as a problem for individual consumers to solve. The center's subsidiary, "Keep America Beautiful," funded by companies including PepsiCo, Coca-Cola, and Philip Morris, partnered with the Ad Council. It produced a legendary television commercial in which an Indian paddling down a polluted river in a canoe began tearing up when he saw a bag of litter thrown into a landfill. "People can start pollution. People can stop it," the announcer growled.

Lesher took over the Chamber of Commerce in 1975, when its coffers, membership, and sense of mission were all at an all-time low. He compared corporate America's indifference to the growth of government to the apathy of the German population that allowed Hitler's rise. He began the work with a crusade against an unobjectionable little bill that would have given $50 million in urban planning grants to cities and states to help them manage suburban sprawl—free money that local governments could spend any way they wished, no strings attached. In Lesher's hands, it was made to sound like a beast out of the Book of Revelation—a law, as Ronald Reagan put it in a radio argument almost certainly informed by Chamber propaganda, that would "replace our nation of small land owners with one in which all property is ultimately vested in the state."

Lesher grew the membership fourfold. His central strategic insight: what was traditionally considered the organization's greatest liability— a querulous membership, with various and opposed interests, scattered across the country—could be its greatest asset. A state-of-the-art computer system could send issue alerts to Chamber members *hurt* by a certain piece of legislation, but not to those *helped* by the same bill, and bury individual members of Congress under heaps of angry mail in a way that looked spontaneous. The practice eventually became known by the epithet "astroturfing": lobbying that looked spontaneous and grassroots, but was actually orchestrated and fake.

Soon after Lesher took over, however, the Chamber fell afoul of IRS regulations that banned groups from mobilizing individuals as "members" if they did not pay dues. In 1976, the organization cleverly lawyered their way around the problem by conjuring up a separate, ostensibly independent, *dues-based* group. Like Richard Viguerie's National Alliance of Senior Citizens, "Citizen's Choice" seemed to have chosen a name designed to mislead: it sounded like the trusted Nader-linked organization Citizen Action. Ronald Reagan conferred his blessings upon the fiction in a radio commentary that November: "Ralph Nader's various enterprises," he said, were "launched with indignant attacks on various straw men," hitching "their indignant wagon to the college student's idealistic star. Very clever—harnessing the idealism of youth to solve their own aims." Citizen's Choice, by contrast, was a "popular citizen's movement."

The chairman of this "popular citizen's movement" was a man named Jay Van Andel, who possessed an estimated net worth between $300 and $500 million—though that figure was disputed: the company he ran, Amway, was not traded publicly. Amway specialized in a controversial business model known as multilevel marketing, in which people paid to distribute its consumer products, but earned most of their income by staking a claim on a percentage of the sales of the "downstream" franchisees they recruited into the scheme. Each new recruit earned a smaller share of the take, unto the vanishing point. Most earned nothing—which was why critics called this business model a "pyramid scheme."

Van Andel was also a Christian fundamentalist who said the economy would collapse in a "day of judgement" unless America returned to the "Christian consensus." Amway distributors attended cult-like rallies that celebrated the company as a patriotic crusader for an American way (that was what "Amway" stood for). Critics said such propaganda distracted distributors from the fraud being perpetrated against them. In 1975, the FTC filed suit against Amway for violating the Commission's new rule against pyramid schemes, which the agency maintained had an "intolerable potential to deceive." Oral arguments took place the day of the Proposition 13 primary. (It was decided that Amway was not, technically, a pyramid scheme, but *was* guilty of price fixing.)

The man who ran Citizen's Choice's day-to-day operations was a Chamber employee named Tom Donohue, who had begun his professional life as a fundraiser, then worked for Nixon's postmaster general—a master of the techniques of mass mailing, that's to say, who, at their base camp a block from the White House, built Citizen's Choice into a sort of pyramid scheme for right-wing public policy. Some members, it was true, joined by their own volition. But others were signed up by their employers, without their permission or even their knowledge. Four hundred thousand Amway distributors were also recruited. The organization then used these membership totals as a blunderbuss to demand policy outcomes (like a law requiring authorization for all government agencies to "sunset" after a certain number of years) decided exclusively by its board, fifteen of the sixteen members of which headed big corporations or trade groups.

The United States Chamber of Commerce also served like a D.C.-based general staff for ad hoc organizations fighting the boardroom Jacobins' wars, like the ones against the consumer agency and labor law reform, providing clerical services, office space, television and radio studios—and strategic coordination.

Other battalions worked beneath the radar. A foundation called the Liberty Fund, bankrolled by a libertarian Wichita, Kansas, petroleum magnate named Charles Koch, began sponsoring free luxury junkets where federal judges learned economics from instructors like Milton Friedman. John M. Olin, a chemical and munitions manufacturer, was recruited into the cause by his neighbor in the Hamptons, William Simon. The Olin Foundation paid economists to get law degrees at the University of Miami under the aegis of a legal scholar, Henry Manne, whose most famous book argued that insider trading was economically efficient and thus should not be illegal; law professors and judges were paid $1,000 plus expenses to attend luxury junkets in which they were indoctrinated in free-market principles. These projects proved enormously influential. They also were not noticed by the media.

Another was the National Legal Center, an umbrella organization for six regional conservative public policy law firms. The Pacific Legal Foundation, in California, fought against regulation of the cancer-causing pesticide DDT. The Mountain States Legal Foundation, in Denver, was run by a man named James Watt, who argued that it was unconstitutional for the federal government to own land other than the "Forts, Magazines, Arsenals, dock-Yards, and other needful Buildings" Congress was given the power to purchase in Article I, Section VIII of the Constitution— which meant it had to give up the 60 percent of the landmass it controlled in Idaho, and 87 percent in Nevada. The branch based in the capital, the Washington Legal Foundation, challenged the Federal Mine Safety Administration's legal authority to punish safety violations. Ronald Reagan loved to boom these groups in his radio commentaries. ("The Foundation's criterion for getting involved is simple: Is it in the public interest?") Beyond a single tiny piece buried one day on page twenty-eight of the *New York Times*, however, hardly anyone else took note.

Instead, the nation's lurch rightward on economics was treated largely as if it were spontaneous. "93% of those surveyed felt govt. is the major cause of inflation," Pennsylvania Republican senator John Heinz wrote in his notes at one meeting with an American Enterprise Institute staffer— apparently unaware that this statistic had been manufactured by sending out a poll to the membership of Citizen's Choice, which was like the Girl Scouts polling its membership about whether children should be allowed to sell cookies door to door, then selling the result to senators as the unadulterated will of the people.

BUT THESE CAMPAIGNS COULD NOT HAVE TAKEN ROOT IF THE PUBLIC wasn't at least partially receptive to the message. And in the spring and summer of 1978, the conservative mood was popping up everywhere— sometimes in the strangest of ways.

Richard Nixon published a memoir. Partially due to a "Don't Buy Books by Crooks" boycott campaign, complete with bumper stickers, T-shirts, and newspaper ads, sales were nowhere near expectations. *Saturday Night Live* depicted the president launching a desperate marketing campaign: buy a book, and "if you're mad at me, kick it around the house for an hour. . . . Why, Pat's already on her fourth copy!" Other Americans thought differently.

In the Appalachian town of Hyden, Kentucky, population five hundred, twice that number waited in line at the airport for two hours in ninety-five-degree heat to get their copies personally signed by the author, in town to cut the ribbon for the new Richard M. Nixon Center public pool and gymnasium. He was welcomed with placards reading "NIXON'S THE ONE FOR 1980" and "NOW MORE THAN EVER." (One young man held "NIXON: ADVOCATE OF HYPOCRICY." "Get that hippie out of here," a local was overheard suggesting. "Or maybe we should beat the hell out of him and burn his welfare check.") For his procession through town, streetlight banners read "STILL THE PEOPLE'S MANDATE." The county executive who had invited him said, "Nixon would carry Leslie County if he ran for president in the morning." In the sweltering gym, a pallid Nixon delivered his first speech since leaving office—"At a time when aggressive dictatorships are stirring up covert subversive action all over the world, the United States should strengthen our CIA to counter their activities," he intoned, as though to the Council on Foreign Relations; when he finished, the rafters literally shook. A *Philadelphia Inquirer* columnist observed that Nixon had also just hosted a Republican fundraiser at his San Clemente compound, and was preparing a book "on the long-term future of the free world and Western Civilization"—and wondered if the Nixon revival signified "an even greater national swing to the right."

Such a swing was also detected in the current president's foreign policy. Jimmy Carter, infuriated at evidence of Soviet intervention in Ethiopia, Angola, and Zaire, began projecting a harder line in his speeches. Arthur Schlesinger complained that it sounded like he wished to "carry us back to the Cold War." Though this perception was actually a chimera, for every time Jimmy Carter tacked right on foreign policy, he almost immediately tacked to the left—sometimes within the same speech.

He signed the Nuclear Non-Proliferation Act of 1978 on March 11. Then, six days later, he began an address at Wake Forest University with a bellicose call to arms: "We, like our forebears, live in a time when those who would destroy liberty are restrained less by their respect for freedom itself than by the knowledge that those of us who cherish freedom are strong." He debunked a series of what he called myths: "that this country somehow is pulling back from protecting its interests and its friends around the world"; "that our defense budget is too burdensome and consumes an undue part of our federal revenues"; that nuclear weapons rendered "tanks, aircraft, infantry, mechanized units" irrelevant—and so, because the Soviet Union was spending more on these things every year, America would, too.

Then, the volta-face: America would "seek the cooperation of the

Soviet Union and other nations in reducing areas of tension," and would "cooperate with the Soviet Union toward common social, scientific, and economic goals," because "old ideological labels have lost some of their meaning."

All thirty-eight Senate Republicans promptly released a statement that after "fifteen short months of incoherence, inconsistency, and ineptitude . . . our foreign policy and national security objectives are confused." They claimed that if they had offered it to Democrats to sign, endorsers would have numbered seventy-five.

The confusion was structural. It dated to President Carter's first big foreign policy decision: naming Zbigniew Brzezinski as his national security advisor and Cyrus Vance as his secretary of state. Vance, a coolly self-possessed WASP, was a true believer in diplomacy. As deputy secretary of defense in 1967, he had talked Greece and Turkey from the precipice of war over Cyprus; in 1968, he resigned in protest at the escalation of the Vietnam War. Under President Carter, he had been instrumental in the Panama negotiations, peace talks in Rhodesia, and in Carter's beloved, apparently quixotic initiatives for rapprochement between Israel and her Muslim neighbors. He saw the Soviet Union's political system as complex and malleable, sought avenues for cooperation wherever American and Soviet interests overlapped, and believed signs of U.S. belligerency only emboldened Kremlin hardliners. "Zbig," a brooding refugee from Communist Poland, believed the opposite: in the 1950s he had been an intellectual architect of the concept of the USSR as a "totalitarian" state, whose implacable will to bury the West rendered any belief that negotiations could reduce tensions naïve. He had advocated *escalation* in Vietnam and, when Vance was quitting the foreign service in protest against that war, argued that student antiwar leaders should be "physically liquidated" or "expelled from the country." He had flirted with multilaterism when he formed the Trilateral Commission—but had since retreated into an old-fashioned orthodoxy. When he looked at the nations of Africa, he saw pawns on the Cold War chessboard. Vance tended to see proud nations defending themselves from re-colonization. By June, one expert observer worried that the feud between the two "opened the door to possible infighting that could wreck the administration."

But the fight was written into the administration's intellectual DNA. A year earlier, when the administration's foundational foreign policy planning document, Policy Review Memorandum 10, leaked, some commentators had described it as blueprint for a new Cold War. Others called it a blueprint for surrender. In fact, it bore elements to support both interpretations. A State Department Soviet expert explained to a congressional committee that the White House's strategic thinking starts "from a frank recognition

that the Soviet-American relationship at this period in history is a competitive one, based upon quite different views of the world and conflicting
long-term aims. . . . At the same time, it is also true that these two countries,
as inhabitants of the same planet, have many overlapping interests. Common sense dictates that we should, while advancing our own interests and
purposes energetically, seek to regulate the competitive aspects to the relationship to reduce the danger of war and at the same time try to enlarge the
areas of cooperation where our interests are not in conflict."

So it was that some days Jimmy Carter acted like a dove: deciding not
to proceed with the B-1 bomber, neutron bomb, or MX missile programs.
Others, he acted like a hawk—for instance, considering a secret CIA
military engagement in southwest Africa even though the law specifically forbade it. He acted this way without fear of being called out for the
contradictions, because he believed the world was a complex place. In the
world of politics, however, it made him look vacillating and uncertain—
both to the Soviets, and to the voters who would have to pick a president
in a little more than two years.

Now the confusion came to a head.

Negotiations were set to resume over the new Strategic Arms Limitation Treaty—"SALT II." Carter asked representatives of the administration's foreign policy factions to submit memos on what he should say
about that at a commencement speech scheduled at his alma mater, the
Naval Academy. He then retreated to Camp David and wrote a draft, a
frustrated White House speechwriter recalled, by "stapling Vance's memo
to Brzezinski's." Carter wrote in his diary that he believed the results were
"surprisingly harmonious." He was the only one.

"I'm convinced that the people of the Soviet Union want peace. I cannot believe that they could possibly want war," he began. "I'm glad to
report to you today that the prospects for a SALT II agreement are good
. . . Improved trade and technological and cultural exchange are among the
immediate benefits of cooperation between our two countries—"

A newspaperman who'd read the text in advance then turned with a
flourish to his colleagues: "And now—war!"

The president launched into a jeremiad about a wicked Soviet Union
"which apparently sees military power and military assistance as the best
means of expanding their influence abroad."

The *Washington Post* headlined its analysis "Two Different Speeches."
Senator Frank Church, chairman of the Senate Foreign Relations Committee, just heard one speech—which he paraphrased, "The Russians are
coming!" Columnist Nicholas von Hoffman called it an invitation for "the
natives to kill each other in the forests." The Soviet newspaper *Pravda*
missed the intended olive branch, too: they described it as "a series of ul-

timatum demands" which "smell of the malicious spirit of the Cold War." Fourteen members of the House International Relations Committee, all but four of them Democrats, posted a baffled letter to the president attesting to their "confusion and doubt." Which was more generous than the editorialists at the *Hartford Courant*, who called the president "dazed," his speech "yet another example of confusion from a national leader who has lost his moorings."

THE OPINION WAS INCREASINGLY COMMON. CARTER'S APPROVAL RATING IN one poll was down to 38 percent. Then another scandal descended.

The previous August, President Carter had given a landmark address on drug policy that included a call to "decriminalize" possession of less than one ounce of marijuana. It bore the imprint of White House special assistant for health issues Peter Bourne, M.D., a psychiatrist who had set up Georgia's first statewide drug treatment program, grown close to Governor Carter, then helped convince him to run for president. In his area of specialization, Bourne was extremely liberal. In a 1976 article, he wrote that cocaine "is probably the most benign of illicit drugs currently in use. At least as strong a case could be made for legalizing it as for legalizing marijuana." In the spring of 1978 he repeated that conviction to a Senate committee.

To be sure, much of American society felt the same way. *Newsweek* reported that coke was frequently present alongside "Dom Perignon and caviar" at smart set parties, quoting a Chicago narcotics detective all but offering a consumer recommendation: "You get a good high with coke and you don't get hooked." Eric Clapton and Jackson Browne both had songs entitled "Cocaine"; Clapton's hit number 30 on the *Billboard* Hot 100. Vodka began outselling whiskey because it went well with the prescription tranquilizer quaaludes. As for marijuana, Rosalyn Carter attracted little controversy on the campaign trail saying that she wasn't worried if her own sons had tried marijuana, "as long as they confided in her." By 1978 half of U.S. high school students said they'd smoked grass, and the pot-fueled comics Cheech and Chong's picture *Up in Smoke* earned $100 million ("Don't go to this movie unless you're high," the poster read). Eleven states, including Nebraska and Mississippi, had made getting caught with under an ounce of the stuff little more consequential than speeding. That's how normal it was.

Which was why the leading pro-pot organization——the National Organization for the Reform of Marijuana Laws—*called itself* "NORML." At Christmastime in 1977, NORML had thrown a massive party in Georgetown that thronged with Capitol Hill and executive branch staffers who acted, said NORML's head Keith Stroup, "as if marijuana were already legalized." Stroup had helped write the president's August 1977 drug policy address while sharing a joint with a White House speechwriter. At that Christmas party, Stroup reported, Dr. Bourne joined him in snorting lines of coke in an upstairs bedroom, alongside Hunter S. Thompson.

A reporter for columnist Jack Anderson heard that story several weeks later. He sought, unsuccessfully at first, to confirm it. Then Stroup, angry at Bourne for refusing to intervene with Carter to end the Drug Enforcement Agency's cooperation with a Mexican government's program to spray the marijuana fields with an herbicide called Paraquat, dropped the dime. Independently, on July 19, newspapers reported that police in suburban Washington had arrested a woman for purchasing quaaludes at a pharmacy with a prescription written for a fictitious name by Dr. Bourne. He denied wrongdoing, claiming the prescription was medically indicated, that using fake names to protect confidentiality was a common clinical practice, approved in the Code of Medical Ethics. He announced his resignation nevertheless to avoid further damage to the administration. Then a scandal that might have been easily contained became a scandal that could not be after Stroup told Anderson's reporter that he had witnessed Dr. Bourne take a sniff of coke, then draw a toke from a joint, at the Christmas party.

Rumors about widespread White House drug use proliferated. At the president's next press conference, the first held in prime time, columnist Daniel Schorr badgered him about whether Bourne had ever prescribed anything to *him*. Headlines like "Bournes Are Known Social Gadflies" sprouted. A source told the media that if Bourne were a woman, "he'd be pregnant every nine months." The president issued a memo demanding his staff "obey the law" whether "you agree with the law or not or others obey the law."

At *that*, comedians started depicting the White House like it was an opium den. So did Ronald Reagan, who added a joke to his mashed potato circuit quiver: no liquor in the Carter White House, but "half the staff is smoking pot—probably the first administration we can call high and dry." Howard Baker demanded a Senate investigation. Syndicated columnist Marianne Means said, "President Carter has given us another White House which views itself as above the law," and noted that, on the way out the door, Bourne claimed that *many* young White House aides used cocaine—a felony that exposed them to the risk of blackmail. The headline punned, "Carter's Really Blown It"—like the president was snorting coke off the Oval Office desk himself. Marijuana decriminalization was hardly heard about again in Washington for another forty years—and Carter's troubles compounded by the day.

The value of the dollar dropped in international currency markets. In an op-ed, Henry Wallich of the Federal Reserve's Board of Governors, argued that inflation had "ended the dollar's role as a trustworthy measure of value." Carter's economic advisors warned him that a further plunge might lead to a stock market crash or a global trade war. The president's next Gallup approval rating was lower than any of the last six presidents at a similar point in office. The same poll had Democrats preferring Ted Kennedy as their 1980 nominee by a margin of 44–20 percent. "Jimmy the Greek," the legendary Las Vegas oddsmaker famous for his appearances on CBS's weekly NFL pregame show, announced two-to-one odds that Carter wouldn't seek reelection, with the same odds against him winning if he did.

And in unrelated news from Tehran, soldiers and helicopter gunships fired into a crowd of twenty thousand demonstrators in Jaleh Square, killing either dozens or hundreds of people, depending on who was counting. According to a later report from an ousted Iranian official, the shah supervised the massacre from a helicopter.

CHAPTER 17

Almighty Politics

THE 1978–79 SCHOOL YEAR BEGAN. IN CALIFORNIA, DISTRICTS DESPER-
ately pared back their spending in anticipation of budget cuts, distrusting
Governor Brown's pledge that Proposition 13 would require none. In
the East Bay town of Newark, a junior high school slashed every single
elective and special-needs program, with supplies so sparse that teachers
began bringing their own. The municipality of Inglewood began sending
property owners bills for fighting fires, according to the amount of water
expended.

Nationwide, another long-brewing controversy involving education
funding came to a history-transforming head.

It involved private schools started by churches. After the Supreme
Court handed down its decision in *Brown v. Board of Education of Topeka*
in 1954, Southern public schools—sometimes entire school systems—shut
down rather than desegregate. Private "segregation academies" sprung up
to replace them. In some states, governments provided grants to subsidize
tuition. The movement accelerated following passage of the 1964 Civil
Rights Act, which prohibited segregation in schools receiving federal assistance and authorized the government to file suit in federal court to enforce *Brown*.

A typical story unfolded in Orangeburg, South Carolina, population
fourteen thousand. In 1965 a legal notice ran in the *Times and Democrat*
newspaper announcing a meeting "for the purpose of organizing an elee-
mosynary corporation to be known as Stonewall Jackson Academy, Inc.,
whose purpose will be to operate a private school system." Its founder,
a local organizer in the George Wallace presidential campaign, told the
paper it would be modeled on nearby Wade Hampton Academy, whose
headmaster advised a conference that he sought to encourage individual-
ity in students, but "not to the point of allowing children to misbehave
in the classroom under the guise of individual freedom or the necessity
for self-expression." The man after which that headmaster had named
his school, Wade Hampton Sr., was the biggest slaveholder in Southern
history; his son Wade Jr. was a leader of the post–Civil War Redeemer

movement that rolled back the Constitution's grant of civil rights to blacks by means of violent terror. The gentleman who intended to establish Stonewall Jackson as its sister institution hoped it would enroll every white student in town. But after an NAACP lawsuit against Orangeburg's segregated schools hit a snag, he said it might not open it all—for what would be the point?

Orangeburg's public schools *were* desegregated, however, and the school named after the Confederate general opened its doors in the fall of 1967. Five months later, as it happened, three black college students were shot to death by police while protesting segregation at the local bowling alley. The historical convergence illustrates a principle: segregation academies, as much as violent state terror, were part and parcel of the South's desperate, last-ditch efforts to preserve white supremacy. Often, this was justified in the language of Christianity. In 1967, Senator Strom Thurmond in South Carolina's constituent newsletter praised "independent, nongovernmental schools" for sustaining both "prayers to God in school" and "regional ideals and values." He needn't specify that the regional values he had in mind weren't the consumption of fried green tomatoes.

The segregation academy movement accelerated again in 1969, after the Supreme Court handed down a thumpingly unanimous decision, in *Alexander v. Holmes County Board of Education*, ordering municipalities to immediately "fashion steps which promise realistically to convert promptly to a system without a 'white' school and a 'Negro' school, but just schools." Mississippi Governor John Bell Williams responded that *he* was leaning toward enrolling his children in a segregation academy—because blacks "all carry switchblades, you know. It's characteristic of the race."

But schools weren't only subsidized by state governments. They were also subsidized by the *federal* government, via the charitable tax exemption in section 501(c)(3) of the tax code. A school launched in 1969 by the White Citizens Council in Lexington, Mississippi, Central Holmes Academy, for example, explained in a fundraising letter that contributions were fully "deductible from your gross income for tax purposes," imploring parents to dig deep—"otherwise, there will be many, many students, whose minds and bodies are just as pure as those of any of their classmates and playmates, who for financial reasons alone, will be forced into one of the intolerable or repugnant 'other schools,' or into dropping out of school entirely." That particular school also took advantage of a loophole opened up in 1970 when IRS Commissioner Randolph Thrower announced he would not apply IRS segregation guidelines to religious schools: they changed their name to Central Holmes *Christian* Academy. And that particular fundraising letter was cited two years later when the

Supreme Court mandated that schools seeking tax deductible status face higher scrutiny if they were opened or expanded in a community following an order for public schools to desegregate.

The civil rights group the Children's Defense Fund began dispatching investigators to Southern towns to see if the ruling was being carried out. In Dothan, Alabama, the investigator was a Yale law school student named Hillary Rodham. She posed as a parent considering moving to town; real estate agents all urged her to send her fictional children to the town's new Christian school. Based on findings like these, the IRS tightened its nondiscrimination guidelines in 1975. They required private schools who wished to keep their tax deductions to adopt a nondiscrimination policy, and announce it in all brochures and catalogues, and in a local broadcast outlet or newspaper ("at least three column inches and captioned in at least 12-point type").

The fight against segregation academies became a key item on the liberal agenda—even as a parallel educational movement complicated the issue. This one was also inspired by a Supreme Court decision: *Engele v. Vital*, which in 1962 outlawed prayer in schools—"kicking God out of the classroom," as conservatives put it. Churches responded by opening up their own schools. In 1967, *Christianity Today* called it "the most exciting development in education today."

The boom was hastened by the breakdown in social mores colloquially known as "the sixties"—which, according to conservative parents, had turned public schools into warrens of drug use, promiscuous sex, faddish humanistic psychologizing, and lax-to-nonexistent discipline. In 1954, there had been 123 non-Catholic church schools in the U.S. Within sixteen years there were almost twenty thousand. Their characteristics sometimes overlapped with segregation academies: they abounded in the South; students were predominantly white. But they were largely a separate phenomenon. Segregation academies were all-but-official civic institutions, teaching nearly identical curricula to the public schools they replaced ("except that we study a lot about the evils of Communism," explained one little girl who'd attended both). Church schools were frequently hardscrabble operations domiciled in church basements, recreation halls, or whatever vacant building was handy; some were part of giant entrepreneurial enterprises, run by megachurch pastors who made good-faith efforts to recruit African Americans; and, to further add to the confusion, sometimes the segregation academies local White Citizens Councils set up as their communities' semi-official white schools *also* met in churches when they were the most suitable buildings available.

Liberals steamrolled these complexities. A study published in 1976 called *The Schools That Hate Built* concluded, "Despite what would seem contrary origins," Christian schools and segregation academies were "indistinguishable." In fact—sometimes—they were *adversarial*. A minister in one Mississippi Delta town scourged the segregationist academies in his area as "private versions of the humanistic public-school system, same textbooks, same curriculum, many times the same children." Local segregationists harassed him because his school enrolled 15 percent black students, 15 percent Native American students, and 5 percent the children of refugees from Vietnam.

Other Christian schools sprung up in the North, in communities without active segregation controversies. The institutions comprising the Philadelphia Association of Christian Schools were mostly black. The superintendent of public instruction in Arizona was a major booster of the movement, for purely theological reasons. ("Western civilization becomes a Western jungle—where might makes right—as soon as we educate our leaders without belief in a supreme being," he said at the dedication of a new building at Phoenix Christian High School; separating religion from government was "the greatest achievement of the devil in America today.") And then there were those church schools formed during local segregation controversies in the South who sought to prove they were not segregation academies by making good-faith efforts to recruit blacks. Though in the South, after hundreds of years of white supremacy, abetted by the institutions of white Southern Christianity, there usually existed far too much racial distrust for that to work. These schools often served the cause of segregation *whatever* their benign intent.

Consider the case in the most racially polarized big city in the nation. In January 1973, a twelve-year legal battle over the segregation of Memphis schools culminated with a judge's order to integrate. The number of private schools soon doubled; public schools were soon 70 percent black. The building boom included an entire Christian school system, known as Briarcrest, that educated twenty-four hundred students in eleven buildings, with a two-thousand-pupil high school under construction. Briarcrest looked like just the sort of illegal "dual school system" the Supreme Court had specifically banned. But the ebullient Baptist preacher behind it, W. Wayne Allen, pleaded to the *New York Times* in 1973 that he was *desperate* to recruit black students—but a black minister friend explained to him that if he recommended their parishioners apply, he would be "ostracized as an Uncle Tom." The executive secretary of the local NAACP, Maxine Smith, retorted, "I sincerely believe that if Briarcrest were required to enroll black students, employ black teachers, or include black people in any of its activities, it would shut down."

Reverend Allen had written in his church bulletin about the capital campaign that allowed him to open Briarcrest, "Nothing is impossible with God. He gave us $1,384,248." Years later, in federal hearings on the issue, the NAACP's Smith, speaking for an impoverished constituency whom God did not favor with seven-figure sums to open schools, pointed out that public schools received government funding proportionate to the number of pupils they educated, so when students fled, public schools rotted as a result, whatever Reverend Allen's intention. A liberal clergyman from Memphis noted in those same hearings that Southern Baptists traditionally *opposed* private schooling, and that this changed only after ambitious, empire-building preachers like Allen (and, he might have added, Jerry Falwell in Lynchburg, Virginia; Don Lyon in John Anderson's Rockford, Illinois, congressional district; and Tim LaHaye, proprietor of the San Diego Christian Unified School System), who "play to the fears and other negative emotions of the general population," and deploy "strict disciplinary methods to control their group," began opening schools to expand their ecclesiastical empires.

Ministers may have sincerely believed that their only aim was to give glory to God. Allen naïvely insisted, "My personal view is that we shouldn't even know whether one of our children is black or white." The effect was frequently segregationist nonetheless. And besides, *all* Christian academies were segregation academies, of another sort: they militantly segregated young minds from any cosmopolitan influence.

One Christian school vogue was *McGuffey's Eclectic Readers*, a textbook series first published in 1836, which included sentiments like "The Jews were pruned for the Gentiles' sake, but they were also pruned for their disbelief"; children studied from them at the for-profit Christian school where Richard Viguerie and Howard Phillips sent their kids. Entrepreneurs began producing textbooks, even entire curricula; the Accelerated Christian Education ("ACE") program was used in more than two thousand schools. (Its units included "Christian Womanhood" and "Authority of Parents.") Science curricula taught that the world was created in seven days, 5,750 years ago. A *New Yorker* writer looking in on the schools operated by Jerry Falwell in Lynchburg, Virginia, concluded, "There is no formal ban on logic, but since analytical reasoning might lead to skepticism, and skepticism to the questioning of Biblical truth, it is simply not encouraged except in disciplines like engineering, where it could be expected to yield a single correct answer."

Some used no textbooks. "The Bible is all we need," explained the headmaster of a school, housed in a prefab steel building in Durham, that advertised "Quality Christian Education" even though its teachers had no accreditation. Robert Billings's *Guide to the Christian School* promised readers everything they needed to know to establish their own in 139 pages. A decade after calling it the most exciting development in education, *Christianity Today* said that many "so-called Christian schools" were "shoddy, racist, superpatriotic pretenses unworthy either of the designation of Christian or of school." And by the Bicentennial year, government officials charged with certifying that Christian academies followed the law began meeting fanatical resistance.

In Drake County, Ohio, the parents of a child named Janice Marie Whisner were charged with truancy for sending their daughter to a school that did not meet the state's minimum standards. The Christian school movement helped the Whisners sue on religious freedom grounds. A fundamentalist press labeled the case "Ohio's Trojan Horse: A Warning to Christian Schools Everywhere." The Ohio Supreme Court decided 6–0 in the family's favor, ruling that the U.S. Constitution's guarantee of religious freedom trumped Ohio's interest in educational standards. A North Carolina superior court judge, however, in a 230-page decision, ruled that the state *could* regulate educational standards—but not textbooks.

Evangelical media followed such stories obsessively. Also the long-simmering case of Bob Jones University, which was founded in the 1920s in Greenville, South Carolina, with a large bequest from the Ku Klux Klan, and was the alma mater of Christian right luminaries like Robert Billings and Tim LaHaye. BJU officials fought in court to save their IRS exemption after the federal government moved to withhold it for their refusal to admit blacks; and then, when they began admitting them, for banning blacks from dating whites. Another case involved little Hillsdale College, a conservative school in Michigan that the Crane brothers had attended. It was proudly racially integrated, with an equal number of male and female students, but like BJU it was refused federal funding—because, as Ronald Reagan raged in a column, "battalions of social engineers" at the Department Health, Education, and Welfare (who "spend all their working hours devising new ways to make schools conform to their view of what education should be") demanded that, since some students accepted GI Bill funds and loans guaranteed by the federal government, administrators had to sign a statement affirming that the school did not discriminate against women. On principle, the school refused to sign.

Such battles metastasized during 1977–78 school term. In tiny Louisville, Nebraska, a Christian school opened with twelve students up to twelfth grade. Except for the kindergarten teacher, it was a literal mom-and-pop operation. Pastor Ed Gilbert's legal battle to exempt it from even filing paperwork with state authorities raged for seven years—by which time the school was operating "in exile" in Missouri, and Gilbert was hiding out like a second-century Christian, his catacomb an Iowa motel room. In Concord, New Hampshire, a judge tried to close the fifty-student Christian Heritage School for violating safety regulations. Reverend

Ray Forrest replied that the rickety firetrap that housed his institution had been "given to me by God," and that "the city does not recognize the school, but the Constitution does," and promised go to jail before bowing down to Caesar. And if city officials pressed the matter, they would discover "that the civil rights movement has been resurrected in a strength never seen before."

So it was that on September 1, 1977, a thousand supporters from as far away as California massed in Concord's town square. "Yes, I must disobey man!" Forrest cried. "Because man's law differs from God's law. I'll never close my school! I'll not obey your law! I'll not obey your judge! I'll not obey your courts!" The "amens," the Associated Press reported, "echoed through the downtown area." Southern Baptist preachers in three-piece-suits took turns at the podium to pledge to join the reverend in jail or even die for the cause. Ministers sent messages from thirty states pledging to descend upon Concord within five hours should the civil authorities arrest Forrest. Among them, the Associated Press reported, was "Rev. Jerry Fallwell" [sic] of Lynchburg, Virginia.

IN JANUARY, JIMMY CARTER'S IRS COMMISSIONER GOT INVOLVED, AND things began to cascade.

Jerome Kurtz gave a speech at an obscure tax conference, promising to answer civil rights activists' long-standing complaints about the vague, ineffectual guidance his agency had provided concerning tax exemptions for schools that discriminated. He thought his remarks innocuous. Evangelical school operators did not consider them innocuous at all.

In May, the U.S Commission on Civil Rights found that seven private schools in Mississippi cited by federal courts for racial discrimination still enjoyed tax exemptions. Congress debated Daniel Moynihan's amendment to the tax bill to include tuition tax credits for private schools, including religious schools. Advocacy for Moynihan's proposal from the likes of Falwell, Billy Graham, and Pat Robertson was noted with surprise by commentators who remembered when Protestant fundamentalists used to talk about the parochial schools Moynihan had in mind as a sinister Papist plot. The amendment lost—mooting another, from Representative Bill Archer, a Republican from Texas, stipulating that federal tuition tax credits could not be "construed as a form of federal aid." Which would have meant, complained Senator Fritz Hollings, a former segregationist who had seen the light, that private schools would have no need of "ever complying with the civil rights laws."

Orrin Hatch introduced a "Protection of Pupil Rights" amendment, which revived a 1973 bill from Representative Earl Landgrebe banning public school actions that "infringe upon or usurp the moral or legal rights or responsibilities of parents or guardians with respect to the moral, emotional or physical development of their young children." That referenced one of conservatives' greatest terrors concerning "secular" schools, that they impinged upon the authority of family patriarchs.

In North Carolina, dozens of schools claimed exemption, as church ministries, from paying unemployment insurance taxes. Next, eleven Tarheel State ministers were hauled into court for refusing to fill out forms affirming that their teachers met state certification requirements. Under cross-examination, one was asked if his congregation voted, paid taxes, and complied with other state laws, given their lawyer's claim that the ministers' "distinct religious community" remained aloof from worldly affairs on religious principle. He responded that they obeyed laws they did not feel "violated their religious freedom." Shortly thereafter, he formally requested that his daycare centers be exempt from licensing, too.

On June 21, the same day an ERA ratification bill in Illinois was pulled several votes shy of passage despite White House lobbying, the administration announced that its planned national conference on family policy — "once seemingly the simplest of President Carter's campaign promises," the New York Times observed—would be postponed indefinitely following enraged responses from conservatives after its name was changed, in a nod to "the diversity of American families," from "the White House Conference on the Family" to "the White House Conference on Families." "Belatedly," a column observed, "it dawned on the administration that a White House Conference on Families just months before the next presidential election could easily turn into a political donnybrook of the first water." Few evangelicals any longer counted Jimmy Carter as one their own.

Eighteen days later, one hundred thousand marched on the National Mall in the largest women's rights assembly in American history, to demand that the deadline for ERA ratification be extended to 1982. Two weeks after that, the Justice Department refused to join Missouri Attorney General John Ashcroft's suit against the National Organization of Women for their boycott of non-ratifying states. Then, just ahead of the new school year, the New Hampshire education commissioner recommended that the Board of Education allow the Heritage Christian School to open in its rickety house in Concord even though Reverend Forrest still refused to file the annual report required of all other private schools. CBS News broadcast a three-part series "Is Anyone Out There Learning?" reporting that 13 percent of seventeen-year-olds were functionally illiterate and that 40 percent of Americans believed their education had been superior to their children's. The two most cited reasons for the decline were drug use and lax discipline.

Minority Leader Howard Baker deleted the private-school tuition credit from the tax bill. *Human Events* howled: the Republican leadership was throwing away not just the votes of Catholics but the " 'Christian school movement,' which has seen the construction of evangelical Protestant schools in unprecedented numbers." It was the marquee conservative magazine's first note of the movement—but far from the last. Connie Marshner of the Heritage Foundation, the lead organizer against the White House family conference, had a new book out, *Blackboard Tyranny*. Its intended audience was conservative-minded but politically neophyte parents, whom she sought to recruit via a powerful metaphor: "Mothers have long observed that after the first child starts school, the rest of the family starts catching more colds and flus. But other forms of disease are not so evident. . . . personality traits that start developing . . . dissatisfaction with family rules and routines . . . off-color language or unfamiliar slang." Parents *could* respond to the presence of a virus by refusing to let their children leave the house—or they could follow her organizing guidelines to attack it at the source.

It was an example of how sophisticated the New Right was becoming at organizing discontent—and came out just as word began circulating in the evangelical world, in the middle of August, that a new set of IRS guidelines for private schools seeking tax exemptions was about to come down. Senator Hatch responded with a statement: "It does not take too much imagination" to envision the IRS demanding "homosexual teachers, the availability of abortion counselors, and the abolition of male and female choruses." Adding to the paranoia, the IRS's Exempt Organizations Division had just ruled that a group founded to "foster an understanding and tolerance of homosexuals and their problems" would henceforth qualify for tax exemptions under 501(c)(3).

Such was the kerosene-soaked landscape upon which Jerome Kurtz was to unwittingly toss his lighted match.

"PROPOSED REVENUE PROCEDURE ON PRIVATE TAX-EXEMPT SCHOOLS" WAS published in the *Federal Register* on August 21. It announced that it would apply to any school "formed or significantly expanded" after the local district began a court-ordered or voluntary desegregation plan—an estimated 3,500 of the nation's 18,000 tax-exempt private schools.

It demanded neither abortion counselors nor gay teachers. It simply required that if a covered school enrolled less than 20 percent of its community's proportion of minorities, that school would have to pass four out of five "affirmative action" tests to demonstrate that it was making a good-faith effort to recruit more. Thus a Christian school of 1,447 that had 5 black students, in a city that was 25 percent black—to take the example of a school in Lynchburg, Virginia, operated by the Reverend Jerry Falwell, which enrolled blacks for the first time that year—would either have to add 68 more, show the feds how it was actively recruiting them, or face further IRS review that might eventually end with donations to that school no longer being tax exempt.

Legally, this should not have been controversial. Despite a widespread misunderstanding that tax deductions for churches was a right bestowed by the First Amendment, Section 501(c)(3) of the IRS code actually exempted all charitable institutions from taxes, under the logic that they rendered services the government would have to provide if they did not. "A tax exemption," a government official defending the rules explained later, "is a matter of legislative grace, rather than one of right."

But Christian fundamentalists had their own ideas about grace—and for them, the IRS's action was yet more evidence that Jimmy Carter, once their civic savior, was now verily delivering the nation unto the Devil.

One figure paying close attention was a thin, balding man with a Texas accent who had pulled his two daughters out of one the most prestigious public schools in D.C.'s Maryland suburbs because he was disgusted with its liberal pedagogy. Though he was himself a Catholic, the far-distant school to which he bussed his children was run by Robert Thoburn, author of *How to Establish and Operate a Successful Christian School*. That parent was Richard Viguerie. He had time on his hands after the Panama Canal fight. He discovered the most useful discontent for the New Right to organize yet.

Why this one, and not ERA, the Panama Canal, or the rest? Robert Billings's son later ventured an explanation: Kurtz had hit the money nerve. "If Christian schools were to lose their tax-exempt status, their tuition could conceivably double. When it becomes not just a moral or a conservative/liberal issue, you definitely take an interest."

A NEW SCHOOL YEAR—AND, BY 1978, ANOTHER ANNUAL CHRISTIAN CONSERVATIVE ritual: protesting the fall TV season. Though this year they were joined by high-minded liberals, grieving the retreat from seriousness in popular culture.

In the early 1970s Norman Lear transformed the face of prime time with radically honest situation comedies like *All in the Family* that featured families negotiating their way through divisive social changes of the 1960s. Liberals loved them; conservatives despised them. Jerry Falwell banned his employees from watching them. Now, however, conservatives and liberals had a TV figure they could calumniate together. His name was Fred Silverman.

As head of daytime programming for CBS, Silverman had turned the fill-in-the-blank quiz show *Match Game* into an afternoon festival of sexual innuendo. (Host Gene Rayburn: "A giant turtle tried to _____ a Volkswagen." Panelist Betty White: "Not with the engine in the rear!") As president of ABC, he presided over the invention of a new sort of programming his critics dubbed "Jigglevision": On *Charlie's Angels*, three sexy single ladies solved crimes for an offscreen boss. On *Three's Company*, two sexy single ladies shared an apartment with a single man. *The Love Boat* chronicled a singles bar on the high seas; its executive producer once fired off a memo demanding "Do we have enough titillating, purely sexual stories?" and another complaining that there weren't enough scripts providing love interests for the ship's pretty cruise director Julie McCoy ("Let the poor girl get laid—please!"). The typical Silverman product married adult situations to stories so simpleminded they could be appreciated by children. Critics dubbed it "kiddie porn"; other networks rushed to copy it. In 1978, NBC snapped Silverman up. *Doonesbury* imagined his first day on the job: "To program for nine-year-olds, you have to *think* like nine-year-olds. If you want NBC to start clicking again, you're going to have to stop acting like grown men! Understood? . . . Good. Now, let's take a look at your cleavage situation."

TV news was increasingly titillating, too. Once, the networks had run their news divisions at a loss, as a signal to the federal government that the networks' precious access to the publicly owned airwaves was morally deserved. Then, in 1977 ABC tapped the head of the *sports* division, Roone Arledge, to simultaneously run the *news* division. Arledge was a television-world P. T. Barnum. He had invented *Wide World of Sports*, which never met a car crash or daredevil motorcycle jump it wouldn't exploit. His *Monday Night Football* borrowed its presentation style from professional wrestling. On Arledge's first day at the news division—in real life, not in *Doonesbury*—he greeted his new underlings wearing a gauche polka-dotted shirt, unbuttoned halfway down to reveal an even gaudier gold chain, and told them their job was to turn news into show business.

Local news was worse. A critic named Ron Powers, in a jeremiad called *The Newscasters*, chose a single WABC-TV *Eyewitness News* broadcast in New York as a case study. In the world beyond, the Labor Department had just announced that the Consumer Price Index grew 1.4 percent in a month; the prime rate charted its biggest increase in a decade; and Afghanistan was on the brink of war; but the lead story on the local news was "Murders in Manhattan! Two men in an expensive East Side apartment . . . an apartment *visited by* Eyewitness News *once before!*" Then came an interview with comic Henny Youngman, the "king of one-liners," then a dispatch from snow-covered Central Park (the giggling correspondent tossed a snowball); then, finally, some economic news—a six-minute segment entitled "Being Rich," the first installment in a promised series of three, documenting socialites cavorting at a charity ball in Palm Beach.

Industry bigwigs told Powers that, after Vietnam and Watergate, people were " 'sick' of unpleasant news" and that the "mood of the country" was " 'People'-oriented"—a word, he wrote, that had "became oracular; it was spoken in hushed italics; it bore the tintinnabulation of cash-register bells." Same in the book trade. At the beginning of the decade, morally serious, public-spirited tomes like *The Pentagon Papers* and Morton Mintz and Jerry S. Cohen's *America, Inc.* filled bestseller lists. Now, seven out of ten titles on the *New York Times* list were self-help books. The most durable was called *Looking Out for #1*, by an Ayn Rand devotee named Robert Ringer—a follow-up to his earlier hit *Winning Through Intimidation*.

In the 1960s, rock stars doted upon their identities as troubadours of social conscience. They were succeeded in the early 1970s pop charts by the equally un-frivolous work of singer-songwriters like Joni Mitchell and Carly Simon, and bands like Fleetwood Mac, who delved deep to map the forlorn geography of modern relationships and personal alienation. Now the hits were all disco, disco, disco; or rock where stars sang bloated odes to the joys and travails of the lives of rock stars; or mellow, genial songs, from a genre comprised of well-groomed, pastel-clad agglomerations like Pablo Cruise, Seals & Crofts, and Ambrosia, that, because they so often involved recreation on the high seas, were later dubbed "yacht rock."

One used to be able to count on college campuses for a bracing dose of youthful idealism. But 1978's surprise Hollywood blockbuster *Animal House* turned drunken fraternity debauches into a hero's quest. It was set in 1962, the year before Kennedy died—before Vietnam, before Watergate. College students embraced it as a how-to guide—thanks in part to a $4.5 million promotional effort from Universal Pictures that organized "toga parties" like the one in the movie on campuses nationwide. It became the second-highest grossing film of the year, behind *Grease*—another pre-sixties nostalgia piece. The alcohol industry seized the opportunity by promoting campus events aimed at persuading students that binge drinking was an integral part of the college experience.

At the University of Wisconsin in Madison, where antiwar students used to fight street battles with police, a twenty-seven-year-old "tenth year" student created an *Animal House*-inspired "Pail and Shovel Party" that won control of the Student Senate on a platform of flooding the football stadium for naval battles and turning parking meters into gum ball machines. The party's accomplishments included a resolution to change the school's name to the University of New Jersey and the planting of a thousand pink flamingos in front of the dean's office. "We're happy that students are apathetic," one of its leaders proclaimed. "If not, we'd be out of office."

ALL, THAT AUTUMN, WAS NOT FRIVOLOUS.

Two weeks into the new school year, Jimmy Carter gathered the prime minister of Israel and the president of Egypt for a diplomatic summit at the presidential retreat at Camp David in Maryland's Catoctin Mountains. It was like something out of the Old Testament: a Solomonic lawgiver called two warring chieftains to the mountaintop to parley; and lo, they descended bearing a miraculous accord.

In the beginning—that was 1973, on Yom Kippur, the Jews' holiest of day, when hordes of Egyptians crossed the Gulf of Suez on rubber boats, and battalions of tanks crossed bridges made of pontoons, nearly overrunning the Jewish state itself. Israel's generals considered a "Samson Option"—atomic warfare—until America rescued Israel with a mighty airlift of arms.

Or perhaps the beginning was 1967, when Israel laid waste to five armies in six days and added great swaths of Arab lands to her dominion.

Or 1956, when Egypt took the Suez Canal from England, who made war to win it back in secret alliance with the Jewish state.

Or 1948, when Israel declared herself a nation and every Arab army invaded, then was defeated, and all the armies were forever more united in a burning hatred at their humiliation by the Jews.

Or perhaps the saga should begin with legends from thousands of years before, when Jews were slaves in Egypt and were freed by an angry God who drowned Pharaoh's army in the Red Sea, and promised them a land of milk and honey for their children and their children's children if they honored their covenant with Him—the story Jews recited each Passover about how "in every generation our enemies rise up against us to destroy us but the Holy One blessed Be He saves us from their hands."

Although, in the Koran's version of the same story, the Almighty had turned away from the Jews to punish them for forgetting their covenant with Him, but commanded Muslims, "You will always find treachery in all but a few them. Overlook this and pardon them."

Which is to say, the enmity between Egypt and Israel was deeper than the mere geopolitics. It was millennial. It was metaphysical. It was as deep as a hatred could be. And the two men that destiny chose to miraculously lead their nations out of this shared bondage of history could not have better exemplified the intractability of the clash.

Menachem Begin's earliest memory was of a Polish soldier flogging a Jew in a public park. He watched his father risk his life by beating off a Polish police sergeant who was humiliating a rabbi by cutting off his beard. As an adolescent, brilliant but frail, he himself was regularly beaten bloody. He always fought back. Then, in 1929, at the age of sixteen, he encountered the man who was born Vladimir Jabotinsky, but renamed himself *Ze'ev*—the Hebrew word for "wolf." Ze'ev Jabotinsky argued that Jews must redeem their suffering by recovering their destiny as warriors, taking back the lands on both banks of the Jordan River, where Arabs outnumbered Jews by a ratio of eight to one. From Jabotinsky, Begin learned to think like a biblical prophet.

Soviet secret police sent him to the gulag, where he was interrogated day and night, but not broken. Miraculously, he "made *Aliya*"—the word shared by Hebrew and Arabic that literally meant "going up," which Zionists adopted to describe the exalted act of settling the Holy Land. There, he organized an underground Jewish army to turn British-mandate Palestine into a Jewish nation. His critics called this madness, because it pulled British resources from its war against the Jew-devouring Nazi war machine. Begin, indifferent to their pleas, responded, "There will be no retreat. Freedom—or death."

Anwar Sadat was simultaneously fighting his own half-mad insurgency against British colonialism, never forgetting that Egypt had been under foreign domination almost continuously since the sixth century BCE. In his struggle, he *collaborated* with the Nazis, and was open in his admiration for Hitler. As a twenty-three-year-old Army captain he single-handedly tried to strike a deal with General Ernst Rommel to lead an army to pin down the British military in Cairo in exchange for Egypt's independence. He ended up in prison as a German spy. He escaped, lived as a fugitive, then joined an underground army that assassinated British soldiers when they were drunk and alone. Then he expanded the army's ambitions, first in an unsuccessful attempt on the life of Egypt's pro-British prime minister, then in a successful one against a top deputy. Arguing his own case in court, he won his acquittal.

Egypt shook free of the British in 1953. Israel had become independent five years before, thanks in part to a vicious campaign of terrorism led by Menachem Begin, whose own underground army, the Irgun, funded by plunder and extortion, pioneered techniques later studied by Palestinian terrorists. like the improvised explosive device, and the bombing of random civilians as a coup de théâtre intended to render occupied lands ungovernable. In 1946 they bombed Jerusalem's five-star King David Hotel, British headquarters, killing ninety-one. Begin declared, "We mourn the Jewish victims. The British did not mourn the six million Jews who lost their lives." During the 1948 War for Independence his troops massacred 248 civilians of an Arab village on the strategic high ground above Jerusalem. Begin, who was far away in Tel Aviv, sent a message to his commanders like he was Moses: "Tell the soldiers: You have made history in Israel with your attack and your conquest. Continue thus until victory. As is in Deir Yassin, so everywhere, we will attack and smite the enemy. God, God, thou has chosen us for conquest."

Arab patriots like Anwar Sadat listened, and decided that a nation of savages was being born in their midst.

Israel won her war; Menachem Begin's violent intransigence continued unabated. In 1951, the Israeli Knesset took up a discussion of cash reparations from Germany for the Holocaust. Begin reared up in horror at the thought of the body, of which he now was a member, negotiating for blood money with the "herd of wolves that devoured our people as prey." He gathered fifteen thousand of his supporters in Zion Square, and commanded—"Go, surround the Knesset, as in the days of Rome. When the Roman procurator wanted to set up an idol in the Holy Temple, the Jews came from all corners of the country, surrounded the building, and said, 'Over our dead bodies!'" Then he threatened his fellow parliamentarians: "You have prisons, concentration camps, an army, a police force, detectives, artillery, machine guns. It makes no difference. On this matter all this force will shatter like glass against a rock." He set his followers loose as a mob.

Begin liked to say, "There is only one thing to which I'm sensitive: Jewish blood." Sadat conceived of his political vocation in much the same way. Both understood themselves as sacred vessels of destiny, sent by divine Providence to redeem their people's historic humiliation. They both spoke in terms of millennia.

And then there was Jimmy Carter, who on this particular subject was half-mad, too. The lands over which they parleyed felt as familiar to him as his native Georgia, where the towns had names like Bethlehem, Hebron, and Goshen. In his campaign memoir, he described his upbringing in biblical terms: "My life on the farm during the Great Depression more nearly resembled farm life of fully two thousand years ago than farm life today." He had sojourned in the Holy Land in 1973, when only those closest to him knew he intended to become president, and he walked where Jesus walked, and bathed where Jesus was baptized, and prayed in a synagogue on the Sea of Galilee.

So when Hamilton Jordan wrote to him in a memo, so sensitive he typed it himself and kept the only copy in his office safe, warning of the gravest possible political risks if he prioritized negotiating a Middle East peace deal, Jimmy Carter ignored it. God would somehow show him a way.

And so he summoned all the power of his office, and risked all the political capital of his new administration, to gather together two men whose hearts had been hardened by ancient hatred, on the mountaintop, with not one thing agreed to in advance, with no plan except to sit them down to talk. Henry Kissinger had warned him that no president should ever personally engage in negotiations where the outcome was in doubt. And here everything was in doubt.

On the first day, the president's wife proposed a prayer, and Menachem Begin read it and made modifications to the text; then they prayed. The text was released to the media—practically the last word to come down from the mountaintop for another thirteen days.

On the second day Sadat handed Carter a lengthy "Framework for a Comprehensive Settlement of the Middle East Problem," and the president despaired: every clause was far beyond what Begin would ever accept. Perhaps Sadat made impossible demands because he was having second thoughts, for rulers of all the Arab lands, stinging from the humiliating losses of 1948, and 1967, and 1973, owed much of their power to their ability to summon the passionate hatred of their people of their permanent enemy the Jews, and dearly wished for Sadat to fail.

The three rulers met. Sadat read his framework aloud. Begin glowered, feeling his nation's very honor traduced. They parted, and Carter once more despaired.

On the third day they met again, and Begin spoke of the treachery of the Egyptian attack in 1973 on the holiest of days, and said, "You address us as if we were a defeated nation." Sadat cried that Israel was pumping oil that very moment from Egyptian wells in the Sinai desert that Israel had conquered in that war. And the two men set off to bickering, until, their faces flushed, they forgot that Jimmy Carter was even there.

"Never! If you do not agree to dismantle the settlements, there will be no peace!"

"We will not agree to dismantle the settlements!"

Anwar Sadat said he saw no reason for the talks to continue, and both men made to leave, but President Carter blocked their path, and successfully begged them to stay only one day more.

That night the president told his wife again and again, "There must be a way." He awoke at five o'clock, played tennis, then returned to his cabin and learned that Anwar Sadat had packed his bags and Menachem Begin was preparing a statement for the press explaining why the summit had failed.

Again and again, the two sides made to pack their bags; each time Carter successfully begged them to keep talking. He played to both men's oversized sense of historical destiny, their patriotism, their egos, their common interest on staying on the good side of the world's most powerful nation, to all the things their nations stood to gain by choosing peace instead of pride. He pushed past the two men's staggering distrust, each side's conviction that what the other actually sought was a window of vulnerability to crush the other side once and for all. He identified points of leverage where others saw none. He found people within each delegation who were able to grasp the bigger picture, and were best equipped to soften their leader's heart, when positions hardened beyond reason. Again and again, those leaders saw what Jimmy Carter looked like when he was very angry—which was, a Camp David chronicler wrote, quite a sight: "He turned icy. His voice would go quiet, his eyes hardened into bullets, and he would smile inappropriately in what looked like a rictus. People who encountered him in this state rarely forgot it."

Jimmy Carter had budgeted three or four days for this reckless diplomatic gamble. On the fifth day Carter, his original plan in tatters, boldly abandoned it and put forth another. It provided the crack of daylight that lit the way to narrowing the gulf between the camps. He had his aides draft a comprehensive single proposal that the American negotiators controlled, at which the two sides hacked and expanded and slashed and shaved, day after day, draft upon draft, each new move providing a new occasion for bickering: twenty-one drafts in all.

Until, on the thirteenth day, the three finally emerged, haggard, with a text in hand all could agree on, and presented themselves before the hundreds of news-starved journalists who had hunkered down in futility in a nearby VFW hall with no one to interview but each other for nearly two weeks.

As the three world leaders announced their miracle, thunderclouds were massing. It looked like the helicopters would not even be able to lift off to ferry the parties back to Washington. Then, they did—and the passengers bore witness to a stunning display of gratitude: homeowners in the flight path had turned on every light in their houses, and the lights in their yards, and the lights on their porches, and the eerie, awesome glow lit the helicopters' way from the mountaintop to the executive mansion, where the arrival of the three men was illuminated by a massive assemblage of television klieg lights.

They sat down in the East Room to sign what history called the Camp David Accords. Seats reserved for the Egyptian delegation were empty: diplomats feared for their lives should their participation become known. This attested to Anwar Sadat's awesome courage.

Jimmy Carter spoke: "When we arrived at Camp David the first thing we agreed upon was to ask the people of the world to pray that our negotiations would be successful. Those prayers have been answered far beyond any expectations." Sadat spoke: "Dear friend, we came to Camp David with all the goodwill and faith we possess, and we left Camp David a few minutes ago with a renewed sense of hope and inspiration. Let us pledge to make the spirit of Camp David a new chapter in the history of our nations." Begin spoke: "The Camp David conference should be renamed. It was the Jimmy Carter conference."

The *New Republic*'s columnist TRB had previously warned Jimmy Carter that if he failed, he risked "reimposition of the oil boycott, more inflation, more unemployment, and possibly war." He faced that down without flinching, producing what others said was impossible. And now TRB reported that the delirious applause following the president's introduction to a joint session of Congress explaining the deal lasted a full nine minutes.

There was still much to be done: completing a formal treaty might take months. But one accomplishment was apparent immediately: Jimmy Carter's approval rating soared seventeen points, to 56 percent. "All the discouraging opinion surveys of the past, all the whispered calculations of politicians, all the cruel judgements of the experts have been declared obsolete by the spectacular success at Camp David," judged Witcover and Germond. "The political slate" was "wiped clean," and with it the doubt that Jimmy Carter was "out of his depth in the presidency."

IT COULDN'T HAVE HAPPENED AT A MORE OPPORTUNE TIME FOR THE DEMocrats. Congressional elections were just around the corner.

One of the final primaries was in Minnesota, on the second Tuesday in September. Two Democrats vied to occupy the seat vacated by the late Hubert Humphrey and now held by his widow Muriel. Donald Fraser was a sixteen-year congressman of towering liberal accomplishment. He had convened a hard-hitting investigation about the ties of the Reverend Sun Myung Moon's Unification Church cult to both Korean intelligence and the conservative movement. "Moonies" descended upon the state to canvass furiously against him door to door. So did anti-abortion activists. His opponent, Robert Short, was a rich businessman who had once owned the Minneapolis NBA franchise. He campaigned against abortion, for a 20 percent across-the-board cut in federal spending and against the "nuts who are taxing the hell out of us," and the environmentalists organizing to preserve the state's million-acre Boundary Waters Canoe Area. Fraser lost. The Democratic Farmer Labor Party (which other states called the Democratic Party) withheld their endorsement from Short—because, exclaimed a DFL official, "How can I possibly support a Democratic candidate who thinks like Ronald Reagan, talks like Spiro Agnew, and campaigns like Richard Nixon?" Dr. Carolyn Gerster, the new president of the National Right to Life Committee, took the occasion of the victory to announce a three-year plan to elect enough pro-life representatives to call a constitutional convention to abolish abortion once and for all.

The following Tuesday, in Oklahoma, the Democratic nod for Senate went to David Boren, a tax-cut obsessive whose opponent called him a "closet Republican." In Massachusetts, Michael Dukakis, a once-promising Democratic superstar, was cut down in a shocking upset. He had won the governorship in 1974 with a "lead pipe guarantee" of no new taxes, and broke the promise. His opponent was the conservative, pro-life Ed King, who dubbed the governor a "limousine liberal," despite his success cutting thousands of poor Bay Staters from the welfare rolls and requiring the rest to perform tasks like painting highway guardrails and picking up litter. King promised a ballot referendum to cap state spending, a slash of property taxes (even though the state was near bankruptcy), and a ban on busing—a potent pledge in Boston, still raw from the violent street clashes that followed an infamous 1974 federal court desegregation plan. Massachusetts's Democratic Party endorsed King. Dukakis lost by nine points. "You gave us a message," King proclaimed in his victory speech. "You said Massachusetts needs a Proposition 13, and now; you said you want capital punishment for premeditated murder, and now; you said you wanted drug pushers to have mandatory jail sentences, and now."

In the Massachusetts Republican senate primary, incumbent Ed Brooke faced Avi Nelson, the conservative talk radio host. Aides implored Brooke to embrace Kemp-Roth or face political death. Brooke declined. Nelson savaged him. Brooke responded with an advertising blitz, a parade of out-of-town worthies from Jesse Jackson to Bill Brock, who broke a party chairman's traditional neutrality to campaign. The Senate's only African American, who had won his previous general election by almost thirty percentage points, survived this primary by only four.

CONSERVATIVES WOULD HAVE PREFERRED THE MEDIA TO FOCUS ON THESE upsets and near-upsets. Instead, commentary focused on how few Americans cared that congressional elections were happening at all—negating any genuine trends. "I thought voter apathy was bad during the last election," a party activist in Alabama was quoted as saying. "But this election has been something." Potential voters "just don't care" a politician in DeKalb, Illinois, agreed. The editors of a small-town Southern newspaper noted, "This year's elections are unusually important and an especially good opportunity for Alabamians, yet many voters are showing little interest." Only 10 percent of eligible Republicans had voted in the New Jersey balloting that chose Jeff Bell. Howard Phillips ran for Senate nomination on the Democratic side in Massachusetts. He had hoped an appearance by Anita Bryant would rally thousands of conservatives. Instead, the event was canceled when only seventy-eight tickets were sold. Phillips tied for fourth.

As the general election approached, the notion of a New Right upsurge was hard to swallow. Their senate candidate in Iowa, Roger Jepsen, scored 40 percent support in a September 24 survey—then 27 percent in one released a week later. In North Carolina, pundits thought it possible Jesse Helms might lose his Senate seat to the state's hard-swinging populist insurance commissioner. In South Carolina, seventy-five-year-old Strom Thurmond, whose calling card had once been his unapologetic racism, was running so scared against his vigorous, handsome forty-year-old challenger he placed his daughter in an integrated public school to impress black voters.

One problem was all the Democrats stealing their signature issue. "To Candidates, Right Looks Right: Both Sides Come Out Conservative on Taxes," *Time* magazine reported after the House advanced a version of the tax bill by a 362–40 vote that lowered the capital gains rate to 25 percent, exempted capital gains from the minimum tax, and exempted proceeds from the sale of a house up to $100,000. Experts estimated that under this version, those making less than $5,000 would receive a 0.4 percent income tax cut, and those making over $200,000, which was ten times the median income, would get back 14.5 percent. Numbers, a critic observed, "unthinkable only six months earlier"—before Prop 13, that is.

As for Jack Kemp and William Roth's proposal for a 30 percent across the board cut for every income tax bracket, Bill Brock said it had brought about "the most complete agreement on an economic issue in modern Republican history." To promote it as the keystone of a coordinated Republican general election campaign, the RNC chartered a 727, painted "REPUBLICAN TAX CLIPPER" across the side, loaded the cargo hold with cartons of pamphlets promising that "Roth-Kemp Is Only the Start," and took off with a cadre of GOP officials aboard on September 20—the day the Senate Finance Committee voted to uphold tax deductions for the business purchase of theater, sports, and opera tickets—for a seven-state tour.

The first stop was New York, where Roth proclaimed, "We have helped the rich, we've helped the poor, but we've ripped off the middle class. We have to change the country in a new direction and help our working people." (Ralph Nader's Tax Reform Research Group said that, actually, under the Republican plan families making $20,000 to $30,000, in the dead center of the middle class, would only receive $16 in savings a year, while those making more than $200,000 would receive an average annual savings of more than $14,000 and 70 percent of package's benefits.) The next day, when the Senate Finance Committee voted 13–1 to exempt the first 70 percent of capital gains from taxation instead of the current law's 50 percent, the Republican Tax Clipper landed in Pennsylvania, where Howard Baker told a cheering crowd, "The Republican tax proposal may be the last chance for the free enterprise system in the United States."

Ronald Reagan joined the entourage in Chicago. In Minneapolis, Democratic Senate candidate Bob Short took advantage of the arrival of the Republican entourage to argue the cut should be 50 percent. The next stop was Detroit. Senator Malcolm Wallop, the Wyoming conservative, faced a tough question: "Everyone wants lower taxes, but how can you cut them *thirty-three percent* without creating huge budget deficits and cutting vital programs?" He responded: "Even the most pessimistic forecasts say it will create four million new jobs—permanent jobs." Minority Leader Rhodes addressed his remarks to Jimmy Carter: "The people of this country want Kemp-Roth. I can't believe any president would veto a tax cut like this, but if he does, he'll pay a terrible price at the polls."

The tour culminated in Los Angeles with a rally starring Gerald Ford, who said it was time to "turn off the federal money machine that robs our paychecks with inflation and higher spending," warning against falling for Carter's merely "token" tax reductions. Reagan wrote a column timed for publication during the road show, pointing to the triumphs of Ed King and Robert Short and arguing that unless more Democrats joined the tax-cut bandwagon, "historians may come to describe 1978 as the Year of the Elephant."

Which, if true, made for an excellent chance that historians might come to describe 1980 as the year of Ronald Reagan—if his people could only get their act together.

CHAPTER 18

Election Season

IN JULY RONALD REAGAN HAD JOURNEYED TO WASHINGTON, RACING FROM one meeting to the next to recruit allies for a presidential race. It proved a frustration—beginning with a lunch in a private Senate dining room with members of the "Kingston Group," the central strategic command for the New Right, joined on this particular occasion by just about every major conservative donor.

The activists and moneymen began grilling Reagan mercilessly for signs of rumored ideological deviations. Some threatened to withdraw their support unless he agreed to cut loose his 1976 campaign manager John Sears. A week previously, at a lunch with reporters organized by the *Christian Science Monitor*'s Godfrey Sperling, "Mr. Sears," according to the *New York Times*, "said that Mr. Reagan's problem with the public was that he was being perceived as being too far to the right." The reporters asked Sears whether the governor would spearhead opposition to Carter's attempts to normalize relations with the People's Republic of China. Sears replied that he didn't expect so—and that he "wouldn't be surprised if Reagan visited China himself. . . . He sees that our main adversary is the Soviet Union," and "believes the fact that China has this same adversary relationship with the Soviet Union makes it apparent that we should be talking to the Chinese leaders." Sears was restating the strategic doctrine of Richard Nixon, Henry Kissinger, and Gerald Ford—what the Reagan forces' "Morality in Foreign Policy" plank at the 1976 convention had been written to oppose. Witcover and Germond called Sears's statement a "tip-off" that Reagan might be abandoning his former disgust for Kissinger, because he had "to start moving toward the center looking to 1980." Members of that base were duly horrified.

To them, Henry Kissinger was Beelzebub, and referring to that big landmass in Asia as "China," full stop, was heresy. They called it *Red China* and considered it an outlaw state, and believed the once-and-future legitimate government of China was the one banished by the forces of Marxist terror in 1949 to the island of Taiwan—whose leaders were Christian, and whose economics were capitalist. In the 1950s, American conservatives had formed a "China Lobby" to advocate for it to be installed in Peking, dreaming of the day when America would finally "unleash Chiang" to take China back for the side of freedom. Men like the ones in the Kingston Group hadn't changed their views since.

John Sears hadn't consulted with Reagan before claiming he was abandoning this pillar of conservative identity; indeed, what Sears said was not true. Just two days before his trip to Washington, as a matter of fact, Reagan had regaled a banquet of anti-Communist Chinese exiles in Los Angeles regarding his recent trip to Asia, "One of the things that struck me most was that the people of Taiwan smile so much. Perhaps that is because they have built a society where they are free to work toward fulfilling the goals they have set for themselves." (In fact, Taiwan was run by a military dictatorship that cemented its rule by massacring ten thousand civilians; under its current, permanent, state of martial law, critics of its single political party were arrested, beaten, and even disappeared; men could be sentenced to prison for having the wrong length of hair.) Reagan went on to explain why he believed President Carter's arguments for normalizing relations with the People's Republic of China were utterly without validity. Now here was John Sears claiming Reagan believed the opposite—what's more, that he was doing so, the *Los Angeles Times* reported, because it "would help soften his right-wing political image, which Sears conceded had been a problem in the past."

Sears had also told the reporters that Reagan would be working to attract ethnic voters—"other than blacks," because of the "bad reputation of the Republican Party" among African Americans. But Reagan himself never would have said such a thing. He always maintained that attracting black voters to the Republican Party would be *easy*, if the party just stuck to its conservative course—that "black Americans want what every other kind of American wants: a crack at a decent job, a home, safe streets, and a good education for their children. And the best way to have those things is for government to get out of the way while we make a bigger pie so that everyone can have a bigger slice."

Sears didn't know his client's mind very well. Deaver and Hannaford, who knew his mind as well as their own spouses'—and who also had the nation of Taiwan as a public relations client—spent the rest of the week doing damage control. And at the meeting of the Kingston Group in Washington, Reagan himself struggled to talk conservatives off the ledge.

"John is not authorized to speak for me," he insisted. "It is absolutely untrue that I am going to Peking. I have not altered one bit in saying this country must not abandon its friends on Taiwan or weaken our mutual defense treaty with them."

He was asked point-blank whether Sears would be his campaign manager. Reagan responded that if he ran for president, "there would be a different campaign organization," with Sears's "talents and abilities" used in some other, undefined, role, promising that these men would be consulted on personnel decisions. He also said that he was hard at work on efforts to clean the liberals out at the Republican National Committee. And that he would never compromise on their shared principles—"to hell with whether they make somebody mad or not."

Tempers cooled—though it was still a "touchy situation," an anonymous attendee told the Associated Press.

AT REAGAN'S NEXT APPOINTMENT, HE WENT FROM THE FRYING PAN INTO the fire. Congressman Phil Crane had been the chairman of Reagan's 1976 presidential campaign in Illinois. This visit was supposed to be a courtesy call. But back in April Crane had let it be known that he might run for president if Reagan did not—and now he informed his friend that he intended to run no matter what.

This slashed at Ronald Reagan's Achilles' heel. Crane was forty-seven. Reagan was sixty-seven. Inauguration Day in 1981 would come sixteen days shy of his seventieth birthday—which was the age at which dear old Dwight D. Eisenhower had *left* office. There was hardly an article on Reagan's prospects that didn't mention the "age problem." Columnist Marquis Childs was typical: "William Henry Harrison, old Tippecanoe, was the only president to be inaugurated at that age, and he died of pneumonia six weeks later." The matter was such a commonplace that even an article about the vogue for plastic surgery in California referenced it: "Let's just say that one fellow might be President of the United States if he'd gotten a facelift."

Reagan's pollster Richard Wirthlin framed the question in all the ways he could think up: ". . . not up to the demands of the presidency . . . too out of touch . . . too tired . . . *too old*?" Most respondents said age wouldn't affect their vote. Nonetheless Wirthlin was petrified: something like forgetting just one dignitary's name on television might change that for good.

Reagan attacked the issue with humor: that he was so old he remembered when a hot story broke and the reporter would run into the newsroom crying, "Stop the chisels!" That watching himself on TV in his old movies was like "looking at a son you never knew you had." That all the wise Confucian leaders he met in Asia thought he was too young to be president. And indeed, his presence belied the impression of decrepitude. He might have been born when William Howard Taft was president, but he hardly looked older than Phil Crane.

A problem remained, however: often Ronald Reagan *sounded* like a doddering old fool.

He had a proclivity for repeating falsehoods, even after being informed that they were false. Like the one about a black cook who manned the guns at Pearl Harbor so heroically the armed services were immediately desegregated. (That came seven years later.) Or a favorite "quotation" he attributed to Vladimir Lenin: "We will take Eastern Europe. We will organize the hordes of Asia. And then we will move into Latin America and we won't have to take the United States; it will fall into our out-stretched hands like overripe fruit." (Lenin never said it, though *The Blue Book of the John Birch Society* claimed he did.) Reagan also had a terrible time remembering names. As governor, it had been press secretary Lyn Nofziger's job to help whenever he drew a blank. (Among staffers, the joke was that Nofziger came home with him at the end of the day: "You remember *Nancy*, don't you, Governor?")

Thanks largely to the age issue, the Republican National Committee meeting that summer bloomed with talk of the presidential prospects of Jack Kemp—a "new face," in the political cliché. "National committee members view as the worst thing that can happen to their party a renewal of the 1976 struggle for the presidential nomination between Ronald Reagan and Gerald Ford," Evans and Novak reported: it would make the GOP seem a party of old men. Sometimes Reagan himself sounded skeptical of his fitness for eight years in the office, telling one interviewer, "Maybe it wouldn't be the worst thing in the world if we had somebody who said, 'What this country needs is a one-term president, who won't have his eye on four years down the road.'"

Phil Crane feared that Reagan would wait until late in 1979, announce that he was retiring, and leave conservatives without a candidate at all. That was why Crane was the first Republican to throw his hat into the ring. But Reagan's recent schedule made his ambitions plain.

There had been a dinner at Stanford at which Reagan grilled Milton Friedman, Bill Simon, Alan Greenspan, and Nixon labor and treasury sec-retary George Shultz about the nuts and bolts of White House operations. A visit to Bohemian Grove, the secret society in the Northern California woods where Republican power brokers frolicked and cut deals. This trip to Washington—then, his first day back, a meeting with a group of fifteen political writers, then individual audiences with reporters from the *Los Angeles Times*, the *Chicago Tribune*, the *New York Daily News*, and the *London Daily Telegraph*; and a tête-a-tête with a friend who owned a hotel in Palm Springs, perhaps for some political intelligence: Gerald Ford lived in Palm Springs, and in a recent poll, Republican voters had pre-ferred Ford to Reagan for the nomination by a margin of 37 to 31 percent.

The next day he pulled a prized Haut-Brion 1947 from his cellar to mark an auspicious occasion: a dinner party for Richard Nixon. Sure, most people considered the former president a disgrace. Reagan still adored him. What's more, Nixon knew a thing or two about winning Republican presidential nominations. And he still had some rich, loyal, powerful friends—like Walter Annenberg, publisher of *TV Guide* and Nixon's ambassador to the United Kingdom, who, with his wife and Pat Nixon, also joined the Reagans that night.

Reagan took his annual August break. Then got to work—hard. On August 27, Ford and Reagan filmed television commercials together for various Republican candidates; the *Washington Post* gossiped, "Republicans who have talked recently with former President Ford say he rarely fails to remark how old Ronald Reagan is looking. . . . The rivalry between the two men that developed during their 1976 race apparently is unabated, which is one reason why many Republicans still think Ford will end up running for the 1980 nomination." In subsequent days, Reagan filmed almost a hundred more campaign commercials for candidates for U.S. senator, congressman, state legislatures, even county boards; his Citizens for the Republic PAC was disbursing hundreds of thousands of dollars to friendly candidates. Not the sort of thing a politician retiree would do. They were building a political machine.

THE DAY RONALD REAGAN RETURNED FROM BOHEMIAN GROVE AND PRE-sented himself to nineteen journalists, he also took a meeting that showed how unpredictable a political figure he could be. It concerned Proposition 6—the Briggs Initiative, the one intended to ban gays and lesbians from teaching in California, which was turning very, very ugly.

An elementary school teacher in the pretty little Sonoma County town of Healdsburg named Larry Berner, a kindly, bearded thirty-eight-year-old Air Force veteran who sounded a little like Mr. Rogers, had written about his experience campaigning against Proposition 6 for the monthly Sonoma County gay newsletter, in which he outed himself. A school board member called him a "moral carcinogenic among the tender treasures of the Heavenly Father." Parents presented the school board with a petition demanding his firing. The board's lawyer said the 1975 repeal of the state's sodomy statute forbade that. The board voted to endorse the Briggs Initiative instead, making of their town a sort of symbolic campaign headquarters—"to protect our children from the rape of their minds before they're raped physically," the school board president explained.

Senator Briggs traveled to Healdsburg, an hour north of San Francisco, for a major speech. "If you let one homosexual teacher stay," he barked, "soon there'll be two, then four, then eight, then twenty-five—and before long, the entire school will be taught by homosexuals." A teacher from the next town over, who was not gay, asked him whether, if his initiative passed, her support of Berner would cost her *her* job. Briggs reassured her: "You don't have to worry. The law is not retroactive." (She would only have to worry if she said something kind about gays *after* it passed.) He told reporters, "Larry Berner is out bragging he's homosexual. We're going to get him." His statement in the official California voter-education pamphlet denounced Berner by name.

Berner responded, "Traditionally, when you call someone a faggot, he runs and hides. Well, this faggot ain't running."

In his defiance, Berner was not just offending his rural neighbors. He was defying the official anti–Proposition 6 organization. It bore the intentionally anodyne name the Concerned Voters of California, and its leader, David Goodstein, argued in his newspaper the *Advocate*, "Almost all gay people could help best by maintaining very low profile. . . . Constructively, we should assist in registering gay voters, stuffing envelopes in the headquarters, and keeping out of sight of non-gay voters, except persuading straight friends and relatives."

Above all, they should *not* come out of the closet. If too many did, Goodstein feared anti-gay pogroms.

Harvey Milk also disagreed. Under his influence, the annual Gay Freedom Day parade in San Francisco on June 25 had taken the theme "Come Out with Joy, Speak Out with Justice." To the Bryant-Briggs "Save Our Children" slogan, signs responded, "We *Are* Your Children." Some marchers even spontaneously flipped over their placards and Magic-Markered their names and hometowns on the back, courageously following the lead of "Harvey Milk / I'm from Woodmere, NY." Among the dozens of marching affinity groups—gay plumbers, gay doctors, gay American Indians, gay department store employees, gay veterans—one carried a metaphorical target on their backs: teachers, who by participating marked themselves, in the initiative's language, "open and notorious homosexuals," subject to termination. Like the one who wore a T-shirt reading, "Would you want Michelangelo teaching your children art?"

They marched beneath a new flag. The movement's best-known symbol had been the pink triangle—like the ones Nazis forced homosexuals to wear. But Milk and his allies wanted their movement to signify *hope*. So he approached a friend, the graphic designer Gilbert Baker, who suggested a rainbow instead. "A rainbow fit us," said the man who became famous as the "gay Betsy Ross." "It is from nature. It connects us to all the colors— all the colors of sexuality, all the diversity in our community."

By the time they strode into Civic Center Plaza behind a giant banner reading "HUMAN RIGHTS ARE ABSOLUTE," they were 250,000 strong. Reporters with microphones were everywhere, which was how America met a white-haired seventy-four-year-old with two gay sons.

One had committed suicide when he learned his local school board was preparing to fire him. "My other son is afraid to be here. . . . I lost one son to the likes of Mr. Briggs and I don't intend to lose another one."

Also interviewed was a colleague of Harvey Milk's on the San Francisco Board of Supervisors. Dan White was a grim, tightly wound former firefighter and cop who had been the only member to vote against adding sexual orientation protections to the city's human rights statute, and also against closing Market Street for this parade. He waved disgustedly at the scene: "The vast majority of people don't want public displays of sexuality."

Harvey Milk mounted the speaker's podium in a blazingly visible white T-shirt with the legend "I'LL NEVER GO BACK" printed next to a closet door marked, "VACANT." He had just received a typed postcard reading, "You get the first bullet the minute you stand at the microphone." He began his speech as he always did:

"My name is Harvey Milk and I want to recruit you!"

When the stupendous roar abated, he continued, "I want to recruit you to the fight to preserve your democracy from the John Briggses and the Anita Bryants who are trying to constitutionalize bigotry." That they could *not* "sit back in silence as 300,000 of our gay brothers and sisters did in Nazi Germany." That they would have you do what Larry Berner did: *come out—*

"To your relatives. I know that it is hard and will upset them but think of how they will upset you in the voting booth": for how could they vote to save their children if they did not know their children were gay?

"Come out to your friends, if indeed they are your friends.

"Come out to your neighbors, your fellow workers, to the people who work where you eat and shop.

"Once and for all, break down the myths, destroy the lies and distortions. . . . For your sake. For the sake of the youngsters who are becoming scared by the votes from Dade to Eugene.

"If Briggs wins he will not stop. They never do. Like all mad people, they are forced to move on, to prove they were right. There will be no safe 'closet' for any gay person.

"Let me remind you what America is," he demanded. "Listen carefully." Then he quoted "Give me your tired, your poor, your huddled masses yearning to be free," and "All men are created equal," and "Oh say does that Star-Spangled Banner yet wave o'er the land of the free."

"Mr. Briggs and Mrs. Bryant—and *all* the bigots out there—that's what America is. No matter how hard you try, you cannot erase those words from the Declaration of Independence. No matter how hard you try, you cannot chip those words off from the base of the Statue of Liberty. And no matter how hard you try you cannot sing the 'Star Spangled Banner' without those words. That's what America is. . . . Love it or leave it!"

And then, another awesome roar from the joyous multitudes. They needed to hear what Harvey Milk said. Because, presently, they had precious little hope.

The president of the political organization founded by Harvey Milk predicted, "We're going to get creamed and it's important that we not deceive people into thinking we can win." Milk's rival David Goldstein editorialized, "We may even lose San Francisco." There was "not one example in the history where a majority has voted for the rights of the minority. . . . The issue is too emotional and there isn't time to change their minds. . . . Our enemies can and will outspend us about 10 to 1."

Milk posted a series of increasingly desperate telegrams to President Carter begging for an anti-Briggs statement. ("How many lives must be destroyed before you speak out?") A new book by the Reverend Tim LaHaye, *Unhappy Gays*, rallied the other side's troops. It warned, inside a cover bedecked with thick iron chains, "You can expect homosexual teachers single-handedly to double the homosexual community within ten years, not by recruiting, but by preparing youngsters mentally for the recruiters," and claimed that "homosexuals are unquestionably more miserable than straight people"—appropriating "gay" as propaganda to becloud the fact.

In Anita Bryant's home state of Oklahoma, Senate hopeful David Boren, accused of being gay, saved his campaign by literally swearing on a Bible that he was not. At the Southern Baptist Convention, Bryant was almost elected as the body's vice president, while thousands massed outside to protest her. President Carter also appeared, though Bryant got more applause. The body unanimously resolved to "reaffirm the commendation of Anita Bryant . . . for her firm stand on the issue of homosexuality."

A poll showed the Briggs Initiative ahead by 61 percent to 33 percent. The American Civil Liberties Union lost a suit asking the court to suspend a California law requiring anyone making a political contribution of $50 or more be listed publicly. Forty-nine-dollar contributions began coming in from terrified, desperate people dwelling in the closet—including Hollywood legend Rock Hudson.

Their chief adversary was an ironic source of hope. John Briggs proved an opportunistic creep who was not even skilled in his opportunism. He had intended for both Proposition 6 and his initiative expanding the number of crimes subject to the death penalty to rocket him to the gubernatorial nomination. But a plan to qualify them for the primary ballot in June to take advantage of Proposition 13 failed from administrative incompetence. The only endorsements he'd garnered were from the Ku Klux Klan, the state Nazi Party—and the Los Angeles County Deputy Sheriff's Organization. His gaffes were even more epic than Howard Jarvis's. Like the time he avowed you could spot a homosexual just by looking at him. (A man who had once dated Briggs's daughter presented himself as a counterexample.) Or the time he said, "One-third of San Francisco's teachers are homosexuals" and "most of them are seducing young boys in toilets." Or when, on television, he ranted so incoherently that the anchor just told him to shut up.

"We can't complain about Briggs," Concerned Voters of California's campaign manager said. "If we had gotten him from central casting, we would have had to double their fee."

Though that was what the Miami campaign had said about Anita Bryant, the anti-Proposition 13 campaign about Howard Jarvis.

But this time, the anti-conservative side began gaining. Teachers inspired public sympathy. Celebrities, and mainstream liberals like George McGovern, who had opposed a gay rights plank in the 1972 Democrat platform, joined the fight. Ads arguing in terms of privacy proved effective. One showed a family forced to live in a fishbowl. Another depicted an eyeball peeking through a keyhole. Brochures said the law would violate due process, that administering it would waste precious government money: "A self-serving politician has dreamed up a moral crusade. And he wants *you* to pay for it," read one. Another featured a cartoon of a giant hand marked with a dollar sign pressing down violently upon a student at an elementary school desk: "THIS AFFECTS ALL OF US."

Which was where Ronald Reagan came in.

IT WAS THE IDEA OF A RECENTLY UN-CLOSETED ANTI-BRIGGS ORGANIZER named David Mixner. As a Hollywood veteran, Reagan likely had plenty of gay friends; and what was Proposition 6 but the ultimate act of big-government meddling? "If we could get that message to Reagan," Mixner implored his colleagues, "he would understand that."

What were Reagan's opinions about gays? Often, quite typical of his times—which is to say, bigoted. In his first year as governor he was asked if he thought homosexuals should be barred from public office. The former lifeguard quipped, "Certainly they should be barred from the Department of Beaches and Parks." He added, "It's a tragic illness." But also that they didn't belong in government. Sometime later, when a dispirited supporter wrote him asking why the Reverend Troy Perry claimed the governor's endorsement for his gay Metropolitan Community Church, Reagan wrote back to protest that the message had been "a routine reply to what seemed to be a courtesy invitation" that "made no mention of the unusual nature of his congregation," and "would not have been sent had all the facts been known. . . . I have never condoned homosexuality, and certainly do not support the abolition of criminal laws regarding sexual conduct." And when his college-age son Ron decided to take up ballet dancing, he wrote a friend, defensively, lest anyone suspect a *Reagan* was gay: "I hasten to assure you he is an athlete and all man."

But his views could also be more tolerant and compassionate than was the norm. Also in his first year as governor, a cabal of aides sabotaged a colleague named Phillip Battaglia by bugging a hotel room to catch him having sex with a man. Battaglia and his companion, also a Reagan aide, resigned. The reason was leaked to columnist Drew Pearson, who wondered luridly "whether the magic charm of Gov. Ronald Reagan can survive the discovery that a homosexual ring has been operating in his office." Reagan refused to respond, protecting his aides' privacy, then refused cooperation when the plotters attempted a purge of other alleged gays in his administration. "They're not contagious," he said.

This was a Reagan pattern: often strikingly unempathetic when it came to the effects of policy on millions of people, he could be achingly so in defense of individuals, especially those he could identify with or knew personally. Though he also joked that since Truman Capote was about to visit the Capitol, they could "tie a rope about him and troll him down the hall to see what they could catch."

Getting a meeting with Reagan turned out to be easy: Mixner met a gay former Reagan official at the man's home—when his wife was out of town. Intrigued, this man approached another, more senior former advisor, who was even more fearfully discreet: they met at an outlying Denny's restaurant, where he begged repeatedly for anonymity, and insisted he review any agreement they arrived at with Reagan. But he also agreed to secure a half hour for them in Reagan's schedule.

Mixner arrived on the appointed day in a brand-new, über-respectable suit. He was startled at Reagan's receptiveness. The governor appreciated his argument that Proposition 6 would obliterate privacy protections (Michael Deaver once said the best way to convince Reagan to do something was to argue that not doing it would "hurt people.")—and that it would waste taxpayer money. He was downright animated—"stirred in his chair," Mixner remembered—by the idea that if Proposition 6 passed, students could blackmail teachers, and "the kids will control the classroom." School discipline was a hobby horse for Reagan: "Obey the rules or get out" was his blunt answer to the plague of student protest in the 1960s.

The half hour stretched to an hour. Reagan's advisors subsequently telephoned Mixner to say their boss would not endorse Proposition 6. He might even consider campaigning against it if they provided their arguments to him in writing. This they did. The endorsement that came back staggered them. They could have written it themselves—though, on second thought, they could not, so stamped was it with Reagan's distinctive voice:

"This measure has nothing to do with those so-called gay rights issues in Florida and elsewhere. Instead, it has the potential of infringing on the basic rights of privacy and even constitutional rights. What if an overwrought youngster disappointed by bad grades imagined it was the teacher's fault and struck out by accusing the teacher of advocating homosexuality? Innocent lives could be ruined."

(Locating politically useful moral distinctions where others saw none was a characteristic Reagan skill. So was his tendency to cast social policy in terms of stories. And "youngsters" was a favorite Reagan word.)

"It could be very costly to implement and has the potential for causing undue harm for people. . . . Whatever it is, homosexuality is not a contagious disease like the measles. Prevailing scientific opinion is that an individual's sexuality is determined at a very early age and that a child's teachers do not really influence this."

(This, as it happened, rhymed with the conclusions of the denomination Reagan had grown up in, the Disciples of Christ, which had voted at their general assembly the previous fall in favor of a liberal position on the subject.)

"I don't approve of teaching a so-called gay life-style in our schools," he concluded. But there "is already adequate legal machinery to deal with such problems."

(It was unclear what legal machinery he was referring to. But once Ronald Reagan convinced himself of something, no one was better at crafting a rhetorically persuasive case for it, even if it was based on evidence that existed mostly in his imagination.)

Concerned Citizens of California knocked his words into a TV commercial, excerpted them in campaign pamphlets alongside endorsements from college deans, union leaders, San Francisco's Catholic archbishop, Republican attorney general candidate George Deukmejian, and the owner of the San Francisco Giants. William F. Buckley joined in with a sympathetic column: "The sensible solution . . . is to permit the community to establish its own criteria for the teachers hired to teach that community's children." Gerald Ford called it an "un-conservative expansion of state power." Four weeks before Election Day, Senator Briggs gave an angry interview. "That one endorsement—Ronald Reagan's—turned the polls around. . . . For Ronald Reagan to march to the drums of homosexuality has irrevocably damaged him nationally."

CONGRESS RACED TOWARD ITS SCHEDULED OCTOBER 14 RECESS WITH A DISconcerting number of loose ends. The biggest one was energy. The Senate had taken up the president's bill after Labor Day. It was now a mere stub of his original plan. Its original centerpiece, a tax on crude oil, was gone. A proposed requirement that industry switch from gas and oil to coal had become voluntary; its conservation demands were nugatory. Still senators from both the left and the right sought to kill it outright. Conservative Republicans were livid that it didn't abandon price controls on natural gas immediately. Liberal Democrats—who "now see Jimmy Carter as a Republican at heart," a columnist said—were outraged it kept controls until 1985.

As weak as the bill was, the president cajoled legislators for support with apocalyptic language. The vice president once more practically moved into his Capitol Hill office. But only months after Carter had declared the challenge of weening Americans off foreign energy the "moral equivalent of war," there had arrived a glut in world petroleum supplies that made him sound like Chicken Little. Now, a year later, the sky *still* had not fallen—and no one cared to listen to his warnings. On the second day of Senate consideration, Mondale counted only forty in favor, forty opposed, and the rest undecided. Concessions offered to win over one senator would alienate another—sometimes two. By the time of the Camp David summit, the air was filled with filibuster threats from every side. Energy Secretary James Schlesinger called the process "a descent into hell."

On September 27, the parties reached a compromise on natural gas deregulation. The president gloated at a press conference that this "proves to our nation and the rest of the world that we, in this government, particularly Congress, can courageously deal with an issue that tests our national will and ability." Newsmen, unimpressed, paid more attention to the darker, more "serious" suit he wore when he made the statement, apparently at the suggestion of Gerald Rafshoon.

He hit the road to campaign for Democratic candidates. At one stop, he spoke on behalf of North Carolina's rip-roaringly populist insurance commissioner John Ingram, who had won the nomination to run against Senator Jesse Helms in an extraordinary upset. The favorite in the Democratic primary, Luther Hodges, the son of JFK's commerce secretary, had quit running one of the state's biggest banks to enter the race. He received the most votes by far in a six-candidate field. But since he hadn't cleared 50 percent, Ingram, who came in a distant second, exercised his legal option to call for a runoff. Ingram had six weeks to campaign, with a budget one-eighth of his wealthy opponent's. So he turned that to his advantage, hammering the banker as the "million dollar man"—"The issue of issues in this campaign is who will represent the people, not the special interests!"—and handing out gold-colored tokens, promising, "If you elect me your senator, this will be money in your pocket." Hodges countered that with his banking expertise, he could help balance the budget. In choosing Ingram and rejecting Hodges, in other words, the Democratic voters of North Carolina had issued a stinging rebuke to the fashionable new Democratic politics of austerity.

Then Jimmy Carter arrived at an Ingram fundraiser, and delivered an austerity sermon.

"There are no problems more serious in our country than inflation, the high tax burden on our people, and waste in government," he said, imploring attendees to support Democrats "to get the government's nose out of the people's business." Then, he vetoed a $10.2 billion public works bill, with a message that mentioned inflation eight times in three hundred words.

Heretofore, the notion of a Democratic killing a massive job-creating disbursement from the public purse during election season was inconceivable. *This* was why many Democrats now saw Jimmy Carter as a Republican at heart. And that was becoming a serious problem.

THE HUMPHREY-HAWKINS BILL SURVIVED IN NAME ONLY, ITS FORMER CALL to create government jobs if unemployment rose above 3 percent now a mere goal of "working toward" 4 percent unemployment—relying "primarily on private enterprise." Carter might have killed it altogether had not Stuart Eizenstat warned him that it was "one of the few bills in which we are clearly aligned with our major constituencies—labor and the minority community."

On the last Monday in September, black legislators met with the president and vice president. The subject was supposed to be about turning out the vote in November. Instead, Representatives John Conyers and Ron Dellums dwelled on Humphrey-Hawkins and the crisis of black unemployment. Mondale said inflation and energy were more pressing. Voices were raised. Conyers stalked out of the room, past the glaring television lights and cameras set up outside to record what was supposed to be a display of Democratic unity.

That weekend the Congressional Black Caucus hosted the biggest black political convention in history, to conclude with an eight-thousand-guest banquet spread over two giant ballrooms in two separate Washington, D.C., hotels, connected by closed-circuit television. Senator Bob Dole worked one of the rooms for three hours, reminding anyone who would listen that Jesse Jackson had recommended blacks "give the GOP a try." Senator Ted Kennedy began with a nice joke—"I have my differences with President Carter, but I didn't think they would put us in different hotels"—then gave the kind of speech a presidential candidate challenging Jimmy Carter from the left might give: "Some say that a different tide is running in this country now. They say the Bakke case and Prop 13 are the wave of the future. They tell us to slow down, to take a rest, to let things be. But I am here tonight to tell you they are wrong! Our trumpets do not know how to sound retreat." The audience roared.

Rumors were that President Carter might be disinvited. Instead he reminded Democrats why they had fallen in love with him in the first place. "Members of the Black Caucus," he began, "distinguished religious leaders, ladies and gentlemen, *brothers and sisters*—"

That brought cries of delight.

"I think in the last two days, everyone knows how I stand on the Humphrey-Hawkins full employment bill. I want to make sure that the chairman of the Black Caucus is with us. So I brought tonight a big button that says, 'Justice through Jobs, Pass Humphrey-Hawkins.'"

Which delighted the crowd yet more.

He rolled on, call-and-response style. ("Can we afford to be satisfied when we've got hundreds of thousands of young black men walking the streets looking for jobs?" "*Noooo!!*") He called up to the stage "the mother of the movement," Rosa Parks; then his United Nations ambassador, a former Congressional Black Caucus stalwart, Andrew Young—"a man who is not afraid to speak out when he sees something wrong. . . . As long as I am president, and Andy Young is willing to stay there, he'll be UN ambassador"—which brought eight thousand people to their feet. He finished with the words "Right on!"—and a black-tie assemblage that included Nat King Cole, Dick Gregory, Coretta Scott King, and Jesse Jackson cried "right on!" back.

Others demurred. While nursing a drink at the bar, an out-of-town politician muttered about "black folks like to applaud." At the post-banquet concert, Stevie Wonder got the crowd to its feet with his ghetto anthem "Living for the City," then, noodling quietly on his electric piano, addressed the watered-down version of Humphrey-Hawkins that the administration was pushing, saying, according to the *Washington Post*, "what everyone else was too polite to say": "4 percent ain't good enough. For a country that's the richest in the world. . . . I call bullshit." The audience roared louder than they had for the president.

It was around then that AFL-CIO chieftain George Meany called Carter "the most conservative president since Calvin Coolidge." A key White House aide pronounced himself delighted: Meany was "doing the president's work for him"—advertising the White House's intent to squeeze federal spending mercilessly. He must have missed the part of Meany's remarks when he hinted unions might not support Carter for reelection. A United Auto Workers spokesman said that, after November, they "will tell Ted to get off his swivel chair and flatly declare himself a candidate against Jimmy Carter for the Democratic party presidential nomination."

GALLUP RELEASED ITS LATEST PRESIDENTIAL APPROVAL RATINGS: SIX POINTS down from the post–Camp David surge. The Senate Finance Committee voted to lower the maximum rate on capital gains. The next day the full Senate voted down an amendment offering modest reform of "tax expenditures"—backdoor benefits to special interests that Ted Kennedy said "subsidized low-priority, unjustifiable, and wasteful programs." Other votes canceled a 1976 reform that raised taxes on the sale of property by wealthy heirs, and added deductions for companies fighting product liability claims.

Kemp-Roth itself was rejected by the full Senate, but on October 9, a Democrat from the president's state, Sam Nunn, introduced a version cutting income tax rates 25 percent over five years if spending growth was kept below 1 percent annually and the budget was balanced by 1983. He recruited a bipartisan coalition of twenty-one cosponsors, including William Roth. It passed with sixty-five votes on October 11. The next morning, a photo appeared above the fold on the front page of the *Washington Post*: William Roth, the proud papa, flanked by Senator Howard Baker and the ranking Republican on the House Ways and Means Committee, offering giant cigars from a box illustrated with a Republican elephant and marked "Son of Kemp-Roth."

THE HOUSE AND SENATE TAX BILLS HAD TO BE RECONCILED IN CONFERENCE in a form the president wouldn't veto. The *Washington Post* called it "the last big poker game of the 95th Congress." On Friday, October 13, the House passed the natural gas compromise by a single vote. Carter signed a civil service reform bill into law, but Congress had to work past its scheduled adjournment to thread the needle on airline deregulation, transportation funding, bank reform, college aid, veterans' pensions—and also on the long-suffering energy package. "This day has been a nightmare," Carter wrote in his diary, noting also the intransigence of Menachem Begin in following through on the agreements reached at Camp David. The next day, the president's son Chip was confronted by chanting Iranian students protesting the shah.

Senators passed Humphrey-Hawkins with so many denuding amendments from Utah's junior senator that it earned the nickname the "Humphrey-Hawkins-Hatch Act." Representative Robert Taft Jr. of Ohio said, "I do not think any Republicans need fear voting for the bill because of any apprehension that there is a victory in the passage of the full employment bill, because there is no full-employment bill anymore."

The energy bill was called up next. A new sword of Damocles emerged: a surprise "mini-filibuster" from Senators Abourezk and Proxmire in protest of its tax breaks for industry. The two chambers had been working twenty hours straight through the weekend, missing game four of the World Series. At 1 a.m. Monday morning the liberal filibuster was finally broken, and the National Energy Act was ready for the president's signature, projected to save an estimated 2.5 million barrels of imported oil by 1985. The president's goal had been 4.5 million barrels. The conference committee on taxes was still at work.

The sun rose to news that the "Son of Kemp-Roth" had been sacrificed to veto fears, replaced with a resolution that a future across-the-board income tax cut was Congress's "intention." The House adjourned at 6:46 a.m., the Senate thirty-one minutes later—in time to read a *Washington Post* piece setting down the 95th Congress's accomplishments for posterity: An "overwhelmingly Democratic congress" had increased Social Security taxes. It had "willingly voted large increases in defense spending, but shied away from expensive domestic initiatives and concentrated on cutting the federal budget deficit." It passed a "tax reform that included $3.5 billion in corporate tax cuts, a $2.1 billion cut in capital gains taxes, socked it to lower-income tax payers by eliminating the deductibility of state and local taxes, and blended in a series of narrow-interest amendments that would benefit specific countries and industries, including a provision of granting a tax break to the heirs of the Gallo wine estate." It "gave the oil companies a natural gas price deregulation bill they had sought unsuccessfully for twenty-five years," and "rejected virtually every proposal put forward by organized labor."

All in all, the "American business class clearly displaced the agenda of social and economic issues that has dominated Congressional politics since the inauguration of the New Deal forty-five years ago."

Carter's pledge to reform the American tax code—a "disgrace to the human race"—had been his most-repeated campaign promise. The bill that landed on his desk, however, let a millionaire who lived off investments pay a lower tax rate than a salaried worker earning the median income, gave the upper half of taxpayers 79 percent of its benefits, and raised the baseline for inheritances subject to estate taxes from $147,000 to $161,000. He considered a veto. He decided that was politically impossible. He signed the bill. The supply-side economists had promised that just on news of a capital gains cut the stock market would soar into the stratosphere. Instead, during the two weeks that followed, the Dow Jones Industrial Average dropped 10 percent. The problem, a key Charls Walker deputy, the chief economist of the Securities Industry Association, patiently explained for an article about Wall Street's continuing woes six months later, was that "the capital gains tax cut was not really strong enough to attract people into the equity market": next time, it would just have to be bigger.

CARTER TRAVELED TO MINNESOTA, BEMOANING IN HIS DIARY THE LACK OF enthusiasm among Democrats for their senate candidate Bob Short, the businessman calling for an immediate 50 percent income tax cut and 20 percent across-the-board slash in federal spending. Carter called the liberals opposing him "the one group of Democrats with whom I feel uncomfortable. They have a commitment to political suicide in order to prove some far-left philosophical point. It's really disgusting."

He returned home for a televised speech: a "frank talk" about "our most serious domestic problem"—inflation, now, at 8.9 percent, almost three points higher than when he took office. It was informed by advice from Gerald Rafshoon: "It is impossible to overestimate the importance of the inflation issue to your presidency." Failure to "demonstrate some control over inflation would make it very difficult for most Americans to be enthusiastic about their President."

Carter's argument was the one conservatives made: inflation was caused by big government. He boasted that "the Occupational Safety and Health Administration, sometimes called OSHA, eliminated nearly 1,000 unnecessary regulations." He promised to "redouble our efforts to put competition back into the American free enterprise system" by "cutting away the regulatory thicket that has grown up around us and giving our competitive free enterprise system a chance to grow up in its place," and to "slash federal hiring."

"I don't have all the answers," he intoned earnestly. "Nobody does. Perhaps there is no complete and adequate answer." A partial answer, however, was for Americans to make do with less. So he would "oppose any further reductions in federal income taxes." He implored "all employers in this country to limit total wage increase to a maximum of 7 percent per year." He announced the formation of a new Council on Wage and Price Stability, or COWPS, to establish voluntary price guidelines for businesses to follow. He insisted that "whether our efforts are successful will finally depend on you as much as me." He concluded, "Reducing the deficit will require difficult and unpleasant decisions. We must face a time of national austerity. Hard choices are necessary if we want to avoid consequences that are even worse."

"*Hard choices*," "*austerity*": you wouldn't have known he was about to sign a tax cut for millionaires. Would *business* follow the president's request to voluntarily hold the line on prices? They had no incentive to do so, nor legal sanction if they did not. Would they honor his plea to limit wage increases? They surely would be glad to, with the claim that they were only following the president's advice.

Carter had promised, "If we meet these standards, the real buying power of your paycheck will rise"—but when? He said that no one could be *sure* whether what he was trying would work, that all he could really promise was avoiding "consequences that are even worse." Nobody shoots Santa Claus? Democrats returned to the campaign trail with President Scrooge having just plugged Santa in the gut.

RIGHT-WING CANDIDATES WERE NOT SETTING THE WORLD ON FIRE, EITHER. In Iowa, vicious attacks against Senator Dick Clark for his vote in favor of the Panama Canal treaties, in a state that had polled 56 percent to 30 percent against them, seemed to be having little effect: a *Des Moines Register* survey had him up by nine points; private polling had him ahead by thirty. In New Hampshire, the New Right activist and former airline pilot Gordon Humphrey was also behind in a mid-October poll by thirty points. The Republican running for Wyoming's single House seat, Dick Cheney, President Ford's right-wing former chief of staff, was grounded for weeks by a heart attack. In North Carolina, the *New York Times* reported, John Ingram might swing an upset against Jesse Helms. And, according to the *Washington Post* reporter writing the series following the contest for the open seat in Illinois's bellwether 22nd Congressional District, surprise Republican nominee Dan Crane appeared to be in for a drubbing.

In that race's first televised debate, Crane jabbered like Joe McCarthy about a monolithic world Communism on the march. His Democratic opponent, Terry Bruce, a dynamic up-and-comer who had never lost an election, noted calmly that there were differences among European, Soviet, Asian, and African Communists. Crane was asked about Africa policy. He launched into an attack on the anti-apartheid movement as a Soviet front, then ranted about Jane Fonda. Calmly, Bruce returned with "I think the situation in Africa is more complicated than you might have just heard." Crane's advisors decided that the more the voters saw of their candidate the more frightened of him they became, and pulled Crane from the next debate. So on October 20 Bruce addressed an empty chair, hammering his opponent's "confusion" and "simplistic worldview."

Crane, desperate, called up Falls Church, Virginia. He told Richard Viguerie it was time to unleash what a RAVCO staffer called "the most potent single piece of mail in American political history": the Wife Letter. "I don't know who thought it up—probably Viguerie, he's the genius— but every place we use it, that wife mailing is the most effective thing that anybody's seen."

Crane had already sent a Wife Letter in the primary. The process began with the candidate's spouse writing a chatty text out in longhand, light on issues, from guidelines RAVCO provided; Judy Crane's began, "Dear Friend . . . With the family and all (we have four small children and are expecting our fifth in July) . . . I haven't had too much time to myself. But I made up my mind today to sit down and write you." It went on for four pages, about Dan's concerns as a family man, about inflation, taxes, energy, and farm problems. It concluded, "The baby's crying so I must close for now. . . . P.S. If you would like to chat with me about Dan's campaign, please feel free to call me at my home at 217-443-0085."

The manuscript was then shipped to Falls Church, embossed onto creamy, "feminine" stationery, mechanically folded, and stuffed along with several family pictures into "personalized" pastel envelopes, upon which a worker affixed a stamp by hand—slightly crooked. The unit cost was double the typical direct mail letter, but it was worth it. Knocking on doors before primary day, again and again, Crane would hear, "I got a real nice letter from your wife," and "You have a real nice family—thanks for the pictures." He was still hearing about it around about Labor Day, six months later: "It was so nice hearing from Judy."

Now it was time to go back to the well, for a version targeted at one hundred thousand Democrats and independents. It went out the week before the general election—a bit earlier than planned, but this was an emergency. And it was working. A night watchman whose wife had voted Democratic in every election since 1948 told the *Post*'s T. R. Reid, "All of a sudden it seems like she's talking about this here Crane. . . . My wife got this letter. It's that picture, that's what. I told her to throw it away, but she's still got it, keeps it right there on the TV."

"ALL OF A SUDDEN."

That was precisely the magic of the man the *Atlantic Monthly* crowned "The King Midas of the New Right." Direct mail done right, Viguerie said, was "like having a water moccasin for a watchdog—silent but deadly": by the time opponents saw it coming it was too late. Though the Democratic establishment *had* finally taken notice. It was hard not to, what with an underdog like Dan Crane outspending his opponent four to one. The UAW's political chief estimated that Viguerie "had the capacity to generate as much money for a campaign as the entire American labor movement."

The DNC aimed a counterstrike at 359,000 Democrats: "The ultra-right will do everything in its power to subvert arms limitation," they would "repeat many of the attitudes and policies which led to America's involvement in the Vietnam War"; and they "*could succeed* . . . let's face it: *change frightens people.*" Their letter documented that the five biggest conservative political action committees, the ACU's Conservative Victory Fund,

Viguerie's Committee for Responsible Youth Politics, Reagan's Citizens for the Republic, and Weyrich's Committee for the Survival of a Free Congress, had amassed $2,957,587 in 1977, compared to $420,029 raised by the biggest liberal PACs—all but one of which, the DNC did not note, belonged to single-issue groups like the Sierra Club, who didn't concentrate on elections. "Not since the heyday of the House Un-American Activities Committee, blacklisting, and the late Senator Joseph McCarthy," the letter concluded, "have the ultra-conservatives organized across the country with as much intensity and vehemence as they are doing right now."

Jesse Helms controlled his own Viguerie-style operation, the Congressional Club, with a hundred full-time employees; its head, Thomas Ellis, had been the architect of Ronald Reagan's crucial victory in the 1976 North Carolina primary (and also directed an organization, the Pioneer Fund, that sought to prove the biological superiority of Caucasians). Ellis had begun pumping out appeals for his boss two years earlier, raising $2.3 million before Helms even landed an opponent. By the time John Ingram was nominated, donations had risen to almost twice that—so Ingram dubbed Helms "the Four Million Dollar Man." Then, after the next Federal Elections Commission report came out, "the Five Million Dollar Man." And, finally, "the Six Million Dollar Man"—just like the hit TV show. Though that turned out to be an understatement. Helms ended up cadging $7.7 million, a Senate record, including three hundred thousand donations from out of state. Ingram raised $264,000. When the *Post*'s Reid, covering Dan Crane's race, knocked on the door of one Illinois farmer, the vexed yeoman pulled out a direct mail piece and quizzed the out-of-town expert: "Who's this 'Jesse Helms'? Why's he sending me all this postage?"

Helms's most powerful weapon was printed on the letterhead of Ronald Reagan, aimed at every donor to Reagan's 1976 presidential campaign. It included a Reagan photograph, suitable for framing—because, the text over Reagan's signature explained, "I was so overwhelmed by the kindness and generosity of people like you everywhere I went that I want to somehow express my appreciation." But "I must admit I have another reason for writing. . . . Senator Helms is a good friend of mine and was of tremendous help to me during my campaign." Democrats, and the "big labor bosses," had made him "their #1 target for defeat in the entire U.S. Senate. I'm not going to sit on the sidelines and let this happen."

ANOTHER PORTENTOUS DEVELOPMENT WENT UNNOTICED BY DEMOCRATS. It was a bold strategic shift from the nation's boardroom Jacobins.

During the boom years, corporations' political donations reflected their de facto partnership with government: the lion's share went to incumbents, mostly members of committees considering legislation affecting the corporations, or representing districts where the corporations had facilities. Most of these incumbents faced little or no chance of defeat, and most were Democrats. Backing challengers seemed counterproductive: Why would you want to give offense to someone who could help or hurt you in Washington?

Ronald Reagan complained about that in his newspaper column, using his favorite Churchillism about the danger of appeasing Hitler: giving to politicians "regardless of an individual lawmaker's overall voting pattern or attitude toward private enterprise, big government deficits, and bureaucratic regulation" was like "feeding an alligator, hoping he would eat you last." Echoed a conservative congressman: "The irony here is that although the public perceives us as carrying business's water, much of big business is really supporting our enemy. Many of these groups are more about buying access to incumbents than to any philosophical principles." Another right-wing congressman put it more bluntly: "Corporate managers are whores. They don't care who's in office, what party or what they stand for. They're just out to buy you."

These critics did not notice a shift afoot. Sometime that summer, at the home of Richard Viguerie, an extraordinary meeting happened. A representative from the National Republican Congressional Committee was there, and Roger Stone of the Young Republicans National Federation; two members of the House of Representatives' Republican Study Committee; leaders from the American Conservative Union, the Conservative Caucus, Reagan's Citizens for the Republic, and Young Americans for Freedom; and Paul Weyrich and Howard Phillips attended; and a staffer from a new anti-abortion group, Life PAC, and the manager of Anita Bryant's Save Our Children campaign, Mike Thompson, and a man from the American Enterprise Institute.

So far so typical; Viguerie summoned New Right coordinating meetings like these all the time. The reason this one was special was that it also included corporate lobbyists and representatives of trade organizations, and business groups like the United States Chamber of Commerce and the Business and Industry Political Action Committee. These Chamber and BIPAC representatives had begun aggressively guiding corporate PACs to sharpen their ideological focus: the Chamber opened an offshoot to which 59 percent of corporate PACs paid a $400 annual subscription for access to its evaluation of the most promising "opportunity races" (conservative challengers); BIPAC, an offshoot the National Association of Manufacturers, began rating candidates 1 to 100 according to their anti-regulatory aplomb.

And that was what this meeting was all about. Viguerie, Weyrich, and Phillips had previously bragged about their contempt for "big business"; big business kept the New Right at a distance, as extremist yahoos. Now they would be working in harness.

What happened next was inscribed in the ledgers of the Federal Elections Commission. Prior to the fiscal year beginning October, approximately half of corporate PAC contributions went to Democrats. In the month of October, however, 71 percent went to Republicans. A subsequent analysis in Viguerie's *New Right Report* newsletter compared the 1976 and 1978 donations from the Chicago & Northwestern Transportation Company, the National Forest Products Association, and the timber companies Weyerhaeuser and Georgia-Pacific. In 1976, they had given approximately 75 percent of their campaign contributions to what *New Right Report* designated as "liberal" candidates. In 1978, it was 25 percent. Corporations were suddenly risking bets on conservative challengers.

Maybe, at that obscure but historic meeting, someone pointed to an instructive precedent. In 1976, when Orrin Hatch defeated Frank Moss—author of the Magnuson-Moss Act, which turned the Federal Trade Commission into a regulatory juggernaut; and the 1975 "lemon law" regulating warranties on appliances and automobiles; and the ban on advertising tobacco on TV—he had received little help from business PACs. Now that Hatch could claim responsibility for crushing labor law reform and denuding the Humphrey-Hawkins full employment law, perhaps CEOs recognized an accomplishment worth repeating.

One result, in the final days before the general election, was a flood of unprecedentedly negative campaign commercials. Which, in turn, helped explain the "rampant negativism" one pollster observed among the electorate, marked by a "classic feeling of powerlessness, that nothing makes a difference." People who feel powerless don't vote. A depression in turnout can make a campaign season wildly volatile. Which helped explain what the *New York Times* reported the Sunday morning before Election Day: "An exceptional number of major contests for office were going down to the wire with experts in doubt about the outcome. As a result, major party shifts seem possible."

ANOTHER VARIABLE FEW ELECTION TOUTS THOUGHT TO RECKON WITH: THE private jet Citizens for the Republic leased to deliver Ronald Reagan to twenty-six states in the final six weeks.

A new version of his standard speech was drafted by William Gavin. Peter Hannaford explained the goal in a memo to the governor: to sound "themes to which this fall's audiences will respond," while "looking beyond to the coalition-building that is necessary to finally take advantage of its new-found opportunity to be the party of 'More'; the party of hope." He was referring to a strategy for the 1980 presidential election—one taking advantage of Carter's insistent wallowing in the message that Americans had to learn to make do with less. At its heart would be a formulation Reagan would repeat so often in the years ahead that staffers referred to it by the shorthand "the five words": "Five simple, familiar, everyday words," Gavin called them in the cover note to his draft. "No sermons of political philosophy. Just five short words: FAMILY. WORK. NEIGHBORHOOD. FREEDOM. PEACE." The new speech would conclude with a quote from Thomas Jefferson—because Jefferson "is usually thought of as the property of the Dems."

Reagan liked Gavin's draft—then improved it. "On an occasion like this," Gavin's text began, "the speaker is expected to raise his party's standard, point with alarm at the other party's policies, embrace our party's principles, and grasp the central meaning—all at the same time." It continued, "It sounds like a job for an octopus rather than a speaker. But I'll try my best to meet those expectations." Reagan slashed that through, substituting language that sang: "That's a little like the old ventriloquist who sang Yankee Doodle Dandy while drinking a glass of water at the same time." Inflation "rising at a rate of twelve percent" became "Today"—more insistent, immediate—"inflation continues to hover at the double-digit level."

Then: "Jimmy Carter tells us everything is fine. We all feel like that prizefighter who was getting a terrific beating. After each round, his manager would say, 'Don't worry kid, he hasn't laid a glove on you.' After a few rounds of this, the fighter finally said to the manager, 'Well, maybe you better check with the referee because somebody in there is beating the living daylights out of me.'"

That became "That's a little like the prizefighter who was backpedaling around the ring trying to keep from getting killed. Every time he passed his corner his manager yelled, 'Stay with him, kid, he hasn't laid a glove on you.' Finally, as he came around again, the fighter said, 'Well keep your eye on the referee because someone in here is beating my brains out.'"

Then, he slashed out that entire throat-clearing exercise, and nine more paragraphs besides, to get straight to the point:

> *What is it that unites all Americans of all faiths, creeds, races, political persuasions and economic backgrounds? What is the common denominator of Americans?*
>
> *I believe it is a simple, single four-letter word. The word is hope. We who call ourselves Americans hope to see a better more peaceful world tomorrow, and we expect to make steady, measurable progress toward the fulfillment of this dream.*
>
> *Now, it is not merely hope that defines an American. It is the practical success in seeing our dreams fulfilled. It is this unique combination of aspiration and accomplishment, dream and deed, that truly sets the American apart.*

Or so it did throughout our national history until the last couple of decades. Since the mid-1960s, we Americans have suffered a succession of heavy blows to our self-confidence. We have known defeat in war, betrayal at home, and contempt everywhere we once commanded respect. We have almost lost sight of the combination that made our nation great. Hope, guts, and—above all—hard work. These have been in short supply in Washington, where politics-as-usual prevails, while our nation drifts.

But the winning combination is still strong among the American people. And especially strong in my party.

Dreams, progress, fulfillment, hope, success, aspiration, accomplishment, deeds, guts, hard work—what *truly sets the American apart*—these were the ideals Republicans upheld. *Defeat, betrayal, contempt, drift*—such was the Democrats' portion—a betrayal of the "workers, savers, and investors in our society—of those who hope and who attempt to build their personal dreams. . . . Americans of all creeds, classes, and colors" who "are struggling to hold their families together in a time of moral anarchy and social disintegration. . . . In 1980, America will have a clear cut choice between them."

Thus armed, Ronald Reagan hit the road.

A LARGER STAFF PAVED THE WAY, WORKING FROM AN EXPANDED ADVANCE manual specifying everything from the banquet furniture ("Make sure the chair he will be using is solid and that no table legs are in his way") to security procedures ("2–3 plain clothes officers . . . An unmarked police vehicle will be requested as a follow-up car. . . . The limo is to be driven by a law enforcement officer . . . place two officers at the front tables to either side of RR facing the audience. Other men can be positioned in the rear of the room or backstage"). There were explicit provisions to avoid public contact at the airport ("For a commercial aircraft this involves obtaining clearance to drive RR's car on the field and parking below the jetway until RR arrives. . . . The greeting party should be limited to 2–3 people"); and instructions for the master of ceremony to tell the audience that the guest of honor would leave immediately following his remarks ("Make sure you have a quick back exit to use"), and that the audience must remain in their seats until he left. Reagan also holstered a memo from Hannaford listing statistics of all the appearances he'd made for the party since the 1976 convention, to answer those still howling that he had tanked Gerald Ford.

Reagan also received advice from foreign policy advisor Richard Allen, who worried that Carter was beginning to sound too hawkish. Yes, Allen wrote, he should criticize "the growing public concern with Carter's weakness and mismanagement." But if he used phrases like "declining U.S. military might," and criticized Carter's work toward a new strategic arms limitation agreement with the Soviet Union, or came off sounding like a "'saber rattler,' a 'button pusher' or as too willing to send in the Marines," that would provide chum to "hostile press which feels you lack depth in 'complex' issues."

This advice Reagan ignored. He would say it was time to stop "spending all our time trying to figure out ways to demean our nation, disarm as quickly as we can, and make the rulers of the Third World happy." He published a column extolling the dictator Anastasio Somoza García, whose family had ruled Nicaragua with an iron fist and grasping hands for forty years, dismissing criticism of him for violently putting down protests. "Somoza is the elected president of the country," he said, which made him the commander of its army. "One thing armies do is put down rebellions." Another slammed Secretary of State Vance for refusing to meet with Ian Smith, prime minister of Rhodesia's white-minority government, on his visit to the U.S. Reagan gladly met with him, then praised the strongman for leading the former colony to independence from Great Britain: "remember some other colonies which did that in 1776?"

It was just as he had insisted in his first major speech after Nixon's resignation, to the Conservative Political Action Conference in early 1975, back when the conservatives were talking about bolting to form a new party: "Is it a third party that we need, or is it a new and revitalized second party, raising a banner of *no pale pastels*?"

REAGAN MADE ONLY TWO NONPOLITICAL STOPS THAT FALL—ONLY MARGINally nonpolitical. One was a black-tie dinner at the Waldorf Astoria, for the New York Investors Association—preceded by a private audience with "Senior Executives at major Wall Street firms" and a meeting with financier Maxwell Rabb, who, a briefing memo explained, had "great influence in the New York business community," was "the most influential Republican within the Jewish community," and had "access to senior management at Philip Morris, and there is reason to believe he has the same access to senior management of other Fortune 500 companies." The other stop was before the Association of American Physicians and Surgeons. The doctors' group was beginning lobbying efforts against a possible future national health insurance bill, and published Reagan's speech as a pamphlet to distribute to members. Its key line read, "Government is not the answer. Government is the problem."

The *Los Angeles Times* chief political reporter, Richard Bergholz, tagged along for a leg of his electioneering tour. "The whole thing is so familiar," he wrote: Reagan ringed by adoring fans in a holding room. The band striking up "California Here I Come." Reagan striding forth, beaming, as if this were the first time he had ever heard the tune. A bevy of yellow-clad cheerleaders, chanting "Rea-*gan*! Rea-*gan*! Rea-*gan*!" The jokes were the only part that changed; they kept up with current events.

The president's no-account brother had just taken a suspicious trip to Libya. He was quoted by the Libyan news agency that he hoped to find "new forms of effective cooperation between the American and the Libyan Arab peoples"—which didn't sound much like how Billy Carter talked. Jabbed Reagan:

"Jimmy Carter's in the White House."

Pause.

"Amy Carter's in the tree house."

Pause, titters.

"Billy's in the doghouse."

Roars.

"They say Billy's earning five times what the President is. That's ridiculous. He's only worth maybe twice as much."

By that point, Bergholz wrote, "Reagan could recite the alphabet and have the audience listening."

He returned home and filmed another passel of candidate ads. ("I think we can keep the number to under thirty-five spots," an aide promised.) He recorded eleven radio commentaries. (A six-part series praised an anti-SALT speech by Committee on the Present Danger's founder, Eugene Rostow—and "there is no way Eugene Rostow could be called a Hawk or a tool of the military interests." Another reported the riches America could be reaping from the sea bottom, were the United Nations not "pushing us around." Others argued against D.C. statehood, Amtrak subsidies, bilingual education, and the Environmental Protection Agency.) Then he gave half a dozen more speeches across Southern California.

He was working so hard, it was hardly surprising that he began to answer a familiar question in a different way: "Ask me next year. I'm not going to close any doors now." And when a particularly insistent group of supporters in Albuquerque just wouldn't stop pestering him, Bergholz reported, Reagan "finally nodded, sighed, and told them to 'hang loose,' as if to say they are on the right track."

AN ILLUSTRATION OF THE INTENSITY OF HIS AMBITIONS CAME IN ILLINOIS. In 1976, Reagan and the Republican senator Charles Percy had exchanged barbs in the press after the senator said that "a Reagan nomination and the crushing defeat likely to follow could signal the beginning of the end of our party as an effective force." Reagan snapped back, "Moderation should be taken in moderation." Ever since, Senator Chuck Percy had been fighting for the ERA, and providing key votes to Jimmy Carter on issues like the Panama Canal treaties. Now, however, Percy was fifteen points behind a vicious opponent simultaneously attacking him from the left as a supposed pal of the racist former agriculture secretary Earl Butz and from the right as a tax-and-spend liberal. Percy responded with commercials on black radio stations featuring endorsements from Jesse Jackson and Muhammad Ali, and on TV with a heavy-rotation spot apologizing for helping "Washington go overboard" with all that spending.

Reagan was scheduled to appear at a Republican fundraiser for a House candidate in suburban Elgin. The Percy people got wind of the appearance. They begged permission for Percy to show up, and for Reagan to say something nice. Some aides wanted Reagan to refuse: Percy was anathema to Reagan's conservative base. Others, however, argued Reagan needed to prove himself a loyal party man. That was the argument which prevailed.

In Elgin, Reagan invited Percy onto the dais and announced in his best stem-winding style, "When you added it all up there are more things we agree on than disagree on! . . . And we have got to *work*, on the *day* in which they count the noses in the new Congress and Senate, so that there are more Republicans than Democrats, so *we* are the majorities on the committees, and *we* have the chairmen of the committees!" He pulled Percy beside him and held his arm up like a heavyweight champ's. He repeated the ritual at four more Chicago-area stops. This, after all, was how Richard Nixon had done it in 1966—building the foundation for his presidential nomination by speaking for any Republican candidate who'd have him, collecting chits to cash in two years hence. Though Reagan could also take advantage of a strategy that the campaign laws in 1966 did not allow: by the end of the year, Citizens for the Republic had showered $3 million on friendly Republican candidates—the most of any PAC on the right.

A WEEK BEFORE ELECTION DAY, WALL STREET WAS ROCKED BY THE NEWS that the dollar had plunged to record lows on international exchanges. The Federal Reserve hiked interest rates by a full percentage point, the highest onetime raise since 1933. Brother Billy was subpoenaed to testify before an inquiry into the criminal allegations against Bert Lance. He asserted his Fifth Amendment right against self-incrimination—and told the press "it wasn't any of their damn business."

In California, ads simultaneously hyped Senator Briggs's anti-gay Proposition 6, and his pro–death penalty Proposition 7, a two-for-one deal: "You can act right now to help protect your family from vicious killers *and* defend your children from homosexual teachers." Reagan published a column reminding readers that the "overwhelming majority" of sexual abuse cases were "committed by heterosexual male adults against young females." Jerry Falwell sent Briggs Amendment letters to fourteen hundred California churches, and told NBC's Tom Snyder, on his *Tomorrow Show,* that if it did not pass it would "bring the wrath of God down upon our nation."

In Iowa, conservative Roger Jepsen repeatedly claimed that Senator Dick Clark exhibited a "total commitment to an unrestricted abortion policy." Clark responded only once: "I don't advocate abortions. I find them very wrong. I would not advocate to a young woman that it's the best alternative. It's the least attractive alternative." He didn't see the issue as particularly important—especially since his pollster Peter Hart, one of the most distinguished in the nation, had him running thirty points ahead, and Evans and Novak quoted a despairing Jepsen county chairman in an October 23 column articulating his only hope: "Maybe Dick Clark will goof up before the election." They then suggested Iowa as the best evidence "why the midterm election nationally is shaping up as another exercise in Republican futility."

But Peter Hart was beginning to wonder whether things were otherwise.

He worried that he was overestimating the Democrat loyalty of Catholics. The pro-lifers certainly thought so. They were busy, the Sunday morning before Election Day, wedging pamphlets beneath every last windshield wiper in every parish parking lot, and evangelical church parking lots, too. The pamphlets were a version of the brochure that had proved so successful in the primary back in June. It reproduced a famous 1965 *Life* magazine photograph by the science photographer Lennart Nilsson of an eighteen-week-old fetus suspended in a diaphanous amniotic cloud, looking for all the world like an angel (ironically, Nilsson's model was likely a *dead* fetus). It reprinted an ad from a local clinic announcing the availability of abortion services through twenty-four weeks. It was headlined, in stark red and white letters, "SEE WHY THIS LITTLE GUY WANTS YOU TO VOTE TUESDAY, NOV. 7TH." Three hundred thousand were distributed—one for every 2.5 voters in the election. "The pro-abortion people had no equivalent," a journalist mused: "there were no Yellow Pages listing the buildings in which thousands of pro-abortion voters might be counted to gather over a three-hour period exactly two days before the election."

That morning Dick Clark got a call from his brother, a Catholic, describing the scene in his parish parking lot, and the senator feared he might not be a senator very much longer.

He received only 395,066 votes to Roger Jepsen's 421,598. An estimated 14 percent of Jepsen's vote came from pro-life Democrats. Peter Hart later returned to Iowa to re-interview voters who had previously reported their intent to vote for Clark. He found that one-quarter had switched in the final fortnight, and that 19 percent stayed home. One-half had changed their mind because of the Panama Canal, the other over abortion. "Jepsen's pitch on these emotional subjects evidently paid off," the *Register* lamented in an editorial called "Best Man Lost." (It was later discovered that the previous year—before he made a "personal commitment to Christ," he insisted—Jepsen had applied to join a spa advertising "nude modeling, nude encounters, and nude rap sessions," whose owner pleaded guilty to "keeping a house of ill-fame.")

Carolyn Gerster of the National Right to Life Committee claimed credit for nine new pro-life votes in the House and six in the Senate, and announced a three-year plan to elect enough pro-life members to enact the Human Life Amendment by 1983. CBS's Roger Mudd reported from Iowa that the moral intensity of these activists reminded him of civil rights marches he'd covered in the 1960s. "Abortion," he said, "could be the most volatile single political issue in the country today, and the right-to-lifers the most powerful single issue block."

ABORTION ACTIVISM WAS ONE OF THE REASONS TUESDAY WAS A REASONABLY good day for Republicans: all told, they won 3 Senate seats, 12 House seats, 319 state legislature seats, and 6 governorships, about the normal turnover for the first off-year outing after a presidential election. The Equal Rights Amendment was another reason. ERA referenda failed in Nevada and Florida by margins of two to one—though a pre-election poll had the Florida measure *ahead* by two to one. Really, it was a great day for conservatives.

William Armstrong beat Senator Floyd Haskell in Colorado by almost twenty points. Jesse Helms would be returning from North Carolina, Strom Thurmond from South Carolina. South Dakota Democratic populist James Abourezk retired, replaced by conservative Republican Larry Pressler. Gordon Humphrey beat Thomas McIntyre with the help a last-minute Hail Mary: The New Right leaders who met to discuss which candidates to support wanted to throw him over the side, until Terry Dolan devised the innovation that may have closed the gap: running commercials on Boston TV, which every previous statewide campaign in New Hampshire history had considered too expensive to try. And Thad Cochran was elected the first Republican Senator from Mississippi in a century. In 1974, conservatives in the Senate had numbered four. Now there would be eleven.

In Wisconsin, a colorful outsider, Lee Dreyfus, spent only $10,000 to defeat the incumbent Democrat governor with a battle cry that the federal government should limit itself to only three activities: "defending our shores, delivering our mail, and staying the hell out of our lives." Dan Crane was chosen to join his brother Phil in the House of Representatives (though their other brother David lost in Indiana). And, in a harbinger of things to come, Dr. Newton Gingrich was going to Congress as the first Republican in history to represent his district.

Gingrich had been campaigning for the seat since 1974, with a "fanaticism," the *Atlanta Journal and Constitution* said, "that only a starved dog can understand when it spots a foundling lamb." His first run had been as a fashionable post-Watergate, good-government post-partisan with liberal leanings; he said he wanted to be the kind of congressman David Broder would like, and he took out all the references to God in the announcements staff wrote for him. In 1976, he went after the ethical lapses of the incumbent John Flynt (who happened to be chairman of the House Ethics Committee). This time around, Flynt had retired, Gingrich's erstwhile good-government liberalism was nowhere to found—and, finally, he prevailed.

His Democratic opponent, State Senator Virginia Shapard, was moderately conservative. A Gingrich flyer pictured her with State Representative Julian Bond, who was black, and read, "If you like welfare cheaters, you'll love Virginia Shapard." A commercial went after her vote against a tax bill introduced by a showboating colleague that hadn't received a single vote besides its sponsor's; the commercial depicted a fat woman's arm (Shapard was "a touch on the heavy side," a Gingrich campaign official noted), on which was a thuggish looking iron bracelet ("like it belonged to *Ilsa, She-Wolf of the SS*"), stamping the word "NO" on a page: "Virginia Shapard had a *chance* to reduce your taxes . . ." Another addressed Shapard's refusal to advance a bill to force recipients of public aid to pick up their checks in person every month at distant welfare offices instead of having them mailed. She remembered it bitterly years later: "just hands reaching out—black hands, white hands, black hands—reaching out and grabbing up dollars and saying, 'Virginia Shapard is for welfare fraud . . .' "

Shapard also was president of Atlanta's Health Systems Agency, a nonprofit authorized by a modest 1975 federal law to coordinate medical resources within regions. Gingrich cried, "We don't need North Atlanta bureaucrats wasting our tax dollars and making decisions about our local health care!" He ran a newspaper ad picturing himself with his two daughters and wife next to a photograph of Shapard, depicted alone: "Newt will take his family to Washington and keep them together; Virginia will go to Washington and leave her husband and children in the care of a nanny." It identified him as "a deacon of the First Baptist Church of Carrollton," Shapard as "a communicant of the Church of the Good Shepherd in Griffin." That particular ad ran only in the rural hinterlands, where, an aide reflected, "'communicant' sounded like a bunch of Catholics to Georgians." (The church in question was Episcopalian.) His last two runs, the *Atlanta Constitution* had enthusiastically endorsed him. This year, the newspaper said, "The Gingrich approach seems to have gone beyond vigor and into demagoguery and plain lying." He managed fine without the paper. In January he began his first of ten terms.

The commentators pointed to prominent Republican losses, like young George W. Bush's in Texas, and said that the party's performance had been only average. What that assessment neglected was context: in the summer of 1977, they were saying that the party was about to go the way of the Whigs. One of them, Everett Carll Ladd, saw his series of articles about the Democrats and Republicans in *Fortune* a year earlier published in book form—which meant that, after reading in your morning newspaper about Senators-elect Armstrong, Jepsen, Humphrey, and all the rest, you could read in Ladd's book that "the GOP today is in a weaker position than any major party since the Civil War."

Many Democratic victors were conspicuously conservative—like the supply-side economist from Texas, Phil Gramm, who won a House seat; or Ed King in Massachusetts, who aped George Wallace's famous campaign slogan—"Send them a message!"—in his primary victory speech over Michael Dukakis: "You gave us a message: You said Massachusetts needs a Proposition 13, and *now*!" Other Democratic successes came from candidates who ran to their Republican opponents' right on economics. In Michigan a Democratic Senate challenger named Carl Levin defeated a powerful Republican incumbent, Bob Griffin. Levin was a liberal on issues of war and peace and civil liberties, but not on taxing and spending. On the other hand, wrote one observer, "his message differed somewhat from the antigovernment rhetoric of Ronald Reagan and other right-wing conservatives intent on dismantling the federal government, but sometimes one had to listen very carefully to make the distinction."

In Delaware, there was Joseph Biden—who, after his 1972 Senate election at the age of twenty-nine as a liberal, became the senator from outside the deep South who did the most to stymie busing to achieve school desegregation, and pioneered the imposition of mandatory sentences for federal crimes. (He said drug dealers were "potential killers " who should be tracked down "like we track down killers.") He boasted in full-page ads that he was "one of the stingiest senators"—the sixth most conservative, according to the National Taxpayers Union (having long ago reversed his previous conviction that balancing the budget "would have a minimal effect on inflation while potentially worsening the economy"). He voted against Humphrey-Hawkins and for the capital gains tax cut of his Delaware colleague William Roth, whom he outflanked from the right with an even more stringent bill to sunset federal programs if they were not specifically reauthorized. He even won Howard Jarvis's endorsement ("You have shown yourself to be in the forefront of the battle to reduce government spending"). He glided to reelection.

As, in California, did Jerry Brown, thanks to one of the most neck-snapping about-faces in modern political history: from scathing critic of Prop 13 to fervent champion, so much so that 47 percent of Californians believed he had always been for it.

CALIFORNIA, THEY LIKED TO SAY, WAS WHERE THE NATION'S FUTURE WAS born. If so, what did November 7, 1978, there foretell?

A colorful Republican named Mike Curb was voted the first California lieutenant governor in history from a different party than the governor. A pop songwriter, record producer, and anti-drug crusader, Curb campaigned in between producing Debby Boone's hit song "You Light Up My Life" and managing the career of teen heartthrob Leif Garrett. Lyn Nofziger recruited him to run for lieutenant governor so they could have an ally running the state if Brown traveled outside it to campaign for president—to keep Brown from "running around the country trashing Ronald Reagan's record," as Curb put it. Score a point for the conservatives.

But then there was Proposition 6. During an election eve visit to Sacramento, President Carter concluded an outdoor speech for Jerry Brown, stepped away from the podium, and Brown whispered something to him—which a hot microphone picked up: "You'll get your loudest applause. It's going to be defeated and Ford and Reagan have come out against it, so I think it's perfectly safe."

Carter returned to the podium: ". . . I also want to ask everyone to vote against Proposition 6!" He got, indeed, his *only* big burst of applause. Then Briggs's initiative failed by more than a million votes. It even lost in Briggs's Orange County. San Francisco's liberal mayor George Moscone at the victory celebration called it "a victory over the despair that has fallen on gay people. It's a victory of intellect over emotion." Larry Berner, the gay Sonoma County elementary school teacher, said, "There's a real message for gay people to come out of our closets, because that's how we won this election . . . we talked to our neighbors and friends, and they accepted us as *human beings*." Harvey Milk tearfully promised that this was only the beginning: next, he announced, he would be organizing a huge gay march on Washington.

Two other California initiative campaigns were not much noticed nationally. One, John Briggs's Proposition 7 expanding the death penalty, passed comfortably. The other, Proposition 5, sought to ban smoking in public places unless they had designated smoking sections, on pain of a $50 fine. After easily qualifying it for the ballot, proponents raised $500,000 for the campaign, airing brilliant commercials starring the sort of handsome movie stars—John Forsythe, Charlton Heston, Gregory Peck—who had taught generations to think of smoking as glamorous in the first place. It led by a wide margin in early polls.

Then, opposition to Prop 5, "Californians for Common Sense," got to work.

The organization was a fully owned subsidiary of the tobacco industry, leveraging the successful campaigns against the FTC and the federal consumer agency by framing Prop 5 as yet one more example of the nanny state: slogans included "They're at it again!"; "Let's stop them before they stop us"; "What will the regulators try to regulate next?" Some of their mass-media ads didn't even mention what *product* Proposition 5 intended to regulate.

Mail pieces, on the other hand, were *targeted* to smokers. A brochure described how Prohibition-era Chicago became a playground for black-market-booze mobsters like Al Capone, then claimed that in modern-day Chicago, under a tough anti-smoking law that had passed in 1975, eight hundred people were convicted for smoking in train cars a year, with "dozens" spending a night in jail. "What has happened in Chicago is the forefront of a new Prohibition movement." Except that the claim was completely false.

An ad aimed at black smokers claimed the initiative was the doing of racists because black people smoked more; another featured Greg Morris, the black actor from *Mission: Impossible* arguing in the show's trademark clipped tones that Prop 5 was unpatriotic. Californians for Common Sense also commissioned a study claiming the state would lose $43 million annually in lost productivity during employee smoking breaks. They said buying "No Smoking" signs would cost the state $20 million. Which wasn't all that much more, as it happened, than this $6.5 million campaign against it cost.

The campaign was the product of the Tobacco Institute, a twenty-year-old lobbying powerhouse that boasted of kicking Frank Moss out of the chairmanship of the Senate Commerce Committee's consumer subcommittee in favor of Senator Wendell Ford of Kentucky, an affable old-fashioned glad-hander who appeared to love nothing more than sipping bourbon, chain-smoking—and doing the Tobacco Institute's bidding. Over the past two years, the institute had doubled its staff, which now included four full-time spokesmen who logged 170,000 miles a year spreading Big Tobacco's case to local Elks Clubs, Rotary Clubs, and radio and television reporters.

Ronald Reagan made his contribution for free. "Here is a piece of mischief cooked up by Big Government fans," Pete Hannaford wrote him in the summer, attaching an article on the initiative from the *Christian Science Monitor*. "Shades of Newspeak in Orwell's *1984*," Reagan wrote in the same election-eve column in which he made his final argument against the anti-gay Briggs initiative. "That reasonable smokers and non-smokers can use a little common courtesy in working out their differences seems not to have occurred to the proponents of Proposition 5. If it passes, it won't be the first time a false assumption found its way into law and made government grow."

"We just have never lost anything in Congress," the Tobacco Institute's president had recently bragged to the Associated Press. He could now brag that they had never lost an initiative campaign. Proposition 5 went down by five hundred thousand votes. The boardroom Jacobins had a perfect record on the year.

CHAPTER 19

Basements

NORMAN ROCKWELL DIED. THE DAY AFTER THE ELECTION, FIFTEEN DAYS before Thanksgiving, and ten days before the State Department relayed to the world, on November 18, that a congressman from California named Leo Ryan had been shot dead in the South American nation of Guyana.

Ryan had gone to investigate a bizarre San Francisco minister named Jim Jones, who had recruited thousands of fanatically devoted followers—a mix of poor, uneducated African Americans and whites from the professional classes—to his "Peoples Temple," whose doctrine joined Marxism with Pentecostal-style faith healing. Jones then impelled hundreds of them to follow him to a barren "agricultural mission," in the jungle, that he had christened Jonestown.

A little-noticed story had gone out over the UPI wire months earlier about a twenty-five-year-old former resident named Deborah Layton. She said Jonestown was patrolled by two rings of khaki-uniformed armed guards who had access to hundreds of rifles, twenty-five pistols, and a homemade bazooka. She described how "an elderly woman was humiliated by being forced to strip, how younger members had fists ground into their foreheads, and how others were ordered to an underground 'box' where they sat for a day at a time." She said acolytes were forced to work from 5:30 a.m. to 6 p.m., then listen to Jones's frenzied sermons until midnight. Most astonishingly, she claimed that one day more than a thousand residents agreed to drink a potion which Jones *told them* would make them pass out, and that they then would be shot. "Jones called it off just before the community was to drink the phony potion." Layton's mother and brother were quoted in the article from an interview via shortwave from the settlement. They called her claims "too ridiculous to refute. We are treated beautifully." Twelve days after that article appeared, the newspaper covering the area where Jones had once headquartered his church in Ukiah, California, gave over an entire page to Jones to respond. In 1973, that newspaper had accepted a $300 gift from the Peoples Temple commending its "position on the First Amendment." He had garnered a similar influence with public officials and media outlets, using similar methods, in his next home base, San Francisco.

By the fall of 1978 Jones had begun receiving further negative attention, as more apostates and their families approached officials with horror stories. The Justice Department began looking into suspicious deaths of members. Congressman Ryan, responding to pleas that the U.S. State Department had mostly ignored, arranged a thirteen-person delegation to travel to Guyana and investigate the settlement where some twelve hundred Americans, according to a church news release, were working to "erase oppression of the poor, eradicate class distinction, and prove that people from various backgrounds could live together."

Church security forces attempted to assassinate the delegation. The congressman, a defector, an NBC News reporter and his cameraman, and a *San Francisco Examiner* journalist all died. Then came reports that some three hundred commune residents, including many children, had ingested Kool-Aid mixed with cyanide in a mass suicide rite. Subsequent reports raised the death toll to nearly a thousand. "They started with the babies," one eyewitness said. Bodies so badly decomposed in the jungle sun they had to be picked up by military teams wearing gas masks began returning home for burial in time for Thanksgiving. That Monday, images of rotting bodies, interviews with anguished family members, and analyses and investigations took up more than half of each of the three network evening newscasts. Every question journalists answered generated more they could not. Allegations began emerging that liberal public officials in San Francisco, including Mayor George Moscone, had relied on the volunteer labor of this cult in order to win election, and that one of Jones's acolytes, Tim Stoen, had even managed to get named deputy district attorney, in charge of investigating election irregularities for which the Peoples Temple was in fact responsible.

Ronald Reagan was asked about Jonestown in Bonn, Germany, where he was embarked on a weeklong European tour. He said Jim Jones "supported a number of political figures but seemed more to be involved in the Democratic Party. I haven't seen anyone in the Republican Party having been helped by him or seeking his help."

Tasteless, ill-timed—and also not true: Jones had also proven adept at seducing the *Republican* power structure up in Ukiah. *Saturday Night Live*'s "Weekend Update" segment responded to Reagan: "Richard Speck, who killed eight nurses, was a Republican precinct chairman in Chicago. . . . Juan Corona, the California machete killer, was a speechwriter for Barry Goldwater . . . and David Berkowitz, the Son of Sam slayer . . . a Youth for Nixon."

They missed Ted Bundy, the 1968 Rockefeller convention delegate. But the unfunny joke raised the obvious question: just how sick was Norman Rockwell's nation, that it kept raising up monsters like these?

ANOTHER HORRIFYING MURDER IMMEDIATELY FOLLOWED.

After the failure of Proposition 6 in California, a new tolerance toward gays appeared to be aborning. Larry Berner, the gay teacher, told a reporter what it was like to finally feel free to hold hands with his partner in restaurants: "It's been a joyous experience, being out of the closet. I expected that something horrible would happen to me if people knew, but the most amazing thing is that absolutely nothing has happened."

On November 19, an ABC made-for-TV movie sympathetically portrayed a lesbian mother's attempt to get custody of her children from her abusive ex-husband. In Wichita, a fundamentalist minister named Michael Schepis wrote ABC and its local affiliate, "In view of Wichita's 83 percent vote last May 9 which repealed the pro-homosexuality 'gay rights' ordinance, your pro-lesbian version of *A Question of Love* is a serious affront to prevailing community standards in our city." Other ministers sermonized their congregations to flood the station with calls of protest. A station receptionist subsequently told the Associated Press she had received ninety-three such messages—but 130 messages in support.

And another cheering development for gay rights supporters was that in San Francisco, the conservative city supervisor Dan White, the former cop and firefighter who had campaigned against gays as "deviants," decided to quit.

Then, however, White changed his mind, begging Mayor Moscone to allow him to reverse his decision. Harvey Milk approached the mayor, too, arguing that only White's vote stood in the way of their shared progressive agenda, and that he would lead gays out of Moscone's column if he allowed White back in. The mayor sided with Milk. The Tuesday after Thanksgiving, Dan White slipped through a side window at City Hall carrying a .38-caliber revolver. He entered the mayor's private office and shot him four times. White reloaded with special hollow-point bullets that explode with particular violence inside the body, walked into Supervisor Harvey Milk's office, and murdered him with five shots.

On his televised *Old Time Gospel Hour*, the Reverend Jerry Falwell said that the "people of San Francisco had better awake to the fact that the judgement, the wrath that is falling upon the city, is of divine origin."

THE POLLSTER BOB TEETER HAD BLAMED "RAMPANT NEGATIVISM" FOR THE fact that only 34.9 percent of eligible voters had bothered to vote in the election that just passed, though more money had been spent to persuade them than in any other election in history. Negativism grew more rampant as the holiday season advanced.

On front porches in nine cities, there appeared tabloid-style pamphlets whose covers screamed in green ink: "THIS INFORMATION IS YOUR KEY TO SURVIVAL." Inside were instructions about evacuating to the countryside in the event of a nuclear war. It was part of a federal pilot program that President Carter was considering expanding to four hundred communities. The information was based on the Pentagon's "Doomsday Atlas," a study outlining survival procedures for communities across the nation—including plans for an airlift of 1.5 million New York City residents to western New York State, and instructions as to how much earth each refugee from heavily populated southern New England would be required to pile up outside walls and on roofs for fallout protection in the relocation areas in sparsely populated northern New England. (Eighty to a hundred bucketfuls per person, it turned out.)

A more immediate apocalypse arrived in Niagara Falls, New York. In 1894, a manufacturer named William Love built a canal beside the Niagara River to support what he hoped would become a utopian industrial development. He ran out of money. The sixteen-acre site was purchased by the Hooker Chemical Company. Between 1942 and 1953 they used it as a dump for wastes, including a clear viscous chemical called polychlorinated biphenyls, or PCBs. Hooker then sold the Niagara Falls school board the site, around which a bucolic residential neighborhood sprang up, where odd things began happening, like die-offs of plants, trees, and pets, and spontaneous fires. The canal was paved over, because children were swimming in it; kids then enjoyed hurling chunks of that pavement into the air to watch them explode upon impact. Streets began buckling, then sinking. After the killer winter of 1977–78, black sludge began seeping into basements. Reporters documented terrible diseases. That summer, the New York State Department of Health found massive concentrations of ten carcinogenic substances in the air.

Governor Hugh Carey offered to buy out the homes of 239 families living in Love Canal's "inner ring." The process of sealing the area was accompanied by headlines like "Pollution Victims Told of Liver Disorders," "An Olfactory Niagara," and "New York Survey Lists Industries' Poisons: 'Anything, Anywhere, Any Time.'" A syndicated article appeared across the country around Thanksgiving describing a neighborhood that used to look like a 1950s sitcom but now resembled "a stage set for a disaster movie." It quoted the head of the Department of Health: "Nothing like this has happened before in the United States. But I think it will happen again." The Environmental Protection Agency's regional director said, "We've been burying these things like ticking time bombs. . . . We're mortgaging our future if we don't control them more carefully. And the bottom line is—who's going to pay to clean this up?" It felt like the bill was coming due for a generation of economic boom times that had secretly been built on a foundation of death.

ALFRED KAHN, THE CORNELL UNIVERSITY ECONOMICS PROFESSOR THE president appointed as his new anti-inflation "czar," announced to a conference of retailers that unless business adhered to his forthcoming Council on Wage and Price Stability guidelines, "we will have a deep, deep depression." The stock market, which had just enjoyed its first gains after a month of plunging values, suffered a near panic. One Oregon newspaper illustrated a feature about the speech with 1930s-era photographs of an emaciated farmer puffing out the empty pockets of his overalls, an unemployment line, and a Civilian Conservation Corps work camp.

At least Americans could be grateful their situation was not as bad as Great Britain's. In 1976, the nation that had once boasted an empire upon which the sun never set became the first developed country to take a loan from the International Monetary Fund. The IMF's conditions demanded brutal austerity, and by the summer of 1978, the Labor prime minister, James Callaghan, asked the national Trades Union Confederation to hold down raises to 5 percent. Unions struck instead. Emergency rooms closed to all but the worst cases. Uncollected trash piled up in the streets. Bread was rationed. Crops rotted without truckers to move them—with little gasoline to fuel them in any event. England entered what became known as its "Winter of Discontent."

In Iran, the shah's government was collapsing day by day at the hands of a many-tentacled revolutionary coalition. Oil strikes brought production from five million to two million barrels a day. One demand was the expulsion of all foreign workers and their dependents, including forty-one thousand Americans. By November 18 at least four thousand Westerners had left "after incidents," UPI reported, "in which their homes were firebombed or ransacked and their cars destroyed. Some foreign workers had narrow escapes dodging Iranians speeding toward them in cars." An American executive was riddled with bullets while driving to work in the city of Ahwaz—"a very well-planned operation, not a bunch of kids playing around," said an anonymous source.

It had something to do, Americans began learning, with a mysterious figure called Ayatollah Ruhollah Khomeini, the exiled spiritual leader of Iran's Shi'ite Muslims, who lived in a residential neighborhood of Paris, subsisting on the simplest of meals, receiving worshipful visitors all day. The *New York Times* profiled him: "Dressed in a black turban and a black robe and white shirt, the Ayatollah sat cross-legged and leaned against a wall, his small intense eyes usually cast down and only occasionally darting a quick glance at his visitor. The interviewer was also asked to kneel on the floor after removing shoes and covering head and shoulders with a white cotton square drape so that only the eyes show." This was because the interviewer was a woman.

The *Times* ran up to six articles a day on the crisis: on the curious anti-shah coalition of secular radicals and religious zealots; about a wave of arson against banks, movie theaters, and liquor stores that was brought to a halt when the shah extended martial law to the entire country; how the shah was buying time for his teetering government with mass arrests of corrupt businessmen and his own officials.

He formed a new cabinet that included opposition figures, which was followed by relative calm—until a November 26 general strike protesting SAVAK's latest massacre. On December 10, an estimated one million protesters marched through the capital chanting "Death to the American cur." An Associated Press analysis the next day observed, "The Carter administration has given full backing to the Shah of Iran without explaining why his survival is so important to national security. The reason, one official said, is simple: Some of the alternatives to the shah are so bleak that public discussion of them could alarm the American people."

How bleak? How alarming? Three weeks earlier, a Senate delegation visiting Tehran had been lectured by former CIA director and ambassador to Iran Richard Helms that the shah's position was secure, that Iran was on the verge of becoming a major world power, and that "Americans should be reassured in having a powerful, loyal ally in such a vital part of the world." The delegation enjoyed a banquet hosted by the shah and his empress in their honor. ("Our visit earlier to view the Crown Jewels," Senator Paul Laxalt remembered, "should have conditioned us to the opulence of the shah's regime, but it didn't prepare us for this. . . . The dinner, with gold service, exquisite crystal, and individual waiters for each of us, was unlike any we'd ever attended.") But they also kept on hearing stray machine gun fire. And they weren't allowed to leave their hotel. Senators Laxalt, John Glenn, and Richard Lugar took a side trip by plane over the Strait of Hormuz, the choke point for 70 percent of Europe's oil supply and 90 percent of Japan's. Laxalt said it "confirmed our worst fears: If the Strait of Hormuz was ever endangered, the seeds of a third world war would be quickly sown."

AN ECCENTRIC SOUTHERN BAPTIST MINISTER FROM TEXAS FINISHED AN EPIC twenty-month, sixteen-hundred-mile journey, avidly reported in the media for years, crawling to the White House on his knees, pulling a cart reading "PRAY AMERICA" and bearing thousands of signatures from well-wishers, to "dramatize the message that America has to get back on its knees before the Lord to keep itself free"—but when he arrived at the White House gate, newspaper readers around the country learned, he was callously told the president was too busy to see him.

Carter traveled to New York for a dinner honoring the outgoing mayor. He opened with a joke. "Several people have asked me why I would leave the White House and come to New York this evening. As a matter of fact, Alfred Kahn was supposed to come." The punchline: his new inflation fighter had responded, "Mr. President, I've just discovered that a meal and an opera ticket in New York is now up to $2,500. And I think this is one situation you ought to handle personally."

Perhaps Carter laughed to keep from crying. No one knew how to handle the "Great Inflation" of 1970. Even decades later, economists didn't agree about what had caused it.

Most believed it had something to do with "guns and butter": Lyndon Johnson's refusal to raise taxes to pay for the Vietnam War, while simultaneously increasing spending for his Great Society. Richard Nixon's venality could have played a role: in August of 1971, facing a stubborn recession and an upcoming reelection fight, he ordered a radical package of economic reforms that included a ninety-day freeze on wages and prices—which he kept on extending for another three years, during which high prices gushed forth like water breaking through a failed dam. Another part of Nixon's radical reform was ending the convertibility of dollars into gold, which greatly increased currency speculation, which may have contributed to inflation as well. And the economy was still suffering from the 1973 Arab oil embargo, which had emboldened OPEC to keep increasing the price at regular intervals: a barrel cost $3.60 in 1972, approximately what it had in 1948, but fetched $25.10 at the end of 1978. OPEC's example inspired other Third World nations to jack up prices for the treasures beneath *their* soil, like Jamaica's bauxite. The success of unions in winning automatic "cost of living" raises contributed to inflation, as, probably, did the trade imbalance, though in complicated ways economists could not quite explain. The coming of age of the children of the postwar "baby boom" might have thrown some previous equilibrium out of whack. Or maybe not. But even if it were possible to grasp precisely the mix of these causes of inflation, that wouldn't necessarily make ending it any easier, for none of these bells could be un-rung.

There was, however, *another* theory of what caused inflation, and it was simple, and suggested a simple remedy to boot. It was the one conservatives believed. Its most eloquent spokesman was the former governor of California: inflation happened when the government spent too much money.

Back when he was a liberal, in 1948, campaigning for Harry Truman, Ronald Reagan had explained inflation as a cruel imposition upon ordinary people by greedy business: "The profits of corporations have doubled, while workers' wages have increased by only one quarter. In other words, profits have gone up *four times* as much as wages. . . . High prices have *not* been caused by high wages, but by *bigger* and *bigger* profits." Now, as a conservative, he argued that greedy government was responsible: "Inflation occurs when the growth of the nation's money supply outstrips the growth in the nation's productivity," he said in a 1976 radio commentary, ventriloquizing Milton Friedman. "The federal government controls the nation's money supply, and is therefore the primary source of inflation. . . . In truth, inflation is simply another tax imposed by Washington in the name of easy money." Inflation was "deliberately planned."

But what was the motive? Buying votes, via goodies paid for from an artificially inflated federal treasury—though the government never actually paid for them at all. Inflation was how the bill for such government profligacy came due—"the direct responsibility of a spendthrift Democratic-controlled Congress that has been unwilling to discipline itself to live within our means."

And what of Jimmy Carter's claim that he intended to force Congress to do precisely that? Answered Reagan: "For Democrats to warn against inflation is like getting a lecture on fire prevention from Mrs. O'Leary's cow. . . . There hasn't been a day in the last two decades that they couldn't have curbed the spending, ended the inflation, and in so doing reduced unemployment, if they wanted to. But this would have gone counter to their doctrinaire liberalism."

The striking thing was that Jimmy Carter seemed to agree. "If we are to overcome the threat of accelerating inflation," he lectured in one speech, "the government will simply not be able to do as much as it has in the past": nothing about OPEC, Vietnam, currency speculation, or any other such complexity. The way to stop inflation was shooting Santa Claus.

Carter didn't seem to recognize the danger in this to Democrats' political fortunes. But Ronald Reagan did: "For Democratic politicians long used to harvesting votes by dispensing nearly unlimited amounts of middle-class dollars, the new reality is going to be hard to get used to," he wrote in a column analyzing the congressional elections. "No wonder there were some sweaty Democrat brows the other night." Representative Tom Foley, a Watergate baby from Washington State, grasped it, too: "Tight budgets strain all the natural fault lines of the Democratic Party. The pressure will intensify as we approach the presidential election year and each group starts pressing its claims."

And how. It was already happening.

Word leaked that Carter budget proposals for FY 1980 would include cuts to federal rail subsidies that an Amtrak executive said "would probably wipe us out west of Chicago." They would also reportedly slash the federal government's biggest jobs program, the Comprehensive Employment and Training Act. A dozen black leaders told the president they might be "unable to contain the urban unrest that would follow that decision."

Alfred Kahn admitted to another group of black leaders that reducing budget deficits was an "inefficient" way to fight inflation—but "until you show me there is a better way, I have no choice." He implored them to help promote compliance with his Council on Wage and Price Stability guidelines, pleading, "We cannot hope to devote the additional resources you and I would like to rebuilding our cities, to resuming our progress to four percent unemployment, and to provide decent medical care to everybody in this country until we somehow restore the balance between what we want and what we can afford," he said. "The prescribed medicine is restraint. The goal is to put the brakes on inflation in a matter of months or a few years at least." If we don't, "we are courting a recession that could be to the last one what pneumonia is to a cold."

Although, in one of those wicked ironies history so enjoys delivering, several decades and many recessions later, the *coincidence* of record budget deficits and record low inflation demonstrated that budget-balancing was in no way necessary to arrest inflation. But that was for a future generation to discover. Now, President Carter's ironclad conviction that it was brought the Democratic Party to the verge of civil war.

THE WEEKEND OF DECEMBER 10, THE PARTY OF JEFFERSON, JACKSON, AND Jimmy Carter convened for a "mini-convention" in Memphis, Tennessee. The president laid a wreath at the site of Martin Luther King Jr.'s assassination; then his opening speech was introduced with a film, produced by Gerald Rafshoon, that was so heavy-handed in its encomia that even Carter partisans appeared embarrassed. In the speech, Carter called his party "the most open, honest, progressive, compassionate political organization in the world today"—before saying it was "an illusion to believe that we can preserve a commitment to compassionate, progressive government if we fail to bring inflation under control . . . sacrifices must be made."

Activists who traveled to Democratic conventions tended to be liberal. Many liberals thought fighting inflation by cutting budgets was the *opposite* of compassionate, progressive government. Liberal policy experts said that fighting inflation by cutting budgets didn't even work. No wonder the crowd—many wearing "KENNEDY FOR PRESIDENT" buttons—applauded so tepidly.

The White House brought resolutions for the delegates to rubber-stamp. One pledged the administration's "every effort" to comply with Humphrey-Hawkins. "That's a hell of a concession," UAW president Douglas Fraser grumbled, "to say we're going to try to comply with the law of the land." Fraser's speech attacked the president: "We are told that times are changing and we must change with the times. I hope the Democratic Party never changes in its commitment to those who are most in need of a helping hand from their government." In the back rooms, he lined up votes for a competing resolution committing the party to a budget "adequate . . . to human needs, in no case less than the current services budget for human and social services for fiscal year 1980." It took a concerted White House whipping operation to defeat it.

These quadrennial off-year mini-conventions, which began in 1974, were supposed to help unite the party faithful. The one in 1978 served instead to put the Democrats' disunity on display for everyone to see.

Carter attended two policy workshops, sitting in the audience like some ordinary county commissioner; *Time* said it felt like Carter wasn't president at all. At the one on inflation, speakers lectured him, until the chair finally asked if anyone had any questions to pose to him *directly*. The room fell silent—until people started walking to the microphones to hector him some more. Through it all, Carter smiled liked he was "St. Sebastian," Garry Wills wrote in the *New York Review of Books*, "pretending he likes nothing more dearly than arrows."

At the workshop on defense policy, Carter was asked about his nuclear arms nonproliferation efforts. He graciously turned the floor over to Senator John Culver of Iowa, "who's been in the forefront of that effort." But Culver took the opportunity to hector the president, too, for increasing the arms budget when a dollar spent on weaponry was "the most inflationary dollar of all." His dig was particularly interesting to the hundreds of reporters present. They all knew Senator Culver and Senator Kennedy had been college roommates.

At the workshop on healthcare, Carter's secretary of health, education, and welfare Joseph Califano delivered a dry presentation on the constraints inflation threats imposed on increased federal spending. He was warmly applauded only by loyalists with which the White House had papered the house.

Then, Ted Kennedy rose to speak.

"I am proud to be with you here today," he began, reading from a text. "I am proud of our country, proud of the Democratic Party, and proud of the dream we have for America and the future. Since the time of Jefferson and Jackson, the Democratic Party has always held its standard high. As a party, we have stood for action, hope and progress in meeting the people's basic needs. We are not a party of reaction or retreat. . . . At our best, we have had leaders with both the vision to see the path, and the skill to guide the nation forward, to bring us closer to our historic goals." He cited Wilson, Roosevelt, Truman, his brother, Lyndon Johnson, Hubert Humphrey—and Jimmy Carter, who "has led us to the threshold of peace in the Middle East and given America world leadership in the cause of human rights." Though it soon became plain he was there not to praise Jimmy Carter but to bury him.

"We meet, however, at a time of caution and uncertainty in the land. The hopes and dreams of millions of citizens are riding on our leadership. Sometimes a party must sail against the wind," he said. Heads began nodding.

"We cannot afford to drift or lie at anchor. We cannot heed the call of those who say it is time to furl the sail.

"We know that some things in America today are wrong. It is wrong that prices are rising as rapidly as they are.

"It is wrong that millions of our fellow citizens are out of work.

"It is wrong that cities are struggling against decay. It is wrong that women and minorities are denied their equal rights. And it is wrong that millions who are sick cannot afford the care they need.

"I support the fight against inflation. But no fight against inflation can be effective or successful unless the fight is fair. The party that tore itself apart over Vietnam in the 1960s cannot afford to tear itself apart today over budget cuts in basic social programs. There could be few more divisive issues for America and for our party than a Democratic policy of drastic slashes in the federal budget at the expense of the elderly, the poor, the black, the sick, the cities, and the unemployed."

Fifteen hundred delegates and a thousand media personnel had arrived in Memphis wondering whether Kennedy would openly take on the president—perhaps even to announce his own presidential bid. Now they heard him articulate what sounded like a presidential platform. Its centerpiece was national health insurance—"the great unfinished business of the Democratic Party," a lacuna on which "America now stands virtually alone. . . . With the sole exception of South Africa, no other industrialized world leaves its citizens in fear of financial ruin because of illness."

National healthcare had been a Carter campaign promise. In 1977, he dodged it. Early in 1978, he made a promise to provide a comprehensive blueprint before Congress's October adjournment—then broke it. Instead, that summer, he forwarded a modest plan for federal coverage of catastrophic hospital expenses, phased in gradually, with a "self-destruct" clause canceling it if cost-containment benchmarks were not met. Kennedy had accused Carter of a "failure of leadership," promising to introduce his own health bill. Joseph Califano responded, "We are committed to proceeding in a prudent manner which does not fuel inflation."

Kennedy's pace quickened and his volume crescendoed as he described the tax favors enjoyed by the rich for money they spent on healthcare, the luxury care enjoyed by members of the Senate and the House, and how the health insurance industry had become "the fastest-growing failing business in America" by charging more and more for less and less. He described how the elderly were forced to decide whether to pay for rent or pills, how young people were gambling on their health by not carrying insurance because they couldn't afford the premiums.

Then, he pushed aside his prepared text and took off his glasses, the better to look his audience in the eye. He appeared to lose himself, drifting some distance from the microphone. But his voice boomed with such righteous fury that no one missed a word.

"I had a father who was touched by stroke, and sick for seven years!"

(Joseph Kennedy, the mightiest patriarch in American history, everyone knew, had been rendered mute and incapacitated, almost entirely locked in with his own thoughts from December 1961 until his death in 1969.)

"We were able to get the best in healthcare. Because we were able to afford it! It would have *bankrupted* any average family in this nation! Any average family that is represented in this hall! And the millions of people you represent all over this nation of ours!"

(He stabbed the air rhythmically at the words.)

"I had a son that was touched by cancer."

(This was Edward Kennedy Jr., born just before his grandfather's stroke, whose leg had to be amputated the day Edward Kennedy Sr. walked his cousin Kathleen down the wedding aisle, before rushing to the hospital to be at his son's side. Everyone knew about this, too.)

"*Extraordinary* health bills that we received, and we were able to afford, and we received, the very best. It would have *obliterated* the savings of any family!"

(He was shouting.)

"Seven months I was in the hospital with a broken back," he said. That brought awed silence. Kennedy rarely talked about the time seven months after his brother's assassination when he survived a plane crash after Birch Bayh pulled him from the wreckage, and the pilot and an aide died next to him. Plane crashes were a family curse: his eldest brother had died in one during World War II, his sister in 1948. This one family's ordeal had structured the political unconscious of an entire generation of Americans. Now he was deploying these recollections to blast away at the president's reputation as a decent, caring man.

He waved his hands: "We've got the very best, all of us at the tip of the iceberg. But I want every delegate at this convention to understand. That as long as I have a vote in the United States Senate it's going to be for that *Democratic! platform! plank!*"—he pounded on the podium—"that provides decent! quality! healthcare! *North* and south. *East* and west. *As a matter of right and not of privilege!!*"

He walked away to an ovation that had begun while he was still speaking, a vortex of energy that the session's chairman, the young governor of Arkansas, Bill Clinton, said was greater than any he had experienced in his life.

Vice President Mondale was the weekend's final speaker. "It is not just the domestic programs that will be analyzed. So will the defense budget," he promised defensively. "Don't worry about the compassion of this president." But he also warned that if Democrats "don't end the ever-rising cost of living, we will be driven out of office as we were by the Vietnam War."

So *not* cutting budgets to end inflation would have the same political consequences for Democrats as the Vietnam War. But Ted Kennedy said *cutting* budgets to end inflation would have the same political consequences for Democrats as the Vietnam War.

That was how the Democrats ended 1978.

CLEVELAND ENDED 1978 ON THE VERGE OF BANKRUPTCY. ONCE UPON A time, Ohio's largest city—which had just fallen off the list of America's ten largest cities—had been one of those brawny industrial meccas whose hard toil had won World War II and built the postwar economic miracle. But manufacturers had been fleeing places like Cleveland to the non-union Sun Belt. Chicago, Pittsburgh, Philadelphia, and Boston all lost more than a third of their manufacturing bases in a decade. Those with the means fled for the suburbs, leaving behind economically vulnerable African Americans, a phenomenon known as white flight. Cities could not tear down abandoned buildings fast enough; blocks became hollow shells; empty factories became playgrounds for vandals and arsonists. Once glittering central business districts became ghost towns. Cities like these were labeled the Rust Belt.

Cleveland seemed on its way to becoming the most forlorn of them all. The mayor, desperate for cash, sold off the sewer system to a private corporation and was trying to do the same with the Port Authority and electrical utility. Then, a baby-faced city council member named Dennis Kucinich, who was thirty-one but looked like he was thirteen, won the mayoralty in his ninth attempt, campaigning against the "fat cats" and "bosses" selling off the city by the pound. In the spring of 1978, a few months after he was inaugurated, the fat cats struck back by organizing a recall election. Kucinich prevailed by 216 votes, helped by a television commercial depicting them cutting up a cake shaped like City Hall—like the Mafiosi carved a cake shaped like Cuba in *The Godfather Part II*.

The Boy Mayor had prevailed with the voters. But it was the fat cats who controlled the city's delinquent loans. They made the mayor an offer they hoped he could not refuse: come up with $15.5 million by midnight, December 15, 1978, or those loans would be called in.

National reporters descended to see what would happen next. They exchanged jokes: "the Mistake by the Lake." "What's the difference between Cleveland and the Titanic? The Titanic had a better orchestra." Kucinich said he might have no choice but to lay off police and sanitation workers—who threatened to strike in turn.

In not-unrelated news, bankers were affixing tags on Cleveland water trucks in preparation to seize them when, seven thousand miles away in the principality of Abu Dhabi, OPEC oil ministers, the new lords of the global economy, bickered over whether to exploit the supply-squeeze brought on by the troubles in Iran to increase the price of a barrel of crude by 5 percent, 15 percent, or 25 percent. Price hawks pointed out that this was only fair, given how America's weakening dollar was draining OPEC members' purchasing power. Doves, led by America's Saudi friends, said a 25 percent hike would "ruin the economy of the world." On December 17 the Associated Press reported that negotiators seemed to be settling for a 10 percent increase. The next day, OPEC announced it would be 14.5 percent, with predictions of more hikes to come.

This was precisely the sort of thing that the White House had said their controversial arms sale to Saudi Arabia would prevent. The arms deal was also supposed to vouchsafe peace in the Middle East. But Cyrus Vance returned home after shuttling between Jerusalem and Cairo to report that his efforts to formalize the deal at Camp David into a peace treaty that Egypt and Israel could sign had ended in shambles.

In Chicago, a news story hit the wires concerning a crime that might have been the most lurid in history were it not for the events a month earlier in Jonestown: "The badly decomposed bodies of three young people and the skeletal remains of as many as five more were uncovered today in a crawl space of the northwestern suburban Chicago home of a bachelor building contractor in West Norwood Park Township. One police source said the number of bodies, believed to be those of young boys, could reach as many as thirty-two."

It took a University of Illinois forensic anthropologist employing "techniques used by archaeologists to uncover ancient ruins" to sift through the bones, teeth, garments and hair to begin identifying bodies. The suspect was described in news reports as a "twice-divorced admitted homosexual."

He shared a name with the figure who, next to Norman Rockwell, most symbolized America's exalted ideal of itself: John Wayne Gacy.

Gacy's modus operandi was hiring local teenage boys to do odd jobs around his house. He would then deploy skills honed as a clown-costumed magician at children's birthday parties to bind them. Then, he would strangle and sodomize them. He was arrogant when police began closing in. "You know," he told one officer after cordially inviting him to breakfast, "clowns can get away with murder."

Clowns, and also, apparently, Chicagoans with clout. Teenage boys had been disappearing for years in Gacy's neighborhood. A ghastly smell had been emanating from his basement. But Gacy had been able to evade suspicion, in part because of his closeness to the local political power structure. The minister, the cop and fireman who'd won office on a law-and-order platform, the children's birthday party entertainer—it was hard not to interpret the third ghastly killing spree in a month as one more parable about all the rot hiding underneath the floorboards of a nation that liked to think of itself as innocent.

On December 22, the White House said it would recommend restoring funding to the Comprehensive Employment and Training Act, the main government jobs program, and other threatened social programs as well, in what was described as Jimmy Carter's "Christmas present to liberals." It was followed five days later, however, with a White House announcement that Carter's budget proposal would include a 10 percent *increase* in defense spending. Christmas presents *to* the president included inklings of the first national gasoline shortage since 1974; the sudden outbreak of a destabilizing war between Vietnam and Cambodia—and an excruciating case of the hemorrhoids. *Time* helpfully explained treatments available to the Leader of the Free World. One involved "dilating, or widening, the anus with stretching devises." Another, "cooling the affected area with liquid nitrogen," was painless but "produces a foul-smelling discharge that requires wearing a sanitary pad for a few weeks."

The *New York Times* reported from Love Canal, "A Joyless Noel for the Niagarans Still Remaining." The UPI said, "State officials have disclosed more chemical dumps, some containing the deadly 'dioxin' that forced the evacuation, are located in the Love Canal area."

As the new year approached, you had to wonder what manner of leader could possibly set things right.

BOOK FOUR

1979

CHAPTER 20

Conventional Wisdom

A HISTORIAN ONCE CALLED HIS BOOK ABOUT THE 1970S *IT SEEMED LIKE Nothing Happened.* Certainly it seemed so compared to the 1960s, when new revolutions seemed to burst forth every month. But in fact enormous things were happening. They just weren't always the sort of things that made for bold, clear headlines. Corporations withdrew their support for the liberal state and politicians embraced capital gains tax cuts; fundamentalist ministers inched their way into partisan politics and conservatives crept ever closer to control of the Republican Party; the Democrats fell into ideological confusion and the electorate became increasingly finicky—such things were, in a word, *complicated*: the sort of developments that rewired the invisible structures that order a society.

The year 1979 would be simpler. It was the year when everything, right there out in the open, just started going wrong. Already by February, calamities like the San Francisco City Hall and Gacy murders, Jonestown and Love Canal, and Cleveland's near bankruptcy no longer felt like aberrations. They just felt like the news.

On January 12, after a manhunt stretching back to 1977, Los Angeles police apprehended a criminal known as the "Hillside Strangler," who had tortured and murdered a dozen women and girls. His name was Kenneth Bianchi, and he and a partner had evaded detection by committing their crimes while posing as undercover police officers. Once, Bianchi even persuaded cops to let them ride along while they *searched* for the Hillside Strangler. A neighbor described Bianchi as friendly and well mannered: "I don't think Kenny could be the strangler." A psychopath could be living next door to you, too.

It snowed in Southern California. Fifty-two whales simultaneously stranded themselves on a Mexican beach. An eighty-five-ton American space station, Skylab, was falling out of the heavens. It would hit sometime in spring. Or possibly summer. Experts said they couldn't be sure.

On January 27, Nelson Rockefeller's publicist announced that the former New York governor, working alone late the previous night in his Rockefeller Center office on a book about his art collection, had died of a heart attack. The next day, the spokesman issued a correction: the magnate had actually expired five blocks away, in his Manhattan apartment. "It's one of those stupid goofs," he apologized. "I had the wrong office." Next, it emerged that he hadn't been alone; he was with his thirty-one-year-old "staff assistant and coordinator of his art books," Megan Marshack. Then that Marshack was "out of town and unavailable for interviews"; and was not thirty-one but twenty-five; and that Rockefeller had hired her away from a $15,000 job as a night editor at AP Radio at a salary of $60,000 even though she had no apparent expertise in art, and afforded her a $45,000 interest-free "loan" to buy an apartment two doors down from his town house; and, finally, that one of the wealthiest and most powerful men in America had died naked amid boxes of unfinished Chinese food and a bottle of Dom Perignon, found by authorities wearing pants but no shoes. His panicked mistress had tried to put some on the corpse. But the feet were already too swollen.

That Saturday, a woman claiming to have "enough nitroglycerine with me to blow this plane up" hijacked a 747 on its way from Los Angeles to New York. She demanded that her plan to save the world be read on all three networks by either Lindsay Wagner, Charlton Heston, or Jack Lemmon. On Monday, in San Diego, a dead-eyed sixteen-year-old named Brenda Spencer took the .22-caliber rifle she had received as a Christmas present and began opening fire on children streaming to class at the elementary school across the street, killing the principal and a custodian, wounding eight children and a policeman. She barricaded herself inside her home, holding scores of police at bay for hours, before a negotiator finally persuaded her to surrender, but not before a *San Diego Tribune* reporter phoned and asked why she had done it. She answered, "I don't like Mondays—this livens up the day." She rang off: "I have to go now. I shot a pig, I think, and I want to shoot some more."

The year 1979 also marked the emergence of a fad for "slasher films" drafting off the success of *Halloween* the previous fall—movies about psychopaths stalking and viciously murdering random people. Also, ten films and TV shows about vampires. In one, *Salem's Lot*, based on a novel by Stephen King, a writer returned to his hometown after an absence to discover his neighbors turning into bloodsucking beasts. Which was what America would have felt like to a real-life Rip Van Winkle now.

A BACKGROUND TO ALL THIS DREAD WAS ECONOMIC.

Between 1945 and 1973, the real incomes of ordinary American families doubled. A high school dropout who had grown up with an outhouse could retire with a vacation house. When that rosy picture began cracking in the wake of the Arab oil embargo, it was possible to see that as a onetime aberration. Then the crack was revealed as a chasm. During the 1950s and '60s, U.S. economic growth averaged almost 4.5 percent each year. In 1969, the chairman of the White House Council of Economic Advisors told President Richard Nixon that he could expect "unusually rapid basic economic growth" for at least another decade. But from 1970 through 1978, growth averaged less than 2.8 percent, and the notion that Americans lived in an era of scarcity became consensus opinion. Inflation, which had averaged about 3 percent annually in the 1950s and '60s, raged at nearly 10 percent—16 percent when it came to food. The postwar boom now seemed a onetime trick, and it was hard for economists to imagine dependable growth of the American economy with nominal inflation *ever* returning. That would require steady growth in productivity. But, beginning in 1973, productivity growth had mysteriously ground to a standstill.

This transformed society at the cellular level. People had grown up learning that you bought things when you had money to buy things—and that if you wanted nicer things, you saved to purchase them later; debt was a marker of poor character. Such values no longer made sense: smart consumers purchased *today*—because next year the object of desire might be prohibitively expensive. "Consumer revolving credit" exploded: inflation made Americans fear the future, and credit cards helped salve that fear. Between 1944 and 1976, when the U.S. population grew 44 percent, credit card debt increased 1,300 percent. One in five holders never paid off their balances in full. And on December 18, 1978, came another of those quiet revolutions that helped rewire the invisible structures that govern the world: the United States Supreme Court, in *Marquette v. First of Omaha*, let banks charter themselves anywhere, rendering state laws capping credit card interest rates moot—meaning that not paying your credit card would cost more than ever before. And yet, people kept charging. "The brake is off," the director of the Gallup Poll economics division observed. "Inflation doesn't slow people down the way it always has. That's a rather historic change."

That change, however, did not bring celebration from a grateful citizenry. "It would be necessary to go back to the 1930s and the Great Depression to find a peacetime issue that had the country so concerned and so distraught," pollster Daniel Yankelovich said about inflation.

The White House's response to the vertigo—*austerity*—left economic liberals bereft. The AFL-CIO's chief lobbyist said that when he was working for the labor federation following LBJ's 1964 landslide, helping usher in Medicare, Medicaid, the first major provision of federal aid to education, and much more besides, "I couldn't figure out why they were paying me. All we did was help the president get his programs through—and it wasn't that hard." Now, he rued that "we will be in opposition to a Democratic president. . . . We've never been in this position before."

Labor liberals thought they had at least one friend in the White House: Stuart Eizenstat, Carter's policy director, who had been nursed in the bosom of Hubert Humphrey's Senate staff. Then, in a January 4 speech to the Women's National Democratic Club, Eizenstat said that while he *hoped* Democrats could "continue to build on the traditional beliefs and commitments of our party and continue to extend hope to those in need," Carter "must face the new reality he inherits; he must govern based on facts and situations handed to him. He cannot recreate the 1960s when he must govern with the far different problems of the 1970s"—an "era of constraints."

That same week, Carter's rival Governor Jerry Brown of California gave an inaugural address that squeezed the president from the right. He referenced his switch on Proposition 13. ("I may learn slow, but I learn real good.") He said, "Simply put, the citizens are revolting against a decade of political leaders who righteously spoke against inflation and excessive government spending but who in practice pursued the opposite course." That was why, he announced, he intended to introduce a resolution in the California legislature to call a national convention to amend the United States Constitution to require a balanced federal budget.

This was radical even among conservative Republicans; so much so that the right-wing group that spawned the movement Brown was joining, the National Taxpayers Union, was alarmed. They had won approval in twenty-six out of the thirty-four state legislatures the Constitution required to convene such a convention by organizing under the radar. Now that Brown had flushed the idea into the open, other conservatives came out of the woodwork to denounce it. Robert Bork said constitutional conventions were "the last resort of foundering nations, not the casual practice of a successful one." Barry Goldwater called the idea "a tragic mistake." President Carter, for his part, called it "extremely dangerous."

Brown harbored ambitions to do what Ronald Reagan had: challenge a sitting president from his own party. Carter advisors dismissed him as an attention-starved fool. That was hubris. Brown's political success overseeing a smooth transition to post–Proposition 13 budgeting had been impressive: less than 0.1 percent of state employees had lost their jobs, and not a single teacher. A new poll had 12 percent of Democrats preferring him as their presidential nominee. In the same poll, 57 percent wanted Teddy Kennedy. With 10 percent undecided, that meant barely a quarter of Democrats wanted the hero of 1976 on the ballot in 1980. Bill Winpisinger of the Machinists Union was asked what Jimmy Carter could do to redeem himself. He answered, "Die."

THE JUSTICE DEPARTMENT WAS FINISHING UP A PROSECUTION MEMO OUT-lining the alleged crimes of Bert Lance. It was reported that the investigation would include Billy Carter, who was just then squiring a delegation of Libyan officials though Georgia. Colonel Gadhafi's government funded terrorist groups like the Japanese Red Army and the Palestinian Liberation Organization, staged state funerals for the "martyrs" who murdered eleven Israeli athletes at the 1972 Olympics. Billy was asked whether he wasn't hurting Jimmy by giving offense to Jews. He responded, "There's a hell of a lot more Arabians than there is Jews." And that Libyans were "some of the best friends I have in the world." And that anyone who objected "can kiss my ass as far as I'm concerned." (It was also reported that he had urinated on the side of a building at the Atlanta airport. He confirmed the report, but insisted that it had been "secluded.")

On January 14, the *Washington Post* said that the Secretary of the Treasury was predicting "continued high inflation," and perhaps a recession. The Teamsters Union defied the president's inflation guidelines by threatening a trucking strike. On January 17, the shah fled Iran, which once again fell to chaos, as the world awaited news of whether the Ayatollah Ruhollah Khomeini would return.

The president handed off his 1979 spending proposal to Congress. "The budget commitment will be to control inflation," he said. "It will be a very austere, stringent, tough fiscal policy." He was hammered from all sides. A tasteless political cartoon imagined the president as a brainwashed member of a cult, only the guru was not Jim Jones but Howard Jarvis. Bill Armstrong, the New Right senator from Colorado, emphasized the proposal's projected $29 billion deficit: "To describe the budget as 'lean and austere' is like talking about a crash diet that permits banana splits and lemon cream pie." Democratic pollster Peter Hart observed that Carter's hair-shirt abstemiousness was having no effect on the party's image: "When you ask voters about the Democrats, you get answers that are forty years out of date. You get the New Deal stereotypes."

On Tuesday evening, January 23, the president gave his State of the Union Address. Preparing it had sorely rattled the speechwriters. Worried about complaints that Carter failed to inspire and had "no clear idea of where he is leading the country," they decided it was past time to devise a catchy two-word slogan—Kennedy's "New Frontier," Johnson's "Great Society," Roosevelt's "New Deal." Their dilemma, however, was simultaneously inspiring clarity and credibly acknowledging the intractably complex, interlocking problems the nation faced. It was compounded by the fact that those problems' conceivable solutions all lay in the distant future, with no political dividends to be harvested from the work required to get there. They decided to try to convince the public that the essence of Carter's accomplishments was initiating a *process*. They tried out phrases like "New Groundwork" and "New Building Blocks." Someone suggested "New Foundation." "Can't we do better?" one speechwriter carped.

Apparently not. Some form of "new foundation" appeared in the speech thirteen times. "Sounds like a lady's undergarment," said one commentator. Daniel Patrick Moynihan pointed out the phrase appeared in the first stanza of the Communist anthem "The Internationale."

Carter had insisted in the speech, "The problems that we face today are different from those that confronted earlier generations of Americans. They are more subtle, more complex, and more interrelated. . . . The challenge to us is to build a new and firmer foundation for the future—for a sound economy, for a more effective government, for more political trust, and for a stable peace—so that the America our children will inherit will be even stronger and better than it is today." He then insisted, "We cannot afford to live beyond our means," promising to "get control of the bureaucracy," "scrutinize the overall effect of regulation on our economy," and "sunset" federal programs that had "outlived their usefulness." The reviews from liberals were scouring. Ted Kennedy said that Carter "asks the poor, the black, the sick, the young, the cities and the unemployed to bear a disproportionate share for the billions of dollars in reductions in federal spending." Tip O'Neill said, "I did not become Speaker of the House to dismantle the programs that I've fought for all my life or the philosophy I believe in. I'm not going to allow people to go to bed hungry for an austerity program." Carter was asked at a news conference three days later if he thought the New Foundation moniker would stick. "I doubt it," he responded. He was right. For the president also, 1979 was the year that everything started going wrong.

IT WAS A COMPLEX TIME IN FOREIGN AFFAIRS. IN MID-DECEMBER, CARTER made a sudden and unexpected announcement that the United States was establishing full diplomatic relations with the Communist government in Beijing, breaking diplomatic ties with the anti-Communist one in Taipei, Taiwan. That recognized, he said, "a simple reality": Beijing was "the sole legal government of China." A group of fifteen conservative lawmakers sued the president for unconstitutionally altering the terms of a treaty with Taiwan. Barry Goldwater called it "one of the worst power grabs in history." Ronald Reagan called it another example of "Uncle Sam putting his tail between his legs and creeping away" and cabled a personal apology to Taipei. But it wasn't just conservatives who objected. "In what he clearly takes to be a major coup," the liberals at the *New Republic* editorialized, "Carter has now just about told the Chinese government in Peking that Taiwan is theirs for the taking."

A state visit from the premier of China, Deng Xiaoping, sealed the deal. It proved a tonic for the battered president's soul. "He's small, tough, intelligent, frank, courageous, personable, self-assured, friendly, and it's a pleasure to negotiate with him," Carter wrote in his diary—something he'd never say of the congressional leadership of his own party. The first state dinner honoring a Chinese leader since Franklin Roosevelt's day brought an unexpected lagniappe: the premier invited the president to share any personal desires he had regarding China; Carter recalled a childhood memory—donating five cents a week in Sunday school to send to Christian missionaries to China—and asked if Deng would consider softening his country's policies regarding freedom of religion; Deng, surprised, laughed pleasantly that he would reply the next day—when he agreed to do just that. Carter called the visit "one of the delightful experiences of my presidency." Deng was equally moved. He got to dance with Mickey Mouse at Disney World and wear a cowboy hat while blazing away with a six-shooter at a Texas barbecue. And, after observing the awesome productivity of American industry, he redoubled his determination to liberalize China's command economy.

But warmth with Beijing brought international complexities. The president hoped to head into the election year with a foreign policy trifecta, capping off his successes with Panama and at Camp David by winning Senate approval for a new Strategic Arms Limitation Treaty. The first such treaty, known as SALT, had been ratified in 1972. Richard Nixon said it heralded "a new era of international relations," and Henry Kissinger called it "one of the greatest diplomatic coups of all time." The self-congratulation was warranted. The treaty established, for the first time, specific ceilings on strategic nuclear weapons, what both sides agreed was nuclear "parity." This made the world a much safer place, because neither believed itself to have the greater ability to survive a nuclear war—and thus had no reason to start one.

Achieving what JFK called in his inaugural address "that uncertain balance of terror that stays the hand of mankind's final war"—known colloquially as "mutually assured destruction"—had taken years of meticulous trust-building. Agreement on verifying compliance had been equally challenging. It was, however, only a five-year deal. In November of 1974 Gerald Ford and Leonid Brezhnev agreed on a framework for an eventual SALT II. It was to include even more aggressive ceilings, including on non-missile "intercontinental delivery vehicles"—airplanes—and limits on the number of "multiple independent targeted reentry vehicles"—warheads—

each missile could carry. In America, this stirred fervent ideological debate. On the right, critics claimed that the Soviets' bulkier missiles, which each carried ten MIRVs, gave them an advantage over the U.S.'s smaller missiles, which only carried three. Defense experts to their left said the deficiency was mitigated by the technical sophistication of America's intercontinental ballistic missiles, and also by a class of short-range, small, mobile, and highly accurate American weapons known as cruise missiles.

President Carter's State Department continued Ford's negotiations. Then, late in 1977, the Soviets deployed their own cruise missile, the SS-20, capable of hitting any target in Europe. Meanwhile, conservatives flayed Carter's negotiators for not seeking to limit a Soviet aircraft known as the Tu-22, or Backfire, bomber, which they argued could be outfitted with nuclear weapons to reach the American mainland. They also bemoaned negotiating with a nation sponsoring insurgencies in Ethiopia, Angola, and Zaire. Critics on both the left and the right criticized Carter's negotiators for not bring up the Kremlin's trial of human rights activists Natan Sharansky and Aleksandr Ginzburg, ridiculously accused of being "spies." Senators on both sides saw the Soviets' desire for an arms deal as leverage to improve such Soviet behavior—a doctrine known as "linkage." The controversy grew so intense that by summer 1978 Carter even considered changing SALT II from a treaty to a mere "agreement," which would need only half of the Senate's votes instead of two-thirds. He decided against it. Popular opinion was on his side: 69 percent of Americans favored détente in the abstract; 72 percent wanted a new SALT treaty; and a strong majority rejected linkage as a predicate for a deal.

Conservatives worked to pulverize this consensus. A new group, the Coalition for Peace Through Strength—whose headquarters in rural Virginia appeared to consist mostly of a giant printing plant—began pumping out propaganda. They sponsored a speakers bureau of retired generals, and booked a melodramatic documentary ("They are spending three times as much of their gross national product on the military as the United States. . . .") on two hundred local television outlets. The American Conservative Union's *Soviet Might/American Myth: U.S. in Retreat* kept showing on TV, importuning viewers four times in half an hour with pleas to call a toll-free number to contribute money to show it even more. It eventually aired on more than 370 stations. "The pro-SALT lobby got a later start than the treaty opponents," NBC News reported. They also had only a quarter of the right's budget.

Scoop Jackson loosed his neocon army of renegade leakers. Eugene Rostow of the Committee on the Present Danger delivered a major address, excerpted in the *Washington Star* under the title "Slipping Toward Impotence Across the Globe," likening SALT II to the Washington Naval

Treaty of 1922, which limited the number of warships America could build, and thus "led straight to Pearl Harbor." The present-day version, he said, would back a future president "into a corner where he would have to choose between the surrender of vital national interests and nuclear holocaust."

Ronald Reagan devoted six straight radio commentaries to summarizing Rostow's arguments. In another, he advanced a conspiracy theory that the Soviets' enthusiasm for SALT II was a ruse to distract the United States while they built up parts of their arsenal not covered in the negotiations—so that "by 1985 they could exert their will whenever they wanted." (He acknowledged that there was no visible evidence this was taking place. But that was the point: "It's always quiet when you are feeding the alligator—when you throw him an arm or leg every now and then—when you drop Angola or Somalia over the side. . . . Will places like Iran or Norway be fed to the alligator when the time comes?")

The elections stalled SALT's progress. Noted the *Economist*, "as the dust settled one conclusion seemed even clearer: in the area of foreign policy, the United States Senate has moved significantly to the right." Senators who had taken risky votes for the Panama Canal treaties weren't likely take a similar risk for their president again. Those "THIS INFORMATION IS YOUR KEY TO SURVIVAL" pamphlets landing on front porches were, in part, a response to this political reality: they signaled to conservatives that the president took seriously Team B's accusation about lagging civil defense preparedness. Though Reagan was unconvinced: "Whether the administration's newfound concern for civil defense represents an awakening or just a bit of Rafshoonery," he columnized, "remains to be seen."

CARTER ANNOUNCED HE WOULD MEET BREZHNEV TO SIGN SALT II SOMEtime in the middle of 1979. But China normalization complicated the matter. China and Russia, once revolutionary comrades in arms, were now bitterest of rivals—and Carter had just taken a side in the rivalry. He had precious little room for maneuver. Events soon provided him less.

On January 7, Vietnam, backed by the Soviet Union, invaded Cambodia, which was backed by China, overthrowing Cambodia's Khmer Rouge government within weeks. Deng, who needed to show strength to his comrades to shore up his new regime's risky course of economic liberalization, bucked up by America's show of confidence in him, prepared to invade Vietnam. Carter's embrace of Deng might end up an unforgivable blunder—or possibly a brilliant coup, forcing Russia's hand to complete SALT before the international situation became too chaotic. Meanwhile Cyrus Vance was shuttling between Israel and Egypt, trying to formalize the Camp David Accords into a peace treaty. This had been proving hopeless even before Israel reinvaded southern Lebanon on January 19, pushing past United Nations peacekeeping forces put in place to prevent them from doing exactly that.

The day after his State of the Union Address, President Carter met with a bipartisan delegation of senators recently returned from meeting with Brezhnev in the USSR. Howard Baker, who led it, made clear that, unlike on the Panama Canal, he was no longer open to allying with the president. He pressed, in fact, a milder version of Ronald Reagan's argument: that the Soviets were using the talks to buy time to secure strategic advantage. He said his vote would be contingent on Russian concessions on Backfire bombers and cruise missiles. At the same meeting, liberal senators said *their* votes were contingent on Soviet improvements in human rights. Carter replied that if SALT was rejected in the Senate, America would be branded a pariah state.

Then, on February 4, at their annual retreat at the Tidewater Inn on the Eastern Shore of Maryland, Republicans voted almost unanimously for a resolution that argued, in a *New York Times* paraphrase, that the "Republican Party should abandon its traditional bipartisanship in foreign policy." The next day, the Senate Foreign Relations Committee's Democratic leadership opened hearings on a bill slapping back at President Carter for abandoning Taiwan. Four weeks later, the Republican National Committee passed a resolution that claimed "an eerie parallel" between the policies of Jimmy Carter and those of Neville Chamberlain in the 1930s: both hoped, "based on an obstinate denial of unpleasant facts," that "a dictator's good behavior will compensate for its own inadequacy."

Senators in both parties were questioning a president's traditional prerogatives to decide foreign policy, and Carter's political hand was weakening day by day—not just because of events overseas. Power, on Capitol Hill, is fungible: anything that leads to questions about an actor's ability to command events in any realm weakens his ability to command in others. And just then, it became all too easy to perceive the president as lacking command. The capital city was about to be overrun by militant farmers. If the president couldn't control the streets of Washington, D.C., what *could* he control?

MORE THAN ANY OTHER ECONOMIC SECTOR, AGRICULTURE DEPENDS ON forces beyond the individual producer's control: the weather, of course; but also geopolitics, monetary policy, international trade—even changing tastes in food. This is the reason why, starting with the New Deal, the federal government established agricultural price supports: so farmers could have the confidence to put crops in the ground every spring in the first place. The system relied on a concept known as "parity," which measured the degree of federal price intervention for each commodity. "One hundred percent parity" signified that a crop's price provided the same purchasing power that it did around the year 1910. The level of support was determined by Congress. Corn and wheat, currently, were at 54 percent parity, soybeans at 70 percent, milk at 81 percent, and cattle at 88 percent.

Farmers demanded more. They had been particularly hard hit by recent economic transformations—especially small family farmers, the sort most likely to think of themselves as no mere "economic sector" but as America's spiritual backbone, just like Thomas Jefferson said: "Those who labor in the earth are the chosen people of God, if he ever had a chosen people. . . . They are the most vigorous, the most independent, the most virtuous, and they are tied to their country and wedded to its liberty and interests by the most lasting bands."

In 1977, a group of them gathered at a restaurant in Campo, Colorado, and decided to agitate around a radical demand: 100 percent parity for *all* crops. They chose a name that announced that they meant business: the American Agricultural Movement, which evoked the American Indian Movement, whose occupation of Wounded Knee, South Dakota, four years earlier had descended into fatal gun battles between protesters and federal law enforcement.

Their first idea, a harvest strike, went nowhere. So in January 1978, three thousand farmers decided to clog the nation's highways, pointing their tractors—maximum speed fifteen miles per hour—toward Washington, D.C. They called it the "Tractorcade," and it proved quite successful. Agriculture Secretary Robert Bergland met them en route to hear their grievances. In Washington, congressmen poured out of their offices to meet them. A third of the protesting farmers stayed through spring to lobby, winning a moratorium on Farmer Home Administration foreclosures, significant reforms in the farm loan program, and an Emergency Farm Assistance Act increasing price supports by an average of 11 percentage points. "We thought we owned the damned town," one leader said. Which was the start of more trouble.

Moderates, satisfied with the half loaf, peeled off. That left a hard core of militants—who decided that the Emergency Farm Assistance Act, by falling short of their 100 percent demand, had been designed to buy their silence. Over the next year, they staged rallies across farm country. These could be frightening. Tractors caravanned through rural downtown business districts during peak shopping hours as burly janissaries combed the sidewalks, ostensibly to recruit participants but also to intimate violence toward those who got in their way. Plans began for a second Tractorcade. It kicked off on January 18, 1979, in states from Texas to Kansas to

Colorado to Alabama—during a record cold snap. "Never saw sunshine in those 17 days," a farmer from Burton, Kansas, remembered.

They affixed signs to their grilles for oncoming motorists:

"FARMERS AREN'T DOLLY PARTON THEY'RE FLAT BUSTED."
"I PUT MY HEART INTO FARMING AND LOST MY HEMORRHOIDS."
"ANOTHER FAMILY FARM IS LOST EVERY 63 SECONDS."

One massive cotton-picker from Arkansas's sign read "POLITI-CIAN EATER." A truck towed a wood chipper labeled "POLITICIAN GRINDER." The processions sometimes stretched for twenty-five miles. TV news eagerly followed the drama. ("How are you going to get your tractors back from Washington?" a reporter asked a farmer, who responded, "We may leave 'em up there with them! Most of these tractors are already hocked to the gills with the government. They keep on feeding us loan programs—but you can't borrow yourself out of debt.")

Things grew tense. The Missouri Highway Patrol banned them from I-70; "farmers indicated they might not cooperate," the AP reported. They converged on county fairgrounds, public parks, and parking lots just beyond Washington—where police suited up in riot gear.

The previous year, farmers honored a request to park their vehicles at a local stadium. This time, they barged into the center of town, tying up traffic and blocking Pennsylvania Avenue; the president could not get to an important meeting. One group threw thresher parts as big as motor-cycles over the White House fence. Others started throwing stones and slashing tires. Police motorcycles were crushed beneath their massive machines—by accident, organizers claimed. Cops began breaking the windows of tractors whose drivers refused to budge, then attacked them with billy clubs. A protester from Mississippi suffered permanent eye damage.

And Congress ignored them.

Farmers, the insurgents discovered, no longer enjoyed exalted moral standing as virtuous yeomen; they were just one more "special interest group"—the fashionable Washington term of art for clamoring citizens driving inflation and making the nation ungovernable by unappeasable demands for ever-growing pieces of an ever-shrinking pie. The Secretary of Agriculture went on *Good Morning America* and said the Tractorcaders were "driven by just old-fashioned greed." Alfred Kahn mocked them: If they were so broke, how could they afford to waste all that fuel? The po-lice invited them to camp overnight on the National Mall—then double-crossed them, barricading the perimeter with cop cars and garbage trucks. Bergland announced, "President Carter has no plans to comment on their demands for more government help." Flyers depicting crosshairs over the secretary's visage were tacked to lampposts; he began traveling with three bodyguards.

It began to rain. Then snow. By Presidents' Day, a record two feet had accumulated. Stranded on the Mall, farmers began breaking up park benches for firewood. A tractor crashed through the ice of the reflecting pool. AAM leaders consulted lawyers for a way out of their predicament. A Texan told a reporter, "If that doesn't work, we'll have to come up with something more dramatic."

Farmers and cops reached a compromise: two hundred tractors would be let through the barriers to parade through the streets. But the operator of one twelve-ton behemoth broke loose from the pack and lumbered toward USDA headquarters, stopping only inches from staving through the ornate front doors. The "SAVE U.S. FARMS, EAT AN ECONOMIST" sign on his rig made for a dramatic picture in the next morning's papers.

ALFRED KAHN ANNOUNCED THAT EVEN THOUGH BUSINESS AND LABOR HAD met their voluntary guidelines a week ahead of schedule, the consumer price index had not budged. With the record cold, home heating oil prices in the Northeast headed into the stratosphere; an eight-month-old child froze to death when the gas company in Queens cut off the heat of a family that hadn't paid its utility bill.

In Nicaragua, an escalating civil war between leftist guerrillas aligned with Cuba, called the Sandinistas, and the ruling strongmen of the Somoza family was coming to a head. On February 8, the administration announced the termination of financial aid and military assistance to the Somoza government, whom America had backed for generations, another unilateral move that drained the trust in their president from senators, who began demanding Carter wrest new SALT concessions from the Soviet Union. Which the Soviets, having watched their nuclear rival China fêted at the White House, were in no mood to give. Everything was connected—on the grand international chessboard, on the streets of Washington, D.C., and in the United States Senate: crisis upon crisis upon crisis. It began to look impossible for the president to manage it all.

On top of all that came Iran.

A *DOONESBURY* CARTOON RAN IN THE MIDDLE OF FEBRUARY, ONE OF A weeklong series mocking Jimmy Carter's already-discarded "New Foundation" metaphor. In the strip, speech balloons emanated from the White House:

"Mr. President? Sorry to disturb you, sir. . . . it's the workmen, sir. The ones installing the new foundation."

"Yes?"

"Well, they were downstairs picking through the rubble of three generations of American foreign policy."

"And?"

"They found Iran, sir. . . . It looks bad, sir. You'd better come quickly."

You might date that inglorious saga to 1872, when the British banker Baron de Reuter, who was Jewish, agreed to pay Nasir al-Din, the shah of Iran, £14,000 annually and a 25 percent cut of the profits for the right to control most of Persia's roads, telegraphs, mills, factories, public works, and natural resources for fifty years. The baron also promised to build a railroad. The Islamic clergy heard a rumor a Jew was planning to lay down tracks through a Shi'ite shrine, leading a coalition of outrage that saw the deal canceled within a year. No railroads were built in Iran for another four decades. But Reuter emerged with a charter to operate the Imperial Bank of Persia. That set the pattern for the next eighty years: potentates sold off Iran's wealth to foreigners, leaving their country a feudal backwater; a tenuous coalition of clerics, educated liberal-minded urbanites, and members of the traditional petty merchant class known as *bazaaris* futilely resisted.

In the 1930s, the potentate was Reza Shah Pahlavi and the foreigner was Adolf Hitler, whose governing style Pahlavi admired. During World War II, Great Britain and the Soviet Union invaded to keep Iran's oil fields from the Nazis. The shah died in African exile. His twenty-one-year-old son Reza was installed as a figurehead ruler. President Truman persuaded the Soviet Union to remove its troops from northern Iran, and the young shah took over with massive American backing, agreeing to put his nation's oil resources under the control of the Anglo-Persian Oil Company, with Britain receiving almost two-thirds of the revenue. Iran—with its two-thousand-mile border with the Soviet Union—became a lynchpin of Cold War strategy.

In 1951, a Paris-educated legal scholar named Mohammad Mosaddegh took power and nationalized Iran's oil—a "a defiant challenge that sprang out of a hatred and envy almost incomprehensible in the west," *Time* said, "one of the worst calamities to the anti-Communist world since the Red conquest of China." (Mosaddegh was neither a Communist nor allied to the Soviet Union.) The United States and Great Britain responded by refusing to buy Iranian oil. Britain drew up plans to invade. A new American president objected, for Dwight Eisenhower wanted to test out a more economical idea. CIA agents recruited friendly elements within the Iranian Army, the BBC's Persian Service spread propaganda of a chaotic popular uprising, and toughs were hired to agitate in the streets to simulate it. The entire operation had been seeded by only five Americans, aided by six Iranian allies, and had cost only $1 million. It ended with Shah Reza Pahlavi restored to the throne as an American client.

In 1973, the Italian journalist Oriana Fallaci traveled to Tehran to interview him. She asked what he thought of democracy. He replied angrily: "You'll see, in a few years, where your wonderful democracy leads. . . . To get things done you need power, and to keep power you shouldn't have to ask permission or advice from anybody." She asked how many political prisoners he had jailed. He replied, "If you're speaking of the Communists . . . I don't consider them political prisoners because it's forbidden by law to be a Communist." He spun out bizarre mystical visions, suggesting he was literally immortal. Fallaci asked him about a rumor he was about to take a second wife. He launched into an angry tirade about the entire female sex: "You're schemers, you're evil. All of you."

Then she asked about those who called him a dictator, and he lost all self-control.

"What would you criticize or attack me for? For my foreign policy? For my oil policy? For having distributed land to the peasants? For allowing workers to share in profits up to twenty percent and be able to own stock up to forty-nine percent? For fighting illiteracy and disease? For having brought progress to a country where there was little or worse?"

He had a point. The vicious dictator was also an accomplished modernizer. He called his program the White Revolution. Beginning in 1963, it brought economic growth above 9 percent for ten straight years, and state-of-the-art hospitals, hydroelectric dams, modern communications and transportation networks. Neighbors began looking upon Iran as a model for their own development.

Another of his innovations was cutting into the power of Iran's Shi'ite clergy, the ulama, which maintained itself as a society apart, headquartered in the sacred city of Qom. The shah dismissed clerics as "a stupid and reactionary bunch whose brains have not moved . . . for a thousand years"—they were the Black Reaction to his White Revolution. He made the nation's school system officially secular. Women were granted the vote and equal treatment from the literacy corps sent out into the countryside and encouraged to pursue careers. Islamic faith was eliminated as a prerequisite for office. The shah also took away the clergy's traditional land holdings, as he did with all major feudal landholders.

This brought unintended consequences. Rural folk poured into cities for factory jobs—leading to decrepit shantytowns, undermining the power of the bazaaris. The bureaucracy grew rotten with kleptocrats. There were major intended consequences, too. The shah's secret police, SAVAK, which experts said exerted a greater control over the population

than the KGB did in the Soviet Union, became infamous the world over
for its macabre methods of torture.

The population grew restless—especially, in 1971, after the shah hosted
a staggering celebration to mark the 2,500th anniversary of Cyrus the
Great's Persian Empire. Upon the ruins of the ancient city of Persepolis
sprung up a city of mansion-like tents, dressed by Jackie Kennedy Onassis's White House decorator. Eighteen tons of food were shipped in to
feed a guest list that included sixty monarchs and heads of state (the emperor of Ethiopia brought a seventy-two-person retinue); a procession
starred seventeen hundred soldiers in ancient costume; they paraded past
fifteen thousand newly planted trees. Dom Perignon 1959 and Château
Lafite Rothschild 1945 were quaffed from custom Baccarat crystal goblets.
Maxim's of Paris brought eighty chefs. (The nation's per capita income
was then $250. A case of Château Lafite Rothschild 1945 went for $500.)
As the shah toasted to a world "free from fear, anxiety, and the constant
threat of annihilation," to the chirping of fifty thousand imported song-
birds, students approaching the site to protest were savagely beaten. Some
of the country's worst slums were just out of view. Estimates of the cost
ranged from $100 million to $200 million.

Ayatollah Ruhollah Khomeini protested from afar. In 1964, he had
been exiled to Iraq after criticizing a treaty granting U.S. military personnel immunity from Iranian law. But his sway over regime critics only
grew. It derived not merely from the ulama but from another, more ironic
source. Tens of thousands of the kingdom's best and brightest had been
sent abroad to train in foreign universities. At home, the number of students doubled. College graduates multiplied faster than even the most
dynamic economy could provide for—and unemployed, educated young
men had always made for history's most fertile recruiting soil for revolutionaries, most especially in authoritarian countries where outlets for
legitimate political expression were few.

The dynamic intensifies when a traditional society sends its children
abroad. In cities like Paris and New York, Ann Arbor and Austin, the
lonely, alienated children of a secularizing middle class found in the religious traditions of their homeland a psychic balm. They breathed in
campus radicalism—and devoured a remarkable body of Islamist thought
from back home that synthesized it with Islam. The brilliant sociologist
Ali Shariati, for example, argued that the thought of a seventh-century
Shi'ite patriarch anticipated the teachings of Marx in his arguments about
how a transcendently just society could be built upon the foundation of
sharia, or Koranic law. They returned home as dedicated theocratic revolutionaries.

But the leader they revered the most was Khomeini, who believed all that was required to administer an entire society was contained within the four corners of the classic Shi'ite texts. He said he would gladly have his own children executed if they acted counter to the laws of God. He was the scion of a long line of mullahs, whose father was executed for protesting abuses from the local nobility when Khomeini was an infant and whose mother died of a cholera epidemic when he was a teenager. The orphan attained the highest rank in Islamic jurisprudence at the unusually young age of thirty-four. He was also a devoted mystic, a student of Sufism, the Christian cognate of which might be Pentecostalism—faith inflamed by a passion for a direct, almost narcotic experience of the divine. And, like the new breed of American fundamentalist in the Jerry Falwell mold, he rejected the older tradition of theological quietism to insist that religious leaders must involve themselves directly in politics—even though, under the shah, that could lead to prison or exile. Khomeini's placid courage in the face of that threat was mesmerizing.

In 1962, when the shah's cabinet passed a law allowing non-Muslims to hold office and women to vote, Khomeini decried it as "the first step toward the abolition of Islam." The following year, when the shah held a phony referendum on his reforms, Khomeini persuaded mullahs to boycott. The shah responded by raiding a leading seminary in Qom, injuring dozens, killing one. Defiant, Khomeini proclaimed, "I will never bow my head to your tyranny." His awed students greeted his arrest with riots. The shah pondered whether to execute him—until one of Khomeini's quietist rivals reached out to save his life by awarding him the title of "grand ayatollah." The Iranian constitution forbade executing anyone with that exalted title—and even the shah dared not violate that.

Soon Khomeini earned another honorific: *marja-e taqlid*, one of about a half dozen "models of emulation" to Shia all over the world—and then, unprecedentedly, "the imam," a description Shi'ites had previously reserved for the twelve successors of the Prophet Muhammed. The fatwa he issued in response to the shah's exorbitant celebration of the pagan King Cyrus in 1971 galvanized the gathering resistance. The next year the president made Iran the centerpiece of the "Nixon Doctrine": in a nutshell, the proposition that, since the Vietnam War had devastated Americans' appetite for sending troops overseas to contain Communism, the U.S. would send weapons and encouragement to allies abroad like the shah to do it for us. Nixon and Kissinger visited Tehran in May of 1972, following devastating military defeats in Vietnam. They asked the shah to be America's "protector" in the Persian Gulf. The shah asked for access to the most advanced American weaponry in return. His wish was granted—and he received even greater access after Iran refused the Soviets permission to use its airspace to resupply Egypt during the 1973 Yom Kippur War, then refused to join the OPEC oil boycott. The shah began spending money on U.S. armaments like a kid in a candy store.

One effect was to make him seem even more the American puppet to his simmering critics. Ayatollah Khomeini, sitting serenely on his prayer rug in Iraq, began issuing taped denunciations of the shah that Iranians around the world inhaled—responding, Oriana Fallaci wrote, "as if they had taken a kilo of drugs."

All the while, the shah refused timid American requests to liberalize his regime. As he gloated to Fallaci: "To reach the rest of the world, oil doesn't go through the Mediterranean, it goes through the Persian Gulf. . . . If the Soviet Union were to attack us . . . we'd probably be overcome, and then the noncommunist countries would hardly sit there with their hands folded. And, they'd intervene. And it would be the Third World War. Obviously, the noncommunist world couldn't accept the disappearance of Iran, because it knows that to lose Iran would mean to lose everything. Have I made myself clear?"

He had. In 1975 Defense Secretary James Schlesinger worried to President Ford whether "our policy of supporting an apparently open-ended Iranian military buildup will continue to serve our long-term interests." President Ford tuned out that advice. In 1976, Jimmy Carter complained in their second debate that Iran got shipments of new fighter jets before the Air Force did, and warships "much more highly sophisticated than the Spruance Class destroyers that are presently being delivered to our own Navy." Ford lectured him like one would a naïve child: "I believe that Governor Carter doesn't realize the need and necessity for arms sales to Iran. . . . The Soviet Union and the Communist-dominated government of Iraq are neighbors of Iran, and Iran is an ally with the United States. It's my *strong* feeling that we ought to sell arms to Iran for our own national security and as an ally, a *strong* ally, of the United States."

Khomeini began instructing his young devotees to mobilize the politically untouchable network of 180,000 mullahs in 9,000 mosques to organize to overthrow the shah. Two liberal Democratic senators, John Culver of Iowa and Thomas Eagleton of Missouri, traveled to Iran shortly after the 1976 election and reported that "massive arms sales may not contribute to regional stability and continuing flow of oil," and warned that "relations with Iran are far too dependent on personalized relationships with the shah," whose government was "antithetical to American values." But theirs was the minority report of a delegation whose other eight senators recommended maintaining the status quo, claiming the shah "appears receptive to international concerns" about human rights. Soon afterward, Nelson Rockefeller stood next to the shah to dedicate a museum of modern art, remarking, "Never have a people gone through such a complete metamorphosis so rapidly, so smoothly, and with so little dislocation." Jimmy Carter toasted the shah the following New Year's for building "an island of stability in one of the more troubled areas of the world."

THE INSURGENTS ORGANIZED UNDERGROUND, USING THE CELL STRUCTURE they had learned from the Communists with whom they were jailed. Iraq expelled the Ayatollah, who removed himself to a small country town outside Paris called Neauphle-le-Château; his red-shingled plaster house became a pilgrimage site. In August 1978, the CIA reported that "Iran is not even in a revolutionary or even a pre-revolutionary situation." That was the month that a movie theater fire in the oil city of Abadan killed more than four hundred people. The shah said it had been started by militants. Militants said it had been started by the shah. Either way, revolutionary fervor spread. Then came the massacre of September 8, 1978, in Tehran's Jaleh Square, the massacre the shah allegedly supervised from a helicopter. That instigated a devastating strike by oil workers. Zbigniew Brzezinski wanted Carter to advise the shah to impose martial law. Cyrus Vance counseled democratic reforms. Carter took Brzezinski's advice, calling the shah with words of encouragement. Pahlavi put twelve cities under army control.

New York magazine published a shocking exposé of SAVAK's activity in the United States. They would arrest a student in Iran for a minor infraction, ruin his life, then tell him he could get back on his feet by working in the U.S. as a spy, one of the many students reporting directly to the head of SAVAK's American operations at Iran's embassy in Washington — where hash-filled orgies were held for the benefit of American senators, to blackmail them. The article also claimed that SAVAK kept American professors on their payroll to spy on Iranian students. And that Iran had delivered $1 million to Richard Nixon's reelection committee in a diplomatic pouch. ("Now we own Nixon," a source said he heard the ambassador brag.) And that Iran had begun building a massive operations center to house and transmit records "on Iranians in America and Iranian and American opponents of the shah," which was abandoned after the media started wondering why a massive construction project was sprouting up at an isolated 420-acre former dairy farm in Upstate New York.

Such revelations did nothing to dampen the enthusiasm of the foreign policy establishment. On November 3, 1978, National Security Advisor Brzezinski called the shah personally to convey the message that the U.S. would "back him to the hilt . . . without any reservation whatsoever, completely and fully in the present crisis." The next day, the shah's security forces massacred students on the campus of Tehran University. According to a book later published by the National Security Council's top Iran expert, for a foreign policy official to express doubts about the shah was "heresy that could destroy a career." He concluded, "It is not an exaggeration to say that America approached Iran from a position of almost unrelieved ignorance."

Riots and strikes once more brought oil production to a standstill. The shah conveyed to President Carter his intention to abdicate. Carter discouraged him, promising support for whatever action he took—"including setting up a military government." America's ambassador to Tehran, William Sullivan, tried to get a memo to the president called "Thinking the Unthinkable" that game-planned scenarios for a post-shah Iran. Brzezinski blocked it.

American intelligence insisted the Soviet Union was behind all the trouble—even as petrified Soviet oil-field technicians joined Westerners on packed airplanes out of the country. Western intellectuals believed the phrase "Islamic revolution" to be an oxymoron: revolution was the business of secular modernizers, not clerics seeking a return to the Middle Ages. Iran's Communist Party believed the same thing. They treated their religious coalition partners as useful idiots, easily pushed aside once the work of overthrowing the monarchy was complete. Actually, it was the other way around.

The *New York Times* got it wrong, too. One of six articles about Iran in the November 6 edition reported that the National Front, the rebels' umbrella organization, had "no identifiable leader." This was at the same time that Khomeini, in Paris, directed two members of his retinue, Mehdi Bazargan and Ebrahim Yazdi, to begin choosing personnel for a cabinet.

The shah began behaving erratically. On November 22, Carter sent Treasury Secretary Michael Blumenthal to meet with him in Kuwait. America's priority was plain to see from the account he cabled back. The shah had insisted that "progress is being made toward restoring full oil production." Blumenthal responded that "this was very encouraging. . . . The USG is very concerned about world production and price developments." The shah, plainly fearing that Blumenthal had been sent to lower the boom, launched into a desperate soliloquy. He described Jimmy Carter–style efforts to fight inflation by cutting spending (even defense spending, "which I am so fond of"). He promised continued efforts to hold down prices at the next OPEC meeting. He mentioned "that clergyman in Paris," who "has such a hold on people for reasons we don't understand."

He pulled the red ace from his sleeve, the card that had set presidents since Eisenhower to do his bidding: he reminded Blumenthal of what Nikita Khrushchev had once supposedly told Walter Lippmann, that "Iran will be like a rotten apple falling into Russia's lap."

It wasn't working. So he pulled out his other trump—warning that OPEC's Arab members might turn off the oil spigot, bringing annual world production from 60 billion to 25 billion barrels. "The world surely cannot survive on a production level of 25 billion barrels a year."

He sounded terribly desperate. Perhaps he had in mind the fate of a previous dictator favored by the U.S., Ngo Dinh Diem of Vietnam, who in 1963 had ended up with a bullet through his head, the result of a coup led by generals that America supported. A delegation of conservative Republican congressmen was ushered into the meeting room. Perhaps fearing in advance that he might not win the sympathy of his first audience, he had held back this potentially more receptive one in reserve. He began unspooling stories about the cunning Communists, whom he insisted just *posed* as mullahs in order to trick "eleven- and twelve-year-old pupils to demonstrate" against him. He complained about Muslim fanatics who "love to destroy" and were "exploited by Communists and the KGB." The conservative congressmen were no more impressed than the treasury secretary.

Senator Richard Lugar asked about the threats to stability posed by the upcoming period of Islamic mourning that would begin in December. He asked why so many Iranians who had prospered so much from the White Revolution were nevertheless following Ayatollah Khomeini.

The shah tried one more time. Didn't they understand that 70 percent of Europe's oil supply and 90 percent of Japan's passed through Iran's Strait of Hormuz? Didn't they understand that unless America did something, "the Soviets will succeed in subverting Iran through the underground"?

The State Department's note-taker recorded "a long period of silence during which the shah stared directly at the floor." His kingdom was slipping away.

THE END CAME IN THE MIDDLE OF JANUARY. THE IRANIAN PARLIAMENT overwhelmingly voted to declare a moderate member of the revolutionary coalition, Shapour Bakhtiar, the country's legitimate ruler. The shah and his empress boarded a plane—"on a vacation," said the statement read over the radio, "because I am tired."

A hushed awe fell over the streets—quiet for the first time in months. Then, delirium. Candy rained from windows. Carnations were stuffed into soldiers' gun barrels. An equestrian statue of the shah's father was toppled. The crowd parted for a woman whose four children had died fighting the regime. "Salute to the mother of martyrs!" a regiment of black-veiled mothers chanted. *Bazaaris* cut the shah's face out of banknotes. They replaced them with images of Khomeini.

One of the chants ran, "After the shah, it's America's turn."

When Khomeini was informed of the shah's final flight, he simply proclaimed, "God is great." He walked across the street and told the assembled press this was only a "preface to our victory": that would come with the establishment of an Islamic republic he himself would "supervise and direct." He then issued "Revolutionary Order No. 1" ordering members of the parliament to flee the country, calling for the greatest national demonstration in Iranian history for Friday, January 19, the Shia holiday of Arba'een.

Experts dismissed this as bluster. Prime Minister Bakhtiar predicted Khomeini would retreat to Qom, several dusty hours by car from the capital, where Khomeini would take up "a Gandhi-like role"; President Carter, who hoped to keep Khomeini out of Iran altogether, wrote in his diary that he seemed "receptive to friendship with the U.S." Khomeini's spokesman, a Baylor University–educated chemistry PhD, insisted to reporters that what Khomeini meant by "Islamic republic" was "a republic as you have in France." He might have believed it. Both the revolution's liberal and Marxist factions expected that superstitious clerics seeking return to the seventh century would soon be swept away by the tides of history.

Diplomatic sources in Washington said the shah's destination was Walter Annenberg's estate in Palm Springs, near where Gerald Ford lived. A newspaper there said Secret Service agents and State Department officials had been spotted. Zbigniew Brzezinski still hoped to restore the shah via a military coup. CIA director Stansfield Turner thought it would be so easy it wouldn't even require a military: "First of all, we need a good PR man," he told an associate, "someone who could get the shah good coverage in the media. It's really an image problem out there." On the ground in Iran, however, America's ambassador, William Sullivan, whom President Carter distrusted and despised, argued desperately that this ship had sailed, that preparations had to be made to deal with the Ayatollah, the nation's only truly popular voice. That conclusion was denied—until it was impossible to deny.

Arba'een arrived—and a river of people eight miles long, a million or more, poured down Reza Shah Boulevard, carrying pictures of the Ayatollah and screaming "death to the shah." At the march's terminus, the ultramodern triumphal arch the shah had erected to commemorate the 2,500th anniversary of the nation he no longer ruled, marshals distributed handbills announcing the illegitimacy of the Bakhtiar government—which President Carter promptly recognized. With America's blessing, Bakhtiar closed Tehran's airport and guarded it with tanks to block the Ayatollah's return. But Carter appeared to be wavering. Early in January, he had sent a carrier group to the Persian Gulf—then pulled it back. ("The first example of no-boat gunboat diplomacy," William Safire wrote.) "We have no intention, neither ability nor desire, to interfere in the internal affairs of Iran," he told the press the day after the shah's retreat. "We've tried this once in Vietnam. It didn't work well, as you know." Simultaneously, he *did* interfere in the internal affairs of Iran, shipping two hundred thousand barrels of fuel to the army, maneuvering to keep the shah out of the United States and Khomeini out of Iran.

Khomeini returned on February 1, on a chartered 747 flight during which he slept on the floor like a humble pilgrim. His final statement upon leaving Paris was "I will be trying to set up a society in which there will be no violence." He was borne to a cemetery to honor the martyrs of the revolution, to the accompaniment of the screams of millions of roadside celebrants. He announced, "I beg to God to cut the hands off all those foreign advisors and helpers in Iran." President Carter wrote in his diary, "Khomeini returned to Iran with a minimum of violence. The military is keeping its powder dry."

Actually, all hell was breaking loose. Policemen, bureaucrats, elders, officials, and anyone else considered tainted were hunted down for assassination. In Tabriz, Iran's ancient capital, the local prison was "liberated," the main military base attacked, its armory looted. The Ayatollah established a command post in a former Tehran elementary school; on its roof, a firing squad methodically executed SAVAK agents, military officers, and those associated with Americans. In the streets, former underground cells became de facto kangaroo courts, and began piling up corpses, too—sometimes for offenses like playing chess.

In New York, United Nations Ambassador Andrew Young predicted that "Khomeini will be some kind of a saint when we finally get over the panic of what is happening there." Two days later, on February 10, mutinying military personnel joined by left-wing and fundamentalist militias easily defeated the Iranian Army's most elite unit, the Imperial Guard. They then overran all the military bases still loyal to the Bakhtiar government. The next day, the army surrendered. The revolutionaries' first move was to shut down oil exports. Energy Secretary Schlesinger said this was likely to lead to a greater crisis than the Arab oil embargo of 1973–74.

ON FEBRUARY 14, MEN IN IRANIAN AIR FORCE UNIFORMS BREACHED THE walls of the American consulate in Tabriz. They took as prisoners its only remaining American employee, and eight other terrified Westerners hiding out in the compound, who soon found themselves confined with other prisoners in a crowded room in a former government office building, waiting interminably, as if it were some Department of Motor Vehicles facility in Duluth. Only in this government building, after a name was called, a body was soon seen dangling from a tree in the yard. Miraculously, the American official was able to negotiate for his party's safe retreat.

Some four hundred miles away in Tehran, around a hundred Marxist street fighters clambered over the gates of the U.S. embassy. In Washington, audio from an open telephone line was fed through loudspeakers in the State Department's seventh-floor crisis room. They heard machine gun fire. "My God," someone uttered, "the embassy's under siege."

Nineteen Marine guards attempted to fight back, armed only with tear gas and bird shot. Two hours later, they were led out of the building with hoods over their heads, kicked and punched by an angry mob. Embassy personnel were holed up in the building's most secure room, the communications center on the second floor of the complex's main building, the chancery, frantically destroying classified documents and coding equipment. Then, the room was breached, the entire American staff of more than a hundred was marched out at gunpoint, hands in the air, to the cheers of the assembled crowd. Ambassador Sullivan managed to place a call through the only remaining working channel of communication—a hotline to the shah's former palace. An Islamic revolutionary picked up. To rescue the Americans the Khomeiniites dispatched a ragtag militia, which then took up permanent positions at the complex gates to guard it on America's behalf. The Ayatollah sent a personal note of apology to Ambassador Sullivan.

The next morning, in the *Arizona Republic*, the banner headline was "Ayatollah Followers Rescue U.S. Envoy." In the Lansing, Michigan, *State Journal*, it was "U.S. Citizens Told: Flee Iran." A State Department spokesman said he did not know whether any of the attacking forces were still in the compound, or the precise whereabouts of all embassy personnel. The State Department announced a goal of evacuating five thousand of the seven thousand Americans still left in country—although Army secretary Harold Brown said that when it came to *securing* that evacuation, "this is not the type of situation in which U.S. military force is likely to be productive." ABC News reported that there was very little that could be done to protect the Americans, "except to hope for the cooperation of the Iranian government."

IF THE HUMILIATION IN IRAN ON VALENTINE'S DAY HAD OCCURRED IN ISO-lation, perhaps the political fallout for the president would have been containable. Except that this was 1979, when everything was going wrong.

At almost exactly the same time marauders were hurling themselves over the gates in Tehran, in Kabul, Afghanistan, four men in official-looking uniforms stopped an armored limousine carrying American ambassador Adolph "Spike" Dubs, gestured for the driver to open his bulletproof window, then a stuck pistol in his face. They kidnaped the ambassador in plain sight of a policeman, who did nothing, and confined him in a room in the nearby Kabul Hotel. American officials urged the Afghanistan government not to endanger Dubs's life with a rescue attempt. They sent the same message to the Soviet Union, with whom Afghanistan's government was aligned. A shot was heard from inside the room. Afghan police stormed inside, blazing gunfire. Ambassador Dubs died from a bullet in the head at point-blank range. And no one ever really figured out why. Frank Reynolds opened ABC's news broadcast with "Good evening, this has been a dark, indeed a devastating day for the United States." The next morning, the *Indianapolis Star*'s headline—right below the one reading "U.S. Planning Mass Iran Airlift"—was "Carter, Vance 'Mad' About Dubs Slaying."

Mad: that'll show them.

Vance and Carter had been ill-disposed to manage the twin crises. They were en route a state visit to Mexico, which Carter had decided not to cancel. There, Carter suffered his third Valentine's Day humiliation.

President José López Portillo y Pacheco was enraged that energy secretary James Schlesinger had canceled a deal to buy a large amount of Mexican natural gas. At the welcoming reception, he lifted his glass and leveled barely concealed insults: "Among permanent, not casual neighbors, surprise moves and sudden deceit and abuse are poisonous fruits that sooner or later have an adverse effect." Then he mentioned his country's newly discovered petroleum reserves, in which his powerful neighbor to the north had shown more than casual interest: "Mexico, because of a non-renewable resource and the financial self-determination it provides, has been given the opportunity of becoming the free, secure, and just nation envisaged by its great leaders in the past." It "suddenly found itself the center of American attention—attention that is a surprising mixture of interest, disdain, and fear, much like the recurring vague fears you inspire in certain areas of our national subconscious."

He concluded with barely diplomatic hints that the United States might soon learn what Mexico knew all too well: what it felt like to fear a powerful neighbor that held your economic fate in its hands. President Carter returned a toast that was even more embarrassing—to President Carter.

"President López Portillo and I have, in the short time together on this visit, found that we have many things in common. . . . We both have beautiful and interesting wives."

(That was odd, ogling a foreign leader's wife.)

"We both run several kilometers a day. As a matter of fact, I told President López Portillo that I first acquired my habit of running here in Mexico City. My first running course was from the Palace of Fine Arts to the Majestic Hotel, where I and my family were staying. In the midst of the Folklorico performance, I discovered I was afflicted with Montezuma's revenge."

The assembled dignitaries grimaced. Mrs. Carter, the UPI reported, "covered her face with her hands in embarrassment." Subsequent negotiations with President López Portillo got nowhere. A big part of how Carter had sold the Panama Canal treaties to the Senate was a promise that they would heighten the respect and esteem of the nations of Latin America for the United States. So much for that.

THE PRESIDENT RETURNED TO NEWS OF A CHINESE INVASION OF CAMBODIA with the Soviet Union's assistance, just the sort of Soviet action the SALT II process was supposed to be discouraging: so much for *that*.

Now two nuclear powers were locked in a regional confrontation—and the Soviets blamed Carter's pro-China attitude for encouraging the Cambodia invasion. They were only half-correct. Deng had indeed informed Carter of his plans. And Carter had tried to dissuade him. He had just been unable to do so.

White House spokesman Jody Powell was pressed about what the president's serial humiliations might mean for senators' support for SALT II. "The SALT treaty has to be voted up or down on its merits," he responded unconvincingly. Conservatives clamored that the "loss of Iran" put American radar and signal monitoring devices on the Soviet border out of reach, rendering it impossible to monitor Soviet compliance. The administration responded that listening posts in Turkey could serve just as well. The former head of the Defense Intelligence Agency, Lieutenant General Daniel Graham, the New Right's premier military voice, called that claim "essentially fraudulent," that Soviet compliance was now unverifiable. The president knew this not to be true: he had accepted an offer from Deng to move such devices to China. But he couldn't tell senators that secret. More impotence.

Then, more impotence after that. A new poll was out from Gallup: 62 percent of Americans believed a recession was "very likely" or "fairly likely" in the next year, only 9 percent "not at all likely." And 46 percent said it would be worse than the one in 1975—the severest since the Great Depression. "Public expectations of an economic downturn are in clear conflict," Gallup explained, "with predictions of the Carter administration." They insisted there would not be any recession at all.

Tom Wicker of the *New York Times* weighed the simultaneous assassination of an American ambassador, the non-defense of the American embassy in Iran, and the alleged Soviet complicity in the outrages in both Iran and Afghanistan, and concluded, "The supposed might and majesty of the United States probably have not been so variously assaulted at one time since the rooftop evacuation of the embassy in Saigon."

Add in Carter's floundering anti-inflation campaign. And his recent anemic, even comical recommendations—*carpool! close gas stations on Sunday!*—for how America could weather diminished oil supplies from Iran. David Broder claimed on the same day as Wicker's column that Washingtonians were "quoting Machiavelli," who taught that the prince must never allow himself to be "rendered despicable by being thought changeable, frivolous, effeminate, timid and irresolute." In some news-papers, the columns from the liberal Wicker and the centrist Broder ran side by side, under twin headlines like "An Image of Weakness" and "It Is Time to Show Some Backbone."

Newsweek reported the chatter in Washington: a Ford foreign policy official said, "We're going down the tubes." A Democratic senator said he was "sick at heart. I couldn't sleep last night." The article was entitled "Feeling Helpless." The next issue's White House report was entitled "Small-Stick Diplomacy." It observed that Carter's political aides were pining for some hostile foreign power to detain some Americans so Carter could order a rescue, like Gerald Ford had when Cambodia nabbed an American merchant ship, the *Mayaguez*, in 1975: even though more people died in the raid than had been saved, Ford had been treated like a hero. "No journalist I know has questioned the wisdom of restraint in the handling of the siege of our embassy in Tehran," Gerald Rafshoon wrote the president. "Yet many of them have cited that event as if it were further evidence of a failure of leadership."

In Washington, they called such convergences *conventional wisdom*: conclusions the press corps considered so self-evident they might as well have been chiseled on tablets.

CHAPTER 21

Superman

REPUBLICANS DREAMING WHITE HOUSE DREAMS RESPONDED TO JIMMY Carter's ordeals as the opportunity of a lifetime.

There were eight of them. Or thirteen. Or fourteen. Or, by the loosest manner of counting, seventeen—an Anderson, a Baker, and a Bush; a Weicker and a Schweiker; a Crane, a Connally, a Kemp; a Ford and a Fernandez; a Stassen and a Richardson; a Reagan, a Simon, a Pressler, a Thompson, and a Haig. Not to mention the two likely Democratic challengers, Kennedy and Brown. These men, and their supporters, used the same words to describe why they deserved the prize: words that described what conventional wisdom said Jimmy Carter lacked. *Backbone. Decisiveness. Strength. Resolve.* And the one that became the political word of the year. In Howard Baker's first campaign circular, it comprised more than a quarter of the nouns. It even became the name of Ronald Reagan's campaign plane: *LeaderShip '80.*

A brochure advocating NATO commander General Alexander Haig promised "stronger and more effective leadership." A Bush campaign piece said, "What are needed today are not labels, but leadership—forceful leadership." John Anderson labeled the Democrats "putative leaders." George Bush flayed Carter for failing "to provide the strong, inspiring leadership that we so badly need"; Jerry Brown, for his "leadership of ruin, leadership of defeat." Ted Kennedy sealed his break with the president by charging America's problems stemmed from "failure of leadership at the very top"—the stuff his late brothers used to emanate, though he didn't have to mention their names, because his hauntingly similar brogue raised the association every time he opened his mouth.

The brand of leadership the public demanded, it seemed, was the opposite of the Jimmy Carter they fell for in 1976, all flannel shirts and plain-spoken decency: voters wanted a *hero*. Talk of heroes had only recently been unfashionable. When *Senior Scholastic* magazine asked its audience of schoolchildren in 1977 who their heroes were, the most common response was Farrah Fawcett-Majors, the jiggly star of *Charlie's Angels*. The fourth most popular answer was "no hero at all." Now, however, hero-longing was everywhere. Just look at the corny movie to which Americans were flocking in the cold weeks of Jimmy Carter's Götterdämmerung: *Superman*.

This new rendition of the old comic book opened in the year 1948, when the infant Kal-El was swaddled by his father and sent to earth just before his planet was destroyed. He was raised by a kindly, childless old couple, the Kents, in a bucolic little farm town. After high school, he found his way to a mysterious arctic fortress, where the ghost of his father trained him to harness his remarkable powers in order to redeem a fallen America.

Chronology was central to the film's logic. Clark Kent had not been around during the 1960s. He thus returned to 1978 not just with superpowers, but his Norman Rockwell values intact. They were intertwined: nostalgia *was* a superpower.

The setting he returned to was central as well: he was a newspaper reporter. *Superman*'s bustling newsroom scenes were filmed to precisely recall *All the President's Men*, the Oscar-winning portrayal of the *Washington Post* reporters investigating Watergate, part of a veritable new genre of film that introduced a new hero into American cinema: the crusading, idol-smashing, counterculture-flavored investigative reporter, powerful precisely because he or she looked below the deceptively placid surface of Norman Rockwell's America to reveal the rottenness underneath. Into this bustling 1970s newsroom, Clark Kent entered as a Rip van Winkle. He was ostentatiously square and deferential, complete with comically unfashionable trilby—the sort of male accoutrement that legend said John F. Kennedy had single-handedly made passé.

This made him the polar opposite of the wised-up star reporter Lois Lane. "How do you spell 'massacre'?" she asks before triumphantly ripping her "sex maniac profile" from the typewriter. "Nine to five it's a Pulitzer Prize winner, what do you think?" she barks to her editor, a dead ringer for Jason Robards as the legendarily curmudgeonly *Post* editor Ben Bradlee in *All the President's Men*'s, who replies, "There's no 'z' in 'brassiere.'"

Clark Kent stammeringly invites her on a date. She turns him down, because she is off to report on the president—"to make sure you-know-who answers a few questions he'd rather duck." She boards a helicopter for the airport, which malfunctions, dangling precipitously over a rooftop ledge—a shot that recalled images from America's shameful 1975 retreat from Vietnam. Superman swoops in to save the day—then, in the next scene, saves Air Force One, too.

"Why are you here?" Lois breathlessly asks. He answers, in a line that drew derisive laughter from moviegoers: "I'm here to fight for truth, justice, and the American way." Lois's response is derisive, too: "You're gonna end up fighting every elected official in the country."

Except that, lo and behold, by the next reel, she—and *we*—have fallen in love with this godlike visitation from a more innocent time. He cleans up the Hieronymus Bosch–like chaos of the city of Metropolis—played in the movie by real-life New York, home Son of Sam and the 1977 blackout riots. The film ends with Superman saving Lois Lane by deploying every ounce of his power to push the earth backwards on its axis—literally turning back time. The allegory was intentional.

Explained director Richard Donner, "He's a lot of what America once was a long time ago. I'm a very liberal human being in my philosophies and my politics. And I find myself, in an odd sort of way . . . respecting the conservative attitudes of what Superman stands for now. Because I think I see a lot of my philosophies in application now and I'm not happy with them. And I almost wish I could go back to what once was, and what America once was." Christopher Reeve, who played Superman, said, "We wanted to know if a man from the innocent '30s could survive in the post-Watergate '70s."

The picture became the most profitable of the year. Maybe, just maybe, a nostalgic hero *could* set things right. Maybe it just took the proper faith in truth, justice, and the American way.

THE MEN RISING TO CHALLENGE JIMMY CARTER DID NOT GENERALLY RE-semble superheroes. Most were painfully bland. No surprise, then, that the first to emerge from the pack was the most charismatic of the bunch—who practically had *leadership* tattooed his forehead.

He was often photographed on his ranch, astride a horse. He grew up poor in the hinterlands, became a big man on campus in college, took a Hollywood screen test at the height of the Depression, and a served as a governor in the booming Sun Belt. He appeared the exact match for what a dejected nation desired in their president—not least in the way he held himself aloof from Washington, which he called a "jungle."

Editors sent journalists to capture him for their readers in profile after profile after profile, which all turned out almost exactly the same. They talked about his "carriage," and how he was "always absolutely in control of himself." How he bore an "actor's control over his body," and was "never out of character." ("Even in an airplane or an automobile he sits so erect that he resembles one of those inflatable dummy passengers used in safety tests.") Producers of television commercials particularly admired him. In his memoir of the 1976 campaign, Gerald Ford's adman Mal MacDougall told of cutting a Ford commercial with this exemplary specimen under trying conditions at a state fair. The first take was virtually perfect—except that it ran four seconds long. MacDougall offered to cut a few words from the script.

"No," the performer answered. "I'll just shorten my drawl."

The director called "Action!" The performer recited his lines precisely four seconds more expeditiously. MacDougall recorded his awe at how good he looked, "that tanned Texas face, the silver hair, the clean white shirt."

The man was not Ronald Reagan. He was John Connally of Texas. Ronald Reagan was the front-runner among Republicans in every presidential poll. But pundits said this was misleading—that in the earliest innings of a presidential race, first place was a bad place to be. George Romney had been in first place for the Republican nomination in 1967. Edmund Muskie in 1971, and Scoop Jackson in 1975, had been the first-place Democrats. All fell on their faces early in the election year. Ronald Reagan, all agreed, was if anything more vulnerable. At sixty-eight years old, any gaffe, any utterance too far out in right field, any wire-service photo of him falling asleep at some interminable Republican banquet, would be all it would take to finish him. That, said the conventional wisdom, was when the superhero known as "Big John" would swoop in to save the day.

JOHN BOWDEN CONNALLY JR. WAS BORN ON A TENANT FARM IN STARK AND unforgiving South Texas, in a house with neither indoor plumbing nor electricity. The soap was fashioned at home from lye and bacon crackling. His mother cooked on the woodstove that also heated the house. Connally was his parents' second son. Their first burned to death after falling into that stove.

Politicians, of course, love to recite stories of hardscrabble beginnings. But in John Connally's case, they were not exaggerated. He began working in the fields alongside his sharecropper father at the age of five. Not too long after, the family moved to San Antonio. John got his first formal job, delivering milk. He arose to do it at two o'clock in the morning.

As is often the case in the homes of boys who become politicians, the family dinner table functioned like a debating society. John Jr. held his own nearly as soon as he could talk. Then he began "exclaiming" long, dramatic orations like the "Siege of the Alamo" in public. In high school he won the district declamation championship. He matriculated at the age of sixteen at the University of Texas in Austin, where he became a glamorous, gorgeous, and impeccably dressed campus star renowned for his facility arguing either side of the nonsense propositions presented in debate contests (like "There is no such thing as a virtuous woman") with equal aplomb—a lifetime habit, some would say.

The University of Texas in the 1930s contained an extraordinary concentration of men who went on to become nationally prominent politicos.
With Jake Pickle and Joe Kilgore, both future congressmen, and Bob
Strauss, a future Democratic Party chairman, Connally chartered a new
fraternity, which challenged the incumbent clique of high-class snobs so
effectively that in 1936 Pickle became student body president. Two years
later, Connally ran. In the first round he fell short by eighteen votes. In
the second, he won by eleven hundred. It was said that the young man in
the three-piece suits was on a first-name basis with 60 percent of the student body.

Then, however, another lifetime habit revealed itself: he grew bored
with his achievement. He was removed from the presidency for not enrolling in enough classes. With brazen aplomb, he resigned with what
sounded like a victory speech. ("Perhaps I can best explain by quoting
Pétain at Verdun: 'Here I stand. I can do no other.'") Then as ever, some
saw him as a phony. And a bully: "He'd kick the shit out of you and later
he would laugh about it," said rival Maury Maverick, who became a liberal populist congressman. "To him, politics was a game, and he meant to
win." Connally did not apologize. Winning was his religion—and when
you won, you were entitled to the spoils.

After law school he applied for a job with the already-legendary Texas
director of the New Deal's National Youth Administration, Lyndon Johnson, whom he followed to Washington as a congressional aide. There, he
assembled a veritable political machine of his own, parceling out jobs to
friends as Capitol elevator operators, policemen, and doorkeepers, winning election as speaker of the "Little Congress" organization of congressional aides—just as Lyndon had.

Connally acquired his mentor's ruthlessness and cunning. He served as
Johnson's campaign manager in 1941 for a Senate special election, an excruciatingly close defeat, then used his mentor's influence to win his protégé a prestigious Navy berth working for the lend-lease program, where
he acquainted himself with the basics of international trade alongside such
future Washington heavyweights as Phil Graham of the *Washington Post*,
Eugene Rostow, and Lloyd Cutler. He was brilliant, detail-oriented, indefatigable—and vain: awed by General de Gaulle in a triumphant procession into Algiers, he became conspicuous for his insistence on wearing his
starched Navy uniform in the unforgiving desert heat. Then, on a combat
assignment aboard an aircraft carrier, he won a Bronze Star for valor directing the defeat of a kamikaze attack. He turned down a hopper full of
promising postwar job offers—join a local law firm, manage an oil and gas
company, run a private utility—to establish an Austin radio station with
his college friends. Congressman Johnson helped secure the FCC permit.

Connally made his first million. In 1948 he ran Johnson's second try for the senate. The stakes were extraordinarily high: a loss might spell LBJ's political death sentence. His protégé did not intend to let that happen. A participant said of the campaign that followed, "It would be illegal now. It wasn't then." This was overgenerous.

To win, they needed nearly 100 percent of the Latino vote. In cities, this meant showering money on bosses who paid voters' poll taxes, with a fat bonus for delivering their precincts—with the help of hundreds of unnecessary "poll workers" hired on Election Day, and paid-off election judges who locked the doors after Election Day, checked the rolls for absentees, then tallied them for LBJ. According to one expert, Johnson picked up some five thousand votes from San Antonio in this way.

In the countryside, votes were bought wholesale. In the five counties along the South Texas border, the man to see was named George Parr. He earned his price by delivering 99 percent of the vote in his territory—which, however, still was not enough. Following a statewide recount, Johnson was two hundred votes behind. So it was that in a bank building in Jim Wells County, Connally and two associates added names to the rolls from the local cemetery. After a two-day meeting of the state executive committee, which saw John Connally rushing from room to room with purposeful abandon, Lyndon Johnson was certified as Texas's senator-elect by a grand total of eighty-seven votes. The legend of John Connally as a political fixer of nearly superhuman capacity was secured.

He spent the 1950s as the top political operative for the legendary Forth Worth oil wildcatter Sid Richardson. Among Connally's accomplishments on his behalf was helping to convince Dwight Eisenhower to run for president, then helping him win—even though Connally and Richardson were Democrats. Then Connally helped maneuver Robert B. Anderson, another Fort Worth oilman, into an appointment as Eisenhower's secretary of the navy. He successfully lobbied for a bill to shift the tideland oil reserves off the Texas coast from federal to state control, to great benefit for Texas oilmen, at great expense to American taxpayers. He also shepherded to passage a bill to end price controls on petroleum. Then, however, came a surprise veto after one legislator displayed on the floor of the Senate an envelope containing $2,500 he had been given in exchange for his vote, and another demonstrated that the nine hundred telegrams for decontrol had been faked by the organization headed by Connally—who left Washington under cover of night, just ahead, it was said, of an indictment for lobbying without a license. This ability to wriggle free from impossible jams only enhanced his legend.

Supporters hoped he would run for the Senate seat vacated when LBJ became vice president. The Senate was too slow for Connally's style. Instead, he won appointment as President Kennedy's naval secretary—an extraordinary coup considering that the previous summer Connally had led an underground attempt to sabotage JFK's nomination at the convention in favor of LBJ, by mainlining smears about Kennedy's poor health. At Connally's confirmation hearings, outraged liberals complained about his directorships in twenty-seven major corporations (who better, Connally responded, to take command of one of the world's biggest employers?), many with interests in the Navy's petroleum reserves, among the largest in the world. ("My experience," he brazenly replied, "will stand me in good stead.") The Washington press corps was dazzled—and took to this swashbuckler in a way they never had his bumptious mentor. Some noted that two men named Roosevelt began their roads to the White House in the Department of the Navy, followed by gubernatorial runs in their home states. And in 1962, Connally did run for Texas governor. He started the race at 4 percent. He won by a hundred thousand votes.

It was then that the most dramatic element in John Connally's legend emerged. He arranged President John F. Kennedy's whirlwind tour of Texas to heal the accelerating civil war between the Texas Democratic Party's liberal populists and Connally's business wing, a crucial political task because the former one-party state was turning increasingly Republican going into the presidential election year. On November 22 in Dallas, one of the bullets that killed Kennedy broke three of Governor Connally's ribs, punctured a lung, shattered a wrist, and lodged in a leg. The sling he wore for years afterward became part of his political uniform—just like his dozen pairs of custom handmade cowboy boots. The Texas Republicans' rise was stopped dead; the Democratic Party's liberal wing was paralyzed. A *Houston Chronicle* poll had previously given Connally a fifty-fifty chance of reelection. Instead, he served three two-year terms—after promising in his 1962 campaign to pass a law limiting governors to two.

Texas populists, naturally, despised him: he had absorbed his mentor's cunning, but none of LBJ's sympathy for the oppressed. (President Johnson rued that he "should have spent more time with that boy," as Governor Connally established himself as a thorn in the side of the War on Poverty. "He likes those oak-paneled rooms too much.") Critics pointed out things like how the members of his Texas Ranger guard detail were required to be at least three inches shorter than he—to ensure, a former assistant said, his "John Wayne look." They noted that after promising to slash state spending by 10 percent, he doubled it. (His favorite beneficiaries were higher education and business development grants; his goal was turning Texas into a hub for aerospace and high tech.) National political reporters began looking on him, you might say, like a superhero.

Consider the safari. In 1967, after deciding not to run for a fourth term, he accepted an invitation from the ABC network to spend the month of August in Africa for the series *The American Sportsman*. The traveling party included TV toughs Clint Walker and David Jannsen. The crowning moment came when a nine-thousand-pound bull elephant loomed menacingly. The governor leveled his .458 Winchester Magnum rifle. The producer exulted: "It was one of the finest kills we've ever had. He caught it with a fantastic brain shot." He also parleyed with leaders of Namibia and Rhodesia—as befitted a bored governor with higher ambitions.

He returned home, announced his retirement, was hosannaed by the *Dallas Morning News* for his "innate honesty." At the tumultuous 1968 Democratic National Convention in Chicago he led the opposition to an antiwar plank; articles bloomed with speculation concerning the possibility of nominee Hubert Humphrey choosing Connally as his running mate—a ritual that would repeat itself three more times across two parties. He left office as the most popular governor in modern Texas history. And, next, a Republican president fell in love with him. "Connally's swaggering self-assurance," Henry Kissinger once said, "was Nixon's Walter Mitty image of himself." Richard Nixon was particularly impressed by the way Connally sat out nearly the entire campaign, then bound together Texas Democrats' wounded wings to carry the state for Humphrey—moving for his party's nominee only after the polls suggested he might have a chance. Then, after Humphrey lost in the general, Connally insinuated himself within the winning party—the sort of cynicism Richard Nixon could *really* respect.

He appointed Connally to a commission studying ways to reorganize the executive branch. They frequently met at Nixon's "Western White House" in San Clemente, California, where Connally was always finding opportunities for private time with Nixon, plying him with delicious gossip about Jack Kennedy and Lyndon Johnson. In November 1970, the group presented the president with its final recommendations. Their chairman, a corporate executive, got bogged down in bureaucratic intricacies. Connally took over, presenting the same information in a manner far more compelling to the boss: emphasizing how the proposed reforms would increase Richard Nixon's power. Smitten, Nixon invited Connally to stay the night. The next morning, he offered him a cabinet job. Connally said he would only consider Treasury or State. Nixon's chief of staff Bob Haldeman wrote up talking points for Nixon to use when he called Connally to persuade him to take the Treasury job. They included, "P feels you're the only man in Dem party that could be P," and, "If you come in, you will be the closest confidante."

The nation was suffering the first inklings of the inflation that would define the decade. In order to embarrass the Republicans, Democrats had passed legislation giving the president authority to institute wage and price controls—something Nixon had pledged to never do. When the bill was put on the president's desk for the inevitable veto, Treasury Secretary Connally shocked Nixon by urging him to sign it: an executive should never refuse a grant of new power. "Put it in the corner like an old shotgun. You never know when you might need it."

No matter that Nixon had heretofore called wage and price controls a heresy. No matter that, as Nixon's economists patiently explained to him, the federal government imposing prices was like shoring up a weakening dam by temporarily plugging the cracks, and once the controls were removed, as they inevitably would have to be someday, inflation would gush forth worse than before. Connally advised him to pursue the "bold stroke." That summer, in what the head of his Council of Economic Advisers called "the most important weekend in the history of economics" since the New Deal, Nixon gathered a team at Camp David for a secret meeting and emerged with his "New Economic Policy." This included ending the convertibility of dollars into gold, single-handedly upending the entire international monetary system—and instituting wage and price controls. *There is no such thing as a virtuous woman.*

In May 1972, bored again, Connally left the Treasury. Nixon extolled him—"never has one cabinet member done more for his county in a year and a half"—and sent him on an eighteen-nation tour as his personal emissary. Touts surmised Nixon would replace Vice President Spiro Agnew with Connally on his reelection ticket. In fact, Nixon had even grander plans: grooming Connally as his designated successor at the head of a "new majority" political party to encompass everyone on the political spectrum save liberal Democrats—perhaps for all time.

Connally headed Democrats for Nixon, in charge of attack ads (and also certain dirty tricks). In May of 1973, with great fanfare, he announced that he was formally joining the Republican Party. With Nixon just beginning to drown in Watergate, the press reported it as a magnanimous act. Next, he returned to Washington as what a journalist described as "unpaid White House consultant on anything and everything." He left after sixty-nine days, his political finger in the wind. Vice President Spiro Agnew was under investigation for bribery, and Nixon might soon be in the market for a replacement.

In a city full of timorous trimmers, admiration for Connally's "toughness" became almost cultish. Georgetown elites loved his stories—like the one about LBJ calling him from the White House in tears: "John, why do they hate me so?" Johnson was *weak*, he instructed his appreciative audiences. This John Connally would never be. LBJ, they hated. Sleazy Richard Nixon, they despised. But *John Connally*: he had style. "His Tex Ritter tuxedo was two tones of azure and delphinium," Maxine Cheshire's social column observed breathlessly of his appearance at a Johnny Cash concert in the White House East Room.

Agnew resigned. Connally set up a war room in the Mayflower Hotel to prepare for his vice-presidential investiture. Democrats, however, pledged that this time, they would finally make *stick* the litany of objections raised at his confirmation hearings in 1961 and 1971. So Nixon called Gerald Ford with the offer instead, with a condition: "I want to make one thing clear. I'm supporting John Connally for the nomination in 1976." Connally had already met with rich backers to begin planning the campaign.

Then, a roadblock.

Eleven days before Richard Nixon's resignation, Connally was indicted for allegedly taking $10,000 in cash as treasury secretary from a lobbyist for the dairy industry shortly after the Nixon administration raised dairy price supports—an "illegal gratuity," according to an indictment that seemed to nail him dead to rights, laying out evidence that, two years after the alleged $10,000 bribe, Connally, fearing discovery, gave that exact sum back to the same lobbyist, then after realizing the $10,000 included currency printed *after* the alleged event, exchanged it for another payout containing older bills.

Connally's defense lawyer was the legendary Edward Bennett Williams. He persuaded the judge to bar the prosecution from playing for the jury White House tapes of Connally pressing Nixon to raise the price supports, including explicit instructions on how to make sure the White House got public credit. He impeached the credibility of the key prosecution witness, a convicted felon. He pointed up his client's fantastic wealth as an argument for his innocence: Why would a man with three houses including a mansion overlooking Montego Bay in Jamaica risk everything for a piddling $10,000? (In fact, at that same Oval Office meeting Connally discussed the possibility of working the grift with the much larger beef industry.) And he dazzled the jury with a stream of character witnesses, including Robert McNamara, Dean Rusk, the legendarily principled black congresswoman from Texas Barbara Jordan, Lady Bird Johnson—who said "John is a man of integrity, a man of honor"—and the Reverend Billy Graham, whose turn on the witness stand earned, from one of the jury's ten African Americans, an earnest "Amen." Connally was acquitted—in both the courts of law and elite opinion.

A testimonial dinner for him at the Hyatt Regency Washington three months later drew four thousand, who paid up to $1,000 to attend. With the proceeds, Connally chartered "Vital Issues of America," which convened high-minded symposia around the country, providing its benefactor a platform as a serious man of ideas, and the John Connally Citizens Forum, a political action committee to shower cash on politicians whose loyalty might someday come in handy. The following year he hosted twenty-two Republican state chairmen and vice chairmen at his nine-thousand-acre cattle ranch (which had its own airstrip) to lecture them on how the party could win in 1976. The officials described it to the waiting press like a religious experience. "I was invited down to discuss Republican strategy," Vermont's chairman said, "but I would have gladly come down just to discuss the vice-presidential nomination of John Connally." Though Connally, he added, "was probably too good for politics." At the Republican convention, he was treated like a giant among men, and once more was discussed as a possible running mate. He hit the campaign trail for Ford. At one stop, the MC introduced the pair as "the President of the United States and John B. Connally." "The only thing Connally didn't like," an observer joked, "was the word 'and.'" After he failed to *deliver* Texas for Ford, the suspicion was that he had *sabotaged* Texas for Ford, the better to set himself up for 1980. His Citizens Forum raised the seventh-biggest haul of any PAC in 1977 and 1978—but distributed only 10 percent of the take. He held the rest back for himself.

In the fall of 1978, he appeared in a string tie on the cover of the *Saturday Evening Post*: "John B. Connally: *Strong* for 1980." The prose was Harlequin romance: "A mild South Texas breeze eased through the open ranch wagon, leaving wisps of the driver's silvery hair in disarray," like cowboys' "when they get thrown in a rodeo or when they have trouble calming a stallion." The thesis was that "to growing numbers of Americans he seems the man most capable of restoring greatness to the White House." John F. Kennedy's national security advisor described him as a man "who always puts the interests of the country and of free society ahead of any political expediencies."

On January 24, 1979, John Connally jutted forth his great chin from behind a National Press Club podium to cowboy whoops from his supporters and become the second Republican to officially announce his presidential campaign. His speech invoked Washington, Lincoln, Franklin Roosevelt—and himself: "We need someone in charge who knows what he is doing and why." The nation itself was fine. "The only missing ingredient is *leadership*."

He was asked whether his bribery indictment might hurt him. He scoffed. "I was tried before a Washington, D.C., jury—ten blacks and two whites—and they gave the answer for all time . . . and that was, simply 'not guilty.'"

His ties to Richard Nixon?

"When I was Secretary of the Treasury I served the nation, not him."

What about Ronald Reagan's ovewhelming lead in the polls?

"I don't envy him that position."

The experts agreed. "The country is hungry for strong leadership, and no one better projects a sense of confidence and masterfulness like Connally," the historian and JFK advisor Arthur Schlesinger Jr. wrote in his diary. The secretary of energy, a Republican, told the president that Connally's "charisma and its effect in the Republican primaries" made him the most likely nominee. One straw in the wind was that more and more *conservatives* were doubting Reagan—who, because he was the front-runner, was not really the front-runner at all. Richard Viguerie was asked his opinion about Connally. He answered that he was "very eager to do anything for him."

THE RIGHT-WING COALITION WAS THRIVING. "IT'S REALLY EXCITING," A young woman with a Dorothy Hamill do gushed to a reporter covering the annual Young Republican Leadership Conference that March. "For a long time Democrats coasted on the New Deal tactics. But the Roosevelt coalition is starting to crumble. There's nothing left in the liberal Democratic philosophy."

A University of Missouri undergrad chimed in: "What this girl is saying is good stuff!"

She continued: "Republicans are saying, 'Hey, we've got programs, we can give new jobs!'" . . . and burbled and burbled until she apologized: "Oh, I'm sorry. I get so excited about this."

She wasn't alone. The meeting was a celebration of conservatism triumphant. John Rhodes was introduced as the "next Speaker of the House." Young Republicans president Roger Stone noted of the presidential field, "All are running as conservatives." The hospitality suite operated by the Ripon Society, the venerable liberal Republican group, was invaded by right-wingers who harassed them with made-up doggerel. "Basically," one of the Riponites recollected, "the message was, 'You're all commie pinkos and we're the wave of the future.'"

That second part seemed about right. "Right-Wing Students Exert Growing Influence on Campus," the *Chronicle of Higher Education* reported. Such students were awash in support institutions: operative Morton Blackwell, who edited Richard Viguerie's newsletter *New Right Report*, opened a political boot camp called the Leadership Institute—"a crash course on how to win." M. Stanton Evans's National Journalism Center trained conservative college newspaper staffers. The Institute for Educational Affairs, established the previous year by William Simon and Irving Kristol with gifts of $100,000 each from Bechtel, Coca-Cola, Dow Chemical, Mobil, and Nestlé, began distributing grants to promising conservative undergraduates and PhD candidates, and subsidized conservatives to take otherwise unpaid internships at activist organizations, periodicals—and even unsuspecting federal agencies.

Organizations for grown-ups were thriving, too—like the American
Legislative Exchange Council, which, along with what *New Right Report*
called a "coalition of pro-life, pro-Right-to-Work, pro-Defense, pro-gun,
pro-free-enterprise, pro-balanced-budget, pro-tax-limitation, pro-farmer,
and anti-left activists," helped crush a constitutional amendment granting
statehood to the heavily Democratic District of Columbia.

The Senate Republicans convened without two of their most liberal
members, Clifford Case, who had lost his primary to the New Right's Jeff
Bell, and Ed Brooke, who lost to the fiscally conservative Democrat Paul
Tsongas. Chuck Percy had only hung on by apologizing for his liberalism
and bringing in Ronald Reagan as a ringer. Orrin Hatch came within a
single vote of becoming chairman of the caucus's campaign committee—
and it had been chutzpah for a freshman even to run. (He had only lost,
according to a senator quoted in *New Right Report*, due to arm-twisting
from Henry Kissinger and "major N.Y. bankers." Hatch had "played
the game by the rules, and the liberals gave him the shaft," the Viguerie
newsletter explained. "His experience is an important lesson for conservatives.") Ted Stevens of Alaska, a onetime moderate, joined the conservative
Senate Steering Committee, quitting the weekly breakfast club for moderate Republicans—which began fading nearly to nothingness.

And on the House side, one Republican freshman plotted a sort of
right-wing reign of terror.

Every two years, two respected scholars of congress, Norm Ornstein
and Thomas Mann, invited new members to off-the-record dinners to
help acquaint them with how the body worked. They were astonished
when one of these new members, the former professor Newt Gingrich,
instead began lecturing them, about how the body *should* work. Then he
unfolded for them a fully formed multiyear plan for the Republican Party
to take control of the lower chamber for the first time since the Hoover
administration. Upon his swearing in, Gingrich wasted no time beginning
to put it into place.

An African American congressman from Detroit, Charles Diggs, had
been convicted for demanding salary kickbacks from his underlings, then
was reelected to a fourteenth term nonetheless. Gingrich announced plans
for a roll call vote to expel him. Thirteen fellow freshmen signed on. Leaders
in both parties tried to explain to these young hotheads how these worked:
action by the full House must follow an Ethics Committee investigation.
No House member had been expelled since 1861, and that had been for taking up arms against the United States. For, according to the Constitution,
voters, not members, decided who served. Congressmen began defending
the body's "regular order" in the press; as Parren Mitchell, the leader of
the Congressional Black Caucus, put it, "The will of the people is what the

House is all about and if people want to elect a Hitler or a Klansman, that is their right, and you and I do not have any right to quarrel with it."

Thus had Newt Gingrich successfully lured congressional Democrats into his briar patch.

"It's time we convinced the American people that there's no double standard for justice—one for them and one for Congressmen," he responded through the media—and soon House leaders were receiving letters that said things like, "My hat is off to the courageous congressman from Georgia."

He referred to his strategy as a long-term game of three-dimensional chess. If he chipped away the public's trust in the House, and with that the party that controlled it, the public would throw the rascals out—and Republicans would inherit the wreckage. The brazenness was remarkable—especially since Gingrich was carrying it out by prioritizing attacks on black members. He even joined a panel pursuing the absurd claim of an obscure candidate of a third party run by the political cultist Lyndon LaRouche that Parren Mitchell had won his fifth term through fraud. This even though Gingrich had won his margin of victory back in his Georgia district through aggressive appeals to black voters, winning the enthusiastic endorsement of the local black newspaper.

But since *no other* Republican even hinted at the possibility of their party attaining a House majority, the media began writing about Gingrich like *he* was a leader. "I am a national politician," he told the AP. "My concerns are national. The agenda we have to confront in my party is national." On his office wall, they reported, Gingrich showed off a movie poster he kept in his office of Robert Redford as a dashing young office seeker in *The Candidate* who famously asked, after his victory, "What do we do now?" No such doubts from Newt—nor from conservatives anywhere.

IN JANUARY REPUBLICANS MET AT THE TIDEWATER INN FOR THEIR ANNUAL retreat. For the second year in a row, they left in a warm glow of unity after passing a slate of resolutions that leaned far to the right. They overwhelmingly rejected the proposal of the radical National Taxpayers Union to call a constitutional convention for a balanced budget amendment—but overwhelmingly endorsed a bill drafted by Milton Friedman and Robert Bork to achieve the same result through the normal legislative process; and Washington conventional wisdom on fiscal policy ratcheted several clicks to the right. George Will gloatingly compared the Maryland resort to where the Bolsheviks plotted their overthrow of the Romanov dynasty: "Comes the revolution, the Tidewater Inn here will be regarded as America's equivalent of the Smolny Institute."

Irving Kristol's face smiled out from the cover of the February 13 issue of *Esquire*. "This unknown intellectual," it read, "is the godfather of the most powerful new political force in America—NEOCONSER-VATISM." Inside, the package of articles, charts, and lists began with an epigraph from Karl Marx—"The ruling ideas of each age have ever been the ideas of its ruling class"—and continued on for twenty lavishly illustrated pages. One essay described neoconservatives as "The Reasonable Right"—a radical reasonableness, however, because neoconservatives were the first conservative cadre in generations that fit comfortably within America's *true* corridors of power, the places where the nation's cultural common sense was formed: the university seminar room, the Manhattan dinner party, the nonprofit foundation boardroom. Liberalism was "going through an intellectual menopause": a hoary, snobby, Ivy League aristocracy. Defending unfashionable values like family, tradition, religion, and unfettered capitalism was *rebellion*. And anything but crazy: Irving Kristol even "*looks* like a man of reason; arrogance is missing from his makeup."

Esquire was the sort of magazine hip young men bought to learn what they needed to know to stay hip, and how to signal that knowledge to others. "Trust us," they now were instructed. "This is the inside dope. . . . The neocons are now in the center ring—the Red Hot Center. Places, everyone. Dress left. Eyes right. Will this lead to the new Anarchy? You bet. More Freedom. Less Government. We *guarantee* you'll like it."

It was an exciting time to be a conservative Republican.

AND ALSO A BOARDROOM JACOBIN.

The Federal Trade Commission lined up an extraordinarily ambitious agenda for 1979. The deadline for public comment on its used-car warranty rules was February 13. (They projected it would add $15 to the price of the average vehicle but would boost sales by restoring confidence in the industry. The National Independent Automobile Dealers Association claimed it would add from $100 to $300, and ruin them.) The five commissioners voted through new rules to take effect in 1980 requiring vocational schools receiving federally guaranteed loan money disclose their job placement rates, and refund course fees on a prorated basis if students dropped out. They asked Congress to change the message on cigarette packs from "Warning: The surgeon general has determined that cigarette smoking is dangerous to your health" to "Danger! Tests prove cigarettes can kill you." They were investigating the high-pressure techniques of door-to-door insurance salesmen, whose policies sometimes paid out death benefits of $10,000 for premiums adding up to . . . $10,000. In their final stages of preparation were rules that would strike down the American Medical Association's limitations on, and the American Dental Association's outright ban of, advertising by members and price-fixing tactics among Realtors; require disclosure of the energy efficiency of insulation and appliances, and ban phony nutritional claims for protein supplements. One was put into operation holding celebrities liable for deceptive marketing of products they endorsed. (The first celebrity snared was Pat Boone, who got 25 cents for every bottle sold of an acne cream he claimed in commercials had cleared up all his daughters' skin.)

After four years of staff research and hearings in six cities, the commission hoped to publish proposed new regulations for funeral homes in April. Funerals were a family's third-greatest single expense behind a home and a car. A 1963 bestseller, *The American Way of Death*, had documented the ways undertakers routinely manipulated grieving families. The new rules would end many of these practices, requiring funeral directors to provide itemized price information upon request, banning the requirement of caskets when customers requested cremation, outlawing embalming bodies without families' permission, punishing them for lying about phony "legal" requirements, and preventing the use of threats to keep competitors from starting new funeral homes.

That list had already been greatly trimmed down over the course of the rule-making process; staff even scrapped a proposed rule against body snatching. Even so, backlash was furious. The conservative columnist James J. Kilpatrick called it a "war against funeral directors." Undertakers rang their congressmen's phones off the hook. With considerable success so far. "You know, a funeral director can kill you," a representative explained to a reporter. "I go to forty or fifty funerals a year. He decides whether you sit next to the widow or at the back of the room." The business backlash against all of this was furious—nowhere more so than against the revived fight over kidvid.

The FTC had been seeking comment for a year on three possible responses to TV commercials pushing unhealthful products to children: banning those addressed to children younger than eight; limiting those aimed at children under twelve; and requiring advertisers to subsidize public service messages promoting nutrition. The public response, overwhelmingly in favor of regulation, filled twenty feet of shelf space at FTC headquarters.

What did the other side have? A war chest estimated at $15 to $30 million, directed by super-lobbyist Tommy Boggs.

Administrative hearings opened in San Francisco on January 15, followed by hearings in Washington in March. In San Francisco, the business coalition spent $500,000 on a lavish press operation at the St. Francis Hotel, distributing to journalists daily summaries of the proceedings with elaborate rebuttals of every pro-regulation witness. The consumer groups, on the other hand, sent out their occasional press releases mimeographed on both sides of the page to save their limited funds.

The consumerists' witnesses were powerfully compelling. A pediatric cardiologist outlined how the relentless promotion of unhealthy food was producing "almost epidemic obesity." A professor from the Harvard School of Dental Medicine demonstrated that a link between sweetened cereals and tooth decay was "beyond any question." A scholar from the University of Pennsylvania demonstrated how children under the age of eight could not distinguish programming from commercials. A spokesman from the Consumer Union cited estimates that the average child watched two hundred thousand TV commercials every year, riveting the room by describing how ads for breakfast products like Cap'n Crunch and Cookie Crisp purveyed "a lie that they should shove candy into their mouths" by calling it "nutrition." "The issue is American business trying to con four- and five-year-olds," he said. The "abuse of young children in the marketplace has never existed in such a degree as it does today." Then he explained how reining that in was licensed by Supreme Court First Amendment precedent going back to the early twentieth century. The hearing judge was rapt.

The arguments from the other side were out of *Alice in Wonderland*.

The president of the Cereal Institute insisted "no dental research study has ever shown that the consumption of breakfast cereals by children . . . increases the incidence of tooth decay." A lawyer for Mattel claimed academic sanction for the conclusion "If presently virtually all television advertising of toys were prohibited"—which no one was suggesting—"the consumer price penalty can be roughly estimated at $840 million annually." A production company said that its *New Mickey Mouse Club* had to be shut down because it could not guarantee stations any advertising for the upcoming season. (In fact no FTC rule would go into effect for three years or more.) A representative from Kellogg said that 95 percent of their commercials *promoted* good health—because they showed cereal being eaten with milk.

When the hearings picked up again in Washington, one expected participant was conspicuously absent. Since his debut on the public stage as the nation's would-be nanny, a flurry of journalistic profiles that cast him as a charming, scrappy underdog had almost turned FTC chairman Mike Pertschuk into a celebrity. "Consumer's Man at FTC," said a handsome spread in *Newsday*, which pictured our hero at home helping his nine-year-old stepson with his homework. "FTC Is Becoming the Consumer's Aggressive Crusader" in the *Washington Post* showed him perched on his desk, rumpled and bespectacled, ready to take on the bad guys from his platform at the head of "the 'biggest public interest law firm in the country.'"

Which helped explain the other side's next guerrilla maneuver: success-fully convincing a federal judge that, because of his speeches advocating kidvid regulation, Pertschuk should be recused from the proceedings.

His side hardly suffered from his absence. A breakout villain emerged: the clownish vice president for scientific affairs for the Grocery Manufac-turers Association, who claimed "government diet commissars" intended to "impose a new national diet ... based upon the personal tastes and fears of a few individuals" demanding foods with no more than 20 percent sugar—which, since "nutrition-oriented groups" meant they planned to ban fruits, vegetables, and dairy products, because these groups suppos-edly believed "there is no relevant difference between natural sugar and sugar added to manufacturing—"

On that cue, aides wheeled in carts laden with foodstuffs representing the daily consumption of the typical American youngster. With a flour-ish, the witness began removing what the bureaucrats were supposedly about to snatch from the family table, in rhythm with his presentation, until there was practically nothing left. "Is this progress or a return to the seventeenth century?" he cried triumphantly. "Is this diet acceptable to—or even edible to—a typical nine-year-old?" The hearing judge practi-cally mocked him outright. When the turn came for Kellogg's manager for children's advertising, she would respond to even the most basic questions by turning around for a whispered huddle with lawyers—then emerge to report that "trade secrets" prevented her from answering. Then, they stirred audience titters by suggesting that curbs on advertising on kids' TV wouldn't work because, after all, sometimes they also watch "Johnny Carson and soap operas."

Peggy Charren of Advocacy for Children's Television stuck in the dagger. The networks claimed "self-regulation" overseen by the National Association of Broadcasters had taken care of the problem. She pointed out that until an FTC order ended it, advertisements for medicines that were by law required to be labeled "Keep Out of Reach of Children," but which talked about them like they were delicious candy, were approved by the NAB as "appropriate." Kellogg's CEO had arranged to be the last wit-ness in the hearing. He canceled. In this particular forum, his side realized they had already lost.

They recouped their advantage elsewhere. Their elaborate press kits had been crafted by the coalition's advertising-industry arm. Editors proved alarmingly susceptible. A *Washington Star* investigation later dis-covered that they had workshopped language to flush out the most "sal-able" phrases—like "national nanny," which was now something like a household phrase.

A week later, Pertschuk testified before the House Commerce Committee on the FTC's FY 1980 appropriation request. He arrived with a platoon of budget officers, program managers, administrators, and lawyers, confident his agency could win its first formal budget authorization in two years. He began with an appropriately bland opening statement. A congressman asked him if he had any thoughts about the previous year's debate over the "legislative veto"—that unprecedented proposal to give Congress power to kill any FTC regulation. Pertschuk responded with almost absurd deference. "We do recognize that there is strong sentiment for it, and we will try to work with the authorizing committees, to the extent that they believe it is necessary, to identify the most workable and responsible form of the legislative veto if that is their wish," even though "it might have several kinds of deleterious effects." He gingerly offered some examples of those effects: since FTC rules took three to five years of highly technical work to gestate, producing records in the tens of thousands of pages, Congress would be overwhelmed. Companies facing regulation might seek to influence lawmakers unduly.

But, asked if he had any compromise to recommend, Pertschuk responded that it wasn't his business to intervene in the legislative process.

Smooth sailing. Then, however, came questioning from a Worcester, Massachusetts, Democrat named Joe Early, and things started going berserk.

Early asked whether the FTC wasn't ill-serving the cause of freedom by "getting so broad." Pertschuk calmly explained how his agency strived to promulgate regulations that were *not* broad by taking advantage of the self-regulating power of the marketplace. Concerning inflated prices for eyeglasses, for example, instead of *setting* prices, the FTC used existing antitrust law to ban trade organizations from keeping eyeglass prices out of ads, making merchants and consumers *more* free by allowing the competitive marketplace to do its work. He then cited studies showing how eyeglass prices were 35 to 40 percent lower in states that had permitted advertising than in those that did not.

He continued, "We have also cut back on rules—"

Early angrily interrupted:

"I don't think the FTC initiated any cutbacks at all. . . . I would like to see for example that the cost of a head of lettuce is 20 percent less because of that FTC action."

Pertschuk replied to the non sequitur, again calmly, by citing the FTC's recent success in winning a judicial consent order against Levi Strauss for fixing retail prices: "the price of Levi's has dropped, and dropped substantially—"

"You say that! I have eight kids. Believe me, prices aren't going down. I don't know where you people shop."

Then he held Pertschuk personally responsible for the fact that the

FTC budget request counted the number of positions it sought to fill in "work years," instead of the number of workers. Pertschuk replied that this was a government-wide innovation undertaken to allow agencies to increase efficiency and cut staffs by hiring more part-time and temporary employees. Early followed up: If they were so concerned about efficiency, why were they asking for more staffers at all?

"We are," Pertschuk complained, "really, with all due respect, a pretty small agency . . ."

"You know, we don't *have* one big federal agency, not one, if you listen to witnesses!" Early then demanded to know why "instead of tilting at windmills" the FTC wasn't doing anything about beef prices.

"We have," Pertschuk responded, then once more attempted deference: "You are quite right in asking. . . . We have had a preliminary investigation, and the Commission has authorized a full investigation—"

"You could have about five calf crops in the time it has taken!"

Minutes earlier, he had called the FTC giant and aggressive. Now it was too timid and small. Then, however, in the next breath, it was too aggressive again, and Pertschuk tried to answer . . . until Early changed the subject, again. Then again and again—until, by the time he was finished with his time, he sounded like a drunk ranting on a street corner.

FTC staffers were baffled by the onslaught—until they learned that the Massachusetts backbencher had been coached for the confrontation in the lobbying offices of Patton Boggs. And also after Early's Federal Election Commission filing came out. It listed fat contributions from the PACs of the optometrists, dentists, the insurance industry, and agricultural cooperatives—the most famous of which, Sunkist, was being prosecuted by the FTC as a monopoly.

Pertschuk was received more politely a few days later before Senate Appropriations. Really, his arguments were hard to answer. He cited the results of a study from the Business Roundtable that found that of all the federal regulatory agencies the FTC had accrued the least cost to consumers. He held up the eyeglasses rule as a real-world success in countering inflation. He noted that of the 152 "trade practice rules" that had existed when he had entered office, 145 had been eliminated. He listed the regulatory inquiries his staffers had recommended that he had decided *not* to pursue, boasted of the entire new division he had opened to minimize regulations' costs to consumers and burdens to business. He itemized the many ways the FTC had succeeded in making the economy freer and more competitive.

Perhaps such sound arguments would have an effect in the fight to come. Or perhaps they would not. It was an exciting time to be a boardroom Jacobin. They had their prey on the run.

CHAPTER 22

Christian Soldiers

MOST OF ALL, IT WAS AN EXCITING TIME TO BE AN EVANGELICAL CHRISTIAN.
After Jimmy Carter's presidential campaign, *Newsweek* magazine declared
1976 "The Year of the Evangelical." 1978 outpaced it by a country mile.

The Christian Broadcasting Network, Pat Robertson's bid to compete
with ABC, NBC, and CBS, was "well on its way to becoming a global
presence," the *New York Times* reported in July. Two other televangelists'
shows, Rex Hubbard's *Cathedral of Tomorrow* and *Oral Roberts and
You*, matched the ratings of Merv Griffin on daytime TV. Robertson's
former television sidekick, a cherub-faced young preacher named Jim
Bakker, broke ground in South Carolina for a "Total Living Center" he
called Heritage USA, with a reported budget of $100 million, to comprise
several "residential villages," including "Old New England," "Polyne-
sian," "California contemporary," and "Swiss chalet"—even, eventually, a
Disney-style amusement park. Bakker said it would "never be finished . . .
until the coming of the Lord." Six years earlier, he had been living with his
wife Tammy Faye in a trailer.

Christianity Today reported that one out of every seven American
radio stations was "Christian-owned and operated," a new one opening
every week. *Newsweek* said that Christian book companies were "threatening to match, dollar for dollar, the sales figures of some of the commercial publishing houses." Oilman Nelson Bunker Hunt and Holiday Inn
founder Wallace Johnson raised $100 million of a projected $1 billion for a
media campaign to "evangelize every man, woman, and child on Earth in
preparation for the millennium."

A delegation announced their pilgrimage to the Holy Land with a
full-page ad in the *New York Times* signed by fifteen leading evangelicals
including W. A. Criswell and Pat Boone. It averred, "The time has come
for evangelical Christians to affirm their belief in Biblical prophecy and
Israel's Divine right to the Land by Speaking out anew." An organizer
explained, "American evangelicals constitute a pro-Israel body far greater
in size than the Jewish community." Prime Minister Begin addressed the
event's opening session. The closing one was held on the legendary moun-

taintop where Jewish martyrs had committed mass suicide rather than submit to Roman rule. Under a banner reading "Masada Shall Not Fall Again," the delegation founded International Christians for Israel, vowing, "The nation of Israel . . . has been established by God and shall stand forever."

THAT JUNKET WAS A CRUCIAL EPISODE IN THE MOST IMPORTANT DEVELOP-ment of all for evangelism: its coming out as a political movement. The most important figure in this development was Jerry Falwell.

Falwell liked to tell the story about how his mother, Sunday mornings, would switch on the radio to Dr. Charles E. Fuller's *Old-Fashioned Revival Hour*—because she knew his alcoholic father would be too lazy to switch it off. He related how Fuller's preaching proved so compelling to him that at the age of eighteen he attended church for the first time in his life. He pulled his blue Plymouth sedan into the parking lot of Park Avenue Baptist Church on a cold January night in 1952; plunked down in the front row with his drinking buddy Jim Moon; and listened to a sermon about hell and the Second Coming, admiring both the preacher's style and the piano player, Macel Pate, who wore a black dress with white trim (and whom Falwell eventually made his wife). Then, he answered the call to the altar and accepted Christ as his savior.

He had been an honor student and a football star. He gave up sports (and, he claimed, an offer to play professional baseball), drinking, smoking, dancing, and movies, to attend Bible college in Missouri, where he studied Scripture from dawn until dusk. A turning point, he said, came his sophomore year, when he was assigned to teach a Sunday school class with only a single student enrolled. As the school's top student, Falwell asked to be assigned to a more desirable section. The administrator refused. So the young seminarian scraped up fifty-five more students by soliciting door to door. "It had been a test," wrote one of the untold number of reporters who called upon Falwell in the years to come, "and Falwell passed it."

Preaching and entrepreneurship were intertwined. He related how he returned to Lynchburg in 1956 at the age of twenty-two and was approached by some laymen who'd raised $1,000 to start a new church. The only affordable building was a one-room semi-shack on Lynchburg's Thomas Road once owned by the Donald Duck Bottling Company. "It was so dirty," he told a reporter, "that when people tried to walk across the encrusted Coke syrup on the floor, their shoes stuck." But within a year he had his own radio show—and soon after that, one on TV.

One reason for his success might have been a skill increasingly in demand in the South after *Brown v. Board of Education*: justifications for racism. He argued in one 1958 sermon, published in the first issue of a newspaper he began publishing in conjunction with his new TV broadcast, the "racial problem in this country is not one of hate—but one of Biblical principle." Biblical principle was foursquare on the side of segregation, as one could see by studying Acts 17:26, in which the Lord sets the "bounds of their habitation" for the nations of the earth. God condemned Noah's son Ham and his brethren for all time to be "servants of servants." "Reading Genesis 10:6–20, and by searching your Bible dictionary and concordance you will find that Ham was the progenitor of the African, or Ethiopian, or colored race.... The mistake we have made is simply this: We have left God out of our decisions altogether. If Chief Warren and his associates had known God's Word and had desired to do the Lord's will, I am quite confident that the 1954 decision would never have been made. What could possibly have worked out in a scriptural and orderly way, now has become a touchy problem." For the "true Negro ... does not want integration. He realizes his potential is far better among his own race. Who then is propagating this terrible thing? First of all, we see the hand of Moscow in the background.... It boils down to whether we are going to take God's word as final."

Then he noted what a fine organist his wife, Macel, was, and the sermon was over.

Twenty years later, Falwell's *Old Time Gospel Hour* was on 327 television stations, his schools educating thousands of students from kindergarten through college. Chartered jets sent him proselytizing all over the world—including, most recently, to Israel and Egypt. Thomas Road Baptist Church boasted sixteen thousand members, in a city with sixty thousand people who had 124 other churches to choose from. "No one is safe here anymore," a Lynchburg Catholic complained. "He sends hundreds of student ministers out to knock on doors to save souls. And when we turn them away, they go after our children. The kids come home all upset, crying all night because they are afraid that unless they join Jerry's church they are going to hell."

TO COSMOPOLITAN ELITES LEARNING ABOUT FALWELL FOR THE FIRST TIME, he seemed just another cornpone country preacher. Closer observers saw crucial distinctions: "Jerry will replace Billy Graham as the leading proponent of evangelism," Graham's biographer explained. "He is less emotional than either Billy or Oral Roberts. He is friendlier, and much less divisive." "His method," *National Review* appreciatively observed, "is not to harangue, but to marshal witnesses."

A remarkable thing to say of a man who claimed in 1977 that homosexuals would "kill you as quick as look at you." It wasn't what Falwell said but how he said it. TV was a "cool" medium, as the theorist Marshall McLuhan famously put it. Compared to other Southern fundamentalists, Falwell was a *cool* preacher—none of the "subliminal sex, fire and excitement or rock-tinged music of a Jimmy Swaggart," in the words of another profile. Packaging, in a pleasingly modern form, the sort of traditional values that millions of upwardly mobile but anxious country-bred Americans left behind when they sought their fortune in the wider world—whether to Lynchburg, Virginia, or Orange County, California, or Concord, New Hampshire—was Falwell's greatest gift.

A long profile of Falwell ran in *Esquire* magazine, shortly before the one on Irving Kristol. It was entitled "The Next Billy Graham." The subtitle observed, "He may be the first preacher to become a political leader." The reporter noted she had been asked to dress modestly for the interview—just like the female *New York Times* writer who interviewed the Ayatollah. She wrote, "The women look like members of the same family. Medium height, brown bouffant hair, deep-blue eyeshadow, and pure-white skin that has never been flushed with the effects of alcohol." One of the men sheepishly admitted he enjoyed watching *Charlie's Angels* and *Three's Company*. "But I wouldn't tell Jerry."

The article was illustrated by the billboard at the threshold of the 3,200-acre Virginia mountaintop where Falwell was building his mighty empire: "WELCOME TO THE THOMAS ROAD BAPTIST CHURCH / WHERE THE OLD TIME GOSPEL IS STILL PREACHED." And Falwell puffing out his chest, thumbs in the vest of his double-knit three-piece suit; Falwell boarding a Learjet; Falwell holding forth before a blackboard in a boardroom; Falwell reviewing blueprints at a construction site stretching as far as the eye could see—and a giant room, with row upon row of desks, that a caption described as the outfit's "countinghouse," where "a crew of reborn Christians open letters with the speed and efficiency of assembly line workers. They pulled checks from the mailbags in sums as large as $450 and as small as $14. The day's total was $339,000. The week's take was $1.2 million." Material wealth, Falwell believed, was "God's way of blessing people who put him first."

Falwell was asked about the lawsuit filed against him by the Securities and Exchange Commission in 1973 for "fraud and deceit" during a $6.6 million bond drive to fund his Bible college. "His jaw tightens, his voice gets louder, but he doesn't pause": it had all been a big misunderstanding. They hadn't filled out a form they hadn't known was required; and the settlement he arrived at "helped me employ the necessary management controls. So my view is that without the SEC investigation, in which we were cleared of all fraud, we could never be where we are today. I believe God meant it for our good."

Which was all just a little bit absurd. Jerry Falwell didn't need lessons from the SEC on how to run a business. A portion of his ministry was even devoted to instructing allied pastors in the use of such spiritual instruments as IBM mainframes and digital mailing lists. A book he wrote with his associate Dr. Elmer Towns in 1973, *Capturing a Town for Christ*, cited the modern shopping mall, "the greatest innovation of business in the last twenty years," as a model: everything a family could need, all in one place—just like Falwell's burgeoning mountaintop empire.

Government was a model, too. He ran a home for recovering alcoholics, hired drug counselors, sent ministers out as de facto social workers, ran what he termed "agencies" for child rearing help and even financial assistance—like the Church of Jesus Christ of Latter-day Saints had been doing for over a century: building a private government for those who believed; which made it all the easier to scourge the actual government as an alien imposition.

Especially the government's schools. As Falwell put it in a sermon published in 1979, "I hope to see the day when, as in the early days of our country, we won't have public schools. The churches will have taken them over again and Christians will be running them. What a happy day that will be." He opened his first, an elementary school, in 1967, in the autumn Virginia first integrated its public schools. The *Lynchburg News* announced it as a "private school for white students." He preached his famous 1965 sermon aimed at Martin Luther King Jr.: "Preachers are called to be soul-winners, not politicians. Nowhere are we commissioned to reform the externals. We are not told to wage war against bootleggers, liquor stores, gamblers, murderers, prostitutes, racketeers, prejudiced persons, institutions, or any other existing evils as such. . . . Love cannot be legislated"—but, two years later, observed of the Supreme Court, "When a group of nine idiots can pass a ruling down that it is illegal to read the Bible in our public schools, they need to be called idiots."

In 1975, he sought to get out from under the crushing debt from his Liberty Baptist College project by taking its chorus on the road for seven months. He said he was inspired to press on after he and his students ventured next door one night to catch the end of a concert by Led Zeppelin, whose caterwauling had disturbed them the previous evening. He wrote: "Thousands of young men and women were lying on the floor, engaged in every filthy act imaginable. The discordant sounds were deafening. On the stage the rock star hero of thousands of American young people stood with outstretched arms in front of a cross"; and Falwell suddenly "felt in a small measure the tremendous weight of sin that was placed on Jesus Christ at the cross." He pledged to work even harder to help young people "turn this country upside down for Christ."

The Lord was working in mysterious ways. The SEC suit, his near-bankruptcy, the satanic vision he stumbled upon at a rock concert—all of it, Jerry Falwell became convinced, was part of His plan—he was being called for something beyond mere soul-winning. He launched his Bicentennial tour of state capitals. He raised his voice against Jimmy Carter's *Playboy* interview. What was "soul-winning," what was "politics"? Falwell played fast and loose. In 1976, he avowed, "This idea of 'religion and politics don't mix' was invented by the devil to keep Christians from running their own country." But he also oftentimes insisted fighting for "morality" wasn't political at all. In 1977 and 1978, he traveled to Florida to join forces with Anita Bryant and to California for John Briggs—then told *Esquire,* "I stay totally on spiritual issues."

He was no longer a racial segregationist. His understanding of the Devil's work on earth was different now: it was gays seeking civil rights. He also liked to quote "a man from whom I took great inspiration": "Fellows, if you're going to be successful, see a fight going all the time. You do pretty well at that." Just like Howard Phillips said: *organize discontent.*

THE DISCONTENT THAT JERRY FALWELL AND HIS BRETHREN DID BEST WITH reached its apotheosis on December 5, 1978, when Christians descended on Washington to testify against IRS commissioner Jerome Kurtz's new regulations for private schools seeking tax exemptions. The four days of hearings were the Christian right's modern Pentecost—the moment of the Bible's augury that "your sons and daughters will prophesy and your young men shall see visions and your old men shall dream dreams."

Kurtz's announcement in August had been met by an onslaught. First, word spread that the IRS had tried to *sneak* the new rules onto the books—that a single eagle-eyed Christian spotted the item in the *Federal Register* of August 21, 1978, "hidden" between a docket notice of inspection of freight cars and a pension and welfare benefit plan. Word went forth to the multitudes: flood the Internal Revenue Service with missives of protest.

In fact, the agency had gone out of its way to publicize the process. And there would have been plenty of protest against the IRS rules in any event. But the rumor helped heighten the passion. Evangelicals thrived on legends. This one inflamed a central component of evangelical identity: *martyrdom.* A cabal of Caesarian bureaucrats secretly conspiring to silence Christ's messengers: here was a discontent two millennia in the making.

The first to sound the klaxon were the leaders of a small movement that believed the Old Testament should provide the blueprint for American law. They called themselves "Christian Reconstructionists." Most of

the principles laid out by their guru, Dr. Rousas J. Rushdoony, in his colossal treatise *The Institutes of Biblical Law*—for instance, that a "Godly
order" must punish homosexuality with death by stoning—found few
takers. But one was highly influential: that for Christian parents to "surrender their children to the state"—to educate them at public schools—
was "to turn them over to the enemy." On August 15, 1978, Rushdoony's
son-in-law Gary North published "The I.R.S. Attack on the Independent
Schools" in the Reconstructionist journal *Remnant Review* arguing that
the IRS was enacting a conspiracy in league with wicked public school
bureaucrats terrified that the superior education Christian schools offered would put them out of business. "Priesthoods like your tax dollars,"
North explained—citing his other intellectual hero, the libertarian economist Friedrich Hayek. "They would like a monopoly even more. And a
monopoly with compulsory attendance: that would be heaven on earth.
For the priests." And North made another influential argument in the next
issue: that "civil rights" was merely the IRS's pretext. Their *real* war—
"being waged at every level, from every side"—was "against those who
deny the sovereignty of the messianic state." He concluded by imploring
"worshippers of anything except the state" to "write a letter, no matter
how short, and make *six photocopies* (as requested)."

One early letter came from Paul Weyrich, a Reconstructionist fellow
traveler: "By this proposal, the IRS is deciding what is right to think and
what is wrong, and pronouncing a death penalty on wrong thoughts. I
cannot think of anything more totalitarian." He then roused his Committee for the Survival of a Free Congress mailing list to follow his example.

The congressman, presidential candidate, and American Conservative
Union chairman Phil Crane wrote Commissioner Kurtz on September
29. His said it was the *IRS*, by introducing racial quotas, that was guilty
of discrimination—and, since he was "not sympathetic in the slightest
with discrimination on the basis of race," he would be fighting that with
everything he had. On October 5, he introduced a bill to take away the
IRS's power to adopt any regulation governing private school admissions
until 1981, then blustered at a press conference, "What is at stake here is
a basic human freedom—the freedom to choose where one will educate
one's children." He was followed by the Christian school lobbyist Robert
Billings, who predicted the IRS might next seek to crush the Quakers for
their commitment to pacifism.

The ACU sent a legislative alert—"IRS SAYS: GUILTY UNTIL
PROVEN INNOCENT"—to its 350,000 members. By then, the IRS had
received twelve thousand letters. One, from the United States Conference of Catholic Bishops, called the rules "completely unrealistic" and
probably unconstitutional. Many, many letters must have followed a Pat

Buchanan column predicting that federal bureaucrats in their "envy and hatred" would soon order military academies to take girls; and a *Human Events* article quoting Robert Billings from a press conference in front of IRS headquarters, saying that the IRS might soon order Catholic doctors to perform abortions.

The most important letters came from members of Congress. One drafted by Representative Larry McDonald asserted, "There is no rational nexus between the delegated function of the Internal Revenue Service to collect revenue and these punitive procedures. If these regulations are accepted as valid, this implies that we can be forced in the future to conform to the notion of social good proclaimed in Washington, not just as to race but to any matter." Its seventy-eight signatories were all conservatives. But another was signed by two liberal Catholics senators, Thomas Eagleton of Missouri and Edmund Muskie of Maine. It complained that the procedure "casts a very wide net that will undoubtedly bring in a large number of non 'white flight' schools." Another Catholic, Joe Biden of Delaware, shared similar views, and later voted to strike money to regulate private schools from the IRS's authorization.

By December the IRS had received 150,000 letters. Phil Crane claimed that another 60,000 messages of opposition came to members of Congress. The IRS responded by announcing three days of hearings. They received so much interest that a fourth day had to be added. Commissioner Kurtz noted the IRS had never invited so much public comment and instituted so much procedural transparency at any previous time in its 116-year history.

And on the first day, the first witness could not have been more unimpressed.

"Your chosen hearing dates most conspicuously fall just prior to the beginning of the Christmas holy season when pastors and other churchmen of many of the parent schools your regulations will drastically affect are particularly preoccupied," Senator Orrin Hatch railed to the ten IRS bureaucrats arrayed onstage before him. "And you self-conveniently chose as the dates on which to hold the only hearings you wish to hold on this matter during that brief interregnum after the close of one Congress and before the beginning of the next one." He concluded, "most Americans find your proposed regulations repulsive."

The first seven witnesses were members of Congress moved to the front of the line in deference to their office, concluding with Senator Strom Thurmond, who said that while the goal of fighting racial discrimination in American society was "impossible for a reasonable man to argue against," there was not a "shred of authority" for what the IRS was attempting. He got a standing ovation. When it died down, an IRS assistant commissioner named Al Winborne asked, "Do we have any more members of Congress who would like to speak at this time? If we do not, I think since several members apparently have been delayed in some way, that we should take a short recess during which I would ask if there—"

A Southern accent rang out.

It belonged to a woman named Peggy June Griffin. She had been raised in the Church of the Nazarene, a Pentecostal denomination whose 1936 *Manual* enjoined members to fight Communism as a matter of doctrine. In the 1960s, working as a secretary at the University of Kentucky, she organized a petition drive to ban Students for a Democratic Society. Her husband quit his job at IBM after learning, as his wife put it, that the company was "selling computers to the Vietcong" (IBM had transferred technology to Eastern European nations, a cause célèbre among conservatives in 1968). In 1973, they sent their son off to Pensacola Christian Academy, which had recently begun selling its curriculum to other schools. Known as Abeka, it would eventually teach millions of Americans that any Bible translation besides the King James Version was part of Satan's plan to confuse the church, and that rock music violated Ephesians 5:18. ("And be not drunk with wine, wherein is excess; but be filled with the Spirit.")

Griffin heard about hearings "to close down the Christian schools" unless they "accept sodomites." She contacted her senator to get on the witness list. He told her it was too late. She responded, "You *will* get me on. This is God's will." She received a speaking spot for Friday, the last scheduled day of hearings. She arrived on Tuesday for the opening hearing, in an auditorium of the Treasury Department, the ornate and imposing edifice featured on the face of the ten-dollar bill: just the sort of setting a modern-day Caesar could be expected to use to intimidate followers of Christ to render unto the state the fealty only He was owed. She watched, appalled, she later recalled, as "one after another, weak-kneed politicians bowed and scraped in their little speeches hoping for some compassion and a listening ear from this proud, out-of-control agency." She rose up from the middle of the audience:

"Will *we* have an opportunity to ask questions of the Congressmen before they have to go back?"

"I beg your pardon," Winborne responded, startled, his eyes searching the crowd. "I don't understand you. Are you scheduled to speak?"

"I'm scheduled to speak Friday, but I doubt there will be everyone here, and I—"

The crowd rustled and rumbled. Winborne asked, "Does anybody in the audience have any objection if she takes a few minutes at this point in time?"

There was none. Winborne looked down from the stage: "Will this be your testimony? You will speak again on Friday, or not?"

As confidently as Moses handing down stone tablets, she replied, "I *will* speak again on Friday." She marched to the stage and placed herself behind the podium:

"My name is June Griffin, and I'm a taxpayer from Evansville, Tennessee. I get the feeling that Congress is asking these men permission to do this and that. We do not want this proposal ground through the mills of compromise. We want it buried. And the authority that these men have assumed as the law of the land must be buried. We have had it. I know that I speak for the Christians in my area, that we must go back to the law of the land that was established by our forefathers. These men do not have the rightful authority to tell us how to run our schools, our homes, and our churches. Thank you."

She got a resounding ovation. She made it onto the national network news. That set the tone for the next four days.

WASHINGTON HAD NEVER SEEN AN ADMINISTRATIVE HEARING LIKE THIS. Protesters from both sides held up picket signs. ("LET GOD RUN RELIGIOUS SCHOOLS—NOT THE IRS"; "JIM CROW WITH YOUR OWN DOUGH.") Ministers passed out tracts. So did an official from the American Conservative Union—a special Christian-schools-and-IRS issue of its magazine, *Battle Line*. Preachers declaimed as if the podium were a tent meeting pulpit—and received the customary whooping and hollering in return. Probably weeping and gnashing of teeth, too, from the panel of bureaucrats on the stage.

A minister from Spokane said he had traveled the farthest. Winborne corrected him: the president of the Alaska Association of Christian Schools had come, too. They crashed on hotel room couches. They skipped flights, happy to strand themselves for the privilege of staying longer. A radio host from Fort Pierce, Florida, said his listeners had raised a collection to pay his way. A man reported awakening at four o'clock to pray for the panel until the opening gavel sounded. One day, so many clamored to be heard that the proceedings adjourned near midnight. One minister commended the panel: "You'd make a good congregation. You haven't fallen asleep." Then, around 11 p.m., one of the panelists did.

The diversity of the Christian school movement was also on display, like the liberal headmaster of a school in Philadelphia who boasted of how his student body was so integrated that black and white students walked arm and arm down the hall. Then, however, a few spots later, a Baptist minister from rural Florida addressed the man from Philadelphia in a white heat: "In a *real* fundamentalist Christian school, two whites or two blacks cannot walk down the hall with their arms around each other!" He said the Philadelphian wouldn't even have been *allowed* inside his school:

"His hair was six inches too long." But a black mother said that was *why* she sent her child to a twenty-pupil Baptist school: "Young men must cut their hair to a certain length, girls can't wear dresses unless they are a certain length. . . . it teaches boys to be gentlemen; it teaches girls to be ladies. . . . What they do in the public schools—no training whatsoever. In Christian schools, you obey."

A father from Haddonfield, New Jersey, explained, "We're sort of a product of a time in which the good guys wore the white hats and the bad guys wore the black hats. . . . We had a little difficulty when the public school decided that it wasn't proper that a child who lived in our country didn't have to stand in respect for the flag that represented our country." Bob Jones III made note of the date—December 7, the anniversary of the "Day of Infamy" at Pearl Harbor—and cried, "Americans of a different sort today, thirty-seven years after Pearl Harbor, gather in this auditorium to defend our freedoms from a different enemy, the IRS!" He was interrupted for applause. He continued, "No one, regardless of color, is fit material for the classroom of a Christian school who is not a regenerated, redeemed, blood-washed child of God. . . . We will go to jail before we will abandon our God-ordained purpose!" That earned another burst— one of seven in five minutes.

That, in fact, happened *every* time a witness indicated a willingness to go to jail—which happened often: "Is the U.S. government prepared to send thousands of preachers to jail for their Bible-based convictions? Please do not miscalculate, because it is exactly what will happen. We are not a bunch of rednecks trying to defend an indefensible position, that is, the hatred of another race. We are men who believe the Bible to be the Word of God and who believe in constitutional government. We would die for either, but we will not obey government when it conflicts with God."

One time, Winborne, well sick of it, interrupted the president of the Colorado Association of Christian Schools:

"I don't know that we've *ever* put anybody in jail for the mere nonpayment of tax."

"Oh, is that right?"

"They'd have to commit a fraudulent act I think before we would put them in jail."

"But we're *ready* to go that far. This is our trench."

"Well, maybe you're over-prepared."

Another reliable route to audience acclaim was to point out that the panel was entirely white. Perhaps, a principal suggested, *they* should prove their racial tolerance, perhaps by walking out of the auditorium and picking a random black person to treat to dinner. "This is what you are asking the schools to do—to provide free scholarships to prove that we have nothing against minority students." He then told story the story of "a little girl that I love very dearly in our school, a little black girl," whose father had told him, "You know, this is the first school that our daughter has attended where she has not been called a 'nigger.' She came from the *public* schools!"

"Shame! Shame!" the congregation responded as one.

Evangelicals were *proud* of their parallel school system. They recited reams of statistics demonstrating their academic superiority over the public competition. (This was a logical fallacy: public schools were required by law to take all comers. But Robert Billings's instruction manual for creating a Christian school included a proposed sample application that asked—in addition to questions like "Do you have the complete assurance that you are saved?"—"Have you received special tutoring to bring you up to standard in any school subject?" and "Have you ever been required to appear before a judge, a court, or a law-enforcing officer?") They responded to even reasonable criticisms with hair-trigger paranoia, entertaining nearly any rumor concerning their persecution as fact. Robert Billings rushed in late for his turn at the podium on the second day: "I was talking to the White House," he said apologetically. "I heard, as I came in the foyer this afternoon, that President Carter had made a statement and it was on CBS News this morning that regardless of the outcome of these hearings, he intended to promulgate these regulations and settle it in court!"

The panel was baffled; the White House had been silent on their work. Then another witness repeated the claim two days later. An exasperated IRS public relations officer responded that he had reached out to CBS, who said they had reported no such thing.

But who trusted the liberal media? Or the IRS? According to Billings, they were treating Christians like slaves. And "it is better to die than to live as slaves."

ONE DAY, THE PROCEEDINGS WERE RELOCATED TO THE COMMERCE DEPARTment auditorium, where, as a matter of policy, visitors were escorted by security personnel when they left the hall—and their paranoia overfloweth. For instance from a witness from Birmingham. She started in on a soliloquy about the moral decrepitude of secular society: "If man is no more than a machine, as Sir Francis Crick and Freud and many others say, he is expandable—and we will have more cruelty, violence, in the streets, more having to be escorted to the ladies room, as I was today, by an *armed guard . . .*"

That particular witness, as it happened, a former public school administrator, continued on to offer an erudite and eloquent explanation of *why* evangelicals decried modern, "humanistic," public school curricula. "You people say that you want to help minorities," she began. But "we children of the Reformation are the *only* people in America who can give any minority the thing that is eternal because only the Judeo-Christian faith has the basis for the dignity of man. . . . the view that man is created in God's image. A man doesn't have to be redeemed to have value. A man can be destitute or derelict and still have worth and still have value. Any boy or girl made in the image of God has value, has dignity, and I would shudder to think that I were part of a ministry in the name of Jesus Christ who did not view boy, girl, man or woman as having eternal worth."

She continued, "When I was a child in public school and I studied history, I had Christian teachers who told me that history was His story. They taught me how God dealt with men and with nations, as we marched through the Roman Empire all the way across the Middle Ages, the Renaissance, the Reformation, and finally we landed on Plymouth Rock. Now, gentlemen, this is not public education today. Perhaps you were in the same school system that I was in when there was a flow to history, when there was a unity, unified body of knowledge."

But now education was just a string of disassociated facts—and if a teacher closed the door and taught "eternal verities as Biblical truth, as Biblical revelation, they are breaking the law."

One could certainly disagree. But at least this presentation helped clarify where some of the more histrionic witnesses were coming from. In fact, had some national magazine published it, it would have served a useful purpose in closing the gap in empathy between these incommensurate tribes. Alas, for her testimony to have been published, this witness would have had to give her full name. She only identified herself for the record as "Mrs. John B. Aimes"—subsuming herself beneath her husband, as her husband subsumed himself beneath the Lord, just as the Book of Ephesians commanded.

Incommensurate tribes—as a sixty-nine-year-old grandmother from Delaware discovered. She began, "I don't know if the lady on the panel has children, but believe me gentlemen, sixty-nine years is many, many batches of Toll House cookies for the PTA—"

An official from the IRS Exempt Organizations Division interrupted her: "The men on the panel have children."

She retorted, "But they don't make cookies," then reconsidered: "Or they may, I don't know." In this topsy-turvy world, anything was possible.

THINGS GREW FRIGHTENING. R. J. RUSHDOONY TESTIFIED AS IF THE TEN Commandments had been handed down only the previous week. He said that the panelists were *literal* manifestations of the pagan gods who had tempted the Israelites, that "Moloch worship was a form of state worship," and that this was "the ultimate treason to God." He received a thunderclap of applause.

A minister lectured, "I remind you that the mother of Moses refused to obey the king and kill her son. . . . Daniel refused to obey a new law that said no man could pray for a thirty-day period, and he went into the den of lions. . . . Peter, Paul, James, and John were likewise lawbreakers. Peter the Apostle said, 'We must obey God rather than men.' We believe only God deserves unqualified obedience. We obey him without question, whereas we obey parents, policemen, judges, superiors, state legislators, Congress, and even the Supreme Court only as long as their demands do not conflict with God's."

The proprietor of Our Shepard's Academy of Stone Mountain, Georgia, said, "If America's one most avidly law-abiding group begins to see our tax collecting agency as the hired goons of the National Education Association, willingly being used to put muscle on the private Christian school competition which is embarrassing them with vastly superior educational results and cost-effectiveness, when the tax-paying honest law-abiding community is pushed to the point of civil disobedience—"

He paused: "I would rather not finish that sentence." Coming only three weeks after Jonestown, such words must have sounded harrowing indeed.

The bureaucrats had not been prepared for anything like this. They had not, for instance, read Dr. Rushdoony's influential 1963 book *The Messianic Character of American Education*, which argued, "The public school is the established church of today and a substitute for the medieval church, dedicated to the same monolithic conception of society." He did not mean that the modern public school system was a metaphorical religion. His followers in fact held that any school that did not acknowledge the dominion of God as revealed by Scripture—like a science class that did not say the world was created in seven days—endorsed a *literal* religion: "secular humanism." A public school teaching secular humanism thereby violated the First Amendment by advocating for a state religion, discriminating against *all other* religions. But if a public school taught Christianity, it was *not* discrimination—because, as Reverend Billings testified, "this republic is a Christian nation founded by Christian men, Christian people with Christian principles."

This hall-of-mirrors logic was a bedrock belief, rooted in a surreal misreading of a 1961 Supreme Court case, *Torcaso v. Watkins*, that affirmed the right of an appellant who refused to declare a belief in God to serve as a notary public. In an aside, Justice Hugo Black had noted that the state could *also* not discriminate against religions that did not believe in God—

"Buddhism, Taoism, Ethical Culture, Secular Humanism and others," he wrote in a footnote many of these fundamentalists had committed to memory. In reality, "secular humanism" was an umbrella term for a loose conglomeration of traditions of nontheistic ethical reasoning that maintained, as a 1933 "Humanist Manifesto" put it, that humans should seek their "development and fulfillment in the here and now." In the imagination of fundamentalists, however, Justice Black revealed an awful truth: government had not just banished God from the classroom but replaced Him with a *state religion*, whose prophets were John Dewey, Auguste Comte, and Jean-Jacques Rousseau. Government was the *aggressor* in the battle to keep church separated from state. Christians were only fighting back.

This idea received its most authoritative recent formulation in a law review article coauthored by John Conlan, the former congressman, "The Establishment of the Religion of Secular Humanism and Its First Amendment Implications." More casual expressions of it could be found everywhere. A Pat Buchanan column argued that if the new rules succeeded, they would kill any private school which "does not conform with the social values of secular humanism which is the newly established religion in the United States." A correspondent to an Indiana newspaper, the day the hearings opened: "Humanism has been identified as a religion, so why not remove it from public schools, too? Or is it really only Christianity that is supposed to be kept out?" A witness at the hearing: "being required to support the establishment of secularism by our taxes, we are being unjustly penalized and hindered in the free exercise of our religion"—and that was "religious persecution." Ronald Reagan contributed a radio commentary—drafted by himself in longhand with a note to editors requesting it run during the hearings—quoting Justice John Marshall ("the power to tax involves the power to destroy") to claim the IRS "threatens the destruction of religious freedom itself with this action. The Commissioner and your congressman should be hearing from you now."

Similar apocalyptic arguments concerned America's founding texts— "the most precious documents ever written by the hands of moral men, apart from the Word of God." The Declaration of Independence called out the king for creating "a multitude of new offices," for having "sent hither swarms of officers to harass our people and eat out their substance"; IRS agents—with the intent, a minister insisted, to "control every facet of the church"—were doing the same thing. Indeed, since American schools, indeed all schools, had begun as religious institutions, the *secular* public school system ("a relic of the dark ages," another minister said) should be forced to justify itself.

After all, a minister insisted, our ancestors all "came into these parts of America with one and the same end, to advance the Kingdom of the Lord

Jesus Christ"—and part of that was the commandment "to educate our children in accord with His will." And yet here they were, lectured another, persecuted by a spiderweb of conspirators insisting on the "indoctrination of America's youth toward totalitarian and world government where individual freedom would be lost for all"—going back to the days of the flamboyant gadfly Madalyn Murray O'Hair, whose legal advocacy had led to the outlawing of prayer in school in the first place, which "may not disturb any of you Caesarian tax collectors, but which offends many of us taxpayers—"

At which Winborne interrupted, for the witness had long ago used up his time: "Excuse me, Mr. Ingram. Are you pretty much through?"

There was a Caesarian tax collector playing to New Testament type, right there.

Back in January, Commissioner Kurtz had taken pains to insist that the IRS had no interest in "any individual's privately held beliefs, just their actions based on such beliefs." But that was the very distinction that ministers considered the heart of the existential threat.

"You cannot say to me or to my church that my bus ministry is a church ministry and my educational ministry is not," one argued. "There's no dichotomy in the church. We have tried very patiently through many hours and you've sat many hours listening to a bunch of preachers trying to say something to you that we feel very strongly about."

Which made for quite the policy dilemma. One witness was Supreme Court litigator William Ball, who had argued such landmark cases as *Wisconsin v. Yoder* (1972), which ruled that the state could not mandate compulsory education for Amish children beyond the eighth grade, and *Meek v. Pittinger* (1975), which struck down a Pennsylvania law mandating what textbooks nonpublic schools must use—and had more recently been developing the argument that Christians' religious liberty was violated when states required their schools to comply with teacher certification requirements, zoning laws, truancy laws—really, any civil law to which they objected. Ball testified that the IRS's "unfamiliarity with the subject it seeks to regulate is no more clear" than when it demanded that Christian schools recruit a certain class of students. "The fundamentalist schools do not 'recruit.' They evangelize; and evangelization is not a thing subject to governmental direction."

So telling them whom to teach was equivalent to telling them how to preach. It was Caesar telling Christians: *We own you.*

Kurtz had boasted in that January speech that his commitment to the First Amendment was so ironclad that "churches today have only minimal demands made on them": just a modest form asking basic questions to demonstrate they were bona fide religious organizations. He had said in his opening statement, "This is a proposal, not a decision. Our minds are open." Then he heard preachers describing those "minimal demands" as if they were Roman imperial decrees ordering Christians to the Colosseum to battle lions. And these Christians did not intend to hide in catacombs. Said one, "You have done something that is incredible: awaken Christendom from one side of Texas to the other." Promised another, "We're really going to be coming here to Washington quite often and we're going to clean house quite a bit."

BUT THE HEARINGS WERE NOT ALL THEOLOGICAL MELODRAMA. THEY WOULD have been easier to ignore if they had been. Instead, at several points, well-informed witnesses, some secular, others religious, spoke dispassionately to the bureaucrats in the language of bureaucrats, undermining the soundness of the proposed revenue procedure on the bureaucrats' own terms. They helped illuminate another aspect of these fundamentalists' world-shaking anger nonetheless: their feeling of being unfairly accused of racism.

John Anderson argued convincingly that the rules fell afoul of the Supreme Court's ruling five months earlier in *Regents of the University of California v. Bakke*, which outlawed numerical quotas for minority admissions—but the IRS appeared to be enforcing them on churches without a second thought. Representatives of liberal-learning private school operators like the National Association of Waldorf Schools—who practiced an educational philosophy so humanist it would make Dr. Rushdoony's hair stand up on end—testified that the procedural hurdles might put them out of business. It was the same argument made by smaller, shoestring Christian schools: that the requirements for certifying their "operation in good faith in a racially non-discriminatory basis," like offering scholarships, were simply beyond their reach, and that for mere financial deficiencies the IRS could find them not in "good faith operated on a non-discriminatory basis." It was humiliating—akin, one anguished official complained, to being an innocent bystander to someone else's crime who was forced to prove they had not committed it.

The most convincing bearer of such an argument was the man who had devised the very 1971 guidelines that Kurtz believed himself to be improving upon, whose liberal bona fides were unimpeachable. IRS commissioner Randolph Thrower had been fired by Richard Nixon for refusing to audit everyone on his "enemies list." As a young lawyer in Georgia, he had demonstrated extraordinary courage as one of the few white lawyers willing to represent black men accused of rape; in 1956, he ran an anti-segregationist campaign there for Congress. Now Thrower testified about a Georgia Christian school that had approached him to help with a dilemma. They had welcomed African American students ever since they opened in 1969, investing considerable resources to recruit them. But they never received a single application. They had approached Thrower in some distress to help defend the good faith of these integrationist efforts. He commissioned a researcher to survey local African Americas to find out why they were not applying. That research discovered that they shared a "very high-level reported satisfaction with the public schools," and were "strongly committed to and supportive of the public-school system" as a matter of principle. And that "the peer pressure against parents and students evidencing an interest in the private school could be overwhelming." Thrower eloquently concluded that the reason was the basic facts of Southern history: blacks reasonably associated white evangelicals with the power structure that had oppressed them for centuries. Attending integrated public schools was both symbol and substance of their proud accomplishment in fighting that oppression. There was simply no way, Thrower explained, for four pages of rules in the *Federal Register* to erase the "perception, whether justified or not as of today, based upon 150 years of history of enforced segregation terminated only recently."

To arguments like these, the IRS listened, deliberated, weighed, and considered. Which, after all, was what they had been hired to do. And so, on February 9, little more than two months after the hearings, Kurtz published a revised proposal. It directed local IRS agents to evaluate school compliance on a "case-by-case," rather than "mechanical," basis. It shifted the burden of proof to the government, not the schools. It softened its former statistical threshold from a trigger for ordering remedial action, into a mere suggestion for investigation by field agents—whose recommendations would be subject to automatic review by himself.

In practical terms, that is to say, nearly every one of those fundamentalists' perfervid anxieties about government *komissars* sabotaging their sacred commission had now been rendered moot.

Which had no apparent effect on subsequent political developments at all. As Peggy June Griffin said: They did not want the rules ground through the mills of compromise. They wanted them buried.

Angry letters continued unabated. Editorials kept horsewhipping the out-of-control IRS. On February 18, Kurtz faced a two-day bipartisan scolding before a congressional subcommittee. A Democrat from Delaware called the rules a "massive attack against the policy of noninterference in the work and goals of charitable institutions," a "full-scale challenge to the First Amendment." John Anderson said they still went "far beyond anything required by the Constitution, the courts, or Congress." A Republican from Florida said they were an attack on the South. Kurtz had to request Secret Service protection because of all the death threats.

The objections were about much more than the law. They were tribal. The New Right had found its most powerful organizing discontent yet.

CONSERVATIVE MOVEMENT ACTIVISTS HAD BEEN WORKING TO RECRUIT PREACH- ers at least since 1962, the year of the Supreme Court's landmark school prayer decision, when John Conlan persuaded oilman J. Howard Pew and General Electric CEO Charles E. Wilson (a "choice fundraiser" who "loves the Lord") to fund the training of ministers to "infiltrate and cap- ture the organs of elective machinery in their respective communities." They never got far. Gun-shy divines had three broad objections. First, they feared giving offense to congregants: supporting candidate X was a great way to chase supporters of candidate Y out of your pews. Second, fundamentalist doctrine discouraged such "worldly" concerns as ungodly. (Colossians 3:2: "Set your affection on things above, not on things on the earth.") And finally they feared the icy objections of that outside world— an especially pregnant concern for ministers with empire-building ambi- tions, who had witnessed the decimation of Billy Graham's reputation after Watergate for his close association with Richard Nixon.

In 1976, the New Right tried again. It was Richard Viguerie who had spurred the congressional run of Robert Billings, who was also the trea- surer of Weyrich's Free Congress Research and Education Foundation, and also that of Robert Thoburn, proprietor of the Christian school where both he and Howard Phillips sent their children—proclaiming, "The next real major area of growth for the conservative ideology and philosophy is among evangelical people."

But both those candidates lost—as did John Conlan for Senate, against a Jewish opponent, after it was revealed that he said, "A vote for Conlan is a vote for Christianity. We need to elect a Christian Congress," making Conlan famous as a bigot. The exposé of their efforts in *Sojourners* maga- zine then made evangelicals look like venal scammers. So ministers had tried taking Richard Viguerie's advice before—and reaped only humilia- tion.

Then, however, came success after success: Anita Bryant in Dade County; a winning campaign electing Thoburn to the Virginia House of Delegates; Phyllis Schlafly nearly breaking the back of the ERA, and her triumphant rally countering the National Women's Conference in Hous- ton; Francis Schaeffer's documentary series *How Then Shall We Live*; the preacher-led antisodomite triumphs in St. Paul, Wichita, and Eugene; the election of evangelical senators in Iowa, Colorado, and New Hampshire—

then, four weeks after that 1978 election, the four-day evangelical Woodstock confronting the IRS in Washington, D.C. It was easier to recruit the reluctant into a political crusade when that crusade was winning. The walls were tumbling down. And, over the next seven headlong months, the modern Christian right was born.

IT BEGAN, IN FACT, THE VERY NEXT DAY.

Robert Billings secured an unused Senate hearing room for Paul Weyrich to make a pitch to ministers before they left town. "I didn't know what to expect," Weyrich remembered. "But I went over there and explained to them what was going on . . . and these people jumped to their feet and started cheering. I was absolutely astounded. I'd never encountered an audience like that, because conservatives are rather reserved."

But their ardor cooled when he began discussing actually organizing their flocks for the 1980 election; they worried their parishioners might abandon them. "You're dead wrong," Weyrich remembered responding. "And moreover, you are going to pay to prove it." He enacted a familiar church ritual—though he himself had learned it watching rallies for Israel bonds: going around the room, calling out each attendee to pledge a $1,000 donation. He raised enough to hire a top Republican pollster, Lance Tarrance, to survey the evangelical grass roots nationally.

Or at least that was Weyrich's version of the genesis of Tarrance's poll. In another account the pitch came the following June, following a rally in Dallas, and the heroic donor was a single wealthy Houston homebuilder named Bob Perry. Evangelical America thrives on legend.

Though at least one legendary event from that week in Washington left an actual, confirming document: a handwritten note from Billings to Weyrich thanking him for convening a "smashing" reception introducing the preachers to the three new evangelical senators-elect. "Paul," he wrote, "we did something that no-one has done in years. . . . I believe something was started last night that will pull together many of our 'fringe' Christian friends. . . . Thank you for your important part. God bless you!' "

Within days, Billings had chartered a new organization, the National Christian Action Coalition, whose name signaled a far greater ambition than his previous group's, which had been called merely Christian School Action. In January other foundational groups emerged, from Southern California—where mixing politics and preaching was *not* unusual. Orange County was a haven for evangelical transplants from Dixie. Since the 1950s, they had been agitating against heretical textbooks, dirty movies, sex education in the schools—and, the year of Barry Goldwater's presidential loss, for a successful ballot initiative to repeal a ban on racial discrimination in housing, which they feared as an opening wedge for government encroachment on their right to build churches where they wished—"only a short step to being told *what* we can preach," one wrote in the *Californian Southern Baptist.*

The founding legend for one of the groups was that Beverly LaHaye was snuggled up on the couch with her husband, Tim, one evening in 1978 watching Barbara Walters interview Betty Friedan, who was claiming to speak for American women. She leapt up and cried, "Betty Friedan doesn't speak for me and I bet she doesn't speak for the majority of women in this country!" (In fact, Barbara Walters didn't interview Betty Friedan in 1978.) The specialty of Concerned Women for America was political rapid response organized via "prayer chapters"—cells—of fifty women each. Within eighteen months, the organization claimed 110,000 dues-paying members and a mailing list larger than Phyllis Schlafly's.

The other new California group was Christian Voice, founded by two ministers, Robert Grant and Richard Zone, who had been active in the Briggs Amendment campaign, and organized via the mailing list from the Catholic, Cleveland-based antipornography organization Citizens for Decency Under Law, provided to them by Jerry Falwell's personal direct-mail expert. The pitch read, "We're *tired* of seeing the federal government trample all over our time-honored and sacred Christian values. We're *tired* of seeing our nation's wealth squandered on crazy, vote-buying welfare schemes, and of seeing our sustenance being destroyed by inflation and big government spending. We want to return to the old values of hard work, thrift, and obedience to the laws of God. In other words, WE WANT OUR COUNTRY BACK!"

Christian Voice's greatest coup was hiring away from the American Conservative Union's "Stop OSHA" campaign a Washington legislative director, Gary Jarmin. He recruited a congressional advisory committee including Senators Hatch, Jepsen, Humphrey, and James McClure of Idaho. Weyrich welcomed Christian Voice to the fold with a meeting that included officials of the ACU, the National Conservative Political Action Committee, the Republican Study Committee of the House of Representatives, Reagan's Citizens for the Republic, and the National Association of Manufacturers. Their first project was distributing *The Internal Revenue Service vs. Christian Education and the First Amendment: A Handbook for Church and Community Leaders,* by a lawyer for the Heritage Foundation. It said that the IRS school hearings had been "providential" in demonstrating why getting "involved in the political process as Christians" was "a duty." By 1981 Christian Voice's political action committee was the eighth-biggest PAC in the country.

Jarmin had previously been a hippie rock drummer, then an official in the Reverend Sun Myung Moon's Unification Church. He later explained a secret to Christian Voice's success. "The beauty of it is that we don't have to organize these voters. They already have their own television networks, publications, schools, meeting places, and respected leaders who are sympathetic to our goals."

A NEW FILM STARRING ORSON WELLES BEGAN APPEARING IN MULTIPLEXES in January that brought to the screen one of the most spectacular publishing sensations in history. *The Late, Great Planet Earth*, by the evangelist Hal Lindsey, had sold nearly ten million copies since its original appearance in 1970. By March, the movie version was one of Hollywood's top ten moneymakers.

"Seventy percent of the prophesies written in the Bible have already been fulfilled," Orson Welles boomed. "If the visions of the prophet John are truly prophetic, the remaining visions will be fulfilled in our lifetime. . . . What are these perils that could mean the end of life on planet earth?"

Out stepped a mustachioed Hal Lindsey, a former missionary with Campus Crusade for Christ, in a blue jumpsuit and giant gold Jewish star hung around his neck, with the answer: "As the world staggers from one crisis to another, I believe we are reaching the end of history as we know it."

The reels that followed tacked between gauzy biblical reenactments, terrifying footage of the awful events haunting the evening news, interviews with respected scientists predicting worse (it's hard to imagine many knew what kind of film they had agreed to participate in), and exegeses of the Bible verses that saw it all coming. Like, for instance, the two hundred million men China now had under arms—"the exact figure predicted in Revelation"—who would soon pour over the River Euphrates to usher in seven years of martial conflagration unlike any seen so far in human history. Israel would sign "a pact with the anti-Christ," who would be falsely "hailed as the savior of mankind" for " 'solving' the Middle East Crisis." (There came a numerological analysis, computer reels whirring in the background, of whether the prophesy referred to Jimmy Carter, Ted Kennedy, or Ronald Reagan.) The seven-year countdown to Armageddon would begin—"the final battle of history . . . multitudes, multitudes, the Valley of Decision, for the day of the Lord is near, in the Valley of Decision. . . ."

And lo, the screen filled with a mushroom cloud, but not before many multitudes of gratuitous, titillating shots of women on beaches in bikinis.

The film was made for a not inconsiderable $11 million, the most for any religious picture ever. (The second most expensive, the movie version of Watergate felon Charles Colson's memoir *Born Again*, had come out in October.) In April it played on the new pay TV service HBO. A similarly themed film, *A Thief in the Night*, had been screened continually in churches since its release in 1972. It centered on the biblical prophecy that the righteous would be "raptured" to heaven, and that those left behind would fight a seven-year battle of Armageddon between the forces of good and evil. Decades later, grown-ups testified of their panic as children every time they saw a weird cloud formation, or when they arrived from school and no one else was home. One boy in Norfolk, Virginia, whose church had a mural of a pilotless plane smacking into a skyscraper, would call his pastor's house. "I'd ask to speak to his wife. I knew there was no way the pastor's wife would be skipped on Rapture Day. Wasn't so sure about the pastor."

A fear of not being raptured was a matchless spur to righteousness. And, now that ministers were instructing their flocks that righteousness demanded supporting the correct political candidates, it was a marvelous spur to political action, too.

THAT JANUARY ALSO SAW THE MARCH FOR LIFE, WHICH THE ORGANIZERS said drew a hundred thousand participants, on the most bitterly cold day of the six annual marches so far. The United States Park Service said it was only sixty thousand—but no one could dispute that their number included more evangelical Protestants than ever.

As the crowd milled before stepping off, a reporter asked organizer Nellie Gray whether she intended to accept the National Organization for Women's renewed invitation to forty groups on both sides of the abortion debate to discuss matters of mutual concern. Gray responded, "Pro-life people will not negotiate with baby killers." Carolyn Gerster of the National Right to Life Committee answered the same question by saying she would accept just as soon as the National Abortion Rights Action League admitted that abortion was "the greatest violence afflicting our society today."

Feminist outreach for peaceful dialogue in 1978 had failed. This time, they followed up the original approach with painstaking negotiations, and probes for common ground—as when NOW's Eleanor Smeal asked Nellie Gray whether she might support more effective sex education to help reduce the incidence of unwanted pregnancy. Gray replied that sex education was a scheme to teach children "how to become fodder for the abortion industry."

Other pro-life activists, however, took the chance. On Valentine's Day, about fifty activists evenly divided between the two sides gathered at a Washington hotel meeting room, in sessions closed to the press in order to minimize ideological posturing. They also agreed in advance that anyone mentioning abortion itself as opposed to areas of potential mutual agreement would be gaveled into silence. There followed several tense but productive hours of work. Women began stepping up to the microphones to convey their appreciation for the common ground that had been reached.

Until three young women marched to the front of the room, read a statement—"We came in respect and not to disrupt this meeting. However, for those of us who love the unborn and for those who do not know the unborn, here is our sister killed by abortion"—then pulled back a blue receiving blanket, revealing an actual dead fetus. The meeting adjourned in pandemonium.

Several of the moderate pro-lifers, though insisting they had not known about the stunt in advance, said that they did not disapprove of it. The National Right to Life Committee said, "Those offended by the visible evidence of the violence done to children in abortion clinics should reexamine the reasons for their objections." Eleanor Smeal stoutly insisted she still believed that the conclave had been a "very big first step" in defusing the issue's tensions. After all, according to the Gallup Poll, only 19 percent of Americans agreed that abortion should be illegal under all circumstances: maybe the issue wasn't so polarizing after all.

Except that, also on Valentine's Day, in Hempstead, Long Island, a twenty-five-year-old man walked into a crowded abortion clinic carrying an antifreeze can full of gasoline, lit a torch, and announced, "Don't anyone move. This place is going up." The Bureau of Alcohol, Tobacco, and Firearms counted it as the fourteenth act of antiabortion terrorism over the previous twelve months.

Passions like these were why ABC News called abortion "the hottest single peacetime issue since prohibition." The Gallup Poll only measured opinions, after all—not how many citizens were willing to sacrifice just about anything to see their righteous cause prevail. "One side sees abortion as a crime," Mary McGrory wrote. "The other regards it as a right. There is no middle ground."

FOR AN EVANGELICAL NAMED ED MCATEER, THE SACRIFICE WAS BRAVING the same vicious Mid-Atlantic Presidents' Day blizzard that had trapped the Tractorcade in Washington, D.C., to attend a crucial meeting in Lynchburg, Virginia.

"Do you really have to go?" he remembered his anxious wife asking.

"I've got to go," he responded.

It was February 17. The weather was so fierce that his plane couldn't make it. McAteer rented a car to drive the rest of the way. At 5 a.m. the next morning, an icy wind still howling, he got a call from Howard Phillips, who wondered if it was necessary for him to show up, too. Phillips was a dear friend, so McAteer spoke frankly: "Howard, I think it's absolutely essential."

McAteer was the nascent Christian right's most indefatigable organizer. A traveling salesman in Colgate-Palmolive's toilet articles division who had worked his way up to sales manager for the entire Southeast, in the early 1970s he had pulled his children out of the public schools because, he said, "they were bringing in the 'sensitivity training program.' That was where teachers and students sit around and feel all over and excite the basic instincts of people." His next step up the corporate ladder brought him to California, where he volunteered with Wycliffe Bible Translators, making contacts with evangelicals all over the world. In 1976, John Conlan and Bill Bright offered him a new job as *their* traveling salesman for their efforts turning preachers into precinct organizers. After it folded, McAteer became field director for Howard Phillips's Conservative Caucus. But he missed working with religious folk.

"So what I did was I got on my pony and started out seeing these high-powered preachers." That was what he was up to now. It was six months after the IRS hearings, and this cadre hoped to recruit Jerry Falwell to lead a mighty national organization.

Falwell had not attended the IRS hearings. He may have just been too busy. He was publishing a weekly newspaper, the *Journal Champion*, which ran articles date-lined from places like South Korea (governed by a military dictatorship, though Falwell's assistant Dr. Elmer Towns wrote that it was "one of the best showplaces for Democracy and Christianity in the world"). He had just helped win a campaign against horse-track betting in Virginia. He was pursuing a new fundraising scheme, the "I Love America Club," whose membership premium was a Bicentennial-themed Bible, left over from a similar effort in 1976. He was on and off the road with a new multimedia presentation—"America, You're Too Young to Die!"—which would eventually visit almost 150 towns.

Now, however, these New Right leaders had managed to secure an extended block of the great man's time to deliver a pitch that, legend had it, he had rejected in 1977. They were confident that this time, after the IRS hearings, he could not refuse. In fact, he proved so enthusiastic, McAteer remembered, that he sent his own Learjet to Washington to fetch Phillips. But the blizzard grounded that plane, too. So, while they waited for Phillips to arrive by car, McAteer asked Weyrich to fill Falwell in on "the political situation."

Weyrich, it was recalled, began with some fateful words:

"Out there is what you might call a moral majority—people who agree on principles based on the Decalogue, for example—but they have been separated by geographical and denominational differences and that has caused them to vote differently—"

He continued on, spinning out an elaborate explanation of what it would take to unite these querulous elements into an effective electoral force when Falwell interrupted:

"Go back to what you said earlier."

So Weyrich began to repeat his analysis. Again, Falwell interrupted: "No, you started out by saying, 'There is something out there—'"

"Oh, I said there was a moral majority—"

"*That's it!* That's the name of our organization!"

Although, in other accounts, it was *Weyrich* who was late and Phillips who delivered the presentation. Still others remembered it being in January—which made for a less dramatic story, for there had been no major Mid-Atlantic blizzard in January. In his autobiography, Falwell claimed he convened the meeting himself, in May; another version dated the founding of the Moral Majority to a March meeting of lawyers for the Conservative Caucus. Another said Robert Billings had issued the summons, another that the whole thing had been the brainchild of Representative Robert Bauman of Maryland. A particularly unflattering version had it that Falwell was recruited to placate Reverend Richard Grant of Christian Voice—after he had complained that any movement to politicize evangelicals "controlled by three Catholics and a Jew"—Weyrich, Viguerie, Terry Dolan, and the *former* Jew Howard Phillips—was "a sham." One chronicler even claimed that this was the first time Falwell was introduced to the issue of abortion—even though "ABORTION-ON-DEMAND" had been one of the liberal outrages listed in Falwell's *TV Guide* ads the previous spring. A particularly dramatic version had the brilliant "Moral Majority" moniker smiting all the participants in the meeting all at once, the spirit moving them during a brainstorming session at which they had already rejected such limp options as "People for a Stable America."

In a culture that thrives on legend, the legends, naturally, sometimes conflict.

The historical record documents this at a bare minimum: Jerry Falwell's next column after Presidents' Day in the *Journal-Champion* announced a political crusade "against abortion-on-demand, pornography and sex and violence on television, and government intervention. . . . But I am especially concerned about the IRS attempt to legislate regulations that will control Christian schools." Robert Billings wrote, "The cost of political negligence is slavery! As our government increases its crippling pressure on the Christian home, school and church, the need for Christian action becomes increasingly critical. If Christians do not master politics, we will, most certainly, be mastered by those who do." The *Journal-Champion* was rechristened the *Moral Majority Report*, and began its new life with a readership of more than a million names from Richard Viguerie's mailing lists.

THE NEXT CATALYST SPARKED TO COMBUSTION IN TEXAS. THE MAN AT ITS center was perhaps the most stupendously charismatic TV preacher of them all.

James Robison, according to his own telling, was born in a charity ward after his alcoholic father deserted his forty-one-year-old mother, who feared that giving birth at such an advanced age would kill her. She was talked out of an abortion, and advertised in the newspaper for a home for her infant son. Baby James was taken in by a Southern Baptist preacher and his wife in Pasadena, Texas, and at age fifteen, as a 1980 front-page profile in the *Minneapolis Star-Tribune* related, "seated in a pew of his foster father's church, while all around him members were praying he would answer the call," he was born again.

Robison began his preaching career specializing in outdoor revivals, becoming one of the most effective "crusade evangelists" in America. Women thought he looked like a cross between Burt Lancaster and James Dean. Men admired him as a proud hunter, outdoorsman, and sports fan—a man's man. His TV show *James Robison, Man with a Message* hit the air in 1970, funded by the Texas oil magnate H. L. Hunt. By the summer of 1978 it was syndicated on sixty-four stations, and began airing in prime time.

One of Robison's affiliates was the ABC station in Dallas–Forth Worth, WFAA. The show was produced there, and the station provided him local airtime for free. The Sunday after Presidents' Day, Robison recorded a sermon describing the gay rights movement as a "perversion of the highest order," citing a *National Enquirer* article that claimed gays were systematically recruiting little boys and (here he cited "police sources" as his authority) murdering them. He also asserted that God had passed His judgment on Harvey Milk by seeing to his assassination. The Dallas Gay Political Caucus asked WFAA to invoke the fairness doctrine, a stipulation of the Federal Communications Act that mandated that holders of federal broadcast licenses provide equal time to balance controversial expressions on issues of public importance. The group insisted that it would not have made the request had Robison limited his rant to biblical teachings that homosexuality was religiously proscribed: *that* was not political. But, "He left the Bible theme and tried to associate us with anything that is negative in any society, and that is slanderous"—and with gay rights legislation pending in Congress, his slander was thus a *political* statement. The station consulted its lawyers, who agreed. WFAA gave the Dallas Gay Political Caucus a half hour to respond, meanwhile suspending Robison's show.

WFAA had suspended Robison several times before, including when he attacked Jimmy Carter's *Playboy* interview, then after he flayed the gay-friendly Metropolitan Community Church, and when he called Christian Science and Mormonism "false faiths." This time, Robison decided he had had quite enough. He reached out to Jerry Falwell—who had run into similar trouble in 1976 when Carter campaign operatives got about a hundred of Falwell's affiliates to not air an episode of *The Old Time Gospel Hour* on which Falwell preached against the *Playboy* interview. Back then, Falwell's response had been an ineffectual news conference at the National Press Club. This time, Christians had a political machine—which promptly cranked into gear. Wallie Criswell led members of his massive First Baptist Church in a march around the WFAA building. Tim LaHaye pitched in from San Diego, announcing, "Doesn't it seem strange that the U.S. government is lenient on Communists, criminals, drug pushers, illegal aliens, rapists, lesbians, homosexuals, and almost anyone who violates the law, but is increasing its attacks on Christians?"

Robison barnstormed. The Sunday after the canceled broadcast, a standing-room-only crowd at North Phoenix Baptist Church heard him denounce the cancelation as an example of the growing "satanic" movement to silence "righteous voices," comparing the equal time request to "giving the Ku Klux Klan two weeks' prime time after *Roots*." He hired a dogged young publicist, a seminary dropout named Michael Huckabee, who arranged a news conference the next Sunday; Robison's remarks got picked up by dozens of newspapers. Then they landed a feature on the controversy in the *New York Times*. Robison also retained one of the most effective and flamboyant lawyers in the country, Richard "Racehorse" Haynes, to appeal his FCC case. Haynes said Robison's was a moral statement, not a political one. (The Bible said wife-swapping was a sin, after all. "No one claimed that would merit wife-swappers as a class to have equal time under the fairness doctrine.")

It also happened that Robison had a TV special in the can, *The End of Outrage . . . A Call to Arms!* It was booked for broadcast on more than seventy stations around the country starting the second week in April, heralded by full-page ads. ("World War II to Jonestown—40 Years of Hell" was the headline for a collage of combat imagery, antiwar protesters, and children's dead bodies splayed on the ground in Guyana: "Concerned Americans, and especially Christians, must see this frank program that confronts us with shocking reminders of the disintegrating society we live in and in which James Robison calls all of us to turn back before it's too late from National Self-Destruction.")

And Robison booked the Dallas Convention Center for a massive rally in pursuit of his cause on June 5—timed for just before the initial pleadings in his case before the FCC in Washington.

SUDDENLY, EVANGELICALS WERE EVERYWHERE. THEY PUSHED A BILL THROUGH the Iowa Senate mandating that "whenever the origin of human kind or the origin of the earth is taught in the education program of the public schools of this state, the concept of creation as supported by scientific research" be taught, too; at Iowa State University, fundamentalist students complained of harassment at the hands of biology professors who refused to respect their religious views.

In California, a rumor circulated—untrue—that Bob Dylan had been baptized in Pat Boone's backyard swimming pool. It *was* true, however, that the countercultural icon had accepted Christ as his personal savior, via the ministration of the pastor of Debby Boone's church, a close friend of Hal Lindsey's. At his concerts, he began refusing to play his most famous songs, instead singing lyrics like "There's a man on a cross, and he been crucified for you / Believe in his power, that's about all you've got to do." Stickers reading "FREEDOM OF SPEECH, THE RIGHT TO PREACH" blossomed on bumpers. Jesse Helms reintroduced legislation to amend the Constitution to restore prayer in schools. Jerry Falwell held an "I Love America" rally on the Capitol steps in Washington on April 27. It was advertised as an effort "to demonstrate to Congress and the American people that this country is ready for a moral revolution," but was not, Falwell hastened to assure journalists, a "political rally." The nonpolitical preacher then thundered to a claimed ten thousand attendees (the Christian right, it seemed, always claimed ten thousand attendees for its rallies), "We are crusading against abortion on demand, against pornography, against sex and violence on television, and against attempts by the Internal Revenue Service to control religious schools." He also said, nonpolitically, that the SALT II treaty "may compromise the safety" of the nation, and Senator Helms spoke, nonpolitically, about his new legislation to overturn the Supreme Court ban on school prayer.

It started raining. Then it stopped. At that moment, Paul Weyrich wrote to Falwell, "Tears came to my eyes. . . . I believe we are on the right track and that together we may work for the Lord's glory to preserve our great nation."

On May 4, Weyrich hosted one hundred activists at a Pro-Life Political Action Conference to plant a New Right flag within the anti-abortion movement. The opening speaker was a Catholic priest. A PR expert formerly in Richard Viguerie's employ gave a media training seminar. Clay Smothers, the black Texas state representative who had been the breakout star of the conservative counterrally to the National Women's Conference in Houston in 1977, pronounced, "Never thought we'd get to the point in this country where the government would condone the mass slaying of the unborn. . . . It is the press which has made pro-lifers look like radicals."

On May 11, Weyrich wrote to James Robison to offer his services: "It is obvious that we share fundamental values. I look forward to a long and productive relationship. I am confident that the Lord has seen to it that we can work together for His purposes." On May 14, James Robison wrote back: "I am convinced that we will be of much help to one another, as we join forces and strength together in the battle for the conservation of a free America. . . . I anticipate a very profitable relationship with you, as we work together for a great cause."

On May 24, for the fourth time, the Florida senate failed to advance the ERA. Schlaflyites had sent their allies bottles of Elmer's Glue-All with a note to remind them to "please stay glued to your seat" if White House officials tried to lure them off the floor to twist their arms.

On June 2, on the eve of Pentecost, twenty-seven athletic stadiums around the nation hosted "Jesus '79" rallies. In Washington, the crowd gave a standing ovation to a woman who walked from the stands to home plate, her now useless wheelchair trailing behind her. A former convict told the *Washington Post*, "I was hooked up with the rackets," then "found Jesus," and "gave up my shylocking and all that." A lady with long braids and an acoustic guitar and a floppy hat, like a 1960s folk singer, sang "The Old Rugged Cross." Day turned into night. The scoreboard flashed "Tonight's Score: Jesus 30,157, Devil 0."

Three days later, the Freedom Rally in support of Pastor Robison took place at the Dallas Convention Center. The crowd was counted at ten thousand—though when it had looked like there might not be enough attendees to claim that number, a last-minute call was placed to Paul Weyrich, who managed to rouse the Catholic dioceses to fill out the crowd.

Howard Phillips spoke first. He was what was known among evangelicals as a "completed Jew." His conversion to Christianity had come, he once said, after reading a tract by Dr. Rushdoony opposing socialized medicine from a biblical perspective. He said, "The founders of our great country knew that our rights did not come from government, they came from God." Falwell spoke, intimating that the order to punish Robison originated in the White House. When Pastor Robison was introduced by Wallie Criswell, Robison fixed his gaze at the TV cameras—and at the WFAA executives monitoring the proceedings via a direct feed—and preached so passionately, to such frenzied response, that Mike Huckabee worried, "If someone had gotten to that microphone and said, 'Let's go four blocks from here and take Channel 8 apart,' that audience would have taken the last brick off the building."

At a press conference, Robison proclaimed, "We want to let people hear from the Christians—the moral majority." It was the first recorded use of the phrase in the media—and also the day of incorporation for a legal trinity: the Moral Majority Foundation, a nonpolitical tax-exempt foundation; Moral Majority, Inc., a legislative lobby; and the Moral Majority Political Action Committee, to raise funds for candidates. Jerry Falwell was named president, Robert Billings executive director; his Capitol Hill brownstone became the Washington headquarters. The board of directors included Robert Thoburn; Tim LaHaye; former Southern Baptist Convention president Charles Stanley; and Florida televangelist D. James Kennedy, a veteran of the Anita Bryant campaign. Connie Marshner of the Heritage Foundation liked to complain that the pro-family movement resembled a "floating crap game"—no headquarters, no spokesman, no center. Now it had all of these.

And soon it emerged that the Moral Majority just might have a presidential candidate. John Connally called Billings, Falwell, Robison, Pat Robertson, and seventeen other leading evangelicals to his ranch in August—around when Richard Viguerie announced he was officially going to work for the Connally campaign.

One order of business was abortion; in March, Connally had given an interview to a magazine in which he said he was opposed to the Human Life Amendment. At this meeting, however, he suggested that after a consultation with Ed McAteer on the "biblical basis for the anti-abortion cause," he had changed his mind; and also implied that he no longer supported the ERA. "At the end of the meeting," a participant told *U.S. News and World Report*, "some of those guys were ready to carry Connally out of there on their shoulders."

CHAPTER 23

The "Front-Runner"

POOR RONALD REAGAN. FOR MONTHS, IN COLUMNS, COMMENTARIES, AND speeches, he had been hurling thunderbolts at "one Jerome Kurtz, Mr. Carter's Commissioner of Internal Revenue," "driving a large number of private schools out of business" from his "granite and marble palace" by means of "arbitrary quotas" that threatened "the destruction of religious freedom." He promoted the lawsuit of the Christian Reconstructionist group Foundation of Law and Society (which he identified as "a public interest law firm in Washington") to make the revenue procedure subject to the mandatory cost-benefit review the White House required of all "substantive regulations." Fat lot of good that did him with the televangelists who filed into John Connally's ranch house in Texas, then reportedly marched out ready to hoist him on their shoulders.

Though that particular setback delighted Reagan's chief campaign strategist, John P. Sears. He considered right-wing voters mostly already in the bag. What they needed now were moderates, and the Republican and business establishment—which was why he considered Reagan's ties to these zealots the most dangerous impediment to the Oval Office that Ronald Reagan faced.

Sears had managed Reagan's 1976 presidential campaign. He began his political career a decade earlier as a brilliant twenty-six-year-old lawyer at Richard Nixon's New York City law firm. When he showed himself a cunning strategist, Nixon recruited him to help drive his political comeback that culminated in the White House. Sears was "unusually perceptive," one of his journalistic profilers observed, "in spotting quick-moving trends," and unusually creative at devising just the tactics to take advantage of them—so good, in fact, that Nixon's 1968 campaign manager John Mitchell jealously chased him out of Nixon's orbit entirely when Mitchell became attorney general. Sears "was a born principal with an ego to match," one Nixon campaign veteran recalled. He was also a penetrating and cynical psychological observer. Before Richard Nixon's post-resignation speech to White House staffers, he bet a friend that the president would say something lachrymose about his mother. He won the bet.

Shortly afterward, a Reaganite approached him to ask if he could imagine the retiring governor winning the 1976 Republican nomination. Everyone else thought Reagan was washed up—but Sears said he might have a chance. Perhaps it was Sears's early faith in him that caused Reagan to retain so much faith in Sears now, even though many of his conservative associates called him "John P. Satan," and blamed him for Reagan's 1976 loss.

Round-faced and plump, Sears looked a little like a cherub—if cherubs scowled and wore suits. He had no discernible ideological beliefs (he was skeptical that ideology played much of a role in elections at all). He was a consummate intriguer, never letting anyone in on his true thoughts ("sphinxlike" was a frequent description). He viewed others like chess pieces to move around in the service of mysterious aims, and held local politicians and activists in particular contempt. His preferred method of communication was the political koan. Like "Power of any kind is like physics; you can't create it or destroy it. It's there somewhere. So when you take it from some hands that have it, it doesn't just disappear. . . . It falls into other hands." Or—his favorite one—"Politics is motion." His method of getting things done involved identifying subtle, almost invisible points of leverage, then finding just the right butterfly wing to flap into motion to bestir the political air to force a cascade of events that would resolve in ways favorable to his candidate.

He also, it appeared, had had a drinking problem and had, politicos gossiped, disappeared on lengthy benders at key moments during the 1976 campaign. But he also, that year, almost achieved a political miracle: Reagan went into the Republican convention within striking distance of retiring a sitting president.

Then, Sears devised a delicate political maneuver that involved having Reagan announce a liberal Republican as his running mate, to try to force Ford to prematurely announce *his* running mate, to disturb the political atmosphere in a manner sufficient to shake loose a decisive number of Ford delegates without shedding too many of Reagan's. It didn't succeed. Ford may have already been too far ahead in any event. Nonetheless, conservatives came away utterly convinced: Sears had snatched defeat from the jaws of victory. That cemented their enmity toward him for all time.

One of them was Lyn Nofziger. Sears had fired Nofziger as campaign press secretary in 1976 in favor of a Sears associate, Jim Lake. In the spring of 1978, Nofziger tried to stab Sears in the back with an attempt to recruit Gerald Ford's presidential campaign manager James Baker to run Reagan's 1980 campaign. (Baker wasn't interested; he was planning to work for his friend George H. W. Bush.)

But Michael Deaver, Nofziger's California rival for Reagan's affections, had already sought to hire Sears, though in a subsidiary role. Deaver thought of him as "a brain for hire who wanted to play on a winning team." Sears responded to that overture, however, that he would only be interested in *running* the campaign—and if offered anything less he might try Senator Howard Baker.

Adding to the intrigue, Nancy Reagan called Sears out to Rancho del Cielo to take his measure, coming away convinced by his argument that he was the *only* person who could make her husband president. That came as a sore disappointment to her dear friend Michael Deaver, who wanted to manage the campaign himself. Then, however, Sears seduced *Deaver* into concluding the same thing. Though Sears did not succeed in persuading Senator Laxalt, who believed Sears's role should be limited to the Northeast, working on selling Reagan to the media establishment—which treated Sears like a political god.

Reagan himself, meanwhile, who hated interpersonal conflict, let the matter settle into a surreal ambiguity, and by the summer of 1978, no one was sure *who* was in charge—leading to that cock-up when Sears, claiming to speak for the governor, told reporters Reagan was abandoning his right-wing views about China—and Reagan reassured the outraged New Rightists of Paul Weyrich's Kingston Group that Sears would *not* be his campaign manager.

While Sears quietly amassed operational control.

The hand of the wily sphinx was evident, for example, in Reagan's perambulations collecting chits from 1978 congressional candidates, including liberals like Charles Percy—as Sears had helped Richard Nixon do in 1966.

So it was that, beginning at the end of 1978, a series of conflicts brewed that established the template for the next two years, when there wasn't a single campaign kerfuffle that hadn't been prefigured in those of the next two months—starting with Reagan's next big project, which borrowed another page from Richard Nixon's 1968 playbook: a stature-enhancing trip overseas.

THE TRAVELING PARTY, MANAGED BY THE FORMER NIXON FOREIGN POLICY hand Dick Allen, said to harbor ambitions as "Reagan's Kissinger," departed on November 25 for ten days in Europe. The itinerary was mostly meetings with officials and experts whose views accorded with those of Reagan, who then produced a series of columns, speeches, commentaries, and letters to friends affecting to report a consensus of elite European opinion, which happened to sound a lot like his own. "They are extremely concerned and want the solid dependable United States, including the solid, dependable dollar that they once knew," he wrote. "They are very fearful, and I'm afraid that if we don't begin showing some muscle soon, they are going to begin making overtures to the Soviets in a feeling of self-defense."

He filed a column from West Germany reporting that Europe was terrified that SALT II would sell them out. From London he wrote of a "widespread belief that the British bureaucracy was over-large and inefficient." From Paris he reported that "market-oriented reform is moving ahead strongly," and that French leaders were fascinated by Proposition 13. From Bavaria he dispatched a goggle-eyed account of the bustling prosperity of the Munich Christmas Market, where "furs abound," the cars were "spanking new," and "the windows are chockfull of expensive goods"—"a sobering experience for the American visitor, whose instinct in Europe these days is to keep his dollars in his pocket for they buy so little." He contrasted that to what he saw in West Berlin—especially the heartbreaking words he saw spray-painted on the Berlin Wall: "Those beyond this wall live in a concentration camp." Several times, he related a conversation he had had with the American general at Checkpoint Charlie. Reagan had asked why they weren't making it easier for Easterners to escape. "We don't want people to try to escape," the general responded. "We keep the status quo." It "jolted" him, Reagan wrote an old friend. "Somehow that doesn't seem like the America I think we should be."

Another memorable encounter took place in London. At a time of economic collapse under the ruling Labor Party, the Tories had chosen a leader criticized as a right-wing ideologue. Reagan's meeting with Margaret Thatcher went much longer than scheduled. They discussed, Allen's notes recorded, "labor union power," the "decline of British productivity," and "welfare." "I have a hard time not campaigning for her," he wrote his former secretary from his Hollywood days, a Brit. "I think she would make a great prime minister."

THEN, THE NEXT PART OF THE PLAN: LEVERAGING THE TRIP TO MARKET RONald Reagan as a statesman. It began with a major foreign policy speech at a luncheon of the Los Angeles World Affairs Council. The advertising flyer his hosts prepared, perhaps with an assist from John Sears, read, "Is the popular former governor shifting from the right to nearer to the center?"

He began his remarks as Richard Nixon used to: cataloguing all the important global personages with whom he had parleyed. And, also as Nixon used to, he explained the concerns they had confided to him (which he would now confide to *you*): there was "no dispute." Where the United States used to enjoy an eight-to-one strategic advantage over the Soviet Union, Russia had now caught up with us, with a program of weapons development that "exceeds by far any legitimate needs they may have for self-defense," and "if present trends continue, the United States will be assigned a role of permanent military inferiority." He insisted that those who "deal with the reality of Soviet tanks just three hours' drive from West Germany's capital of Bonn; with the threat of Soviet SS-20 missiles being deployed in increasing numbers and with a range to reach every city in Europe; and with the Soviet Backfire bomber, which has a capability of delivering nuclear weapons to any point on the continent" were uniformly terrified of what Jimmy Carter was up to—because "those tanks, SS-20 missiles, and Backfire bombers are not covered by the SALT II agreement now being negotiated."

Such claims had been the backbone of right-wing arguments against SALT II from the beginning. The work of Reagan's speechwriters was re-crafting them in a way the foreign policy establishment could respect, the better to avoid the charge that Reagan was an extremist standing in the way of peace. To do so, they borrowed another Nixon trick. Reagan claimed that his interlocutors had suggested three ways to think about all of this. Some advised "recognition of the Soviet juggernaut" as "a fact of life." Others, while admitting that the Soviets harbored malign ambitions, had boundless faith in "arms control agreements and increased trade as a means to moderate and constrain Soviet ambitions." The first two possibilities were meant to be perceived by the audience as plainly unacceptable *extremes*. The third option—the one, naturally, that Reagan believed—was presented as the center-point of expert European opinion.

Thus having fortified himself as a sensible moderate, he proceeded to scare the bejesus out of his audience about Soviet intentions—then laid out the sensible course thereupon. The Soviets were "pursuing a program to achieve clear-cut military superiority over the West. Once this is accomplished, they will intimidate, 'Finlandize,' and ultimately neutralize Western Europe. Those holding this view believe the most effective response by the West is a reinvigoration of NATO and an explicit military deployments program designed to counter the Soviet threat. They do not exclude the possibility of reaching meaningful arms agreements, but argue that such agreements must be balanced and must contain mutual advantages. . . . A one-sided arms control agreement would be worse than no agreement at all." SALT II as it existed was "one-sided," and thus should be shelved.

Politics is motion. The aim was to leverage the political energy of SALT to elevate Reagan as the president's debating opponent—just as Richard Nixon had rescued himself from irrelevancy in 1966 by turning himself into President Lyndon Johnson's debating opponent on Vietnam.

But that was the easy part. The hard part would be the question-and-answer session.

Reagan's aides had been imploring him to avoid specifics when he talked extemporaneously about foreign affairs. But Reagan *loved* discussing the specifics about foreign affairs—upon which he was a loquacious pedant. His pedantry frequently included wacky John Birch–style conspiracy theories, easily debunked facts, made-up quotes . . . just the kind of thing John Sears feared could stop his ascent cold. Which was why, in a memo to Reagan prior to the event, aides literally scripted answers, as if he were back in Hollywood. The proposed response to questioning like "Governor, you've been quite critical of the Carter administration's SALT negotiations. . . . Do you intend to urge that the treaty be defeated? And do you seriously believe that President Carter and his advisors would actually sign a treaty that is not in our best interests?" ran almost four hundred words.

When the question arrived as predicted, the governor knocked it out of the park. In fact, as was frequently the case with scripts prepared for him by aides, the master storyteller considerably improved upon it. It had been suggested he say, *We have not yet seen the treaty, and I therefore cannot say what my position will be.* In Reagan's version, he was "trying very hard not to be like the guy who, having seen the monkey, thought he could run the circus." Another line had him observe that for a decade now the U.S. had been accumulating agreements with the Soviets, both arms pacts and trade deals, and that *the Senate debate on SALT II would provide an ideal forum for a comprehensive debate on American strategy for the next decade . . . an opportunity to reexamine the very premises of our foreign policy, and should serve as a means of enlightening the public on a crucially important component of our national goals.* Reagan's version punched up that word salad considerably: "Wouldn't this Senate discussion on SALT II be a fine time to . . . say, 'Look, let's discuss the whole strategy position of the U.S. for the next ten years and see how well these fit together, and are they good for the U.S.'?"

The goal had been to evoke headlines like "Reagan Calls for Broad Strategic *Debate*," instead of "Reagan Calls for SALT *Defeat*." It worked like a charm. "Reagan Urges Debate on U.S. Policy," said one. "Reagan Challenges Carter to Foreign Policy Debate," read another: Reagan and President Carter sharing the headline as equals—that was a grand slam.

When Peter Hannaford reported back to headquarters that the boss had handled the Q&A well, however, he also had to admit one exception—one that luckily did not make it into the news reports. Answering a question about Africa, Reagan performed one of his favorite far-right tics: adducing some menacing fake "quotation," which he believed was actually real, that supposedly demonstrated the Reds' unquenchable thirst for world conquest. "He who controls Africa controls the world," he had claimed that Vladimir Ilyich Lenin said. Hannaford fired off a memo to Dick Allen: "Would you advise if this quote is correct or not?"

It was not. The words belonged to French president Valéry Giscard D'Estaing, speaking in 1978.

This was John Sears's dilemma. For the next two years, he would have to sell "Ronald Reagan," sensible statesman, while keeping the actual Ronald Reagan in check. What happened next demonstrated just how narrow a needle that would be to thread.

ONE OF THE QUESTIONS SCRIPTED FOR THE GOVERNOR'S RESPONSE AT THE Los Angeles speech was whether the U.S. should establish full diplomatic relations with the People's Republic of China. The proposed answer began, "*This is a very complex issue...*," and ran on for another 350 words. The very next day, President Carter *did* announce that America was establishing full diplomatic relations with the People's Republic of China. And Reagan's response was not complex at all.

His next column in Nofziger's *Citizens for the Republic Newsletter* predicted Communist China would invade Taiwan with Jimmy Carter's permission. An accompanying article called Carter's move "a shameful and totally unnecessary act of appeasement" just like Neville Chamberlain's cave to Adolf Hitler. The following issue compared *Time* magazine's choice of Deng Xiaoping as 1978 Man of the Year to their pick of Hitler in 1938 and Stalin in 1939, the two men "most responsible for the most devastating war the world had yet seen," and asked, "And what of 1980? Will America have someone to call on to lead it out of danger? Someone who believes not in appeasement but who will seek, in Churchill's words, 'Victory at all costs, victory in spite of all terror, and victory however long and hard the road may be, for without victory there is no survival.'"

In a world with thousands of thermonuclear warheads ready to launch, "Victory at all costs, victory in spite of all terror" was not precisely the message with which John Sears wished Reagan to be associated.

Reagan's next newspaper column argued that Deng had fleeced Carter like he was a rube at the state fair. The one after that predicted that the Chinese Communists would leverage diplomatic recognition to initiate "slow, subtle economic and political warfare that could lead to strangulation" of Taiwan, and that by the time "the White House adds two and two and figures out Peking's game" Taiwan would become to Jimmy Carter what the Sudetenland was to Neville Chamberlain.

Even as these columns were being drafted, Jules Witcover and Jack Germond reported that Reagan was "getting advice from his principal political strategist, John Sears, to avoid making the China-Taiwan issue any sort of centerpiece in his next bid for the Republican nomination." Peter

Hannaford contacted Dick Allen in Washington and assured him that the piece was "gratuitous nonsense." But five weeks later a column appeared under Reagan's byline in the mighty *New York Times* arguing that America should proceed with a diplomatic program to "seek friendship, commerce and other mutually acceptable goals" with Communist China.

Sears clearly had not consolidated his hold. One side of the Reagan operation sounded like Joseph McCarthy. The other aped Henry Kissinger. Which Ronald Reagan would prevail? The question would reassert itself again and again over the next twenty-three months.

THE GOVERNOR RETURNED TO THE ROAD. TO SAN DIEGO FOR A NATIONAL Turkey Federation luncheon. ("Breeding of turkeys is a very specialized science," a poultry executive briefed the aspiring commander in chief. "Specialized crews of 'inseminators' take the semen from the toms and artificially inseminate the hens. . . .") To Palm Beach to accept a "Torch of Learning" award from the American Friends of Hebrew University, then address ten thousand members of the American Farm Bureau Federation, then attend a luncheon with a rich auto dealer in Tampa. Then a hop over to Georgia for the annual banquet of the Valdosta Chamber of Commerce.

Perhaps some in the audience in Palm Beach would remember his visit there, two years earlier, when he claimed that "the experts are telling us is that the Soviet Union now believes that they could absorb a blow from us—a nuclear blow—with fewer casualties than they took in World War II—twenty million dead and wounded, unofficially—and that it could be acceptable to them." He claimed that was why the Kremlin had sent twenty million of their young people into the countryside—to practice reconstructing Russian society. "In other words, a nuclear conflict in their view would not be unthinkable as it is to us." For they had also "dispersed their industry," and "hardened their nuclear sites to make them defensible against attack from us." He predicted that "as early as next year and at least by 1981" America could expect an ultimatum: surrender or suffer a nuclear exchange. Because the Soviets believed "that if there was such a nuclear exchange, they could destroy us and we couldn't destroy them."

None of this was remotely true. He sounded like a character in *Dr. Strangelove*. And John Sears was terrified he could sound like that again, only with the national news cameras running, on any given day.

HOW NARROW WAS THAT NEEDLE SEARS HOPED TO THREAD? TAKE A PEEK behind the curtain.

One of the campaign-in-formation's strategic initiatives went by the acronym PTWWT. That stood for "People to Whom We Talk": a continually updated list of distinguished foreign policy personages like Henry Kissinger, NATO commander General Alexander Haig, and Harry Rowan of the RAND Corporation. A related effort was called the "SP Program": a formal process for staffers to draft letters to molders of establishment opinion for the governor to "Sign Personally." These missives frequently praised books and articles the recipient had written, establishing their signatory—despite what you might have heard—as a cosmopolitan intellectual, well within the mainstream of respectable opinion.

On December 14, for example, the day of that marquee speech to the Los Angeles World Affairs Council, an SP letter went out to the *New York Times'* most liberal columnist, Anthony Lewis, responding to his piece about a famous Kennedy assassination conspiracy theorist, Mark Lane, who turned up in the news as the late Reverend Jim Jones's spokesman. "It is probably safe to say that over the years, had we compared notes, we would have found ourselves in disagreement on many issues," the letter ran. "But when your column 'The Mark of Zorro' caught up with me on my return from Europe the other day, I found myself in agreement with every paragraph. Perhaps we can become co-chairmen of the Ad Hoc Committee to Tune Out Mark Lane. . . . Thanks for saying what needed saying. . . . Sincerely, Ronald Reagan."

Neoconservatives were a special focus of the program—for instance an SP letter that went out to "Norman and Midge": Norman Podhoretz, editor of *Commentary*, and his wife Midge Decter, of *Harper's*. It had Reagan claiming to have "finally caught up with the Sunday *New York Times* of June 11 and your article 'The Cold War Again.' I think you made an excellent point about the semantic differential in the U.S. and Soviet interpretations of agreements such as SALT I and SALT II." Recipients frequently responded to such letters in effusive, highly personal terms. So it was that several rounds of correspondence with "Nat"—the neoconservative Harvard sociologist Nathan Glazer—followed an SP on the subject of subway graffiti and urban disorder, then "the relative attractiveness of welfare to work." Another special focus was moderate Republican elected officials. "Dear Pete," a letter ran to Delaware's Governor Dupont: "I saw an item the other day about your signing into law a bill which allows Delaware motorcyclists to ride without helmets. I agree with your remark that anyone who does so is 'damn foolish,' but I agree wholeheartedly with your action. We went through the same thing in Sacramento, with the same conclusion—it just wasn't any of government's business."

The more naïve among these correspondents would have been mightily disillusioned if they saw the sausage being made. One SP letter thanked a think tank intellectual for sending along his "absorbing but sobering" book. It was sent to Reagan for his signature with a cover note: "Please do not feel obligated to read the attached book." By contrast, the cover note for a letter to one of the most liberal GOP senators, Charles "Mac" Mathias of Maryland, praising an op-ed he had authored, specified that it was "OK" for Reagan to "see article." After all, Reagan was likely to soon *meet* Senator Mathias. It wouldn't do for him to be backfooted if the senator asked him what it was that he liked in particular about the piece. Another SP went to the Catholic intellectual Michael Novak, praising him in a way that suggested Reagan had just newly encountered his work—even though the standard speech Reagan was then delivering included a line about how liberalism these days was a creed that only the rich could afford, quoting none other than Michael Novak.

Another went to the author of an article in *Commentary* magazine. It praised her, saying, "Your approach is so different from ordinary analyses of policy matters that I found myself reexamining a number of the premises and views which have governed my thinking in recent years." The article, by a neoconservative Georgetown professor named Jeane Kirkpatrick, was entitled "Dictatorships and Double Standards," and argued that Jimmy Carter systematically ignored human rights violations by Communist nations while singling out the alleged violations by anti-Communist allies. Having Reagan sign a letter praising it as a novel argument was downright comical: for years, he had constantly said the same thing, using exactly the same language—that human rights policy must follow "a single, not a double standard," as he put it, for example, in a 1977 speech at New York's Waldorf Astoria Hotel to three thousand people, covered in the *New York Times*.

Be that as it may: flattery worked. The SP to Kirkpatrick, drafted by Richard Allen, and physically signed, as it happened, by Reagan's secretary, concluded, "If it is possible, I should like very much to have the opportunity to meet with you and to discuss some of the points you have raised." That began a relationship that eventually led to Kirkpatrick—who in another *Commentary* article derided the New Right as a political menace, especially for its "conviction that there exists out there in the electorate a permanent conservative majority," which happened to be Ronald Reagan's conviction, too—becoming one of the campaign's foreign policy advisors.

But successful politics is about building coalitions. Jeane Kirkpatrick was a Democrat. Democrats like her who disagreed with their party's post-Vietnam drift left on foreign policy were valuable recruits to that coalition. And it was hard to argue with success—such as the remarkable success they scored with an SP Reagan signed to a close associate of the late Hubert Humphrey, the Washington lawyer Max Kampelman, praising an article he had written in *Harper's* called "The Power of the Press:

A Problem for Our Democracy." ("For me, the key point is on page 10 . . ."). Kampelman's response was effusive. He noted that he would soon be in Palm Beach for a dinner of the American Friends of Hebrew University. He said, "I now serve as National Board Chairman of the organization and will make an effort to attend the dinner that evening. I understand a private session with a few of our people is being planned to follow the dinner. . . ."

Richard Allen underlined that part of Kampelman's response before sending it back to Peter Hannaford with a note: "This SP thing is working well!" Kampelman later became Reagan's advisor on arms control—and a key node in the campaign's outreach to Jewish donors.

But there was also another, entirely separate file for letters signed by Reagan: for letters he dictated personally to his secretary. The difference between them was stark—and, potentially, quite humiliating.

These letters went to people like dear friends from his Hollywood days, and Iowa, and Illinois pals to whom he reminisced about past sports glories—but also such embarrassing figures as the far-right newspaper publisher William Loeb, and Reagan's friend the newspaper psychic Jeane Dixon. Many went to apparent strangers, answering correspondence that piqued the governor's ire—most often, by complaining that he appeared to be moving to the ideological center. No accusation vexed him more; preserving his sense of himself as a person of pure motivation was Ronald Reagan's strongest psychological drive. Had John Sears and Dick Allen enjoyed access to *these* letters, they might have fainted straightaway.

In one, he wondered how "the Old Testament prophesies that would foretell Armaggeddon" related to recent events in the Middle East. Another concurred with a friend's worries about the damage subversive textbooks were doing to young, impressionable minds. The recipient, Dr. George S. Benson, was a notorious McCarthyite fundamentalist minister who in the 1950s had turned his tiny segregated Bible college in Searcy, Arkansas, into a factory for hysteric propaganda pamphlets and films about Communist infiltration of the U.S. Reagan dictated that one, as it happened, the same day a Kissingerian telegram drafted by Dick Allen went out under his name congratulating the newly elected prime minister of Japan and proposing a back-channel political alliance.

The same day the governor received his instructions on how to convince reporters at that Los Angeles World Affairs Council luncheon that he held respectable opinions on arms control and relations with China, he dictated a letter to a correspondent who had flayed him for endorsing Senator Charles Percy. "I realize there were some who thought it was betraying the faith to do that," Reagan said, reassuring him that he would never do such a thing. A similar response, which in dictated form ran for almost three double-spaced pages, went to one Alistair M. Reid, whom Reagan reassured, "If it ever becomes necessary to have an additional law denying homosexuals the right to advocate their lifestyle I'll be the first in line to support it." He denied the charge that he "did all I could as governor to disarm citizens," and said that "I always have been unalterably opposed to gun control." (This was not true: he signed a strict gun control law in 1967, after armed Black Panthers visited the Capitol building in Sacramento.) He insisted defensively that the only action he had taken toward school integration in California was "a law giving authority over schools to the local school boards in an effort to keep the decisions from being made by judges in our courts. Unfortunately, since then decisions are being made in federal courts, thus getting around our state law."

Then, he got *really* defensive. Again, the subject was that last-minute endorsement for the Republican heretic Chuck Percy, upon which he uttered a falsehood that he had only appeared with Percy once, and that one time because he had been veritably ambushed to do so: "This was the extent of my campaigning for Senator Percy. . . . I'd be very interested, if you don't mind, in finding out where you received this erroneous information. . . ."

Which was interesting, because as he dictated that, he was about to embark on his next big political trip, his most important of the year by far. The destination was Washington, and the agenda was winning over the likes of Chuck Percy that he should be the party's consensus pick for the nomination. The goal was locking up the contest before it began—selling his nomination as an inevitability, giving pols one last opportunity to get on the train before it left the station.

HE ARRIVED ON JANUARY 21. THE MOST IMPORTANT STOPS WERE THE OF-fices of Ford loyalists from 1976: "We want to shake the idea," a strategist told a journalist, "that there is all that Ford support out there and that some stop-Reagan candidate can fall heir to it." They also hoped to win commitments to serve on Reagan's presidential exploratory committee so the pickings would be slim for the other candidates when they came calling in the capital—which both George Bush and John Connally would be doing just after Reagan left.

He addressed a luncheon of Republican governors in town for the annual RNC meeting. It was hosted by Illinois's James Thompson—an aggressive advocate for public funding of abortions, who had previously said that if Reagan were the nominee "we wouldn't recover politically for a generation." Representative Trent Lott of Mississippi coordinated a reception for House members. John Sears handled a sensitive situation involving Jack Kemp: the supply-side gang hoped to induce him to run for president. According to Witcover and Germond, Sears approached him with what could be interpreted as a Mafia-style ultimatum: that "considering his youth, he should weigh carefully all the options." Reagan also met with every Republican senator, the most liberal ones individually.

Could it work? On the one hand, when Gallup asked Republicans whom they wanted as their presidential nominee, 40 percent named Reagan. Ford was in second with 24 percent, with Senator Baker in third with 9 percent. Among *all* voters, however, Reagan lost to Carter by twelve points—but Gerald Ford came quite a bit closer. It was the classic dilemma in America's two-party, winner-take all system: the party rank and file preferred someone the full electorate considered extreme. All the more reason to convince everyone that Reagan was *not* extreme.

Which helped explain why two other important meetings on Reagan's Washington schedule were kept quiet. The first was a briefing with Paul Nitze, Charles Tyroler II, and Gene Rostow of the Committee on the Present Danger—the extremists arguing that SALT II was 1938-style appeasement. The second was a speech to two hundred corporate lobbyists, to whom Reagan reiterated his argument that business PACs should fund right-wing challengers, including his favorite Churchillism: "Perhaps you can keep the alligator happy by feeding him. It might even seem that you are acting in self-interest. But the best you can hope for is that he'll eat you last." Notably, in that day's iteration of the metaphor the alligator stood for the same moderate incumbents he had just tried to recruit to his presidential campaign.

The eye of that needle John Sears was trying to thread—it would be very narrow indeed.

THE DAY AFTER REAGAN LEFT WASHINGTON, THE CAMPAIGN'S ACHILLES' heel flared up with a vengeance. Nelson Rockefeller died of a heart attack. That brought up the age issue. Rockefeller, until that day apparently hale and hearty, was seventy years old. Reagan was only two years younger.

Their political lives had always been intertwined. Reagan first came to national political prominence campaigning for Goldwater against Rockefeller in the 1964 California presidential primary. In 1968, they both ran last-minute contests for the nomination. Then, in their final terms as governors of the nation's two largest states, Rockefeller, long synonymous with Republican liberalism, drifted to the right, especially on issues of criminal justice, and they became occasional allies. And more recently commentators had taken to mentioning them in the same breath—as over-the-hill also-rans who should step aside so their party wouldn't enter the eighties saddled with an old-man image. Rockefeller's fatal heart attack was a stark reminder of that.

Jules Witcover and Jack Germond turned their next column to the subject. They noted that a state rep in New Hampshire had turned down an offer to chair the Reagan campaign because he thought Reagan was too old, and that an unnamed Republican leader had observed of George Bush, "I don't see where he's a damned bit different from Ronald Reagan, but he is fifteen years younger," and that the reason so many had emerged to challenge Reagan, even though he had nearly twice as much support in polls as the second-place contender, was the expectation that he might keel over—politically if not literally: "a seventy-year-old man cannot become sixty no matter how many primaries he wins."

The timing of the setback was particularly unfortunate because John Sears was beginning to show success convincing the Washington establishment that Reagan wasn't a dangerous right-winger. One of the capital's most influential pundits, Godfrey Sperling of the *Christian Science Monitor*, reported speculation that a President Reagan might consider Henry Kissinger for secretary of state, quoting "one Reagan aide" who also said, "When Reagan announces the formation of his presidential-exploratory committee, probably in March, you . . . are going to find that a number of very prominent Republicans who have been associated with Gerald Ford will be on that list." The source was almost certainly Sears, with whom Sperling was close. Then the newsmagazine *U.S. News & World Report*'s "Washington Whispers" column reported, "Increasingly heard among Republican politics is talk of a Ronald Reagan–George Bush ticket for 1980. Such a pairing, the reasoning goes, would link the party's conservative and moderate wings and enhance the GOP's chances of capturing California and Texas." It was hard not to imagine that John Sears had done the whispering.

Reagan headed east again, this time to line up money. The first stop, Columbus, Ohio, included a meeting with seven prominent Midwestern Jewish leaders. ("Sixty percent of Nixon's 1972 support," Reagan's campaign finance lawyer Loren Smith claimed to Ed Meese, came "from the Jewish community.") This was followed by several days in New York City, where he attended an off-the-record luncheon with wealthy business publisher Malcolm Forbes, a $2,500-a-ticket fundraiser for Citizens for the Republic, a meeting at the headquarters of the United Jewish Committee, a lunch with Walter Wriston of Citibank, America's most influential banker—and a luncheon at the legendary Manhattan power restaurant 21 that was truly extraordinary.

The host was the financier the Reagan team had been courting since autumn, Maxwell Rabb. Reagan's traveling assistant Jim Stockdale observed that Rabb was "a total pragmatist" who had been "aligned with the Rockefeller group during their reign." They noticed that Rabb seemed to have "developed an attraction" to Helene von Damm, Reagan's longtime executive assistant, so von Damm became the point person in recruiting him, working to persuade him to host a luncheon with Reagan and the city's power elite. "If he would accept," Stockdale said, "it would rock the New York Republican establishment."

Rabb did—then asked whether the campaign wanted the guests to be "strong Reagan types" or "some of the real leadership in New York." That was an easy question to answer. The guest list was the cream of "that exceedingly minute segment of our country that can truly be characterized as opinion-makers." They included the chairman of the board of Lehman Brothers, the president of Columbia University, the former chairman of the Chase Manhattan Bank, the chairman of the board of Freeport Minerals, a *Time* senior editor, and a "dean of Wall Street investment bankers." There was also Franklin Roosevelt's son John ("the Republican Roosevelt"); Louis Lefkowitz, the former state attorney general; and John Oakes, the retired editorial page editor of the *New York Times* who was also nephew of the publisher. Many were Democrats—Oakes, Rabb explained in a letter to Reagan, was "a strong liberal" who had "recently written an article condemning Carter's rejection of Taiwan": perhaps a neoconservative in the making?

Rabb announced that he would join the Reagan for President exploratory committee. Reagan's thank-you note included his home phone number and an invitation to call him day or night. But a thank-you note to Rabb from a Lehman Brothers partner and undersecretary of state under Eisenhower suggested that the event's success only went so far. It read, "I shall be glad to work for him if he is nominated." Not "I shall be glad to work for him *to be* nominated."

This was no surprise. Most big money was behind John Connally. When he had begun gearing up his presidential campaign, Connally wrote in his memoir, "My staff and advisers were concerned that I would be labeled the candidate of big business. I never saw it as a liability." For instance, one of his campaign promises was to repeal the law making it a federal crime for American corporations to bribe foreign officials—a rather brazen position for a man indicted on charges of receiving a bribe himself.

It must have felt for Ronald Reagan like when those fundamentalist ministers were ready to carry off Big John on their shoulders. *No one* had cheered on big business's crusade against government more enthusiastically than Reagan. But chairmen of investment banks didn't tend to be gambling men. A candidate with the unfortunate tendency to pop off with anti-Communist conspiracy theories—or so old he might keel over from a heart attack—did not seem a safe political bet.

THEN, ANOTHER REAGAN WILDCARD FLOATED TO THE TOP OF HIS DECK: those feuds within his political organization.

Building a presidential campaign is among the strangest of organizational efforts. You construct the equivalent of a major national corporation, hiring hundreds of employees and persuading thousands more to work for free, but one built to last little more than a year. Then, if you win the nomination, you effect a total reorganization, including a merger with all the *other* organizations that only the previous week you were fighting tooth and nail.

The first and most crucial task was recruiting, from a very limited and highly in-demand talent pool, a national network of professional organizers, locking in their loyalty as early as possible to render them unavailable to all the *other* organizations—all on the gossamer promise that their loyalty will be rewarded once their man wins the ultimate prize. A lot of faith is required of those who make the commitment. It doesn't help if the campaign doing the pitching appears in complete disarray.

Potential Reagan recruits would likely have heard rumors of John Sears's alcoholic benders during the 1976 campaign. And that Sears demanded unquestioned control, had a terrifying temper, and hardly communicated directly to his underlings at all. They would have been obsessively following inside-baseball reports from political journalists about the states of the various campaigns—like one headlined "Power Struggle Grows" which appeared the day after Reagan's speech to the Los Angeles Council on World Affairs speculating that Sears and his deputy Charlie Black, who had left the RNC to work for Reagan, were entertaining offers from Robert Dole, and that Nofziger and Deaver were both jockeying to replace Sears.

That particular report was not quite true, but it was in the ballpark. Sears had struck a deal with his three closest deputies from 1976, Jim Lake, Charlie Black, and David Keene, to stick together as a team, in order to keep the Californians Hannaford, Deaver, Meese, and Nofziger from control. But by February, the campaign's simmering resentments had grown so unmanageable that on Presidents' Day weekend all the principals met in St. Louis—halfway between the campaign's split power centers in California and the East—to hash them out. Sears reported back to his deputies that their side had won—but with a "casualty": David Keene would not be named the campaign's spokesman in Washington, as had been expected, but would be demoted to research assistant at Deaver and Hannaford's offices in L.A. Word of Keene's dissatisfaction leaked. Jim Baker called

Keene down to Houston to offer him a job as the Bush campaign's political director.

Keene agonized for weeks. Some of his conservative movement fellow-travelers, a band of brothers since the Goldwater days, urged him to accept: a Reagan nomination was no sure thing, and having a conservative in the camp of the ideologically suspect Bush could be useful should Bush somehow emerge from the pack. (Though admittedly, that seemed unlikely: a December Gallup Poll recorded that the national name recognition of the man *Time* labeled "the thinking man's candidate" was less than the margin of error.)

Nofziger begged him to stay. Nofziger had earlier proposed a campaign structure putting himself and Michael Deaver in charge; when Sears emerged on top instead, he had punished Nofziger by pushing him from his longtime role as Reagan spokesman into fundraising—setting him up to fail, Nofziger believed, because fundraising was a task for which he had no experience and was constitutionally ill-suited. He wanted a conservative ally in the Reagan organization.

Keene, torn, proposed a deal: that he and Nofziger would meet with Reagan. If Reagan, unbidden, asked Keene to stay, he would—even if his job was sweeping the floor. Nofziger agreed, but he was being a good sport. He knew Reagan was too uncomfortable with interpersonal conflict to take a side. The trio spent an hour in Reagan's hotel suite during his Washington visit, drinking and making small talk. Nofziger fidgeted, agonized, waiting for the governor to bring the issue up. He never did. Keene joined Bush.

For America's most widely read political columnists, the Reagan soap opera was an ongoing fascination. Evans and Novak's piece on Keene's defection appeared eight days before the scheduled March 7 announcement of Reagan's presidential exploratory committee. "Keene is so highly esteemed in the conservative movement that his decision in itself is significantly a gain for Bush and a loss for Reagan," they wrote. His decision revealed "potentially poisonous disputes among the rivals for control of the Reagan campaign." They observed that a main reason for the collapse of front-runner Edmund Muskie's 1972 campaign was feuding at the top, and that "Republican insiders have forecast that Reagan's downfall, like Muskie's, could evolve from internal power struggle"—but that the "fascinating, enigmatic Republican strategist who ran Reagan's 1976 campaign," John Sears, was "praised by the press as a miracle worker."

As if on John Sears's cue, the *Christian Science Monitor* chimed in with an editorial, in the sort of voice-of-God passive tense that bespoke Washington conventional wisdom: "It unquestionably will not be a fringe operation if John Sears, the announced chief strategist, performs as he did in 1976. And when it is recalled how close the Reagan team came to over-taking a Republican president, the prospects for interesting politics going into 1980 cannot be discounted." They pointed out, however, that Sears was "anathematized by grassroots conservatives as Reagan's undoing" in that 1976 campaign.

The drama at headquarters was repeated at the grass roots. One activist from suburban Detroit fired off a three-alarm letter to the campaign chairman: "Dear Senator Laxalt: A rumor has ramped up here in Michigan which is most disturbing to me. . . . This rumor states that a 'moderate' will be appointed chair in Michigan for the 'Committee to Elect Ronald Reagan President' in 1980. . . . I know that you, sir, and Governor Reagan are above such dishonorable maneuvers. . . . It would sadden, disappoint, and disillusion me."

All of this made Keene's hiring a remarkable coup for Bush. The editors of *Human Events* pronounced their blessing over the formerly dreaded Yankee globalist they now judged "several notches to the right of Ford." Keene began claiming that he had talked to conservatives all over the country who questioned whether Reagan could win but considered Bush "a good second choice." Keene himself told *Human Events* that Reagan was too old to win, that "the front-running position is not always an envious one, as George Romney and Edmund Muskie can attest," and that all it would take for Reagan to fade for good was to "make a mistake during the campaign, say the wrong thing"—just once.

That had been the conventional wisdom in the "liberal media." Now that the conservative activists' journal of record was endorsing it, it was safe for wavering Reagan fans to think it, too.

ON MARCH 6, THE CAMPAIGN RECEIVED A POLL REPORTING THAT 31 PER-cent of Republicans wanted Reagan, down nine points from December. Gerald Ford was in second with 26 percent. If the former president did not run, Ronald Reagan would *need* his moderate supporters—even while, according to the gossip, Ford was doing everything in his power to stop his despised rival's ascent.

Which explained why, at the ceremony announcing the Reagan for President exploratory committee the next morning, former Ford cabinet members stepped up to the podium one after the other to proclaim Ronald Wilson Reagan the rightful heir not just to their former boss, but President Dwight David Eisenhower.

To appreciate the irony, a little recent history was useful. In 1957, President Eisenhower, fresh from a reelection in which he had campaigned as a "modern Republican," explicitly deriding his party's conservative traditions, announced a budget Barry Goldwater called a "siren song of socialism" that was the opening battle cry of the modern conservative movement. That movement's first great milestone had been Goldwater's own presidential nomination in 1964. But that campaign's emotional high point was a televised speech from Reagan on Goldwater's behalf. Reagan hoisted the banner for Goldwater's supposedly discredited conservatism with such unapologetic eloquence that David Broder proclaimed it the greatest national political debut since William Jennings Bryan's "Cross of Gold" speech in 1896.

In other words, Ronald Reagan entered politics by yoking himself to a movement founded in the rejection of Dwight D. Eisenhower. Gerald Ford was the lineal descendent of Eisenhower's ideology. This March 6 ceremony announcing the Reagan exploratory committee—which not accidentally took place in a room in the National Republican Club of Capitol Hill, which was called the Eisenhower Lounge—comprised an almost Orwellian attempt to shove this history down a memory hole.

It began with Senator Laxalt proclaiming, "Not since General Eisenhower's first election almost 30 years ago has there been such a perfect fit between the man and the public mood as there is today with Governor Reagan and the American people." Laxalt then pronounced himself "especially pleased that our committee has so many members from President Ford's administration, and from his campaign."

Reagan was giving a paid speech at a finance conference in New York. He "sent" a statement of appreciation to be read: "I am honored and pleased that so many friends in the Republican party have expressed their confidence in me by forming the Reagan for President Committee. . . . I await their findings with great interest." This particularly strange ritual was an artifact of recent campaign finance law. "Exploratory committees" were legal shells allowing a presidential aspirant to raise and spend money while not officially declaring himself a candidate. The instant Reagan officially declared, the exploratory committee—"admittedly a joke, a sham," an anonymous Reagan official, who sounded a whole lot like the rumpled old Lyn Nofziger, told the Associated Press—became a campaign committee. But the sham was of particular importance to Reagan, because it allowed him to continue his radio broadcasts without his opponents claiming the right to equal broadcast time, and to accept payments for his speeches and columns without the fees being counted as campaign contributions. The federal government would match contributions to a presidential campaign—but only if the candidate agreed to keep campaign spending under a legally specified ceiling.

The sham was also an important media event. It trumpeted the Reaganites' success recruiting 364 members into an exploratory committee that included several senators; twenty-five House members; dozens of Republican National Committeemen; celebrities like John Wayne, Frank Sinatra, Pat Boone, Jimmy Stewart, James Cagney—as well as Ford cabinet members Caspar Weinberger, Stanley Hathaway, William Simon, and Earl Butz, who filled out four of the seven slots on the steering committee. "About one fourth of the committee members," a press release trumpeted, "were Ford supporters in 1976."

Equally newsworthy for savvy political reporters poring over that list were the names it did *not* include: for instance, none of the rich California businessmen who served as Reagan's gubernatorial "kitchen cabinet"— symbols of Reagan's Goldwaterite past Sears hoped to shed. (It was also important to Sears to keep them at arm's length because they alone had the legitimacy to challenge his authority with Reagan himself.) Senators Helms and Thurmond were missing, too—they both leaned toward Connally.

On one hand, the event was a success: the last time around, the only "names" Sears had been able to drum up for Reagan's campaign committee were a former Kentucky governor; Laxalt, then in his first year in the Senate; and a retired right-wing congressman who had been a buddy of Reagan's when they both worked at the same Iowa radio station in the 1930s. This time, UPI called Reagan's list "by far the most impressive put together by any 1980 contender." On the other hand, Earl Butz—the guy who'd resigned as agriculture secretary after telling a racist dirty joke— was hardly the glimmering prize among Ford cabinet members, and William Simon was the sort of right-wing ideologue Sears had hoped to avoid.

At the Capitol Hill Club podium, the speeches were protesting far too much. One claimed that Reagan's coalition was "by far deeper and broader than any of the challengers for the nomination," cutting "across every partisan or ideological boundary." Sometimes, they strained credibility: That Reagan would restore "the carefully constructed Republican foundation for a peaceful world which was built in the first half of this decade" (an odd claim considering that the 1976 party platform Reagan constantly identified himself with was specifically written to repudiate the Nixon-Kissinger foreign policy from the first half of the decade). That Reagan "raised money unselfishly for his party and its candidates" (that asked reporters to forget that a little more than a year earlier Reagan had announced he was boycotting Republican fundraising to protest the RNC's refusal to come out against the Panama Canal treaties). One reporter cornered Paul Laxalt, quoting back at him his claim that on "virtually all major issues Governor Reagan's position and the position of the American majority are the same": Did that mean Reagan was *moderating* his positions? Laxalt responded, "I think the American people have pretty much moved to where Ronald Reagan is"—then plaintively added, protesting too much: "Our is not a fringe campaign."

THAT WAS TRUE IF YOU COUNTED THE EFFORT OF PHIL CRANE, WHOSE fringe campaign seemed to be going nowhere. Though not so much that it didn't have William Loeb of the *Manchester Union Leader*, one of Ronald Reagan's most influential fans, sorely concerned.

Bill Loeb was the most notorious clown in American politics. How clownish? Consider his romantic history. In 1926, at the age of twenty-one, he married a Smith College professor eight years his senior; in 1932 they divorced. In 1941, he bought two newspapers in Vermont with the money of a married woman with whom he was having an affair; in 1946 she helped him buy two more newspapers in Manchester, the *Union* and the *Leader*, which he merged; she withdrew her backing after discovering that he was secretly married to someone else. He divorced in 1951, then took a third wife. Now consider the attack he aimed at Nelson Rockefeller that helped end his chances in the New Hampshire primary in 1964: that he was a "wife swapper."

Such political vendettas, carried out via histrionic front-page editorials in the *Union Leader*, were regular features of the quadrennial first-in-the-nation primary in New Hampshire—even though Loeb actually lived and voted over the border in Massachusetts. Four years later, his target was George Romney; four after that, Edmund ("Moscow") Muskie. Both underperformed in the New Hampshire primary, and flamed out soon after. Political experts estimated his blessing upon a candidate could move anywhere from 3 to 15 percent of New Hampshire voters.

What positions of Loeb's might a candidate consider adopting to win his favor? That Senator Joseph McCarthy had not in fact died from hepatitis but "was murdered by the Communists as surely as if he had been put before a wall and shot." Or they could join Loeb in calling Richard Nixon and Gerald Ford's national security advisor "Kissinger the Kike." Or agree with him that the New Hampshire National Guard ought to be provided its own nuclear arsenal. Or echo Leob's affection for the neo-Nazi eugenicist Dr. William Shockley, or his front-page observation about South Africa's apartheid government, "When the Russian Communists lead hordes of black terrorists to slaughter whites in South Africa on a large scale, the American white population will have been so brainwashed that instead of reacting to support their fellow whites in South Africa they will sit by and do nothing. . . . IN SHORT, THE RUSSIANS ARE PREPARING THE AMERICAN MIND TO ACCEPT THE RUSSIAN BLACK CONQUEST OF SOUTH AFRICA. IT IS AS SIMPLE AND DIRECT AS THAT."

Loeb was a frequent recipient of Ronald Reagan's friendly dictated letters—the only media figure with that honor (unless you counted newspaper psychic Jeane Dixon). And in January 1979, he was so worried that Phil Crane would cut into his friend's New Hampshire vote, and provide a path to victory for George Bush, that he recommended to Michael Deaver that Reagan skip the primary altogether. That advice was not taken. So Loeb trotted out his very own Plan B.

Phil Crane arrived in New Hampshire with his wife and his eight children on March 7 to a headline in the *Leader* advertising "The Two Faces of Congressman Crane: Clean Cut Conservative? Or Party Playboy?" It quoted an unnamed source claiming that Crane "was committed in this life to bedding down 1,000 different women." A second article claimed he and Mrs. Crane, "deeply involved in the Washington cocktail circuit," were perpetually drunk. A third said that Crane was a lazy congressman. An accompanying editorial, signed by Loeb—who looked like a much shorter version of Daddy Warbucks, where Crane was exceptionally handsome—insisted he had not run this exposé "solely because we are supporting former Gov. Ronald Reagan for the Republican nomination for the presidency," but out of journalistic duty, reluctantly. The *Union Leader* also printed Crane's reaction when he was confronted with the charges—"I challenge anyone to give me some single incident that would indicate that any of this is true." No one did. But by March 9, it was a national story. The New Hampshire House of Representatives passed a unanimous resolution of apology for the "134 inches of totally unsubstantiated allegations."

The paper said its sources were Reagan "aides and supporters"—which covered a lot of ground. Crane, noting that the smears had run "within 24 hours of the announcement of a Reagan for President Committee," demanded that Reagan "investigate your staff to find the person or persons involved and dismiss them." Reagan, indignant, responded, "I informed Congressman Crane that none of my staff is in any way responsible for the article. . . . I told Congressman Crane that if he had any evidence to the contrary, it was his responsibility to get it to me personally." Richard Viguerie's *New Right Report* also blamed Reagan's campaign. (That suggested a hint of intrigue, given Viguerie's support for Connally.) The Crane campaign claimed that it was being deluged with support from disgusted former Reagan supporters. Unlikely: by the end of the month, it was nearly $1 million in debt, and less than a quarter of survey respondents said they knew enough about Crane to evaluate him. At the end of May, the chairman, executive director, and press secretary quit; and Crane's campaign was little heard from again—while Reagan was saddled with suspicions of a Nixon-style dirty tricks operation.

• • •

GIVEN ALL THAT, HOW DID THE REPUBLICAN RACE STAND?

The weekend after the Reagan exploratory announcement, six hundred party activists from thirteen states gathered in Indianapolis for the Midwest Conference of Republican Leaders. Six candidates or potential candidates gave short speeches; their deputies worked the back rooms; when it was over, CBS News collected straw-poll ballots. It was the first of several similar such events scheduled throughout 1979. One reporter joked that they were like Miss America pageants for presidential candidates. Another called them "cattle shows." That was the moniker that stuck.

Howard Baker spoke first. Becoming president had been something the Tennessean longed for ever since he emerged as the breakout star of the Senate Watergate hearings in 1973. His campaign was being organized by the Republican establishment's most distinguished consulting firm, Bailey, Deardourff & Associates. Jimmy Carter and Fritz Mondale, many of Baker's fellow senators, and many leading Washington operatives—including John Sears—considered him Carter's most formidable potential general election foe. But the highest-level Republican official he'd been able to recruit in a primary state so far was a lowly county commissioner. For he wouldn't even consider beginning his campaign until the close of the congressional session.

Baker was the "Washington candidate." He had recently led a delegation to Moscow to discuss the SALT II negotiations with the general secretary of the Communist Party, Leonid Brezhnev—but hadn't met yet with a single New Hampshire GOP county chairman. High diplomacy in the service of his nation's international interests, not boozy backslapping, was at the center of his political being. He intended to lead with his strength: campaigning as the distinguished solon, a foreign policy sage—the "Great Conciliator," as his Senate nickname had it. In Indianapolis, he called SALT II the "most important single foreign policy debate we have had since World War II," and proposed, referring to the recent unpleasantness between Messrs. Reagan, Crane, and Loeb, that a tribunal of respected senior Republicans referee disputes between camps, "to keep us all in line, as tempers are frayed, as the pitch and heat of this campaign increases."

When Kansas Senator Bob Dole's turn came, he dismissed that idea with a snarl: "Are we going to be able to control what the press writes by appointing a committee? I hope not." That played to *his* strength: Dole was the nasty one, the political assassin—the guy who could *really* stick it to the libs. But some Republicans considered Dole's sour, lackluster performance as Gerald Ford's running mate a contribution factor to Jimmy Carter's victory. Despite visiting forty-two states in 1978, Dole was at 2 percent in the polls. He insisted to an Indianapolis reporter, "If Carter proved anything he proved early polls don't mean a great deal." But he didn't impress anyone at this cattle show podium, either.

George Herbert Walker Bush did better. He turned to Indiana's popular governor, Otis Bowen, a physician, and drafted him to contest an Indiana Democratic senator up for reelection: "I don't want to set Doc's political agenda, but can you think of anything better than to have Doc Bowen whip Birch Bayh in 1980?" The crowd went wild. This was politics the old-fashioned way, and Bush was working it hard. He had to. He was the son of a senator himself—but the sort of senator that these conservative Indianans, their coats cut from respectable Republican cloth, had grown up despising. Prescott Bush had been a partner in Democrat Averell Harriman's Wall Street bank; a member of Skull and Bones at Yale; a critic of Joe McCarthy; a dear friend of Nelson Rockefeller and golf partner of President Eisenhower; a champion of international law and the United Nations. Conservatives called that sort of thing "globaloney."

The apple didn't fall far from the tree. George Herbert Walker Bush was Skull and Bones, too. His wife, Barbara, was a descendent of President Franklin Pierce and the poet Henry Wadsworth Longfellow. (Her family Christmas card list was one of the campaign's important organizing tools; it contained 8,500 names.) He had a brother nicknamed Bucky; his own was Poppy. And though he had resettled the family from his natal Connecticut and made an independent Texas fortune as a builder of offshore oil platforms, his background as a New England preppy had always proven an impediment to his political rise. In 1964, he tried and failed to win a congressional seat as a Goldwater conservative. In 1966, he won the seat in a campaign in which he said virtually nothing about policy but was marketed on TV like a shiny automobile. Then he was retired by a crushing defeat for Senate in 1970.

He was redeemed by an outstanding record loyally serving his party and president in thankless, appointive jobs. His post as United Nations ambassador had been offered to him by Nixon virtually out of pity after his 1970 loss. He became chairman of the Republican National Committee just as Watergate was breaking, skillfully balancing the nearly impossible tasks of upholding the reputation of the party while maintaining as much loyalty to the doomed president as circumstances allowed: at precisely the correct moment, Bush released a precisely correct letter, which read, "Dear Mr. President: It is my considered judgement that you should now resign." He was the nation's second envoy to the People's Republic of China, where the thankless task was balancing America's divided loyalty to Taipei and Beijing. Then he accepted President's Ford nomination as director of the CIA—a supreme act of loyalty, given that the agency had recently suffered humiliating and debilitating investigations about its dark past. (His distinguished service there nearly earned him a nomination as Gerald Ford's running mate.)

The Bush calling card was devotion to duty—had been ever since he volunteered to fight in World War II and became the youngest bomber pilot in the history of the Navy. He was the candidate of noblesse oblige—for which he made no apology: "Listen, I believe in it. It was inculcated in me by my father. My kids believe in it. Maybe it has eroded in this country, but with me and with my family it is traditional."

But he was also the candidate of globaloney. He arrived in Indiana following a visit to China at the personal invitation of Deng Xiaoping. The trip had been a success; Deng toasted Bush as "old friend" and his petroleum company won a breakthrough deal allowing them to prospect for oil off the Communist state's seacoasts. But it was not exactly the kind of thing you wanted on your résumé if your aim was seducing the conservative grass roots.

That was why Bush's campaign manager, Jim Baker, who had run Gerald Ford's presidential campaign in 1976, intended to build out a grass-roots organization surpassing all others. It would be concentrated not in New Hampshire but in Iowa, which held the first caucus, in January—and where, in 1976, "Jimmy Who?" was elevated to viability with his showing after a year of painstaking spadework. At the podium in Indianapolis, Bush began by insisting that he *was* a conservative—"but one with compassion."

He had no compassion for John Connally; the two men despised each other. Way back in March of 1977, William Safire had noted of the 1980 race, "Most of the behind-the-scenes action will begin in Houston," where the two Texans sought to cut into the far greater support Reagan already enjoyed. Safire pointed out how Bush and Connally were rushing to line up the bigwigs of the town's two contending factions of the super-rich, "'Old Cattle Money' versus 'New Oil Money' . . . Alamo versus Mayflower." Connally—the Alamo's man—called Bush "Little Lord Fauntleroy" and a "bedwetting Trilateralist," reveling in referring to him as "Poppy." Bush thought Big John a crook. When Bush's new aide David Keene joked he would look for Connally at his regular table at Houston's elite Petroleum Club, Bush shot back, "You don't really understand me, do you? The clubs I belong to wouldn't have John Connally as a member."

In Indianapolis, George Bush went straight for his rival's jugular. He promised to work to "somehow lower the level of cynicism about government" by making a full disclosure of all his personal holdings and assets when he officially announced his candidacy in May—something he knew Connally could not do without risking a second federal indictment.

But Bush's punch didn't land. Big John stole the show. His theme, naturally, was leadership. America was being "pushed around by third-rate countries." There was "never a time in the long history of the United States when we had less influence, or suffered a greater loss of prestige." In foreign policy, "the world perceives us as weak and vacillating and indecisive"; in trade, America was "letting our allies and our friends take advantage of us."

Each of these sallies received a burst of applause. The biggest came when John Connally said that if *John Connally* had been president when Iranians attacked the U.S. embassy, "every single Iranian in this country who overstayed his visa would have been sent home right quick." At that it sounded like a high school football stadium on a Friday night in Texas when the hometown boys scored a last-second touchdown to win the big game. When Republicans captured the White House, he continued, and—why not?—maybe the Senate, too, "America could finally rebuild *respect*."

THIS WAS THE STORY RONALD REAGAN HAD BEEN TELLING FOR YEARS. SO what, at that Indianapolis cattle show, was Reagan's response?

There was none. Sears had claimed a "scheduling conflict." He made the same excuse for forthcoming cattle shows in Iowa, New Hampshire, Florida, and Maine.

Reagan was in New York. That morning, he made a pitch to nine African American political leaders. He lunched with the lieutenant governor of Pennsylvania, William Warren Scranton III, a most-un-Reagan-like devotee of the Beatles' meditation guru Maharishi Mahesh Yogi and a man whose father had run against Barry Goldwater by calling his platform a "crazy-quilt collection of absurd and dangerous positions"—not exactly a natural Reagan ally. Reagan was interviewed by the executives from a syndicate of black-owned radio stations. Then he flew to a lucrative engagement before an investment conference in Miami hosted by the TV stock-picker Louis Rukeyser, booked instead of accepting an offer for Reagan to be grand marshal of Washington, D.C.'s, St. Patrick's Day Parade. This was the soul of Sears's strategy for the early innings: no politicking. Let the also-rans tire each other out; the front-runner would coast, risk-free, making his move in his own time.

The Indianpaolis attendees filled out their ballots—choosing Connally over Reagan to be their nominee by a margin of 31 percent to 22.8 percent.

Next came Bush with 18.6 percent; Baker, Crane, and Dole each got around 13 percent, and there were a few votes for Jack Kemp. Delegates also voted on which Republican was most electable. Connally came in first for that, too. In a vote on who was best on the issues, Reagan came in last. Which was ironic, because, on those issues, everyone else was saying what Ronald Reagan had been saying for months: Bush said that on the China deal America "gave all and gained nothing," then quoted Milton Friedman; Baker said he feared the SALT II deal would "lock into place a distinct superiority on behalf of the Soviet Union"; all the speakers called Jimmy Carter a phony budget cutter, spending America into the grave.

Evans and Novak passed their judgment: "If Ronald Reagan ends up dissipating a seemingly insurmountable lead for the Republican nomination, the decline may have started at last weekend's Midwest Republican Conference here when an absent Reagan left the stage open for a rampaging John B. Connally." They reported chatter that Ted Kennedy would be the Democratic nominee—and that "many believe only Connally can defeat him." They debunked the absurdly transparent spin from Reagan operatives about their man's embarrassing straw-poll results, and reported that conventioneers interpreted Reagan's absence as "an intentional message that he holds himself aloof from lesser presidential hopefuls."

"You can't put up forever with someone who stays aloof," a Midwestern county Republican chairman said. Washington society humorist Mark Russell happened to be performing that weekend at the Waldorf Astoria in Manhattan. One of his jokes was "Pat and Debby Boone have just endorsed Ronald Reagan. Therefore the Republican convention is just a meaningless charade." To heartland Republicans, Ronald Reagan was an aloof snob. To the sort of Northeastern elites John Sears had him chasing around New York trying to impress, he was a joke. To other Republican officials, he was a political wrecking ball.

The "front-runner" had a long way to go.

CHAPTER 24

Energy

PRESIDENT CARTER WAS IN THE MIDDLE EAST TRYING TO SALVAGE THE CAMP David Accords, on the verge of collapse at a time when he could not afford a defeat.

Shortly before departing, he had planned to headline a party fundraiser in Los Angeles. Then a full-page ran in local dailies: "We are Democrats who supported Mr. Carter and believe him to be a hardworking and decent man. He has tried his best to be a good president. It pains us to say that he has not succeeded. . . . As a result of this *CRISIS OF LEADERSHIP*, Americans everywhere are feeling more isolated, less connected to each other and to their government." It was signed by Norman Lear, Burt Lancaster, Jane Fonda, and dozens of other prominent Southern California liberals, and begged him not run for reelection. Carter canceled his trip.

The *New York Times* and CBS polled Americans about whether they thought President Carter had "strong leadership qualities"; 55 percent said he did not. *Doonesbury* ran a week of cartoons on the "liberal cult," "under the guidance of its charismatic leader, 'Ted,'" then two weeks mocking the president. (Carter: "The Army's still with us, right?" Hamilton Jordan: "I can check.") Jordan wrote President Carter a memo laying out strategy for 1980. It began: "Over the 200-year history of our country the myth developed and was sustained by events that incumbent presidents were always reelected"; time, he argued, to retire the myth. Indeed, he focused almost exclusively on how to beat fellow Democrats—and also how they should seek to underhandedly pressure state parties to adjust their primary calendars to do so.

Ted Kennedy repeated a standard line whenever he was asked if he was running. Reporters labeled it "E, E, and I": "I expect Carter would be re-nominated, I expect he'll be reelected, and I intend to support him." Jerry Brown *was* preparing to run. Scuttlebutt was that Representative Mo Udall and Senators Daniel Patrick Moynihan and Adlai Stevenson III might, too. Arthur Schlesinger Jr. predicted that Carter would, in fact, withdraw from contention, because he "must be aware, since he is an intelligent man, that he is miscast in his job." At a Reagan campaign planning meeting, John Sears suggested Carter might be challenged by his own vice president—and that whoever opposed him would win.

The attorney general prepared to appoint a special prosecutor to investigate government loans brokered by Bert Lance for the Carter family peanut warehouse. Billy Carter took the Fifth Amendment rather than answer investigators' questions, then checked into rehab. House majority leader Jim Wright told the *New York Times*, "No one is big enough for the job. So we have to settle for what we've got."

THEN, IN THE MIDDLE EAST, CARTER PROVED HIMSELF . . . A LEADER.

The treaty signing had originally been penciled in for December 1978—a fantasy, as it turned out. Accord at Camp David had only proven possible because the deal indefinitely postponed the most intractable problem: self-government for Palestinians in Israeli-occupied Gaza and the West Bank. When Cyrus Vance visited Egypt at the end of 1978, President Anwar Sadat demanded that the question be addressed immediately. Vance persuaded him push that deadline to the end of 1979. Then, in Jerusalem, Prime Minister Menachem Begin roared that he would accept self-government for the Palestinians precisely never, accusing Carter of selling him out. Further talks were shelved until late January—by which time the war in Southeast Asia, the impasse on SALT, and the debate over aid to Nicaragua left the White House with a very weak hand to play. Carter's Middle Eastern visit was a trip into a diplomatic lion's den.

Carter emerged after two days in Cairo with Sadat's respect and confidence. His landing in Jerusalem heralded difficulty: the protest signs were stinging, including one reading "WELCOME BILLY'S BROTHER!" At the prime minister's private residence, Begin pulled a fast one, claiming that he would have to submit any agreement to his cabinet for approval, then to an eight-day debate in the Knesset. Carter stood up and threatened to get right back on Air Force One. Begin stood up, too; they argued nose to nose for another forty-five minutes. Carter left near midnight, nearly as disgusted as he had ever been in his life. The next day, he met with Israel's president, Yitzhak Navon, who told Carter that this was the first *he* had heard about submitting anything to the Knesset.

Carter attended a cabinet meeting. Begin asked him to preside—then kept interrupting. At a banquet, Begin's toast was a patronizing lecture. Carter spoke to the Knesset, returned to his hotel room as exhausted as he had been in years, then Cyrus Vance and Zbigniew Brzezinski arrived to tell him that they had made no headway with the cabinet, either—though Begin claimed "substantial progress."

At breakfast the next morning, Begin said that of the seven questions

Carter had come all the way from Washington to resolve, he could only agree on four. Carter stood up once more to leave—but this time his bluff worked. Begin backed down, agreeing not just to all seven items but to come to Washington with Anwar Sadat to sign the treaty on the White House lawn.

Then, rather awkwardly, the elevator bearing them and their wives to the King David Hotel lobby stopped between floors, and, after a twenty-minute wait, technicians had to pry open the door so the heads of state and their wives could climb down on a ladder to appear before the press. "Mr. President," Tip O'Neill told him in a call to Air Force One, "you're not just a deacon"—Carter's Secret Service code name—"but a pope."

And so, on March 26, 1979, schoolchildren around the world were pulled from classes to assembly halls to watch on TV as two ancient enemies signed their enmity away. On the front page of the *Washington Post*, a White House advisor observed, "This will have a long-lasting benefit for Jimmy Carter. It will make him look presidential." Pat Caddell was quoted: "This is the kind of thing we can come back to—always. Great presidents are measured by great events. And this will have an impact."

The pollster began gathering data to measure that impact. He learned that the president had received a bump of only 4 or 5 percentage points, which dissolved within days, as the next national crisis began.

A NEW THRILLER WAS SHOWING ON 543 MOVIE SCREENS. THE SCREEN-writer, a former New Leftist named Mike Gray, had intended to write a script about greedy oil companies. Then he started to research the nuclear power industry, and decided that that would better serve his muckraking intentions instead.

The picture starred Michael Douglas in a role that had become cliché in the popular antiauthoritarian cinema of the 1970s: the lone-wolf, truth-telling journalist. He is a freelance cameraman, hired to film a puff piece about nuclear power—that "almost magical transformation of matter into energy that experts tell us may be our best shot at energy self-sufficiency," bubbles the pretty local TV correspondent played by Jane Fonda. Then, inside a plant called Ventana—the word looked a little like "Vietnam"—they capture on film a cover-up of a safety deficiency that, a nuclear scientist tells them, suggests "we may have come very close to the China syndrome":

"The what?"

"If the core is exposed, for whatever reason, the fuel heats beyond core heat tolerance in a matter of minutes. Nothing can stop it, and it melts right down through the bottom of the plant, theoretically to China."

In the real world, Americans had been instructed for decades that there was nothing dangerous about splitting the elementary particles of the universe to produce electricity. In a famous speech to the United Nations in 1953, President Eisenhower unveiled an "Atoms for Peace" initiative dedicated to finding ways "by which the miraculous inventiveness of man shall not be dedicated to his death, but consecrated to his life." Nuclear power—the use of the word "nuclear" was deliberate, to distract from the martial associations of the word "atomic"—was at the center of this vision: "the new symbol of the more abundant life, the radioactive key to industrial independence," a *Saturday Evening Post* article promised, "suited to any task—from moving mountains to curing cancer." Radioactivity was *good*; or at least not bad: a fearsome natural force, to be sure—but so were water and wind. "Radioactivity. It's been in the family for generations," ran one power company ad from 1972 picturing a happy family at play, and promised, "a person living next door to a nuclear power plant for a year would be exposed to less additional radiation than by making one round-trip coast-to-coast flight." The Nuclear Regulatory Commission said the likelihood of a citizen dying from a nuclear reactor accident was less than the chance of being killed by a meteor.

But in 1976, three General Electric nuclear engineers quit their jobs to campaign for a ban on nuclear power. "You can't expect these things to run flawlessly for forty years," they said. "There are too many people, too many steps, too many weaknesses in the whole chain." A safety coordinator at the Nuclear Regulatory Commission resigned because his recommendations were being ignored. Protesters committed civil disobedience at the site of a plant under construction in Seabrook, New Hampshire—to angry defensiveness from the industry's supporters, including Ronald Reagan, who had learned to love nuclear power as a spokesman for GE in the 1950s. He called the Seabrook protesters "pseudo-environmentalists" and "Luddites," and repeated industry claims that "nuclear plants can't become bombs."

Nuclear critics also obsessed over the events in 1974 around a plutonium plant in Oklahoma owned by the Kerr-McGee Corporation. An employee named Karen Silkwood contracted radiation contamination, then died in a mysterious car accident on her way to deliver documents about safety violations to a *New York Times* journalist. Jane Fonda had hoped to buy the rights to that story. She was unable to do so. Then she read Mike Gray's *China Syndrome*, and produced that instead.

Jack Lemmon played another stock character from 1970s antiauthoritarian cinema: the earnest mid-level bureaucrat who becomes a hero simply by paying attention and doing the right thing—a dangerous choice in a corrupt, fallen world. Lemmon begins the story as a dedicated company man. When confronted with the evidence, he insists that nuclear plant quality control is so thorough, with so many built-in redundancies, that what they had witnessed in fact *proved* the plant's invulnerability: "We stopped it in time. And we stopped it in time for one simple reason. And I told you that: *the system works, goddamn it!*"

And every critically aware viewer who had paid attention during Vietnam knew precisely how to interpret *that*.

The China Syndrome opened on March 16. In an uncanny coincidence, only two weeks earlier, twenty radioactive dump sites were discovered around Denver, with more unearthed every day—a nuclear Love Canal. And a judge was hearing the Silkwood family's lawsuit against Kerr-McGee. Still more uncannily, on March 13, the Nuclear Regulatory Commission ordered five plants in the East shuttered for a month for inspections after it was discovered that the computer code used to design their emergency cooling systems underestimated earthquake stresses by as much as a factor of six. (An engineer from the massive construction company Bechtel said that the concern was as unwarranted as "requiring snow tires in Hawaii.") The government had also just sued a small Wisconsin-based left-wing magazine, the *Progressive*, to enjoin publication of a harrowing article about how hydrogen bombs were constructed. Simultaneously, a long-simmering story hit critical mass. It concerned deadly "cancer clusters" citizen researchers had been documenting in Nevada and Utah near disused 1950s atomic test sites, now earning front-page headlines like "Fallout Danger Kept Secret."

For the producers of *The China Syndrome*, who included Douglas and Fonda, these interlocking scares invited just the sort of public discussion they hoped their film would inspire. But they were sorely disappointed. The picture did only moderate business despite a massive $6 million promotion budget. In the era of *Superman* and *Star Wars*, the post-Vietnam, post-Watergate conspiracy genre felt exhausted.

Until the uncanniest coincidence of all: *The China Syndrome* became nonfiction.

ON WEDNESDAY, MARCH 28, AT 4 A.M., A MAN LOOKED OVER AT THE COOL-ing tower of the nuclear plant on a little island in the Susquehanna River thirty miles as the crow flies from Harrisburg, Pennsylvania. He described it like a prophet from the Book of Revelation: "I saw a plume of steam rise several hundred feet in the air. . . . And it roared. . . . I looked out the window and I saw this huge column going up in the air and roaring."

A worker had mistakenly left open a valve, which stuck, displacing the water required to cool the core of Three Mile Island's Unit 2. Several minutes of confused frenzy followed—thanks to an unintended consequence of a design feature actually described by Jack Lemmon in *The China Syndrome*: " 'Defense in depth.' That means backup systems to backup systems"—more than one hundred alarms shrieking at once. Each represented a single failed backup system. Since so many were sounding, it was impossible to determine which required attention.

The first official word from a representative of the utility company Metropolitan Edison, or Met-Ed, was "Everything is under control. There is and was no danger to public health." The next day, Lieutenant Governor Scranton said, "There was a small release of radiation to the environment." But he seemed to contradict himself two sentences later: "No increase in normal radiation levels has been detected."

The media personnel swarming the scene, outfitted in breathing devices and gear, discovered differently. A Met-Ed spokesman told them, "We do not refer to it as a nuclear accident because it was not that." A reporter responded, "How can you say it's not a nuclear accident when radiation is being detected as far away as sixteen miles—*excess* levels of radiation?"

"Well, that does not constitute an accident. It wasn't an accident. It was a failure of a piece of machinery."

That "there was no accident"—only, yes, a stuck valve—was precisely what Jack Lemmon assured Jane Fonda in *The China Syndrome*. To which, understandably, audiences were now flocking.

Scranton accused the company of releasing confusing and contradictory information. But government released confusing and contradictory information, too. On Thursday an NRC official wrongly announced that the reactor would be in a safe "cold shutdown" within a day. The next day—"Black Friday"—an independent expert detected radiation levels fifteen times normal, suggesting pregnant women and young children should leave the area immediately. Governor Richard Thornburgh arrived, and said that they should not: the situation was "stable and under control." Which was right around the time a massive hydrogen bubble developed in the container housing the core, which if not reduced could create a real-life China syndrome, for federal regulators—after calling experts around the country in a panic—discovered that if oxygen levels rose, too, the bubble might cause an explosion: just the thing the industry had been insisting for decades was impossible.

Thornburgh now advised pregnant women and young children to "leave the area within a five-mile radius of the Three Mile Island facility until further notice." Walter Cronkite gravely intoned, "The world has never known a day quite like today. It faced the considerable uncertainties and dangers of the worst nuclear power plant accident of the atomic age. And the horror tonight is that it could get much worse." On Saturday, March 31, the NRC's director of systems safety recommended a general evacuation. The highways became a scene from a disaster movie; by Sunday night, fifty thousand citizens had fled.

The reactor cooled, the bubble shrank, and the threat abated. The distrust remained. "I don't know about that stuff, that nuclear," an old-timer told the press. "Seems to me so powerful, man can't tame it right."

LEADERSHIP. IN HIS FIRST PRESS CONFERENCE, LIEUTENANT GOVERNOR Scranton had been asked to explain the Three Mile Island alarm system. He responded, "I am not a nuclear engineer." The President of the United States, however, *was* a nuclear engineer—a former officer in Admiral Hyman G. Rickover's nuclear submarine fleet. So Jimmy Carter put on his engineering hat, consulted with Rickover and Dr. Harold Denton, the Nuclear Regulatory Commission's chief official for power plants, and concluded that the danger was minimal. In his diary, he blamed the fuss on "the news media, led by the *Washington Post*, engaged in irresponsible scare tactics designed to terrify the public and, not incidentally, sell newspapers."

With time to reflect, Denton subsequently showed considerably less confidence. He said his agency had had a "*Titanic*" mentality, believing that Three Mile Island "was so well-designed that you couldn't possibly have serious core damage." His agency, so overwhelmed with applications for new plants that they joked about hiring new evaluators off the street, approved reactors "with an extremely small audit." A local reporter, upon further investigation, reflected that they should have called it the Nuclear *Promotional* Agency. Even at the time, the NRC chairman, whose personnel had no legal right to enter the plant, and didn't possess mobile equipment to make independent readings of radiation levels, compared the authorities on the site to blind men. As for the representatives of the industry who had spent the last twenty-five years telling the public that what had just taken place could not take place, they sounded like the bad guys in Watergate: "We have more important things to do than tell you every little step we take," one Metropolitan Edison spokesman snapped to reporters.

The mayor of Middleton, a town three miles away, had been informed about the accident more than four hours after it took place, by a Met-Ed official who told him it was not serious and no radiation had been released, then turned on his car radio twenty seconds later and learned that radioactivity *had* been released—intentionally. "Now how are we to believe anything?" he asked. The mayor of a town twenty-three miles away complained, "No person was available to answer our basic questions." Met-Ed seemed never to have even considered the problem of communicating with the public in the event of an emergency. There was only a single phone line into the plant, which rang in the manager's office. Plans for emergency evacuation were nonexistent. A *New York Times* editorial on Friday, March 30, called this the "credibility meltdown."

Met-Ed brought in the slick Washington public relations firm Hill &

Knowlton. It suggested that the utility set up a telephone number for the public to call for updates. "But we don't have anyone who could man the telephones," an executive responded. "And we don't know what to say." Hill & Knowlton, known for its work with tobacco companies, answered, "Take the phone off the hook."

The president flew to the site after church on Sunday. Yellow plastic boots on his feet, he visited the control room, where he was pleased to learn that he and the first lady were receiving about a third as much radiation as a passenger on an airplane flight at thirty-five thousand feet. He delivered a short statement from the Middleton town hall—commending the governor and local officials for their leadership, praising the cool professionalism of all involved and the outstanding communication between private and public officials—and assured the public of the same thing the men in suits had: that they had never been in danger, and everything was under control.

Shortly after that, witnesses told a Senate subcommittee that on the day of the malfunction, Three Mile Island's uranium fuel had gone fifty minutes without any cooling water—information Met-Ed had withheld. Denton testified, "It's still too early to say how close we were to a meltdown, but the core clearly reached very high temperatures." Because of the way the instruments in the control room were shielded from radiation, technicians never had any idea *how* to calculate whether it was too hot or not. "We did not have, from the very first day," Denton admitted, "the kind of things we needed to get from the licensee to judge what had occurred and what to do about it. This utility was not prepared to cope with this kind of accident."

IN *ANOTHER* UNCANNY COINCIDENCE, NINE DAYS AFTER THE ACCIDENT THE president was scheduled to deliver his fourth major speech on energy.

The problem, he said, "is very serious, and it's getting worse. We're wasting too much energy, we're buying too much oil from foreign countries, and we are not producing enough oil, gas, or coal in the United States. . . . In order to control energy prices, production, and distribution, the federal bureaucracy and red tape have become so complicated, it is almost unbelievable. Energy prices are high, and they're going higher, no matter what we do."

The speech was meant to announce his decision to do for petroleum what the National Energy Act of 1978 had done for natural gas: "decontrol" it, over thirty-one months, until its price reached market level. This was intended both to spur domestic production, which totaled half of the oil America used, compared to almost 80 percent in 1970, and to encourage Americans to conserve.

Arriving at this proposal had been a politically excruciating decision. Inflation was above 13 percent. The day before Three Mile Island, OPEC had taken advantage of the cessation of imports from Iran by announcing a 9 percent price hike. The price on the international "spot market" had doubled in three months. And here was the president, announcing his intent to deliberately escalate prices further. "This is a painful step," he told the nation, "and I'll give it to you straight: Each of us will have to use less oil and pay more for it." The alternative was a nation "dangerously dependent on a thin line of oil tankers stretching halfway around the earth," from "one of the most unstable regions of the world."

The spoonful of sugar to make this medicine go down was a "windfall profits tax": a 50 percent levy on the estimated $107.9 billion in increased revenue American oil companies would begin reaping annually for doing precisely nothing, just because prices would rise. The revenue was to be earmarked for mass-transit subsidies; a federal corporation to develop synthetic fuels and alternative energy sources like wind and solar; and energy subsidies for the poor. The decontrol decision had been the president's to make, but the windfall profits tax would have to be approved by Congress.

There was a certain elegant karma to the idea. Energy companies received huge tax favors: since the 1913 Revenue Act they could write off more than a quarter of their costs as a "depletion allowance"; in 1950, the State Department began letting them shelter profits earned overseas. But, because industry simply considered those favors its due, explained Carter, "as surely as the sun will rise tomorrow, the oil companies can be expected to fight to keep the profits which they have not earned." He concluded with a stab at Churchillian gravitas to spur them to stand down: "The future of the country we love is at stake. We Americans have met equal challenges in the past. Our nation has endured and prospered. . . . We must recognize the urgency of this challenge—and we must work together to meet it. Then we, too, will endure. We, too, will prosper. We, too, will triumph."

But the speech barely gestured to Three Mile Island, even as the panic still spread. A nearby cow gave birth to a stillborn calf; that was recorded in newspapers as far away as El Paso. The county mental health agency reported a 25 percent increase in visits from children. One told them, "See, our door has a crack in it, in the screen. I dream that stuff's coming in and trying to get us." Women's clinics couldn't handle all the requests for pregnancy tests.

"I SURVIVED THREE MILE ISLAND," read the T-shirts. In fact, scientists said they couldn't know *what* the long-term effects might be. A government committee had been scheduled to release a report in the fall of 1978 about the health effects of radiation exposure. The project bogged down after scientists couldn't agree on recommendations—because, a newspaper explained, "it is impossible to distinguish a cancer caused by radiation from any other kind of cancer." There were "no flames," a reporter noted from the scene, "no people dropping like flies"—just an odorless, invisible, silent *something*, undetectable except by expensive equipment. "I hate being a guinea pig," one young housewife remarked.

JIMMY CARTER KEPT ASKING PEOPLE TO TRUST HIM. IT DIDN'T WORK. TWO days after his speech *Saturday Night Live* performed an elaborate sketch called "The Pepsi Syndrome." Bill Murray played a worker at "Two Mile Island." He spilled a soft drink in the control room—right next to a sign reading "NO SOFT DRINKS IN CONTROL ROOM." A smarmy publicist, whose name was "Denton," said the resulting meltdown was no more dangerous than "drying your hair in toaster oven." President Carter visited the control room with the first lady. With that grin that had once felt so charming but now felt simpering and smug, he pronounced, "Well of course *ahm* familiar with nuclear facilities. As you know, *ahm* a nuclear engineer." He triumphantly deduced the cause of the accident, then declared, "I'd like to go inside and check it out. I've never seen the core of a water-cooled reactor!"

Rosalynn responded: "Oh, look, Jimmy, why don't we just visit the Hershey factory!" That got the most rollicking laugh from the studio audience so far.

Carter, yet more smug: "Please. I think I know how to handle myself around a nuclear facility! Besides, I'm protected! I got my little yellow boots on! I want to go in and take a peek." The PR man asked the plant engineer if it was safe to go it, and he answered, "You're asking the wrong guy, I don't really know." That got the second-biggest laugh.

The smug PR guy suggested the first couple should have brought Amy—"she would have had a ball." The laughs grew shorter, a little bit nervous.

"Well, you know, Jimmy really wanted to bring her," Rosalynn said, "but I thought, 'Well, she's got school, and besides'"—said with a half sob—"'what if one day Amy wants to have children?'"

That got no laughter at all.

The final scene was another press conference: "Mr. Denton, is it true that the president is one hundred feet tall?"

"No! Absolutely not!"

"Is the president ninety feet tall?"

"No comment."

A ninety-foot-tall president stuck his head through the window:

"First, let me say that this experience has not changed my commitment to nuclear power. . . ."

Two years earlier, when *SNL* parodied the "Ask President Carter" radio call-in program, Carter's pedantry, micromanagement, and uncannily even-keeled affect in a crisis—when he calmly talked down a caller overdosing on LSD—were depicted with touching affection. Two years later, these same qualities just seemed creepy.

THE ADMINISTRATION HAD BEEN WARNING OF AN IMPENDING ENERGY SHORT-age since the Ayatollah Khomeini took control of Iran. By the time of Three Mile Island, oil companies had announced between 5 and 15 percent less in projected fuel deliveries than from the same time in 1978. Energy Secretary James Schlesinger considered ordering gas station hours shortened. Congress considered printing rationing coupons. In Maryland, gas stations began closing on Sundays; in California, weekend blocks-long filling-station lines became routine. In Oregon, manufacturers of steel drums and storage tanks, useful for hoarding oil, couldn't keep pace with demand; in Minneapolis, an advertisement from a dealer in gas-guzzling customized vans promised "If *There Is A Gas Shortage* This Spring, You Can Just Turn In Your Trans Van & Walk Away!"

Industry leaders called this a "premature panic situation." Congress apparently agreed. On April 25, the House Commerce Committee voted 23–15 to deny the president the authority to close service stations on weekends in the case of a supply emergency; on April 26, 22–20 to deny his request for such power to ration gasoline.

As for the windfall profits tax, liberal Democrats were almost as angry with it as the oil companies—with Senator Kennedy calling it "a transparent fig leaf over the vast new profits the industry will reap." The president at his press conference the next day called Kennedy's critique "a lot of baloney." The press room erupted in laughter. But the president wasn't joking. His face was grim as he turned his attention to the House Commerce Committee, which had scheduled an imminent second vote on rationing authority: "It would take us six or seven months to prepare such a plan if we were faced with a severe shortage of gasoline brought about by an interruption of supplies."

Then, once again, the committee spurned him. They even came within a single vote of stripping his authority to decontrol gasoline altogether.

In an Associated Press/NBC poll, 70 percent of the public said that the notion of a gas shortage was an industry hoax. A conspiracy theory from 1974 resurfaced. An advisor related it to the president: Exxon and Mobil had parked full tankers just off the coasts, then, "when gas gets to be 'X' dollars a gallon," they would dump the high-priced stuff on the public, because "the oil companies are just trying to rip us off, and Carter is letting them get away with it."

So Carter's pleas to conserve fell on deaf ears. Only one in five Americans said that they had driven less in the previous month. Only 25 percent said that they would drive less if gas reached a dollar a gallon—which was already happening in California. This refusal to change habits in the face of rising prices was a stinging rebuke to a main rationale for decontrol: that higher prices would spur conservation.

Maybe people kept driving in spite of expert warnings about an imminent shortage because it felt like experts didn't have a clue. Or maybe people kept driving in spite of expert warnings because it was something you could control, when it felt like everything else was spinning out of control. Like what happened on Friday, April 27, in San Antonio, Texas. A sixty-four-year-old man opened fire with a fully automatic machine gun on a crowd gathered for the city's annual Battle of Flowers parade. More than four thousand people were in range of his fusillade; fifty-three were hit, two fatally, before the gunman shot himself. Investigators found "no discernible motive."

"IT FINALLY HAPPENED."

That was how *Newsweek* described the scene when blocks-long gas lines began sprouting up in California on Wednesday, May 2. A manageable weekend annoyance was suddenly an everyday thing, cars converging from all directions like locusts on any service station still open, queues up to five hundred cars long snarling traffic for blocks—some drivers, after running out of gas in line, *pushing* their cars to the pump. Assaults on service station attendants were common. A pregnant woman was beaten by a burly man after an argument about who had cut in front of whom. Hospitals reported an epidemic of gasoline poisoning from grifters sucking fuel out of gas tanks with hoses. The number of people hoarding gas inside homes, even car trunks—just one rear-end tap away from a fireball—"curdles my blood," a doctor in the county health department said. People began carting gasoline in everything from plastic milk jugs to knapsacks with makeshift plastic liners; firemen were "scared witless." A survey of gas retailers suggested that by Memorial Day Weekend—service stations' busiest time of year—virtually every underground tank in California would be dry.

What had happened? Why had *this* Wednesday been apocalyptic, when last Wednesday had been fine?

Some held a newspaper article responsible—a small one, at the bottom of the *Los Angeles Times* front page on May 1. "Most Major Oil Firms Cut May Gasoline Allotments" explained that "to conserve supplies for the heavy summer driving season, when President Carter has warned that serious shortages may occur," and to honor the president's request to preserve crude for winter home heating oil, Exxon would be delivering only 80 percent of the amount to stations in May 1979 as they had in May 1978, and Texaco and Mobil would deliver 85 percent. These cutbacks hadn't actually happened when the story ran; objectively, there was no less gas than the day before. And when those smaller allotments did in fact go into effect, gas lines were not 15 or 20 percent but several hundred percent longer. Why? One author called it "a study in the sociology of unreason." Fearing no fuel tomorrow, people filled up today—even if they had just done so yesterday. Since the average purchase was now three gallons instead of eight, that already meant over twice the people in gas lines—and then, when people saw long lines forming, they joined them, lest the gas run out before they needed it. Service station owners, who received their stocks in a monthly allotment, began closing earlier to make sure the gas lasted through the month—and the sight of closed stations spread the panic even more than the sight of clogged ones did, spurring that locust-like convergence on the ones that were open still.

This run-on-the-tanks phenomenon was called "topping off"—soon a household phrase. As soldiers used to say in wartime when they lucked upon a cigarette: *Smoke 'em if you got 'em.* When Jimmy Carter called for an attitude toward energy consumption that was the moral equivalent of war, this was not what he'd had in mind.

IT HAPPENED THAT THE PRESIDENT OF THE UNITED STATES WAS SCHEDULED to arrive in California on Saturday, May 5. Which one might think was fortunate. If there had ever been a time and place that called for presidential leadership, this was it.

He began the trip in Iowa, promising farmers the same amount of diesel they'd received the previous year. He also promised "adequate supplies of heating oil for New England."

The political press made note: the Hawkeye State held the first presidential nominating contest, and New Hampshire held the second. They noticed, too, that Carter had changed the part in his hair ("The result is a lower, more youthful looking hairline," the *New York Times* observed). And that his weight was down to 198 pounds ("largely a result of his jogging and a new diet stressing fish, vegetables, and fruit"). And that his speaking had become punchier, and that, unlike last year, he hadn't snubbed the annual banquet of the White House Correspondents' Association—and "repeatedly brought the house down with well-paced one liners," like the one in which he called Jerry Brown's nascent presidential campaign "California's way of celebrating the UNESCO's Year of the Child." Press Secretary Jody Powell denied the *Times* theory that these were signs of a pre-election-season tune-up from Gerald Rafshoon. Powell was lying.

Rafshoon had just reminded the president in a memo, "In politics—or at least 1980 presidential politics—style is everything. . . . *You're going to have to start looking, talking, and acting more like a leader if you're going to be successful—even if it's artificial.* Look at it this way: changing your position on issues to get votes is wrong; changing your style (like the part of the hair) in order to be effective is just smart, and in the long run, morally good. Your ability (or lack of it) to move an audience and a nation by your words is no longer a minor matter of personal concern to you. It is the greatest reason (under your control) why your Presidency has not been more successful than it has."

But if the president was playing demagogue, he did an incomplete job of it. At an Iowa press conference, a reporter pointed out that oil company profits in the first quarter were twice that of other corporations, and asked: Was that too high? Carter responded that they were "*not* higher than other corporations." Then, in the next sentence, he acknowledged they were; then, in his third, he said that the incentive of high profits for oil companies was a "sound thing for the country."

Then, he descended upon the angry city of Los Angeles, where fire trucks were unable to respond to calls because of gas lines blocking the streets.

The situation bore some similarity to what confronted Franklin Delano Roosevelt when he was inaugurated in March of 1933. Then, the virus was bank lines formed by panicked citizens desperate to grab cash before the reserves ran dry. It inspired the famous line in Roosevelt's inaugural address that "the only thing we have to fear is fear itself." That week, Roosevelt took the unprecedented step of declaring a "bank holiday" of unspecified duration, which stopped the run on the banks in its tracks. Forty-six years later, it may have been that there *were* no words that President Carter could have uttered, no policy formula he could have announced, that could in like fashion have restored the nation's confidence at a time of epidemic distrust. Be that as it may, what President Carter did say and do in Los Angeles fell indisputably wide of the mark.

He didn't even give a speech. He released a statement. It opened less *the only thing we have to fear is fear itself* than *I told you so*: "Although this particular crisis came on suddenly, we have known since 1973–74 that something like this was bound to happen. . . . The reason for the gas lines and terrible inconvenience here—and the rest of the nation faces similar problems later this summer and maybe worse next year—is that we have failed to be prepared." He listed all the proposals of his that Congress had not acted upon. He implored Congress to make progress on the windfall profits tax. (Which was peevish, for whatever its merits as policy, the tax had nothing to do with ameliorating the present emergency.) He flayed legislators: "Too many people are afraid to vote for steps that may be a little unpopular. As a result, we continue to dream while our problems grow worse and worse. . . . The fact of the matter is that once a shortage is on us, there is no way to create more gas out of thin air. By then, it is too late for immediate relief." Which was misleading. It was *not* too late for immediate relief in California: people could stop topping off. Yet this was buried so far down that few news reports mentioned it.

The statement ended with Carter in his engineer's voice: "Immediate causes of the problem seem to be. . . ." There followed a series of numbered points. If a political cartoon were to have illustrated the press release, Jimmy Carter would have been wearing a scientist's lab coat, gesturing with a pointer at a set of blackboard equations, while outside the window, drivers in gas lines attacked one another with baseball bats.

The first cause named was the revolution in Iran. The second complained that Americans kept increasing their fuel consumption. The third cited his "decision that priority in a time of shortage must be given to heat for homes, hospitals, etc., and to food production." Which was where the contrast was most stark with Franklin Roosevelt—who had said of the American people that he was merely "the present instrument of their wishes," and that the "*people* of the United States have not failed." Carter suggested the opposite: that the people *had* failed the nation, with their selfishness—in contrast to himself, busy providing for the cold, the sick, and the hungry.

He said his energy secretary would be looking into the situation. But that things would get worse before they got better: "That is the truth. To imply otherwise, to waste more valuable time looking for a painless way out can have only one result: more weekends like this here in southern California—and all over the country." Then, as if he could not resist clobbering his political adversaries one last time, he concluded: "It is time for responsible national leaders in the Congress and elsewhere to forget about extending controls or taking away my power to begin phased decontrol. Those proposals will never pass. They offer no solution to the problems faced by people here in southern California, and they are a waste of time and a distraction from the real task we face."

He made only one other utterance on the subject during his two days in California, ad-libbed during a speech praising the contributions of Mexican immigrants: "The supply and shortages are going to be worse.

There's less fuel in the future and you'll pay more for it." Which might have just stoked more panic.

OTHER POLITICIANS HAD OTHER EXPLANATIONS FOR CALIFORNIA'S WOES. At a hearing on the windfall profits tax, Senator Long, owner of all those Louisiana oil leases, blamed the president, whom he addressed directly: "America would remain at the mercy of the Arabs as long as you remain in government . . . which may not be that long."

Congress's most prominent consumer advocates, Representatives Toby Moffett of Connecticut and Senator Howard Metzenbaum of Ohio, blamed oil companies: "It is our suspicion," they wrote in a letter to the Government Accounting Office, that "the shortage is contrived, not real, and that the purpose is to justify the higher prices that have spiraled relentlessly upward since January."

Howard Baker warned that unless the companies started using their profits to produce more instead of paying out so much in dividends, the public might demand that they be broken up, or even nationalized.

John Connally counseled patience—the crisis would pass in mere months, just like in 1973–74—and added a line to his stump speech: if he were president he would demand Japan stop selling so many goods here so cheaply, "or your people better be ready to sit on the docks in Yokohama in their own Toyotas watching their own television sets." It always got a standing ovation. Blaming Japan for dumping was easier than reckoning with the American auto industry's shortsighted refusal to produce little but gas-guzzlers.

And Ronald Reagan said what he always said: everything would be fine if Washington would just get its foot off the free market's neck. Also that this was no time to back away from nuclear power. "Some catastrophe!" he cried in one of three commentaries minimizing Three Mile Island. "No one was killed, no one was injured, and there will not be a single additional death from cancer among the two million people living within a fifty-mile radius of the plant." And the only fallout was "a beneficial kind to one small group of Americans—the cast, crew, and investors in the movie *The China Syndrome*."

Jerry Brown revived a big-government solution Governor Reagan had instituted during the 1973–74 crisis: a rationing system limiting service to vehicles whose license plates ended with even digits one day, and odd ones the next. (California's latest fad—personalized license plates—was accommodated by assigning a numerical value to each letter of the alphabet.) Then Brown winged east to speak at a massive antinuclear protest in Washington, D.C. The leaders were the first protesters in Washington history to be granted a personal audience with the president—who told them shutting down nuclear plants was out of the question. The next day, May 8, the *Los Angeles Times* wondered whether in the future "people will remember this as the time the car—the symbol of Los Angeles—changed from necessity to albatross."

THE PRESIDENT REINTRODUCED HIS STANDBY RATIONING PROPOSAL. THE House, including more than a hundred Democrats, rejected it overwhelmingly—despite Carter's intensive personal lobbying, an impassioned appeal to his caucus from Speaker O'Neill, and a series of amendments to appease farmers, cabdrivers, and truckers. Carter called reporters into the Oval Office and unloaded: "Yesterday, I was shocked and embarrassed by our nation's government." Tip O'Neill said he was "shedding a tear for America." An unnamed White House official, who sounded a whole lot like Hamilton Jordan, told the press: "The time is past when people can try to excuse their votes on grounds that somebody at the White House didn't have his shoes shined or his tie on straight, or that we didn't invite them to a cocktail party three months ago."

Carter implored Congress, if they wouldn't vote for his emergency plan, to come up with their own within the next ninety days. No one came forward to, as Chicago political parlance put it, "wear the jacket": to risk responsibility for potential failure. That was borne by Carter alone—upon whom it was becoming all too easy to blame everything.

The capital was atwitter over the cover article in the June issue of *Atlantic Monthly* by a twenty-nine-year-old former White House speechwriter named James Fallows. Entitled "The Passionless Presidency," it explained the mysteries of the Carter presidency better than anyone had before. Suddenly, it became easier to understand why the president was so poor at explaining what he was doing and why: this was because the "subject that most inspired him" was "not what he proposed to do, but what he was," and displaying to the rest of the world "that he is a good man." (Like in that bizarre statement on May 5 from Los Angeles about all the hospitals he was heating.) But Carter lacked "the passion to convert himself from a good man into an effective one, to learn how to do the job." And, Fallows insisted, "Carter and those closest to him took office in profound ignorance of their jobs."

The article also provided a way to understand Carter's inability to stick to a course once he announced it; and the wildly incommensurate way so many of his policies jostled with one another; and why his speeches sounded stapled together. Also, his failure "to explain his goals and thereby to offer an object for loyalty larger than himself": "Carter believes fifty things, but no one thing. . . . The only thing that finally gives coherence to the items of his creed is that he happens to believe them all. . . . Carter thinks in lists, not arguments; as long as items are there, their order does not matter, nor does the hierarchy among them." His self-defeating inability to delegate and prioritize: he acted on "everything that reached his desk. He believed in the clean-desk philosophy. During his first month, he said, 'Unless there's a holocaust, I'll take care of everything the same day it comes in.'" And, finally, his almost chilling determination to entrust the most difficult jobs only to the narrow circle of associates he knew in Georgia—because they were the ones "devoted to nothing more than what their boss has decided to do."

An exceptionally embarrassing portrait. Perhaps even more embarrassingly, Carter seemed not to understand that it was embarrassing. At a press conference after its publication, a reporter asked about the amazing detail obsessing all of Washington: Did the Leader of the Free World *really* arrange the schedule for the White House tennis court? "I have never personally monitored who used or did not use the White House tennis court," Carter replied—then robotically elaborated, "I have let my secretary, Susan Clough, receive requests from members of the White House staff who wanted to use the tennis court at certain times so that more than one person would not want to use the same tennis court simultaneously unless they were either on opposite sides of the net or engaged in a doubles contest."

In a poll of New Hampshire Democrats, 58 percent now wanted Ted Kennedy to be their presidential nominee. And in a May 12 commencement address at Howard University, the senator from Massachusetts piled on. He called it "incredible," referring to petroleum price decontrol, that a Democratic White House would push a program that would most adversely affect low- and middle-income Americans," and earned a thunderous ovation from his mostly African American audience asking, "Is it fair to ask poor elderly citizens in northeast Washington to shift to cat food so they can afford to pay their heating bills?" Pity Jimmy Carter. Back in California, he was being blamed for the gas lines because he held back crude oil so poor little grandmas in the Northeast *wouldn't* have to eat cat food in winter.

IN THAT 1933 INAUGURAL ADDRESS, FRANKLIN ROOSEVELT HAD REFERRED to the "warm bath of national unity" abroad in the land. Those waters were rather frigid now. Despite the president's insistence, the rest of the country didn't see what was happening in California as their problem. Although, to be fair, it was hard to know *what* Jimmy Carter insisted. His California statement had warned that the crisis would spread to the rest of the states at any moment. Then, in his angry jeremiad from the Oval Office after losing standby rationing authority, he said, "I am not predicting that we will have a shortage."

Some public officials acted as if the emergency was imminent. In Illinois, Governor Thompson ordered state troopers to issue speeding tickets to every driver they caught going over fifty-five miles an hour, with even the highest-ranking officers placed on ten-hour shifts to catch them. In Ocean City, Maryland, whose population was 3,500 in winter and 250,000 in the summer, the P. T. Barnum–like mayor, Harry W. Kelley, boomed what he claimed was an ironclad promise: "If you get to Ocean City, we'll get you home." How? "I can't reveal my secret," he said, flashing a mischievous grin. "But when I have to do it, you'll know." This portly gent was soon a minor celebrity, showing up on the *Today* show and in *Time* magazine, a chauffeur's cap on his head and an "I'VE GOT A SECRET" button on his lapel, gesturing to the camera with a gas nozzle.

Most officials, however, acted like there was nothing to fear. A newspaper in Allentown, Pennsylvania, contacted resort towns within a three-hundred-mile radius and found them all "ardently optimistic" that no shortage would occur. Mostly, the rest of the nation just looked to California and gawked. California—where citizens struggled, to the rest of the nation's amusement, with exotic new conveyances like "walking" and "buses."

Oddball California.

Where the governor usually slept on the floor on a mattress, but for most of April slept in a tent in Africa on a romantic safari with pop star Linda Ronstadt, and where a majority of voters told pollsters that was just fine, and 12 percent said it *improved* their opinion of him.

Where the lieutenant governor was a right-wing record producer who took advantage of the governor's convenient absence by appointing his own judges and trying to call special elections for constitutional amendments banning mandatory busing and imposing a ceiling on government spending.

Where, according to one report from an all-night gas station, drivers "spent their time drinking wine, smoking marijuana, talking with people in other cars, flitting between the tailgate parties"—and "cursing President Carter."

Where a fitness instructor bounced up and down gas lines, distributing a Scandinavian Airlines pamphlet of exercises you could do sitting down—perhaps working off the calories accumulated from the snacks sold by sexy young ladies in hot pants zooming up and down the lines on roller skates.

Where a kid cruised to classes at UCLA on a lawnmower, and a couple rode to their Pacific Palisades law office on horseback, tying their mounts to parking meters. Where superagent Lew Wasserman started driving his Mustang to work instead of his gas-guzzling Porsche—leaving underlings nervous whether they should fall in line and abandon their status-symbol autos as well.

Where a Union 77 station owner directed gas-line traffic dressed up as a sheik, with a real .44-caliber Magnum holstered on one side of his waist, a gas nozzle on the other.

Where gas was $1.19 per gallon, when in fall it had been around 80 cents.

Where silly suckers fell for guys posing as gas station attendants who asked for "deposits" from the drivers waiting in line.

And where an unmarked tanker truck began parking over underground gas tanks and "pumping unleaded gasoline out of the station's tanks, not into it," and a man brandishing a pistol held off a gas station manager and a queue of frightened motorists and filled up his Cadillac for free.

California's state motto, presidential press secretary Jody Powell mocked callously, should be "Give me mine and to hell with the rest of the country." Senator Percy of Illinois chimed in that California had been "creating their own problems," and welcomed the fact that its citizens were finally suffering the consequences for "depending continually on automobiles."

California: home of the late Jim Jones's Peoples Temple, the "I don't like Mondays" teenage homicidal maniac the Hillside Stranger—and the former San Francisco city supervisor, cop, and fireman who had climbed through a back window at City Hall with his police revolver and shot the mayor and a fellow city supervisor dead. Which provided the next California spectacle for the nation to gawk at: the trial of Dan White.

THE NEWFOUND CONFIDENCE OF GAYS HAD BROUGHT VIOLENT BACKLASH in nearly all the communities where they settled and made themselves visible. In Key West, in early January, a gay landscape architect was shot dead in his home. Then, the gay playwright Tennessee Williams's house was broken into. A local Baptist minister took the opportunity to run an ad in the newspaper: "If I were the chief of police, I would get me a hundred good men, give them each a baseball bat, and have them walk down Duval Street and dare one of these freaks to stick his head over the sidewalk. That is the way it was done in Key West in the days I remember and love." Subsequently, Tennessee Williams and a friend were exiting a gay disco off Duval Street, harmonizing on an old Christian hymn—"And He walks with me / And He talks with me"—when men leapt out of the shadows and sent America's greatest living playwright to the sidewalk.

"Let's run!" cried his companion. Answered Tennessee Williams: "I am not in the habit of retreat."

In the San Francisco neighborhood formerly known as Eureka Valley, once a quiet Irish neighborhood anchored by the Most Holy Redeemer Catholic Church and convent, longtime residents mourned the loss of their turf in like manner. That neighborhood was now known as the Castro, and in one recent incident, ten men crashed into a lesbian bar known as Peg's Place, yelling "Let's get the dykes!" "Call the police!" the bouncer cried to the bartender. Answered a marauder, "We *are* the police. We can go anywhere we damn well please."

This encounter was symbolic. Even as it was transforming into a mecca of live-and-let-live hedonism during the 1960s and '70s, San Francisco was governed by a staid WASP elite, with Catholic "white ethnics" granted the police force and fire departments as consolation prizes. The civic structure that rendered this arrangement ironclad was a city board of supervisors elected "at large"—that is, without districts, shutting out anyone lacking resources to campaign citywide. Meanwhile, the city changed. Middle-class Irish and Italians moved out to the suburbs, like whites everywhere. The handsome wood-frame Victorians in which they were raised fell to decrepitude. Hippies who came to San Francisco with flowers in their hair planted roots in the decaying old neighborhoods. They were joined by a mass migration of gays and lesbians, impelled to settle in San Francisco almost as if according to the biblical precept of the "city of refuge," where those falling afoul of the priestly code could live in peace. One remarkable consequence of this was that, where "rust belt" cities like Cleveland rotted, San Francisco was revitalized. One impressed witness was a former Californian governor who, in one of his radio commentaries in 1975, praised the entrepreneurial grit of the young San Franciscans restoring those grand old Victorians. "Ironically," Ronald Reagan said, "this comes from the so-called 'counterculture.' A college student of the '60s who may have scoffed at the work ethic of the time now finds rich satisfaction turning out an intricately made molding or door."

Who knows whether Reagan understood that he was praising, if implicitly, the new gay migration. Those San Franciscans most likely to *vote* for Ronald Reagan increasingly found themselves at the wrong end of the transformation. Conservative white ethnic families who stayed found themselves priced out of their neighborhoods. They began to feel themselves aliens amid this unholy triumvirate of liberals, libertines, and real estate speculators.

The first gay bar opened in the Castro in 1963; the first gay bar with plate glass windows opened soon after. One gay migrant marveled at that development: in particular that "you were in the *daylight*." Gay softball leagues, choruses, newspapers, movie theaters sprang up—and with them, anguished Irish Catholic parents, like the father whose confused son ran up to him one day and implored, "Am I going to be gay? Am I going to be gay?"

The Castro settled into a sort of low-grade civil war. A bar called Toad Hall, next to the convent, was torched by arsonists three times in three months. The San Francisco branch of the Reverend Troy Perry's gay-affirming Metropolitan Community Church was burned twice. Gay men fought back by other means. A former maternity shop became a boutique called All-American Boy. Watering holes opened with names like the Hustle Inn, the Tool Box, and the Rear End Bar. At the neighborhood's 1920s movie palace, Disney pictures and Hollywood blockbusters were replaced by events like the debut of *Tricia's Wedding*, an outrageous X-rated farce produced by a drag troupe called the Cockettes, and Bette Davis movies where the audience shouted out all the lines. The traditional family Halloween parade, established by a beloved local plumber, was taken over by a collective called the Sisters of Perpetual Indulgence.

Though in the Castro perpetual indulgence didn't have to wait for Halloween. There, one resident later remembered, it was "Mardi Gras every weekend."

Meanwhile the city's sclerotic political structure stayed frozen in place—until 1975, when a successful initiative campaign transformed the board of supervisors into a body elected by district. This was a political revolution. In 1977, the gays of the Castro were able to send one of their own to City Hall: the camera store owner Harvey Milk. So were the Irish Catholics of the Outer Mission neighborhood: the former cop and firefighter Dan White, who had campaigned by telling the story of how his parents were priced out of the city in which they had toiled all their lives by skyrocketing taxes and rents—and "social deviants." He promised, "We've got to stand up to the criminal element in this city and tell them we're not going to take it. . . . By choosing to run for supervisor, I have committed myself to the confrontation which can no longer be avoided by those who care."

His trial for murder began on May 1.

DURING JURY SELECTION, DEFENSE LAWYERS HAD STRUCK MEMBERS OF THE pool who answered yes to questions like "Have you ever supported controversial causes like homosexual rights?" The prosecution, inexplicably, offered few objections; the all-straight jury ended up including four elderly Catholic women active in their churches, and a retired cop; and six of Dan White's neighbors, but none of Harvey Milk's.

The jury sat behind a bulletproof acrylic-glass wall and listened to an opening statement by the prosecuting attorney, Thomas F. Norman, who narrated the events of the crime with straightforward blandness. Curiously, though he was supposed to be seeking a conviction for first-degree murder—murder that was willful and premeditated with malice afore-thought—he said nothing about what White's forethoughts might have been.

The defense's opening was far more evocative. White's lawyer Douglas Schmidt admitted the obvious up front—that White had shot and killed Supervisor Milk and Mayor Moscone. But "good people, fine people, with fine backgrounds, simply don't kill people in cold blood. It just doesn't happen, and obviously some part of them has not been presented so far." He depicted White as an exemplary citizen—star athlete, Vietnam veteran, father, police officer, and a fireman "decorated for having saved a woman and her child in a very dangerous fire"—who had tragically fallen prey to an undiagnosed manic depression, which caused "radical changes to the diet, compulsive difficulty in sleeping, low energy, withdrawal from du-ties, withdrawal from job, and withdrawal from others, and sometimes bizarre behavior." But Dan White "was the type of man that was not a complainer. He didn't complain about physical injuries, didn't complain about a disease he didn't know he had." Dan White, the defense suggested, was a man from another time.

The kind of ideal they were depicting, in fact, sounded a lot like a fa-mous American then very much in the news: John Wayne. "The Duke" was dying, slowly and painfully—and, naturally, uncomplainingly—of cancer, and talk of what that meant for America was everywhere that spring. A sculptor with the John Wayne–like name of Brett-Livingstone Strong was hewing a seven-foot likeness of John Wayne's face out of a twelve-ton boulder. The president took time out to sit with Wayne on his trip to California. At the Academy Awards ceremony in April, Wayne made his first public appearance in months. The orchestra struck up the theme from *The High and the Mighty* (1954), in which the Duke played a pilot who calmly sets down an ailing jetliner while his copilot panics. His famous weather-beaten face gaunt, his once-powerful body emaciated, he nonetheless nimbly descended a winding onstage staircase like he was Fred Astaire. The audience at the Dorothy Chandler Pavilion went wild. "That," the legendary superpatriot croaked, "is just about the only medi-cine a fella really needs."

Which was a lot like the Dan White depicted by his lawyers at his trial—an individual who "had an attitude that he developed through his life, perhaps because of his father, a man that he had admired the most in his life, that if you weren't succeeding, weren't coping . . . then you simply had to try harder." White, his lawyer continued, "was deeply endowed with and believed very strongly in the traditional American values, family and home. I think he could be classified as almost rigidly moral, but above that, he was an honest man, and he was fair, perhaps too fair for the politics of San Francisco. . . . He believed that a man's word, essentially, was his bond, and with respect to being fair."

So what had happened to lay him so low? He was beset, his lawyer suggested, by wicked forces beyond his control—just like old San Francisco itself.

"The evidence will show that Dan White came from a vastly different lifestyle than Harvey Milk. Harvey Milk was a homosexual leader and politician." White had won his race for supervisor "with no political prowess, with no connections," merely through the sweat of his brow, and thereupon, then came face-to-face with tricksters like Harvey Milk, and was flummoxed to discover "that in politics one does not always vote one's conscience, rather one votes, on occasion, because it's expedient and politically sound."

The lawyer finally turned to the strange events of November, when White suddenly resigned his supervisory position, citing financial hardship, then suddenly asked for it back. That Mayor Moscone had at first been inclined to grant him his request; then, after lobbying from Milk, Moscone thought better of it. The lawyer argued White had come to City Hall that fateful morning intending nothing more than to plead his case, and ended up shooting Moscone and Milk in a sort of bout of mania triggered by the trauma of rejection—and, because of this "diminished capacity," could not be guilty of first-degree murder.

Demonstrating that White's acts showed neither premeditation, deliberation, nor malice was a steep hill to climb. He had, after all, brought his .38-caliber revolver with him to City Hall—but that was only because, his lawyer claimed, "in addition to the usual threats to public officials" from the city's left-wing terrorists groups, who had kept up a steady stream of bombings all decade, there "were 900 bodies lying in Guyana to indicate that, indeed, people were bent on murder, and of course, as to Peoples Temple, and I think it will be shown that was tied more to the liberal elements of San Francisco and not so much to the conservative elements."

He had also brought with him a package of special hollow-point bullets, which expand inside the body to shred flesh. And, after shooting Mayor Moscone, he had reloaded with these bullets to shoot Supervisor Milk. A defense psychiatrist insisted that this frightened soul had carried these implements with him as a sort of "security blanket." And that he had had no special animus against Harvey Milk. In fact, White's lawyer argued—again, "though they were from vastly different lifestyles"—that White had "sought to befriend" Harvey Milk.

He had, yes, crawled through a back window, evading a metal detector—but that, another defense psychiatrist testified, was because White "didn't want to embarrass the police officer at the door" by forcing him to confront a politician. Dan White was a *gentleman*—which indeed explained, said a defense psychiatrist, why he *shot* the two men, in fact a confused, twisted expression of a finely developed sense of honor that prevented him from doing what a typical person might have done in his situation: punch his rivals in the nose. Shooting felt to him a much more impersonal, and therefore moral, means of retaliation. "It seems to me he takes special consideration not to hurt their feelings," the psychiatrist said.

THE PROSECUTION'S CASE WAS SO WEAK THAT LEGAL OBSERVERS WERE BAF-fled. The state played a tape of White's confession, which he made after walking into a police station an hour after the crime, to Patrolman Frank Falzon, a friend of his since grammar school and an activist in his campaign for supervisor. On the tape, Falzon seemed to take pains to coach White to confess in a way that would create a record that would make it difficult for a prosecutor to win conviction for first-degree murder. When his friend began to lose focus just as he was about to describe the crime, Falzon even helped him out by changing the subject, skipping him ahead to what he had done *after* the crime, and at one point repeating something White had said as if to bring it to the attention of whoever might listen to it later: "You turned yourself in. I wasn't aware of that." But there was no way he could not have been aware of that.

White went on and on, pitiably, about his supposed victimization at the hands of the media and investigators looking into allegations he was working in the council as a front for a local real estate developer building a waterfront tourist development, who had rewarded White with a valuable food-stand concession; and about the way his City Hall colleagues only saw a "political opportunity and they were going to degrade me and my family and the job that I had tried to do and, and more or less hang me out to dry"—and then the confession finally arrived at the violence in Mayor Moscone's office, which White described dazedly as if it were an event that had happened to *him*, not the other way around: "I just kinda stumbled in the back, went, went, went in the back room and he sat down and he was all, he was talking and nothing was getting through to me. It was just like a roaring in my ears."

Then to Milk, who "just kind of smirked at me as if to say, too bad, and then and then I just got all flushed, and hot, and—I shot him."

He reloaded his gun, "out of instinct . . . it's just the training I guess I had, you know." He complained in a whiny tone, "I never really intended to hurt anybody. It's just, this past several months, it got to the point I couldn't take it and I never wanted the job for ego or you know perpetuate myself or anything like that, I was just trying to do a good job for the city."

It was then, their work apparently complete, that officers had turned off the recording machine.

Playing that tape for the jury worked—for the defense: it supported at almost every turn their argument of manslaughter by reason of diminished capacity. Four jurors, overcome with sympathy, broke into tears. The prosecutor never followed up to ask Falzon how his long friendship with the accused might have compromised him. (He would never humiliate an officer like that, he later told a reporter, while his "family was in the court-room.") He didn't point out that, in the weeks leading up to the crime, the FBI had begun investigating White; or challenge this strange depiction of Harvey Milk as a venal power-mad pol. (One of Milk's signature initiatives, in fact, had been a tax to discourage real estate speculation.)

The prosecution didn't really do much of anything. In response to defense cross-examination, Falzon said that he had only seen White lose his temper once, that the person he interviewed in Northern Station was "not the Dan White he had known at all"—who, before the politicians got to him, had been a "man among men." On subsequent days, Falzon, who should have been the *prosecution's* star witness, sat beside his old friend at the defense table.

A former New Left radical named Warren Hinckle, now a writer for the *San Francisco Chronicle*, suspected the city was throwing the case. He interviewed the man who had accompanied White for seventy-two hours after his arrest, Undersheriff Jim Denman, whom the prosecution had inscrutably neglected to call as a witness, and heard an astonishing tale: Dan White had arrived at the jail calm, controlled, and purposeful—like a person who set out a difficult task for himself and had accomplished it. There, he received chummy pats from other cops, who joked about the shootings and delighted at his apparent lack of shame. They sang "Danny Boy," and whistled the Notre Dame fight song over the police radio frequency. "To a lot of those cops," Denman told Hinckle, "Dan White was a hero. . . . The more I observed what went on at the jail, the more I began to stop seeing what Dan White did as the act of an individual and began to see it as a political act in a political movement."

Then, at the trial White transformed himself for his daily court appearances into a zombielike shell, the better to suit the "diminished capacity" defense.

A cornerstone of that defense were the psychiatrists called as expert witnesses. The testimony of one became legendary. Dr. Martin Blinder was an expert in "diagnoses of the hysterical personality." Under questioning, he described the cycles of despondency that marked Dan White's depressive episodes. First, he would turn "resentful and quarrelsome." Then White "would abandon his usual program of exercise and good

nutrition and start gorging himself on junk foods: Twinkies, Coca Cola."
That would cycle him further into depression: "The worse he'd feel, the
more he'd gorge himself, and so on, in a vicious circle," until White spent
the ten days leading up to his visit to City Hall "just sitting in front of the
TV . . . binging on Twinkies." Blinder then cited unnamed studies "where
they have taken so-called career criminals and taken them off their junk
food and put them on milk and meat and potatoes, and their criminal records immediately evaporate . . . individuals who are susceptible to these
noxious stimuli, when given these noxious stimuli will undergo complete
change and engage in behavior they normally would not." That physio-
chemical change, he concluded, was one of three factors contributing to
the crime.

The prosecution did not challenge this. Just like it never challenged
the parade of character witnesses depicting Dan White as a paragon of
virtue. Once he began digging, however, Hinckle discovered a very different story. White's first campaign manager said she quit because she was
afraid of him. A political observer described his "uncanny ability to stoke
people's insecurities. He helped people hate. He's the scariest person I've
ever met." Another said, "I'm not sure whether he thinks he's George
Patton or Adolf Hitler, but he sure makes me nervous. . . . He was like a
spring ready to go off." Gay activists visiting Milk at City Hall dreaded
White's menacing glares. He had beaten up black kids integrating his high
school—then, campaigning for supervisor, opportunistically recruited a
black street gang to disrupt other candidates' events. One community
leader described his relationship with these enforcers as "like Jim Jones
with his bodyguards." Another said, "The whole thing was out of *Clock-
work Orange*." White had even won the support of local Nazis; four
showed up at a candidate forum wearing swastikas and "UNITE AND
FIGHT WITH DAN WHITE" shirts. When one of his opponents asked
White to request that they leave, White refused. Then, in the supervisory
chambers, one of White's aides manhandled two social service workers
there to testify against one of his projects. "I told White he was inciting
people and that it could lead to violence," one of the victims told Hinckle,
"and he said something like, 'Well, if that's the way it is, then that's the
way it is.'"

None of this came out at trial. Nor did the reason Dan White first
began despising Harvey Milk—a political dispute over a psychiatric treatment center that was to open in his district, over which White felt Milk
had double-crossed him.

Hinckle drafted an article he called "The Witness the Prosecution Isn't
Calling." His editors at the *San Francisco Chronicle* wouldn't run it. They

said it would prejudice the jury—despite the fact the jury wasn't allowed to read newspapers.

WHAT WAS GOING ON? WAS THE SAN FRANCISCO DA'S OFFICE TAKING A dive? Was the city's liberal newspaper abetting them? Yes, concluded Warren Hinckle: "A prolonged debate over White's character and political motivations would have brought out matters the San Francisco Convention and Visitors Bureau—and not a few prominent politicians—would have undoubtedly preferred to leave in the closet." It also might have opened up the fact that Jim Jones's brainwashed minions had been instrumental in the mayor's victory in 1975, and Harvey Milk's in 1977. In sum, local boosters feared that exposing the city's festering divisions might push it past the brink of violence.

Mayor Moscone's first act upon his 1975 inauguration had been to hire a liberal police chief, Charles Gain, with the mandate to reform an ossified institution where promotions were based on what parish you belonged to and cops joyfully busted up gay bars with impunity. He announced, "We'll hire gays the same as we hire everyone else," encouraged them to come out of the closet, and patronized the Castro's bars. Officers also took offense at his decision to change the color of the cop cars to a soft powder blue. They mocked him as "Gloria," spat on his car's windshield, defiled precinct house elevators with nasty graffiti directed at him. After he attended a fundraiser for the prostitution decriminalization organization COYOTE called the "Hooker's Ball" ("the social event of the year for heterosexuals, bisexuals, trisexuals, nonsexuals, homosexuals, and other minorities who feel discriminated against"), he was depicted on bulletin boards inside crosshairs. Then, in 1978, Gain announced a recruitment campaign for gay officers. At that, Hinckle wrote, threats of bodily harm to him became "almost as commonplace as bathroom pornography."

Mayor Moscone pressed for a tough settlement in a racial discrimination lawsuit against the police force. Discrimination against black cops was greater in San Francisco, one study said, than in Montgomery, Alabama. Supervisor White said this was part of a conspiracy to methodically decimate the city's bulwarks against anarchy: "The radicals are currently after the judiciary and the police department. They are trying to crack the judiciary through challenging incumbents for reelection. They are after the Police Department through enforced racial quotas that will destroy the department's non-radical middle management. Once they've taken over the law enforcement mechanisms of San Francisco, they've got the city cold."

San Francisco's liberal sheriff Richard Hongisto was a former San

Francisco cop—the first white to join the minority police officer association, which was now suing the force for discrimination. He traveled to Miami to campaign against Anita Bryant. Upon his return, he began carrying a pistol at all times—not to protect himself from prisoners, but to protect himself from assassination by fellow officers. He also kept a sealed letter in his desk to be read in the event of his death. Harvey Milk had had one of those, too. It read, "Let the bullets that rip through my brain smash through every closet door in the country." Such was the fear gay advocates in San Francisco lived with—even before Harvey Milk's self-prophesy came true.

Then came those assassinations, then Jonestown, within the space of ten awful days. "What scares me about the City Hall murders," a gay journalist observed, "is that they were so much like Jonestown. They were both cult murders. In Jones it was a suicide cult. In San Francisco it was a cop cult."

The new mayor, Dianne Feinstein, who had mentored Supervisor White, appeared to side with the cop cult. She gave an interview to *Ladies' Home Journal* arguing against too much gay visibility: "It's fine for us to live here respecting each other's lifestyles, but it doesn't mean imposing them on others." Castro Street began referring to her as "Ayatollah Feinstein." She fired Chief Gain, hiring an old-line Irish cop to replace him. Cops declared open season on gays: violent raids, random ID checks at bars, wearing T-shirts reading "FREE DAN WHITE" visible under their uniforms. One man who attended the trial every day wore a swastika and a medallion reading, in Hebrew, "Hitler was right." He explained, "We call him 'Gentle Dan.' All over the city you see signs that say 'Free Dan White.' He did what he had to do." He was a hero who had rid the town of bad guys with his six-shooter, just like John Wayne in *Rio Bravo*.

On May 20, the judge in Dan White's case handed down his instructions to the jury. It was "DAY NO. 11" of the California gas shortage, as the headline of the *Los Angeles Times* daily gas-line roundup read. ("Things weren't much worse," the paper reported, which "is sort of like saying it's a nice day in hell.") Governor Brown ordered gas stations to stay open one day each weekend, and was ignored. Rowdy motorists camped overnight on gas lines. Cops mistakenly arrested a man on suspicion of car theft when they noticed one license plate on the car overlaying another. Actually, he had just borrowed his brother-in-laws's plate, which ended with an even number, to buy gas.

The jury deliberated for thirty-six hours. The gays of Castro Street steeled themselves. The foreman announced the verdict: manslaughter, meaning Dan White might be eligible for parole in two years.

Stunned reporters froze. The retired-cop juror shook the defense counsel's hand heartily. Another juror told an interviewer, "It just all came together as if God were watching over us, as if God brought us together." A third called White "a moral man," and said he particularly appreciated the testimony that he was too moral to punch his victims in the face. A fourth said that the verdict "must be God's will or it would not have turned out this way." Every juror who gave interviews emphasized that the prosecution had done nothing to convince them White harbored malice toward his victims—it was not premeditated murder with malice aforethought but merely the act of "panic, brought on by stress."

As it happened, in 1984, during Dan White's term in prison, he told his friend Frank Falzon, "I was on a mission. I wanted four of them. Carol Ruth Silver"—another supervisor—"she was the biggest snake of the bunch. And Willie Brown"—an African American assemblyman—"he was masterminding the whole thing."

IN THE SUMMER OF 1977, BACK WHEN HARVEY MILK WAS JUST A CAMERA store owner and thrice-failed supervisory candidate, he came into his own as a community leader after Anita Bryant's victory in Miami by grabbing a bullhorn and talking an enraged crowd out of rioting.

But Harvey Milk was dead, and there was no one to stop a riot now.

A group of lesbians led the way (though Mayor Feinstein, like a Southern sheriff, blamed "outside agitators"). They stormed out of the bars and thronged angrily downtown, battling police all the way. At the crime scene—City Hall—people staved in windows, vandalized offices, stoned police, and torched cop cars, whose sirens wailed forlornly through the night. Three hours later, sixty-one police officers were in the hospital, and four thousand demonstrators straggled back home to the Castro—where, at 11 p.m., another group of marauders got to work. The first stop for police officers seeking retribution was the Elephant Walk, the bar Harvey Milk loved for its big plate glass windows, which they smashed, pummeling the "cocksuckers" and "dirty faggots" at random. Before it was over, they sent a hundred gays to the hospital. By the time tear gas finally cleared, new graffiti became visible on Castro Street walls. "FEINSTEIN WILL DIE." "DEATH TO DAN WHITE." "ISLAMIC JUSTICE—AN EYE FOR AN EYE." It joined another massive scrawl on a concrete wall a few blocks over at Mission Dolores Park that read "KILL FAGS! DAN WHITE FOR MAYOR." An American neighborhood had become a war zone.

Neighborhood was one of the "five simple, familiar, everyday words" that Reagan argued in his standard stump speech must be the foundation of every Republican campaign message. Michael Deaver had recently scrawled a note during a planning meeting for Ronald Reagan's presidential campaign: "Neighborhoods = good potential issue incl neighborhood schools; concept of ability to control situation (as opposed to impotence to ctrl own affairs)." The insight was a sound one. Just look at how many people were willing to spill blood for their neighborhoods in San Francisco. Just look at how, in 1979, impotence to control one's own affairs spread day by day.

ON MAY 22 THE HOUSE OF REPRESENTATIVES VOTED ON WHETHER TO CANCEL the president's authority to decontrol gasoline. John Anderson told a reporter, "The president is virtually in the position of a lame duck. He has lost that much credibility with members of his own party." John Sears called him a "political hemophiliac. Once scratched he'll probably bleed to death." Representative Toby Moffett of Connecticut, asked when he would begin supporting Ted Kennedy, answered, "Immediately." Then Moffett whipped his colleagues to vote for the anti-decontrol resolution, which he called "a choice between this and three-mile lines at the gas stations and shootouts at the pumps, California style." It went two to one against the president. The majority included an enormous number of Democrats, both left (one said the windfall profits tax would still allow "embarrassing" profits), right (Phil Gramm, the former supply-side economics professor, called the tax anti-capitalist "demagoguery"), and center (Al Gore of Tennessee said that it "would add 1.5 percent to the inflation rate for benefits that are almost illusory")—and also the entire Democratic leadership.

The next day, after what Carter called in his diary "a depressing breakfast with economic advisors, who don't know what to do about inflation or energy," a grand jury indicted Bert Lance on twenty-two counts of conspiracy and violating banking laws. Carter had never distanced himself from him—even in the midst of headlines that spring like "Lance Greased White House for Tycoons," which reported that the former budget director lobbied for White House access for two crooked friends seeking an oil concession in Qatar. And the exasperated D.C. commentariat had had enough. The indictment, one respected veteran pundit wrote, was "more than just a blockbuster news story." It was a "telling commentary on the character of Jimmy Carter himself, and the weaknesses of his troubled presidency." In "clinging to his old friend Bert," Carter "shows himself to be a moralizing hypocrite," making it "doubly difficult for the public to discern that there is a difference between his personal loyalty to Lance and that of Richard Nixon—in the early 'Stonewall' days of Watergate—to the likes of John Mitchell, Bob Haldeman, and John Ehrlichman."

At a speech two days later to the Democratic National Committee the president got a good reception. Perhaps because its subject was "American hopelessness"—of which there was plenty to go around.

On Friday morning, May 25, a six-year-old boy named Etan Patz, dressed in a "Future Flight Captain" pilot cap, corduroy jacket, and sneakers with glow-in-the-dark stripes, left his family's Manhattan apartment to walk for the school bus alone for the very first time. His cherubic face and halo of flaxen hair would remain a haunting fixture in newspapers and newscasts for years.

And that afternoon, at O'Hare International Airport in Chicago, an American Airlines DC-10, fully loaded with fuel for a flight to Los Angeles, appeared to lift off normally, stalled a few hundred feet in the air, rolled ninety degrees to the left, started shaking, then exploded upon impact in a field. The four-hundred-foot-high fireball could be seen eight miles away; firefighters couldn't approach the scorching site for an hour because of the heat. Two hundred seventy-three passengers and crew had died instantly, in the worst air disaster in United States history. It had almost been far worse: a gas storage facility, and an adjacent trailer park with one thousand units heated by oil, came very close to going up in flames.

The left engine of the three-engine craft had separated from the wing as it sped down the runway, after a three-inch fastening bolt cracked in half. The National Transportation Safety Board announced that this bolt had been failing for some time, unnoticed by American Airlines mechanics—but that that alone couldn't have caused the crash; DC-10s were designed to fly with only two engines. The Federal Aviation Administration grounded the nation's 138 DC-10s for inspection. They concluded that when the engine sheared off, it also severed the hydraulic lines that controlled the wing's flaps—which revealed a potential deadly design flaw: DC-10s had only three hydraulic systems, whereas the other planes in the DC-10's class, Lockheed's TriStar and Boeing's 747, had four and five onboard hydraulic systems respectively. And the systems on these planes were located on the wings' *rear*, protecting them from such accidents. The DC-10's hydraulics were located dangerously at the wings' front.

Less than twenty-four hours after the nation's DC-10s were once more cleared to fly, the FAA ordered American Airlines DC-10s grounded, this time because of dangers introduced by a flaw in how American had *inspected* its planes after the accident. Executives at American and McDonnell Douglas got into a public sniping match about who was responsible. Meanwhile, FAA administrator Langhorne Bond, assuming the crisis was behind him, galivanted off to the biannual Paris Air Show—where engineers had to track him down to inform him about a new crisis: the danger believed to have been introduced by flawed inspections was discovered in planes inspected *not* using that flawed method, and every DC-10 might be as vulnerable as before the whole ordeal had begun. Bond took the Concorde supersonic jet back home. Though he might have avoided the rush had he taken action a week earlier, after the *Chicago Tribune* reported that McDonnell Douglas internal documents warned of just such vulnerabilities.

Then, he announced at a packed press conference that new developments had "changed my certitude from the position of high likelihood of no risk to a sufficient likelihood of risk," so he was re-grounding the entire fleet again, for how long he couldn't say.

As American airports shuddered to a near standstill for all the grounded jets, an NTSB investigator told *Time*, "We have no handle on this one yet. . . . And if we find out, what kind of fix can we ask to have made? We don't know." Veteran aviation reporters recalled another design flaw in the DC-10: its cargo hatches blew open in mid-flight, accounting for a 1974 Turkish Air crash that killed 346 people. The Airline Pilots Association accused the FAA of "lethargy." At a congressional hearing, Administrator Bond's responses were so inadequate that the committee chairman bolted up and shouted at him: "Jesus Christ, just who is in charge over there anyway?" President Carter ignored calls for Bond's resignation. American DC-10s were out of service a total of thirty-seven days—then, over the following five months, DC-10s around the world suffered two *more* catastrophic crashes, one killing 74 in Mexico City, another 257 after crashing into a rocky slope at the edge of Antarctica.

"There have been few heroes in the distressing developments since the accident," *Time* magazine concluded on July 11: so few heroes anywhere; and so much impotence, too. Like Three Mile Island all over again—system breakdowns everywhere you looked. Among the stories relegated to inside pages of O'Hare International Airport's hometown newspaper that might have made the front page any other week were predictions of another OPEC price hike; congressional testimony from an assistant United States attorney and a Department of Energy official about what they said was a DOE cover-up of "illegal transactions by oil companies that drive up the price of oil"; threats by both independent gasoline retailers and independent truckers to go on strike to protest what they said were unfair government fuel allocations; and a feature on a chemical called 2,4,5-T, known as "Agent Orange" when it was used as a defoliant in Vietnam. Scientists noticed an epidemic of liver cancers in areas where it had been used. Even though the Army eventually suspended its military use, (long) after scientists warned it caused birth defects, it was still being manufactured in places now suffering an excess of miscarriages.

The president gave his fiftieth press conference, announcing an executive order granting emergency powers to governors to impose minimum purchase requirements, mandatory opening hours at gas stations, and odd-even license plate rationing. But Memorial Day came and went with few gas lines outside of California. Experts had no firm idea why—any more than "experts" knew when the nation's DC-10s would take off once again. The *Los Angeles Times* ran an explanatory article sorting out "the intricate web of factors" that had caused gas lines; it took up almost two and a half full pages. Some factors were unique to California. The vast majority, however, were not. Soon after that, an expert the White House had appointed to study the gas situation said that even though the Department of Energy had previously reported that the nation's supply shortfall was a mere 7 or 8 percent, it actually was closer to 20 percent.

So maybe the problem *wasn't* just panic-buying, or topping off—or a single car-crazy state chock-full of selfish oddballs. The problem was broader than that. And could arrive at a gas station near you any day.

CHAPTER 25

To the Mountaintop

THE GAS LINES STARTED SURGING EAST IN JUNE—ALONG WITH SUCH SUP-posed only-in-California oddities as commuting on horseback and trading sex for fuel. And in Ocean City, Maryland, Mayor Harry Kelley was in utter panic. His scheme to fuel the return trip of any tourist who made it to his resort town had proven too successful. "People said, 'we'll fill up when we get to Ocean City,'" a resident explained. Ocean City had its busiest June weekend ever. Mayor Kelley's secret—a 41,000-gallon un-derground tank meant to last the entire summer—went 87 percent dry. A strange man approached him with a promise to provide the city's service stations all the gas they needed. Kelley presented him with the key to the city. What he didn't do was check his background. The *Baltimore Sun* did, and discovered he was a con man with a long history of jail time for fraud.

The mayor was learning the same lesson as the president: managing an energy shortage was no simple thing. Carter called fifteen oil executives from various sectors of the industry to the White House to demand why, with crude imports increasing, the oil supply was decreasing. The retail-ers blamed the producers. The producers blamed OPEC. Consumer and environmental leaders, called in the next day, blamed Carter's decontrol policy. The president, in turn, blamed Mobil—"the most irresponsible company in America." All were partially right, all were partially wrong— and nobody had a solution that wouldn't solve one part of the problem by introducing another somewhere else.

Around then, the president's reelection campaign chairman said a curi-ous thing: "Every issue that Jimmy Carter has taken on has lost us votes." He meant that as a boast: the president was politically selfless. But Con-gress certainly wasn't trusting him as politically selfless: they approved a resolution calling on Carter to prove that the gasoline shortage was not cynically contrived—the very thing he had been futilely endeavoring to do since February of 1977. The public didn't trust him, either. His approval rating was now 29 percent, around where Richard Nixon's was after the Saturday Night Massacre.

His inflation policy was in shambles. On May 31 a federal judge, ruling in a lawsuit brought by the AFL-CIO—which was supposed to be one of Carter's allies—struck down the only part of the "voluntary" COWPS guidelines that actually worked, because it was the only part that wasn't voluntary: denying federal contracts to companies that defied the guidelines. Carter had to send his bureaucrats back to the drawing board—even as inflation was at an annual rate of 14 percent, five points higher than when he unveiled COWPS in October.

Precious metal prices surged; gold and silver were what investors stocked up on when the world seemed out of control—a pretty safe bet, that. In Texas, the judge in the nation's biggest drug conspiracy cases was shot dead. In Sacramento, four twelve- and thirteen-year-olds were convicted of trying to kill their teacher for giving them failing grades. In Kansas City, the roof of the city's architectural jewel, Kemper Arena, site of the 1976 Republican National Convention, collapsed in a storm. The roof at the Hartford Civic Center in Connecticut had collapsed seventeen months earlier, hours after a sold-out basketball game. Architects publicly worried the computer models they relied on to make large structures safe were to blame.

Add in Love Canal, Three Mile Island, the DC-10 debacle—and Skylab. The 75.5-ton space station was set to reenter the atmosphere in fragments weighing more than one thousand pounds, at speeds up to 270 mph, "sometime between July 7 and July 25," according to the latest prediction from scientists. *Sometime.*

Also: *somewhere.* "The space agency is moving ahead with plans to try to maintain some control over Skylab so engineers might be able to keep the space station debris away from the most populous areas when it falls to Earth next month," UPI reported, though all scientists could predict was that it would impact somewhere within a range between 50 degrees north latitude and 50 degrees south latitude, a band that included all of the United States, Africa, and South America, and most of Europe, India, and China. At least, those experts said, "a person inside a home or automobile" would be safe from "most" Skylab debris.

Originally, nobody had even conceived such a possibility. Skylab was supposed to have been outfitted with extra rockets to keep it in orbit indefinitely—then those rockets were dropped from the design to save money. On its first mission, in 1973, a meteoroid ripped away an enormous section of the heat shield, then a prematurely extended solar wing sheared off; the second wing would not extend at all. On the next mission its thruster engines sprang leaks. On another, astronauts almost weren't able to repair the radar antenna, without which they might have drifted in space incommunicado, forever. Also, Skylab was already supposed to have been joined by a "space shuttle"—but NASA's decade-old project for a reusable airplane-like craft was years behind schedule.

It was the tenth anniversary of the 1969 moon landing, when the machines built by the world's most confident nation conquered the very heavens. Now one was about to rain down in ruin. The ancient Greeks used to write myths about this sort of thing.

ON THURSDAY, JUNE 7, INDEPENDENT OWNER-OPERATORS OF CARGO TRUCKS, who moved 85 percent of the nation's food, went on strike to demand the right to charge more, carry heavier loads, and get 100 percent of their 1978 allocation of diesel fuel—just like Jimmy Carter had given the farmers. "Six years ago it cost me $38 to fill my truck," a striker explained. "Now it costs $140." Strike leaders said that if current trends continued, truckers would lose money every time they accepted a job.

On the first day, three hundred trucks blocked the Indiana Toll Road, closing the deepwater port on Lake Michigan adjacent to Bethlehem Steel. In Bismarck, North Dakota, drivers blocked access to almost all truck stops within thirty miles. A strike leader said they would be "as non-violent as possible—but you can't police everyone." Non-strikers in Iowa began driving alongside police escorts just in case.

On the third day, snipers started firing on "scabs." Beef processors cut orders for cattle, fearing that they couldn't get their perishable product to market. Farmers started plowing under crops. On the fourth day, an empty cattle truck was torched to cinders in Wisconsin; on the fifth, truck traffic on the Dairy State's interstates was virtually nonexistent.

When the gunfire had started, a spokesman for the Independent Truckers' Association had said, "If I find out who fired the shots I'll turn him in myself." Leaders were now less conciliatory. "In another week, we'll see something dramatic," one said. "If those people want any lettuce or produce, they better get to the store."

John Wayne died. President Carter eulogized, "It was because of what John Wayne said about what we are and what we can be that his great and deep love of America was returned in full measure." A letter writer wrote to *Time*, "Somehow I just don't feel as safe without the Duke around anymore." Others felt unsafe from the encomiums. They recalled the Duke on display in a 1971 *Playboy* interview, the one who said, "I believe in white supremacy until the blacks are educated to the point of responsibility," and, regarding Indians, "Our so-called stealing of this country from them was a simple matter of survival. There were great numbers of people who needed new land, and the Indians were selfishly trying to keep it for themselves." Wrote a minister to *Time*, "To represent him as an example of what American manhood ought to be is rubbish, a disturbing sign of the turn toward reactionary conservatism."

On June 12, with the greatest fanfare, Carter unveiled his long-promised proposal for national health insurance—the one whose absence a year earlier Teddy Kennedy had labeled Carter's signature "failure of leadership." By historical standards, it was a sweeping step forward. Employers would be required to pick up two-thirds their employees' insurance, and both employees and employers would receive subsidies to help. Medicare and Medicaid would be merged into a single program, with access to both greatly expanded. Pregnant women and infants would get treated for free. Doctor fees would be fixed by the government. If the plan went into effect on schedule in 1983, 80 million more Americans would be insured, at a cost of $24.3 billion.

By Ted Kennedy's standards, however—his proposal gave free care to everyone, at the cost, said White House experts, of $63.8 billion—it was piddling. Kennedy called a press conference a few hours after the president's. "This step is a regressive one," he said. "By perpetuating two *separate* and *unequal* systems of care, the President's plan may well become the straw that breaks the back of the American health care system."

"Separate and unequal" was a provocation against the president, who doted on his image as an anti-racist Southerner. For "separate but equal" was the formulation by which the Supreme Court's 1897 decision in *Plessy v. Ferguson* justified the South's system of legal segregation. The president responded to the insult to his honor that evening at a White House dinner with sixty House members: "If Kennedy runs, I'll whip his ass."

A startled congressman responded, "Excuse me, what did you say?"

The president repeated himself: "If Kennedy runs, I'll whip his ass."

Toby Moffett interjected: "I don't think the president wants to repeat what he said."

"Yes I do," replied Carter, then repeated it more firmly.

White House advisors told attendees to have no compunction about repeating what they had heard—which could not have been more widely reported if it were a foreign invasion. Tom Brokaw, introducing an interview with Kennedy on the next morning's *Today* show, delicately said the president had referred to a "three-letter part of the anatomy that's somewhere near the bottom." He then asked his guest the inevitable question. Kennedy laughed: "Well, if I were to run, which I don't intend to do, I hope to win."

The price of gas had gone up 55.1 percent since January. Fifty-eight percent of American service stations didn't have any to sell at any price.

And the president absented himself from the nation for twelve of the next seventeen days.

ON JUNE 14, HE TRAVELED TO VIENNA FOR A SUMMIT WITH SOVIET LEADER Leonid Brezhnev to conclude SALT II. As it stood, the treaty obligated the USSR to build a third fewer nuclear vehicles in 1985 than it would have in the treaty's absence—and now the two discussed possible negotiations for a SALT III, which they hoped would not just slow growth but cut deeply into existing stockpiles, perhaps even prohibit new weapons entirely. Brezhnev, officially an atheist, startled Carter by telling him, "If we do not succeed, God will not forgive us." He also made a verbal promise to limit the production of the Tu-22 Backfire bombers, the plane whose exclusion from the deal had so dismayed conservatives. A triumphant signing ceremony was held on the morning of June 18, then Carter rushed home to address a joint session of Congress that night.

Were it not for the energy emergency, the speech would likely have been judged a triumph. A government study called *The Effects of Nuclear War* had just been released. Tens of millions of people would die instantly, tens of millions more in days from nuclear fallout, then tens of millions *more* without factories to manufacture antibiotics, without hospitals and doctors. Then, mass starvation would set in. The study received enormous coverage; "Better To Be Dead," one headline ran. No surprise, then, that by a margin of two to one, the public overwhelmingly supported what their president had just achieved in Vienna. *Newsweek* called Carter's speech the best he had ever delivered. But White House logs recorded that of the 493 citizens who contacted the White House afterward, only 113 wanted to talk about nuclear weapons. "I saw the president on TV the other night," a trucker told a switchboard operator. "All he could mention was that SALT II agreement. That doesn't do a damned bit of good for us—we've got a national emergency out here in the country. People are getting killed in the streets."

The governors of Alabama, Kentucky, North Carolina, Minnesota, and Florida deployed phalanxes of Guardsmen to protect tanker trucks and freight convoys; snipers found unescorted rigs to shoot instead. Narrow canyon roads in Utah were rendered impassable by roofing nails. The Interstate Commerce Commission announced that owner-operators could now collect a 5.6 percent fuel surcharge; the president of the Independent Truckers' Association called that "crumbs off the table," and said the strike would continue. Supermarket managers said perishable products would start disappearing from shelves by the end of the week. Connecticut truckers shut down the waterfront terminal that handled 70 percent of the state's gasoline. Violence spread to thirty states. Getty Oil began installing bulletproof windows in its tankers.

And those inclined to insensitivity no longer made fun of those car-crazy Californians. Instead, they slapped stickers on their bumpers like "NUKE THEIR ASS AND TAKE THEIR GAS" and posters on their walls reading "How much is the gas now?" with a grinning American GI standing over a prostrate Arab, a mushroom cloud forming in the background.

THE FIRST TRUCKER TO DIE FROM GUNFIRE WAS A TEAMSTER FROM ALABAMA on Wednesday, June 20. The Independent Truckers' Association responded that it had no intention of backing down from plans, effective midnight, to escalate enforcement efforts to increase participation in the strike beyond the present 40 percent of independent truckers. Governor Fob James announced that he would put those responsible "under the jailhouse," and told a meeting of trucking executives, "The law of the land gives you the right to defend yourself." One asked, "Are you giving us permission to shoot somebody?" The governor answered, "Shoot somebody that stops you? Absolutely." Then, that, 'It's time to put the billy back in the billy-stick. I'd put a shotgun beside me and go . . . I'd kill anybody that tried to stop me.'

The president responded passionlessly. He extended Congress's mandate limiting government buildings to eighty degrees for summer cooling and sixty-five degrees for winter heating to almost all places of public accommodation. In a ceremony on the roof of the White House, he dedicated a set of solar panels and announced his recommendation that Congress create a "solar bank," funded from the windfall profits tax, to work toward deriving 20 percent of American energy from renewable sources by the year 2000. But he didn't say anything about the trucking strike. Administration sources said his options were "limited" in any event; Jody Powell said he might increase truckers' allocation of diesel fuel by cutting off farmers' extra share earlier than intended, and might have a decision by the weekend. Or perhaps he might not.

The news said Jody Powell himself had recently spent an hour in line to fill up his battered old Volkswagen—though Energy Secretary James Schlesinger managed to obtain a tankful after only twenty-five minutes, surely a disappointment to many: Schlesinger's back-and-forth feck-lessness on the crisis had made him the most cursed man in America. "It's really a psychological problem," his spokesmen said at first. Then, Schlesinger claimed that "the worst of the problem is over," now that he had no idea whether it was or not.

On June 21, the president *did* give a speech about trucking—a statistics-laden presentation introducing his plan to deregulate the industry. The only nod to the crisis turning the nation's interstates into shooting galleries was an oblique reference to the "precious diesel fuel" that would be saved—eventually—when Congress passed the bill. Perhaps realizing his political error, he showed up in the White House briefing room two hours later. He praised the "vital role" independent truckers played in the economy and said that his administration was "trying" to "meet their legitimate grievances," that some things had "already been announced" or "will be announced soon." He vowed, "Murder, vandalism, and physical intimidation are criminal acts, and they will be treated as such." Then he turned the podium over to the FBI director to answer questions, and disappeared, making no more public appearances until two days later to offer a few words on the White House lawn on "this difficult time for our nation" before stepping into the helicopter for his next overseas jaunt. Advisors had considered scheduling a fireside chat. But they couldn't think of anything useful for him to say.

ON SATURDAY AFTERNOON, JUNE 23, AIR FORCE ONE WAS WINGING THE president and the first lady to Tokyo when a convoy of truckers in an industrial suburb northeast of Philadelphia lumbered slowly through the center of town. Locals, angry that service stations had stopped pumping for the day, followed afoot, cheering as the truckers maneuvered their rigs into a massive intersection known locally as "Five Points," then refused police orders to move as yet more citizens gathered to cheer their defiance.

Such sympathy was not unusual, despite the hardship the strike had brought; at least the over-the-road cowboys were *doing something*. This was an area hit hard by the crisis; a DJ in nearby Trenton became a folk hero by locking himself in the booth and playing for eleven hours straight the hit new country ditty "Cheaper Crude or No More Food," which proposed American farmers avenge the Mideast by starving it. "I think it's about time to unite," said a local housewife who rallied with her husband and two children. "If we wait any longer, we won't be able to heat our homes this winter." Another said, "Anyone who owns anything operated on gas is on the truckers' side."

Soon the high-spirited throng resembled a small-town Fourth of July. Local authorities called in reinforcements from nearby municipalities, state troopers, and Philadelphia's corps of police dogs. When another service station shuttered, the dozens in line joined the protest, chanting "More gas! More gas!" At six-thirty, a trucker honked his way into the center of the intersection, climbed out of his cab, and started taunting the cops, who wrestled him down and tossed him violently into a squad car.

Darkness fell. The crowd numbered more than a thousand. They were ordered to clear the streets. Some sat down instead. Other started throwing bottles at cops. Officers started making arrests, and the protest broke up. But the trucks were still there the next morning. That afternoon, a hundred or so teenagers, bored on a hazy Sunday, joined the drivers, smoking pot and drinking beer. At nightfall there was a fight over a girl.

Someone dragged an abandoned mattress and sofa into the intersection and set them aflame, then a junked 1974 Grand Torino, then a van. Kids smashed the plate glass windows at a closed Mobil station, vandalized its pumps, and started pouring looted motor oil into the blackening flames, which shot higher and higher. The crowd topped two thousand. Cops in riot gear waded in with nightsticks and dogs. Some kids fought back—many calling the cops "pigs." It looked a lot like the corner of Michigan Avenue and Balbo Drive in Chicago during the 1968 Democratic Convention. "I have to say," a witness recollected, "it was a miracle there was no fatality." The next morning, Americans around the country beginning the last work week before the Fourth of July saw a picture on the front page of their local newspapers of a long-haired shirtless youth leaping exuberantly at the sight of a burning car illuminating eight-foot-high graffiti reading "MORE GAS NOW!"

But the most striking thing about the riot was not that it happened. It was *where* it happened: a town called Levittown—a word that had become a veritable shorthand for America's prosperous postwar mass middle class. The first Levittown, on Long Island, was built between 1947 and 1952 using such efficient mass production techniques that almost any white World War II veteran could take advantage of federal lending programs to be able to afford a single-family home. (Nonwhites were excluded, formally at first, and then informally after the Supreme Court banned restrictive covenants in 1948.) This second Levittown, built just down the road from a new U.S. Steel mill, had been a significant improvement over the ticky-tacky original: winding streets, irregularly shaped subdivisions, and extensive landscaping and recreational facilities created a community atmosphere.

It also, however, followed the unquestioned postwar pattern: it rendered residents automobile-dependent. And why not? The cost of petroleum *declined* in real dollars between 1950 and 1973—a period during which the number of cars and trucks on American roads quadrupled. Levittown, Pennsylvania, had ninety-seven miles of streets for only seventeen thousand residents. Its outdoor mall, "Shop-a-Rama," the largest east of the Mississippi, had spaces for six thousand cars. The formerly cheap oil that had lulled the nation into its thrall had become an instrument of virtual mass house arrest. No wonder a conspicuous feature of the Levittown riot was the ransacking of a shuttered service station, looted motor oil fueling a pyre built to ritually sacrifice two gas-guzzling carcasses. It was like some strange religious rite—a potlatch devouring the instruments of their suffering, which had once been the agents of their liberation.

Symbols of middle American normalcy kept rearing up and strangling

America's sense of itself as decent, prosperous, and safe. The Kool-Aid that Jim Jones used to poison his followers. The Twinkies that supposedly turned Dan White into a homicidal maniac. Family farmers invading Washington, D.C. A necrophile birthday clown. The year 1979 was when the pure products of America went crazy.

THAT SATURDAY, JUNE 23, THE AMERICAN AUTOMOBILE ASSOCIATION SAID that fewer than half of the gas stations in America were open. In New York, where 95 percent were closed, truckers blocked rush hour traffic on the Long Island Expressway for thirty miles. Nationwide, it was the most violent day of the trucking strike yet. And President Carter was in Tokyo.

He was there for a summit of the "G7," the world's seven biggest capitalist economies. That meeting, however, began in five days. First, he enjoyed a state visit—which he had decided not to cancel. And so, as Levittown burned, TVs broadcast the sumptuous ceremonies at Akasaka Palace, modeled on the Palace of Versailles; the president striding down a red carpet past an honor guard outfitted in blinding whites to the strains of a military band; Carter greeting the Japanese diplomatic corps beside Crown Prince Akihito, who was clothed in a traditional *hakama* skirt; Carter reviewing rank upon rank of crisply uniformed schoolchildren waving little paper Stars and Stripes and Rising Suns. He posed with one of the white-faced performers after a kabuki play, lunched with Japanese celebrities, made a pilgrimage to a Meiji shrine. (He refused the priests' request to bow and say a prayer. "Afterwards," he wrote in his diary, "my interpreter said he was a Christian and was proud that I did not worship heathen gods.") He held a televised town hall meeting. "Suppose you are not married and suppose you fall in love with a colored girl," a local asked. "What would you do?" Carter answered with an unstinting, unsentimental lesson about slavery and racial discrimination in the United States, and the halting, incomplete progress Americans had made in the years since. He concluded, sweetly, "As far as intermarriages are concerned, I've never been in love with any woman except my wife. But I would hope that in the true spirit of equality and in an absence of racial prejudice that I would not let the color of a woman's skin interfere with my love for her if I felt that way."

He glanced playfully at his wife: "It is a hypothetical question, Rosalynn, and I have no intention to leave you for another woman."

"Thank you very much, Mr. President. I like the U.S. more because of your answer."

He smiled like he hadn't a care in the world. He had plenty. In Belgium, General Alexander Haig, retiring with a hero's honors from his posting as supreme commander of allied forces in Europe (some said to run for the Republican nomination) was riding to work at NATO headquarters when an explosion detonated by remote control lifted his limousine several feet in the air, leaving a five-foot crater. An attempted assassination of the commander of 4.5 million men under arms, by forces unknown, had come within a split second of success.

Time featured shots of rotting crops in the field for want of truckers to transport them. *Newsweek* said, "Like some Biblical plague, the nation's energy problems keep multiplying." Then, they multiplied some more.

The leaders of the Free World were donning black tie for dinner with Emperor Hirohito when word came from Geneva that OPEC's oil ministers were hiking the price of a barrel of crude oil 16 percent—60 percent more than in December, up 1,000 percent since the start of the decade. Commentators suggested that this latest hike was owed to anger at America for the peace it had brokered between Israel and Egypt—as if it were Jimmy Carter's fault. In Tokyo, Carter wrote in his diary that it was "one of the worst days of my diplomatic life."

Just like the U.S. states, these seven nations had incommensurate energy interests. Canada was energy independent; Japan was 100 percent reliant on imports. Some countries had spare cash to pay producers a premium above the posted price, rate-busting that enraged the United States—which itself had enraged many of these same countries by subsidizing diesel and heating oil imports. And when it came to demand, the average Japanese and Italian burned sixteen barrels of fuel per year, whereas the average American required thirty. Europe and Japan taxed gas so highly that it cost multiples of what it did in the United States, so they had little sympathy for American officials whining that the hike would increase prices four or five cents a gallon at American pumps. They thought America childishly selfish concerning energy—much as the rest of America had once looked upon California, before the crisis spread their way. Just before the summit, President Valéry Giscard d'Estaing of France said that America "hadn't even started" to curb its wasteful habits—enraging Jimmy Carter, who for two years had been doing everything in his poor powers to get his fellow citizens to do exactly that. Under these inauspicious conditions, seven willful leaders sat down at the twenty-seven-foot mahogany table in the gilded cage of Akasaka Palace, tried to devise a collective blow against the power of OPEC—and failed. The press dubbed the fiasco "Khomeini Summit."

Back home trucker violence grew worse: six shootings in one day in Illinois, a fourteen-year-old boy wounded in Arkansas, the major fuel terminal for independent truckers in Birmingham, Alabama, brought to a standstill despite Governor Fob James's tough talk. "There's no way we're giving up," a strike spokesman in Connecticut insisted.

Gas lines grew. On PBS, *The MacNeil-Lehrer Report* broadcast from a gas station in Queens. "For God's sake," cried the owner, casting his eye down blocks of drivers baking under the morning sun, "if they want to enforce this rationing or whatever they want to do, can't somebody supply a *policeman* or somebody." Then he announced he was out of gas. The guy at the head of the line shouted, "I'm in line two hours and I just can't get gas? That's baloney! Carter doesn't get my vote next year"—then shifted blame to the oil companies: "Just you wait, once it gets up to a dollar and a half a gallon, you'll have all the gas you want and there'll be no more lines." Drivers converged upon the poor put-upon owner, who threw up his hands: "You tell the goddamned governor he's got to police this goddamned gasoline situation! I will not take this crap from customers. Let him police it or *stop selling gas*!" He turned to the camera, flushed with shame: "I lose control of myself." He sighed. "My wife says I've become very grouchy."

The president left Tokyo lamenting twelve hours of negotiating wasted, telling reporters that the OPEC decision would make a recession "much more likely." He deplaned in Seoul for more ceremonial pomp and circumstance—then more frustration at the negotiating table, with South Korean dictator Park Chung-hee. The Commerce Department reported negative economic growth for the previous quarter; three more like months and the country would officially be in recession. A motorist imprisoned in a gas line yelped to a reporter, "What in the hell is Carter doing in Japan and Korea when all the problems are here?" Mu'ammar Gadhafi, Billy Carter's friend, was quoted threatening to shut down Libya's oil imports, setting off a mini-panic on Wall Street. Presidential advisors began sinking into what the *Washington Post* called "genuine political despair, perhaps unmatched in any modern White House, except in those very last days of Nixon." Stuart Eizenstat and Walter Mondale sat down with members of Congress to describe the commitments the G7 had arrived at to control oil imports through 1985. The congresspeople only wanted to discuss how they were "literally afraid" to face their constituents' anger during the July 4 recess.

Carter's next stop was supposed to be in Hawaii, to readjust to the time shift and recover from the exhaustion. Eizenstat sent him a long memo addressing the awful things happening back home. It ended with a series of recommendations. The second was "Skip Hawaii." So he did.

"People were pulling guns on each other in gas lines," Carter's chief speechwriter Hendrik Hertzberg recalled. "The idea of Carter lounging on the beach while this was going on was just—it was just *inconceivable*."

THE WHITE HOUSE ANNOUNCED INSTEAD THAT CARTER WOULD GIVE A speech.

According to an unflattering article about that decision and its wide-ranging consequences in *Time*, it happened shortly after leaving Asia, on Sunday morning, July 1, after Gerald Rafshoon told the president that Harris was about to announce a 25 percent presidential approval rating. *Time* scolded him for making that call while he was "obviously too weary to consider the decision carefully, let alone give much thought to what he might say," then for mobilizing the West Wing to promote it—for instance, calling cameramen into the Cabinet Room at 6:45 a.m. "to film him in rolled-up shirtsleeves."

He still had a quarter of the general public on his side. But with the mandarins of the political press, he was just sacrificing competency for Rafshoonery.

A speechwriter named Gordon Stewart began bashing out a draft. It felt more inadequate with each new sentence he wrote. The gist was a series of technical policy ideas about how to solve the problem of energy misallocation in the short term and the crisis of dependence on the Middle East in the long term, larded with jargon like "geothermally pressured methane." It was, that is to say, much like Carter's four *previous* energy speeches—each delivered to successively smaller audiences. Patrick Caddell found this approach so excruciatingly wrongheaded he was nearly going out of his mind. For two years now, he had been imploring the president to deliver a speech aiming much higher—to address the nation's "crisis of confidence."

Caddell was despised by a faction of White House policy mavens as a melodramatic, self-absorbed fool—which was an easy thing to conclude. Instead of joining the White House, Caddell advised Carter as a sideline, simultaneously marketing his access to attract deep-pocketed clients like Exxon, Merck & Co. pharmaceuticals, and the government of Saudi Arabia. Many had interests directly opposed to the White House's. He presided over a Georgetown bachelor pad whose pool became known "R Street Beach," for its role as a gathering spot for D.C.'s hip young coked-up social set; he squired Lauren Bacall to an inaugural ball; he dated Hugh Hefner's daughter—and became a media darling. ("Pat Caddell, 27, Is the Whiz Kid Pollster Who Plays Good News–Bad News with the President," *People* magazine entitled a profile.) His indifference to traditional Democratic constituencies exceeded even Carter's—sometimes to the extent of sabotaging the White House. In the spring of 1978, for instance, while Carter was making phone calls to try to break the labor law reform filibuster, Caddell was all over the media trumpeting his firm's poll showing that most Americans thought labor unions were "too powerful already."

In January of 1979, in the run-up to the president's State of the Union,

Caddell made his most aggressive attempt so far to monopolize the mind of the president, in a frenzied memo conveying what he called a "chilling," "dangerous," "debilitating," and "staggering" finding: for the first time, half of Americans were "long-term pessimists." The figure had only been 30 percent in 1975, just after Watergate, around the time of the humiliating fall of Saigon, and the worst recession since the 1930s. He implored Carter to take advantage of his captive State of the Union audience to wrestle "this immense and ethereal monster" to ground. He had been elected, Caddell reminded him, "to restore trust, restore values." This was his chance to "deal with this spiritual malaise in America." Helpfully, he enclosed his own draft. "I fear if we fail to address this crisis of confidence that history will severely judge our inaction." His thrust was parried by another trusted advisor, Stu Eizenstat, the owlish policy hand, who succeeded in persuading the president to deliver a traditional address instead.

Caddell tried again in April. He was a man given to uncontrolled excitations. A journalistic critic once described the "splutter of words" that emitted from his "thunderous visage" as if he were in a "perpetual state of self-electrocution." He was particularly self-electrocuted now. He had become besotted with a *Time* magazine article entitled "The Deluge of Disastermania," which dilated upon the runaway success of books and films like *The Late, Great Planet Earth*, *The Towering Inferno*, and *Earthquake*. The public was drawn to intimations of apocalypse, Isaac Asimov pointed out in the article, even though the disasters depicted were "either very low in probability, or very distant in the future." But Caddell interpreted that as *confirming* his fundamental intuition: America's soul-sickness was no mere objective response to recent events, but far more deeply rooted. He agreed with a professor quoted in the piece who said, "We must prepare ourselves for the mass psychological hysteria, the conscious or unconscious sense of terror that may build to a climax."

Caddell was also prone to cunning bureaucratic end runs to get his ideas in front of the boss—another reason staffers despised him. He wrangled a one-on-one breakfast with the first lady. He recited the litany of woe: 50 percent of Americans were "long-term pessimists"; an unprecedented 30 percent expressed pessimism about their own future, including privileged people who logically should have the least reason to fear; a strong plurality said it made no difference who got elected; barely anyone believed politicians cared about inflation or taxes, or intended to do anything about them. He also showed the first lady his rejected State of the Union draft that he believed could have helped reverse this psychic drift, and, two hours later, Rosalynn Carter, in her own state of excitation, had Caddell repeat the presentation to Jody Powell, and directed Caddell to write it up for her husband.

At this point, Caddell was so jittery he could hardly compose coherent sentences. This task he delegated to a friend named Wayne Granquist, a statistics expert at the Office of Management and Budget whom he had met while helping plan the 1980 Census. Like a Pentecostal infused with the Holy Spirit, he dictated while Granquist typed. West Wingers took to calling the seventy-five-page jeremiad that resulted the "Apocalypse Now" memo—after the Francis Ford Coppola film Caddell was helping promote on the side.

It began, "America is a nation deep in crisis. Unlike civil war or depression, this crisis, nearly invisible, is unique from those that previously have engaged Americans in their history. Psychological more than material, it is a crisis of confidence marked by a dwindling faith in the future"—where, unlike the traumas of the 1960s, "there are no armies of the night, no street demonstrations, no powerful lobbies."

Caddell entered flattery mode: "This crisis is not your fault as President. It is the natural revolt of historical forces and events which have been in motion for twenty years. This crisis threatens the political and social fabric of the nation."

(Granquist hit the underline key on his typewriter.)

"... *the pessimism has spread to the elites; the young, the college educated, and the higher income groups. ... Everywhere there is a groping tentative swirl of discussion among the most intelligent elites from many fields. ... 1 out of 3 Americans see their own lives going straight downhill ... a psychological crisis of the first order.*"

Caddell discussed Alexis de Tocqueville, the economist John Maynard Keynes, the journalist Tom Wolfe, and the political scientist and biographer James MacGregor Burns, whose recent book *Leadership* articulated a schema of "transactional" presidents, who merely manage the government, and "transformational" ones, under whom "leaders and followers raise one another to higher levels of motivation and morality." Caddell argued that Americans suffered an "ennui of affluence"—on the verge of a recession, at a time when average incomes had been stagnant for some six years. He mentioned his latest object of intellectual excitation, a curmudgeonly history professor from Rochester also quoted in the "Disastermania" article named Christopher Lasch, who was on the cusp of an odd bout with national celebrity himself, thanks to a dense, abstract treatise whose original title was *Life Without a Future* that had somehow become a national bestseller. Its highly theoretical psychoanalytic argument concerned transformations in parenting styles and cultural ideals over the course of the twentieth century that Lasch believed had produced the sort of psychologically insecure adults he saw all around him now. A typical sentence ran, "Because the intrapsychic world of these patients is so thinly populated—consisting only of the 'grandiose' self in Kernberg's words, 'the devalued, shadow images of self and others, and potential persecutors'—they experience intense feelings of emptiness and inauthenticity." The published title was *The Culture of Narcissism*, though Caddell misintroduced it to the president as *Narcissism in America*.

Carter read the memo at the end of April. He pronounced it a "masterpiece." Eizenstat labeled it "bullshit." Walter Mondale thought it was almost insane.

When the gas crisis hit California, Caddell began sending the president and Mrs. Carter selections from intellectuals and activists who had inspired him. One evening, the Carters, Walter Mondale, Hamilton Jordan, Gerald Rafshoon, Caddell, and former DNC chair and special ambassador for Middle East negotiations Robert Strauss had cocktails on the Truman balcony. (The president said, "This country is going to hell. This government has fucked up from end to end." Then he apologized for swearing in front of a lady.) Caddell persuaded him to schedule a dinner with some of these figures, including Lasch.

Jesse Jackson said that people watched too much television. John Gardner, a former LBJ cabinet member who had started the group Common Cause to attenuate the power of Washington interest groups, said that there were too many interest groups. Sociologist Daniel Bell lectured on the "limits of the mundane." Bill Moyers, the president complained, was too "preacherly." Carter told Lasch he had read *The Culture of Narcissism*—then explained that he read a whole lot, thanks to a speed-reading course he had taken. The president then asked how the professor might apply the lessons of his book to heal America's spiritual drift. Lasch responded that he had no idea.

"All I can say," he wrote to a friend, baffled by what it was in his book that Pat Caddell imagined had any practical political application, "is that subsequent events confirmed my own prejudice against speed reading." After he had time to think about it, Lasch followed up with a letter to the president worrying that calls for sacrifice were meaningless in an increasingly corporate-controlled society where sacrifice was ever more unequally distributed, advising Carter to concentrate on *that*. Daniel Bell made a similar argument in a letter to Jody Powell. Lasch subsequently lamented, "The president does not seem terribly responsive."

Carter traveled to Vienna, then Tokyo and Seoul. Skylab sank lower in the heavens. Carter made his decision to give the televised speech. Thursday, July 5, at 9 p.m. EST was appointed as the time. Caddell contributed his most feverish memo yet, advising that since the public had stopped listening to him, the president should attempt a drastic "breakthrough." He suggested leaking that Carter had absented himself to an "unknown destination"; the press would go "bonkers"; Jody Powell could then incite outright "pandemonium" to "build our audience" by announcing that "(a) the President is gone, (b) that there is no national crisis, etc., (c) that the president is doing something that he views as crucial and has wanted to do for a while, (d) and, no questions will be answered." Meanwhile Carter would be secretly traveling the country, meeting with ordinary Americans—"to help you capture your 'ear' for America." Powell would then announce that Carter would deliver an address of "grave national importance . . . rumors will be flying . . . you are going to resign, that you are going to announce you are not going to seek reelection, that you have gone crazy."

He also said the president should call a "second Constitutional Convention"—upon which Vice President Mondale wondered whether Caddell wasn't *literally* crazy.

ON INDEPENDENCE DAY JIMMY CARTER HELICOPTERED TO CAMP DAVID FOR what appeared to be a vacation. CBS News said New York streets were so empty from the unavailability of gas that Hollywood could have shot *The Day the Earth Stood Still* there. John Denver, the beloved troubadour famous for his protests against building highways across unspoiled wilderness, emerged as a national villain after it was reported he had secreted a tank beneath the lawn of his Colorado home of a size large enough to hoard gas to fuel a car for six years.

The president did some fishing. He read Gordon Stewart's most recent draft for the next night's address, and a memo from Walter Mondale pronouncing that draft dour and depressing, suggesting he give an uplifting JFK-style speech instead. He read Caddell's 107-page memo, and described it in his diary as "one of the most brilliant analyses of sociological and political interrelationships I have ever seen. The more I read it along with Rosalynn, the more I became excited." He called in to Robert Strauss's office in Washington, where Jordan, Mondale, Rafshoon, and Deputy Press Secretary Rex Granum were working over Stewart's draft. He ordered them to stop. He did not, he said, want to "bullshit the American people."

An alarmed Rex Granum asked what he should tell the press.

"Just say I cancelled the damned speech."

With that, the value of the dollar began collapsing on world exchanges. Blumenthal reached Carter at a trout stream, on an Army field telephone, and told him he had to say *something*. So Carter authorized Powell to announce that he would propose measures to restrain U.S. demand for imported oil. The Federal Reserve started buying up dollars. The slide abated, as jokes began rocketing around Washington: That the president was off on a fishing trip, but he was just standing there without a pole. That Marine One would fetch him back to Washington anytime now, just as soon as they could find his pants. *Time* spluttered that he "seemed strangely unaware of the uproar that his decision would touch off." Senator Abraham Ribicoff, the liberal Democrat from Connecticut, blurted, "Why, the man doesn't deserve to be president!" Washington's afternoon newspaper the *Star* reported that the administration was in "chaos." "No one knows what the President is up to," an exasperated aide was quoted as saying.

But the next day was when things *really* started getting strange.

HAMILTON JORDAN AND JODY POWELL WERE RELAXING AROUND PAT CADdell's pool when they were called to report ASAP to the helicopter pad at the vice president's Naval Observatory home. They were ferried along with Eizenstat and Rafshoon to the president's private summer camp in the Catoctin Mountains. The forty-minute flight was virtually silent—but for when Hamilton Jordan muttered, "We gotta fire people."

They were deposited at Laurel Lodge, where the Camp David Accords had been hammered out. Jimmy and Rosalynn appeared, and explained that they all would be there for at least a week.

The president alone was cheerful, spouting jokes. The subsequent debate hardened battle lines. Walter Mondale and Stuart Eizenstat maintained that a speech addressing the nation's psychic wounds was lunacy, that the Washington establishment would destroy them. Jody Powell supported Caddell and said bidding for the media's affections was futile. The vice president, to cut the tension, blamed the tempers on residual jet lag. The president snapped back, "I feel fine."

Mondale gave back as good as he got. He called Caddell's memo loony and said that the citizenry's misery was the result of *real* problems, addressable by *real* policies, not airy sermonizing, and that Caddell's idea for a new constitutional convention could literally put the republic at risk. Eizenstat was his tag-team partner. He pointed to the desperate attempts to prop up the fallen dollar, barking to the commander in chief, "I hope you're happy."

Another Caddell memo was passed around. The word *bullshit* was once more heard. As the congregation broke for dinner after three hours, the president informed them that he was with Pat Caddell "100 percent," and that their job was to devise a speech centering on his "brilliant memo."

He hiked a forest path with a distraught Walter Mondale, talking him down from resigning, distracting him with a request to help brainstorm public officials and private citizens to call to Camp David for consultation—"political wise men and women," the president said: pregnant words. He had told Emperor Hirohito that a conclave of "wise men" could have prevented World War II. "The Wise Men" was also the name given the council of outside advisors who had persuaded Lyndon Johnson to begin negotiations to end the Vietnam War. Which, one could observe, had immediately preceded Johnson's decision to quit the presidency.

MARINE HELICOPTERS BEGAN SHUTTLING WISE MEN FROM WASHINGTON LIKE airborne Greyhound buses. Upon their arrival at what the gawking, shut-out media invariably referred to as the "mountaintop," Ham Jordan handed them copies of Christopher Lasch's *The Culture of Narcissism*. So many made the pilgrimage that stewards feared that they would run out of the glasses stamped "Camp David" that people kept snagging for souvenirs.

The first platoon consisted of seven governors. Carter welcomed them with the same poignant introduction he would deliver to each assemblage to come: that he was deeply concerned with the restlessness, the anxiety, the uncertainty, the collapse of trust in institutions and the credibility of authority, which he attributed, following Caddell, to the traumas America suffered as a result of the assassinations of JFK, RFK, and Martin Luther King Jr.; the Vietnam War; and Watergate. He used a favorite Caddell word to describe it: "malaise." Accounts filtering out repeated that word, which began showing up in news reports.

The malaise that concerned him most, the president told his guests, was Pat Caddell's finding that for the first time ever, Americans thought their children's lives would be worse than their own. He said that he believed that this was what was making it difficult for Americans to respond to his calls for sacrifice. He indicted his own leadership, too—for letting himself drift into an identity merely as the head of the government, not the head of the nation, as he said he had promised to be in 1976. He then asked what *they* thought might be done to help him reach the American people—then sat back down, sometimes cross-legged on the floor, saying pretty much nothing. Usually his wife sat beside him. Both took notes.

The governors informed him of a sense of concern, even panic, at the speech cancellation, of speculation that he was depressed or even losing his mind. The evidence of their senses, however, showed a man who was serenely upbeat. His diary from the time, in fact, suggests a happy customer at some coastal spiritual retreat in Big Sur.

A complement of celebrated private citizens swept in, consulting with Carter until dinner, then until one in the morning at the Carters' quarters, then through breakfast on Sunday morning. Two firsthand accounts of those meetings emerged.

The first, from Clark Clifford, trusted counselor to Democratic presidents since Truman, speaking on the record, was low-key. ("I think he believes as I do that he's not getting across to the people.") The other, attributed to an unnamed participant who sounded like he was describing a kidnapping, was more alarming: "Tell me what is wrong with my administration," Carter was reported to have said after Jordan, Powell, Rafshoon, and Caddell had left the room—then he received the sort of assault that might ensue if ravens were released from locked trunks. Someone told him he was being ridiculed all over the country—and Carter responded as if he were hearing it for the first time. Clark Clifford "abandoned the deliberate, wise man style he has become famous for" and asked incredulously how it was possible that he hadn't fired a single incompetent over the course of his entire administration. They hammered the Georgia mafia as incompetents, imploring him to bring in an experienced Washington hand to take over his communications shop. Hedley Donovan, the former editor in chief of Time, Inc., was available, someone suggested; all agreed he would be perfect. That advice became easy to ignore when next morning's *Time* magazine arrived.

The lead article, "Carter Was Speechless," was illustrated with a picture of a bewildered-looking Jimmy Carter, and suggested that the entire spectacle was a giant con—possibly cover for negotiations with Ted Kennedy concerning the 1980 nomination, maybe for preparations to resign. Hugh Sidey, whose weekly *Time* column "The Presidency" had been imperiously lecturing chief executives since Lyndon Johnson's day, wrote that the "chilling conclusion was echoed even in the ranks of his friends and supporters: he may not be up to the challenge." It was the gathering conventional wisdom—that, as Tom Wicker said in the *Times* the next morning, Carter had "reached the low point not only of his Administration but perhaps of the postwar presidency."

Carter seemed perversely to almost relish the abuse—heaping plenty of it on himself. "I worked hard all week, some of the most strenuous mental work of my life. . . . It's not easy for me to accept criticism and to reassess my ways of doing things, to admit my mistakes," he wrote one night in his diary. "This was a week of intense reassessment. I ran every day from three to seven miles and swam afterward." It was almost the language of a flagellant. A senator observed that he seemed to view the energy crisis almost as a gift—"the cutting edge in an effort to revive ourselves as a nation."

ON THE SEVENTH DAY, THE ASSOCIATED PRESS REPORTED THAT WHEN Carter would leave his "seclusion" was "a matter of conjecture." He received a group of congressmen, his first contact with the legislative branch in a week. His diary claimed, dubiously, that the advice of legislators from both energy-producing and energy-consuming states was "remarkably compatible." (The only "dissident," he journaled, was Speaker Tip O'Neill, "who cannot accept the idea that the Great Society days are over, and that all the problems of the nation cannot be solved with massive spending programs, public works, etc.")

He met with a group of economists, which left him annoyed. The next day, he met with a group of religious leaders, which left him over the moon.

The meeting began with a prayer asking Christ to bestow wisdom and strength upon "this Christian fellowship to enable us to come to grips with the great issues of our time." Rabbi Marc Tanenbaum joked to his colleagues at the American Jewish Committee that he wasn't too offended. "In keeping with the 'fairness doctrine' . . . the President asked me to offer the closing prayer," which he did—starting in Hebrew.

The men referred to one another by first names. Most had been friends for years from ecumenical gatherings: the Catholic cardinal from New York City, the head of the National Council of Churches, the patriarch of the Greek Orthodox Church, a Methodist bishop, a leading black Baptist, the outgoing Southern Baptist Convention president. Their fellowship symbolized an ideal of public religiosity scholars called the American "civil religion," exemplified by President Eisenhower's much-mocked avowal that "our form of government has no sense unless it is founded in a deeply felt religious faith, and I don't care what it is." It represented, in other words, an older, gentler ideal of public religiosity—from back before the likes of Jerry Falwell came to prominence. The group's only non-clergyman, Robert Bellah, a Harvard sociologist with a preacherly bent, had coined the phrase *civil religion*, and had recently published an essay on America's "covenantal" tradition, by which he meant a commitment to the communal public good that persevered alongside America's less elevated ethic of market-based self-interest. Bellah argued that America's covenantal side must be restored in order to transcend the "mood of vindictiveness and repression rather than generosity of spirit," which "could lead to the end of free government in America." The imprint of that essay was far more evident in Carter's final speech than Christopher Lasch's thinking—although, just as with Lasch and Daniel Bell, the president ignored the part of Bellah's argument that said national revival was impossible until corporate power was checked.

Carter gave his spiel. "In the early round of responses," Rabbi Tanenbaum recorded, "there was a certain amount of pietistic sycophancy." Soon enough, however, the preachers got down to the nut cutting. Terence Cardinal Cooke scoured the nation's "rampant materialism" and "self-indulgence." Rabbi Tanenbaum and Professor Bellah riffed back about "the systematic malaise which is a consequence of living in a nuclear age where universal annihilation is now conceivable for the first time in history." (Tanenbaum quoted a recent speech of Billy Graham: "We are the first generation to be told that we may be the last.") The "death of symbolic immortality" at Auschwitz and Hiroshima was brought up; also "the anxieties over Skylab and DC-10s, the widespread poisoning of the atmosphere and earth through toxic waters." All agreed that the panicked response to the energy crisis was a symptom of "an anxiety overload that has been accumulating from these developments since World War II," and that the understandable, if regrettable, public reaction—an "escape into personal pleasure"—would not have been so dangerous in an era of abundance ("the American cornucopia for the last two hundred years," was what someone called it); but now that America had crossed the Rubicon from abundance to scarcity, the preachers told their president, it was time for him to lead "a massive effort to realize restraint, modest consumption habits, discipline in an era of stringency."

Instilling an ethic of scarcity in a nation whose habits were formed in an age of abundance, all agreed, would be a challenge. The president's task, they said, was thus to lead the nation to appreciate the possibility of a *deeper* abundance, grounded in spiritual terms. The room thrummed with fellow feeling. It was easy to imagine the president crying *Amen*. Rabbi Tanenbaum made to give the closing prayer. Carter suggested they clasp hands, as brethren.

He had been spending long moments alone, literally wandering in the wilderness, resting upon benches scooped out of giant tree trunks, pondering what he would say in the speech, now scheduled for Sunday night, July 15. He and Rosalynn compared notes, collecting pertinent quotes. He read memos: Rafshoon insisting that "if we give the speech Caddell has proposed," which was "BS," it "could even be a disaster. . . . People are not turning to Kennedy or Connally because they are attuned to the crisis of confidence in the country but are turning to them because they look like the solution to the crisis"; Mondale imploring him to stop castigating the public in the mode of the Puritan divine Jonathan Edwards's sermon "Sinners in the Hands of an Angry God." At another meeting with governors, thirty-two-year-old William J. Clinton of Arkansas, the youngest governor in the nation, suggested, too, that he had been coming off too much like a "17th century New England Puritan." Carter disagreed. The divines had just given him permission to do what he had always wanted to do in the first place. He would deliver a *sermon*.

CARTER SIGNED A DECLARATION OF AN OFFICIAL "NATIONAL ENERGY SUP-ply shortage," ordering all places of public accommodation, effective Monday morning, to keep their air conditioners no lower than 80 degrees. He consulted with Speaker O'Neill about the progress of his bill to in-augurate a Department of Education, which passed the House and was sent to the Senate on Wednesday, July 12. Meanwhile the ordinary, surreal business of 1979 continued.

Skylab crashed in the western desert of Australia. The Somoza government in Nicaragua neared collapse, and thousands of "boat people" continued desperately setting out on the high seas in rickety vessels to escape war-torn Southeast Asia. (At the Tokyo summit, Carter had promised that America would take in seven thousand more refugees per month, an increase of about 70 percent.) In Durant, Oklahoma, the "Dick Barrett Fiddlers Super Bowl" country fiddling championship was canceled because, said the head of the local chamber of commerce, tourists couldn't afford the gas to get there.

In Miami, Ted Bundy was on trial for the bludgeoning murders of two sorority sisters—a trial that a new Florida law allowed to be recorded for newscasts. More than two hundred TV crews from around the world descended on a makeshift courthouse pressroom, more cluttered with gear than a hoarder's basement. A nonstop clatter of well-coiffed news personalities filmed "stand-ups" and narrations to accompany footage like jurors reviewing crime scene photographs ("indescribably gruesome") and oversized blowups of bite marks on the twenty-year-old victims and the inside of Bundy's mouth, and testimony from the likes of the maintenance man who first stumbled upon the crime scene. ("I could see insider her skull.") Though Bundy was not a lawyer, the judge made the shocking decision to allow him to run his own defense. One day, one of his lawyers was very effectively cross-examining a witness when Bundy, apparently jealous of all the attention his lawyer was getting, kicked the lawyer out of the courtroom and continued the cross-examination himself.

Reporters were mesmerized by the thirty-two-year-old former law student, an "articulate, intelligent man with boyish good looks," "personable," and possessed of a "quick, disarming smile." He was allowed to wander the courtroom freely, winking and smiling, and to give unlimited interviews. ("Yes, I intend to complete my legal education and become a lawyer, and I'll be a damned good lawyer.") His jokes kept reporters in stitches. (One headline: "Jail Hasn't Robbed Bundy of His Humor.") They were particularly fascinated by all the women from as far away as Seattle—"attractive, young, and single" according to one feature—who lined up for hours to attend. "I don't know what it is he has, but he's fascinating. He's impressive. He just has a kid of magnetism," said one. A giggling teenager described a thrill akin to watching a slasher movie: "You try to imagine yourself in his place, and how he's feeling, looking at the pillows, with blood stains and everything, if he really did it or not!" Another spectator identified herself as Bundy's fiancée. It was all extremely disturbing. Then, one day, Bundy kept asking a police officer on the witness stand to repeat his description of the crime scene, again and again and again—as if he were relishing the opportunity to revisit his handiwork.

Another circus to gawk at unfolded in Chicago. On July 12, hordes of young people streamed into a standing-room-only doubleheader between the White Sox and the Detroit Tigers at Comiskey Park, enticed by an eccentric local rock DJ named Steve Dahl, locally infamous for his songs parodying John Wayne Gacy and Skylab, who, enraged that his former station had fired him after changing its format from rock to disco, announced that anyone bringing a disco record to the game could get in for 98 cents, and that during the break between games he would blow up those records. It was the low point of a cultural movement known as "Disco Sucks," born after a country band in Tucson improvised a song of the same name when a polyester-clad concert patron wouldn't stop shouting "Play some disco!" Their record soon became the only country number that rock stations played. Many of those same stations fielded streams of abusive phone calls every time they played a song by a black artist. "White males eighteen to thirty-four," a *Rolling Stone* writer commented, "are the most likely to see disco as the product of homosexuals, blacks, and Latins, and therefore they're the most likely to respond to appeals to wipe out such threats to their security."

And at Comiskey Park, as he exploded crates of disco records the response from Dahl's drunken fans, who looked a whole lot like the drunken youth setting cars on fire in Levittown, Pennsylvania, was to break out into a riot, tearing up the stadium with such abandon that the home team had to forfeit the second game.

Call it homophobia, or racism, or only a bunch of kids letting off steam on a hot day. Or maybe just call it malaise.

THAT NIGHT, AN ASSOCIATION OF EIGHT THOUSAND INDEPENDENT SERVICE stations in Pennsylvania and Delaware went on strike, demanding a change in the federal government allocation formulae they said unfairly favored oil company affiliates. The day before, Pennsylvania's Governor Dick Thornburgh had been one of Jimmy Carter's visitors. He'd implored the president to at least announce the *possibility* of reforms that might avert this catastrophe. Instead, Thornburgh became one more visitor who emerged baffled that every time they brought up the subject of energy policy, the president, in the words of another mystified pol, would begin reflecting "on the content of *People* magazine, on the 'malaise' gripping the country, and the 'decline of the American family.'"

And, that same day, a Mr. and Mrs. Bill Fisher, a machinist and housewife from Carnegie, Pennsylvania, were told by someone named Patrick Caddell that "an important man from Washington" would be visiting their home that evening. Caddell directed them to scrounge up some neighbors, and handed Mrs. Fisher $100 to buy refreshments. Two hours later, the President of the United States arrived. He delivered the same introductory remarks he had to the cardinal, the congressmen, Clark Clifford, and all the rest. Then, for two hours, he once again sat back, listened, and took notes. The press was informed of what was transpiring only after one of them wondered to press aides where in the world the suddenly absent president was. "We told him there needs to be a return in this country to the strength of the family unit. People need to start going back to church again," Bill Fisher told inquiring reporters. Why did he think the president had chosen *them*? "We're the people at the bottom of the pole. We support the rich and poor, I guess that's the way I see it"—which sounded a whole lot like something you'd read in *Human Events*. The next day, Carter made a similar jaunt to a coal town in the Eastern Panhandle of West Virginia. The sixty-one-year-old retired Marine who hosted him said he hadn't "the remotest idea" why he was picked.

The *Pittsburgh Press*'s article about the meeting with the Fishers ran beside a list of the few service stations open in the city, and an article on how those that stayed open received telephoned threats of violence and had their hoses slashed.

THE FINAL CONSULTATION SESSION AT CAMP DAVID WAS WITH NATIONAL newspaper columnists and network news anchors. It was the first time the media had set eyes on the president in eleven days. "They were pleased to come and impressed, I believe, with what I had to say, and interested in the procedure I had followed on" was the president's impression. Jack Germond's, on the other hand, was that it was "unsettling to the point of being almost frightening."

Then came a final meeting between Carter and staff. The speechwriting team was stuck. Staffers kept on sabotaging one another, trying to convince the speechwriters that they represented the opinions of higher-ups. Perhaps, the theory went, if all the president's men could just sit down together, they might finally make the whole thing work. Instead they tore each other apart, as Jimmy Carter looked on as placidly as the Buddha.

Finally, someone started lecturing Stuart Eizenstat that his technical mumbo jumbo about geothermally pressured methane and the like would put the nation to sleep. Eizenstat responded with focused rage. It *wasn't* mumbo jumbo, he said—then set out to prove his point. He had been working on these ideas with such intensity for so long that he was able to reduce his policy suggestions to a series of simple points. He began reciting them, one after the other, in a staccato exhalation that left his listeners in awe.

There emerged a sort of miracle. The policy lecture and the spiritual sermon, the abstract and the material, *the spirit and the flesh*, resolved into the same story, and the congregation realized they weren't on different sides at all. The impasse passed; like in an inspiring movie scene, a speech started coming together. Hertzberg and Stewart pulled the second and third sections of the text together in an hour. The first section they left to Carter himself. It would be unlike anything ever attempted before in a presidential speech.

The staff was dismissed. Carter repaired to the Camp David movie theater, tricked out as a mock Oval Office, to practice his delivery. Gordon Stewart, left behind with the task of editing it into a version to deliver at two appearances the day after the TV address, was in the room, too.

Stewart had taken an unusual route to the job. By profession, he was a theater director. The previous winter he had been rehearsing the Broadway debut of *The Elephant Man* when his lung collapsed, and he had to withdraw. Hertzberg had been looking for someone to join his staff after James Fallows quit. Stewart was an old friend and neighbor with speechwriting experience. He joined the White House in April. Now, two months later, he sat quietly off in a corner in a fake log cabin with a notepad as the Leader of the Free World sat at a fake desk in front of fake cameras, once more grinding his speechwriters' hard work into dry dust, in the manner that had once moved a Democratic senator to describe this way what happened when the television set in the Democratic cloakroom was tuned to a Carter speech: "Inside ten minutes or less we're all gossiping to ourselves and ignoring him. Hell, if we don't listen, who will?"

Stewart muttered something; Carter shot him an angry glare.

Stewart muttered again, more intelligibly: "I'm sorry, I didn't hear that."

Carter repeated the line, only louder. Stewart started talking, as if to an imaginary palooka sitting on a barstool: *I don't know what this guy is talking about, something about a sickness. . . .*

Carter got pissed.

Then, he started to listen.

"Others had tried to coach Carter before," Hertzberg later explained, "usually by telling him not to do things (don't grin so much, knock off the sing-song)," sometimes with "technical tricks, such as double- or triple-underlining words to be stressed." It took a theater director to finally succeed where others had tried and failed:

"Mr. President, what I'm trying to suggest is that you are not just *telling* me to hear you. I am going to get up and start walking out the door, and I would like to see if you can stop me."

Carter started again. Stewart started leaving.

Carter changed.

"*Now* you've got it. I don't *have to* listen to you just because you're the President. If I'm in a bar, I can and will change the channel."

JIMMY CARTER CAME DOWN FROM THE MOUNTAINTOP. HE ATTENDED SUN-day services, then rehearsed some more. At six o'clock eastern time Roger Mudd opened the news on CBS explaining, "It is rare indeed that an American president should acknowledge publicly and beforehand that a particular speech or event is a turning point for him. It simply makes the stakes too high for comfort. But that is exactly what President Carter has done, and it is an indication of how deeply he believes he is in trouble. His speech tonight from the Oval Office of the White House, on leadership, on energy, and on what he describes as the national malaise could very well determine who governs the country for the next four years."

Then it was ten o'clock—when an episode of the miniseries *Moses the Lawgiver* in which the patriarch descended from Mount Sinai bearing stone tablets, clever media wags observed, was preempted by . . . whatever this was going to be.

Jimmy Carter began with a twinkle in his eye and a hint of the grin Americans had fallen in love with in 1976, and an ingratiating invocation of happier times.

"Good evening. This is a very special night for me. Exactly three years ago, on July 15, 1976, I accepted the nomination of my party to run for President of the United States. I promised you a president who is not isolated from the people, who feels your pain, and who shares your dreams and who draws his strength and wisdom from you."

He recalled all the other times he had spoken to the people—speeches, he lamented, that had become "increasingly narrow, focused more and more on what the isolated world of *Washington* thinks is important . . . more and more about what the *government* thinks or what the *government* should be doing. And less and less"—he gently chopped the air in front of him—"about our nation's hopes, our dreams, and our vision of the future."

His lips pursed, his head bowed, and he almost blushed, as if he felt a flush of shame at the ridiculousness of it all. *The people versus the government*: Carter returned to that opposition over and over. He would let none mistake which side he was on.

Energy, he allowed, and what the government should do about it, had been the original reason for tonight's address. Then, "I began to ask myself the same question that I now know has been troubling many of you: Why have we not been able to get together as a *nation*"—his fist punched the air—"to resolve our serious energy problem? It's *clear* that the true problems of our nation are much deeper—*deeper!*—than energy shortages. *Deeper!* than inflation, or recession. And I realized more than ever that as president I need your help." So he had invited to Camp David "people from every segment of society," and also—his eyes twinkled again at the pleasing thought—had ventured abroad in the land "to *listen* to *other* Americans, men and women like you."

He pulled out notes, to share "a few of the typical comments that I wrote down." It was hard not to imagine sixty-five million Americans hanging on the edge of their seats.

He quoted the "southern governor" who told him, "Mr. President, you are not leading this nation. You're just managing the *government.*" (He looked into the camera searchingly.)

"You don't see the *people* anymore." (He blushed again.)

"Don't talk to us about politics, or the mechanics of *government*. But about an understanding of our common good. Mr. President, we are in trouble. Talk to us about blood, and sweat, and tears."

He paused, fixing his gaze at the camera: "If you lead, Mr. President, we will follow."

He quoted a "young woman from Pennsylvania" who said "I feel so far from government. I feel like ordinary people are excluded from political power."

A "young Chicano": "Some of us have suffered from recession all our lives." Came a particularly soulful pause. "Some people have wasted energy. But some people haven't had *anything* to waste."

A black female mayor from Mississippi ("I like this one particularly"): "You can't sell anything on Wall Street until someone else digs it up somewhere first."

A religious leader: "No material shortage could touch the important things, like God's love for us, and our love for one another. . . ."

"This kind of summarized a lot of other statements: 'Mr. President, we are confronted with a *moral*, and a *spiritual* crisis.'"

As for energy, "there will be other cartels and other shortages." But the true problem was deeper. He raised his voice: "*All! The legislation! In the world!* Can't *fix* what's *wrong* with America!"

His eyes no longer twinkled. They locked solemnly with the viewers'. The camera had been pulled in close for intimacy. Now it drew back for drama. It was galvanizing. This was the man with whom, back in 1976, the American people had fallen in love.

"I want to speak to a subject even *more serious* than energy or inflation. I want to talk to you, *right now!* About a *fundamental—threat—to—American—democracy*. I do not mean our political and civil liberties.

They will endure. And I do not refer to the outward strength of America, a nation that is at peace tonight everywhere in the world, with unmatched economic power and military might. The threat is nearly"—he paused, appearing to be sincerely searching for just the right word—"*invisible* in ordinary ways. It is a *crisis*—of *confidence*. It is a crisis that strikes at the very heart and soul and spirit of our national will."

That paragraph felt both perfectly formed and achingly spontaneous, like all truly great political speeches. The next paragraph did, too:

"We can see this crisis in the growing doubt about the meaning of our own lives and in the loss of a unity of purpose for our nation. The erosion of our confidence in the future is threatening to destroy the social and the political fabric of America."

He swelled to a sincere, grand crescendo:

"The confidence that we have always had as a people is not simply some romantic dream or proverb that we read just on the Fourth of July. It is the idea which founded our nation and has guided our development as a people. Confidence in the future has supported everything else—public institutions and private enterprise, our own families, and the very constitution of the United States. Confidence has defined our course and has served as a link between generations. We've always believed in something called—progress! We've always had a *faith* that the days of our *children*— would be better than our own."

He grew somber: "Our people are *losing that faith*."

It was remarkable, unprecedented, the depth at which the president worried this grand, abstract, existential theme: "Human identity is no longer defined by what one *does*, but what one *owns*. But we've discovered that owning *things*, and consuming *things*, does not satisfy our longing for meaning. We're learning that piling up material goods *cannot* fill the emptiness of lives which have no confidence, or purpose. . . . For the first time in the history of our country a majority of our people believe that the next five years will be worse than the past five years. Two thirds of our people do not even vote! The productivity of American workers is actually dropping, and the willingness of Americans to save for the future has fallen below that of all people in the Western world. . . . And as you know there has been disrespect for government. *And for churches*. And for schools, the news media, and other institutions."

The camera again pulled close.

"This is not a message of happiness or reassurance, but it is the truth, and it is a warning."

He reviewed recent history: the assassinations that shattered the faith that "ours was a nation of the ballot, not the bullet"; the war that eviscerated the faith "that our armies were invincible and our causes were always just"; Watergate's theft of Americans' bedrock conviction that the "presidency was a place of honor"; the inflation that turned the venerable phrase "sound of a dollar" into a joke—and the way the 1973 energy crisis revealed the fallacy of Americans' belief "that our nation's resources were *limitless.*"

(He almost laughed: *Can you believe how naïve we used to be?*)

"Those wounds are still very deep. They have never been healed."

Yes, "the gap between citizens and our government has never seemed so wide." Yes, Washington seems incapable of action. Congress seems "twisted and pulled in every direction by hundreds of well-financed and powerful interests," and "every extreme position defended to the last vote, and often the last breath."

"You don't like it. And neither do I. What can we do?"

He picked up his notes and read a citizen's advice: "We've got to stop crying. And start *sweating.*"

He paused a very long time.

"Stop cursing. And start praying."

He paused again.

"Stop talking. And start walking.

"We know the strength of America. We are *strong.* We *can* regain our unity, we *can* regain our confidence. We're the *heirs* of generations who survived threats *much* more powerful, and *awesome,* than those who challenge us now. Our fathers and mothers were *strong* men and women, who shaped a *new* society during the Great Depression. Who fought world wars. And carved out a new charter of peace for the world. We *ourselves* are the same Americans who just ten years ago put a man on the moon. We are the generation who dedicated ourselves to the pursuit of human rights, and equality. And we are the generation that will win the war on the energy problem and in that process *rebuild* the unity and confidence of America. . . . That path leads to *true freedom.* For our nation and ourselves. We can take the first steps down that path. As we begin to solve our energy problem. *Energy!* will be the immediate test of how we unite. And it can also be the *standard around* which we rally. On the battlefield of energy we can build a new confidence. And we can seize control again of our common destiny."

How? Six simple ways.

By setting a clear goal—"beginning this moment"—of never using more foreign oil than we had in 1977.

By imposing quotas on that imported oil.

By devoting "the *most massive—peacetime—commitment—*of funds and resources in our nation's history to develop America's *own* alternative source of fuel." (Announcing a federal corporation to issue $5 million in energy bonds, Carter shrewdly harkened back with nostalgia for

America's all-encompassing civic mobilization during World War II: "I especially want them to be in small denominations so that average Americans can invest directly in America's energy security.")

By mandating that utility companies switch to other fuels to cut their use of oil by half within the next decade.

By creating "the nation's first solar bank, which will help us achieve the crucial goal of 20 percent of our energy coming from solar power by the year 2000"—again, "just as a similar synthetic rubber corporation helped us win World War II."

And finally, with "a bold conservation program to involve every state, county, and city and every average American in our energy battle. . . . Working together with our common faith, we cannot fail."

HE HAD FINALLY SUCCEEDED IN EFFECTIVELY ARTICULATING WHAT HE HAD been trying to say since the first weeks of his presidency: the struggle for energy independence was the moral equivalent of war. And Carter had had available to him much easier political paths out of his political crisis than a speech like this. He could have boasted that he had just successfully jawboned a promise from the Saudis to increase their oil output by enough to wipe out half of the current shortage. Or point to the end of the trucking strike, accomplished without any disruptive concessions, and the dissipation of gas lines nationwide.

Carter easily could have blamed big oil—for he knew they were about to announce for the quarter profits 68 percent greater than the same period in 1978. Senator Metzenbaum had recently said, "I don't think an industry could ever have a lower image in the American people's eyes than the oil industry this moment," despite massive sums spent on laundering its tattered reputation. ("*Funding for this program,*" began each episode of PBS's evening newscast, "*has been provided by . . . grants from the Exxon Corporation, Allied Chemical Corporation, and the Corporation for Public Broadcasting.*") He also could just as easily have blamed OPEC. That was what Stuart Eizenstat had wanted him to do.

Instead he took the harder path: what he called "honest answers, not easy answers." Amazingly, it *worked*: he immediately reaped just about the greatest public opinion dividend in the history of presidential rhetoric, an eleven-point bump in approval ratings in one poll, and seventeen points in another.

Then, as he began working to pass his new energy plan into law, he squandered his gains with a single colossal mistake.

UPON THE MOUNTAINTOP, THE DISTINGUISHED WASHINGTON PERSONAGES had been unanimous: he *must* discipline his White House by purging disloyal and less-than-competent officials and hiring a chief of staff. He had never had one, considering it an impediment to direct communication with key members of his administration.

And so, the Tuesday after the speech, he called the White House meeting heard round the world.

Around the table sat eighteen top White House staffers and his sixteen cabinet secretaries. They were informed that Hamilton Jordan would henceforth be his chief of staff. Carter lectured them about the importance of loyalty. Then he assigned homework: provide a written evaluation of the loyalty of staffers in their employ; and tender him letters of resignation, which he would subsequently decide whether to accept or reject.

A president firing people was routine. Doing it en masse and without warning was shocking. "Had a purge like the president's taken place in the Soviet Union," the *Nation* observed, "Kremlinologists would have been pontificating about the problems of transition in a totalitarian state."

The next forty-eight hours were a deathwatch. Speaking of Kremlinologists, NPR brought in *Izvestia*'s Washington correspondent to study where officials were standing in photographs of public events to discern who was in President Carter's favor and who was not—like American Soviet Union experts did on May Day in Moscow. Then, on Thursday—in Chicago the dispatch broke into a rerun of *Laverne and Shirley*—a black-backgrounded "SPECIAL REPORT" logo appeared as Charles Gibson of ABC News revealed the first firing with the agitated gravity of a tornado sighting: "The first of the shakeups of President Carter's cabinet is in the works. Secretary of Health, Education, and Welfare Joseph Califano . . ."

Califano had been Lyndon Johnson's right-hand man on domestic policy. A figure of highest esteem within the Washington establishment, he had used that independent power base to sustain a crusade against the tobacco industry—with political consequences in the mid-Atlantic states that terrified Carter. So his firing came as no surprise. The way the passionless president handled it, however, shocked Washington. Califano was summoned into the private study off the Oval Office and told, "You've been the best secretary of HEW." But he had to go, Carter said apologetically, because of "friction with the White House staff." Then he invited him to vacation the next weekend at Camp David. Califano, extremely proud to be running an agency whose flourishing he had supervised under LBJ, was crushed. Carter didn't seem to notice—and repeated the invitation as Califano was walking out the door. ("Bring your children along.") Califano leaked the whole story to reporters. Jody Powell denied that Carter had praised him, thus accusing one of the most respected figures in Washington of lying.

Next to go was Michael Blumenthal as secretary of the treasury; then attorney general Griffin Bell; then finally, energy secretary James Schlesinger and transportation secretary Brock Adams. Califano, Schlesinger, and Adams made sense on policy or performance grounds; Bell had been preparing to leave in any event, with a replacement already named. But the whispers in Washington were that Carter's beef with Blumenthal was sheer pettiness: that he was an attention-hog, and that his department had investigated Bert Lance. Washington conventional wisdom hardened: that the entire operation resembled the petulance of a tin-pot dictator.

The promotion of thirty-four-year-old Ham Jordan calcified the impression. Since returning from service in Vietnam in 1970, he hadn't had any other job besides serving Jimmy Carter. Just that week, the newspapers were full of pictures of his automobile immobilized by a "Denver boot" because he hadn't paid his parking tickets. Jordan even doubted his own administrative abilities; which were superior, in any event, to his diplomatic ones. He had publicly called senators wavering on the Panama Canal treaties "bastards." He allegedly threw a drink at a woman at a bar, groped the bosom of the Egyptian ambassador's wife. With his baby face, he seemed about as intimidating as a teddy bear. *This* was who Jimmy Carter tapped to put his White House in order? "Good grief! They're cutting down the biggest trees and keeping the monkeys," Representative Charlie Wilson of Texas pronounced. A Chicagoan wrote him to complain about the insult to monkeys, who in fact "demonstrate wondrous political acumen and sophistication."

Jordan attempted a charm offensive, exchanging blue jeans for three-piece suits, apologizing to legislative leaders for past slights. It didn't work. "We're looking at another Nixon," said Senator Ted Stevens. "I told reporters that some of us are seriously worried about the president. We feel he's approaching a period of some sort of mental problem."

The backlash was overwhelming. The "midsummer massacre," *Newsweek* said, "signaled to survivors that political loyalty has priority over professional competence," and "sent a spasm of anxiety around the world about the stability of his reign." In fact, the backlash was *so* overwhelming, that, like an errant missile in wartime, it brought collateral damage: his successful speech was *retroactively* evaluated as a failure. One newspaper called "everything since July 4" an "exercise in Rafshoonery." A cartoonist depicted the president as a magician shooting his rabbit after a trick had failed. His old friends at *Time* said the purge "provoked new doubts about Carter's understanding of the federal government and about his own leadership ability." Hugh Sidey wrote of the "deep sadness in Washington this week. Concern about Jimmy Carter and his administration has gone beyond anger. The immediate shock of the graceless cabinet changes will wear off, but doubts about the presidency will grow even larger and seep out across the world. Ultimately, they are doubts about America."

Later, an advisor suggested that the miscalculation was an unintended consequence of the speech's very popularity: they never imagined it would have that kind of impact. So they had built in a plan for an immediate, bold follow-up to accentuate the intended image of command. Instead, it sent the opposite signal: an image of panic.

Which Carter immediately compounded.

He called reporters to an off-the-record briefing. He read a ninety-second statement pronouncing the changes "constructive" and "positive." He turned on his heel and left. The next day, reporters were invited to the White House for hamburgers. They were expecting an apology. Instead, the president strode in and announced he was reneging on his promise of twice-monthly press conferences, and that "I think it is time for you all, if you don't mind me being blunt, to look at the substance of what I have done rather than having as a permanent consideration how much it has shaken the so-called Washington establishment."

Recalled Walter Mondale, "It went from sugar to shit right there." The president's approval rating went back to pre–Camp David levels, and in one poll dipped to 23 percent.

THE MARKETS HAD SENT JITTERY SIGNALS DURING JIMMY CARTER'S FORT-night on the mountaintop. Wall Street hoped the big speech would include reassurances that he would keep inflation in hand. Whatever else it was, in an economy reliant on consumer debt, a jeremiad to buy less did not fit the bill. Following the cabinet firings, currency traders—"thinking of the European model where governments fall," Eizenstat tried to comfort the boss—dumped dollars for yen, francs, pounds, and deutschmarks. Banks raised interest rates. An ounce of gold, which a decade earlier had cost $35, went above $300 for the first time in history—up 50 percent in just the last year: "Once a 'Barbarous Relic,'" a New York Times headline explained, "Gold Feeds on Anxiety."

But Wall Street's confidence returned following a surprise announcement on July 26. The president had let go of his treasury secretary without a replacement. He offered the job to David Rockefeller of Chase Manhattan, then the CEOs of General Electric and DuPont. All refused; quite the business no-confidence vote. The idea surfaced of tapping Federal Reserve chairman William Miller. Miller accepted. Now the administration needed a Fed chair.

Carter had just appointed as *vice* chairman an obscure banking entrepreneur, former state legislator, and Jimmy Carter fundraiser from Florida named Frederick Schultz. Because he struck the Senate Banking Committee more like a glad-handing used car salesman—or a marionette hired to undermine the Fed's political independence—than someone qualified to stabilize the world's biggest economy, he had barely been confirmed. And now, with Miller's move to Treasury, Fred Schultz was acting Federal Reserve *chairman*. The Dow dumped more than 7.5 percent that day in heavy trading. Gold soared to $303.95. The panic in the markets made this a perilously sensitive job to fill.

Which was why, seeking the most reassuring possible appointment, a politically comatose president almost accidentally ended up making one of the most influential government appointments of the twentieth century.

Paul Volcker was the president of the Federal Reserve Bank of New York. Because he was a leading "inflation hawk," Wall Street exhaled. In London, the announcement came as an aide to Margaret Thatcher's chancellor of the exchequer had finished drafting a detailed memo outlining the perilous state of the U.S. Now he appended a P.S.: "The news has just come through of the nomination of Paul Volcker to the Fed. This is excellent. . . . He is well-respected in the banking community and well-known and liked abroad. He is known to have been in favour of a rather tighter policy on money recently. It will do something, on the economic side, to counter the ill-effects of last week's events." *Time* headlined, "Volcker to the Rescue."

WHAT HE DID NOT RESCUE WAS THE PRESIDENT'S POLITICAL FORTUNES.

The *New Republic* called him "a failure, and a cowardly failure at that." The *Washington Post* observed, "However much the president might have done in the past two weeks to corner the malaise vote, you have to concede that he has also done wonders in uniting his party"—against him from the right, Scoop Jackson blasted him for creating the malaise he claimed to be curing, and from the left, George McGovern gave a speech to his Senate intern alumni that argued, "We can recover from our present malaise by setting the stage" for a presidential run by "the most logical candidate for our party." That would be, of course, Ted Kennedy—who was presently embarked on a long vacation, sailing around Cape Cod and pondering whether he should run.

Evans and Novak hired Pat Caddell to go door to door to canvass 1976 Democratic primary voters about their choice for 1980. He found that Kennedy beat Carter six to one—*before* Carter's ill-fated cabinet shakeup. ("He's in over his head," said a factory inspector. But Kennedy appeared to a salesman as "strong, experienced, knowledgeable.") In New York, both Senator Moynihan and Governor Carey announced that they would support Ted Kennedy if he ran. Howard Baker suggested Carter save his failed presidency by not running for reelection. Jerry Brown was growing more serious about a challenge: enough so that Garry Trudeau, who appeared to despise him, devoted a week of *Doonesbury* to flaying the governor for dodgy real-world donations he had received from the Chicago mob fixer Sidney Korshak. The strips were so nasty that lawsuit-shy newspapers refused to print them.

The president hit the road, seeking solace from a public he remained convinced loved him as much as ever. On July 31, he landed in the coal-mining town of Bardstown, Kentucky, where he hammered Washington as "insulated" and "isolated." Then Washington hammered back.

Georgetown's least favorite Carterite was Andrew Young, the tart-tongued United Nations ambassador, and what everyone now wanted to know was why Carter didn't get rid of *him*. Hamilton Jordan responded that Carter considered Young indispensable. Just then Young was hard at work shepherding a pet project of the president's: persuading the Palestine Liberation Organization to accept UN Resolution 242, adopted after the 1967 Arab-Israeli War. One of its stipulations was accepting Israel's right to exist as a sovereign state. Once that happened, Carter hoped to press Israel to accept 242's *other* stipulation: withdrawing from the territories it conquered in that war. Then, Young discovered that the United Nations Division for Palestinian Rights was about to call for the creation of a Palestinian state—an ill-timed move that would have imploded Carter's delicate diplomacy. So Young sought to convey the danger to the PLO's UN representative in a meeting at a private apartment. But that fell afoul of an administration promise to Israel never to meet with the PLO. Israeli intelligence leaked a transcript of the meeting; Carter was forced to fire Young—even while calling him "the best man I have ever known in public life." The response was yet more ridicule.

Perhaps that was why the president left town again—steaming Mark Twain–style, for his annual August vacation, 650 miles down the Mississippi River aboard the tourist paddle wheeler the *Delta Queen*. Though if this was an exercise in Rafshoonery, at least it was a successful one. "I didn't think we'd be able to get close to him," enthused one of the first family's 150 fellow passengers, a mailman from St. Louis. "He's just like one of us." He wore jeans and jogging shoes, or gray slacks that fit loosely at the waist, carrying out official business on a wrought-iron table and writing letters in longhand. He told affectionate stories about Billy Carter and said kind things about Andrew Young—insular, isolated Washington be damned. He lapped up river lore from the crew while eleven-year-old Amy ran free about the deck with a newfound pack of friends. The first family freely provided autographs, shook every hand, and gave the nation a charmingly intimate peek into their eccentric everyday habits. Like reading constantly, even while eating: "My father was the only member of my family for two or three generations who didn't read at the table," Carter explained. His current favorite, he said, was Robert Ludlam's thriller *The Gemini Contenders*.

He gave speeches selling his energy plan at stops along the way. He was elated by the enthusiasm of the crowds. Or, at least, most of them. When the *Delta Queen* docked in Davenport, Iowa, the reception was merely "polite," said the *Washington Post*. "He's lost popularity around here," a Democratic state representative explained. "There's a general feeling of lack of leadership. . . . Teddy Kennedy would be good for the ticket. This is a Catholic, Democratic town. He'd bring out the vote." Sixty-two percent of Democrats nationally agreed the party should nominate Kennedy. Only 34 percent wanted Carter.

Carter also jogged every day, even if he had to do it on deck. Jogging was his new obsession. The way he did it betokened his obsessively competitive nature—the "I'll whip his ass" Jimmy Carter, the Jimmy Carter who, in his most fervent private prayers, asked God to grant him humility. The Jimmy Carter who boasted in his diary of finding more Indian arrowheads than his wife when they took a walk in the woods, or that Rosalynn had been chosen "among the ten women in the world who have the most sensuous and elegant legs," or of the "very narrow victory" scored in softball in a game between his team composed of Secret Service agents and Billy's composed of reporters. Recently, he'd jotted down his regret after he and White House physician Dr. William Lukash had notched a sluggish time on a difficult, hilly ten-kilometer course he was to run in an amateur road race in a few weeks. The next day, he was thrilled to record that they carved three minutes off their time.

He returned home, swore in his new energy secretary—and was greeted by an ugly front-page *Post* headline: "FBI Investigating Alleged Cocaine Use by Jordan." The allegation was that on June 27, 1978, in the basement of the New York City celebrity disco Studio 54, in the presence of club owner Steve Rubell and a drug dealer, Carter's chief of staff had approached a publicist and asked, "Where do you get coke?" All three supposed witnesses appeared on ABC's *20/20* to relate their recollections in detail. Jordan furiously denied it. The following spring, after a thorough investigation, a special prosecutor would conclude that Rubell had made the whole thing up in a desperate attempt for leverage to get a federal tax case against him dismissed. For now, however, the president said he had "complete confidence" in Jordan, as much as if the denial had come from his own wife or children. The charge lingered in the air for almost a year, draining yet more trust in the White House—for Carter's vote of confidence for his Georgia mafia associate, after all, sounded a hell of a lot like what he had said about Bert Lance, who was now on trial in federal court.

On August 28, Jody Powell told an Associate Press reporter a funny little story about the time back in April when the president was fishing near Plains and a hissing, frantic rabbit, or something, bore its teeth, flared its nostrils, and appeared to make a run at him. Carter, traumatized by rodents ever since a field mouse ran up the leg of his father's trousers when he was a boy, beat it away with a paddle. Aides hadn't believed the tale— "Everybody knows rabbits don't swim"—so the president got hold of a photograph of the encounter. "You could see him with his paddle raised, and you could see something in the water," the AP quoted one of those doubting aides. "But you couldn't tell what it was. It could have been anything." Another aide, however, called it "a killer rabbit," and added, "The president was swinging for his life."

Now *this* was important news, decided the editors of the *Post*. They ran the AP piece on the front page under the headline "Bunny Goes Bugs: Rabbit Attacks President." But the White House had refused to release the photograph. So the *Post* ran a cartoon in its stead: a sweating president in a canoe approached from below by a cute floppy-eared bunny, like the famous poster for *Jaws*—only the legend read "PAWS." The next day, the AP quoted Bob Dole insisting the president should apologize to the bunny, who after all was "doing something a little unusual these days— trying to get aboard the president's boat." Jerry Falwell said he should have slaughtered the beast, because the Book of Revelation associates swamp rabbits with the Devil.

The *Washington Star* published a poll showing Republican front-runner Ronald Reagan ahead of Carter 42 percent to 38 percent in a general election matchup, Baker tied with him, and John Connally ("thought by many political professionals and opinion makers as a major threat") behind him by four points; "Carter is not strong" beat "Carter is strong" by 41 percentage points.

On September 8, at a Reagan campaign meeting to discuss public policy, two distinguished Republican economists, Alan Greenspan and George Shultz, game-planned political scenarios should the economy fall into a depression. On September 13, an NBC News poll showed the president with a 19 percent approval rating. Two days later, the president strapped on running togs and pinned the number "39" to his breast for that hilly ten-kilometer race in the Catoctin Mountains. It was so hot that a hundred entrants dropped out. "I've got to keep trying," the president gasped to a Secret Service agent who begged him to quit. Seconds later, he collapsed in an unpresidential heap. The picture of Carter looking ashen-faced and gaunt as a Third World refugee monopolized the next day's front pages. It seemed like the president kept getting smaller.

CHAPTER 26

"Refusing to Fan the Flames of Moderation"

FOR CONSERVATIVES, PERHAPS THE ONLY THING MORE INFURIATING THAN President Carter signing SALT II was that he had done so after exchanging the traditional Russian greeting with the Soviet head of state: a lip-smacking embrace. Upon his return, he had announced that he was green-lighting a $30 billion project to build a new missile with ten warheads, the MX, built atop a sixty–ton tracked vehicle that would move around to evade Soviet detection. It earned him no credit on the right.

The New Right's Morton Blackwell, Howard Phillips, Paul Weyrich, Terry Dolan, and General Daniel O. Graham met at Richard Viguerie's Virginia mansion for a buffet supper, balancing plates on their laps, to discuss how to leverage SALT as a means, as Terry Dolan put it, of "*exposing* those people"—Senate liberals—and "get rid of them in the long run." They decided to hold rallies in all fifty states, partnering with Jerry Falwell's new Moral Majority. They flooded the solid gold mailboxes:

> *Dear Friend,*
>
> *I think you will appreciate, more than most Americans, what I am sending you.*
>
> *I have enclosed two flags: the red, white, and blue of Old Glory— and the white flag of surrender.*
>
> *I want to show you, by these two flags, what is at stake for America under the SALT II Treaty with Russia. . . .*

It was a coalition effort. Neoconservatives held fortnightly strategy sessions at Washington's Madison Hotel, packed with young Senate staffers with the highest security clearances and led by the formidable former head of the Securities and Exchange Commission William Casey, a World War II–era spy. Scoop Jackson, whose speeches were normally plodding, gave an electrifying address abjuring fools seeking "accommodation with a totalitarian superpower" in a manner "ominously reminiscent of Great Britain in the 1930s." The American Conservative Union's *Soviet Might/*

American Myth was taken out of the vaults for several hundred more syndicated showings. Another group's documentary, *The Price of Peace and Freedom*, was scheduled for viewings on 850 stations. A third organization produced *The SALT Syndrome*, for a hefty $300,000. (The two competing liberal productions, *War Without Winners* and *Survival or Suicide*, had budgets of $175,000 and $75,000, respectively.)

A key argument concerned something called the "window of vulnerability": the theory that, under the treaty, the combined "throw weight" of the USSR's strategic forces would be so superior that a preemptive strike by only 15 percent of *theirs* would destroy 90 percent of *ours*, rendering a counterstrike impossible, thereby greatly increasing the Russians' incentive to strike first, which would make it all the more likely that they would try. Decades later, when Russian archives were opened to scholars, these claims were debunked. Even in 1979, there were hard-to-answer counterarguments. Deputy CIA Director Herbert Scoville, in the pro-SALT film *War Without Winners*, complained, "The myth of U.S. inferiority is being spread to try and panic the public. The taxpayer is being raked off on this deal by a very few corporations and individuals," increasing the likelihood humanity would be "wiped off the face of the earth."

But conservatives had already won over the most important target. At an event in Mississippi, Minority Leader Baker declared—with, Evans and Novak noted, none of the "diffidence and compromising stand that have become Baker's trademark"—that "we must awaken those Americans who have been lulled to sleep by foolish liberals and leftists here and abroad who believe peace can be procured by granting the Soviets strategic superiority." He said this even though the treaty merely codified agreements that Gerald Ford reached with the Soviets, back when Baker was pro-détente. Then, the next day in Little Rock, the senator who was supposed to be the moderate in the GOP presidential field praised the "flood tide of conservatism" sweeping the nation.

IN A SURPRISING DEVELOPMENT, THAT FLOOD TIDE THREATENED TO ENgulf one of the Senate's proudest liberals.

Frank Church became the first Democratic senator in Idaho history in 1957, replacing a devotee of Joseph McCarthy. His dream was restoring his state's nearly forgotten progressive tradition. He championed the normalization of relations with Communist China, was one of the earliest and most eloquent congressional doves on Vietnam, and became a household name in 1975 by leading the Senate's yearlong investigation into abuses of power by the FBI and CIA. Present Carter sent him to Cuba to discuss normalizing relations with Fidel Castro. Then he served as Carter's stalwart floor leader in the Panama Canal fight—by which time bumper stickers circulated in Idaho reading "FRANK CHURCH FOR A STRONGER RUSSIA." In 1979, he earned the gavel as chairman of the Senate Armed Services Committee—another dream—where he hoped to leave behind a legacy worthy of chiseling upon his gravestone: leading the ratification of SALT II. That spring, in perhaps the finest speech of his career, he called the treaty instrumental to "the survival of our people and our system," imprecating the "abstract mumbo jumbo of the nuclear priesthood" as the "great moral blindness of our time."

But Frank Church was also up for reelection in an increasingly right-wing state. On July 17, his Democratic colleague Richard Stone, who was also up for reelection—facing a Florida electorate full of Cuban-American anti-Communist diehards—said at the SALT II hearings that he had learned that a Soviet combat brigade some two thousand troops strong had recently arrived in Cuba. The charge was particularly sensitive because, that same day, Nicaragua's anti-Communist strongman Anastasio Somoza Debayle surrendered Managua to a government backed by Cuba. Church and his ranking Republican colleague Jacob Javits issued a joint statement denying the brigade's existence, and Church returned to his work presiding over the hearings with a diligence and passion longtime Capitol Hill watchers described as awe-inspiring.

Soon, however, they noticed a certain nervousness creeping into his performance. Back home, a savage television commercial had begun running. "You see," a narrator gravely intoned as the camera panned over an abandoned Idaho missile site, "Senator Church has *almost always* opposed a strong national defense. . . . *If Senator Church wins, you lose.*"

It was quickly pointed out that those empty silos had housed missiles deactivated in 1965 as obsolete. Church called it Nazi-style "big lie" propaganda. When the group responsible, the National Conservative Political Action Committee (NCPAC, pronounced "nikpack"), pulled the ad after howls of outrage from the local papers, its leader Terry Dolan was unapologetic: "He says we filmed the commercials in front of the wrong missile. We don't think that's important."

Terry Dolan was a name to remember. Trim, handsome, and fashionably mustachioed, the twenty-eight-year-old son of the manager of a Sears outlet in a blue-collar part of Connecticut, his New Right colleagues knew, secretly enjoyed having sex with men. They considered Dolan indispensable nonetheless. The reason was that his brazenness was unmatched. He openly reveled in exploiting loopholes in campaign finance laws—especially the one allowing PACs to raise and spend unlimited amounts, saying whatever they liked, so long as they did not formally coordinate with any candidate. His aim, he said, was a federal budget that spent 99 percent on defense, "and 1 percent on delivering the mail. That's it. Leave us alone."

On August 16, Dolan stepped up to a news conference podium to announce a program unlike any in the history of Senate campaigning: NCPAC would spend $700,000 on attack ads against a "hit list" comprising Church and his fellow senators Birch Bayh of Indiana, John Culver of Iowa, George McGovern of South Dakota, and Alan Cranston of California—though none of these men yet had an opponent. A traditionally timed campaign, Dolan explained, made it difficult to get the target's "negative numbers up.... We're going to do it for an extended period of time, and hope it will stick"—even if, by Election Day, voters "may not remember *why* they're so upset."

He screened his commercials. "Sweet Georgia Brown" played in the background of one, which featured a basketball player in a red, white, and blue uniform. " 'Globetrotter,' " the announcer explained, "is a great name for a basketball team. But it's a terrible name for a senator. . . . While the energy crisis was breaking, George McGovern was touring Cuba with Fidel Castro. He took a one-month junket to Africa. All at taxpayer expense. No wonder he's lost touch with South Dakota. With so many problems at home, we need a senator, not a globetrotter. . . . *Because if McGovern wins, you lose.*" Another spot saw a housewife slice into a giant log of deli meat at a supermarket: "One very big piece of baloney is Birch Bayh telling us he's fighting inflation." A $46 billion price tag popped up: "That's how much deficit spending Bayh voted for last year alone. So to stop inflation you'll have to stop Bayh first. . . . *Because if Bayh wins, you lose.*"

Dolan had been planning the ads since January, when he blithely told an interviewer, "The beautiful thing about this campaign is all you have to do is change the names of the liberals and fill in the blanks." He was asked why he had chosen these particular Democrats out of the nineteen up for reelection. He answered, "We picked them because they're the most distasteful, the most liberal, the most radical, and the most vulnerable." Also because they were important votes on arms control: "We may win SALT because of this."

What he did not say was that they were mostly from states with small populations. As an early fundraising appeal from NCPAC's "Target McGovern" subsidiary explained—below a caricature of George McGovern with a bull's-eye over his heart, and a claim that the "radical left-wing extremist" had cosponsored a fundraiser for the head of the Congressional Black Caucus with "U.S. Communist Party leader Gus Hall"—how purchasing ads during the Super Bowl on Houston TV cost between $4,000 and $10,000, whereas the same ad in Sioux Falls cost $220. "Yet, both Texas and South Dakota have EQUAL votes in the U.S Senate."

Billboards started popping up across the prairies depicting a caricature of a smiling George McGovern passing a box full of missiles labeled "SALT II" to a Soviet general (*"McGovern sells out the U.S. . . . again! If McGovern wins, you lose"*). In newspaper ads, the cartoon McGovern handed over the United States and Taiwan to a caricature of a Chinese man. Idaho and South Dakota were NCPAC's proof of concept. Evidence that the concept was sound soon arrived.

ON AUGUST 30, FRANK CHURCH WAS REPAIRING A FENCE IN HIS BACKYARD when his wife summoned him inside. A State Department officer was on the phone, who revealed that, any day now, the media would be reporting leaked intelligence that a Soviet combat brigade had indeed been spotted in Cuba—precisely what he had denied the previous month.

Church sighed—"Well, SALT is dead"—and returned to work. Then he rushed back inside, so agitated that his wife feared he had struck himself with a hammer. He had been seized by a fright that his own career would die with SALT. Defying a request from the State Department briefer to keep the intelligence private, he began arranging a press conference for that very night to get out ahead of the story. He announced that he had just learned of a "buildup of Soviet ground forces to brigade strength" on Fidel Castro's island, and urged President Carter to demand "an immediate withdrawal of all combat troops from Cuba."

But the crisis was a noncrisis, borne of a bureaucratic snafu. President Carter's hawkish National Security Advisor Zbigniew Brzezinski had ordered intelligence agencies to review the Soviet Union's military presence in Cuba. On August 28, a top-secret National Intelligence Digest, circulated to four hundred government officials, reported the Soviet "combat brigade." This was a semantic mistake. The troops were members of a pre-existing "advisory mission" whose presence accorded with understandings between the three countries in operation since the Cuban Missile Crisis. The State Department believed they posed "no threat to the United States." The mistake was the fault of NSA staffers who had ventured to interpret information that they were only supposed to report. That set into motion the cascade of misunderstandings that culminated with the State Department's call to Church.

Patient diplomacy could have easily neutralized the situation, had cooler heads prevailed. But Frank Church was not in a cool state of mind. He was haunted by a soul-searing political flashback: to October 1962, when he had reassured his constituents that they need not fear military threat from Cuba, just days before pictures of the Soviet nuclear missile installation on the island were beamed to the world. That November, he was barely reelected. Sometimes, he reflected, you can walk the plank once and survive. Perhaps even a second time. When it came to sounding "soft" on Communism, however, this was something like Frank Church's fourth, fifth, or sixth.

President Carter marched to the pressroom on September 7 to offer a typically ambiguous statement: the brigade was not a threat, but its purpose was "not clear"; Americans should not worry because the troops had been there "for some time, perhaps for quite a few years," but "this status quo is not acceptable." No such equivocation from Church. He told reporters there was "no likelihood whatsoever" of ratifying SALT until the brigade was removed.

Doonesbury soon imagined Church convening new hearings called "Operation Manhood." In the comic, Scoop Jackson waved a parchment copy of the Monroe Doctrine, demanding Jimmy Carter face down the Soviets "eyeball to eyeball, like a real man." A beribboned general reported surveillance footage of a requisition form "for nearly 1500 Czech staple guns" and warned of an imminent invasion of Florida, Alabama, and "parts of Mississippi," then profusely thanked Frank Church: "By refusing to fan the flames of moderation, a calm, negotiated solution has been narrowly averted! Thanks to you, the American people have been given another chance to show they're still number one!"

A GOOD-OLD-FASHIONED COLD WAR PANIC, JUST LIKE IN JOSEPH MCCARthy's day. Howard Baker was right: a floodtide of conservatism *was* sweeping the nation.

In Los Angeles, a county school board member named Howard Miller had cosponsored a resolution in 1976 opposing busing students to achieve racial integration. In February 1979, as the body's president, he followed a judge's order to submit a plan to do so. Anti-busing activists in the San Fernando Valley filed enough signatures to put his recall on the June primary ballot. They aired a blitz of expensive TV commercials unprecedented in a school board election. Miller protested that his recall would backfire, spurring the courts to act *more* forcefully. Los Angeles County did not listen: he was replaced by a Proposition 13 activist who claimed that Miller's "destructive busing program threatens the very social fabric that binds our cherished diversity."

The United States Chamber of Commerce chose as its new president Jay Van Andel of Amway, the head of the Chamber's front organization Citizen's Choice. Together with J. Willard Marriott, he announced a drive for an "immediate $25–$30 billion 'tax return' to the taxpayers," warning Congress, "The American taxpayer has established a superb record of voluntary tax payments to the nation's treasury," but "tax law inconsistencies, IRS harassment, an inflated tax rate and any number of other factors could break down the willingness of the American people to comply with IRS regulations"—a veritable threat of a tax strike if the boardroom Jacobins did not get their way.

A coalition joining Richard Viguerie and Charls Walker killed another attempt at public financing of congressional elections, persuading eight Democrats on the House Administration Committee to defect at the last minute. Then Walker reconstituted his old American Council for Capital Formation coalition for a new raid on the U.S. Treasury: the Jones-Conable Capital Cost Recovery Act, which would speed up companies' ability to claim depreciation deductions on equipment—the one item on the boardroom Jacobins' wish list left out of the 1978 tax law. Even though an estimated 80 percent of its benefits would go the biggest tenth of American corporations, Walker persuaded the National Federation of Independent Businesses to get behind it, and a majority of members of both houses to cosponsor it. He gloated, "At the rate we're winning, I'm worried about working us out of business."

As the Federal Trade Commission's budget authorization came up before Congress, the House and Senate seemed almost to compete to one-up each other in their attacks on the benighted agency. Senator Harrison Schmitt of New Mexico introduced an amendment to let either house of Congress rip up new FTC rules by majority vote—the "legislative veto," which the Senate had scrupulously decided was unconstitutional when the hotheads in the House sent it their way last year, but which now seemed certain to pass both houses. Another Republican Senate freshman, John Danforth of Missouri, went to war over a modest little program subsidizing public interest groups to serve as witnesses so that industry wouldn't dominate regulatory hearings: a "boondoggle," he insisted, because "if groups really represent 'the public'—or even a particular sector of the public—it would seem to me they could raise the money on their own." Other senators introduced amendments to ban the FTC from touching entire industries, aggression unprecedented in the history of congressional authorizations—the mirror image, in fact, of the 1975 Magnuson-Moss Act *requiring* the FTC to regulate entire industries. By June, almost 150 anti-FTC bills had been introduced. By Labor Day, the *Chicago Tribune* recorded, the agency was "fighting for its life."

A Democratic Watergate baby in the House, Marty Russo, sought to ban the FTC from regulating funeral homes. "Overregulation is already enough of a problem in the nation," he wrote to colleagues. "Productivity is being harmed." (Pertschuk replied sardonically, "It is a little difficult to grasp the concept of productivity in funeral production.") "A federal law covering the funeral industry will no doubt lessen competition." (Pertschuk: "It is hard to comprehend how enhanced opportunities to compare prices could do anything but strengthen competition.") A Republican piped up during the debate, "Must this country be like Sweden, where it is against the law to spank your child?" The amendment passed 223–147, which the *Washington Post* called "stunning." Mike Pertschuk was not stunned: "No congressman needs to be told that a funeral director whose customers begin to select $350 funerals in place of $3,500 packages will remember nothing else as the next election approaches."

Similar assaults sought to ban the FTC from investigating door-to-door insurance sales. ("If this doesn't work, I don't know what will," Senator Danforth said in support of an amendment introduced by the Democrat Howard Cannon—"maybe criminal sanctions.") And used car dealers. And the manufacturers of products whose names had fallen into common usage, like American Cyanamid's "Formica," which a 1946 law required the FTC to remove from trademark protection. (Formica's CEO labeled Mike Pertschuk "one of the most dangerous men in America," a "complete socialist.") And to cancel the FTC's monopoly suit against Sunkist, which legal experts said was the first time Congress had interfered with ongoing litigation in history. And regulations to make it easier to sell generic drugs; and to end antitrust proceedings against Exxon and Mobil (which David Obey of Wisconsin said would be "the most inflationary and anti-consumer actions yet offered in the Ninety-Sixth Congress"); and the "shared-monopoly" case against the cereal companies—and, of course, kidvid, the crusade against which had been so successful discrediting the FTC with the public in 1978, the *New York Times Magazine* explained, that in 1979 "major economic forces smell victory and are moving in for the kill" against the agency itself.

As the Senate Consumer Subcommittee began FTC hearings, *People* magazine profiled "The Bureaucrat Who Makes Business Turn Blue." "Once," reported the glossy that more frequently featured Barry Manilow, Farrah Fawcett, and the "10 Sexiest Bachelors in the World," "Pertschuk got an idea for a new TV series. The plot of his show revolved around the Senate Commerce Committee. 'I thought we could show the committee as a kind of public-interest guerrilla organization, with staff members in tension with special-interest corporations,' Pertschuk now laughs. His heroic Senate investigators would roam the country 'defeating the forces of evil—sort of like the Scarlet Pimpernel.'" The flight of fancy had been inspired by the committee during its consumerist heyday under his mentor Senator Magnuson. Now, however, it was run by the former head of the Tobacco Institute, Wendell Ford of Kentucky. Testifying before it, Pertschuk suffered another bloodbath—*People*, and the people, be damned.

A man named Ernest Pepples, vice president and general counsel of Brown & Williamson Tobacco, testified. He had recently scored an anti-FTC public relations coup after his company exhausted its legal options attempting to block a subpoena for corporate records about its advertising strategies dating back to 1964: he arranged for a truck to back up to the agency's Pennsylvania Avenue doorstep, dumping 13,845 pounds of paper for the benefit of TV cameras. Now Pepples demanded that the FTC be abolished because of its "reckless bullying." Pertschuk responded that Brown & Williamson had claimed to the secretary of health and human services that it had "a strict policy against promoting cigarettes to persons under twenty-one years of age"—then produced documents outlining a detailed marketing plan aimed at "the young smoker," for whom tobacco "is not yet an integral part of life," recommending cigarettes be depicted "as one of the few initiations into the adult world, as part of the illicit pleasure category" including "'pot,' wine, beer, sex, etc.," and crafting language that would offer "a means of *repressing* their health concerns about smoking a full flavor Viceroy." Pertschuk also read out searing testimony from agency hearings on other matters, like that from a Connecticut woman who chose cremation for her late husband because she couldn't afford a funeral, but paid $600 for a casket that the funeral director lied was the least expensive available; and an old lady in Grand Rapids whom a hearing aid salesman had taken for $485 even though she was deaf.

He also extended his customary deference. He apologized for staffers who exhibited a "vendetta" against the industries they were investigating, explaining he had fired them before their rulemaking processes got far. He described a committee he had convened, headed by a respected state attorney general, to work out compromises between regulators and industries. He detailed the eight hours he had spent sitting around a table with funeral industry representatives listening to their concerns. When a senior Democrat nonetheless threatened he would keep on investigating the FTC "with a thoroughness no agency had ever experienced before," Pertschuk responded: "I accept the rightness of what you said."

Fat lot of good deference did him. Two months later, when Chairman Cannon gaveled open the full Commerce Committee to consider the FTC authorization bill, ironically entitled the "FTC Improvements Act," an astonished *Washington Post* correspondent wrote, "The various senators could hardly wait to propose their amendments, with Senator Howell Heflin twice offering his before the appropriate sections of the authorization were brought up."

The measure that Heflin, a Democrat from Alabama, was so eager to introduce would strip the commission of authority to break up monopolies. FTC commissioners said that was akin to banning the IRS from auditing tax returns. The measure only failed because critics discovered its text was borrowed directly from a brief written by lawyers for General Mills. Amendments stripping the FTC of its power to regulate life insurance, kidvid, and professional organizations passed overwhelmingly. The House's version of the bill had a ban on regulating savings and loans. There would now be a House-Senate conference committee to reconcile the bills—no earlier than four months into the fiscal year the authorization was supposed to fund.

That fall, several investigative articles came out that totted up receipts from the boardroom Jacobins' crusades that had spurred this remarkable turn of events. Nine members of the U.S. Chamber of Commerce's "FTC Victims' Alumni Association" had spent $5,494,063 in donations to political candidates. The funeral industry expended more than $850,000 on lobbying. The tobacco industry's spending since the FTC had ordered health warnings on cigarettes in 1964 was a staggering $850 *million*. Also, that fall, the White House released the second edition of the *Calendar of Federal Regulations*, part of President Carter's effort to hack back government red tape, which rated dozens of federal agencies according to a number of objective measurements. The FTC tied for third place in both benefit to the public compared to cost and transparency; the kidvid proceeding was singled out for particular praise. The study's author was asked how the FTC could simultaneously be the most competent regulator and the most anathematized. "Maybe," he responded archly, "there's a correlation between the two."

A LETTER WENT OUT VIA THE FIRM OF A VIGUERIE PROTÉGÉ TARGETING senators including Church, Bayh, and McGovern—as well as Congressman Robert Drinan of Massachusetts, a Catholic priest—from Weyrich's group Americans for Life:

Dear Friend,

. . . Help me STOP THE BABY KILLERS by signing and mailing the enclosed anti-abortion postcards to your U.S. Senators. . . .

Abortion means killing a living baby, a tiny human being with a beating heart and little fingers . . . killing a baby boy or girl with burning deadly chemicals or a powerful machine that sucks and tears the little infant from its mother's womb. . . .

If you think I'm too harsh when I refer to these Members of Congress as Baby Killers, stop and think a minute. Recall during the Vietnam War when hypocrites like McGovern and these others piously wrung their hands and denounced the brutal slaying of Vietnamese children. . . . If a little baby boy or little baby girl has a real, live beating heart and is developed enough to have toes and fingers and eyes and ears, can't these holier-than-thou politicians give them the right to life, too . . . ?

It was signed by Donald "Buz" Lukens, an Ohio state senator and veteran conservative activist (later convicted of soliciting sex from an underage prostitute). Reporters asked him whether using the words "baby killer" and "murder" forty-one times wasn't a little bit much. "Brutal," he agreed. "But we had to get contributors' attention or we would have lost our money." Responding to a complaint from Senators Bayh and McGovern, the United States Postal Service ruled that they had no power to stop the letter. Its sponsors responded by promising to mail it to sixty thousand additional homes. Organizing discontent was the name of the game, and its most ruthless practitioners were followers of the Prince of Peace.

In Dallas, at the annual meeting of the Southern Baptist Convention, conservatives replaced a leadership they insisted was "liberal" in a coup like the one at the National Rifle Association in 1977. Its two plotters had been working for this moment for more than a decade—first traveling from church to church making theological arguments about Baptist seminaries whose teachings violated the doctrine of "biblical inerrancy"; then, when those proved ineffectual, making their pitch via issues like abortion, the ERA, and homosexuality.

Veteran delegates complained that they could not recognize their beloved church gathering: it felt instead like a party convention. James Robison bellowed that "if we are a denomination that tolerates liberalism in any form, and continues to support it, we will be guilty of the suicidal death of countless millions of people through the world," and called the existing SBC leadership "snakes," "termites," and "devils." (And, worse, "like government bureaucrats.") Reverend Charles Stanley, a Moral Majority board member, scourged "demonic" humanism, liberalism, abortion, the United Nations, the ACLU, and the 1977 National Women's Conference—"spawned . . . in socialism and communism and that's a fact. . . . Unless we stand up, we are going to lose this republic." Their candidate for SBC president, a handsome young Floridian named Adrian Rogers, beat out six other contenders—then launched an "impartial" investigation of "liberal" Baptist seminaries one target described as a "witch hunt." He paid a visit to the home of another prominent Southern Baptist. "I hope," he claimed to have told Jimmy Carter, "you will give up your secular humanism and return back to Christianity."

Richard Viguerie solemnized the marriage between the New and Christian rights with a special issue of *Conservative Digest*, "Mobilizing the Moral Majority." It profiled Rogers, Robert Billings, Pat Robertson,

James Robison, and Jerry Falwell, running articles by Paul Weyrich, who stated, "The family will be to the decade of the 1980s what environmentalism and consumerism have been to the 1970s and what the Vietnam war was to the 1960s," and Billings, who said "Jerome Kurtz has done more to bring Christians together than any man since the Apostle Paul."

In Richmond, in September, Falwell publicly unveiled the Moral Majority with a rally on the steps of the Virginia State Capitol. In Washington, Ed McAteer chartered a new organization, the Religious Roundtable, modeled on the CEOs' group the Business Roundtable, to organize ministers—especially those not yet ready to surface aboveground as political activists. (McAteer modeled its governing "Council of Fifty-Six" on the fifty-six signers of the Declaration of Independence—who knew that if the Revolution was defeated, "they would face the hangman's noose as traitors," keeping their names secret for six months.)

The Senate voted 47–43 on a Jesse Helms amendment that Senator Metzenbaum described as locking in "the tax-exempt status of private schools in perpetuity." The House voted to deny the IRS funds to enforce the private school regulations. Christian Voice launched its signature effort, a "Biblical Scorecard" rating legislative candidates on a "morality scale" from 0 to 100 on issues including homosexuality, pornography, national defense, and sanctions against the white-minority government of Rhodesia (the "moral" position was to be against the sanctions). *U.S. News & World Report* published an article on "Preachers in Politics," which quoted Pat Robertson: "We have enough votes to run the country. And when the people say, 'We've had enough,' we are going to take over."

Also in September, Dr. Francis Schaeffer, the evangelical theologian behind the doctrine of co-belligerency, went on tour with a new film series focused entirely on the issue he had been reluctant to include in his 1977 production. His partner was a charismatic and heroic Philadelphia surgeon named C. Everett Koop, famous for performing the first successful separation of conjoined twins, who also considered abortion the greatest moral outrage of our time.

The images in *Whatever Happened to the Human Race?* were galvanizing. The opening sequence depicted a mother and her children, clad in white gowns, their skin stained white, painting the main title on a massive pane of glass, which then shattered into shards. Its most memorable one saw thousands of black and brown baby dolls floating upon the Dead Sea as a narrator described abortion methods in nauseating clinical detail. Then Dr. Schaeffer spoke, perched upon a rock, surrounded by those infant effigies: "This is the site on which the city of Sodom once stood. . . . Sodom comes readily to mind when one contemplates the evils of abortion, and the death of moral law. . . . These theories of so-called 'liberation from Biblical absolutes' are bearing their bitter fruit . . . at least six million unborn babies have been aborted." At that invocation of Hitler's Holocaust against the Jews, the wind howled melodramatically—the soundtrack's first break from a sumptuous score recorded by the London Symphony Orchestra with a children's choir.

The project lost a million dollars, but its benefactors, which included the Knights of Columbus, were repaid in kind by thousands of new recruits to the cause. The *New York Times* did a long feature on Dr. Schaeffer and Dr. Koop. By the end of their twenty-city tour, recalled the film's director, Dr. Schaeffer's son Frankie, "we were calling for civil disobedience, the takeover of the Republican Party, and even hinting at overthrowing our 'unjust pro-abortion government.'" The Christian soldiers were feeling their oats.

THEIR LEADERS BEGAN INTERVIEWING REPUBLICAN PRESIDENTIAL CANDIdates—and John Connally walked into a snafu. Reverend James D. Kennedy asked him, "What reason would you give God for letting you into heaven?" He answered: "My mother was a Methodist, my pappy was a Methodist, my grandmother was a Methodist, and I'd just tell Him I ain't any worse than any of the other people who went into heaven."

This was a test. John Connally had failed it.

Bill Bright subsequently visited him at Harvard's Kennedy School of Government, where he was teaching a course, and asked him about his "relationship with Christ." Connally said that this was a "personal matter." Bright said, "Governor Connally, with all due respect, Jesus Christ died on the cross in a very public way for you." Connally apologized; Bright began tutoring him in Evangelical Christianity 101.

Reagan's Catholic speechwriter Bill Gavin sent a *U.S. News* article on Christians in politics to Pete Hannaford and policy advisor Martin Anderson, writing, "I am told by Bill Gribbin (with whom I worked in Buckley's office and who has many contacts among the New Right) that this is a legitimate grass roots phenomenon, not the front-group for any New Right types. Because of the rhetoric and the 'moral' angle, a lot of the New Right types have been attracted to the TV preachers, but Bill tells me that they are not in the bag to any one candidate."

Ronald Reagan was not a habitual churchgoer. But he was plenty serious about his Christianity. He loved reciting a line from his favorite book, Whittaker Chambers's *Witness*, in which the former Communist described watching his daughter sleep and deciding he could no longer be an atheist. Reagan spoke constantly of his hope America would undergo a "spiritual revival." His evangelical fans doted upon a story from 1970 of gathering with the Reagans at the Sacramento home of a Charismatic Lutheran named Herbert Ellingwood, who replaced Edwin Meese as the governor's legal affairs secretary. The group, including Pat Boone and his wife, held hands and prayed for the Reagans. A minister and retired Learjet executive named George Otis began an offering.

"The Holy Spirit came upon me," Otis related. "There was this pulsing in my arm."

And Reverend Otis addressed to Governor Reagan the words the Lord laid upon his heart: *"If you walk uprightly before Me, you will reside at 1600 Pennsylvania Avenue."*

Reagan had long enjoyed bringing up a certain subject among those he thought would be sympathetic: how biblical prophecies about the end of the world were coming to pass. In 1971, he brought it up with someone who turned out *not* to be sympathetic: Democratic state senate leader James Mills, a Bible-believing Baptist, who told him these ideas were heretical. Then, "like a preacher to a skeptical college student," Mills remembered Reagan vigorously endeavoring to set him straight. ("Ezekiel says that fire and brimstone will be rained upon the enemies of God's people. That must mean that they'll be destroyed by nuclear weapons.")

But Reagan's familiarity with the folkways of evangelicals could be spotty. Chuck Colson remembered the time a reporter held up a copy of Colson's memoir, *Born Again*, before Reagan and asked if *he* was born again. "Reagan shrugged, like the fellow had landed from Mars. He didn't know what he meant."

Which may be why, the night before Reagan was to speak before the convention of the National Religious Broadcasters—the day after he spoke to the board of the New York Stock Exchange and dined with a former Federal Reserve chairman—John Conlan gave him a tutoring session. He was, before speaking in the ballroom, to be interviewed by many of the same figures as Connally had been. There, James D. Kennedy asked Reagan the same thing he had asked Connally. This time, Reverend Kennedy received the correct answer:

"I wouldn't give any reason for letting me in. I'd just ask for mercy, because of what Jesus Christ did for me at Calvary."

Then Reagan recited from the Gospel of John: "For God so loved the world that he gave His only begotten Son, that whoever believed in Him should not perish, but have everlasting life." He strode into the full convention, participated in a question and answer session, and proceeded to knock 'em dead.

Many of the people organizing his campaign were indifferent to the accomplishment. At a planning meeting around the time of the Moral Majority's incorporation, John Sears reported gossip that Paul Weyrich had landed in John Connally's camp—and concluded, "Viguerie and Weyrich can go to Connally without harm to us." Some had been warning him against too close an association with Bible-thumpers for years. And when *U.S. News & World Report*'s September feature on "Preachers and Politics" was sent by Bill Gavin to Hannaford as a subject of possible interest, Gavin wondered how "we can show the movement we are with them on the social issues without, at the same time, alienating those who might be turned off by the 'style' of the movement's people, which seems to be a bit blunt at times." Hannaford responded, "I agree with you that we need to be careful. Fundamentalists—at least the ones I've run into over the years—tend to be rigid, not very tolerant *and* highly tendentious." By way of comparison, that very same day, Hannaford warmly accepted an invitation for Reagan to meet a delegation of the National Association of Arab Americans—a less controversial association, apparently. Later that fall, Hannaford sent Ed Meese a sheaf of newspaper clippings headed "SUBJECT: 'gay issues, revisited.'" He noted "a very thin line to tread between getting the support of fundamentalists, on the one hand, and people who need to know how strongly RR is opposed to bigotry, on the other. The latter, in my opinion, are much more potent politically and in terms of swaying the opinions of others."

CHAPTER 27

"Do You Ever Feel That We Might Be the Generation That Sees Armageddon?"

RONALD REAGAN WAS EITHER DOMINATING THE PRESIDENTIAL FIELD OR going nowhere fast; it was hard to tell. He beat every other challenger in polls of Republican voters by margins of two to one or better. But people still had a hard time taking him seriously.

Insomniacs were regularly reminded that the man hoping to lead the Free World had once been a middling Hollywood contract player; one week in July he was a lawyer helping the Dead End Kids out of a jam in 1939's *Hell's Kitchen* at 3:30 a.m. on Channel 51 in Orlando; the "Gipper" in *Knute Rockne, All-American* at 12:40 a.m. in Miami; a high-spirited military academy cadet in *Brother Rat* (1938) at 10:30 p.m. in central Wisconsin—and, in a rare daylight appearance, on Channel 45 in Lebanon, Pennsylvania, a Klan-hunting district attorney in *Storm Warning* (1951). In August, three comedians from Milwaukee shot a disaster movie send-up called *Airplane!* The script included the line, "I haven't felt this awful since I saw that Ronald Reagan film." (Howard Jarvis made a cameo.) A columnist for the newspaper in Petaluma, California, ran a piece consisting of open-ended questions on "Heroes Past and Present." Like "Whose voice will be most listened to in the next century, Bing Crosby or Frank Sinatra's?" And "Will Ronald Reagan be best remembered as a politician or a movie actor?"

When the Reagan for President executive committee prepared to hear pitches from advertising agencies, one unexpectedly dropped out. Perhaps they agreed with the syndicated conservative James J. Kilpatrick, who insisted that "the polls are wrong . . . voters who have been dismayed by Jimmy Carter are bound to reflect before long, having lived with one amateur in the White House, on the prospect of two in a row." Or the liberal Richard Reeves, who jabbed with "A number of otherwise respectable men have been attracting suspicion these days by hanging around golf courses and locker rooms": Republican leaders stalking the former president after seeing polls showing that "only Ford can prevent Reagan from walking away with the Republican nomination."

When John Sears occasionally let Reagan attend events with the other contenders, he was suffering from the comparison. At the National Federation of Independent Business's convention, Evans and Novak reported that those "hounding him for autographs" also agreed that "Reagan lacked the punch of two earlier speakers: Jack Kemp—and more significantly, Connally." ("He looked awfully pale; maybe he could use some suntan oil.") At the National Federation of Republican Women's conclave in Indianapolis (where Connally's organization delivered its man at the head of a two-block-long parade featuring cheerleaders on roller skates and a marching band), the columnists said attendees treated Reagan like the guy who had once been their "favorite boyfriend" but now were enjoying "being wooed by all the other good-looking guys in town." And in Lancaster, Pennsylvania, a young congressman pulled Reagan aside to beg him to pledge to serve only one term. Reportedly, Reagan's handlers had considered the idea, which Sears rejected because it would only call attention to his age, though another advisor said it was "something we might consider at a later date."

One problem was that Reagan was delivering pretty much the same speech he had since the Kennedy administration. When he started in once more to shuffling those now famous yellowed index cards, the traveling press would groan, brace themselves for the same dubious statistics, corny one-liners, and bromides they had heard so many times before—and dismiss what one called the "docile Chautauqua circuit lecture campaign of tried-and-true one-liners" as sheer laziness. But this was a key component of John Sears's strategy: doing the exact same thing he always did was supposed to insinuate the conclusion that Reagan's victory was so predetermined, he needn't even campaign.

Unfortunately, this played into the stereotype that Reagan was lazy and incurious. It also made him look greedy. (A Federal Communications Commission ruling that Reagan could continue giving radio commentaries, without stations being forced to provide equal time for opponents, was followed by a rash of reports about all the income he was raking in by *not* officially campaigning.) And, also, deceptive—like the time NBC News took viewers inside a warren of jangling telephones and busy clerks drafting letters on preprinted stationery to solicit donations from a 400,000-name mailing list: the Reagan "exploratory committee" headquarters, which didn't look like it was exploring a thing.

But Sears's strategy suited the noncandidate just fine. The new system of political nominations, in the wake of both parties' post-1968 reforms eliminating the role of backroom wheeling and dealing, meant more and more early caucuses and primaries. Ronald Reagan despised it.

Jimmy Carter had brilliantly exploited the new reality, trudging from farmstead to farmstead many months ahead of Iowa's first-in-the-nation caucus. The system was still more "front-loaded" now. Puerto Rico saw how Iowa and New Hampshire leveraged their status to earn political favors, and scheduled a primary before New Hampshire's. A Republican official was asked what effect this might have on the election. He answered, "Both nominees will probably be Puerto Rican." It was supposed to be a joke—but in actuality, a dark-horse candidate, a former ambassador named Ben Fernandez, *was* building his strategy to become the first major-party Hispanic presidential contender on pulling off a miracle in Puerto Rico. George Bush had sent his son Jeb to campaign there in Spanish. But Ronald Reagan wouldn't play the game. Whenever he was asked when he would finally drop the pretense and officially announce, he repurposed a political saw—no one paid attention to politics before the World Series in the election year—and kept to the same old routine.

And so, one Monday in May, when the other contenders ate rubber chicken at an Iowa banquet keynoted by Henry Kissinger, Reagan was in Reno entertaining the In-Flight Food Service Association. The next day, he taped a TV interview—in Canada, where no delegates were to be had. Three days later, he was in Washington for the annual Republican Senate-House fundraising dinner, then attended a breakfast honoring Gerald Ford. "Anyone who leaves Gerald Ford's name off the list of potential nominees is crazy," RNC chairman Bill Brock observed—which made Reagan's appearance a veritable advertisement for an opponent.

All this helped explain why Reagan's operative on Capitol Hill reported that the scuttlebutt there was that Reagan "might not even run again."

IN FACT, HIS CANDIDACY ANNOUNCEMENT DATE HAD BEEN SET: NOVEM-ber 13. And a Reagan appearance now usually included a meet-and-greet with donors willing to pay $50, $100, or even $1,000 for the privilege. Unfortunately for the campaign, not many attendees were recruited. Self-respecting presidential campaigns were supposed to have a *Fortune* 500 executive as finance chairman to recruit donors. Searching for one, Team Reagan struck out again and again.

One problem was the man Sears had kicked upstairs to run fundrais-ing. Lyn Nofziger, a dab hand with happy-go-lucky journalists, couldn't have been worse with the tycoons and socialites. So he nearly gave up: stopped making the requisite phone calls, and at Reagan appearances jab-bered with his reporter pals instead of sucking up to guests. Helene von Damm tried to draft one of the big wheels from Reagan's old guberna-torial "kitchen cabinet," pharmaceutical magnate Justin Dart, to work through his Rolodex. Surely insulted at how they had been sidelined,

Dart turned her down. Another prospect, a dehydrated onion and garlic tycoon, refused after studying the balance sheets. Meese's notes from that meeting: "Lack of ctrl + direction + morale."

Fundraising ideas like selling T-shirts with a Norman Rockwell portrait of Reagan failed. A direct mail letter to their 408,000-name house list cost them $76,000 to pull in $36,000 in checks. Richard Viguerie charged them $45,000 to reach 225,000 addresses—which earned only $7,300. (Meese: "Bad list. Hate Mail, people dead.") And time was running out. The non-campaign would soon face a difficult decision. Under the new finance laws, a presidential campaign could accept matching funds if it agreed to abide by mandatory spending caps in each state, a total of $17 million for the nomination period. If a campaign forwent federal support, it could spend unlimited amounts. To take that risk required a faith that at least *twice* that $17 million could be raised, to make up for the missing matching funds. It wasn't likely they would come close. In May, they debated whether to sell their three telex machines. (They already had given up their coffee machine.) In June they began talks with a Houston banker who had kept Reagan's hopes alive in 1976 with a well-timed loan. It must not have gone well, for soon they began sending out termination notices to staffers in Iowa.

They had taken in $1.4 million. John Connally had raised $2.2 million. Rumor was that Big John was going to reject federal funds and shoot for the moon. "Connally's intentions: buy election," Meese wrote in his notes.

THE BAN ON REAGAN APPEARING TO BE RUNNING FOR PRESIDENT DIDN'T include appearing presidential. A week after the March exploratory announcement, Reagan's strategists began planning stature-enhancing junkets to the Middle East, Mexico, Canada, South America—and even, possibly, the USSR. Only the Mexican and Canadian trips came off. Perhaps that was all they could afford. And perhaps that financial desperation explained certain suspicious activities concerning Reagan's Mexico jaunt.

Nine days after meeting with President José López Portillo in July, Reagan sent this letter:

Dear Mr. President:

> *If it should be the Lord's will that I attain the office I am presently seeking . . . let me assure you I will be asking for another meeting to discuss and hopefully implement the kind of fair and open relationship that should exist between us as neighbors. . . . In the meantime, may I be so presumptuous as to mention another matter which I did not think should be brought up in the brief time we had*

*together. I am aware that some time ago your government made an
inquiry of ours about obtaining delivery of the F-5E Northrop fighter
plane. Since I am a Californian, of course, I am very familiar with
the Northrop Company and with that aircraft, I believe the situation
is presently on hold at your government's request.*

Reagan then pitched like a used car salesman: "I have taken keen interest in the F-5E and followed closely the activities in Washington on the
provision and support of this fine airplane. . . . I happen to have learned
that Northrop could make an almost immediate delivery, which, I'm sure,
would mean a lower price than if the planes had to be constructed at the
ever-increasing rate of inflation in our land." He concluded, "I have no
connection with Northrop and only mean to be helpful if your government is still interested in this aircraft."

It was not true that he had no such connection. One of Nancy Reagan's best friends, Ruth Jones, was married to Northrop's president.
Immediately prior to Reagan's trip, Thomas and Ruth Jones had each
donated the maximum allowable $1,000 individual contribution to his
exploratory committee. Immediately afterward, Jones joined the governor
for lunch. He had a sordid history of using money to influence politics:
during Watergate, he admitted to falsifying donations to one of Richard
Nixon's political slush funds; in 1975, he signed a Justice Department consent decree after Northrop allegedly paid $30 million in bribes to foreign
officials—part of what led Congress to pass the Foreign Corrupt Practices
Act two years later.

Though to be fair, that $2,000 from the Joneses couldn't keep up with
the $1 million the chairman of Lockheed directed to John Connally, who
had organized a federal $250 million loan guarantee for that company
when he was treasury secretary.

Another unusual recent episode involved the Republic of South Africa. Reagan had been invited to visit there in 1978 under the auspices of
something called the South African Freedom Foundation. The invitation
was transmitted by a longtime Reagan supporter and associate of South
Africa's and Rhodesia's prime ministers (both of whom "respect and admire you and were greatly disappointed when you were narrowly defeated
in your bid for the Republican nomination for the presidency"). Peter
Hannaford persuaded Reagan to decline. Then, in March 1979, Reagan
was offered $10,000 to address three hundred "top American CEOs" at
a seminar on investment opportunities in South Africa. This offer Reagan
was prepared to accept. Gerald Ford and William Simon had keynoted the
same event in previous years.

Then it emerged that both the putatively private organization sponsoring the seminar, and the South African Freedom Foundation, were government fronts at the center of a metastasizing scandal rocking the African nation, involving millions in laundered funds, and even a secret attempt to purchase the *Washington Star* to turn it into a secret South African propaganda organ. On June 4, South Africa's president was forced to resign for his complicity in the scandal.

That did not, however, prevent Reagan and Hannaford from receiving South Africa's deputy secretary for information in Reagan's office on June 18. The next week, Reagan published a column on "how strong the winds of change are blowing in South Africa." It reported glowingly on the investment seminar he had declined to address, quoting approvingly what a Pretoria official had said there: "not to rest until racial discrimination has disappeared from our statute books and everyday life in South Africa."

At the time, every South African was classified into one of four racial groups to determine access to education, property, employment, and residence. Blacks had to carry passbooks at all times, to enforce the ban on spending more than three days in any area where they were not born and raised or had not lived for fifteen years or had not worked continuously for ten. None of this changed for over a decade. The first election open to blacks would not take place until 1994.

A THIRD DELICATE PROJECT INVOLVED OUTREACH TO SUPPORTERS OF ISrael. The claim of the campaign's lawyer that 60 percent of the money raised for Richard Nixon's reelection had come from Jews was surely exaggerated. But the Reagan campaign acted like they believed it. During one early meeting, Meese scrawled an arrow connecting "Middle East" to "Financial Support." After the signing of the Israel-Egypt peace treaty late in March every single member of the campaign's seven-man executive committee worried over a project to get *just right* a response to all the fans writing in hoping that Reagan would speak out against the money the U.S. was committing to help implement the deal: excessive foreign aid was a foundational conservative complaint, but aid to Israel was of paramount concern to most Jews. And when the committee reached out to individual supporters, the vast majority of the time they were Jews—like Max Rabb, or Max Kampelman, the late Hubert Humphrey's friend, whose orchestrated correspondence with Reagan had inspired Richard Allen to exclaim, "This SP thing is working well!"

Kampelman helped coordinate a meeting Reagan participated in after accepting an award from the American Friends of Hebrew University. The attendees, and other Jewish leaders in contact with the campaign, advised him to publish "an article favorable to Israel." That launched an elaborate four-month process. An April draft from a think tank intellectual was marked up by many hands on the staff (one early cut was a line that America must be "prepared to contain Israel to the 1967 lines"—anathema to American supporters of Menachem Begin's right-wing government). It was then sent to outside reviewers, including the chairman of the National Republican Jewish Coalition. Only on July 31 did Reagan learn of the project, scrawling the words "OK—RR" on the text. Then, staffers got four more days for final tweaks.

"Recognizing the Israeli Asset" ran in the *Washington Post* on August 15. To staffers' delight, it was republished in the *International Herald Tribune* and the *New York Post*. "The American Israel Public Affairs Committee (AIPAC) will also undertake a distribution to 15,000 people on its mailing list it describes as 'opinion makers, political activists, and "doers," '" Dick Allen crowed. "The impact of the article, I am told, was excellent in Israel . . . Numerous calls were received in California. . . . Bill Safire spoke with several of us, and in his conversation with me made a pitch for a second article, hopefully to appear in the *New York Times*."

It was their last success for some time.

ANOTHER PERSONNEL CRISIS ERUPTED. ON FRIDAY, AUGUST 24, LYN NOFZIGER submitted his resignation. The boss, vacationing on his ranch, was beside himself; Nofziger, with him since 1966, was one of his dearest associates — about the only person he ever christened with a nickname: "Lynwell." He begged him to reconsider, or at least do nothing until Reagan got back to town. That Monday, at Reagan's home, Sears, his loyalists Charlie Black and Jim Lake, and also Michael Deaver, argued that Nofziger should go. Ed Meese and the governor were the only ones arguing that Nofziger should stay.

As usual, the meeting leaked. Spokesman Lake was asked whether disputes over moderating Reagan were responsible. "That simply isn't true; there was no disagreement," he spun. But Nofziger refused to follow the script, complaining via the next morning's *Los Angeles Times* that Sears was keeping conservative Reagan loyalists at arm's length. The *Star* called it "the outcome of the 'East-West' tension that was long evident." The *Post* said it was the product of "tensions that may cause future problems for the Reagan organization"—not exactly the sort of things that wavering potential big-ticket Reagan contributors wanted to hear. The *Washington Star* asked Sears if Nofziger had resigned. "He may have, and he may not have," he responded. "I can tell you he wasn't fired."

He had been fired—"made an example of what could happen if you stood up to Sears," Nofziger told the world. Sears celebrated his coup in a brash interview with Al Hunt of the *Wall Street Journal*, who dutifully relayed Sears's boast that he had chosen to run Reagan's campaign only after being courted by many other hopefuls—and that his plan was for Reagan to "burst on the political scene in November with a half-hour television address officially announcing his candidacy. This will be followed by a series of policy statements that are being carefully researched by experts," with the goal of "avoiding the types of gaffes that plagued the 1976 Reagan campaign." Then, Hunt wrote, Sears would "present the sixty-eight-year-old Mr. Reagan as a thoughtful but vibrant political leader."

Reagan had been made to sound like Pinocchio to Sears's Geppetto. A Nofziger ally on the staff sent a copy to the governor, annotating all the ways Sears had insulted him.

Jim Lake assured the press that "virtually all the people working on planning Reagan's campaign" agreed with Sears's strategy. The candidate, it appeared, was not one of them: he continued dictating antsy letters defending his right-wing bona fides. "I am as opposed as you to homosexuals being able to advocate their lifestyles," he wrote in one, assuring the recipient that he was "unalterably opposed to the effort on the part of gay rights organizations to demand recognition as they are presently doing." Another debunked a column describing him as "once 'ultra-conservative,' now suddenly ultramodern." His commentaries and columns were hardly less moderate; "DC-10s have replaced Three Mile Island as the source of panic in our daily ration of news but the anti-nuclear forces are still beating the drums," said one describing antinuclear demonstrators as "modern Luddites" who "behind the scenes . . . are being manipulated by forces sympathetic to the Soviet Union." He kept wandering into staff meetings, interjecting right-wing nostrums about how "no nation can survive under fiat money," or how it supposedly cost the Department of Health, Education, and Welfare three dollars to deliver each dollar of benefits.

Many of those meetings were dedicated to crafting policy positions that, Sears promised columnists Witcover and Germond, were marked by their "Nixonian thoroughness." Germond was skeptical. He had recently dined at the Reagans' home at Sears's invitation. The would-be statesman kept going off on bizarre tangents—wondering, for instance, whether Gerald Ford had staged fake assassination attempts to win sympathy for his renomination in 1976, and expressing incredulity that anyone could believe General Eisenhower had had an affair during World War II. Each time, Germond assumed Reagan was joking—until he "looked at Sears and found him staring at the ceiling. Lake seemed preoccupied with his watch." Germond decided to do Reagan the favor of assuming the evening was off the record. "He was always a man with a very loose hold on the real world around him," he wrote of the experience, much later.

Before Reagan's candidacy announcement, there was to be one preparatory effort to display his alleged Nixonian thoroughness on public policy: an address on SALT II to the state Republican convention in San Diego on September 13. Treaty hearings had moved from Frank Church's liberal Foreign Relations Committee to Scoop Jackson's conservative Armed Services Committee, where an entire session was devoted to vituperation directed at Jackson for all the leaks coming from his neoconservative minions. The anti–SALT II campaign, nonetheless, was succeeding: Howard Baker announced his opposition, predicting "another Cuban missile crisis" should the treaty be ratified.

While Reagan's staff labored over the speech, Reagan gave Sears an awful scare. He traveled to Colorado, descending two thousand feet beneath Cheyenne Mountain to the headquarters of the North American Aerospace Defense Command, indulging, with a schoolboy's awe, his fascination with the minutiae of nuclear strategy. "All the way to Los Angeles we were talking about the briefing and what we learned," he wrote in a thank-you note to the general who'd hosted the "enjoyable, interesting, and exciting experience." He was especially delighted by the technology that was tracking thousands of objects in the sky—even "a glove lost by an astronaut that is still circling the earth"—and dismayed that, despite all this technology, there was no way to *protect* against an incoming nuclear weapon. It struck him that the whole terrible business could somehow be made moot if only America could build a gargantuan space shield in the sky. He wanted to mention this unconventional proposal—which some later suggested had lurked in the back of his mind since his star turn in a 1940 B-movie serial in which the Navy devised an "Inertia Projector" that shot rockets out of the sky and "promises to become the greatest force for world peace ever discovered"—in his SALT II speech.

Sears was horrified. The whole point was making Reagan sound *conventional*. Dick Allen hastened to reassure the executive committee that the text was being carved to the finest tolerance to avoid any such provocations—that Reagan had agreed to convey his ideas in a "'respectable,' predictable manner." But, Allen felt obligated to add, "not with any measurable degree of enthusiasm" from Reagan. "I spoke with him at least ten times on the matter, and always had the impression that he was going along with the 'strategy' but didn't think too much of it."

The "Soviet combat brigade" burst into the news. Allen scripted a response should reporters ask the governor about it: "Until we have the answers, SALT II should be set aside." Reagan delivered it flawlessly in an interview with John Sears's favorite media conduit, Godfrey Sperling. But he apparently couldn't help himself in a stroll with reporters around his old stomping grounds, the capitol in Sacramento—where, the UPI reported, the "two-term former governor of California, now 68," who has "spent much of the summer in seclusion at his Santa Barbara, California ranch where aides said he was studying the issues" (because his "handlers" thought "it would be 'foolish' for him to become too visible while he has a commanding lead in the polls"), had blurted out that America should break off *all* communication with Russia until its troops were sent home. A *Philadelphia Enquirer* editorial replied, "It is bad enough that Mr. Reagan projects a shoot-from-the hip image in his view of foreign affairs. It is even worse that he seems to project that image deliberately and apparently considers it a political plus. That is really frightening."

He delivered his speech, calling for nuclear "adequacy" where he had once demanded superiority, and for "shelving" the treaty where he had previously called outright for its defeat. Such Jesuitical distinctions were duly noted by conservatives who called Reagan a sellout, and media commentators who called him a marionette. *Time* published "Candidate Reagan Is Born Again: His Staff Is Grooming Him as a Middle-of-the Roader." The *New York Times* called it "a moderately worded speech today that appeared to reflect efforts by his advisors to make him appear less vehement." The response inspired a flurry of staff memos about the futility of crafting a moderate image when—William Gavin underlined for emphasis—"*it is the fact of the moderation that becomes news.*"

REAGAN MADE MORE NEWS FOR HOW HE WAS GOING BROKE. ONE ARTICLE, "The Big Money's for Connally," reported that the Reagan for President Committee was $500,000 in debt, quoting an embittered Lyn Nofziger: "I think corporate America has simply decided that John Connally is a tougher and bigger and a better candidate."

And what *about* John Connally? *He* was either dominating the field or going nowhere fast; it was hard to tell which.

He rented a house in New Hampshire, intending to stay a spell. But already on the first leg of his "Leadership for America" tour in March, it had become plain those hard-shell Yankees wanted nothing to do with him. So Connally's campaign manager, a shrewd and well-connected operator named Eddie Mahe, called an audible. The nation's second, third, and fourth primaries were all in the South, where a staggering number of 1976 Reagan bitter-enders were defecting to Connally. So that was where Connally would make his stand.

They put the most chips down on Florida, where the party had initiated an especially front-loaded process: a series of sixty-seven county conventions, beginning in August, to elect delegates for the state convention in Orlando on November 11, where a presidential straw poll would be held and the first-round delegates for the national convention chosen. Just like Jimmy Carter in Iowa, they hoped to do so well there that the media would credit Connally's account with that most mystical of political currencies: *momentum.* All it would take, they decided, was a strong second at the state convention. The media would call it a "two-man race"—whereupon Connally could finish off Old Man Reagan once and for all in the South Carolina, Alabama, and Georgia party primaries in March.

His strategy ran on two tracks. Track one, spellbinding oratory before Republican audiences in hotel ballrooms, was going off without a hitch. Connally spoke at an auctioneer's pace, gesticulating like politicians used to do before the age of amplification. When he decried the way other nations supposedly took advantage of the United States—"We're the most vulnerable nation on earth. This country is a hostage!"—respectable Republicans would stand up and scream like he was Ringo Starr and this was 1964. Their greatest delirium followed his signature line demanding that Japan lower its trade barriers or "be prepared to sit on the dock in Yokohama in your Hondas and your Toyotas." (In Florida he added the line "eating your own orange.") They went particularly nuts, one day in Florida, when he stared down a Japanese TV crew while delivering the line.

At a cattle show in Chicago, an awed observer said, his "bubbly confidence had Illinois Republicans shrieking their appreciation." In San Diego, the Kiwanis gave him five standing ovations. ("Normally our speakers receive a polite reception and some clapping.") At one meeting he got a standing ovation before he began. He even got a standing ovation from a meeting of House Republicans. Journos went nuts, too. His crowds, one marveled, veritably "applaud or laugh at his command."

He was capturing something these elites clearly longed for. What was it?

It seemed to have something to do with never apologizing—like when he baited all the goody-two-shoes about Richard Nixon's Oval Office tapes, "They ought to have been burned," or tut-tutted all the "small and bigoted minds" who refused to accept his acquittal on his 1974 corruption charges by an overwhelmingly black and female jury: "What more do you want? Do you want blood?" At one gathering, when he said that, the crowd reportedly "stood and whooped for joy."

They loved his response to what was supposed to be an insult—that he was a "wheeler-dealer": "If you mean someone smart enough to deal with Congress . . . and tough enough to deal with other countries and not give everything away, I'm a wheeler-dealer. If it means someone smart enough to not get caught in a shell game, I'm that smart."

Also, when he answered those who said he was buying the election: he would just say he planned to spend *more* money.

"There's no question in my mind that the man is qualified to be president," said one dazzled state party official. "I think he's shifting the mood of the country," said another. The other candidates were dumbstruck in the face of it. "I remind you that they're one of the best customers Illinois has," Bob Dole said in Chicago about Connally's Japan-baiting, and "very important to rural America." Tepid applause. *Yawn.*

There was only one problem with track one: ordinary voters didn't see the appeal.

Reagan pollster Richard Wirthlin asked respondents to name the first three things that came to their mind at the mention of John Connally's name. The most popular responses were "I don't like him," "Switching parties," and "Not honest/sincere." Only 6.8 percent thought he had "high moral character"—a quality only 1.6 percent thought "not very important" in a president. More than a third of Republicans told pollsters they would never vote for him under any circumstance. The gulf between elite and mass opinion was strikingly revealed when *Newsweek* said one reason Carter had scooted to Camp David in July was because polls showed him losing to "Reagan or Connally." An annoyed public opinion expert wrote a letter to the editor: he wasn't aware of a single poll that gave Connally a chance against Carter.

Maybe plain folks were better at spotting phonies. Nowadays, Connally mocked Jimmy Carter for calling for sacrifice and claiming this was an age of scarcity—but in 1974 he had said scarcity and sacrifice were things "we will have to live with for the rest of our lives." He decried détente—but had previously praised Henry Kissinger to the skies. He called himself a free-market conservative but favored the reestablishment of a version of the Depression-era Reconstruction Finance Corporation to bail out cities and government-approved businesses. He was especially pliant on social issues—first calling himself pro-choice, then telling those ministers who visited his ranch he had seen the light once he'd been shown where in the Bible it said he was wrong. Concluded a conservative skeptic, "Figuratively speaking, Connally wants to sleep in every bed. He cannot be everything to everybody."

But when it came to one issue in particular, John Connally was not flexible at all—and this was surely the biggest source of his popularity deficit. Connally seemed poised to hand over the White House keys to the most despised institutions in America: energy companies. His answer to Carter's July 15 "crisis of confidence" speech was that there would be no crisis if Washington would "immediately deregulate all oil and gas." He then proposed to hand over $5 billion to industry to develop synthetic fuels, no strings attached.

Opinions like these were why Connally had commitments from the top officers of 114 *Fortune* 500 companies; why the chairman of one oil company said, "I'm very fond of the governor. He's my man"; why William F. Buckley said that comparing his energy policy to Carter's was like "Secretariat versus the milkman's horse." (Buckley, after all, sat on a family fortune built by his father's oil wildcatting in Mexico.) But they were also why Garry Trudeau drew a series of particularly mocking *Doonesbury* strips imagining Connally running a therapy group for lachrymose energy titans. According to one poll that spring, 63.8 percent of ordinary voters believed that industry invented the energy crisis to line their pockets. "Connally's gamble that the anti–oil company backlash won't hurt him is a high-risk one" with voters, *Business Week* ventured.

Which helped explain track two of the Connally strategy: fixing it so ordinary voters had as little role in picking the Republican nominee as possible.

Results were mixed. In June, Connally's people successfully packed a party meeting in Arkansas deliberating over replacing the party primary with a caucus; that turned out to be easy, for Sears's asleep-at-the-switch Reagan organization was nowhere to be found. On the other hand, in Texas, in another attempt to put in the fix, Connally loyalists in the legislature introduced a bill to help him by moving the presidential primary from May to June. Hilarity ensued: a dozen Democrats from the thirty-one-seat state senate, dubbed the "Killer Bees," worried that conservatives would be able request a Republican ballot in March and vote for Connally, then declare themselves Democrats in May to vote against *them*. So they hid out to prevent a quorum, evading the Texas Rangers sent to fetch them by hiding in an un-air-conditioned garage apartment with only two beds, three miles from the Capitol. It was funny for everyone except Connally: even after the fugitives were collared, his side was crushed in the vote.

One shrewd media analyst concluded that what his efforts added up to was a "magnificently outfitted battleship with a wooden hull." This was demonstrated when the battleship pulled up alongside Florida. It pounded the state with fusillade after fusillade of broadcast spots, trumpeting a toll-free number to call to learn how *you, too,* could become a delegate at a county Republican convention near you. At the first big county convention, however, in Pinellas, Connally captured only thirty delegates to Reagan's seventy. He purchased a full-page "SPECIAL MESSAGE TO THE PEOPLE OF FLORIDA" in the regional edition of *Time* on September 3. The next week, his wavy-haired visage graced *Time*'s cover ("Very few people know how to handle power, how to keep it from overcoming them," he was quoted observing modestly in the seven-page spread). He won forty of sixty delegates in Sarasota County that day—by, Reagan supporters complained, dragging confused senior citizens from nursing homes. But he still only had about half the Florida delegates Reagan did.

Then, the battleship ran aground.

The governor styled himself the master of the "bold stroke"—like the one in 1971 where he single-handedly persuaded the president to upend the entire international economic system. Now he would venture a bold stroke to humble Reagan. The subject was the Middle East; no grander canvas than that. John Connally believed he knew something about the Middle East. He had many business relationships there. He had purchased a Houston bank in partnership with two Arab sheiks.

And of course he believed he knew something about politics.

In secret, not even telling his campaign manager, Connally began devising an Arab-Israeli peace plan, far more ambitious than Camp David, with his chief policy advisor, Sam Hoskinson, a former CIA and National Security Council staffer—a career civil servant with no political experience, one might wish to note. They worked through some fourteen speech drafts. They worried over whether to consult Henry Kissinger, whom all the contenders were courting (George H. W. Bush promised him secretary of state). They decided to approach him—but Kissinger wouldn't return their calls. So Hoskinson flew to New York and showed up on his literal doorstep. The cagey old operator scowled, ushered Hoskinson inside, read the speech, and advised him to tear it up.

A week before Connally was to speak, he finally showed the text to his staff. Press secretary Jim Brady said it would be a political disaster. Others pointed out that donations from Jews would dry up. His campaign manager, Eddie Mahe, was on a cruise with his wife, a fundamentalist Christian. She read the speech, and announced that she could no longer support her husband's boss. After the governor reassured him that he had reviewed one of its main proposals with King Hussein of Jordan, who hadn't raised any objection, Mahe signed off, reluctantly.

Connally spoke on October 11, at the National Press Club. His "new approach" was based, he said, on "American interests"—not those of Israel or the Arabs. It would have Arab nations, Israel, and the Palestinians sign a peace treaty affirming Israel's right to exist, renouncing violence, and forgoing the use of oil—"the lifeblood of Western civilization"—as a tool to force political changes, in exchange for a Palestinian homeland and for Israel ending its "creeping annexation of the West Bank."

This last was the same delicate subject that Ronald Reagan's advisors had nervously excised from their Israel op-ed two months earlier. Connally's bold stroke was an attempt to show he was not nervous: "A clear distinction must be drawn by the United States between support for Israel's security, which is a moral imperative," he said, "and support for Israel's broader territorial acquisitions." The settlement, and the unimpeded flow of oil, would be vouchsafed by a massive new concentration of American airpower on the bases Israel had given up on the Sinai Peninsula, and a new Fifth Fleet stationed near the Strait of Hormuz. (The fleet idea had been too much for Hoskinson, who said it might sound like the suggestion of a crazed militarist. The old navy secretary, however, insisted.)

Connally exited the Press Club that afternoon in a state of exaltation — "as if," a biographer recorded, he had "become the U.S. president *in abstentia*, showing the way for the stout-hearted to what *had* to be done." That night, speaking in Alabama, he floated as if on a narcotic high. The next day, he had the whole speech printed on a page he had purchased in the *New York Times*; and prepared to reap the veneration that had customarily been his due.

Then, the reviews came in.

A *Times* editorial equated Connally with Jesse Jackson, last seen embracing PLO chairman and terrorism advocate Yasser Arafat. Both Connally and Jackson were attempting to broker Middle East peace, the *Times* said, via "a wicked and dangerous diplomatic bargain" marked by an "unspoken assumption that the United States has an oil problem mainly because American Jews somehow prevent American politicians from forcing a quick West Bank deal on Israel. What else does Mr. Connally mean when he says the country must 'now' base policy on 'American interests'? These are ugly code words that have the effect of blaming Israel and Jews for gas lines." Thirty-four Jewish organizations called the speech a "disservice to the cause of peace." George Will labeled it "extreme, reckless, and self-defeating." The *New Republic* flung what must have been a stinging charge: *naïve.* Did not Connally "know from his Saudi friends that they don't really want an independent Palestinian state in the West Bank"?

A rumor emerged that Connally would be doubling down on the proposal by baiting Israel, delivering a statement from the steps of its embassy in Washington. William Safire said Republican supporters of Israel "made a reassessment of Ronald Reagan and decided he looked ten years younger." David Rockefeller had been expected to attend a Connally dinner; he withdrew his RSVP. Republican grandees and Republican grass roots were finally united in their contempt for John Connally — none more so than Christian conservatives, like Mrs. Mahe, who cherished Israel as the sacred landing pad for the prophesied return of Christ. In the next Gallup Poll, Connally finished fourth, behind Howard Baker.

Florida Republicans met in Orlando, where they could enjoy not one, not two, but three offers of hot air balloon rides from campaigns salivating for their technically meaningless straw-poll votes. Reagan won 36 percent; George Bush, whom many assumed had already dropped out, came in a surprisingly strong third with 22 percent; and Connally got 27 percent, having spent $1,500 per vote, leaving behind box after box of unclaimed free T-shirts reading "CONNALLY—LEADERSHIP FOR

AMERICA." Soundings before the Israel speech had had Connally and Reagan neck and neck.

Among those most disappointed must have been the editors of the *New York Times Magazine*, whose issue for the following Sunday was at the printers. It included a fulsome eight-thousand-word Connally profile, full of grandiose Connally quotations like "They just put speeches in front of Reagan to read" and "Bush sat on his butt in those appointed jobs," and now hilarious editorial judgments like "Behind the swagger is one of the fastest, most experienced minds in national politics." It concluded that if, as was likely, Ronald Reagan suffered George Romney and Edmund Muskie's fate, "Connally would emerge as the Republican to beat—an irresistible choice for those frustrated by a well-meaning but paralyzed presidency, those who want a country that swaggers again the way this candidate does."

AROUND THEN A REMARKABLE EVENT TRANSPIRED IN CONNALLY'S HOME state, at a hotel adjacent to the Dallas–Fort Worth International Airport.

Were some future scribe to set down upon parchment some holy book recording the rise of America's religious right, hotel meeting rooms would surely be overrepresented among its most sacred settings. Though this time, it was an entire hotel floor, cordoned off for a rarified congregation that included Billy Graham, Pat Robertson, Paige Patterson, Charles Stanley, a Notre Dame professor, an Anglican priest, and an Orthodox rabbi. Paul Weyrich had called them there to implore them to join the New Right's crusade. There followed some forty-eight hours of sweaty prayer and earnest discussion. Robert Novak, invited to watch, wrote that this was the point at which he decided "Jimmy Carter's goose was cooked because I saw the intensity of those people." Pat Robertson called it "one of the most moving things I've ever seen." "Minister after minister," Weyrich recalled, stood up and testified: "I was part of Carter's team in 1976. I delivered my congregation for Carter. I urged them all to vote for Carter because I thought he was a moral individual. I found out otherwise." Billy Graham was said to have announced, "I believe God has shown me that unless we have a change in America, we have a thousand days as a free nation"; and Bill Bright to have responded, "I know. I do not believe we'll survive more than three years as a free nation. It's that serious"; and Pat Robertson to have chimed in: "I believe the same thing."

Then—"and I can just remember so well," Robertson related— "Charles Stanley slapped his hand on a table and said, 'I'll give my life to solve this. I'll give everything I've got to turn this country.'" Robertson said, "Me too. I'll die to turn this country. Whatever it takes. We can't lose the country."

Almost every man joined this political altar call—all except for tel-evangelist Rex Humbard, who was still uncomfortable getting involved in elections, and Dr. Graham, still stung by his bad publicity from Watergate. The participants would tell this story in sermons again and again and again; for evangelical culture thrives on legend. Though one fact was always excluded in the telling: the data that clinched their decisions.

Weyrich had raised his $30,000 goal for the massive survey he had dreamed up, of the evangelical rank and file, from the top Republican pollster Lance Tarrance, whose firm spent six weeks in the field inter-viewing hundreds of Christians around the country. For Weyrich's use, questions probed what *issues* were most salient to them—pinpointing the most fruitful discontents to organize. For the benefit of ministers, Tar-rance polled congregants about whether they would continue to support them—spiritually *and* financially—should they become political activists. Now, at the hotel next to the airport, Tarrance presented the results. They were overwhelming. Not only would parishioners accept their ministers' political activity, they were clamoring for it. They wanted to reach into their own wallets to help—"without cutting back on their usual tithing," Tarrance reported. "By the end of the meeting," he remembered, "I had people tripping over themselves to come to me and say, 'What do we do? Tell us what to do.'" Thy will be done, on earth as it is in data.

SO: WHAT *TO* DO? THE ANSWER WAS BECOMING INCREASINGLY CLEAR: DE-vote themselves to the election of Ronald Reagan.

A few months earlier, Reagan posted an impassioned public letter to Henry Hyde—forwarded to any potential supporter who asked about his position on abortion—praising "Henry" for his "courage, determina-tion, and articulate championship of the vital cause of the unborn child in America today." Next came Connally's gaffes concerning the theology of redemption, and his heretical proposal for the Middle East. Then, eight days before Reagan was set to appear on national TV to announce his campaign, the former California governor gave an interview that erased any further doubts.

The interviewer was TV preacher Jim Bakker. "Mr. Carter *said* some things that are right," he intoned softly to his guest. "But he doesn't *ap-point* an evangelical Christian, and he doesn't *act* like an evangelical Chris-tian." Reagan nodded his head in agreement. Bakker continued, "And this has bothered us all. But your stand all the way back, on *all* these issues that are so important to our, so important to us—"

Reagan interrupted. "Do you ever feel that if we don't do it now, if we let this become another Sodom and Gomorrah, that we might be the generation that sees Armageddon?" He was practically whispering—aching with sincerity.

Bakker agreed. "This is the most important election ever to face the United States. I really believe that. And with the *controls* on religion—I don't think anyone knows what has happened in our leadership. In the *crushing* of religion in this country . . ."

And Ronald Reagan nodded some more.

CHAPTER 28

Shocks

SOMETIMES GREAT EVENTS THAT CHANGE HISTORY UNFOLD ON TELEVISION screens for all the world to see. Other times they are effected by tiny groups, working secretly behind closed office doors. That autumn, two events had epochal impacts not just on the presidential year, but on the course of world history. The first one happened behind closed doors.

On Saturday, October 6, 1979, the new Federal Reserve chairman convened a press conference—a rare event, even more so for taking place on a Saturday night. Earlier in the day, Paul Volcker had informed his colleagues, "If I may be so crude, the patient has been constipated for a long time and Ex-lax will no longer work. I'm suggesting an enema." At the press conference, Volcker announced that, in addition to the expected hike in the discount rate the Fed charged to member banks, he was making two changes in the way it fulfilled its mandate to control the nation's money supply. One of those changes was relatively minor—an increase in the amount banks would be required to keep in their vaults in reserve. The other change, however, was colossal, amounting to a radical shift in how the American economy worked. But it was also sufficiently esoteric, and so blandly presented, that most outlets buried it at the bottom of their stories, with UPI not mentioning it at all.

The Federal Reserve System is a peculiar institution. Entirely foreign to any article of the Constitution, answerable only to itself, its job is to set the terms by which banks acquire money, to endeavor to maximize employment, stabilize prices, and moderate long-term interest rates—veritably, to control the economy. And since the first two of those goals are often in tension, affecting different classes of Americans in completely different ways, that job is inherently political.

There was a cliché frequently repeated by politicians. It described inflation as the "cruelest tax," because, as Ronald Reagan put it in 1975, it hits "those hardest who can least afford it." But this is not so. Inflation taxes investors: if a bond matures when inflation is high, the bondholder's profit is diminished. Inflation also taxes corporations: they lose money if their rate of profit does not keep up with the inflation. And, of course, inflation also taxes the ordinary schlub who has to pay ten bucks for a tank of gas that used to cost six.

But. If that same schlub belonged to a union that negotiated a cost of living adjustment in his employment contract, as was the case for most factory workers, inflation hardly hurt him at all. (It didn't necessarily hurt nonunion workers much, either: employers tended to raise wages in concert with the best union contracts, to keep workers from fleeing, or seeking to unionize their workplace, too.) And if that same schlub was paying down a fixed-rate mortgage, he was better off if inflation *increased*: he had borrowed dollars that were dear, but would pay back the loan with dollars that were cheap.

For people like this, the biggest financial problem caused by inflation—"bracket creep"—was easily fixed by indexing tax rates to inflation, which required no intervention in the broader economy. For Americans further down the income scale, many government social insurance payments were already indexed. As a New York University economist named Edward Wolff summarized the data in a 1978 study in the *Review of Income and Wealth*, inflation was like "a progressive tax, leading to greater equality in the distribution of wealth." That was why Federal Reserve policy was political. It effected distribution by stealth.

According to Arthur Burns, the Federal Reserve chairman appointed by Richard Nixon in 1970, who served through 1978, the Fed could have easily ended the Great Inflation of the 1970s at any time: "it could have restricted money supply and created sufficient strain in the financial and industrial markets to terminate inflation with little delay. It did not do so because the Federal Reserve was itself caught up in the philosophical currents that were transforming American life and culture." He was referring to the notion all that Americans had a right to share in the nation's growing prosperity—the obligation central bankers felt to maximize employment and increase access to credit. But as Burns bemoaned, this introduced "a strong inflationary bias" into the economy.

Burns said this in a speech called "The Anguish of Central Banking." Conservative economists described this anguish with blunt honesty. The libertarian James Buchanan complained that inflation, by encouraging borrowing, "prompts behavioral responses" in which "'Enjoy, enjoy!'—the imperative of our time—becomes a rational response in a setting where tomorrow remains insecure and where the plans made yesterday seem to have been made in folly." Milton Friedman wrote that when politicians purchased votes by cheapening dollars, "prudent behavior becomes reckless and 'reckless' behavior becomes prudent." This, according to a conservative thinker named Henry Hazlitt, whose book *Economics in One Lesson* had profoundly influenced Ronald Reagan, made people *immoral*. "During every great inflation," he said in 1978, "there is a striking decline in both public and private morality." What allowed this disastrous state of affairs to continue, a former Federal Reserve economist said in the *Wall Street Journal* in June 1979, was "the almost universal commitment to the objective of 'full employment'" and the "welfare-state idea which holds that government ought to have a continuing active concern with the poor, the sick, the aged, and the chronically unemployed."

Conservatives made such arguments to little avail: Arthur Burns's anguished central bankers kept on responding to popular pressure to pump more money into the system. Then, the economic events of 1979 rendered these arguments persuasive further left on the ideological spectrum. Manic financial speculation—*reckless behavior becoming prudent*—was being indulged in as never before, up and down the economic ladder, accelerating the inflationary spiral as never before. Farmers bought more land and fancy new equipment on borrowed money, putting up land as collateral, which increased the price of land, providing them more collateral to borrow more. Southern Californians scooped up extra houses as investments, also on credit. During the month of September, economic growth was about 2 percent—but bank lending increased by 22 percent.

The Federal Reserve had been responding by gradually raising interest rates—which is to say, increasing the cost of borrowing. The way it would know if this was working was that investors would indicate their "confidence" in the dollar by investing in dollars. Instead, the opposite was happening. Up in the empyrean heights of the international currency markets, the Mexican peso, of all things, was becoming a favorite of traders; down on the ground, anyone who could was trading dollars for precious metals. Which was why the price of silver had tripled since January, gold had climbed 29 percent in a month to $411 an ounce—and the owner of a precious metal exchange in the Empire State Building in New York had to hire a security guard to handle the crowds who slept outside his store to be the first ones in line every morning to trade in family heirlooms, bags of pre-1964 quarters, and in the case of one dentist, $3,000 worth of gold and silver fillings.

But at the Federal Reserve's grand, columned marble palace in Washington, D.C., whose bronze ceremonial doors facing Constitution Avenue never opened, the chairman whom Jimmy Carter had installed practically by accident had an idea about how to make it stop.

Raising interest rates was not working. The inflation rate was now 13 percent and climbing, but economic activity was not slowing. That was because everyone kept making bets that buying now and paying later would pay off. They rationally expected that the dollar would keep getting weaker—a self-fulfilling prophesy, for the more these bets compounded, the weaker the dollar became.

The reason this behavior could not be quieted simply by jacking up interest rates was that the expectation that interest rates would *soon* rise compounded the frenzy to buy more on credit now. One Federal Reserve governor compared it to a traffic signal turning yellow: it just caused people to speed up before it turned red. Paul Volcker called this the "froth of inflationary expectations." By October 1979, there was so much froth that one of the Federal Reserve's governors, Henry Wallich, who had grown up in Germany in the early 1920s when deutschmarks were so devalued that people had to cart them around by the wheelbarrow, was terrified that, just possibly, it could happen here.

And maybe it could. Maybe Paul Volcker had little choice—politics be damned. Or maybe not.

When Jimmy Carter had first met this inflation hawk in July, he was surprised to discover he was a Democrat. Not, however, the sort of Democrat who scrupled too much about causing high unemployment. He said as much in his confirmation hearings: curbing inflation would be his paramount priority. He would "call the shots as we see them." What had anguished his predecessors did not anguish him at all.

Paul Volcker also deeply admired Milton Friedman. He especially admired what had previously been considered one of Friedman's most radical ideas. As things presently stood, the central bank's Open Markets Committee met every six or eight weeks, poring over zillions of indicators to recommend changes in the money supply on a continual basis, taking an active and ongoing role in adjusting the economy month by month. Milton Friedman's idea was that the Federal Reserve should act *all at once* to contract the money supply, then *fix* the rate at which it grew—*forever*. No more active adjusting of the economy to ensure its smooth functioning. *That* was the colossal technical fix in the Federal Reserve's operating system that Volcker had decided to institute: instantly turning the traffic signal red.

When he first explained it to others inside the marble temple, they were horrified. Wallich, the survivor of Weimar hyperinflation, protested that traders would hysterically overreact if the Fed removed themselves from an active role in setting interest rates and had the market do it instead. The underlying economy would be destabilized in wrenchingly unpredictable ways, for who knew how long. Creating stable markets, Wallich insisted, was what they were being paid to do. He called it "a pact with the devil."

"Sometimes," Volcker replied, "you have to deal with the devil."

Over several days in late September, Volcker worked to convince his seven-member board of governors. On September 29, he boarded a plane with Treasury Secretary William Miller and White House Council of Economic Advisers Chairman Charles Schultze for Belgrade, Yugoslavia, to join representatives of 138 other nations at the triennial conference of the International Monetary Fund. There, for the first time, a select few public officials learned how the American economy was about to be upended. Miller, the previous Fed chairman, roared back that the price of credit would skyrocket, the economic gears would grind, and that inflation would, at first, *increase*—possibly for years. Schultze agreed—adding that when recession descended, there would be nothing the self-manacled Fed could do to abate it.

That, Volcker responded, was precisely the point. "What I hoped," he later explained, "was that there would be a strong reaction in the markets. Interest rates would rise sharply at first, but that would have a favorable impact on inflationary expectation, so that long-term rates would start coming down. The sign of psychological success was whether long-term rates would stabilize and start coming down."

What these two political appointees understood was that there was no way this would happen before the 1980 presidential election. Volcker allowed that he understood their concerns, would think them over, and let the administration review the plan before he announced it. All present knew that legally he didn't owe Carter that much—or, really, an explanation. In Belgrade, Volcker seemed to consider himself more accountable to the likes of the chancellor of West Germany, Helmut Schmidt—who lectured that unless the United States acted effectively to combat inflation, Germany wouldn't repeat its action of a year earlier, when Schmidt had led international efforts to rescue the dollar. As the *New York Times* colorfully put it, "The Europeans all but backed him up against the Berlin Wall to tell him squarely that, although America may take some perverse pleasure from its perpetual inflation, its chief trading partners and allies do not."

Such international considerations were another way inflation policy was inherently political. Europe squeezing the U.S. in *its own* manufacturers' interests. Thus, in addition to the recession it was intentionally inducing, would the "Volcker shock" screw American workers twice over.

That IMF meeting was where Arthur Burns delivered his "Anguish of Central Banking" speech. Most who heard the Nixon appointee insist that it was "illusory to expect central banks to put an end to the inflation that now afflicts the industrial democracies" had no idea that those words were already moot.

Schultze and Miller failed to dissuade Volcker from leaving Belgrade early to finalize his plan. On October 4, the Department of Commerce announced that wholesale prices had shot up 1.4 percent in the previous month. Gold hit $444 per ounce. On October 6, Volcker summoned the Federal Reserve's Board of Governors, its Open Markets Committee, and the leaders of the system's five regional banks to the marble palace—"and none of us knew why," the president of the St. Louis Fed, Larry Roos, said. Then, brilliantly and methodically, Volcker outlined why this radical scheme was imperative. "Damndest thing," said Roos. "I nearly fell out of my chair when I observed that all of my colleagues, many of whom had been disdainful, were now all supporting a monetarist approach."

The financial press was hastily summoned to the Fed's opulent two-and-a-half-story-high conference room. Volcker entered through a side door, lowered his six-foot, seven-inch, 240-pound frame into a chair at the head of the massive table in front of a black marble fireplace, an American eagle statue looming dramatically above his head. "His colleagues," a journalist recorded, "were barely visible through the cloud of pipe and cigar smoke."

Volcker's message was cloudy, too. He said his measures would bring "credit under surer control" (it was the opposite). In a dispatch the AP wired to its thousands of client newspapers—it ran on the same front pages as news of the capture of a sniper threatening to blow up six San Francisco blocks—he was paraphrased as having insisted that the Fed would not "completely cut off credit" (the word *completely* was the only thing that kept it from being a fib); and that the Fed's new plan would place "less emphasis on confining short-term fluctuations in the federal funds" (which was true only if "less emphasis" meant "no emphasis"). He also said that "the flow of money from banks to consumers will stabilize," which would "avoid uncertainties about the outlook for prices," and "that these actions will ultimately have a settling effect on the financial markets"—a deception, because he knew the "settling effect" would take years. He also said that "the best indications that I have now, in an uncertain world, is that this can be accomplished reasonably smoothly." That was the biggest deception of all.

Jimmy Carter had been promising all year that "we will not try to wring inflation out of our economic system by pursuing policies designed to bring about a recession." But this was precisely what the Volcker shock would do. Schultze and Miller had tried to persuade President Carter to jawbone Volcker into reconsidering his announcement, or at least criticize it to distance himself from the political consequences. Carter refused. Maybe because Volcker had been deceptive with him—as indeed he had been deceptive about his plans ever since his confirmation hearings in July. Or maybe Carter simply decided he liked what Volcker was up to.

Once, a preference for low interest rates had been a Democratic article of faith, a token of the party's New Deal populism. (Squeezing credit, Harry Truman once cried after his Fed chair raised interest rates, "is exactly what Mr. Stalin wants.") *This* Democratic president, however, seemed to welcome Volcker's shock as a contribution to the ethic of sacrifice he so revered. He sent out spokesman Jody Powell to announce in time for the next day's papers that the president expected the Federal Reserve's actions would "help reduce inflationary expectations, contribute to a stronger U.S. dollar abroad, and curb unhealthy speculations in commodity markets," and that "success in reducing inflationary pressures will lead in due course both to lower rates of price increases and to lower interest rates."

In due course. In Milton Friedman's estimate, offered in a thrilled review in his *Newsweek* column, his acolyte's plan, "if strictly adhered to," might "end inflation in the next five years." It actually took only four—by which time the economy had lost 2.4 million manufacturing jobs, with a far greater proportion of the national income flowing to investors than to Americans who worked for wages. By which time President Jimmy Carter was no longer president.

THE IMMEDIATE EFFECTS OF THE "VOLCKER SHOCK" WERE ILLUSTRATED ON the cover of *Time*: a portrait of the Fed chair surrounded by a squiggle of economic indicator arrows heading off maniacally in every direction—ending up mostly pointing sharply down. The Dow fell more than 10 percent in two weeks. The federal funds rate—the interest rate over which the Fed used to have the most direct control—jumped 15 percent in a day. IBM had had the bad luck to put out a bond issue that week; the syndicate that underwrote it lost a quick $50 million. Traders dubbed it the "Saturday-night special"—the nickname for the cheap pistols crooks used to commit criminal mayhem. That Wednesday, on PBS's *MacNeil-Lehrer Report*, Volcker called traders' response "constructive": the *point* was to "capture their attention. . . . A lot of people were skeptical about whether we could deal with inflation. I hope they're less skeptical now." Although, in a speech the day before, Volcker suggested that the responsibility belonged merely to impersonal market forces, not him—"after years of inflation, the long run has caught up with us."

Tremors rippled through the "real economy." Like when a credit union in Portland decided to restrict loans to "non-luxury items": no money for recreational vehicles, furniture, boats, vacations—or stock purchases. Chemical Bank used to require an income of $8,000 for those seeking consumer loans. They raised that to $10,000. It became harder to buy a home even if you could afford the higher interest: some savings and loans stopped taking applications for new mortgages altogether; others lowered the maximum amounts they would lend, or limited loans to existing customers, or demanded larger down payments. In Dublin, California, a car dealer fired a third of his staff, and struggled to keep his business operating at 50 percent capacity. In Portsmouth, Virginia, a previously successful homebuilder decided to up and liquidate his business. A wise decision: one of his colleagues sold only a single house in the next two years.

In a *New York Times* feature on the fiftieth anniversary of the 1929 Wall Street crash, the legendary eighty-year-old libertarian economist Friedrich Hayek said, "We are much too afraid of another depression to really fight inflation. I think you could stop it completely by just keeping the money supply and money wages where they are. It would cause a short, severe depression, but it might be over in six months." Paul Volcker offered similar sentiments in testimony to the Congressional Joint Economic Committee on October 17: "The standard of living of the average American has to decline. I don't think you can escape that." He was followed by Treasury Secretary Miller, who defended him: "High and persistent inflation has become deeply embedded in our economic structure and is a clear and present danger to our national wellbeing. Containment of inflation is fundamental to a restoration of sound economic growth."

An unheeded minority protested that nothing good could come of this pain. Two economists from the investment research firm Sanford C. Bernstein & Co. wrote a report complaining that a technical claim at the foundation of Volcker's plan—that the size of "non-borrowed reserves" determined the money supply—was objectively false; they were ignored. Some members of the Fed governing committee, after joining the unanimous vote in October, changed their minds by November. The president of the Federal Reserve Bank of Minneapolis argued at a meeting of the now neutered Federal Reserve Open Markets Committee that no one could predict whether the program would have the intended results. The president of the American Economic Association, Robert Solow of MIT, said that a "monetary policy designed to stop inflation by inducing a downturn" was "disproportionately costly": "The effect on prices is small and long delayed. . . . It is burning down the house to roast the pig." There was no policy discussion about how the transition might be eased for those whose economic houses had been incinerated through no fault of their own, to roast somebody else's pig. There couldn't have been: it had been sprung as a complete surprise.

But elite opinion was largely ecstatic. *Newsweek* praised a long-overdue "radical shock treatment for the economy." Alan Greenspan enthused that "if adhered to, it would be the most important change in monetary policy in a generation." The hosannas came from liberals, too. Nicholas von Hoffman, a journalist who first came to prominence for his sympathetic reporting on hippies in San Francisco, published an extended panegyric in the *New York Times Magazine* that placed Arthur Burns's "anguish of central banking" narrative at its center. "The forces that will be working away at Volcker," von Hoffman wrote, were "deep, and enormously powerful. In the modern era, no Fed chairman or his board has been able to resist the political pressure—the demands for 'accommodation,' as the bankers call it—for long." In von Hoffman's description, Chairman Burns had been a veritable ninety-eight-pound weakling, Volcker a "stubborn mule, the intellectual activist, the rock of integrity," whose "mettle needed to end the costly price climb" was only matched by his selflessness: he had, after all, taken a $53,000-a-year pay cut from his previous job.

The cult of the swaggering John Connally had passed. The cult of Volcker replaced it practically without missing a beat.

AMERICANS LONGED FOR A MAN ON HORSEBACK—EVEN IF HE WORE A CASsock. Pope John Paul II received a delirious reception visiting the U.S. On October 5, he said mass in Chicago's Grant Park before an estimated 1.5 million pilgrims, by no means all of them Catholic, terrifying city officials that the ground might buckle beneath the weight and collapse into the underground garage. The reverence partly owed to the pontiff's world-shaking visit that June to his native city of Warsaw, which had achieved what no American president, let alone Jimmy Carter, ever had: making the Kremlin shudder in fear of losing hold of one of their satellite nations.

Newsweek's Meg Greenfield called it "leadership chic"—"this season's motherhood and apple pie." Her main exhibit was Volcker's "bash on the head" announcement, the "damn the side effects and costs" manner in which he made it, and the near-universal acclaim it received. She noted, as well, Jimmy Carter's new habit of pounding his fist while delivering speeches, and his "manly imprecation, 'I'll whip his ass,'" concerning Senator Kennedy. He was giving the public what it wanted, a *New York Times*/CBS poll suggested. Voters were asked whether they would "be more likely to vote for someone who would step on some toes and bend some rules to get things done." Two-thirds said that they would.

The writer Victor Gold published a satire about this longing for strongmen in *Washingtonian* magazine: It is 1980, and the American people, dissatisfied with the failure of Lyndon Johnson's Texas mafia (who "botched a simple contract hit in Southeast Asia"), Nixon's California mafia ("couldn't even handle a third-rate burglary")—"and the less said about the Georgia mafia, the better"—turned over the White House "to the real thing—the *Mafia* Mafia." America's energy concerns immediately abated, once "the Ayatollah Khomeini and Muammar Qaddafi each woke up with a sacred ram's head at the foot of their beds." The new president's first State of the Union address ("The only thing you have to fear is *me*") was followed by his only press conference. ("That's a good question," he replied to a *Washington Post* reporter who asked him to spell out his agenda. *"Don't ask it again."*) The Supreme Court, Congress, the Brookings Institution, Harvard University, Common Cause, the IRS, "and the entire cast and crew of *Sixty Minutes*" all disappeared—and impressed pundits gave their seal of approval, Joseph Kraft having taken the temperature of the electorate and discovering that "the current resident at 1600 Pennsylvania Avenue has the support of the American people in whatever enterprise he chooses to undertake." The president's two sons, asked how they would help their father's reelection, replied, "Lean on a few people and keep our noses clean."

Was the satire a little broad? Possibly not. Even Meg Greenfield didn't *blame* Paul Volcker for having to step on a few toes and bend some rules to get things done; she mostly regretted that American society had fallen to such dissolution that the shock was required. The editors of the *New York Times Magazine*, in the same issue as Von Hoffman's ode to Volcker, published an essay, "The Looming 1980s," arguing that the " 'no-fault' attitudes of the past decades . . . must yield to a new era in which Americans will rediscover 'personal guilt'—the acceptance of individual responsibility."

One of the bizarre things about this new conventional wisdom concerning American softness was how closely it resembled what Jimmy Carter had been saying—even though Carter himself was being held up as the exemplar of how American leadership had failed.

Then, on November 4, the next event that changed history going into the presidential election year burst onto the TV screens—and made all too plain that leadership chic would not be abating anytime soon.

IRAN WAS GOING BERSERK. LATE IN THE SUMMER, ORIANA FALLACI WAS RE- ceived there like a conquering hero because of the 1973 interview she had published revealing Shah Mohammad Reza Pahlavi as a power-hungry madman. She found herself less welcome when she revealed the purpose of her visit: to "interview this Khomeini, to ask him how he dared to call his bloodbath a revolution."

Khomeini had installed as chief jurist Ayatollah Mohammed Sadeq Givi Khalkhali, who had spent time as a youth in a mental hospital for strangling cats, a hobby in which it was said he still indulged. Among his jurisprudential innovations was the concept of "obvious guilt"—which was how he did away with testimony and defense lawyers, skipping straight to gigglingly pronouncing sentences of execution in five minutes or less. When he ran out of former government officials, Fallaci wrote, "the firing squads turned on adulterers and alleged adulterers, on homosexuals or alleged homosexuals, on young lovers caught showing their affection, on women who went around with their heads uncovered or partially uncovered, on the absent-minded who were caught drinking a beer or a glass of wine."

Through the personal intervention of the prime minister of the provisional government, Mehdi Bazargan, Fallaci miraculously received permission to interview the imam. Bazargan was universally respected even though he was a defender of secularism. He dreamed of establishing Iran as a Western-style representative democracy. He even had the courage to shake Fallaci's hand.

She set out for Qom, a borrowed chador hidden away in her purse; for a woman to present herself in the holy city not draped hair to toe in black was inconceivable. The only problem was where to put it on. The desert highway was bereft of a single gas station. She asked her handler if she might change in the car. He answered, "In the name of Allah! Are you joking!"

They approached the bustling city; Fallaci hid beneath window level until they found an inconspicuous spot on the sidewalk. As she wrestled the thing over her clothes, her hair became momentarily visible; "I was cursed fearfully." They tried a hotel, were immediately hustled out. The handler entered another establishment alone, and managed to secure a room key; Fallaci was ejected the moment she crossed the threshold. At a third hotel she got twenty feet inside—but the only employee who would speak to her refused a bribe to allow her use of a bathroom.

They found their way to the mayor's office. A kindly officer allowed them access to a chamber that was empty except for a single ornate gold seat—the throne room, unused since the shah's abdication. Then someone happened into the room. Her handler unleashed "the groan of a creature who has lost all hope." The intruder dutifully delivered them to a mullah, who ruled that a married man alone in a room with a woman was guilty of adultery. The handler saved their skin in the only way he could think of: he fetched an official, and Oriana Fallaci became the man's second wife.

She searched in vain in *The Commandments of Ayatollah Khomeini*, the guidebook to daily living sold in every Tehran street stall, to learn how she might gain an annulment. Given that she suffered neither from insanity, madness, leprosy, blindness, skin disease, lameness, or sexual defects, and her new husband was neither mad nor, as best she knew, missing a genital organ, for all she knew she was married to him still.

PERHAPS THE SITUATION WOULD NOT HAVE GROWN SO FRENZIED HAD THE Ayatollah's forces not felt so besieged. The course of their revolution had not run smooth. It began in a bloom of ideological pluralism, sidewalk vendors sold publications from Islamist to Marxist, even Marxist-Islamist. Then, Khomeini loyalists began a bid for complete control.

One of the most important was Sadegh Ghotbzadeh, a veteran anti-shah activist educated at the Georgetown School of Foreign Service, placed in charge of state television and radio, where he undertook a purge of leftists—these via execution—and women, and instituted worse censorship than the shah's. In March, twenty thousand women took to the streets to protest. Several thousand more, in chadors—"wingless bats," Fallaci called them—protested the protesters. One of the liberals shot at Ghotbzadeh's limousine and another injured a bodyguard with a knife.

On April 1, Khomeini claimed he had received a 97 percent mandate in a referendum to institute an Islamic republic, declaring "the first day of a government of God." This was followed two weeks later by protests from thousands shouting "Down with Khomeini," carrying portraits of Tehran's most popular liberal clerk, Ayatollah Mahmoud Taleghani, who said that Khomeini was worse than the shah. His sons were then kidnapped and tortured.

The following week a general was murdered. At his funeral procession, a man in an air force uniform failed to assassinate Prime Minister Bazargan with a machine gun. A week later, his faction successfully cut down the chairman of the Revolutionary Council. Khomeini responded by establishing an Army of the Guardians of the Islamic Revolutionary Council—his very own SAVAK.

The last independent newspaper suspended publication. Anti-Khomeini forces announced a breakaway National Democratic Front. Unemployment was estimated between 35 and 50 percent. Farms were left unattended, the transportation infrastructure to get crops to markets having collapsed. Fallaci estimated that 80 percent of the stores in big cities were closed. Government agencies were paralyzed. Tehran's once-gleaming airport fell to greasy, graffiti-covered ruin. Given these manifest practical failings, the Islamists' most effective weapon of control became the stoking of hysteria. Almost daily street processions; mobs burning any building that contained liquor to the ground; fatwas pronounced against regime enemies.

And scapegoats, many, many scapegoats—like the United States, which Khomeini labeled the "Great Satan." And the Kurds seeking autonomy in the northern territories, against whom Khomeini declared a holy war. The Ayatollah Khalkhali set up itinerant kangaroo courts in the Kurdish regions, which inaugurated nearly random executions, sometimes more than sixty in a day. Since Iran's army was a shambles, vigilantes commandeered taxis, buses, motorcycles, and trucks and headed north to kill Kurds themselves. The thin regular forces shot into these mobs, which pressed on nonetheless, carrying out massacre after massacre, insisting they were acting on the authority of the imam.

And, also, the shah—no matter that the former king was living like a high-class mendicant. He alighted at a resort in Egypt; then was forced to leave with his massive security retinue after a week for a "visit" to Morocco, where he was kicked out after ninety days by a king who feared revolt from *his* nation's Islamist revolutionaries. Then it was to the Bahamas, where the shah's sixty-day visa was not renewed; and, finally, Mexico, where he reposed in an eleven-bedroom villa, idling away the hours at the Cuernavaca Racquet Club. In the imagination of Iranians, he was plotting with the Central Intelligence Agency for his return, just like in 1956—even though the CIA now had no more power to control events than the shah did.

There were four CIA agents in the entire country. One, who had arrived shortly before the revolution, was on his first tour, and knew almost nothing about Iran. Another, in March, was beaten within an in inch of his life by a mob. In May, after the Senate unanimously passed a resolution condemning the government slaughtering Jews, Baha'is, and political opponents, the Manhattan apartment of its sponsor, Senator Jacob Javits, had to be placed under twenty-four-hour armed guard. For in Iran the resolution was taken as self-evident proof that the U.S. intended to begin the restoration any day.

In fact, Jimmy Carter hoped to achieve a diplomatic accommodation with the revolution, not least in the hopes of protecting Americans still living there. In late February Khomeini had sent an emissary pledging friendship and cooperation should the U.S. not interfere in Iran, and Carter gave him that assurance.

Shortly afterward, Carter sought to further protect Americans by recruiting two emissaries whom the shah trusted to request that he not seek shelter in the United States. But Carter was tragically unlucky in his choice of emissaries. "Don't worry about another embassy attack," a Washington CIA official had recently reassured one of his colleagues in Iran. "The only thing that could trigger an attack would be if the Shah was let into the United States—and no one in this town is stupid enough to do that." That would make Henry Kissinger, and Kissinger's dear friend David Rockefeller, very stupid people indeed—for instead of fulfilling Carter's request to tell the shah *not* to come, they set up a veritable lobbying office in a tony Manhattan town house to pressure Carter to change his mind. Their effort had a code name: Project Eagle. It even extended to efforts by David Rockefeller to find suitable living quarters for the shah in the United States. ("Not large enough for my very special client," he wrote a Realtor who had pointed him to two estates worth $2 million each.)

Rockefellers and Pahlavis had long enjoyed terms of intimacy. Nelson Rockefeller had first visited Iran as a guest of the last shah's father, in 1931, and had enjoyed a particularly convivial visit with the son in 1977 dedicating a majestic new museum of contemporary art. David Rockefeller's Chase Manhattan Bank held Iranian deposits from the monarchy exceeding $1 billion and had financed $1.7 billion of Iranian public works projects, and held $2.5 million of the shah's personal fortune. As for Kissinger, the sort of high-flying Middle East shuttle diplomacy that made him famous would have been inconceivable absent Mohammad Reza Pahlavi's good offices. Both believed hosting the shah was America's unquestionable duty.

They prevailed upon Howard Baker, whom Carter still hoped would come around on SALT II, to help. They won over Gerald Ford ("I told him why this was a problem, with potential kidnapping of American diplomats," Carter wrote in his diary on April 11 of his meeting with the former president); perhaps they influenced George Will, who wrote in his *Washington Post* column that denying the shah sanctuary was "inconsistent with a great nation's self-respect." Richard Nixon joined Operation Eagle, visiting the shah in Acapulco. John J. McCloy, the eighty-four-year-old dean of foreign policy mandarins, wrote the State Department's second-highest official, Warren Christopher, that to bar him "could seriously impair our ability to obtain the support of those of whom we might well stand in need."

The president was unimpressed. On April 19, the shah was informed he was not welcome in the United States. Three weeks later, Ayatollah Khalkhali pronounced a death sentence upon his entire family, which he said could be legally carried out anywhere in the world. The Iranian government offered $135,000 and a free trip to Mecca to anyone who killed the shah—though Khalkhali announced that the former empress could spare herself by doing it herself.

AS ALWAYS, ADVICE TO THE PRESIDENT FROM HIS FOREIGN POLICY OFFI-cials was divided. The hawks were at Zbigniew Brzezinski's National Security Council, who reported, "Khomeini is his own worst enemy. Left to his own devices, he will destroy himself," that while Minister Bazargan's rational secularists "lose more often than they win, they are buying time and giving Khomeini a chance to discredit himself by his extremism." So Brzezinski advised covert aid to the secularists, and that Carter should fear violent backlash from the hapless Islamists should he succor the shah. But at the State Department, Vance warned of "possible dangers to American people" if he took that course; *his* Iran expert warned that confidence the U.S. could muster *any* control over Iranian events was hubris—"We simply do not have the bios, inventory of political groups or current picture of daily life as it evolves at various levels in Iran. Ignorance here of Iran's events is massive."

For the time being, the president decided America was best served by goodwill toward the revolution. When terror attacks by Arab separatists in Iran reduced oil refinery capacity by 80 percent, for instance, he authorized emergency shipments of kerosene and home heating oil. *Diplomacy*: this was how normal states behaved with one another, after all.

But in Iran, normal was nowhere to be found.

In July, Ayatollah Khomeini banned music on radio and TV. A new press code prescribed three years in jail for journalists spreading "insults, calumny, or falsehoods" against religious leaders, banning them from interviewing Iranians outside the presence of the Ministry of National Guidance. In August, he announced that a planned constituent assembly would be entirely filled by his loyalists, mostly clergy; the next day, militants guarding the United States embassy compound, having lost Khomeini's favor, were usurped by another squad of revolutionaries in a machine gun battle. Then protests against the new press law led to the worst riots since January. Nonetheless, on September 4, the Associated Press office was ordered closed; four days later, the government shut down all publishers expressing disagreements with the regime. The next evening, a popular mullah who had been protesting massacres of Kurds fell facedown onto his supper plate, dead. Publicly, Khomeini cried crocodile tears—not least, Fallaci said, because "his death provided an excuse for the umpteenth procession, attended by hundreds of thousands, men on one side and veiled women on the other, paralyzing the city from sunup to sundown ... human magma that extended for miles like a shroud."

Now Khomeini had no credible opposition. On September 12, the body drafting a new constitution approved a clause granting supreme power to mullahs. On the 14th, Khomeini declared that candidates for parliament had to be clergymen. The secular interim government was supposed to be running the country. Khomeini was supposed to be a figurehead. Instead, it was the other way around.

Foreign Minister Ebrahim Yazdi traveled to New York to lead Iran's delegation to the new United Nations session. He met with American officials to insist spare parts and kerosene weren't enough: America must return both the shah's monetary assets and all shah loyalists to Iran—and to their deaths.

A complication developed. An assistant of David Rockefeller's insisted to the State Department that the shah was so gravely ill with cancer that he could only be treated at Memorial Sloan Kettering in New York. "Whether the shah might have received comparable treatment in Mexico City," a historian later wrote, "remained controversial for years to come."

At that, Cyrus Vance reversed himself: he said the shah should be admitted for treatment on "humanitarian grounds." He told Carter that if he was not, Kissinger might abandon the SALT II ratification fight. (Mostly, he already had.) Hamilton Jordan raised the specter of what Kissinger might say if the shah died: "that first you caused the shah's downfall and now you've killed him." Walter Mondale, the voice Carter perhaps trusted most, had long advocated offering sanctuary; back in July, Carter had snapped back, *Fuck the shah! He's just as well playing tennis in Acapulco as he is in California.*" The health situation, however, weighed on him. Carter, after all, doted upon his image as a humanitarian. On October 19, he asked his national security team point-blank: "Does somebody here have the answer as to what we do if the diplomats in our embassy are taken hostage?" There followed an interval of silence.

"I gather not. On that day we will all sit here with long, drawn faces, and realize that we've been had."

He nonetheless scrawled "OK" on the face of a memo from Vance reading, "If we decide to permit the shah to come to the United States for treatment, we would want to inform the Iranians that we were doing so for humanitarian purposes and to leave open any question of future residency."

The next day, a CIA agent at the Tehran embassy stared incredulously at a cable announcing that decision. America's chargé d'affaires in Iran, Bruce Laingen, informed Prime Minister Bazargan and Foreign Minister Yazdi, with whom his relations were warm, of Carter's plans. Yazdi responded, "You're opening Pandora's box with this." The shah entered the U.S. on October 22; "The eagle has landed," David Rockefeller's chief of staff reported, as if rejoicing. On the 24th, Vance told Carter that at the embassy in Tehran, "the past two days have been calm." Two days later, Bazargan and Yazdi arranged a short meeting with Brzezinski on the sidelines of a ceremony in Tangiers celebrating the twenty-fifth anniversary of Algerian independence, relaying Iranian fears that the shah was in New York to plot his restoration. Brzezinski assured them the shah was too sick to try any such thing, and encouraged Iran to sue in United States courts to recoup his assets, and was so delighted to find the leaders of Iran's government intelligent and competent that he advised Washington that normalization with a stabilizing Iran was reasonably on track.

IT HAD NOT BEEN PARTICULARLY DIFFICULT FOR A CABAL OF IRANIAN STU-dents to set all that on its ear.

Their idea to sit in at an embassy was arrived at by the core group in the third week of October. The main dispute was *which* embassy to seize: Two preferred the Soviet Union's. Two wanted the United States'. America's decision to take in the shah ended that argument.

On Friday, November 2, around a hundred students from Tehran's four big universities—though many were so busy with politics they hadn't attended classes for a year or more—attended a meeting at which a civil engineering student outlined a plan. "What we are proposing is a peaceful occupation of the American embassy—without arms," he explained. "This will mean taking the embassy personnel hostage, not as diplomatic personnel, but as agents of the American government. They are deeply involved in their government's conspiracies in any case." A colleague displayed crudely drawn maps, explaining how a few hundred students might penetrate, then occupy, the main building. Perhaps they could even stay overnight—like American students used to do in university administration buildings in the 1960s.

The action would come Sunday morning, when embassy activity was at a minimum, during a procession to honor the first anniversary of a massacre at Tehran University, which Khomeini had declared as National Student Day. Several hundred would break off from the line of march, wearing red armbands to identify one another, and laminated placards with pictures of Khomeini on their chests. That way, if they were martyred, the imam's bloodied image would be flashed electronically before the world. They called themselves "Muslim Students Following the Imam's Line." That distanced them from the revolution's Marxist remnant, which they despised. What few guns they carried were to fight off any rival group that might horn in on their accomplishment. They would bring enough food, they agreed, for three days.

On Saturday they won an audience with a top cleric they admired, asking him to inform Khomeini of their plans; perhaps the imam might even pronounce his blessing. A few hours later, they gathered around their radios for the Ayatollah's National Student Day speech, and heard him say, "All our problems come from America. . . . It is, therefore, up to the dear pupils, students and theological students, to expand with all their might the attacks against the United States and Israel so they may force the United States to return the deposed and criminal shah." They were elated: they believed this was a message to them. In fact, it was a coincidence. Khomeini had never received word of their plans. The drama that followed would be compounded by many such ironies.

The next day at 10 a.m., the memorial procession shrieked its way past the U.S. embassy, and a young woman—most of this cadre were women— hoisted a banner reading "*Allahu Akbar.*" That was the signal.

Revolutionary Guards complied with a request to step aside. Bolt cutters emerged from beneath chadors. The names of individual plotters were carefully checked off a master list; once all were safely inside the grounds, the gates were locked from the inside—which didn't keep more than a thousand exuberant fellow travelers from spontaneously scaling the fences themselves, many just high school students. When embassy personnel in the various buildings scattered around the parklike compound noticed the unusual sight through their windows, some locked their office doors, but most weren't particularly concerned. Back in February, the marauders had machine guns. These were kids, and only carried signs. They read, "We do not wish to harm you. We only wish to set-in [sic]."

It was only because of a Ralph Nader–like concern for employee safety that the invaders were able to get inside the main embassy building, the chancery. Following the February breach, its windows had been fitted with steel bars and sand-filled bullet-traps. One basement window in the battleship-like building was secured only with a simple lock, to serve as a fire exit. The students were able to breach it. The CIA station chief called to alert the embassy's dozen Marine guards. He also reached the chargé d'affaires, Bruce Laingen, who was just finishing up a cordial meeting at the foreign ministry. Laingen instructed the station chief not to allow Marines to open fire under any circumstances, and to use tear gas only as a last resort.

The last resort very soon arrived.

Students began breaking windows, sabotaging security cameras, and battering locked doors, including to the same second-floor "secure" communications room embassy staff had holed up inside in February. Some but not all of the staff had made it inside. They worked to destroy documents in a balky paper-pulper—until it seized up with a *chonk* and they had to continue the job using an ordinary office shredder. Students with bullhorns circulated to announce in English and Farsi that they intended no harm, while outside, the chancery was ringed with thousands of revelers screaming for the Americans' deaths.

It was 2:30 p.m. in Tehran—3 a.m. in Washington—when the Americans in the secure room got word from Laingen that he had assurances from the government that they need only be patient a little while longer, until official forces arrived to rout the students and restore the embassy to U.S. control. And, around that same time, the embassy's political officer spoke to a secretary in the office of the prime minister, who greeted the Americans cordially—"It's so nice to hear from you! Tell me, are those visas we sent over ready?"—and assured the officer that in twenty minutes or so a force of Revolutionary Guards would arrive to save the day.

Within the next ninety minutes, after speaking with a contact within the police force, a Marine realized that, somewhere, a decision had been made—and that this would no longer be the case. The embassy's security chief ventured outside the chancery to try to negotiate. He ended up blindfolded, with a pistol to his head. Soon blindfolded Americans were being led outside one by one, each accompanied by a student, some of them cruel ("Vietnam, Vietnam, Vietnam," one repeated with each step), some of them kind ("Don't be afraid, don't be afraid"). At least one American thought he was being led to a firing squad.

Brzezinski woke the president at Camp David. He spoke reassuringly: no hostages had been shot, which suggested that they were in the clear, since "such actions were usually most violent in the first hours."

Foreign Minister Yazdi drove to Qom. He was ushered in to sit on a floor cushion beside Khomeini just as the imam was beginning his customary evening audiences. He was apparently hearing the news for the first time. He asked Yazdi who was responsible and what they wanted. Then, he gave a blunt and unambiguous order: "Go and kick them out."

The foreign minister, exhausted from the trip to Algiers from which he had only that morning returned, didn't act with any particular haste— best, he reasoned, to wait a few hours to let the crowds disperse and tempers cool. He was therefore rather shocked when he turned on the radio that evening. In the interim, the Ayatollah had apparently flipped on a radio or TV himself—now saturated with images from the embassy of jubilation and veneration for himself. He sent his cleric son Ahmed in a helicopter to report back from the scene. There, Ahmed was deliriously borne aloft and hoisted bodily over the gates. He was led on a tour of "the great nest of U.S. espionage," paraded before the subdued, blindfolded Americans, and shown seized documents and electronics equipment. He returned with a glowing report. Which was apparently what persuaded the Ayatollah to go on the radio to endorse the captors and announce that Iran should build "a Great Wall of China between itself and the United States," and all citizens should do "whatever is necessary" to force the shah's return.

No official anywhere was sure what would happen next, nor even whether this event was all that important. Hamilton Jordan, at Camp David, remarked, "It'll be over in a few hours, but it could provide a nice contrast between Carter and our friend from Massachusetts"—Teddy Kennedy—"in how to handle a crisis." One of the hostages was still thinking of it as "a sit-in that got out of hand." State Department spokesman Hodding Carter said, "We expect the government of Iran to secure the release of the Americans and to return the embassy compound to our control."

But that government's nominal leaders, Prime Minister Bazargan and Foreign Minister Yazdi, wondered whether they would survive in their jobs another day.

NO SUCH AMBIGUITY REIGNED ON AMERICAN TV SCREENS. "GOOD EVE-ning," ABC's Sunday anchor Sam Donaldson began the newscast, lips pursed, beside a yellow outline marked "IRAN." "The American embassy in Tehran has been invaded and occupied by Iranian students. The Americans inside have been taken prisoner."

Cut to footage: tens of thousands of voices thundering as one, chanting an inscrutable chant. An American in a business suit, hunched defeatedly, an American in combat fatigues, erect and scowling, and an American in a casual gray turtleneck were led through an apoplectic crowd. At their feet, a picture of a ridiculously costumed shah, medals covering his breast, a regal purple sash across his chest, curled up in flames. An American burned.

The network recited bare facts: Khomeini's anti-American speech that had spurred on the marauders; Khomeini's post hoc expression of approval; the three-hour battle the Marines fought only with tear gas; the lack of apparent violence so far against the captives; the American chargé d'affaires's ongoing dialogue with the Iranians; assurances the State Department had received that "the Iranian government would do its best to resolve the matter"; Iranian officials' insistence that the U.S. had been warned something like this might happen if Americans admitted the shah.

And also, the briefest of observations that to "hundreds of thousands of families" in Iran, the shah was a symbol of misery and death.

Newspapers the next morning and through the week filled out some of the geopolitical complexities. In American living rooms, however, blunt televised images spoke louder. By the fourth day of the crisis—by which time it had become clear this wasn't to be a blip like last time—all three network newscasts devoted more than half of their airtime to Iran. Only in the fourth week of the crisis did Iran begin occupying less than a third.

Among the stories that were crowded out by this saturation coverage was the development of the worst famine in modern world history, in Cambodia. *Time*'s massive cover story that went to the printers before the hostages were taken, which appeared in mailboxes on November 5, described a "grisly cavalcade of specters, wrapped in black rags" staggering into Thailand by the tens of thousands, "children with death's-head faces, their bellies swollen, their limbs as thin and fragile as dried twigs," the consequence of a numbingly tragic history in which a peaceful nation became the unwitting base for Communist insurgents from Vietnam, then "the target of savage U.S. bombings," then "four years of mass terror and murder under the Khmer Rouge," then of invasion from Vietnam in January 1979. Cyrus Vance said, "I can think of no issue now before the world community and before every single nation that can lay greater claim to our concern and our action." That claim promptly atrophied, for Cyrus Vance as much as everyone else. *Time*'s next four covers were on Iran.

Never did a single story monopolize so much mass-media oxygen for so long. There was nothing like this, for instance, after North Korea seized the merchant ship the USS *Pueblo* in 1968, killing one crew member, starving the rest and torturing them with mock firing squads, holding them for eleven months. American diplomats were held for more than a year in China in 1949 with hardly any publicity at all. But those ordeals had not starred street frenzies that the news cameras could linger upon for minutes on end—homing in on things like a giant banner depicting a befuddled Jimmy Carter and reading "US CAN NOT DO ANYTHING."

The network that was third in the ratings provided the most galvanizing coverage. By coincidence, for the first four days, ABC was the only outfit able to get a news crew to the embassy gates. And, in another coincidence, ABC was the network that had been so eager to lure viewers to its newscast that in 1978 it had elevated the creator of *Wide World of Sports* to head its news division.

When the hostages were taken, Roone Arledge happened to be in Lake Placid, New York, where the Winter Olympics were opening in four months, producing a special to promote ABC's coverage. He discovered that the hotel staff, the sports reporters, the training athletes—*everybody*—was concerned with nothing else. The next day, in New York, "My elevator operator, the taxi driver . . . All these people care about now are the hostages of Iran." So that was what he intended to give to them.

He had been casting about for a network show to fill the slot after the local news that affiliates gave over to reruns of cop shows and situation comedies, but which NBC dominated with *The Tonight Show Starring Johnny Carson*. The affiliates balked, but Arledge got his way:

"*Police Story* will be seen forty-five minutes from now so that we may bring you the following special program from ABC News. . . ."

It was 11:30 p.m. eastern standard time on November 8. Anchorman Frank Reynolds began: "Look at this!" (The screen froze on an image of embassy press attaché Barry Rosen, a blindfold covering nearly his entire face like a shroud.) "One American. Blindfolded. Handcuffed. Today, in the courtyard of the American embassy in Tehran. He and sixty-some others, still held hostage"—the fist-waving crowd, braying their chant—"and threatened in a country gone out of control. The pictures, exclusive, as are so many more in this broadcast."

Cut to the burning American flag, then Uncle Sam hanged in effigy. When the cameras finally trained on the anchorman, who began his plodding explanation of the politics that had led to this point, the same yellow Iran outline in the background was accompanied by that image of the shrouded Barry Rosen, which became the nightly series' visual signature.

By the end of the month, the ratings for TV news in general had climbed by 3.8 percentage points. The ratings for ABC's new late-night broadcast, christened *America Held Hostage: The Crisis in Iran*, were stratospheric. A news director at a CBS local affiliate expressed his frustration that his own network was superior at *explaining* the crisis. But "ABC has been more attuned to what really grabs the public." The *Los Angeles Times* TV column reported, "ABC has finally found someone who can beat Johnny Carson: Khomeini." Soon, having divined that late-night news attracted a more affluent viewership than talk shows or sitcom reruns, ABC made the broadcast permanent, changing its name to *Nightline* in anticipation of the time—surely not too far in the future—when there would be no more hostage crisis to exploit.

THE ATTENTION OF THE WORLD MADE IT ALL TOO EASY FOR KHOMEINI'S forces to recognize the extraordinary political leverage they now possessed. Within forty-eight hours, the political position of anyone who might advocate for the Americans' release became untenable; Bazargan and Yazdi resigned. That left only theocrats in charge. State television began providing an uncensored video feed of the mania at the embassy gates—the crowds, a British journalist lamented, serving almost "like professional extras," beginning their chants when cameras were trained on them and ending them when they were turned off.

The political consequences were unmistakable in America, too. The images slotted effortlessly into the long-gathering narrative of American malaise, humiliation, and failed leadership. It spurred the poor sap at the center of that narrative into a portentous decision. Hundreds had begun assembling spontaneously before the Iranian embassy, armed with chants and American flags. President Carter and Hamilton Jordan, on the first Tuesday of the crisis, happened to drive past in the presidential limousine. Jordan was spellbound. "I was glad that the people cared," he later reflected—but "bothered they cared so much." It suggested to him that, politically, they could not stick to the quiet diplomacy that had marked the *Pueblo* crisis. The president would have to be seen by the public as actively and persistently confronting the issue.

Carter announced that Ramsey Clark, a former attorney general who had paid a sympathetic visit to Khomeini during his Paris exile, would travel to Iran bearing a personal letter from Carter appealing to the Ayatollah to free the hostages. (When Clark arrived in Turkey, the regime announced it would not receive him. "Humanitarian appeals to Khomeini," he reported back, "are unlikely to be productive.") Carter announced that he was canceling a long-planned diplomatic trip to Canada to concentrate on the crisis. Enraged by all the Iranian students protesting in solidarity with their brothers and sisters occupying the embassy—in New York they draped a twenty-foot banner reading "THE SHAH MUST BE TRIED AND PUNISHED" over the arm of the Statue of Liberty—he announced that the Immigration and Naturalization Service would require all fifty thousand Iranian students to report their locations and visa status at the nearest INS office, and would immediately initiate deportation proceedings ("in accordance with constitutional due process requirements") against those out of status, an unprecedented act. In a major speech before the annual convention of the AFL-CIO, he announced that he was freezing Iran's assets held in U.S banks. "We have done nothing for which any American need apologize," he said. "The actions of Iranian leaders and the radicals who invaded our embassy were completely unjustified. They and all others must know that the United States of America will not yield to international terrorism or to blackmail."

Then, he traveled to National Cathedral, was followed by the TV cameras down the center aisle to the front of the congregation, and joined a thousand State Department employees in a prayer service led by a rabbi, an imam, and a priest.

"THE DECISION WAS MADE FOR THERE TO BE A VERY VISIBLY CONCERNED president who said in effect that the hostages' fate is a paramount concern of the president of the United States," an administration official recalled. Perhaps the citizenry was simply too aroused to allow any other course. Consider the scene that unfolded that first Friday in tony Beverly Hills, California.

A group of Iranians announced their intent to march past Rodeo Drive's famous upscale boutiques in support of the embassy students. A housewife and activist for both Proposition 13 and Greenpeace's "Save the Whales" campaign had already joined the movement to drive during the day with her headlights on to show solidarity with the hostages, but wanted to do more. She set up a phone tree to organize a counterdemonstration against them, and within hours, had commitments from seven hundred people.

Police feared a riot. People "want the Iranian students in this country put into concentration camps," reported an aide to California's U.S. senator Alan Cranston of the phone calls they were receiving. So officials banned both the march and the planned counterdemonstration. The Iranians insisted they would march nonetheless. "We'll be ready for 'em," the Beverly Hills police chief promised. The Jewish Defense League, a vigilante organization responsible for a number of terrorist bombings, promised to show up as well.

At 10 a.m. on Friday, November 9, about thirty Iranians began striding down Wilshire Boulevard. They got about twenty feet. "Get out of America now, you filthy Iranians!" the JDL's local leader cried as his followers began pummeling them and ripping up their "DEATH TO THE SHAH" placards. Then several hundred more people waded in to join the attack.

An Iranian was wrestled to the ground. "Kick him! Kick him!" someone screamed; those nearby got in satisfying wallops. Two Iranians were chased down the street. "My friend just jumped out of a car and knocked out six of the guy's teeth with a hammer," one of the pursuers boasted.

Others began grabbing heavy pipe fittings from a contractor's parked truck and throwing them at Iranians' heads. A terrified young man clung to his elderly mother, looking up pleadingly at a cop: "We're from Romania." The officer responded, "You'd better move on. These people aren't asking questions." Though that was not precisely true: one man in army fatigue pants and a T-shirt asked a swarthy-looking man, "Are you Iranian?" "Yes," came the reply; he was kneed in the groin. A police officer arrested two Iranians, including the one who had just been kicked in the groin, letting the guy who kicked him go. A woman shook his hand. "Boom! Boom!" he replied. "It felt great. And I'm not pissed off yet. You wait. All I ask is that I can get into the ring with one. I'll have a good time." A passerby told a cop he had just watched an American cold-cock an Iranian and wanted to testify against him. The officer shot back, "We saw it too," and walked away while a second officer picked up the witness's bicycle and hurled it onto the sidewalk.

"They'd cut off your goddamn hands if you tried to pull this shit in Iran! Why don't you go home?" a man screamed. He was answered, earnestly, "The shah is an international criminal. It is not in the best interests of Americans to defend him."

A man from Simi Valley bellowed, "Go back to Israel!"

(The man next to him whispered something in his ear.)

"I mean Iran!"

A man with a thick mustache made the CBS News. His shriek—"I'm sick of being stomped on!! We're not going to take it anymore!! America!! America!!"—was so loud it must have overdriven TV speakers.

One hundred thirty-six Iranians were arrested. Many chanted "Long live Khomeini" as they were led away. So were fourteen of the Americans who assaulted them. They sang "God Bless America" as the police bus hauled them off. The *Los Angeles Times* noted the diversity of the crowd that had joined in this gleeful communion: "motorcycle riders with Harley-Davidson wings emblazoned on their jackets; elderly, gray-haired men wearing brown military caps; blonde young men and women from college fraternities and sororities wearing Greek Week T-shirts; homosexuals wearing Gay Power T-shirts and a number of persons wearing buttons that said, 'Turn on to Jesus' and 'Smile God Loves You.'" They bore signs reading things like "NUKE IRAN!," "MAKE THE PIG KHOMEINI PAY," "I LOVE THE SHAH," "THIS THANKSGIVING, ROAST AN IRANIAN," and "IRAN IS THE ARMPIT OF THE

WORLD." One kid in bell-bottoms watched from atop a street sign, waving a 1976 Bicentennial flag. Two students from Northrop University awkwardly held an eight-foot-long Old Glory over their heads. "We thought we'd come down and show some good old American patriotism. It was the biggest flag we could find at school."

As it happened, an American icon was present that day in Beverly Hills: boxer Muhammed Ali, who interrupted several assaults. "Islamic religion means peace," he told reporters afterward. "I think it's my duty to make a move to offset some of this bad publicity." He then took advantage of the media attention to announce his willingness to exchange *himself* for the hostages, and that he would fly to London to await word from the Iranians. He never made it. An Iranian called in to WBBM news radio in New York, claiming to be conveying the hostage-takers' official response: "There will be no substitutes, no negotiations. We want the shah."

CHAPTER 29

Kickoffs

ON THE DAY THE HOSTAGES WERE SEIZED, TWO SPECIAL BROADCASTS COM-peted for viewers' attention. One was the TV debut of *Jaws*. It received the highest ratings of any movie on network TV ever. Which was a good thing for Senator Kennedy, because the other special was an hour-long profile of him on CBS that proved so unflattering it made political history.

Kennedy was scheduled to declare his presidential challenge three days hence, on November 7. But he had made the decision in his heart back in July, while watching Jimmy Carter's "crisis of confidence" speech, which he experienced as an insult to everything he cherished most about his family's political legacy—its vision of America as a land of progress and hope. At the time, according to a *New York Times*/CBS poll, 53 percent of Democrats wanted Kennedy as their nominee, compared to 16 percent for Carter and 7 percent for Jerry Brown. In Gallup's head-to-head matchup against Reagan, Carter lost by ten points, but Kennedy won by eighteen. On July 30, the *New York Times Magazine* published an article conclud-ing that "Kennedy could become president without really trying."

But two obstacles stood in the way of an *official* decision. The first was family. Kennedy would never run without the blessing of his mother, Rose; "Teddy" was the only son she had left. And there was his wife, Joan. She was in an alcoholism treatment program, and they spent so little time together that it made news whenever they did.

So Kennedyologists watched obsessively for if they began to do so more—for any sign, really, of an impending announcement. The senator's rhetoric. His legislative maneuvers. His figure. (He lost twenty pounds, supposedly from giving up ice cream: for many, that clinched it.) The travel itineraries of what was alternately termed the "Kennedy camp," "Kennedy old hands," and "Kennedy family retainers"—media shorthand for the seemingly inexhaustible number of operatives and officials who it seemed would abandon their own children should Senator Kennedy only ask.

Some of those Kennedyologists were in the White House. The Army Signal Corps was dispatched to videotape Kennedy's public appearances;

the president's daily news summary became a Kennedy news ticker. One day it reported on Massachusetts labor leaders and liberals staging a draft-Kennedy protest, the next the executive director of the NAACP's avowal that Kennedy would get more black support than Carter. And by Labor Day weekend, the president had decided that he had finally had enough. He telephoned Kennedy on Cape Cod, summoned him to lunch, and asked for a categorical statement of noncandidacy. The *Atlanta Constitution* reported that Kennedy's response was to ask *Carter* for such a statement. Actually, Kennedy said he was still thinking it over.

A political cartoon depicted a banner across an urban storefront reading "KENNEDY FOR PRESIDENT" in enormous letters—with "*might not run*" scrunched in between the first and second words. Then, the word went forth to friend and foe: Rose Kennedy had told her son that she had no objection to a run. Rowland Evans and Robert Novak had a sizable advance to write a book about the president's reelection campaign. They returned it. For now the idea of Jimmy Carter as the 1980 Democratic nominee began to seem almost absurd.

Newt Gingrich predicted that it would be "a mean, cruel, brutal campaign." In fact, it already was. At a dinner with Wall Street heavies a presidential assistant said that Kennedy's "not going to survive the primaries"—a very rude joke indeed. Carter began spraying favors on key constituencies: $3.1 million in public housing grants to Dade County just before the Florida state Democratic convention; a promise to Chicago mayor Jane Byrne to relocate an Air Force station from O'Hare to pave the way for the airport's expansion. (She endorsed Kennedy anyway.)

On October 20, at the dedication of the John F. Kennedy Presidential Library, before Jacqueline Kennedy Onassis, Lady Bird Johnson, Coretta Scott King, and a veritable battalion of Kennedy cousins, brothers, sisters, uncles, and aunts, Carter backhandedly taunted his would-be opponent as a pathetic Rip Van Winkle, pining for the day when his brother was alive: "The world of 1980 is as different from that of 1960 as the world of 1960 was from that of 1940," he sniped. "Fiscal restraint has become a matter of simple public duty."

It was the latest in a long line of slights: Carter neglecting to invite Kennedy to the state dinner for Deng Xiaoping; Carter refusing to appoint Kennedy hand Archibald Cox to a federal judgeship; Carter not returning his calls; Carter promising to "whip his ass." Now, the wind whipping dramatically off Boston Harbor, salt air filling his nostrils, Kennedy had to be restrained from seizing the podium and improvising a cutting response. "At the ceremony's conclusion," a political reporter wrote, "the most sought-after man in the audience was Carl Wagner, Ted Kennedy's political aide, who was hiring for the upcoming campaign."

A Harris Poll now showed 72 percent agreeing that Kennedy had "the personality and leadership qualities a president should have." In an eloquent series of campaign-like appearances in late October and early November, he flayed the hide off the president in tones redolent of the most famous speeches of JFK. He thrust his fists for emphasis behind the podium at a labor convention in Boston: "There are those voices! In this country today! Who would have us believe! That we cannot come to grips with the leading problems that are facing our nation today! Well I don't believe that to be the case!" (JFK in 1960: *It is a contest between the contented and the concerned! Between those who wish to stand still! And those who wish to move ahead!*) He cried in Philadelphia, "There are some who say we can no longer meet these challenges with the same confidence and skill we had in other days!" (You could almost hear his brother answering back across the bridge of years: *Let them come to Philly!*) After that one, the *New York Times* called it "all but official."

But something curious was happening. The closer the official moment, the more inarticulate the would-be candidate became—comically so. There he was, before one of the white clapboard houses of the famous "Kennedy compound" in Hyannis, press conference microphones poking at his big chin like silver batons, (not) answering the simple question of when and under what circumstances he might become a candidate for the presidential nomination:

"Well, I, not, I have no, uh, at the present time, ah, clearly I am ah, uh, I am not, um, I am not, I am not—"

"When will you make up your mind, Senator?"

"Well, I am not, ah, I don't have any, uh, particular time, uh, uh, frame, or any uh particular time, uh, uh, date."

His calling card was supposed to be charisma. He was supposed to be Democrats' consensus choice to raise the fallen leadership standard. So what to make of *this*?

Perhaps it had something to do with that second obstacle to Kennedy's official announcement. It went by the name "Chappaquiddick."

THE NOVEMBER 4 CBS SPECIAL OPENED WITH A MONTAGE INTERSPERSING contemporary and classic moments in the American political religion that went by the name *Kennedy*: Ted, just three years out of law school, in a famous debate in his first Senate campaign when his opponent cried that if his name were Edward *Moore* he would not even be there; Rose in black mourning clothes at Robert Kennedy's funeral; 1972 Democratic nominee George McGovern recalling when an attractive young woman almost knocked him over to tell Teddy, "Oh senator! I just can't wait to get to 1976."

The next clips included a Cadillac nearly submerged in Nantucket Sound, and Kennedy sitting at in a book-lined study asserting, "There is no truth, no truth whatever, to the widely circulated suspicion of immoral conduct . . ."

Flash to the present. Teddy and Rose purposefully supervised a happy young brood packing for a camping trip. Two of Rose's dozens of grand-children tossed a football on the lawn—just as Ted, Jack, Kick, and Bobby used to do in the famous home movies. Offscreen, correspondent Roger Mudd said, "This is probably how a mother whose son is running for president would like a documentary about him to begin: a nice walking shot of the two of them as she sets off with her grandchildren on a sum-mer camping trip."

That was a tip-off: what was to come next, no mother would want to see.

Mudd and Kennedy sat on Adirondack chairs for an outdoors inter-view, in casual blazers, Mudd asking increasingly probing questions—like whether he was afraid of assassination; Kennedy kept retreating to some far-distant place. Mudd asked, "What's the present state of your mar-riage, Senator?" Kennedy stiffened, then, approximately twenty *uh*s and *um*s later, formed a few inauthentic-sounding words. Mudd asked if he ever thought about the "purported Kennedy family curse." The sena-tor, framed so tightly that the famous chin nearly filled the bottom of the screen, referred blankly to "a sudden sequence of circumstances, uh, that happened in fairly, uh, rapid sequence, at that time, which I think, ah, probably helped me to reach that observation, ah, probably in the last ten years. . . . I wouldn't say that viewpoint is mine any longer?"—raising his pitch like he was asking a question.

The commercial break was a welcome reprieve. But the second seg-ment was near to a political execution.

It began with an aerial shot of a famous rickety wooden bridge. Mudd narrated, "The mystery of what happened at Chappaquiddick ten years ago still hangs over Martha's Vineyard like a summer ground fog, and still is impenetrable. . . . By his own account, Kennedy had come to Martha's Vineyard on July 18, 1969, to race in the Edgartown Regatta and to host a cookout for half a dozen women who had worked for his late brother Robert. The cookout would be held on Chappaquiddick Island, separated from Edgartown by 500 feet of water and a brief ferry ride. . . ."

The way the program recounted what happened next resembled one of the "slasher" movies that had become a Hollywood craze. The events that night were reenacted, beginning with an establishing shot of the cottage in the woods "which Kennedy's political aides had rented and stocked with food and drink."

The camera panned to an adjoining road: "It was 11:15, everyone later agreed, when Kennedy left the party, feeling tired, he said, and wanting to catch the ferry back to Edgartown to his motel. He rarely drove himself, but this time got the keys from his chauffeur and started down Chappaquiddick's main road toward the ferry."

Then—a slasher film visual signature—the action leading to the fatal climax was depicted from a killer's point of view: in this case, from a camera mounted in the backseat of an Oldsmobile, though the windshield of which a yellow median strip glowed flourescent—

"With him was twenty-eight-year-old Mary Jo Kopechne, who had complained that she wasn't feeling well and had asked Kennedy for a ride back to her hotel."

A reflector sign unmistakably indicated that the road veered left, but the car turned sharply right, onto a very bumpy dirt road—

"Kennedy later testified that he became generally aware that the road was unpaved, but he kept going for approximately half a mile until he hit the dike bridge. Only then, he said, did he realize that he took the wrong road, and that it was too late."

The sequence lasted little more than a minute before segueing into Mudd standing next to the bridge in daylight, relating, "Senator Kennedy did not report the drowning of Mary Jo Kopechne until the next day, ten hours later—conduct that he said was irrational, inexcusable, inexplicable, and indefensible. In addition, the judge who presided at the inquest thought Kennedy was not telling the truth—that he had *meant* to turn toward this bridge. Because he chose to drive himself and did not use his chauffeur, because Mary Jo Kopechne told no one she was leaving, and because she brought with her neither her hotel key nor her purse, Judge James Boyle said that Kennedy and Kopechne were *not* heading toward the Edgartown Ferry."

The next segment continued the interview on the lawn. Kennedy attempted to explain away the evidence in a way that made his previous answers sound like a model of concision and confidence.

But the segment after that was a striking contrast. It followed the senator through a typical workday, beginning at seven-thirty in the morning with a briefing from an expert on an upcoming hearing on abuse of over-the-counter tranquilizers, then another in the car on the way to the Capitol, Kennedy asking probing questions all the while. He arrived at his office and was swarmed by reporters, where the white glow of TV lights followed him every time he stepped out the door. And yet he retained an astonishing focus. He parried a silly question from a foreign reporter ("What do you think of the Cuban situation? What would you think your brother President Kennedy would have done?"), juggled phone calls, ab-

sorbed a constant stream of information from aides buzzing in and out—
one literally jogging to keep up as Kennedy dashed to a meeting. Kennedy
even kept his sangfroid at a fundraiser while one person after another—including Bob Hope—wiggled through the scrum to grasp a hand, share a
word, or just make eye contact. Then he was shown crying thunder from
a podium to an electrified labor convention. *This* Kennedy looked like a
man who could be not just president, but a *great* president.

The program then wrapped up with another interview segment, in
his office. Mudd tossed a softball: "Why do you want to be president?"
Kennedy was silent for four seconds, then took nearly two minutes and
128 words, not counting the proliferation of *ah*s and *um*s, to say virtually
nothing at all.

Strikingly, it wasn't until three-quarters of the way through that he
managed to say the word *I*. And the few coherent fragments made for
quite the psychological study. Kennedy spoke choppily of America's
abundant resources, its great technology, its productivity, its "energy and
resourcefulness"; lamented that so many other countries were "doing better than us"; then concluded, "And, uh, I would uh basically uh feel uh
that it's imperative for this country to either move forward, that it can't
stand still, or otherwise that it would go backward." It sounded like an
exceptionally clumsy paraphrasing of what his *brother* said in one of the
most effective moments in the annals of political TV: his opening statement in his first debate against Richard Nixon—which went down in history for erasing the electorate's doubts that this callow young senator was
up to the job. The bowdlerization nineteen years later included a Freudian
slip: he said that America must "be focused on problems in a way that
brings a sense of restoration to this country."

Why *did* Teddy Kennedy want to be president? Maybe because Kennedy men were expected to rule, and he was the only Kennedy man
left—*restoration*. Maybe because he was *supposed* to want to be president.
Maybe because he had let his father down when he was alive, and now he
could put things right. Maybe because his brothers had all proven their
manhood under fire, but when his time came, he had not. JFK had *saved*
eleven crew members from his Navy PT boat from drowning, with staggering valor and ingenuity—a feat that EMK, at Chappaquiddick, uncannily inverted.

No wonder Ted Kennedy stammered. The burden had to be overwhelming.

The reviews were savage. A Senate colleague said, "If you can wind
him up and program him with a speech with words from his staff, he is
terribly effective. But when you put him on his own, he is really at a loss
for words." Tom Wicker wrote that anyone might wilt under such tough

questioning—"but the rest of us aren't running for president on a platform of leadership." The next week, on his first official campaign tour, a review in Chicago came in the form of a hurled rotten egg.

In the last Gallup sounding, Kennedy had beaten Carter among Democrats by a ratio of two to one. In the first poll after his candidacy announcement, it was only three to two. In another survey, he dropped ten points among independents. In the straw poll at the Iowa Democratic Party's annual Jefferson-Jackson Dinner in Des Moines four days after Roger Mudd's interview, Jimmy Carter won with 70 percent.

THE FAMILY RETAINERS INSISTED THAT KENNEDY HAD FUMBLED THE QUES-tion on why he wanted to be president only because the interview had been filmed on October 12, when he was only "exploring" a run, and feared putting his federal matching funds at risk by suggesting he *was* running. Maybe. But in spring, Ronald Reagan had no problem hitting a similar question out of the park.

"Governor," Bill Moyers of PBS had asked him as they strolled about on his ranch, "why would a man who could spend his retirement years serenely and peacefully in a beautiful place like this want to plunge back into the maelstrom of presidential politics?"

"*Welllll*, maybe there are some things I can do that might be of service," Reagan answered sweetly. "I love this ranch. I don't know, though, that I could be very happy spending all my time here. I look forward to it, I miss it when I'm away from it, but I also think—I want to participate. I'm very concerned about what I think is going on in this country. . . . I never wanted to hold public office in the first place, never set out to seek it, was persuaded to do what I did; but I must say that I found it the most fulfilling thing I'd ever done in my life, the eight years that I was governor of California. But again, I think you have to pay your way, I think."

"What do you mean?"

"Well, for all the good things that have happened, you have to put a little back, you have to help if you can. I've always felt that way."

The interview ranged amiably across biography, philosophy, and political analysis for another pleasant forty-five minutes, Reagan holding his own against tough questions all the while. Moyers, the former preacher, was particularly taken by the casually un-defensive way Reagan responded when challenged for naming "materialism" as a source of America's greatness: that just meant "individuals wanting better things, more comfort, and there being people with ideas who are free to say, 'Hey, I'll bet the people would like this, I'm going to make it.'" Then, eyes shining, he offered a panegyric to the inventor of a device to solve the perennial problem of too-warm soft drinks in summer: "You're serving people a cold drink in the can, you just clamp the—snap the handle onto it, and people hold it by the handle and the drink doesn't warm up. *And he's going to make a million dollars!*"

Reagan's announcement was scheduled to happen six days after Kennedy's, and five days after Jerry Brown's. His fundraising was looking up, the campaign having discovered a nifty election law loophole: labor donated by entertainers didn't count against the matching fund ceiling. Frank Sinatra, a former JFK intimate, had already given the maximum amount of money allowable by law. "Now I'm going back to Boston to sing for Reagan," he told a reporter. "I can already hear them saying, 'Oh, there he goes changing sides again.' But, hell, Reagan's been my friend for years and I'm singing for him."

The first Sinatra event was in September. Helene von Damm had recruited as hosts two New Jersey construction company partners, Jay Schiavone and Raymond Donovan, who owned a country club named Fiddler's Elbow, by appealing to the Garden State's inferiority complex vis-à-vis New York: they could be the first in Jersey history to host a $1,000-a-plate political event. It grossed an estimated $400,000. (Donovan later became secretary of labor.) Two sold-out Wayne Newton concerts on October 28 and 29 in Houston and Fort Worth grossed $190,000. The big kahuna was November 1 at Boston Music Hall with Sinatra and Dean Martin. A fan wrote to Reagan complaining about the $250 ticket price. Reagan figured out a way to blame Washington: the campaign was *forced* to charge an exorbitant price, because "the strict limitation on soliciting contributions now imposed on candidates by the government" meant that "raising sufficient funds to campaign is extremely difficult. . . . I can assure you they are not very helpful to the democratic process—namely in allowing the candidate to get their message to the greatest number of people."

As was often the case, the campaign disagreed with the campaigner. They wanted their man as *far away* from the greatest number of people as possible; high-dollar events suited them just fine. The *Washington Post* called him "the shrouded candidate." In Boston, he was more shrouded than ever before.

A Mercedes pulled directly onto the tarmac at Logan Airport. Reagan's body man David Fischer held an umbrella over his head and led him to the car. Reagan broke away to shake hands with the cops who would guard him. Fischer grew visibly agitated.

The party made its way to the glassed-off Presidential Suite on the Colonnade Hotel's eleventh floor. Reagan only left it to pass through a connecting door to another suite set up for TV interviews. At the theater, security officers were briefed by a burly man with a wire curling from his

In the spring of 1978, in conservative Wichita, a fundamentalist preacher organized a successful crusade to repeal the town's gay rights ordinance. Then, the same thing happened in two cities, St. Paul, Minnesota, and Eugene, Oregon, that prided themselves on their liberal tolerance. Approaching the general election, attention turned to California. An ambitious Orange County state senator named John Briggs (right, in confrontation with a gay rights activist) had visited City Hall Plaza in San Francisco—a "moral garbage dump," he said—to announce he had gathered enough signatures to place a referendum on the November ballot, Proposition 6, which would ban "open and notorious homosexuals" from teaching in public schools, as well as those "advocating, soliciting, imposing, encouraging, or promoting private or public homosexual activity." By fall his initiative was ahead in the polls two to one.

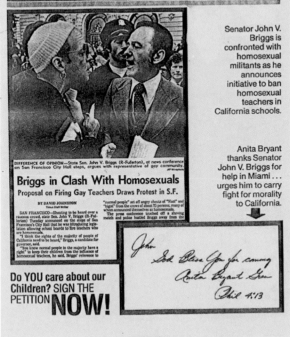

50

A prominent anti–Prop 6 campaign leader, fearing pogroms, urged gays to maintain "a very low profile" in the effort to defeat it. Instead, two brave men who disagreed became its face: a rural schoolteacher named Larry Berner (above left) and San Francisco City Councilman Harvey Milk (above right), who in grand-marshalling the annual San Francisco gay pride march (slogan: "Come Out with Joy, Speak with Justice") defied a postcard reading "You get the first bullet the minute you stand at the microphone." They won a surprising ally: Ronald Reagan, who decided Prop 6 represented unwarranted government intrusion, while reassuring angry conservatives, "If it ever becomes necessary to have an additional law denying homosexuals the right to advocate their lifestyle I'll be the first in line to support it."

A self-serving politician has dreamed up a 'moral' crusade.

And he wants you to pay for it.

San Francisco City College

"This measure has nothing to do with those so-called gay rights issues in Florida and elsewhere. Instead, it has the potential of infringing on the basic rights of privacy and even constitutional rights. It could be very costly to implement and it has the potential for causing undue harm to people." **Ronald Reagan**

"A vote for Proposition 6 is not a vote for morality but an act of discrimination. I am opposed to Proposition 6 and this is in line with the National Conference of Catholic Bishops who stated, 'Homosexuals, like everyone else, should not suffer from prejudice against their basic human rights." **Msgr. James B. Flynn**

53

Taxes were another dominant issue in 1978. Conservatives had long carped, concerning the goodies liberals voted citizens from government coffers, "No one shoots Santa Claus." Then new-fangled "supply-side" economists like Arthur Laffer (above, with his famous curve) insisted that across-the-board income tax cuts performed fiscal miracles. Other economists, even conservatives like Milton Friedman, called that absurd. But Republican politicians loved it: now they had their own Santa Claus. And, following the Proposition 13 landslide, ambitious Democrats—including California's governor Jerry Brown (below with Howard Jarvis, whose measure Brown had previously called an "unworkable and crazy" "fraud")—leaped onto the tax-revolt bandwagon too. Brown began being talked up as a possible challenger to Jimmy Carter for the 1980 Democratic nomination.

54

The pundit class cited relatively small Republican gains in 1978 as a lukewarm endorsement of the status quo. That ignored what they had been saying months earlier: that "the GOP today is in a weaker position than any major party since the Civil War." The most common explanation as to why was that right wingers were coming to dominate it. But in November, the most impressive victories came from conservative candidates. Dick Cheney won Wyoming's congressional seat even though a heart attack grounded him for weeks.

And Iowa's Roger Jepsen came back from 30 points behind to win a Senate seat. The pollster for the losing Democrat credited pro-life activists for the margin of victory. On the Sunday before the election, they blanketed windshields in church parking lots with pamphlets featuring a famous 1965 photograph of a fetus in the womb with the message: "This little guy wants you to vote."

Conservatives also benefited from New Right "direct mail" campaigns (*"act right now to help protect your family from vicious killers"*) and the nonstop electioneering of Ronald Reagan, building a bank of favors for a presidential run. He even, controversially, endorsed a liberal, Senator Chuck Percy of Illinois, who saved his seat by apologizing on TV for helping "Washington go overboard."

Democrats winning office in 1978 also struck conspicuously conservative positions: a supply-side economist, Phil Gramm; a tax-revolt zealot, Edward J. King, who vanquished Massachusetts governor Mike Dukakis in a primary; a socially liberal Michiganander, Carl Levin, who "differed somewhat from the anti-government rhetoric of Ronald Reagan," but "one had to listen very carefully to make the distinction." They were only following their president. Since his first big televised speech, on energy, in front of a White House fireplace wearing a cardigan sweater (above), Carter's watchword was "sacrifice"—a word he had never used on the campaign trail against Ford. As 1979 approached, Carter boasted of the "austerity" of his proposed budget, which he believed, incorrectly, would stanch runaway inflation. When his campaign promise of a national healthcare plan failed to emerge by the party's midterm convention in Memphis, Senator Edward M. Kennedy gave a rip-roaring speech attacking him from the left that many believed augured a run for the 1980 Democratic nomination.

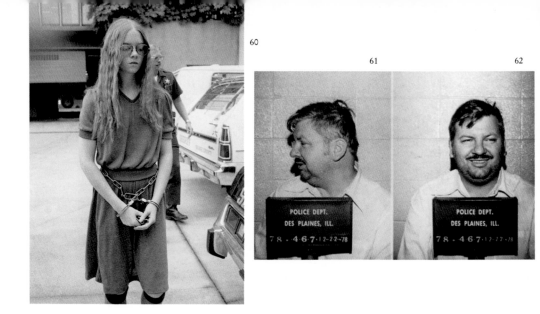

The news was a banquet of terrors. Clockwise from left: a teenager shot up an elementary school, declaring, "I don't like Mondays"; John Wayne Gacy buried thirty-three teenagers' corpses in his basement; serial killer Ted Bundy represented himself, taking delight in describing the crimes he was accused of; the "Hillside Strangler" murdered twelve; Harvey Milk's assassination in San Francisco City Hall set off riots when his killer was convicted only of manslaughter; a DC-10 crash killed 271, revealing a trail of bungling; Jim Jones's cultists committed mass suicide; a nuclear plant nearly melted down, and authorities seemed to have no idea how to respond; toxic waste oozed from basements in a bucolic Niagara Falls neighborhood; gas-line riots broke out in Levittown, Pennsylvania.

63

64

65

66

67

68

71

Jimmy Carter seemed to get smaller every day in the face of these challenges. The press learned about a strange incident in which he was menaced by a rabbit while fishing; when the White House refused to release the photo (above), the *Washington Post* ran a humiliating caricature on the front page of the president swatting at a bunny rabbit like it was the shark from *Jaws*. When Carter collapsed during a 10-kilometer road race, pictures of the president appearing pitifully gaunt appeared in newspapers across the land.

Voters were in the market for the opposite of the plaid shirts and plain-spoken decency they fell for in 1976: they wanted good-old-fashioned heroes, like the one in the throwback film that was the second highest grossing picture of 1978 (left). Pundits agreed it couldn't be the aging GOP front-runner, Ronald Reagan; he would fade once he made his first gaffe or fell asleep on camera. Then, they agreed, "Big John" Connally (right) would swoop in to save the day. Only the voters disagreed.

74

Ted Kennedy was the designated hero for the Democrats. He was way ahead in the polls—until a CBS special featuring a reenactment of Chappaquiddick, filmed like a horror movie, and an interview in which he stuttered uncomfortably when asked why he wanted the job.

Connally fell by the wayside. Pundits then boosted George Bush, whose managers made his youthful athleticism a central part of his appeal. In New Hampshire, Ronald Reagan crushed him, dominating from then on out.

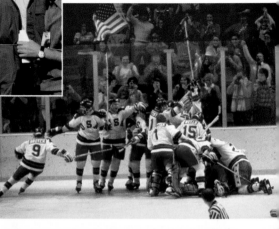

77

One reason the public longed
for heroes was the seizure of
fifty-two American hostages
in Iran, a humiliation revisited
every night on the news.
Another was the Soviet
invasion of Afghanistan. One
reaction was a resurgence of
old-fashioned patriotism, like
the nation's ecstatic response
to America's victory over the
Soviet Union in ice hockey at
the Winter Olympics. Another
was a lust for revenge

Reagan's strategists told him that George Bush was his smartest choice for running mate. But Reagan considered Bush a weakling. At the convention, rumors swirled that Reagan might try something unprecedented: choose a former president. Gerald Ford told Walter Cronkite that he might be willing, if the intent was something like a "co-presidency"—which was precisely what Reagan's and Ford's representatives were busy negotiating. An astonished Carter aide replied, "It would look as though Reagan's own party didn't think he could handle the big job without supervision." Reagan advisors had long shared just that concern. They spent considerable resources persuading the establishment that they had nothing to fear from a Reagan presidency.

82

Dear Frank,

Thank you for your letter of July 18 and the copy of The Evolution of Soviet Security Stragety. I apologize for the delay in responding these days, I carry my but with so much time spent on the road, I carry my reading about in my briefcase and use the time on airplanes to catch up. I found Mr. Haselkorn's book absorbing but sobering reading. I only wish some of those administration officials who seem to think that just under the surface, the Soviet negotiators ████████████ are nice, Christian gentlemen would pay attention to this report.

Thank you also for your help with contacts in France. Dick Allen has kept me abreast of matters.

Sincerely,

RR

They wrote fawning letters to pundits and policy intellectuals for Reagan to sign. The one at left had the governor warmly praise a book on foreign policy that a cover note instructed him to "not feel obliged to read". . .

RR   4/17   gp
Richard James Whalen   2

Dear Dick: Just a quick line between trips to thank you for the material you sent, particularly the analysis of the middleast situation. It truly is frightening, and I found after I had read it that I couldn't keep from ~~~~~~ *heartening* back to the Old Testament prophecies of the events that would foretell Armageddon. Maybe the United States couldn't head off what seems to *be* building up there, but surely we ~~~~~~ could have made a better try than this man has made.

Again, my heartfelt thanks and very best to your lovely partner.
Sinc. Ron

. . . while the Reagan they hoped would never see the light of day dictated his own letters to fans and friends, articulating extremist notions like the role "Old Testament prophecies of the events that would foretell Armageddon" might play in the Middle East.

83

84

Newborn Republicans fled the Democratic coalition for Reagan. Evangelical Christians had been flirting with the Republicans since Carter's *Playboy* interview. At a rally of preachers in August, Reagan cemented the alliance alongside Jerry Falwell: "I know you can't endorse me. But I endorse you and what you're doing."

Reagan's muscular patriotism and tax-cut promises—and Carter's embrace of austerity and neglect of labor—peeled off blue-collar Democrats. Reagan was also on his way to winning 71 percent of voters most strongly opposed to government efforts to help blacks.

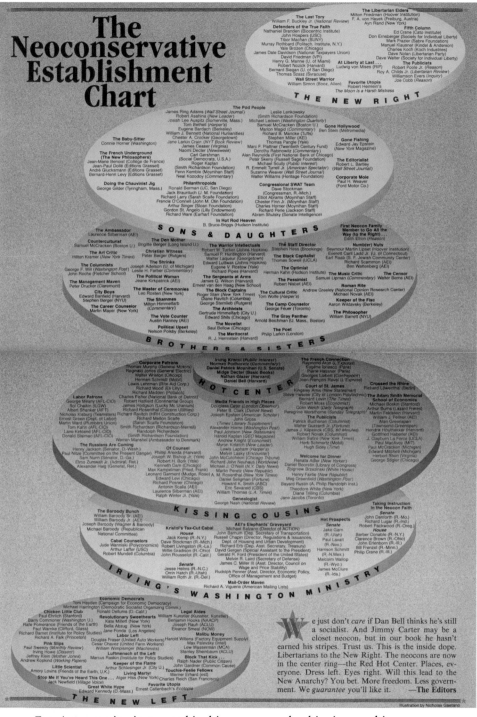

Esquire magazine instructed its hip young readership, in a gushing twenty-page package heralded by Irving Kristol on the cover, that liberalism was going through "menopause," while neoconservatism was the "the Red Hot Center."

"They tell us we must learn to live with less, and teach our children that their lives will be less full and prosperous than ours have been," Reagan cried in his acceptance speech. "I don't believe that. And I don't believe you believe that either." He won in a landslide, even though only 21 percent of voters agreed with him that "too much" was being spent on the environment, urban programs, and health, education, and welfare. Reaganism felt joyous, inspiring, free (above, in Jersey City on Labor Day; right, in South Carolina with Senator Strom Thurmond). Carter seemed dour, doubting, and—in the judgment of pundits scolding him for articulating his fears about Reagan—mean.

Republicans' congressional performance was an equally significant story. They took the Senate for the first time since 1954 and upset several Democratic House leaders. One reason was dirty campaigning by the National Conservative Political Action Committee, a New Right group whose head, Terry Dolan, a closeted gay man, trumpeted the pleasure he took in exploiting a loophole in the post-Watergate campaign finance law allowing unlimited spending by outside groups that didn't "coordinate" with a candidate. The law's intent was idealistic: to make elections more democratic. Dolan interpreted it differently: "A group like ours could lie through its teeth and the candidate it helps stays clean."

Jimmy Carter had followed a precedent set by Gerald Ford: he was inaugu-rated in an ordinary business suit. Reagan went back to formalwear. All the corporate jets flying into the airport that would come to be named for him caused congestion unlike any air traffic controllers had ever seen. First Lady Nancy Reagan's wardrobe for the day cost an estimated $25,000, including a dress it took four weeks to hand-embroider. At the inaugural balls, fur coats so overloaded the coat racks that they resembled great lumbering mastodons out of the prehistoric past.

ear: "I want all nine of you around the governor when we go in there to-night. We don't want any ordinary people coming up and touching him."

The Reagans, the Sinatras, and Dean Martin filed into the foyer for a photo op. Sinatra did the talking:

"What cabinet posts has he promised you guys?"

"Liquor."

Somebody asked why he was switching allegiance from the Kennedys to Reagan. Sinatra fingered his cigarette pack in irritation. "I had an allegiance with President *Jack* Kennedy. Jack had presence and aptitude." Teddy was another story altogether.

REAGAN'S ANNOUNCEMENT WAS TWELVE DAYS LATER. A TICKET COST $500, but it featured no such musical draw—and as the event approached, the planners were mortified that news cameras might pan around a half-empty room.

The setting was not exactly Reagan Country: New York City, whose image was frozen in scenes of marauders burning down corner groceries, subway cars slathered with graffiti, and garbage. Gotham had begun fighting back by retaining the graphic artist Milton Glazer to devise an "I ♥ New York" promotional campaign. *Saturday Night Live* answered with the cast singing "I Love Sodom" to the tune of the campaign's theme song.

The summer of 1979 saw a record epidemic of bank robberies. The typical perpetrators were not the efficient professionals authorities were used to, but desperately poor young men acting spontaneously. Since 1970 the poverty rate in the Bronx had risen from 19.5 percent to 27.6 percent; in Brooklyn, it almost tripled. The police force began a training program to deal with this new breed of desperado—then suspended it because lay-offs had produced a shortage of officers. Mayor Koch responded by suggesting bank guards should start shooting bank robbers themselves.

New York was short of police despite President Carter signing its second federal bailout into law in August 1978. Though it might be more accurate to say that there was a shortage of cops *because* of that bailout—for Mayor Koch persuaded Congress to pass it with a promise of austerity that ended up with the city's workforce cut back a fifth, several hundred thousand being kicked off welfare, transit fares bumped up by almost half, the city's public colleges charging tuition for the first time, and nineteen fire companies closed and twenty-seven daycare centers closing. The streets were filthier; the number of city employees sweeping them fell from 2,700 in 1975 to 500, a hundred-year low. The subways were more crowded with beggars; the homeless population increased for the first time since the 1930s. Felonies increased 70 percent in a year. A band of vigilantes in red berets calling themselves the Guardian Angels, described as "a cross between a special forces military squad and a street gang," began patrolling the trains.

No surprise, then, that when Helene von Damm, tasked with organizing Reagan's announcement gala, learned that it was to take place in Manhattan—possibly because, as Reagan told an interviewer, "every time I cross the Mississippi River and come East I find there is this picture of me as some kind of Neanderthal who is going to put people up against the wall"—it sounded insane.

But the kind of people who bought $500 tickets to political events were not taking subways or buses. And, way out at Reagan headquarters next to the Los Angeles International Airport, von Damm was hardly aware that a new Manhattan was arising from the ashes of the old.

Theorists of capitalism called this "creative destruction": investors, sometimes unsavory ones, swooped in to buy depreciating assets, redeveloping them to create fantastic new sources of wealth. A paradigmatic example was the Commodore Hotel on East 42nd Street, across from the Chrysler Building, down the street from Grand Central Station. In 1976, the elegant pile, opened right after the First World War, was near ruins. It hadn't paid real estate taxes to the city for six years, after its owner, the Penn Central Railroad, went bankrupt. It was slated to close. But in the run-up to hosting the 1976 Democratic National Convention, the city was terrified of a landmark building on Manhattan's marquee street falling to blight. So the Commodore became the first experiment in a new strategy: making redevelopment more attractive by promising the developers future tax relief. The beneficiaries would then be required to share future profits with the city; everyone would win.

The hungry young killer who emerged to save the Commodore was profiled fawningly in the *New York Times*. He was "tall, lean, and blond, with dazzling white teeth, and he looks ever so much like Robert Redford. He rides around town in a chauffeured silver Cadillac with his initials, DJT, on the plates. He dates slinky fashion models, belongs to the most elegant clubs, and at only 30 years of age, estimates that he is worth 'more than $200 million.'" His favorite word, the *Times* related, was "flair." He also said that he was "publicity shy." The *Times* was so glad to find a folk hero to celebrate in the depressed metropolis that they didn't look too closely. Their reporter joined Donald Trump while he inspected all the construction sites he claimed to be developing around the city: "a typical workday," he said. In fact, they all belonged to, or were financed by, his father; same with the limousine. That "more than $200 million" in net worth? He was counting his dad's money—telling the IRS that his taxable income that year was only $24,594.

"So far," he boasted, "I've never made a bad deal." The Commodore project, at least, was a good deal—for Donald Trump. To gain the property, and the opportunity to flay off its landmark brick façade in favor of the gaudy bronze-tinted glass he preferred, he put up no money of his own, receiving $100 million in bank loans by negotiating an extraordinary labyrinthine deal with the New York Urban Development Corporation to forgo real estate taxes in which the city was supposed to earn its money back within forty years, though Trump said that day would come in twenty-five. Critics scoffed. They calculated that the deal would leave New York City $160 million in the lurch. That prediction proved conservative. Trump's lawyers had written the contract so that money only counted as "profit" when Trump received it, while expenses were deducted immediately, and, years later, after Trump's business partner the Hyatt Corporation dropped out of the deal and sued him, New York City claimed they had been defrauded, and auditors discovered that the hotel was missing the most basic financial records and had brazenly violated generally accepted accounting principles.

But while these shenanigans were taking place Trump was held up as just the tonic a depressed city needed to get its swagger back. And at least in its tonier precincts, the swagger *was* returning. The summer of epidemic bank robberies, Manhattan hotels enjoyed their highest levels of occupancy since 1965. Harry Helmsley was building a fifty-one-story luxury behemoth down the street from Trump's, also with a tax abatement deal. Financial deregulation opened new sorts of speculative opportunities, and down Wall Street way, the young beneficiaries—who soon would be labeled "yuppies"—took Donald Trump as a role model. The month Ed Koch told bank guards to shoot bank robbers, Trump's wife showed off the couple's apartment in the *Times*. (" 'I wanted a very dramatic *galleria*,' she said in her Austrian accent, 'so I put in dark marble floors with little lights around the mirror like a waterfall.' ") Her husband meanwhile bought the Bonwit Teller building ("the best piece of property in the world"), promising that the sixty-five-story "Trump Tower" with which he intended to replace it would be "the most spectacular building ever built."

The Staten Island Express bus had begun traveling thirty-five miles per hour on the freeways because their tires burst if they exceed that, and officials had finally promised to add fire extinguishers to the half of buses that didn't have them—with "fingers crossed," the news said, "because they expect a number would be stolen." A quarter of Bronx and Brooklyn residents were living in poverty. Bank customers were taking their life in their hands every time they withdrew cash. But by the fall of 1979, midtown Manhattan was doing spectacularly. Which was why it made sense for Ronald Reagan to announce his presidential campaign there at a $500-a-ticket gala.

OR MAYBE IT DID NOT.

Helene von Damm arrived from Los Angeles. "I didn't anticipate what a different world the East Coast is," she recollected. "No one knew of his record as governor, but everyone seemed to know that he had 'co-starred' with a monkey in *Bedtime for Bonzo*." Another thing she discovered was that the possessors of most of this flashy new money were, like Donald Trump, Democrats.

Her partner in party planning, a financier and former producer named Charles Wick (he was responsible for the 1961 movie *Snow White and the Three Stooges*), turned for help to old Republican warhorses from the Eisenhower era. William Casey, the mumbling, unkempt sixty-six-year-old former head of the Securities and Exchange Commission under Richard Nixon, agreed to serve as chairman. They booked a suite at the Mayfair Regent Hotel on Park Avenue as their war room—which they would not have been able to afford at all had Wick not been friends with the manager. They were able to reserve the appropriately grand International Ballroom at the Hilton next to Rockefeller Center without a down payment, because Wick was college pals with Hilton's CEO—who nonetheless stipulated that if some wedding, bar mitzvah, or sales conference that could pay in advance wanted the slot, the Reagan for President Committee would have to come up with cash on the barrelhead.

Fortunate that the ballroom had partitions to configure its size. Charlie Wick had suggested a $1,000 ticket price. His comrades at the Mayfair patiently explained that the New York City social scene was so crowded with galas (like the casino night for cerebral palsy five nights before their shindig, hosted, the *Times* society column reported, by "Mrs. Edgar M. Bronfman, Arlene Francis, and Mrs. Donald Trump") that they could only ask $500. Still they had so few takers that they had to, as they said on Broadway, paper the house: a telegram was sent to every ticket holder inviting them to "bring a young person (18 years or younger) as a guest." Though that still was not fetching enough bodies, and they fretted about the $35-a-plate cost.

A press release went out. It contained a typo: "New *Your*" instead of "New York." They hired a fundraiser whose fees were higher than the money he raised. A backer in Pennsylvania, Drew Lewis, offered to buy $50,000 worth of tickets, on credit: "I can give you bodies. In a few months you'll get the money. That's all I can offer right now. Take it or leave it." They took it. The bad publicity from unfilled seats was worse than finishing in the red. (Lewis later became secretary of transportation.)

The plan was also to run a prerecorded version of Reagan's announcement speech that night on national TV as he gave it in the ballroom. But the networks wouldn't sell them time. So Los Angeles hired a syndication company that promised "no less than forty out of the fifty top markets." Shortly before go time, the company had lined up only 66 percent—at a cost twice as much as network time. Cities not represented included Houston and Dallas. Each syndicated station would be broadcasting it at a different time of the day; or, in the case of Cleveland, the next day, at 12:30 a.m.

AT HEADQUARTERS IN LOS ANGELES, THE CHALLENGE WAS CRAFTING A speech that would both be inviting to the masses and satisfy media expectations—because when reporters complained that Reagan kept saying the same old things, John Sears's excuse was that he'd unveil bold new policy ideas just as soon as he officially became a candidate.

They did their work with the help of an astonishingly ambitious survey from Dick Wirthlin. His interviewers had posed hundreds of questions to two thousand people—two groups of people, actually: one was also asked questions about John Connally; another gave their opinions about Howard Baker (whom Sears had considered Reagan's second most formidable challenger, though by then Baker's campaign had been dashed on the rocks). In a 773-page volume, answers were cross-referenced according to two dozen variables, including whether Spanish was spoken in the home (5.5 percent); whether respondents were born-again Christians; and whether they were "white," "black," "oriental," or "other." The index listing cross-tabulations was eighty-seven pages alone. Ronald Reagan might have a reputation as a straight-from-the-shoulder truth-teller, but if the handlers scripting that truth-telling needed to know the difference between how union and nonunion members gauged the importance that their president "inspire confidence," the answer was at their fingertips; just turn to page 347. Episcopalians' feelings toward Governor Jerry Brown? That was page 295.

Quite a haystack. The problem was that there were hardly any encouraging needles within.

Only 22.1 percent thought Reagan "cares about people" (compared to 38.6 percent for Carter). Just over 23 percent said he was "trustworthy" (Carter: 38.9 percent). Only 27.1 percent thought he "knows national-world problems," a quality 93.8 percent thought was important in a president (Carter: 40.7 percent). As for thinking Reagan had a "high moral character," 18.7 percent. Asked what came to their mind at the mention of his name, one of the most common answers was that he was an unqualified movie actor. Also high up was "He's too old."

Respondents were invited to list the nation's three biggest problems.

The most popular answer by far, with a 52.6 percent response, was "inflation." But "government spending"—which, for years, Ronald Reagan had been instructing the public *caused* inflation—was listed by only 2.8 percent. Only 1 percent were vexed by "government control," 0.7 percent by "national defense," 0.9 percent by "too much welfare," 0.4 percent by "high property taxes." "Decline of moral values" was tied with "unemployment" for the second most cited problem, but it appeared few conceptualized it as conservatives did; the only social issue cited was abortion, by only one in a thousand respondents—2.5 percentage points less than those who cited "utility costs." Almost 55 percent said it was acceptable to "terminate pregnancy at any time" (and only 0.1 percent listed it as a top issue). Nearly 64 percent favored the Equal Rights Amendment. More than 40 percent thought solar was the "best future energy source," only 15.4 percent nuclear power—most surveyed *before* Three Mile Island.

Thus did the people planning Ronald Reagan's campaign discover that the nation shared his opinions hardly at all.

THE PARTY PLANNERS COULD REPORT PROGRESS, OF A SORT: HOUSE MInority leader Robert Michel, who had a lovely voice, agreed to sing the national anthem. A famous political cartoonist, whose daughter was dating Charlie Wick's son, would draw caricatures for free. Two of Nancy Reagan's dear friends, Betty Wilson and Marion Jorgensen, came bearing tablecloths left over from a benefit in Palm Springs. If the planning for the Reagan debut had been a movie, it would have been one of those musicals where a bunch of plucky kids put on an amateur theatrical in a barn, with the Mickey Rooney and Judy Garland parts played by seventy-year-old Wall Street financiers and the socialite wives of oil-field equipment manufacturers, a happy ending anything but assured.

Before the big day, profiles introducing the candidate piled up in newspapers. The one in the *Detroit News* spent its first twenty-two paragraphs dwelling on Reagan's age. The *Washington Post*'s revealed that Reagan was a devoted reader of his horoscope, that his columns were drafted by "a public relations firm," that he called his wife "Mommy," and that he bristled when a reporter observed he never got the girl in the movies. The one in the *Wall Street Journal*, by a 1976 Reagan delegate, said Reagan had first "studied statesmanship and, when that proved ineffectual, raucous jingoism," and labeled John Sears his "stage manager."

Sears seemed to deliberately court the description, topping himself with increasingly arrogant pronouncements. Asked why Reagan skipped events with other candidates, he said, "I'm not going to take this beautiful horse out of the stable and risk breaking his leg." Asked why a cash-strapped campaign was renting a private jet for $1,700 an hour, he said,

"When you're a front-runner you must go in style." And: "When you're the front-runner, everybody returns your phone calls. It gives you a great utility to communicate and shape the course of the campaign." (For the "race usually can't start until the front-runner lets it.")

Reagan occupied himself dictating letters. He answered a correspondent concerned about his conservation record by endorsing a maximalist version of the ideas of a cadre of legal scholars and legislators in the Mountain West, like James Watt and Anne Gorsuch in Colorado, who called themselves the "Sagebrush Rebellion": that the Constitution only allowed the federal government to own a tiny bit of land. (Their critics in the Colorado legislature called them "the Crazies.") He told an enthusiast for returning to the gold standard that he was searching for "a plan as to how this could be accomplished." Backing money with gold—"hard" currency, "real" money—had been a shibboleth of conservative populists since the days when manly frontiersmen carried heavy ingots around to pay their debts and signal their disgust at the effete, Eastern Bank of the United States. It hadn't been American policy since 1933. Almost all economists considered returning to it an insane idea. But Reagan reassured this correspondent, "I am not changing my positions one bit nor is anyone in my organization trying to change me."

Though presently, his staff was busy trying to fine-tune respectable new positions for him to utter on every issue under the sun.

Richard Allen had just sent Reagan an unusually frank memo imploring him to "drop quoting Marx (died in 1883), Lenin (died in 1942), or Stalin (died in 1953)" when delivering what Allen delicately described as his "frank and direct" answer about why he opposed détente, which typically explained that the Soviet Union had not "retreated one inch from its determination to one day have the Marxian dream of a one-world Communist state." Allen was worried that this scared audiences to death.

Reagan's last stop before heading east was a fundraiser at the former estate of Douglas Fairbanks and Mary Pickford, where he said, concerning the hostage crisis, "I think the situation that we are in right now could have been prevented, had we had a consistent policy of supporting the shah." Then he stopped at Jim Bakker's Virginia studio, predicting that the battle of Armageddon might come any day.

Then it was off to New York, to introduce himself as a candidate to lead the Free World.

REAGAN DID INTERVIEWS WITH THE NETWORK MORNING SHOWS. ON NBC'S *Today*, he told Tom Brokaw, "If I become president, other than perhaps Margaret Thatcher, I will probably be younger than almost all the heads of state I will have to do business with."

Brokaw pointed out that Valéry Giscard d'Estaing was much younger than he. Reagan responded, "Who?"

Reagan had met with the fifty-three-year-old president of France a year earlier—and also the forty-year-old president of Canada. Press Secretary Jim Lake insisted that *of course* Reagan knew who the president of France was; he just couldn't hear what Brokaw had said. A *Washington Post* reporter joked that they could run that correction. Lake sighed: "We'd rather have you say he's too ignorant than too old."

Reagan sat in on interviews with two potential admen, one responsible for coining Pepsi's slogan "The Choice of a New Generation," the other, "Four Out of Five Dentists Recommend Trident." They went with the latter. He taped his TV speech. He made the rounds of gatherings in the city, accompanied by a new set of companions: Secret Service agents. (He chose the code name "Rawhide." Nancy Reagan went with "Rainbow.") At one, he was introduced by the right-wing radio call-in host Barry Gray, who said that Reagan should be elected because "the nation cries out for desperate leadership." *Oops.*

At the Hilton Helene von Damm worked until three in the morning arranging the seating, scattering the handful of Hollywood stars around the room to maximize the number of guests who could brag about meeting a celebrity. Robert Stack and his wife arrived early. She escorted them to their table. The man who played the unflappable Eliot Ness on TV erupted, because it wasn't near the center. Max Rabb arrived in a huff because his favorite rabbi would not be doing the invocation. Von Damm broke into tears, retreating to the ladies' room. "Men can swear without being labeled unprofessional," she told herself, "so why can't women cry?"

Her spirits turned as the ballroom began to fill. Then, it grew veritably crowded. There were hundreds of Republican officials from near and far, many of them still neutral. There was William F. Buckley, several fantastically wealthy businessmen, scores of camera-friendly young people ("invited as special guests of Governor Reagan," the brand-new *Reagan Country* campaign newsletter fudged). Soon 1,800 were bustling about, sipping cocktails, while the balcony above filled with 225 media personnel from around the world.

The lights dimmed. The curtains swept open. From the rafters descended a screen, upon which Jimmy Stewart appeared. The beloved Hollywood superstar introduced a snippet from Reagan's tear-jerking speech following Gerald Ford's nomination at the 1976 convention. Then he narrated his dear friend's subsequent adventures crisscrossing the country for his party, including the time he was stuck in Cut Bank, Montana—"The Coldest Spot in the Nation"—during a Lincoln Day blizzard.

"In fact, if you added up the hours he has spent on the road, they total thirty-four solid weeks since 1976 . . . far from a vacation trip."

A shot of Reagan working with his shirt off:

"Ronald Reagan built not only the fences, but also the house and dock, as a form of exercise. . . . Part of any day on the ranch also involves a daily flood of phone calls and paperwork, as seen in this news photo taken during the 1976 campaign. . . . And then it's on to the next city . . . speech after speech, banquet after banquet . . . though some are not so easy."

The film was officially entitled *1980: Time for Reagan*. At Reagan headquarters, they called it *Tarzan Reagan*.

The candidate emerged in a blaze of klieg light. The electrified crowd cheered and cheered. Reagan made it official with his speech in the ballroom, and on TV, following an introduction from Michael Landon of TV's *Little House on the Prairie*, he was beamed simultaneously into . . . 50 percent of American homes.

THE TEXT BORE THE IMPRESS OF WIRTHLIN'S RESEARCH. SO 22.1 PERCENT of voters thought Reagan did not care about people? He told a favorite story about his family during Great Depression, "when those with too little to eat outnumbered those who had enough." So 68.3 percent said the energy shortage was invented by the energy companies to jack up their profits? For the first and possibly the last time, Reagan poked at the energy companies: "In recent days, there's been a lot of talk about excess oil company profits. I don't believe we've been given all the information we need to make a judgment about this. We *should have* that information. . . . It is government's function to determine whether we are being unfairly exploited, and if so to take immediate and appropriate action"—not exactly Reagan's line in the consumer agency fight the year before.

But mostly, it was unadulterated Reagan, exuding an inheritance he attributed to the influence of his mother, whom he once wrote had "a sense of optimism that ran as deep as the cosmos."

"To me, our country is a living, breathing presence, unimpressed by what others say is impossible, generous—yes, and naive. Sometimes wrong. Never mean. And always impatient to provide a better life for its people, in a framework of a basic fairness and freedom. You know, someone once said that the difference between an American and any other kind of person is that an American lives in anticipation of the future, because he knows it will be a great place.

"Others fear the future as just a repetition of past failures . . . who would have us believe that the United States, like other great civilizations of the past, has reached the zenith of its power; that we are weak and fearful, reduced to bickering with each other and no longer possessed of the will to cope with our problems. . . .

"They tell us we must learn to live with less, and teach our children that their lives will be less full and prosperous than ours have been; that the America of the coming years will be a place where—because of our past excesses—it will be impossible to dream and make those dreams come true.

"I don't believe that. And I don't believe you believe that either. That's why I'm seeking the presidency. I cannot and will not stand by and see this great country destroy itself."

He turned to his customary liturgy of absolution:

"Our leaders attempt to blame their failures on circumstances beyond their control, on false estimates by unknown, unidentifiable experts who rewrite modern history in an attempt to convince us our own high standard of living, the result of thrift and hard work, is somehow selfish extravagance which we must *renounce* as we join in the sharing of *scarcity*." But "the crisis we face is not the result of *any* failure of the American spirit."

He was standing beside an American flag, in a carefully dressed office set, with paintings of America's natural beauty on the wall, photos of the American flag planted on the moon, and the famous "Earthrise" taken from the first NASA orbital mission. Occasionally he sat behind a desk covered with family snapshots.

But when he did, the leather chair squeaked. Meanwhile, in the ballroom, the public address system kept dropping out, and the lights randomly brightened and dimmed.

He turned to policy proposals—and in the balcony, reporters raised their pens, remembering John Sears's promises about the "Nixonian thoroughness" they would entail.

But on inflation, it was four straight minutes of the same old *lower taxes, slash spending*. Same with energy: less government, more drilling, "putting the market system to work."

Then, however, he said that if Puerto Ricans voted in favor of statehood in an upcoming referendum, he would expedite their wishes—that was new. And next he introduced a rather startling idea.

"A developing closeness among Canada, Mexico, and the United States—a North American accord—would permit achievement in each country beyond that which I believe any of them, strong as they are, could accomplish in the absence of such cooperation." It was "time we stopped thinking of our nearest neighbors as foreigners." A North American union could update America's achievement two hundred years ago when "we taught the world that a new form of government, created out of the genius of man to cope with his circumstances, could succeed in bringing a measure of quality to human life previously thought impossible."

The details were vague. But the ideal as he summarized it was crystalline: a North American continent "in which the peoples and commerce of its three strong countries flow more freely across their present borders than they do today."

Borders more porous not just for money and goods but people was anathema to many conservatives. Reagan thought the opposite way. He'd been pondering the idea since spring, when he dictated a rare letter about policy, tasking advisor Richard Whalen to work on what he referred to as the "open border project." One component, Whalen's resulting white paper suggested, could be work permits for Mexicans seeking residency. It quoted a consultant suggesting the Roman ideal of universal citizenship as a model, or Britain's Commonwealth of Nations. Another said, "The simplicity of the idea, and its generosity, cannot fail to work its way among the poor, the hopeless *and* among the educated and more affluent." One advised not worrying too much about objections from the "establishment in the Southwest": the advantage "of cheap labor with no questions asked" would trump the white Protestant elite's concerns about "cultural dilution."

In July Reagan discussed the idea with the leaders of Mexico and Canada; in August, the campaign's executive committee game-planned a strategy to "pre-sell" it to think tanks, columnists, editors, and academics; Richard Wirthlin sent his interviewers out to gauge public support. There was something quintessentially Reagan about it, this luminous melding of misty-eyed pride that immigrants still saw the United States as a beacon of hope, his bedrock belief in America as the world's magnanimous steward, alongside bottomless faith that freer markets were always a humanitarian boon.

In the speech, the North American union section seamlessly flowed into a soaring concluding peroration, filled with his favorite patriotic quotations. One was from Thomas Paine, who said, "when Washington's men were freezing at Valley Forge, 'We have in our power to begin the world over again.' We still have that power." The other came from the Puritan divine "John Winthrop, standing on the deck of the tiny *Arabella* off the coast of Massachusetts," who "told the little band of Pilgrims: '*We shall be as a city upon a hill.*'"

He closed with his most cherished reference of all, a paraphrase from Franklin Roosevelt's 1933 inaugural address: "I believe that you and I together can keep this rendezvous with destiny."

The crowd erupted. He plunged into their midst, exuberantly shaking hand after hand, while in the balcony, reporters began composing their reviews.

They were terrible.

The *Wall Street Journal* called it "a speech patently put together by a political packager." The *Rocky Mountain News*, in a piece headlined "Reagan Announces His Candidacy—Again," found little of interest in the announcement of "a 68-year-old former movie star" other than that he was "the tenth man to declare his candidacy for the 1980 GOP nomination." (Then it cut away to Teddy Kennedy.) The *Washington Post* called it "a muted restatement of familiar Reagan themes," and accompanied their review with a feature on Reagan's refusal to debate his rivals. The *Chicago Tribune* ran its dispatch on page eight, paired with a feature on the failed campaign of 1972 front-runner Edmund Muskie. The *New York Times* front page showed him studying note cards, like he couldn't utter a word without them. A news analysis compared it to his 1976 demand that the Republican Party "erect a banner of bold colors, no pastel shades": "Last night, he seemed to choose pastels."

THE NEXT MORNING REAGAN HIT THE ROAD—MUCH TO THE CONSTERNA-tion of Charlie Wick, who had secured the attendance of several fat cats by promising them an audience with Reagan.

The first stop was a press conference in Washington, where the campaign's newly announced head of policy development, Jack Kemp, called Reagan the "oldest and wisest candidate." Oops again. (The press corps started referring to Reagan as "O&W.")

The oldest and wisest candidate took the podium, and again ignored the national moratorium on politicizing the hostage crisis, claiming that the Iranian revolution was Jimmy Carter's fault for not having "encouraged the shah to separate some of the more incendiary leaders from their followers." Then he ignored Richard Allen's advice, averring that "the Soviet Union has never strayed one inch from its determination to one day have the Marxian dream of a one-world Communist state." And he insulted the president for his collapse in the road race in September: "If I were a betting man, I'd bet that I won't have to be helped off the track."

He swung through nine cities in the next five days. A briefing on his first stop explained that his event was being held in a union hall in South Boston, "known as Southey . . . an Irish/Catholic, working class, Democratic area. . . . To avoid excluding any ethnics, a Polish band will appear." It listed among the most pressing local issues the price of home heating oil, taxes and inflation, layoffs at the Quincy shipyards—and "BUSING" and "CRIME AND VIOLENCE."

These observations, and the fact that a legendary old Irish Democratic pol named Albert "Dapper" O'Neil appeared alongside him, revealed this opening tour's theme. Dapper O'Neil was the designated successor on the city council of Louise Day Hicks, the legendary leader of the violent opposition to the integration of South Boston High School; he called integration supporters "Communist dupes," the federal desegregation order "a Communist plot against Boston," was an adamant supporter of South Africa's apartheid government, and famously never went anywhere without a gun.

Then it was off to a rally alongside Congressman Henry Hyde in Cicero, Illinois, a white ethnic working-class suburb of Chicago whose history of racist violence rivaled South Boston's. The last time a black person tried to live there was 1951; the ensuing riot warned anyone against trying again for decades. A little more than a dozen years before Reagan's visit, a black kid was beaten to death just for crossing into Cicero to look for a job, and Martin Luther King Jr. gave up on a plan for a housing march there after the Cook County sheriff called it "awfully close to a suicidal act." Reagan's briefing explained that the top issue was a sales tax increase to expand the Regional Transportation Authority (lest it be made easier for outsiders to penetrate the white citadel), and a "recent HEW decision to force a busing program on the city of Chicago and surrounding suburbs." Next Reagan visited the most racially segregated city in America: Milwaukee, where the segregationist George Wallace had performed shockingly well in the 1964 Democratic presidential primary campaign, and the "hottest issue," his briefing read, was resentment over the reopening of the 1955 case of a police officer who shot an unarmed black man.

Ronald Reagan doted upon his lack of racism, even as he opposed antiracist public policies. When people criticized him for opposing the 1965 Voting Rights Act, he protested that his objection had only been that the law was "humiliating to the South." When they pointed to his opposition to California's open housing law in 1966, he said that the overriding moral issue was the sacred nature of property rights.

He kept a quiver of anecdotes at hand to explain how the heroic actions of individuals had *already* solved America's racial ordeal, like the sports announcers, himself included, who successfully organized against the official Major League guidebook's assertion, "Baseball is a game for Caucasian gentlemen," integrating blacks into the league. (There was no such guidebook, and he stopped broadcasting a decade before baseball desegregated.) He would claim that his best friend—William Franklin Burghardt, "Burgie," a college football teammate—was black (they exchanged letters occasionally), and cite the fact that Los Angeles elected a black mayor in 1975 as proof that racism was a thing of the past. In 1968, he said that the only reason race remained a political issue was because Democratic demagogues made it one, whipping up racial grievance in order to lure the black man "onto a federal plantation and ignore him."

Others in the Reagan campaign had a more sophisticated grasp of the issue.

"Reagan voters," Dick Wirthlin's firm concluded in a June "Survey of Voter Values and Attitude," scored highest on "respect for authority, individualism, and authoritarianism—and a low score on egalitarianism," especially if they were over fifty-five years of age, or were members of "Eastern European ethnic groups living in large cities." Wirthlin thus identified the richest seam of new Reagan voters as "Democrats, head of household, employed, 35 years and older, earning less than $15,000." He didn't bother to add the obvious point that he was referring only to whites.

They were the voters most strongly affected by the late 1960s "Philadelphia Plan" enforcing quotas for minority workers on federal construction projects. And by 1972 amendments to the Civil Rights Act that made it easier for the Justice Department to sue fire departments and police forces for racial discrimination—like Dan White's police force in San Francisco. Also, by the Supreme Court's 1976 decision in *Franks v. Bowman Transportation* specifying "retroactive seniority" as a remedy for past workplace discrimination. Establishing time-on-the-job as the key determinant of pay and benefits, Justice William Brennan wrote in his decision, meant that a black employee "will perpetually remain subordinate to persons who, but for illegal discrimination, would have been, in respect to entitlement to the benefits, his inferiors." But Justice Lewis Powell wrote in his dissent that if black workers leapfrogged longer-serving white ones on seniority lists, the benefit was "derived not at the expense of the employer, but at the expense of other workers." They were the kind of voters about whom, the *New York Times* noted in 1972 (on page 47), the pollster Daniel Yankelovich had discovered "a dirty little secret that is neither little nor secret but central to current politics": when asked, "Do you feel that minority groups are receiving too much, too little, or just about the right amount of attention," 80 percent who answered "too much" voted for Richard Nixon.

In Cicero, they read the *Chicago Tribune*—which referred in eighty different stories between 1974 and 1980 to "welfare queens": women, usually black, who supposedly grew comfortable ripping off the public purse, abetted by naïve liberals who made it all too easy to get by without working at all. Now, according to a National Election Studies poll of Americans' perception of the parties, 68.8 percent of voters believed Democrats were "likely to aid minorities," up from 59.4 percent in 1972, compared to 27.33 percent who said that about Republicans. The number of Americans who supported increased spending to improve the conditions of blacks was at a record low, 24 percent. Americans maintaining that blacks and other minorities should "help themselves" was at an all-time high of 41 percent, up five percentage points since 1976.

People like these were the target audience for a board game released that fall called Public Assistance: "This is going to be a fun Christmas for Republicans. Republicans love this game," its creator enthused. Players circled around a track, Monopoly-style, picking from two piles of cards: "WELFARE BENEFITS" ("While in welfare office parking lot, you syphon gas from social worker's Pinto into your Lincoln. Collect $200"; "Your spouse or live-in lands government job, takes first turn on Government cake walk") and "WORKING PERSON'S BURDEN" ("You are up for high-paying promotion, but Government 'Affirmative Action' rules require that a 'disadvantaged minority, homosexual, Buddhist female' be promoted over you. Lose $500"). The object was to accumulate the most money without working; the most efficient way to do so was to collect "illegitimate children."

Reagan's managers were targeting voters who felt victimized by government actions that cost them the privileges their whiteness once afforded them. In Cicero, they clamored six-abreast in line waiting for the FBI to complete its bomb check to enter the Morton Community College gym to celebrate what city fathers had officially declared "Ronald Reagan Day." Inside, they chanted, "Reagan's right! Reagan's right!" in eager anticipation. They cheered lustily when Reagan described Jimmy Carter's new Department of Education as a plot to replace neighborhood schools with a system directed from Washington. They gave him a standing ovation when he bellowed, "The Carter administration's principal argument for signing SALT II is that *no one will like us if we don't*. His argument for giving away the Panama Canal was that *no one would like us if we didn't*. . . . Isn't it about time that we stopped worrying whether anyone likes us and decide we're going to be respected in the world—respected to the point that never again will any dictator dare to invade an American embassy and hold our people hostage?"

In Milwaukee, he blamed corporate tax rates for industrial decline, and promised as nominee to attract "the millions of patriotic Democrats across the country who feel just like we do about what it happening in this country." Then Gerald Ford's hometown of Grand Rapids, where auto jobs were disappearing by the day; then Atlanta, where his briefing read "Crime is the most biting local issue"; then Orlando to vanquish John Connally at the Republican convention.

Then to Cedar Rapids and Des Moines—a rare foray into the state where the first official nominating contest was to take place in thirty-seven days, on January 21. In the *Des Moines Register* poll, Reagan had 50 percent support, more than three times George Bush in second place.

HE DID MUCH WORSE WITH THE MEDIA. THE *WASHINGTON POST*'S ACE REAgan watcher, Lou Cannon, on the beat since his first gubernatorial campaign, reported from the tour that Reagan's bobbles in response to reporters' questions raised "new doubts about his capacity to serve as president." Reagan subsequently looked back on that first week on the trail, "So far as I can tell, when we started out in the morning, the goal of many of the reporters was simply to catch me fouling up my speech or to trap me into a minor error about an obscure inconsequential topic that had nothing to do with the campaign." But the one he bobbled worst, during his Michigan stop, was neither minor, obscure, nor inconsequential: the fate of American manufacturing.

It was once a profound source of patriotic pride. Now, anxieties over its decline suffused every TV commercial break. They were filled with foreign accents. When admen required a semiotic shorthand to signify quality, style, and dependability, a European read the copy—because "American-made" now signified "unreliable crap." A Harvard professor had just published *Japan as Number One: Lessons for America*, and even though the Japanese considered its idyllic portrait of them virtually unrecognizable, the book was widely read from Washington to Wall Street, where a perception of Japanese virtue as mirror image of American failure had become near to common sense.

Patriotism had once kept that image from solidifying; people had a nagging suspicion that there was something wrong about buying cars manufactured in countries against which their fathers had fought. Japanese companies deployed the best Madison Avenue had to offer to shake that prejudice. Honda achieved it with commercials featuring the curmudgeonly but charming voice of actor Burgess Meredith. Subaru ran brilliant ads starring the thirty-eighth president's daughter, Susan, with the Capitol dome in the background. ("Take it from a Ford. Drive Subaru." What could be more stolidly patriotic than the Ford family?) By the autumn of Reagan's debut, such campaigns had succeeded so admirably that a commercial in heavy rotation (it ran during Roger Mudd's November 4 broadcast on Ted Kennedy) practically begged Americans, as a patriotic duty, to at least *consider* the possibility that there might be exceptions to the trend. It starred a soaring American eagle and a John Wayne soundalike who allowed how the ideals of our fathers had been "threatened by the slipshod, the second rate"— but "Whirlpool Corporation believes in one simple idea. To continue to design, build, and service home appliances the right way—with pride. . . . If we can't keep this simple idea alive, then indeed we are the endangered species."

By then, the percentage of all manufactured goods on the American market that were imported rose to 40 percent; in 1970, the figure had been 14 percent. Japanese cars captured a quarter of American sales—because

American carmakers were the most conspicuously slipshod and second-rate domestic manufacturers of all. "Come on home to Chevrolet, come on home!" General Motors jingled. Americans refused the invitation.

In 1978, U.S. automakers sold 9.3 million units. In 1979, they moved only 8.3 million. The economic consequences were colossal, for one out of twelve manufacturing jobs—in sectors like rubber, steel, and aluminum—were tied to the industry. Factory layoffs were one of the reasons voters in Southey, Cicero, and Milwaukee were so angry—and blamed racial scapegoats for their plight. The truth, however, which Ralph Nader had been arguing since 1965, was that the decline was almost entirely of American industry's own making. America's Big Three automakers—General Motors, Ford, and Chrysler—were so sclerotic, stupid, and arrogant that if they did not exist, a Soviet propagandist might wish to invent them, as glaring counterdemonstrations to the proposition that capitalism was the most efficient economic system.

The Big Three insisted on producing what one of the few dynamic executives in the industry—George Romney, who retired as president of American Motors in 1962 to go into politics—called "gas-guzzling dinosaurs." At the time he said that, the Big Three's fleets averaged twelve miles per gallon, and ingenious engineers at NASA were busy putting men on the moon. By the time the first energy crisis hit in 1973, the not-so-ingenious engineers in Detroit were only able to increase that figure to 13.4 mpg. Automakers in both Europe and Japan produced smaller, more efficient front-wheel-drive cars. When a member of Ford's board of directors who lived in California said they were catching on among young people there, a top executive snapped back that they "probably all lived in communes." Such indifference to customers reached a sort of apotheosis when Ford went on trial for reckless homicide in the deaths of three teenage girls after the fuel tank on their Pinto, located behind the rear axle, burst into flames when their car was hit from behind. Ford was acquitted of all charges—three years after an exposé in *Mother Jones* magazine proved its executives were aware of the deadly flaw but decided not to fix it because a "cost-benefit" analysis suggested that it made more financial sense to chance lawsuits rather than expend the eleven dollars per automobile that would require.

Of all the big American manufacturers, Chrysler was the worst. During American capitalism's golden years in the 1960s, their executives systematically cheated the firm's future by skimping on research and development, pushing artificially high production quotas in order to make the stock appear more attractive. Tens of thousands of excess vehicles were stored in a "sales bank"—giant warehouses, even giant parking lots where they rusted outside in the Detroit winters. In 1976, Chrysler re-

leased two smaller models, the Aspen and the Volare, which the Center for
Auto Safety named the "lemons of the year"; then two more, the Omni
and the Horizon, which were rated "too risky to drive" by Consumers
Union—though since they had contracted with Volkswagen to build them
rather than recommit factories to building smaller cars, they couldn't meet
demand in any event. Their corporate research division suggested sterling
opportunities for a new sort of vehicle called a "minivan." But that went
nowhere—because by then, bold innovation had become inconceivable.

The company lost $159 million in 1978. CEO John Riccardo asked
Washington for temporary relief from federal regulations. He was denied.
After shuttering his biggest factory in May of 1979, Riccardo approached
President Carter, hat in hand, to ask for another relief package, to no avail.
In August, congressmen with Chrysler factories in their districts came up
with the idea of a federal grant with future taxes as collateral—the kind of
deal Donald Trump enjoyed. The White House refused that, too. Finally,
Jimmy Carter reluctantly settled on a $1.5 billion loan guarantee package,
with ruthless austerity terms attached—because a Congressional Budget
Office study suggested that if Chrysler went under it could cost up to
three hundred thousand jobs. The UAW had already announced for Ted
Kennedy, so Carter needed all the remaining affection he could muster
among industrial workers if he were to be renominated—and if he were to
be *reelected*, he would have to prevail in crucial Michigan, which the Republicans had chosen as the site for their 1980 convention.

The package worked its way through Congress in the fall. On Octo-
ber 31, Chrysler posted a numbing $460 million loss for the third quarter.
Hearings in the Senate Banking Committee began on November 4. The
House Banking Committee approved the package 24–17 on November 14.

So where would Reagan stand on the Chrysler bailout: on the principle of governmental noninterference in the free market, or for saving
jobs in a key electoral state during a recession? At his press conference in
Washington he had dodged. When he landed in Grand Rapids, Michigan,
reporters pressed him again. Reagan replied haltingly: "I don't believe
I'm in agreement with the plan that was presented by the president"—
though he didn't seem to understand what the plan entailed. "There are
other things that can still be done which would not run the risk that this
plan runs," such as renegotiated labor contracts and "realignment of the
company itself"—but the deal *already included* these provisions, and, as
for those "other things" that could "still be done," Lou Cannon pointed
out, Reagan did not "appear to have a clue as to what these other things
were."

Reagan's worried handlers began canceling planned appearances. "By
the second week of December," a journalist wrote, "the pace was so lei-

surely that a baggage call in South Carolina was listed on the campaign schedule as an 'event.'"

TO BE FAIR, HE HAD A DIFFICULT PERSONNEL ISSUE ON HIS MIND—JUST THE sort of thing that always caused him the most stress. The ever-roiling rivalries among "the fellas"—what Reagan called his close staff—had crystallized along regional lines: the men who had come up alongside their hero in Sacramento, and called their favorite newspaper by one word, the *Times*, and the ones on Sears's side, for whom the only newspaper by that name was published on 43rd Street in New York. And by November, the feuding between the "Easterners" and the "California Cronies" had grown so acrimonious that an attempt at reconciliation at their hotel in Washington after the announcement descended into a shouting match, with Nancy Reagan sobbing in the background.

Reagan returned home for Thanksgiving. He caught up on his dictation. ("I envy you your visit to South Africa," he wrote an old Hollywood friend. "They must be the ally with which we line up in any world strategy that we are going to follow for our own security.") On November 26, he met with the fellas at his home.

The last to arrive was Michael Deaver, who was confused to find himself ushered into a bedroom while the rest of the group conferred in the den. Deaver had been an ambitious young publicist when he took his first political job, in the successful 1964 Senate campaign of George Murphy, a star of old MGM musicals. His job was tailing Murphy's opponent and handing him a cigar every time he got out of a car, so Murphy might be photographed looking like a corrupt political boss. That was how Deaver learned the importance of what he called "visuals"—his political specialty.

He hadn't supported Ronald Reagan for governor in 1966; he thought only a moderate could win. But he got a job on the new governor's transition team, then rose to be the assistant to the chief of staff, in charge of the governor's schedule, public appearances, and travel; that was how the two became close. Deaver was especially trusted by Nancy Reagan. They shared a passion, he wrote: "helping her husband do the best he could and to look good while doing it"; that was how he became the most important figure in Ronald Reagan's political life.

Countless times, Deaver was the first person Reagan saw in the morning and the last person he saw at night. Long conversations kindled between them a greater intimacy than they had shared with any other man. "Everything I was to do for Reagan in Sacramento and after," he later said, came "from a burning desire never to disappoint the man, no matter how insignificant the job at hand. As a boss, there was just something about him that made you want to please him and to do your best."

It was almost mystical how precisely he grew to know his boss's habits. He could enhance Reagan's performance—without threatening his ego—so effectively, it was almost magical. How to improve upon a rare poor first take at an important TV taping? Since Reagan drank decaf, make "a pot of real Navy coffee, double the caffeine." ("He understood my thinking when I handed him the java. No words needed to be exchanged. . . . As he sat before the camera a second time, he was the old Reagan, animated and lively. . . . Of course the coffee was just a reminder that he could and would have to do better.") Lacking that "usual glow" in the hours before an important debate? Leave a bottle of fine French wine by his place at dinner beforehand. ("Being a wine lover—one glass only, of course—Reagan would inspect it. If the year and vintage passed muster with him, he was sure to pour himself a glass while reviewing his notes. . . . After a glass of a fine French red, Reagan seemed to get his color back. His eyes sparkled, and his cheeks turned red.")

He knew to be especially careful with what Reagan was given to read; "it would be entered into his mental computer and could be spit out at any time in the future." He knew how to convince him not to do something: don't call it "political death." Tell him it would "hurt people." He knew to keep him disciplined during interviews. "He's too relaxed when he's sitting. He's not careful. He's controversial." And to never, ever let him talk to the press from his ranch. Once, public outrage rained down upon Reagan after he claimed that South Africa's new "reformist administration" had "eliminated the segregation that we once had in our own country." At that particular time, Michael Deaver was not on Reagan's staff. "They should have protected him," he observed. "He's so much the product of his environment. He's all alone out at his ranch, nobody with him. He's probably dreaming about riding his horse. Maybe the horse went by at that moment. And he's on the phone, talking to one person and not thinking that hundreds of thousands will eventually be in the audience. He's relaxed . . ."

How in the hell could John Sears ever learn to understand Reagan like *that*?

THE GOVERNOR USHERED DEAVER BACK INTO THE LIVING ROOM: "MIKE, the fellas here have been telling me about how you've been running the fund-raising efforts, and we're losing money."

Deaver remembered the pained look on Reagan's face as he relayed an accusation: that Deaver was padding the bill for the rent he charged the campaign for the use of his public relations office—an enraging claim, given that Sears's extravagant spending habits were a big reason the campaign was in such financial pain.

Deaver boiled over. *Of course* others in Reagan's orbit resented him for his intimacy with Reagan. (Pat Buchanan mocked him as the "keeper of the royal chamber pot.") *Of course* John Sears would seek to purge a major obstacle in his drive for total control. But forcing *Reagan himself* to wield the ax was simply too much.

"If these guys are going to sink to these tactics now, what would we do if we ever got to the White House? I'm leaving."

Reagan followed him: "No, this is not what I want."

"Sorry, sir, but it's what I want."

Reagan stomped back inside: "Well, I hope you're happy. The best guy we had just left. . . . You are small, petty men."

He turned to Nancy: "They'll be in here again and next time they'll be after Ed Meese. And goddammit I'm not going to let that happen."

Research director Martin Anderson, also with Reagan since the 1960s, quit in solidarity. Nofziger, then Deaver and Anderson: he was losing the people he most trusted. And of course, Evans and Novak reported the whole thing. All in all, an inauspicious start to the front-runner's presidential campaign.

CHAPTER 30

Patriotisms

AMERICAN FAMILIES HAD MUCH TO FRET OVER THAT THANKSGIVING. DUR-
ing the past twenty-four hours, Sunni militants in Saudi Arabia had taken
thousands of pilgrims hostage at the Grand Mosque in Mecca; on the
radio, Ayatollah Khomeini blamed the U.S. "and its stooge Israel," which
was why, in Karachi, Pakistan, mobs overran the American consulate,
and in Islamabad, mobs screaming "kill the American dogs" torched the
embassy, trapping hundreds in an upstairs vault, leaving two American
soldiers dead. In Tehran, the largest mass march yet thundered past the
embassy, roaring the familiar chants that all began "*marg bar*"—"*death
to*": "Death to the shah," "Death to America," "Death to Carter."

In the U.S. in the weeks since November 4 anti-Iranian melees had broken out in more than a dozen cities and college campuses. In Houston, office workers streamed out of skyscrapers to surround the Iranian consulate
behind hand-scrawled placards reading things like "WHY NOT AN IRA-
NIAN HOSTAGE?" The next day, the ritual was repeated, less spontaneously: ringleaders brought American flags (to hold) and Iranian flags (to
burn), and the front row marched behind posters with images of the late
John Wayne, like a Roman phalanx bearing shields. On Thanksgiving Day,
a Molotov cocktail was thrown through the window of the Islamic Student
Center at the University of Oklahoma, and an interview with Barry Goldwater was published: if Khomeini "hurts one American," America should
obliterate Iran's oil fields "and let them sit there and starve to death."

On a family coffee table one might find new issues of *Time*, with an
irresolute-looking President Carter on the cover ("Test of Wills"), or
Newsweek, with an eagle shedding its feathers ("Has America Lost Its
Clout?"), cataloguing recent blows to America's "power of effective action": from "Soviet and Cuban forces marching unhindered across large
parts of Africa" to "oil sheiks raising their prices recklessly" to "staunch,
if unsavory friends" losing power in Nicaragua and Iran, to the plunging
dollar, the plunging standard of living, and the struggle of the American
armed forces, "which once held a nuclear monopoly, to maintain something called 'parity.'"

Effective action. The previous week, *Time* had interviewed twenty-four military experts about whether America could do what tiny Israel had done in 1976 when its commandos heroically rescued 102 hostages held by Palestinian militants at the Entebbe, Uganda, airport. Retired admiral Elmo Zumwalt spoke for the consensus: "I think it's pretty much out of the question." In a speech in Des Moines, another retired admiral said it would ignite World War III: if "the Russians didn't like it, which they probably wouldn't, they might come in from the north," North Korea might invade South Korea—and "the lid is off."

So America was helpless—even, NBC News reported, as "sources are telling the White House that the hostages are being subjected to harsh methods of brainwashing . . . tied up 24 hours a day and forced to remain seated without the opportunity for exercise." This was greatly exaggerated: these students were far too unsophisticated to brainwash anyone. But still, America was helpless.

Helpless as hostage Jerry Miele, shrouded in a blindfold, was led to the embassy gate, and hectored at earsplitting volume by a crowd eager to tear him limb from limb.

Helpless as the students threatened to put the hostages on "trial" as a prelude to their execution.

Helpless to begin negotiations, because the Iranian government was so chaotic and America's intelligence so poor that no one had any idea with whom to negotiate.

Helpless as more than half the hostages were said to have signed a petition demanding the shah's return to Iranian custody: "I did sign and I'm glad I did," read a letter from a nineteen-year-old Marine guard to his parents, which raised visions of Patricia Hearst. The Ayatollah announced, "in the name of Islamic mercy," that blacks and women would be released "unless they were proven spies," apparently the result of the work of PLO negotiators. At a press conference, a female returnee said, "If the American people were put in touch with the developments in the Third World and America's interference in the internal affairs of other countries, we would certainly protest the American government," and an African American Marine described how the education he had received in "American imperialism" helped him grasp how "a lot of people are suffering for a few people on top": "in a way, I kind of hate to leave them."

By December, Muslims marched on American embassies in Kuwait City and Manila, burned Jimmy Carter in effigy in Calcutta, bombed the embassy in Thailand, and overran the consulate in Libya, forcing the Americans to flee out the back—in Tripoli, the city invoked every time the Marines hymned their world-beating can-do dominance. Not, it appeared, anymore.

A man in the street told a network correspondent, "Carter should get off his duff."

"What do you think he can do?"

"I don't know."

A woman offered, "Force should be used."

"But what if responding militarily would mean the hostages would be harmed?"

"No, then we shouldn't use force."

An ABC reporter was able to finagle a phone call with one of the captors. He asked how long they could keep the Americans if the shah was never returned. "Time is not important for us," the student replied.

"But you cannot keep them forever."

"Okay, why not?"

From Foggy Bottom, Marvin Kalb reported, "There is a very deep frustration that we have tried everything and most of our efforts have not borne fruit," and quoted a State Department official: "We don't have the Shadow or Superman in our employ."

Helpless. CBS rounded up all the anti-Iranian violence that had occurred in Sacramento, California, where printed banners had begun appearing above restaurant doors—"WE RESERVE THE RIGHT TO REFUSE SERVICE TO IRANIAN CITIZENS." A service station's windows were smashed, a tow truck's tires slashed. ("Do you see yourself as American?" the correspondent asked the owner. He answered, "*Yes, sir!*") Someone shot out a hardware store's plate glass windows. (The owner put up a sign: "We are *Chaldean Catholicks* From BAGHDAD [*MOSOPO-TEMIA*].") A trembling Iranian woman pleaded, "We are innocent. We are living with fear where there is supposed to be law and order."

In Washington, a federal district judge ruled that the government could not ban demonstrations on public land by Iranians. President Carter appealed, fearing violence across the street from the White House. He implored Americans not to scapegoat Iranians in America. The message apparently didn't reach Senator Robert Byrd, the Democratic Senate leader, who liked to affect a good ol' boy image (he played old-timey bluegrass fiddle from the podia at political events). He told the *Charleston Daily Mail* he wouldn't blame anyone for "throwing eggs or anything else at Iranian students demonstrating in this country. I wouldn't mind taking a punch myself if I could get to them." (His staff subsequently released a statement clarifying that he did not "advocate or condone any form of violence.")

Nor the citizens in Columbus, Ohio, who chanted "Nagasaki, Hiroshima, why not Iran?" while marching through downtown.

Nor the high school students in the nearby college town of Oxford, who burned an Iranian flag as a class project, while parents and teachers proudly looked on.

A Birmingham, Alabama, gospel quartet released a song called "Message to Khomeini" that a radio station in Oklahoma said was requested 150 times in a day—even after it had already been spun a dozen times. It began in mocking imitation of the Muslim call to prayer, continued with spoken couplets concluding, "You think you're so darned bad, but when Uncle Sam gets mad, there's gonna be an oil slick right where Iran used to be," then chorused, "'Cause we can take our bb guns and blow your buns to the sun / Just our boy scouts could wipe you out." (Then a harmonica blew a military fanfare.)

In 1968, sporting one of the "FREE THE PUEBLO" bumper stickers distributed by the John Birch Society on your car marked you as a right-wing kook. Now vigilantism had gone pop. Though one difference from 1968 was that, this time, the bloodlust provided a distraction from the most precipitous industrial decline since the Great Depression. Five days after Thanksgiving, U.S. Steel announced it was closing sixteen plants. Two days later, they announced a 2.6 percent price hike, helping drive the fourth-quarter inflation rate to 13.3 percent. The prime rate neared 13 percent—which meant that in the twenty-two states that banned mortgage rates above 12 percent, the only way to buy a house was in cash. Bills were coming due, too, from the Great Tax Revolt: in Cincinnati, the public schools closed for three weeks for lack of funds.

Cincinnati's students returned to class on December 3. That night, the Who was playing at Riverfront Coliseum. There were, however, no reserved tickets. When doors opened there was such a mad dash for seats that eleven concertgoers were crushed to death. The city's Republican mayor, Ken Blackwell, suggested banning rock concerts. An editorial in a college newspaper in Buffalo—the next stop on the British band's tour—noted the profusion of American flags, anti-Ayatollah banners, and Nuremberg rally–like chants at the Who concert at Buffalo Memorial Auditorium and took note of what psychologists called the "blurring effect": when individuals surrender their identity to mobs. They concluded, "this 'blurring effect' has been sweeping the nation like a new fad." Blame *rock concerts*? "When Midwestern high school students march and burn Iranian flags because 'that's how the Iranians are treating us' . . . who's fooling whom?"

SOME PEOPLE HAD A WORD FOR IT.

"Iran Spurs Rebirth of Patriotism in U.S.: Crisis Unites Nation as Few Events Have," ran the banner across the entire front page of the *Akron Beacon Journal* on December 9. The jump on the inside page was illustrated with a photo of a man with a "NUKE IRAN" sign. The article, reprinted from the *Washington Post*—which called it "The Greening of Patriotism in America"—reported, "Hawks and American flags are suddenly 'in' on American campuses; doves and anti-Americanism are 'out.'" "God Bless America" was breaking out at college football games. The denizens of a Waterloo, Iowa, coffee shop agreed that a company of Marines could end the crisis right quick; a religion professor in North Carolina who described himself as "more than a dove on Vietnam," who had "never known war to solve the issues that ostensibly lead to war," now thought "Iran must be taught a lesson." Seven Iranian students had been beaten at Southern Illinois University, one in the middle of class, and on the reception desk at the biggest daily newspaper in Oklahoma, red, white, and blue stickpins impaled an Ayatollah Khomeini voodoo doll. "Nuke 'em Till They Glow. It worked in Japan. It'll work in Iran" posters were popular at the University of North Carolina, "Nuke the Ayatollah" T-shirts at Arizona State.

Patriotism. After Statesville, North Carolina, merchants lined the two busiest downtown commercial blocks with American flags, the head of the local chamber of commerce enthused, "What if every town did this? . . . This country has been split since Vietnam. It may sound corny, but it may be the best thing ever to happen to America." A Disciples of Christ minister in Cleveland took a different view: "There is a John Wayne mentality emerging in the U.S. today. It is a macho spirit that insists that in any time of international difficulty, the U.S. government should wield force."

The shah's medical treatment wound up in New York. Mexico would not readmit him. Ronald Reagan, flying from Minnesota to Seattle on his campaign charter jet, told the press gaggle, "If you read those words on the Statue of Liberty, we have a history of being an asylum for political exiles. And the shah certainly was as loyal an ally for a great many years as this country could possibly have had. . . . I think this country should make it plain that he is welcome to remain." Asked whether this wouldn't endanger the hostages, he offered an unorthodox interpretation of the militants' one unambiguous demand: "They have told us it would make *no difference* if we let him leave the United States. They have said they would still consider that we have sheltered him by letting him go."

EITHER THEY HAD TOLD RONALD REAGAN THIS PERSONALLY, OR EVERY other news outlet in the world had neglected to report it. In fact, President Carter would have loved nothing more than to let the shah leave, if anyone would have him. But the only nation that would was Egypt—an invitation the shah refused. So it was that the former monarch was slipped under the cover of darkness to Lackland Air Force Base in San Antonio, which boasted both tight security and an advanced cancer clinic. Not for good, insisted State Department spokesman Hodding Carter—but "we're not going to put a man in a rowboat and send him out beyond the continental shelf if he has no place to go."

The White House reiterated their warning of unspecified consequences if the hostages were harmed, as now seemed more likely—though the State Department said it was "beyond our capacity to know" because their captors had barred outside observers, and "the possibilities of what may be happening to those prisoners" were "infinite." The safety of Lackland's civilian neighbors was also a concern, for Iranian students in America were hardly uniformly pacific; in St. Paul, four armed Iranians had been arrested during a reception at the governor's mansion for plotting to kidnap the governor.

Ted Kennedy was asked about Reagan's remarks on the shah by a TV interviewer in San Francisco on Sunday night, December 2. The senator responded, "The shah ran one of the most violent regimes in the history of mankind, in the form of terrorism, in basic and fundamental violations of human rights, in the cruel circumstances to his own people. How do we justify in the United States on the one hand accepting that individual because he would like to come here and stay and his umpteen billions of dollars that he's stolen from Iran and at the same time say to Hispanics who are here legally that they have to wait nine years to bring their wife and their children to this country?"

The interviewer asked if the shah's history of looking out for U.S. interests should count for something. Kennedy cocked his head earnestly: "I think he was looking out for one person—himself. To tie American fortunes . . . on one man rather than a whole nation and a people is a policy—that's bankrupt." He then called for "open debate" on the subject.

Previously, Kennedy had consistently offered the opposite opinion. ("I don't think looking to the past or anticipating the future enhances the opportunity for the safety and security of the hostages.") He appeared to be making a strategic pivot—perhaps in response to a new ABC/Harris Poll that had Carter ahead for the first time; or a *Wall Street Journal* report that when voters were asked to agree or disagree with the statement "Because of what happened at Chappaquiddick, he does not deserve to be president," they answered yes 27 percent of the time. A year earlier, only 19 percent had said so. Or perhaps he decided it was time for the media to think of Reagan, not Carter, as Kennedy's opponent. Or he was seeking to raise himself in the esteem of Mexican American voters in California. Or maybe he was just sick of America's sordid history with Iran being tossed down the memory hole. Whatever the motivation, it backfired. Exactly one prominent columnist criticized what Ronald Reagan had said about the shah: irascible Mike Royko of Chicago. (He argued that he had signed "the hostages' death warrants"—though he was "grateful to Reagan for once again reminding us the kind of pea-sized brain he has.") Everyone else went after Ted Kennedy—*hard*.

The San Francisco interview led two of the three network newscasts. On NBC, illustrated with the graphic the network used for its broadcast-leading block of bitter Iran news—an American eagle, wrapped in an American flag, inside a birdcage: "Senator Kennedy was on the defensive today. . . ." On ABC, whose nightly Iran graphic had added a ticker of the hostages' days in captivity to the picture of the blindfolded hostage: "During the first weeks after the hostages were taken, major presidential contenders refrained from making any substantive comments on the crisis. All that has changed."

That wasn't so: both Connally and Reagan had regularly used the crisis to flay the president. Connally nonetheless now weighed in with relish about this supposedly shattered taboo: "I am sure the Ayatollah Khomeini is pleased to hear Senator Kennedy's remarks." Henry Hyde cried on the House floor, "Mr. Speaker, I wonder if the senator from Massachusetts has considered *registering* as an agent for the government of Iran." The RNC chairman pointed to the joint statement he had just issued with the DNC chairman pledging bipartisan unity on the subject—which "the senator's comments would seem to erode."

From the State Department briefing room, Hodding Carter stated gravely, "The secretary of state regrets any such statement which shifts the focus away from concern for the hostages and may interfere with delicate negotiations." (There were no negotiations.) Robert Strauss, before the green-and-white "Support President Carter" legend of the soon-to-be-announced reelection campaign he was to chair, said that it was "an *error* to inject anything into his campaign that in *any way* could endanger the lives of the people over there." And in the Senate, the number two ranking Republican, Ted Stevens of Alaska, said politicians should not be "making statements that might echo the feelings of the mob which is holding our hostages in Tehran."

The newscasts also quoted the delighted reaction of Sadegh Ghotbzadeh, who now was foreign minister: "This is the kind of statement that should be taken in the United States, on the side of justice, to expose the shah to the American public." That certainly added fuel to the bonfire beneath Ted Kennedy's feet.

He toggled between apology and defiance: "Throughout the day," a reporter revealed, "the senator's aides called Washington to check reaction to Kennedy's statements, and to prepare new ones." And in politics, as they say, when you're explaining, you're losing. The *Washington Post* editorial opining that his words "must have looked like an engraved invitation in Tehran" ran next to a picture of Kennedy smilingly shaking hands with the shah in 1975. The *New York Post* did it up tabloid style: "TEDDY IS THE TOAST OF TEHRAN!"

The timing couldn't have been better for Jimmy Carter. He was scheduled to officially announce his campaign the day after Kennedy's interview. He did so in a solemn event in the East Room. He said he would have preferred not to have to do it at all, if campaign law did not require it. It was, he told a small number of close associates (and a large number of reporters), "a somber time. . . . Fifty Americans continue to be held hostage in Iran, hostages of a mob and a government that have become one and the same. . . . At the height of the civil war, Abraham Lincoln said, 'I have but one task and that is to save the union.' . . . I must devote my considered efforts to the Iranian crisis." So his campaign announcement was also an announcement that he would not campaign: just stay in Washington to "lead our response to the ever-changing situation of the greatest sensitivity and importance." Which was far more effective than any ordinary whooping-and-hollering, balloon-dropping, fireworks-exploding extravaganza ever could have been.

He had also just received splendid news: Gallup had his approval rating at 54 percent. Their last pre-hostage sounding had him at 29 percent, his lowest ever. The pollsters at NBC found that 67 percent of the public approved of his handling of the Iran crisis, with 71 percent maintaining that he was doing the most he possibly could. Call it patriotism, call it leadership chic. But three days after Kennedy's remarks, 100 percent in a much smaller survey—the fifty state Democratic chairmen—said Carter's handling of Iran was helping his political standing.

"I'M SORRY . . . I'M SORRY YOU FEEL THAT WAY. . . . *NOW LISTEN, YOU DON'T have to . . .*"

The secretary at the former car dealership in downtown Washington that housed Ted Kennedy's campaign headquarters sighed: "That's the third time in the last five minutes that someone called in to say they wouldn't vote for him for dogcatcher."

At least she could be grateful that they *had* telephones; in the first several days after Kennedy's announcement, there were none. The "old hands" and "Kennedy family retainers" were *supposed* to be political maestros—"You don't have the tooling up time with Kennedy," one veteran of the supposed "well-oiled Kennedy machine" had boasted to Witcover and Germond back in October. Instead, his campaign had begun in incompetence. Media hand Charlie Guggenheim, a legend for his work on Bobby and Jack's campaigns, began shooting commercials in a style that hadn't changed *since* Bobby and Jack's campaigns. Another hire, Herb Schmerz, an old family friend, depleted morale for the simple fact of his presence: he was the Mobil Oil vice president responsible for crafting propaganda to advance energy policies Ted Kennedy despised, and his only previous presidential campaign experience was with John Connally. "These guys would walk in 9:30, 10, they'd make a couple of phone calls, and then they'd go to lunch," a bemused witness to the farce recalled later to a veteran Washington operative.

Kennedy's next big speech after the Iran debacle was at a famous civil rights church in Washington. The Communist Workers Party launched a volley of heckling as he began. In a *New York* magazine article called "Camelot Collapsing," reporter Joe Klein wrote, "The crowd whipped around, half-expecting a flash and shot and tragedy again." The hecklers were contained; but Kennedy began repeating the same sentence—*"From that beginning to that day, Shiloh has been a center of Christian education and social action. . . . And I say to you, from that beginning to this day, Shiloh has been a center of Christian education and social action. . . ."*—like a robot who'd blown a fuse.

A half dozen campaign veterans parachuted in as emergency reinforcements. Rick Stearns, George McGovern's ace delegate hunter from 1972, was appalled to discover that no organizers were in the field for the Iowa caucuses on January 21. He quickly raised a cadre of a dozen—impossibly tasked with finding at least one volunteer for each one of the state's 2,531 precinct caucuses by the time they took place eighteen days later. Another ringer, the lobbyist for the Boston diocese, had hardly done any campaign work since 1968. "What's different?" he barked when it was suggested his skills might be somewhat out of date.

Kennedy traveled to Iowa. Enormous crowds, electric with expectation, encountered a "fortuitously named cipher," Joe Klein wrote, who seemed "clumsy and uncertain even in his best moment." And yet the senator had a crutch: that old reliable Kennedy aura, the strange, cultic fantasy of a mythic deliverance to a *time before everything went wrong*, was always there for the senator. ("You *shook his hand*? Well then, can I shake yours?") He frequently yielded to the temptation to lean on it. *"President Kennedy* rolled backed steel prices!" he cried in Davenport, which got a standing ovation—as if nostalgia alone could cripple inflation.

Ironically, he proved sharpest on the issue that was now supposed to be his weakest. In one small Iowa town, a citizen asked about Reagan's argument that America should take in the shah, because America was a beacon for those tossed politically adrift. Kennedy returned calmly, "We pride ourselves on being a country of asylum for those who have been persecuted or prosecuted, but we've never been a dumping ground for despots or dictators or people who have plundered a nation. I think there is a balance."

Sound arguments didn't help. Voters told reporters they would have come to cheer Kennedy on were it not for his "unpatriotic" comments. Many who did show up bore signs like "SENATOR, KHOMEINI HAS YOUR SPEECH READY. PLEASE CALL IRAN." In the twelve days after his shah remarks, Kennedy lost a dozen points in the polls.

IN THE MIDDLE OF DECEMBER, PRESIDENT CARTER FROZE $5 BILLION IN Iranian assets and persuaded Panama to take in the shah, whom Ayatollah Khalkhali promptly promised once more to hunt down with death squads. It would have been a good time for the media to review the complicated shared history that had brought America and Iran to this pass.

A special on the events of 1953, when the CIA overthrew the Iranian president for nationalizing the nation's oil fields, would have been helpful in explaining to the public why Iranians despised America so. The agent in charge, Franklin Delano Roosevelt's nephew Kermit, had first tried paying off corrupt Iranian newspapermen to write awful things about Prime Minister Mosaddegh, and prominent Muslim clerics to denounce him in the mosques. That failing to do the trick, Roosevelt hired one gang of thugs to start a riot, then another gang to attack the first, until the streets were sufficiently chaotic for paid-off army officers to rumble up to the palace in tanks and persuade the baffled prime minister to flee. "All in all," a historian wrote, "only five Americans, with a half-dozen Iranian contacts, had organized the entire uprising." Then the king toasted the spy: "I owe my throne to God, my people, my army—and to you!"

Perhaps some thoughtful commentator could have debunked President Carter's assertion in his announcement speech that fifty Americans were "hostages of a mob and a government that have become one and the same." He could have reminded Americans that the Iranian *government* hadn't taken these hostages, and that the relationship of Iran's chaotic shambles of a government to the actual hostage-takers better resembled a state of civil war. That there was a man named Abolhassan Bani-Sadr, the former foreign minister, now running the economics ministry, who was maneuvering to persuade the students to release their captives in exchange for face-saving concessions about past mistakes from the Americans. And Foreign Minister Ghotbzadeh, once an ally to the theocrats, who had now switched sides, and so was denounced by the students as "filthy and satanic ways"; and some of the clerics who opposed the Ayatollah so aggressively that they had been snatched up and tortured. That even Khomeini's hanging judge the Ayatollah Khalkhali said that to put the hostages on trial as spies was ridiculous because every nation has spies—and that, far from pulling the strings, Khomeini himself did little else but pray on his rug on the floor in Qom, saying almost nothing about anything.

The news could have focused coverage on educating the public how, in Iran as it actually existed, the left hand wasn't just ignorant of the right; the fingers on the hands were incommunicado, including with the hapless students inside the embassy, who were so naïve and foolish that they kept responding with earnest, head-scratching bafflement over why they weren't received more sympathetically in America—which had fought its own revolution against an unjust foreign Goliath, after all, and was ruled by a president who said he prioritized human rights.

Instead, as the holiday season advanced, the coverage evolved in an opposite direction.

A new sort of visual storytelling joined images of burning American flags and manic *"Marg bar America"* roars. It featured weeping wives, stoic fathers, and anxious children; patriotic anthems and religious hymns; sweeping shots of amber waves of grain, and candles, and ribbons, and flags. The ABC Thanksgiving-night newscast reported from the home of a Waterloo, Iowa, hostage family. The correspondent noted their conviction that "Kathryn would have wanted them to continue their Thanksgiving rituals." The family's minister was shown delivering a sermon to packed pews. The hostage's mother, who looked uncannily like the gray-haired, round-faced matriarch holding out the turkey above her family's plentiful table in Norman Rockwell's famous *Freedom from Want* painting, served roasted goose and turkey, sweet potatoes, and oyster dressing. Her brother offered grace (*"Thank you for this successful harvest..."*). Her mother promised that there would be "a lot of laughter. But the laughter turns to tears."

"Susan King, ABC News, with the Koob family in Waterloo, Iowa."

It was surely no coincidence that the storytellers at Roone Arledge's ABC News chose a place like Waterloo for the tableau; or that the hostage whose family's grief they chose to dramatize was a woman. Such storytelling was a centuries-old American tradition. Menacing outsiders had been taking Americans hostage since before there had even *been* a United States of America. Then, the hostage takers were those who'd inhabited the soil before it *became* America, fighting their own dispossession. One response was the invention of a unique American literary genre that became known as the "captivity narrative." These seventeenth- and eighteenth-century stories about inscrutable savages seizing innocent maidens salved guilty consciences by blurring moral complexity. So did the twentieth-century version.

Ted Stevens had scourged Ted Kennedy for "echoing the feelings of the mob which is holding our hostages in Tehran." Sharing that interpretation was now all but an official civic commandment. So was fuzzing distinctions between the Iranian mob and the Iranian government—who were, after all, "one and the same," Jimmy Carter had said from the White House East Room, before invoking Abraham Lincoln.

Stories depicting the crisis through the lens of the victims who were unquestionably *innocent*—the hostages' families—were the stereo accompaniment of narrative calls to vigilante violence. It was a way to occlude the discomforting stories of those who might reasonably see these captives as, at least a tiny bit, *guilty*: someone, say, whose brother, father, or son was one of the demonstrators mowed down by one of the shah's helicopter gunships in Jaleh Square. Harder news might have forced harder questions: about the *American* brothers, fathers, and sons who were in Iran carrying out a policy of supporting the shah's regime "without any reservation whatsoever," as Zbigniew Brzezinski explained to the monarch two months after that massacre, and the day before another one at Tehran University.

Innocents here, savages there: listen to Roone Arledge. Note the title he gave his new nightly ratings bonanza: *America* was being held hostage. Note that image he threw up on the screen to introduce the hostage portion of every night's newscast: an anonymous American swathed in muslin. It could have happened to *any of us*. No. It had happened to *all of us*. No: all of *what was best in us*. That was what was being held hostage.

Now, of course the ordeal of hostages, and the grief of families who'd had their loved ones stolen, was genuinely newsworthy. And the public's outpouring of passionate sympathy was a necessary subject to portray. It had come straight from the grass roots. Beginning the Sunday following Thanksgiving, a weekly candlelight vigil cropped up in front of the Iranian embassy. The bell towers of Lawrence, Massachusetts, massed every noon in chorus, fifty chimes in slow succession, one for each hostage. Ten thousand cabdrivers drove with their lights on in honking vigil in New York; in Charleston, South Carolina, when a radio disc jockey announced his station was giving away fifteen thousand armbands with "50" printed on them to wear "today and every day 'til all fifty Americans are returned home safely," they were gone within a few hours. Forty thousand more were quickly produced, and they were worn by black and white and rich and poor. On December 16, a moving ceremony took place in which two of the hostages' children laid a wreath before the massive statue at the Lincoln Memorial, then three more laid a placard next to it with a quote from the Great Emancipator: "Those who deny freedom to others deserve it not for themselves, and under a just God, cannot long retain it." Secretary of State Cyrus Vance stood behind them, the only sounds the commander

barking orders to a Marine honor guard. Shortly afterward, Penne Laingen, whose husband, Bruce, the American attaché in Tehran, had been arrested and held prisoner at Iran's foreign ministry, and a sister of Kathryn
Koob, carried a wreath to the Iranian embassy with a ribbon around it
reading "Let our people go. Set our people free" as a hundred supporters
across the street held candles and sang Christmas carols.

All this was remarkable. A reasonable amount of coverage would
have gone a long way. Instead, such images *dominated* the news—at least
the part not being dominated by ululating Iranian mobs. And the White
House gladly drafted off these sentimental energies. Twelve days before
Christmas, the president presided over the traditional dedication of the
giant White House tree—this year left symbolically unlit, surrounded by
fifty smaller trees emitting a soft, holy glow. "We will turn on the other
lights on the tree when the American hostages come home," he said with
feeling. A local news brief reporting on that ceremony also noted that the
OPEC nations had raised the price of a barrel of crude oil by $6, and gold
had shot up to $461 an ounce upon the news. No wonder Americans wel-
comed sentimental distractions.

Carter proclaimed December 18 "National Unity Day." He urged all
Americans to display the American flag in a statement that, once again,
asserted, "a mob and a government . . . have become one and the same."
A second Lincoln Memorial ceremony attracted seven thousand communicants on December 22—five thousand of them State Department
employees given the afternoon off. William Safire, the former professional
image-manipulator, called it a White House conspiracy to shame Carter's
political rivals from criticizing his "six-week period of appeasement."
"This is an election campaign? This is a farce. . . . Only if candidates start
acting like candidates will the president be forced to start acting like a
president."

Safire would be disappointed. A force perhaps more powerful than
even the White House amplified the sentimentality: the lust for readers
and ratings.

WHAT WAS WRONG WITH THIS? LET A HOSTAGE WIFE EXPLAIN.

Barbara Rosen, who was married to embassy press attaché Barry
Rosen, later wrote eloquently about the damage that issued from turning her and her fellow sufferers into characters in a "public affairs soap
opera." A sharp strategic thinker herself, Rosen realized immediately that
the best way to protect the hostages' safety was preserving their anonymity, because that denied the hostage-takers the ability to single out captives
as differentially culpable individuals—say, if they had worked for the CIA.
Then it was falsely reported that her husband, Barry, *was* that blindfolded

hostage in the first news footage out of Tehran. So a right-wing New York City talk radio host tracked down Barry Rosen's mother, who bragged on the radio like any proud Jewish parent about how her son spoke fluid Farsi and had attended a Yeshiva—intelligence, his wife feared, that might cost him his life when it made it back to Tehran. Then, the radio host managed to *call* the embassy—and began burbling that America could erase Iran from the map whenever it chose. Barbara Rosen felt so helpless and angry while listening that her own mother feared she'd have a stroke.

Tehran wouldn't release a list of hostage names. Washington was cagey about their identities, too, in part to protect the fact that six Americans who'd escaped during the initial chaos were living secretly inside the Canadian embassy. Reporters, however, proved too enterprising, and on December 12, the *New York Daily News*, which had the largest circulation of any newspaper in America, printed mini-profiles with a photograph of each one. That set off a frenzy: television news producers—especially local ones—went on the hunt for grieving families to depict at their hearths. Shots of crying women were particularly prized. "They milked her for tears," a heartbroken Barbara Rosen wrote of her mother-in-law, "which made for dramatic viewing."

Rosen herself was recruited by the White House's Iran Working Group to represent family members on TV. She became livid at broadcasters' insensitivity. The producers of Tom Snyder's *Tomorrow Show* on NBC tried to sell her a tape of her interview for $150. Another time she blurted out that the hostage-takers were "terrorists," then begged a producer to cut that part out—"What if my slip hurt Barry? Can't you *please* do something about that one word?" They lied and told her that the edit was technically impossible. Even worse was the way that insensitivity melted once the camera blinked to life, and the interviewers snapped into character:

"We wonder what you are really *feeling* now that Barry has been held captive for fifty-four days?"

(She found it especially excruciating how everyone always asked how long the hostages had been held, though everyone already knew: it was part of the ABC News graphic with the shrouded hostage; after January 16, it even became an appendage of Walter Cronkite's traditional nightly "and that's the way it was . . ." sign-off: ". . . *on the forty-seventh day of captivity for the American hostages in Iran*.")

"Self-absorption was the rule," Rosen wrote; "few interviewers raised serious questions. Few seemed able to because most had done little homework on Iran." And when an insufficient degree of sensitivity was being *feigned*, directors told correspondents what expression to affect during the cutaway shots: "No, no—furrow your brow a little more . . . now look straight ahead, and a little more serious." ("The serious look," Rosen reflected, "was often requested of interviewers who had asked ridiculous questions.")

She started complaining to the interviewers themselves. "Respected correspondents with reputations for exposing other people's failures" responded, "It's what they want. If we don't show it, the other channels will," and "Who's going to pay if we don't get the ratings?" She wrote, "If they weren't selling advertising time, they were selling the network itself, which promoted its own stars and crowed praise for its own work in the same-pitched tone as ordinary advertising." But when one segment was "devoted to a publicity-puff chat with a Hollywood personality," the next "to a demonstration by a snake charmer or fashion designer, how seriously could the audience take the third segment's conversation about Iran?"

"Now on this Christmas eve, trapped as we are between the traditional spirit of the season and concern for our country in Iran, the words 'Merry Christmas' carry a special poignancy. So we offer for you tonight words from two letters. The first, from an Iranian student in Kentucky. 'I don't know how to write a letter to show my feelings because my English language is so poor. I pray every day for all the hostages to return to the United States.'"

That was Frank Reynolds of NBC, who then read a letter from Bruce Laingen on "the basic decency of every human being" and the "power of prayer." Both, Reynolds concluded, "are really telling us the same thing. So, on this Christmas eve, maybe we ought to think back only a few months ago, to a much happier time. Luciano Pavarotti, in Chicago, singing to the Pope, the people. *All* the people." The newscast closed with five straight minutes of the opera singer's rendition of "Ave Maria."

They might better have devoted that airtime to analyzing developments on the border between the Soviet Union and Afghanistan, which was where the last awful news event of an awful year was about to explode.

SOME YOUNG AMERICANS HAD ONLY RECENTLY VIEWED AFGHANISTAN AS A sort of earthly paradise: it was a stop on the "hippie trail," the transnational belt of destinations for spiritual seekers and drug-experimenters stretching from Europe to the Far East. Afghanistan's westernmost major city, Herat, a hundred miles from Afghanistan's border with Iran, was especially cherished: "You could always find someone who was willing to take time off for a friendly chat—or for a shared sampling of the fine local hashish," one writer observed.

Afghanistan had always been a crossroad of empires. During the Cold War, the Soviet Union and the United States competed to confer benefactions upon a country that, viewed from the ground, appeared barren of value, but which a mere glance at a regional map demonstrated was a crucial geopolitical prize. In the end, however, that fact removed the Afghan government's incentive to develop the capacities of *its own* people, whose communities remained underdeveloped and isolated.

American aid declined when Nixon and Kissinger began prioritizing ties to Afghanistan's neighbors Pakistan and Iran. Moscow picked up the slack, drawing closer to the indigenous Communist organization, the People's Democratic Party of Afghanistan—whose members, like Marxists all over the Third World, admired the USSR as a model for the rapid industrialization of a backward, feudal society, which liberal democracy seemed too gentle to accomplish. Then the Kremlin watched with frustration as Afghanistan's leader hedged his bets and drew closer to the Muslim Middle East, especially Iran, which drew him objectively closer to the U.S.

A precipitous chain of events began in the spring of 1978. A Communist leader was mysteriously assassinated; a brilliant and cunning party leader named Hafizullah Amin, who had spent years patiently honeycombing the Afghan military with loyalists, executed a nearly bloodless coup. Amin installed a figurehead named Nur Mohammad Taraki as president. Both were from a faction within Afghanistan's Communist party known as "Khalq," whose Marxism was frenetic and extreme. Like Joseph Stalin, who supposedly said one had to break eggs to make an omelet, they sought immediate, radical transformation of a deeply traditionalist society. Their rivals in the "Parcham" faction were gradualists: like Karl Marx himself, they believed that a society must first achieve industrialism before socialism could be achieved.

These divisions became increasingly fraught in the new regime, as President Amin and his commissar-behind-the-throne Taraki got to work breaking eggs: seizing land, granting civil rights to women, sending cadres of teachers into the countryside to modernize by brute force—often teaching at the literal point of a gun. The government removed green, the color of Islam, from the new national flag. Reckless land reform destabilized tightly knit rural social structures whose intricacies went back centuries—not entirely unlike what the Khmer Rouge had done in Cambodia.

Their putative partners in the Kremlin looked on in dismay. They had learned of the "April Revolution" through a wire report, and had not been pleased: their relationship with the pre-Communist government had been smooth, and they had no interest in instability on their southern border. Their commitment to the new government was halfhearted. They grew increasingly irritated as it broke more and more eggs.

Sporadic rural rebellions against the regime began in June 1978, following rumors that the government was outlawing the Koran, and possibly marriage. A tribal army numbering in the tens of thousands formed. Itinerant counterrevolutionaries were soon traveling from village to village, recruiting the fighters known as the Mujahideen, who assassinated government officials, spread mayhem, and conquered territory in a war to take back Afghanistan for Allah. One of its most successful recruiters, Ahmed Shah Massoud, was something novel within Afghan society: an *Islamist*. A child of the professional middle class, much like so many of the young revolutionaries in Iran, he had been educated abroad, in Egypt, where he fell under the sway of the political evangelists of the Muslim Brotherhood. Other recruits, including the son of a wealthy Saudi family whose name was Osama bin Laden, poured in from abroad. In fact, the makeshift army's greatest success came in Herat, where the most valiant soldiers were laborers who had worked on the shah's infrastructure project in Iran, had stayed for the revolution, and now sought to export jihad to their native land.

Neither the USSR nor the United States made allowance in their strategic calculations for this new factor in global affairs. The State Department's top Iran expert judged a month after the shah fell, "Pan-Islam is not likely to become a significant international force. There are too many regional and cultural divisions within the Muslim world for united political action." At approximately the moment he said it, Islamic political solidarity inspired by the Iranian revolution helped Herat insurgents fight so effectively that the Afghan military lost contact with Kabul for a week. Taraki desperately cabled the Kremlin, begging for men and materiel. This set off anguished days of emergency debate in the Soviet Politburo.

The debate strikingly paralleled that between Zbigniew Brzezinski and Cyrus Vance—and also the debates among American policymakers in the mid-1960s about Vietnam. KGB chief Yuri Andropov led the hawks: "We cannot afford to lose Afghanistan under any circumstances." Foreign Minister Andrei Gromyko was the diplomat: "The Afghan army is unreliable, and our army could become the aggressor. With whom will it fight? With the Afghan people! Our army would have to shoot them! The negative factors would be enormous. Most countries will go against it. . . . We would ruin everything we have constructed with such great difficulty, détente above all." Brezhnev's aide Alexei Kosygin said "it would be a fatal mistake to commit ground troops"—just like the 1950s American general who warned Eisenhower not to get bogged down in a land war in Asia.

They decided to send guns, some helicopter gunships, and seven hundred paratroopers, disguised as technicians, to be advisors. But the insurgents routed the Communists. Thousands of government soldiers mutinied, joining the rebels. Soviet advisors were chased through the streets; Soviet corpses were paraded on pikes. A glorious city fell to ruins. Twenty-five thousand people may have died.

And a little like in South Vietnam in 1963–64, despite laments from their far-off sponsors that their Cold War proxies engaged in "extreme measures and unjustified repression," Moscow felt they had no choice but to involve themselves deeper.

So did President Carter. In July, he authorized the CIA to supply covert assistance to the mujahideen, acting on the advice of Zbigniew Brzezinski, who hoped it would escalate the violence to the point that the Soviet Union directly intervened.

Khalq zealots moved against Parcham moderates. At the end of August, the intriguer behind it all, Hafizullah Amin, moved against the figurehead president, Nur Mohammad Taraki, when he was away in Moscow begging for assistance. When he returned, what the Soviet ambassador in Kabul hoped would be a meeting of reconciliation turned into a gunfight. In September, Amin assumed control. The Soviets smuggled Taraki into the Soviet Union, hoping to restore him as leader—a plot Amin got word of, murdering Taraki upon his return.

Cooler heads in the Red Army pleaded for disengagement before it was too late. Then, however, Amin signaled that he might do what Anwar Sadat did in 1972: expel Soviet advisors, switching sides in the Cold War to the United States.

That did it.

On December 9, ABC News reported that advance elements of a Soviet mechanized division were moving into Afghanistan. On December 12 the Politburo teetered between counsels of withdrawal and invasion. One of the arguments deployed by the hawks was that the United States Senate's reluctance to ratify the SALT II treaty proved the U.S. had never been interested in peace—an argument similar to the one American hawks pressed against the Soviet Union.

By coincidence, that same day, NATO approved the deployment of cruise missiles that could reach the USSR in minutes. That strengthened the hand of Kremlin hawks. As did (accurate) suspicions that America was already covertly involved. Andropov claimed it was the opening bid by America to seize a "new Ottoman empire" in Central Asia. Another hawk argued that failure to act to preserve the Marxist government in Afghanistan would shake the confidence of Communist regimes everywhere in the Soviet Union—a position with tragically uncanny echoes of a March 1965 memo from an assistant secretary of state about why America must press on in Vietnam: 70 percent of the reason, he argued, was to "avoid a humiliating US defeat (to our reputation as guarantor)."

The Politburo's most respected dove, Alexei Kosygin, was absent with an illness. High oil prices instilled unwarranted confidence in the resilience of the USSR's battered command economy. The final decision technically belonged to Leonid Brezhnev—who was near his deathbed, and too drunk to fully participate besides. When a participant excoriated Amin, Brezhnev pounded the table, cried "Dirty man!" and exited the room.

The clinching argument appeared to come from Andropov and Defense Minister Dmitri Ustinov, who wore enough medals on his uniform to stop a bullet. They argued that in the absence of bold action, the U.S. would install short-range missiles in Afghanistan on the Soviet border— phantom fears of a reverse Cuban Missile Crisis, though one with no evidence to support it. It was no less absurd than the interpretation of much of the U.S. security establishment concerning what happened next: that this was a calculated act of Soviet imperialism—perhaps the first step in a drive into Iran, them Saudi Arabia, in order to seize the lion's share of the world's oil reserves in a brazen drive for world conquest unmatched since the days of Adolf Hitler—and not what it actually was, a chaotic, ambivalent, and desperate attempt by a Soviet leadership cadre gasping for life to stanch the bleeding from a series of political accidents.

The first convoys from the 40th Soviet Army crossed the border on Christmas Day. They were followed by tens of thousands of motorized infantry troops. It was the first time during the Cold War that the Soviet Union had invaded an officially neutral border outside the Warsaw Pact. On December 27, the Red Army overran the presidential palace in Kabul. President Amin was already half-dead from a KGB poisoning attempt. Ironically, the reason he was not *entirely* dead were the desperate ministrations of an intrepid Soviet doctor, who apparently hadn't received the signal that Amin was meant to die. Such was the fog of Cold War.

The National Security Council's top Soviet expert reported to the president, "The invasion sharply increases the prospect of eventual Soviet military domination of the Greater Middle East and the U.S. exclusion from the region." Carter stepped up to the podium in the White House briefing room on December 28 and said it "gives rise to the most fundamental questions pertaining to international stability." In a New Year's Eve TV interview, he averred, "My opinion of the Russians has changed more dramatically in the last week than even the previous two and a half years. . . . The action of the Soviets has made a more dramatic change in my opinion of what the Soviets' ultimate goals are than anything they've done in the previous time that I've been in office."

As for Leonid Brezhnev, he told his ambassador to the U.S., "It'll be over in three to four weeks."

It was not. Though something else happened in three weeks: the Iowa caucuses, the long-anticipated first showdown in the presidential race.

Heading into it, the American Enterprise Institute's *Public Opinion* magazine reported, "Every scrap of evidence from opinion polls that have been taken in recent weeks—and the pollsters have had a field day—attests to the fact that Americans are in a much more assertive, even jingoistic mood, stiffer than at any time since the early days of Vietnam." NBC found that 81 percent of Americans were "personally angered" by the hostage crisis. Eighty percent told ABC that it was "one of the most serious crises since the Vietnam War." *Then* came Afghanistan—and about two-thirds of Americans told pollsters they wanted an increase in defense spending. Before, it had been 50 percent; in 1971 it had been 11 percent.

These were cheering numbers for Ronald Reagan. Maybe he could *really* become the front-runner now.

BOOK FIVE
1980

CHAPTER 31

"The Imam Does Not Often Respond"

GEORGE BUSH WON THE IOWA CAUCUSES. FEW SAW IT COMING EXCEPT George Bush. "How can anyone with such impressive credentials, who has served his country for so long, achieve such widespread anonymity?" Dan Rather asked him on *60 Minutes* eight days before the contest—then accused him of actually being a stalking horse for Gerald Ford.

Back in 1978, the *Washington Post* reported from an Indiana political event at which Bush was the keynote speaker. "Who's George Bush?" a woman asked; concerning the who was standing right beside her. The article was entitled "A Truly Unannounced Candidate," and identified him as "a Texan who has been elected to only one office—representing a rich white Houston district in the House. An improbable candidacy, you might say." Eight months later, to the same newspaper, Bush said something even more improbable: "I will win." He gave three reasons. The first was, "We are the most well-organized campaign in the field." The second and third were ... well, those didn't much matter. In Iowa, organizing was the name the game. And if you won it in Iowa, as Jimmy Carter had proven, miracles were possible.

Bush had officially announced his campaign at the National Press Club in May. Jules Witcover joked then that it had just peaked. David Keene, however, promptly dispatched a twenty-nine-year-old kid named Rich Bond to work for two full weeks to flood an Ames Republican dinner holding a straw poll. Bond had come up in the Republican machine that ran Nassau County, New York, as thoroughly as the late Richard J. Daley's machine ran Cook County, Illinois. He organized a 13.5 percentage point victory for Bush at the Ames dinner, even though in a telephone poll of Iowa Republicans, Bush only came in sixth.

The state's strange system of picking convention delegates involved gathering activists—typically fewer than 10 percent of the state's registered voters—on a cold January day to 2,531 separate precinct caucuses, many in individuals' homes. The media would credit whichever candidate managed to corral the greatest portion into his corner with "momentum"— and with some forty separate state primary elections *following* Iowa's caucuses, more than could possibly be deeply organized, momentum was everything. Just look at Jimmy Carter in 1976.

Bond got married—then returned with his new wife to Iowa, leaving his new love nest in Ames every morning at seven for the hour's drive to a lonely office in an old insurance building in Des Moines. Then, he picked up the phone. His plan was to build an Amway-style pyramid structure, in which the first recruits recruited the next recruits, and so on. But first he had to recruit the first recruiters—for a candidate that showed up in some polls beside an asterisk indicating *"less than one percent support."*

Bond had a list of 1976 Republican caucus-goers. He started on page one.

"I'm Rich Bond. I'm calling for George Bush, and he's running for president. You may not have heard of him. May I send you some information?"

This frequently proved a frustration, precisely because some he reached *had* heard of him: Bush was the Yankee globalist quisling who belonged to the Trilateral Commission—Moscow's American headquarters, according to a conspiracy theory that had taken root on the right, pushed by the political cult leader Lyndon LaRouche. Bond kept a drawerful of returned Bush literature marked with obscenities, or messages like "drop dead" and "Reagan for President." One recipient sent back the postage-paid return envelope with a brick inside, and a note reading, "We'll never vote for a Trilateralist."

But Bond also *believed* in George Bush—had believed in him ever since he'd watched him fight tirelessly for the good name of the Republican Party as RNC chair during Watergate. And Bond wasn't afraid of hard work. When he had grown tired of Nassau County politics in the early 1970s, he bought a nineteen-foot clam boat and worked for two years as a commercial fisherman.

His indefatigability was shared by his candidate. "I will always be working harder than anyone else," Bush said. "I want to be president more than anyone else." His political director, David Keene, put it more bluntly: his boss "would kill his mother for the main chance and Iowa is the main chance." By caucus day he had spent twenty-seven days there; Reagan had spent thirty-four hours. By the end of 1979, Bush had suffered the serial humiliations of the campaign trail for three hundred days— nationwide. One day, the humiliation came at a six-dollar-a-plate party fundraiser in Chilton County, Alabama. He was presented with a Possum Growers and Breeders of America membership card, and a license plate reading "Eat more possum"—and then, a squiggling baby possum, which he gamely dangled by the tail. "Everything I do now must be focused on leaving behind people who are willing to get involved and work. That will eventually result in name identification and I know it will result in votes," Bush told a reporter in Chilton County—perhaps still stinking of possum.

ONE REASON THE WORK WAS SO HARD WAS THAT BUSH WAS AN AWKWARD FIT with the party he wished to lead. Reagan's campaign chief in New Hampshire, a bluff Jewish businessman named Jerry Carmen, drew this contrast: "Most us are the first generation of our community or family to go to college. . . . Bush has the elite, the Yankee aristocracy of the valley." He was a "preppy," to cite the pop culture term for his tribe. A plaid-covered satire called *The Official Preppy Handbook* came out that year. Bush's campaign committee could have formed an appendix: it was a bramble of names with roman numerals after them, winners of international yachting competitions, veterans of Yale University's legendary a cappella singing group the Whiffenpoofs, to which his father, Prescott, once belonged. That was a problem. "The first thing we should do in this campaign," a Bush hand said, "is get rid of everyone who calls our candidate 'Poppy.' "

From these meager materials, Bush strained to style himself a populist. "Now some of you know that Barbara and I lived in a communist country," he speechified at a November cattle show in Maine. "The first few months we lived in China were fantastic—remember Boswell's Johnson, you're not a man until you've seen the Great Wall of China—then we woke up and we recognized that the freedoms we've taken for granted all our lives simply don't exist. . . . And I came back to this country blessed with experience that no other candidate has, blessed with a family and sons with a sense of service to their country."

Then he did, however, bring the crowd to its feet by crying that it was time to "stop wringing our hands and apologizing for our country."

Like any self-respecting WASP, Bush's superpower was family bonds. ("Mummy and Daddy make certain that he or she will not stray from the family fold because he or she won't know that other folds exist," Chapter One of *The Official Preppy Handbook*, "The Preppy Value System," instructed.) His youngest son, Marvin, moved to Iowa for almost a year, speaking anywhere he could find a handful to listen. His son Neil worked New Hampshire. John Ellis ("Jeb") moved to Puerto Rico with his Mexican-born wife. His daughter Dorothy—"Doro"—took leave from Boston College to attend secretarial school to make herself more useful. (His oldest son, George W., the failed congressional candidate, was a bit of a wastrel. He didn't do much of anything at all.)

Bush also benefitted from his right-wing political director's taste for the jugular. "I don't question Reagan's health or stamina or his intellectual capacity to handle issues," David Keene told *Time*. "But he *may* be able to field tough questions and develop sophisticated positions under the pressure of a campaign." And Bush's mismatch with the modern Republican Party was hardly total. His campaign committee also included a number of Sunbelt entrepreneurs like himself—he *had*, after all, succeeded on his own in Texas oil, which was one reason his fellow preppies admired him. He was aptly described as "the crossover candidate, embodying more than any other the shift within the party from East to West, from dominance by moderates to dominance by outspoken conservatives."

Bush's performance at the podium at that Maine cattle show, and doubts about Reagan, and indefatigable organizing—and a thorough scouring of their famous 8,500-name family Christmas card list for neighbors of their summer cottage in Kennebunkport—gave Bush a 466 to 335 straw-poll victory. Howard Baker had pegged his entire strategy on winning that vote. In his speech he had pledged "a revival of the honorable profession of politics"—to limp applause, and an even limper vote. The rejection in Maine knocked him out of serious contention.

Then, however, in Florida two weeks later, Bush slid to the middle of the pack, and "Bush has peaked" was once more heard in the land.

A CONVERSATION THERE BETWEEN TWO LEFT-WING REPORTERS FROM THE *Village Voice*, Alexander Cockburn and James Ridgeway, and a "bulky Florida businessman, sunning himself by the pool," helped explain Bush's frustration. Reagan and Crane, he snapped, were "the only two men here who truly care about this country," while Bush was a Trilateralist: "The Trilateral controls and orchestrates what is going to happen in the world. George Bush represents nothing but the elitists. . . . The Bolshevik Revolution was literally underwritten by the Chase Manhattan Bank. It's provable. Go look it up . . . I'm not a stupid person. I went to a fine school and I got a master's from Harvard. . . . At the rate we're going, my kids are going to live in some form of dictatorship. When a couple making forty or fifty grand can do nothing but pay their bills, that isn't freedom."

William F. Buckley had supposedly affected a purge of such lunacy from the conservative movement following Goldwater's loss, on the theory that conservatism could never prosper unless it was considered respectable. The purge didn't take; conservatism was prospering nonetheless. Bush tried to protect himself by quitting the Trilateral Commission, and also the Council on Foreign Relations. Theodore "Teddy" White, the *Making of the President* chronicler, was impressed that he went no further than that. "As a civilized person," Bush "could not, or would not, court the Moral Majority, the right-to-life movement, the National Rifle Association." This, however, was a mistaken impression. As Dick Wirthlin observed in a Reagan strategy memo, "Bush's reputation as a moderate" was "founded largely on stylistic criteria." When a clever Reagan aide sought to demonstrate this by stripping off the identifying headers on speeches by Phil Crane and Bush before showing them to Orrin Hatch, Hatch guessed that Bush's speech was Crane's.

It wasn't helping him with the party's right. Stylistically, Bush seemed almost to relish opportunities to disassociate himself from the Republican rank and file's *anger*. (A caller to a Keene, New Hampshire, radio show said the president should turn Iran into an oil slick, just like the song said. Bush replied that this was no time for "rattling the saber," or seeking "political advantage.") He condescended to his party's base of *arriviste* entrepreneurs. (He concluded a contrast of his foreign policy experience to Reagan's by crying, "I've *been there*—not lecturing on the Republican free enterprise circuit"). He fetishized rule-following. ("Absolute international *anarchy* out there. Dealing with people like the Ayatollah, who has absolutely no concept of *order*." Sentence fragments were another Bush verbal tic.)

Right-wing positions he could adopt—no problem. Organizations he could quit. The preppy habits of a lifetime: those were harder to shake. Fortunately, in Iowa, there were other avenues to pursue.

BY JANUARY, IOWANS COULDN'T TURN ON A TV OR RADIO WITHOUT RUNning into a campaign ad.

John Connally's were lame. His own campaign manager called "Coffee with Connally"—which reprised a format from his 1962 gubernatorial run—"probably the worst political television that had ever been made." Reagan's were weak, too. The ad firm they'd chosen was run by a seventy-four-year-old whose breakthrough work had come on the *I Love Lucy* show. His corny spots made Reagan look like a 1950s pitchman, complete with phony sets and props.

Howard Baker's radio ads featured the tagline, "The hostages can't vote, but we can." One on TV featured footage of his answer to an Iranian student at the University of Iowa who asked him why he was so concerned with Iran's violation of international law, but had demonstrated no such concern "when the Shah was killing Iranian people with U.S. weapons, and—"

Baker interrupted: "Because, *my friend*, I'm interested in fifty *Americans*, that's why, and when those fifty Americans are released I'm perfectly willing to talk about it" . . . and a thunderclap of applause drowned out the rest. The ad segued into his campaign song, "Welcome Back America. You've Been Away Too Long."

Desperate for a miracle, his campaign ran it twenty times a day.

George Bush's commercials, also run constantly, were the most art-ful of any candidate's. One featured grainy footage of him clambering up the side of a ship, then gazing coolly into the camera, as a narrator with the flat, stern, matter-of-a-fact tone associated with World War II docu-mentaries recited, "This is not a professional film. It was made September 22, 1944, by a crew member on the USS *Finback*, an American submarine that surfaced in Japanese controlled waters to rescue a downed American flyer." That faded into a photograph of Bush at his CIA desk as the an-nouncer attested to his commitment to "maintaining a *strong* national defense." For another, Bush's adman (the candidate called him "my Cecil B. DeMille") choreographed Bush to climb down the wing of a propel-ler plane into a crowded hangar—a fiction: it was raining too hard to fly; Bush had been driven to the airport—with a crowd coached to chant "We want Bush! We want Bush!" and the candidate interrupting to cry, "I bring you word from all across America! We're going all the way!"

A third opened on the candidate in profile, his Yankee face angular and determined: "Strong leadership? George Bush!"

He punched the air from behind a podium: "I think one of the great *shortcomings* of our president—and I don't take any pleasure in this. He *is* my president! I want to see him succeed!"

(A little grin: "At least until the next election!")

"But one of the things that is *plaguing* our country is that he's not doing what I know I can do: bring *excellence to government*. Get the best in America! And you watch the United States. Excellence renewed! Solve these problems!"

"George Bush. A president we won't have to train."

AS IT HAPPENED, THE ACTUAL PRESIDENT, THE ONE WHO PUTATIVELY STILL needed training, was then aggressively—but self-effacingly—managing a harrowing onslaught of overseas challenges with creativity, discipline, and skill.

There was Iran. At a January 8 briefing to members of Congress he said that a rescue attempt "would almost certainly end in failure and al-most certainly end in the death of the hostages"—a handsome little poker bluff, for he had already green-lighted a bold CIA operation to rescue eight American personnel living secretly in the Canadian embassy. (They were disguised as a film crew working on a science fiction picture called *Argo*.) With steely discipline, the president had never even hinted of their existence. On January 27, they crossed over Iranian airspace to freedom. Carter let it appear to be an entirely Canadian operation.

Then there was Afghanistan, where a Soviet armored division had rumbled into Herat, raising fears that they would next take Iran's oil fields, then, perhaps, Saudi Arabia's—in which event the Iranian hostage crisis would go down in history as but a footnote. U.S. intelligence took that contingency seriously enough that Carter was given the option to render the border impassable with tactical nuclear weapons. He rejected that counsel. Using nuclear weapons would have been tragedy in any instance, but particularly in this case, for the Kremlin did not dream of pressing beyond Afghanistan.

He did, however, agree to another radical proposal, pressed by Zbigniew Brzezinski.

Over the past two months, his hawkish national security director had seemed determined to single-handedly turn the Cold War hot. He had sent a top-secret questionnaire to all U.S. ambassadors asking them to describe all Cuban activities in their areas, hoping to base a propaganda campaign on their responses. In December, he pronounced his satisfaction that the hostage crisis had ended the "Vietnam complex"—America's alleged neurotic hesitancy to project force abroad. ("Fritz raised hell," the president wrote in his diary. "He thought this was a psychiatric analysis of people like him who had been against the Vietnam War.") Now, Brzezinski proposed a massive increase in secret military aide to the mujahideen, with the Pakistan government as intermediary.

This was illegal. In April, President Carter had ruled that Pakistan fell under a law prohibiting assistance to countries developing nuclear weapons. Which was why, when Brzezinski went on the ABC News show *Issues and Answers* the Sunday after the invasion, he insisted that any aid would be transmitted to the rebels "in keeping with our constitutional principles."

It was not. Instead, the president whom all those Republicans in Iowa were accusing of lacking the mettle to do what needed to be done authorized CIA operatives to scour international arms bazaars to procure *Soviet* weapons to send off to Pakistan, the better to hide the origin of that assistance in the United States.

His first big public statement on Afghanistan was a televised speech on January 4. He called the Soviet incursion a potential threat to the stability of "much of the world's oil supplies." He asked the Senate to shelve SALT II indefinitely, just like Ronald Reagan had once recommended (it did, and ended up never voting on it at all). He said, "Although the United States would prefer not to withdraw from the Olympic games scheduled in Moscow this summer, the Soviet Union must realize that its continued aggressive actions will endanger both the participation of athletes and the travel to Moscow by spectators who would normally wish to attend the Olympic games." And he announced an embargo of seventeen million tons of American grain that the Soviet Union had already ordered.

At *that*, given that he was taking billions in business away from Iowa farmers, his political aides were in a sweat. Ted Kennedy seized the initiative: "The American farmer will pay the price for an ineffective foreign policy," he said. Nonetheless, the president's speech had received the highest television ratings of any of his addresses, scoring an approval rating approaching 100 percent.

As he spoke, United Nations Secretary General Kurt Waldheim prepared to return home a day early from a catastrophic diplomatic mission to Iran. He had hoped to meet with Khomeini. Instead, he was frog-marched through a tourist itinerary from hell, including a cemetery of martyrs of the revolution, a meeting with "victims of SAVAK torture sessions" (actually people with congenital disabilities), and a press conference at which the embassy students called him an "American pawn." Three times, his presence caused riots that made him fear for his life. His exit was celebrated with a march of a million demonstrators shouting for his blood. He reported back to President Carter that "there is no government there, the terrorists are making the decisions, Khomeini is unapproachable," and "the Revolutionary Council is ineffective and timid." Then, the Revolutionary Council expelled all American journalists.

Foreign Minister Ghotbzadeh was anguished at how unhinged student militants had become the tail that wagged the revolutionary dog, monopolizing world attention with weekly press conferences "exposing" competent public officials, one after another, as "traitors" and "spies." He was desperate to see their reign of terror end. Then came a possible breakthrough. Ghotbzadeh approached an unlikely pair, an Argentinian exporter of Cuban cigars named Hector Villalon and a French human rights lawyer named Christian Bourget, to undertake a diplomatic mission to Panama to deliver a pro forma request to President Omar Efrain Torrijos Herrera to extradite the shah—with, however, no hope of success. Villalon and Bourget suggested another plan: reach out to the Americans to set up *fake* extradition talks as cover for negotiations to free the hostages.

President Carter authorized Hamilton Jordan to fly to a Florida Air Force base to make first contact. The week before the Iowa caucuses, talks began in a London hotel room. Jordan, representing Carter, and Villalon and Bourget, representing Ghotbzadeh—who at first, having placed his life in the balance by going this far, cautiously refused to speak to Jordan when handed the phone—began delicately shadowboxing their way to agreeing upon some harmless public concessions the U.S. might make to persuade the students to declare victory, free the hostages, and ride off into the sunset as revolutionary heroes.

Ghotbzadeh told Jordan that he had outlined the plan to the Ayatollah. Jordan asked about Khomeini's response. "The imam does not often respond," Ghotbzadeh said. "He listened to our explanation and nodded. . . . If he had objected to our proposal he would have said so." Which was better than nothing—and would have served as a useful rebuke to the arguments of the president's opponents that the White House was incompetent, had anyone been allowed to know about it.

IN IOWA, A *LOS ANGELES TIMES* REPORTER SAID, "THE RICH BLACK EARTH seems ready to tremble under the weight of visiting White House aspirants." It did not, however, tremble under the weight of a presidential entourage. Carter insisted that duty demanded he stay behind in Washington. Fritz Mondale campaigned in his stead, traipsing through basketball gyms where he used to compete for his high school across the border in Minnesota. His burden was explaining to farmers why the president chose to embargo their grain.

A half hour of nationally purchased television time campaigned for Carter as well—a cinema verité montage collected over three days of candid filming of the president and his aides outfitted with wireless microphones. On one of the days, not coincidentally, the president met the Pope, whom he addressed in his native Polish, an attempted seduction of those Catholic Democrats who had jumped the aisle in 1978 to vote for the pro-life Senator Roger Jepsen.

The Sunday before the caucuses, Carter appeared on NBC's Sunday-morning interview program *Meet the Press*. It was just the kind of tough display a nervous electorate might wish to see from a president in something like wartime. He called the Afghanistan crisis "the most serious threat to world peace since the Second World War." Columnist Carl Rowan jabbed back: "Your critics say the reason the Soviets are moving is that they've seen weakness on your part." Judy Woodruff of PBS thrusted: "Why did it take almost three years for you to discover the true intentions of the Soviet leadership?" Carter deflected, nonplused, that no president since Truman had faced a Soviet incursion into a nation not already in their orbit, with their own troops—in a "buffer state between the Soviet Union and Iran and the world's oil supplies and the Hormuz Straits and the Persian Gulf": no time to be changing horses in midstream.

David Broder—"with all due respect"—threw a roundhouse from the right: "We are still at 5.8 unemployment. Inflation has risen from 4.8 percent to 13 percent. We still don't have a viable energy policy. Russian troops are in Cuba and Afghanistan. The dollar is falling. Gold is rising. And the hostages, after seventy-eight days, are still in Tehran. Just what have you done, sir, to deserve re-nomination?" Carter deftly parried that, too—as he did another question, about why he had come on NBC but "refused to appear any place where your challengers could confront you directly": "Mr. Broder, in a time of *crisis* for our country I believe it's very important for the President *not* to assume, in a public way, the role of a partisan campaigner."

Jerry Brown disagreed that this wasn't partisan campaigning; he filed suit for equal time. He lost. Brown had spent December accusing Carter of a "Nixon-type" campaign of "hiding behind the hostages." That failed. He lobbied frantically to be included in a *Des Moines Register* televised debate—which was canceled after Carter refused to participate. Mary McGrory said that this was par for the course for Brown, "a child of television . . . notoriously disdainful of the nitty gritty of precinct organization." But there was another reason Iowa did not tremble under Jerry Brown's weight: the California Supreme Court had ruled that California lieutenant governor Mike Curb, the Reaganite record producer, could do whatever he liked as acting governor whenever Jerry Brown set foot outside the state. So, having exhausted his options for an electronic campaign, Brown removed his name from caucus ballots.

Neither was Iowa trembling beneath the weight of Ronald Reagan. When Iowa Republicans complained, John Sears responded with his customary arrogance: "It wouldn't do any good to have him going to coffees and shaking hands like the others. People will get the idea he's an ordinary man like the rest of us." The candidate was forced to do damage control. He was "*proud* to be an ordinary man," he told a radio host, on the phone, from a fundraising trip to New York, repeating his dubious excuse for nonparticipation in the *Register*'s Republican debate: it would only exacerbate party divisions.

THE SHOW WENT ON, NONETHELESS. BUSH, BAKER, CONNALLY, CRANE, AND Dole canceled one another out with their equivalent conservatisms. This proved a boon to the sixth debater, who had recently been the butt of a *Saturday Night Live* "Weekend Update" gag from Jane Curtin: "*Anyone who has seen Congressman John B. Anderson of Illinois, please call 800-555-1212.*"

Anderson gibed: "I must confess to this audience that I am not a younger Ronald Reagan with experience"—for the rest seemed to be arguing precisely that. He continued that, unlike Ronald Reagan, he recognized "a genuine role for the federal government when it comes to advancing the cause of human rights or civil rights in this country." The media, if not the Iowa electorate, proved charmed. They began paying considerably more attention to the eloquent odd duck from Rockford. *People* magazine called him "a potential spoiler—if not winner—in New Hampshire." (He wasn't. He got 10 percent.) The editors of *Time* invited him to a private lunch. The

New York Times published an editorial entitled "Why Not the Best?"—the title of Jimmy Carter's 1976 campaign memoir.

Walter Cronkite was particularly entranced. "The Republican presidential candidate once spoofed as the missing man of the campaign, now has been found!" he pronounced with sparkling eyes after the Iowa debate. So were the producers of *Saturday Night Live*, after Anderson's representatives proposed Anderson participate in a skit. The media's affection for the only nonconservative Republican standing was a development with consequences.

IOWA TREMBLED BENEATH THE WEIGHT OF TED KENNEDY'S ENTOURAGE nearly literally: he traveled to appearances, the AP reported, with "an assortment of seven planes and helicopters chartered by the reporters trailing behind him." An ambulance usually followed his motorcades.

He might have been better off staying home. One of his campaign lines was that he would never support anything as foolish as a Soviet grain embargo; then the *Des Moines Register* reported that he had advocated one in 1973. *Reader's Digest*, America's second most popular magazine behind *TV Guide*, published a cover article, "Chappaquiddick: The Still Unanswered Questions," claiming that Kennedy could not possibly have swum across the channel as he claimed given the currents at that particular time. Joan Kennedy was drafted to stand by his side and claim, "I believe my husband's story which he told me right after the incident"—rather unconvincing for anyone who knew that they hardly spoke to one another. An CBS News poll gave him a 38 percent approval rating, finding that only 39 percent thought he told the truth most of the time. One-fifth said they would never vote for him under any circumstances. The pressure seemed to make him stammer more. Mary McGrory said, "The flame under the charisma has been turned down so low it seems to have gone out."

THE BUSH CAMPAIGN WAS SO FRENETIC THAT ONE DAY BARBARA AND George unexpectedly ran into one another at the Des Moines airport. "How long are you going to stay out campaigning?" a reporter asked—to which he replied, "Until I run out of underpants."

(Another reporter: "Did he just say . . . *underpants*?")

On the big day, staffers in Rich Bond's once-lonely insurance-building office pored through massive binders to tell first-time caucus-goers which private home, school gym, or Rotary club to report to, to declare their allegiance to Bush, as fifteen newly installed phone lines rang 120 times an hour. It was their first sign that they might just pull it out.

The final total was 31.5 percent for Bush and 29.4 percent for Reagan. The Republicans' also-rans were Baker (15 percent), Connally (9 percent),

Crane (7 percent), Anderson (4 percent), and Dole (1 percent). On the Democratic side, 59 percent caucused for the commander in chief, 31 percent for Senator Kennedy. It was only the second election a Kennedy had lost.

The biggest loser might have been the political scientists who had spent the last four years dilating upon the plague of voter apathy. In January of 1976, 38,600 Democrats and 21,000 Republicans had caucused in Iowa. This year, the respective figures were approximately 100,000 and 125,000. "One theory," John Chancellor offered on NBC, "is that they were reflecting the frustration of all Americans with the hostages and Afghanistan. They wanted to make some kind of civic statement—to *do* something."

Americans all over were making civic statements supporting their president, whose approval ratings would never again dip as low as they had before the hostages were seized. Later that week in Salem, Oregon, a thousand stood outside City Hall in subzero temperatures for a candlelight vigil—"especially difficult for the high school musicians, many of whom were protected only by their uniforms," the local paper noted proudly. "If communities throughout the state and nation were to follow Salem's example and were to make their outpourings of community support known to President Carter, it would help sustain him as he faces the difficult decisions that will lead to the release of the fifty hostages."

Middle schoolers adopted hostages as pen pals. A new symbol joined the church bells, the candlelight vigils, and the armbands, overwhelming them all: the yellow ribbon. Penne Laingen, the wife of the imprisoned American attaché, had a giant oak tree on her front lawn. Around Christmastime, she remembered a seven-year-old hit song by Tony Orlando that told the story of a prisoner who asked his lover to tie a yellow ribbon around an old oak tree to let him know that she didn't love him any less than when he went away. So Mrs. Laingen started hanging ribbons around *her* oak tree. She recruited the college students abusing Iranian anti-shah demonstrators on her street to tie ribbons instead—and they did. A reporter who interviewed her for the *Washington Post* began tying them around trees in her suburb. Another foreign service wife began tying them up and down Embassy Row. The fifty little Christmas trees on the White House lawn memorializing the fifty hostages began sporting ribbons. The craze spread nationwide, then to Tehran, where hostages started getting yellow ribbons in the mail. They remembered the song, and teared up. One student captor dumped a pile of them at a hostage's feet: "What does this mean?" The guard didn't believe him when he replied, "It just means they haven't forgotten me." Bruce Laingen placed one in his window. A guard assumed it was a signal to commandos to launch a raid. Though they worried that a deposit of bird excrement on the window was a signal, too. "I'll be darned if I'll wash that window," Laingen decided.

CHAPTER 32

"Do You Believe in Miracles?"

GEORGE BUSH JUMPED FROM 6 PERCENT SUPPORT TO 27 PERCENT NATION-
ally after his Iowa win, which was good news to the boys on the press
buses in New Hampshire. It proved them right: Ronald Reagan *was*
George Romney in '68 and Edmund Muskie in '72 — an early-inning flash
in the pan.

"After First Blush, Reagan Losing Bloom" said a headline in the *Washington Post*. A longtime Reaganite was quoted: "The old fire doesn't seem
to be there now." His latest gaffes were reviewed, a new one reported. Lyn
Nofziger was brought out of mothballs; he suggested that Reagan seemed
so desperate to be president that maybe he didn't deserve to win: "They
have him so intimidated, so convinced that he shouldn't be speaking out
for what he believes, that he's not Ronald Reagan."

A Reagan internal poll found a thirty-point swing to Bush in New
Hampshire in a week. The new conventional wisdom was that all Bush
need do was hold that lead for the traditional first presidential campaign
showdown to, this year, be the last.

Fawning Bush profiles bloomed: George Bush, heroic teenage bomber
pilot; George Bush, uprooting himself from his Connecticut life of ease
to reinvent himself as a rough-and-tumble Texas oil prospector; George
Bush, man of duty, who stood and saluted and took the truly difficult jobs
when the other guys ran and hid. They formed a perfect counterpart to
the new Bush commercials — tagline: "The man America turns to when a
tough job has to be done."

In his post-Iowa press conference, Bush introduced himself in his
inimitably goofy way to Americans just starting to pay attention to the
presidential race. "Now they will be after me, *howling* and *yowling* at
my heels. What we will have is *momentum*. We will look forward to *big
mo* being on our side, as they say in athletics." *Big mo* became one of the
year's catchphrases. Mike Royko did a series of columns depicting himself trading campaign intelligence in primary-state saloons with his pal
Big Mo.

A Bush campaign theme was his athleticism. Bush jogged so frequently in front of cameras that *Newsweek*'s cover coming out of Iowa—"Bush Breaks Out of the Pack"—seemed almost inevitable. It displayed him in full stride, looking like he was storming Omaha Beach in 1945 in running shoes and baggy sweats. A similar image hung at the threshold of the house in a run-down Manchester neighborhood that served as Bush headquarters. The poster read "Join the Frontrunner"; cards reproducing it were passed out to every visitor.

Bush's New Hampshire chairman, Hugh Gregg, a well-regarded retired governor, insisted that *age* wasn't the issue in this campaign—"stamina" was. "My candidate goes six to midnight—seven major rallies a day. He's a bundle of energy. Reagan doesn't have the physical stamina to be president and wouldn't survive it." The "Great Conciliator," Howard Baker, conciliated out of one side of his mouth—"I'd like to say Reagan is too old, but I won't say it because I don't believe it"—and insinuated Reagan's decrepitude out of the other.

Ronald Reagan also exercised every day, if less photogenically. He knelt down with his rump in the air, extending a little wheel with handles sticking out of the center like a baker rolling out dough, until his stomach was flat on the ground, waited a beat, then rolled himself back, over and over again for half an hour. Once, visiting Reagan's hotel room during the Republican convention, Bush—fifteen years Reagan's junior, star of two Yale College World Series teams—asked to give the little wheel a go. He collapsed unceremoniously on his belly on the first try.

PRESIDENT CARTER DELIVERED A SOMBER STATE OF THE UNION ADDRESS the day after Iowa. "This last few months has not been an easy time for any of us. As we meet tonight, it has never been more clear that the state of our union depends on the state of the world. And tonight, as throughout our own generation, freedom and peace in the world depend on the state of our union. The 1980s have been born in turmoil, strife, and change. This is a time of challenge to our interests and our values and it's a time that tests our wisdom and our wills. . . . The Soviet Union must pay a concrete price for their aggression. While this invasion continues, we and the other nations of the world cannot conduct business as usual."

He thus drew a line in the sand known as the Carter Doctrine: Any "attempt by any outside force to gain control of the Persian Gulf region will be regarded as an assault on the vital interests of the United States of America, and such an assault will be repelled by any means necessary." He backed the threat with a naval deployment to the Indian Ocean, having arranged for American use of naval and air facilities in northeast Africa and the Persian Gulf. He said that even though "our volunteer forces are adequate for current defense needs, and I hope that it will not become necessary to impose a draft," he was sending legislation to Congress—paralleling a bill the Senate Armed Services Committee had been considering since spring—to register males between eighteen and twenty-five for the selective service system, to prepare to "meet future mobilization needs" more expeditiously, should they arise.

He formalized his call for an Olympic boycott. And demanded "a strong defense budget for 1981, encompassing a 5 percent real growth in authorizations, without any reductions." (He had run for president promising cuts of 5 to 7 percent.) He called for removing "unwarranted restraints on America's ability to collect intelligence." (He had argued the opposite point four year earlier, and in 1977 cut the CIA's covert operations staff from twelve hundred to fewer than four hundred.) The next day, friendly senators introduced legislation making it easier to keep CIA operations secret.

RONALD REAGAN WAS NOT IMPRESSED. CAMPAIGNING IN SOUTH CAROLINA, site of the second big primary, he called the Carter Doctrine "a vague threat that if *further* aggression transpires in the Persian Gulf he *might* do something. . . . We are in a power poker game with the Soviet Union. . . . Grain embargoes and threats to refuse to attend the Olympics are not responsive to the Soviet call of our hand." He growled, "In Iran, fifty innocent Americans are still being held hostage as a result of an act of war on our embassy. I cannot doubt that our failure to act decisively at the time that this happened provided the Russians with the final encouragement to invade Afghanistan. . . . The Iranians bet that Mr. Carter would be weak in responding to an act of war. They are right."

Then, Reagan laid down the marker that he would repeat up to Election Day: "Mr. Carter is encouraging the belief that this nation will not risk war no matter what the provocation. In doing so he is *increasing* the challenge of a nuclear confrontation"—just like "when Mr. Chamberlain was tapping his cane on the cobblestones of Europe."

In L.A., Reagan held his first press conference since his defeat. The *New York Times* said he appeared "tense and, at times, crestfallen"—a sight as rare as a four-leaf clover. He dismissed Iowa as a "straw vote" (it wasn't), said he won sixty-one Iowa counties to Bush's thirty-two (irrelevant: Bush won the heavily populated ones), and that draft registration was "a meaningless gesture."

The next day, Saturday, January 26, taping a *60 Minutes* interview to run the following evening, he said that were he president, and enfeeblement "were a possibility, I'd be the first to recognize it, and the first to step down." (This was a proposition with which anyone with an enfeebled parent who insisted upon keeping his or her driver's license might wish to quibble.) He insisted that he "directed" his own campaign. (A friend told Edwin Meese that this part sounded particularly unconvincing.) Hammering Jimmy Carter as a weakling, he said America should institute a military blockade of Cuba to punish the Soviet Union, and that Cuba's Caribbean neighbors wouldn't mind: "They are more concerned with our apparent weakness in the face of the Soviet Union than they are about us once again being big old Uncle Sam." He reiterated his call for America to arm Pakistan (he couldn't know this was already happening), even to possibly send troops—"We have every reason to be there"—and called for new American naval bases in East Africa, Southwest Asia, and the Middle East.

Then he said, "I am not a warmonger." He was just worried what could happen if the Soviet Union came to believe "there is no place with which we would risk war to stop them."

This was part one of Reagan's new strategy, devised at an intense Chicago meeting the day after Iowa: make a different newsworthy attack on Jimmy Carter's foreign policy every day. (Though the *New York Times* did not consider it newsworthy: they buried their report on page twenty-three.) The second part of the strategy was to campaign like the dickens, to prove he had more stamina than anyone else in the race.

Reagan doubled his scheduled events for the next five weeks—the last extended interval between major showdowns. At every stop he emphasized how eager he was to debate. ("I can't be the only person concerned with unity. If no one else is concerned with it, I'm going to have to think in terms of self-survival.") On Monday, in Milford, New Hampshire, he plunged headlong into a crowd of one thousand, "because Nancy and I would like to come down and meet each of you personally." The curtain closed at his last event, the ninth of the day, at midnight, with the temperature down in the teens. On Tuesday, he did eleven. Then he flew down to South Carolina, where the next day he did several more.

The blitz was timed for his birthday. "Some people ask me how I feel," he said at every stop. "And all I can say is, compared with the alternative, I'm very happy." He was drowned out by laughter before he could finish the sentence. Before seven hundred in Anderson, South Carolina, he received his fifth birthday cake in three days. It carried three candles—one, he joked, for every decade of the thirtieth anniversary of his thirty-ninth birthday.

Then he turned serious.

"I was in Taiwan dealing with Chiang Kai-Shek while Henry Kissinger was in Peking making the final arrangements for President Nixon's visit to China," he said. He compared that to Bush: "one brief term as ambassador to the UN, special representative to mainland China, and director of the

CIA—which I don't think is exactly an education in good foreign policy." He recalled that he reassured Taiwan that America would never betray them. Then, Jimmy Carter *did* betray them. "I would like to be the president who takes the message to the world that there will be no more Taiwans, no more Vietnams—that there will be no more betrayals of friends by the United States."

His received his seventh cake at a chamber of commerce banquet where his South Carolina campaign chairman introduced him by claiming that nations traditionally "turned to mature leadership in times of crisis." Then Reagan lamented how the USSR, "fueled with American capital, run by American computers, and fed with American grain," kept playing America for the fool, and that Jimmy Carter bowed to "Kremlin propaganda" on arms control, until, after the Afghanistan invasion, he *finally* realized that "the Soviets can't be trusted."

The strategy was working. The *Boston Globe* poll of New Hampshire Republicans showed Reagan and Bush neck and neck.

BUSH'S BIG MO KEPT RUNNING INTO THE VERY SAME SNAG.

Just before Iowa, Reagan had sat down with the new president of the National Right to Life Committee, Dr. Carolyn Gerster. He had received their endorsement, Gerster said, in exchange for pledging to appoint only anti-abortion justices to the Supreme Court.

Her movement was more aflame than ever. Federal District Court Judge John Dooling, a practicing Catholic, had just handed down a 642-page ruling striking down the Hyde Amendment with an argument that stung: that by *singling out* a certain medical procedure to be denied federal funds, the Hyde Amendment *imposed* a religious view. The court thus deprived the Christians of their cherished martyrdom; they were the religious persecutors. Noted *Time*, "Although an amendment outlawing all abortions has received little support so far, Dooling's decision could have the unintentional result of fueling the movement."

And how: just look at what happened everywhere Bush's campaign bus stopped.

George Bush *supported* the Hyde Amendment. He was no fan of abortion; "talking about his moral opposition," the *Washington Post* reported from his campaign kickoff, "his voice breaks." But he also had a past to contend with. As a member of the Ways and Means Committee during his two congressional terms, he was such an enthusiastic booster of birth control—once a pet issue among his class—that Chairman Wilbur Mills nicknamed him "Rubbers." Unlike Ronald Reagan, he had opposed the Human Life Amendment. So in New Hampshire, pro-lifers bird-dogged him everywhere he went. That summer, he had muttered, "How am I going to get rid of them?" Robert Novak, overhearing, piped up: "Change your position." So Bush did: he wrote in a January questionnaire from the Republican Women's Task Force that he would support a constitutional amendment "to give the states authority to regulate abortion within their boundaries." Too little, too late. Given a foot, the zealots demanded a mile. These days, the Christian right had big mo, too.

The Moral Majority's first promotional mailer suggested a secret of their success where four years earlier they had failed. "What Is the Moral Majority?" opened, "Moral Majority, Inc. is made up of millions of Americans, including 72,000 ministers, priests, and rabbis." *And rabbis*: In 1976, John Conlan and Bill Bright named their group the "Christian Freedom Foundation." They circulated a manual on electing "real Christians." Conlan campaigned against his Jewish opponent pleading "We need to elect a Christian congressman." They were crushed in the press. The Christian right learned from that: it loudly insisted it was ecumenical. Thereupon, it received remarkably friendly press. A *New York Times* feature on Falwell, for instance, noted how he was "sunburned from visits to refugee camps in Thailand last week." They neglected the more unsavory elements of his appeal.

He was back on tour with his multimedia revue. At Trinity Christian Academy in Jacksonville, Florida, a teacher was so riled up after Falwell's preachments about the dangers of homosexuality that he told his class, "In my day, we knew how to deal with faggots. . . . We knocked a guy's head into the side of the fountain! He was bleeding like a squashed tomato." When a student complained to another teacher about this un-Christlike utterance, the concern turned on him, not the teacher: "Are *you* thinking of turning gay, Dwayne? A gay person cannot be saved."

Paul Weyrich kept up a busy schedule of political bootcamps for ministers. At Charles Stanley's megachurch in Georgia, it got so rip-roaring that when someone mentioned something about baptism, the hefty Melkite Greek Orthodox Catholic was introduced bodily to the Southern Baptist practice of adult full-immersion baptism, via the pool in the back of the church. The first issue of the *Moral Majority Report* neared completion. It included an article by Robert Billings: "Out of the Pews, Into the Precincts." With Richard Viguerie's help, it would go out to a mailing list approaching a million people.

And the White House began taking notice.

For years, a moderate Southern Baptist minister named Robert Maddox had been lobbying for an administration job stanching Carter's bleeding among his former evangelical base. Finally, Hamilton Jordan hired him. He persuaded Carter to address the National Religious Broadcasters convention in Washington on the day of the Iowa caucuses, and arranged, for the next morning, a White House get-together for evangelical leaders, including Falwell, over at the White House, for grits. There, however, the president equivocated on abortion, and reiterated his support of the ERA. "I was hanging onto the black iron gates at the White House," Tim La-Haye subsequently related, "and we prayed that God would help us to do everything we could to keep him from being elected."

NO DOUBT NOW WHOM THEY WISHED TO ELECT TO THE PRESIDENCY IN-stead. On January 30, Ronald Reagan appeared to a delirious reception in the auditorium of the Christian institution of higher learning in South Carolina wrapped up in federal litigation to preserve its right to exclude African Americans: Bob Jones University—a "great institution," Reagan proclaimed. Regarding the IRS guidelines, he said, "You do not alter the evil character of racial quotas simply by changing the color of the ben-eficiary." The crowd was particularly ecstatic when he said that the U.S. should not observe "SALT II or SALT I until the Soviet Union withdraws its troops from Afghanistan." And when he repeated a favorite line about Vietnam—"never again will we allow men to fight and give their lives for a cause that we're not intending to win"—he got a standing ovation. The *New York Times* called it "one of the warmest receptions of the cam-paign." Bob Jones III told his students to "take the word to family" to pray for a Reagan victory. Then they massed in the rain to catch a glimpse of him. "Do you think he'll sign my Bible?" one asked a Secret Service agent.

A couple of weeks later, Jerry Falwell traveled to Alaska at the behest of a minister named Jerry Prevo, who had defeated Anchorage's gay rights ordinance, then requested Falwell's help in his Moral Majority chapter's first big project: flooding the state's Republican caucuses for Reagan. Prevo believed that "in this country, Christianity has been discriminated against." In his speech to his flock, Falwell recounted his recent White House breakfast:

"We were discussing the national defense and all these things and I asked the president, 'Sir, why do you have known practicing homosexuals on your senior staff here at the White House?'"

Carter replied, according to Falwell, "Well, I am president of all the American people, and I believe I should represent everyone."

"So I said, 'why don't you have some murderers and bank robbers and so forth to represent!'"

The audience cried their delight. Reagan won the Alaska Republican preference poll 58 percent to 26 recent, at caucuses, thanks to stealthy Moral Majority organizing, with twice the turnout of 1976. His field director, stunned, proclaimed, "We never dreamed we'd win by this margin."

In New Hampshire, a new subsidiary of the California-based Christian Voice, "Christians for Reagan," began its work. "Do you believe America was destined for the avalanche of pornography, abortion, homosexuality, murder, rape and child abuse that has befallen us?" their circular asked. "Your destiny as a Christian and an American calls you to join with me in this great Crusade to Save America. Bring God Back to American leadership and elect Ronald Reagan President of the United States."

Reagan escalated his daily jabs at Carter. On February 7, it was an evidence-free accusation that Soviet T62 tanks and MiG-23 fighters had been positioned in Yemen for an invasion of Oman by the Soviet combat brigade in Cuba, and called for a total boycott of trade with the Soviet Union—which would not spur retaliation because "the Soviet Union is not ready for that all-out confrontation." He covered his bases when he made claims like these, however, by noting that he did not have all the information a president would have at his disposal, so he couldn't speak with complete authority. The *Washington Post* pointed out that this was his campaign's fault: aides refused offered State Department briefings, to leave Reagan free to back away from any statement perceived as overly bellicose "by treating it as just another alternative."

In Tallahassee, he blamed the hostage seizure on the "ease with which the administration abandoned its support of the shah," and said Carter's "continual failure to give the Soviet Union clear and unmistakable signals concerning our vital interests is driving the country closer to a nuclear confrontation." (So much for last week's claim that they weren't ready for confrontation.) In Jacksonville he said that, though "I am not opposed to the policy of trying to hold down nuclear proliferation," he might allow Pakistan to develop nuclear weapons if they allowed America to base troops there; and he would be sorry to see a new country develop a nuclear arsenal—but "I don't think it's any of our business." An hour later, aides called in reporters to stress that Reagan *supported* efforts to stop nuclear proliferation, and only meant to say that it was difficult as a practical matter. A week later, however, Reagan repeated the same thing.

He was not even speaking to John Sears by then. Which perhaps was the reason the brake appeared to be off. The *Washington Post* noted with distaste that he had even been "dusting off his references to the woman in Chicago who received welfare checks under 127 different names." He joined John Connally in calling for the repeal of the Foreign Corrupt Practices Act. He said that nineteen key members of the Carter administration were members of the Trilateral Commission—only because that might lead, Ed Meese clarified to reporters suspicious why Reagan was trawling these fever swamps, to a "softening of defense," because Trilateralists believed commerce "should transcend, perhaps, the national defense." Then, the campaign released a statement headed "GUN CONTROL DISARMS THE HONEST CITIZEN, NOT THE CRIMINAL." This had no impact on the race. For, in an eye-opening display of how far to the right the Republican Party had gone, every candidate appeared at a gun-rights rally in Concord to one-up the others with their enthusiasm—except John Anderson. He said, mildly, "There is a case that can be made to limit the availability of concealed handguns"; he was booed. He continued, "We license automobiles. What's so wrong with telling the law-abiding citizens of this country that we will license certain handguns." Someone shouted, "Shut up!"

BUSH RETAINED A THREE-POINT EDGE IN THE LATEST NATIONWIDE HARRIS Poll—eleven points among independents. Independents were particularly crucial in New Hampshire, where citizens could on Election Day choose which party primary they would vote in. So it was fortuitous for Ronald Reagan that, even as his public statements became increasingly right-wing, aspects of how he saw the world were presented as entirely mainstream in three separate phenomena saturating TV. The first was a documentary miniseries on PBS that ran on ten consecutive Friday evenings beginning on January 11. It was called *Free to Choose*, and it was hosted by Reagan's friend Milton Friedman.

Friedman had retired from the University of Chicago in 1977 after winning his Nobel Prize, and taken a fellowship at the Hoover Institution at Stanford University. The week he began, he received a call from the head of the PBS affiliate in Erie, Pennsylvania, a rare conservative in the liberal world of public broadcasting, who was offended by a fifteen-part BBC economics series, hosted by the liberal economist John Kenneth Galbraith, that was about to run on PBS. Friedman agreed, reluctantly at first, to host a program in response. The original idea was a modest series of filmed Friedman lectures. It soon became fantastically more ambitious—ten state-of-the-art half hours of gorgeous visual storytelling in which the nation's premier laissez-faire economist explicated the magic of the unfettered marketplace from exotic locales all over the world.

To demonstrate the exponential growth in federal regulation, clerks at the Library of Congress Jefferson Building stacked every volume of the *Federal Register* chronology since its inception in the 1930s in piles around the building's landmark rotunda until a single year's stack was too high not to teeter and fall. Friedman traveled to the University of California at Los Angeles, and Dartmouth in New Hampshire, to contrast public and private education. (Dartmouth students were hardworking because they paid high tuition, and thus appreciated the value of their education; UCLA students slept in class, played pinball, and lolled by the pool because their state-subsidized tuitions were so cheap.) He explained the gold standard inside the Federal Reserve Bank of New York's giant vault, perched upon a bench of gold bars; illustrated the perils of rent control and government jobs programs on a burned-out block in the Bronx. (That episode, like the one on public schools, mimicked Ronald Reagan's practice of casting African Americans as those most harmed by government.) At the Bureau of Engraving and Printing he pushed the button that started the currency printing presses that his monetary theory said were responsible for inflation; in a Las Vegas casino, he delivered a discourse on the importance of risk in a free society. Then it was off to a series of overseas shoots: to contrast East and West Berlin; to Cambridge to talk about John Maynard Keynes; to a soulless government housing project in Manchester; to the Greek island where Hippocrates practiced medicine. No expenses were spared. They were charged to such deep-pocketed benefactors as Bechtel, General Mills, General Motors, and William Simon's Olin Foundation—whose vice president had talked Friedman into the project when he'd been skeptical.

These travels served a simple theme, established in episode one, which opened with a sweeping helicopter shot of the Manhattan skyline as Friedman explained the promethean power of the market. ("Once all of this was a swamp, covered with forest. . . .") In Manhattan's Chinatown, he stood inside "exactly the kind of factory that my mother worked in when she came to this country for the first time at the age of fourteen, almost ninety years ago. And if there had not been factories like this here then at which she could have started to work and earn a little money, she wouldn't have been able to come. . . . Of course, she didn't stay here a long time, she stayed here while she learned the language, while she developed some feeling for the country, and gradually she was able to make a better life for herself."

Next it was off to Hong Kong, where that same miracle was happening *now*: a "laboratory experiment in what happens when government is limited to its proper function and leaves people free to pursue their own objectives." On the ferry crossing the harbor, he described how "the power of the free market has enabled the industrious people of Hong Kong to transform what was once barren rock into one of the most thriving and successful places in Asia." At a clangorous factory, workers churned out plastic trinkets at a furious pace, "free to work what hours they choose, free to move to other jobs. The market gives them that choice": a modern version of his mother's sweatshop. Which, in the next scene, gave way to a spotless laboratory-like facility: "Competition from places like South Korea and Taiwan have made cheap products like this less profitable, so Hong Kong businessmen have been . . . developing more sophisticated products and new technology that can match anything in the West or East—and their employees have been developing new skills." If government only stayed out of the way, ran the argument, sweatshops *inevitably* evolved into microchip factories.

"This miracle," Friedman marveled, "hasn't been achieved by government action," but by "impersonal forces of the marketplace"—which he then demonstrated by walking down a bustling Hong Kong street to the little shop of "Mr. Chung, who makes metal containers. Nobody's ordered him to; he does it because he's found that he can do better for himself that way than by making anything else. But if demand for metal containers went down, or somebody found a way of making them cheaper, Mr. Chung would soon get that message." To the establishment of a "Mr. Yu, who has been making traditional Cantonese wedding gowns for forty-two years. But the demand for these elaborate garments is falling. The firm has already gotten that message"—Mr. Yu smiled broadly—"and is already looking for another product."

It all worked seamlessly, Friedman said, because the people on that barren rock understood what Americans had back during the nineteenth century—which schoolchildren mistakenly learned was the age of robber barons, but whose unregulated economy actually had made it America's golden age. "We've been squandering that inheritance," the genial little gentleman softly rued.

The narrative was exceptionally seductive: economic utopia was within America's grasp, if only government would get out of the way. It was also a thoroughgoing fantasy—starting with that harbor ferry, without which the barren rock's economy could not exist. It had been built by government, subsidized so heavily that tickets were practically free. Hong Kong's housing was among the most government-subsidized and -regulated on earth. Its businesses could not operate without the sufferance of criminal gangs. What's more, the residents of Friedman's bastion of liberty could not *vote*: they were subjects of the British crown, with greatly limited free speech rights.

The second episode was even more fantastical. It attributed the present-day prosperity of Japan to the Meiji Dynasty's opening to international trade in 1868, in contrast to the squalor of India, supposedly caused because its government adopted fashionable ideas about "central planning" upon independence in 1948. What that ignored was that Japan's postwar industrial development, whose main economic architect had been a Communist, was as state-directed as any outside the Communist orbit, and that India's two centuries as a British colony had played an enormous, continuous role in keeping it poor, and that the process of breaking down its traditional system of agriculture in favor of production for international trade during the Victorian period produced famines that killed millions.

Each episode then featured half-hour debates between Friedman and his allies and an equal number of his ideological adversaries. But the leftists didn't stand a chance against Friedman's cunning in debate. In the first one, the socialist Michael Harrington derided "the *myth* of free enterprise which disguises the *fact* of state capitalism," pointing out that in the "real world" America's biggest businesses were "welfare-dependent," receiving billions in various kinds of subsidies from the federal government. And, cheerfully, Milton Friedman agreed. He *despised* such corporate welfare—which need only abate for America to thrive as never before. (The show's corporate sponsors had apparently missed the message that Friedman was not on their side.)

PBS originally resisted handing over airtime to such a partisan figure—until pressure was brought to bear on network officials by the Pennsylvania PBS executives, who argued that it was necessary as a balance for Galbraith's "clearly ideological series." *Free to Choose* was far more ideological. One producer wrote to Friedman that the goal was "changing attitudes rather than explaining principles . . . to make a whole new audience, hundreds of thousands—perhaps millions—of reasonably intelligent laymen suddenly think in a new way about their old assumptions. Then, they can go to read your books and articles and grasp the facts and the logical arguments that you build in them and the conclusions you reach, and be genuinely convinced and converted."

In that, they assuredly succeeded.

The ratings were better than for PBS's *Masterpiece Theater*. Fan mail poured in. "Our family is so excited by your show. As far as I am concerned, there hasn't been a more important show in the history of TV." The series' home station, WQLN, averaged two hundred to three hundred such messages a day, receiving only six negative ones by the time they began forwarding them to Friedman, who was so overwhelmed he had to respond with an apologetic form letter. An accompanying volume, *Free to Choose: A Personal Statement*, became one of the bestselling books of the year.

The last episode to air before the New Hampshire primary took on one of Ronald Reagan's favorite villains, the Consumer Product Safety Commission—which neither Reagan nor Friedman bothered to mention was budgeted at less than the cost of a single fighter jet. The show featured scenes so ridiculous they could have been scripted by Buster Keaton: government bureaucrats in suits and helmets, peddling bicycles ("even though 80 percent of bike accidents are caused by human error"); in safety goggles, firing tiny pistols ("to prevent toy guns from making too big a boom"); and rocking playground swings back and forth ("No matter how many tests there are, children's swings are never going to be totally safe. You cannot outlaw accidents!"). "Spendthrift and snooping government," Friedman harrumphed, "deciding what *they* think is good for us. They are taking away *our* freedom to choose."

The message was that not capitalists but public officials were the *real* greedy malefactors. It was an auspicious time to be selling it. The story most dominating the news besides Iran and Afghanistan was "Abscam," the FBI's shorthand for a series of sting operations, beginning in 1978, in which undercover agents dressed as Arab oil sheiks nabbed several white-collar criminals—then, the mayor of Camden, New Jersey, who dropped the dime on several members of Congress, including one senator, who were recorded on camera accepting suitcases full of cash in exchange for favors. Reagan's own campaign could hardly have planned it better themselves—though the next TV phenomenon that came to Reagan's aid was one of their own productions: his New Hampshire commercials, which were strikingly effective—rather to the surprise of the Reagan high command, who had not really planned them at all.

SHORTLY BEFORE IOWA THE REAGAN CAMPAIGN FIRED ITS MADISON AVENUE agency. This was partly for financial reasons: the Reagan for President Committee was being so poorly managed that it was perilously close to hitting the FEC's spending ceilings in the various primary states. Their media buyer knew a guy in Philadelphia, Elliott Curson, who had never done a national campaign, but might work cheap; John Sears liked his stuff for Jeff Bell's Senate campaign in New Jersey. Curson and Bell, who had grown close, flew out to Iowa for a meeting, as a team. Reagan loved Curson's offbeat whimsy. His mangers loved that Curson promised to film eleven commercials for $18,000. They hired him even though he supported the ERA and abortion rights. His firm wrote the scripts over two days based on a sixty-page issue paper. Curson and Bell flew out to L.A. for a weekend shoot. Their first stop was Reagan headquarters by the airport. Ed Meese told them that they had just missed the candidate, who had *just* stopped to cheer the staff up after the Iowa loss. Bell thought this was quite something: usually, it was the *staff* that cheered up the candidate.

The man Hollywood used to call "One Take Reagan" lived up to his reputation, shooting the eleven ads in a few hours. Curson was amazed that no higher-ups reviewed the scripts or the shoot. The reason was that John Sears still didn't think advertising was all that important. He assumed that the media would give the front-runner all the attention he needed for free.

Curson's ideas for the commercials proved brilliant. Later, in the general election, the campaign hired another top-drawer agency, which conducted the most elaborate focus-grouping and market-testing in the history of electioneering to arrive at the same conclusions Curson had by intuition. He reflected that what most people knew about Reagan was that he was old, was right-wing, spent too much time on his ranch, and had been a movie star and governor of California—but not the effective and relatively moderate record he had established as governor. So many of the ads simply had Reagan, without makeup, straightforwardly *explaining* that record, speaking directly to the camera, unadorned by fancy lights, music, animation, or sets—to say, as Curson explained later that spring to a radio interviewer in Philadelphia named Terry Gross, "Okay, here's what we're gonna do, don't worry, I've done it before." Curson reasoned that if the Reagan in the commercials looked better that the Reagan on the news, a stereotype would be confirmed: he was a Hollywood phony. Indeed, that was the flaw in *George Bush's* commercials: "He looked pretty."

Reagan's ads didn't even sport catchy taglines. Instead, each ended with a punctuating thought from Reagan; then a simple white "REAGAN" lingered on the screen for several seconds—"a pause to underline what he's said," Curson explained, to "separate Reagan from the soap commercial coming up."

One bore the impress of Jeff Bell's supply-side passions. The announcer stated, "Ronald Reagan believes that when you tax something you get less of it. We're taxing work, savings and investment like never before. As a result we have less work, less savings and less invested." Then Reagan, straight to the camera: "I didn't always agree with President Kennedy. But when his 30 percent federal tax cut became law, the economy did so well that every group in the country came out ahead. Even the government gained $54 billion in unexpected revenues. *If I become President, we're going to try that again.*"

Another ad was referred to in-house as the "Good Shepherd." The announcer said, "In the past few years, our income has been eroded by the worst peacetime inflation and the largest tax increases in history. Our leaders tell us that in order to help energy consumers, we have to tax energy producers. And to have lower prices, we have to keep federal tax rates high. Ronald Reagan doesn't believe that." Reagan spoke: "If there's one thing we've seen enough of, it's this idea that for one American to gain, another American has to suffer. When the economy is weak . . . everybody suffers . . . especially those who have the least. If we reduce paperwork and unnecessary regulations . . . if we cut tax rates deeply and permanently, we'll be removing many of the barriers that hold everybody back. Those who have the least will gain the most. If we put incentives back into society, everyone will gain."

Then, the punctuating thought: *"We have to move ahead. But we can't leave anyone behind."*

The staff in California were sure they were far too primitive to be effective. One appalled aide told *Time* magazine that the Good Shepherd made Reagan sound like a liberal. Jude Wanniski read that and fired off a frantic letter to Peter Hannaford: "It doesn't imply that Reagan is a liberal!!! It implies that he's a leader!!" He noted, "I had lunch yesterday in Newark at the Essex Club with six of the biggest GOP financial supporters in the state, and they uniformly told me that Reagan can't win, that he's another Goldwater, and I told them to watch Reagan win in November by a landslide—because he is a conservative populist where Goldwater was a conservative elitist."

Alexander Cockburn and James Ridgeway made a similar observation: this way of framing the supply-side message "enabled Reagan to stare an unemployed worker unflinchingly in the face in the spring, summer, and fall of 1980 and tell him that the Republicans, not the Democrats, were the real advocates of growth and would put him back to work. This, plus a 4 percent real decline in living standards in the last two years of the Carter administration was what gave Reagan the edge. What had the Democrats got to offer in return?"

Evidence supported this. Dick Wirthlin found that 80 percent of New Hampshire voters rated Curson's ads positively. The Good Shepherd and the JFK supply-side ad were particular favorites with Democrats, whom focus groups showed were frequently viewing Reagan more favorably than Ted Kennedy or Jimmy Carter.

THE THIRD TELEVISED PHENOMENON HELPING REAGAN ALSO GAVE CARTER a boost. It was the Winter Olympics—one of the most effective advertisements for American patriotism ever.

Four years earlier ABC News had run a poignant report by Peter Jennings decrying the "rampant nationalism" marring the games in Innsbruck, Austria: the Olympics, once a "festival of life and sport," were becoming a fight about "the superiority of one political system over another." He particularly chided American fans who "see hockey as an extension of the Cold War on ice."

That, however, was then. Now the man who produced the 1976 Olympics broadcast, Roone Arledge, was also in charge of ABC News. And now, patriotism was *chic*.

A book called *The Right Stuff* was riding its twentieth week on the bestseller list—battling it out with dour titles like *Aunt Erma's Cope Book* and *How to Prosper During the Coming Bad Years*. The book was a celebration of an unadulterated American triumph: the Mercury manned space program. Its author, Tom Wolfe, who wore blindingly white cus-tom-tailored suits, boasted of his "civilized" inability to find the gas tank when he rented a car, and longed to return to the days when "guilt" was in fashion—a self-identified gentleman, "not of this age." The *Times* called his ecstatic testimonial to the stoic heroes who volunteered to cheat death by perching themselves atop rockets with 7.6 million tons of thrust, which kept exploding during tests, "nostalgic, worshipful, jingoistic"—and "su-perb." It was equally nostalgic concerning their loyal wives—he called them "death angels," and the hyper-competent NASA engineers who contrasted so refreshingly to those who built and maintained Three Mile Island, Skylab, and American Airlines DC-10s. When he had begun the project in 1972, Wolfe got little interest from publishers—but that was back when only 11 percent of the public wanted higher defense budgets, not 50 percent like now: *patriotism chic.*

And in Lake Placid, Roone Arledge played it to the hilt. He packaged the Olympics and the hostages together seamlessly, leading into *America Held Hostage* each night with a Lake Placid wrap-up, sending news personnel for the first time to do Olympics coverage, including the "Up Close and Personal" profiles of (American) athletes that he had pioneered for ABC's 1972 Olympics coverage from Munich. The broadcast even had a disco-flavored theme song, performed by smooth-jazz flugelhornist Chuck Mangione.

There was plenty of sentiment to exploit. On February 15, a hand-some, corn-fed twenty-one-year-old from Wisconsin named Eric Heiden won the first of five gold medals in speed skating, a record; his sister Beth won a bronze. Two twin brothers from Yakima, Phil and Steve Mahre, competed against each other in skiing. Phil won a silver in slalom. But that was nothing compared to what was happening on the hockey rink.

The Soviet hockey team had won every gold medal since 1964. (Amer-ica had once won a silver, in 1972). In 1976, they won every game. Going into the 1980 tournament, the Soviets scored a surreal fifty-one goals in five contests, including a 10–3 drubbing of the Americans in an exhibition game at Madison Square Garden—and it "could have been higher," the *New York Daily News* said, "if the Soviets had exerted themselves a bit." The Soviet coach was asked if the game indicated anything about their readiness for the Olympics. He thought not. "To know the real strengths of a team, you must play against strong opposition."

Some of the Soviets had been playing together for fifteen years: this was their life. Conventionally, American teams were pickup outfits, some-thing college stars did as a lark before signing lucrative contracts with the National Hockey League—and since individual showboating on national TV might help them win a *more* lucrative contract, the teams functioned terribly as *teams*. If this was a Cold War allegory, the implied narrative was the inability of greedy capitalists to sacrifice for the common good.

The American coach, Herb Brooks, was determined to try a different way. Choosing his team, he sacrificed more skilled individuals for ones he thought would work well together. (Hockey experts wondered if any of them were good enough individually to *make* the Soviet squad.) He greatly expanded preparation time, all the way back to the summer of the long gas lines. They started out a tangle of college and regional rivals, toothless misfits with Boston and Minnesota accents; Brooks forged them into a well-oiled machine within which individual heroics were *punished*. He drove them mercilessly, despite the fact that as the opening whistle approached, no one was sure whether the Soviet Union would be boycotting Lake Placid as retribution against America's likely summer boycott of Moscow.

In their first game the Americans achieved a surprising last-minute tie against Sweden. Their next, against silver-medal favorite Czechoslovakia, was tied at two when the U.S. somehow pulled ahead, then piled up four more goals while giving up none. ABC announcer Al Michaels said they were now the second-best hockey team in the world.

People who'd never watched a hockey game started tuning in, thrilling to the stories—*up close and personal*: the unrelievedly grim coach who had been cut from the last American team to win a gold medal, in Squaw Valley in 1960; Mike Eruzione, the twenty-five-year-old minor-league washout, whom Brooks had named captain; goalie Jim Craig, whose sickly mother told him on her deathbed that her dream was for him to play in the Olympics; their best offensive line, three guys who grew up playing on frozen New England ponds and were called the Coneheads because they seemed to communicate telepathically, like aliens.

They trounced the Norwegians 5–1. Then, the Romanians, 7–2. On February 20—the deadline Carter had imposed for a Soviet withdrawal from Afghanistan, when America's summer Olympic boycott became official—they clinched a medal with a 4–2 defeat of West Germany.

Surpassing expectations was fun. But it was time for reality to intrude, against the team that had just beaten them 10–3 without half trying.

With one second left in the first period, the Americans put the puck in the goal to tie the Soviets at two, and Herb Brooks, in his customary unfashionable checked blazer, smiled for perhaps the first time in the tournament. Eruzione scored late in the third period to give the U.S. a one-goal lead. Al Michaels said, "The creased smile of Herb Brooks became a wide grin."

"Twenty-eight seconds and the crowd is going insane!"

But the Soviets were controlling the puck, hammering at the goal again and again.

"Nineteen seconds. Johnson over to Ramsey ... the puck is still loose ... eleven seconds. You've got ten seconds! The count is going on right now. ... Five seconds left in the game—*do you believe in miracles???* YES!!!*"

The frenzy that followed resembled the crowd at the embassy gates in Tehran. No one would leave. The crowd started changing "USA! USA!"

In the gold medal game against Finland a shorthanded goal put the Americans ahead 4–2. Seven seconds. Michaels: "The crowd going insane at the moment! Bedlam here, stomping! Five seconds to the gold medal, four to the gold medal—*this impossible dream comes true!*"

A kid skittered onto the ice with a big flag. Jim Craig draped it around himself with, the *Boston Globe* wrote, "only his head and the tail ends of his fat goalie's stick poking through, and as he skated, glided, shook the row of hands, he was a symbol, a hope, a promise ... he looked like the Statue of Liberty on skates."

Vice President Walter Mondale joined the team in the locker room, where a phone had been wired to the White House—and ABC's sound truck. Millions of Americans heard the president invite the players glee-fully to the White House. Each ascended, one by one, up the steps to the South Portico, where Carter embraced them. He said that the entire West Wing had stopped work in order to attend.

It was the day before the New Hampshire primary.

THE PREVIOUS SUNDAY, SOMETHING STRANGE HAD HAPPENED AT A REPUB-lican debate. It was a political moment about as only-in-New-Hampshire as a flinty old man in a mackinaw shouting "Live Free or Die" in the shadow of the Old Man of the Mountain—and what made it the most only-in-New-Hampshire moment of all was the stakes: who might end up the next Leader of the Free World.

The little city of Nashua, population 67,865, had a little newspaper, the *Telegraph*. It invited the two Republican front-runners to debate in the high school gym. Both accepted. Bob Dole, running a distant fourth, pro-tested to the Federal Election Commission that excluding the other candi-dates was an illegal in-kind corporate contribution from the *Telegraph* to Reagan and Bush. On the Thursday before the debate, the FEC agreed. So the paper approached Reagan and Bush to ask if they would split the cost, to moot the corporate-contribution issue. The Bush campaign wouldn't pony up. The Reagan campaign did. John Sears, as was his wont, had a trick up his sleeve.

On Friday, Sears and his deputy Jim Lake called the other campaigns to inform them that *Reagan* was now the debate's sponsor, and that he wished to invite them to participate. Candidates from across the fruited plain—except for John Connally, who hoped to score his Hail Mary in South Carolina, where he was campaigning day and night—booked last-minute flights to Boston, then drove up to southeast New Hampshire for the chance to pull off *their* miracle. One campaign was *not* informed of this development, however: George Bush's. He entered the building suspecting Reagan had backed out of the debate because he didn't want to face Bush one-on-one—as he believed the *Telegraph* was still demanding.

At midday, a Reagan advance man named Rick Ahearn asked the freelance local soundman working the event if they could accommodate one more position on the dais; yes, they could. How about two? Yes. Four? They could manage that, too. Ahearn stashed four extra chairs behind the stage. Lake then showed the soundman a check made out in the amount of his fee. That way, Lake later explained, he could say, if he had to, "Remember now, you're working for us, you get it at the end of the night. I didn't tell him what was going to transpire, I just showed him the check."

In a public poll, Reagan had pulled close to even; in Wirthlin's private poll, he approached a 10 percent lead. He had been nine points back after Iowa. William Loeb had helped: one day the giant banner atop the *Manchester Union Leader* read "REAGAN VOTERS MUST TURN OUT TUESDAY"; another day, it was "REAGAN IS OUR REPUBLICAN HOME."

But Reagan had landed himself in a political jam.

Riding on his campaign bus on Saturday the 16th between Keene and Milford after a hard day of campaigning, Reagan told his campaign companion Senator Gordon Humphrey an ethnic joke. It was the kind of humor he sometimes favored, in private; back in his childhood, his mother, a local thespian, loved to tell jokes in ethnic dialects.

This was the one about how you could tell the Polish guy at a cockfight. (He brought a duck.) And how you could tell the Italian. (He bet on the duck.) And whether the mafia was there. (The duck won.) A reporter who hadn't heard the joke asked him to repeat it, which Reagan obligingly did—then the journalist reported on it. Reagan tried, lamely, to claim that he had only told it as a sort of pedagogical lesson on the *offensiveness* of ethnic jokes, which of course he abhorred. "I plead that I was the *victim* of something that was done," he insisted.

His backfilling was sabotaged inadvertently that same day by his wife, who was campaigning in the Chicago suburb of Rosemont. The loudspeakers picked her up telling her husband on the phone that she wished he could be there to see "all these beautiful white people." She later claimed that she was referring to the snow—although when she realized people could hear her, she had turned pale and added, "beautiful black and white people." There were no black people present. Not in a white suburb like Rosemont.

In Nashua, some twenty-five hundred people crunched across the snow to the gym, inside the monstrously bland mid-century redbrick high school that looked just like hundreds of other monstrously bland mid-century redbrick high schools around the country. They were primed for political combat. The crowd also included the lion's share of the quadrennial alien invasion known as the political press—eagerly flushed out for the occasion by Reagan's advance team, who were told they would see something they could not afford to miss.

Reagan's campaign was stationed in a classroom at one end of a long hallway—"Corridor D." Bush was on the opposite end. Five minutes before the scheduled start time, Bush was told that Reagan wanted to meet with him. Bush sent James Baker down Corridor D. John Sears told Baker that the governor was ready to begin. Bush's man said that that was for the *Telegraph* people to decide: this was their debate, after all.

A door to an adjoining room opened, and the presence of the *other* four candidates was revealed. James Baker was shocked.

It was already twenty-five minutes past the scheduled start time. Bush was summoned to the stage. On his way, he was met by Senator Humphrey, delegated by his five opponents to confront him for—as Dole, John Anderson, Phil Crane, and Howard Baker had been given to understand by Reagan's representatives—having intentionally shut them out. Humphrey demanded Bush meet with the other candidates: "If you don't come right now, you're doing a disservice to party unity."

Bush was enraged at being lectured on party unity by the New Right firebrand who had been emceeing blistering Reagan rallies across the state. He snapped, "I've done more for this party than you'll ever do," turned on his heels, and marched testily to the stage—where he vainly tried to strike an air of command amid the confusion.

He was followed by Reagan, the other four candidates behind him in train. The gym was packed tighter than a Lake Placid hockey arena. Reagan shook Bush's hand; they exchanged a word or two, then Reagan shook the hand of the *Nashua Telegraph* editor, a mild-looking, balding man named Jon Breen, who was moderating. Reagan and Breen tried to confer amid the steadily mounting roar of a crowd whose mood grew increasingly electric as word spread that what had been billed as a two-man debate might become a six-man battle royale—if only their local newspaper would let it.

Reagan asked if he could make a statement. Moderator Breen, adamant that the agreed-upon two-man format continue as scheduled, barked,

'No." Reagan spoke into three microphones bundled in front of him on the table: "I am the *sponsor*, and I supposed I would have some rights."

The newspaper's publisher tried to restore order: "This is getting to sound more like a boxing match. . . . In the rear are four men who haven't been invited by the *Nashua Telegraph—*"

He was answered by a wall of boos. A lady cried "Get them chairs!" An offstage voice attempted to begin a two-man debate: "If we may have the first question, Mr. Breen."

Reagan wagged a finger.

"Excuse me. You asked me if you could make an announcement first. And I asked you if I could make an announcement myself."

The offstage voice: "Would the sound man please turn Mr. Reagan's mic off for a minute?"

Reagan bolted out of his seat, lips pursed. The crowd started pumping their fists. The "Nashua Four" stood stock-still behind the table like lampposts. Reagan, his face flushed, his eyes fierce, extended his left index finger, saying something off-mic. George Bush looked pained, staring blankly like one of the townsmen in *High Noon* desperate to get out of town before the desperadoes rode in.

Breen: "Will the sound man please turn Mr. Reagan's mic off?"

Reagan looked incredulous. He pursed his lips again. An American flag framed in the news shots behind him, he tried to stand up, but had to hunch a little bit so the microphone cord would reach all the way. He demanded sternly, "Is this on?"

"YES!" the crowd cried back, and the old trooper was now loaded for bear. He sat down and snapped, *"Mr. Green—"*

"Would you turn the microphone *off.*"

"You *asked* for me," Reagan began responding, and as Breen began to interrupt him, a chant emerged from all way back in the bleachers: *"Let him speak! Let him speak!"*

At that, Reagan roared the line everyone remembered: "I am *paying* for this microphone, Mr. Green!!"

A monstrous ovation erupted. Bush looked shell-shocked. The other four contenders clapped appreciatively. Reagan gave a satisfied nod.

And sharp observers noticed something familiar about the tableau.

There was a Frank Capra picture that came out in 1948, a fraught time in Reagan's own life: he was divorcing; his movie career was floundering; he was getting more and more involved in politics, which was why his estranged wife had grown weary of him. The movie was called *State of the Union*, and it, too, centered on a marriage troubled by politics. Spencer Tracy depicted Grant Matthews, a principled, bighearted airplane magnate drafted to run for president by a political boss; Katharine Hepburn played his estranged wife, who falls back in love with him as he heroically rises above the corruption and demagoguery of politics as usual in his bracingly truth-telling campaign. Then, however, she falls back *out* of love as her husband surrenders more and more to the temptations of demagoguery the closer he gets to the prize. Until, in the melodramatic conclusion, as his wife reluctantly reads from a sappy script to introduce her husband for a live radio broadcast, the Spencer Tracy character decides to reclaim his soul and his wife's respect. He steals away the microphone—"Ladies and gentlemen, this is Grant Matthews. I'm sorry to interrupt but I can't take any more of this"—and a scuffle breaks out as the corrupt political boss, seeing his meal ticket slipping away, tries desperately to shut down the broadcast, and Tracy cries, *"Don't shut me off! I'm paying for this microphone!"*

He proceeds to deliver an emotional patriotic sermon as his tearstained-faced wife looks on in adoration.

Reagan understood drama—in Hollywood black-and-white terms. There were many instances in his career when men far more cynical than he understood that if they could manage to cast Reagan in his own mind, with his rigidly moralistic way of seeing the world, as a corruption-fighting hero, he would rise up for their side with roaringly sincere indig-nation, like in a Frank Capra movie—even if the truth was actually rather gray. For instance, in 1945, when Reagan was president of the Screen Ac-tors Guild and the studio heads convinced him that persuading his mem-bers to cross a picket line in a nasty jurisdictional strike was the heroic thing to do, because the strike was part of a Communist plot to take over the motion picture industry. (It wasn't.)

Was this situation a little like that, with John Sears as the cynical ma-nipulator?

Reagan didn't *appear* to be playacting. But either he *knew* his cam-paign had intentionally staged this confrontation with the sponsoring newspaper in order to trick Bush into looking like the heavy—in which case Reagan *was* performing an act, and perhaps had been rehearsing *State of the Union* in his mind all day. Or *he himself* had been deceived on this question, led to believe by his own deputies that the newspaper had inten-tionally double-crossed the other contenders, and was sincerely angry at the paper and Bush for breaking a deal.

Either way, it played magnificently—even though he muffed a line (He said "Mr. *Green*," not "Mr. *Breen*.") George Herbert Walker Bush was rendered purely and simply the Hollywood villain: a snob excluding the lesser breeds from his exclusive club, refusing to engage in a fair fight, timidly backing down from risk. On the other side, at center stage, stood Ronald Wilson Reagan, *leader*—a hero standing tall for the American principle of fair play.

The reporters were rousted from the filing center—the cafeteria—to the band room, where Dole, Anderson, Baker, and Crane gave statements amid the tympani and glockenspiels, the double basses, woodwinds, and brass, that played into the Reagan campaign's narrative. Baker, the candidate of conciliation and open government, was so mad his nostrils flared. He called what he believed Bush to have done "the most flagrant effort to reinstitute closed-door politics I have ever seen." John Anderson said, "Clearly, the responsibility of this whole travesty rests with Mr. Bush." Dole said Bush "wants to be the king."

John Sears, for his part, leaned against a hallway locker, grinning mischievously: "We're just party unifiers."

George Bush retreated to Houston and was seen jogging in the Texas sun on the same newscasts in which Reagan shook hands in the snow—and which also ran and reran the footage of Reagan taking steely command of the Nashua debate. (Media critics counted seventeen minutes of network coverage of "I'm paying for this microphone," and zero of the actual debate that followed.) A subsequent poll discovered that 70 percent of New Hampshire Republican voters knew Reagan was sixty-nine years old, but 83 percent didn't care. And in the only poll that mattered, Reagan won the New Hampshire primary with more votes than all the other candidates combined. He appeared at a victory party in front of a red, white, and blue banner inscribed with the slogan devised by the jettisoned Madison Avenue ad agency, which the campaign had decided to stick with: "LET'S MAKE AMERICA GREAT AGAIN."

THAT WAS FEBRUARY 26. THE NEXT PRIMARY, IN SOUTH CAROLINA, WAS ON March 8. But before turning their eyes south, the Reagan team had a piece of business to attend to. Ed Meese put out a statement that had been prepared for release after the vote, win or lose:

"WASHINGTON, D.C., FEB. 26, 1980—Ronald Reagan today announced that William J. Casey has been named executive vice chairman and campaign director of his presidential campaign, replacing John Sears who has resigned to return to his law practice. . . . In announcing the change in his campaign organization, Reagan said, 'The campaign requires a sharp reduction in expenses and a restructuring of our organization to intensify the people-to-people type of campaigning I have been doing here in New Hampshire. Bill Casey has my complete confidence and full authority to carry out that work.'

"Reagan has also accepted resignations from Charlie Black, national political director, and Jim Lake, press secretary, who are returning to private business. Reagan expressed appreciation 'for the effort John Sears, Charlie Black, and Jim Lake have put into my campaign.'"

This had long been in the cards. "There was a feeling," Reagan complained after it was over, "that I was just kind of a spokesman for John Sears." Given Reagan's disinclination to fire anyone, even those with whom he was not speaking, perhaps it was not surprising that the final decision apparently came down to his wife. Once, shortly after Iowa, Jim Lake had told Reagan that his disappointment from that loss was showing up in his speaking. Nancy Reagan took Lake aside and snapped that *knocking him down* was the worst way to handle her husband: *you built Ronald Reagan up*.

Sears had been knocking him down from the beginning. Reagan said he gave him "knots in his stomach." He had to go.

Sears got his revenge at a ninety-minute press conference at the National Press Club. He announced that, despite rumors that he would be joining Howard Baker's moribund campaign, he would not go "directly to work" for any other candidate—and promptly, from that podium, went to work for *every* other candidate. Reagan's campaign, he said, was a shambles. Reagan was "a very competent person in many respects," but he displayed a "certain casualness" concerning "matters of substance for which people hold him to account." He himself, Sears insisted, "didn't want the governor to change his positions"—only "to show greater depth of understanding on the issues." Though Reagan was, he allowed, "a very kind human being."

CHAPTER 33

"Jimmy's Depression Is Gonna Be *Worse* than Herbert's"

AFTER IOWA, TED KENNEDY ANNOUNCED THAT HE WOULD DELIVER A MAJOR speech at Georgetown University. His campaign funds were all but depleted. Jimmy Carter let himself hope that he was bowing out. Instead, Kennedy doubled down.

He had been enraged at Carter's hawkish State of the Union. After he denounced it on the record, an aide called it politically ill-advised. Kennedy responded: "If I'm going to stay in this race—and I am—I am going to do it on my own terms." This speech was that declaration of independence—and his belated answer to Roger Mudd about why he was running in the first place.

He began with a demand for "fairness" on Chappaquiddick, because his speech giving his defense on TV in 1969 was "the only truth I can tell because that is the way it happened." He called for a six-month freeze on prices, profits, dividends, interest rates, and rent. He bemoaned Carter for "moving toward the brink of sending another generation of the young to die for the failures of the old in foreign policy," ridiculed him for calling Afghanistan the gravest threat to peace since World War II, and blamed him personally for both the hostage crisis and the Soviet incursion. He concluded by calling him a hack: "It is easy to bend to the political breezes. But as I said a year ago, sometimes a party must sail into the wind."

The *Washington Post* printed the entire thing. It became his stump speech in New Hampshire. Where, however, on February 26 (which Carter's congressional allies had declared a "National Day of Prayer and Meditation" for the hostages) he was trounced—"in his own backyard," as the political reporters liked to say—49 percent to 38 percent, with 10 percent for Jerry Brown. It suggested the political power of patriotism. The Gallup Poll published that day had Carter's national approval rating above 50 percent, even though the economy was falling apart, and even though, in response to that, Carter proposed yet more sacrifice. In his

State of the Union Address, his only gesture toward domestic priorities had been a short austerity sermon, repeating his favorite quote from Walter Lippmann on the eve of World War II: "You took the good things for granted. Now you must earn them again. For every right that you cherish, you have a duty which you must fulfill. For every good which you wish to preserve, you will have to sacrifice your comfort and your ease. There is nothing for nothing any longer."

Six days later, interest rates on long-term treasury bonds reached 11 percent, higher even than during the Civil War, and the Federal Reserve again raised the discount rate a once-unprecedented full percentage point. Nervous traders began dumping thirty-year bonds, which by February 19 had lost 20 percent of their value since the beginning of the year. Corporate bonds saw a similar plunge. The *Wall Street Journal* estimated portfolio losses since October at $400 million. The inflation rate hit 18 percent, the highest since World War II. The unemployment rate ticked upward, too, led by attrition in auto and steel. In January, "Dodge Main" in Hamtramck, Michigan, and Ford's Pico Rivera plant in Southern California had both shut down. In February Chrysler posted $375 million in losses for the fourth quarter, more than $1 billion for the year, both records. The UAW announced that it would start picketing Toyota, Honda, and Subaru dealerships to persuade the White House to slap import limits on Japanese cars.

And still, the complaint from opinion-molders was that Carter was not pumping enough lead into ol' St. Nick's gut.

"If President Carter wants to move fast on inflation he has only one lever that will make much difference," the *Washington Post*'s editors urged on February 24. "He will have to start cutting his budget, rapidly and severely"—not just next next year's, "but the current one." The next day, Paul Volcker amplified that message in testimony to the Senate Banking Committee: "We've reached the point in this inflation situation where decisive action is necessary," he said, recommending "as much progress as we can . . . in balancing the budget." He also said he agreed with one of John Anderson's central campaign proposals: a fifty-cent-per-gallon increase in the federal gas tax.

Carter convened a budget-cutting task force of economic advisors and Democratic congressional leaders from across the party spectrum—"so we can walk the plank together," Senator Byrd said. The *Post* reported the day of the New Hampshire primary that cuts might total between $8 billion and $10 billion. The goal, the *Post* said, was "to reassure the nation's skittish financial markets that it is serious about fighting inflation." The next day's edition brought news that the task force was considering ending cost-of-living increases to Social Security benefits, capping future budgets at a set percentage of the economy, and slapping an excise tax on imported gasoline (surely confusing those wondering how increasing prices for a major household expense *contained* inflation).

What they would *not* consider, Carter insisted, was government price controls, the solution favored by Teddy Kennedy and 64 percent of the public, but which economists, businessmen—and Carter—considered anathema.

On March 1, major banks raised their prime lending rate to 16.75 percent, a record. The rumor now was that the budget task force was seeking $20 billion in cuts. Representative Richard Gephardt of Missouri said they had no choice: "When you have bank executives come in and say, 'We're getting close to bank lines,' people get frightened. If ever there was a time in recent history to balance the budget, this is it."

Perhaps these leaks were strategic, to make the task force look generous when it finally asked for less. Or perhaps they were intended to quiet the braying voices like *Newsweek*, which said "a balanced budget would have almost magical significance," quoting a Citibank executive for support; and Martin Feldstein of Harvard ("Milton" Feldstein, the *Chicago Tribune* misidentified him, perhaps confusing him with the Nobel Prize winner preaching the evils of government spending on TV every Friday night), who said Volcker "hasn't tightened enough." The *New York Times* even ran an extraordinary editorial demanding a balanced budget to slow inflation, admitting that "nobody any longer knows for sure" how to slow inflation, but insisting the budget should be balanced nonetheless, "even if the economy maintains its strength and produces a surplus. The extra revenue could be used to fight inflation further, through tax cuts."

ANOTHER RUMOR WAS THAT THE WHITE HOUSE MIGHT IMPOSE SOMETHING called "credit controls." That could mean lowering credit limits on charge cards; requiring minimum down payments for car and home loans; or shrinking the maximum time frame for paying loans back. Paul Volcker opposed credit controls. He said they would induce a recession. In fact, Carter *intended* "to keep squeezing the American economy until it cries 'ouch' and falls into a recession," the *Washington Post* explained. Though a mild one, of limited duration: "Nothing short of that will spell success for their latest anti-inflation push," the *Post* summarized the administration's thinking.

On March 14, banks raised their prime rates another half point, and Jimmy Carter went on TV from the East Room. He announced that he was tearing up the budget proposal he had called "lean and austere" when submitting it two months earlier, and which was projected to lower the deficit by 60 percent, in favor of revisions that, he said, further "cut spending in the 1981 budget by more than $18 billion."

Apparently, he had gotten carried away. The press office made a correction: he actually meant *$13 billion*.

Cuts included $1.7 billion from revenue sharing aid to states and cities, $859 million from welfare spending, $265 million from mass transit, and unspecified amounts from highways, foreign aid, mental health, and law-enforcement grants—but nothing from Pentagon spending. There would be a federal hiring freeze, and an excise tax on foreign oil estimated to increase gas prices by ten cents a gallon. (Carter attempted to clear up confusion over how a price increase cut inflation by claiming that the revenue the tax produced would lower the national debt, which would contribute to *eventually* reducing inflation. Then he reintroduced the confusion by saying it would encourage people to purchase less gas—which if they did would counteract that contribution .)

He also announced credit controls—because "just as our governments have been borrowing to make ends meet, so have individual Americans," and "when we try to beat inflation with borrowed money, we just make the problem worse"—in the form of changes in bank rules to make it harder for individuals to get credit cards, and more expensive to defer paying off the debts. Jimmy Carter had found a *new* Santa Claus to shoot—and convinced Volcker to go along.

"Carter Budget Cut Draws Fire from All Directions," a newspaper summarized the reviews. Mayors who'd filed their budgets based on Carter's January spending plan felt the floor drop out from underneath them: in the post–Proposition 13 climate, they would have to lay off city workers. Energy experts said OPEC would react by hiking prices even more. William Proxmire said Carter had gone "not nearly as far as needed," recommending a "misery loves company" slash of $12 billion more. The editorial suites were also concerned that not enough blood had been squeezed from the stone. "President Carter's new and improved anti-inflation program is not much of either," the *New York Times* said, complaining that the president had "yielded much too quickly to the demands of organized labor." Though organized labor heard a different speech. "Cut through the rhetoric," union leader Jerry Wurf said, "and what you have here is a return to the economic philosophy of Herbert Hoover."

The meanest headline appeared in the *Boston Globe*. Its editorial page editor had originally wanted to savage Carter, then acceded to his colleagues' recommendation for a "kinder, collegial" commentary instead—but vented his frustration in the form of a dummy headline he knew would be removed before publication. It was not. So 160,000 copies of the *Globe* hit Beantown with an editorial page topped by the headline "More Mush from the Wimp."

Carter still had Democratic voters on his side. On March 11, he swept a string of Southern primaries. On March 18—the day he announced he would not be imposing import limits on Japanese cars, because he valued their superior fuel economy—he crushed Kennedy in Illinois by a margin of two to one, receiving 165 delegates to Kennedy's 14. A *New York Daily News* poll indicated a similar margin against Kennedy for the New York primary on March 25. His nomination now all but inconceivable, Jacqueline Kennedy Onassis called a meeting of the clan to discuss graceful ways to persuade Uncle Ted to withdraw.

THE *NEW YORK TIMES* HAD AN ELECTORAL EXPLANATION OF CARTER'S NEW budget cuts: "Not only to rescue the nation from runaway inflation but also to rob his political opponents of what is potentially the most explosive issue in the 1980 presidential election"—balancing the budget—in order to "steal the thunder of any Republican candidate that Mr. Carter, if re-nominated, would face in the fall." The *Times* was clearly not paying attention to Ronald Reagan's press releases. One, responding to the increased prime rate, said that "President Carter is forcing the very people who have been hurt most by inflation—the poor, the working men and women, and small business—to bear the greatest burden for controlling it. . . . It is time for this nation to abandon Jimmy Carter's economics of despair." Neither were the *Times* editorialists paying attention to his commercials. Elliott Curson's ads kept showing through the primaries, including the Good Shepherd one saying that the way to arrest inflation was to "cut tax rates deeply and permanently," with nothing about budgets, except implicitly in its accusation that Carter believed "that for one American to gain, another American has to suffer."

Ronald Reagan was playing Santa Claus to Jimmy Carter's Scrooge. Which made for a marvelous contrast to George Bush, whose chief economic advisor was that very Harvard professor, Martin Feldstein, who said Volcker wasn't squeezing the economy enough.

It was also quite the contrast to a *new* likely contender for the nomination.

Jerry Ford, whose own much-mocked "Whip Inflation Now" program had been launched in 1975 with a similar call to national sacrifice, had invited Adam Clymer of the *New York Times* to his compound outside Palm Springs and entrusted him with a quote that ran in the Sunday, March 2, edition: "A very conservative Republican can't win a national election." Clymer asked if he was referring to Reagan. Ford answered, "That's right." His associates began expeditiously researching state ballot access requirements; he gave a big speech in Florida, where the primary was March 11, then a press conference at which he declared himself available for a draft as the "most electable Republican"; he boasted on CBS

News, "When I came into office, the inflation rate was 12 percent, and my policies brought it down to 4.8 percent." He was even consulting with his old pollster Bob Teeter—presently on the payroll of George Bush, which rather gave the game away: should Bush collapse, the Republican establishment was gearing up to wheel in Ford as his replacement.

An ABC/Harris Poll said that Ford would beat Carter 54 percent to 44 percent, while Carter would beat Reagan 58–40, and that Republicans favored Ford for the nomination over Reagan 33–27. The March 4 primary in Massachusetts was thus stand or fall for Bush. He did well, winning 3,000 votes more than Reagan—though John Anderson did better, with 327 votes over Bush. That same day in Vermont, Anderson finished only a thousand votes behind Reagan for a strong second. Walter Cronkite exulted, "Good evening. Campaign '80 took an abrupt turn tonight just six weeks after the first votes were cast in Iowa. In Massachusetts and Vermont, a little-noticed candidate came out of nowhere to become a factor in the race for the Republican nomination"—like it was the biggest campaign news so far.

Never mind that Vermont was not exactly a bellwether of the modern Republican Party; *Walter Cronkite*, CBS's anchorman since 1951, "Uncle Walter," "the most trusted man in America," the man who had nursed America through its traumas of assassination and war: *he* certainly was seen as a bellwether. And a George Washington University study subsequently discovered that Cronkite's CBS network gave Anderson more coverage than John Connally, three times more than Phil Crane, and six times more than Robert Dole—all of whom bested Anderson in the polls. So Anderson *must* be important.

Cronkite led his media brethren in celebrating the Illinoisan as a "forthright," "honest," "articulate" "breath of fresh air"—as, the *Post's* Myra MacPherson wrote the week after the New Hampshire primary (where he got 10 percent), "the thinking man's candidate." "There should be a button on the typewriters for reporters to punch in the phrase 'with the exception of John Anderson,'" she wrote in lamenting the dreary similarity between the conservatism of Bush and Reagan—whom Anderson labeled "Tweedledee and Tweedledum."

The press loved his willingness to shoot merrily at Santa Claus—with a bazooka: just look at his signature 50-cent-a-gallon gasoline tax proposal, or his own *Playboy* interview, in which he said the next president "is going to have to wear something of a hair shirt. He may have to be a little reminiscent of the prophet Jeremiah, in the sense that he issues a few lamentations about what can happen to the country and to the world if we don't exhibit a willingness to endure some measure of sacrifice."

They thrilled to his un-politician-like passion for specifics. (When an interviewer in *Doonesbury* asked for details about the 3,830 government jobs he would cut in California, Anderson began reciting: "Mr. T. J. Hooton of Sherman Oaks, Mr. Newton Longbottom of . . ."). He bucked trends in his party by embracing gun control and decrying the supply-siders' insistence you could both raise defense spending and balance the budget at the same time, scourged the Moral Majority from a position of Christian authority, quoted Emerson, filled college auditoriums to the rafters. He fulfilled a plot requirement of the media's campaign-season narrative-building: a *wildcard*. And also fulfilled a fetish among pundits for men-beyond-party—a *maverick*.

SNL's producers figured out a way for him to make a cameo without the other candidates demanding equal time. The sketch depicted them knocking one another out until Anderson was the last man standing. At which the camera swung to the audience and trained on—John Anderson, who said nothing, but flashed a charming grin. Thanks in part to the ministrations of the savvy media advisor David Garth—the man who had made gnomish Ed Koch mayor of New York—people began looking at John B. from Rockford as *hip*.

His big chance would come in his home state on March 18. With all the donations coming in from his media moment in the sun, he could even afford TV commercials. ("Think about the ANDERSON difference!") And, once he was up on TV, Anderson began wondering why he needed a party at all.

SOUTH CAROLINA VOTED ON SATURDAY, MARCH 8; THEN ALABAMA, FLORida, and Georgia on Tuesday—and they *were* bellwethers of the new Republican Party. John Connally hoped he could whip up a miracle in the Palmetto State. But Reagan's side had a secret weapon.

Richard Nixon used to say that if you wanted a sensitive political job done, get a "good healthy right-wing exuberant" to do it. This year, the most exuberant were all with Reagan. There was Roger Stone, the Watergate bit player who had been elected as Young Republican president in 1977 by depicting his opponent, a 1976 Reagan delegate, as a captive of "Rockefeller liberals." Stone was Reagan's organizer in the Northeast, in charge of crucial primaries in Pennsylvania (April 22) and New York (April 25).

The manager for Stone's cutthroat YR campaign, Paul Manafort, ran the South. Before spring was out, Stone, Manafort, and John Sears's fired aide-de-camp Charlie Black had formed their own PR firm, hoping to capitalize on their closeness to Reagan should he capture the White House.

And then there was an insouciant young fellow named Harvey LeRoy Atwater in South Carolina—the most conscienceless gut-gutter of them all. Atwater was a rogue among rogues, eating cornflakes doused in Tabasco sauce for breakfast, always picking away at blues guitar—sometimes even during interviews. "Reporters ate it up," a journalist noted. "Who among them had so effortlessly crossed America's bitter racial divide? Atwater traded licks with B.B. King!"

The charm hid a gift for devising cunning ways for his candidates to exploit Southern racism without appearing to do so. He was particularly proud of his work in 1978 reelecting Senator Strom Thurmond, the former segregationist whom Atwater claimed had won 38 percent of South Carolina's middle-class black vote. (It was his idea for Thurmond to place his daughter in an integrated public school. After his victory, he enrolled her in a private school.) All the same, Thurmond's white base remained undisturbed. How?

Atwater explained the secret to an inquiring political scientist in 1981—though he asked not to be quoted. The trick was "how abstract you handle the race thing. . . . You start out in 1954 by saying, 'Nigger, nigger, nigger.' By 1968 you can't say 'nigger'—that hurts you, backfires. So you say stuff like, uh, forced busing, states' rights, and all that stuff, and you're getting so abstract now, you're talking about cutting taxes, and all these things you're talking about are totally economic things and a byproduct of them is, blacks get hurt worse than whites. . . . And if it is getting that abstract and that coded, we're doing away with the racial problem one way or another. You follow me? Because obviously sitting around saying, 'We want to cut taxes, we want to cut this,' is much more abstract than even the busing thing, uh, and a hell of a lot more abstract than 'Nigger, nigger.' So any way you look at it, race is coming on the back burner."

Strom Thurmond had longed to unleash Atwater's dark arts on behalf of *his* candidate—Connally. Atwater, however, performed an unsentimental analysis of the polls, and signed on with Reagan. During one of the governor's visits, Atwater crammed an appearance with so many friends he was able to inform the press that folks were being turned away by fire marshals. He got a South Carolinian named *Reid* Buckley to tape radio ads labeling George Bush as a liberal—crafted to make it seem like his famous soundalike brother *Bill* Buckley was endorsing Reagan. Then, in the candidate debate, George Bush reduced John Connally to spluttering by pressing him to answer a charge that he was buying black votes with $700,000 in "walking around money." Atwater was responsible for the smear, passing it on to Bush's advisor Harry Dent—so it was traced back to Bush's campaign, not Reagan's. Sewing such acrimony between one's opponents, known as "ratfucking," was a specialty of the young Republican milieu that incubated all the healthiest right-wing exuberants.

In that debate, Reagan struck the tone he did in his dictated letters—

with John Sears no longer around to persuade him otherwise. Marijuana was "probably the most dangerous drug in America today." (More dangerous than heroin?) The government should leave cleaning up nuclear waste—a major issue in South Carolina—"in the hands of the private power companies." Presidents should threaten "a very unpleasant action" anytime American hostages were taken and not released by a specified deadline: "This is where we have failed in Iran." Bush, incredulous, replied, "You can't make a generalized judgement on *any hostage situation*!"

The next day, Reagan came out against federal disaster-area declarations as so much socialism: "When Chicago burned down, they didn't declare it a disaster area. They just rebuilt it, the people of Chicago, and this is the kind of America we can have again." (In fact, the Secretary of War in 1871 did something functionally identical, with Washington sending rations, tents, supplies, and millions of dollars in aid.) He said that he could balance the budget by cutting forty-one "totally unnecessary" items cited by a document the General Accounting Office had transmitted to the Congressional Budget Office, "adding up to $11 billion in spending." (GAO and CBO spokesmen said that they had never heard of any such document, and $11 billion wasn't close to the full budget deficit.)

The *Los Angeles Times* published a full-length interview with Reagan by Robert Scheer, the left-wing journalist whose colloquy with Carter had set the 1976 campaign on its ear. Reagan loved having wide-ranging philosophical discussions with liberals, when his handlers allowed him. "Why are you speaking to me? Why aren't you more uptight?" Scheer had asked on the campaign plane. Reagan paused, then smiled: "*Welll*—why does a preacher speak to a sinner?"

Scheer asked Reagan whether his opposition to abortion didn't contradict his objection to government intrusion into family life. Reagan replied that the *problem* with abortion was the government intruding into family life: "In some of our inner cities, there are actually cases, many more of them than you would believe, that young girls, under age, who deliberately go out to have a baby so that they can get what they call 'a pad of their own' because getting the baby, unmarried, they can become put on the Aid to Dependent Children program. . . . Being on the welfare program makes her eligible for Medicaid. So she then goes and gets rid of the baby, and the government pays for it with tax dollars and the government is bound by law to protect her privacy and not let her own parents know."

Reagan said his objection to the minimum wage was that it allowed organized labor "to kind of keep a monopoly to itself and to its own membership at a much higher standard of living." (This was the opposite of true.) He called abortion "murder," but also "a whim that many women may have, like cosmetic surgery." There followed a long exchange over

Reagan's contention that Americans' belief in God gave Americans "a different regard for human life than those monsters"—Communists; Scheer returned that Iran's godly ayatollahs had no problem holding human life in contempt; Reagan replied that this was "*misuse* of religion," then veered into a passionate recounting of his fight against the Reds in Hollywood: "There was no blacklist in Hollywood. The blacklist in Hollywood, if there was one, was provided by the Communists." (In fact, one actor Reagan named as a Communist in the 1940s never played in another movie until 1964.) Scheer finally gave up.

South Carolina's conservative electorate found no reason to find fault with any of this: they gave Reagan 55 percent to George Bush's 15 percent. John Anderson recorded 0 percent. John Connally, with 30 percent, decided his cause was hopeless and dropped out. His campaign chairman, Alabama construction magnate Winton Blount, moved on to his next project—building a university for the Saudi royal family.

THREE DAYS LATER, 114 DELEGATES WERE AT STAKE, IN GEORGIA, ALABAMA, and Florida. Bush conceded the first two—but hoped to demonstrate his national appeal by winning diverse Florida. His play was attacking Reagan on the issue of greatest sensitivity to Florida's surfeit of retirees. In the South Carolina debate, after Bush promised to fix budget growth at the level of inflation, Reagan did him one better, promising to freeze spending entirely. Bush said that would starve grannies on Social Security: "A person who has saved all his life for retirement should not be wiped out by inflation!"

When Barry Goldwater questioned Social Security in New Hampshire in 1964, he was hounded so mercilessly that he never mentioned it again. That October, Reagan's nationally televised speech for Goldwater came within an inch of getting canceled by Goldwater's nervous operatives because Reagan suggested in it that adding "voluntary features" to Social Security "would permit a citizen who can do better on his own to be excused upon presentation of evidence that he had made provisions for the nonearning years," and that conservatives were "against forcing all citizens, regardless of need, into a compulsory government program."

Political reality had set in by the time he ran for president in 1976, when he brought out his biggest gun—Jimmy Stewart—to reassure seniors, in full *Mr. Smith Goes to Washington* mien, that his friend Ronald Reagan would "*strengthen* and *improve* Social Security and guarantee that those who are counting on it will always get their benefits." This time, in 1980, Reagan indignantly howled that he would *never* freeze *Social Security*—just "other areas."

Otherwise he sounded as extreme as he ever had. Gas lines had shown signs of returning in South Florida; Reagan said Carter had "singled out" the region for that punishment. He claimed, "there has been an attempt to harass those who are sympathetic to Cuba." Pressed for specifics, he admitted he had "no examples," then fled. He also discussed the gold standard. The supply-side priesthood considered it sacramental. Most other economists called it nuts. One of the commercials Jeff Bell wrote with Curson had Reagan averring, "We're never going to get price stability until we return to some form of gold." Following the taping, Reagan apologized to Bell that the ad had been shelved because "some people here in California"—Bell suspected Milton Friedman—"might be upset." Now, however, in Birmingham, Reagan said he was directing his economic advisors to plan a return to gold, because "no nation in history has ever survived fiat money—money that did not have a precious metal backing—and why we should suddenly think that we can be different from any other nation in thousands of years of civilized history, I don't know."

He won Alabama with 70 percent, Georgia with 73 percent, and Florida with 56 percent. Gerald Ford's associates had already placed his name on every ballot that did not require the candidate's personal assent. Now that Reagan was on the cusp of nomination, on March 13, Ford signed a document declaring his intent to run in those states that did require his assent—telling the aides who witnessed his signature, "You have to make sure if we don't do this, these documents don't ever see the light of day." Two days later, however, he gathered his people in his Palm Springs living room and called it all off. Immediately after saying that, he launched into a tirade against Jimmy Carter, stalked out of the room in frustration, and held up his thumb and forefinger with but a sliver of daylight between them:

"And Reagan is about *that* much better."

NOW THAT REAGAN WAS PRACTICALLY THE NOMINEE, THE PRESS BELATEDLY started examining some of the claims from the campaign that had gotten him there.

On *Issues and Answers* on March 16, host John Laurence noted his commercial claiming that John F. Kennedy "helped almost everybody in the country" with a 30 percent tax cut. Laurence pointed out that the 1960s cut had only averaged 19 percent, was not uniform across the board but progressive, and had not closed the budget deficit as claimed. Reagan replied, "I don't remember saying that, because I honestly don't know what the rate of tax cut was."

Laurence asked if he read his scripts before reciting them.

"I read them," Reagan said. "And I suppose in the process of a whole afternoon, as you know, sitting in front of the camera and doing these things and each one several times over that I maybe just went by that without thinking."

The *Washington Star* took apart a commercial trumpeting Reagan's supposed reduction of California's welfare bill by $2 billion without cutting assistance to the truly needy and found four factual errors in thirty seconds. *Time* considered his claim that "history shows" that "when the taxes of a nation approach about 20 percent of the people's income, there begins to be lack of respect for government": "History shows no such thing. Most Western European nations have long had tax rates far higher than that, and higher than U.S. rates, but with lower crime rates."

And, at the same time, the financial masters of the universe, who had already swung their loyalty from Connally to Bush, contemplated whether they could stomach switching to Reagan now.

Some didn't find the problem difficult. Charls Walker jumped ship from Connally effortlessly, writing a memo advising Reagan that he needn't scruple about calling for both a balanced budget and a massive increase in military spending. Donald Rumsfeld, now CEO of Searle pharmaceuticals, had long ago shocked *Newsweek*'s board of editors by revealing that he was "comfortable" with Reagan—something they had never heard any other *Fortune* 500 executive say.

Others, including several Rockefellers, the chairman of *Time*, the president of the Oppenheimer fund, the director of Lehman Brothers, financier Felix Rohatyn, and foreign policy sage George Ball, declared for Anderson. Perhaps some admired his new commercials; one focus-group subject sardonically observed that they seemed to say, "if somebody would only tell me what hard decision to make, I'll make it."

He was now, his friends at CBS reported, "cloaked in the symbols of a big-time candidate. Bigger crowds. Bigger airplanes. Secret Service motorcades, and big money to back him. Yesterday alone, campaign mail produced $117,000!" Also, bigger TV audiences. On March 13, Reagan, Bush, Anderson, and Crane debated on TV in Illinois, sitting in modish chairs with mushroom bases and little round plastic tables beside them, like guests on *The Dick Cavett Show*. Reagan made a characteristic gaffe—that America's first Supreme Court chief justice, John Marshall, "wasn't even a lawyer." Few noticed. His stagecraft stole the show.

The other candidates were ganging up on Anderson over his suspect Republican loyalties; Anderson hemmed and hawed when asked to pledge support for the eventual nominee. Reagan floated above the fray, looking presidential, letting his rivals assault one another with unseemly cross talk. He was finally asked to weigh in. He did so in mock sternness: "John!" he said, then drew a *Tonight Show*–style studio audience roar with the perfectly timed punch line, "You *really* would prefer Teddy

Kennedy to *me*?" Anderson nearly doubled over, then patted his rival appreciatively on the arm.

Six nights later, Walter Cronkite had the sad duty to report on Illinois: "On the Republican side, that widely anticipated challenge to Ronald Reagan from John Anderson did not materialize." He got 36 percent, Reagan was just a hair shy of 50, and George Bush lagged far behind with 11 percent.

Now boardroom Jacobins no longer could evade *their* duty. The *Wall Street Journal* editorial crew dubbed their dilemma "Learning to Live with Reagan"—though, for entirely different reasons, they seemed to be having a tough time themselves. "Why," Robert Bartley's supply-side scribes mused, "do so many people who agree with his positions still find themselves unenthusiastic about his candidacy?" After all, he was elected twice in an overwhelmingly Democratic state, where he established "an excellent record," and his "recovery from the stumble in Iowa suggests he has the flexibility necessary to correct mistakes." The *Journal* decided it was his louche affection for "those who view the burning issues of the day as opposing gun control, making abortion unconstitutional, and outlawing homosexuality"— that "Mr. Reagan has indulged these supporters rather than educating them." More conventional Republicans thought the problem was his louche affection for the loopy economic theories of the *Journal*. So it was that Reagan's new campaign manager made selling them his first major project.

BILL CASEY WAS SOMETHING OF A RIGHT-WING EXUBERANT HIMSELF. BORN in 1913 to a modest family in Queens, as a hotshot young lawyer during the Depression he helped invent the idea of "sheltering" income from New Deal tax levies on the rich—then grew rich himself writing guidebooks teaching others the tricks of the trade. He rose to head secret intelligence in Europe at the Office of Strategic Services, the swashbuckling World War II spy agency that evolved into the CIA. He spent time in Washington, D.C., where he was close to the head of the RNC under Eisenhower, Leonard Hall. ("A lot of us thought he was Len Hall's brains," his friend F. Clifton White told a doubter when Casey was tapped to run Reagan's campaign.) In 1955, he wrote the investment prospectus for *National Review*. Under Nixon, he served as chairman of the Securities and Exchange Commission, then ran the Import-Export Bank under Ford, then settled back into an exceptionally lucrative career helping rich people avoid paying taxes.

Meanwhile he kept a hand in politics. He chartered a think tank called the Manhattan Institute. He dabbled in economic development policy in his suburban town, founding a group, the Action Committee for Long Island, that envisioned an almost total blurring of the line between private fortune and government. He was a particular admirer of a California libertarian named Robert Poole, who theorized turning over to for-profit companies municipal services from garbage collection to firefighting. Casey pitched local bankers to think of loans to his group "not as a contribution to some worthwhile cause, but as an investment in proving a market." When the campaign season began gearing up, he was working to create a "Committee for Responsible Healthcare" to advocate against national health insurance on the model of the Committee on the Present Danger. In common with most of his Wall Street comrades, he wasn't enthusiastic about Reagan; he hedged his bets, donating the maximum to the Reagan, Bush, and Connally exploratory committees, before finally deciding he preferred Reagan for president with Bush as his running mate, signing on to chair the November 13 announcement dinner.

Nancy Reagan thought him grotesque: a sartorial unmade bed, with crooked ties and crooked teeth, a mumbler even from a podium, with table manners like a hobo. Campaign chairman Paul Laxalt, however, called him a "godsend." He was a morale-building manager, who governed like a chairman of the board, not a dictator like Sears. He lowered overhead, firing people left and right, and developed a state-of-the-art cash-flow management system. He relocated to Los Angeles, where the campaign was based. (John Sears never did.) He consulted his old friend Clif White, who told him that the campaign could not skimp on a full-time media coordinator. They considered a brooding figure named Roger Ailes, but settled on an advertising executive named Peter Dailey—he was based in L.A. Casey also reversed a decision by the staff in L.A. to spend a pile on new ads to replace the allegedly "technically inferior" Curson commercials.

But Casey's most important preconvention project was persuading Wall Street to learn to live with Reagan.

His chief of staff, Ed Meese, recruited establishment economists and executives like Milton Friedman and Arthur Burns; George Shultz, the CEO of Bechtel and a board member at Morgan Guarantee, Sears, and the Alfred P. Sloan Foundation; Charles Schwab; Don Regan of Merrill Lynch; and Caspar Weinberger, general counsel at Bechtel (and a member, *shudder*, of the Trilateral Commission). He brought in a cadre that the *Washington Post* described as having been "young program-oriented aides in the salad days of the Nixon administration when people talked about welfare reform rather than Watergate." From their work, sayeth the *Post*, "new themes and proposals are beginning to make inroads into Reagan's stock antigovernment speech."

But Meese was rather a right-wing exuberant, too. He had first caught Governor Reagan's attention as a fearsome prosecutor in Alameda County, targeting antiwar protesters and black power militants. He became Governor Reagan's legal secretary, then chief of staff. In 1969, he helped turn a protest over Berkeley's "People's Park" into a military occupation. One hundred and twenty-eight people were sent to the hospital with gunshot wounds. One lost his life. Robert Scheer had recently pointed out to him that no evidence ever emerged that the man who was shot to death was more than a bystander. Meese responded, "James Rector deserved to die."

So which side *was* Meese on—the internationalist quislings or the conservative hard core? With Reagan nearly the presumptive nominee, such questions about who the "real" conservatives were and who the squishes, who the true Reagan loyalists and who the Trojan-horse opportunists, were becoming increasingly fraught.

One of those young Nixon "program-oriented" aides, Peter Flannigan, hosted a dinner for the former president, where, Richard Allen wrote confidentially to Casey and Meese, a major agenda item was "the need for RR to 'broaden the base,' especially with the business community." One of the guests was Alexander Haig, the retired NATO commander and Nixon's final chief of staff, now president of a multinational manufacturing conglomerate. He had "promised to be helpful . . . within the constraints of his company activities," Allen reported—though Allen was suspicious that Haig "could be playing a 'double game,'" worming his way into Reagan councils in league with Henry Kissinger.

Conclaves like these especially panicked the supply-siders, who were terrified Reagan would be seduced from the true religion just as they were beginning to taste victory. Two congressmen, Republican David Stockman of Michigan and Democrat Phil Gramm of Texas, were pushing an alternate budget that joined the Kemp-Roth income tax cut, Charls Walker's plan for corporate tax cuts via greater depreciation allowances, and meat-ax cuts to programs like job training ($900 million), food stamps ($1.1 billion), and school lunches ($300 million). Stockman was certain his party was finally grasping the Truth—that it was "possible to cut taxes, raise defense, and balance the budget all at once." He was particularly dismayed that Reagan was "aligning himself with Jerry Falwell, the anti–gun control nuts, the Bible-thumping creationists," folks obsessed with "the threat of unisex toilets, the school prayer amendment and the rest of the New Right litany." Irving Kristol, for his part, wrote in the *Wall Street Journal*, like a right-wing Joseph Stalin, that the political advantage tax cuts would provide Republicans was so historically imperative that they should be blasted through *whatever* the effect on the budget. "The neoconservative is willing to leave those problems to be coped with by liberal interregnums. He wants to shape the future and will leave it to his opponents to tidy up afterwards": now was no time to go wobbly.

Business Week called this moment in the campaign "The Battle for Ronald Reagan's Mind." Though maybe it wasn't so dramatic as all that.

Neither hairsplitting debates about the fiscal effects of tax cuts, after all, nor concerns about Reagan's killjoy Christian friends, seemed to bother the hordes of Wall Street traders who, when he visited the floor of the New York Stock Exchange on March 23, surrounded Reagan and stomped their acclaim, hooting and whistling and tossing trading slips in the air, even grasping for the hem of Reagan's garment. (An "unbelievable mob scene," one witness said.) Then, two hundred attended a $200 fundraiser at the NYSE's Luncheon Club, bombarding Reagan with questions about everything under the sun—"and he was great," one attendee gushed.

Fact-checkers disagreed. "The U.S. Geological Survey has told me that the proven potential for oil in Alaska alone is greater than the proven reserves in Saudi Arabia," he had enthused to the traders. The Geological Survey said they had no idea what he was talking about.

ON MARCH 24 THE LABOR DEPARTMENT ANNOUNCED A RISE IN UNEMPLOY-ment far in excess of predictions. This was a sign that Carter's credit controls, which one economist had dismissed as merely "symbolic" and another said would have "marginal impact," had not opened a *mild* reces-sion, as intended, but a fiscal Pandora's box. And the next day Ted Ken-nedy celebrated an electoral miracle.

Kennedy had been crushed in Illinois by twenty-six points. He was supposed to do even worse in New York. Carter had Rupert Murdoch, for one thing. Murdoch had been awaiting a favorable decision from the Ex-port-Import Bank on financing for an airliner deal he was involved in, and got it two days after a February 17 meeting with Carter. Both before that and afterward, his *New York Post* kept putting nasty Kennedy stuff on the cover like "TEDDY IS THE TOAST OF TEHRAN" and "TEDDY'S SECRET PARTIES."

Then Kennedy reaped a stroke of luck. America's United Nations ambassador cast a vote in the Security Council for a resolution calling for Israel to dismantle settlements in the West Bank and in Arab East Jerusa-lem. The two previous times the resolution had come before the Security Council, America had abstained. Carter explained that he *thought* he was instructing his ambassador to vote for a resolution from which all refer-ences to Jerusalem had been struck—an admission of carelessness that only made him look, to New York's sizable Jewish electorate, even worse.

Kennedy also had a living legend in his corner. Carroll O'Connor played Archie Bunker on *All in the Family*, a character intended by his creator, Norman Lear, to represent the quintessential ignorant, racist working-class clown. Ironically, however, white working-class men adopted Archie as a *hero*. In 1972, some sported "Archie for President" buttons. O'Connor's commercials for Ted Kennedy deliberately played to this misreading, in an attempt to reach out to white ethnics in the outer boroughs. Sporting an Archie-like canvas jacket, sounding far more Queens-like than he usually did off-camera, O'Connor fixed the viewer's gaze and said, "Friends, Herbert *Hoi*-ver hid out in the White House, too, responding to *desperate* problems with patriotic pronouncements. And we got a *helluva* depression. But I'm afraid Jimmy's depression is gonna be *worse* than Herbert's. . . . I trust Ted Kennedy. I believe in him. In *every* way, folks."

The New York City subway system campaigned for Kennedy, too. He took a ride for the cameras the morning before the balloting, promising money for the dilapidated system if he became president. The news footage that night ran alongside images of a roof collapse at *the very spot* he had traversed only hours before. The next morning, he won 58.9 percent to 41.1 percent over the president. He beat Carter in Connecticut, too—where there also were a lot of Archie Bunker Democrats.

JERRY BROWN HAD YET TO HIT THE 14 PERCENT MARK. IN CONNECTICUT HE finished behind a devotee of Lyndon LaRouche. *His* miracle, he hoped, would come in Wisconsin, on April 1.

"My principles are simple," he had declared behind a bright white podium reading "WOW!" at his campaign announcement: "Protect the earth, serve the people, and explore the universe." He was supposed to be the candidate of the future. In a swing-for-the-fences gambit in Wisconsin, an independent-minded state where he polled well, he brought in Francis Ford Coppola to direct a thirty-minute live television extravaganza from Madison's Capitol grounds. Coppola said he hoped it would be remembered as a capstone of his career.

It was a cold night; students warmed themselves around bonfires. Brown stepped up before a "blue screen" that was to carry synchronized footage as background to his speech, which was entitled "The Shape of Things to Come." Things went off the rails right away.

The "chyron"—the words onscreen—was typed out live: first, "LIVE FROM MADISNO," then "MADISOO," then "MAIDSON," then "MADISON, WISCO," before finally coming out right. Coppola cued a dramatic helicopter shot, which however was blotted out by a spotlight beamed from below. Brown strode to the podium to the sound of technicians barking out nervous instructions. All the while, the helicopter's *swoff swoff swoff* was so distracting you almost expected it to belt out Wagner's "Ride of the Valkyries" like in *Apocalypse Now*.

The podium microphone kept cutting out. The live audience cried, "We can't hear you! We can't hear you!"—which the TV audience could hear just fine.

Someone passed Brown a hand mic, which worked—but now, with

him untethered from his mark behind the podium, the blue-screen process to project images behind him was thrown terribly out of whack, and
Madison's stately Capitol could be seen through electronic gashes carved
into the side of his head, which changed shape in the most fascinating way
as the light hit at different angles.

He launched into a halting, jerky, pedantic explanation of how he believed America had arrived at the plight it was in now (by borrowing from
the future during the golden years with printing-press money to pay for
both guns and butter); and then, as he was discussing the reasons for the
collapse of the auto industry, the slide show began, images with no rhyme
or reason at all (a gleaming white building, a junkyard, a freeway inter-
change, an astronaut turning somersaults in zero gravity . . .).

He began offering his policy prescriptions: exempt personal savings
from taxation, and also the first $5,000 in dividend income; tax incentives
for "rebuilding what society really needs, and getting off this mounting
debt"—or did he say *death*?—"and waste, and packaging, and excessive
advertising"; "reindustrialization bonds"; increased funding for research
for "the Thomas Edison or Marconi of 1980" to "revolutionize the world
and make this planet a very small global village where we can begin to
sense that we are a global family on a very small speck in this universe"; a
bullet train from Milwaukee to Madison.

And then suddenly, he stopped, as people milled around wondering if
the event were over.

No: he took a question from the audience. A woman wanted to know
what he would do to pass the ERA, and what would make him a good
president. Of the former, he said he would "bring all those recalcitrant legislators who have been voting against ERA to Washington and keep them
there until they to change their minds." Of the latter, he said something
about his time in a Jesuit seminary where he wasn't allowed to speak.

"And so just let me conclude with one thought. . . . As we look to the
future, let us pledge allegiance to that future."

Then he recited the Pledge of Allegiance.

He sniffed from a cold. The lapels of his overlarge tan overcoat flopped
about in a whipping wind, like a weatherman reporting on the advance of
a storm. He said, "Thank you and good night." The techs shouted things
at each other. The announcer told the audience, "It's gone much, much
better than we ever dreamed of."

The shape of things to come: on primary day he got 12 percent, and
dropped out.

THE DAY BEFORE THAT PRIMARY, THE PRESIDENT OF THE DOLOROUS PRES-
ent did something unusual: he personally briefed network anchormen, the

editor of the *Washington Post*, and several prominent pundits off the record on an announcement he would make the next morning. It concerned the hostages in Iran, toward whom Americans' emotional attachment continued to grow.

On *The 700 Club*, Pat Boone debuted "The Hostage Prayer," a gospel song accompanied by an angelic choir that drowned out a Tehran mob chanting "Death to America." A radio station serving Fort Killeen in Texas debuted a single called "Bomb Iran"—one of at least seven separate records to come out in 1979 and '80 by that title, each more or less inspired by the Beach Boys, competing to be the most vicious. One invited listeners to throw rocks at mosques and ended with what sounded like an atomic bomb blast. "The phones lit up like a Christmas tree," a DJ in Anchorage, Alaska, said of the time he first played it. "We logged more than 20,000 calls in three days."

Behind the scenes, the negotiation between Hamilton Jordan and the odd couple Hector Villalon and Christian Bourget had come tantalizingly close to a deal. The pair visited the White House at the end of January, informing Jordan that Foreign Minister Sadegh Ghotbzadeh had authorized them as his official representatives. The day after that, Abolhassan Bani-Sadr won 70 percent in Iran's presidential election, and announced that it was time to end the embassy siege. Khomeini blessed the outcome of the vote—suggesting, implicitly, that he also endorsed ending the Americans' captivity.

Over the next days, the negotiators ironed out a road map: the United Nations would name a commission to study Iran's historic grievances against the United States. The White House would publicly oppose the panel, to enhance its credibility in Iran. Their official report would condemn hostage-taking as "un-Islamic," giving the students political cover for letting the hostages go. As this was happening, Khomeini entered a hospital for heart trouble, and gave a speech—"Be without fear, no matter whether a person comes or a person goes"—that appeared to prepare his followers for the passing of the Khomeini era.

One of the things that drove Carter's New Hampshire victory was the dribble of news suggesting that the end might be near. His public statements cautiously prepared the way for a possible breakthrough. Then, on the eve of the five-person UN commission's departure for Tehran, hopes were extinguished when Khomeini delivered a surprise edict praising the captors as "heroes of our revolution" and announced that the decision to release them could only be made by Iran's parliament, the "Majlis," which didn't yet exist, and wasn't expected to for a month or more. When the UN commission arrived, they so feared for their safety that they refused to open a package the students said contained incriminating American documents. They thought it might contain a bomb.

On March 13, amid news footage of the commission members leaving Tehran in defeat, Bani-Sadr flip-flopped, calling the hostage-takers "young patriots." Jordan responded by posting him a handwritten three-page letter that concluded with a barely veiled threat: "From the outset, President Carter had pursued a policy of patience and restraint. However, the atmosphere of restraint, cannot last forever."

Republicans clamored for a show of force. Bush first accused Carter of "pussy-footing around," calling on the president to cut off all diplomatic contact, then, on the Thursday before the Wisconsin vote, he shredded Carter for "a policy of empty bluff and essentially meaningless symbolism," the kind of "appeasement" that "has always been an incentive for aggression." Kennedy insisted, "I'm not going to be silenced in making what I consider constructive recommendations."

The clamor inside the White House was worse. At one meeting, Zbigniew Brzezinski argued that the diplomatic track was a fool's errand, that the Iranian coastal island housing the world's largest offshore crude oil processing facility should be seized. He was joined by Secretary of Defense Harold Brown and Joint Chiefs of Staff Chairman General David C. Jones. Cyrus Vance objected to even considering military action, arguing that "Khomeini and his followers, with a Shi'ite affinity for martyrdom, actually might welcome American military action as a way of uniting the Moslem world against the West"—to which Carter snapped, "Should we wait another year?"

Then, sunshine broke through. President Bani-Sadr somehow persuaded the Revolutionary Council that the hostages must be transferred to the foreign ministry. The students appeared not to object—to have finally surrendered to the forces seeking to turn Iran into a normal member of the community of nations. *That* was the announcement about which Carter had briefed the journalists on March 31—and which he delivered to a group of reporters called into the Oval Office at the unusual hour of 7:18 a.m.

His words were cautiously vague: "This morning, the President of Iran has announced that the hostages' control would be transferred to the Government of Iran, which we consider to be a positive step"—then he added a fillip that implicitly credited for the breakthrough his threat of economic punishment: "In light of that action, we do not consider it appropriate now to impose additional sanctions." The plain implication was that once the hostages were shifted to the custody of Bani-Sadr's government, they would soon be on a plane home.

Wisconsin Democrats went to the polls, visions of the hostages' homecoming (and Jerry Brown's zombie-eaten face) dancing in their heads. Carter got 56 percent. On the Republican side Reagan won with 40 percent, Bush got 30 percent, and Anderson got 27 percent. The candidates in both parties scored similar results the same day in Kansas.

The next big showdowns: Pennsylvania Republicans and Democrats voted on April 22, and Michigan Democrats voted on April 26. Neither Kennedy, Anderson, nor Bush quit, despite the near-mathematical certainty they couldn't be their party's nominee.

CHAPTER 34

"Feed Your Faith and Starve Your Doubts!"

ON MARCH 27, AN ORDINARY CITIZEN SENT HIS PRESIDENT A LETTER: "WE are supporting you, sir, one hundred percent. Your inflation fighting program has forced us into alternatives that we are not finding hard to live with. We are spending with more wisdom and not as frequently. We are drawing closer to each other more and more during this fight against inflation. . . . We have once again discovered parlor games, sing songs, and lengthy walks and other means of old-fashioned entertainment."

For three years now Jimmy Carter had been calling for sacrifice in the manner of a wartime president—so much so, the venerable humor columnist Art Buchwald wrote, that all his talk of "pain" and "discipline" was beginning to sound kinky. The message was beginning to take—all too well, unfortunately. Credit controls helped slow consumer spending so much that the economy was grinding to a standstill. Housing starts were at their lowest in twenty years. Ford Motor Company announced that it was closing three more plants and laying off twelve thousand workers at seven others. GM announced eighteen thousand layoffs. Wisconsin Steel did not give its more than three thousand workers even a day's warning before shutting its massive plant on the Southeast Side of Chicago for good on March 28; the workers received only $700 of their promised $4,200 in severance pay. The prime rate hit 20 percent. Gold topped $900 an ounce. "There had never been anything like it in modern American history," said *Newsweek*, "and even veteran moneymen stood in awe." One Fed governor said, "We are in a South American inflationary environment now."

Veteran moneymen also presumed that, as a politician fighting for reelection, Jimmy Carter would transform into a William Jennings Bryan–style populist any day now. They were wrong. The day before the Wisconsin primary, Carter signed a sweeping banking deregulation package. It removed most restrictions on banks operating across state lines, allowed instant electronic transfer of funds—and, most epochally, phased out "Regulation Q."

Regulation Q was the centerpiece of a suite of rules created by the

Banking Act of 1933 to tamp down the rampant financial speculation that helped cause the Great Depression. It banned banks from paying interest on checking accounts, and capped interest rates on savings accounts. Banks, basically, were no longer able to compete for customers by *bidding* for them—an expensive proposition that incentivized banks to seek out high-risk, high-return investment, and also something only big banks could afford. The banking business stayed modest and conservative; banks stayed small, competing instead to best serve their local communities. Americans enjoyed a decades-long run of stability unprecedented in the history of modern capitalism. Big bankers despised it—especially Walter Wriston, the CEO of Citibank, who was so passionate for financial deregulation he fantasized about Citibank buying its own nation, so it could write its own laws. They had been leaning on reluctant presidents to strike Regulation Q from the books for decades.

And now, in Jimmy Carter, they finally found one who would. He signed the bill in a public ceremony, handing out signing pens to a number of banking CEOs. Arthur Schlesinger declared him "not a Democrat—at least in anything more recent than the Grover Cleveland sense of the word." Carter couldn't have cast himself as a better foil for Ted Kennedy if he were writing a script.

BUT HOLLYWOOD COULDN'T HAVE COME UP WITH A BETTER PLOT TWIST than what happened next: for mysterious reasons, Iran's Abolhassan Bani-Sadr announced that the hostages would *stay* with the students, joining the Ayatollah in insisting that their fate belonged to the not-yet-convened Iranian parliament and demanding that President Carter refrain from "hostile statements" about Iran. The media questioned whether Carter's Oval Office announcement the morning of the Wisconsin primary had just been a cynical Election Day ploy.

On April 12, Kennedy won the Arizona caucuses 55–45 with a surprise last-minute endorsement of Cesar Chavez's United Farm Workers. He was spending so much time in Pennsylvania that people joked that he might be eligible to vote there. Before a convention of the American Federation of State, County, and Municipal Employees there on April 13, he chuckled darkly: "I think yesterday that Jimmy Carter found that there's a little *cactus* there in the Rose Garden. *Arrrrrre* we gonna do as well in Pennsylvania? Let's hear it!!!" (He heard it. AFSCME was another of his union endorsers.) The next morning, on ABC's *Face the Nation*, Senator Frank Church of Idaho said, "If high interest rates don't begin to come down ... we're going to begin to see what the Eastern papers like to call a 'recession' turn into a deep depression."

Carter was ahead two-to-one in delegates. But if Kennedy could win in great big diverse Pennsylvania it would suggest that he would be a better *general election* candidate than the president, which might spur a stampede among Democratic activists for Carter to bow out. Carter fought back by announcing enhanced unemployment benefits for forty-eight thousand laid-off autoworkers—but also ran a historically awful TV commercial. It featured himself at the plate during a softball game, patiently letting bad pitches go by. Apparently, this was meant to fore-ground his maturity and patience. But the baffling tagline—"Do you want more of the same? Cross your fingers"—was a softball for Ken-nedy's ad men, who responded, "On housing, interest rates, even foreign affairs, his attitude was 'I'll keep my fingers crossed.' . . . Kennedy for president. If you believe we can do better." Though Carter also had ef-fective ads. In these, carefully edited to *just barely* not cross the line into a direct attack over Chappaquiddick, proverbial men and women in the street pronounced their doubts about Kennedy's character. These, how-ever, were neutralized by the announcement of a surprise Kennedy en-dorser: the parents of Mary Jo Kopechne.

Carter called on a ringer from next-door Delaware, the latest in a long line of Democratic up-and-comers to be tagged with the coveted sobri-quet "Kennedyesque." Joe Biden, thirty-seven years old, had been the first senator to endorse the *last* Democratic up-and-comer to earn that label: Jimmy Carter. Biden, "popular among ethnic Democrats and young women," a Wilmington newspaper noted, was besieged by requests to campaign for vulnerable Democrats all year. "As he campaigns for others, he ingratiates himself," the paper noted, "dropping remarks about running for—and some day becoming—president." An exquisitely well-calibrated difference-splitter, in a restaurant banquet room appearance for Carter in which forty of seventy chairs were empty, he managed to drop such a remark without a word of criticism for Kennedy ("If you're looking for an Irish Catholic Democrat to support, wait until 1984 and one of us will be back"), and give an endorsement for Carter so lukewarm it was practi-cally an apology: "Jimmy Carter is not the finest thing since wheat cakes; he's not the second coming. . . . He's not going to go down in the history books . . . but he is doing a good job."

Anything more enthusiastic just wouldn't have sounded credible. On April 25, Chrysler said it was eliminating 20 percent of their non-produc-tion jobs. The Federal Reserve's Open Markets Committee met, agreeing that Carter's deliberately induced recession would "be somewhat larger than had been anticipated a month earlier," "accompanied by a substantial increase in unemployment." Retail sales were falling faster than any time in three decades because the credit controls had "curbed considerably spend-ing in anticipation of price increases." The committee's consensus recommendation, however, was to stay the course: "An easing of monetary policy could have very undesirable repercussions on inflationary psychology."

Then, about 558,000 Pennsylvania Democrats cast their ballots for Kennedy, 3,000 more than for Carter. But 80,000 marked "no preference," and 30,000 voted for the already-withdrawn Jerry Brown. An exit poll revealed that a majority of Kennedy voters said that the nation was in "an economic emergency that is more dangerous than any military threat abroad." The same poll found that two of five Bush voters admitted they were not voting *for* Bush but *against* Reagan, and that over a third of Republicans would never vote for Anderson—with reasons divided between those believing his ideas were "impractical" and those who found him "too liberal." Fifty-seven percent of Democrats expressed impatience with the president for failing to win the hostages' release—and a startling 31 percent would defect to Reagan if Carter was their party's nominee.

Carter also managed to win fifty-four of Missouri's sixty-four convention delegates that day. The score stood at 1,207 for Carter to 667 for Kennedy. Which meant that Kennedy's nomination was impossible under the convention rules presently in place.

So those rules, the Kennedy people began thinking, would just have to change.

THE CARTER ADMINISTRATION'S INABILITY TO HELP BLUE-COLLAR WORKers made Ronald Reagan's economic message—*tax cuts for everyone*—sound better all the time. A longtime Democrat in West Allis, Wisconsin, who had crossed over in that state's open primary to vote for Reagan, explained to *Time*, "Inflation is eating us up, welfare is a mess, we don't have any power in this country—why shouldn't we switch?" Besides, Reagan "would return us to this country's true meaning."

In the six major primaries so far, nearly half of wage workers had voted for Reagan. He was promising that his tax cuts would lower inflation, interest rates, and unemployment; tax cuts as radical as these had never been tried, so he could promise anything he pleased. Which was pretty darned irritating for George Bush. Who, in Pennsylvania, decided to attack the problem head-on.

His aide Pete Teeley had seen an editorial that condemned Carter's economic policies as the product of "witch doctors." Teeley liked the sound of that. He tried out a similar phrase on his tongue to describe Reagan's economic policies. His boss tried it out on the stump in Pittsburgh on April 10: Reagan's plan to cut between $70 billion and $90 billion in taxes *and* balance the budget—with "no mention of where and how he would make budget cuts"—was "voodoo economics." He then ventured an unsupportable prediction of his own: voodoo economics would cause

30 percent inflation by 1982. "Frankly, I'm very surprised that the leading candidate for the Republican nomination could even be contemplating such economic madness during this crucial period in our country's economic history."

Success. He won 50 percent to Reagan's 43 percent, and chose to press on to Texas two weeks later.

EARLY ON APRIL 24, A PHONE CALL WOKE HENDRIK HERTZBERG. PAT CADdell told him to turn on the TV. Every channel depicted a desert graveyard of twisted, molten metal. Hertzberg immediately knew what this was about: some sort of rescue mission in Iran had failed. He darted to the White House to begin working on one of the saddest speeches he would ever write.

As best the first Western journalist to arrive at the scene could piece together, at least six giant Sea Stallion helicopters, and several hulking C-130 Hercules transport planes, had landed in a remote desert flat outside the city of Tabas, apparently to refuel the helicopters, and when a C-130 tried to take off, a swirl of dust from one of the Sea Stallions' rotors may have rendered the chopper invisible, and the plane crashed into it. Or perhaps it had been the other way around. Either way, there was a massive explosion, far too hot to drag clear any American bodies, of which it turned out there were eight. The survivors fled in an undamaged plane.

This was Operation Eagle Claw. It had been under consideration since autumn, carefully rehearsed by ninety Delta Force commandos, planned out on an elaborate eight-by-eight-foot model of the United States embassy compound—which in real life they never got near. Zbigniew Brzezinski had been pressing for Carter to green-light it all year, with added intensity following the successful "Canadian Caper" rescue in January, then after Bani-Sadr's double-cross on April 1. "In my view," a memo Brzezinski presented the president on April 10 read, "a carefully planned and boldly executed rescue operation represents the only realistic prospect that the hostages—any of them—will be freed in the foreseeable future. Our policy of restraint has won us well-deserved understanding throughout the world, but it has run out. It is time for us to act. Now." Indeed, Brzezinski was *so* eager for action that he had a staffer leak the plan, including a battle map, to Penne Laingen, in the hopes the hostage families would pressure Carter to move forward. (Instead, Laingen implored Carter not to.) Brzezinski also stated his desire to ride in one of the helicopters that would deposit the commandos outside the city. A colleague convinced him that might be a bit too much.

Carter approved the operation at a meeting on April 11 from which Cyrus Vance had been deliberately excluded. Vance tendered his resignation, effective whether the rescue operation succeeded or not. Carter accepted it. On the evening of the 24th, Walter Cronkite cocked his head somberly like he had on November 22, 1963: "This was a tragic loss. The loss may not be limited to lives. At stake in this mission was American prestige. It will be a while yet before we know the full score there. At stake also was the Carter administration's credibility."

Carter, haunted and sallow, appeared on TV to take full responsibility, promising further diplomacy, explaining that the fatal collision had occurred as the craft were preparing to retreat after he had called off the mission because of an equipment failure. The Ayatollah Khomeini attributed the collision to God, who had sent forth a miraculous sandstorm. Then he dispatched the Ayatollah Khalkhali to the crash site, where he posed for cameras poking at eight Americans' charred remains with a stick. Jimmy Carter's next Gallup approval rating fell to 38 percent.

BUT THE REPUBLICANS' NEAR-NOMINEE WAS NONE TOO POPULAR, EITHER— even among some on the right. On the day of Eagle Claw's failure, conservative New York City radio host Barry Farber polled his listeners about whether they preferred Richard Nixon over the available alternatives; fifty-five of eighty-three callers said yes. "Cesspool countries like Iran wouldn't push us around," remarked one. CBS News reported their own poll that night: only 48 percent said they were "satisfied" with the available presidential alternatives.

That would have made for auspicious timing for an announcement John Anderson made that day, had the news from the Iranian desert not knocked it off the front page: he was dropping out of the Republican race to begin the arduous task of getting on all fifty state presidential ballots as an independent. Polls suggested that he would start with an impressive 17 to 21 percent of likely voters. The *New York Times* found that he would draw equally from Reagan and Carter, but a *Washington Post* poll said he would hurt Carter more. His decision received surprisingly little attention—until a *New Republic* reporter named Morton Kondracke reached Walter Cronkite to ask him about rumors that Anderson was considering him as a running mate. Cronkite, who had announced plans to retire at the end of the year, answered, "I'd be so honored to be asked. I wouldn't turn it down. It would be the right party. I've been an independent all my life." Requests for confirmation bombarded CBS News, but Cronkite was on an overnight sailing voyage, so no one could confirm or deny it. Anderson was on the front page for several days—until, that is, the newsman weighed anchor, insisting that, though Kondracke had quoted him correctly, he had been "misinterpreted": he "had no interest in entering politics in any capacity." Anderson returned to the inside pages.

The Democrats voted next in Michigan, where unemployment was five points higher than the national average. The United Auto Workers had endorsed Ted Kennedy. Carter extended special benefits to 131,000 more idled autoworkers. Kennedy edged him by 1.4 points. Pat Caddell suggested that one reason for Kennedy's recent victories was that voters knew he couldn't win—and thus felt comfortable lodging the symbolic protest against Carter without fear it might elevate Kennedy to the White House.

Republicans wouldn't vote in Michigan until May 20, but the Reagan campaign took advantage of the attention being paid it now by issuing a statement blaming a 25 percent drop in automobile sales on "a deliberate policy of the Carter administration to squeeze the nation into recession—at the expense of working men and women, who are paying the price of Carter's economic game plan by losing their jobs . . . trying to balance the budget, in effect, by putting people out of work." Reagan therefore demanded an immediate review of all regulations affecting the industry; and, of course, tax cuts.

It was the kind of statement one might find in a general election campaign—which Reagan and his campaign were itching to embark on, if only George Bush would let them. Instead, Bush plowed forward in the hopes that a sufficiently thumping home-state victory on May 3 would tar *his* opponent as unelectable in the fall. The media dubbed it the "Texas Shootout." John Connally was campaigning with the Reagans. Nancy Reagan snapped to him, "Why can't you get him out of the race? He's doing nothing but costing us time and money and energy." Connally doubted that his opinion cut much ice with the human being who despised him most in the world, but he agreed to call James Baker to try. He also addressed Nancy's husband: "I hope when it's over that you won't reward him with the vice-presidency." Reagan shook his head: "Don't worry. I'll never do that."

ON APRIL 28, THOUSANDS OF PILGRIMS BEGAN STREAMING TO THE NA-tional Mall for the Christian right's most extravagant coming out so far. It was organized by a Puerto Rican charismatic Christian, the Reverend John Gimenez, who had once been an incarcerated drug addict. He had told his Virginia Beach neighbor Pat Robertson of the vision God had given him for a great gathering of Christians on the Mall. Robertson approached Bill Bright, who happened to have received a *similar* vision—though his was for a conference in Washington of twenty-five thousand ministers. So Bright wasn't sure if this was the *same* vision. Bright was, after all, a Presbyterian, and they traditionally considered charismatics heretics. He decided to take a chance, honoring the spirit of cobelligerency by signing on as Giminez's cochairman. They also recruited the president of the Southern Baptists, the president of the SBC's pastors conference, and Presbyterian televangelist D. James Kennedy. They chose April 28 and 29 for the two-day affair because, one of the anchors for the live broadcast on Robertson's Christian Broadcasting Network explained, April 29 was the date when the Puritans had arrived on these shores and "dedicated this country to God."

Actually, they landed on April 26. But who was counting?

The signs that Eastertide had been propitious. Forty-two members of a single Southern Baptist congregation in Gainesville, Florida, were elected to the 122-member Alachua County Democratic Executive Committee. (Their pastor was running for the state senate seat—because, his wife told columnist Richard Reeves, God told him to in a vision.) Bob Dylan was interrupting concerts with rants about "specific things, in the Book of Daniel and the Book of Revelation, which just might apply to these times here." ("Just look at the presence of the Soviet Union in Afghanistan.") On April 21, the Supreme Court heard oral arguments on the Hyde Amendment, with pro-lifers cautiously optimistic.

The lobbying group Christian Voice put out its first Biblical Scorecard rating of congressmen, based on their votes on fourteen issues. (It got enormous media attention, most of it mocking: Senator John Glenn of Ohio, the former astronaut, Eagle Scout, and current Sunday school–teaching Presbyterian elder, got a score of 0, as did Robert Drinan, the Jesuit priest who was also a Democratic congressman from Massachusetts—while Representative Richard Kelly of Florida, who was a conservative Republican, got 100 even though he had taken $25,000 in bribes from the FBI's fake sheik in the Abscam sting.) Tim LaHaye's new book *The Battle for the Mind* was flying off the shelves of Christian bookstores. It was "dedicated to explaining humanism in simple terms, so that the man on the street can both understand its danger and be motivated to oppose it at the place it can be defeated—the ballot box," and argued that until 1979, "we did not have a tax supported religion in America," until Jimmy Carter, "a humanist masquerading as a Christian," opened the Department of Education. Now, "since humanism is an official declared religion, we find the government establishing a religion and giving the high priest a position in the president's cabinet."

And now the Christians were on the humanists' doorstep.

The proceedings began with a women's meeting that packed the Daughters of the American Revolution's Constitution Hall, chaired by Mrs. Strom Thurmond, Mrs. Roy Rogers, and Mrs. Pat Boone. That evening the visitors enjoyed a rainy gospel concert at RFK Stadium, where

Jim Bakker set forth the usual litany of evidence that the nation was turning its face from God—"and you wonder why we haven't been winning any wars lately?"

The next morning, a coalition of Washington, D.C., priests, ministers, and rabbis released a shaken statement: "It is arrogant to assert that one's position on a political issue is 'Christian.' . . . There is no 'Christian' vote or legislation"—as communicants in everything from hooded sweatshirts to deacons' three-piece suits, and even nuns in habits, began gathering around a stage with the cathedral-like Smithsonian Castle at the speakers' back, gazing skyward as the sun broke miraculously over the Capitol dome, making the usual observations of the favor God had plainly bestowed upon them.

A CBN anchor desk overlooked the audience, where a former NBC News correspondent named Cal Thomas and his partner, Kathy Asbeck, bantered like Tom Brokaw and Jane Pauley on the *Today Show* about the tens of thousands of people who had already arrived, "not to ask man for anything, but to ask God to heal our nation."

(Actually the audience was grouped by congressional district, marching in disciplined ranks, state by state in alphabetical order, on the sidewalks around the Mall; and were enjoined to head up Capitol Hill to lobby after the event; and at the last minute organizers withdrew a statement of purpose directing "political leaders" to remember that "you are first, servants of God, then servants of the people," their job to "frame laws, statues, and ordinances that are in harmony with God's word" and repeal those "which have offended Him.")

". . . And also the *unity* that's here this morning—blacks, whites, and Chicanos, charismatics, non-charismatics, evangelicals, *every* kind of religious background . . ."

(That was another official line, vouchsafed by the two black holiness preachers who would be speaking, and the way CBN's cameras trained constantly on the crowd's tiny number of nonwhites.)

Bill Bright was the first speaker. He predicted that if America's military decline were not arrested it would set the world "aflame." He was followed by some of the most spellbinding orators alive.

Charles Stanley, who had the mien of a game show host, cried, "*No nation has survived the collapse of its home life.* . . . Because of this, those who are the *enemies* of the nations, those who would like to *replace* our philosophical ideas, *know* that in order to conquer America, *the home must be destroyed.* So is it any wonder that *Satan* has launched an all-out attack against the American home?" (He named, in addition to divorce, pornography, and homosexuality, "different ideas" as among Satan's weapons, then thanked Jesus "for the privilege of being loved by our wives and our children.")

A blond preacher recalled his recent trip to a refugee camp in Thailand, where "God is moving on the hearts of those people in the most unusual way." When Cambodia fell to the Khmer Rouge in 1975, he reported, there were but three thousand Christians in the country, but *in this one camp* there were over twenty thousand Christians! Over the last five years, two and a half million people—*at least*—have starved, been annihilated in one of the greatest genocides in the history of modern man. And yet God has used this atrocity to bring tens of thousands of people to the foot of the cross."

Reverend Lester Sumrall, a sixty-seven-year-old veteran of missionary tours of Tahiti and South America, who was "not afraid of *any* of the devil's isms," had the crowd chanting with him: *"Feed your faith and starve your doubts! Feed your faith and starve your doubts!"*

Sumrall was the author, most recently, of *Demons: The Answer Book.* In 1960, the year of John F. Kennedy's presidential campaign, he had published a fearsome tract entitled *Roman Catholicism Slays*, whose bright orange cover depicted a heretic being burned at the stake. Now, however, bygones were bygone: after a hymn, Pat Robertson took the stage to roars, spoke of "the ecumenical spirit of love we have for one another," and called up Father John Randall of the diocese of Providence, Rhode Island, a pioneer in the Catholic charismatic movement, who prayed in a New York accent for the Catholic bishops at their national convention that day in Chicago. Robertson gave him a bear hug. And the most honored time slot was reserved for the long-haired and bearded Father John Bertolucci of Albany, who paced the stage with a handheld microphone: "As we approach the three o'clock hour, I am reminded that my king, my Lord, my master, my savior, Yeshua Emmanuel, one with us, one who saves, God with us, *shed his blood* centuries ago at this hour on the cross, that you and I *might be free*! . . . *Do you need a Catholic to tell you that?*" (He was later banished from the ministry for molesting boys.)

According to the National Park Service, some two hundred thousand people heard him say it. They held up American flags, signs with slogans like "LET THIS GREAT NATION RETURN TO GOD AND PRAY OR BE JUDGED—PITTSBURGH" and "GOD BLESS AMERICA" and "I PRAY FOR MY PRESIDENT EVERY DAY," one depicting the "HOLY BIBLE" above the words "IT'S TRUE," another declaring "THEY SHALL RISE UP AS EAGLES" from the book of Isaiah— Phyllis Schlafly's watchword. When the men—and one woman—behind the plexiglass podium asked them to pray, they dropped their signs and joined hands in small circles, or held palms up to the sky in supplication, sign language interpreter and the massive choir, too—all male, in white shirts and ties, arrayed in ranks behind the stage. Pat Boone called it "one of the greatest days in human history." Tears flowed.

During lulls, CBN crews did roving interviews. Representative Bob Dornan marveled from atop the Capitol steps that with all the crises wracking the nation and world the administration "has *time* to engage in so much *mischief* against the American family," and enthused about how thrilling it would be to see the pilgrims march up Capitol Hill to lobby. ("I only wish they could come for several weeks!") A uniformed leader of Cops for Christ—"representing lawmen who are now under grace!"— described in a working-class Italian accent a vision he had received of this very event two years earlier. A black mother who'd ridden a chartered bus from North Carolina said it was "going to bring our nation together." And a gentleman from Florida whom the Lord had given "a vision calling for the Christian people to get out of the churches and stand up for Jesus Christ" rued that "there's only nineteen million of us Christians who have registered to vote. There's an estimated twenty-three to fifty million of voter age who have not registered, and this is *pitiful*. Because 98 percent of the bartenders are ready to vote; twenty million homosexuals are ready to go to the polls this year, Lord knows how many of the abortionists are ready to go. And if us Christians do not line up and let the holy spirit move upon us . . ."

He trailed off, harrowed. November would tell. But Jerry Falwell was confident. He called April 29, 1980, "the greatest day for the cause of conservatism and American morality in my adult life."

ONE MILE TO THE NORTHWEST, IN THE WHITE HOUSE PRESS ROOM, THE president reiterated the desolation he felt for the failed rescue mission. Then he said, "There is a deeper failure than that of incomplete success, and that is the failure to attempt a worthy effort, a failure to try." Later in the year, the National Council of Teachers of English awarded that dubious phrase—"incomplete success"—their annual Doublespeak Award, a dishonor also bestowed upon his opponent for Reagan's campaign oratory, "filled with inaccurate assertions and statistics and misrepresentations of his past record." Reporters peppered the president with questions about the resignation of Cyrus Vance—who on the way out the door, the *Washington Post* reported the next morning, blamed "those pygmies in the White House" for America's woes. Then in an afternoon question-and-answer session with community leaders, Carter said "the responsibilities that have been on my shoulders in the past few months have now been alleviated to some degree," and were "manageable enough now for me to leave the White House for a limited travel schedule, including some campaigning."

(Reagan offered an acid response from Texas: "If he feels freed, I wonder if he thinks now that the hostages have been somehow freed.")

Then, Carter noted the challenge of landing aircraft at night in "an isolated area of the jungle." The press office clarified that, of course, he meant "desert." A jungle was where the *last* foreign debacle crushed a Democratic presidency. Sigmund Freud, take note.

ONE OF THE BURDENS THE PRESIDENT SAID HAD BEEN LIFTED FROM HIS shoulders that let him leave town to campaign was passage of the windfall profits tax, sent from Capitol Hill for his signature nearly a full year after he proposed it. The *Wall Street Journal* spoke for the boardroom Jacobins in greeting the news with a black-bordered editorial called "The Death of Reason." Though boardroom Jacobins could also celebrate a victory.

All through April, a contentious conference committee couldn't arrive at a compromise between the House and Senate versions of the authorization bill for the Federal Trade Commission—which was still operating on a continuing resolution. House leaders gave the committee a deadline of May 1 to complete its work. They were not able to—so for the first time in U.S. history, a federal agency was forced to close its doors.

The shutdown only lasted twenty-four hours. But the FTC Improvements Act that President Carter signed contained something unprecedented for any federal regulatory body: a provision for Congress to veto its work. It limited (but did not close down) FTC activities on kidvid, used cars, and insurance sales. Its action to end the trademark protection for Formica was scotched. "All told," a Harvard School of Public Administration case study concluded, "the FTC rose from the pillory battered and wobbly, but still standing." But many of its best staffers had already quit in frustration. The message to other regulators had been sent: do your work efficiently and effectively, and you might face the guillotine, too.

The Heritage Foundation certainly hoped so. The think tank Paul Weyrich had chartered in 1974 was confident enough that a conservative would replace Jimmy Carter that it had committed $100,000 so far to a compendium of recommended actions for him to follow once he got to the White House: *Mandate for Leadership*, which eventually comprised twenty volumes and three thousand pages, with two thousand individual executive suggestions. The section on the FTC, composed by the director of the Regulatory Action Center of the U.S. Chamber of Commerce, proposed eliminating its role in fighting antitrust violations, and a "new philosophical underpinning" for its regulatory process, which, he argued, currently ambushed business with arbitrary and capricious regulations as "investigator, grand jury, judge, jury, and prosecutor, with all of the inherent unfairness entailed in this arrangement."

Hollywood continued its conservative trend. *The Empire Strikes Back*, the sequel to *Star Wars*, the 1977 movie whose director, George Lucas, promised would "tell the kids, 'Hey, this is right and this is wrong,'" was a runaway success. It partook of a hot film-world trend: making profit more predictable by pumping out new installments of blockbusters: *Jaws 2*; *Rocky II*; *Smokey and the Bandit II*; *Oh, God! Book II*—and also *Superman II*, which was filmed simultaneously with *Superman I*. A new sort of weekly variety show began its second season, a lighthearted look at the charms of ordinary Americans, like the guy who played a fiddle using a toothpick for a bow, and the detective for missing pets who called himself "Sherlock Bones." It was called *Real People*—and one of its themes was that real people held government bureaucrats in contempt. ("It's nice that at least one person in Washington is being funny on purpose!" a host responded to a segment on the debut episode starring capital humorist Mark Russell; another rather sympathetically portrayed a sweepstakes winner who went to jail rather than pay any taxes on his winnings, presenting one of his fellow prisoners as the voice of commonsense wisdom: "If I had my way, I'd turn him loose.")

Patriotic music was enjoying a revival. A song by the Charlie Daniels Band, "In America," hit number 11 on the Billboard Hot 100 (*"Yeah, we're walking real proud / and we're talkin' real loud again . . . You never did think / That it ever would happen again"*). A hit song by Kenny Rogers, "Coward of the County," told the story of a man whose father taught him to always turn the other cheek, until, "twenty years of crawling bottled up inside him," he took down an entire bar room to avenge the rape of his girl, because "sometimes you gotta fight when you're a man": an allegory to write *finis* to the Vietnam syndrome. (The song came out in the fall of 1979; the TV movie version two years later.) Neil Diamond prereleased the theme song of a film due out the next year, *The Jazz Singer*. It was called "America," and it was an ode to immigration as the highest form of patriotism—a sentiment with which both Reagan and Bush strongly agreed.

At a debate between them in Houston, time was allotted for audience questions. A young man leapt up and asked, "Do you think that children of illegal aliens should be allowed to attend Texas public schools for free, or do you think their parents should pay for their education?" Bush, Reagan, and moderator Howard K. Smith each awkwardly waited for someone to speak.

Bush finally broke in to ask to whom the question was addressed. Smith said the questioner was looking "straight at you."

"I was afraid he was," Bush replied, lips pursed, understanding that his intended answer might not be entirely welcome. He nevertheless launched into it passionately: America had "made *illegal* some kind of labor that I'd like to see made *legal*. . . . We're creating a whole society of *really, honorable, decent, family-loving, people*, that are in violation of the law."

He turned earnest: he didn't "want to see a bunch of six- and eight-year-old kids, being made, you know, totally uneducated, and made to feel they were living outside the law! Let's address ourselves to the fundamentals. These are *good* people. *Strong* people. Part of my family is Mexican."

Reagan was equally passionate: "Rather than talking about putting up a fence, why don't we work out some recognition of our mutual problems, and make it possible for them to come here legally with a work permit, and then while they're working and earning here, they pay taxes here?" He said he wanted to "open the border both ways," and was for "understanding their problems": the Mexican economy was in trouble, and immigration to the U.S. was "the only safety valve they have right now."

He received an impressed round of applause. Reagan got lots of applause that evening in Houston. Howard K. Smith's first question had been to Bush: Was Reagan overpromising to the American people? The man Smith referred to as "Ambassador Bush" eagerly launched into an exhaustive critique, full of facts and figures, about the irresponsibility of Reagan's budget-busting tax cut and described his own more prudent, targeted tax cut, a third of Reagan's size.

The audience greeted his answer with silence.

Reagan took his turn, claiming that *every* time a big across-the-board tax cut had been instituted, "there was such an increase in prosperity that the government, even in the first year, got *increased* revenues, not less!" He followed that falsehood with a parable about a spendthrift son: "You can lecture him day after day about saving money and not being extravagant, or you can solve the problem by cutting his allowance!"

The crowd burst into delighted laughter and applause. George Bush looked stunned.

Smith challenged Reagan about all the dubious figures he had been using, like the one about the Kennedy-Johnson tax cut being the same size as his 30 percent tax cut "when it was only 18 percent"—and Reagan interrupted with another sheer invention: "That was only the first year! It was a two-year tax cut, and it was a 27 percent tax cut, and I think that's close enough to round up to thirty."

That got another round of applause—and even Smith appeared delighted by the response.

He then challenged Reagan about another old standby: that every dollar of federal aid granted by the Department of Health, Education, and Welfare costs three dollars to administer. For HEW, he pointed out, said the real figure was twelve cents—and Reagan got one of his *Tonight Show*–sized thunderclaps of laughter by interrupting, "And I wouldn't believe HEW if they were here in the room!" Though, to be fair, he also *did* have an answer—an impossible-to-follow blizzard of arithmetic, which received *another* burst of applause.

Reagan, in fact, had an answer to everything—delivered so forcefully that, each time, the audience was spellbound.

Bush said *something something something* about the economy . . . concluding "I don't believe in an economic total soft landing." No response. Reagan said, "I brought along some facts and figures because I thought they would come in handy. . . . If Americans since 1950, in the last thirty years, had been able to save and invest, if our economy had been able to grow at only one and a half percent more a year, our incomes would be 50 percent higher, jobs would be plentiful, we'd have a balanced budget, lower payroll taxes instead of higher, a solvent Social Security program, and our industrial program would be three times as great as that of the Soviet Union. And we would have unquestioned military superiority."

What was he responding to? What was he arguing for or against? That wasn't clear. The audience didn't care; they just applauded.

Reagan repeated his demand, long ago walked back by his aides, for an embargo on Cuba to punish the Soviet Union. Bush yelped helplessly that *Cuba* hadn't invaded Afghanistan, maundered about "hemispheric problems," pointed out that within the international community an "embargo" was considered an act of war, which was why Kennedy had insisted on the word *quarantine* during the Cuban Missile Crisis . . . but Reagan kept saying *embargo*, and getting still more applause.

Bush gave a forgettable closing statement. Reagan said that "in the eighteenth century we created here in this land the freest and most unique society that has ever been known to man. In the nineteenth century, we built the greatest industrial power that the world has ever seen. And we spent most of the twentieth century—apologizing. And I don't know what we're apologizing for!"

And who could forget hearing something like that?

Bush lost Texas with 46 percent of the vote. Since Texas rewarded its delegates in winner-take-all fashion, Bush's chances edged closer to mathematical impossibility.

JIMMY CARTER HARVESTED MORE BAD LUCK.

At their debate, both Bush and Reagan had excoriated him for failing to provide aid to the Afghan rebels via Pakistan—precisely what he was already doing, in secret. They flayed him for his profligacy—as if he had not just announced emergency budget cuts. No good deed of Jimmy Carter's ever went unpunished—like his credit controls, which were scaring people away from stores, and which one market analyst now said probably "weren't needed in the first place" because interest rates were going down on their own.

Then, with the "freedom flotilla," a Carter good deed was punished like none before.

Carter's policy of outreach to Cuba was *succeeding*—despite the Republicans' consensus that it made him a pathetic appeaser. His tender of better relations, and his reorientation of American foreign policy around human rights, had prompted Fidel Castro to allow Cuban exiles to return to visit their relatives, and to release thousands of political prisoners. Unfortunately for Castro, flooding the population with witnesses to their government's inadequacies served to intensify resistance to his regime. So he opened a political safety valve: he withdrew military guards from the Peruvian embassy. His expectation was that a few hundred of the most determined regime critics would take advantage of the sanctuary. Instead, more than ten thousand Cubans from all walks of life quickly crowded into the compound.

Acting quickly, the shrewd revolutionary declared that those gathered there were the "scum" of Cuban society anyway—and good riddance. He ordered a group of loyalists to travel to the nearby port of Mariel and set sail for America, hoping thousands would follow their tutelary example. Quick-thinking entrepreneurs in Miami saw what was happening and chartered fishing craft and parked them in the temporarily opened harbor—and *tens of thousands* of Cubans promptly fled. The "Mariel boatlift" was on. Carter said the Thursday after winning the Texas Democratic primary, "We'll continue to provide an open heart and open arms to refugees seeking freedom from Communist domination"; and more came. By the following Tuesday, as many as seventy thousand Cubans had arrived in Florida.

This wasn't unprecedented; in 1965 Castro had opened a similar safety valve by inviting Cubans with relatives in the U.S. to depart. This time, however, people packing little vessels shoulder to shoulder needn't claim family connections—which meant that many, upon landfall, had nowhere to go.

To process the arrivals, the government opened tent cities in underutilized military bases, much as it had for thousands of impoverished "boat people" fleeing Haiti after 1972. The experiment began hopefully. At Camp Eglin in the Florida Panhandle, a Cuban declared in wonderment, "America is like a paradise, just like they say in the Bible." The day before the first Cubans arrived at "Camp Liberty," inside Fort Chaffee in Arkansas, Governor Bill Clinton announced cheerfully, "I know that everyone in this state sympathizes and identifies with them in their desire for freedom." The president and the governor would soon have reason to reconsider their welcoming attitudes.

Fidel Castro, both to embarrass Carter and to render credible his propaganda that the *Marielistas* were "scum," had made sure to include in the exodus a small population from Cuba's jails—less than 2 percent of outflow, the vast majority "guilty" of "crimes" like trafficking in the all-pervasive black market so their families would not starve. For once, however, Communist propaganda was taken as gospel. On May 11, the front page of the *New York Times* carried the headline "Retarded People and Criminals Are Included in Cuban Exodus." Two days later, UPI reported that two hundred Cubans, "some of them reportedly hardcore criminals, have in fact been transferred to a federal prison in Alabama." That number represented but 0.56 percent of the arrivals thus far. But many residents from the areas around the military bases—all in conservative regions—were not interested in doing the math.

A plane soared above Fort Chaffee, dragging a banner: "THE KU KLUX KLAN IS WATCHING HERE." A Klansman in full regalia was arrested after using his Marine ID card to wriggle his way onto the tarmac to scream at them as they got off the airplane. Motorists bellowed "Cubans go home" as they drove past the gates. Others picketed them. One fifty-six-year-old woman in a red, white, and blue outfit and a hand-lettered "God Keep America Free" sign "dabbed a tear away from her eye with a white-gloved hand," Gannett reported, and said, "I'm just a homegrown citizen of the United States. My objections to these Cubans are too numerous to mention—fuel, jobs, water, that's just a few of them." The reporter asked if she had borne similar objections to the fifty thousand Vietnamese who had passed through Fort Chaffee in 1975. She claimed she had not. A nearby demonstrator, however, admitted he had: "The president and the governor said when the Vietnamese came out here that they were only going to stay a little while. Now they live here, they've got our jobs. They've got our tax dollars."

Another worried observer was Colorado's Democratic governor, Richard Lamm. He said he hoped no refugees would be coming to *his* state: "It seems to me the evidence is clear and overwhelming that Castro is emptying out his prisons and mental institutions. I think this country is sadly mistaken if we feel we can be the reservoir for all of the displaced people in the world. There are too many of them. The numbers are overwhelming."

ON SUNDAY, MAY 18, AN EARTHQUAKE TRIGGERED THE ERUPTION OF Mount Saint Helens, a volcano in Washington State, shooting a plume of ash sixteen miles in the sky, killing fifty-seven. In the Liberty City neighborhood of Miami, a protest following the acquittal of police responsible for the death of a black former Marine erupted into a riot. On the first day, three died; then as the violence spread to three more sections of the city, fifteen more. The fires burned for six days.

A new memoir came out from the unapologetic architect of the Watergate burglary. In *Will*, G. Gordon Liddy revealed he had also hatched plans to assassinate columnist Jack Anderson on behalf of the White House, perhaps via "aspirin roulette"; had volunteered to be assassinated if it would help preserve the Nixon presidency—and also admitted that he rather admired Adolf Hitler, who made him feel "like a God." Reviewers labeled him a fascist. The one in the Kosciusko, Mississippi, *Star-Herald* allowed that perhaps this was the case—but that even so, this was the "kind of man the USA needs badly," and "the lack of them, more than anything else, may prove yet to be our downfall."

At Love Canal, the government had bought out the homes of the 223 families closest to the dumping grounds. The Environmental Protection Agency now released the results of a study of the seven hundred residents who remained. Almost a third of the sample had chromosomal abnormalities that might portend cancer, birth defects, and miscarriages. An EPA spokesperson called it "startling, much worse than we had expected"—but added that the results were not conclusive. The day of the Mount Saint Helens eruption, the leader of the Love Canal activists, Lois Gibbs, sent a telegram to the president demanding that he declare it a federal disaster area so that the remaining residents could qualify for low-interest loans. She argued, "Our government has gone out its way to assist the boat people and the Cuban refugees. Please, President Carter, help your loyal tax-paying United States citizens." But the EPA said action would have to await a review set to conclude on Wednesday. Gibbs responded, "We've been dealing with Wednesday for two years!" Her cadre took two EPA representatives hostage in one of their homes—a "Sesame Street picnic," one of them warned, compared to what might come next. A neighbor poured out gasoline to spell out "EPA" on a front lawn, then set it ablaze. Carter made the disaster declaration.

That, however, was followed by reports that there likely were at least thirty thousand similar hazardous chemical waste sites elsewhere in the country. Carter, spurred also by a horrifying, fifteen-hour fire the previous month at a chemical waste dump that came within six hundred feet of an explosion that might have flattened Elizabeth, New Jersey, renewed his advocacy for a "superfund" combining industry and government money to clean them up.

And the primaries ground on.

Oregon Republicans gave Bush 58.3 percent and Reagan 54 percent on May 20—but Michigan handed Reagan a resounding defeat. The Bush campaign now calculated that if they ran the table in the remaining contests, they could keep Reagan under the 998-delegate threshold for a first-ballot convention victory. They celebrated a *Time*/Yankelovich finding that 55 percent hoped "it won't come down to a choice between Reagan and Carter," and Gallup's that just 34 percent of Reagan voters "strongly supported" him. Their jubilation lasted only until that evening's newscasts, when two of the three networks counted 998 delegates for Reagan.

Bush called key supporters to an emergency meeting at his house to hash over the possibilities. ("Bush's longtime housekeeper," it was reported, "performed miracles.") He agonized for days. Finally, in a Houston hotel ballroom on May 27, he announced that he was quitting: "I see the world not as I wish it were, but as it is," he said, which could be read as a backhanded dig at Reagan. He called a *New York Times* reporter to his home for an exclusive interview, and pointed to a periodical on the coffee table—the Yale alumni magazine: "That's the first time we've been able to put that out for months." He indicated another on an end table. "I guess we can put this away now." It was *National Review*.

TED KENNEDY WOULD NOT THUS CONCEDE TO REALITY. HE SET HIS SIGHTS on "Super Tuesday"—June 3, when a third of the total convention delegates would be chosen in states from Rhode Island to California, the nation's most populous, which awarded its delegates winner-take-all.

Events continued grinding Carter down. The day after Oregon, inside Camp Liberty in Arkansas, three Cuban refugees, out of the population of thousands, were arrested for sexual assault. Six more were scooped up trying to escape. Governor Clinton announced that state police would join forces in a twenty-four-hour patrol and asked the federal government for additional help. The deterrent failed.

The *Marielistas* had thought they were fleeing to freedom. They had been told it would take forty-eight hours to check their backgrounds, evaluate their health, and send them on their way. But the Cuban government had stripped them of all pieces of paper before they left, making it impossible for even those with relatives eager to receive them to be processed efficiently. Refugees who had already languished for weeks at the Peruvian embassy now languished on cots in squalid tents in temperatures approaching one hundred degrees. Then three hundred decided they had had enough. Crying *"Liberdad!"* they stormed Fort Chaffee's gates—and were rounded up just shy of success. Governor Clinton activated sixty-five National Guardsmen. A spokesman for the Federal Emergency Management Agency warned, "If you wanted to tightly clamp down on this place, it would take a battalion of troops." So Clinton promised to mobilize more.

The next week at Fort McCoy in Wisconsin a refugee died from either falling or jumping from a tree. At Camp Liberty, six more days of mounting tension erupted into a riot. This time, pelting guards with rocks and fighting their way forward with clubs fashioned from cots, the refugees successfully breached Fort Chaffee's gates. It ended after state troopers opened fire. A picture made front pages around the country—including in Eau Claire, a ninety-minute drive from Fort McCoy: hundreds of sweating, angry Latino men, some shirtless, shoulder to shoulder as far as the eye could see, appearing to be marauding their way down a thoroughfare.

Governor Clinton first blamed Cuban agents: "They want Fidel Castro to be able to laugh at us." Then, he blamed Jimmy Carter, for not telling guards that they could use "riot procedures." By this time, local would-be vigilantes were so fired up that shops were running out of ammunition, and the nation's youngest governor's reelection was in jeopardy. "Everyone knows we're getting Cuba's trash," a resident told a reporter from his porch, a twelve-gauge shotgun in his lap.

The Fed relaxed credit controls considerably—after the Commerce Department's first-quarter numbers showed economic growth 0.6 percent below expectations. The unemployment rate was almost 8 percent. Inflation was 14.4 percent. Though in a separate report, Commerce revealed that after-tax profits were *up* 5.9 percent since 1979.

Ted Kennedy's commercials exploited economic anger. In one, Carroll O'Connor growled, "Carter equals Reagan equals Hoover equals depression." In another, over Jimmy Carter's smiling face, the announcer intoned, "This man has led our country into the worst economic crisis since the Depression. . . . Let's join Ted Kennedy and fight back against four years of failure."

Jimmy Carter won five of the eight Super Tuesday contests. But Kennedy won California, though with an unresounding 45 percent, and 11.4 percent of Democrats voting for "un-pledged." The senator accelerated his schedule for the run-up to the August convention—where, though all told he had received only 38 percent of primary and caucus votes to Carter's slight majority, his strategists were devising a plan to seize the nomination, nonetheless.

ANOTHER BIG POLITICAL STORY LEADING UP TO THE CONVENTIONS WAS the impact of the National Conservative Political Action Committee's airwave assault on its "hit list" of five, then six, liberal senators.

Ever since their cookie-cutter ads began appearing, locals poured rage at these Eastern carpetbaggers who "could care less about the real interests of the folks who live and work there," as the chairman of the government department at a small Lutheran college in George McGovern's South Dakota complained: they just poured poison through South Dakotans' TVs because they recognized a "golden opportunity" in a "remote, rural state." From NCPAC's sprawling headquarters, which took up an entire floor of an Arlington office building, Terry Dolan responded to such complaints insouciantly as ever: "We're interested in ideology. We're not interested in respectability."

They simultaneously tried to uphold a fiction that they were but humble servants of local "middle-of-the-road conservatives" who had begged their assistance against the "ultraliberal" senators who had bamboozled humble yeomen into sending them to Washington, where they forced "a host of radical positions" down unwitting constituents' throats. NCPAC operationalized this part of the strategy by naming suitably pliant state legislators as "state coordinators." That gambit faltered in Iowa, however, when they misspelled the name of the state legislator in question, Senator Roger Jessup, in the press release announcing his appointment—and because Jessup *learned* of his appointment from that same press release. He said he had just told these visitors from Virginia that he was willing to "help out."

Locals also huffed that in *their* states, negative campaigning backfired. Stumping for John Culver, Representative Tom Harkin insisted, "Iowans are too independent to believe much of what they say." In Indiana, that same message even issued from a local operative *hired* by NCPAC: Hoosiers would never respond to "name calling" and wouldn't buy claims that Birch Bayh was "radical," he said, securing a promise from Terry Dolan that he could raise the $146,000 ad budget himself, and control the message, to avoid charges that Bayh was getting crucified by "outside money."

The promise wasn't kept. A NCPAC letter went out to forty thousand Indianans signed by Senator Gordon Humphrey labeling Bayh a "radical." A friend of Bayh's denounced the "breach of senator courtesy." The New Right senator replied that he had meant "nothing personal." Dolan said nothing. What the New Right understood was that whatever people *claimed* about higher cognitive functions influencing political decision-making, ugly, endlessly repeated messages firing up visceral emotions like disgust worked whether voters knew it or not.

The underlying charge the NCPAC ads deployed to spur that disgust was that of *deception*: these senators need to be "exposed," for claiming to answer to the home folks when they actually served leftist puppet-masters in New York and Washington. In one of their ads, for instance, a mock game show contestant, "Verna Smith from Sacramento," was asked how she thought the National Taxpayers Union (a name that sounded neutral, but actually belonged to a far-right group) rated Senator Alan Cranston on "protecting the dollar." Mrs. Smith answered instantly:

"One hundred percent!"

"I'm sorry. You lose." (It was actually 8 percent.)

In another, "Verna Smith of Indianapolis" struck out—"I never knew Birch Bayh voted like that!"—on inflation, national security, and farm issues. On "farm issues," NCPAC derived its benchmark from the ratings by the business-oriented National Farm Bureau—which counted congressmen's positions on several right-wing pet issues that had little or nothing to do with agriculture at all.

Their audiences didn't realize they were being deceived by NCPAC; they thought they were being deceived by their congressmen. And a natural response to being deceived is rage. Like the rage felt by a citizen of Fort Worth, Texas, after NCPAC started running ads against Congressman Jim Wright, the House majority leader. He burst into a Wright campaign office, shrieked that his congressman was a "liar," and threw a potted plant at the wall. Wright was not an "extremist," nor an "ultra-liberal"; in fact, the onetime progressive populist had moved so far to the right that the AFL-CIO, which had once rated him a 95 percent, gave him a 59. The U.S. Chamber of Commerce had boosted him over the course of his career from 20 to 41 percent.

Neither was Thomas Eagleton of Missouri. He was an aggressive budget hawk and one of the few remaining pro-life Democrats in the Senate. That did not spare him, in May, from becoming the sixth member of the NCPAC hit list. According to a study, before their ads hit the air, 42 percent of Missouri respondents thought their senior senator was doing a good job on national defense. Subsequently, 10 percent did. In Idaho, where NCPAC had been hammering Frank Church since the summer of 1979, his polling lead over his not-yet-named opponent went from seventeen points in November to five points in February.

The deceptions were systematic and overwhelming. Their fundraising letters said donations would "cost very little" because donors "COULD claim A TAX CREDIT" equal to one-half of contributions up to $50 per person or $100 per couple. The IRS was asked to issue an opinion on the letter, and clarified that it was false: the relevant statute clearly stated that the tax credit was limited to donations for *candidates*—not campaigns against incumbents who might not yet even *have* an opposing candidate. On April 3, the Democratic National Committee asked the Federal Election Commission to take action to inform potential donors of the ruling. But it was far too late for that to do any good.

In Idaho, in April, Congressman Steven Symms, the NCPAC board member, announced that he was officially running against Frank Church. The reason Symms had held out so long was that political action committees weren't allowed to "coordinate" with candidates; if he wasn't a candidate, he couldn't be accused of coordination. In Indiana, thirty-three-year-old congressman Dan Quayle was running an optimistic John F. Kennedy–style campaign against fifty-two-year-old Birch Bayh, called NCPAC's ads "disgusting," and said that he rejected their support.

Though Terry Dolan made it all too easy to view such avowals as cynical. As he told one interviewer, "A group like ours could lie through its teeth and the candidate it helps stays clean."

THE MOST DRAMATIC LEGAL TEST OF THE "COORDINATION" ISSUE WAS South Dakota, where George McGovern was running scared. A state electorate suspicious that the former presidential candidate had become too big for his britches had barely returned him to Washington in 1974. Republicans were keen to snatch the vulnerable seat, pouring resources into recruiting a promising opponent. Here was another of those quiet, behind-the-scenes developments rewiring the politics of the nation in the late 1970s: where the Democratic Party had hardly any effective infrastructure for recruiting, training, and fundraising for candidates, the Republicans had built out such resources to a remarkable degree.

One of the best-oiled components of the machine was the Senate Republican Campaign Committee. Run by a figure who couldn't have been more establishment—Pennsylvania senator John Heinz, heir to the ketchup fortune—the SRCC were concerned with victory, not ideology, judging candidates strictly as horseflesh. ("Mickelson is about 38 years old, six-foot-four-inches, 220 pounds, and a lawyer.... His father was Speaker of the House ... and was a popular governor as well," noted a staff memo on possible South Dakota recruits.) But none of the prospects they judged most promising would run. The next two possibilities down the line, the state's attorney general and treasurer, were disqualified when they were caught playing blackjack in a bar in a remote town that turned into a prairie Las Vegas during pheasant season. (When the law enforcement officer approached them, they smiled at the familiar face and asked if he was there for business or pleasure. Not many people lived in South Dakota. That's what made it so useful for NCPAC's purposes.)

Terry Dolan couldn't care less about the SRCC's exquisite electoral algebra; he considered the Republican Party a "social club" where bloodless wimps went to "pick their nose." His preferred candidate was a far-right member of the state legislature named Jim Abdnor. NCPAC representatives buttonholed him at the 1979 state fair and showed him a survey by their pollster Arthur Finkelstein that they claimed demonstrated he would crush McGovern. Dolan then requested Orrin Hatch and Gordon Humphrey advise Abdnor that a seat beside them in the Senate was his for the taking—a prima facie violation of the law against coordination between PACs and candidates. Abdnor, for his part, appeared baffled by the whole thing. So did many South Dakotans.

McGovern kicked off his campaign in February at the famous Corn Palace in his hometown of Mitchell with Senator Robert Byrd in tow. McGovern held up a full-page newspaper ad that NCPAC had taken out across the state the day before, showcasing six of his votes to claim that "GEORGE MCGOVERN DOESN'T REPRESENT SOUTH DAKOTA."

He tilted his half-glasses charmingly:

"I have some questions I want to ask these dudes! If they can find only six mistakes in seventeen years and 1,000 roll calls, we must have been right 994 times! . . . These people do not represent the interests of ordinary citizens of South Dakota. I say they don't understand the principles of fair play and decency!"

His audience huzzahed their approval. A farm wife wondered earnestly to an out-of-town reporter how her beloved senator, with responsive constituent offices in just about every little South Dakota town, could be the cat's-paw of out-of-town extremists: "He's the son of a South Dakota minister!"

But as spring advanced, McGovern was forced to perform an unexpected duty: campaigning in the Democratic primary. Pro-lifers recruited to run against him a South Dakota–born math teacher who'd lived in Texas since 1961. Dead-fetus leaflets accusing him of voting "tax dollars to kill pre-born children" appeared on car windshields in church parking lots across the state the Sunday before the primary. Huffed the preacher's son, "I resent it when I come out of God's house on Sunday morning and find that some misguided political agent has put a leaflet on my car accusing me of being anti-family and a killer of babies. . . . A lot of right-to-lifers are being used by the right wing without realizing they're sort of political dupes." His no-name opponent, who hardly campaigned, got a shockingly hefty 26,850 votes to McGovern's 44,690.

McGovern started returning home very frequently, constantly harassed by accusatory questions. ("Is it true you're a pal of Fidel Castro?"

". . . that you sold the Panama Canal to the Communists?" ". . . that you want to kill the unborn?") "It's all these off-the-wall right-wing ideas. They've been running this stuff for two years," McGovern sighed. He called NCPAC "fanatics."

He also said, "I am a liberal Democrat. I always have been. And I'm too old to change now."

Which was one way NCPAC's targets responded to the smears—trusting their neighbors to recognize tricksters when they saw them. This was the approach of Senator John Culver in Iowa, running against Congressman Chuck Grassley. The *New Yorker*'s Elizabeth Drew had recently published a little book about Culver called *Senator*, which chronicled his work hour by hour for ten days during the summer of 1978. "Each of the one hundred members of the Senate at some point establishes a reputation within the institution by which his colleagues judge him," the book opened. "Some become known as mediocrities, some as well-meaning but ineffective, some as phonies, some as mavericks . . . a few are dismissed as jokes, and a few are taken seriously. . . . In 1978, at the age of forty-five, John C. Culver, a Democratic senator from Iowa, still in his first term, which had started in 1975, had already established himself a reputation as one of the most effective members of the Senate." Drew praised his firm principles, his pragmatism, and his willingness to do "the hard work of legislating, of putting together coalitions, of mediating among the conflicting interests of this country, of making the whole thing go."

Like McGovern, Culver refused to run from his liberal record, telling the press that he trusted Iowans to tune out those making a "simplistic, slanted appeal to fear and prejudice"; to interpret his signature opposition to "reckless" defense spending not as extremism but down-home common sense; and respect the sincerity of his pro-choice views even if they disagreed. He had seen his former senior colleague Dick Clark trim his sails in response to the New Right onslaught in 1978, after all; and Clark was his colleague no more.

Frank Church, in Idaho, meanwhile, stuck with the opposite strategy—first in his demagogic response to the Soviet brigade in Cuba, then by voting for an amendment to restore school prayer. It made for a nice little natural experiment: come November, which approach to the fear-brokers would prevail?

ANOTHER OPEN QUESTION WAS WHETHER THIS NEW CHRISTIAN RIGHT were paper tigers or a genuine force: Could they accomplish, for instance, the simple blunt task that Democratic political machines had been mastering for generations—extricating supporters from their warm houses on cold Tuesdays to *vote*?

A test of their organizational mettle emerged in the final weeks before the party conventions. The White House Conference on Families that Jimmy Carter had promised on the campaign trail in 1976 was now such a political minefield that holding it at the White House was out of the question. There would be regional gatherings instead: in Baltimore the weekend of June 1, in Minneapolis beginning June 19, and in Los Angeles starting July 10. A more politic politician might have quietly scuttled the project altogether, for preliminary meetings made plain that a political donnybrook like the National Women's Conference in Houston in 1977 was in the making.

At one to elect delegates from Virginia for the conference in Baltimore, Connie Marshner's National Pro-Family Coalition loaded up the church buses and emerged from the aptly named Grant Battlefield Ballroom at the Sheraton in Fredericksburg with twenty-two of twenty-four delegates. An advocate for the needs of single mothers—who noticed many of the buses had signs reading "Lynchburg"—was flabbergasted: every time a productive discussion got going on issues like divorce courts that took over a year to resolve child custody disputes, or the "marriage penalty" in federal income tax laws left over from a time when few women earned money outside the home, or the poor regulation of nursing homes, the self-described "pro-family" cadre bogged them down in acrimonious side-debates over abortion, the ERA, or why the organizers referred to plural "families" instead of "*the* family." "It was one of the most frustrating experiences I ever had," she exclaimed. "We've lost all rationality."

New York City brought a victory for the other side—electing what the *Daily News* termed an "awfully Abzugian" delegation that included activists from Catholics for Free Choice and Lesbians Over the Age of Forty. Responded Paul Weyrich in *Conservative Digest*, "Throughout history, many of the more successful revolutionaries . . . spelled out their plans in advance but were not taken seriously until it was too late." He held up Hitler's *Mein Kampf* as his example. "If ever the moral majority needed to take a revolutionary's advance plans seriously, this is it," he wrote. Though it was not one of these supposed liberal fascists, but a representative of Weyrich's side, from a pro-life group called the Morality Action Committee, who left in police custody after punching a member of a Catholic pro-choice group in the gut.

What was "morality"? What was a "family"? In an election for a spot representing Washington, D.C., a candidate from the National Pro-Family Coalition, a Catholic priest named Father Joaquin Brazan, faced off against a bisexual social worker, Billy S. Jones, who had helped organize the first gay and lesbian march on Washington and the National Third World Lesbian and Gay Conference. The "pro-family" priest won. Six years later, the priest was sentenced to a twenty-five-year prison term after admitting to sodomizing ten boys, while Jones was in a committed relationship that would last for another forty years, in which he and his partner raised five children.

The delegates elected to the three meetings were predominantly conservative. They would be joined, however, by delegates appointed by public officials, who were mostly family service professionals. Since fall, they had been eagerly participating in hearings across the nation convened by the WHCF's executive director, John Carr. Many were standing-room-only. They produced an aching, honest record of the breadth of family function and dysfunction in the United States. "I had no idea wife-beating would surface that heavily," Carr remarked to a reporter for *Washingtonian* magazine. "This was the real stuff. . . . Whatever your feelings about adolescent pregnancy or the issue of family planning are, this was not an abstract discussion." It needed to be prioritized at the regional meetings.

Christian conservatives, naturally, disagreed.

They derided the appointed delegates as "the professionals," and "secular humanists" only there because they had "a vested interest in getting more federal funds for their programs." They gnashed their teeth over the conferences' $3 million congressional subsidy as if it were all the gold in the world. The first lady of Alabama—the wife of the governor who had authorized truckers to shoot scabs—wrote to conference director Jim Guy Tucker that her state "would not participate in this or other such conferences which do not establish traditional Judeo-Christian values concerning the family, the foundation of our nation under God." The governor of Indiana withdrew his state, too, predicting "divisiveness." Safe bet.

At the Baltimore meeting on June 5, President Carter gave a moving— to some—speech: "When we think of families we ordinarily think of brothers and sisters, and a father and a mother." But "the essence of family life is the universal need for mutual support, for nurturing a safe haven for children and for old people, and for love . . . love can be found, obviously, in many different circumstances." But these were fighting words for the conservatives: proof that what this was *really* all about was the state ramming a *redefinition* of "family" down Americans' throats. On the second day, the National Pro-Family Coalition's Larry Pratt, who ran Gun Owners of America, wrestled the microphone from Jim Guy Tucker and announced that "the conference is stacked and we should walk out"—and they did.

In Minneapolis, the right organized particularly shrewdly, thanks to the presence of Phyllis Schlafly, who arrived straight from the Illinois capitol, where her forces had scored their latest triumph against ERA ratification. They won resolutions excluding homosexuals from the definition of the family and opposing "the imposition of secular humanist philosophy in public institutions."

The "professionals" were bereft: How did miring a once-in-a-lifetime chance to reform broken family policies in swamps of polarization help those who needed support keeping their elderly and disabled loved ones at home and out of institutions, strengthen incentives for businesses to provide more flexible schedules for parents, reform Social Security to provide better for homemakers, combat drug and alcohol abuse—*help families*? Marshner was unapologetic: "In a political battle," she told *Washingtonian*, "first you have to polarize people in order to get their attention. . . . What do you do with people who have spent 12,000 hours sitting in front of TV before they've graduated from high school, people who aren't used to reading or thinking or paying attention to what's going on around them? You have to make a big stink." The next week she organized a counter-conference in Washington. By its close, attendees could celebrate plans for a new "pro-family" think tank, the Family Research Council, headed by Dr. James Dobson, and a Supreme Court decision upholding the Hyde Amendment.

And, while it was going on, a letter went out to 160,000 ministers signed by Ed McAteer, James Robison, and the Dallas Cowboys coach Tom Landry inviting them to a much more massive two-day conference, the "National Affairs Briefing" of the Religious Roundtable, at Reunion Arena in Dallas, on August 21. They promised "knowledge about what is really going on in the erratic swings of the economy, the intrigues of international affairs and the domestic crisis which is morally enslaving our country," and strategies to "inform and mobilize your church and community in this non-partisan effort to do something that can determine the moral character of America."

Invites also went out to the three presidential candidates. Only Reagan accepted—though, to be sure, his invitation was far more fulsome than the rest. "I am thrilled with the progress you are making toward the Presidency of the United States," the Reverend James Robison wrote him. "As one seeking to know and do the will of God, I stand firmly convinced that you are the best candidate to lead us during these crisis days in American history. I will do everything possible within the limits of my ministry to help you."

IN JUNE, COLUMNIST ELLEN GOODMAN RECORDED A PET PEEVE: WALTER Cronkite's nightly practice, "delivered in the well-known, well-punctuated, well-modulated, properly authoritative manner—rather like a benediction," of ending his newscast ". . . *and that's the way it was, on the*"—on the day Goodman's column appeared, it was *"221st"—"day of captivity for the American hostages in Iran."* She called it an implicit editorial whose message was "do something! do something!" and "a subtle and powerful daily reminder of our impotence or incompetence, helping no one, not even the hostages." She protested to CBS executives. They claimed to have no idea what she was complaining about.

July 4 was the 244th day. Jimmy Carter addressed a town meeting at a high school in Merced, California—"where Boy Scouts still proudly wear their uniforms, where the old values of hard work and patriotism still run deep, where people still respect their president," Frank Reynolds of ABC said. The president shucked his jacket, to delighted cheers. A wall of American flags stood sentry behind him. He talked about how proud he was that exiles sought refuge in the United States. A farmer asked him why the government had canceled a 1950s program of temporary visas for Mexican farmworkers while letting in these "boatloads of people . . . who in some cases will never work." Carter made a calm, patient defense of his policy of welcoming refugees. Then, he stopped himself and grinned:

"There are loafers in my own family. I hate to admit it. Maybe even in yours!" The audience veritably exploded with delight.

This Independence Day was for the hostages. At the Prince of Peace Church in Jacksonville a fifty-three-hour vigil began with choruses of "America the Beautiful," then a mass was said for each hostage individually. Two hundred and forty-four American flags flew in Hermitage, Pennsylvania (and one Canadian flag, on the eighty-sixth pole, symbolizing the day that country helped eight hostages escape), and a flame flickered for Pennsylvania's native son Michael Metrinko, to burn until he himself put it out. In St. Louis, celebrants released a cloud of balloons carrying tags ferrying heavenward sweet wishes that those finding them were to send to the family of local hostage Rodney Sickman. In Wye, Maryland, Penne Laingen tied a yellow ribbon around an old oak tree—the four-hundred-year-old official state tree—while the governor looked on.

Elsewhere, Independence Hall in Philadelphia a rabbi offered the invocation, "Bless our fellow Americans, hostages of a new, but familiar fanaticism who will not be forgotten." The beloved Philadelphia Orchestra conductor Eugene Ormandy, an émigré from Hungary, said, "Everybody asks me where I was born, and everybody gets the same answer—'I was born in America,' and after a short stop I say, 'at the age of twenty-one.'" Then Vice President Mondale spoke: "Wherever people are oppressed, they know that there is freedom in America."

Elsewhere, a New Orleans–based oldies band premiered "Their New Smash Single 'BOMB IRAN'" (*"Old Uncle Sam / is gettin' pretty hot / trying to turn Iran / into a parking lot."*) The group's leader complained, "We're not making any money because some Iranian has gone and bought up the rights to the tune 'Barbara Ann,'" and said that a mob of Iranians had jumped him. "Just how long can this go on? Now is the time for us to have some pride in our country again."

And in Clarksburg, Massachusetts, another of those cities where the old values of hard work and patriotism still ran deep and Boy Scouts still wore their uniforms, the annual woodpile erected by the fire department was topped by a four-foot-tall drawing of the Ayatollah Khomeini by a local eighth-grade girl. "I wish the real one was up there," the fire chief said after the ceremonial bonfire was touched off at midnight.

THE FINAL WHITE HOUSE FAMILY CONFERENCE OPENED ONE WEEK LATER IN Los Angeles. Conservatives agitated for a resolution endorsing the Family Protection Act, a legislative package introduced by Senator Roger Jepsen and Reagan's campaign chairman, Senator Paul Laxalt, that would explicitly declare spanking children protected by the Constitution and ban federal legal aid for abortion, school desegregation, divorce, and homosexual rights litigation. Phyllis Schlafly's deputy Rosemary Thomson attended a luncheon at which, she complained, the feminist minister's invocation was "interspersed with Women's Lib buzzwords like 'liberating parental arms,' 'fearful conformity,' 'interdependence,' " and " 'the process of birthing something new' " — this last phrase, she clarified, being code for secular humanist curricula in schools.

She wasn't discouraged. This was a useful organizational tune-up. Christians, she wrote, now "will be ready to register to vote, work for, and elect pro-family candidates next November. God may be giving us our greatest opportunity to change the direction of America. The White House Conference on Families is the trigger that will fully awaken the Silent Majority!"

The Republican National Convention began in three days.

CHAPTER 35

Conventions

THE REPUBLICANS MET IN A BRUTALIST CONCRETE PILE CALLED JOE LOUIS Arena in 63 percent African American Detroit. That had been at the urging of the RNC's Bill Brock, who still hoped the party could attract more black voters. *National Review* publisher William Rusher said that for insisting that the party "lift its skirts and show its ankle to Detroit inner city blacks," thus slighting "right-to-life people, pro-gun people, pro-energy people," Brock ought to be fired.

The headquarters hotel, the Detroit Plaza, sat atop the shiny glass Renaissance Center, which had opened in 1976 with federal financing as part of an effort to revitalize a city that had lost over a third of its population since 1950. "A Spark of Spirit, a Riverside Renaissance in Motor City," the *Washington Post* had exulted then—a goal undercut by the spiritless new building itself, surrounded as it was by a fortresslike thirty-foot concrete wall. Republicans weren't much interested in exploring the city anyway. A joke circulated at the RNC meeting that chose Detroit: "There's good news and there's bad news. The good news is that the convention hall is only a block away from the headquarters hotel. The bad news is that nobody's ever made it."

One of the city's two dailies, the *Free Press*, was on strike. A walkout by nine thousand city garbagemen, sewage workers, and bus drivers was settled sixty hours before the opening gavel—but not before a burst water main went unrepaired for days. City officials anxiously awaited official word from the Census Bureau confirming estimates that the city had shrunk by a fifth since 1970, which would trigger devastating cuts in federal aid. Japan announced that for the first time in history they had surpassed America in auto production. Local congressman Charles Diggs lost his final appeal and was ordered to report for a three-year jail term. The streets were "one big traffic jam," ABC reported—"but not quite as big as it might have been. Michigan's Governor William Milliken had his car stolen this morning at the Detroit airport."

Prostitutes weren't concerned. One told the *Detroit News* she expected to earn at least $1,000 from the week's twenty thousand visitors. Nor were businesses that dealt in party supplies. The manager of one said that the Reagan campaign had ordered more red felt cowboy hats than they could possibly provide, and that they'd sold out their stock of flags. Though she hadn't moved as many inflatable elephants as she would have liked. "The manufacturers tell us it's a petroleum product and the price has risen considerably."

Fifteen thousand media personnel arrived, including six hundred from each network, who spent a combined $50 million on their broadcasts, three times more than the convention cost the Republicans. Roone Arledge assigned his best man to direct—a veteran of *Monday Night Football* and *Wide World of Sports*. NBC's John Chancellor, an actual journalist, wondered what they were doing there in the first place. "Maybe we shouldn't cover these things gavel to gavel," he reflected. "We know how the story will turn out."

Which was why, with dozens of hours of airtime to fill, the networks obsessed about the one story that they *didn't* know how it would turn out. The Reagan campaign didn't know, either.

THE WORK OF SELECTING A RUNNING MATE HAD BEGUN IN APRIL WHEN THEY clinched the nomination. The key player was pollster Dick Wirthlin, who tested the performance of not just tickets with the names on their short list—Howard Baker, William Simon, Jack Kemp, Richard Lugar, Paul Laxalt, and George Bush—but *everyone* publicly mentioned as a possibility: eighteen potential tickets in all. No campaign had done this before.

Some were weeded out for reasons of compatibility, others for questionable character (Donald Rumsfeld, for example, was judged so freakishly ambitious that a Reagan aide joked that if he became vice president Reagan would need a food taster). Jack Kemp and Richard Lugar campaigned furiously for the job—though Lugar scotched his chances when he answered a question about whether Reagan had the intellect to be president, "I'm not sure that is what's called for. What's called for is his ability to harness people who are very bright." Howard Baker and George Bush insisted that they weren't interested: "Take Sherman and cube it," Bush said, referring to General William Tecumseh Sherman's famous 1884 statement refusing a presidential draft, "I will not accept if nominated and will not serve if elected." But both also campaigned, if quietly. Bush, for example, reworked his speech scheduled for the third night of the convention from a generalized attack on Carter to a panegyric to Reagan, and denied to a reporter that he had ever uttered the phrase "voodoo economics"—even after the reporter played him the videotape.

Following these wisps of news gave the talking heads and camera crews plenty to occupy their time—when they weren't on the hunt for the goofiest hats (probably the three-foot-tall elephant-head-in-an-Abe-Lincoln-stovepipe balanced atop a stocky fellow in a leisure suit), or searching out the nuttiest delegate to interview. The prizewinner here might have been a delegate from Alaska, where the Moral Majority had virtually taken over the state party, who explicated her theory for the White House's acceptance of homosexuality: "The first step in Communists taking over is getting the government to control everything. If we let everything be controlled by Washington, all they have to do is take over that one city. There *must* be Communists in Washington right now."

EXTREMISTS WERE A PROBLEM. "THE MESSAGE WE WANT TO GET ACROSS," ED Meese told the *New York Times* the day before the opening gavel, was Reagan as "essentially a problem solver, that he is not rigid and doctrinaire," and wished "more than anything else" to unify the country. The platform he would be running on, however, knocked out in Detroit over the previous week, ran the other way.

Key members of the drafting committee were Jesse Helms, Jack Kemp, and Congressman Trent Lott, Reagan's campaign chairman in Mississippi, who cochaired. David Stockman later wrote with satisfaction in his memoir that Lott "bent over backward to appoint supply siders. Senator Roth got the (crucial) economic policy committee, and Brother Kemp was given the Defense and Foreign Policy chair. It was a coup, and another link in Wanniski's chain."

That would be Jude Wanniski, the supply-side propagandist who, during platform week, called a meeting to draft the inflation plank at a restaurant with Stockman, Jeff Bell, and Kemp—"a supply-side central committee," Stockman wrote. (A former Communist sympathizer, Stockman shared with many on the right a fondness for Soviet political language.) "With his eye toward history," Stockman recalled, "Kemp immediately grabbed a napkin and started taking notes."

They knew they couldn't explicitly call for returning to gold—a "four-letter word" to the establishment. So they got the gold standard in via a side door: "The severing of the dollar's link with real commodities in the 1960s and 1970s," the plank read, "in order to pursue economic goals other than dollar stability, has unleashed hyper-inflationary forces at home and monetary disorder abroad, without bringing any of the desired economic benefits."

Stockman drafted the energy plank himself, cutting to ribbons what he liked to call Carter's "Soviet-like energy '*Gosplan*.'" The text made reference to the anti-Carter resolution at the 1977 NAACP convention on energy—the one for which infiltrating energy executives were responsible—in order to decry the supposed impact Carter's "no-growth energy policy will have on the opportunities of America's black people and other minorities." It blamed "60 percent of the world oil price increase since 1973" not on OPEC, but on the depreciation of the American dollar. It called energy taxes "punitive," dismissed the federal fifty-five-miles-per-hour speed limit as "counterproductive."

There had been a spirited debate in the energy subcommittee on the speed limit. But the economic planks passed largely without controversy—even though Alexander Cockburn and James Ridgeway of the *Village Voice* observed that fulfilling their promises "would require nothing less than a miracle from the Almighty God to whom the convention prayed almost without cease." The defense language was devised in consultation with John Singlaub, the major general cashiered for criticizing Jimmy Carter's foreign policy. Since then, with Congressman Larry McDonald, he had founded, "Western Goals," a private database of alleged domestic subversives—the "first and only public foundation," they claimed, filling "the critical gap abused by the crippling of the FBI, the disabling of the House Committee on Un-American Activities, and the destruction of crucial government files." Singlaub also had become the leading advocate for schemes to arm irregular guerrilla forces in nations like Nicaragua to overthrow their Communist governments, paid for by private donors as a way around the squeamish qualms of feckless politicians. Several times, with another consultant on the defense planks, General Daniel O. Graham, he had recently visited Central America—"battered by the Carter Administration's economic and diplomatic sanctions linked to its undifferentiated charges of human rights violations" the platform said—to discuss such a project with Guatemala's violent right-wing government.

The previous year, Singlaub had been talked up by right-wingers as a presidential prospect. Now he was a perfectly contented Reagan surrogate—boasting that the candidate had told him on the trail, "General, you give me more material for my speeches than anyone else." Singlaub said Reagan was "the only national politician who really understands what I am talking about." His party now, apparently, concurred: the defense planks, which also advocated a passion of General Graham's—antimissile weapons deployed in outer space—passed with little opposition.

THE SOCIAL ISSUES PLANKS WERE A SUBJECT OF GREATER CONTROVERSY— especially in the streets. Upon news that the platform committee was to scotch the Equal Rights Amendment for the first time since 1940 in spite of the fact that 52 percent of Reagan supporters wanted it, Republican feminists erected a mock family home in the protest area with thirty-eight displays celebrating all the states that had ratified the ERA.

In the same poll, only 32 percent of Reagan supporters wanted a full ban on abortion. But conservatives had stacked that subcommittee, too. *"Fascist baby-killer!"* one of them screamed at the single member to vote against a plank reading, "We affirm our support of a constitutional amendment to restore protection of the right to life for unborn children. We also support the Congressional efforts to restrict the use of taxpayers' dollars for abortion. We protest the Supreme Court's intrusion into the family structure through its denial of the parent's obligation and right to guide their minor children."

Both passed the full platform committee by voice vote. The RNC's vice chairman, a feminist named Mary Crisp, who had won the job in 1977 against Ronald Reagan's candidate Dr. Gloria Toote, had been stripped of her position, replaced by a woman named Betty Heitman, who promised that she would "avoid controversial issues." The day of the ERA and abortion subcommittee defeats Crisp gave what ABC News said was "*supposed* to be the 'nice Republican lady' exit speech," but was instead an angry exhortation: "Although our party has presented the outward appearance of vibrant health, I'm afraid that we are suffering from serious internal sickness. . . . We are about to bury the rights of over a hundred million American women under a heap of platitudes. Even worse is that our party is asking for a constitutional amendment to ban abortions. I personally believe that these two actions could prevent our party from electing the next President of the United States." Her words were followed by a shocked silence.

(*"Is Mary Crisp just a woman scorned? Not so, say party leaders who admit, only off the record, they fear conservatives have gone too far. Susan King, ABC News, Detroit."*)

The platform crackled with New Right buzzwords, neocon buzzwords, Christian right buzzwords, supply-side buzzwords, boardroom Jacobin buzzwords. "Voluntary prayer" in schools. "The continuing efforts of the president's administration to define and influence the family." Their "unilateral cancellations" of weapons systems. "The unconstitutional regulatory vendetta . . . against independent schools." "Regulatory burden." "Overregulation." "Excessive regulation." "Regulatory costs."

And also a call to "oppose federal registration of firearms" and strike down provisions in the Gun Control Act of 1968 that served "to restrain the law-abiding citizen in his legitimate use of firearms." That had been inserted right before a paragraph decrying the "murderous epidemic of drug abuse" which "Mr. Carter, through his policies and his personnel, has demonstrated little interest in stopping." It was strengthened from a draft merely opposing federal firearm registration.

The last lines the committee approved were a scriptural-sounding preamble: "And so, in this 1980 Republican Platform, we call out to the American people: With God's help, let us now, together, make America great again." Senator Lowell Weicker of Connecticut called the platform "disgraceful," sending a letter to constituents promising to campaign against it. An "Anderson Republican" told the press, "I've lived through 1964. I didn't like it, but I find this much worse. I feel they just don't want the moderates in the party."

RONALD REAGAN ARRIVED FOLLOWING A FLIGHT WHERE THE MOOD WAS so buoyant that for the first time even Nancy joined in the ritual bowling game played with an orange during takeoff. ("I had a sneaking likeness for the Reagan plane," Theodore White told his diary. "There's no fun in the Carter entourage.") He released a statement about the three hundred thousand automotive jobs that had been lost—"The problems weren't made in Japan or Europe but in Washington"—and demanded the repeal of the law under which Carter had instituted credit controls. He met privately with Jerry Ford. He had earlier been asked by reporters about the ERA donnybrook. He responded with the same defensive huff he always did when accused of enabling bigots: "I have been in the *forefront*, when I was governor, of equal rights for women! . . . Mary Crisp, I think, should look to herself and *find out how loyal* she's been to the Republican Party for some time!"

In the news, Jimmy Carter's brother, Billy, agreed to register as a foreign agent, in a deal with the Justice Department to avoid charges for failing to do so despite having received a quarter million dollars in gifts and "loans" from the Libyan government. In Detroit, breakfast for a thousand delegates began with a prayer for "the protection of all life, especially for the unborn." The opening gavel sounded in Joe Louis Arena, followed by a moment of silence for the hostages; Pat Boone recited the Pledge of Allegiance; country stars Glen Campbell and Tanya Tucker sang the National Anthem. Then, another prayer was recited.

A procession of ten thousand protesters passed the arena chanting for endorsement of the ERA. An hour afterward, the platform committee officially transmitted their work to the full convention without a single plank having met the twenty-seven-vote threshold it would have required to debate revisions on the floor.

The big event at the first evening session was a speech by Gerald Ford—"the person the polls say would most help Ronald Reagan as his running mate," Bill Moyers noted. "But the former president has said *no*, *no*, a thousand times *no*." It was the former president's birthday, July 14. At the podium, behind a wall of red, white, and blue carnations, above the giant letters reading "TOGETHER . . . A NEW BEGINNING," he surprised everyone who recalled him as a bland timeserver by knocking it out of the park.

"Some call me an elder statesman. I don't know . . . I don't mind telling you all that I am not ready to quit yet." (That raised eyebrows.) " 'Elder statesmen' are supposed to sit quietly and smile wisely from the sidelines. I've never been much for sitting. I've never spent much time on the sidelines. Betty'll tell you that. This country means too much to me to comfortably park on the bench. So when this convention fields the team for Governor Reagan, count me in."

This was impressively conciliatory, considering he was pledging his heart to the man many still held responsible for him losing the White House; and considering that when Ronald Reagan gave his concession speech at the 1976 convention, he hadn't even whispered a reference to Gerald Ford.

Then Ford reportedly tried to rush back to Palm Springs, worried some fool would try to draft him for vice president. Reagan addressed a late-night reception for delegates from talking points reminding him to observe "no one knows the hurt of unemployment more than black Americans and other minorities" and that he was "pleased the Republican Party has a strong plank addressing needs of black and Hispanic Americans," and to mention the party's "historic commitment to equal rights for women." He also carried with him an alternate set of remarks, so sensitive that only one copy existed, to read if he wished to make a certain surprise announcement. He chose to keep it in his pocket.

ON TUESDAY REAGAN MET WITH UNEMPLOYED AUTOWORKERS, THEN DELegates upset about the ERA—who left impressed with his promise to consider women for high positions, including the Supreme Court.

An Illinois delegate caucus got bogged down in acrimony over the platform language promising that a Reagan administration would "work for the appointment of judges at all levels of the judiciary who respect traditional family values and the sanctity of innocent human life." Senator Percy called the plank "the most outrageous" he had ever seen. A judge from Cook County, Illinois, wondered how the litmus test had gone from "Do you support the United States Constitution?" to "If you're not against abortion you can't be a judge." A pro-life delegate replied angrily, "The platform says *nothing* at all about a litmus test, says nothing at all about abortion!" The delegation was polled. The pro-choicers lost overwhelmingly. In a New York caucus, a motion to work to restore the ERA was shouted down.

Reagan attended a luncheon at a Polish American club to honor his delegation liaison team, which turned awkward: he was seated between Jack Kemp, a vice-presidential possibility whom Reagan looked upon like a son, and, *oops*, George Bush. "There was no hiding the tension," a network correspondent observed. "Bush appeared eager to please, listening to Reagan's stories while munching kielbasa, but the two have never developed a real friendship."

That was an understatement. The last time they had seen each other was the Texas debate, which had concluded with Reagan seeming almost to laugh at Bush while answering a question about his running-mate deliberations: "It goes without saying that anyone you would recommend to the convention would have to carry out the programs that you have promised the people you were going to implement. They will have to agree with the Kemp-Roth tax bill!"

But Reagan's grievances with Bush extended far beyond that. Bush's radio ads compared Reagan's inexperience and cluelessness to Carter's— "Can we afford the same mistake twice?" Bush's performance in the Nashua debate convinced Reagan that the man who volunteered to become one of the youngest fighter pilots in the World War II Navy was a coward. (Future campaign chroniclers collected quotations Reagan was said to have uttered on the subject: *"If he can't stand up to that kind of pressure, how could he stand up to the pressure of being president?" "George froze that night. That haunts me." "How would this guy deal with the Russians?"*) Aboard *LeaderShip '80*, Stuart Spencer, a veteran Republican strategist who had worked both on Reagan's gubernatorial campaign in 1966 and Gerald Ford's presidential campaign in 1976, made the mistake of arguing that George Bush was really the only logical running mate, as a moderate counterbalance to a conservative platform, as a strong performer in key swing states, as an experienced government official, as a loyal team player, as an indefatigable campaigner. He received a rare flash of Reagan temper: "Why should I? Voodoo economics!"

Spencer realized he had ventured too far. Burying a hatchet was one thing. This was a Viking-sized battle-ax. As for Bush, the Texan was said to still be simmering from Reagan's snub of his son's 1978 congressional campaign. Even if he was offered the job, would he take it?

YES, IT TURNED OUT, HE WOULD.

A *New York* magazine reporter named Michael Kramer flew to Detroit with Bush to shadow him through convention week—the only writer who thought he merited such attention. Perhaps Kramer had in mind a tragic portrait of a man who'd sacrificed his life, his fortune, and his sacred honor to win the White House and ended up with a $500,000 campaign debt to show for it.

He immediately learned that Bush was in fact desperate for the nod— and fairly confident he would get it. He had an ace in the hole in the form of Gerald Ford, whom James Baker had convinced to make Bush's case to Reagan. Bush intended his performance during convention week as an audition. "I'm pretty damned nervous," he told his Boswell, then giggled.

He settled in on the nineteenth floor of the Hotel Pontchartrain, accompanied by a handful of family and retainers. He got to work soliciting invitations to hosanna Reagan before as many state delegations as would have him. He jogged for the cameras to display his youthful vigor. But courtesy calls to his suite were sparse. Sitting beside Reagan eating Polish sausage was a torment. Maybe James Baker's intelligence was wrong. "If this doesn't work out, I'm gonna be the pissedest-off guy around," he told Kramer. The stress of his lonely pseudo-campaign, he said, was causing him "a peristaltic contraction in the lower colon."

MORMON POP STARS DONNY AND MARIE OSMOND STARRED IN A YOUTH FOR Reagan rally at the 2,920-seat Henry and Edsel Ford Auditorium. Beforehand, the rally coordinator coached the crowd. ("We're going to raise some pandemonium for Governor Reagan.... We're going to have all kinds of hell raising.") Twenty-two-year-old Donny's script said that they had "just returned from an extensive world tour" where they had witnessed "the decline of the United States' prestige and respect through the world.... I think we can safely say that all of us want to make America great again.... I am buying a home just like everyone else and I am paying the same high interest rates."

ABC News paid a visit to the trailer the Reagan campaign had set up for Clif White, a nostalgic throwback to the setup he used as the nerve center to secure Goldwater the 1964 nomination in San Francisco. In case of floor fights, the correspondent said, "it's rumored that Reagan's floor leaders have loads of information about their delegates, including, so they say, their blood pressure, their favorite beer, the name of their bookie, and their last dental checkup."

That was a little joke: There would be no floor fights. There would be no public controversy at all. Conservatives didn't even bother to boo Henry Kissinger when he delivered his speech.

ABC also reported that "although top advisors insist Bush, who has been greeting enthusiastic audiences in Detroit"—he was shown bellowing, *"I look under Governor Reagan for a foreign policy that will restore respect"*—"would be the best vice presidential candidate, Reagan is reluctant to go with him."

Then they showed Reagan saying, "I haven't ruled anyone out," and Ford avowing, "My opinion now is as it had been for the last six weeks and I have no reason whatsoever to change my opinion."

The evening session ran two hours behind schedule. The keynote speech by Representative Guy Vander Jagt of Michigan was postponed until the next day. The order had come from a certain gentleman watching attentively on the sixty-ninth floor of the Renaissance Center. Ronald Reagan knew something about television, and he didn't want the show extending past prime time.

NOMINATION DAY BROUGHT A THUNDERSTORM AND EIGHTY-MILE-PER-hour winds, leaving outdoor vendors hip-deep in murk. Hotels lost power, delegates caucused by candlelight—or, if they were important enough, by TV lights powered by backup generators. The show must go on.

This inspired a labored metaphor from a network correspondent about the "storm" in the personal relations between Reagan's and Bush's wives. It also caused the plane carrying Howard Phillips to land an hour late—though the New Right honcho somehow managed to secure a police escort for his limousine, and was able to arrive on time for a meeting with Reagan in his suite, alongside Paul Weyrich, Phyllis Schlafly, and Jerry Falwell. There, they warned Reagan that the right absolutely could not accept George Bush, whom Phyllis Schlafly had told reporters would be "very hurtful to the ticket. There would be a great deal of people who would not vote." Reagan assured them his pick would be suitably conservative.

It was one of two times in Detroit that Falwell conferred with Reagan. At the other, Falwell reportedly said that he would "vote for him even if he had the devil on his ticket," but would "prefer Representative Jack Kemp or Jesse Helms." To the media, however, Falwell insisted that he was only in Detroit chaperoning his "I Love America" singers: "I'm not a Republican or a Democrat. I'm a noisy Baptist."

In Jesse Helms's suite, at a meeting with the very conservative head of the Texas delegation, a shouting match erupted over whether to push Helms, Crane, or Kemp—terrifying all involved that if they couldn't agree on one, Bush would wind up with the job. Which could get ugly, for a movement was forming among conservative delegates to walk off the floor if he did.

Boardroom Jacobins were not slighted. Michael Deaver and Reagan's personal secretary, Nancy Reynolds, had recruited William Agee, chairman of the board of the Bendix Corporation, a multinational construction firm, to arrange meetings between major executives and Republican power players in Detroit. Perhaps Agee did some recruiting for a program he enacted later in the fall, a pyramid-style scheme to "enlist as many American business leaders as we can to join with us in spreading the message to every business leader in every city, town, and village in our great country" to send chain letters to executives with the message that corporate money could be spent in "unlimited amounts" to contact their shareholders, executives, and administrators to get out the Reagan vote. "There are more than 25 million stockholders in this country," Reagan's campaign lawyer wrote in a letter promoting the scheme. "Corporations can reach their stockholders with a letter from the president in quarterly reports or enclosed with dividends. Not only is this a huge free mail program, it is targeted to a group very concerned about the issues discussed."

Businessmen were also plied for contributions by a Texas oilman named Robert Mosbacher and a Nashville legal developer named Ted Welch, in charge of weaponizing a novel legal interpretation. In 1979 Carter had signed a revision to campaign finance law allowing national parties to transfer funds to the states—"closer to the people," as Ronald Reagan liked to say; the amendment was intended to subsidize political activities by ordinary folks at the grass roots, things like passing out signs, calling neighbors, organizing voter drives. It also, however, provided an unintended vehicle for corporations to achieve by other means something that was intended to be illegal: campaign contributions from corporations. In its "hard" form, it still was. Selling the benefits of these newfangled "soft money" gifts, Mosbacher and Welch, who liked to say, "Instead of playing golf, I raise money," did land office business.

ON ABC, FRANK REYNOLDS MUSED OVER THE DILEMMA OF THE SIGN-MAKERS: "Until Reagan announces his choice, they can't fill in the blank space." Meanwhile a curious rumor concerning that was whipping about. When Bush heard it from a loyalist with his ear to the ground, he remembered thinking, "That's crazy. That'll never happen."

The previous night, Bush was up in his nineteenth-floor aerie, melancholically padding about in khakis and a polo shirt, drinking a beer, his only company that one determined *New York* magazine reporter, when, at 3:48 in the afternoon, a walkie-talkie squawked to life with possible news: "Stay close."

Bush ate popcorn, watched the tube ("The first thing I'm gonna do as vice president is crusade to stop the commercial from increasing in volume"), cast occasional timid glances at the phone like a teenager hoping for a date for the prom.

5:18. The walkie-talkie squawked again: "False alarm."

Kramer brought up Kansas City in 1976, where Ford suffered a similarly agonizing wait. Bush had enough Stroh's in him to wax philosophical: "You know, it builds character."

If the TV happened to be tuned to ABC, he would have received a sting even worse than too-loud TV commercials: his own voice. *"Though he spent months criticizing Reagan for being too simplistic, Bush is willing to stand by the GOP man. 'I feel very comfortable and enthusiastic about his views on foreign policy . . .'"*

He calmed his nerves with a jog around an indoor track, then returned to his room to prepare for his evening speech. Now the TV was tuned to CBS. Walter Cronkite had managed to finagle a surprise guest into his booth—the subject of the absurd rumor that had just astonished Bush, which now was ricocheting around the convention hall: the thirty-seventh President of the United States.

What would happen, Cronkite asked, "if they got up there on that platform and said, 'It's gotta be Gerald Ford'?"

Ford conceded that it "would be tough" to turn down a draft to run for vice president. But he shook his head in a manner suggesting "no way" while he said it.

Then, however, Ford did something astonishing. Reagan and Bush were both watching in their hotel suites. Both were reported to have veritably gasped as Ford started laying down *terms:*

"I really believe that in all fairness to me, if there is to be any change, it has to be predicated on the arrangements that I would expect as a vice president in a relationship with the president. I would not go to Washington . . . and be a figurehead vice president. If I go to Washington, and I'm not saying I am accepting, I have to go there with the belief that I will be playing a meaningful role across the board in the basic and the crucial and the important decisions . . . so I have to, before I can even consider any revision in the firm position I have taken, I have to have responsible assurances."

This was something. Cronkite pressed: "What about the question of pride?"

There came an indecipherable response. Seeking to clarify, Walter Cronkite coined the word soon on everyone's lips:

"So it's got to be something like a *co-*presidency?"

Gerald Ford seemed to like the sound of that. Power is a powerful drug.

"That's something Governor Reagan really ought to consider. . . . Neither Betty nor myself would have any sense that our pride would be hurt if we went there as Number Two instead of Number One."

Betty, sitting beside him, raised no objection.

"We've been around this city a long time, Walter, and I think we're big enough, we're self-assured enough that that problem wouldn't affect us in any way whatsoever. But the point you raised is a very legitimate one. We have a lot of friends in Washington. And the president-to-be—and I would hope it's Ronald Reagan—he also has to have pride. And for him not to understand the realities and some of the things that might happen in Washington is oblivious to reality."

And that *really* was something.

A LOT HAD BEEN HAPPENING BEHIND THE SCENES. THAT FIRST DAY, MEET-ing Ford in his suite at the Detroit Plaza Hotel, one floor above his own in the Renaissance Center, Reagan surprised his old rival by handing him a gift-wrapped package: an authentic Native American "peace pipe." Ford was touched. Then, that evening, came Ford's warm words for him in his speech, and it was Reagan's turn to be delighted.

Dick Wirthlin was also delighted. It wasn't long after Reagan clinched the nomination that he persuaded Ed Meese and William Casey that a Reagan-Ford ticket, which polled better than any other, could make the difference in a close election, especially in the big swing states where Ted Kennedy had proven Carter was weak: Pennsylvania and Gerald Ford's Michigan. Casey and Meese were sufficiently impressed to have Wirthlin repeat the argument to Reagan. Wirthlin knew his quarry well enough to fold in the sort of appeal to patriotic duty that was always the surest route to Ronald Reagan's heart: he reminded him how, after the 1976 conven-tion, even though he publicly stated that he would never accept a spot on the ticket with Ford, he later admitted that he hadn't meant it, that if Ford had implored him that the country needed him, he could not have said no. Wirthlin argued that Ford should not be denied that *same* opportunity to do *his* duty if that was the only way to rescue the nation from another di-sastrous Carter term.

Reagan conferred with his old kitchen cabinet, who approved the no-tion, and gave Wirthlin the green light to investigate further.

Reaganites sent feelers to Fordists to sound out the former president. But at a tête-à-tête in Palm Springs, Ford gave what Reagan thought was a firm refusal. Nonetheless associates of both men kept the idea alive. The most aggressive was Henry Kissinger, as a route to returning to the center of power. *No permanent friends, no permanent enemies*, as the old politi-cal saying goes. In 1971, in the Oval Office, Henry Kissinger agreed with Richard Nixon when he said, "With a Reagan in here, you could damn well almost get yourself in a nuclear war." ("He has no judgement," Kis-singer concurred.) During the 1976 primaries, Reagan aimed his campaign rhetoric almost more at Kissinger than Gerald Ford. In January of 1980, Kissinger was reported to have called Reagan "an intellectual lightweight"; in February, Reagan pledged in New Hampshire not to name Kissinger to a cabinet post.

Now a frequent joke in Detroit was that Kissinger was just one more of the city's thousands of hopeless job-seekers. Cartoonist Pat Oliphant depicted him backstage, looking pathetic, holding up a sign that read "AVAILABLE." Mary McGrory called him "an unemployed Metternich." They had no idea that Henry Kissinger was actually at the white-hot center of the action—negotiating, with Alan Greenspan and Representative Richard Cheney at his side, with Casey, Meese, and Wirthlin to accomplish something unprecedented: make a former president a *vice* president, with more power than a vice president had ever previously enjoyed.

The Ford side's negotiation points included making Kissinger secretary of state and Greenspan secretary of the treasury. Talks were far enough along by Reagan's first public appearance on Monday that the very sensitive document he held in reserve in his coat pocket was a text by Peter Hannaford, full of cross-outs and typos, reading, "There is one person more than any other I want as my running mate. He is a man uniquely qualified in terms of experience; a man of ability, compassion, and commitment. That man is Gerald Ford."

On the Reagan side, the principals were working so intensively to make what was dubbed the "dream ticket" work that at a Wednesday-morning breakfast they didn't notice when the Secret Service evacuated the governor to a lower floor for fear that the windows would crash in from the storm. Unspecified "Reagan supporters" were reported to have donated $600,000 to the proposed Ford presidential library. By Wednesday night, a teleprompter text was prepared just in case Reagan needed it for his acceptance speech on Thursday. (". . . THERE ARE FEW ACTIONS YOU CAN TAKE THAT WOULD HAVE A GREATER IMPACT ON OUR ABILITY TO CHART THE COURSE OF OUR NATION'S FUTURE THAN TO BRING GERALD FORD TO THE TICKET.")

What was more astonishing were the evolving terms: a thoroughgoing redefinition of the customary role of vice president. A text recording their understanding proposed that a Vice President Ford would head a White House "executive office," supervising both the Office of Management and Budget and the National Security Council—serving, Greenspan explained, like a corporate "chief operating officer" with Reagan as the nation's CEO. It *would* have been a veritable "co-presidency," just like Ford told Walter Cronkite on TV.

Talks were proceeding furiously, emissaries bolting between Reagan's sixty-ninth-story suite and Ford's on the seventieth, newly minted jokes rocketing around the floor at Joe Louis Arena ("Ford will be president before nine, after five, and on weekends"), when a stagehand locked eyes with George Bush, waiting in the wings to deliver his prime-time speech:

"I'm sorry, Mr. Bush, really sorry. I was pulling for you."

"Sorry about what?"

"You mean you haven't heard? It's all over. Reagan's picked Ford as his running mate."

Bush was nothing if not a man of duty. He delivered his remarks enthusiastically. (*If anyone wants to know why Ronald Reagan is a winner, you can refer him to me. I'm an expert on the subject!*) He received an enthusiastic response. He returned to his hotel, had half a beer in the lobby with his eldest son, then restlessly brought the rest up to his room, where he learned that there had been no such announcement—only one more rumor.

But ABC News had already suggested it as fact. A segment opened blaring an opera aria: "This is Susan King. George Bush always said the opera wasn't over until the fat lady sang. Well, she sang last night. And this morning there was a final note in the Bush campaign for the presidency: *'And I plan to enthusiastically support Governor Reagan and encourage you to do exactly the same thing.'* "

Always the bridesmaid. Bush had been considered by Barry Goldwater in 1964; by Richard Nixon both in 1968 and after Spiro Agnew's resignation in 1973; and by Ford. Now his two-year presidential journey had shrunken down to a round of speeches releasing his delegates to a man he despised, loyally giving credit to him for all his best ideas.

THREE BLOCKS UPRIVER AND SIXTY-NINE FLOORS IN THE SKY, THE NEGOTIA-tions were still ongoing as the Reagan family gathered around the television set to savor the nomination roll call.

The signs waved. ("WASHINGTON STATE ERUPTS FOR REA-GAN"; "RON TURNS US ON"; "SHELL THAT PEANUT"). The band played. And the radios and portable television sets blared rumors. That the Secret Service was tracking down George Bush. Or Representative Vander Jagt. That Bush had been spotted at the barbershop. Or Reagan had been seen meeting Ford.

At 11:13, the great state of Montana put Reagan over the top. The rest made their ceremonial declarations of fealty in alphabetical turn. A stubborn thirty-seven delegates cast votes for Anderson, thirteen for Bush, one for Ambassador Anne Armstrong. A legend sprung up that one delegate even stood up for John Connally, which made for a too-good-to-check detail for posterity: the fictional Connally loyalist was dubbed the "$10 Million Delegate," which was how much Connally squandered on his once-so-promising campaign.

At approximately thirty minutes to midnight, Walter Cronkite asked one of his correspondents whether Reagan would be coming to the arena with an announcement or would be "leaving them hanging overnight."

They were estimating the precise time it would take a Secret Service motorcade to travel the distance from the Renaissance Center to the Joe Louis Arena loading dock when Leslie Stahl appeared amid the waving flags and banners and bellowing delegates and blaring band and announced, "I am just being told by a high lieutenant that the choice is" — her eyes bulged out — "*Bush!*"

Walter Cronkite mock-buried his face in his cuff links: "Well who's writing the script for this one that's what I wanna know!"

THE PREVIOUS HOURS HAD BEEN THE KIND OF HISTORICAL HINGE MOMENT that every participant memorializes, each confidently putting snatches of dialogue within quotation marks that never match with one another (complete with precise facial expressions) of negotiations whose ebbs and flows shifted minute by minute, and different straws that broke the camel's back. The upshot was the same: Ford entered Reagan's suite and told him that the whole thing just couldn't work. After Ford left, according to one account, Reagan asked for the phone. According to one account, he also "grimaced."

Ford as running mate "played right into our argument that Reagan couldn't be trusted with the presidency," Gerald Rafshoon later noted. "It would look as though Reagan's own party didn't think he could handle the big job without supervision, without somebody around to make sure he wasn't too quick on the trigger." The remarkable thing was that by letting the discussion get as far as it did, those closest to Ronald Reagan seemed to be entertaining that idea themselves.

From the adjoining room, the Bush retinue heard their man eagerly pledge to support every jot and tittle of a platform containing all manner of propositions he had been running around the country denouncing as absurd. Then he put down the phone. His whoops mixed with those of his staff and friends suddenly rushing into his suite, which was lonely no more.

DOZENS OF AIRHORNS SPLIT EARS. THOUSANDS OF PEOPLE HOLLERED AT the top of their lungs. State standards and red, white, and blue "Reagan/ Bush" signs bobbed up and down — and the rosy-cheeked man of the hour grinned from ear to ear, then cried with more than a little sincere concern:

"We're losing *prime time!*"

He tried quieting the crowd with two more thank-yous; then listened as a grand old ritual from conventions past broke out: "*Viva!!*" the California section roared, hoisting their cowboy hats skyward; and the Texas section did the same while they cried out "*Olé!*" The nominee tried a couple more thank-yous, then couldn't contain a chuckle: "You're singing *our* song!"

He quipped, "Well, the first thrill tonight was to find myself for the first time in a long time in a movie on prime time!" Nancy, radiant in pale yellow, shook her head in mock embarrassment and giggled.

"But this, as you can imagine, is the second big thrill. Mr. Chairman, Mr. Vice President-to-be, this convention, my fellow citizens of this great nation: with a *deep* awareness of the responsibility conferred by your trust, I accept your nomination for the presidency."

This speech had been drafted by Peter Hannaford late in June, though the second next utterance—it came after his pledge to "build a new consensus with all those across the land who share a community of values embodied in these words: family, work, neighborhood, peace and freedom"—Reagan wrote himself, and it had been inserted into the text only two days earlier. It was a politically brilliant deflection of the ERA controversy:

"I know we have had a quarrel or two, but only as to the method of attaining a goal. There was no argument about the goal. As president, I will establish a liaison with the fifty governors to encourage them to eliminate, where it exists, discrimination against women. I will monitor federal laws to ensure their implementation and to add statutes if they are needed."

Then came the meat. For years, Reagan had been pressing upon his party a lonely counsel that conservatism could be the basis of a new majority of Republicans, Democrats, and Independents—not by borrowing the popular nostrums of liberalism but by proudly defying them. Now his vision had triumphed—at least among Republicans. He was more convinced than ever it would triumph with *Democrats*. It was why he always bragged of being the first presidential candidate who had also been a union president, and that he still carried with him his union card. It was why the platform committee breakfasted with labor leaders in Detroit—and though the UAW's Douglas Fraser had called that meeting a "charade." But when a reporter for a Chicago-based socialist newspaper wandered forty miles up I-94 to the industrial suburbs of Macomb County, the unemployed Chrysler employees he met in a workingman's bar were all voting for Reagan; the Democrats, they said, were just interested in handing out welfare to lazy blacks instead of helping people like them. His editor refused to print the dispatch. He didn't want to believe his beloved proletariat could "think like Archie Bunker."

Union Democrats were now watching Ronald Reagan in bars like that around the country. And, to the white ones, at least, what he was saying sounded pretty good.

"The major issue of this campaign is the direct *political*, *personal* and *moral* responsibility of Democratic Party leadership—in the White House and in Congress—for this unprecedented calamity which has befallen us.

They tell us they have done the most that humanly could be done. They say that the United States has had its day in the sun; that our nation has passed its zenith. They expect you to tell your children that the American people no longer have the will to cope with their problems; that the future will be one of sacrifice and few opportunities."

He tilted his head:

"My fellow citizens, I utterly reject that view. The American people, the most generous on earth, who created the highest standard of living, are not going to accept the notion that we can only make a better world for others by moving backwards ourselves. Those who believe we can, have no business leading the nation."

He reminded them that in 1976, "Mr. Carter said, 'Trust me.' And a lot of people did. Now, many of those people are out of work. Many have seen their savings eaten away by inflation. . . . And, today, a great many who trusted Mr. Carter wonder if we can survive the Carter policies of national defense."

(The audience was solemnly, respectfully silent.)

He made sure, too, to play the good shepherd—it was "essential that we maintain both the forward momentum of economic growth and the strength of the safety net beneath those in society who need help. We also believe it is essential that the integrity of all aspects of Social Security are preserved."

(Amid the very mild applause this received, a scattering of boos could be heard.)

"When those in leadership give us tax increases and tell us we must also do with less, have they thought about those who have always had less— especially the minorities? This is like telling them that just as they step on the first rung of the ladder of opportunity, the ladder is being pulled out from under them. That may be the Democratic leadership's message to the minorities, but it won't be ours. Our message will be: we have to move ahead, but we're not going to leave anyone behind."

(A cameraman panned the audience, apparently searching for a black face. None was found.)

This was Reagan's familiar liturgy of absolution, his decades-long argument why liberals were wrong when they said the things *you* believed were immoral—that, actually, *they* were the immoral ones.

He turned to energy, said that nuclear power ("under rigorous safety standards") "must not be thwarted by a tiny minority opposed to economic growth," nor the right to explore oil be infringed—because "the economic prosperity of our people is a fundamental *part* of our environment."

(That got some of the biggest applause of the speech.)

He came to a section on foreign policy: "The Carter Administration lives in the world of make-believe. . . . But you and I live in a real world, where disasters are overtaking our nation without any real response from Washington. . . . We are not a warlike people. Quite the opposite. We always seek to live in peace. We resort to force infrequently and with great reluctance—and only after we have determined that it is absolutely necessary. We are awed—and rightly so—by the forces of destruction at loose in the world in this nuclear era. But neither can we be naive or foolish. Four times in my lifetime America has gone to war, bleeding the lives of its young men into the sands of beachheads, the fields of Europe and the jungles and rice paddies of Asia."

(That was one of several parts of the speech Reagan's own edits rendered far sharper and more evocative than his aides' drafts.)

He uttered a now-signature nostrum: "We know only too well that war comes not when the forces of freedom are strong, but when they are weak. It is then that tyrants are tempted."

(Someone hoisted an American flag into the frame.)

He pursed his lips worriedly: "We simply *cannot* learn these lessons again the hard way without risking our destruction."

(At that, the cheers and the applause and the airhorns peeled on and on—and the crowd began a rhythmic chant—some viewers of the broadcast thought it was *"Win! Win! Win!,"* others *"Strength! Strength! Strength!"*—accelerating into a lusty roar that almost sounded, well . . . *warlike.*)

He made the now-requisite implicit avowal that his age would not slow him—that some say presidential elections impose "difficult and exhausting burdens on those who seek the office. I have not found it so." He added a splendid patriotic fillip: "It is impossible to capture in words the splendor of this vast continent which God has granted as our portion of this creation. There are no words to express the extraordinary strength and character of this breed of people we call Americans."

He launched into his final peroration quoting a political hero—who once said, Reagan noted, "For three long years I have been going up and down this country preaching that government—federal, state, and local—costs too much. I shall not stop that preaching. As an immediate program of action, we must abolish useless offices. We must eliminate unnecessary functions of government . . . we must consolidate subdivisions of government . . . and, like the private citizen, give up luxuries which we can no longer afford."

That, he triumphantly pointed out, was Franklin Roosevelt, in *his* first presidential nomination acceptance speech. It was a brilliantly conceived invitation for lifelong Democrats to do what Reagan had done long ago—

change parties—framing his defection from the Democrats as a response to that party's betrayal of *its own* principles.

Then he cast his eyes downward, almost shamefacedly. "I have thought of something that's—not a part of my speech. And I'm worried over whether I should do it," he said in apparently nervous fits and starts.

He looked down again, as if gathering his courage . . . then lifted his eyes with resolve.

"Can we doubt that only a Divine Providence placed this land, this *island* of freedom, here as a refuge, for all those people in the world who yearn to breathe free?"

He recited a roll call:

"Jews and Christians enduring persecution behind the Iron Curtain.

"The boat people of Southeast Asia, of Cuba, and of Haiti.

"The victims of drought and famine in Africa.

"The freedom fighters of Afghanistan.

"And our own countrymen held in savage captivity."

This part was a deception, that all this was "not a part of" his speech. It was right there in its first draft, and worked over carefully ever since. (The first clause had originally only mentioned Jews enduring persecution behind the Iron Curtain; Reagan added in "Christians." He also crossed out "victims of drought and famine in Africa"; it was subsequently restored.) But it sure *sounded* spontaneous. Reagan had been honing these skills for a very long time.

He next intoned something even more softly, haltingly—a bit they had decided not to include in the official text distributed to reporters or to put on the teleprompter, the better to make it look like he pulled it straight from his heart:

"I must confess that I've been a little afraid to suggest what I'm about to suggest."

(He looked like he was about to mist up.)

"I'm more afraid not to. Can we begin our crusade, joined together, in a moment of silent prayer?"

Ten seconds later, he said, "God bless America," and the ovation went on and on and on.

The *Washington Post* spoke for the conventional wisdom: "The Cloud in '64 Goldwater Speech"—*"Extremism in defense of liberty is no vice! Moderation in pursuit of justice is no virtue!"*—"Yields to a Rainbow in '80."

Dick Wirthlin took out his calipers. Before the convention, he had asked voters whether they could state "something bad, from their personal point of view" that would result from a President Reagan, a measure he predicted would be "key to the election"; 85 percent could. During the convention, nearly a fifth of America forgot those fears: now only 67 percent could name "something bad"—compared to 66 percent for Carter, up from 45 percent in June. The Harris Poll gave Reagan a 61–33 lead, the second-largest campaign-opening jump start in history. Before the convention, the Reagan-Carter matchup had been 51–44. Even though, Robert Teeter reported, reproducing his famous finding from 1977, the number of voters who called themselves "Republican" was still below 20 percent.

There was some grumbling among Republicans concerning the choice of running mate. It soon abated: Bush had given his commitment to the platform, Jerry Falwell said, sounding like a political boss promising discipline from his machine, "and if he meant that and will practice it, he'll have no problem from our people."

THERE IS A SAYING: CONSERVATIVES SEEK CONVERTS, LIBERALS SEEK HERetics. And: Democrats fall in love; Republicans fall in line. Of course, who falls in love can fall out of love. And presently, the man Democrats had fallen in love with in 1976—the president who was still not quite the Democratic Party's presumptive presidential nominee—was now seen by many of them as a heretic. Senator Kennedy, accepting an endorsement in New York from the International Union of Police Associations the day after the Republican convention insisted there was still time before the Democrats' opened on August 11 to pick him. He also said, "Democratic policies have not failed these last four years. They have not been tried."

Six days later, the precise method by which Kennedy intended to snatch victory from the jaws of defeat was revealed. There was a meeting between the two campaigns to head off a divisive fight over the platform. There, Kennedy's side revealed their intention to seek a vote on the first day, when delegates approved procedures for the convention, to revoke "Rule F-3C," which bound delegates to vote for the candidate they had actually been selected in their state's primary or caucus to represent.

Kennedy spent the next weeks calling delegates to get them to accede to this "open convention" idea. He surely reminded them of Carter's 22 percent approval rating in a recent Harris Poll. He might also have pointed out that if they agreed to become one of the three hundred delegates that it would take to peel off from Carter if they were to win on F-3C, they needn't exercise their newfound freedom by nominating *him*.

There had by then emerged an exploratory committee for Senator Scoop Jackson, led by Hubert Humphrey's 1972 national finance chair (Kennedy promptly announced he was putting the neocon standard bearer on his list of potential running mates). The Harris Poll surveyed the possibility of Carter's new secretary of state, Edmund Muskie. (He beat Reagan by a margin of 51–44. He also hadn't *quite* given a Sherman Statement.) Even Walter Mondale's name was being floated—much to the vice president's chagrin.

The leader of the open convention movement in Congress claimed, "My phone has not stopping ringing with Democrats calling from all over the US, elected officials, non-elected officials, saying, 'Let's do it. Let's open up this process . . . let's turn this thing around. Let's beat Reagan!' " In New York, both Governor Carey and Mayor Koch announced that they supported the idea; then Senate Majority Leader Byrd. But ABC News kept an ongoing tally: even though Harris found 58 percent of Democrats and independents nationwide wanted someone other than Carter as the Democratic nominee, they couldn't find a single delegate who'd say on the record that they intended to vote down Rule F3-C.

ON AUGUST 1 CARTER CALLED HIS CONVENTION DELEGATES TO THE WHITE House East Room and fumed, "It's almost incomprehensible how a brokered, horse-traded, smoke-filled room convention could be labeled 'open,' and a decision made by twenty million Democrats in the open primaries and the open caucuses could be called 'closed.' " But another series of political setbacks for Carter was strengthening the argument for anyone but Carter day by day.

At his next press conference, all the reporters wanted to talk about was Billygate. The American Agriculture Movement threatened to roll a Tractorcade up to Madison Square Garden to protest agriculture policies they claimed would lead to a depression. Two nights of race riots broke out in Orlando. And at an army base in Indiantown Gap, Pennsylvania, hundreds of Cuban refugees reacted to the violent arrest of a pregnant woman, and the 105-degree heat, by breaking windows, throwing garbage can lids like Frisbees, and taking over a camp building.

They represented the *Marielistas'* most desperate, dwindling remnant—those who couldn't find sponsors in the U.S. The rioters were dwarfed by camp residents who signed a petition denouncing them; the ringleaders had all been arrested; fifteen hundred riot-equipped MPs and National Guardsmen were now patrolling the perimeter of the camp. All the same, the panic of local residents did not abate. A member of the township board of supervisors reported, "I'm telling people, 'If you see them on your property, shoot them.'" The full board came within a hairsbreadth of authorizing vigilante patrols to do so on sight. But the township's part-time prosecutor refused to press charges against the rioters, noting that his court didn't go into session until November, and that by October 15 the Cubans scattered at bases around the country were scheduled to be consolidated at Fort Chaffee. Which was another source of Jimmy Carter's political ordeal. Bill Clinton swore up and down that Carter had promised they wouldn't be relocated there, then double-crossed him. And Arkansas, like Pennsylvania, was a key swing state.

Iranian students were arrested during violent clashes between pro- and anti-Khomeini protesters in Washington, D.C., and Manhattan. Some were jailed in upstate Otisville, New York, after refusing to give their names to arresting officers. Tehran described the arrests as "barbaric," engendering fears that the American hostages might face retaliation. Then, in Otisville, Iranian prisoners were reportedly beaten. That inspired solidarity marches from Iranians, which spurred so much vigilante violence that more than a hundred Iranians had to hide out in a New York City mosque like cornered rats. The State Department suspected that the entire fiasco had been cooked up from Tehran to distract from the fallout of a failed coup attempt by Iranian exiles, a frenzy of executions, purges, and street processions having failed to restore the revolutionary government's stability—and now the fear was that the Ayatollah might order some sort of violent action against the incarcerated "American spies" to shore it up.

The *drip drip drip* of Billy Carter news became a deluge. An infamous convicted securities fraudster always referred to in the papers as "fugitive financier Robert Vesco," who had secretly funneled $200,000 to Richard Nixon's reelection committee then fled the country when bribery failed to win him exoneration, was being mentioned in connection with the money Libya had loaned to the president's brother. Billy also reportedly told investigators he had received State Department briefings useful to Libya "from Jimmy," and said of an official who said he wasn't being truthful in Justice Department interviews, "Lisker is full of shit."

A Senate panel announced that they would begin Billygate hearings six days after the Democratic convention. This was a crushing political blow even if the president were absolved of any wrongdoing. For wasn't the shimmering implied promise that elected Jimmy Carter in 1976 that under his presidency, America could *transcend* the sordid corruption of the Nixon years? Instead, scandals kept on erupting like Mount Saint Helens. On August 9, a jury at the Manhattan federal courthouse watched on videotape as Abscam defendant Michael Myers, a former longshoreman elected to Congress from Philadelphia when he was only thirty-three—a onetime Democratic bright light—told the FBI's undercover sheik, "I'm going to tell you something real simple and short: money talks in this business"—he meant politics—"and B.S. walks." Then he walked away with an envelope containing $50,000 in cash. On August 10, *Time* magazine reported that Jeff Carter, the president's twenty-seven-year-old son, was a 50 percent partner in a consulting firm that had been paid $200,000 by the corrupt, violent dictator of the Philippines.

Then, it was August 11—time for the Democratic convention to begin.

THE HOST CITY LINED THE HIGHWAYS FROM THE AIRPORTS WITH GERANIUMS— Potemkin-village illusions, just like in Detroit.

The social scene was certainly better. A committee of eighty volunteers, recruited from the glitterati to host delegations, competed to one-up one another. Songwriter David Rose bet he could offer more sumptuous hospitality for his state than *Sesame Street* producer Christopher Cerf could offer his, with a date with *The Muppet Show*'s Miss Piggy going to the winner. Alaska's host served two hundred pounds of seafood, mounds of fresh produce and cheese. ("They tell me they don't have fruit and they don't have tomatoes and they never get any decent cheese.") The delegates from North and South Dakota partied at the Dakota, where John Lennon and Yoko Ono lived. Donald Trump—whose Grand Hyatt opened in time to house delegates, though his promised "most spectacular building ever built" on Fifth Avenue was so badly beyond schedule that two hundred undocumented Polish immigrants worked demolition in twelve-hour shifts without gloves, hard hats, or masks—cohosted the Texas delegation with the founder of *Ms.* magazine, Elizabeth Forsling Harris. They treated their guests to a "hoedown" in Greenwich Village's Lone Star Cafe. But New York was not necessarily *safer*, the Midtown boom having skipped the area around the Garden: three thousand police from the city's austerity-wracked force were detailed there, advising egress from the Seventh Avenue exits on its east side rather than risk contact with all the derelicts, street workers, bag ladies, pickpockets, and degenerates who congregated on Eighth. Nor friendlier: "the cabbies were so much fun in '76, wearing Jimmy Carter masks and all that," a Texan reported. "Now they give you lectures on how great Ronald Reagan is."

Attendees gossiped about a blockbuster new revelation: Ronald Reagan was an astrology enthusiast. The candidate himself had recently told an interviewer, "80 percent of the people in New York's Hall of Fame are Aquarians"—like himself. (He told the same interviewer, "The greatest leaders in history are remembered more for what they said than for what they did. When you think of Lincoln, how many people know what decisions he made here or there? But the Gettysburg Address . . .") His friend Jeane Dixon claimed that she was an informal Reagan advisor. Southern Californians in the know whispered about the monthly celebrity parties Reagan hosted where the *Los Angeles Times* astrology columnist Carroll Righter held court; he once introduced him with "I'd never even think of making an important decision without calling Carroll first." The *Chicago Tribune*'s seer, Joyce Jillson, said Reagan aides paid her $1,200 to work up charts on eight vice-presidential prospects (Bush had a "tremendously lucky chart for election day"); then, in response to Lyn Nofziger's denial that Reagan had anything to do with such nonsense, she said that he had held his 1967 gubernatorial inauguration at midnight because that was when the stars best aligned.

Yet more evidence that this Hollywood refugee would be easy to whip.

Hollywood. Carter's image-makers studied the Republicans on how to craft an effective show. They noticed that the networks never trained on the podium for more than eight minutes before cutting away to reporters interviewing famous people on the floor. So they strewed administration luminaries throughout the arena to distract the cameras from all the glamorous Kennedy relatives and celebrity friends. During the first session, the interviews were mostly concerned with the "open convention" debate; as in Detroit, the networks were desperate to stir up drama—even though the Kennedy camp's most optimistic predictions suggested they had no chance of success.

"Governor Clinton, you are going to vote with President Carter on the adoption of F3-C, but you're not happy about it, are you?"

"Well, I wish it hadn't come to this. . . . But I still believe after it's over that we'll get back together and be able to win."

—cut to Illinois delegation: *"Now we have heard reports that there will be slippage, as many as twenty to twenty-five votes away from the Carter position on the rule!"*

Each side got a half hour to make their case. The famous litigator Edward Bennett Williams and Congresswoman Maxine Waters of Los Angeles spoke for Kennedy: he said that Carter was asking delegates "to vote themselves into bondage"; she said, referring to the hundreds of White House operatives reported to be whipping delegates, "I cannot support a rule which tells me that I am not permitted to answer to the people who elected me in Watts but only to the staff aides of a candidate in Washington." Mayor Maynard Jackson of Atlanta, speaking for Carter, intoned soulfully that "we have marched on Selma, Alabama, to get the right to vote. Let us now not violate the sanctity of that ballot. Nineteen million voters participated in our—*our!*—process, in reliance on our promise that we would respect their choice. Let's keep our word to America right there."

Kennedy people and Carter people, decrying with equivalent passion the betrayals of truth, justice, and the Democratic Party way being practiced by mountebanks on the other side: not exactly an augury of party unity.

The vote to change the rule fell 546 delegates short. Kennedy retreated to his headquarters at the Waldorf Astoria. He conferred with family and staff. Then he called the president, who was fishing at Camp David, to concede defeat.

But only in the presidential race.

He made his way to a ballroom, his wife (who for once appeared happy to be there) and a floppy-haired son by his side. The waiting crowd chanted *"We want Ted!"* He said in a simpering tone, "Well, I'm deeply gratified by the support I received in the rules fight tonight, but not *quite* as gratified as President Carter. Huh?" Then, to cries of *"No! No! No!"* he announced, "My name will not be placed into nomination. But the efforts for Democratic principles must and will continue."

He told his staff not to make any further compromises on platform language until he got his speech the next night into the convention record. His war would continue, by other means.

GEORGE MCGOVERN HAD ALSO TESTIFIED FOR KENNEDY. HIS REMARKS IN-cluded a joke about his own nominating convention, when the Democrats' fetish for open debate had caused him to deliver his acceptance speech at three o'clock in the morning: "Finally at a Democratic convention I have gotten on in prime time!" But 1980 wasn't much better than 1972. The first two days adjourned around midnight. The Wednesday session that nominated Jimmy Carter ran until 12:56 a.m.

The convention directors had been afraid that if Kennedy's minority caucus used every tool at its disposal to demand debates and roll call votes for its proposals, the convention would run at least seventy-nine hours— a full week. It had taken round after round of discussions just to limit floor debates to seventeen hours. Even then, just in case, credentials were printed for a fifth day, should they be required.

It was a political war of position, both sides pressing for advantages to potentially embarrass the other on live TV. In the preliminary negotia-tions, the bone of contention was which of the many left-leaning *minority* planks that Kennedy wished to replace Carter's more right-leaning *major-ity* planks would be debated on the convention floor, with speeches from both sides, followed by roll call votes—creating a noisy public record of how much support each side had on each issue. Or, alternately, one side could concede a plank to the other, with a voice vote—*aye* or *nay*—cer-tifying a predetermined outcome, skipping a floor fight. The more, and more intense, the floor fights, the more divided the party. It was just such a floor fight, over whether the Democratic Party should call for an end to the Vietnam War, that had led to literal violence in the convention hall, and then a general election defeat, in 1968.

At the arena, the war footing was symbolized by the six heavily se-cured trailers the Carter side parked outside in a tight circle like wagons on the Oregon Trail, and Kennedy's eighteen-hundred-square-foot command post inside. Each operation ran with military discipline, beaming instantaneous, secure communication to their delegates—who sometimes sat next to each other within states—on how to vote, when to pass, whether to abstain, and what to say. Carter had fourteen roving floor leaders and ten regional leaders commanding 200 floor whips, who wore shiny green vests. Kennedy's side had 120 floor whips. They wore blue baseball hats—sartorial signifiers in an intraparty civil war.

One of the planks the two sides had agreed to pass through voice vote was Kennedy's minority report for the platform to oppose reductions in the funding of any program whose purpose "is to serve the basic human needs of the most needy"—quite the Carter concession: it appeared to put the Democratic Party officially on the record against the impassioned budget-slashing speech that Carter had delivered in the White House East Room just five months earlier. The first floor fight was over Kennedy's national health insurance plan—for Carter, a concession too far.

A Kennedy witness spoke of nearly dying in a head-on collision with a drunk driver, the $20,000 debt she was in fourteen years and four operations later, even though she had thought she had *good* health insurance: "I can't tell you what it's like to be a mother and watch your children grow and not be able to hold them the way a mother wants to," she said tearfully. A Carter witness from the National Council of Senior Citizens reminded the convention that "a fifty-three-year-old horse-opera actor named Ronald Reagan" had campaigned against Medicare as "socialized medicine," and that if John F. Kennedy had followed Edward M. Kennedy's advice and tried for full nationalized healthcare then, instead of trying first for coverage for the elderly, Ronald Reagan's side would have won—and millions of his organization's constituents would be dead.

Vote for the Carter plank, the audience watching at home could conclude, and you were for keeping mothers from holding their children. Vote for Kennedy, and you were kicking Grandma out of the hospital.

The Carter whips went to work. The vote went against Kennedy, 1,573 to 1,349.

It went on like that for two straight days. Speaking for Kennedy's plank that legislation "to guarantee a job for every American who is able to work" must be the "single greatest domestic priority," to "take precedence over all other domestic priorities"—for instance, inflation—found Congressman Louis Stokes shouting his incredulity that Jimmy Carter could be so callous: "Why are we *debating* this issue? . . . Never before in our history and our heritage have we established priorities that required the sacrifice of *jobs*!" Carter's side put up Governor Jim Hunt of North Carolina, who noted, "The banner headlines today may be about recession, not inflation, but let us not doubt for one minute what our people are still feeling. Do we want to tell them in this convention that fighting inflation is not important anymore? Do you want to say that to the young couple in your states who cannot buy that home because of high interest rates?"

And one could not help but notice an ugly cleavage that wasn't just ideological. *"Our people"*: Jim Hunt was a White Southerner. Stokes was an African American congressman representing the Cleveland ghetto—and *his* people, for whom mortgage rates were not exactly a paramount worry, were suffering 40 percent unemployment.

Each of these fights ripped scabs from the party's ravaged body. One fight was over a Kennedy minority report to repeal $5.5 billion in tax breaks for the energy industry, which Carter said were imperative to stimulate domestic production to make America energy independent. Right-leaning Democrats from energy-producing states called Kennedy's plank insane. (A Louisiana congressman: *"Mr. Chairman, the minority report would punish our own small American domestic energy production!"*) Liberals from energy-consuming states said the same thing about the other side. (A Chicago union president: *"There are ten million Americans out of work today . . . who literally have to choose between heat for their homes and food for their families. . . . How much would five and a half billion dollars mean to them?"*) Another energy fight was over a key proposal from Carter's 1979 "crisis of confidence" speech: a federal corporation to subsidize the development of synthetic fuels, which Carter, begging the nation to trust him, had called imperative to America's very survival—and which was now up for an up-or-down, Kennedy-versus-Carter vote.

ON MONDAY, THE CARTER SIDE WHIPPED AND WHIPPED, AND WON EACH and every time. The Tuesday session was yet more acrimonious—especially over two planks regarding what Paul Weyrich described as the Democratic Party's Achilles' heel: *sex.*

Feminists had organized to introduce a minority report to refuse party funds and technical assistance to candidates who opposed the Equal Rights Amendment. Their speeches, especially the one from Sonia Johnson, a former Mormon excommunicated from the church for advocating for the ERA, were emotion-drenched, soul-stirring, overwhelming—the sort people told their grandchildren about, about the time they were present when the moral arc of the universe at long last bent toward justice.

But the party establishment despised it. The mayor of Miami testified that "taking reprisals against a fellow Democrat for his or her belief" was an outright travesty. A national committeewoman from Virginia said such a "litmus test" for candidates running in conservative districts would just hand more seats to Republicans.

Jimmy Carter felt the same, pragmatic, way. But the mood of the room was overwhelmingly with the moral arc of the universe.

Speakers on both sides were interrupted by *"ERA! ERA!"* chants. Their passion grew, and grew, and grew—until whips for the National Education Association shocked the assembly and instructed their three-hundred-delegate bloc to vote for the minority report. Carter decided that he had no choice but to let this one go. Word was sent to the session chairman, K. Leroy Irvis, the speaker of the Pennsylvania House of Representatives—a civil rights hero himself, the first African American to lead any state legislature since Reconstruction—to scotch the planned roll call. He called a voice vote and announced the *ayes* had it. It was one of the very few genuine surprises during the four-day convention, an overwhelmingly jubilant moment. In a congratulatory gesture, the chairman gave the floor to Bella Abzug, who loosed one of her trademark foghorn blasts: "Mr. Chairman! In view of this unanimous acclaim, I shall not ask for a roll vote, and I join with you in expressing our great satisfaction that this convention has gone on record as being prepared to take some meaningful action in support of ratification of the Equal Rights Amendment!"

Ah, but it would not be so easy. After some commotion, Irvis clomped his gavel.

"The chair has been advised that the state of Alabama requests a roll call vote."

Alabama's delegation, not incidentally, had been sent to New York by Governor Fob James with instructions to serve as a firewall against the party's liberal turn, to work for planks abolishing the Department of Education, instituting a corporate tax cut, and affirming "strength and respect" as America's foreign policy priority.

Irvis called the required vote to judge whether the required 20 percent threshold for a motion for a roll call had been met. He announced that it hadn't. Conservative Democrats did not agree. They decried a liberal power play. Their bitterness poured yet more fuel on the even nastier fight that came next, over the feminists' *other* minority report—for a plank recognizing "reproductive freedom as a fundamental human right," and ending "restrictions on funding for health services for the poor that deny poor women especially the right to exercise a constitutionally guaranteed right to privacy." A Missouri bloc of pro-lifers, all Carter supporters, had threatened to walk out of the convention if *that* abomination were not given a full debate and a recorded vote. Carter decided, again, he had no choice but to accede.

The debate turned particularly ugly over a clause denouncing sterilization without informed consent, still occasionally practiced against poor minority women, especially in the South and Puerto Rico and on Native

Americans: in 1977, a Cheyenne tribal chief judge visited Geneva to present evidence to the United Nations Convention on Indigenous Rights that perhaps a quarter of Native American women of childbearing age had been sterilized by physicians abusing the federal Family Planning Services and Population Research Act of 1970. Virginia's law authorizing sterilization for those judged "anti-social" and "feebleminded" was still on the books and had just become national news. Early in 1980, a scholar researching the case of Carrie Buck—the plaintiff in the 1924 Supreme Court case in which Justice Oliver Wendell Holmes, upholding Virginia sterilization law, had infamously written, "Three generations of imbeciles is enough"—discovered that Buck's sister was still alive, and had tried for most of her married life to have children, but had also been sterilized without her knowledge because the state had judged her "socially inadequate." The researcher determined that thousands of persons were sterilized in this Virginia program, which remained active all the way up to 1972. Meanwhile, the New York–based feminist group Committee for Abortion Rights and Against Sterilization Abuse had grown concerned that, under the Hyde Amendment, welfare recipients unable to afford abortions might find themselves coerced into government-financed sterilization. So feminists added "involuntary and uniformed sterilization for women and men" as an example of the "government interference in the reproductive decisions of Americans" that the Democratic the plank abjured.

Congressman Roman Pucinski, a Catholic pro-lifer from Chicago, apoplectic, called it a dirty trick, a smear intended to imply that pro-lifers were *pro*–involuntary sterilization. Another speaker for the pro-life side, Congressman Dick Gephardt of Missouri, said the plank itself, by labeling abortion a "fundamental human right," was calculated insult intended to label pro-lifers as *anti*–human rights, too. The pro-choice witnesses were equally impassioned. One, a doctor who had been convicted of manslaughter for ending pregnancies, told gripping stories of women who had become sterile from incompetent abortion procedures before *Roe v. Wade*. Another was a woman from Texas whose best friend became pregnant because she was unable to take oral contraception for medical reasons. Six months from graduating college on a scholarship, and already raising three children, too poor to get an abortion at a clinic, she sought a cheaper, back-alley one. The witness intoned softly, "I held Rosie's hand as she died a most horrible death."

During this debate, pro-life Missourians positioned themselves next to the podium and tried to raise a massive banner with a picture of a darling little girl and reading, "KILL HER NOW, IT'S MURDER—KILL BEFORE BIRTH, IT'S ABORTION." Members of the adjoining California delegation tried to stop them from doing so. Two pro-lifers, one a state senator and the other St. Louis's city clerk, violently tried to wrap the massive banner around one of the Californians. There was a scuffle. A United States congressman named Harold Volkmer, best known for his opposition to gun control, knocked a Californian to the floor.

The roll call vote went on. The pro-choicers won, 2,005 to 956.3. And there still was another divisive debate to come that day.

IT CONCERNED A KENNEDY MINORITY REPORT FOR A PLANK SPECIFYING $12 billion in "job-creating spending," committing the party to renounce any government policy that would increase unemployment (which pretty much covered Carter's entire anti-inflation program), and a program of wage and price controls (which Carter considered lunacy). A pollster discovered that 80 percent of delegates wanted it to pass. Jimmy Carter was desperate for it not to. This, he decided, was where he would make his stand.

So did Ted Kennedy.

One Kennedy witness's presence was a particularly stinging rebuke to the president: civil rights leader Julian Bond of Atlanta, one of his first prominent black supporters. He called Carter's opposition a "cowardly and callous retreat from the principles of this party."

But that was nothing compared to the witness everyone was waiting for. The previous day, a mere rumor that he was approaching the convention hall was enough to bring all other chatter to a standstill. Now Ted Kennedy approached the podium. But he couldn't speak for a good twenty minutes. The tumultuous reception just wouldn't die. When it did, Kennedy didn't say anything about the plank. He delivered the equivalent of an acceptance speech. People still talked about it decades later as one of the greatest addresses ever delivered at a national party convention.

One part was exactly what you might have expected if Kennedy were accepting the Democratic nomination—flaying the hide off of the Republican nominee:

"We must not permit the Republicans to seize and run on the slogans of prosperity! We heard the orators at their convention all trying to talk like Democrats!" Then he repurposed the old preacher's saw about the Devil: all that the other party's convention proved was that "*even Republican nominees* can quote *Franklin Roosevelt* to their own purpose."

The crowd once more went wild.

"The same Republicans who are talking about the crisis of unemployment have nominated a man who once said, and I quote, 'Unemployment insurance is a prepaid vacation plan for freeloaders.' *And that nominee is no friend of labor!*

"The same Republicans who are talking about the problems of the inner cities have nominated a man who said, and I quote, 'I have included in my morning and evening prayers every day the prayer that the Federal Government not bail out New York.' *And that nominee is no friend of this city and our great urban centers across this nation!*

"The same Republicans who are talking about security for the elderly have nominated a man who said just four years ago that 'Participation in social security should be made voluntary.' *And that nominee is no friend of the senior citizens of this nation!*

"The same Republicans who are talking about preserving the environment have nominated a man who last year made the preposterous statement, and I quote, 'Eighty percent of our air pollution comes from plants and trees.' *And that nominee is no friend of the environment!*

"And the same Republicans who are invoking Franklin Roosevelt have nominated a man who said in 1976, and these are his exact words, 'Fascism was really the basis of the New Deal.' *And that nominee whose name is Ronald Reagan has no right to quote Franklin Delano Roosevelt!*"

That part, however, came seven and a half minutes after Kennedy began. The rest of the speech was the most effective oration delivered against the policies of Jimmy Carter by any candidate during the 1980 campaign—advocating, one by one, every platform plank that the Carter-whipped convention delegates just defeated.

"Let us pledge that we will never misuse unemployment, high interest rates, and human misery as false weapons against inflation. . . .

"Let us pledge that employment will be the first priority of our economic policy. . . .

"The poor may be out of political fashion, but they are not without human needs. . . .

"We must meet the pressures of the present by invoking the full power of government to master increasing prices. . . .

"We can be proud that our party stands for investment in safe energy, instead of a nuclear future that may threaten the future itself. . . .

"We are the Party of the New Freedom, the New Deal, and the New Frontier. We have always been the Party of hope. So this year let us offer new hope, new hope to an America uncertain about the present, but unsurpassed in its potential for the future. . . .

"*For all those whose cares have been our concern, the work goes on, the cause endures, the hope still lives, and the dream shall never die!*"

There followed an astounding thirty-eight-minute ovation—five minutes longer than the speech itself, which had been already interrupted for cheers forty-four times.

As the acclaim for the rival he thought he had vanquished rose to a frenzy, President Carter became terrified he was on the verge of a runaway convention. And vague language on priorities was one thing. A blunt commitment to wage and price controls was another. And so, during those thirty-eight minutes of communal ecstasy, Carter's men initiated furious negotiations with Kennedy's. "When the chants of 'We Want Kennedy' finally subsided," UPI reported, there was agreement: Carter would yield on the jobs program if Kennedy would on price controls. Chairman Tip O'Neill called the question; whips whipped; the revision was shouted through in a voice vote. Thus did Jimmy Carter agree to run for reelection on a platform that asked for $12 billion in new *spending*, which he believed to be at direct cross-purposes with his fundamental economic goal—balancing the budget to fight inflation—which he had argued for as a national imperative in a speech six months earlier that announced $13 billion in new *cuts*. He had no choice, reflected DNC Chairman John White. "The mood of the house—well, it's Kennedy's night."

AND THERE WAS YET ANOTHER DAY OF PLATFORM ACRIMONY TO COME.

On Wednesday morning, conventioneers were talking about the strike of thousands of Polish workers at the Lenin Shipyards in the Polish city of Gdansk, and the news that the democratic socialist African American congressman from Berkeley, Ron Dellums, was abandoning his symbolic run for the nomination, and that civil rights leaders had called off a planned walkout by black delegates—a quarter of the total—during the president's acceptance speech. That left only one planned walkout, by the Machinists Union. Because, one of their leaders said, "Jimmy Carter walked out on us shortly after he was inaugurated."

It was the eighty-second birthday of the president's mother. ("He's crazy," Miz Lillian told rapt reporters, noting that her son had gotten up at 6 a.m. for a jog. "I feel so sorry for the Secret Service men.") In other Carter family news, the Senate subcommittee investigating Billy Carter was revealed to have obtained documents, photographs, and hours of taped conversations suggesting that Robert Vesco was willing to spend $11 million on a project to bribe or blackmail Carter administration officials on behalf of Libya's attempts to obtain American C-130 cargo planes. A new poll said that almost three-quarters of the nation Reagan had just called the most generous on earth regretted welcoming Cuban refugees. The news also took note of the fifteenth anniversary of the Watts riot. One veteran Los Angeles anti-poverty activist reflected, "The job problem is greater in the black community than it has been since the Civil War." And that John Anderson, recently returned from a trip to Israel, was stalking New York City seeking support from disillusioned Kennedy fans.

It was also reported that Ted Kennedy was still mulling over whether to appear on the platform with Jimmy Carter after his acceptance speech:

unless Carter explicitly promised not to "tear out" the just-passed Kennedy platform planks, Kennedy political director Paul Kirk said, "it might be tough."

Willie Nelson stepped to the Madison Square Garden dais in his trademark T-shirt, long braid, and bandana to sing the National Anthem. He messed up the lyrics: no "rockets' red glare," or "bombs bursting in air." The bombs came from the podium instead: a perilous fight indeed.

Carter had proposed a 27 percent increase in military spending by the end of his second term. Meanwhile, the *Washington Post* and the *New York Times* were reporting on a leaked top-secret new nuclear strategy document, Presidential Directive Number 59, said to "give priority to attacking military targets in the Soviet Union rather than destroying cities and industrial complexes," placing "less emphasis on all-out retaliation against Soviet cities in the event of a Russian attack"—which in the paradoxical logic of nuclear warfare appeared to some media commentators to suggest the possibility that Carter was making atomic warfare more likely, by making it easier to launch an attack that pulled up shy of Armageddon.

Like the "Soviet brigade in Cuba" story, however, media discussion was confused: it reported as new something that was old, with little or no understanding that the "limited" options still entailed millions of projected deaths. But it *also* came in the context of rumors that Carter might take the opportunity of his acceptance speech to unveil plans to develop a new strategic bomber—which reports said would be called the "Stealth" in reference to its ability to hide from enemy radar—to shore up his right flank for the coming campaign. Henry Kissinger was accusing the White House of leaking PD-59 itself, for the very same reason. All this maximized liberal suspicions that Carter intended to out-Reagan Reagan in the fall—pouring gasoline on two *more* platform fights: one over a Kennedy plank to cancel the MX missile system, and another calling for a nuclear freeze.

And these fights Carter was even more determined to win than the others.

Liberals hoisted signs reading things like "BAN THE X-RATED MISSILE" and "MX: DISASTER ON WHEELS." Carter's witnesses, Secretary of Defense Harold Brown and General George M. Seignious, spoke in what Frank Church had once decried as "the abstract mumbo jumbo of the nuclear priesthood," the "great moral blindness of our time": they claimed these massive new weapons systems would "reduce the risk" of "the Soviets' deployment of 6,000 intercontinental missile warheads capable of destroying our fixed Minutemen missiles in their silos" and that "if we abandon our land-based missiles . . . we would invite the Soviets to concentrate their resources on defeating our missile submarines and this could eventually threaten this vital backbone of our nuclear deterrent."

Then, in another humiliation for Carter, one of the *Kennedy* witnesses was Carter's own former arms negotiator, Paul Warnke, who had retired after the signing of SALT II. Warnke said all this was nonsense, an effort to divert "billions upon billions of dollars" from necessary priorities in support of the "delusion that we can have a limited little nuclear war in which the good guys win."

Delegates were ushered in clumps into a Carter trailer for lectures from Secretary Brown. They had already all received copies of a handwritten letter from Carter on presidential stationery imploring Democrats to "demonstrate to our nation and to the world that we are committed to defending our country" by voting against the Kennedy defense planks. Union delegates received one imploring the same from the leaders of the AFL-CIO. The question was called. Carter won by about the same margin as the F3-C fight on Monday. Carter had won the battle to take a Democratic Party into the fall election as hawks.

But he had already lost the political war. Shortly afterward, eighty members of an elite organization of Democrats, formed after George McGovern's loss made them despair of their party's retreat from the Cold War, gathered at a poolside dinner buffet at the Washington home of Max Kampelman, the associate of the late Hubert Humphrey that the Reaganites had been assiduously recruiting.

Senator Moynihan took the floor: "The question is, should CDM endorse the Democratic nominee this year?"—a rather startling question for an organization called the Coalition for a Democratic Majority. "Just out of curiosity: a show of hands. How many in this room are thinking of voting for Ronald Reagan?"

One person raised his hand, then three, then a dozen—then, after some hesitation, almost everyone.

"My, my," said the senator who had just figuratively held his nose at the podium in Madison Square Garden and endorsed Carter's foreign policy performance after months spent savaging it. He waggled his chin. "I am surprised—and yet, not surprised." He scanned his audience for their reaction. Most of them were surprised, too.

AFTER THE PRESIDENT OF THE UNITED STATES WAS OFFICIALLY RENOMInated by his party by a margin of 2,129 to 1,465, Tip O'Neill read a four-sentence statement from Ted Kennedy congratulating him, promising to work for his victory. He mustered all the sincerity he could manage: "And so, united we stand."

The next afternoon, the day of his acceptance speech, President Carter told a joke at a luncheon about Ronald Reagan: "If a catastrophe should befall our country" and Reagan should represent the U.S. at the next G7 meeting, "people will have to go around with labels on their chests saying, 'Hello, my name is Helmut Schmidt. I'm from Germany.'"

Outside, police clashed with thirty-odd members of the Communist Workers Party, who sprayed cops with Mace. Elsewhere, speechwriter Hendrik Hertzberg made last-minute revisions on the president's speech, suturing its mismatched parts together in work he compared to an emergency room trauma surgeon's after a gas main explosion.

The delegates watched a biographical film that made note of the ridicule even Abraham Lincoln suffered: "No president has been entirely beloved in his own time. Putting them down is one of the favorite pastimes in American politics."

At 9:45, as Carter was about to begin, the hall was five thousand six hundred over capacity—so police closed the doors, shutting out many dignitaries and delegates—because to assure a capacity crowd convention managers had let in thousands of people without the proper credentials.

The president took the podium. There were no welcoming chants. And the most memorable parts of what followed were the things that went wrong.

He looked nervous, even scared. It turned out that the teleprompter blinked out, so his opening sentences were improvised. When he launched into a determinately spirited *"And we're going to beat the Republicans in November!"* a string of firecrackers went off next to the platform, courtesy of another Communist Workers Party member who had managed to sneak onto the floor. Carter grew more rattled. His eyes darted about as he called the roll of Democratic heroes past, his trademark grin barely evident. He finally began gathering a bit of steam, then called out "a great man who should have been president, who would have been one of the greatest presidents in history—Hubert! Horatio! Hornblower!"

A short pause. He tried a faux-confident fist-slash; then, twice as loud as before—

"Humphrey!!!"

—which made the blunder sound worse.

He called out Senator Kennedy's name—and got his most spirited ovation so far. He looked bereft pretty much the whole time after that.

Television reaction shots kept landing on stone-faced audience members—including, at one point, his own mother. Seventeen minutes in, a news camera caught a delegate yawning; twenty-six seconds later, a sleeping kid. You could call that media bias—except that once, when the cameras trained in on two *appreciative* audience members—Johnny and June Carter Cash—the frame also happened to capture a downcast woman pressing her palms to her chin like she was recalling a root canal. Four minutes later, the president's reference to draft registration was angrily booed. The contrast to Kennedy was unmistakable. When he'd spoken, people looked downright awed.

The ordeal concluded thirty soporific minutes later, Carter's face shiny with Nixonian sweat. The cameras trained skyward—and the traditional boxcar-sized bundles of balloons refused to release, until one bundle finally dribbled out a desultory couple of dozen. All three network anchors made a point of calling attention to the metaphor.

The worst part came next. Carter held his new baby granddaughter, surrounded by family, while party grandees started filling the stage—except someone conspicuous was missing.

Kennedy watched the speech on TV in his hotel. Then he got caught up in traffic. He belatedly took the stage, and dignitaries immediately began peeling off from Carter and gravitating toward him. "It looks a little bit backwards," an anchorman said. "It's almost as though the man who lost is waiting on the platform for the man who won!" his partner replied.

Carter passed Kennedy with his back to him. Finally, the two men were pushed together. Kennedy offered a desultory handshake. Amy Carter looked at Kennedy like he was a ghoul. The crowd started chanting: *"We want Teddy! We want Teddy!"* Rosalynn Carter leaned valiantly into a microphone, failing to raise a "We want Jimmy!"

Walter Mondale subsequently told a reporter, his tone unconvincing, "It was very comfortable. It was not difficult for anyone. Everything went fine." The first post-convention Gallup Poll came in. Carter received a break: with John Anderson at 14 percent, Carter was within a single point of Reagan, 38-39. Maybe people appreciated how the Democrats aired their differences in public. Or maybe it was because the Reagan campaign was off to a such a ghastly start.

CHAPTER 36

"Meanness"

IN JUNE, DICK WIRTHLIN COMPLETED AN UNPRECEDENTEDLY DETAILED 176-page week-by-week plan for selling Ronald Reagan to the nation. It deployed state-of-the-art computer modeling, digesting data from surveys taken before and after the primaries, historical voting patterns, and financial analysis, to set forth various conditions under which the required 270 electoral votes could be achieved. Called the "Black Book," in December of 1980 it won Wirthlin *Advertising Age* magazine's coveted prize for Adman of the Year.

The models were, in the social science term of art, "dynamic." In 1970, polling for Reagan's gubernatorial reelection campaign, Wirthlin had invented something called a "tracking poll," in which the same question was asked of the public again and again; in a quantum advance for *this* campaign, tracking poll results could be iteratively fed back into this statistical matrix on an almost daily basis, pinpointing the precise direction and intensity of public attitudes as they *changed*, down to the county level. They could help determine which formulations for Reagan and his surrogates to utter; which ads hit hardest and which fell flat; which locales demanded additional surrogate or candidate visits, or "media buys"; which tactics to repeat and which to discard.

A new twenty-four-hour cable news station, CNN, had just begun broadcasting; staffers monitored it every minute for possibly relevant developments. This was to help inform another pioneering Wirthlin innovation: "simulation modeling"—the scientific study of *what-ifs*. Like, *What if Carter managed to free the hostages?* What were Reagan's potential routes to political recovery?

Their 23,000-square-foot headquarters in an Arlington office building formerly occupied by John Connally's campaign was a hive of activity in which nothing was left to chance. No voter subgroup, no issue position, no dollar spent, no mile traveled, no campaign stop's pros and cons went unaccounted for. Naturally the choice of where to launch the campaign received particularly intense consideration. They chose for his first big speech after the convention an August 2 gathering of the National Urban

League, the venerable African American civil rights organization. "We weren't expecting to pick up any black votes in New York," an advisor later noted. "We just wanted to show moderates and liberals that Reagan wasn't anti-black." The target audience, Wirthlin explained, was suburban whites.

But what the campaign said was a scheduling problem arose, and the Urban League appearance was postponed to the next day—the sort of development, in a crowded campaign, that was neither particularly unusual nor consequential. Except that this made his *first* campaign stop what was originally supposed to be his second, and Reagan ended up actually opening his campaign marveling, wide-eyed, to a T-shirted crowd of thousands standing under a hot Southern sun, "I think you all know without me telling you that Nancy and I have never seen anything like this—because there isn't any place like this anywhere on earth! . . . How did you ever accomplish this without a federal program?" The Mississippi crowd roared in appreciation. And it was true. There *was* nothing like the Neshoba County Fair.

Every July, farm families from across the middle of the state moved into elaborate on-site two-story cabins for a week, enjoying card games, bull sessions, and romancing on the front porch and balcony all night long, after spending long days enjoying the midway, the livestock displays, country and gospel music, mule races, beauty contests, pie-eating contests—and the only legal horse racing in the state.

White families, that is. Blacks only participated as employees.

In the 1950s and '60s, the fair was the place where state and local politicians competed to outdo each other with nasty imprecations at the evil federal government and civil rights organizations like the Student Nonviolent Coordinating Committee and the NAACP—an acronym that Paul Johnson said in his successful run for governor in 1963 stood for "Niggers, Apes, Alligators, Coons and Possums." In 1964, the fair opened as planned on August 8 even though six days earlier, the bodies of three SNCC voter-registration workers were discovered buried in an earthen dam a few miles away. They had been assassinated by the Ku Klux Klan, with the assistance of the local sheriff, Lawrence Rainey.

And now Ronald Reagan was raising the curtain on his campaign there. Which raised more than a few eyebrows.

White supremacist organizations like the KKK had been making increasingly frequent appearances in the news in recent years. In 1977, a small Klan unit led by Grand Wizard David Duke received a great deal of publicity for patrolling the Mexican border on horseback with weapons in an effort to halt border crossings, setting "punji traps," camouflaged pits filled with sharpened sticks, for migrants to fall into, a technique borrowed from the Viet Cong. In 1978, six thousand robed Klansmen rallied in Morgan County, Alabama, after a nineteen-year-old black man with an IQ of thirty-nine was charged with raping three white women; the next year, during his trial, ten thousand rallied, and a gunfight broke out between Klansmen and black demonstrators. That November, Communists in Greensboro, North Carolina, were preparing with residents of a housing project for an anti-Klan march when a caravan of Klansmen and Nazis rolled up, gathered shotguns and rifles out of the trunk of a blue Ford Fairlane, and began firing. Eighty seconds later, five were dead. The women who disrupted Jimmy Carter's acceptance speech were widows of two of the victims.

In April of 1980, robed Klansmen had brazenly fired shots from their car while cruising down the main thoroughfare in Chattanooga's black neighborhood; a week later, Klansmen marched through downtown Kokomo, Indiana. In May, an avowed Nazi got 43 percent of the vote in the Republican primary for North Carolina attorney general, winning forty-five of 100 counties, coming only seventy-five votes from taking the county encompassing Winston-Salem. ("There are many closet Nazis in the Republican Party. Most conservatives are closet Nazis," he said. "If you scratch a conservative, you'll find a Nazi underneath, just as if you scratch a liberal, you'll find a Communist.") That was during the period in which white sheets became a veritable fixture at demonstrations in Arkansas against the Mariel boatlift. A month later, in California, Klansman Tom Metzger won the congressional nomination from the San Diego area as a Democrat. He promised to "get into Congress and have a fistfight every day."

Then, the head of the Urban League, Vernon Jordan, was shot while riding in a car with a white woman (it was the first story broadcast by CNN). African Americans suspected a racial motive, correctly: it turned out the shooter was a white supremacist who had shot several other interracial couples, firebombed one synagogue and shot at the members of another, and attempted to assassinate pornographer Larry Flynt because his magazine *Hustler* depicted interracial sex. Klan membership was believed to have gone from 6,500 to 10,500 in the previous five years. The openly racist magazine the *Spotlight*, published by a Holocaust denier named Willis Carto, had three hundred thousand paid subscribers, many times more than *Human Events* or *National Review*. Gallup found that 13 percent of Americans (and 20 percent of Southern whites) approved of the KKK; in 1965, it was 7 percent. The sort of open racists that the civil rights revolution had supposedly vanquished now seemed almost ubiquitous—

and they were history conscious: in Winston-Salem, North Carolina, the Federated Knights of the Ku Klux Klan even curated an exhibition of nineteenth-century Klan artifacts: "our version of 'Roots,' " a leader said.

And here was Ronald Reagan, ducking in on what you might call one of their sacred sites. What was his campaign thinking?

It was part of a strategy to signal that Republicans intended to seriously contest the South for the first time in over a century. Jimmy Carter's Atlanta was considered first, until the Mississippi Republican Party suggested a rural audience would be more receptive. That suited Wirthlin's plan just fine: a county fair checked off two of the Black Book's four most important target groups: Southern white Protestants and rural voters (the other two, which overlapped, were blue-collar workers in industrial areas and urban "white ethnics").

Reagan would be the first presidential nominee ever to address the fair. Previously, it would have been a waste of time: for most of U.S. history it was taken for granted that Mississippi went to the Democrats. This year, however, Mississippi seemed up for grabs.

Reagan was fetched at the airport in Meridian by his state chairman, Congressman Trent Lott. Lott had been president of the fraternity that stockpiled a cache of weapons used to riot against the federal marshals protecting a black student seeking to enter the University of Mississippi in 1962. Later, a defensive state party official insisted it was Lott—and certainly not *them*—who suggested that if Reagan really wanted to win this crowd over, he need only fold a certain two-word phrase into his speech: *states' rights.*

These were the most reliable code words Southern demagogues could deploy to activate their audiences' most feral rage against African American civil rights. Ronald Reagan, whose unshakable belief in his own purity of motivation was his defining trait, surely got to immediate work persuading himself that in uttering them, he was referring to *all* federal intrusion into local affairs, from the Occupational Safety and Health Administration to the Department of Ed—the same thing he *always* excoriated. He seemed anxious about taking the suggestion all the same. For, as Reagan speeches went, this was a strange one. He took less than ten minutes, an unusually large portion of that spent buttering up his audience: praising the fair, praising the state, telling an uplifting story about the time he watched the Ole Miss football team upset Tennessee while sitting next to their governor, telling joke after joke after joke (*"Now, I know that people keep telling me that Jimmy Carter's doing his best"*—pause—*"that's our problem!"*): almost as if he was reluctant to get to the point. Halfway in, he finally did. He began reciting his familiar litany of federal government failure, though a little more wobbly than was customary:

"Over the recent years—with the *best of intentions!*—they have created a vast bureaucracy, or bureaucratic structure, bureaus and departments and agencies, to try and solve all the problems and eliminate all the things of human misery that they can. They have *forgotten* that when you create a government bureaucracy, no matter how well intentioned it is, almost instantly its *primary priority* becomes—preservation of the bureaucracy."

He had started rushing, like he was nervous, far shy of his usual level of energy, when he delivered the payload:

"I believe in states' rights; I believe in people doing as much as they can for themselves at the community level and at the private level, and I believe that we've *distorted* the balance of government."

Then, he returned to his usual boilerplate. Far from the usual Neshoba County Fair demagoguery, the way he carried out Trent Lott's suggestion doused the enthusiasm of a previously energetic crowd. He did far better with the jokes and the football story. And it was hardly worth it. The backlash was immediate and caustic.

Jimmy Carter organized a passel of Southern politicians to demand a collective apology that framed Ronald Reagan as a modern-day carpetbagger. Andrew Young penned a moving essay for the *Washington Post* about stopping in Neshoba County during Martin Luther King Jr.'s 1966 March Against Fear.

> *Sheriff Lawrence Rainey and his posse were nightriders in good standing, and a black man's life wasn't worth much once he decided to approach the courthouse with voting on his mind.*
>
> *I remember Martin standing on the Neshoba County Courthouse steps in 1966, describing how the bodies of the slain civil rights workers had been found buried in a dam two years earlier. He said, "The murderers of Goodman, Chaney, and Schwerner are no doubt within the range of my voice." A voice rang out: "Yeah, damn right. We're right here behind you."*

Young noted, too, that Reagan had just been endorsed by the imperial wizard of the Invisible Empire, Knights of the Ku Klux Klan—who praised his platform for reading "as if it were written by a Klansman." Carter's only African American cabinet member, Health and Human Services Secretary Patricia Harris, observed that Reagan had taken weeks before disclaiming that endorsement, and that now, when she heard Reagan speak, she saw "a specter of white sheets." As for the intended audience, many white Mississippians who might have once been proud of their state's reputation as the most fearsome bastion of resistance, were now ashamed to find the nation pointing it out. Which was why, claimed an embarrassed Mississippi Reagan fan in a letter to Bill Brock, in Neshoba County, the Republican candidate had screwed the pooch. "Three weeks ago Reagan had a landslide victory in Mississippi. Today it is a tossup."

REAGAN'S SPEECH BEFORE THE URBAN LEAGUE THE NEXT DAY, FOLLOWED BY a hospital visit to Vernon Jordan, might have proven a political coup, were it not for the Neshoba controversy—and the opening that day of the trial in the Greensboro Klan/Nazi murders. The Urban League was the most conservative of the major black organizations. At the convention, its vice president for political affairs had presented a report criticizing affirmative action and the "permanent civil rights enforcement bureaucracy" supporting it, in favor of a strategy of "expanded black business ownership"—just what Reagan endorsed, in a speech sketching out Jack Kemp's idea of "enterprise zones" with tax advantages and reduced regulations in depressed minority areas. But he was met with stone-faced silence.

He hopped into a limousine for the same South Bronx block Jimmy Carter visited in 1977 to promise federal disaster assistance. Reagan pointed reporters to the surrounding rubble, "DECAY" spray-painted on one abandoned building, "BROKEN PROMISES" and "FALSE PROMISES" on another: a paradigmatic example of failed big government solutions. Local residents pinned behind barriers across the street, their every move watched by police snipers on surrounding rooftops, did not appreciate being cast as Reagan's props. They started booing and yelling for him to talk to *them*. Reagan walked over, reporters and TV crews with their heavy equipment lumbering behind like a herd of buffalo, to do just that. He *hated* being accused of racism.

A woman shouted: "*What are you going to do for us?*"

Reagan cried back, hoarse, almost at the top of his lungs: "*I am trying to tell you!* That I know of no *program*, or *promise* that a president can make that the *federal government* can come in and *wave a wand* and do this! And I can't do a *damned thing* for you if I don't get elected."

"No, but afterward! What are you—?"

The exchange continued fruitlessly, cameras clicking and whirring, until the crowd converged in an angry chant: "*You ain't gonna do nothing! You ain't gonna do nothing!*"

The next day a former Nazi and Klansman named Gerald Carlson won the Republican nomination for the congressional seat representing the depressed automotive city of Dearborn, Michigan. He had spent only $180, had no campaign headquarters or phone number, and electioneered mostly by handing out leaflets comprised of mug shots that appeared in newspapers during National Auto Theft Week. A few weeks later, ABC News followed him canvassing voters for the general election:

"I'd like to get to Washington to see if we can't get back some of the civil rights that the white majority of this country once had."

A woman: "I agree with that."

"The blacks will not perform the same way that white people do. They don't have that much respect for white society, for the white civilization that we have here."

Another woman: "I personally find it frightening."

REAGAN SEQUESTERED HIMSELF IN PACIFIC PALISADES TO PREPARE FOR THE campaign ahead, then emerged on August 16 for a press conference with George Bush at his side.

His advisors were hard at work threading John Sears's needle. One day, an economic advisor pleaded to a reporter that "while the governor likes Kemp . . . he's going to listen to the big boys—Shultz, Burns, Greenspan, Weinberger, Simon, and Friedman. . . . None of them believes that simply cutting taxes or balancing the budget" would magically end inflation. He insisted that Reagan's beliefs in that regard had been reformed by these distinguished personages.

Another day, the candidate sat for a briefing by foreign policy experts, then Reagan went off to do something else, while the experts presented themselves for the press. Lyn Nofziger was asked how many belonged to "CPD." "What's that? A gasoline additive?" Nofziger tried quipping, in distraction from the question's implication: that the candidate was in harness with the extremists of the Committee on the Present Danger.

CPD was fearmongering as aggressively as ever. Member Norman Podhoretz had just published a book called *The Present Danger*, which argued that the U.S. should have seized Arab oil fields when it had a chance in 1973, complained about "the prominence of homosexuals in the literary world," and argued, Goldwater-style, that "incessant harping on the danger of confrontation and nuclear war, all of this is part of a culture of appeasement." A *Washington Post* letter-writer called attention to an article that Reagan defense hand William van Cleave had published in *National Review* in 1968 recommending a nuclear strike against China. (Van Cleave howled that he had only discussed "options"—a claim undermined by the cover image teasing the piece, which depicted a missile reading "Bomb the Bomb" pointed at "Red China.")

Richard Allen followed Nofziger. He insisted that the briefing was but "another indicator of our intention to wage a broad and responsible campaign appealing to people of all parties and persuasions."

Then, however, CPD founder Eugene Rostow took the podium and recommended "a program of considerable rearmament." Perhaps after a nervous look from Nofziger, he clarified that he wasn't speaking for the campaign. A reporter asked if they could question someone who *did* speak for the campaign. Allen began ambling to the podium. Nofziger pushed him aside: "I think we'll just leave it."

Washington's foreign policy mandarins worried about Ronald Reagan. What worried them most was what he might do about China. That was why Reagan was standing beside George Bush now. The head of America's liaison office in Beijing in 1974 and 1975 was about to travel to the People's Republic of China to reassure its government that they—and, implicitly, the foreign policy establishment back home—needn't fear the Republican nominee. Which would be a tricky argument to make.

Ever since Richard Nixon's historic 1972 trip to the People's Republic of China, when Nixon, Kissinger, and Zhou Enlai crafted a precisely worded "Shanghai Communiqué" to mark the two nations' new diplomatic understanding, America's China policy had hung on an abstraction as difficult to explain as the Holy Trinity: that though there might *appear* to be two nations, the Republic of China (Taiwan) and the People's Republic of China, there actually was only *one*, which happened to have two *governments*. Things became yet more esoteric when Carter normalized relations with the *People's Republic* of China, breaking off formal diplomatic relations with the *Republic* of China. At that point, the American embassy in Taiwan became a *liaison office*, sponsored by a "private foundation," even though it was funded by the U.S. government and staffed by foreign service officers— who, however, resigned their government positions for exactly as long as they worked in Taipei, then resumed their former status the moment they left. America's former liaison office in Beijing became an *embassy*.

At the Republican convention, the attempt to preserve this status quo while placating the conservatives who despised "Red China" added yet another level of complexity—like explaining how energy was a wave and a particle at the same time. The platform promised that President Reagan would both "continue the process of building a working relationship with the PRC" and "deplore the Carter Administration's treatment of Taiwan," while simultaneously working to strengthen relations with both. But passing that language had required a side deal with Senator Jesse Helms in which Reagan promised to work to return a *real* embassy to Taiwan. Reagan himself was so emotional on the subject of Taiwan that in 1971, when a bloc of nations, including African nations (but also European nations), voted for Beijing to occupy China's United Nations seat instead of Taiwan, he raged at President Nixon, "To see those monkeys from those African countries—damn them, they're still uncomfortable wearing shoes!"

Now, in Los Angeles, Ambassador Bush was asked, naturally enough, "Do you suggest that as a ticket you no longer advocate establishment of any kind of formal government-to-government relationship with Taiwan?"

Bush deferentially referred the question to his running mate. Who wasn't nearly up to the task.

Reagan's answer was interminable, and so muddled that media outlets reported slightly different words. Though all translations converged in noting that Reagan had said that he wished for an "official" relationship with Taiwan. In a follow-up, he clarified that he meant "government-to-government" relations with Taiwan—which the government in Beijing would inevitably interpret as a grave insult. George Bush, standing nervously beside him, must have wondered what the hell he had gotten himself into.

He landed in Japan to news that the *People's Daily* had blasted Reagan as "brazen" and "irresponsible," out to "destroy the basic principle of normalization of U.S.-China relations." Bush tried to insist that "Governor Reagan hasn't proposed a two-Chinas policy, nor does he intend to propose such a policy. We don't advocate diplomatic relations with Taiwan, nor have we." He arrived in Beijing. Premier Deng Xiaoping, upon their greeting, called him "old friend"—and said, "Since we are old friends, we must be very frank." Bush responded, "Returning to Peking is like a pleasant homecoming."

Not so pleasant.

Foreign minister Huang Hua, as they were about to disappear into a private meeting, took the unusual step of browbeating Bush before the press for "remarks that have the effect of retrogressing from the current state of Sino-American relations"—adding, "I would like to make it clear that China on its part has no intention whatsoever of involving itself in the presidential election in the United States between the two parties." Bush responded, "I certainly respect your views on wanting to stay out of the American election. I'd like to stay out of it myself sometimes."

Probably never more than at present. They emerged, Bush claiming that their talks had been "very positive"; Xinhua, the official Chinese news agency, distributed a dispatch that seemed to suggest that Beijing agreed. Then, the next day, Reagan was asked, "Are you still for 'official relations' with Taiwan, yes or no?" He replied, "Um, I guess it's a yes." Xinhua said that meant that his original remarks were "absolutely not a slip of the tongue." Bush said, "No comment."

Another day, another gaffe: next Reagan referred to Taiwan as the "Free Republic of China"—and Xinghua said Reagan's words "cancelled out" Bush's visit, and that those who believed "that China, to maintain its relationship with the U.S., will eventually swallow the bitter pill prepared by Reagan, are daydreaming."

The next day, Reagan tried, "I don't know that I said that." Bush tried outright lying: "He did not say that"—which crossed signals with his running mate, who finally just allowed, "I misstated."

Bush returned home to a round of nasty articles and editorials. One called Reagan an "ideologue, living in a bygone past, insensitive to the complexities and nuances of the world," noting the "troubling ties of two senior Reagan aides, Michael Deaver and Peter Hannaford, whose public relations firm has been on Taipei's payroll since 1977." Others wondered how Reagan could continue delivering his lusty applause line "No more Vietnams! No more Taiwans!" and expect to work with Beijing as president. The *New York Times* wheeled out John Sears, who said that Reagan "does have a difficulty in being disciplined in what he says," and that it was challenging to campaign with the burden of "explaining every day why you're not an idiot."

THE MEDIA WAS SIMULTANEOUSLY ATWITTER CONCERNING TWO MORE AL-leged Reagan disasters. The fullness of time would yield more nuanced evaluations.

The Veterans of Foreign Wars broke with eighty years of precedent and endorsed Reagan. On August 18, he addressed their convention in Chicago. The speech Richard Allen had drafted for him included a proposal for renewed arms control talks with the USSR. Reagan judged it boring. The staff pumped out a second attempt, this one focusing on the treatment of veterans. Reagan scotched that, too—then drafted his own. Built upon a quote from Will Rogers—"I've never seen anyone insult Jack Dempsey"—it explicated his doctrine of peace through strength. There was nothing surprising about it—except for one section near the beginning.

He described the calamities that had befallen war-torn Southeast Asia: "Tens of thousands of boat people have shown us there is no freedom in the so-called peace in Vietnam. The hill people of Laos know poison gas, not justice, and in Cambodia there is only the peace of the grave for at least one-third of the population slaughtered by the Communists." He cited the now-familiar coinage of Gene Rostow—"For too long, we have lived with the 'Vietnam Syndrome'"—which he blamed on the Communists' plan "to win in the field of propaganda here in America what they could not win on the battlefield in Vietnam."

Then came words almost universally judged a calamitous mistake: "It is time we recognized that ours was, in truth, a *noble cause*."

He explained this with an analysis that once upon a time had been embraced by virtually all Americans, back when Marines were landing in Da Nang: "A small country newly freed from colonial rule sought our help in establishing self-rule and the means of self-defense against a totalitarian neighbor bent on conquest." The VFW audience gave this an enthusiastic ovation—an even more enthusiastic one when he continued, "We dishonor the memory of 50,000 young Americans who died in that cause when we give way to guilt as if we were doing something shameful."

The response from the commentariat, on the other hand, was baffled dismay.

Joseph Kraft decried a "wholly gratuitous reference to Vietnam," serving only to "re-divide the country on a subject famous for fostering the most furious discord." Haynes Johnson of the *Washington Post* said Reagan "deliberately stirred the fires with the old trigger words." Evans and Novak took readers behind the scenes to describe how this "stunning" "self-inflicted wound" came about: aides had written a wise speech, but the candidate insisted upon replacing it with something foolish. Mary McGrory wrote, "Jimmy Carter is anxious to pin the warmonger label on him, and Reagan is backing right up to him." She said his new slogan, "Peace Through Strength," was bad enough. "But Reagan didn't leave it at that. He opened up the subject of Vietnam again. What, pray, is the audience for that?" The *New York Times* news report led, in self-evident tones betokening conventional wisdom on the march: "Despite his decline in the polls and the Democratic accusations that he is warlike, Ronald Reagan stuck to his military preparedness themes."

This was myopic. The shift in public attitudes toward preferring greater military preparedness after the taking of the Iran hostages and the Soviet invasion of Afghanistan had been unmistakable. And who was the audience for reopening the subject of Vietnam? The evidence emerging from every quarter suggested: a considerable portion of Americans from all walks of life.

In May, the Senate had passed an authorization cosponsored by all one hundred members for a Vietnam Veterans Memorial in Washington, D.C.; in July, Congress authorized three acres on the National Mall as the site. Conservatives including Ronald Reagan embraced a revisionist volume, *America in Vietnam*, by Guenter Lewy, which argued that "the sense of guilt created by the Vietnam war in the minds of many Americans is not warranted," that "moral convictions are not the exclusive possession of persons in conscience opposed to war." On the left, many were reconsidering their former belief in the nobility of the victorious side: in 1979, following an Amnesty International investigation, the legendary folk singer Joan Baez published an "Open Letter to the Socialist Republic of Vietnam," appealing to her former comrades "to end the imprisonment and torture—to allow an international team of neutral observers to inspect your prisons and re-education centers." It was signed by veteran antiwar activists including Peter Yarrow of Peter, Paul, and Mary, Allen Ginsberg, and Father Daniel Berrigan.

In Hollywood, a brilliant director of the ninth most profitable film of 1978—which enjoyed a second, successful run in 1979—demonstrated the existence of a big audience indeed for reopening Vietnam. *The Deer Hunter* was densely symbolic and visually overpowering. Its plot, which involved of a group of young men from a hardscrabble Pennsylvania steel town who eagerly went off to fight a war in the old John Wayne manner, and came back with their innocence shattered, defied simple summary. But the most striking thing about it was easy to see, once someone pointed it out: director Michael Cimino re-presented the indelibly famous media images of the "television war" of actual atrocities committed by America and its South Vietnamese ally, only inverted, as if committed by the *enemy*, against *us*. A Communist soldier threw a grenade into an underground shelter full of women and children, another mowed down an escaping woman and her baby—images that rhymed with famous photographs of the My Lai massacre. In a jungle prison, Americans were held in a cramped bamboo cage—which looked just like the "tiger cages" depicted in *Life* magazine in which our South Vietnamese allies tortured *their* often-innocent prisoners. (One sharp-eyed critic noted that the American prisoners' headbands resembled Christ's crown of thorns, and that the placement of their bodies resembled crucifixion.) The most disturbing revision of all came in the most famous scene, in which barbaric Vietnamese tormentors force brainwashed prisoners to play Russian roulette. When one refused, his captor held the gun to his head in precise imitation of one of the most harrowing images from the war, from 1968, in which a South Vietnamese military policeman pressed a pistol to the head of an alleged spy and carried out his summary execution in the middle of the street.

During *The Deer Hunter*'s concluding homecoming scene, the characters joined in a spontaneous, soulful "America the Beautiful." Something fascinating happened at many screenings of the film: the audience began joining in—singing along, metaphorically, with a version of the Vietnam War in which Americans were the only victims. The critic Peter Biskind saw in this "the very worst aspects of American culture, those that led to Vietnam in the first place. Its popularity and warm reception by the critics indicate a failure to consolidate whatever progress was made in the '60s toward confronting the underside of our national life." He concluded, "It is tempting to call Cimino our first home-grown fascist director." An essayist in the *New York Times* labeled the picture "The Gook Hunter," describing its gestation thus: "For three years there was virtual silence:

Then Hollywood sensed that a lot of money could be made with a movie that appealed directly to those racist instincts that cause wars . . . a movie that reincarnated the triumphant Batman-jawed Caucasian warrior . . . the Vietnamese as Oriental brutes and dolts."

Such opinions didn't keep it from sweeping the 1979 Academy Awards, where the ailing John Wayne presented Cimino with the Best Picture statuette. And it was *The Deer Hunter* that inspired a veteran named Jan Scruggs to launch the personal crusade that led to Congress authorizing a Vietnam memorial on the National Mall.

Whether Vietnam was a noble cause was in the eye of the beholder. But many more Americans than prominent pundits supposed would gladly embrace a politician who encouraged them to believe it was.

"REAGAN TO ALTER STYLE: CANDIDATE TO END EMBARRASSING SLIPUPS," a headline read on August 22, a day when Reagan, allegedly, made several more. The location was Dallas—a place that had recently seized the American imagination.

A television program debuted as a limited-run miniseries on CBS in the spring of 1978 and proved so popular it had a twelve-year run as the most popular by far of a new crop of evening soap operas about rich, feuding families. *Dallas* chronicled the intrigues of the brood sired by an unscrupulous oil wildcatter, John Ross "Jock" Ewing Sr., whose equally diabolical son J.R. epitomized what was also in real life the wildest and wooliest faction of the business world: independent oilmen. A season-ending cliffhanger in March, in which J.R. was shot by a mysterious assassin, had so galvanized the nation that it strengthened the bargaining position that summer of television writers who threatened the timely opening of the fall television season by striking. When Jimmy Carter showed up for a fundraiser there during the TV work stoppage, he grinned and confessed, "I came to Dallas to find out confidentially who shot J.R. If any of you could let me know that, I could finance the whole campaign this fall." At the Republican convention, you could buy a button reading "A DEMOCRAT SHOT J.R."

It just so happened that the event Reagan was attending in Dallas had been financed by the real-life inspiration for J.R. In 1977, T. Cullen Davis, whose wildcatter father bequeathed him America's eighth-largest privately held company, was acquitted, barely, of the execution-style murder of his estranged wife's boyfriend and that man's daughter, and two others, thanks to an audacious defense from the flamboyant Texas attorney Richard "Racehorse" Haynes. In 1979, Haynes steered Davis to another unlikely acquittal, this time for allegedly hiring a hit man to murder fifteen people including the judge presiding in his divorce—with the alleged execution order preserved on tape. The *Austin American Statesman* ran a cartoon: a masked burglar stood over a dead liquor-store clerk, smoking gun in hand, protesting his innocence to a cop, who asks, "Who do you think you are—Cullen Davis?"

Haynes, as it happened, also represented the Reverend James Robison in his case before the FCC after his Fort Worth affiliate pulled him off the air for claiming that gay men recruited little boys. In June, Pastor Robison stood with Cullen Davis on the grounds of his 181-acre estate while a thousand of his employees and their families looked on as he stepped forward to accept Jesus Christ as his personal savior. Unrepentance might be beyond God's power to forgive. But the televangelist was proud to welcome the probable murderer as a regular on his TV show. Davis wrote a sizable check to stage the Religious Roundtable's National Affairs Briefing at Dallas's Reunion Arena, where Reagan would be speaking on August 22. So did another morally questionable Texas oil scion: Nelson Bunker Hunt, whose father, H.L., was said to have been the richest man in America, and in November of 1963 had welcomed John F. Kennedy to Dallas by announcing on the radio that the thirty-sixth president intended to form a "dictatorship" where "no firearms are permitted." H.L.'s sons had just embroiled the nation in another genuine Texas soap opera: they lost their shirts, and threatened the stability of world commodity markets, in an attempt to illegally corner the market in silver, backed by Arab sheiks and aided by Representative Steven Symms, Representative Larry McDonald, and Senator Jesse Helms, who helped block a Pentagon plan to sell excess silver from the nation's strategic reserve in order to purchase commodities deemed more strategically necessary. Though Nelson Bunker Hunt still had enough money left over to write a sizable check to the National Affairs Briefing.

It was, after all, a nice charitable tax deduction: the Religious Roundtable insisted that their two-day extravaganza featuring all of the Christian right's Southern Baptist superstars (and one Pentecostal, Pat Robertson) was not political at all.

Jerry Falwell arrived following a rally in Harrisburg, Pennsylvania, where his sermon was accompanied by a slide show of images including Charles Manson, porn theater marquees, canoodling young men, a murderous quote attributed to an American Communist Party leader dreaming "of the hour when the last Congressman is strangled to death on the guts of the last preacher," bloody fetuses in ceramic hospital pans, and a mushroom cloud (which happened to illustrate the theme of his recent pamphlet, *Armageddon and the Coming War With Russia*, reading the signs of the times to predict an imminent nuclear war, which, "considered from a positive viewpoint," would culminate in the return of Jesus Christ.)

Falwell was in a bit of trouble over his claim before that Alaska Moral Majority chapter that he had confronted Jimmy Carter in the White House that if he was hiring homosexuals, he might as well hire murderers and bank robbers, too. The former Southern Baptist Convention president Bailey Smith, Jimmy Carter's friend, had also been in the room, and said Falwell hadn't said it. Smith was soon proven right—by the audiotape Falwell had made of the meeting and sent to the White House as a courtesy. Falwell apologized, sort of: "I have stated as clearly and emphatically as I know how that my recent statement was not intended to be a verbatim report of our conversation with President Carter. Instead, my statement was intended to be, and was, an honest portrayal of President Carter's position on gay rights." He was now asked about the lie every time he spoke with a mainstream journalist. In flag-draped Reunion Arena, however, he had nothing to fear.

The opening address came from Representative Guy Vander Jagt, who urged a vote for Ronald Reagan because, "For too long, Christians have seemed to think that politics was too dirty and messy for them to be involved in. . . . It's time to go out and get yourself a bar of soap and roll up your sleeves and make politics clean again." A famous black preacher from Watts, E. V. Hill, earned one of his three standing ovations preaching on a recent news story about the Navy: "When a woman who is accused of lesbianism is given an honorable discharge, something should be said! In a day when teachers look and smell worse than those they are teaching, something should be said!" Tim LaHaye spoke, and Connie Marshner, and Southern Baptist Convention president Adrian Rogers, and Amway's Richard DeVos, Dallas Cowboys coach Tom Landry, Representative Phil Crane, and Senators Bill Armstrong and Jesse Helms. Fob James of Alabama, too. He said it was "nonsense" to separate church and state. He later became the only Democratic governor to endorse Reagan.

Two generals were on the program; one so impressed a previously apolitical minister from Spartanburg, South Carolina, that he pledged to set up an Election Day phone bank inside his church. The crowd of 16,000 included 4,500 pastors who stood and recited a pledge to participate in a church-based voter registration drive on Sunday, September 28, dubbed "Christians Are Citizens Too Day." Despite the Dallas organizers' claims of nonpartisanship, the event had been conceived within the Reagan campaign's Christian-outreach operation.

Nonpartisan indeed. Congressman Vander Jagt might plead for Christians to clean up politics. Paul Weyrich, on the other hand, lectured that "many of our Christians have what I call the 'Goo-Goo Syndrome'— 'good government.'" He scowled: "They want *everybody* to vote! I don't want everybody to vote. Elections are *not won* by a majority of people:

they never *have been* from the beginning of our country, and they *are not now.*"

He grew agitated: "As a matter of fact our leverage in elections goes up as the *voting populace goes down.*"

He complained about ministers who registered their congregants to vote without telling them who the "good guys" were, and he attacked critics who said that the New Right simplified complicated issues: "Ultimately, everything can be reduced to right and wrong. *Everything.* . . . We see everything in black and white perspective because Scripture sees thing in black and white perspective."

Then, there was "God's Angry Man," Dallas's own James Robison. His national profile was being boosted by a new $1.5 million TV special, *Wake Up, America: We're All Hostages!*, which was scheduled to air in two hundred markets by the election. It featured many of the figures onstage at Reunion Arena—and also Aleksandr Solzhenitsyn and Jack Kemp. Robison explained, "One of the most awesome and destructive idols of all is the government. . . . This god is out of control and will destroy us all." A sort of commercial break interrupted: "A vote this year is a vote for survival. That's why we've organized a listing of candidates . . . showing their voting records, to tell you that the record speaks. . . . *The wicked and the Godless are most active.*" Viewers were also implored to "send gifts and contributions," with a gold-plated "V-O-T-E" stickpin with the "T" in the form of the cross on Calvary as a premium.

Many were wearing them now as Robison, perhaps the most awesome oratorial talent since William Jennings Bryan, rose from his seat on the dais to take the podium.

"It's time for Christians to crawl out from under pews. . . . You read about the Savior. They say He didn't get involved in politics. Well, I ask you then: *Who crucified him?* . . . Not voting is a sin against *Almighty God*!"

Among those who rose to their feet in exultation was Ronald Reagan, who had arrived at his appointed time to begin his speech—which was actually quite some time ago. But Robison wasn't nearly ready to stop. And, in a demonstration of the Christian right's power, he had no problem making a presidential nominee cool his heels.

He cited Proverbs: "*When the righteous are in authority the people rejoice. But when the wicked beareth rule, the people mourn*"—that meant that "there is *no* possible way you can separate God from government and have a successful government. . . . If the *righteous!* the *pro-family!* the *moral!* the *Biblical!* the *godly!* the *hardworking!* and the *decent!* individuals in this country stay out of politics *who on this earth does this leave* to make the policies under which you and I live, and struggle to survive?"

He launched into his final crescendo—which began at what would be the pinnacle for most preachers: "*We! Must! Begin!* To *literally penetrate* every area of our society!" Government was "a *confiscator*! And a *consumer*! And a *disperser* of your wealth. *It! Produces! Nothing!* And it functions *best* when it functions *least!*"

And at that he leaned forward, practically through the podium, to address the guest of honor:

"I thank *God*—Mr. Reagan was willing to come here tonight. Because it took a *lot* of concern about what you think, and a *lot* of courage for him to walk in here tonight and speak to you. And I wanna thank him for coming. May *God* bless America, because America once again blesses God."

Yet it was not yet Ronald Reagan's turn to speak.

D. James Kennedy explained why "1980 could be America's last free election." He was then supposed to introduce W. A. Criswell, who was to introduce his old friend Ronald Reagan . . . but then Jerry Falwell, who had already spoken once, wriggled his way behind the podium. He said that the event was $100,000 in the red, they had to take a collection—and "the doors are locked." Organizers claimed they summoned that $100,000 in the next ten minutes: quite a useful display for a constituency seeking respect from a political candidate.

Finally, he introduced the man who, in offering his pulpit to Gerald Ford in 1976, had done more than anyone else to get this movement started. Falwell called Wallie Criswell the "Protestant Pope of this generation." Criswell quickly welcomed Reagan to "one of the greatest assemblies of the twentieth century," then stepped aside, and the governor finally squared himself away behind the podium to speak.

THE TEXT HAD BEEN DRAFTED BY A VETERAN CONGRESSIONAL STAFFER WITH religious-right contacts named Bill Gribbin, who explained to Bill Gavin and Ed Meese that he had included "*an awful lot* of code words, religious allusions, and whatnot . . . which might be missed if one is not close to evangelical religion"—a useful gambit to evade accusations that Reagan was mixing church and state. "It is important, however, for the speaker to understand each and every one of them. His audience will. Boy, will they ever!"

Reagan got the first of many bursts of acclaim with a clever piece of plausible deniability—which, just to be safe, was *not* included in the pamphlet version produced for wider distribution: "You know, a few days ago, I addressed a group in Chicago and received their endorsement for my candidacy. Now, I know this is a *non-partisan* gathering, and so I know that you can't endorse *me*, but I only brought that up because I want you to know that I endorse you and what you're doing." He got another when he said, "You know, I'm told that throughout history, man has adopted about four billion laws. It's always seemed to me, however, that in all that time and with all those laws, we haven't improved by one iota on the Ten Commandments!"

He said that "traditional Judeo-Christian values based on the moral teaching of religion are undergoing what is perhaps their most serious challenge in our nation's history." He accused their common enemies of "a new and cynical attack . . . to remove from our public policy debate the voice of traditional morality" through "intimidation and name-calling." He got interrupted for applause when he said, "If we have come to a time in the United States when the attempt to see traditional moral values reflected in public policy leaves one open to irresponsible charges, then the structure of our free society is under attack and the foundation of our freedom is threatened." He signaled his sympathy with a key tenet of Christian reconstructionism: "Under the pretense of separation of church and state, religious beliefs cannot be advocated, but atheism can." He cracked a classic Reagan-joke-with-a-message: "You know, I've often had a fantasy: I've thought of serving an atheist a delicious gourmet dinner and then asking he or she whether they believed there was a cook."

Sixteen thousand Christians roared their delight. They roared even more loudly when their guest pronounced himself "shocked" that the First Amendment was being "used as a reason to keep traditional moral values away from policy making," when all truly educated observers understood that "the First Amendment was written not to protect the people and their laws from religious values, but to protect those values from government tyranny."

Peter Hannaford had inserted a few statesmanlike paragraphs on the importance of working with international allies, intended for media ears as damage control for the VFW speech. It came and went with little notice. Next, Reagan checked off a series of signature Christian right discontents: against a social studies curriculum sponsored by the federal government called MACOS that invited students to think about religion in relativist terms; the FCC hounding preachers but not "the drug propaganda poorly concealed in the lyrics of some recorded songs"—and, of course, the IRS, which "without approval of Congress" had determined "that tax exemption constitutes federal funding" (it always had), forcing "all tax-exempt schools, including church schools, to abide by affirmative action orders drawn up by—who else?—"IRS bureaucrats." Then he said that the book he would want with him if he were shipwrecked on a desert island was none other than the Bible—because "it is an *incontrovertible fact* that all the complex and horrendous questions confronting us at home, and worldwide, have their answer, in that single book." The response was so rapturous that he had to wait a minute before he could continue.

IT DID NOT IMPRESS THE REAGAN STAFFERS WHO WISHED THAT HE wouldn't show up to anything like this at all. One of those staffers had told Robert Billings, after he was hired away from the Moral Majority to become the campaign's religious outreach director, "I'm afraid of you people. You are making the Republican Party a religious organization and chasing off many of our supporters." And at one of Reagan's next stops, a group of governors *begged* him to stick to economic issues and stay away from the divisive Christian stuff. "He just won't let go of those things," an aide complained.

Who knows how nervous voices like these would have been had they seen what happened backstage.

Gary North, the son-in-law of Dr. R. J. Rushdoony, expressed his consternation that the Christian Reconstructionist guru—the one who advocated stoning as the proper punishment for homosexuality—had not been offered a spot on the program. Reagan's new religious-outreach chief, Billings, responded diplomatically: "If it weren't for his books, none of us would be here." North complained, "Nobody in the audience understands that." "True," Billings assured him, "but *we* do."

EDITORS NEWLY WRAPPING THEIR MINDS AROUND ALL OF THIS MADE UP for lost time by ordering up massive coverage from Dallas. The *New York Times* did a major profile of Falwell. Articles about the Christian right took up most of the front page of the August 25 *Minneapolis Star*—and all of pages four, five, and eight. But there was one story the four hundred journalists in attendance almost entirely missed: the meeting with which Reagan's day in Dallas began. More than two hundred religious leaders, politicians, and businessmen—with independent oilmen like Cullen Davis and Bunker Hunt overrepresented—enjoyed a meet-and-greet with the candidate at the Hyatt Regency Hotel, where Reagan told them, "We have God's promise that if we turn to Him and ask His help, we shall have it. If we believe God has blessed America with liberty, then we have not just a *right* to vote, but a *duty* to vote." Cullen emerged to tell the local paper, "I'm for him. I hope he gets elected. Ronald Reagan represents the majority of the people in this country. Everything I've seen about him has been great."

It wasn't until a year later that reporters—actually, only one reporter, David Rogers of the *Boston Globe*—noticed the subterranean new development in American politics that this meeting exemplified: the flood of money in the 1980 elections to conservative Republicans from Christian independent oilmen. Many of them were fundamentalist Christians. They had previously donated, and in much smaller amounts, mostly to Democrats. And only one reporter, from a Houston paper, seemed to have noticed the private meeting at the Hyatt. Instead, the reporting from Dallas largely concentrated on the narrative that Reagan's serial gaffes and mistakes were setting him up for disaster. They especially dwelled on Reagan's answer to a press conference question about whether the theory of evolution should be taught in schools. He looked down, reflected, then said quickly, "Uh, I have a great many questions about evolution. And I think the recent discoveries over the years have pointed out great flaws in it."

Conventional wisdom congealed: an extremist like this would have a hard time winning a national election. A close observer of Texas politics begged to differ: "I think a lot of people look at this conference and assume these are right-wingers who were involved anyway." Not so: "most of them are hearing a lot of this for the first time . . . I don't think they're going home and forgetting all this. You've got to remember these people do know how to organize around their churches. If they're told what to do, I'm betting they'll get it done." And they *would* be told what to do. "People want leadership," Robert Billings was once overheard saying. "They don't want to think for themselves. They want to be told what to think by some of us here, close to the front."

IT WAS ALL QUITE A BIT ODD. WHAT POLITICAL TOUTS WHO CALLED REAgan's adventure in Dallas an inexplicable mistake seemed not to notice was that these were the people who had stopped ERA ratification dead in its tracks, despite the fact that polls showed that upward of 60 percent of Americans favored it year after year, despite the fact of consistent presidential lobbying for it. What no one in the political press seemed to notice was that Reagan's right-wing activist base *knew what it was doing.*

Another feature that was mostly invisible in the coverage of the presidential campaign was Reagan's career as a radio commentator—recognition that Reagan had been crafting his five-minute homilies about why liberalism was driving America astray since 1975, picking up more radio affiliates every year, with millions of listeners ever day—that *Reagan* knew what he was doing.

Like this. Four days after Dallas, Reagan traveled to Columbus to accept an endorsement from the International Brotherhood of Teamsters, the biggest union in the country. But out in the crowd, policy director Martin Anderson and economist Alan Greenspan, who'd helped draft his speech on the plane, were losing their minds. Their text had him point to Carter's responsibility for "one of the major economic contractions of the last fifty years." Instead, he referred to "a new depression—the Carter depression." *Depression*, Greenspan had patiently explained to him, was a technical term in economics, and technically, the United States was not in one. The candidate listened, and added a refrain to his stock speech:

"His answer to all this misery? He tries to tell us we are 'only' in a recession, not a depression, as if definitions—words—relieve our suffering."

(In point of fact Carter hadn't said any such thing.)

"Let the record show that when the American people cried out for economic help, Jimmy Carter took refuge behind a dictionary. Wellll, if it's a definition he wants, I'll give him one. A recession is when your neighbor loses his job. A depression is when you lose yours. And recovery is when Jimmy Carter loses his!"

The crowds would roar. That was when he really stuck in the knife: *"Let Mr. Carter go to their homes, look their children in the eye, and argue with them that it is 'only' a recession that put dad or mom out of work!"* He had adopted it from something he remembered from Harry Truman. It became one of the rhetorical signatures of the campaign.

BUT FOR NOW, THE REAGAN CAMPAIGN WAS TREADING WATER, WITH THE media *and* in the polls. Carter enjoyed good economic news for once. New numbers showed inflation had flattened out in July for the first time in thirteen years. The consumer confidence index ticked up; the recession was reported to be on its way out; there was a brief burst of euphoria on Wall Street. Carter also scored nicely with the economic press when his experts ran Reagan's economic proposal through computer models and estimated that the revenue lost from his tax cut would devour almost half the discretionary federal budget. *Newsweek* reported that alongside a cartoon taking off on a ridiculous Saturday-night ABC program, the one where suave Ricardo Montalbán, garbed in an immaculate white suit, and his four-foot-high sidekick, hosted visitors on a magic island where wishes came true. The cartoon depicted a pompadoured Reagan in his own white suit carrying a briefcase reading "RR tax proposal" beneath a banner reading "FANTASY ISLAND."

Bush's return from China inaugurated another round of editorials about Reagan's foolishness. It got worse when Reagan gave an interview blaming a rabid press for his campaign's woes. The campaign invested enormous effort in rolling out an elaborate conspiracy theory that the White House had leaked the existence of the top-secret Stealth bomber project to bolster Carter's national security bona fides, but Reagan's claims didn't hold together, and it didn't take with the press or the public.

Top staffers were summoned to the rented Virginia manse where the Reagans stayed between campaign trips—called Wexford, it was secluded by a long, winding driveway, and had been built by John F. Kennedy—for an emergency meeting. One told waiting reporters, "The way things are going now, we are going to lose." Another grumbled, "Nobody mentioned that the candidate himself was causing a lot of the problems." The only adjustment was adding a staffer with presidential campaign experience to *LeaderShip '80*. Reagan's usual companions, Nofziger, Deaver, and Meese, had none.

Carter's Southern-states manager reported "dramatic" gains "across-the-board regionally, anchored in less-educated, lower income Democrats"—voters Wirthlin pegged as Reagan's most important quarry. In Alabama, Carter jumped from sixteen points behind to five points ahead. "RR has lost major ground on cars, risk crisis, vision & shoots from the hip," a Carter memo reported, while Carter's "competency ratings have jumped considerably and are now a bit positive."

On August 28, the Thursday before the Labor Day weekend, the president stepped up to the microphones in the East Room and announced a new $25 million economic program—his fifth economic program so far—which he claimed would create a million jobs and stifle inflation. Reagan issued a statement from Wexford: "This program has nothing to do with the economy—it has everything to do with the election." In fact, Carter's wonky congeries of refundable tax credits, rejiggered depreciation schedules, targeted energy subsidies, regional assistance grants, and modernization grants for industry could not have been *less* demagogic—certainly compared to an untested 30 percent tax cut across the board.

America looked at their president and yawned. They looked at the Republican nominee and blanched. The candidates traveled to their Labor Day weekend kickoff events just about tied.

CARTER SPOKE TO FORTY THOUSAND AT A FAIR IN THE NORTHERN ALABAMA town of Tuscumbia, famous as the birthplace of Helen Keller, where he offered a panegyric to the brave "working men and women of Poland." Reagan was in Jersey City, New Jersey, becoming the first Republican presidential candidate to campaign in that Democratic city since 1968. He insisted on coming here, he said, "because I believe today that in this country there are millions of Democrats who are just as unhappy at how things are going as the rest of us are." He spoke in the shadow of the Statue of Liberty, in one of the most visually spectacular and rhetorically inspiring political events ever staged. His white linen shirt set off his summer tan gorgeously. New York harbor rippled in the gentle breeze. Then—"under the gaze of the Mother of Exiles," as he put it—he hymned the golden door through which so many millions "first stepped foot on American soil. Right there"—he pointed to it—"on Ellis Island."

"These families came here to work. They came to build." He gestured thoughtfully to those others who "came to America in different ways, from other lands, under different, often harrowing conditions—but this place symbolizes what they *all* managed to build, no matter where they came from or how much they suffered." Then he called out to those suffering *now*, under Jimmy Carter—who "tells us that the *descendants* of those who sacrificed to start again in this land of freedom may have to abandon that dream that drew their ancestors to a new life and land."

It was a masterpiece presentation of his grand political dream: to permanently enfold beneath the Republican tent masses of patriotic, tradition-minded blue-collar Americans. Those who had had enough of Jimmy Carter's "litany of despair, of broken promises, of sacred trusts abandoned and forgotten," his "no-growth policy, an ever shrinking economic pie with smaller pieces for each of us." He reminded his audience that he was the only union leader to run for president. He quoted the late AFL-CIO president George Meany, speaking a year earlier, on the "climate of economic anxiety and uncertainty" midwifed by the Carter administration. He said: "I pledge to you in his memory that the voice of the American worker will once again be heeded in Washington"—promising regular consultation with union leaders—"and that the climate of fear that he spoke of will no longer threaten workers and their families."

He turned his eyes heavenward: "I want more than anything I've ever wanted to have an administration that will, through its actions at home and in the international arena, let millions of people know that Miss Liberty still 'lifts her lamp beside the golden door.' . . . Let us pledge to each other, with this great lady looking on, that we *can*, and so help us God, we *will* make America great again." It was cut into one hell of a campaign commercial. Maybe he could put the whole slump behind him.

Then he flew halfway across the country for a stop at the Michigan State Fair, where at an end-of-the-day "ethnic picnic" in a working-class suburb of Detroit called Allen Park, all those hopes were dashed.

HIS BIZARRE EXCUSE FOR THE STRANGE UTTERANCE THAT WAS SOON DOMI-nating the news was that he had been distracted by a heckler wearing a Jimmy Carter mask, whom he had jokingly addressed *as if* she were Carter—"I thought you were in Alabama!" He lamely tried to explain that the jolt of this strange sight had been the cause of the incorrect, off-the-cuff claim that followed: "I am glad to be here where you're feeling firsthand the economic problems that have been committed, and he's opening his campaign down in the city that gave birth to the Ku Klux Klan."

He said that he had seen a news story that mentioned Carter and a KKK connection, which was probably true—there had been articles mentioning that a Klan group based in Tuscumbia intended to *picket* President Carter. What surely also explained it was that Reagan never got more rattled than when he thought he was being accused of racism—like when he lost his temper in the Bronx. After Neshoba, he was being lumped in with "states' rights" demagogues from Mississippi's ugly past. It also so happened that this backyard barbecue was taking place in the district where the Republican white supremacist congressional nominee Gerald Carlson was campaigning to plentiful national publicity—surely on his mind, too.

He lost himself—and Jimmy Carter pounced at an opportunity right in the wheelhouse of his general election strategy. "In an economy in which real per capita disposable income had plunged 6 percent since Carter took office and inflation had not fallen below 14 percent all year," a campaign planner told Teddy White, they "knew if we had to fight this campaign in the trenches, talking about the consumer price index and the economy, we would not be in good shape." Instead, the work became getting the public to question whether Reagan was, in the words of campaign chairman Robert Strauss, "a man of presidential caliber."

And so, with swift dispatch, came the barrage.

DNC Chairman John White proclaimed that Reagan "now has no chance of carrying any state in the South" after having "slurred the entire region." Six Southern governors sent a joint telegram demanding an apology: "America cannot afford as its president a man who has such a limited, uniformed, and simplistic view of this great region of our united country." The area's Democratic congressman telegrammed that Reagan had committed "an insult to Tuscumbia and the people who live there." The president called Reagan's remark "slurs and innuendo," and said that "as an American and a southerner, I resent it." Now all anyone wanted to write about was Reagan's rhetorical carelessness—"a continuing symptom of foot-in-mouth disease that in his case seems incurable," an AP reporter wrote.

Within Reagan's camp, one faction advised ignoring it—to "stay on the offensive." Instead, they split the difference, crafting an "apology" equally as confused as the original offense. It blamed *Carter*: "I intended no inference that Mr. Carter was in any way sympathetic to the Klan and in no way did I intend to disparage the city of Tuscumbia or the state of Alabama. Nor do I believe there is any place for the Klan in the hearts of the people in the South. . . . The issue of the Ku Klux Klan was first injected into this election season several weeks ago by Mr. Carter's former appointee, Andrew Young, when he criticized me for attending the Neshoba County Fair in Philadelphia, Mississippi, and by Carter's Secretary of Health and Human Services, Mrs. Patricia Harris, who referred to the Klan in an attack on my candidacy."

George Bush contributed that the Democratic Party was guilty of "groin kicking." Bush's former campaign manager Jim Baker wrote Reagan a letter, which, after much respectful throat clearing, warned, "If you are to achieve a position to put your beliefs into practice, every word you say will be picked apart, or rather 'nitpicked' apart. All you have to do is be aware of that, accept it, and otherwise be yourself."

Easier said than done.

BUSH APPEARED ON *MEET THE PRESS*, AND WAS GIVEN LITTLE TIME TO DO anything but answer for Reagan's gaffes—snapping at incessant pestering over Reagan's views on the theory of evolution: "I'm not going to answer peripheral questions that do nothing but divert the American people from the number one issue. . . . It's the economy."

Reagan spoke to the B'nai Brith convention in Washington, winning a standing ovation from an overwhelmingly Democratic audience by hitting Carter for refusing to refer to the PLO as a terrorist organization. He traveled to Jacksonville, Florida, where he tried to inflame a crowd of retirees with his accusation that Carter had destroyed the usefulness of the Stealth bomber program by leaking its existence.

Then, in a press conference, he claimed that he had never wished to make Social Security voluntary—"never in my life."

Robert Strauss again did the honors: "I am sure that Governor Reagan did not intentionally misrepresent his record yesterday in Jacksonville, Florida, when he said he had 'never in my life' proposed making Social Security voluntary," Strauss said—adding with some nice passive aggression that he nonetheless felt "compelled," for the sake of accuracy, to observe that Reagan had urged just that before a national TV audience sixteen years earlier.

And on the Reagan trail, adjustments were made.

He flew to Philadelphia—the one in Pennsylvania, the first stop in a tour of overwhelmingly Democratic cities in six industrial states. He breakfasted with the archbishop, then spoke on the steps of the museum made famous by Sylvester Stallone in *Rocky*, from a text hastily adjusted to attest to his passion for preserving Social Security.

Naturally, the press corps was eager to follow up with questions. They found themselves physically restrained, with an aggressiveness unfamiliar to veterans of the Reagan beat, where daily press "avails" had always been de rigueur, from getting anywhere near the candidate. *This* strategic necessity had in fact been forecast in Dick Wirthlin's Black Book as one of its nineteen "Conditions of Victory": *"The candidate and/or campaign avoids self-inflicted blunders."*

They also had to thread John Sears's needle. In Chicago, after touring a Lithuanian neighborhood and meeting with Polish American leaders, Reagan spoke to the International Business Council, unveiling calculations that he said proved he could produce a budget surplus by 1983 without "altering or taking back necessary entitlements already granted to the American people."

Implicitly, he was answering a new analysis from Jimmy Carter's budget director that compared Reagan's economic program to a Hollywood fantasy. Those calculations concluded that (1) if Kemp-Roth passed, (2) America did not default on its debt, (3) Social Security and Medicare were fully funded, and (4) the defense budget was increased by Reagan's intended amount, only $10 billion would be left over, out of a budget of half a trillion dollars, for everything else. So in Chicago Reagan introduced a *new* set of numbers, which he promised had been vetted by "any number of distinguished economists and businessmen," including George Shultz, William Simon, Alan Greenspan, and Gerald Ford's budget director. The *New York Times* praised Reagan for having "emerged from Wonderland." A critic later pointed out that these new numbers projected an ability to raise more tax revenue than the old numbers only because they were premised on a still-astronomical 8.7 percent inflation rate through 1985—but were part of a plan that simultaneously promised to *lower* inflation. "In other words, a policy that promised to balance the budget in order to reduce inflation was going to attain budget balance by assuming the very inflation that balance was supposed to eliminate."

The governor was still in Wonderland. Only now he was willingly joined there by some of the most distinguished mainstream economic figures in the Republican Party.

THE LEAGUE OF WOMEN VOTERS ANNOUNCED THAT THERE WOULD BE A candidate debate on September 21. Carter said he wouldn't participate. The League said that John Anderson could if he surpassed 15 percent in enough polls by September 10—which he did. So Reagan would be debating Anderson.

John B. needed the boost. One poll from the *Washington Star* found that Reagan and Carter were tied at 39 percent—but that 60 percent said they weren't excited about any of the candidates. Broken down by those with a preference, however, 57 percent of the Carter supporters and 56 percent of the Reagan supporters—and a whopping *72 percent* of Anderson voters—said that they weren't excited by their pick. That scotched notions that Anderson could become some sort of post-partisan catch basin for disillusioned voters on both sides: Anderson was just one more candidate not to like. After the League of Women Voters warned they might place an extra chair onstage to represent the absent Carter, Johnny

Carson won a big laugh in his monologue: "You know what bothers me? Suppose the chair wins."

Reagan and Bush landed in Washington for an unusual joint campaign event with more than two hundred Republican members of Congress on the Capitol Steps. Before two thousand spectators, they collectively committed to five promises: slashing Congress's budget and bureaucracy, passing the first year's Kemp-Roth tax reduction, weeding out $34 billion in government waste, instituting enterprise zones, and strengthening defense. The architect of the gathering was first-term firebrand Newt Gingrich, who called it a "historic moment."

Gingrich's ambitions were no less vaulting than they had been when he sketched out a "three-dimensional chess" long-term plan for the Republicans to take over Congress. The previous fall, insisting that Washington's "gatekeepers" were "trying to prevent the rule of the majority," he attempted a plan to corral the votes of both conservative Republicans and Democrats to take the speakership from Tip O'Neill. And now he was scripting words for his party's presidential nominee.

"Within a year from today, by September 15, 1981, these five goals will be accomplished," Reagan said—thanks to this "contract with the American people."

THE CARTER CAMPAIGN HIT SNAGS.

On September 12, his campaign manager Tim Kraft quit to fight allegations that he had used cocaine. This was a strange and unfair development. When Hamilton Jordan had been falsely accused of snorting coke in the basement of Studio 54, a feature of the ethics package the president proudly signed into law in 1978 kicked in: an independent council was appointed, as required anytime there was evidence that a high-level executive branch official might have committed a crime. But on the way to exonerating Jordan, a witness told independent counsel Arthur Christy that he had once seen Kraft using the drug, and another time observed events that *suggested* he might have used it. Much to Christy's dismay, legal duty required him to deploy the full weight of his office's power to investigate Kraft—for an alleged peccadillo in which millions of Americans had indulged. With Jimmy Carter, no good deed went unpunished.

The next day, Carter received more bad luck—if luck had anything to do with it.

Under New York State's unique electoral rules, candidates could appear under more than one "party line" on a ballot. The Liberal Party, the Conservative Party, the Right to Life Party—all developed loyal constituencies that voted for whichever candidate party brass "cross-endorsed" to run on their line. For instance, every six years many liberals voted for

Senator Jacob Javits on the Liberal line, even though he was a Republican. Which could have explosive possibilities for the presidential election in November, observed the *New York Times*: if the Liberal Party gave its line to John Anderson "for disgruntled Democrats to vote for" instead of Carter, "most believe that Mr. Carter would lose the state and, without the state, lose the nation."

The Liberal Party was by then neither liberal nor a party; it was run with an iron hand by a shifty operator named Ray Harding—who defensively denied the *Times* theory that he held the presidential election in his hands, and insisted his organization's endorsement would be based strictly on the merits. Reagan's northeast regional coordinator Roger Stone was both an unscrupulous and boastful man, and what he boasted to a journalist many years later was that, in 1980, he approached the city's famously reptilian Republican fixer Roy Cohn, a Reagan fan, for advice on persuading Harding to slate Anderson.

"You need to visit his lawyer and see what his number is."

"Roy, I don't understand you."

"How much cash, you dumb fuck."

His number was $125,000. The problem, Stone responded, was that the campaign didn't have that kind of cash lying around. Barked back Cohn, "That's not the problem. How does he want it?"

Cohn gave Stone a suitcase ("I don't look in the suitcase. . . . I don't even know what's in the suitcase," Stone later recollected), with instructions for its delievery; Stone paid Cohn's law firm a "legal fee"; and on Saturday, September 13, at its annual convention, the Liberal Party nominated John Anderson to appear on their ballot line.

THEN CARTER'S PROBLEMS GOT WORSE.

On Monday, September 15, before thirteen hundred sweltering voters in a high school gym in Corpus Christi, he noted before taking audience questions that this was his twenty-fifth town hall meeting. Then he took a little swipe at Mr. Reagan: "The campaign staff of my opponent have put him under wraps. He's not having meetings like this. He's not having press conferences anymore, because when he has spoken on his own the last few days, he's gotten himself in trouble. In the Oval Office, as president, that's where the most difficult questions come, perhaps to any human being on earth, and you've got to be able to respond accurately, in a way that doesn't embarrass you personally and does not embarrass our Nation." At a fundraiser in Houston, he gibed that Reagan had been "muzzled."

He wasn't supposed to be doing this. The *Wall Street Journal* had usefully termed Carter's campaign strategy a "shoebox war": painting Reagan "as an insensitive incompetent, the kind of man who got his right-wing views from nothing but shoeboxes full of old newspaper clippings." For it to work, however, the campaign had to leave the dagger thrusting to surrogates—like Robert Strauss. If Carter did it, it would not be "presidential"—and he'd surrender the last vestiges of the sturdy foundation of his political capital since 1976: his *image as a decent man.*

But Carter longed to speak his mind. He was irritated—beyond irritated.

He couldn't believe how seriously Reagan's economic mumbo jumbo was being taken. He couldn't believe that Reagan got away with so much saber rattling. And it was astonishing that Reagan emerged untouched from a serious staff scandal, after *Mother Jones* magazine discovered that Richard V. Allen had been paid $60,000 in 1972 for six months of work for the lawyer of "fugitive financier" Robert Vesco, and had been in the room when that lawyer pleaded for Vesco's exoneration to the chairman of the Securities and Exchange Commission, then somehow forgot to mention this after being asked under oath to disclose all his associations with, and knowledge of, Vesco's activities. They also reported his work as a registered agent of the Portuguese government to help them defend their colonialism in Mozambique. Two hundred copies of that exposé had been hand-delivered to top journalists in Washington before the Republican convention. It received hardly any attention—and none in the *New York Times.* All the while, evidence that this very same Vesco had been involved in Libyan influence peddling poured gasoline on Billygate—the subject of over fifty *New York Times* articles over the previous month, even though the best efforts of nine senators had yet to reveal anything worse than a few instances of "poor judgement" on the part of anyone but Billy.

"We assumed," Hendrik Hertzberg later said plaintively, "that they would cover him like they might cover us." The *Times* never did, for instance, call out Reagan's continued insistence that he had never suggested that Social Security be made voluntary. To the president and his men, it felt like the media's obsession with "balancing" the news between left and right had killed simple journalistic good sense.

Their fears were not unfounded. To take a recent example, the far-right outfit Accuracy in Media bought shares in the New York Times Company in order to harass its executives at shareholder meetings. To make peace, publisher Arthur O. "Punch" Sulzberger invited its president, Reed Irvine, to regular conclaves at the newspaper's corporate suite—a courtesy extended to no other shareholder. The relationship soon advanced to a first-name basis: "Dear Punch," Irvine wrote after a meeting in July, "One area that we did not get into to the extent that I had wanted was the defense that exists to protect the *Times* and its readers from the Soviet disinformation and propaganda operation. . . . We lost in Vietnam because of our inattention to this area." Sulzberger dutifully delegated his second-in-command to ride herd on the paper's Paris bureau regarding one of Irvine's complaints. Executive editor Max Frankel fumed to Sulzberger, "I think it's more fitting to tell such people to practice their judgement of us in their publication and to let us manage and write ours as we see fit. I would be ashamed if we ever did pass muster with such nitwits." Yet the back-channel correspondence between the right-wing gadfly and the publisher continued—as if the nitwit deserved more influence with the *Times* than the White House.

But Jimmy Carter wasn't supposed to complain.

He had dipped a toe in those dangerous waters by weighing in on the Tuscumbia flap, and accusing his opponent of having been "muzzled." Then, on Tuesday, September 16, he waded in hip-deep. He was among friends, speaking at Ebenezer Baptist Church, the Atlanta congregation of his friend Martin Luther "Daddy" King, the father of the civil rights martyr, whose closing prayer at the 1976 Democratic National Convention had been one of the most memorable moments of the campaign. On his way in, answering a reporter's question about the Ku Klux Klan's sudden emergence in political discussions, Carter said that Reagan had started it—then reiterated, "Governor Reagan has been, in effect, muzzled by his campaign workers. He's not talking about China or evolution or the Ku Klux Klan, and I don't believe that the Klan will be any significant factor in the future."

He stepped inside, and heard Congressional Black Caucus Chairman Parren Mitchell slashing Reagan: "I'm going to talk about a man . . . who seeks the presidency of the United States with the endorsement of the Ku Klux Klan."

Then, the president took to the pulpit, stained-glassed light streaming in upon his face; and he preached:

"If it hadn't been for Daddy King, and his beloved wife, I would not be president. Had it not been for his Martin Luther King Jr., I would not be president. Had he not been a man of courage and vision and tenacity and faith, I would not be president."

He recalled a time on the campaign trail when something he said was interpreted as racist—a remark expressing sympathy for those who desired "ethnically pure" neighborhoods. He thanked Daddy King for his support in the days that followed, holding his hand on camera at a rally in Atlanta.

Then, Carter departed from his text.

"You've seen in this campaign the stirrings of *hate*.

"And the rebirth of *code words* like 'states' rights.' In a speech in Mississippi! And a campaign reference to the Ku Klux Klan relating to the South. *That*—is a message—that creates a *cloud* on the political horizon. *Hatred*—has no place in this country." An ovation began to swell. Carter rode the wave: "*Racism* has no place in this country!!"

It took only until four o'clock for Hamilton Jordan to issue a nervous clarification that Carter was not calling *Ronald Reagan* racist. It didn't work. Jimmy Carter had crossed a line. At his next White House press conference, running live on all three networks, the media set upon him like sharks. A journalist sanctimoniously demanded: "Do you think that Governor Reagan is running a campaign of hatred and racism? And how do you answer allegations that you are running a mean campaign?"

"I do not think he's running a campaign of racism"—he shut his eyes, as if this were painful—"or hatred. And I think my campaign is very moderate in its tone."

A reporter practically stared him down: "You've accused him of interjecting the Ku Klux Klan into the campaign."

The figures in the pressroom came to attention; then, Carter lied:

"The only thing I said Governor Reagan has injected into the campaign was a use of the words 'states' rights' in a speech in Mississippi."

James Reston of the *New York Times*, one of those masters of that genre of commentary where personal opinions are handed down like truths from Mount Sinai, wrote, "President Carter must know that, despite his recent rise in the popularity polls, many of his supporters—even many members of his own administration—are deeply disappointed by the mean and cunning antics of his campaign. . . . For among many of the people who wish him well and have serious doubts about Governor Reagan, there is a growing feeling that Carter is trying to be too shrewd, too clever and calculating, and that, in his confusion of ends and means, he is negating the principles and ideals that helped bring him to the White House in the first place." Hugh Sidey of *Time*, Reston's number one competitor for the job of press corps referee in chief, said "The past few days have revealed a man capable of far more petty vituperation than most Americans thought possible even in a dank political season." He said he feared a second-term President Carter unchecked by the requirement of reelection might draw up enemies lists in the manner of Richard Nixon. "The wrath that escaped Carter's lips about racism and hatred when he prays and poses as the epitome of Christian charity leads even his supporters to protest his meanness."

Carter's *meanness* was now a certified campaign issue. The conventional wisdom was now that he was taking, in the words of a headline on a front-page City Section column in the *Philadelphia Inquirer*, "The Low Road to High Office."

NANCY REAGAN CUT A COMMERCIAL: "I *DEEPLY, DEEPLY* RESENT, AND AM offended by, the attacks that President Carter has made on my husband—

the *personal* attacks he has made on my husband. . . . He is not a warmonger. He is not a man who is going to throw the elderly out in the street and cut out their social security. . . . That's campaigning on fear!" (Then she raised fears about Carter's "vacillating, weak foreign policy.")

Jimmy Carter made a spin through California, where Reagan's 50 percent negative rating in their internal polls had Carter campaign officials thinking he might win Reagan's home state. Californians, it turned out, were especially concerned about *Reagan's* vacillating foreign policy: that the newborn dove was a warmonger still. Carter's people remembered a high-impact ad that Gerald Ford ran in his primary in 1976. A voice pronounced the tagline with motherly concern: "*Governor* Reagan could not start a war. *President* Reagan could." They had something in mind like that now—Reston and Sidey be damned.

In Knoxville that day, Reagan reminded listeners that in 1976 the Carter campaign had hammered Jerry Ford with something called the "Misery Index": the rate of inflation plus the rate of unemployment. "It was 12.5 percent. Today, after three and a half years, that Misery Index has grown to 20.3 percent. . . . By every way we have of measuring failure, his policies have failed. . . . By the very standard Jimmy Carter used to define failure, he has failed."

Reagan pinned every problem but the weather on the president. So why shouldn't Carter take off the gloves, too?

He stood at the podium bearing the presidential seal at a town hall meeting in Torrance. The press tended to ignore his introductory remarks at these things. This time, however, the words he uttered played on TV again and again:

"Six weeks from now our nation will make a very critical decision. This decision will set the course of your life and of our nation's life not just for the next four years but for many generations to come. It will help to decide what kind of world we live in. It will help to decide whether we have war or peace. It's an awesome choice."

And Reagan yelped like a struck dog. "I think it's inconceivable that anyone and particularly a president of the United States would imply, as this is another incidence that he is implying and has several times, that anyone, any person in this country would want war, and that's what he's charging. And I think it's unforgivable."

Hamilton Jordan tried a halfway apology: "It was an overstatement of the case. However, Governor Reagan has repeatedly advocated the use of U.S. troops in crisis situations." But at an outdoor rally at Louisiana State University, Reagan departed from his text: "I think to accuse that anyone would deliberately want a war is beneath decency."

Carter, engineer-like, began adding example after example to his speeches of times Reagan had advocated threatening military force to resolve conflicts, from suggesting that a violent ultimatum to the North Koreans would free the crew of the USS *Pueblo* in 1968, to proposing Cuba be blockaded to punish the Soviet Union over Afghanistan.

Martin Anderson was quoted smugly in the *Washington Star*: "Carter's biggest asset is the aura of the presidency. When someone starts tarnishing the office, people don't like it." And this was now Washington conventional wisdom. Which was pretty convenient for Reagan. Now, when he said something daffy—like, in Buffalo, that "approximately 80 percent of our air pollution stems from hydrocarbons released by vegetation, so let's not go overboard in setting and enforcing tough emission standards from man-made sources"—Carter could not hit back without it confirming his "meanness" to the press.

Reagan's handlers, just to make sure, worked even harder to protect him from himself. After the LSU speech, a scrum of reporters clustered around Reagan. Lyn Nofziger plunged in like a halfback, crying, "We ain't got a press conference!"—which, indeed, Reagan ain't had in three weeks. Nofziger's regular refrain, after Reagan read prepared remarks from his portable podium—"No questions! No questions!"—became, among the traveling press corps, almost an informal campaign slogan.

Then, cowed by all the "muzzling" talk, his handlers backed off and let reporters on *LeaderShip '80* question the candidate. They even promised a bona fide news conference when they landed in Washington, D.C. At that press conference, a reporter brought up something Reagan had said in Harlingen, Texas, in the wilting heat, following a performance by a mariachi band to entertain the largely Mexican American crowd: that he would grant visas to undocumented Mexican immigrants "for whatever length of time they want to stay. . . . You don't build a nine-foot fence along the border between two friendly nations." The fence had been a Carter administration proposal back in December 1978—the "Tortilla Curtain," the notional twenty-seven-mile barrier had been dubbed by horrified human rights activists, though Reagan's host in Texas, Republican governor Bill Clements, whom Reagan had helped elect that fall, thought that solution wasn't nearly harsh enough. So, now, naturally, a reporter sought to clarify their apparent differences. Reagan replied that, actually, applause had swallowed up a subsequent clarification that their visas should have a stated termination date.

After that howler, it was back to the old block and tackle.

Like the time, visiting Lincoln's tomb in Springfield, he performed an Illinois political tradition for the cameras: rubbing the Great Emancipator's bronze nose for luck. He began answering a pool reporter's question about the hostages—and Nofziger nearly knocked them over hustling the great man away. On the bus, another press officer, James Brady, defended the practice. "We have our own agenda. We don't want a story to break before we were ready to communicate it to the market."

CHAPTER 37

"A Shabby Business"

THE DAY PRESIDENT CARTER MADE HIS ALLEGED BLOOPER IN CALIFORNIA, his fear for an unsteady hand at the tiller in the White House situation room was especially intense. Saddam Hussein, who had seized power in Iraq the previous year by executing hundreds of high-ranking members of his own Ba'ath Party, had just launched a series of air strikes in an attempt to take out the Iranian Air Force, which failed; the next day, he tried to finish off the weakened Iranian Army with a ground invasion, which met unexpectedly strong resistance. Iran and Iraq were at war. That threatened the peace of the Strait of Hormuz—which were it to become a battlefield, Senator Laxalt had realized with a start while flying over it in 1978, might sow "seeds of a third world war."

In Torrance, Carter had acted quickly and shrewdly to seize a strategic opportunity. He said during the town hall that Iraq's invasion could "convince Iran that they need peace with their neighbors, they need to be part of the international community, they need to be able to have a strong and viable economy, they need to get spare parts for their military weapons, and so forth, and therefore induce them to release the hostages. I'm not predicting that, but it's a possibility." The press corps, amid the kerfuffle over Carter calling Reagan a warmonger, hardly noticed. The intended audience surely paid closer attention: Carter was tendering Iran a feeler for a new round of negotiations.

The Reagan campaign paid close attention, too. For this was crucial intelligence for one of *their* most important strategic opportunities.

They had been laying down markers for it since spring, when Bill Casey told the *New York Times*, "That was a shabby business about the Iranian hostages on the morning of the Wisconsin primary, the act of a man with no nerve. We expect that Carter will try everything to get reelected. So we'll be ready for everything." The project was named in Wirthlin's Black Book. He had discovered that, if Carter managed to spring the hostages, it would be worth ten points in the polls. So he enshrined as one of his nineteen Conditions of Victory, "*We can neutralize Carter's 'October Surprise.'*"

The Reagan plan to minimize the political boon Carter would harvest from a hostage release had two components. The first was an intelligence operation. The security establishment was already honeycombed with supporters—including a complement of "Spooks for Bush," current and former Central Intelligence Agency personnel who had informally volunteered in the former CIA director's campaign. Now they helped man a twenty-four-hour operations center at Reagan headquarters, monitoring chatter from the field to keep abreast of possible hostage-release developments. Retired military personnel monitored airplane tail numbers at Air Force bases for hints arms might be on their way to trade for hostages. So thorough was their penetration, so many-tentacled their connections to shady arms dealers abroad that might broker an exchange, that it eventually inspired detailed (but unsubstantiated) conspiracy theories that the former spook Bill Casey had *directly* negotiated with Iran to hold the hostages until after the election. Mostly, however, this intelligence operation was a waste of time. Once, its supervisor spotted mounds covered by black tarps at McGuire Air Force Base in New Jersey. He had a local check on them every single day. "It never moved!" he told an interviewer more than ten years later. "It may still be there!"

No, the real jackpot came from the operation's other wing: disinformation.

It was run by an exceptionally well-connected and shrewd professional media manipulator named Robert Keith Gray, on leave from the Washington office of the public relations firm Hill & Knowlton. The aim was to sow public suspicion that Carter would even sell out America's security in order to win—so if the miracle actually happened, the public would suspect it all was a cynical ploy. Gray's first success might have come on August 18. Jack Anderson published the first of a series of columns claiming that Carter was planning an invasion of Iran, timed, for maximum political gain, in mid-October. This was not true. National Security Agency Iran hand Gary Sick came to believe it was the work of Gray's disinformation team—a suspicion underlined by an utterance immediately afterward, as if in coordination, in which Reagan expressed his fear Carter might be "tempted to take reckless actions designed to reassure Americans that our power is undiminished."

The operation attempted to nest the hostage-cynicism narrative within a larger one: that Carter was no high-minded idealist, but actually a power-mad fiend. On September 11, Bill Brock called a press conference to announce that the RNC was filing twenty-nine Freedom of Information Act requests to investigate "to what degree the administration is using the taxpayers to finance their own reelection campaign." Paul Laxalt provided examples of this "continuing and unbridled abuse of incumbency," like the time the head of OSHA said that Reagan wanted to abolish the agency.

As if the OSHA head could not come up with this inference on his own. Reagan had called the agency part of an effort "to minimize the ownership of private property in this country." And said: "I bet everyone in this room has, at one time or another, climbed a ladder. . . . How we did it without their 144 rules and regulations about ladder climbing I'll never know." OSHA had two regulations about climbing ladders. The insinuation failed to take root.

The campaign had more success with another—the one that, by the middle of September, was capital conventional wisdom: that Jimmy Carter was *mean*. That work had begun in earnest on August 29, when Laxalt released a seven-page letter to editorial writers. Like a basketball player "working the ref" to goad him to into calling fouls on the opposing team, it yelped that offensive remarks from Patricia Harris and Andrew Young tying Reagan to the KKK "went largely unnoticed" by editors ("Can you imagine the outcry from the other side if it was reported that a Republican official had engaged in similar tactics, say by comparing the Democrats to the Communist Party?") The document then laid out several research files' worth of alleged incidences of racism in Jimmy Carter's campaigns in 1966, 1970, and 1976. Laxalt concluded, in a more-in-sorrow-than-anger tone, "You and I have a vested interest in civilized debate. It's up to you to keep this campaign a clean one and not let fear tactics go uncriticized or unchallenged."

By the time of the Ebenezer Baptist Church speech and Torrance town hall, the media had proven itself quite up to Laxalt's demands.

THE OCTOBER SURPRISE TEAM PROBED FOR OPPORTUNITIES. IT HELPED that, for months, the public had heard so many contradictory rumors that cynicism concerning hostage-release news was already rampant. A typical episode unfolded in July. A Saudi newspaper quoted "well-informed sources" who said they would be home within three weeks. Those hopes were then promptly dashed by news that the Ayatollah had said, "Islam cannot be implemented with men with minds trained in Europe"—an expression of no-confidence in precisely those Western-educated officials working for the hostages' release.

Another apparent break came a few weeks later: the shah died, mooting the students' main demand, that he be returned to Tehran. The problem was that there wasn't yet a functioning Iranian parliament, or Majlis, to decide what should happen next. News that the Majlis would be impaneled was followed by news that it had gotten bogged down over choosing a prime minister, followed by news that the prime minister they'd picked, an unqualified former schoolteacher named Mohammad Ali Rajai, did not satisfy President Bani-Sadr, who blocked the installation of the cabinet full of clerics Rajai had named. Finally, on September 1, the Majlis got its act together, issuing two demands for the hostages' release: return the wealth that the shah held in the U.S. banks and acknowledge past interference in Iran's internal affairs. (Later the Majlis added the condition of unfreezing all Iranian assets in U.S. banks.)

And at Reagan headquarters, the ref-working began.

Campaign cochair Anne Armstrong was sent out to give a luncheon for the press. In her remarks, she added to the usual charge that Carter was "breaking new ground in the use of incumbency to get elected" that Americans' joy if the hostages were released shouldn't dispel concerns "about the continuing, spiraling decline of American prestige." Nor should "an October Surprise be sufficient to meet Carter's basic problem—the economy."

Assistant Secretary of State Warren Christopher began active negotiations with Tehran—first with optimism, because the Majlis had not demanded a deal-breaking apology for America's past interference in Iran, then with hopes shattered after the Ayatollah *added* that demand. Then came the September 22 Iraq incursion, and Carter's hopeful feeler from California—followed, in the Reagan camp three days later, by an apparent ratchet upward in the influence operation. Pat Buchanan, a sometime Reagan advisor whose sister was the campaign's treasurer, wrote in his syndicated column that the "oft-predicted 'October surprise,' a media event to blot out the memory of four forgettable years, may well be the release of hostages in exchange for American concessions." The next day, President Carter told an interviewer in Wisconsin, "We will do whatever is necessary to keep the gulf open." ABC's Sam Donaldson relayed the quote with a knowing arch of the eyebrow: "It's campaign time, and Carter is talking tough." On October 1, in Pittsburgh, Teddy White answered a confident prediction of victory from Michael Deaver, "But what about an October surprise?"

The message was getting through.

REAGAN WAS IN PITTSBURGH TO VISIT A STEEL MILL THAT HAD JUST LAID off hundreds of workers. One of the employees who remained told a journalist that he hated "the fucking Japanese" as much as he did the "fucking buttercup-yellow politicians you can't trust." Reagan alighted upon the depressed coal town of Wilkes-Barre armed with a research memo attesting to the popularity of firearms there, and the latest news on Senators Jesse Helms and James McClure's plans to filibuster a five-hundred-page bipartisan crime bill fourteen years in the making if it included a gun control amendment, and a selection of his own previous pro-gun positions, and a reminder to mention that the local Democratic congressman was for gun control; also that northeast Pennsylvania's unemployment rate was 12.3 percent. Wilkes-Barre's proletariat proved no less angry at politicians than Pittsburgh's—one party's in particular: a reporter heard from Democratic activists that calls to *their own* precinct lists were turning up more Reagan than Carter voters.

Reagan had come to Pennsylvania after New York, where on September 30 he had costarred with Frank Sinatra in a fundraiser beamed on closed-circuit TV to Republicans around the country, then addressed five hundred small business owners, calling for the estate tax exemption to be increased. (It just had been, in the tax bill Carter signed in 1978.) Next he donned a hard hat at a subway construction site (subsidized by the federal government to the tune of $800 million) where the banners included "SANDHOGS FOR REAGAN," "ITALIANS FOR REAGAN," and "BRING HOME OUR HOSTAGES." He announced that he had changed his mind and now favored federal aid to New York City. He caught a football.

The campaign judged those two days a success. Teddy White explained one reason why: a New York local newscast "carried three 'bites' of the morning's work"; the NBC network news showed him thrilling the sandhogs; and the Wilkes-Barre stop made the news in Pittsburgh. But there was also was another reason, one he could not be aware of: the October Surprise operation had shifted into its next gear, from the surrogates to the principals. Reagan, in an interview with the AP, answered a question about how he would handle the hostage crisis by saying that he "wondered whether they will be there in January. . . . The president has been pretty industrious in using the incumbency in this campaign, more so than any president that I could recall. So, as I say, I'm just bracing myself for an October surprise." And his running mate made the same insinuation: "One thing that's at the back of everyone's minds is, 'What can Carter do that is so sensational and so flamboyant, if you will"—*that's Jimmy Carter, Mr. Flamboyant*—"to pull off an October surprise. And everybody kind of speculates about it, but there's not a darned thing we can do about it, nor is there any strategy we can do except possibly have it discounted."

OCTOBER 1 WAS ALSO THE FIRST DAY OF THE FISCAL YEAR. THE COMMERCE Department reported that the economy had contracted by a tenth during the second quarter. Citibank raised its prime rate to 13.5 percent, then added another half point the next day. Carter fumed that the Federal Reserve was doing nothing to keep the economy moving. Arthur Burns sternly lectured him in the press: "The president's criticism of the Fed is regrettable. The basic reason for the rise of interest rates is that fears of inflation are increasing. If the Federal Reserve acted on the president's advice, these fears would intensify, international confidence in the dollar would be weakened, and interest rates would almost certainly rise sharply further."

Another statistic related to the economy was released that day by a group of media critics: over the previous month, Carter's "meanness" tied with the economy as the fourth most covered subject on ABC News. And the *Wall Street Journal* ran a front-page article on the role of economic news in the campaign. It featured an interview with a young Reagan operative who, with his typical cunning, had managed to get both himself and the campaign's narrative into the lead:

"WASHINGTON—A candidate seeking reelection, wrote PhD candidate Lee Atwater in 1978, can exploit built-in advantages of office, ranging from his ability to attract instant press attention to his chance to distribute political plumbs. Today, the 29-year-old political scientist is getting a first-hand glimpse.... From his vantage point as Reagan political director in the Southern states, Mr. Atwater is 'doing a real good job' of proving his observations correct. 'Jimmy Carter is blatantly political, and he's using every perquisite at his disposal,' Mr. Atwater contends."

CARTER WAS IN MICHIGAN, DEMONSTRATING HOW FLAT-FOOTED A DEMA-gogue he actually was.

He was there in answer to a taunt from George Bush during his appearance in the state—that "it would take a lot of guts for him to come to Flint." The city was the site of several massive General Motors plants. Its unemployment rate was 9.6 percent when Carter took office. It was 25.9 percent now. The president impressed approximately no one by putting on an inspector's lab coat and driving a new, fuel-efficient model off the line, claiming that America's cars were as good as anything Japan made—an assertion undercut on ABC that night by reporting on a defective Ford model whose wheels were nearly impossible to remove, and GM's recall of 372,000 faulty Cadillacs. In Washington, Carter's proposal for a government-industry "superfund" for chemical waste cleanup unexpectedly stalled. The House had overwhelmingly approved a $1.2 billion package in August, after DuPont's CEO Irving Shapiro endorsed the idea. Then, a historian later discovered, "a number of chemical firms, now sensing that Ronald Reagan would soon be elected, decided to hold firm in the hope that no legislation would be enacted."

October 1 was also a busy day at the Federal Election Commission, which had a deadline the next day to make a major decision. John Anderson was seeking bank loans as collateral for the federal matching funds he *might* receive if his campaign did well enough. They had to decide if this was legal. The answer they arrived at was ambiguous—which for Anderson was as bad as an outright refusal. "We must *know* that we'll be repaid before we'll commit to a loan," as one banker noted. Anderson was rarely cracking 10 percent in polls. Still, he refused to quit.

That drama intersected with another. On September 25 the League of Women Voters, in a concession to President Carter's insistence on a three-way debate, announced that they would stage, first, a debate between the major-party candidates, then one including Anderson—but that they would "under no circumstances consider sponsoring a debate between Governor Reagan and President Carter unless they agreed to participate in a multi-candidate debate." Carter quickly accepted the twin invitation. Reagan turned it down. The Carter campaign baited Reagan as a chicken. Still, the pundits gave the win in this particular round of shadowboxing to Reagan, on points for his tactical cleverness.

Anderson had begun tearing into Carter, and cozying up to Reagan. He accused the president of campaigning by fear, saying that claiming Reagan would divide the country was a sign of "*his own* fear that he is now not going to win the election." As if obliging the characterization, Carter ads began running on the radio saying a vote for John Anderson was a vote for Reagan. Anderson replied with bumper stickers—"A vote for Anderson is a vote for Anderson"—then ripped Carter even harder: he was a "near total failure." He was neither the liberal he pretended to be nor a conservative, but "an opportunist." "Mr. Carter's administration has been incompetent. It has been incoherent." His campaigning has "been offensive to many thinking Americans and really harmful to the political process. . . . I wish he would open that heavy Bible that he so ostentatiously carries on Sunday morning as he goes to and from the classroom of the Sunday school at the Baptist church."

They called Anderson an antipolitician. But he was a shrewd enough politician to know that his only chance to reverse the spiral of bad-polls-causing-bad-fundraising-causing-bad-polls-causing-bad-fundraising was harvesting Carter defectors—and screaming caustically enough to grab the attention from a fickle media. Which could only have added to the metastasizing number of citizens for whom Wednesday, November 5, could not come soon enough.

Among them was Teddy White. The author of *The Making of the President 1960*, *The Making of the President 1964*, *The Making of the President 1968*, and *The Making of the President 1972* had not produced a *Making of the President 1976*—perhaps because he was so sickened by the duck-nibbling rituals presidential campaigns had become. His diary suggested he was almost to the point of a nervous breakdown—or a breakdown, at least, in his democratic faith. "It's gone on too long," he wrote on September 30. "How long can you stay interested in the problems of inflation and the tax cut? There were five national elections in Germany the year before Hitler came to power in 1933; the last, which Hitler won, showed a sharp drop-off in votes. We've had politics up to our ears, are gorged with it."

NOT ALL VOTERS WERE APATHETIC.

In Boston, the conservative newspaper the *Herald* gave over an entire front page to a proclamation from the city's archbishop: "Those who make abortion possible by law . . . cannot separate themselves totally from that guilt which accompanies this horrendous crime and deadly sin," and that those "for true human freedom—and for life" must "follow your conscience when you vote." Howard Phillips said that the cardinal had just "joined the Moral Majority."

Jerry Falwell's face beamed out from the cover of *Newsweek*. The head of Christians for Reagan was quoted inside: "Christians gave Jimmy Carter his razor-thin margin of victory in 1976. We plan to reverse that in 1980." His name was Colonel Doner ("Colonel" was his first name, not his rank). When ABC News subsequently visited him for an interview, they asked if his group had TV commercials. "I was a little slow on the uptake," Doner later remembered—before it dawned on him that they wanted to *show* his commercials in a report. So he whipped some together. An excerpt of one ad, for which he hadn't even purchased airtime ("I'm duty-bound as a Christian and a mother to vote for Ronald Reagan," said a sweet matron with four children beside her on a front porch) showed up all the same, for free, during the first of a three-part series on "politics and the pulpit."

Christian Voice distributed five hundred thousand of their congressmen-rating Biblical Scorecards. A film called *Politics—A Christian Viewpoint* aired in churches, featuring interviews with figures like Jesse Helms and Paul Weyrich explaining holy offices like voter registration and precinct organization. A thousand evangelicals arrived in Jerusalem for a conference celebrating the opening of a "Christian embassy" in the city where they expected Christ's return. A *700 Club* personality named Jeremiah Denton, running at Jesse Helms's urging, won the Virginia Republican Senate primary. (Viewers of the TV movie on his life story the previous fall knew him as the Vietnam prisoner of war who heroically blinked T-O-R-T-U-R-E in Morse code when paraded before a film camera and ordered to attest to his good treatment.) In an Alabama Republican primary, the Moral Majority's candidate defeated a congressman who not only was a Baptist minister but had authored a constitutional amendment to return prayer to the schools. He also, however, had some liberal positions, and disagreed with Christian right leaders on strategy—so he had to go. "They beat my brains out with Christian love," he said.

The *Los Angeles Times* gave Falwell space on its op-ed page to publish "Enforcing God's Law in the Voting Booth." He was identified as the author of a new book, *Listen, America!*, in which, of South Africa, he wrote, "The many Christian believers of that great nation need our prayers that their doors remain open to the Gospel. If we are not careful the United States will be next." Its economic teachings came from Milton Friedman's *Free to Choose*; its argument that "it is time for our welfare program to be examined and much of it done away with" was illustrated via an un-Christ-like parable about adopting two dogs whose former owner instructed him to feed them fresh meat. Instead, Falwell bought "a big bag of brown nuggets. . . . They did not eat luxuriously, but they did eat."

Falwell toured the upper Midwest. In St. Paul, he introduced the crowd to a half dozen members of the Minnesota legislature's "Pro-Decency Caucus." Introducing him in Neenah, Wisconsin, the state Moral Majority chairman explained, "Moral Majority intends to give you the information of which candidates live by the ten commandments. You take that information to the polls and vote for God." A pastor said that "our country is no longer Christian and it's time we took it back." The latest edition of the *Moral Majority Report* came out featuring a Falwell editorial entitled "Moral Majority Opposes 'Christian Republic.'"

ABC's cameras recorded a meeting of Iowa church folks organizing to distribute dead-fetus leaflets on windshields in church parking lots to defeat Senator John Culver:

"Does John Culver represent Iowa when he votes to kill innocent babies with taxpayer money?"

"NO!!!"

"If just each one of you will reach ten churches with the truth on Chuck Grassley and John Culver—"

"It means that we will win the election hands down in this state."

Culver and Grassley were tied. But maybe not for long. The Sunday after that was the "Christians Are Citizens Too Day" voter registration drive—an idea hatched within the Reagan campaign.

Liberals poured out rage at what they were witnessing. HHS Secretary Patricia Harris said that she was "beginning to fear that we could have an Ayatollah Khomeini in this country." The president of Yale University decried the "radical assault on pluralism." The Reverend William Sloane Coffin opened his sanctuary to TV cameras for the first time ever to record him preaching that "the Bible is something like a mirror: if an ass peers in, you can't expect an apostle to peer out." Norman Lear chartered a membership organization called People for the American Way to fight "this alarming new movement" who were "teaching people to hate, but in a 'Christian' way." Iowa congressman Tom Harkin said that if churches wanted to measure a politician's morality "on the basis of his vote on the B-1 bomber or the creation of the Department of Education, they ought to be taxed." The University of Chicago religion scholar Martin Marty, a devout Lutheran, said on one of ABC's "Politics and the Pulpit" broadcasts that the Moral Majority seemed to believe that "if you aren't their kind of Christian, you're a second-class citizen," and that if they really *were* a majority like they claimed, "logically they are going to impose their particular brand of theology and lifestyle on the rest of us."

Which further inflamed evangelicals' martyrdom, making them work all the harder.

ON OCTOBER 3, REAGAN SPOKE TO AN ECSTATIC CROWD OF EIGHT THOU-sand at the National Religious Broadcasters forum in a still-under-construction auditorium at Jerry Falwell's Liberty Baptist College. He received the most resounding of his many ovations for avowing, "I think the government should get out of the family. It can't be a parent. It doesn't know more about raising children than a parent does," and that "I don't think we should have ever expelled God from the classroom." Although, interestingly enough, the ACLU later discovered that God—or at least organized prayer—had been expelled from *Illinois* classrooms before Reagan had come of school age.

The press pack had the August Religious Roundtable gathering on their minds. For there, the executive director of the north Texas branch of the American Jewish Committee had recorded Southern Baptist Convention president Bailey Smith telling a press conference (to "particularly enthusiastic response," a witness observed), "It's interesting to me at great political battles how you have a Protestant to pray, and a Catholic to pray and then you have a Jew to pray. With all due respect to those dear people, my friends, God Almighty does not hear the prayer of a Jew. For how in the world can God hear the prayer of a man who says that Jesus Christ is not the true Messiah? It is blasphemy. It may be politically expedient, but no one can pray unless he prays through the name of Jesus Christ." The AJC official distributed the transcript to Jewish leaders around the country. It caused a stir. And, now that Ronald Reagan was fellowshipping with the Moral Majority's leader, after enthusiastically endorsing the gathering where Reverend Smith had uttered those words, journalists naturally were eager to learn what he thought of them—the moment he stepped off the plane.

He answered, "Since both the Christian and Judaic religions are based on the same god, the God of Moses, I'm quite sure those prayers are heard. But then, I guess, everyone can make his own interpretation of the Bible and many individuals have been making different interpretations for a long time"; not quite the full-throated disavowal.

He faced the same question at a press conference, Falwell at his side. He reminded reporters that it wasn't *Jerry Falwell* who had made that statement. (Which was true, as far as it went; Falwell had only been quoted the day before exclaiming, "One is redeemed who trusts in God through faith in Jesus Christ!") The *Boston Globe* ran a picture of the pair that looked like they were locked in passionate embrace, noting that 50 percent of Jews were undecided in the presidential election. Shortly afterward, Rabbi Marc Tanenbaum of the American Jewish Committee suggested that perhaps Falwell was simply "ignorant" about Judaism, and proposed a meeting—from which Falwell emerged to announce that "God is a respecter of all persons. He loves everyone alike. He hears the heart cry of any sincere person who calls on Him." For the media, this awkward business was over; Jerry Falwell had apparently been redeemed. No one asked him about his recent pamphlet with the mushroom cloud on the cover, *Armageddon and the Coming War With Russia.*

The fate of another New Right figure was up in the air. The same day Reagan was in Lynchburg, Representative Robert Bauman of Maryland, the chairman of the American Conservative Union and the possessor of a 100 percent score on Christian Voice's Biblical Scorecard ratings, was arrested in a Washington, D.C., park and pleaded not guilty to soliciting sex with and "performing oral sodomy on" a sixteen-year-old boy. His lawyer blamed alcohol, and the prosecutor agreed that he need not be tried if he entered a treatment program for alcoholism. His doctor, on the other hand, said that he did not think Bauman was an alcoholic—just that "something terrible happened to him." He had also, the *New York Times* reported, "sponsored legislation specifically authorizing employers to discriminate against gays and another measure to deny veterans' benefits to those discharged for homosexuality."

JIMMY CARTER GAVE AN INTERVIEW AT THE AIRPORT ON THE WAY OUT OF Flint, Michigan. He said that one of the things that worried him about Ronald Reagan was that "in a troubled world, with the closest possible margin of decision, there is the option of the use of weapons or the commitment to try to resolve a dispute peacefully." Whether that disqualified his opponent for the presidency was "a judgement that the American people would have to make."

His daily intelligence briefings had grown almost inconceivably weighty. Crises were flaring up across the Middle East: Egypt's Anwar Sadat was increasingly isolated in the region, his hold on power within his own country increasingly fragile, because of the peace deal he had signed with Israel. The Gulf kingdoms were obsessively monitoring any danger in the Strait of Hormuz, determining whether or not to intervene. Carter had somehow to affirm America's neutrality between Iran and Iraq lest the war escalate into a regional one should America tip its hand to one side; at the same time, it behooved him to somehow signal to the Iranians that American help *might* be on its way, should they just do the right thing concerning the hostages. Meanwhile nuclear-armed Israel watched warily, as did the USSR, which had signed a fifteen-year friendship pact with Saddam Hussein, similar to the one with Afghanistan—where war still raged, too. He also negotiated an end to the Mariel boatlift.

Given all this, the ads Carter was running were about as accurate as political commercials could be. At one, he sat at his desk, intently marking up papers, his glasses atop a nearby pile. (*"Each day, the most important information flows into the Oval Office."*) He read documents in the presidential limousine, peering out the window with evident concern. (*"And when the chief of state travels out into the world, as our principal representative . . ."*) He strode purposefully up the steps to Air Force One; on board, navy-blue briefing books covering the table, he lectured a note-taking aide (*". . . about nations, relations, and people."*) He sat with world leaders around a table in ornate gold high-backed chairs. He was heard speaking—"This will be the fourth economic summit conference, and I approach it with optimism. . . ."—then shown at a formal dinner in the East Room, then laying a wreath at the funeral of the Japanese prime minister, then walking with Deng Xiaoping.

"President Carter represents this nation with intelligence, and dignity. He has built a working relationship with the People's Republic of China. And he has established a working relationship with a range of world leaders."

The next shot was a close-up of the White House portico, which pulled back to reveal a crowd on the lawn, then a close-up of the waving president, first lady, and Pope John Paul II—the spiritual leader of all those sturdy white ethnic proletarians Dick Wirthlin had Ronald Reagan working so hard to persuade.

"Like many Americans, they have come to respect the dedication, the humanity, and the good sense of President Carter."

The tagline was the campaign's simple slogan: "RE-ELECT PRESIDENT CARTER." Because he knew how to be president. And what did Ronald Reagan know?

PRACTICALLY THE ONLY TV COMMERCIAL REAGAN WAS RUNNING SOUGHT TO answer that question—actually, several iterations of the same ad, which sometimes ran its full five minutes, other times in thirty- and sixty-second chunks. It was premised on the most foundational of the Conditions of Victory from Wirthlin's Black Book: "The conservative Republican Reagan base can be expanded to include a sufficient number of Moderates, Independents, soft Republicans, and soft Democrats to offset Carter's natural Democratic base and his incumbency advantage." The data points most crucial to this conclusion rhymed with Elliott Curson's intuition from back in February: 90 percent of voters had heard of Ronald Reagan. But only 40 percent—and higher east of the Mississippi—knew what he had done.

So it was that adman Peter Dailey, refining the work in round after round of focus-group interviews after each new cut at the problem, endeavored to instruct them.

The ad was a mini-biography. It bore a strong resemblance to Jimmy Carter's in 1976. It told the story of a boy raised "in America's heartland, small-town Illinois. From a close-knit family, a sense for the values of family, even though luxuries were few and hard to come by." (It had not been, of course, actually quite so bucolic, given his father's frequent alcoholic benders.)

Next, it was off to Hollywood, where his "appeal came from his roots, in his character. . . . He appealed to audiences because he was so clearly one of them." (This was closer to the truth.)

He had been "a peacetime volunteer army officer, and with the outbreak of World War II, he signed on for active duty." (You couldn't expect a campaign commercial to explain that the main reason he signed up for peacetime reserve duty, cheating on his vision test to do so, was for the chance to ride horses; nor all the wartime deferments Warner Bros. hustled for him before finally managing to land him a cushy posting at "Fort Wacky" in Culver City, California, making training films.)

"Captain Reagan returned to Warner Bros. and to one of the most challenging periods of his life." (This was a clever way to acknowledge, and evade, his 1947 divorce.)

Then came his work as a "dedicated union man"; his work as a corporate pitchman was skipped. Then his swearing in as governor of California—"next to president, the biggest job in the nation."

This was where a one-minute version of the ad began, with the narrator booming, "This is a man whose time has come. A *strong* leader. With a *proven* record." He was said to have inherited a "state of crisis," a deficit at $194 million and counting, a state near bankruptcy, then "became the greatest tax reformer in the state's history. When Governor Reagan left office, the $194 million deficit had been transformed into a $550 million surplus. The *San Francisco Chronicle* said Governor Reagan 'has saved the state from bankruptcy.' The time is now for strong leadership. *Ronald Reagan* for president."

Those words—*tax reformer*—did a lot of work. They suggested he was a tax-cutter. This was no less than a foundation of one of his campaign's most crucial claims: he could balance a budget while cutting taxes *because he had done it before*. The *Los Angeles Times* demonstrated why this was false. It "omits the fact that the tax refunds he boasts of were made possible only because his administration imposed three large tax increases that raised billions of dollars more than any of the experts imagined they would."

But that analysis appeared in April—with, apparently, little impact; the biography ads ran and ran and ran. They kept on running into October, so often that one governor deeply involved in the campaign called Reagan to complain that if he saw the documentary on TV one more time he was going to throw up. They would keep on running, the campaign managers replied, until polling confirmed that the message was getting through to undecided voters.

BUT IT WAS CARTER'S MESSAGE THAT APPEARED TO BE GETTING THROUGH. More and more, men and women in the street were telling interviewers that they were afraid of Reagan.

The election polls still had them just about tied. But Carter's *personal* approval rating—as opposed to his job performance rating—remained high. So he continued to press the attack. He said that Reagan's tax proposal was "a monstrous, ill-conceived giveaway to the very rich." He reminded voters, "My opponent was against Medicaid and Medicare. When Chrysler Motor Company was just about to go under, I and the Congress were working to guarantee loans—not to give away a nickel but just to give Chrysler the right to borrow money. And my opponent, who is a Republican"—a useful reminder, given that still only a fifth of the country *identified* themselves as Republicans—"said, 'I don't see anything wrong with bankruptcy.'"

Commentators pressed forward on the attack, too—against Carter. Mary McGrory asked, "Is our president really the man who preached morality in 1976?" A political cartoonist drew Jimmy Carter as Dr. Jekyll, pouring fluids into beakers—"*A small charge of racism . . . A touch of hate . . . Some oil of sanctimony . . . A little drop of viciousness . . . A pinch of pettiness . . . A modicum of meanness . . .*"—then turning with a *poof* into Richard Nixon, arms in a double V-for-victory salute.

Reagan's standard stump speech insisted that Carter's "economic policies have put two million Americans out of work," and that "no amount of rhetoric can obscure the disaster those policies have inflicted." New

York Lieutenant Governor Mario Cuomo responded plaintively: "Why is it mean for Carter to say that Reagan is imprudent, and therefore dangerous, when it isn't mean for people to say that Carter deliberately put people out on the street?"

FOUR MONDAYS BEFORE THE ELECTION, CARTER WAS IN CHICAGO, WHERE, at a gathering in the backyard of a private home, he spoke eloquently of his fears about Reagan moving into the White House. "It's not a place for simplistic answers. It's not a place for shooting from the hip. It's not a place for snap judgements that might have serious consequences." He once more cited all the crises when Reagan had advocated sending troops, in Angola, in Cyprus, in Lebanon, in North Korea, even in Ecuador for a recent dispute over fishing grounds. "That's as a governor or as a candidate for president. What he would do in the Oval Office, I don't know."

He reminded his listeners that presidents "literally decide the lives of millions of people in our country and indeed throughout the world." He referred to Reagan's remark back in February that Pakistan's efforts to build nuclear weapons weren't "any of our business." He noted Reagan's reaction, in 1977, when SALT II talks in Moscow broke down: he welcomed it, enthusing that now the "one trump card that has never been used" could be thrown—threatening an arms race, for if the Russians know they "have to compete with us, I'm sure they'll come running to the table and say 'wait a minute,' because they know they can't." Regarding *that*, Carter was downright indignant: "I don't believe this country needs a president who believes that the best way to control nuclear weapons is to start a nuclear arms race and play a trump card against the Soviet Union."

Jules Witcover and Jack Germond were alarmed, too—about Carter. They detected "stridency, a note of desperation and pleading" in Carter's voice. And when he attacked Reagan "specifically by name," they reported, "in the roped off press section, jaws fell."

Next Carter spoke at a fundraiser downtown. Reverend Bailey Smith's remarks in Dallas, and Falwell's response to them, were at the top of his mind. He couldn't believe that a presidential candidate would stand with a man who questioned another person's worth in the eyes of God. He pleaded with his audience to expend more energy registering voters—because who wins would "determine whether or not this America will be unified, or, if I lose the election, whether Americans might be separated black from white, Jew from Christian, North from South, rural from urban; whether this nation—"

The press hardly heard the rest. "There were only looks of disbelief as the words 'black from white . . .' sank in," Witcover and Germond observed. "Jimmy Carter was back on the low road . . . outdoing himself."

Ronald Reagan sorrowed the next morning, "I can't be angry. I'm saddened that anyone, particularly someone who has held that position, could intimate such a thing. I'm not asking for an apology from him. I know who I have to account to for my actions. But I think he owes the country an apology." Carter organizer Greg Schneiders, touring college campuses, discovered that the first or second question he now got after every recruiting speech concerned Carter's alleged "meanness." He said he had "never seen an issue seep down from the press in Washington to the local level so fast. . . . It yanked the safety net from under him."

Gerald Rafshoon had seen this coming. In July, he had written in a strategy memo, "People would feel more comfortable if they could get their thoughts and perceptions about Jimmy Carter straight. Either: 'Yes, he is a good man *and* a good president,' or 'He's a lousy president and he's not a particularly nice man either. He tricked us.'" Rafshoon theorized that their job would be to "make it easy for people to change their minds about the competence issue."

The media preferred to dwell on the question of whether he was a nice man. So it was that Jimmy Carter was called to answer for his sins to Barbara Walters, whose ABC News interview program had become a sort of modern American electronic confessional. She asked him to answer for the way he had become so "mean, vindictive, hysterical, and on the point of desperation." He answered, jaw clenched, eyes flashing steel: "Well, those characterizations are not accurate, Barbara. I think it's true that when Mr. Reagan says that I am desperate or vindictive or hysterical, he shares part of the blame that I have assumed that the tone of the campaign has departed from the way it ought to be between two candidates for the highest office in the land."

"No more name-calling?"

"I'll do my best."

"Mr. President, are you apologizing?"

"*Well.*"

Ronald Reagan, in Lacrosse, Wisconsin, informed that Carter had told Walters that both candidates had made comments "that are probably ill-advised" and was ready to get back to the issues, said, "Well, I think that would be nice if he did." Then he blasted away: "You mean he's really going to talk finally about how his administration has caused runaway inflation, unemployment beyond anything we've known since the '30s, credit rising to the highest since the Civil War? . . . I can stay home maybe then." Then, at a "Save Our Steel" rally in Steubenville, Ohio, he tossed a bomb in the direction of the Environmental Protection Agency, "who, if they had their way, you and I would have to live in rabbit holes or birds' nests." Nobody asked him to apologize for being mean.

At Reagan headquarters in Alexandria, Virginia, two big decisions were taken: to switch out the bio ads for the next phase of advertising; and, with Wirthlin's tracking polls suggesting Carter's base in the South was weakening, to move resources from their previous battleground states in the Great Lakes, the foundation of a model projecting a relatively close election, and shift them to states like Georgia and Louisiana, part of a model projecting a rout.

AS JIMMY CARTER CONFESSED MEANNESS TO BARBARA WALTERS, JOHN ANderson accused the president of exploiting the hostages "to secure his re-nomination" because his "gaze extends no further than the next public opinion poll," and Jesse Jackson gave a speech begging Anderson to withdraw, because there was "no time to waste with fascism about three weeks away." Election season was certifiably ugly.

Although, actually, Reagan's new commercials were rather gentlemanly—"kind of dull," an *Advertising Age* industry survey concluded. Both Bill Moyers and the media critic Ron Powers were astounded by their marginal quality. The lack of sheen was intentional. It was driven by research—especially with independent voters—which once again dovetailed with Elliott Curson's intuitions from the winter, and Lyn Nofziger's going back years: Reagan was most successful when he spoke directly to voters. Reagan's base, Peter Bailey said, "enjoyed stylized associations—the Statue of Liberty, 'God Bless America,' waving wheat, farmers around a table, the governor choking up while speaking—but for the 15 percent we were targeting, the slightest hint of that kind of production would have been distracting, invalidating everything we did." Among everyone else, "We found that if we presented Reagan as anything but a competent former governor offering solutions, we reinforced that level of perception we wanted to avoid—actor."

So it was that Americans were presented endless iterations of Ronald Reagan sitting in a study looking directly into a camera, explaining what he had done as governor of California and how that augured what he would do as President of the United States.

The candidate himself was said to be "champing at the bit" to go negative. The October Surprise strategy afforded him the thrill by proxy—with the added advantage of spurring the president to continue blowing his stack. The nation's emotional attachment to the captives in Tehran was reaching a new pitch of intensity; on October 8, a hostage wife began a campaign to erect a thousand billboards around the country asking, "Have you thought about the hostages today?" The fighting between Iran and Iraq was reaching a new intensity, too, with the nations of the Middle East, and even North Korea, beginning to choose up sides. Iran warned it might begin mining the Persian Gulf and the Strait of Hormuz—a state of chaos not exactly conducive to manipulation by even the most cynical president. Reagan officials told the *New York Times* to brace themselves for "some kind of dramatic actions during the next two weeks." Carter replied in consternation: "There is no way you contrive some sort of false surprise to be sprung on the American people just before the election!"

REAGAN HAD HIS OWN PROBLEMS: HE REQUIRED PROTECTION FROM HIMself. After he addressed the steelworkers in Steubenville—who booed him—a reporter wedged in to inquire about the time he said that "approximately 80 percent of our air pollution" stemmed from hydrocarbons released from vegetation. Irritated, he replied, "First of all, I didn't say 80 percent. I said 92 percent—93 percent, pardon me. And I didn't say 'air pollution,' I said oxides of nitrogen. And I am right. Growing and decaying vegetation in this land are responsible for 93 percent of the oxides of nitrogen." Climate scientists cleared up the confusion, somewhat; they explained that *industry* was responsible for approximately that percentage of oxides of nitrogen, a pollutant, and that the stuff trees emitted was harmless. (*Factories, trees*: who wouldn't confuse them?)

Southern California happened to be undergoing its worst smog emergency in years; and that was where Reagan alighted next. At Claremont College, protesters comprised a tenth of the audience. Their signs included "MUTANTS FOR REAGAN" and "NUKE THE TREES." A protester even *dressed* as a tree—with a sign reading "CHOP ME DOWN BEFORE I KILL AGAIN." Reagan addressed the demonstrators: "It isn't true that I suggested that we should let up and not do anything about smog! . . . I am an environmentalist. . . . We passed the strictest air pollution laws. . . . We have the cleanest water act that has been passed in the United States!" He also, however, said air pollution had been "substantially controlled." At one of his next stops, a scrawled placard read, "WE'RE CHOKING ON SUBSTANTIALLY CONTROLLED SMOG." Often, his words weren't audible above heckling.

The man who coined the phrase "let Reagan be Reagan" honored his advice in the breach. "He's talking, Lyn, he's talking!" an aide cried one day when Reagan was spotted unaccompanied in the presence of reporters; Nofziger skedaddled thither posthaste to remove him. The *San Francisco Chronicle* ran a feature on "Nofziger's Wall Around Reagan." It quoted him stating unapologetically, "Q-and-A's tend to defuse what we want to talk about. One guy stands up and says, 'Explain your position on abortion or the Panama Canal.' Shit"—"S - - -," in the paper's family-friendly rendering—"I don't want to see stories on abortion or the

Panama Canal. Why should we talk about abortion when his position is known and there are no votes to be gained from that?"

Nofziger contributed to the election's ugliness. When a rumor spread that Reagan had suffered a heart attack, he went on New York talk radio and insisted the White House planted it. "Now I'm going to start a rumor. Write this. Jimmy Carter has the clap."

But Walter Mondale contributed also. He said that Reagan's muzzling reminded him of how one dealt with a pet dog: you only let him excrete under supervision.

THE ELECTION SEASON'S UGLIEST ACTOR, HOWEVER, WAS THE NATIONAL Conservative Political Action Committee.

"It's the dirtiest campaign I've been involved in," complained one of the targets of their Senate hit list, George McGovern. Even his opponent Jim Abdnor said he wished he had never heard of NCPAC—though he also claimed, rather dubiously, "I wasn't aware this was going on." Another target, Frank Church, also called it the dirtiest campaign he'd experienced. His race against Steve Symms was tied—but the days when he dreamed of restoring Idaho's progressive populist heritage were but a memory. A visiting Eastern reporter stopped into a store to get his luggage repaired. The proprietor told him, "I personally think it doesn't make much difference who's president; get rid of these labor bastards is what I'm after." The reporter was admiring the gorgeous snowcapped peaks rimming Boise when he overheard a citizen say that the nation's problems could only be solved if all the homosexuals were rounded up and shot.

In a state in which 60 percent of the land was owned by the federal government, Idaho's Sagebrush Rebellion activists were particularly vehement. Symms's unqualified endorsement of their agenda—opening up thirty thousand acres of public lands for cobalt mining, dredge mining in rivers, breaking ground for a new phosphate mine in a national forest, storing nuclear waste in exchange for federal money—explained why the Independent Petroleum Association of America grew his campaign coffers from $32,061 at the beginning of the year to nearly $400,000 by spring, of which $154,000 alone was raised in a single two-day swing through Texas. "It's really scary," said an environmentalist working to preserve the Snake River. (He was voting for Anderson.) "I feel I'm being overpowered by all this rightist propaganda, all these people backed by big bucks." NCPAC spent $200,000 bombarding the state with new mailers on Church's "anti-taxpayer, anti-defense, anti-family votes." Symms didn't even try denying a connection to NCPAC; he was a member of its board.

Idaho's conservative junior senator, James McClure, hit the road with him, holding Church personally responsible for the assassination of a CIA agent in Greece, repeating a debunked story invented by CIA propagandists to discredit his 1975 investigation of the agency. Scoop Jackson, the single person most responsible for burying Church's beloved SALT II, loyally campaigned for his Senate Democratic neighbor nonetheless—but couldn't believe the poison he was hearing: "Here *I* have to go around and defend my record on national defense because some lunatics are running loose!"

As for Ronald Reagan, he visited Idaho Falls for Symms on October 14, and said that when he became president, "The next administration will reflect the values and goals of the Sagebrush Rebellion. Indeed, we can turn the Sagebrush Rebellion into the Sagebrush Solution."

AN EVEN NASTIER CONSERVATIVE WAS TRYING TO BEAT AN INCUMBENT REpublican, though one even more liberal than many Democrats. Jacob Javits was the longest-serving senator in New York history. In May of 1979, direct mail recipients received a mailing proposing they flood the office of the "allegedly Republican United States Senator" with these "birthday cards":

"DEAR SENATOR JAVITS:

"HAPPY 75TH BIRTHDAY.

"WHY DON'T YOU QUIT WHILE YOU'RE AHEAD?"

Now he was seventy-six—and looked older. A *New York* magazine article the previous year about the jockeying to replace him had mentioned twelve possible candidates, including the Democrats' eventual nominee, Watergate hero Elizabeth Holtzman, and a Republican long shot, Henry Kissinger—but not the person who emerged as the true force in the race: a far-right town supervisor in the town of Hempstead, a Long Island suburb, named Alfonse D'Amato, who beat Javits in the September Republican primary in a campaign masterminded by NCPAC's pollster Arthur Finkelstein, an acolyte of Jesse Helms—an unlikely one, given that he was Jewish and gay. D'Amato's TV campaign was the first anyone could remember that consisted *only* of negative commercials; D'Amato didn't appear in them. "He was completely irrelevant to the campaign," Finkelstein later boasted. Javits appeared in one, however, looking haggard, as a narrator made reference to his heretofore little-known diagnosis with Lou Gehrig's disease. (*"And now, at age seventy-six and in failing health, Jacob Javits wants six more years...."*) Another ad featured the candidate's mother, hefting a grocery bag, speaking of an old lady's economic travails in Jimmy Carter's America, urging, "Vote for my son, Al." That humanized him. "We had to prove Alfonse had a mother," Finkelstein said. Otherwise he was just a feral ball of reactionary rage. "Do you realize if we got the *welfare monkey* off our backs how many policemen we could hire and put on the streets?" he told one gathering. "How we could fight that fight against what's taking place and ravaging our streets and the fact is we need a *death penalty* today in this state if we ever needed one."

But a *Newsweek* rundown of races ten days before the November 4 balloting didn't mention D'Amato, predicting that "Javits, running as a Liberal, won't catch Holtzman." They also observed that all the "REAGAN/CHURCH bumper stickers on Idaho highways reflect ticket-splitting that may save Church." Birch Bayh "may fall"; John Culver was "fighting hard against a conservative backlash"; "a vulnerable McGovern is in the fight of his life"; and "Clinton, the nation's youngest governor, will probably win."

November would tell.

ON OCTOBER 15, WITH WIRTHLIN'S TRACKING POLLS SHOWING HIM BEHIND Carter for the first time, Reagan toured ravaged industrial towns in Ohio and Michigan, labeling himself an "old union man" and ratcheting up the economic attacks: "A few weeks ago, I said Mr. Carter's policies have resulted in an American tragedy. Nowhere is that tragedy more evident than in cities like Lima, where men and women willing to work and help their families prosper are out of work—and out of hope." Then, the press corps followed him to a redbrick church in a ramshackle inner-city neighborhood in Detroit.

He was racking up astonishing endorsements. There was legendary civil rights lawyer Morris Abrams, whose landmark 1962 Supreme Court victory had banned electoral rules giving disproportionate influence to rural whites in House elections, and Edward Costikyan, a towering liberal reformer of New York City's corrupt Democratic machine. Franklin Delano Roosevelt's son James. The national president of the American Agriculture Movement, the farmers who had descended in tractors upon Washington, D.C., in 1978. Watergate special prosecutor Leon Jaworski announced that he would head Democrats for Reagan, admitting that he had once called Reagan extremist—but better a "competent extremist than an incompetent moderate."

Reagan was also about to receive the nod from the seventeen-thousand-member Professional Air Traffic Controllers Organization union, who said Carter had "mismanaged" the air traffic control system, while Reagan understood "the vital role of the professional controller": the endorsement came in exchange for a pledge to appoint a new FAA administrator who had their approval—and might also have been motivated by knowledge that President Carter had a plan on the books to undermine their union should they strike when their contract came up for renegotiation the following year.

Reagan even got an endorsement from a national vice president of the American Federation of Government Employees, which represented federal workers, who called Reagan's positions "a breath of fresh air after the inept policies of the last four years"—and some grudging warmth from an even more surprising quarter after he announced three Mondays before the election that "one of the first Supreme Court vacancies in my administration will be filled by the most qualified woman I can possibly find." He even impressed Eleanor Smeal of the National Organization of Women. She told the *New York Times* that Reagan was "finally waking up to the fact that this issue is a lot hotter than he realized," repeating campaign talking points that he had supported fourteen civil rights bills as governor.

A particularly nifty little endorsement appeared in the *Times* edition of Tuesday, October 15. Every four years since 1972, the paper had looked in on Dewey Burton, an automotive worker from Michigan. In neatly allegorical fashion, every four years, the self-identified New Deal Democrat became more disillusioned with his political party—make that, now, his *former* party. "If Reagan wins," he said, "you can bet we'll throw a party." That same day, Reagan was blessed by Virginia senator Harry Flood Jr., who had inherited both his father's senate seat and his statewide political machine. This was the first time a member of the family had endorsed a presidential candidate in more than forty years.

The most astonishing endorsement came the next day, from the pulpit of that church in Detroit: Ralph Abernathy, former president of the Southern Christian Leadership Conference, who identified himself as "the man in whose arms Martin Luther King died," and said he was "totally committed to rebuilding . . . a nation that is sensitive to the poor and the downtrodden." He recalled campaigning for Jimmy Carter, then watching as Carter broke his promises, until, now, "black people cannot make it." He said he would have loved to have been able to back Senator Kennedy; but, since he could not, "I have been praying and I have been studying and today I have had an opportunity to come to a decision after a private meeting with Governor Reagan. And after we discussed certain issues, I am thoroughly convinced that I should make this announcement. . . . I endorse the candidacy of Ronald Reagan as the next president of the United States!"

Then, following a chorus of *amens*, he called two "bosom buddies" from the civil rights movement to the altar. Reverend E. V. Hill had spoken at the Religious Roundtable rally in Dallas. Hosea Williams, another legatee of Dr. King, said, "I was the closet black to Governor Carter when he was governor of Georgia"—but now he said that "Jimmy Carter did not do as much for the black people of Georgia as governor as Lester Maddox"—a segregationist—did, and that Ronald Reagan had done more for blacks as governor of California than Carter had in Georgia, too. He said the Democrats were "taking black people for granted"—comparing them to white Southerners who "never got nothing out of Washington until they broke with the Democratic Party during the Goldwater campaign."

When Dick Wirthlin was conceptualizing Reagan's outreach to African Americans as a way to reassure white suburbanites, he surely never imagined success like this. Later that day, the National Association of Police Associations—the organization of police unions—announced that their organization, like the Veterans of Foreign Wars, was making Ronald Reagan the first presidential candidate they had ever endorsed.

CHAPTER 38

"Carter Is Smarter Than Reagan"

LEADERSHIP '80 SET ITS COURSE NORTHEAST. EVERY YEAR SINCE 1945, POLI-ticians from both parties donned formal dress and descended upon the Waldorf Astoria on Park Avenue in Manhattan for the Al Smith Memorial Foundation Dinner, to honor the first Catholic major-party presidential nominee and raise money for Catholic charities at the invitation of the cardinal himself, a ritual especially beloved in presidential years: since 1960, the Democratic and Republican nominees sat side by side and poked fun at themselves and each other only weeks before the election.

There was giddiness that day in the Reagan campaign—and it wasn't only over all the new endorsements. A new Gallup Poll had Reagan ahead by three points. Two nights earlier, he had done a marvelous job on Barbara Walters, especially in deflecting questions concerning anything but Jimmy Carter's economic failures. Then came their biggest October Surprise coup so far.

It was October 16, and, as it happened, Prime Minister Mohammad Ali Rajai of Iran was *also* in New York, to plead his country's case against Iraq's aggression to the United Nations, where President Carter had said he would be willing to meet with him to discuss the hostages' release. The previous night, the Chicago ABC affiliate WLS, citing information from unnamed "military reserve pilots," reported that American cargo planes loaded with spare parts were ready to depart for Iran, and that the American hostages, reportedly spread out over various locations, were returning to the embassy in preparation for "a trip home for all but four of them, as part of an arms deal in Iran." None of this was true. Gary Sick of the National Security Council became convinced that it was another Reagan plant, timed for a possible Carter-Rajai meeting—a meeting that never came off, perhaps thanks to this sabotage. The story that Carter might be willing to compromise American security by trading arms for hostages, on the other hand, reverberated for days. A subsequent Harris Poll revealed that Americans opposed releasing the hostages in exchange for spare parts by a margin of 46 percent to 39 percent. *"Backlash,"* Reagan campaign researcher Annalise Martin scrawled in a memo recording this evidence that the October Surprise plan was working.

The final reason for the high spirits within the campaign was the resolution of a tense conflict within its high command. Reagan had been heavily criticized for refusing to join a debate that didn't include Anderson. It had brought about, in fact, the only awkward moment in that Barbara Walters interview—some squirming after she noted that "many people say" his motivation was not fairness but that he was "either afraid to debate him" or that he had wanted to build up Anderson to "siphon off the Carter votes."

Then, however, Reagan zipped through Ohio and Michigan, and the League of Women Voters changed position, announcing a debate limited to the major-party nominees. That called Reagan's bluff—and the campaign had a tough decision to make.

Debate preparations were mind-bogglingly thorough. The research files were voluminous, the strategizing about when and how to deploy them meticulous. ("FYI: Use only if have to," one pre-debate memo advised: *"Some have criticized RR's 'noble cause' remark, but in 1976, Carter said Vietnam was a 'racist war.'"*) Almost since the day after the convention the candidate had been undergoing extensive videotaped drills of practice Q&As—*tough* ones—the game-film logged down to the second for review:

TIME	NO.	QUESTION
7:07		Joke
7:11:58	1	President Carter's rating is now the lowest it has been. How would you restore trust of voters? . . .
7:11:58	2	The Carter Administration has no long term plan for economic problems. What would the Reagan Administration do come January 20 . . .
7:30:55	7	Why should blacks and other minorities feel you'll do more for them than the present administration? . . .
7:50:44	16	You labeled Bush as a "Tri-lateralist." How can you justify having Bush on your ticket? . . .
7:52:16	17	If you're for women's rights why are you against the ERA?
7:54:42	18	What is your position regarding the PLO and Israel's possession of occupied Arab lands, Jerusalem? . . .

These preparations intensified with the agreement to debate Anderson on September 21. A TV studio was erected in the garage of Reagan's rented mansion. Congressman David Stockman was recruited to impersonate Anderson, whom he had once served as administrative assistant. But

Reagan performed miserably. "He couldn't fill up the time," Stockman recalled. "And what time he could fill, he filled with wooly platitudes."

Although, it was true, when the time came on September 21 and the red light blinked on, Reagan rose marvelously to the occasion as ever, turning in a smooth, charming, and effective performance.

So: To debate, or not to debate? That, now, was the question.

Their latest poll had their man seven points ahead—so Dick Wirthlin advised against the risk and just run out the clock. Lyn Nofziger, after two fretful months spent jawboning away Reagan gaffes, agreed. But Stu Spencer, who coached Reagan on the campaign plane, and James Baker, who commanded the pre-debate operation, argued the other way—not least because the media would rub their face in their hypocrisy if they ducked. During that September 21 debate with Anderson, they had run a spot depicting an empty podium as a narrator with an official-sounding tone one might associate with a spokesman for the League of Women Voters scolded, "*Women voters* invited President Carter to join in the 1980 debates. He refused the invitation. Maybe it's because, during his administration, as inflation has gone as high as 18 percent . . ." Quite the easy attack angle, should they refuse the League's invitation now.

The Carter side, meanwhile, was licking their chops. As Gerald Rafshoon wrote in his July campaign media plan—in capital letters— "CARTER IS SMARTER THAN REAGAN. The president is a man who grasps what is going on. We must show Carter as a man who comprehends the facts." Putting him *onstage* next to Reagan while the old man pulled keepsakes from his mental shoebox, uttered some alarming nuclear provocation—or simply forgot his lines: that was the royal road to setting up the costar of *Bedtime for Bonzo* for a Barry Goldwater–sized rout.

And on the Reagan campaign plane, many shared that fear.

They were on the way to New York for the Al Smith Dinner, hashing out these pros and cons for the umpteenth time, when the candidate butted in. He said that he and Nancy had already decided: he would debate.

President Carter arrived at the Waldorf Astoria, and promptly violated the spirit of the event: he sequestered himself in his suite and stayed there until it was time for him to speak. Reagan arrived and eagerly launched into the same glad-handing rituals that he had mastered working thousands of hotel ballrooms before.

Terence Cardinal Cooke took the podium, joked that joining these two men together "demonstrated a power even greater than the League of Women Voters," and introduced Carter, who spoke first—and again violated the spirit of the event: he skipped the self-mockery. "For the last three and a half years I have faced the awesome pressures known only to those who occupy the Oval Office," he began. Then, he indulged his tendency to sanctimony to the hilt, telling a story from the previous day's town meeting in Pennsylvania. A Jewish boy named Avi Leiter had asked him if he believed that God heard the prayers of a Jew. He recalled how at Camp David, "I was sure that God heard all our prayers, Christian, Jewish, and Muslim, because thirteen days later we had an agreement." He concluded with a hosanna to "little Avi Leiter," whose "question no American child should ever have to ask his president," that was actually a snipe at Ronald Reagan: "We've come through difficult and bitter times in this country. We've done well. But we cannot pause on a plateau of self-congratulation while Avi Leiter and other potential future Al Smiths of America struggle against the sheer walls of intolerance that are still all too evident."

In the audience, heads shook in disapproval: *mean.*

Then Reagan did what he did best: he slayed 'em with jokes. His best was that there was no truth to the rumor that he had attended the original Al Smith Dinner. In fact, he never felt younger. The trick was "riding older and older horses." By that point, like the man once said, Reagan could have recited the alphabet and had the audience eating out of his hand. And at that, doubts within Reagan's traveling party were erased: they were ready to put their man in the ring.

The two sides negotiated staging. Team Carter wanted extensive time for rebuttal, so the president could debunk Reagan's massacred facts and misunderstandings. To which the Reagan side was glad to accede: nothing went over worse on TV than pedantry. Stockman returned to the garage studio, this time as Carter. Their work was helped by a remarkable ace up the Reaganites' sleeve: a Carter briefing book on national security and foreign affairs that had somehow turned up at Reagan headquarters and let Reagan anticipate exactly what Carter might say in the debate.

It wasn't the first time the campaign had received unauthorized materials from within the bowels of the government. Earlier in October, an Army sergeant walked into headquarters in Arlington, said he did not approve of Carter's military budgets, and left behind a large envelope. Its contents included White House budget documents and economic analyses, and also a handwritten "Dear Jimmy" note from Anwar Sadat. A communications staffer wrote an op-ed, "Little White House Lies," based on information contained in a document called "Guidance on Unemployment Rate and Producer Price Index in September," to appear under William Simon's name, a contribution to yet one more of the campaign's media-influence operations: claims that Carter was "Jimmying" economic statistics. Several weeks later, the sergeant returned with Carter's itinerary for the home stretch of the campaign.

ON THE TRAIL, THINGS GREW NASTIER. ON OCTOBER 21, CARTER AN-nounced that he was prepared to consider unfreezing Iranian assets in exchange for the release of the hostages. Reagan was in Louisville celebrating another astonishing endorsement: the antiwar 1968 Democratic presidential candidate Senator Eugene McCarthy, who Reagan said he hoped would help convince people "I don't eat my young." Then he made his most direct attack in the Iran issue so far: "I don't *understand* why fifty-two Americans have been held hostage for almost a year now!"

Leaving his hotel, he was asked why he had decided to politicize the crisis. Defensive, he began spluttering—"I was simply remarking that with the election day, unless they suddenly are released, will be one year . . ."—then composed himself: "I believe that this administration's foreign policy helped create the entire situation that made their kidnap possible. And I think the fact that they've been there that long is a humiliation and a disgrace to this country." In blackjack, this was called "doubling down."

TV commercials for Reagan were nasty, too—at least the ones cut by political action committees, uncoordinated with the campaign. One of the National Conservative Political Action Committee's lingered over photos of Carter appointees, first and foremost a certain African American one: "In 1976, Jimmy Carter said 'Why not the best?' Now let's look at what he gave us. Andrew Young, Carter's UN ambassador, who called Iran's Ayatollah Khomeini a saint, forced to resign after lying to the president. Bert Lance, also forced to resign. Dr. Peter Bourne, the Carter drug expert, forced to resign after supplying drugs to a White House staffer. And the list goes on." The ad aired predominantly in the South, where Gerald Rafshoon imagined lingering on Andrew Young's black face was proving particularly effective.

The American Conservative Union's Citizens for Reagan in '80 PAC tracked down Carter ads from 1976 that his campaign had neglected to copyright, such as one in which Carter howled about Ford doing nothing about a 6.5 percent rate of inflation. That ran; then the announcer said, *"He did do something about the inflation rate. He more than doubled it."* A scholar of political advertising thought another NCPAC ad was the most damaging of the season. It aired an excerpt of Carter promising in his debate with Gerald Ford to bring unemployment down to 3 percent, inflation to 4.5 percent. The actual numbers flowed across the screen, then Carter's face appeared as his voice was distorted with a disturbing echo effect: *"I keep my promises . . . promises . . . promises . . . promises . . ."*

Others caused Carter personal anguish: the ads from Christians for

Reagan. There was the one with that matron sitting beside her children on a porch: "As a Christian mother of four, I want my children to be able to pray in school. I don't want them being taught that abortion and homosexuality are perfectly all right. I was sorry to learn that President Carter disagrees with me on all of these issues. . . . Because of this, I'm duty-bound as a Christian and a mother to vote for Ronald Reagan, a man that will protect my family's values." Another featured a gay pride parade in San Francisco: "Flexing their political muscle, they elect a mayor. . . . Now the march has reached Washington. . . . Carter advocates acceptance of homosexuality. Ronald Reagan stands for the traditional American family." It concluded on a freeze-frame of two men kissing in a park. A third excoriated the Democratic platform's promise to "affirm the dignity of all people" and "protect all groups from discrimination based on race, color, religion, national origin, sex, or sexual orientation."

At first, they ran in only seven cities in the South—including Atlanta, where Rosalynn Carter was confronted by a clutch of church women who told her, "Jimmy's anti-Christ." Then, they ran everywhere—in news reports conveying the controversy. Gary Jarmin of Christian Voice told the *Washington Post*, "We decided it was necessary to run these ads because our information indicates that the vast majority of evangelical Christians are totally unaware of President Carter's support for homosexual rights. . . . We believe that there is no issue which will cause evangelicals to defect from Carter more than this one." A Reagan spokesman said, "We don't take a position on what they do. We're completely separate and don't have input with these people."

Town hall–style question-and-answer sessions were now Carter's predominant campaigning format. At one in Memphis five days before the election, a mother and teacher said, "It seems to be the popular thing these days for . . . those of us who support our new Department of Education, to be charged with being immoral. . . . How are you reacting to these charges from our *moral* opponent?"

It touched a nerve.

Carter noted that he was speaking in a state that housed the headquarters of his religious denomination—the one whose latest president had declared his hope the president would give up his secular humanism and return to Christianity. "We're kind of one family in the South. We share a common background. We share a common set of values about patriotism, about family, about hard work, about neighborliness, and we share, many of us, a common religious faith."

He grew exceptionally earnest. "I grew up as a little boy who went to Sunday school every Sunday morning," he said. "From the time I was three years old, I never missed going to Sunday school. When I went to the U.S. Naval Academy as a midshipman for three years, I taught Sunday school."

He still did—whenever he possibly could.

"My religious beliefs are very precious to me, and I've never tried to criticize those who worshiped differently from me. But until this year, I have never had anybody question the sincerity of my belief in God and my commitment to my life as a Christian believing in Jesus Christ as my savior. Lately I have heard about—I have not seen them—some very vicious television advertisements questioning my religious beliefs, insinuating all kinds of damaging things to me within the region that I love so much. I'm not going to dignify these attacks by answering them specifically."

Which ended up only giving the ads more exposure—for now the news had to show just what the president was carping about.

THE ACU HAD HOPED JIMMY CARTER WOULD SUE OVER THEIR USE OF HIS old ads: then, the news would have to show their commercials, too. They were punching a pillow. The Carter campaign just wasn't aggressive like that.

They *thought* of suing the PAC responsible for an ad in which the face of John Anderson appeared while an announcer sneered about the positions he shared with Ted Kennedy: *"Ted Kennedy. John Anderson. Ted Kennedy. John Anderson. We defeated one. Now we must defeat the other."* For the line "we defeated" implied that *Jimmy Carter* had taken out the ad, and Carter headquarters was promptly flooded with calls from voters protesting yet more evidence of the president's meanness. Which was a nice little ratfuck, for the ad actually came from Jesse Helms's Congressional Club, and didn't, Carter's campaign lawyer complained, "adequately identify its source, as required by the FCC." But as Jesse Helms's minions well knew, by the time they filed the paperwork, it would have been too late—so nothing could be done.

The good-government group Common Cause had tried something like that in July, filing suit with the Federal Election Commission against a Republican PAC called Americans for Change headed by Senator Harrison Schmitt of New Mexico, whose ads featured voters trying in vain to remember one campaign promise Jimmy Carter had kept—though Common Cause wasn't suing about the content (which was actually pretty accurate: even though Carter *had* kept lots of promises, a poll found that only 10 percent of voters could remember one). They were challenging the "independent expenditure" strategy itself: the loophole that allowed donors to PACs to exceed the $1,000-per person limit on contributions to candidates. But their lawsuit was still wending its way through the courts over a year later—when they lost in the Supreme Court, after, along the way, a lower court decision was overturned suggesting that the very *principle* of campaign contribution limits was unconstitutional.

Independent groups spent more than $9 million trying to elect Ronald Reagan. There was virtually no PAC spending for Jimmy Carter at all.

THE REAGAN CAMPAIGN PLANE PASSED OVER A FOREST FIRE IN LOUISIANA. A speechwriter and a press aide began a mocking, rhythmic chant: "Killer trees! Killer trees!" Reports were now that Reagan's polls no longer showed him comfortably ahead. Ed Meese testily denied it. *Everyone*, now, was testy.

Team Reagan finally decided voters were familiar enough with Reagan and his record to haul out their negative ads. One featured a graph of prices four years ago and now, with the final bar erupting as if through the top of the screen. In another, a jittery, slasher movie–style camera closed in on a pretty yellow Victorian—then, as if by a ghost, the door slammed. Reagan's voice: *"Once upon a time, four long years ago, most Americans could dream of owning a home. . . . Jimmy Carter's inflation, with record interest rates and a lack of mortgage money, have slammed the door on that dream."* Another reprised the image of an empty podium reserved for Carter that ran during Reagan's debate with Anderson: *"Bread up over 74 percent. Hamburger up over 114 percent. Milk, up over 86 percent. Sugar, up over 156 percent. Thanks to Carter's runaway inflation, we pay more and the farmer makes less. Can we afford four more years of this?"*

The nastiest ran in states that Ted Kennedy had won. It featured campaign trail footage of the hoarse-voiced senator savaging Carter at the top of his lungs: *"I! Say! It's time to say! No! More! American hostages! No! More! High interest rates! No! More! High inflation! And No! More! Jimmy Carter!"* Wirthlin worried that voters would find them *too* nasty. So he tested them. "I was so amazed by the results I had them tested again. The reaction was 'That's what Senator Kennedy said about Carter. It's not dirty.'"

The Carter campaign did not test its own ads—but the Reagan campaign did, the better to counter them. They found that viewers judged them "considerably more negative in tone." Which, Wirthlin observed, was interesting precisely because they *weren't* more negative in tone. Most, in the final weeks, were testimonials from celebrities like Henry Fonda and Mary Tyler Moore, from Ted Kennedy, from ordinary Americans. ("I think he cares about the people. That's my impression of him.") Wirthlin's focus groups found many convinced they must be paid actors.

"By election day," he marveled, "Ronald Reagan was viewed as more 'presidential' than the president."

One reason was certainly ads like these: What kind of president required character witnesses?

Another was the debate, which took place in Cleveland on Wednesday, October 28, exactly six days before the balloting.

The polls were tied. The TV confrontation was anticipated as the tiebreaker—"the world heavyweight championship and the Super Bowl combined," Elizabeth Drew of the *New Yorker* wrote. "The only thing missing is Howard Cosell." Though really the loudmouth ABC Sports personality wasn't necessary: his shoes were filled by reporters and politicos, handicapping, gossiping, and filling in color commentary like it *was* a heavyweight bout. Reagan's cornerman even worked the refs: "I think Governor Reagan has to anticipate some show of the typical Carter meanness," Gerald Ford said, "the typical Carter vindictiveness."

The president took a jog in the driving rain. "I run every day I can," he said into an ABC microphone.

"Is there anything new about the hostages?"

(The Ayatollah had just given a speech in which he only mocked President Carter once, which was taken as a positive sign.)

"No. See you later."

He disappeared into his hotel room for the rest of the day to bone up; his challenger made himself readily available, saying charming things for the cameras. ("If I seem a little uptight, *welll*, I was always that way when I ran the quarter mile too!") Reagan wouldn't be doing much studying: not his style. Alan Greenspan had recently accompanied him on a cross-country flight, charged with making sure Reagan worked his way through a half-inch-thick briefing book. Martin Anderson kept shooting the economist dirty looks, to no avail. ("I think," Greenspan remembered, "I heard more clever stories during that flight than in any other four- or five-hour period in my life.")

Reagan just didn't seem nervous. Back in 1976, Carter told Walter Cronkite that *he* was nervous—"as a farmer from Georgia"—about even *addressing* the President of the United States on terms of equality. No such worries from Reagan. "He doesn't see him as the president," Stu Spencer told Witcover and Germond. "He sees him as a little shit."

He also had that ace up his sleeve. David Stockman even bragged about it, to a luncheon of his constituents in Cassopolis, Michigan: "I just spent the weekend as Carter," he said, noting the pilfered briefing book that had helped him master the role. The revelation that Reagan was cheating was not reported on any network—including on ABC, where the conservative columnist George Will, who saw the stolen document while helping coach

Reagan, was commenting on the debate—and only in one newspaper, covering Elkhart, Indiana.

AT 9:30 EASTERN STANDARD TIME MORE THAN HALF THE COUNTRY—120 million viewers—flipped on their TVs, some with their phones at the ready: ABC had organized a poll, one fifty-cent 900 number to dial to "vote" for Carter, another for Reagan. The candidates crossed the big empty stage. Reagan continued past his podium to shake Carter's hand. The president hadn't been prepared for that. He appeared taken aback.

Reagan won the coin flip, and chose to take first crack at the opening question: "What are the differences between the two of you on the uses of American military power?"

Perhaps it was the ruddy cheeks from the pre-debate glass of wine that Michael Deaver had slipped him that imparted charm to an answer that might otherwise have sounded slashing: "I don't know what the differences might be because I don't know what Mr. Carter's policies are!" He then launched into a soulful avowal of his passion for peace. These were lines he had been honing all fall. They included "America has never gotten into war because we were too strong," then a sorrowful fillip: "We *can* get into a war by letting events get out of hand, as they have in the last three and three-fourth years under the foreign policies of this administration, until we're faced each time with a crisis."

Then he cocked his head intently: "I have seen four wars in my lifetime. I'm a father of sons; I have a grandson. I don't *ever* want to see another generation of young Americans bleed their lives into sandy beachheads in the Pacific, or rice paddies and jungles in Asia, or the muddy, bloody, battlefields of Europe."

This was *not* the blathering mad bomber that his campaign had prepared the public to expect. Jimmy Carter was already on his back foot.

When his turn came, he established a theme: he cited the "thousands of decisions" he had made as president, said he was "a much wiser and more experienced man than I was when I debated four years ago against President Ford." Which happened to contradict his appeal against President Ford four years ago, which was that he was better qualified to serve than mere Washington timeservers.

He looked sour. His sentences were choppy. He searched the sky before answering questions, blinked often, shifted his gaze. His collar didn't quite fit; his tie was tied in an unsightly pinch. (If there was one thing Ronald Reagan had mastered since the 1930s, it was tying knots that met his collar as sharply as the facet of a diamond.) Conspicuously, he looked down at his notes. Reagan's delivery had been smooth, well modulated, and exquisitely paced—and during reaction shots, he gave off an effective air of bemused incredulity while Jimmy Carter explained and explained and explained.

Many of Carter's answers were me-too arguments. For instance, boasting of his "steady, methodical increase for defense." Which opened him up to a nice cheap shot from Reagan, who observed that Carter's promised new mobile strike force "does make me question his assaults on whether *I* am the one that is quick to look for the use of force." (*Grin.* If you wanted a hawk in the White House, why not vote for the one who would throw a tax cut into the bargain?)

Harry Ellis of the *Christian Science Monitor* asked Carter to admit responsibility for the economic ordeal facing the nation. The question, taxing in any event, was made even more so when Ellis added: ". . . and wouldn't it be an act of leadership to tell the American people they're going to have to sacrifice to adopt a leaner lifestyle for some time to come?" It encapsulated the strange dilemma that had boxed the president in all year: no credit for all the times he did precisely that—ever since he donned a cardigan sweater in front of a White House fireplace in the third month of his term, for which he was mocked. Carter answered as he always did, bragging about shooting Santa Claus: "We have demanded that the American people sacrifice, and they've done very well."

When Carter said it, his eyes smiled brighter than they did for the entire debate. Which couldn't have been a better setup for the refrain Reagan had been perfecting for years. As he had recently delivered it at a campaign rally: "We don't have inflation because *the people* are living too well. We have inflation because the *government* is living too well."

Reagan now recalled something Carter said in 1976: *I pledge that if I am elected, we will never use unemployment and recession as a tool to fight inflation. We will never sacrifice someone's job, his livelihood, for the sake of an economic plan.* Carter had broken that promise. Reagan, on the other hand, the Good Shepherd, insisted that "you can lick inflation by *increasing* productivity and by decreasing the cost of government."

He noted that the Social Security reform Carter signed included "the single biggest tax increase in our nation's history," but would "only put a Band-Aid on this and postpone the day of reckoning by a few years at most" (a few decades, actually). That all the budget cutting that was required could easily be accomplished by eliminating waste and fraud. That the only reason he had ever questioned the minimum wage was because it crushed the hopes of black teenagers, "doing away with the jobs that they could once get."

He said cities would bloom under Jack Kemp–style development zones, that Jimmy Carter's approach to the problem had been well on display on Charlotte Street in the South Bronx. He almost seemed to choke up when he described it: ". . . like a bombed-out city—great, gaunt skeletons of buildings, windows smashed out. . . . And this was the spot at which President Carter had promised that he was going to bring in a vast program to rebuild this area!" (Actually, Carter had promised nothing of the kind.)

He said that in 1976 Jimmy Carter had "invented a thing he called the misery index. He added the rate of unemployment and the rate of inflation, and it came, at that time, to 12.5 under President Ford. And he said that no man with that size misery index had a right to seek reelection to the presidency." (Carter hadn't invented it, and never said Ford did not have a right to seek reelection to the presidency.) "Today, by his own decision"—a useful Freudian slip; Reagan must have meant "definition"— "the misery index is in excess of 20 percent, and I think this must suggest something. . . . And that's why I believe there are going to be millions of Democrats that are going to vote with us this time around, because they too want that promise kept. It was a promise for less government and less taxes and more freedom for the people."

For people who hadn't been paying much attention, it sure made Jimmy Carter look foolish when he kept claiming *this guy* was the uncaring Scrooge.

IT WAS THE STRANGEST THING. NO ONE ON THE CARTER TEAM SEEMED TO have noticed that Reagan had well-practiced answers for all these attacks; no one had thought to do the work of preparing *new* lines of attack with which to effect ambushes. For a campaign strategy based on exploiting their opponent's past rhetoric, opposition research was strikingly weak— in part because, for years, anytime White House assistants tried to interest Carter in preparing for his reelection, he pushed the task away with distaste.

They hadn't tapped anyone from Washington's deep pool of accomplished dirt hunters; "oppo" was run by a twenty-nine-year-old Princeton political science graduate, who worked out of the George Washington University library. His team concentrated on news coverage of Reagan's gubernatorial terms and 1976 presidential campaign, and complained that the work had been easier when Carter's opponent was Kennedy, with seventeen still-ongoing years in the Senate to comb. It seemed never to have occurred to anyone in the White House that Reagan had years and years of rhetoric *outside* his campaigns and terms in elected office from which to compile ordnance to throw at him at just this moment. His biweekly newsletter columns, for instance, which included chestnuts like "Nuclear 'Wastes' Have Valuable Uses." Or that newsletter's endorsement of Laetrile ("an extract of apricot kernels which many think may be efficacious against cancer but which government in its wisdom wants to keep people from using")—which was medically useless, and killed many of those who traveled to Mexico for the treatment, but was a pet cause of John Birch Society stalwart (and Citizens for the Republic endorsee) Congressman Larry McDonald.

Neither did the White House assign some low-level staffer to monitor the utterances of the man who had been the front-runner to replace Carter for more than two years. If they had, they could have weaponized gems like Reagan's claim in a radio commentary that all the world's projected atomic waste through the year 2000 could fit on a single football field (actually that statistic was for one nuclear plant), or the 1976 speech in which he argued that teachers' unions were following a script laid down by Hitler—just for a start.

They didn't take their adversary seriously enough for that. They presumed the public would see what they saw. Which was that Carter was smart and that Reagan was stupid. And that therefore Reagan would lose any debate. Which overlooked the fact that Reagan had *won* practically every debate he had participated in—going back at least to 1967, when he appeared on the same TV hookup with Robert F. Kennedy to discuss the Vietnam War, and twisted his opponent in such knots that Kennedy subsequently yelled "Who the fuck got me into this?" and ordered staffers never to pair him with "that son-of-a-bitch" ever again.

A former speaker in the California assembly had warned them about that. But Jimmy Carter was an arrogant man. His political staff had staged their own rounds of practice debates, with a young political science professor playing Reagan—who did a credible enough imitation that Carter was soundly defeated. His response to that was to cancel the scrimmages. He was *president*, after all. He dealt with these issues all the time. He could handle the actor. There was no one around him willing or able to penetrate the bubble to persuade him otherwise—of Reagan's extraordinary skill, perfected over decades, at sounding neither extreme nor ill-informed (even when he actually was) but kindly and shrewd.

In 1979, his speechwriter Bill Gavin observed in a memo, "The television coverage we will ultimately be getting will be of great advantage. He simply cannot be perceived as 'harsh' when people see him and listen to him over a long period of time." And now here were the American people, seeing and hearing him for a long period of time, proving Gavin's prophesy correct—as Carter sounded harsher with every question.

He answered one about Social Security: "Although Governor Reagan has changed his position lately, on four different occasions he has advocated making Social Security a voluntary system, which would, in effect, very quickly bankrupt it." Reagan responded indignantly, locking in on the camera with a mild scowl: "We cannot frighten, as we have with the threats and the campaign rhetoric that has gone on in this campaign, our senior citizens, leave them thinking that in some way they're endangered and they would have no place to run." Then he launched into a fantastical story about how "the voluntary thing I suggested"—well, the elaborate tale that followed had something to do with a young orphan whose aunt died who could not receive Social Security benefits because his aunt was not his mother, and had no resemblance to what Reagan had stated perfectly plainly before a massive TV audience in 1964, that it was preferable to add "voluntary features" to Social Security in order to let citizens get a better return on their investment, oblivious to the simple actuarial fact that thus thinning out the pool of Social Security contributors would collapse the program. This was exactly what the Carter side had *hoped* Reagan would do: make things up.

So Carter pushed further. "As a matter of fact," he said gravely, "Governor Reagan began his political career campaigning around this nation *against* Medicare"—a reasonably accurate summary of the facts. In 1961, Reagan had recorded a speech for a record album distributed around the nation by the American Medical Association, to be played at gatherings resembling Tupperware parties, arguing that President Kennedy's proposal to extend Social Security to cover medical care for the elderly represented an opening wedge to a government takeover of "every area of freedom as we have known in this country," predicting that if it were passed, "we are going to spend our sunset years telling our children and our children's children what it was like in America when men were free." Reagan was fired from his job of hosting *General Electric Theater* in part for so prominently advocating this radical position.

"Now," Carter continued, "we have an opportunity to move toward national health insurance, with an emphasis—"

As he spoke, the camera cut to Reagan, who was rocking back and forth in his place, beaming like a boxer whose opponent had just lowered his gloves—

"An emphasis on prevention of disease—"

The frame pulled back to encompass both men, Carter discoursing earnestly, no idea of the roundhouse punch being prepared for him, Reagan's face betraying a hint of pity—

"An emphasis on outpatient care, not inpatient care. An emphasis on hospital cost-containment, to hold down the cost of hospital care"—Carter was getting a little bit animated, striking the podium softly with his hands for emphasis—"for those who are ill."

Reagan smiled.

"An emphasis on catastrophic health insurance for a family that's being wiped out because of a very high medical bill. . . . Governor Reagan, again, was, typically, against such a proposal."

The moderator: "Governor?"

He delivered the knockout blow with an easy chuckle: "There you go again!" A burst of delighted laughter from the audience: Jimmy Carter was being *mean* again.

Reagan's face never shined brighter than during what he said next: "When I opposed Medicare, there was *another* piece of legislation meeting the same problem before the Congress. I happened to *favor* the other piece of legislation and thought that it would be better for the senior citizens and provide better care than the one that was finally passed. I was not opposing the *principle* of providing care for them. I was opposing *one* piece of legislation as versus another."

Backstage, Carter people high-fived one another. "Because we knew that was a lie," Hendrik Hertzberg remembered. "And we thought that now the press would take him down." Instead, he was lauded for his snappy comeback.

REAGAN KNEW HOW TO DEBATE. TELLING RESONANT STORIES WAS THE MOST important part. Which President Carter was about to be reminded of, in the next part of the debate, when he tried to do some storytelling of his own.

When Jimmy Carter argued that his forty-five months in the Oval Office had brought him an extraordinary ensemble of skills for meeting the requirements of the presidency, he was surely correct—when it came to his role as Engineer in Chief. Another capacity, however, had rather withered during that time: his gifts as a preacher. At one point in the debate, Reagan, affecting to speak of America's progress on civil rights, naïvely recalled "the days when I was young and when this country didn't even know it had a racial problem." And Carter's response—"Those who suffered from discrimination because of race or sex certainly knew we had a racial problem"—was decent enough, for an engineer. But he could have told a *story*—like the unforgettable one he related in his 1976 campaign book, *Why Not the Best*. The black champion Joe Louis fought a rematch with Adolf Hitler's favorite, Max Schmeling, after getting pummeled by the German two years before:

All of our black neighbors came to see Daddy . . . they asked if they could listen to the fight. We propped the radio up in the open window of our house—for it was inconceivable for a white family in rural Georgia to allow a crowd of African Americans inside their house—*Louis prevailed. My father was deeply disappointed. . . . There was no sound from anyone in the yard, except a polite "Thank you, Mister Earl." . . . Then our several dozen visitors filed across the dirt road, across the railroad track, and qui-*

etly entered a house about a hundred yards away, out in the field. At that point, pandemonium broke loose inside that house, as our black neighbors shouted and yelled in celebration of the Louis victory.

The beaten-down president's sense of an audience—a strength, back in 1976—had atrophied. At the podium in Cleveland, he *did* try for a more emotional connection with his listeners, and failed badly. It came during a long colloquy about terrorism, describing his greatest fear as president: that terrorists would gain control of a nuclear device. He repeated Reagan's disturbing avowal that it wasn't "any of our business" if Pakistan, full of militant jihadists, got the bomb. And during Reagan's turn to respond, he simply ignored what Carter had said. So the president tried another tack:

"I had a discussion with my daughter, Amy, the other day, before I came here, to ask her what the most important issue was. She said she thought nuclear weaponry and the control of nuclear arms."

You could hear giggling. Amy Carter had just turned thirteen. These days, she rarely appeared in the media—so the image of her people had in their heads was frozen in 1976, when she was eight. The next day she was interviewed, and said perfectly reasonable things about why nuclear proliferation was such a dangerous problem. Be that as it may. In the last week of the campaign, Amy Carter, nuclear expert, became America's favorite joke. Even Ronald Reagan joined in the fun: "I know he touched our hearts, all of us, the other night. I remember when Patty and Ron were little tiny kids, we used to talk about nuclear power." His crowds would chant: "*Amy! Amy! Amy!*" in response.

Still, Carter people weren't worried. They counted up all the things Reagan said that weren't so, which Carter could continue correcting through Election Day, and scored him the winner. A Freudian slip suggested that their boss better understood what had just taken place. He began his closing statement thanking the good people of Cleveland for their hospitality "during the last few moments of my life."

Reagan's closing statement was a masterpiece. He posed a memorable question: "Next Tuesday all of you will go to the polls, will stand there in the polling place and make a decision. I think when you make that decision, it might be well if you would ask yourself: Are you better off than you were four years ago?" Rupert Murdoch's *New York Post* the next morning led with their fifty-cent-per-vote survey: "REAGAN WINS TV POLL 2–1."

Which the Carter campaign shrugged off: surely the only people who'd waste good money on so silly an exercise were rich Republicans. Even though more respectable instruments achieved similar results. For instance, according to Richard Wirthlin, 42 percent had previously agreed

Reagan had the traits of a "strong leader." By Election Day, that number was 61 percent.

IN IRAN, AN HOUR-BY-HOUR MELODRAMA UNFOLDED.

The day after Carter and Reagan's debate, the Majlis announced that it would finally hold a long-awaited public session to deliberate over the hostages. Chatter was that a deal might involve an exchange of military materiel—and, from the Reagan camp, Gerald Ford was put forward to warn that if Carter supplied weapons and spare parts for Iran to use against Iraq "to manipulate the release of the hostages to get back in the White House," it might end in a catastrophe greater than the Vietnam War.

The next day, Ayatollah Khalkhali, the "hanging judge," said that the goal was to free the hostages before the American election. Enough hawkish members of the Majlis boycotted in protest that a quorum couldn't be called.

Then, CBS reported that fifty American fighter planes previously purchased by Iran had been delivered to Israel, and that Swedish transport planes were "on standby," suggesting that Israel was helping to broker a deal. Maybe it was true—or maybe the news was disinformation planted by the October Surprise project.

Meanwhile Reagan surrogates laid down markers. Senator John Tower warned, "We have never released arms to hostile countries. Those arms were sold to the shah of Iran. It is clearly unwise for us to position ourselves on one side of this war." Henry Kissinger said that the Iran-Iraq War was Carter's fault for allowing a power vacuum to emerge after the shah's fall, and that trading arms for hostages was "a very worrisome phenomenon" that suggested "the U.S. can be blackmailed." Robert Teeter publicized a poll showing that 55 percent of the country feared that Carter would give away too much to get the hostages returned. The project had moved public opinion. It had moved media opinion, too. "Carter has repeatedly turned the hostage situation to his political advantage in the campaign," the *Minneapolis Tribune* said in reporting the Teeter poll.

Two more epic endorsements came, both from outfits that had never backed a presidential candidate before: *TV Guide*, circulation 18.9 million, whose publisher, Walter Annenberg, called voting for Reagan a "matter of conscience," and the National Rifle Association, which praised Reagan as "a long-time member of the NRA" who had promised them that his Justice Department would "pursue and prosecute those in government who abuse citizens for the political ends of gun control."

The last day of October was a Muslim holy day, so there was no parliament in Tehran. But a tantalizing radio commentary ran in Arabic: "We have achieved what we set out to do. We have exposed America's long criminal history in Iran and the release of the hostages should not be interpreted as either unjust or cowardly." Though that part was excised from rebroadcasts; and, yet more confusingly, the state broadcast in English included this line from the Koran: "Surely unto God all things must come home."

Speech language was prepared for Reagan and Bush to deliver should the hostages be released. Bush's text read, "Finally, the year-long nightmare is over for America and for these brave and good families. As they make their way home, we must hope and pray that never again will our nation suffer the humiliation and despair of these past months. . . . We must ask what commitments Mr. Carter has made. Are we being drawn into a 'quagmire' in the Middle East—into the conflict between Iran and Iraq? . . . This is not the time for secret agreements and secret diplomacy. The first step is to ensure the safe return of the hostages. Then, when that is accomplished, we should consider the resumption of normal relations with Iran." They also had an emergency TV commercial in the can: "In a copyrighted story in the *New York Times* on October 27, William Safire wrote, 'The smoothest of Iran's diplomatic criminals was shown on American TV this weekend warning American voters that they had better not elect Ronald Reagan. Ayatollah Khomeini and his men prefer a weak and manageable U.S. president and have decided to do everything in their power to determine our election results.' A reminder from Democrats for Reagan." The headline the *Times* used for Safire's piece—"The Ayatollah Vote"—filled the screen.

The next day, the Saturday before the election, it emerged that Reagan might have to use these emergency materials.

The Majlis finally began its deliberations, Reagan researchers monitoring developments minute by minute. Noon: "Hostages: No Change. Muskie: 'In Washington Sec. of State Muskie told reporters that no deal had been made for the hostages and such rumors may be politically motivated.'" 12:08 p.m.: "no deal, final terms have to be set, and Secretary of State Muskie denied domestic political considerations were informing the State Department's work . . . 'Anybody with an ounce of political brains would not wait until the Sunday before the Tuesday of elections.' . . . Some demands dropped, other added." 12:48 p.m.: "Secretary Muskie, wearing a yellow 'Free the Hostages' lapel pin, gave a tense press conference: 'There is no deal. We don't even know what conditions the parliament is debating . . . having dealt with the Iranian leaders for six months now, I don't exclude anything.'" 1:00 p.m.: "Muskie said that negotiations were probable and denied that he apologized to Iran's Prime Minister in a letter received by Iran."

Carter flew to Chicago for a campaign event. ABC's 7:00 newscast reported polls showing that a third of likely voters believed that Carter was exploiting the hostages for political reasons. At 8:43, Evans and Novak reported that some sort of handshake deal had occurred two weeks earlier between White House counsel Lloyd Cutler and Iranian emissaries in Geneva, which was followed by movements of military materiel. Skeptical reporters pestered Walter Mondale: "Is this another Wisconsin caper?" Carter paid a surprise visit to an Italian-American Sports Hall of Fame dinner and told childhood stories about his "great heroes" Phil Rizzuto and Joe DiMaggio. Then, the next morning, he made an unscheduled fight back to Washington, upon news that the Majlis was about to make a declaration.

The Sunday newspapers were full of illustrated features anticipating the first anniversary of the November 4 embassy seizure—Election Day. George Bush, on *Face the Nation*, lectured sternly: "There are certain terms the United States *must not* and *cannot* pay." Gerald Ford oozed on *Meet the Press*: "I don't allege that he *kept* them there. I'm sure that they have, behind the scenes and otherwise, sought to take certain action to get their release.... There are many reliable rumors to the effect that there has been much, much more activity, not only in Washington but elsewhere, in an attempt to achieve some concrete results by November 4. That's a matter of record, not only statements by the departments, but also from other sources." Ed Muskie, also on *Meet the Press*, insisted that the United States would never accept "just any proposition," that any deal would preserve America's honor and interests—but that he had no deal to report.

That evening, the president broke into a football game, saying pretty much nothing, concluding: "I wish I could predict when the hostages will return. I cannot. But whether our hostages come home before or after the election, and regardless of the outcome of the election, the Iranian government and the world community will find our country, its people, and the leaders of both political parties united in desiring the early and safe return of the hostages to their homes, but only on a basis that preserves our national honor and our national integrity." The next night, Walter Cronkite played "Tie a Yellow Ribbon Round the Ole Oak Tree" on his evening news broadcast.... *"And that's the way it is, Monday, November 3, 1980, the three hundred and sixty-sixth day of captivity for the American hostages in Iran."*

One could easily argue that the Reagan project to neutralize the political boon to Carter of a hostage release before the election, by sabotaging the delicate balance of trust such high-stakes negotiations required, could easily have shaded into having the effect of helping *keep* the hostages in Iran until after the election. Which the October Surprise project principals, sophisticated in the ways of the world, had to know it might. Though in any event, the Ayatollah was surely glad to humiliate a president who had provided aid and comfort to his life's sworn enemy, the shah; and so the hostages remained where they were for another two and a half months.

DICK WIRTHLIN, WHOSE SURVEY TEAM WAS DOING FIVE HUNDRED INTER-views a day and compiling rolling averages every three days, told his insiders their man was ahead. Pat Caddell had it just about tied. Then a late-inning scandal burst: a massive report in the *Wall Street Journal* that Reagan's foreign policy chief Richard Allen had passed government trade secrets to a Japanese business associate in 1970, and that Allen was *presently* on the payroll of a Japanese carmaker even as Reagan was busy wooing unemployed American autoworkers. Allen responded with a non-denial denial (the article was "filled with inconsistencies, inaccuracies, and allegations that are . . . totally false"); then, a threat: "When we get to the bottom of it, it may even be more unpleasant for someone else." Leon Ja-worksi sent a letter to the attorney general calling for an investigation—of whoever it was leaked the evidence against Allen. Ronald Reagan said he hadn't read the report, so he wouldn't be commenting.

On Thursday, October 30, the campaign announced Allen was taking a "leave of absence"; and the scandal talk faded into the mist.

Just in time for some more to emerge on the other side.

Late Wednesday, the UPI reported alleged details—leaked, Jody Pow-ell said, by the Reagan campaign—of an interim report from the Jus-tice Department's Office of Professional Responsibility on Billygate. "Sources familiar" with the document said it characterized the president as "remarkably uncooperative," and raised the possibility of "compulsory processes"—subpoenaing a sitting president to testify under oath for the first time in history. The report's author implored, to preserve the integ-rity of an ongoing investigation, that his report be kept secret. Senator Richard Lugar, a member of the special Senate committee investigating Billy Carter, implored that it be released—though that was for Senator Birch Bayh to decide: "He's the chairman of the committee." Thus did a Republican cleverly trap a Democrat in the final innings of a fight for his political life into a choice between appearing to countenance a presidential cover-up, or throwing President Carter under the bus.

Reporters cornered Bayh in the wings before a big speech for a re-sponse. Nervously, he said he hadn't read the report, that it should be up to the committee counsel, a respected former federal judge, to decide whether it should be released, or perhaps should require a unanimous committee vote. (And: "I didn't ask for this crazy job.") Lugar called that a dodge. Senators Howard Baker, Strom Thurmond, and Robert Dole piled on. James Baker solemnly intoned, "A presidency built upon trust and integrity should fear no investigation by the Justice Department. We call upon the president immediately to end his uncooperative tactics and cooperate fully as he has promised to do."

The Reagan campaign had discovered a *November* surprise: fill a room full of smoke, and maybe, by Tuesday, voters would imagine a crime into existence. No report emerged; nor in the fullness of time, any wrongdoing by President Carter—who nonetheless, sweating to Election Day, was forced to shout defensively "We've cooperated!" to reporters hounding him for a response.

A REAGAN SWING THROUGH TEXAS. IN DALLAS, FOR AN APPEARANCE BROAD-cast across the state: utter, joyous pandemonium. The announcer boomed him into a giant sports arena like a beloved heavyweight champion— *"The! Next! President! Of! The! United! States!"* Cowboy-hatted cheer-leaders parted the crowd, glittering red, white, and blue. Nancy and the governor strode forth beneath a banner reading "THERE HAS NEVER BEEN ANY DEBATE—REAGAN IS THE WINNER," past heralds holding placards ("HOW DO YOU SPELL RELIEF? R-E-A-G-A-N"; "AMY FOR SECRETARY OF STATE"; "THIS IS REAGAN COUN-TRY"), like a party, the ovation pealing on and on and on. Behind him onstage a gaggle of public officials (not a few of them Democrats), an American flag as high as a three-story house; out front, near the stage. There appeared a black face. He served as a human Moebius strip: to sub-urban moderates, who likely would not recognize who he was and what he believed (he was the only person wearing name tag), he was reassurance that supporting Reagan could not be an act of bigotry. For the people who *did* recognize him—right-wing evangelicals—he marked Reagan as one of their one own. It was Clay Smothers, the state legislator who at the Na-tional Women's Conference counterrally complained that he had "enough civil rights to choke a hungry goat" and now just wanted to "segregate his family" from the "misfits and perverts."

Reagan squared himself behind the podium, waiting patiently for the "We want Reagan! We want Reagan!" chant that had fallen into rhythm with the drum-and-bugle corps to fade, then delivered the speech he'd been honing since the convention—with the help of Richard Wirthlin's research—to a perfect, crowd-pleasing sheen. It included a promise: "Re-member that my tax cuts will *not* reduce the government to less money than it is presently getting. . . . The government will continue to have *more* money." And one of those glorious Reagan perorations, delivered this time to an awed hush, to a crowd full of glistening eyes:

What is it that we as Americans really want? It isn't power. If we only wanted power, we long ago could have dominated the world. It isn't world leadership as an end in itself; we've had world leadership thrust upon us by events. We've never pursued it. In my view, what we want is so simple. . . . We want to live in freedom, and in peace. To see our children have at least the opportunities that we had . . . to worship God in our own way . . . to live in our own way, in our own community, without hurting anyone, or anyone hurting us. . . . I'm talking about the very essence of what it is to be an American. . . . A signer of the Declaration of Independence said that what was important wasn't that we left wealth to our children. It was important that we left them liberty . . . The leadership that I envision in Washington, if I should win enough of your support, is to take the government off the backs of the people of the United States and turn you loose to do what you do so well. Thank you very much!

As one, they leapt to their feet. This was the state where Reagan's absence in 1976 earned him the most blame for Gerald Ford's defeat: Carter nabbed Texas in 1976 by three percentage points. This time, the Republicans would win it by fourteen.

Carter swung through New Jersey. He'd almost won it last time, coming only two points shy against Ford. He entered a banquet hall for a speech intended to inspire the party workers of Essex County to knock on doors until their knuckles bled. It included, naturally, a paean to Franklin Roosevelt, his "compassion for the people," his vision providing farmers with electricity ("The Republicans were against it"), a federal minimum wage ("The Republicans called it socialism . . . 'How could the government possibly interfere in the private enterprise system . . . ?'"), a federal retirement system ("These kinds of concepts . . . are still the commitments of our party.")—and then, a few minutes later, an even more passionate avowal that if you loved Franklin Delano Roosevelt, well, maybe Jimmy Carter's just your man after all:

And we believe that we ought to get the Government's nose out of the private enterprise of this country. We've deregulated rail, deregulated trucking, deregulated airlines, deregulated financial institutions, working on communications, to make sure that we have a free enterprise system that's competitive.

Ronald Reagan went on to win New Jersey by almost as much as he did Texas.

• • •

THE NATION VOTED. OR RATHER, 52.8 PERCENT OF ELIGIBLE VOTERS DID—
the fewest since 1948, even though the candidates had spent more to woo
them than in any election in American history. According to one poll, 60
percent said they weren't excited by any of the candidates. Forty-three
percent of Reagan voters said they were just voting *against* Carter. Thirty-
four percent of Carter voters said that they were just voting *against* Reagan. A political cartoonist depicted one voter's reaction to his choices: his
feet could be seen dangling beneath the voting booth curtain.

But a vote is a vote, no matter with how much passion it is cast. Reagan won a bare majority of them, about 51 percent, with Anderson getting less than 7 percent. But on the electoral map, Reagan's triumph was
overwhelming: Carter and Mondale won only Hawaii, Maryland, West
Virginia, Rhode Island, the District of Columbia, and their home states
of Georgia and Minnesota, a mere forty-nine electoral votes; even Barry
Goldwater had received fifty-three.

In the week following the debate, millions of minds had changed
toward Reagan, like a dam burst: "Basically," Massachusetts congressman
Paul Tsongas said, "the New Deal died yesterday."

But had it? The truth was more muddled.

After all, 84 percent of Reagan voters gave "time for a change" as their
major reason for choosing him—not any ideological reason at all. Indeed,
since 1975, the Opinion Research Corporation, a Republican firm, had
asked whether citizens favored keeping "taxes and services about where
they are." The results were consistent ever since, at about 45 percent, with
only 21 percent saying "too much" was being spent on the environment,
health, education, welfare, and urban aid programs.

So what sort of economic mandate had Reagan received, what in Carter's economic program had been rejected?

A CBS/*New York Times* exit poll, which canvassed a staggering 12,782
voters nationwide, produced a surprising conclusion. Voters were asked
which was the more important problem, unemployment or inflation. Ever
since inflation began ticking up over 10 percent, both Carter's advisors
and political pundits had been adamant: the public was veritably *consumed* with concern over inflation—that, as Carter's public opinion expert
Gerald Rafshoon wrote to him in September 1979, "it is impossible to
overestimate the importance of the inflation issue to your presidency. . . .
It would be difficult to err on the side of too tough a program." Turned
out it *was* possible: that advice informed Carter's headlong rush toward
austerity policies that sacrificed jobs upon a deflationary altar, but on
Election Day, voters by a margin of 45 percent to 39 percent told the exit
pollsters that they were more concerned with unemployment. That was

the "liberal" answer to the question—the focus of all of Ted Kennedy's passionate efforts to pledge in the Democratic platform that "a guarantee of a job for every American who is able to work" must "take precedence over all other domestic priorities," meaning fighting inflation; the plank against which a conservative Southern Democratic governor thundered, "Do we want to tell them in this convention that fighting inflation is *not important anymore?*"

Well, Jimmy Carter had implored the electorate that nothing was more important to him. But of that 45 percent plurality who said jobs were *more* important, 60 percent voted for Reagan.

Carter's frenzied efforts to cut spending didn't avail him much, either. "Balancing the federal budget" was named as the third most important issue, behind "inflation and economy" and "jobs and unemployment," which clustered together closely. Twenty-one percent of voters cited that as their voting issue. But of those voters, a decisive 65 percent preferred Reagan—who *avoided* talking about cutting the budget, claiming tax cuts would take care of the problem on their own. And the Republican presidential candidate gained thirteen points from four years earlier among voters most concerned about jobs. George Bush had once called Reagan's promise that uniform across-the-board tax cuts would both deliver jobs *and* a balanced budget "voodoo economics." A plurality of the electorate, however, seemed to trust that Reagan's promise was perfectly credible.

THE REAGAN CAMPAIGN'S EFFORTS TO SHAPE THE PUBLIC'S PERCEPTION that Carter was *mean* succeeded, that was for certain: asked to name which candidates made "especially unfair" charges during the campaign, 23 percent cited Reagan, 40 percent Carter. Another development cut against the victor: for the first time, there was a recognizable "gender gap" between the two parties. Carter got a slight majority of female voters; Reagan got 55 percent of men. This pattern proved enduring.

Reagan also ran fifteen points ahead of Ford's results among manual laborers, twenty points ahead among labor-union families, and twenty-one points among Democrats overall. Tax-cut promises surely contributed to this spectacular success, which also suggests an electoral toll taken by Carter's austerity economics. But the government services Reagan voters *did* wish to see diminished helps clarify the picture. Reagan got 71 percent of the vote of those who most strongly opposed government efforts to improve the social and economic position of African Americans. Carter received 93 percent of the votes of those who supported them. Given that the percentage of respondents saying minorities should "help themselves" was at an all-time high, eight percentage points greater than four years earlier—and the fact that there was no diminished support for spending on things like education, Social Security, crime control, and the environment—racial animus helps explain part of this electoral bounty; and also why, while in 1976 the Republicans managed no electoral votes in the South, this time they nabbed all but Georgia's twelve.

One of the victims of Reagan's coattails in the South was Governor Clinton—who soon began puzzling out how, in this apparent era of conservative hegemony, Democrats in the South might rise again.

IN THE YEARS TO COME, A PIECE OF CONVENTIONAL WISDOM HARDENED like anodized steel: Carter lost his reelection because he was unable to do anything about the hostages. And indeed, in the CBS/*New York Times* exit poll, "U.S. prestige around the world" was voters' fourth most important issue—and those who cited it as their *most* important went for Reagan 61 percent to 31 percent—a sixteen-point gain for the Republicans since 1976. But another foreign policy result was strikingly counterintuitive. The 17 percent of voters who cited the crisis in Iran as the most important issue preferred *Carter*—by a heaping a margin of two to one. Carter *won* the hostage issue. The ironclad conventional wisdom was wrong. Perhaps, more than posterity appreciated, people respected Carter's grinding, sedulous efforts to negotiate a favorable outcome with people who appeared to be lunatics, keeping the hostages alive and unharmed. Maybe they admired his rescue gamble in April. Or perhaps voters were terrified that Reagan might do *anything* to punish Iran. Start another Vietnam. Or worse. "What's green and glows?" began a joke whose punch line was "Iran fifteen minutes after Ronald Reagan's inauguration."

IN DADE COUNTY, FLORIDA, GOVERNMENT FORMS HAD BEGUN BEING printed in English, Spanish, and Creole to accommodate its population of Cuban and Haitian exiles. A Russian immigrant named Emmy Shafer grew irritated when someone addressed her in Spanish at the mall. Even more easily than Anita Bryant before her, she had no trouble gathering six times the required signatures for a referendum to ban tax dollars from "promoting any culture other than American, or any language other than English"—including in advertising for tourists. And now, with 60 percent of the vote, a city harrowed by the Mariel boatlift made English their "official language."

The previous year, at the Libetarian Party convention, the forty-year-old heir to a Kansas-based oil-refining fortune named David Koch, whose father was a founder of the John Birch Society, successfully campaigned for the 1980 vice-presidential slot by pledging to donate "several hundred thousand dollars to start" to the campaign, hoping a strong Libertarian showing would place him at the center of a long-term effort to reduce the role of the federal government far more than Ronald Reagan dared dream. The ticket made the ballot in all fifty states, but hardly a dent in the vote—1.06 percent. Soon after, Koch decided to pursue his political crusade by other means instead.

The left-wing Citizens Party made twenty-nine state ballots. Its organizers hoped to reach the 5 percent threshold to qualify the party for matching funds in 1984. But their candidate, a beloved ecological writer named Barry Commoner, was receiving virtually no media attention. Then Commoner's campaign manager came up with an idea. Section 315 of the Federal Communications Act prohibited censorship of political advertising. So they raised enough money for a single radio commercial. It began with the noise of a bustling restaurant. Then a man cried, "Bullshit!"

A woman, shocked: "*What?*"

"Carter, Reagan, and Anderson—it's all bullshit."

Then Commoner came onscreen and made his pitch.

They received the attention they hoped for. Commoner's campaign manager used it to point out that it is "a serious problem in this country that the only way we can attract attention is to remind people that this campaign is a hollow sham"; a *Los Angeles Times* columnist used it to perform an unscientific experiment. He called twenty phone numbers randomly, asking the recipient to fill in the blank: "The presidential election campaign so far has been mainly _____." Sixty percent used the same word as Commoner's commercial.

The Citizens got even fewer votes than the Libertarians. Though in the college town of Burlington, Vermont, a Marxist gadfly with a thick Brooklyn accent named Bernie Sanders won an unlikely mayoral victory. Although, on the other side of the country and the ideological spectrum, the new state senator from the western San Fernando Valley would be Ed Davis—the sheriff of Los Angeles County who published a pro–death penalty open letter declaring "all-out war against you who have been literally getting away with murder," proposed "hang 'em at the airport" as a solution to hijacking, and complained that the "federal government was out to force me to hire four-foot-eleven-inch transvestite morons" when he was sheriff of Los Angeles County.

LOU HARRIS WAS THE ONLY POLLSTER TO SEE THE REAGAN LANDSLIDE COMing. Not coincidentally, he was the only pollster doing careful work measuring the impact of the new Christian right. He found that, in 1976, two-thirds of white fundamentalist Protestants had gone for Carter. In 1980, 61 percent went for Reagan. Harris's final estimate was that the swing amounted to two-thirds of Reagan's margin. If the election had been close, they would have handed Reagan his victory—just as the Moral Majority had hoped.

On Wednesday, the market pulled out of a three-week slump with record trading volume: the boardroom Jacobins were harvesting their portion. And that evening, Ted Koppel opened a special edition of *Nightline* by wondering why "what seemed too close to call forty-eight hours ago now seems to have been inevitable all along."

Frank Reynolds interviewed Reagan: "Many people believe that you intend to serve only one term, because of your age. Are they right?" He replied, "I have no way of answering that."

Though the main focus of the newscast was not Reagan but the Christian right—part of a surfeit of attention that precisely inverted the dearth of it during their rise. Robert Maddox, the minister from Georgia who had begged his way onto the White House staff to stanch Carter's bleeding among evangelicals, complained, "They're writing their own *Mein Kampf*. They're writing their own *Das Kapital*. They're not being secret about it. You have to give them credit for that. They're saying *we want to take over the country*." Gary Jarmin of Christian Voice was interviewed sitting on a stack of campaign circulars. Paul Weyrich was filmed at a political meeting crying that "in terms of our ability to challenge any presidential bid on his part, or any future that he has," George Herbert Walker Bush was a dead man walking—"if in fact he is not going to accept or espouse those positions that are in fact in the Republican platform."

George McGovern, John Culver, Frank Church, and Birch Bayh were also interviewed. All had lost—a result of perhaps even greater historical import than Reagan's victory: the Republican takeover of the Senate for only the third time since Herbert Hoover and the first time since 1952.

One of the victors was a Georgia office-supply business owner Mack Mattingly, who had run Barry Goldwater's 1964 campaign in Georgia. He knocked off a political legend, Herman Talmadge, who had been both a governor and a senator, as had his father before him. In New York, Al D'Amato squeaked by Elizabeth Holtzman. The incumbent, Jacob Javits, the Senate's most liberal Republican, only got 11 percent. In Wisconsin, one of the New Right's favorite congressmen, Robert Kasten, knocked off one of the founders of the modern environmental movement, Senator Gaylord Nelson. And with the exception of Senator Alan Cranston of California, who appeared never to have been a serious target, and the pro-lifer Thomas Eagleton—who barely held on—all the targets of the National Conservative Political Action Committee's "hit list," George McGovern, John Culver, Frank Church, and Birch Bayh, with eighty years of experience between them, went down—*hard*.

Now here they were on *Nightline* sitting for exit interviews with Barbara Walters, looking stupefied.

Birch Bayh had been taken down by the thirty-three-year-old one-term congressman Dan Quayle, whose resemblance to Robert Redford was frequently remarked upon; indeed, in a livid telegram to the candidate during the campaign's home stretch, demanding he cease and desist, the liberal movie star accused Quayle of spreading that claim himself. Now Quayle answered Redford: "Dear Bob: The 'Sting' operation worked. By sending that telegram endorsing Birch Bayh, I won overwhelmingly. . . . P.S.: I am sending you that personally autographed picture. I think, however, it would be highly inappropriate to use in your promotional materials."

Bayh told Barbara Walters, "The thing that concerns me is how some of these right-wing hate groups have had the taste of blood, and now they're going to be *intimidating*—can you imagine sitting there and listening to *Paul Weyrich* threatening the vice president of the United States—?"

Walters cut him off mid-sentence. It was time to bring on the evening's stars, Jerry Falwell and Paul Weyrich, who got eight full minutes of airtime. "I object to Senator Bayh when he speaks of hate groups," Falwell pronounced smugly. "We have a very deep love for America and everybody in it." He denied a report that a Moral Majority minister had said, "We finally have a Christian in the White House." Jimmy Carter, Falwell insisted, was "a *fine* Christian."

ANOTHER NEW DEVELOPMENT IN 1980 WAS THAT INDEPENDENT OIL producers doubled their spending to $25.7 million, mostly to Republicans—more than was raised by the DNC, the Democratic Congressional Campaign Committee, and the Democratic Senatorial Campaign Committee combined. Reported David Rogers in the *Boston Globe*, "Better than one out of every ten PAC dollars going to challengers last year came from oil." Challengers would be easiest to influence if they won. Chuck Grassley, for example, John Culver's replacement. The next year a Capitol Hill observer told Rogers, "There was a time when people in Iowa could attack oil with impunity. That time has passed."

Democrats kept the House—but lost some of their most powerful members. The toll included people like Public Works Committee Chairman Howard "Bizz" Johnson, for whom highways and interchanges across California were named; both the chairman of the Ways and Means Committee, Al Ullman, and his second-in-command, James Corman, who was beaten by the anti-busing activist responsible for recalling the president of the Los Angeles County School Board the year before. Majority Whip John Brademas was taken down by a twenty-seven-year-old graduate of one of Paul Weyrich's candidate schools.

The neo-Nazi congressional nominee in Dearborn, Michigan, ran without the support of the local Republican party. He still got a third of the vote, against an incumbent whose opponent only got 20 percent in 1978.

• • •

ON DECEMBER 8, JOHN LENNON, ONE OF THE LIVING SYMBOLS OF THE IN-surgencies of the 1960s, performed a sort of sixties-style act of freedom in itself: he appeared, as he frequently did, unaccompanied by a bodyguard, with his young son in the streets of New York. He signed a record album in front of his apartment building across from Central Park for a fan. He joined his wife, Yoko Ono, for a recording session. He returned home, and was walking into his building when that same fan killed him with four shots at close range.

Somewhere in Los Angeles, several women began four weeks' work hand-embroidering beads onto Nancy Reagan's inaugural gown, part of a day's wardrobe estimated at a value of $25,000.

And on January 20, the corporate jets stacked up in the sky in an air-borne traffic jam the likes of which Washington National Airport had never seen.

Ronald Reagan stepped up to the inaugural platform. For the first time, it faced west: to symbolize, aides told reporters, the "new direction opened by a man of the West"—as if Richard Nixon had never been president at all.

He wore formal wear, Gerald Ford's and Jimmy Carter's decisions to take the oath of office in ordinary business attire not having taken as precedent. He was sworn in—and at approximately that moment, custody of the hostages was turned over to the United States.

Coverage toggled between the Capitol and reports from Iran of an Algerian jetliner reportedly bearing the fifty-two American hostages; and America's fortieth president gave his inaugural address:

"For decades we have piled deficit upon deficit, mortgaging our future and our children's future for the temporary convenience of the present. . . .

"In this present crisis, government is not the solution to our problem; government is the problem. . . .

"We will again be the exemplar of freedom and a beacon of hope for those who do not now have freedom.

"With God's help, we can and will resolve the problems which now confront us. . . . And after all, why shouldn't we believe that? We are Americans."

The hostages flew to Frankfurt, and freedom. The news producer overseeing ABC's coverage refused to intercut footage of the landing with inspirational music. Roone Arledge found someone from his sports division to do it instead.

And the revelers moved out to the inaugural balls, where it was observed that fur coats so overloaded the coatracks that they resembled great lumbering mastodons out of the prehistoric past.

Acknowledgments

MY GRATITUDE GOES OUT FIRST TO THE SCHOLARS.

The first I want to recognize is Leo Ribuffo, whose pioneering work on American conservatism had a profound influence on me when I began this journey in the 1990s, as I hope his astringent insistence on evidence over pundit speculation does still. I was very saddened by his death in 2018.

Next come authors of useful second works on the 1970s, like Michael Barone, Edward Berkowitz, Thomas Bertelsmann, Peter Carroll, Jefferson Cowie, Steven Hayward, Philip Jenkins, Laura Kalman, James T. Patterson, Dominic Sandbrook, Bruce Schulman, and Sean Wilentz.

Those whose books helped reconstruct the ins and outs of Capitol Hill include J. Lee Annis (on Senate minority leader Howard Baker), John A. Farrell (on House speaker Tip O'Neill), Julian Zelizer (on everything: I own eight books with his name on the spine), and, especially, Ian Shapiro, whose *The Last Great Senate* is, indeed, great.

On the rise of the New Right, I should recognize Ernest B. Ferguson (for his classic biography of Jesse Helms), Adam Clymer, Richard Vetterli (on Orrin Hatch), and Alan Crawford, an apostate from the New Right to whom it was a kick to reach out to discuss his invaluable 1981 chronicle *Thunder on the Right*. Two more recent apostates, Colonel Doner and Frank Schaeffer, produced useful memoirs. LeRoy Ashby and Rod Gramer produced a benchmark biography of a key New Right victim, Frank Church. Another victim of the New Right was Senator Thomas McIntyre, who from that experience produced the invaluable 1979 book *The Fear Brokers*. Also invaluable is another book produced at the time, journalist Connie Paige's *The Right to Lifers*.

Other useful scholars on the New Right's constituent intersecting discontents include (on feminism and anti-feminism) Donald Critchlow, Susan Faludi, Gillian Frank, Lara Osborne, Robert Self, Marjorie Spruill, and especially the late Ruth Murray Brown; (on abortion) Cynthia Gorney, Linda Greenhouse and Reva B. Siegal, and Stacy Taranto; (on the Christian right) Randall Balmer, Matthew Moen, Joseph Crespino, Darren Dochuk, Seth Dowland, Francis Fitzgerald, J. Brooks Flippen, Dan Gilgoff, Michael Hammond, Susan Harding, William C. Inboden, William Martin, Michael McVicar, Jeremy Rifkin, John G. Turner, Daniel K. Williams, and Michael Sean Winters; and (on anti-gay organizing) Dudley Clenendon and Adam Nagourney, Fred Fejes, the late Warren Hinckle, Carol Mason, and the late Randy Shilts.

On the political economy of the period, important sources include Mark Blyth, the late William Greider, Edward McClelland, the late Judith Stein, and Matt Stoller. On taxes, the tax revolt, and supply-side economics: Jonathan Chait, Robert Kuttner, and Molly Michelmore. On the business revolt against liberalism: Mike Davis, Thomas Byrne Edsall, Elizabeth Fones-Wolf, Lawrence Glickman, Mark Green, Jacob Hacker and Paul Pierson, John Judis, Alyssa Katz, Charles Noble, Michael Pertschuk, Kim Phillips-Fein, and David P. Vogel. On the American Agriculture Movement: William P. Browne, John Dinse, Jo Freeman, and Catherine McNichol Stock. On neoconservatism: Sidney Blumenthal and Peter Steinfels; hats off, too, to Blumenthal's indispensable book of profiles of the era's political consultants, *The Permanent Campaign*.

On political advertising: Kathleen Hall Jamieson. On drug policy: Ryan Grim. On film: Peter Biskind, Thomas Shtatz, and Erik Lundegaard—with Lundegaard and Eric Kleefeld informing my interpretation of the 1978 film *Superman*. On Ted Kennedy: Tim Stanley. On race, and the 1970s "ethnic revival": Matthew Jacobsen. On John Connally: James Reston Jr. On George H. W. Bush: John Meacham. On John Anderson: Jim Mason. On Three Mile Island: Natasha Zaretsky. On Ralph Nader: Justin Martin. On Roone Arledge: Travis Vogan. On conservative think tanks: Jason Stahl. On energy: Daniel Horowitz and Meg Jacobs. On New York City: Jonathan Mahler and Kim Phillips-Fein. On the National Rifle Association: Mark Ames, Jill Lapore, and Riva Siegel. On *The Deer Hunter*: H. Bruce Franklin and Jerry Lembecke. On the 1980 election and the South: Marcus Witcher. On the Sagebrush Rebellion: Jefferson Decker. On Dick Cheney and Donald Rumsfeld: James Mann. On Milton Friedman: Sören Brandes. On Love Canal: Michael Stewart Foley. On Joe Biden: Branko Marcitec. On Newt Gingrich: Justin DeMello, David Osborne, and Craig Shirley. On 1970s TV: Elana Levine. On credit controls: Stacey Schreft. On Patrick Caddell: Jordan Michael Smith.

I couldn't have come up with my interpretation of the crucial subject of Iran without the work of Mark Bowen, David Farber, Gary Sick, Blake Jones, and especially Christian Caryl, whose *Strange Rebels: 1979 and the Birth of the 21st Century* contributed greatly to my understanding of the Soviet invasion of Afghanistan as well.

Authors who were especially useful in reconstructing the run-up to

Ronald Reagan's 1980 presidential campaign include Lou Cannon, Bob Collacello, Ronnie Dugge, William Kleinknecht, and Garry Wills. Standout authors on the Carter presidency include Stuart Eizenstat, Joe Klein, Marc Reisner (on water policy), Robert Schlesinger (on speechwriting), Bob Woodward (on scandals), and Lawrence Wright (on the 1978 Camp David Accords).

I also relied on journalists composing the first draft of this history at the time of these events. One I've particularly cherished over the years is Jules Witcover, whose 1970 *The Resurrection of Richard Nixon* was such an important source for my *Nixonland*, and whose *Blue Smoke and Mirrors: How Reagan Won and Why Carter Lost the Election of 1980*, coauthored with his partner the late Jack Germond, was crucial this time around. Others include the late Alexander Cockburn, Elizabeth Drew, T. R. Reid, and James Ridgeway. Special recognition, too, to Garry Trudeau, who first taught me about this stuff when I was a kid growing up in the 1980s, stealing my big brother's *Doonesbury* books from the 1970s.

Let's venerate, too, the folks who build and maintain online archives. Some do so on their individual initiative, like Douglas O. Linder of the University of Missouri–Kansas City School of Law, whose FamousTrials.com was useful in reconstructing the trial of Dan White; Dave Leip, whose U.S. Elections Atlas provides indispensable statistics; the diehard *Saturday Night Live* fans behind SNLtranscripts.jt.org; and Hawes Publications, which has uploaded every week's *New York Times* bestseller list for easy reference. Brewster Kahle is an American hero for providing a platform for crowdsourced historian preservation through his nonprofit Internet Archive, where, for example, one kind soul uploaded transcripts of all the ABC News broadcasts from 1979 to 1980. Julian Assange remains a controversial figure, but the State Department documents uploaded to Wikileaks.org documenting the fall of the Shah of Iran were indispensable to me. I also cherish Gerhard Peters and John Woolly for building the Presidency Project (Presidency.UCSB.Edu), where just about every public utterance by Jimmy Carter quoted here can be found. Amy Salit of WGYY graciously rescued an ancient Terry Gross interview from the *Fresh Air* archives for me. And I am grateful to Annelise Anderson, the late Martin Anderson, and Kiron K. Skinner for their series of volumes collecting the prepresidential letters, speeches, and commentaries of Ronald Reagan.

Participants in events described in these chapters, or experts on them, who were generous with me in their recollections and expertise, include Theresa Amato, Annelise Anderson, J. Lee Annis, Joan Baez, Sam Bagestos, Jeffrey Bell, the late William F. Buckley, Joseph Burdzinski, Jon Butler, Jameson Campaigne, Dan Cantor, Mary Ellen Chamberlin,

John Comaroff, Joseph Crespino, Elliott Curson, David Dayen, Jefferson Decker, Robert Dreyfuss, Ronnie Dugger, Mickey Edwards, James Fallows, Bill Gluba, Victor Goodman, Mark Green, Peggy June Griffin, Colin Harrison, Dave Heller (who found two veterans of Iowa politics of the period for me to interview on the fly in the middle of a minor-league baseball game), Hendrik Hertzberg, Pia Hinckle (who answered my questions about her late father, Warren Hinckle's, work on the trial of Dan White), Senator Gordon Humphrey, the late Maggie JoChild (who many, many years ago told me stories about the "White Night" riot that I will never forget), ABilly Jones-Hennin, John Judis, Fred Kaplan, Cricket Keating, David Keene, Lew and Joanne Koch, Sharon Lerner, Christopher Lydon, Dr. Stanley Margulies, Joseph McCartin, Bill Moyers, Ralph Nader, Adam Nagourney, Emi Nakamura, Melanie Nathan, David Neiwert, Allen Nichols, Howard Park, Michael Pertschuk, Samuel Popkin, David Rubenstein, Frank Schaeffer, Robert Scheer, Adele Stan, Roger Stone, Lance Tarrance, Meredith Tax, Jeffrey Toobin, Nina Totenberg, Richard Viguerie, Jesse Walker, Dwayne Walker, Pam Walton, Jon Weiner, Christine Alice Westberg, Alan Wolfe, and Brent Wynja. I also would especially like to recognize my dear, late friend Victor Harbison.

Then of course there are the physical archives. The ones I relied on most were the Hoover Institution at Stanford University, the Vanderbilt Television News Archive, and the Ronald Reagan Presidential Library and Museum. Thank you to the institutions that sponsor them and the archivists who steward them. Research assistance along the way was provided by Theresa Berger at the Hoover Institution, Eduardo Medrano at the Ronald Reagan Presidential Library, Jason Stahl, and, especially, by my indefatigable friend Douglas Grant. Important artifacts and documents were also provided to me by Kristina Lapinski, Howard Park, Lucy Knight—and my dear friend eBay.com.

I have enjoyed developing a lively, opinionated, and well-informed community of friends on Facebook with whom I've shared my progress from time to time, who have shared in return their own recollections and expertise. Robert Anderson, who told me a wonderful story about the effects of Proposition 13 in California, was a particularly lively correspondent, and it saddened me greatly to learn of his death in 2019.

I'm grateful to the editor who first signed up my last book, originally intended to cover the years between 1973 and 1980—which metastasized into two books—Cary Goldstein; and my publisher at Simon & Schuster, Jonathan Karp; and the splendid editorial adventurer there who brought the project across the finish line with me, Sean Manning. Sean and Jon's confidence and trust in me have been extraordinary. I appreciate them very much—as I do my agent these last ten years or so, Tina Bennett. Thanks, too, to Jay Mandel for his help.

Several of those nearest and dearest to me aided in, um—perfecting?—the manuscript: my sister Linda Perlstein; my friends Celia Bucci, Allison Miller, Karl Fogel, Meg Handler (Meg was also my brilliant and efficient partner in producing the photo inserts), and Katie Waddell; and last but not least my wife, Judy Cohn. This project, now complete, has covered twenty-two years of American history, and almost twenty-four years of my own history. It has contained volumes: four of them, to be exact. Judy's grace, wisdom, and patience helped make my life as good as it could possibly be. And fortunately for you, her grace, wisdom, and *impatience* helped make these pages as good as they could be. Without the manic music from her red pen—*get to the point!!*—getting to the end could have required a few volumes more.

Shoulder to shoulder now, my love, for all the manic music to come.

Notes

THESE NOTES ARE ALSO ONLINE AT RICKPERLSTEIN.NET/REAGANLAND
-SOURCE-NOTES/ with, wherever possible, links to the documents, articles, and book pages cited. Most newspaper links lead to the best publicly available online archive, Newspapers.com, which requires a paid subscription, as do many of the articles from *Time* magazine. Syndicated columns appear on different days in different newspapers so they may not be cited on the original day they appeared. To maximize the availability of links, I often cite articles from major national newspapers in their syndicated versions, which also may not be cited on the original day they appeared. All general election statistics cited in the text for popular and electoral votes can be found at https://uselectionatlas.org/. Primary election results can be found in the "1980 Republican presidential primaries" and "1980 Democratic presidential primaries" entries at Wikipedia.org. Cited statistics for unemployment rates can be confirmed at http://www.fedprimerate.com/mortgage_rates.htm; monthly inflation rates at http://www.inflationdata.com, under the "Numerical Inflation Data" tab. Unless otherwise noted, President Carter job approval ratings are from the Gallup Organization and can be confirmed at https://www.presidency.ucsb.edu/statistics/data/presidential-job-approval. Date when news reports and campaign commercials were accessed at YouTube.com are cited. Cited television footage from the 1986 documentary *The Made for TV Election* is linked to the exact timestamp in which it appears in the program on YouTube.com, last accessed May 24, 2020. When I cite bestseller statistics, my source is the downloadable *New York Times* lists at http://www.hawes.com. Because of the closure of the Hoover Institution and the Ronald Reagan Presidential Library during the COVID-19 crisis, it was impossible to confirm some of the citations; these will be updated online when it becomes possible to do so, and in future editions. Scholars having problems finding documents cited here should contact me directly at Reaganland2020@gmail.com, for assistance.

ABBREVIATIONS

AA: Annelise Anderson Papers, Hoover Institution, Stanford, California

ABCIA: 1980 ABC News transcripts, Internet Archive

AP: Associated Press newspaper syndicate

APP: American Presidency Project, http://www.presidency.ucbs.edu

BG: *Boston Globe*

CFTRN: *Citizens for the Republic Newsletter*, Ronald Reagan Presidential
  Library, Ronald Reagan Presidential Campaign Papers, boxes
  38–39.

CT: *Chicago Tribune*

DH: Deaver and Hannaford Papers, Hoover Institution, Stanford,
  California

ENIR: Rowland Evans and Robert Novak "Inside Report" column

HE: *Human Events*

LAT: *Los Angeles Times*

MFTVE: *The Made-for-TV Election*, 1986 documentary by William
  Brandon Shanley.

NYT: *New York Times*

RALIL: Kiron K. Skinner, Annelise Anderson, and Martin Anderson, eds.,
  Reagan: A Life in Letters (New York: Simon & Schuster, 2004)

RPV: Kiron K. Skinner, Annelise Anderson, and Martin Anderson, eds.,
  *Reagan's Path to Victory: The Shaping of Ronald Reagan's Vision:
  Selected Writings* (New York: Free Press, 1994)

RRB: Reagan radio broadcast tapes, Hoover Archives, Stanford University

RRC: Ronald Reagan syndicated newspaper column

RRIHOH: Kiron K. Skinner, Annelise Anderson, and Martin Anderson,
  eds, *Reagan in His Own Hand: The Writings of Ronald Reagan
  That Reveal His Revolutionary Vision for America* (New York:
  Free Press, 2001).

RRPL: Ronald Reagan Presidential Library, Simi Valley, California, Ronald
  Reagan Pre-Presidential Files

RVA: Richard V. Allen Papers, Hoover Archives, Stanford University

UPI: United Press International newspaper syndicate

USNWR: *U.S. News and World Report*

VTVNA: Vanderbilt Television News Archive, Nashville, Tennessee

WS: *Washington Star*

WP: *Washington Post*

WSJ: *Wall Street Journal*

W&G: Jules Witcover and Jack Germond syndicated column

CHAPTER ONE

3 **Reagan blamed** "Reagan Ties Ford Loss to Watergate Movie," *St. Petersburg Times*, March 22, 2977; RRB 76-03 track 02, "The Ford Strike," recorded October 18, 1976.

3 **the factor many** See for example "Walter Scott's Personality Parade," December 26, 1976; Robert L. Healy column, BG, November 7, 1976.

3 **"only effective campaign work"** Malcolm D. MacDougall, "How Madison Avenue Didn't Put a Ford in Your Future," *New York*, February 21, 1977.

4 *New York Times* **had concluded** "Reagan Shuns Role in Ford's Campaign," NYT, October 30, 1976.

4 **"No defeated candidate"** AP, December 16, 1976.

4 **"curtain of silence"** Letter to Mrs. Florence P. Moore, RALIL, 233.

4 *Boston Globe*'s **Washington columnist** David Nyhan column, BG, November 7.

4 **"At 65, he is considered"** "Reagan Hints at Active Role in Shaping G.O.P. Future," NYT, November 5, 1976.

4 **"bright, tough young conservative"** Jack Anderson column, November 8, 1976.

4 **"closer to extinction"** "Politicians Find G.O.P. Fighting for Its Survival," NYT, November 24, 1976.

4 **18 percent** Mary McGrory column, April 4, 1977; Phil Crane letter to the editor, WSJ, June 8, 1977; Everett Carll Ladd Jr., "The Unmaking of the Republican Party," *Fortune*, September 1977.

4 **"entrust its future to younger"** "Reagan Hints at Active Role in Shaping G.O.P. Future," NYT, November 5, 1976.

4 **"We give the impression"** J. F. terHorst column, November 15, 1976.

4 **The American Conservative Union** David B. Wilson column, BG, November 14, 1976; UPI, November 6, 1976; "Conservatives Urged to Work to Control Both Parties Rather Than Start One of Their Own," LAT, December 12, 1976.

4 **Reagan himself entertained** David B. Frisk, *If Not Us, Who?: William Rusher, National Review, and the Conservative Movement* (Wilmington, DE: Intercollegiate Studies Institute, 2011).

4 **"You know, in the business"** *New York Times* Service, December 16, 1976.

5 **One day that summer** Malcolm D. MacDougall, *We Almost Made It: President Ford's Adman Tells the Personal Story Behind One of the Most Surprising Campaigns in American Political History* (New York: Crown, 1977), 53–54.

5 **One of them, a rabbi** Howard Singer letter to the editor, NYT, September 26, 1976.

5 **"a new breed of student"** Joseph N. Bell, "Silence on Campus," *Harper's*, March 3, 1976.

5 **College business courses** Bethany Morton, "Make Payroll, Not War," in Bruce J. Schulman and Julian E. Zelizer, eds., *Rightward Bound: Making America Conservative in the 1970s* (Cambridge, MA: Harvard University Press, 2008), 52–71.

5 **college professor gave a speech** Bell, "Silence on Campus."

6 **Jimmy Carter kicked off** Jules Witcover, *Marathon: The Pursuit of the Presidency, 1972–1976* (New York: Viking, 1977), 545; Victory Gold, *PR As In President* (New York: Doubleday, 1977), 206. On Detroit crime see "Detroit to Lay Off 972 Policemen; "357 Others Stay Home, Apparently as Protest," LAT, July 1, 1976; "Governments Cut Services to Save Funds," LAT, August 10, 1976; UPI, "Black Gangs Terrorize Detroit Rock Fans," August 17, 1976.

6 **Ford opened at the White House** Witcover, *Marathon*, pp. 553, 638.

6 **"there were no issues"** MacDougall, *We Almost Made It*, 63.

7 ***"I'm feeling good about America"*** Ibid., 121.

7 **Jimmy Carter's commercials** YouTube.com, accessed April 25, 2020.

7 **Carter's packagers** Elizabeth Drew, *American Journal: The Events of 1976* (New York: Random House, 1977), 145.

8 **former news** Theodore White, *America In Search of Itself: The Making of the President, 1956–1980* (New York: Harper & Row, 1981), 190; Sidney Blumenthal, *The Permanent Campaign: Inside the World of Elite Political Operatives* (Boston: Beacon Press, 1980), 47.

8 **Patrick Caddell** Ibid., 27–57; Joe Klein, *Politics Lost: How American Democracy Was Trivialized by People Who Think You're Stupid* (New York: Doubleday, 2006), 35–56; Caddell Oral History, Miller Center, University of Virginia; Gold, *PR As In President*, 207; Anthony Lewis, "Winter of Discontent," NYT, April 15, 1974.

9 **Ford adman** MacDougall, *We Almost Made It*, 22–23, 44–48.

9 **FBI director Clarence Kelley** Witcover, *Marathon*, 547.

10 **Bob Dole, Ford's hatchet-man** Ibid., 548–49; AP, September 6, 1976.

10 **"body attached to the hand"** "Carter Has Ad Headstart in Pennsylvania," NYT, April 18, 1976.

10 **"spontaneous" presidential stroll** "Ford 'Campaigns' from White House by Signing Bills," NYT, September 8, 1976.

10 **one-third of voters** *Hamilton* (OH) *Journal News*, September 16, 1976.

10 **first person ever to propose** Newton Minow and Craig LeMay, *Inside the Presidential Debates: Their Improbable Past and Promising Future* (Chicago: University of Chicago Press, 2008); email communication with Newton Minow.

11 **"completely controlled"** Gold, *PR As In President*, 225–26.

11 **police penned off** Witcover, *Marathon*, 576.

11 **his first run-in** J. Brooks Flippen, *Jimmy Carter, the Politics of Family, and the Rise of the Religious Right* (Athens, GA: University of Georgia Press, 2011), 90; "Carter Suggests That U.S. Foster Rights Overseas," NYT, September 9, 1976.

11 **"Lousy television"** AP, September 29, 1976.

12 **Until there arrived** Debate, glitch and all, can be viewed at C-Span.org.

13 **Eugene McCarthy** Minow and Lemay, *Inside the Presidential Debates*, 52.

13 **these "two men who were seeking"** F. Clifton White, *Politics as a Noble Calling: The Memoirs of F. Clifton White* (Ottawa, IL: Jameson Books, 1994), 203.

13 **candidates had been trained** Witcover, *Marathon*, 578.

13 **The conservative weekly** HE, September 15, 1976.

13 **Reagan got letters** Reagan to Phillip W. Flannery and Luke B. Schmidt, RALIL, 220.

13 **"reassess our party"** Reagan to Russell Castle, ibid., 221.

14 **Four days later** "Memo to the Media," August 24, 1976, RRPL, Box 17.

14 **One of the commentaries** AP, September 2, 1976.

14 **He was asked** Ibid.

14 **Ford phoned** AP, September 3, 1976.

14 **The *New York Times* said** "Aides Say Reagan Will Campaign for Ford If He Gets Assignments," NYT, September 9, 1976.

14 **Ford's running mate** "Dole Invades Carter-land," CT, September 2, 1976.

14 **Reagan's longtime** "California Typifies Lack of Interest Shown Across Nation in Campaign," NYT, September 19, 1976.

14 **"Hang Haerle"** "California GOP Convenes in Anaheim Amid Claims of United Support for Ford," LAT, September 26, 1976.

14 Texas's "sounded" "Ford Backers Narrowly Keep Control of Texas Republican Party," NYT, September 13, 1976.

14 Reagan's most loyal "Helms Calls for Kissinger to Back Platform or Quit," NYT, September 9, 1976.

14 It was a quintessential Teleprompter text with stage directions, RRPL, Box 21.

16 The next morning "Reagan Is Too Busy to Aid Ford in Five States," September 20, 1976.

16 That summer, Jimmy Carter Robert Scheer, *Playing President: My Close Encounters with Nixon, Carter, Bush I, Reagan, and Clinton—and How They Did Not Prepare Me for George W. Bush* (Brooklyn: Akashic Books, 2006); email correspondence with Robert Scheer.

17 A second front BG, October 3, 1976; Witcover, *Marathon*, 580; MacDougall, *We Almost Made It*, 136.

18 "SMILE IF YOU'RE HORNY" Witcover, *Marathon*, 590.

18 "We've been deeply wounded" NYT, October 1, 1976.

19 "naturalized Martian" Dominic Sandbrook, *Mad as Hell: The Crisis of the 1970s and the Rise of the Populist Right* (New York: Anchor Books, 2012), 201.

19 Boston's mayor Witcover, *Marathon*, 589.

19 In 1972, nonwhites Robert Mason, *Richard Nixon and the Quest for a New Majority* (Chapel Hill: University of North Carolina Press, 2005), 189.

19 Mal MacDougall predicted MacDougall, *We Almost Made It*, 169.

19 a *Rolling Stone* dispatch Ibid., 145–46; AP, October 2, 1976; Witcover, *Marathon*, 592.

20 Dole traveled to Reagan's "Reagan Joins Dole in New Haven and Praises the Republican Platform," NYT, October 3, 1976.

20 "unique in party platform history" RRC, September 26, 1976.

20 MacDougall concluded MacDougall, *We Almost Made It*, 137.

20 The Republicans debuted Ibid. 137, 186; "Pearl Bailey," LivingRoomCandidate.org.

20 family was the "cornerstone" Leo Ribuffo, "Family Policy Past as Prologue: Jimmy Carter, the White House Conference on Families, and the Mobilization of the New Christian Right," *Review of Policy Research*, April 26, 2006.

20 Ford signed APP, October 4, 1976; weather report, October 4, 1976, WP.

21 Ford scrimmaged Witcover, *Marathon*, 594.

21 Carter was drilled Gold, *PR As In President*, 229.

21 He answered the first question Debate at C-Span.org.

21 one of forty-two grins Gold, *PR As In President*, 229.

21 "That stiff, prissy man" Arthur M. Schlesinger Jr., *Journals: 1952–2000* (New York: Penguin, 2007), 370.

22 Had he? Leo Ribuffo, "Is Poland a Soviet Satellite? Gerald Ford, the Sonnenfeldt Doctrine, and the Election of 1976," in *Right Center Left: Essays in American History* (New Brunswick, NJ: Rutgers University Press, 1992), 189–212. See also Gold, *PR As In President*, 535; Witcover, *Marathon*, 594–96, 601–2; MacDougall, *We Almost Made It*, 148; Tom Wicker, *On Press: A Top Reporter's Life in, and Reflections on, American Journalism* (New York: Viking, 1978), 71; Walter Mondale, *The Good Fight: A Life in Liberal Politics* (New York: Scribner, 2010), 168–69; and "His Political Director Looks Back: E. Europe Error Was Crucial for Ford," LAT, December 8, 1976. Stalin quote comes from Karen Underhill, a scholar on Poland.

23 "After twenty-four hours" Witcover, *Marathon*, 601.

23 with the joke circulating Ibid., 606.

23 Back in August MacDougall, *We Almost Made It*, 46.

23 "Evangelicals Seen Cooling on Carter" WP, September 29, 1976.

24 In 1918 Vincent Irvine Masters, *The Call of the South: A Presentation of the Home Principle in Missions, Especially as It Applies to the South* (Atlanta: Publicity Department of the Home Mission Board of the Southern Baptist Convention, 1918).

24 "I Love America" rallies Flippen, *Jimmy Carter*, 81; Susan Harding, *The Book of Jerry Falwell* (Princeton: Princeton University Press, 2000), 119–20.

24 "stage movements" Flippen, *Jimmy Carter*, 195.

24 A Fairfax, Virginia, minister For 1976 Christian right see " 'Vote Christian' Impact on Election Weighed," LAT, November 8, 1976; "Religious Leaders Score Group's Reported Effort to Elect Only Christians," NYT, October 21, 1976; " 'Vote-Christian' Political Drives Assailed," LAT, October 23, 1976; Flippen, *Jimmy Carter*, 82; Martin, *With God on Our Side*, 152; Connie Paige, *The Right to Lifers: Who They Are, How They Operate, and Where They Get Their Money* (New York: Summit Books, 1983), 156-57; and John G. Turner, *Bill Bright and the Campus Crusade for Christ: The Renewal of Evangelism in Twentieth Century America* (Chapel Hill: University of North Carolina Press, 2009), 158–68.

25 "Christian Embassy" "Christian Embassy Opens in Capital, Aims at Reaching Federal Officials," *Toledo Blade*, March 5, 1976; "Campus Crusade Seeks Great Awakening," LAT, July 25, 1976; "Campus Crusade Evangelizes Officials; Christian Embassy in Washington," LAT, March 12, 1977; and WP, November 11, 1978.

25 The cascading damage "Evangelicals Seen Cooling on Carter."

26 At first the president Flippen, *Jimmy Carter*, 98.

26 Ford hosted thirty-four MacDougall, *We Almost Made It*, 140; Daily Diary, September 30, 1976, Gerald Ford Presidential Library.

26 "Don't force me" Chris Ladd, "Pastors, Not Politicians, Turned Dixie Republican," *Forbes*, March 27, 2017; Curtis W. Freeman, " 'Never Had I Been So Blind': "W. A. Criswell's 'Change' on Racial Segregation," *Journal of Southern Religion* X (2007).

26 He also said Billy Graham, *Just As I Am: The Autobiography of Billy Graham* (New York: HarperCollins, 2018), 528–29.

26 "he's acknowledged" BG, October 11, 1976.

26 In 1960 "Texas Baptists Welcome Ford," LAT, October 11, 1976; also for 1972, 1975, and 1976 quotes.

27 "tremendous subjective impact" Transcript, President Ford Library.

27 military-industrial complex Rick Perlstein, *Before the Storm: Barry Goldwater and the Unmaking of the American Consensus* (New York: Farrar, Straus & Giroux, 2001), 124.

28 interior was festooned Pool Report, Gerald Ford Library, October 10, 1976.

28 "I am for him" "Gerald Ford Exits First Baptist Church in Dallas, Texas, with Pastor W. A. Criswell," GettyImages.com.

28 "prior commitment" "Reagan Snubs Ford Campaign in California," CT, October 25, 1980.

29 The final debate Debate on C-Span.org.

29 "nibbled to death" Marvin Barrett and Zachary Sklar, *The Eye of the Storm: The Seventh Alfred Dupont–Columbia University Survey of Broadcast Journalism* (New York: Lippincott & Crowell, 1980), 32.

29 "If Reagan had been" MacDougall, *We Almost Made It*, 164.

CHAPTER TWO

30 **Shortly after Election Day** "About Long Island: So Let's Hear It for Orrin Hatch," NYT, November 28, 1976.

30 **Malcolm Wallop** "Some New Political Figures Have Emerged," NYT, November 4, 1976.

31 **"Last of the Mohicans"** BG, November 7, 1976.

31 **Utah's new senator-elect** Richard Vetterli, *Orrin Hatch: Challenging the Washington Establishment* (Southlake, TX: Gateway Books, 1982); Orrin Hatch, *Square Peg: Confessions of a Citizen Senator* (New York: Basic Books, 2002), both passim.

32 **He approached a stalwart** Orrin Hatch, "Tribute to Cleon Skousen," *Congressional Record: Senate*, January 25, 2006, S114; Cleon Skousen, *The Naked Communist* (1958).

33 **"I'm a non-politician"** "Today in the West," *Deseret News*, May 10, 1976.

33 **"conservatives whose game"** Alan Crawford, *Thunder on the Right: The "New Right" and the Politics of Resentment* (New York: Pantheon, 1981), 290.

33 **"a guerrilla battle"** Robert J. Hoy, "Lid on a Boiling Pot," in *The New Right Papers*, Robert. W. Whitaker, ed. (New York: St. Martin's Press, 1982), 84.

33 **prototypical New Right crusade** Ibid.; Rick Perlstein, *Invisible Bridge: The Fall of Nixon and the Rise of Reagan* (New York: Simon & Schuster, 2014), 306.

33 **"issues that people"** "The New Right: A Special Report," *Conservative Digest*, June 1979.

33 **Pat Caddell** Joe Klein, *Politics Lost: How American Democracy Was Trivialized by People Who Think You're Stupid* (New York: Doubleday, 2006), 56.

34 **"We organize discontent"** Viguerie and Franke, *Right Turn: How Conservatives Used New and Alternative Media to Take Over America* (Lanham, MD: Taylor Trade Publishing, 2004), 128.

34 **Howard Phillips** Blumenthal, *The Permanent Campaign*, 231; Thomas J. McIntyre, *The Fear Brokers* (Boston: Beacon Press, 1981), 71.

34 **Jesse Helms gave** "Thunder from the Right," NYT *Magazine*, February 8, 1981.

34 **Viguerie's story** Sidney Blumenthal, *The Permanent Campaign*, 217–234; author interview with Viguerie, 1998.

35 **"solid gold mailbox"** Viguerie and Franke, *Right Turn*, 88.

35 *Dear Friend* McIntyre, *The Fear Brokers*, 73.

36 **"Achilles heel"** Frances FitzGerald, "A Disciplined, Charging Army," *New Yorker*, May 18, 1981.

36 **"the godfather"** McIntyre, *The Fear Brokers*, 73.

36 **Boston pizzeria** Blumenthal, *The Permanent Campaign*, 230.

36 **"great hulk of a man"** Connie Paige, *The Right to Lifers: Who They Are, How They Operate, and Where They Get Their Money* (New York: Summit Books, 1983), 141.

36 **"By 1980"** AP, December 13, 1976.

36 **"Point A to Point Z"** Blumenthal, *The Permanent Campaign*, 227.

36 **He always claimed** For instance in Viguerie and Franke, *Right Turn*, 129.

37 **former radio newsman** Ibid., 128–29; Martin, *With God on Our Side*, 170.

37 **In 1971, Weyrich** See Jason Stahl, *Right Moves: The Conservative Think Tank in American Political Culture Since 1945* (Chapel Hill: University of North Carolina Press, 2016), 70–77, which debunks Weyrich's own misrepresentations of this history.

37 **"We're not here to be"** Peter G. Brown, *Restoring the Public Trust: A Fresh Vision for Progressives in America* (Boston: Beacon Press, 1994), 6.

37 **Weyrich soon quit** Adam Clymer, *Drawing the Line at the Big Ditch: The Panama*

Canal Treaties and the Rise of the Right (Lawrence: University Press of Kansas, 2008), 131–32.

37 **"Teutonic forebears"** Paige, *The Right to Lifers*, 135.

37 **The legal vehicle** Clymer, *Drawing the Line at the Big Ditch*, 130; David P. Vogel, *Fluctuating Fortunes: The Political Power of Business in America* (New York: Basic Books, 1989), 207.

38 **"diagram of its organization"** Nick Kotz, "King Midas of 'The New Right,'" *Atlantic Monthly*, November 1978.

38 **"We can define it"** NBC News, October 26, 1976, VTVNA.

38 **Weyrich had met him** Vetterli, *Orrin Hatch*, 32–33.

38 **reaching out to Ronald Reagan** Ibid., 44–45; "Hatch Gets Reagan Endorsement in Utah Senate Race," *St. George Daily Spectrum*, September 10, 1976; UPI, September 12, 1976; "The Political Birth of Orrin Hatch," *Salt Lake City Tribune*, January 13, 2012.

39 **Hatch's opponent** NYT, September 26, 1976; Vetterli, *Orrin Hatch*, 53; *Deseret News*, October 5, 1976.

39 **"a continued drift"** "Watergate, Vietnam, and Howe Make Moss Bid in Utah a Toss-up," NYT, October 19, 1976.

39 **In Moss's Utah** Letters to the editor, *West Valley View*, June 17, 1976; *Richfield Reaper*, July 1, 1976; *Ogden Standard-Examiner*, July 16, 1976; *Salt Lake City Tribune*, October 30, 1976; *Provo Daily Herald*, November 1, 1976; UPI, July 8, 1976; "Cancer Society Affirms Stand on Fluoridation," *Saint George Daily Spectrum*, July 29, 1976; "Fluoridation Far from Dead, Backer Avows," *Salt Lake City Tribune*, November 5, 1976.

40 **In Michigan** John Chamberlain column, October 26, 1976; HE, October 30 and November 13, 1976.

40 **"bald little professor"** William Greider, *Secrets of the Temple: How the Federal Reserve Runs the Country* (New York: Simon & Schuster, 1989), 87. See also Sidney Blumenthal, *The Rise of the Counter-Establishment: The Conservative Ascent to Political Power* (New York: Times Books, 2007), 87–121.

40 **neatly summarized** RRB 76-03, track 13, "Milton Friedman #2," recorded October 18, 1976.

41 **In Chicago** "A Wife's View: Friedman's Nobel: It's Late, but Nice," CT, October 18, 1976.

41 **Bellow wrote** Saul Bellow, *Mr. Sammler's Planet* (New York: Viking Press, 1970), 105.

41 **quite the rebuke** "GOP Not in the 20th Century Yet," BG, May 20, 1977.

41 **"our resident fascist"** Thomas M. Sipos, "Ben Stein—Portrait of a Hollywood Republican," *Hollywood Investigator*, September 28, 2003.

41 **Viguerie made a rare** "Group Scores Charges Put Before Vote Panel," NYT, October 28, 1976. The FEC filing can be found here, accessed January 21, 2929.

42 **"frankly because his prices"** "Casey Cash Challenged by Unit Backing Walgren," *Pittsburgh Post-Gazette*, October 26, 1976.

42 **On the same ballot** "Matheson Tops Romney, Hatch Edges Moss, Marriott, McKay Win," *Salt Lake City Tribune*, November 3, 1976.

42 **So did Daniel Patrick Moynihan** For Moynihan as neoconservative see Peter Steinfels, *The Neoconservatives: The Men Who Are Changing American Politics* (New York: Simon & Schuster, 1979).

42 **The formerly Marxist** My interpretation is indebted to Blumenthal, *The Rise of the Counter-Establishment*, 122–165.

43 **It began, naturally** G. B. Kistiakowsky, "Is Paranoia Necessary for Security?" NYT

Magazine, November 27, 1977; "Report on Soviet Nuclear Strategy Says Moscow Emphasizes Victory," NYT, June 25, 1977; Frances FitzGerald, *Way Out There in the Blue: Reagan, Star Wars, and the End of the Cold War* (New York: Simon & Schuster, 2000), 81–84, 93; Blumenthal, *The Rise of the Counter-Establishment*, 140; "Assessing Soviet Strength Is a Team Task," NYT, February 6, 1977. For examples of neoconservative leaks and arguments working their way into political debates see "U.S. Defense Buildup Forces Facing Carter Gain Strength," WP, January 2, 1977, and, in the same paper on the same day, "Carter to Inherit Intense Dispute on Soviet Intentions"; Clayton Fritchey column, *Newsday* Service, January 8, 1977; "Ikle Thinks Soviets Uncertain About Their Strategic Intent," WP, January 15, 1977 (about Senate hearings called in response to Team B claims); Richard Pipes, "Strategic Superiority," NYT, February 6, 1976; "Brezhnev Termed Détente a Ruse, 1973 Report Said," BG, February 11, 1977; Stanley Karnow, "Who's Afraid of the Russians," CT, February 19, 1977; "The Nuclear Arms Debate Reverberates Through Washington," WP, February 20, 1977.

45 **Carter was unmoved** Blumenthal, *Rise of the Counter-Establishment*, 129; Jimmy Carter, *White House Diary* (New York: Macmillan, 2010), 76.

45 **publicly announced** "On U.S. Dealings with the Soviet Union," NYT, January 11, 1977.

45 *Washington Post* **front page** "Carter to Inherit Intense Dispute on Soviet Intentions," WP, January 2, 1977.

45 **mainstream arms control expert** "U.S. Defense Buildup Forces Facing Carter Gain Strength," WP, January 2, 1977.

45 **A liberal Democrat** Clayton Fritchey column, *Newsday* Service, January 8, 1977.

45 **Senator Charles Percy** "Ikle Thinks Soviets Uncertain About Their Strategic Intent," WP, January 15, 1977.

45 **Conservative Caucus** AP, December 13, 1976; "Conservatives Urged to Work to Control Both Parties Rather Than Start One of Their Own," LAT, December 12, 1976.

46 **picking a new party chairman** "Smith Leaves GOP Post," BG, November 23, 1976; "Mrs. Smith Quits Top GOP Post," CT, November 23, 1976; UPI, November 26, 1976; ENIR, November 29, 1976; Frank Starr column, CT, December 8, 1976; "Anne Armstrong Is Sounded Out as GOP Head," WP, December 11, 1976; ENIR, January 5, 7077; "Ford Backs Former Aide as GOP Chairman," WP, January 6, 1977.

46 **"rednecks of Georgia"** Mary McGrory column, January 23, 1977.

46 **compromise pick** "Republicans Select Brock as Party Head," NYT, January 15, 1977.

46 **Republican senators** Vetterli, *Orrin Hatch*, 73.

46 **"most intriguing"** *Congressional Quarterly Almanac* (Washington, D.C.: CQ Press, 1976).

47 **Theodore Sorensen** Peter N. Carroll, *It Seemed Like Nothing Happened: The Tragedy and Promise of America in the 1970s* (New York: Holt, 1982), 209; "Sorensen Defended by Carter," WP, January 17, 1977; ENIR, January 17, 1977; HE, December 25.

47 **Sorensen snapped back** "PostScript," WP, February 14, 1977.

47 **The *New York Times* reported** "Assessing Soviet Strength Is a Team Task," NYT, February 6, 1977.

47 **Pollsters found Americans** "U.S. Defense Buildup Forces Facing Carter Gain Strength," WP, January 2, 1977.

47 *Who's Who Among American High School* "Survey Finds Teenagers Are More Conservative," NYT, November 30, 1976.

47   **"Ball for the Unrepresented"** HE, January 22, 1977.

47   **"March for Life"** "40,000 March in Abortion Protest," WP, January 23, 1977.

CHAPTER THREE

51   **"since Dwight Eisenhower"** "Inaugural Day: Looking Ahead," WP, January 20, 1977.

51   **"The pigs' schools"** Marc Liberle and Tom Seligson, eds., *The High School Revolutionaries* (New York: Random House, 1970), 67.

51   **Richard Nixon worked** Jon Weiner, *Gimme Some Truth: The John Lennon FBI Files* (Berkeley: University of California Press, 2000).

51   **The day broke** "The Denim Inaugural," *Newsweek*, January 24, 1977; Alistair Cooke, *Alistair Cooke's America* (New York: Basic Books, 2009), 231; "Carter Is Sworn In as President, Asks 'Fresh Faith in Old Dream,' " WP, January 21, 1977; Theodore White, *America In Search of Itself: The Making of the President, 1956–1980* (New York: Harper & Row, 1981), 194.

53   **cries of delight** Carroll, *It Seemed Like Nothing Happened*, 266.

53   **"New Spirit Inaugural Concert"** "The Denim Inaugural"; "A Spectacular Television Variety Extravaganza for a President-to-Be," WP, January 21, 1977.

53   **Sally Quinn** ". . . And an Evening of Watching the Carters Watching the Stars," WP, January 21, 1977.

53   **House Speaker Tip O'Neill** "Squaring Off in Washington: Tip O'Neill vs. Jimmy Carter," *New York*, May 16, 1977.

53   **"Snopes clan"** Kevin P. Phillips column, January 21, 1977; Robert Novak, *The Prince of Darkness: 50 Years Reporting in Washington* (New York: Crown Forum, 2007), 296.

53   **"*Gone with the Wind*"** "Carter Associates Get 6 of Top 7 Positions," BG, January 15, 1977.

53   **"tight little group"** Elizabeth Drew, *American Journal: The Events of 1976* (New York: Random House. 1977), 299.

54   **"disdain for members"** "Jimmy Carter vs. Congress?" WSJ, March 25, 1977.

54   **"not too bright"** "Hill Democrats Unhappy with Carter's Emissary," WP, November 5, 1976.

54   **"zero, zip, zilch"** Carroll, *It Seemed Like Nothing Happened*, 207.

54   **in brown ink** "The Denim Inaugural."

54   **on the front page** "Inaugural Events Lists Cause Anger," WP, January 7, 1977.

54   **Gallup found that** "The Denim Inaugural."

55   **"If, after the inauguration"** HE, December 18, 1976.

55   **William Simon** ENIR, November 27, 1976.

55   **Frank Johnson** HE, January 1, 1977.

55   **Ralph Nader** Justin Martin, *Nader: Crusader, Spoiler, Icon* (New York: Basic Books, 2002), 180.

55   **"old-line, money establishment"** HE, December 18. 1976.

55   **redneck brother** "A Brotherly Good Time," WP, January 21, 1977.

55   **"He has to know"** "Problems of a Problem Solver," NYT *Magazine*, January 8, 1978.

55   **biblical prophet** Author interview with Hendrik Hertzberg.

56   **young men who had evaded service** " 'A Proper Thing To Do': President Carter's Pardon of Draft Evaders," article in possession of author; AP, August 25, 1976;

Robert O. Self, *All in the Family: The Realignment of American Democracy Since the 1960s* (New York: Hill & Wang, 2012), 72.

56 **Barry Goldwater** Carroll, *It Seemed Like Nothing Happened*, 213.

56 **"slap in the face"** "10,000 Affected Now," NYT, January 22, 1977.

56 **Governor Meldrim Thomson** UPI, January 22, 1977.

56 **$50 rebate** "Economic Recovery Progress—Message to Congress," January 31, 1977, APP; White, *America In Search of Itself*, 204.

56 **all thought it ridiculous** AP, February 8, 1977; Ian Shapiro, *The Last Great Senate: Courage and Statesmanship in Times of Crisis* (New York: Public Affairs Books, 2012), 46, 50.

57 **price of petroleum** Daniel Horowitz, *Jimmy Carter and the Energy Crisis of the 1970s: The "Crisis of Confidence" Speech of July 15, 1979* (New York: Bedford/St. Martin's, 2004), 7.

57 **a ten-thousand word** Sidney Blumenthal, *The Permanent Campaign: Inside the World of Elite Political Operatives* (Boston: Beacon Press, 1980), 58.

57 **On February 2** AP, February 3, 1977; UPI, February 3, 1977; Knight Newspapers, February 2, 1977; White, *America In Search of Itself*, 203; APP, February 3, 1977. View speech at MillerCenter.org.

58 **legislators over whose head** Shapiro, *The Last Great Senate*, 48.

58 **Paul Warnke** Ibid., 67; Frances FitzGerald, *Way Out There in the Blue: Reagan, Star Wars, and the End of the Cold War* (New York: Simon & Schuster, 2000), 81.

59 **for Micronesia** Sidney Blumenthal, *The Rise of the Counter-Establishment: The Conservative Ascent to Political Power* (New York: Times Books, 2007), 129.

59 **On the morning of** ENIR, February 2, 1977.

59 **Nitze testified** United States Congress, Senate Committee on Foreign Relations, *Warnke Nomination: Hearings Before the Committee on Foreign Relations* (1977); quote on 143, 183.

59 **Senator Robert Byrd of West Virginia** Shapiro, *The Last Great Senate*, 70–71.

59 **president's first press conference** APP, February 8, 1977.

60 **Evans and Novak's third** ENIR, February 23, 1977.

60 **Armed Services Committee** AP, March 1, 1977; AP, March 4, 1977.

60 **The New Right joined in** J. Peter Scoblic, *Us. vs. Them: Conservatism in the Age of Nuclear Terror* (New York: Viking, 2008), 103–4.

60 **Scoop Jackson boasted** Shapiro, *The Great Last Senate*, 71.

60 **failed water policies** Marc Reisner, *Cadillac Desert: The American West and Its Disappearing Water* (New York: Penguin. Books, 1993), 11.

60 **On February 18** Jimmy Carter, *White House Diary* (New York: Macmillan, 2010), 23; Shapiro, *The Last Great Senate*, 48.

61 **"Tucson and Phoenix"** Reisner, *Cadillac Desert*, 316.

61 **Gridiron Club** " 'Marching from Georgia,' " WP, March 21, 1977.

61 **contempt was real** Shapiro, *The Last Great Senate*, 50; "Long Warns Carter on Water Projects," NYT, March 21, 1977.

61 **"gut tells me"** Paul Laxalt, *Paul Laxalt's Nevada: A Memoir* (Reno, NV: Jack Bacon & Co, 2000), 308.

61 **Byrd was not appeased** Shapiro, *The Last Great Senate*, 50; also for Muskie quote.

62 **Mark "The Bird" Fidrych** Mary McGrory column, April 10, 1977.

62 **give up chauffeured limousines** William Safire column, NYT, February 7, 1977.

62 **beloved presidential yacht** UPI, May 21, 1977.

62 **Sunday school** Randall Balmer, *Redeemer: The Life of Jimmy Carter* (New York: Basic Books, 2014), 78.

62 **no hard liquor** AP, January 28, 1977.

62 **His visit to the Department** Reuters, February 11, 1977.

62 **Amy's White House tree house** AP, March 13, 1977.

62 **baptism by total immersion** AP, February 7, 1977.

62 *Ask President Carter* NYT, March 6, 1977; APP, March 5, 1977.

63 *Saturday Night Live* View sketch at YouTube.com, accessed April 25, 2020.

63 **first town meeting** APP, March 16, 1977. View a short clip at C-Span.org.

63 *Day with the President* "Daylong Visit with Carter," BG, April 14, 1977.

63 **Judged David Broder** "Mr. Carter When He's 'Out Front,' " WP, March 23, 1977.

63 **Garry Trudeau's** *Doonesbury* See strips from March 21, 1977; March 22, 1977; March 23, 1977; March 24, 1977; March 25, 1977; March 26, 1977; and March 29, 1977.

63 **"the single most crucial"** "Carter in the Midst of Most Crucial Week of Presidency," WP, April 17, 1977.

63 **"The percentage of those"** Ibid.

63 **"a return of the confidence"** "Carter Up Close," *Newsweek*, May 2, 1977.

63 **On April 18** "Address to the Nation on Energy," APP; Shapiro, *The Last Great Senate*, 54.

64 **"sky is falling" speech** "Carter in Midst of Most Crucial Week of Presidency," WP, April 17, 1977

64 **joint session of Congress** APP, April 20, 1977.

64 **first time in his fifty-two years** William F. Buckley, *A Hymnal: The Controversial Arts* (New York: G. P. Putnam's Sons, 1978), 246.

64 **televised press conference** APP, April 22, 1977.

64 **"television industry by the nose"** "Carter and the Networks," BG, April 18, 1977.

64 **funeral of Chairman Mao** William Safire column, NYT, April 18, 1977.

64 **"MEOW"** D. Zingerg, ed., *Uncertain Power: The Struggle for a National Energy Policy* (Pergamon Press, 1983).

64 **approval ratings ranged** Mary McGrory column, April 10, 1977; Shapiro, *The Last Great Senate*, 35.

64 **Gallup had Congress** George Gallup column, April 18, 1977.

64 **86 percent** Shapiro, *The Last Great Senate*, 35.

64 **"A rash of books"** Cox Newspaper Service, April 11, 1977.

65 **"brutal" and "intimidating"** "Carter's Style Making Aides Apprehensive," NYT, April 25, 1977.

65 **progressively less charming** AP, April 27, 1977.

65 **Another festering problem** CFTRN, April 15, 1977.

65 **"get all paranoid"** "Young Apologizes for Citing British Racism," WP, April 8, 1977; "Young Feels U.S. Is 'Paranoid' on Communist Activities in Africa," NYT, April 12, 1977; "Cuba Called Stabilizer in Angola," WP, April 17, 1977; Peter Masley column, April 23, 1977.

65 **" 'Andrew Young Must Go' Action Kit"** UPI, July 30, 1977; "Conservative Caucus Out to Smear Andy Young," *Jet*, August 18, 1977.

CHAPTER FOUR

66 **Executives had worried** Matthew Delmont, *Making* Roots: *A Nation Captivated* (Berkeley: University of California Press, 2016), 129.

66 **"We couldn't talk"** Sandbrook, *Mad as Hell: The Crisis of the 1970s and the Rise of the Populist Right* (New York: Anchor Books, 2012), 201.

66 **"really identified with blacks"** Roger Wilkins, "The Editorial Notebook," NYT, February 2, 1977.

66 **"significant head start"** "Reaganites Quietly Building for Future; Camp Intact," LAT, April 9, 1977.

66 **"Very frankly"** David Weigel, "Ronald Reagan on the 'Rather Destructive' Bias of Alex Haley's *Roots*," *Slate*, September 8, 2014.

66 **"We're outnumbered"** AP, December 16, 1976.

66 **"New Year's Resolutions"** RRC, December 31, 1976.

67 **Five days before Carter's** "Excerpts of Remarks by the Hon. Ronald Reagan, Former Governor of California, Before the Intercollegiate Studies Institute Banquet, Mayflower Hotel, Washington, D.C., Saturday, January 15, 1977," RRPL, Box 21.

67 **"street corner conservative"** William F. Gavin, *Street Corner Conservative* (New Rochelle, NY: Arlington House, 2015).

67 **"not a cult"** Hannaford to Reagan, December 14, 1976, RRPL, Box 21.

68 **wife's regular appearances** Jody Jacobs columns, LAT, February 2 and September 11, 1977.

68 **"Being a former farmer"** AP, January 2, 1973.

68 **Violent crime was skyrocketing** U.S. Department of Justice, Office of Justice Programs, Bureau of Justice Statistics, "Crime Data Brief: Homicide Trends in the United States: 2000 Update," January 2003.

68 **America had not executed** Wikipedia.org, "Capital Punishment in the United States"; Jimmy Carter, *White House Diary* (New York: Macmillan, 2010), 69; James T. Patterson, *Restless Giant: The United States from Watergate to Bush V. Gore* (New York: Oxford University Press, 2007), 40; UPI, October 4, 1976.

68 **That same year, in California** UPI, June 24, 1977.

68 **Gary Gilmore** UPI, December 14, 1976.

68 **"What about the murderer's victims?"** RRC, January 27, 1977.

68 **"more impressive deterrent"** David Broder column, December 8, 1976.

69 **Arlan Stangeland** "Tapping the Little Guy," WP, March 7, 1977.

69 **"We don't want"** Gillian Frank, " 'The Civil Rights of Parents': Race and Conservative Politics in Anita Bryant's Campaign Against Gay Rights in 1970's Florida," *Journal of the History of Sexuality* 22, No. 1 (January 2013): 126–160.

69 **"news one seldom finds"** Alan Crawford, *Thunder on the Right: The "New Right" and the Politics of Resentment* (New York: Pantheon, 1981), 54.

69 **Reagan's PAC** Ibid., 17; Lou Cannon, *Governor Reagan: His Rise to Power* (New York: Public Affairs Books, 2003), 440; "Side Street Office May Be Reagan's 1980 Launching Pad," LAT, January 28, 1977.

70 **On March 1** UPI, March 2, 1977; AP, March 2, 1977.

70 **The next morning** ENIR, March 2, 1977.

70 **next batch** RRB 76-03, track B1, "England"; RRB 76-10, track B6, "Sports and Religion," in RPV, 103; RRB 76-10, track B7, "Amtrak."

70 **first introduction** RRB 76-11, "Economic Plan."

70 **Ever since 1975** Joel Rogers and Thomas Ferguson, *Right Turn: The Decline of the Democrats and the Future of American Politics* (New York: Macmillan, 1987), 19.

70 **seventy percent said the government** *The Gallup Poll* (Wilmington, DE: Scholarly Resources), 1976, 1092.

71 **government-provided minimum income** Robert Kuttner, *Revolt of the Haves: Tax Rebellions and Hard Times* (New York: Simon & Schuster, 1980), 24-25.

71 **shadow cabinet** Gannett, February 25, 1977.

71 **Deaver and Hannaford advised** ENIR, March 2, 1977.

71 **Spain's fascist dictator** Zach Dorfman, "The Congressman Who Created His Own Deep State," *Politico*, December 12, 2018.

71 **Long Island high school principal** Thomas J. McIntyre, *The Fear Brokers* (Boston: Beacon Press, 1981), 74.

72 **"First CFR Candidate a Winner"** CFTRN, March 1, 1977.

72 **Feminists first proposed** Marjorie Spruill, "Gender and America's Right Turn," in *Rightward Bound: Making America Conservative in the 1970s* (Cambridge, MA: Harvard University Press, 2008), 77–78.

72 **In 1974, George Gallup** George Gallup column, November 4, 1974.

72 **In 1976, *Time* replaced** "Women of the Year: Great Changes, New Changes, Tough Choices," *Time*, January 5, 1976.

73 **best-selling paperback of 1974** Marabel Morgan, *The Total Woman* (Ada, MI: Fleming H. Ravell, 1973); Robert O. Self, *All in the Family: The Realignment of American Democracy Since the 1960s* (New York: Hill & Wang, 2012), 261; Gregory Curtis, "Retreat from Liberation," *Texas Monthly*, June 1975, 63; Andrea Dworkin, *Right Wing Women* (New York: TarcherPerigree, 1983) 25; Barbara Ehrenreich, Elizabeth Hess, and Gloria Jacobs, *Remaking Love: The Feminization of Sex* (New York: Anchor Press/Doubleday, 1986), 40; "Paperback Best Sellers of 1976," NYT, January 2, 1977.

73 **A similar book sold** Susan Faludi, *Backlash: The Undeclared War Against American Women* (New York: Crown, 1991), 251; Robert O. Self, *All in the Family: The Realignment of American Democracy Since the 1960s* (New York: Hill & Wang, 2012), 261.

73 **"truly Spirit-filled"** Faludi, *Backlash*, 259.

73 ***The Secret Power of Femininity*** Self, *All in the Family*, 181; "Femininity Forums Thrive Despite Push to Equality," *Morning Record*, August 9, 1972; "Parents' Love Points to Temple Goals," *Deseret News*, August 12, 1978.

73 ***The Gift of Inner Healing*** Dworkin, *Right-Wing Women*, 21.

73 **"Eve Reborn"** Curtis, "Retreat from Liberation."

74 **Phyllis Schlafly was born** Donald Critchlow, *Phyllis Schlafly and Grassroots Conservatism: A Woman's Crusade* (Princeton: Princeton University Press, 2008); Carol Felsenthal, *Sweetheart of the Silent Majority: The Biography of Phyllis Schlafly* (New York: Doubleday, 1981).

76 ***A Choice, Not an Echo*** Rick Perlstein, *Before the Storm: Barry Goldwater and the Unmaking of the American Consensus* (New York: Hill and Wang, 2001), 349, 477.

76 **"a few secret kingmakers"** Phyllis Schlafly, *A Choice Not an Echo: Updated and Expanded 50th Anniversary Edition* (New York: Regnery, 2014).

77 **"What's Wrong with 'Equal Rights'"** Reprinted in Lyman Tower Sargent, ed., *Extremism in America: A Reader* (New York: NYU Press, 1995), 257.

78 **Within days** Ruth Murray Brown, *For a "Christian America": A History of the Religious Right* (New York: Prometheus, 2002), 29.

78 **William F. Buckley** *Firing Line*, April 15, 1973.

78 **In January** "Equal Rights Amendment Slows Down," WP, January 28, 1973.

78 **phalanx of regional leaders** Brown, *For a "Christian America,"* 87–92.

78 **Tottie Ellis** Robert Hooper, *A Distinct People: A History of the Churches of Christ in the 20th Century* (West Monroe, LA: Howard Books, 1983), 250.

78 **after studying biblical prophecy** Rosemary Thomson, *Withstanding Humanism's Challenge to Families: Anatomy of a White House Conference* (Morton, IL: Traditional Publications, 1981).

78 **Lottie Beth Hobbes** Murray, *A Distinct People*, 39–42, 88, 90.

79 **"Happiness of Women"** UPI, April 2, 1972.

79 **Mississippians for God** Self, *All in the Family*, 294.

79 **Factually Informed Gals** Caroline Bird, "State Meetings: Every Woman Her Say," National Commission on the Observance of International Women's Year, *The Spirit of Houston: The First National Women's Conference*, 99–113.

79 **Utah's HOTDOG** Richard Spong, "ERA—Where She Stands," *Miami Herald*, March 19, 1975.

79 **Operation Wake-Up** Self, *All in the Family*, 294.

79 **Women for Responsible Legislation** Brown, *For a "Christian America,"* 29.

79 **"Schlafly took scattered"** Ibid, 53.

79 **"People wonder how"** Ibid., 38.

79 **"you couldn't get away"** Ibid., 55.

79 **Betty Friedan bellowed** Donald Critchlow, *Phyllis Schlafly and Grassroots Conservatism: A Woman's Crusade* (Princeton: Princeton University Press, 2008), 226–27.

80 **"a thing invulnerable"** Thomas Edward Lawrence, *The Seven Pillars of Wisdom* (London: Wordsworth Classics of World Literature, 1999 [originally 1926]), 182.

80 **"everywhere and nowhere"** Carl von Clausewitz, *On War* (Princeton: Princeton University Press, 1989 [originally 1832]), 480.

80 **homemade bread** Brown, *For a "Christian America,"* 64.

80 **Church of Jesus Christ of Latter-Day Saints** "First Presidency Statements on the ERA," October 22, 1976, ChurchofJesusChrist.org.

80 **"prayer chain"** AP, March 2, 1977.

81 **called ERAmerica** Jane J. Mansfield, *Why We Lost the ERA* (Chicago: University of Chicago Press, 1986), 121–22.; Brown, *For a "Christian America,"* 54.

81 **Elly Peterson** Sara Fitzgerald, *Elly Peterson: "Mother" of the Moderates* (Ann Arbor: University of Michigan Press, 2011).

81 **One reason for their failure** Mansfield, *Why We Lost the ERA.*

82 **"co-sexual penal institutions"** John Birch Society ad in *Bartlesville (Oklahoma) Examiner-Enterprise*, January 13, 1975, in possession of author.

82 **"integrated like the races"** Gillian Frank, " 'The Civil Rights of Parents.' "

82 **Sam Ervin** Self, *All in the Family*, 293.

82 **marry his horse** See for example "The Anger Is Equal in ERA Battle," CT, June 3, 1977. For background see "Love Story," *Aspen Times*, September 28, 2014.

82 **primary reason** Brown, *For a "Christian America,"* 70.

82 **even more crucial** Ibid, 88.

83 **150,000 pieces** *New York Times* Service, April 7, 1977.

83 **Ronald Reagan joined** RRB 76-11, track A2, "Equal Rights Amendment," recorded March 23, 1977.

83 **In the 1950s** David K. Johnson, *The Lavender Scare: The Cold War Persecution of Gays and Lesbians in the Federal Government* (Chicago: University of Chicago Press, 2006).

83 *Homosexuality and Citizenship* Jonathan Harrison, "This Is What Happened to Gay People in Florida Fifty Years Ago. It Should Never Happen Again," *History News Network*, October 19, 2014.

84 **the Snake Pit** Dudley Clendinen and Adam Nagourney, *Out for Good: The Struggle to Build a Gay Rights Movement in America* (New York: Simon & Schuster, 2001), 53.

84 **nearly passed the New York City Council** Ibid., 51–52.

84 **Arthur Goldberg** Ibid., 78–79.

84 Frank Kameny Ibid., 110–124.
84 "Persecution of homosexuals" Ibid., 117.
84 "age of sexual consent" Ibid., 121.
84 Barney Frank Ibid., 125.
84 Minneapolis Ibid., 227.
84 Atlanta Ibid., 80–81, 319–321.
84 Troy Perry Ibid., 175–187.
84 Ann Landers June 25, 1973, column.
85 *Diagnostic and Statistical Manual* Clendinen and Nagourney, *Out for Good*, 199–207.
85 Elaine Noble Ibid., 218–24; Randy Shilts, *The Mayor of Castro Street: The Life and Times of Harvey Milk* (New York: St. Martin's Press, 1982), 124–25.
85 thirty-seven cities Gillian Frank, " 'The Civil Rights of Parents.' "
85 Leonard Matlovich *Time*, September 8, 1975.
85 In 1976, Jimmy Carter Clendinen and Nagourney, *Out for Good*, 272.
85 Midge Costanza Ibid., 270.
85 "The year of the gay" Shilts, *The Mayor of Castro Street*, 155.
85 In Miami For Miami background see Clendinen and Nagourney, *Out for Good*, 290–311; Frank, " 'The Civil Rights of Parents.' "
86 "the best role" Anita Bryant, *Bless This House* (Old Tappan, NJ: Revel, 1972), 13.
86 Now she testified Clendinen and Nagourney, *Out for Good*, 297–99.
87 news from Fort Lauderdale J. Brooks Flippen, *Jimmy Carter*, 302.
87 Dr. Judianne Densen-Gerber Philip Jenkins, *Decade of Nightmares: The End of the Sixties and the Making of Eighties America* (New York: Oxford University Press, 2008), 114.
88 Bryant received a telegram "Topics," NYT, March 14, 1977.
88 "Reuben the Good" Flippen, *Jimmy Carter*, 136; Clendinen and Nagourney, *Out for Good*, 301.
88 Reverend Pat Robertson Flippen, *Jimmy Carter*, 119.
89 Stuart Eizenstat. Ibid.
89 "God wants stability" Jeremy Rifkin and Ted Howard, *The Emerging Order: God in the Age of Scarcity* (New York: G. P. Putnam's Sons, 1979), 103.
89 Francis Schaeffer Garry Wills, *Under God: Religion and American Politics* (New York: Simon & Schuster, 1990), 320; Frank Schaeffer, *Crazy for God: How I Grew Up as One of the Elect, Helped Found the Religious Right, and Lived to Take All (or Almost All) of It Back* (New York: Da Capo Press, 2008).
89 *How Should We Then Live?* View episodes at Youtube.com, accessed April 25, 2020.
91 The series was advertised See for example *Eau Claire Telegram*, October 24, 1977.
91 Arie Crown Theater Rosemary Thomson, *The Price of LIBerty* (Charisma Media,1978), 19.
91 It toured fourteen *Christianity Today*, April 1, 1977.
91 Liberty Baptist College Chris Lehmann, *The Money Cult: Capitalism, Christianity, and the Unmaking of the American Dream* (New York: Melville House, 2016), 312.
91 Costanza was careful Clendinen and Nagourney, *Out for Good*, 288–91.
92 "such a crusade to stop it" Flippen, *Jimmy Carter*, 136.
92 "Bryant is really" Clendinen and Nagourney, *Out for Good*, 300.
92 "civil rights of parents" Flippen, *Jimmy Carter*, 135.
92 Geto and Jim Foster Ibid.
93 At the annual Gridiron "Marching from Georgia," WP, March 21, 1977.

93 **Arthur Schlesinger Jr.** Israel Shenker, "So What's the Bad Word?" NYT, February 24, 1977.

93 **A liberal columnist** William Raspberry column, May 2, 1977.

93 **"make me feel creepy"** Richard Buffum column, LAT, June 19, 1977.

93 **President Carter** "Election Reform Message to Congress," APP, March 22, 1977.

94 **legislators from both parties** "Carter Proposes End of Electoral College in Presidential Votes," NYT, March 23, 1977.

94 **The next issue** "Election 'Reform' Package Euthanasia for GOP," BG, April 2, 1977.

94 **"sky high"** Kevin Phillips column, April 2, 1977.

94 **"eight million illegal aliens"** John Chamberlain column, May 31, 1977.

94 **"take for granted"** John Chamberlain column, May 24, 1977.

94 **"potential for cheating"** RRB 75-06, track 10, recorded March 25, 1975, in RPV, 390–93.

94 **"try reverse psychology"** RRB 77-09, track A4, recorded January 19, 1977, in RRIHOH, 245.

95 **"friendly neighborhood bureaucrat"** CFTRN, April 15, 1977.

95 **"federation of sovereign states"** RRB 76-12, track A3, recorded April 13, 1977, in RRIHOH, 242.

95 **Bill Brock** "Ex-Governor: Conservatives Are in the Majority," LAT, April 17, 1977.

95 **"Democratic Power Grab"** *First Monday* magazine, June 1977.

95 **The RNC passed a resolution** "GOP Starts from Bottom in Preservation Struggle," WP, May 11, 1977.

95 **"unremitting opposition"** "Rhodes Withdraws Support to Register Voters Election Day," WP, May 17.

95 **"LEADERSHIP IN PRESERVING"** "Right On for the New Right," *Time*, October 3, 1977.

95 **veteran Washington columnist** Mary McGrory column, April 3, 1977.

96 **Black had been chosen** ENIR, April 27, 1977.

96 **Howard Phillips soon wrote** Connie Paige, *The Right to Lifers: Who They Are, How They Operate, and Where They Get Their Money* (New York: Summit Books, 1983), 141.

96 **Representative Charlie Wilson** AP, April 11, 1977.

96 **A typical example** Alan Crawford, *Thunder on the Right: The "New Right" and the Politics of Resentment* (New York: Pantheon, 1981), 62–63.

97 **"issues bulletin"** Ibid., 64

97 **John Conlan** Ibid.

97 **"The left"** Sidney Blumenthal, *The Permanent Campaign: Inside the World of Elite Political Operatives* (Boston: Beacon Press, 1980), 226–27.

97 **Citizens Committee for the Right** Jack Anderson column, November 5, 1977.

97 **Ethan Geto and Jim Foster** Clendinen and Nagourney, *Out for Good*, 301.

97 **A month earlier** *St. Petersburg Independent,* "Florida ERA Passage Assured," March 10, 1977.

97 **"fear of legal homosexual"** *Miami Herald*, April 14, 1977.

98 **"The Orange Bowl parade"** Clendinen and Nagourney, *Out for Good*, 303.

98 **"Many parents are confused"** Ibid.

98 **Anita Bryant raised funds** *Who's Who*, CBS, aired April 12, 1977. View at You Tube.com, accessed April 25, 2020.

98 **Muslim extremists** "The Day Terrorists Took D.C. Hostage," WP, March 10, 2017.

98 **same .44-caliber pistol** Jonathon Mahler, *"Ladies and Gentlemen, the Bronx Is*

Burning": 1977, Baseball, Politics, and the Battle for the Soul of a City (New York: Picador, 2006), 247.

98 **PBS documentary** "TV: 'Fire Next Door,' " NYT, March 22, 1977. See clip at Bill Moyers.com, accessed April 25, 2020.

98 **syndicated TV documentary** "Energy Crisis Documentary Sold Like a Hot Potato," April 12, 1977.

98 **Isaac Asimov published** Jenkins, *Decade of Nightmares*, 72.

98 **typical day of news** "From *Times* Wires," *St. Petersburg Times*, March 22, 1977.

99 **"reflect the full diversity"** Public Law 94-167, reprinted in GovTrack.us and National Commission on the Observance of International Women's Year, *The Spirit of Houston: The First National Women's Conference*, An Official Report to the President, the Congress, and the People of the United States, March 1978.

99 **"The heart of all this"** Self, *All in the Family*, 312.

CHAPTER FIVE

100 **Citizens for the Republic** "Reagan Plans Discussions on TV to Raise Money and Followers," NYT, April 28, 1977.

100 *Merv Griffin Show* Letter to Citizens for the Republic members, March 17, 1977, RRPL, Box 17; Hannaford to Governor and Mrs. Reagan, April 6, 1977.

100 *Meet the Press* May 1, 1977, transcript in Ibid.

100 **Nofziger was engaged** See RRPL, Box 85, "D.M.I. (Decision Making Information)."

100 **"We're not in the business"** "Reaganites Quietly Building for Future; Camp Intact," LAT, April 9, 1977.

100 **Jack Cunningham** AP, May 18, 1977; "Cunningham vs. Durning," *Lewiston Morning Tribune*, April 8, 1977; Alan Crawford, *Thunder on the Right: The "New Right" and the Politics of Resentment* (New York: Pantheon, 1981), 55; Nick Kotz, "King Midas of 'The New Right,' " *Atlantic Monthly*, November 1978; McIntyre, *The Fear Brokers*, 71.

100 **On May 20** "Reagan Seeks to Shore Up Support on the East Coast," LAT, May 22, 1977.

101 **"mashed potato circuit"** See, generally, "What's Reagan Aiming For," CT, June 15, 1977; "Familiar Lines: For Reagan, 'The Speech' Says It All," LAT, October 21, 1978; "California Headquarters—Scheduling Files—Invitations/Turndowns," 1978, RRPL, Box 62; speech files, RRPL, Box 21, 22 23; "Advance Procedures," Box 84.

101 **three hundred invitations** ENIR, March 2, 1977.

101 **"look of pleased expectancy"** W&G, October 6, 1979.

102 **"wide-eyed adoration"** "Strong Wives Keeping Pace with Frontrunners," NYT, April 5, 1980.

102 **same jokes** "Familiar Lines"; "Reagan Starts His Race for the Presidency," *London Observer*, January 28, 1979; "Reagan: Soviet Ultimatum Near," *Palm Beach Post*, January 5, 1979; "Reagan's Index Cards of One Liners," CBS News, n.d.

102 **"adversarial relationship"** "Ronald Reagan: What's Happening to Our Dollar," *California Business*, July 1979.

102 **"164 different federal agencies"** "Items," RRB, recorded March 2, 1978; "Inside Ronald Reagan: A Reason Interview," *Reason*, July 1975. For 131 taxes in a loaf of bread see "Bureaucrats Cause Inflation," *Akron Reporter*, June 23, 1976.

102 **can't hit a home run** Michael Deaver, *A Different Drummer: My Thirty Years with Ronald Reagan* (New York: Harper, 2001), 27.

103 **David Frost's televised interviews** James Reston Jr., *The Conviction of Richard Nixon: The Untold Story of the Frost/Nixon Interviews* (New York: Harmony, 2007). The Watergate interview at YouTube.com, accessed April 25, 2020.

103 **In Atlantic City** UPI, May 21, 1977; AP, May 21, 1977.

104 **"Has the governor taken leave"** *Greensboro Daily News*, May 27, 1977.

104 **72 percent** Reston, *The Conviction of Richard Nixon*, 173.

104 **"Watergate was the climactic"** Patrick Buchanan column, May 16, 1977.

104 **A book slated** Victor Lasky, *It Didn't Start with Watergate* (New York: Dutton, 1977).

104 **"secondary McCarthy Era"** William Safire column, *New York Times* Service, April 25, 1977.

104 **"Working Paper on Political Strategy"** "The Scenario: Most of Carter's Early Moves Charted in 1976 Caddell Memo," WP, May 4, 1977.

105 **"All Quiet on the Potomac"** NYT, May 12, 1977.

106 **"You're throwing"** Ian Shapiro, *The Last Great Senate: Courage and Statesmanship in Times of Crisis* (New York: Public Affairs Books, 2012), 89.

106 **completely ethics-happy** UPI, July 15, 1977.

106 **South Korean businessman** John A. Farrell, *Tip O'Neill and the Democratic Century* (New York: Little, Brown, 2001), 481–85.

106 **"Koreagate"** William Safire column, *New York Times* Service, April 12, 1977.

106 **"arm's length"** ENIR, May 21, 1977.

106 *New York Times* **reported** Robert Schlesinger, *White House Ghosts: Presidents and Their Speechwriters* (New York: Simon & Schuster, 2008), 274.

107 *I have a quiet confidence* "Address at Commencement Exercises at the University of Notre Dame," APP, May 22, 1977.

107 **Ronald Reagan called it** RRC, August 12, 1977.

107 **"hurt our allies"** Randall Balmer, *Redeemer: The Life of Jimmy Carter* (New York: Basic Books, 2014), 82.

107 **"so maladroit"** William F. Buckley, *A Hymnal: The Controversial Arts* (New York: G. P. Putnam's Sons, 1978), 246.

108 **major foreign policy address** RRPL, Box 22; "Reagan Is Critical of Carter on Rights," NYT, June 10, 1977.

108 **Amnesty International** Ibid.

108 **CBS News** Thesis Raevis to Peter Hannaford, June 9, 1977, RPP, Box 22.

108 **not entirely flattering** "What's Reagan Aiming For," CT, June 15, 1977.

109 **Paul Manafort** Franklin Foer, "Paul Manafort, American Hustler," *Atlantic*, March 2018.

109 **Walter Cronkite** Alan Crawford, *Thunder on the Right: The "New Right" and the Politics of Resentment* (New York: Pantheon, 1981), 23.

109 **treated Ronald Reagan** AP, June 12, 1977.

109 **Geto and Foster noted** Lillian Faderman, *The Gay Rights Revolution: The Story of the Struggle* (New York: Simon & Schuster, 2015), 347.

109 **But Mike Thompson** Dudley Clendinen and Adam Nagourney, *Out for Good: The Struggle to Build a Gay Rights Movement in America* (New York: Simon & Schuster, 2001), 304.

109 **popular** *Miami Herald* **columnist** Charles Whited, "Taking a Stand on Gay Rights No Easy Task," *Miami Herald*, March 29, 1977.

109 **1950s automobile** Gillian Frank, " 'The Civil Rights of Parents.' " See ads here.

110 **"stable family relationship"** "New Liberal Law on Public Housing," *Southeast Missourian*, May 23, 1977.

110 **Save Our Children rally** Viewed by author courtesy of Kristina Lapinski, collected from Liberty University archives, Lynchburg, Virginia.

111 **"Anita Bryant Versus the Homosexuals"** *Newsweek*, June 6, 1977.

111 **"cesspool of sexual perversion"** For Miami home stretch, Clendinen and Nagourney, *Out for Good*, 305–8.

112 **placards depicting Hitler** Randy Shilts, *The Mayor of Castro Street: The Life and Times of Harvey Milk* (New York: St. Martin's Press, 1982), 164.

CHAPTER SIX

113 **"Ailing GOP May Not Recover"** WSJ, May 25, 1977.

113 **Representative Phil Crane of Illinois** Letter to the Editor, June 8, 1977.

113 **"two Checker cabs could"** NBS News, January 1, 1977.

113 **The *Boston Globe's* David Nyhan** BG, June 5, 1977.

114 **Nyhan's colleague Robert Healy** BG, June 24, 1977.

114 ***New York Times* reported** "Republicans Hope to Rebuild Party in South with 'Working Man' Image," NYT, July 25, 1977.

114 **The *Washington Post*** "Southern Republicans: Their Plight Is Getting Worse," WP, July 12, 1977.

114 **National Rifle Association** Reva Siegel, "Dead or Alive: Originalism as Popular Constitutionalism in Heller," *Harvard Law Review* 122 (November 2008); Jill Lepore, "Battleground America: One Nation, Under the Gun," *New Yorker*, April 16, 2020; "How NRA's True Believers Converted a Marksmanship Group Into a Mighty Gun Lobby," WP, January 12, 2013; AP, May 19, 1977; AP, May 24, 1977; Harry Kelly column, Knight-Ridder Syndicate, June 1, 1977.

115 **NRA cardholder** RRB 75-11, track 7, "Gun Control," recorded June 1975.

116 **"a bare look"** Harry Kelly column, Knight-Ridder Syndicate, June 1, 1977.

116 **the drug PCP** Philip Jenkins, *Decade of Nightmares: The End of the Sixties and the Making of Eighties America* (New York: Oxford University Press, 2008), 127–28; for quote see "PCP: Killer Weed Is 'Status' Drug," WP, July 3, 1977.

116 **sensational hearings** *Sexual Exploitation of Children*, Hearings Before the Subcommittee on Crime of the Committee on the Judiciary, House of Representatives, Ninety-Fifth Congress, First Session, May 23, 25, June 10, and September 10, 1977.

117 ***Hello from the gutters*** "Breslin to Son of Sam: End Your Torment and Give Yourself Up," *New York Daily News*, May 7, 1977; Jonathon Mahler, *"Ladies and Gentlemen, the Bronx Is Burning,": 1977, Baseball, Politics, and the Battle for the Soul of a City* (New York: Picador, 2006), 251.

117 **In the 1960s** Peter Biskind, *Easy Riders, Raging Bulls: How the Sex, Drugs, and Rock 'n' Roll Generation Saved Hollywood* (New York: Simon & Schuster, 1988).

118 **"pure 1930s make-believe"** "Review: 'Rocky,' " NYT, November 22, 1976. See also analyses in Jefferson Cowie, *Stayin' Alive: The 1970s and the Last Days of the Working Class* (New York: New Press, 2010), 326–29; Matthew Frye Jacobson, *Roots Too: White Ethnic Revival in Post–Civil Rights America* (Cambridge, MA: Harvard University Press, 2006), 100–102.

118 **George Lucas** Biskind, *Easy Riders, Raging Bulls*, 98–101.

119 **"I discovered that making"** Ibid, 318.

119 **When Lucas was writing the script** Ibid., 324.

119 **Pauline Kael** "Contrasts: George Lucas's 'Star Wars,' Marguerite Duras's 'Truck,' and Robert M. Young's 'Short Eyes,' " *New Yorker*, September 19, 1977.

119 **"The sad duty"** "A Conversation with Jimmy Carter," NYT, June 19, 1976.

119 **"Presidential Review Memorandum 10"** "Memo Sets Stage in Assessing U.S., Soviet Strength," WP, July 6, 1977; Alan Wolf, "Carter Plays At Hawks and Doves," *Nation*, June 24, 1978.

119 **Evans and Novak's** ENIR, August 10, 1977, and September 12, 1977.

120 **In San Francisco** Clendinen and Nagourney, *Out for Good*, 310.

120 **response in Houston** "Remembering LGBT History: Houston's Stonewall: The Night Anita Bryant Came to Town," *Daily Kos*, March 10, 2013.

120 **Boston Common** Clendinen and Nagourney, *Out for Good*, 313–15.

120 *Dear Friend* "When the Homosexuals Burn the Holy Bible in Public . . . How Can I Stand By Silently," reprinted in Matthew Avery Sutton, ed., *Jerry Falwell and the Rise of the Religious Right: A Brief History with Documents* (Boston: Bedford/ St. Martin's 2013), 102–6.

121 **The Gallup organization** "California Homosexuals Prepare for School Battles," NYT, August 8, 1977.

121 **John Briggs** Randy Shilts, *The Mayor of Castro Street: The Life and Times of Harvey Milk* (New York: St. Martin's Press, 1982), 154, 157; AP, June 10, 1977; Fred Fejes, *Gay Rights and Moral Panic: The Origins of America's Debate on Homosexuality* (New York: Palgrave Macmillan, 2008), 182; "Briggs in Clash with Homosexuals," LAT, June 15, 1977.

121 **That day** "Senate Gets Bill to Ban Bay Marriages," LAT, June 15, 1977; AP, June 14, 1977; AP, June 15, 1977.

121 **Four days later** "Carter Says Plans of Government Should Keep Families Together," NYT, June 19, 1977; J. Brooks Flippen, *Jimmy Carter, the Politics of Family, and the Rise of the Religious Right* (Athens, GA: University of Georgia Press, 2011), 144.

121 **Vice President Mondale** Ibid,145.

121 **White House conference** Ibid, 126.

122 **Robert Hillsborough** Clendinen and Nagourney, *Out for Good*, 636.

122 **Conservatives had been trying** Flippen, *Jimmy Carter*, 192; Robert O. Self, *All in the Family: The Realignment of American Democracy Since the 1960s* (New York: Hill & Wang, 2012), 288; Cynthia Gorney, *Articles of Faith: A Frontline History of the Abortion Wars* (New York: Simon & Schuster, 2000), 280–83; "Garn Bill Would Bar Using Tax Money for Abortions," *Deseret News*, March 24, 1975; UPI, October 8, 1975; *Congressional Quarterly* Service, September 29, 1976.

122 **"a 626-month-old fetus"** Kevin Phillips column, July 26, 1976.

122 **on June 17** UPI, June 18, 1977.

122 **"never seen such joy"** AP, June 18, 1977.

123 **"cruel use of poor people"** AP, June 19, 1977.

123 **"By this time Tuesday"** "Abortion Foes Look to Ultimate Victory," NYT, June19, 1977.

123 **"We, the law abiding"** *Valley News*, May 8, 1977.

124 **TV's Phil Donahue** AP, May 5, 1977.

124 **give up his power to commute** "New Twist in Death Penalty Debate," LAT, May 5, 1977.

124 **"feel it is a deterrent"** "Death Penalty," LAT, May 17, 1977.

124 **Mrs. A. Sullivan** "Encouraging Murder," *Long Beach Independent*, May 23, 1977.

124 **Her neighbor William Tuggle** "The Death Penalty," *Long Beach Independent*, May 27, 1977.

124 **"I am Todd Murray"** Ibid.

125 **"You have more brains"** "To Stop Killers," *Long Beach Independent*, May 22, 1977.

125   **"Todd goes"** "Against Death Penalty," *Long Beach Independent*, May 18, 1977.

125   **Governor Pierre DuPont** AP, May 15, 1977.

125   **"I hope** God" AP, May 17, 1977.

125   **"most agonizing decision"** AP, May 15, 1977.

125   **struck by a poll** "Political Notebook: Mangers Explains Support of Death Penalty," LAT, May 16, 1977.

125   **"nullify every"** AP, May 17, 1977.

125   **harder for convicted murderers** UPI, May 17, 1977.

125   **"pervasive savagery"** "The Legality of Savagery," LAT, May 20, 1977.

125   **Brown's veto message** "Brown Gives Death Penalty Quick Veto," LAT, May 28, 1977.

125   **when Senator John Briggs** "Briggs Looks to '78 Race, Won't Oppose Death Veto," *Long Beach Independent*, June 2, 1977.

126   **begged Briggs to withdraw it** "Briggs to Push Death Penalty Ballot Initiative," LAT, June 14, 1977.

126   **then, failing** "Younger Won't Lead Death Penalty Initiative," LAT, June 13, 1977.

126   **Reagan, panicked** AP, June 16, 1977.

126   **"overthrow the government"** "Death Penalty," *Long Beach Independent*, June 16, 1977.

126   **During debate** "Death Penalty Petitions," LAT, June 24, 1977.

126   **called gays "lepers"** "Davis' Focus on Unconventional Sex Worries Some GOP Leaders," LAT, August 7, 1977; "Retiring Los Angeles Police Chief, in Governor Race, Stresses Morals," NYT, January 14, 1978.

126   **In New York, on June 26** Mahler, *"Ladies and Gentlemen, the Bronx Is Burning,"* 252.

126   **In Washington, D.C.** UPI, June 28, 1977.

127   **On June 29** "Senate Vote Forbids Using Federal Funds for Most Abortions," NYT, June 30, 1977.

127   **"open season"** Flippen, *Jimmy Carter*, 135.

127   **election pamphlet** Shilts, *The Mayor of Castro Street*, 162.

127   **201st birthday** Warren Hinckle, "Dan White's San Francisco," *Inquiry*, October 29, 1979.

127   **On July 5** "Shah of Iran's Wife Honored; Protest Staged," LAT, July 6, 1977.

128   **"There was beaucoup"** Jody Jacobs, "L.A. Party for Iran Empress Farah Diba," LAT, July 11, 1977.

128   **"Christmas tree of exemptions"** *Washington Post* Service, July 8, 1977.

128   **Judge John F. Dooling Jr.** Tanya Melich, *The Republican War Against Women: An Insider's Report from Behind the Lines* (New York: Bantam, 1996), 77.

128   **"Mr. President"** "The President's News Conference," July 12, 1977, APP.

128   **Midge Costanza's phone** Flippen, *Jimmy Carter*, 123.

128   **"Is it moral"** Ibid., 140–41; ENIR, August 1, 1977.

128   **"Carter Discovers 'Life Is Unfair,' "** *Ms.*, January 1978.

129   **"The party told me"** W&G, July 20, 1977.

129   **blackout in 1965** David Nye, *When the Lights Went Out: A History of Blackouts in America* (Cambridge: MIT Press, 2013), 81–94.

129   **In 1977, different sorts** Ibid., 105–6, 121–36; Mahler, *"Ladies and Gentlemen, the Bronx Is Burning,"* 175–206.

130   **Herbert Gutman** Joshua Freeman, *Working Class New York: Life and Labor in New York Since World War II* (New Press, 2001), 282; "Disorders of '02 and '77: Readers," NYT, August 3, 1977.

130 **Midge Decter** "Looting and Liberal Racism," *Commentary*, September 1977.

130 **"It lowers all of us"** *New York State Legislative Annual* (Albany: New York Legislative Service, 1977), 351.

130 **The Democratic primary** Mahler, *"Ladies and Gentlemen, the Bronx Is Burning,"* passim.

131 **"cat into the ring"** *Saturday Night Live*, May 21, 1977.

132 **"Puerto Rico isn't free?"** Bryan Burrough, *Days of Rage: America's Radical Underground, the FBI, and the Forgotten Age of Domestic Terrorism* (New York: Penguin, 2015), 400.

132 **"little hot squat"** *New York Daily News*, April 20, 1972.

134 **"The Added Danger of a Savage Week"** NYT, August 5, 1977.

134 **A Democrat cried** "Brown 'Not Surprised' by Action on Death Penalty," LAT, August 12, 1977.

134 **a painting by Andy Warhol** Mahler, *"Ladies and Gentlemen, the Bronx Is Burning,"* 284.

134 **Ronald Reagan enjoyed** Bob Colacello, *Ronnie and Nancy: Their Path to the White House—1911 to 1980* (New York: Grand Central Publishing, 2004), 268.

135 **Two New Right congressmen** " 'Instant Fraud' Package Faces House Test," HE, July 23, 1977.

135 **Allen was the Senate's** "Senator James B. Allen Dies; Alabamian Led Canal Pact Fight," NYT, June 2, 1978.

135 **Viguerie said** "Doubt Cast on Two Republicans' Support of Canal Pact," NYT, August 22, 1977.

CHAPTER SEVEN

136 **Bert Lance** Shapiro, *The Last Great Senate: Courage and Statesmanship in Times of Crisis* (New York: Public Affairs Books, 2012), 96; Bert Lance, *The Truth of the Matter: My Life In and Out of Politics* (Summit Books, 1991), 137; Kathleen Hall Jamieson, *Packaging the Presidency: A History and Criticism of Presidential Advertising* (New York: Oxford University Press, 1988), 331–34; "Georgia Banker Due for U.S. Budget Job," NYT, November 24, 1976.

136 **"hip deep in debt"** "The Administration: The Budget Chief's Balance Sheet," *Time*, May 23, 1977.

136 **Lance warned Carter** Lance, *The Truth of the Matter*, 133.

136 **extension of Lance's deadline** Bob Woodward, *Shadow: Five Presidents and the Legacy of Watergate* (New York: Simon & Schuster, 1999), 78.

136 **"unofficial assistant president"** *Nation's Business*, May 1977.

137 **William Safire** "William Safire, Political Columnist and Oracle of Language, Dies at 79," NYT, September 27, 2009; Eric Alterman, *Sound and Fury: The Making of the Punditocracy* (New York: HarperCollins, 1992), 35; Garry Wills, "William Safire at the Top of the Heap," *New York*, November 28, 1977.

137 **legendary "kitchen debate"** William Safire, *The Relations Explosion: A Diagram of the Coming Boom and Shakeout in Corporate Relations* (New York: Macmillan, 1963).

137 **inaugural was** "Pedestrian Inaugural," NYT, January 24, 1977.

137 **"the infamous 'Doar Plan' "** "Rejected Counsel," NYT, February 3, 1977.

138 **"Will Mr. Civiletti inform"** "Helping the House Corruption Grand Jury," NYT, February 28, 1977.

138 **"John Mitchell blush"** "President Carter's First Cover Up," NYT, March 3, 1977.

138 **"equating *Hustler* magazine"** "Letters," NYT, March 15, 1977.

138 **Paul Warnke** "Mr. Warnke's Hit List," NYT, April 21, 1977.

138 **"gang of four"** "Inside Justice's Politics," NYT, June 6, 1977.

138 **"halls of mirrors"** "Of Style and Substance," NYT, May 16, 1977.

138 **"If this is an open administration"** "Carter, Coke, and Castro," NYT, July 7, 1977.

138 **a Harris Poll** AP, August 15, 1977.

139 **His first attempt** "Carter's Broken Lance," NYT, July 21, 1977.

139 **"You have been smeared"** "Senators Back Lance and Abandon Inquiry," NYT, July 26, 1977.

139 **"18 U.S. Code 656"** William Safire, *Safire's Washington* (New York: Times Books, 1980), 259–60.

139 **Negotiations had been** J. Lee Annis, *Howard Baker: Conciliator in an Age of Crisis* (Knoxville, TN: Howard Baker Center, 2007); Adam Clymer, *Drawing the Line at the Big Ditch: The Panama Canal Treaties and the Rise of the Right* (Lawrence: University Press of Kansas, 2008); "Canal, Though a Proud Engineering Achievement, Has Caused Serious Anguish for U.S. and Panama," NYT, August 11, 1977.

140 **Senator Goldwater** ENIR, July 9, 1977.

140 **Senator S. I. Hayakawa** "Hayakawa Ready to Back Panama Canal Treaties," LAT, August 19, 1977.

140 **On August 7** Clymer, *Drawing the Line at the Big Ditch*, 49.

140 **"a few nuts"** Jimmy Carter, *White House Diary* (New York: Macmillan, 2010), 80.

140 **But on August 26** Ibid., 86.

141 **"greater than the Tower of Babel"** ENIR, August 19, 1977.

141 **One constituent confronted** "Voters Cite Concern Over Panama Canal," NYT, August 28, 1977.

141 **"first step toward the dismemberment"** Stephen S. Rosenfeld column, *Washington Post* Service, August 9, 1977. The letter was in the July 24, 1977, NYT.

141 **A conservative senator** "Close to Blocking New Canal Pact, Opponents Claim," LAT, August 12, 1977.

141 **Senator Joseph Biden** Branko Marcitec, *Yesterday's Man: The Case Against Joe Biden* (New York: Verso, 2020), 136.

142 **"issue we can't lose"** Clymer, *Drawing the Line at the Big Ditch*, 56.

142 **Howard Phillips said** " 'Keep the Canal' Drive On; Conservatives Rally to Cause," *Atlanta Journal and Constitution*, August 28, 1977.

142 **"Conservative Register"** Clymer, *Drawing the Line at the Big Ditch*, 133.

142 **"with their pocket calculators"** Alan Crawford, *Thunder on the Right: The "New Right" and the Politics of Resentment* (New York: Pantheon, 1981), 58.

142 **Robert Livingston** AP, August 28, 1977.

142 **Weyrich bragged** "Close to Blocking New Canal Pact, Opponents Claim," LAT, August 12, 1977.

142 **"There is NO Panama Canal!"** "Conservatives Map Drive Against the Canal Treaty," NYT, August 16, 1977.

142 *Nashville Tennessean* Clymer, *Drawing the Line at the Big Ditch*, 65.

143 **"Reagan Leads Drive to Halt Canal Pact"** BG, August 12, 1977.

143 **"Reagan Less Adamant"** LAT, August 12, 1977.

143 **The statement** *Atlanta Constitution*, August 20, 1977.

143 **"every bit the same"** "Reagan Less Adamant in Anti-Canal Treaty Stand" LAT, August 12, 1977.

143 **far-right intriguer** John Carbaugh to Peter Hannaford, "Re: Attached Polling Data; Governor Reagan's Possible Testimony Before the Separation of Powers Subcommittee; Other Matters," RRPL, Box 22; "Departing Senate Aide Leaves Trail of Questions," NYT, July 1, 1982; Hannaford to Deaver, July 15, 1977.

144 **One report** "Group Chaired by Reagan Hits Hayakawa on Treaties," LAT, August 23, 1977.

144 **Another the next day** "Reagan Denies Role in Canal Pact Memo," LAT, August 24, 1977.

144 **Evans and Novak reported** ENIR, August 19, 1977.

144 **the president called Reagan** "Ford Says He'll Support Panama Canal Treaties," LAT, August 17, 1977.

144 **That weekend** Clymer, *Drawing the Line at the Big Ditch*, 70.

144 **Young Americans for Freedom** "Excerpts from an Address by the Hon. Ronald Reagan to Young Americans for Freedom," August 25, 1977, RRPL, Box 22.

144 **arrayed the headlines** King Features, "RONALD REAGAN Makes News," September 6, 1977; King Features, "FYI Sales Bulletin," September 6, 1977, RRPL, Box 10.

144 **legendary James Reston** "Reagan on Panama," NYT, August 28, 1977.

145 **"Ronald Reagan ... born again"** Conrad cartoon, LAT, August 18, 1977.

145 **comptroller of the currency** "Lance Defends Financial Transactions," WP, August 6, 1977.

145 **"By not asking"** William Safire column, *New York Times* Service, August 5, 1977.

145 **"Lancegate"** NYT, August 11, 1977.

145 **On August 12** "Lance Had Warnings on Bank Officer's Lending Judgments," WP, August 12, 1977.

145 **The next day came** Lance, *The Truth of the Matter*, 135.

145 **same stock as collateral** Woodward, *Shadow*, 59.

145 **"brung you your cow"** Lance, *The Truth of the Matter*, 145–46; "Lance Testifies: Of Elsie and a Cow Named Spot," *Time*, April 14, 1980.

146 **"This unfortunate incident"** Woodward, *Shadow*, 58.

146 **comptroller of the currency** Lance, *The Truth of the Matter*, 136; "Investigation Clears Lance of Wrongdoing," WP, August 19 1977.

147 **dramatic press conference** "President Dramatically Endorses OMB Director," WP, August 19, 1977; "Remarks of the President at a News Conference by Bert Lance Following an Investigation of His Finances," APP, August 18 1977.

147 **imaginary dialogue** Reston column, *New York Times* Service, August 21, 1977.

147 **"President Carter's embrace"** Letters to the editor, WP, August 29, 1977.

147 **editorial cartoonist Oliphant** For Oliphant and Herblock cartoons, William Safire, "Lancegate: Why Carter Stuck It Out," NYT *Magazine*, October 6, 1977.

147 **secretary of symbolism** *Doonesbury*, September 13, 1977.

147 *Good Times* Season Five, Episode 6, "Willona, the Fuzz," October 19, 1977.

148 **A *Newsweek* poll** John Hohenberg, *A Crisis for the American Press* (New York: Columbia University Press, 1978), 73–75.

148 **Broder connected** Broder column, *Washington Post* Service, September 2, 1977.

148 **The president responded** Carter, *White House Diary*, 87.

148 **hundreds of outraged** Clymer, *Drawing the Line at the Big Ditch*, 57.

148 **Pan American Union Building** Ibid., 50; "Panama Canal Treaties: Remarks at the Signing Ceremony at the Pan American Union Building," APP, September 7, 1977; "Panama Canal Treaties; Remarks at a White House Dinner for Western Hemisphere Leaders Attending the Signing," APP, September 7, 1977.

148 **"Jimmy Carter under pressure"** Joseph Kraft column, WP, September 8, 1977.

149 **"deceptive practices"** Mahler, *"Ladies and Gentlemen, the Bronx Is Burning,"* 288.

149 **"Kill! Kill! Kill!"** Ibid., 261.

149 **Bess Myerson** Ibid., 299–301.

149 **A liberal former friend** Ibid., 270.

149 **"Put your anger to work"** Ibid., 293.

149 **"tough on the side of reason"** Ibid., 297.

149 **"VOTE FOR CUOMO NOT THE HOMO"** Ibid., 316.

150 **U.S. Open tennis** "Spectator Is Shot in Forest Hills," NYT, September 5, 1977; "Queens Was Burning Too," NYT *Magazine*, August 23, 2012.

150 **"talk about perverts?"** Suzanne Marin Levine and Mary Thom, eds., *Bella: How One Tough Broad from the Bronx Fought Jim Crow and Joe McCarthy* (Farrar, Straus & Giroux, 2007), 185.

150 **"that schmuck"** Mahler, *"Ladies and Gentlemen, the Bronx Is Burning,"* 283.

150 **"women from all walks of life"** "Bella Abzug Answers Charges by James Kilpatrick," *Day*, April 11, 1977, published in many newspapers carrying the April 3 column by James J. Kilpatrick.

150 **"I'd like to see Phyllis Schlafly"** "Personalities," NEA Syndicate, July 14, 1977.

CHAPTER EIGHT

151 **"I made the decision"** Mary Thom, ed., *Letters to Ms.* (New York: Henry Holt, 1988).

151 **"When my baby"** Ruth Carter Stapleton, *The Gift of Inner Healing* (New York: Bantam Books, 1977), quoted in Andrea Dworkin, *Right Wing Women* (New York: TarcherPerigree, 1983), 21.

151 **"smoldering resentment"** Beverly LaHaye, *The Spirit Controlled Woman* (Harvest House Publishers, 1976), 89, quoted in Susan Faludi, *Backlash: The Undeclared War Against American Women* (New York: Crown, 1991), 260.

151 **In 1975, Ann Landers** Anne Klingston, "Was Having Kids a Mistake," *Today's Parent*, January 11, 2018.

151 **"I work in an office"** Thom, ed., *Letters to Ms.*

152 **Feminists' redemption** Jane O'Reilly, "Click: The Housewife's Moment of Truth," *Ms.*, Spring 1972.

152 **"become a bible"** Thom, ed., *Letters to Ms.*

152 **A leader might shamefacedly** Ruth Murray Brown, *For a "Christian America": A History of the Religious Right* (New York: Prometheus, 2002), 87.

152 **Schlafly's Illinois deputy** Rosemary Thomson, *The Price of LIBerty* (Charisma Media, 1978).

152 **"lots of Chinese women"** Marilyn French, *The Women's Room: A Novel* (New York: Simon & Schuster, 1977).

153 **height of World War II** Michael Barone, *Our Country: The Shaping of Our America from Roosevelt to Reagan* (New York: Free Press, 1990), 564.

154 **Christian Booksellers Association** Bruce J. Schulman and Julian E. Zelizer, eds., *Rightward Bound: Making America Conservative in the 1970s* (Cambridge, MA: Harvard University Press, 2008), 40.

154   *Christian Yellow Pages* "Born-Again Businesses Listed," *Boca Raton News*, July 8, 1977.

154   **child-rearing help** Dan Gilgoff, *The Jesus Machine: How James Dobson, Focus on the Family, and Evangelical America Are Winning the Culture War* (New York: St. Martin's Press, 2007).

154   **Pat Robertson's** "Evangelical TV Show Picks Up Steam: 700 Club, with 2.5 Million Viewers, Challenges News, 'Soaps,' " LAT, July 31, 1976.

154   **"inner child"** "Walking People Out of Their Past: An Interview with Ruth Carter Stapleton," *Christianity Today*, November 4, 1977.

154   **Stapleton drew her following** "Sister Ruth," *Newsweek*, July 17, 1978.

155   **his daughter Debby** *People*, April 17, 1978.

155   **Christian nightclubs** *New York Times* Service, June 6, 1977.

155   **Turn to Pastor Tim** Barbara Ehrenreich, Elizabeth Hess, and Gloria Jacobs, *Remaking Love: The Feminization of Sex* (New York: Anchor Press/Doubleday, 1986), 147.

155   **"thinks about economics"** Tim and Beverly LaHaye, *The Act of Marriage: The Beauty of Sexual Love* (Grand Rapids: Zondervan, 1976), 42.

155   **Mrs. LaHaye oversaw** "LaHaye Wages War Against Humanists," LAT, February 2, 1981.

155   **According to one study** Brown, *For a "Christian America."*

155   **"liftin' and totin' bill"** "Stop ERA" ad, *Dixon Evening Telegraph*, April 28, 1977.

156   **"These women lawyers"** Donald Critchlow, *Phyllis Schlafly and Grassroots Conservatism: A Woman's Crusade* (Princeton: Princeton University Press, 2008), 244.

156   **"I want to remain"** "Prospects for Equal Rights Plan Dim as Drive Fails in Key States," NYT, May 21, 1979.

156   **Dr. Brothers exclaimed** *Merv Griffin Show*, September 23, 1977. View on You Tube.com, accessed March 17, 2020.

156   **"a harmonious conference"** Brown, *For a "Christian America,"* 103.

156   **More than 130,000** Spruill, "Gender and America's Right Turn."

156   **"Women's Town Meeting"** Ibid., 81; Brown, *For a "Christian America,"* 109.

157   **"Parliamentary procedures"** Rosemary Thomson, *The Price of LIBerty* (Charisma Media,1978), 92.

157   **"want your child taught"** Ibid., 129; Brown, *For a "Christian America,"* 131.

157   **One recipient wrote** Flippen, *Jimmy Carter*, 121.

157   **"roomful of lesbians"** Thomson, *The Price of LIBerty*, 94.

158   **"Levis on and hair on their legs"** Brown, *For a "Christian America,"* 116.

158   **In Michigan** Sara Fitzgerald, *Elly Peterson: "Mother" of the Moderates* (Ann Arbor, University of Michigan Press, 2011), 231.

158   **next was Oklahoma** James J. Kilpatrick column, July 7, 1977.

158   **In Missouri** Brown, *For a "Christian America,"* 109; Thomson, *The Price of LIBerty*, 130; Sarah Diamond, *Roads to Dominion: Right-Wing Movements and Political Power in the United States* (New York: Guilford, 1995), 168; National Commission on the Observance of International Women's Year, *The Spirit of Houston: The First National Women's Conference*, 104.

158   **In Washington State** Ibid., 110; "A Life Changing Event," *Daily Record*, March 26, 2007; Washington State Historical Society, "International Women's Year Oral History Project"; Cassandra Tate, "Washington State Conference for Women, 1977," HistoryLink.org.

159   **Satan was "alive"** Thomson, *The Price of LIBerty*, 118.

159 **"25 lesbian-type workshops"** Ibid., 95.

159 **"Call Off Your Tired Old Ethics"** Nancy A. Hewitt, ed., *No Permanent Waves: Recasting Histories of U.S. Feminism* (New Brunswick, NJ: Rutgers University Press, 2010), 259.

159 **In Utah** "Mormon Turnout Overwhelms Women's Conference in Utah," NYT, July 25, 1977; Spruill, "Gender and America's Right Turn"; National Commission on the Observance of International Women's Year, *The Spirit of Houston: The First National Women's Conference*, 109.

159 **Mississippi's meeting** "The Mississippi 'Takeover': Feminists, Anti-Feminists, and the International Women's Year Conference of 1977," in Martha H. Swain, Elizabeth Anne Payne, and Marjorie Spruill, eds., *Mississippi Women: Their Live, Their Histories* (Athens, GA: University of Georgia Press, 2010), 287–312.

160 **In 1960, Reverend W. A. Criswell** Daniel K. Williams, *God's Own Party: The Making of the Christian Right* (New York: Oxford University Press, 2012), 52.

160 **"turned on my television"** Michael Sean Winters, *God's Right Hand: How Jerry Falwell Made God a Republican and Baptized the American Right* (New York: HarperOne, 2012), 118.

160 *Christianity Today* **advised** Editorial, *Christianity Today*, February 14, 1975.

161 **"movingly encountering"** Flippen, *Jimmy Carter*, 191.

161 **"If I live in a suburb"** Dennis Haack, "Discernment Exercise: Cobelligerency Without Belligerency—Loving Believers Who Are Simply Wrong," RansomFellowship.org, June 2, 2007.

161 **"God used pagans"** Neil J. Young, *We Gather Together: The Religious Right and the Problem of Interfaith Politics* (New York: Oxford University Press, 2015), 172.

CHAPTER NINE

163 **Senator Jesse Helms** Rosemary Thomson, *The Price of LIBerty* (Charisma Media, 1978), 99–100.

163 **meeting in Indiana** Erin M. Kemper, "Battling 'Big Sister' Government: Hoosier Women and the Politics of International Women's Year," *Journal of Women's History* 24, No. 2 (Summer 2012).

163 **Senator Helms convened** Thomson, *The Price of LIBerty*; Marjorie Spruill, "Gender and America's Right Turn," *Rightward Bound: Making America Conservative in the 1970s* (Cambridge, MA: Harvard University Press, 2008), 84.

164 **Allan Bakke** Matthew Frye Jacobson, *Roots Too: White Ethnic Revival in Post–Civil Rights America* (Cambridge: Harvard University Press, 2006), 98–100.

164 **more friend-of-the-court briefs** "57 Law Briefs on Bakke," WP, September 17, 1977.

164 **Supporters of affirmative action** For overview see John David Skrtenty, *The Ironies of Affirmative Action: Politics, Culture, and Justice in America* (Chicago: University of Chicago Press, 1996).

165 *World of Our Fathers* Jacobson, *Roots Too*, 18, 79, 269.

165 **"Everyone wants a ghetto"** Ibid., 18.

165 **Jews, themselves victims** "Rights Groups Divide Over Quotas," NYT, June 12, 1977.

165 **"This wretched contract"** "Moynihan Decries Plan to Assign New York City Teachers by Race," NYT, September 24, 1977.

165 **"the situation of other immigrant groups"** Martin Luther King Jr., *Where Do We Go from Here? Chaos or Community* (Boston: Beacon Press, 1967).

166 **a historian wrote** Jacobson, *Roots Too*, 42.

166 **"So many Jews today"** Ibid., 46.

166 **Michael Dukakis** Ibid.

166 **Academy Award for *Rocky*** Ibid., 100–102.

166 **Youngstown Sheet and Tube** Dominic Sandbrook, *Mad as Hell: The Crisis of the 1970s and the Rise of the Populist Right* (New York: Anchor Books, 2012), 238–40; Michael J. McManus, "Free Enterprise," *Bangor Daily News*, July 24, 1978.

166 **Eighty-three percent of Americans** George Gallup column, May 1, 1977.

166 **"What potentially is the most"** "57 Law Briefs on Bakke."

166 **seventy-four-page *Bakke* brief** Laura Kalman, *Right Star Rising: A New Politics, 1974–1980* (New York: Norton, 2010), 197.

167 **black radio station** "Blacks Tie Up White House Switchboard with Calls to Support Affirmative Action," *Jet*, September 27, 1977.

167 **no common interest** John A. Farrell, *Tip O'Neill and the Democratic Century* (New York: Little, Brown, 2001), 465; Meg Jacobs, *Panic at the Pump: The Energy Crisis and the Transformation of American Politics in the 1970s* (New York: Hill & Wang, 2016), 162–73; Daniel Horowitz, *Jimmy Carter and the Energy Crisis of the 1970s: The "Crisis of Confidence" Speech of July 15, 1979* (New York: Bedford/ St. Martin's, 2004), 7; David P. Vogel, *Fluctuating Fortunes: The Political Power of Business in America* (New York: Basic Books, 1989), 128.

167 **single day in June** *New York Times* Service, June 10, 1977; AP, June 10, 1977.

167 **clever strategy** Farrell, *Tip O'Neill*, 469.

168 **Jimmy called Tip** Ibid., 471.

168 **considerable energy leases** ABC News, *Battleground Washington: Armies of Influence*, August 19, 1979, VTVNA.

168 **And on September 26** Jacobs, *Panic at the Pump*, 184.

168 **moral equivalent** Ibid.

168 **Arthur Schlesinger wrote** *Journals: 1952–2000* (New York: Penguin, 2007), 381.

168 **"With every passing day"** "The President's News Conference," September 29 1977, APP.

168 **stop in the South Bronx** "New York City: Exchange with Reporters Following a Tour of the South Bronx," October 5, 1977, APP.

169 **should have visited Bushwick** "A Presidential Visit," *New York Daily News*, September 29, 1977.

169 **The *Daily News*** James Wieghart, "For Mr. Jimmy, It's Shape Up or Ship Out," *New York Daily News*, October 3, 1977.

169 **"Eptitude Question"** "Can Carter Cope?" *Newsweek*, October 24, 1977.

169 **William Safire thrusted** *New York Times* Service, October 20, 1977.

169 **James Fallows lectured** Robert Schlesinger, *White House Ghosts: Presidents and Their Speechwriters* (New York: Simon & Schuster, 2008), 277–78.

169 **brought in a ringer** Ibid., 279.

169 ***Time*'s Hugh Sidey** "The Presidency: The Trouble with Loose Lingo," *Time*, November 21, 1977.

169 **"moral equivalent of Sominex"** "News Analysis: Energy Clichés and Bromides," BG, November 10, 1977.

169 **Nicholas von Hoffman** "Carter's Energy Speech: Incomprehensible Fumbling and Lethargy," WP, November 16, 1977.

169 **Senators streamed south** Ian Shapiro, *The Last Great Senate: Courage and States-*

manship in Times of Crisis (New York: Public Affairs Books, 2012), 34; Paul Laxalt, *Paul Laxalt's Nevada: A Memoir* (Reno, NV: Jack Bacon & Co, 2000), 226.

170 **"Some of these bastards"** "White House Lobbying to Change Opinions on Canal," NYT, October 13, 1977.

170 **American Conservative Union** Adam Clymer, *Drawing the Line at the Big Ditch: The Panama Canal Treaties and the Rise of the Right* (Lawrence: University Press of Kansas, 2008), 65; McIntyre, *The Fear Brokers*, 123.

170 **"*awful* lot of punishing"** Ibid., 100.

170 **Hamilton Jordan insisted** "White House Lobbying to Change Opinions on Canal."

170 **Democrats comforted** Clayton Fritchey column, *Newsday* Service, September 18, 1977.

171 **Another public opinion** "The Nation: Right On for the New Right," *Time*, October 3, 1977.

171 **A typical contribution** Norman Podhoretz, "The Culture of Appeasement," *Harper's*, October 1977.

171 **Republican National Committee** Novak, *The Prince of Darkness*, 34.

171 **Sheriff Ed Davis** W&G, December 23, 1977.

171 **"Homosexuals are raising millions"** Bancroft Library, University of California–Berkeley, Protest Collection, Briggs folio.

171 **activists importuned** Clendinen and Nagourney, *Out for Good*, 381.

171 **ABC situation comedy** Laura Kalman, *Right Star Rising: A New Politics, 1974–1980* (New York: Norton, 2010), 264; "Memo to Networks: 'Clean up TV!' " *Christianity Today*, December 30, 1977.

172 **"concept of a 'grass-roots' "** Mildred Jefferson, *Right to Life News*, July 1977.

172 **unintended consequence** "Abortion Foes Gain Support as They Intensify Campaign," NYT, October 23, 1977.

172 **Now, in Seneca Falls** "Women Relay the Movement's Torch from Seneca Falls to Houston," NYT, October 7, 1977.

173 **Mason-Dixon line** "A Relay for Women's Rights Runs into Southern Chivalry," NYT, November 4, 1977.

173 **a triumvirate** Edith Grinnell, "The Last Mile," http://www.joefreeman.com/photos/Houstonremember.html.

173 **threshold of the Sam Houston Coliseum** My reconstruction is derived from National Commission on the Observance of International Women's Year, *The Spirit of Houston: The First National Women's Conference*, An Official Report to the President, the Congress, and the People of the United States, March, 1978; Spruill, "Gender and America's Right Turn"; Lucy Komisar, "With the Women at Houston: Feminism as National Politics," *Nation*, December 10, 1977; Prudence Mackintosh, "The Good Old Girls," *Texas Monthly*, January 1978; UPI, November 14, 1977; UPI, November 17, 1977; UPI, November 18, 1977; AP, November 18, 1977; Self, *All in the Family*, 315–21; Flippen, *Jimmy Carter*, 147–53; *Today* show transcript, November 18, 1977; *Daily Breakthrough* newsletter, November 18, 1977, and November 19, 1977; Jane O'Reilly column, CT, December 18, 1977; Joan Beck column, *Chicago Tribune* Service, November 20, 1977; Tanya Melich, *The Republican War Against Women: An Insider's Report from Behind the Lines* (New York: Bantam, 1996), 84–85; Gloria Steinem, "Houston and History," in *Outrageous Acts and Everyday Rebellions* (New York: Macmillan, 1983); Thomson, *The Price of LIBerty*; Carol Felsenthal, *Sweetheart of the Silent Majority: The Biography of Phyllis Schlafly* (New York: Doubleday, 1981); *Ms.* magazine, March 1978; Andrea Dwor-

kin, *Right Wing Women* (New York: TarcherPerigree, 1983); Donald Critchlow, *Phyllis Schlafly and Grassroots Conservatism: A Woman's Crusade* (Princeton: Princeton University Press, 2008); Martin, *With God on Our Side*; and Ruth Murray Brown, *For a "Christian America": A History of the Religious Right* (New York: Prometheus, 2002).

185   **extraordinary geopolitical development** Lawrence Wright, *Thirteen Days in September: Carter, Begin, and Sadat at Camp David* (New York: Knopf, 2014), 26–29.

186   **Meanwhile, in Houston** Brown, *For a "Christian America,"* 117–18.

187   **"small group of intellectuals"** Melich, *The Republican War on Women*, 94.

187   **"Constitutional Convention for women"** Steinem, "Houston and History," 304.

187   **"sort of milestone"** Ibid., 315.

187   **Schlafly left warning** Critchlow, *Phyllis Schlafly and Grassroots Conservatism*, 247–48.

187   **A preacher from Calcasieu Parish** Felsenthal, *Sweetheart of the Silent Majority*, 279.

187   **Tottie Ellis returned home** Robert Hooper, *A Distinct People: A History of the Churches of Christ in the 20th Century* (West Monroe, LA: Howard Books, 1983), 250.

187   **governor of Missouri** Martin, *With God on Our Side*, 165.

187   **"best recruiting tool"** Brown, *For a "Christian America,"* 117.

CHAPTER TEN

188   **Chamber of Commerce** Alyssa Katz, *The Influence Machine: The U.S. Chamber of Commerce and the Corporate Capture of American Life* (New York: Spiegel & Grau, 2015), 27–28.

188   **federal spending doubled** Binyamin Applebaum, *The Economists' Hour: False Prophets, Free Markets, and the Fracture of Society* (New York: Little, Brown, 2019), 11.

188   **"Treaty of Detroit"** Nelson Lichtenstein, *Walter Reuther: The Most Dangerous Man in Detroit* (Urbana: University of Illinois Press, 1997), 279–80.

188   **next GM contract** Ibid., 284.

188   **Advertising Council** Robert Griffith, "The Selling of America: The Advertising Council and American Politics, 1942–1960," *Business History Review*, autumn 1983, 401.

188   **General Electric distributed** Jesse Walker, "Suspicious Minds," *Reason*, December 2014. Download *Road to Serfdom* comic at Mises.org, accessed April 22, 2020.

189   **By 1954** Elizabeth Fones-Wolf, *Selling Free Enterprise: The Business Assault on Labor and Liberalism, 1945–1950* (Urbana: University of Illinois Press, 1995), 204.

189   **only legitimate role** William F. Buckley, "*National Review*: Statement of Intentions (1955)," in Gregory Schneider, ed., *Conservatism Since 1930: A Reader* (New York: NYU Press, 2003), 195–200.

189   **His pitch yielded** John Judis, *William F. Buckley: Patron Saint of the Conservatives* (New York: Simon & Schuster, 1988), 191.

189   **gross domestic product** "US GDP by Year Compared to Recessions and Events," https://www.thebalance.com/us-gdp-by-year-3305543.

189   **In 1960, a conservative polling firm** Sharon Beder, "The Role of 'Economic Education' in Achieving Capitalist Hegemony," *State of Nature* 2 (Sept/Oct 2006).

189   **Lyndon Johnson was interrupted** Rick Perlstein, *Before the Storm: Barry Gold-water and the Unmaking of the American Consensus* (New York: Farrar, Straus & Giroux, 2001), 309.

189   *New Republic* **called it** ; David P. Vogel, *Fluctuating Fortunes: The Political Power of Business in America* (New York: Basic Books, 1989), 25.

190   **almost two-thirds** Ibid., 41.

190   **"As the range of conscious"** Ibid., 25.

190   **"riots and arson"** John David Skrtenty, *The Ironies of Affirmative Action: Politics, Culture, and Justice in America* (Chicago: University of Chicago Press, 1996), p. 89.

190   **remarkable hearing** Michael Pertschuk, *Revolt Against Regulation* (Berkeley: University of California Press, 1983), 67, 36–37.

191   **The following day** Vogel, *Fluctuating Fortunes*, 50.

191   **"truth in lending"** Ibid.

191   **The floodgates opened** "Consumer Interests: Legislative Derby Has Begun," *Toledo Blade*, February 18, 1968.

192   **"Keep the big boys"** Pertschuk, *Revolt Against Regulation*, 25.

192   **remarkable shift** Vogel, *Fluctuating Fortunes*, 54.

192   **"come to be skeptical"** Ibid., 66.

192   **1971 was the first year** Judith Stein, *Pivotal Decade: How the United States Traded Factories for Finance in the 1970s* (New Haven: Yale University Press, 2010), 200.

192   **A manufacturer of cribs** Matt Stoller, *Goliath: The 100-Year War Between Monopoly Power and Democracy* (New York: Simon & Schuster, 2019), 325.

192   **Frederick Donner** Vogel, *Fluctuating Fortunes*, 43.

193   **college seniors** Ibid., 54.

193   **Ralph Nader** Justin Martin, *Nader: Crusader, Spoiler, Icon* (New York: Basic Books, 2002), passim.

194   **"barely contained fury"** Pertschuk, *Revolt Against Regulation*, 32.

194   *New York Times* **acknowledged** "Lawyer Charges Autos Safety Lag," NYT, November 30, 1965.

194   *Times Book Review* "In High Gear," **NYT** *Book Review*, December 5, 1965.

194   **"The American auto industry"** David Halberstam, *The Reckoning* (New York: William Morrow & Co., 1986), 490.

195   **Nader testified** Vogel, *Fluctuating Fortunes*, 44; Pertschuk, *Revolt Against Regulation*, 21.

195   **"nut behind the wheel"** Pertschuk, *Revolt Against Regulation*, 41.

195   **"second collision"** Ralph Nader, *Unsafe at Any Speed* (New York: Dunlop & Grossmans, 1965), Chapter Three.

195   **"written almost exclusively"** "Statement by Ralph Nader Before the Senate Subcommittee on Executive Reorganization," *Traffic Safety: Examination and Review of Efficiency, Economy, and Coordination of Public and Private Agencies' Activities and the Role of the Federal Government*, Hearings before the Subcommittee on Executive Reorganization of the Committee on Government Operations, United States Senate, Eighty-Ninth Congress, First Session, March 22, 25, and 26, 1965, Part I.

196   **Senator Carl Curtis** "Writer Predicts No Law Auto Act; Charges Harassment," WP, February 11, 1966.

196   **While he was working** "Investigators Hound Auto Safety Witness," WP, March 7, 1966; UPI, March 9, 1966; "GM Chief Called to Quiz on Probe of Auto Critic," WP, March 11, 1966; "GM's Head Apologizes to 'Harassed' Car Critic," WP,

March 26, 1966; "GM-Hired Detective Sough to Find a Link Between Ribicoff and Nader," WP, March 26, 1966; "GM's Goliath Bows at David; Individual Conscience Soars," WP, March 27, 1966; Vogel, *Fluctuating Fortunes*, 45; Halberstam, *The Reckoning*, 491.

197 *New York Times* profiled "Man in the News: Ralph Nader," March 23, 1966.

197 **"one of the bedrocks"** "The Corvair Caper," WP, March 26, 1966.

197 **"When they started looking"** Vogel, *Fluctuating Fortunes*, 45.

197 **$425,000 legal settlement** Ibid., 49.

197 **"Nader's Raiders"** Mark Green, *Bright, Infinite Future: A Generational Memoir on the Progressive Rise* (New York: St. Martins, 2016), 51–54; Martin, *Nader*, 75–77.

198 **"Cap the Knife"** Ibid., 81.

198 **Occupational Safety and Health** Katz, *The Influence Machine*, 35–36.

198 **Nor did he veto** Vogel, *Fluctuating Fortunes*, 69–76.

199 **Frank Moss congratulated** Pertschuk, *Revolt Against Regulation*, 76–77.

199 **In 1971 Webster's** Martin, *Nader*, 138.

199 **A book called** Morton Mintz and Jerry S. Cohen, *America, Inc.: Who Owns and Operates the United States* (New York: Dial Press, 1971).

199 **Children begged** Dr. Seuss, *The Lorax* (New York: Random House, 1971).

199 **Gore Vidal published** Gore Vidal, "The Best Man, 1972: Would Ralph Nader Buy a Used Office from this Country?" *Esquire*, June 1971.

199 **Mike Royko's readers** Green, *Bright, Infinite Future*, 59.

199 **Bryce Harlow** "Advertising: Nixon Aide on Consumerism," NYT, February 3, 1970.

199 **borrowed third-hand** Martin, *Nader*, 82.

200 **The neighborhood was pocked** Vogel, *Fluctuating Fortunes*, 60, 103.

200 **sixty-two thousand donors** Amy Handlin, ed., *Dirty Deals? An Encyclopedia of Lobbying, Political Influence, and Corruption* (ABC-CLIO, 2014), 595.

200 **Nearly one hundred thousand** Vogel, *Fluctuating Fortunes*, 94.

200 **attorneys' fees** Ibid., 105. The Consumer Product Safety Act (1972), the Federal Trade Commission Improvement Act (1974), and the Toxic Substance Control Act (1976) all authorized federal money to support suits providing "substantial public benefit."

200 **George McGovern** Green, *Bright, Infinite Future*, 59.

200 **1972 Clean Water** Richard Nixon, "Veto of the Federal Water Pollution Control Amendments of 1972," October 17, 1972, APP.

200 **radical right-wing budget** "Mr. Nixon's Stern New Deal," *Newsweek*, February 12, 1973.

200 **Thanks to Watergate** Vogel, *Fluctuating Fortunes*, 117.

201 **"Until two or three years ago"** Ibid., 120.

201 **paper airplane** Ibid., 133.

201 **A 1964 study** Ibid., 34.

201 **In 1966, when the highway safety** Ibid., 44.

201 **"We don't have a business community"** Ibid., 200.

201 **"codfish catch"** Ibid., 214.

201 **In 1976, Senator Abraham Ribicoff** Ibid., 93; also Abner Mikva.

202 **public interest law firms** Ibid., 94.

202 **The Massachusetts attorney general** Green, *Bright, Infinite Future*, 60.

202 **Nader hosted** *Saturday Night Live* Ibid, 60; Martin, *Nader*, 141.

202 **"We can raise the ante"** Vogel, *Fluctuating Fortunes*, 149.

202 **"most important piece"** Green, *Bright, Infinite Future*, 74.

202 **The idea for a** Lawrence Glickman, *Buying Power: A History of Consumer Activism in America* (Chicago: University of Chicago Press, 2009), 284–98.

203 **"permanently federalizes and subsidizes"** For the fight against the proposal are from George Schwartz, "The Successful Fight Against a Federal Consumer Protection Agency," *MSU Business Topics* 27 (Summer 1979), 45–57.

203 **He was taking advantage** Thomas Ferguson, "Industrial Conflict and the Coming of the New Deal: The Triumph of Multinational Liberalism in America," in Gary Gerstle and Steve Fraser, eds., *The Rise and Fall of the New Deal Order, 1930–1980* (Princeton: Princeton University Press, 1989); Rogers and Ferguson, *Right Turn*.

204 **"Will You Be Free to Celebrate Christmas"** Poster in collection of author.

204 **Jack Brooks of Texas** AP, April 19, 1977.

204 **Conservative think tanks** Heritage Foundation *Issues Bulletin*, "Consumer Protection Act, H.R. 6805," May 9, 1977.

205 **"too dumb to buy"** 75-01, recorded January 8, 1975.

205 **"equate their own"** "Agency for Consumer Advocacy," 75-01, track 01, recorded May 1975, RRB.

205 **editor of the** *National Enquirer* Ronald Reagan, "Professional Consumerists," RRPL, Box 19 or 50.

205 **"apple pie and motherhood"** Glickman, *Buying Power*, 279.

205 *"Henry González"* Walter Guzzardi Jr., "Business Is Learning How to Win in Washington," *Fortune*, March 27, 1978.

206 **In 1950, America's share** Rogers and Ferguson, *Right Turn*, 81.

206 **"state's environmental laws"** Meg Jacobs, "The Politics of Environmental Regulation: Business-Government Relations in the 1970s and Beyond," in Julian Zelizer and Kim Phillips-Fein, eds., *What's Good for Business: Business and American Politics Since World War II* (New York: Oxford University Press, 2012), 212.

206 **fewer than a hundred** Ibid., 223.

206 **Consumer Issue Working Group** Description and quotes from Mark Green and Andrew Buchsbaum, *The Corporate Lobbies: Political Profiles of the Business Roundtable and the Chamber of Commerce* (Washington, D.C.: Public Citizen, 1980); Glickman, *Buying Power*; and Schwartz, "The Successful Fight Against a Federal Consumer Protection Agency."

208 **"Ralph just won't let us"** Ibid., quoting Michael Pertschuk.

CHAPTER ELEVEN

211 **state visit to Washington** Jimmy Carter, *White House Diary* (New York: Macmillan, 2010), 135–36.

211 **This time** UPI, January 1, 1978.

212 **main goal** Carter, *White House Diary*, 155–58; J. Brooks Flippen, *Jimmy Carter, the Politics of Family, and the Rise of the Religious Right* (Athens, GA: University of Georgia Press, 2011), 158.

212 **F-15 fighter jets** Daniel Strieff, "Arms Wrestle: Capitol Hill Fight Over Carter's 1978 Middle East 'Package' Airplane Sale," *Diplomatic History* 40, Issue 3 (June 2016), 475–99.

212   **Islamic scholars** Christian Caryl, *Strange Rebels: 1979 and the Birth of the 21st Century* (New York: Basic Books, 2013), 139.

213   **announced in October** Ian Shapiro, *The Last Great Senate: Courage and States-manship in Times of Crisis* (New York: Public Affairs Books, 2012), 113.

213   **coal strike** Dominic Sandbrook, *Mad as Hell: The Crisis of the 1970s and the Rise of the Populist Right* (New York: Anchor Books, 2012), 232.

213   **"unconditional surrender"** Marc Reisner, *Cadillac Desert: The American West and Its Disappearing Water* (New York: Penguin. Books, 1993), 321.

213   **"blizzard of anti-treaty mail"** "Coalition Politics on the Right," WSJ, January 3, 1978.

213   **Senator Howard Baker** Lee Annis, *Howard Baker: Conciliator in an Age of Crisis* (Knoxville, TN: Howard Baker Center, 2007), 125.

213   **His pollster** Adam Clymer, *Drawing the Line at the Big Ditch: The Panama Canal Treaties and the Rise of the Right* (Lawrence: University Press of Kansas, 2008), 80.

213   **value of the dollar** UPI, January 7, 1978.

213   *Chicago Sun-Times* **series** Aaron Swartz, "Is Undercover Over? Disguise Seen as Deceit by Timid Reporting," *Fair*, March 1, 2008.

214   **welfare funds** AP, January 16, 1978.

214   **twenty-two thousand Cuban troops** *Washington Post* Service, February 15, 1978.

214   **Carter called him** Carter, *White House Diary*, 164.

214   **As introduced in 1974** Robert M. Collins, *More: The Politics of Economic Growth in Postwar America* (New York: Oxford University Press, 2000), 167.

214   **in the spring** Jefferson Cowie, *Stayin' Alive: The 1970s and the Last Days of the Working Class* (New York: New Press, 2010), 272.

214   **Joe Biden complained** Branko Marcetic, *Yesterday's Man: The Case Against Joe Biden* (New York: Verso, 2020), 38.

214   **Congressional Black Caucus** Carter, *White House Diary*, 92.

215   **Nixon made his first** Robert Sam Anson, *Exile: The Unquiet Oblivion of Richard M. Nixon* (New York: Simon & Schuster, 1984), 184–85; Sandbrook, *Mad as Hell*, 201, 231–32

215   **"feel more at home"** Carter, *White House Diary*, 165.

215   **"Government cannot solve"** "State of the Union," January 19, 1978, APP.

215   **long-awaited tax plan** "Tax Reduction and Reform Message to the Congress," January 20, 1978, APP; Robert Kuttner, *Revolt of the Haves: Tax Rebellions and Hard Times* (New York: Simon & Schuster, 1980), 234, 242; Judith Stein, *Pivotal Decade: How the United States Traded Factories for Finance in the 1970s* (New Haven: Yale University Press, 2010), 193; Vogel, *Fluctuating Fortunes*, 174; Molly C. Michelmore, *Tax and Spend: The Welfare State, Tax Politics, and the Limits of American Liberalism* (State College: University of Pennsylvania Press, 2012), 128.

216   **chairman of Carter's Board** Stein, *Pivotal Decade*, 193–94.

216   **Ways and Means chairman** Kuttner, *Revolt of the Haves*, 246; "Ullman Opposes Plan to Tighten Business Expense-Account Taxes," NYT, January 19, 1978.

216   **Robert Packwood** "The Tax Education of Jimmy Carter," *Fortune*, January 16, 1978

216   **"three-martini lunch"** Kuttner, *Revolt of the Haves*, 234; Vogel, *Fluctuating Fortunes*, 174; Virginia Payette column, United Features, May 22, 1978; "Business Or Pleasure?" *Lakeland Ledger*, June 13, 1978.

216   **"how many martinis"** "The President's News Conference," February 17, 1978, APP.

216   **On January 23** George Gallup column, January 23, 1978.

216 **sell Saudi Arabia sixty F-15s** Strieff, "Arms Wrestle."

217 **"If you think the members"** AP, January 30, 1978.

217 **on January 31** Carter, *White House Diary*, 167.

217 **snow removal equipment** "A Reckoning in Bent Blades," NYT, February 4, 1978.

217 **"Hey Washington?"** Oliphant cartoon, *Washington Star* Syndicate, February 5, 1978.

217 **Carter rang up six** Green, *Bright, Infinite Future*, 76.

217 **most comprehensive onslaught** Vogel, *Fluctuating Fortunes*, 162, 204; George Schwartz, "The Successful Fight Against a Federal Consumer Protection Agency," *MSU Business Topics* 27 (Summer 1979), 45–57.

218 **Ralph Nader's hubris** Ibid.; Walter Guzzardi Jr., "Business Is Learning How to Win in Washington," *Fortune*, March 27, 1978, 36; Ralph Nader, " 'Mushy Liberals' Slide Away," *Philadelphia Daily News*, October 3, 1977;

218 **ever since 1962** Vogel, *Fluctuating Fortunes*, 28.

218 **Publisher Katharine Graham** John Judis, *The Paradox of American Democracy: Elites, Special Interests, and the Betrayal of Public Trust* (New York: Pantheon, 2000), 168.

218 **The resulting diatribe** "Representing Consumers," WP, February 7, 1978.

218 **"abolish the U.S. government"** Mark Green and Andrew Buchsbaum, *The Corporate Lobbies: Political Profiles of the Business Roundtable and the Chamber of Commerce* (Washington, D.C.: Public Citizen, 1980).

218 **Explanations from formerly supportive** Ibid.; Vogel, *Fluctuating Fortunes*, 162–63.

219 **"Representatives were listening"** "Defeat of Protection Agency Was a Semi-Mortal Blow," NYT, February 12, 1978.

219 *Chicago Tribune* **editorialized** "A Consumer Bill Gets Consumed," CT, February 13, 1978.

219 **Ronald Reagan celebrated** RRC, February 17, 1978.

219 **newspaper syndication contract** Letter from King Features, January 23, 1978, RRPL, Box 10.

219 **Gallup Poll reported** Lou Cannon, *Governor Reagan: His Rise to Power* (New York: Public Affairs Books, 2003), 444.

219 **top political associates gathered** ENIR, January 16, 1978.

220 **Republican National Committee's annual** UPI, January 20, 1978; UPI, January 21, 1978; Paul Cowan, *Tribes of America: Journalistic Discoveries of Our People and Their Cultures* (New York: New Press, 2008 [originally 1979]), 107–8; "What PUSH's Jesse Jackson Told GOP," *Washington Afro-American*, January 31, 1978; John Lofton column, February 2, 1978.

220 **"I wish we had Republicans"** "Jesse Jackson Tells Receptive G.O.P. It Can Pick Up Votes of Blacks," NYT, January 21, 1978.

220 *Who's Who Among High School Students* RRC, January 13, 1978.

220 **He flayed pedagogical** RRB, no identification number, recorded February 20, 1978, in RRIHOH, 345.

220 **funding of school districts** RRB 78-01, track B1, "Taxes," recorded January 9, 1978, in RPV, 251.

220 **Jesus Christ's divinity** RRB 78-01, track A2, "Christmas," recorded January 9, 1978, in RPV, 247.

221 **philanthropic individuals** RRB 78-01, tracks A1 and A2, "American Farm School I" and "American Farm School II," recorded January 9, 1978, in RPV, 248.

221 **outrageously lenient sentences** RRB 78-01, track B3, "Crime," recorded January 9, 1978, in RPV, 254.

221 "missing in action" RRB 75-01, track A5, "Human Rights I," recorded January 9, 1978, in RRIHOH, 345.

221 oil companies RRB 78-02, track A5, "Oil," recorded January 27, 1978, in RPV, 265.

221 "killer satellites" RRB 78-03, track A2, "Spaceships," recorded February 20, 1978, in RPV, 257.

221 "$57 million an hour" Quoted in Ronnie Dugger, *On Reagan: The Man and His Presidency* (New York: McGraw Hill, 1983), 337.

221 exasperation at conservationists RRB 78-03, track A3, "Redwoods," recorded February 20, 1978, in RPV, 140.

221 Mineral King RRB 78-04, track B4, "Mineral King," recorded March 13, 1978, in RPV, 278.

221 situation in southern Africa RRC, October 22, 1976; AP, May 4, 1977; RRB 76-04, track 6, "Africa," recorded November 2, 1976; "Excerpts of Remarks by the Hon. Ronald Reagan, Former Governor of California, Before the Intercollegiate Studies Institute Banquet, Mayflower Hotel, Washington, D.C., Saturday, January 15, 1977," RRPL, Box 21; RRB 76-09, track B8, "Rhodesia," recorded August 15, 1977, in RPV, 179; RRC, February 27, 1978; *Vital Speeches of the Day*, May 1.

222 energy policy held by the NAACP Reagan to Century 21 convention, January 20, 1978, RRPL, Box 71; RRC, January 25, 1978.

222 petroleum industry propaganda Alexander Cockburn and James Ridgeway, "Big Oil's New Black Ally," *Village Voice*, January 23, 1978.

223 "Mrs. Margaret Bush Wilson" Transcript, Bill Moyers interview, RRPL, Box 59.

223 pollster Dick Wirthlin RRPL, SERIES II: Charlie Black Files, SUBSERIES A: Subject Files, Box 85, "D.M.I. (Decision Making Information)."

223 Bruce Eberle W&G, July 4, 1977.

223 subsidizing the coal strike CFTRN, April 1, 1978.

223 Madame Tussauds wax museum CFTRN, January 11, 1978.

223 "Nuclear 'Wastes' Have Valuable Uses" CFTRN, April 1, 1978.

224 She used to travel Helene von Damm, *At Reagan's Side: Twenty Years in the Political Mainstream* (New York: Doubleday, 1989), 89–90.

224 "description of totalitarianism" Ibid., 39. For her rise up the ranks, 44–60.

224 tender biographical portrait Helene von Damm, ed., *Sincerely, Ronald Reagan* (Ottawa, IL: Jameson Books, 1976).

224 filed 333 letters RRPL, Box 62 "California Headquarters—Scheduling Files—Invitations/Turndowns, 1978.

225 wrong schedule page See RRPL, Box 19, Schedules.

225 "Having seen so many" Speech to Georgia Citizens for the Republican Meeting, January 21, 1978, RRPL, Box 71.

225 change in capital gains Hannaford to Reagan, July 1, 1978, "SUBJECT: Capital gains taxes"; Daniel T. Kingsley to Hannaford, July 17, 1978, DH, Box 2, Folder 7.

225 National Association of Broadcasters Mark Fowler to Hannaford, March 31, 1978; Hannaford to Reagan, April 7, 1978, DH, Box 2, Folder 7.

225 construction executives Hannaford to Reagan, January 17, 1977, "SUBJECT: Your February 1 speech to California Builders' Exchange"; Jim Crumpacker to Hannaford, January 24, 1977, DH, Box 3, Folder 1.

225 California Thoroughbred Breeders Hannaford to Reagan, "SUBJECT: CTBA event, Monday 2/23/78"; Neil Papiano to Michael Deaver, January 14, 1978, DH, Box 2, Folder 7.

225 **standard fee was $5,000** "Aides Say Reagan Will Campaign for Ford If He Gets Assignments," NYT, September 9, 1976.

225 **That January** Schedules, RRPL, Box 19.

225 **"Larry Lennon will be present"** September 19, 1979, schedule file: Von Damm to Stockdale, August 17, 1979; John Erthein to Reagan memo, Box 23, RRPL.

226 **Reagan had signed** Craig Shirley, *Rendezvous with Destiny: Ronald Reagan and the Campaign That Changed America* (Wilmington, DE: Intercollegiate Studies Institute, 2009), 26.

226 **"style of a liberal punk"** Garry Wills, *Reagan's America: Innocents at Home* (New York: Doubleday, 1986), 397.

226 **Reagan and Buckley argued** January 13, 1978, RRPL, Box 71; Heather Hendershot, *Open to Debate: How William F. Buckley Put Liberal America on the Firing Line* (New York: Broadside Books, 2016), Chapter Six. View debate at C-Span .org, accessed March 27, 2020. Buckley opening statement in William F. Buckley, *A Hymnal: The Controversial Arts* (New York: G. P. Putnam's Sons, 1978), 61.

227 **leaked cable** Annis, *Howard Baker*, 127; Shapiro, *The Last Great Senate*, 141–42.

228 **Buckley devoted** William F. Buckley column, March 4, 1978.

229 **did a series** *Doonesbury*, September 26, 1977; September 27, 1977; September 28, 1977; September 30, 1977; and October 1, 1977.

230 **"severe and long-lasting"** "House, Senate, Reach Accord on Abortions," *Baltimore Sun*, December 8, 1977.

230 **in Columbus, Ohio** *New York Times* Service, March 6, 1978; Herman Herst Jr. column, May 15, 1978, *Boca Raton News*, May 15, 1978.

230 **In Akron** Nick Thimmesch column, January 24, 1978.

230 **"Committee of the Silent Majority"** McIntyre, *The Fear Brokers*, 158.

230 **her own** *Firing Line* "Phyllis Schlafly Trumps William F. Buckley in Debate Over Panama Canal," Breitbart.com, January 25, 2016; YouTube.com, accessed April 26, 2020.

230 **"kike bankers"** *Panama Canal Treaties, 1977–1978*, prepared by the Subcommittee on Separations of Powers of the Committee on the Judiciary, United States Senate, Part 2 of 3, February 27 through March 16, 1978, page 2303.

230 **Governor Meldrim Thomson** "Talk Given Before Delegates of the 59th American Legion Convention, Denver, Colorado, August 24, 1977," *Dixon Evening Telegraph*, November 17, 1977.

230 **left for South Africa** McIntyre, *The Fear Brokers*, 291–92; UPI, January 13, 1978; UPI, January 16, 1978; AP, January 17, 1978; UPI, January 17, 1978; AP, January 19, 1978; UPI, January 21, 1978; "President Assails the Absent Thomson," BG, February 19, 1978.

231 **"only American leader"** "Nashua, New Hampshire: Remarks and a Question-and-Answer Session at a Town Meeting with New Hampshire High School Students," February 18, 1978, APP.

231 **New Hampshire's liberal** Clymer, *Drawing the Line at the Big Ditch*, 106–13; Sidney Blumenthal, *The Permanent Campaign: Inside the World of Elite Political Operatives* (Boston: Beacon Press, 1980), 217; UPI, November 13, 1978; author correspondence with Senator Gordon Humphrey.

232 **In New Jersey** E. J. Dionne, *Why the Right Went Wrong: Conservatism: From Goldwater to the Tea Party and Beyond* (New York: Simon & Schuster, 2016), 71–72; HE, April 23, 1977; "Politics," NYT, December 4, 1977; "Trenton Topics," NYT, December 13, 1977.

232 **Representative Bill Armstrong** HE, July 16, 1977, and November 18. 1978; Clymer, *Drawing the Line at the Big Ditch*, 123; author interview with Nina Totenberg.

233 **Dr. Newton Leroy Gingrich** David Osborne, "The Swinging Days of Newt Gingrich," *Mother Jones*, November 1984; "The Millennial's Guide to Newt Gingrich," *Politico*, July 14, 2016; Craig Shirley, *Citizen Newt: The Making of a Reagan Conservative* (Nashville: Thomas Nelson, 2017), 21–22; "After Political Victory, a Personal Revolution," WP, December 19, 1994.

233 **Avi Nelson** "Brooke Running Scared in Primary," WP, September 17, 1978.

233 **"Women are just naturally"** Dr. George Crane, "The Worry Clinic," for example September 1, 1950; June 14, 1951; December 3, 1962; June 28, 1978.

233 **first sibling trio** "Meet the Cornbelt Kennedys; Phil Crane and His Remarkable Family Are Flying High," *People*, September 11, 1978.

233 **TV preacher named Don Lyon** AP, March 12, 1978; W&G, December 3, 1977.

234 **Hawkeye State** HE, June 17, 1978; Connie Paige, *The Right to Lifers: Who They Are, How They Operate, and Where They Get Their Money* (New York: Summit Books, 1983), 190; McIntyre, *The Fear Brokers*, 137; Clymer, *Drawing the Line at the Big Ditch*, 117.

234 **"Hang Sen. Dick Clark"** Randall Balmer, *Redeemer: The Life of Jimmy Carter* (New York: Basic Books, 2014), 101, 142.

234 **"Panama Truth Squad"** Viguerie and Franke, *Right Turn*, 113; McIntyre, *The Fear Brokers*, 122; January 19, 1978, RRPL, Box 71; Clymer, *Drawing the Line at the Big Ditch*, 59–60; Paul Laxalt, *Paul Laxalt's Nevada: A Memoir* (Reno, NV: Jack Bacon & Co., 2000), 231.

234 **Reagan and Laxalt** Shirley, *Rendezvous with Destiny*, 26.

234 **Richard Viguerie raised** Viguerie and Franke, *Right Turn*, 113–14.

234 **The ACU had already** "Panama Treaties at Stake in Bitter Propaganda War," NYT, January 20, 1978.

234 **Citizens for the Republic training** CFTRN, January 11, 1978.

234 **challengers to "regular party"** "Reaganites Quietly Building for Future; Camp Intact," LAT, April 9, 1977.

235 **Weyrich's was** Clymer, *Drawing the Line at the Big Ditch*, 133–34; McIntyre, *The Fear Brokers*, 84.

235 **Youngstown, Ohio** M. Stanton Evans column, February 26, 1978; "New Right Leaders Reach Out to Unions," WP, February 5, 1978; author correspondence with Mickey Edwards.

235 **Viguerie was quoted** *National Journal*, January 28, 1978. See also "Coalition Politics on the Right," WSJ, January 3, 1978; "The New Right's Strong Ambition Is Fueled by Huge Mail Campaign," NYT, December 4, 1977.

236 **in St. Paul, Minnesota** Clendinen and Nagourney, *Out for Good*, 323–24; AP, April 19, 1978; Randy Shilts, *The Mayor of Castro Street: The Life and Times of Harvey Milk* (New York: St. Martin's Press, 1982), 223–26, 215–17.

236 **Wichita, Kansas** Clendinen and Nagourney, *Out for Good*, 322–23; Fred Fejes, *Gay Rights and Moral Panic: The Origins of America's Debate on Homosexuality* (New York: Palgrave Macmillan, 2008), 161, 173–75.

236 **Eugene, Oregon** Fejes, *Gay Rights and Moral Panic*, 175–76; Clendinen and Nagourney, *Out for Good*, 322.

236 **Florida Citrus Commission** Gannett News Service, January 22, 1978.

236 **"done the most damage"** Jackie M. Blount, *Fit to Teach: Same-Sex Desire, Gender, and School Work in the Twentieth Century* (Albany: State University of New York Press, 2006), 147.

236 **fell 70 percent** Clendinen and Nagourney, *Out for Good*, 328.

236 **"rally for decency"** Ibid.

236 **Twin Cities' archbishop** Ibid., 322.

236 **"Talk of property tax revolt"** RRC, January 24, 1978.

237 **Several times, a tax-obsessed** Kuttner, *Revolt of the Haves*, 39–44; Sandbrook, *Mad as Hell*, 278–80.

238 **only 30 percent** "Tax Revolt Building Nationwide," *Newsday*, August 11, 1978.

238 **On February 1** "Address to the Nation on the Panama Canal Treaties," February 1, 1978, APP.

238 **45 percent to 42** Annis, *Howard Baker*, 131.

238 **They did not** AP, February 2, 1978.

239 **Debate opened** Shapiro, *The Last Great Senate*, 146–47; AP, February 9, 1978; LeRoy Ashby and Rod Gramer, *Fighting the Odds: The Life of Frank Church* (Pullman: Washington State University Press, 1993), 542; Annis, *Howard Baker*, 131.

239 **TV across Tennessee** Ibid., 132.

239 **"How can it be both?"** Panama Canal Treaties, page 1464.

240 **"unremitting trickle"** Ashby and Gramer, *Fighting the Odds*, 543.

240 *Alice's Adventures in Wonderland* Ibid, 552.

240 **smashed it to the ground** Ibid.

240 **Ronald Reagan was granted** "Senate Starts Debate on Panama Pact with the Outcome Still in Doubt," NYT, February 9, 1978.

240 **The next morning Senator Byrd** "Senate, with Ears Open to Vox Populi, Again Debates Canal," NYT, February 10, 1978.

240 **"pistol at its temple!"** AP, February 10, 1978.

240 **By the third day** Ashby and Gramer, *Fighting the Odds*, 551. All quotes also available in *Panama Canal Treaties: United States Senate Debate 1977–78, Part 1*, United States Senate, Committee on the Judiciary, Subcommittee on Separation of Powers.

241 **So it was that DeConcini** Shapiro, *The Last Great Senate*, 147–48.

CHAPTER TWELVE

242 **a certain Chief Redbird** AP, February 10, 1978.

242 **mine workers rejected** AP, February 13, 1978.

242 **Tongsun Park** AP, February 24, 1978.

242 **47 percent** George Gallup column, February 21, 1978.

242 **Reporters peppered** "The President's News Conference," February 17, 1978, APP.

242 **United States attorney in Philadelphia** AP, January 18, 1978.

243 **Safire pounced** William Safire column, January 24, 1978.

243 *Doonesbury* mocked March 12, 1978.

243 **Ronald Reagan suggested** RRC, January 31, 1978.

243 **Hamilton Jordan** Bob Woodward, *Shadow: Five Presidents and the Legacy of Watergate* (New York: Simon & Schuster, 1999), 71.

243 **William Safire responded** William Safire column, February 23, 1978.

243 **Amateur hour** RRC, March 2, 1978.

243 **abortion issue grew nastier** *New York Times* Service, March 5, 1978; Herman Herst Jr. column, May 15, 1978, *Boca Raton News*, May 15, 1978.

243 **An ABC News segment** ABC News, August 9, 1878, VTVNA.

244   **National Organization for Women** "NOW Seeking Abortion Summit Talks with Pro-Life Forces," *Pittsburgh Press*, February 8, 1978.

244   **"no exceptions"** "Nellie Gray, Abortion Foe and Leader of Annual March, Dies at 88," NYT, August 15, 2012.

244   **Joseph Califano** "H.E.W. Team Had to Match Intention with Law," NYT, March 5, 1978.

244   **riding herd** David P. Vogel, *Fluctuating Fortunes: The Political Power of Business in America* (New York: Basic Books, 1989), 174.

245   **"sensory experience"** "FTC is Seeking Way to Decide if Pictures in Advertising Convey False Impressions" WSJ, August 11, 1978; "Michael Pertschuk and the Federal Trade Commission," John F. Kennedy School of Government Case Program #C16–81–387.0 (1981).

245   **"shared monopoly"** Ibid.; "The Future of Advertising at the FTC" *Broadcast*, January 1979; Annual Report, Kellogg Corporation, 1979, 18; F.M. Sherer, "The F.T.C., Oligopoly, and Shared Monopoly," Harvard Kennedy School of Government, Faculty Research Working Paper Series, September 2013, RWP13-031.

245   **farthest-reaching initiative** "Michael Pertschuk and the Federal Trade Commission," Kennedy School; Vogel, *Fluctuating Fortunes*, 164.

245   **letter from the senators** Michael Pertschuk, *Revolt Against Regulation* (Berkeley: University of California Press, 1983), 78.

246   **"Tony the Tiger"** Ibid.

246   **"bones bleached"** "Michael Pertschuk and the Federal Trade Commission."

246   **several structural measures** Ibid.

247   **"Every little bitty town"** Robert E. Crew, *Politics and Public Management: An Introduction* (Eagan, MN: West Publishing, 1992), 25.

247   **confident of success** "Michael Pertschuk and the Federal Trade Commission."

247   **A young first-term Democrat** For floor debate see *Congressional Record*, Volume 124, Part 4, February 28, 1978, H5011.

248   **always seemed to have his arm** "Michael Pertschuk and the Federal Trade Commission." Also "extraordinary margin."

248   **"preposterous intervention"** "The FTC as National Nanny," WP, March 1, 1978.

248   **plugged-in Washington** Pertschuk, *Revolt Against Regulation*, 55.

248   **ad hoc campaign** "Michael Pertschuk and the Federal Trade Commission."

248   **reaped nice rewards** Federal Elections Commission reports for Levitas, Broyhill, and American Dental Political Action Committee, FEC.gov.

249   **The dentists hoped** AP, December 3, 1978.

249   **heard his colleague** Thomas J. McIntyre, *The Fear Brokers* (Boston: Beacon Press, 1981), xiii, 127. For full speech see *Panama Canal Treaties*, 2287.

251   **Governor Thomson was unbowed** McIntyre, *The Fear Brokers*, 157–58.

251   **"In 1975, a great many"** Ibid., xxv.

251   **the AP reported** AP, March 12, 1978.

252   **"authority of Jesus Christ"** Jim Mason, *No Holding Back: The 1980 John B. Anderson Presidential Campaign* (Lanham, MD: University Press of America, 2011), 14–15.

252   **save a similar** Ibid., 17–20; Brad Koplinski, *Hats in the Ring: Conservations with Presidential Candidates* (North Bethesda, MD: Presidential Publishers, 2000), 21.

252   **"most tragic error"** Mason, *No Holding Back*, 26.

252   **Reverend Don Lyon's** Ibid, 28.

252   **Adam Clymer** "Right Wing Seeks to Unseat Rep Anderson," NYT, February 16, 1978.

252 **Jerry Ford and Henry Kissinger** HE, March 4, 1978.

253 **G. Conoly Phillips** "Candidate for Senate," WP, February 23, 1978.

253 **Three early installments** "Political Drama in the Heartlands: First, a Candidate Who Didn't Have a Chance, Then Three Who Do," WP, February 5, 1978; "Scaling a Higher Mountain in the 22nd," WP, March 6, 1978; "Name Recognition of Priority in a Race to Succeed Shipley," WP, March 13, 1978.

254 **Reid's article two days before** "Becoming a Money Magnet," WP, March 19, 1978.

255 **Tuesday, March 21** "In the 22nd, It's Down to Two: Crane vs Bruce in November," WP, March 23, 1978; Koplinski, *Hats in the Ring*, 21.

CHAPTER THIRTEEN

256 **Pennies rained** Thomas J. McIntyre, *The Fear Brokers* (Boston: Beacon Press, 1981), 124.

256 **Iowa's liberal senator** Adam Clymer, *Drawing the Line at the Big Ditch: The Panama Canal Treaties and the Rise of the Right* (Lawrence: University Press of Kansas, 2008), 67.

256 **Phil Crane published** *Surrender in Panama* (Ottawa, IL: Jameson Books, 1978); Clymer, *Drawing the Line at the Big Ditch*, 58.

256 **The American Legion** McIntyre, *The Fear Brokers*, 125.

256 **In New Hampshire** Ibid.; " 'Keep Our Canal' Drive Started," *Eugene Register Guard*, February 14, 1978.

256 **Johnny Paycheck** AP, March 2, 1978.

256 **Taft-Hartley** "Miners: No! Carter to Act Today," *Pittsburgh Post-Gazette*, March 6, 1978; *Chicago Tribune* Service, March 10, 1978; AP, March 20, 1978.

256 **Frank Moore** Clymer, *Drawing the Line at the Big Ditch*, 97.

257 **senators ran to the press** "White House Woos Holdouts on Canal," NYT, March 14, 1978.

257 **"Billygate"** "And Now a 'Billygate'?", CT, March 16, 1978.

257 **"worst days"** Jimmy Carter, *White House Diary* (New York: Macmillan, 2010), 177.

257 **delivered an ultimatum** Ian Shapiro, *The Last Great Senate: Courage and Statesmanship in Times of Crisis* (New York: Public Affairs Books, 2012), 148; "Daily Diary of President Jimmy Carter," March 15, 1978, Jimmy Carter Presidential Library.

258 **"100 percent"** LeRoy Ashby and Rod Gramer, *Fighting the Odds: The Life of Frank Church* (Pullman: Washington State University Press, 1993), 548.

258 **"president emphasized"** "Canal," *Orlando Sentinel*, March 16, 1978.

258 **airplane buzzed** J. Lee Annis, *Howard Baker: Conciliator in an Age of Crisis* (Knoxville, TN: Howard Baker Center, 2007), 134.

258 **President Ford called** Carter, *White House Diary*, 178

258 **bang his gavel** Paul Laxalt, *Paul Laxalt's Nevada: A Memoir* (Reno: Jack Bacon & Co., 2000), 234; Shapiro, *The Last Great Senate*, 148; UPI, March 18, 1978.

259 **Carter took the podium** "Panama Canal Treaties: Remarks on Senate Ratification of the Neutrality Treaty," March 16, 1978, APP.

259 **To his diary** Carter, *White House Diary*, 178.

259 **A Gallup Poll** George Gallup column, March 16, 1978.

259 **Bert Lance** "Lance Turns In Diplomatic Passport," NYT, March 22, 1978.

259 **Menachem Begin traveled** "Mideast Outlook Now: Gloom and More Gloom,"

USNWR, April 3,1978; "Visit of Prime Minister Begin of Israel: Remarks on the Departure of the Prime Minister," March 22, 1978, APP.

259 **Conservative Political Action Conference** UPI, March 18, 1978.

260 **Ronald Reagan spoke** RRPL, Box 431, "Speech Files—January–June 1978 (1/2)."

260 **"a mob of racketeers"** RRC, March 26, 1978.

260 **Torrijos's Guardia Nacional** "Paid to Accuse Panama Leader, Man Tells ABC," WP, August 15, 1979; AP, August 15, 1979. I attempted to verify ABC's story independently, disappearing down a far-right rabbit hole. I found one mention of the agent, Alexis Watson Castillo, in a 1977 edition of the intelligence publication *America's Journal*, identified as a defector from Panama's G-2 intelligence service, and claiming that the Guardia Nacional was under Cuban control. In a conspiracy tract by Nevin Gussak, *Noriega and Communism: The Ties That Bind*, the agent is cited claiming that Cuban military figures had selected houses in the Canal Zone for confiscation when it reverted to Panamanian control, when Soviet technicians would supposedly take over operations. In an expurgated transcript of a closed Senate session, Senator Birch Bayh said the agent had been found to have fabricated information in 1961, and contradicted himself in FBI interviews concerning his claims about Torrijos, and that American counterintelligence officials suspected he was a Cuban plant. (See *Panama Canal Treaties: United States Senate Debate 1977–78, Part 2*, United States Senate, Committee on the Judiciary, Subcommittee on Separation of Powers, 2792-95.) Watson's American handler in the affair, General Daniel O. Graham, later became a key broker of private funds to the Nicaraguan Contras.

260 **We are more unified** "Ford Lists Top Six for 1980," CT, April 8, 1978.

260 **"Steiger Amendment"** Robert Kuttner, *Revolt of the Haves: Tax Rebellions and Hard Times* (New York: Simon & Schuster, 1980), 243; Vogel, *Fluctuating Fortunes*, 175.

260 **surprising development** Ibid., 60; Molly C. Michelmore, *Tax and Spend: The Welfare State, Tax Politics, and the Limits of American Liberalism* (State College: University of Pennsylvania Press, 2012), 107.

260 **seven years later** Kuttner, *Revolt of the Haves*, 333–34.

260 **cattle that Ronald Reagan** Rick Perlstein, "Ronald Reagan: Welfare Queen of Montana (or: Tax Tips for Mitt Romney)," RollingStone.com, February 7, 2012.

261 **from 23 to 14.1 percent** John Judis, "Which Side Are the Tax Cutters On?" *In These Times*, July 29, 1981.

261 **Edward Zschau** Kuttner, *Revolt of the Haves*, 243.

261 **Labor productivity** Daniel J. Sargent, *A Superpower Transformed: The Remaking of American Foreign Relations in the 1970s* (New York: Oxford University Press, 2015), 238; Paul Krugman, *Peddling Prosperity: Economic Sense and Nonsense in the Age of Diminished Expectations* (New York: Norton, 1995), 57–59; Thomas Edsall, *The New Politics of Inequality* (New York: W. W. Norton, 1985), 213–14; Rogers and Ferguson, *Right Turn*, 78–80; Judith Stein, *Pivotal Decade: How the United States Traded Factories for Finance in the 1970s* (New Haven: Yale University Press, 2010), 200.

261 **also tantalized** RCC, March 23, 1978.

261 **Walter Wriston** Kuttner, *Revolt of the Haves*, 236.

262 **Ullman complained** Ibid., 245.

262 **"main reason for the vote"** "House Blocks Plan on Election Funds," NYT, March 22, 1978.

262 **Speaker O'Neill** "Corporate Use of Political Action Panels Growing," NYT, April 19, 1978.

262 **In New Hampshire** *New York Times* Service, April 1, 1978.

262 **In Albany** "New York Assembly Votes to Restore the Death Penalty," NYT, March 21, 1978.

262 **"some tittering"** "Candidate Answered 'Call' in Va. Race," WP, April 12, 1978; "Element of Confusion Added to Va. Democrats' Meetings," WP, April 16, 1978.

263 **Pat Robertson** "News Goliaths, Watch Out?" *Christianity Today*, March 10, 1978.

263 **The previous September** "Video Evangelism: How Pat Robertson's Christian Broadcasting Network Is Spreading the Word Like It's Never Been Spread Before," WP *Magazine*, June 4, 1978.

263 *Jerusalem Post* "The American Right Warms Up to Israel," *Jerusalem Post Magazine*, August 18, 1977.

263 **Jerry Falwell traveled there** Flippen, *Jimmy Carter*, 195; Melani McAllister, *Epic Encounters: Cultural, Media, and U.S. Interests in the Middle East Since 1945* (Berkeley: University of California Press [Updated Edition], 2005), 194; Michael Scherer and Ken Silverstein, "Born Again Zionists," *Mother Jones*, September/October 2002.

264 **In Tulsa** "Oral Roberts: Faith in the City of Faith," *Christianity Today*, May 19, 1978.

264 **In Minneapolis** "Economic Enemy Number One," *Christianity Today*, June 2, 1978; AP, March 10, 1978.

264 **The NBC radio network** AP, March 14, 1978; "NBC Radio Ban on Anti-Abortion Sermon Contested," NYT, March 25, 1978; "Stations to Air Anti-Abortion Talk," CT, April 8, 1978; HE, April 22, 1978.

264 **CBS television, however** "TV Review: Moyers Unravels Abortion Issue," LAT, April 22, 1978.

264 **Dr. Mildred Jefferson** UPI, March 14, 1978.

264 **ACTION, the federal agency** AP, February 12, 1978.

265 **Susan B. Anthony's birthday** Flippen, *Jimmy Carter*, 165.

265 **ceremony on March 22** Ibid., 166; National Commission on the Observance of International Women's Year, *The Spirit of Houston: The First National Women's Conference*, An Official Report to the President, the Congress, and the People of the United States, March 1978, 7; "National Commission on the Observance of International Women's Year, 1975: Remarks at a Reception Honoring the Commission," March 22, 1978, APP.

265 **Eleanor Smeal promised** Flippen, *Jimmy Carter* 164–65.

265 **John Ashcroft** Ibid.

265 **capitol in Springfield** Carol Felsenthal, *Sweetheart of the Silent Majority: The Biography of Phyllis Schlafly* (New York: Doubleday, 1981), 243; "ERA Backers, Foes Meet in Rally," CT, April 13, 1978.

265 **William Schneider observed** McIntyre, *The Fear Brokers*, 93. "Quisling traitor" is 154.

265 **calls from the president** Frank Moore, Bob Beckel, and Bob Thompson to president, "RE: Panama Calls," March 28, 1978, Office of Staff Secretary; Series: Presidential Files, Folder 4/4/78 [1], Container 69, downloaded from Jimmy Carter Presidential Library.

266 **Simon Bolívar's tomb** "Caracas, Venezuela: Remarks at a Wreath-Laying Ceremony at the Tomb of Simon Bolivar," March 28, 1978, APP; Carter, *White House Diary*, 181.

266 **In Brazil** "The President's News Conference," March 30, 1978, APP.

266 **sub-Saharan Africa** "Carter's Record Pace in Personal Diplomacy," USNWR, April 3, 1978.

266 **Republican donors** "GOP Parades Its Leaders in 14 Cities," LAT, April 7, 1978; "Cross-Country Jubilee of Eisenhower Nostalgia," WP, April 8, 1978; "Thompson Ranked GOP Contender," CT, April 7, 1978; "Ford Assails President on Defense and Urges Work on Neutron Bomb," NYT, April 7, 1978; "Eisenhower Silver Jubilee" handwritten draft, RRPL, Box 23.

267 **that slur ignored** "President Stresses Welfare Limit Despite Warning," NYT, May 27, 1977; Joseph Califano, "Welfare Reform: A Dream That Was Impossible," WP, May 22, 1981.

268 **a sour mood** Carter, *White House Diary*, 183.

268 **"We have learned at last"** "Inaugural Address," January 20, 1969, APP.

269 **original tax package** Stein, *Pivotal Decade*, 194. White House debate is 195–97.

269 **Only 32 percent** Sandbrook, *Mad as Hell*, 233.

269 **a major address** "Anti-Inflation Policy: Remarks to Members of the American Society of Newspaper Editors Announcing the Administration's Policy," April 11, APP.

270 **"It shall be"** "Presidential Directive/NSC-30," February 17, 1978, in Kristin Ahlberg, ed., *Foreign Relations of the United States, 1977–1980, Volume II, Human Rights and Humanitarian Affairs* (Washington, D.C.: Department of State, 2013), 405.

270 **On March 29** Christian Caryl, *Strange Rebels: 1979 and the Birth of the 21st Century* (New York: Basic Books, 2013), 139.

270 **Nicolae Ceauçescu** "Visit of President Ceausescu of Romania: Toasts at the State Dinner," April 12, 1978, APP; "The Communist Romanian Government Deliberately Irradiated Striking Miners," *Vintage News*, June 15, 2018.

271 **"moral equivalent of imperialism"** RRC, April 13, 1978.

271 **"most magnanimous"** Randall Balmer, *Redeemer: The Life of Jimmy Carter* (New York: Basic Books, 2014), 85.

271 **"throw in the State Department"** "Canal," RRB 78-06, track A1, recorded April 3, 1978, in RRIHOH, 208.

271 **Orrin Hatch** AP, April 6, 1978.

271 **planning this Asian tour** "R Reagan Travel—1978 (Far East/Iran) 1/3," RRPL, Box 28; also for itinerary and accompanying documentation.

272 **Richard V. Allen** ENIR, December 26, 1968, and January 18, 1969; *New York Times* Service, September 11, 1969; " 'Doctor R.V. Allen,' Now Just 'Mister,' Is Leaving White House Staff Post," WP, October 5, 1969; "Former Nixon Aide Denies Soliciting Campaign Funds," NYT, September 16, 1976. For Brookings Institution: Stanley I. Kutler, ed., *Abuse of Power: The New Nixon Tapes* (New York: Free Press, 1999), 2, 7, 12, 37. For Anna Chennault: George Will column, August 6, 2014.

273 **DeConcini situation** Ashby and Gramer, *Fighting the Odds*, 548–49; Shapiro, *The Last Great Senate*, 150–54.

273 **"watch me lose"** Clymer, *Drawing the Line at the Big Ditch*, 110.

274 **tried to enjoy** Carter, *White House Diary*, 185; Ashby and Gramer, *Fighting the Odds*, 552.

274 **"coverage notwithstanding"** "Panama: The Senate's Final Test," NYT, April 18, 1978.

274 **Tax-Weary and Concerned Americans** WP, April 18, 1978, C20.

274 **Debate began** Ashby and Gramer, *Fighting the Odds*, 549.

274 **"prayed night and morning"** Clymer, *Drawing the Line at the Big Ditch*, 182.
274 **In Tokyo** AP, April 19, 1978.
274 **Weyrich told** WP, April 19, 1978.

CHAPTER FOURTEEN

275 **study was released** "Economist Says Capital Gains Tax Reduction Would Benefit Economy More Than a Tax Cut," WSJ, May 5, 1978.
275 **No such skepticism** "Stupendous Steiger," WSJ, April 26, 1978 (included in a *Journal* feature of the newspaper's nineteen most historic editorials for its 125th anniversary).
276 **Ronald Reagan said** RRC, June 13, 1978, and July 5, 1978.
276 **Louis Rukeyser** Rukeyser column, March 20, 1978.
276 **Caspar Weinberger** "We Need Tax Policies to Aid Our Economy, Not Win Votes," CT, May 14, 1978.
276 **"Richer Half"** WP, March 13, 1978.
276 **"Britain's High Taxes"** NYT, March 13, 1978.
276 **"capital formation crisis"** See for example *Capital Formation: Hearings Before the Select Committee on Small Business*, United States Senate, Ninety-Fifth Congress, Second Session, Part 1, February 8 and 10, 1978.
276 **House Ways and Means** "President's Tax Measure May Die Soon at Hands of Democrats on House Panel," WSJ, April 20, 1978.
276 **Jimmy Carter fought** "The President's News Conference," April 25, 1978, APP.
276 **"so anti-reform"** "President and House Democrats Discuss Tax Cut Without Reform," NYT, April 22, 1978.
766 **nineteen supporters** "Stupendous Steiger."
276 **Tom Bradley** Ibid.
277 **veto his own** "Tax Credit Plan for Parents of Children in Private Schools Gains House Support," WSJ, May 5, 1978.
277 **1,930 letters** Molly C. Michelmore, *Tax and Spend: The Welfare State, Tax Politics, and the Limits of American Liberalism* (State College: University of Pennsylvania Press, 2012), 107.
277 **"They were braced"** Robert Kuttner, *Revolt of the Haves: Tax Rebellions and Hard Times* (New York: Simon & Schuster, 1980), 2
277 **American Council for Capital Formation** Ibid., 240.
277 **"far-out conclusions"** "Business: Flash and a Touch of Brash," *Time*, June 25, 1979.
277 **The genius responsible** Kuttner, *Revolt of the Haves*, 238–39; John Judis, *The Paradox of American Democracy: Elites, Special Interests, and the Betrayal of Public Trust* (New York: Pantheon, 2000), 134; ABC News, *Battleground Washington: Armies of Influence*, August 19, 1979, VTVNA; "Charles E. Walker, Tax Lobbyist for Republicans and Big Business," WP, June 25, 2015; Sidney Blumenthal, *The Rise of the Counter-Establishment: The Conservative Ascent to Political Power* (New York: Times Books, 2007), 70–73; Jacob S. Hacker and Paul Pierson, *Winner-Take-All Politics: How Washington Made the Rich Richer—and Turned Its Back on the Middle Class* (New York: Simon & Schuster, 2010), 124–28.
279 **Robert Keith Gray** Kuttner, *Revolt of the Haves*, 239.
279 **"Carlton Group"** Hacker and Pierson, *Winner-Take-All Politics*, 133–34.

279 "consensus is cohering" Ibid.

279 Treasury Secretary AP, May 9, 1978.

279 "entered the Lexicon" Kuttner, *Revolt of the Haves*, 245–46.

279 mainstream economists Robert M. Collins, *More: The Politics of Economic Growth in Postwar America* (New York: Oxford University Press, 2000), 180–81.

280 "limiting the government's" Milton Friedman, "The Kemp-Roth Free Lunch," *Newsweek*, August 7, 1978.

280 "public choice" Dominic Sandbrook, *Mad as Hell: The Crisis of the 1970s and the Rise of the Populist Right* (New York: Anchor Books, 2012), 278.

280 "ramp for the expansion" Paul Craig Roberts, "The Breakdown of the Keynesian Model," *Public Interest*, Summer 1978.

281 Arthur Laffer Jonathan Chait, *The Big Con: Crackpot Economists and the Fleecing of America* (New York: Houghton Mifflin Harcourt, 2007), 14.

281 Robert A. Mundell Paul Krugman, *Peddling Prosperity: Economic Sense and Nonsense in the Age of Diminished Expectations* (New York: Norton, 1995), 87; Bartley is p. 83.

282 Jude Wanniski Robert Novak introduction, Jude Wanniski, *The Way the World Works: Twentieth Anniversary Edition* (Washington, D.C.: Gateway Editions, 1998).

282 In 1973, Laffer Krugman, *Peddling Prosperity*, 95; Robert Novak, *The Prince of Darkness: 50 Years Reporting in Washington* (New York: Crown Forum, 2007), 321; Chait, *The Big Con*, 14.

283 "correct prescription" Jude Wanniski, "It's Time to Cut Taxes," WSJ, December 11, 1974.

284 three months later Michael O'Connor, "Conservatism, Stagflation, and Supply-Side Economics," U.S. Intellectual History Blog, May 13, 2014.

284 "supply-side fiscalists" Collins, *More*, 185.

284 "A few of us at Michael 1" Robert Bartley, *The Seven Fat Years: And How to Do It Again* (New York: Free Press, 1992), 48.

284 textbook neoconservative Peter Steinfels, *The Neoconservatives: The Men Who Are Changing American Politics* (New York: Simon & Schuster, 1979), 85–112.

285 Murray Weidenbaum Jason Stahl, *Right Moves: The Conservative Think Tank in American Politics and Culture Since 1945* (Chapel Hill: University of North Carolina Press, 2016), 83–84.

285 "$102.7 billion" Charles Noble, *Liberalism at Work: The Rise and Fall of OSHA* (Philadelphia: Temple University Press, 1986), 115.

285 early Christmas present Timothy B. Clark, "The Costs and Benefits of Regulation—Who Knows How Great They Really Are," *National Journal*, December 1, 1979.

286 take credit Jimmy Carter, *White House Diary* (New York: Macmillan, 2010), 202.

286 Occupational Safety and Health Administration Vogel, *Fluctuating Fortunes*, 172.

286 Carter had already "Executive Order 12044—Improving Government Regulations," March 23, 1978, APP.

286 sheets of (blank) paper Robert Schlesinger, *White House Ghosts: Presidents and Their Speechwriters* (New York: Simon & Schuster, 2008), 296.

286 the *Public Interest* Steinfels, *The Neoconservatives*, 44–46, 235–36.

286 "Queen Isabella" Jude Wanniski, "The Mundell-Laffer Hypothesis: A New View of the World Economy," *Public Interest*, Spring 1975.

286 "Write it, and I'll run it" Stahl, *Right Moves*, 98–99.

287 "Two Santa Claus Theory" "Taxes and a Two-Santa Theory," *National Observer*, March 6, 1976.

287 Jack Kemp Collins, *More*, 174.

288 "Football fans know" Kuttner, *Revolt of the Haves*, 289.

288 Job Creation Act of 1975 Collins, *More*, 175.

288 "The final and best" John F. Kennedy, "Address and Question and Answer Period at the Economic Club of New York," December 14, 1962, APP.

289 Robert Bartley told Jude Wanniski Collins, *More*, 185.

289 "exhausted and ecstatic" Chait, *The Big Con*, 16.

289 "Dressed in his bathrobe" Geoffrey Kabaservice, *Rule and Ruin: The Downfall of Moderation and the Destruction of the Republican Party, from Eisenhower to the Tea Party* (New York: Oxford University Press, 2012), 352.

289 In 1977, Kemp Collins, *More*, 176–77.

289 what John F. Kennedy Kathleen Hall Jamieson, *Packaging the Presidency: A History and Criticism of Presidential Advertising* (New York: Oxford University Press, 1988), 394.

289 Income taxes hadn't Thomas Edsall, *The New Politics of Inequality* (New York: W. W. Norton, 1985), 209–10.

290 "most unfair tax" Ronald Reagan 1976 campaign commercial, YouTube.com, accessed April 1, 2020.

290 tax employees paid See "Historical FICA Tax Information," Milefoot.com.

290 legislation Jimmy Carter championed Eric Laursen, *The People's Pension: The Struggle to Defend Social Security Since Reagan* (Chico, CA: AK Press, 2012), 44.

290 Conference Board "The Economic Scene," NYT, June 11, 1978.

291 fall of 1977 Patrick Buchanan column, October 25, 1977; "The Tax Relief Act of 1977," *First Monday*, August 1977.

291 next issue of the *Public Interest* Jude Wanniski, "Taxes, Revenues, and the 'Laffer Curve,' " *Public Interest*, Winter 1978.

291 single phone call Stahl, *Right Moves*, 101; "typical review" is 103; Friedman, 104.

292 Gardner Ackley Collins, *More*, 177.

292 Franco Modigliani Collins, *More*, 177; Stein is 186.

292 Alan Greenspan Seymour Zucker, "Massive Tax Cuts Won't Work," *Newsday*, August 9, 1978; also Stigler and *Business Week*.

292 drubbings almost as severe Ibid.

292 passed off in the media Kuttner, *Revolt of the Haves*, 248.

292 Kemp, hunching forward William Safire column, May 4, 1978.

293 dean of Washington pundits David Broder column, *Washington Post* Service, January 21, 1977.

293 Tidewater Inn David Broder column, *Washington Post* Service, May 3, 1978.

293 Major General John K. Singlaub Kyle Burke, *Revolutionaries for the Right: Anticommunist Internationalism and Paramilitary Warfare in the Cold War* (Charlotte: University of North Carolina Press, 2018), 95–96.

293 *Soviet Might/American Myth* Thomas J. McIntyre, *The Fear Brokers* (Boston: Beacon Press, 1981), 132–33; "Singlaub Makes Film, Blasts U.S. Defense," *Deseret News*, June 12, 1978.

293 "I want a trophy" AP, April 20, 1978; Carter, *White House Diary*, 191.

293 White House Correspondents' Ibid., 192; "Press: Adversary Relationship," *Time*, May 15, 1978.

294 sale to Saudi Arabia Strieff, "Arms Wrestle."

294 cedar from Lebanon Carter, *White House Diary*, 192.

294 Gallup reported "Carter Edges Ford and Reagan in Gallup Poll," LAT, May 10, 1978.

294 **"long in the tooth"** Novak, *The Prince of Darkness*, 334; James J. Kilpatrick column, May 6, 1978.

294 **Jesse Helms said** RRC, May 23, 1978.

294 **A Roper poll** Collins, *More*, 178.

295 **"relentlessly wholesome"** "Pat and Debby Show," *People*, April 17, 1978.

295 **In Minnesota** Clendinen and Nagourney, *Out for Good*, 324–36; Fred Fejes, *Gay Rights and Moral Panic: The Origins of America's Debate on Homosexuality* (New York: Palgrave Macmillan, 2008), 173.

295 **"we have been attacked"** Randy Shilts, *The Mayor of Castro Street: The Life and Times of Harvey Milk* (New York: St. Martin's Press, 1982), 223–26, 218.

295 **State Senator John Briggs** Ibid., 219.

296 **Mayor Connie Kennard** ABC News, May 8, 1978, VTVNA.

296 **The reverend leading** UPI, April 29, 1978.

296 **shocking 83 percent** Fejes, *Gay Rights and Moral Panic*, 174.

296 **White House public liaison** "Wichita Repeals Homosexual Law," NYT, May 10 1978.

296 **For her forthrightness** AP, June 1, 1978.

296 ***Old Time Gospel Hour*** *Christianity Today*, June 21, 1978; "The Next Billy Graham," *Esquire*, October 10, 1978.

297 **Three days after Wichita** "Sears, Roebuck: Accounts Closed," *Christianity Today*, June 2, 1978.

297 **Giants Stadium** "Jesus '78," *Christianity Today*, June 2, 1978; Flippen, *Jimmy Carter*, 190; "Remembering Keith Green," PrayerCentral.net; "The Day Jimmy Carter Saved the Jews from Mike Evans," JewishIsrael.com, April 29, 2013; "Andraé Crouch & The Disciples—'Live' At Carnegie Hall," Danelikes.com, August 4, 2012. All accessed April 26, 2020.

297 **That Friday** "Carter Now Seeks a Smaller Tax Cut and a Three Month Delay," NYT, May 13, 1978.

298 **Carter had insisted** "The President's News Conference," April 25, 1978, APP.

298 **his economists** Judith Stein, *Pivotal Decade: How the United States Traded Factories for Finance in the 1970s* (New Haven: Yale University Press, 2010), 194, 199; "Carter, Reacting to Criticism, Is Mulling Whether His Tax Plan Should Be Pared," WSJ, April 21, 1978.

298 **Carter's arms sale** Strieff, "Arms Wrestle."

299 **AIPAC's annual policy conference** AP, May 9, 1978.

299 **"The lobbying pressure"** Carter, *White House Diary*, 194.

300 **emotional Senate debate** Shapiro, *The Last Great Senate*, 167.

300 **"Gang That Couldn't Shoot Straight"** WP, May 18, 1978.

300 **"Can Carter's Presidency Be Redeemed?"** WP, May 16, 1978.

300 **"perhaps the strongest"** "Stampedes on Taxes," BG, May 26, 1978.

300 **Gerald Rafshoon** "The Passionless Presidency," *Atlantic Monthly*, May 1979.

301 **"comes out fuzzy"** Herblock cartoon, WP, May 21, 1978.

301 **which color socks** Meg Jacobs, *Panic at the Pump*, 191.

301 **On May 15** AP, May 16, 1978.

301 **"Wichita and St. Paul"** Fejes, *Gay Rights and Moral Panic*, 177.

301 **Burlington, Vermont** Christopher Hewitt, *Political Violence and Terrorism in Modern America: A Chronology* (Westport, CT: Greenwood, 2005), 118.

301 **angry letters** "Principle of Nonviolent Opposition," *Burlington Free Press*, May 25, 1978.

301 **United Presbyterian Church** UPI, May 6, 1978; AP, May 23, 1978.

301 **Jerry Falwell preached** Daniel K. Williams, *God's Own Party: The Making of the Christian Right* (New York: Oxford University Press, 2010), 152.

302 **Eugene voted** Fejes, *Gay Rights and Moral Panic*, 177.

302 **Milk had enjoyed** Shilts, *The Mayor of Castro Street*, 220–21.

302 **"the lack of *hope*"** "How the Harvey Milk 'Hope Speech' Resonates This National Coming Out Day," *Advocate*, October 11, 2012.

303 **Texas's 19th District** Jean Edward Smith, *Bush* (New York: Simon & Schuster, 2016), 35.

303 **In Iowa** McIntyre, *The Fear Brokers*, 137, 142.

304 **In New Jersey** HE, June 17, 1978.

304 *Chicago Tribune* **columnist** "Nation: GOP New Right Has Money and Much to Learn," CT, May 31, 1978.

304 **enraged conservatives** Colacello, *Ronnie and Nancy*, 471–72.

304 **"Reagan: More Serious Than Ever"** WP, May 16, 1978.

304 **Dick Wirthlin wrapped** See *Selected Congressional Districts*, Vols. 3–17, and *Survey Overview* and *Profiles of Selected California and Texas Congressional Districts*, RRPL, Box 85.

304 **CFR was on its way** Adam Clymer, *Drawing the Line at the Big Ditch: The Panama Canal Treaties and the Rise of the Right* (Lawrence: University Press of Kansas, 2008), 138.

304 **Peter Hannaford met** Novak, *The Prince of Darkness*, 334–35.

305 **"drastic" and desperate"** "The Jarvis-Gann Proposition," WSJ, April 25, 1978.

CHAPTER FIFTEEN

306 **"Sign this"** Peter Schrag, *Paradise Lost: California's Experience, America's Future* (New York: New Press, 1998), 142. Wartime ad is 133.

306 **By the early 1960s** Robert Kuttner, *Revolt of the Haves: Tax Rebellions and Hard Times* (New York: Simon & Schuster, 1980), passim.

306 **Black Panther Party** Robert O. Self, *American Babylon: Race and the Struggle for Postwar Oakland* (Princeton: Princeton University Press), 300–304.

308 **"political Richter scale"** AP, August 26, 1976.

308 **a strange man** "The Puzzling Politics of Jerry Brown," WP, February 5, 1978.

308 **"ecological limits"** Rick Perlstein, *Invisible Bridge; The Fall of Nixon and the Rise of Reagan* (New York: Simon & Schuster, 2014), 687.

308 **decrepit mental hospitals** CBS News, December 22, 1978, VTVNA.

308 **Jesse Unruh** "The Puzzling Politics of Jerry Brown."

308 **less than $36,000** Kuttner, *Revolt of the Haves*, 8.

309 **"split rate"** Ibid., 68.

309 **"*You* are the people"** James T. Patterson, *Restless Giant: The United States from Watergate to Bush V. Gore* (New York: Oxford University press, 2007), 133.

310 **The experts "thought"** Kuttner, *Revolt of the Haves*, 71.

310 **"stupidest people"** Alan Crawford, *Thunder on the Right: The "New Right" and the Politics of Resentment* (New York: Pantheon, 1981), 102.

310 **Proposition C** "Is Tax Limitation a Dead Idea," HE, November 13, 1976.

310 **"It may look good"** Kuttner, *Revolt of the Haves*, 72–73; for gaffes, 77.

311 **experts' bluff** Ibid., 73.

312 "Save the American Dream" KTLA, May 31, UCLA Film and Television Archive, YouTube.com, accessed April 2, 2020.

312 "cotton-picking legislators" "Homeowners Get Tax News, Vow to Back Prop. 13," LAT, May 19, 1978.

312 Tax Limitation Conference AP, May 22, 1978.

313 American Legislative Exchange Council Dan Kaufman, *The Fall of Wisconsin: The Conservative Conquest of a Progressive Bastion and the Future of American Politics* (New York: W.W. Norton, 2018), 133–34.

313 *Newsweek* agreed "The Great Tax Revolt," *Newsweek*, June 19, 1978.

313 "The damn thing" William Safire column, February 27, 1979.

314 "unions are woven" Matt Stoller, *Goliath: The 100-Year War Between Monopoly Power and Democracy* (New York: Simon & Schuster, 2019), 188.

314 Dwight Eisenhower in 1952 "The Text of General Eisenhower's Speech at A.F.L. Convention," NYT, September 18, 1952.

314 "Dunlop Commission" Mike Davis, *Prisoners of the American Dream: Politics and Economy in the History of the American Working Class* (New York: Verso, 1986), 134; Jefferson Cowie, " 'A One-Sided Class War': Rethinking Doug Fraser's 1978 Resignation from the Labor Management Group," *Labor History* 44, No. 4 (2003).

314 J. P. Stevens Jefferson Cowie, *Stayin' Alive: The 1970s and the Last Days of the Working Class* (New York: New Press, 2010), 289–90.

314 The bill introduced Ibid., 292; Thomas J. McIntyre, *The Fear Brokers* (Boston: Beacon Press, 1981), 90.

314 $3.4 million Judith Stein, *Pivotal Decade: How the United States Traded Factories for Finance in the 1970s* (New Haven: Yale University Press, 2010), 184.

315 former labor secretaries AP, September 8, 1977.

315 Stuart Eizenstat argued Cowie, *Stayin' Alive*, 292.

315 "difficult to overestimate" Stein, *Pivotal Decade*, 184–86; also card check, Deering Milliken, and "Cro-Magnon types."

315 J. P. Stevens's headquarters Cowie, *Stayin' Alive*, 290.

315 "crime pays" Tom Wicker column, *New York Times* Service, August 15, 1977.

315 illegally fired See National Labor Relations Board annual reports, 1970–1978.

316 In the first ten years Cowie, *Stayin' Alive*, 289.

316 as Orrin Hatch Hatch column, *Pacific News* Service, June 15, 1978.

316 1970–78 period See National Labor Relations Board annual reports, 1970–1978.

316 big strikes Lane Windham, *Knocking on Labor's Door: Union Organizing in the 1970s and the Roots of the New Economic Divide* (Charlotte: University of North Carolina Press, 2017).

316 "common situs" Davis, *Prisoners of the American Dream*, 134.

316 "venereal disease" "Salute to Reagan," WP, June 10, 1977.

317 policy committee Joel Rogers and Thomas Ferguson, "Labor Law Reform and Its Enemies," *Nation*, January 6, 1979.

317 "could push our country" Walter Guzzardi Jr., "Business Is Learning How to Win in Washington," *Fortune*, March 27, 1978, 36.

318 in his memoir Orrin Hatch, *Square Peg: Confessions of a Citizen Senator* (New York: Basic Books, 2002), 24.

318 "When I first arrived" "Big Business on the Offensive," NYT *Magazine*, December 9, 1979.

318 reported on their progress Mark Green and Andrew Buchsbaum, *The Corporate Lobbies: Political Profiles of the Business Roundtable and the Chamber of Commerce* (Washington: Public Citizen, 1980).

318   "singularly inconsistent" Stein, *Pivotal Decade*, 188.

318   "major economic burden" UPI, April 12, 1978.

319   most restaurants Green and Buchsbaum, *The Corporate Lobbies*.

319   Senator Howard Metzenbaum Ibid., 126; also for Senate post office.

319   "What will happen" Guzzardi, "Business Is Learning."

319   only $2.5 million John Judis, *The Paradox of American Democracy: Elites, Special Interests, and the Betrayal of Public Trust* (New York: Pantheon, 2000), 140.

319   Dale Bumpers " 'Grass-Roots' Lobbying in Full Flower," WP, May 28, 1972; Green and Buchsbaum, *The Corporate Lobbies*; also for Percy.

319   "doesn't even matter" McIntyre, *The Fear Brokers*, 93.

320   "They go computer" "Computer Mail Spews a Blizzard of Influence on Congress," WP, January 29, 1978.

320   cheap air travel Thomas Edsall, *The New Politics of Inequality* (New York: W.W. Norton, 1985), 125; Green and Buchsbaum, *The Corporate Lobbies*.

320   "victims' vigil" *Washington Star* Service, May 10, 1978; "Senators Face Heavy Labor-Bill Lobbying," *Louisville Courier-Journal*, June 4, 1978; "Furious Controversy Falls to Senators," *Des Moines Register*, May 14, 1978.

320   "our macho" Green and Buchsbaum, *The Corporate Lobbies*.

320   George Meany "George Meany Appeals for a New Approach to the Labor Law Reform Bill," WSJ, May 4, 1978.

320   "What are the real" UPI, May 30, 1978.

320   too complex For origins and effects of post-Watergate congressional reform see Julian Zelizer, *On Capitol Hill: The Struggle to Reform Congress and Its Consequences, 1948–2000*, and Edsall, *The New Politics of Inequality*.

322   "holy war" James Gross, *Broken Promise: The Subversion of U.S. Labor Relations Policy, 1947–1994* (Philadelphia: Temple University Press, 1995), 239; Hatch, *Square Peg*, 29; Green and Buchsbaum, *The Corporate Lobbies*, 127.

322   *First National Bank of Boston* John Nichols and Robert W. McChesney, *Dollarocracy: How the Money and Media Election Complex Is Destroying America* (New York: Nation Books), 70–71, 82–83.

322   second was a gut-punch Jefferson Decker, *The Other Rights Rebellion: Conservative Lawyers and the Remaking of American Government* (New York: Oxford University Press, 2016), 50–54; McIntyre, *The Fear Brokers*, 66.

323   "Stop OSHA" "OSHA Undaunted By High Court's Warrant Ruling," *Beaver County Times*, August 15, 1978.

323   "Here's a citizen" RRB 76-08, track B8, "More About OSHA," recorded January 19, 1977.

323   Bob Kasten *Milwaukee Journal*, October 30, 1976.

323   "protects commercial buildings" *Marshall v. Barlow's, Inc.*, 436 U.S. 307 (1978).

323   "thousands of handicapped" KTLA, May 31, 1978.

323   school districts Schrag, *Paradise Lost*, 146.

324   "taxpayers' gravy train" Ibid., 139.

324   press conference KTLA, May 31, 1978.

324   "The black and the brown" Ibid.

324   Blacks disagreed Thomas Edsall and Jane Byrne Edsall, *Chain Reaction: The Impact of Race, Rights, and Taxes on American Politics* (New York: W.W. Norton, 1991), 130.

324   "moochers and loafers" KTLA, May 31, 1978.

324   "New Reactionaries" RRC, May 31, 1978.

324   "New Poor" William Safire column, June 1, 1978.

324 **"consumer fraud"** "Brown Calls Prop. 13 'Crazy,' " *San Francisco Examiner*, May 28, 1978.

325 **Milton Friedman** Joel Fox, "Proposition 13 and Milton Friedman," *Fox and Hounds Daily*, August 6, 2009.

325 **evening before Election** NBC News, June 5, 1978, VTVNA.

325 **In New Jersey** "Bell's Victory: Tax Cut Idea Very Popular," WP, June 8, 1978; author correspondence with Elliot Curson; HE, June 17, 1978.

325 **" 'from the prosperous' "** Molly C. Michelmore, *Tax and Spend: The Welfare State, Tax Politics, and the Limits of American Liberalism* (State College: University of Pennsylvania Press, 2012), 131.

326 **Jules Witcover buttonholed** Jules Witcover, *The Making of an Ink-Stained Wretch: Half a Century Pounding the Political Beat* (Baltimore: Johns Hopkins University Press, 2005), 228; Witcover and Jack Germond, *Blue Smoke and Mirrors: How Reagan Won and Why Carter Lost the Election of 1980* (New York: Viking, 1981), 100.

326 **Jarvis gloated** McIntyre, *The Fear Brokers*, 35.

326 **Paul Weyrich** Adam Clymer, *Drawing the Line at the Big Ditch: The Panama Canal Treaties and the Rise of the Right* (Lawrence: University Press of Kansas, 2008), 126.

326 **Bill Bradley** "Bell's Victory: Tax Cut Idea Very Popular," WP, June 8, 1978.

326 **same day in Ohio** Kuttner, *Revolt of the Haves*, 97.

327 **claimed victories** "Anti-Abortionists' Impact Is Felt in Elections Across the Nation," NYT, June 20, 1978.

327 **New York City court** "Group Fighting Abortion Planning to Step Up Its Drive," NYT, July 3, 1978.

327 **Emma Goldman Clinic** Christopher Hewitt, *Political Violence and Terrorism in Modern America: A Chronology* (Westport, CT: Greenwood, 2005), 118.

327 **Two weeks later** "Group Fighting Abortion Planning."

327 **"Senator Long"** Hatch, *Square Peg*, 32.

328 **pro-labor aide** Cowie, *Stayin' Alive*, 294.

328 **first cloture vote** Ian Shapiro, *The Last Great Senate: Courage and Statesmanship in Times of Crisis* (New York: Public Affairs Books, 2012), 179.

328 **On June 11** "Revolt Against Taxes . . . and Performance," WP, June 11, 1978.

328 **Lou Harris's pollsters** "How the Capital Gains Fight Was Won," *Wharton* magazine, Winter 1979.

328 **House and Senate** "Michael Pertschuk and the Federal Trade Commission," John F. Kennedy School of Government Case Program #C16–81–387.0 (1981).

328 **entire cabinet meeting** Jimmy Carter, *White House Diary* (New York: Macmillan, 2010), 202.

328 **Chairman Brock filed** "The G.O.P.'s Pre-1980 Lawsuit," NYT, August 4, 1978.

328 **state legislative candidates** Connie Paige, *The Right to Lifers: Who They Are, How They Operate, and Where They Get Their Money* (New York: Summit Books, 1983), 189.

328 **the showdown** Hatch, *Square Peg*, 35–40; Shapiro, *The Last Great Senate*, 181–84.

329 **"I think it's just"** NBC News, June 22, 1978, VTVNA.

329 **"Santa Claus"** Dale McFetters column, Scripps-Howard Service, July 3, 1978.

329 **Douglas Fraser** Cowie, " 'A One-Sided Class War.' "

330 **Ray Marshall** Shapiro, *The Last Great Senate*, 183.

330 **"Reagan's Magic"** Tom Wicker column, *New York Times* Service, June 13, 1978.

330 **trip to New York** Schedule, June 12 and 13, 1978, RRPL, Box 71.

330 **"Kefauver Amendment"** RRB, 78-08, track B2, "Drugs"; materials in RRPL Box 246 indicate it was recorded between June 19 and July 7, 1978.

330 **strategy session** Deaver notes, June 14, 1978, RRPL Box 103.

331 **New York State** *Newsday*, August 11, 1978.

331 **In Georgia** "Washington Chatter," Newspaper Enterprise Association, June 17, 1978; Tanya Melich, *The Republican War Against Women: An Insider's Report From Behind the Lines* (New York: Bantam, 1996), 94; W&G, May 22, 1978.

332 **In California** ENIR, June 8, 1978; Robert Novak, *The Prince of Darkness: 50 Years Reporting in Washington* (New York: Crown Forum, 2007), 321–22.

332 **And in Washington** *New York Times* Service, June 18, 1978.

CHAPTER SIXTEEN

333 **fictional congresswoman** *Doonesbury*, August 13, 1978.

333 **cover of *Time*** "Tax Revolt!" *Time*, June 19, 1978.

333 **exact same words** "Tax Revolt!" *Newsweek*, June 19, 1978.

333 **visited Capitol Hill** "Coast Author of the Tax Cut Scouts Capital," NYT, June 20, 1978.

333 **Harris said** Bruce J. Schulman, *The Seventies: The Great Shift in American Culture, Society, and Politics* (New York: Simon & Schuster, 2001), 212.

333 **In Michigan** AP, August 15, 1978.

334 **In Massachusetts** *Newsday*, August 11, 1978. Also for Delaware, Hawaii, Nevada, Indiana, and Utah.

334 **In Idaho** Robert Kuttner, *Revolt of the Haves: Tax Rebellions and Hard Times* (New York: Simon & Schuster, 1980), 148.

334 **Jim Whittenburg** Ibid., 296; AP, December 14, 1977; UPI, April 13, 1983.

334 **"We used to be the kooks"** Kuttner, *Revolt of the Haves*, 276.

334 **"a new kind of class war"** Jason Stahl, *Right Moves: The Conservative Think Tank in American Political Culture Since 1945* (Chapel Hill: University of North Carolina Press, 2016), 104.

334 **"property-owning class"** "Voting for Capitalism," *Fortune*, July 17, 1978.

334 **"Watts riot"** "Calif. Taxpayer Revolt Spreading Like Wildfire," *New York Daily News*, June 5, 1978.

334 **"You certainly had"** Peter Schrag, *Paradise Lost: California's Experience, America's Future* (New York: New Press, 1998), 158.

334 **"a cloven hoof"** Joseph Kraft column, June 13, 1978; also LAT/CBS poll.

335 **George McGovern** "Prop. 13 Stuns Liberal Leaders," LAT, June 25, 1978; "McGovern Asks Stand Against Tax Cut Tide," NYT, June 18, 1978.

335 **Jesse Jackson** Colman McCarthy column, WP, June 23, 1978.

335 **"Joe McCarthy"** "Tax-Cut Issue Dominates State Legislators' Parley," NYT, July 8, 1978.

335 **would not "tolerate"** "The President's News Conference," June 26, 1978, APP.

335 **"millionaire's relief bill"** AP, June 29, 1978.

335 **White House aide** Kuttner, *Revolt of the Haves*, 93.

335 **poll reported** "How the Capital Gains Fight Was Won," *Wharton*, Winter 1979.

335 **"no stopping"** "Momentum for Tax Cut," NYT, July 17, 1978.

335 **helpful context** "The Economic Wind's Blowing Toward the Right—For Now"; "Simon: Preaching the Word for Olin," both NYT, July 16, 1978.

336 **Dr. Richard Lesher** Alyssa Katz, *The Influence Machine: The U.S. Chamber of Commerce and the Corporate Capture of American Life* (New York: Spiegel & Grau, 2015), 40–50.

336 **"Keep America Beautiful"** Sharon Lerner, "Waste Only: How the Plastics Industry Is Fighting to Keep Polluting the World," *Intercept*, July 20, 2019; author correspondence with Finis Dunaway; *Solid Waste Management Act of 1972*, Hearings before the Subcommittee on the Environment of the Committee on Armed Services, United States Senate, Ninety-Second Congress, Second Session, March 6, 10, and 13, 1972.

337 **as Ronald Reagan** RRB 75-08, track 09, "Land Use," recorded April 1975.

337 **greatest asset** Thomas Edsall, *The New Politics of Inequality* (New York: W. W. Norton, 1985), 124.

337 **"Citizen's Choice"** Katz, *The Influence Machine*, 47–51.

337 **Ronald Reagan conferred** RRB 76-05, track B2, "Citizen's Choice," recorded November 16, 1976.

337 **Jay Van Andel** Robert L. Fitzpatrick and Joyce K. Reynolds, *False Profits: Seeking Financial and Spiritual Deliverance in Multi-Level Marketing and Pyramid Schemes* (Herald Press, 1997).

338 **Christian fundamentalist** Connie Paige, *The Right to Lifers: Who They Are, How They Operate, and Where They Get Their Money* (New York: Summit Books, 1983), 124.

338 **FTC filed suit** *In the Matter of Amway Corporation, Inc. et al., Final Order, Opinion, etc., In Regard to Alleged Violations of the Federal Communications Act*, Docket 9023. Complaint, March 25—Final Order, May 8, 1979.

338 **Liberty Fund** Steven M. Teles, *The Rise of the Conservative Legal Movement: The Battle for Control of the Law* (Princeton: Princeton University Press, 2008), 111–15.

338 **Henry Manne** Ibid., 90–91.

339 **National Legal Center** Jefferson Decker, *The Other Rights Rebellion: Conservative Lawyers and the Remaking of American Government* (New York: Oxford University Press, 2016), 95–98.

339 **Ronald Reagan loved** RRB 75-12, track 11, "Pacific Legal Foundation," recorded June 1975.

339 **"93% of those surveyed"** Katz, *The Influence Machine*, 93.

339 **"Don't Buy Books"** WABC-TV News, June 19, 1978, at YouTube.com; *Saturday Night Live*, May 20, 1978, both accessed April 25, 2020.

340 **town of Hyden** Robert Sam Anson, *Exile: The Unquiet Oblivion of Richard Nixon* (New York: Simon & Schuster, 1984), 191–94.

340 **Republican fundraiser** *Philadelphia Inquirer*, August 30, 1978.

340 **"back to the Cold War"** Arthur M. Schlesinger Jr., *Journals: 1952–2000* (New York: Penguin, 2007), 393.

340 **We, like our forebears** "Address at Wake Forest University in Winston-Salem, North Carolina," March 17, 1978, APP.

341 **All thirty-eight** Adam Clymer, *Drawing the Line at the Big Ditch: The Panama Canal Treaties and the Rise of the Right* (Lawrence: University Press of Kansas, 2008), 164.

341 **"physically liquidated"** "Zbigniew Brzezinski, National Security Advisor to Jimmy Carter, Dies at 89," NYT, May 26, 2017.

341 **"infighting that could"** Alan Wolfe, "Carter Plays at Hawks and Doves," *Nation*, June 24, 1978. This essay is the best source for understanding the intellectual tensions built into Jimmy Carter's foreign policy.

342 **"stapling Vance's"** James Fallows, "The Passionless Presidency," *Atlantic Monthly*, May 1979; Robert Schlesinger, *White House Ghosts: Presidents and Their Speechwriters* (New York: Simon & Schuster, 2008), 287–88.

342   **"surprisingly harmonious"** Jimmy Carter, *White House Diary* (New York: Macmillan, 2010), 198.

342   **"I'm convinced that"** "Address at the Commencement Exercises at the United States Naval Academy," June 7, 1978, APP.

342   **"*And now—war!*"** Fallows, "The Passionless Presidency."

342   **"Two Different Speeches"** WP, June 8, 1978.

342   **Senator Frank Church** *Washington Star*, June 8, 1978.

342   **"natives to kill each other"** Nicholas von Hoffman column, June 16, 1978.

342   **The Soviet newspaper** "Pravda Hits 'Cold War' Tone of Carter's Annapolis Speech," WP, June 12, 1978.

343   **Fourteen members** "14 House Members Seek Clarification," WP, June 12, 1978.

343   **"example of confusion"** Wolfe, "Carter Plays at Hawks and Doves."

343   **down to 38 percent** William Safire column, July 3, 1978.

343   **another scandal** Ryan Grim, *This Is Your Country on Drugs: The Secret History of Getting High in America* (Hoboken, NJ: Wiley, 2010), 67–74; AP, July 21, 1978.

344   **Daniel Schorr badgered** "The President's News Conference," July 20, 1978, APP.

344   **"Social Gadflies"** Emily Dufton, *Grass Roots: The Rise and Fall of Marijuana in America* (New York: Basic Books, 2017), 116.

344   **"pregnant every nine months"** Ibid.; "obey the law," 118.

344   **"high and dry"** "Tower Ticker," CT, November 8, 1978.

344   **Howard Baker demanded** AP, July 25, 1978.

344   **"Carter's Really Blown It"** Marianne Means column, *Lansing State Journal*, August 1, 1978.

345   **value of the dollar** Dominic Sandbrook, *Mad as Hell: The Crisis of the 1970s and the Rise of the Populist Right* (New York: Anchor Books, 2012), 233–34.

345   **In an op-ed** "Inflation Undermines Honesty at Many Levels," *Minneapolis Star Tribune*, August 6, 1978.

345   **Jimmy the Greek** " 'Greek' Says It's 2 to 1 Carter Retires," WP, August 13, 1978.

345   **news from Tehran** Christian Caryl, *Strange Rebels: 1979 and the Birth of the 21st Century* (New York: Basic Books, 2013), 141.

CHAPTER SEVENTEEN

346   **East Bay town** Author correspondence with Robert Anderson.

346   **municipality of Inglewood** "Proposition 13, in 5 Months, Has Not Spurred Major Spending Cutbacks," NYT, November 7, 1978.

346   **"segregation academies"** Joseph Crespino, *In Search of Another Country: Mississippi and the Conservative Counterrevolution* (Princeton: Princeton University Press, 2009), chapters 6 and 7; Stephanie R. Rolph, *Resisting Equality: The Citizens' Council, 1954–1989* (Baton Rouge, LA: LSU Press, 2008).

346   **Orangeburg, South Carolina** "Notice," *Orangeburg Times and Democrat*, July 15, 1965; "Independent School Head Pleased with Meeting Here," *Orangeburg Times and Democrat*, March 30, 1966; "Private School Development Issue at Cameron Meeting," *Orangeburg Times and Democrat*, March 23, 1967.

346   **Wallace presidential campaign** "Wallace Will Be in Greenville Tuesday, July 18," *Orangeburg Times and Democrat*, July 10, 1967.

347   **"regional ideals and values"** Joseph Crespino, *Strom Thurmond's America* (New York: Hill & Wang, 2012), 268.

347 **thumpingly unanimous** *Alexander v. Holmes County Board of Education*, 396 U.S. 19 (1969).

347 **Governor John Bell Williams** "The South Fights an Agonizing But Losing Battle," NYT, January 18, 1970.

347 **Central Holmes Academy** *Green v. Kennedy*, 309 F. Supp. 1127 (D.D.C. 1970).

348 **In Dothan, Alabama** "How Hillary Clinton Went Undercover to Examine Race in Education," NYT, December 28, 2015.

348 **IRS tightened** Crespino, *In Search of Another Country*, 253.

348 **"three column inches"** *Tax-Exempt Status of Private Schools*, Hearings Before the Subcommittee on Oversight of the Committee on Ways and Means, House of Representatives, Ninety-Sixth Congress, First Session, Part 1 of 2, February 20, 21, 1979, 16.

348 **"most exciting development"** 1967 article quoted in William H. Willimon, "Should Churches Buy into the Education Business?" *Christianity Today*, May 5, 1978.

348 **In 1954** Crespino, *In Search of Another Country*, 249–50.

348 **"evils of Communism"** Ibid., 244.

348 **study published in 1976** Ibid., 249.

349 **"versions of the humanistic"** "Christian Schools versus the I.R.S.," *Public Interest*, Fall 1980.

349 **Philadelphia Association of Christian Schools** Ronald J. Sider, ed., *The Chicago Declaration* (Eugene, OR: Wipf & Stock, 1969), 14.

349 **"becomes a Western jungle"** "Chief of Arizona Education Says Atheists Have Taken Over," *Arizona Republic*, October 20, 1973.

349 **segregation of Memphis** "School Conflict in the South Is Intensifying," NYT, August 19, 1973; Martin P. Claussen and Evelyn Bills Claussen, eds., *The Voice of Christian and Jewish Dissenters in America: U.S. Internal Revenue Service Hearings on Proposed 'Discrimination' Tax Controls over Christian, Jews, and Secular Private Schools, Dec. 5, 6, 7, 8, 1978* (Washington, D.C.: Piedmont Press, 1982). Testimony from Maxine A. Smith on 43, Kenneth L Dean on 67, and Wayne Allen on 500.

350 *McGuffey's Eclectic Readers* "Less Is More, Preaches Headmaster Robert Thoburn, and the New Right Says 'Amen,' " *People*, June 22, 1981; Skipp Porteous, "Anti-Semitism [III]: Its Prevalence within the Christian Right," ShlomSherman.com, May 1994.

350 **"no formal ban"** Frances FitzGerald, "A Disciplined, Charging Army," *New Yorker*, May 18, 1981.

350 **"Bible is all we need"** William H. Willimon, "Should Churches Buy Into the Education Business?" *Christianity Today*, May 5, 1978.

350 **Robert Billings's** *A Guide to the Christian School* (Hammond, IN: Hyles-Anderson Publishers, 1971 [1st ed.]).

351 **"so-called Christian Schools"** Willimon, "Should Churches Buy Into the Education Business?"

350 **Janice Marie Whisner** "Parents Back Christian Schools as Alternative," NYT, October 26, 1976; Alan N. Grover, *Ohio's Trojan Horse: A Warning to Christian Schools Everywhere* (Greenville, SC: Bob Jones University Press, 1977).

351 **North Carolina superior court** "Christian Schools: Learning in the Courtroom," *Christianity Today*, September 22, 1978.

351 **Bob Jones University** "The Story of *Bob Jones University v. United States*: Race, Religion, and Congress's Extraordinary Acquiescence," *Columbia Public Law & Legal Theory Working Papers*, March 11, 2010.

351 **little Hillsdale College** RRC, February 3, 1978.

351   **Louisville, Nebraska** "Faith Baptist Church Opens K–12 with 16 Students," *Platts-mouth Journal*, August 29, 1977; "Possible Court Case Would Test Right of School To Set Minimum Standards for School Children," *Plattsmouth Journal*, October 6, 1977; UPI, March 4, 1978; "Louisville Baptist Congregation, Pastor Will Defend Their School in County Court," *Lincoln Journal Star*, March 7, 1978; AP, November 16, 1978; "Nebraska Baptists Defy State Over School Control," NYT, January 9, 1984.

351   **In Concord, New Hampshire** AP, August 31, 1977; AP, September 2, 1977; AP, September 3, 1977; UPI, September 7, 1977; UPI, September 13, 1977.

352   **Kurtz gave a speech** "Difficult Definitional Problems in Tax Administration: Religion and Race," speech before Public Law Institute conference, January 9, 1978, reprinted in Claussen and Claussen, eds., *The Voice of Christian and Jewish Dissenters in America*, 1.

352   **noted with surprise** "GOP Blows Opportunity on Tuition Tax Credit," HE, August 26, 1978.

352   **Orrin Hatch** Erling Skorpen, "Another Viewpoint," *Bangor Daily News*, June 4, 1980; "Backing Is Sought for New School Act," Letter to Editor, *Asbury Park Press*, November 9, 1973.

353   **In North Carolina** "Christian Schools: Learning in the Courtroom," *Christianity Today*, September 22, 1978; AP, July 27, 1978; James J. Kilpatrick column, August 4, 1978; AP, September 5, 1978.

353   **On June 21** Carol Felsenthal, *Sweetheart of the Silent Majority: The Biography of Phyllis Schlafly* (New York: Doubleday, 1981), 289; "U.S. Family Conference Delayed Amid Disputes and Resignations," NYT, June 19, 1978.

353   **column observed** Martha Angle and Robert Walters column, NEA Service, July 2, 1978.

353   **one hundred thousand marched** J. Brooks Flippen, *Jimmy Carter, the Politics of Family, and the Rise of the Religious Right* (Athens, GA: University of Georgia Press, 2011), 173.

353   **John Ashcroft's suit** UPI, July 27, 1978.

353   **rickety house in Concord** AP, September 21, 1978.

353   **"Is Anyone Out There Learning?"** "CBS News Examines Public Education," *South Idaho Press*, August 20, 1978.

354   *Human Events* **howled** "GOP Blows Opportunity on Tuition Tax Credit," HE, August 26, 1978.

354   **"Mothers have long observed"** Connaught Coyne Marshner, *Blackboard Tyranny* (New Rochelle, NY: Arlington House, 1978).

354   **Senator Hatch responded** HE, October 7, 1978, quoting Hatch in August 15 debate on tuition tax credit.

354   **"tolerance of homosexuals"** "Tax Report: A Special Summary and Forecast of Federal and State Tax Developments," WSJ, August 30, 1978. See Department of the Treasurer, Internal Revenue Service, *Internal Revenue Cumulative Bulletin 1978-2, July–December*, 172–73.

354   **"Proposed Revenue Procedure"** *Federal Register* of August 22, 1978, 37296.

354   **an estimated 3,500** "Senator Protests Linking of Schools' Race, Tax Status," *Detroit Free Press*, December 6, 1978.

354   **Christian school of 1,447** Daniel K. Williams, "Jerry Falwell's Sunbelt Politics: The Regional Origins of the Moral Majority," *Journal of Policy History* 11, No. 2 (2010).

355   **"legislative grace"** Claussen and Claussen, eds., *The Voice of Christian and Jewish Dissenters in America*, Arthur Fleming testimony, 30. The fundamentalist editors

of a book of hearing transcripts on the subject added "[*sic*]" following the word "grace."

355 **Richard Viguerie** "Speakers Deplore IRS Proposal to Tax Schools Ruled Discriminatory," *Des Moines Register*, December 6, 1978; "Less Is More, Preaches Headmaster Robert Thoburn and the New Right Says 'Amen,' " *People*, June 22, 1981; Claussen and Claussen, *The Voice of Christian and Jewish Dissenters in America*, xv, Thoburn and Viguerie testimony; David Nevin and Robert Bills, *The Schools That Fear Built* (Washington, D.C.: Acropolis Books, 1976), 77; McIntyre, *The Fear Brokers*, 98.

355 **Robert Billings's son** William Martin, *With God on Our Side: The Rise of the Religious Right in America* (New York: Broadway Books, 1996), 152, 173.

355 **Fred Silverman** Elena Levine, *Wallowing in Sex: The New Sexual Culture of 1970s American Television* (Durham, NC: Duke University Press, 2007), passim; James T. Patterson, *Restless Giant: The United States from Watergate to Bush v. Gore* (New York: Oxford University Press, 2007), 46; Michele Hilmes, ed., *NBC: America's Network* (Berkeley: University of California Press, 238).

356 **"your cleavage situation"** *Doonesbury*, May 25, 1978.

356 **Roone Arledge** Ron Powers, *The Newscasters: The News Business as Show Business* (New York: Leisure Books, 1980), 18, 84–87; Travis Vogan, *ABC Sports: The Rise and Fall of Network Sports Television* (Berkeley: University of California Press, 2018).

356 **Local news was worse** Powers, *The Newscasters*, passim.

357 *Animal House* Lisa Wade, "How American Colleges Became Bastions of Sex, Booze, and Entitlement," *Time*, January 6, 2017; Caitlin Flannigan, "Pop Culture's War on Fraternities," *Atlantic*, February 18. 2014; "Toga! Toga! Toga!: The Toga Party, Popping Up on Campuses Across the Country," WP, September 26, 1978; "Business: Bed Sheets Bonanza," *Time*, October 23, 1978.

357 **"Pail and Shovel Party"** " 'Pail and Shovel' Rules the Campus," WP, October 19, 1978; AP, October 14, 1978.

358 *In the beginning* My account of the Camp David Accords relies on Lawrence Wright, *Thirteen Days in September: Carter, Begin, and Sadat at Camp David* (New York: Knopf, 2014).

363 **"political slate" was "wiped clean"** W&G, September 19. 1978.

363 **"Moonies" descended** Paige, *The Right to Lifers*, 117.

363 **Robert Short** McIntyre, *The Fear Brokers*, 26; "Republicans Defend Tax Cut Proposal on Nationwide Blitz," WP, September 22, 1978; Martha Angle and Robert Walters column, NEA Service, October 3, 1978.

363 **Dr. Carolyn Gerster** Paige, *The Right to Lifers*, 117.

364 **David Boren** "Gutter Shootout in Oklahoma," WP, August 12, 1978.

364 **Ed King** Lily Geismer, *"Don't Blame Us": Suburban Liberals and the Transformation of the Democratic Party* (Princeton: Princeton University Press, 2014), 258; "Dukakis Upset, Brooke Leads in Mass.," WP, September 20, 1978.

364 **Avi Nelson** "Brooke Running Scared in Primary," WP, September 17, 1978; Clymer, *Drawing the Line at the Big Ditch*, 127.

364 **activist in Alabama** "Voters' Feelings Undefined," *Anniston Star*, September 1, 1978.

364 **in DeKalb, Illinois** UPI, September 1, 1978.

364 **small-town Southern newspaper** "Editorials from Around the State," *Montgomery Advertiser*, September 2, 1978.

364 **Jeff Bell** McIntyre, *The Fear Brokers*, 30.

364 **Howard Phillips** Patrick Buchanan column, September 7, 1978; Dudley Clendinen and Adam Nagourney, *Out for Good: The Struggle to Build a Gay Rights Movement in America* (New York: Simon & Schuster, 2001), 329.

365 **Roger Jepsen** Clymer, *Drawing the Line at the Big Ditch*, 122.

365 **Strom Thurmond** Crespino, *Strom Thurmond's America*, 280.

365 **"To Candidates, Right Looks Right"** *Time*, September 25, 1978.

365 **Experts estimated** "Tax Bill Conferees Begin Work Today," WP, October 12, 1978.

365 **a critic observed** Robert Kuttner, *Revolt of the Haves: Tax Rebellions and Hard Times* (New York: Simon & Schuster, 1980), 247.

365 **"the most complete agreement"** TRB, *New Republic*, August 19, 1978.

365 **"REPUBLICAN TAX CLIPPER"** "GOP on Tour to Support Tax Cut Bill," *Newsday*, September 21, 1978; "Republicans Defend Tax Cut Proposal on Nationwide Blitz," WP, September 22, 1978; "GOP Brass Blitzes Here for Tax Cut," CT, September 23, 1978; Briefings: Republican Tax Cut Blitz, RRPL, Box 52.

365 **Tax Reform Research Group** UPI, September 22, 1978.

366 **"Year of the Elephant"** RRC, September 26, 1978.

CHAPTER EIGHTEEN

367 **"Kingston Group"** July 26, 1978, RRPL, Box 73; Frank van der Linden, *The Real Reagan: What He Believes, What He Has Accomplished, What We Can Expect from Him* (New York: William Morrow & Co., 1981), 156.

367 **lunch with reporters** "Reagan Weighs Trip to Mainland China; Indicates Move to Political Center," LAT, July 20, 1978; "Crane Weighs Race for President," NYT, July 20, 1978.

367 **"moving toward the center"** W&G, December 21, 1978.

368 **"China Lobby"** A good summary can be found in Kyle Burke, *Revolutionaries for the Right: Anticommunist Internationalism and Paramilitary Warfare in the Cold War* (Chapel Hill: University of North Carolina Press), 13–15.

368 **regaled a banquet** "Address by the Honorable Ronald Reagan to the Chinese Consolidated Benevolent Association and the Committee to Conservative Chinese Culture," July 17, 1978, DH, "Press Releases" files.

368 **massacring ten thousand** Burke, *Revolutionaries for the Right*, 14.

368 **wrong length of hair** "Freddy's Hair," *Savage Minds: Notes and Queries in Anthropology*, January 29, 2016.

368 **"help soften his right-wing"** "Reagan Weighs Trip to Mainland China; Indicates Move to Political Center," LAT, July 20, 1978.

368 **"other than blacks"** "Topics," NYT, July 23, 1978.

368 **that "black Americans want"** Speech to Georgia Citizens for the Republic, January 21, 1978, RRPL, Box 71.

368 **doing damage control** Draft and text of "RR's Statement on U.S. China Relations," July 21, 1978, DH, "Press Releases" files; Deaver to Citizens for the Republic steering committee member, July 21, 1978; Deaver to Allen, Anderson, Hannaford, Keene, Laxalt, Meese, Nofziger, Sears, Whalen, and Wirthlin, July 21, 1878; all in DH, "Press Releases" files; Hannaford to David Leigh of WP, June 30, 1978, DH; Hannaford to Bob Scheer, June 30, 1980, DH.

368 **"John is not authorized"** Van der Linden, *The Real Reagan*, 156.

369 **"touchy situation"** AP, August 4, 1978.

369 **Phil Crane** Van der Linden, *The Real Reagan*, 157; "Rep. Crane Informs Reagan

of Plans for '80 Presidential Bid," WP, July 27, 1978; Paul Laxalt, *Paul Laxalt's Nevada: A Memoir* (Reno, NV: Jack Bacon & Co, 2000), 309.

369 **"old Tippecanoe"** "Reagan: More Serious Than Ever," WP, May 16, 1978.

369 **"gotten a facelift"** AP, February 18, 1977.

369 **Reagan's pollster Richard Wirthlin** Lou Cannon, *Governor Reagan: His Rise to Power* (New York: Public Affairs Books, 2003), 439.

369 **"Stop the chisels!"** Craig Shirley, *Rendezvous with Destiny: Ronald Reagan and the Campaign That Changed America* (Wilmington, DE: Intercollegiate Studies Institute, 2009), 33.

369 **"son you never knew you had"** Michael Deaver with Mickey Herskowitz, *Behind the Scenes: In Which the Author Talks About Ronald and Nancy Reagan . . . and Himself* (New York: William Morrow & Co., 1988), 75.

369 **wise Confucian leaders** "For Reagan, 'The Speech' Says It All," LAT, October 21, 1978.

370 **guns at Pearl Harbor** Thomas W. Cutrer and T. Michael Parrish, "How Dorie Miller's Bravery Helped Fight Navy Racism," *World War II Magazine*, October 31, 2019.

370 **"like overripe fruit"** Richard Reeves, *President Reagan: The Triumph of Imagination* (New York: Simon & Schuster, 2005), 154; Robert Welch, *The Blue Book of the John Birch Society* (Belmont, MA: Western Islands, 1961) 11.

370 **"You remember *Nancy*"** Jack Germond, *Fat Man in the Middle Seat: Forty Years of Covering Politics* (New York: Random House, 1999), 155.

370 **prospects of Jack Kemp** ENIR, July 24, 1978.

370 **"Maybe it wouldn't"** *Los Angeles Times Service, December 7, 1976.*

370 **dinner at Stanford** George Schultz, *Turmoil and Triumph: My Years as Secretary of State* (New York: Scribner, 1993).

370 **Bohemian Grove** July 28, 1978, RRPL, Box 59.

370 **first day back** July 31, 1978, ibid.

370 **margin of 37 to 31 percent** George Gallup column, August 13, 1978.

370 **prized Haut-Brion** Bob Colacello, *Ronnie and Nancy: Their Path to the White House—1911 to 1980* (New York: Grand Central Publishing, 2004), 473.

371 **On August 27** Shirley, *Rendezvous with Destiny*, 34; Cannon, *Governor Reagan*, 444.

371 *Washington Post* **gossiped** "PostScript," WP, August 28, 1978.

371 **elementary school teacher** "Gay Teacher Divides a Town," LAT, October 21, 1978; "California Is Roiled by a New Initiative, Over Homosexuals," WSJ, October 10, 1978; William F. Buckley column, September 19, 1978; Jackie M. Blount, *Fit to Teach: Same-Sex Desire, Gender, and School Work in the Twentieth Century* (Albany: State University of New York Press, 2006), 154; Randy Shilts, *The Mayor of Castro Street: The Life and Times of Harvey Milk* (New York: St. Martin's Press, 1982), 223–26, 239.

372 **"Almost all gay people"** Dudley Clendinen and Adam Nagourney, *Out for Good: The Struggle to Build a Gay Rights Movement in America* (New York: Simon & Schuster, 2001), 382.

372 **Gay Freedom Day** Ibid., 346–47; Shilts, *The Mayor of Castro Street*, 223–26; German Lopez, "Gilbert Baker Created the LGBTQ Flag. Here's What His Creation Stood For," Vox.com, June 2, 2017.

374 **"get creamed"** Shilts, *The Mayor of Castro Street*, 221.

374 **"not one example"** Blount, *Fit to Teach*, 145–46.

374 **"How many lives"** Shilts, *The Mayor of Castro Street*, 244.

374 **A new book** Timothy F. LaHaye, *The Unhappy Gays: What Everyone Should Know About Homosexuality* (Carol Stream, IL: Tyndale House, 1978), 207.

374 **David Boren** "We're OK; How's Oklahoma," *Mother Jones*, December, 1978.

374 **Southern Baptist Convention** Clendinen and Nagourney, *Out for Good*, 329.

374 **A poll showed** "Poll Shows Californians Support Controversial Initiatives," WP, September 20, 1978.

374 **Rock Hudson** Clendinen and Nagourney, *Out for Good*, 385.

374 **only endorsements** Shilts, *The Mayor of Castro Street*, 247.

375 **presented himself as a counterexample** Ibid., 243.

375 **"third of San Francisco's teachers"** Ibid., 388.

375 **"We can't complain"** Fred Fejes, *Gay Rights and Moral Panic: The Origins of America's Debate on Homosexuality* (New York: Palgrave Macmillan, 2008), 205.

375 **Ads arguing in terms** Clendinen and Nagourney, *Out for Good*, 384.

375 **"A self-serving politician"** Bancroft Library, University of California–Berkeley, Protest Collection, Briggs folio.

375 **"If we could"** For a complete account of Reagan and the Briggs referendum see Clendinen and Nagourney, *Out for Good*, 335–38.

375 **"they should be barred"** Mark Green, *Ronald Reagan's Reign of Error* (New York: Pantheon, 1987), 119.

375 **Reverend Troy Perry** Reagan to Reverend Gay, n.d., in RALIL, 233.

376 **"an athlete and all man"** Reagan to Lorraine and Elwood Wagner, June 5, 1979, dictation file, RRPL, Box 1; reprinted in ibid., 66–67.

376 **colleague named Phillip Battaglia** Cannon, *Governor Reagan*, 238–53.

376 **Truman Capote** Shirley, *Rendezvous with Destiny*, 35.

377 **the denomination Reagan** *Christianity Today*, December 5, 1977.

377 **excerpted them in** Bancroft Library, University of California–Berkeley, Protest Collection, Briggs folio.

377 **William F. Buckley joined** William F. Buckley column, September 19, 1978.

377 **Gerald Ford called it** Shilts, *The Mayor of Castro Street*, 243.

377 **"Ronald Reagan's—turned"** "Briggs to Try Antigay Move Again in 1980," LAT, November 9, 1978.

377 **biggest one was energy** For background see Ian Shapiro, *The Last Great Senate: Courage and Statesmanship in Times of Crisis* (New York: Public Affairs Books, 2012), 200–203; Meg Jacobs, *Panic at the Pump: The Energy Crisis and the Transformation of American Politics in the 1970s* (New York: Hill & Wang, 2016), 185–190; "Gas-Price Bill Faces Renewed Resistance," NYT, August 2, 1978; Jimmy Carter, *White House Diary* (New York: Macmillan, 2010), 212, 246, 251.

378 **"descent into hell"** Shapiro, *The Last Great Senate*, 200.

378 **On September 27** UPI, September 28, 1978.

378 **Newsmen, unimpressed** Jacobs, *Panic at the Pump*, 189.

378 **populist insurance commissioner** "Saying No Is Positive for Sen. Helms," *Atlanta Constitution*, February 19, 1978; "Democratic Senate Hopefuls Struggle to Find Issues," AP, March 26, 1978; AP, April 20, 1978; "Luther Hodges Jr. Forced into a Primary Runoff," WP, May 4, 1978; ENIR, October 1, 1978.

379 **austerity sermon** APP, September 22, 1978.

379 **public works bill** Carter, *White House Diary*, 249.

379 **Humphrey-Hawkins** Judith Stein, *Pivotal Decade: How the United States Traded Factories for Finance in the 1970s* (New Haven: Yale University Press, 2010), 191–92; Jefferson Cowie, *Stayin' Alive: The 1970s and the Last Days of the Working Class* (New York: New Press, 2010), 266–86; Robert Carswell to Carter, March 24,

1978, downloadable from Jimmy Carter Presidential Library; Robert M. Collins, *More: The Politics of Economic Growth in Postwar America* (New York: Oxford University Press, 2000), 167–71.

379   **black legislators met** Cowie, *Stayin' Alive*, 285,

379   **Black Caucus hosted** "Tense Politics and Changing Moods," WP, October 2, 1978; "Carter Gives Support to Jobs Bill as Black Caucus Raises $600,000," *Jet*, October 19, 1978.

380   **"since Calvin Coolidge"** "The President's Bet on Retrenchment," WP, November 20, 1978.

380   **"get off his swivel chair"** Victor Riesel column, October 4, 1978.

381   **Gallup released** George Gallup column, October 8, 1978. Compare to Gallup column, September 30, 1978.

381   **"tax expenditures"** Molly C. Michelmore, *Tax and Spend: The Welfare State, Tax Politics, and the Limits of Liberalism* (Philadelphia: University of Pennsylvania Press, 2014), 132; Robert Kuttner, *Revolt of the Haves: Tax Rebellions and Hard Times* (New York: Simon & Schuster, 1980), 231; David P. Vogel, *Fluctuating Fortunes: The Political Power of Business in America* (New York: Basic Books, 1989), 174.

381   **Other votes** "$142 Billion Cut in Taxes Linked to Spending Curb," WP, October 10, 1978.

381   **"Son of Kemp-Roth"** "Tax Conferees Begin Work Today," WP, October 12, 1978.

381   **"last big poker game"** "A Bewildering Deck of Wild Cards for Conferees on the Tax-Cut Bill," WP, October 14, 1978.

381   **"a nightmare"** Carter, *White House Diary*, 251.

381   **"Humphrey-Hawkins-Hatch"** Cowie, *Stayin' Alive*, 285.

382   **"mini-filibuster"** "Snail-Pace Energy Bill Stalls at Session's End," WP, October 15, 1978.

382   **National Energy Act** Jacobs, *Panic at the Pump*, 190.

382   **The sun rose** "Compromise Reached on Key Tax Cuts," WP, October 15, 1978.

382   **The bill that landed** Kuttner, *Revolt of the Haves*, 249.

383   **"not really strong enough"** Ibid., 268.

383   **traveled to Minnesota** Carter, *White House Diary*, 254.

383   **"frank talk"** "Anti-Inflation Program: Address to the Nation," APP, October 24, 1978.

383   **Gerald Rafshoon** Bruce J. Schulman, *The Seventies: The Great Shift in American Culture, Society, and Politics* (New York: Simon & Schuster, 2001), 133.

384   **In Iowa** Thomas J. McIntyre, *The Fear Brokers* (Boston: Beacon Press, 1981), 137–38; Clymer, *Drawing the Line at the Big Ditch*, 112, 117; Cynthia Gorney, *Articles of Faith: A Frontline History of the Abortion Wars* (New York: Simon & Schuster, 2000), 330; *Des Moines Register*, September 24, 1978.

384   **In New Hampshire** Clymer, *Drawing the Line at the Big Ditch*, 115.

384   **In North Carolina** "G.O.P. May Gain Nationally," NYT, November 6, 1978.

384   **Illinois's bellwether** "Dan Crane's Unhappy Dilemma: To Debate or Not to Debate," WP, October 22, 1978.

384   **Wife Letter** "Crane Plays His Ace: Wife's Letters to 100,000 Friends," WP, October 28, 1978.

385   **"The King Midas of the New Right"** *Atlantic Monthly*, November 1978.

385   **"water moccasin"** Connie Paige, *The Right to Lifers: Who They Are, How They Operate, and Where They Get Their Money* (New York: Summit Books, 1983), 133.

385   **"entire American labor movement"** Schulman, *The Seventies*, 198.

385 **The DNC aimed a counterstrike** John White to Carter, September 1, 1978, downloadable from Jimmy Carter Presidential Library.

386 **Jesse Helms controlled his own** "Thunder from the Right," NYT *Magazine*, February 8, 1981; Ernest B. Ferguson, *Hard Right: The Rise of Jesse Helms* (New York: Norton, 1986), 115, 145–50.

386 **Pioneer Fund** "From Eugenics to Voter ID Laws: Thomas Farr's Connections to the Pioneer Fund," *Hate Watch*, Southern Poverty Law Center, December 4, 2017.

386 **"Who's this 'Jesse Helms'?"** "Crane Plays His Ace."

386 **letterhead of Ronald Reagan** Ferguson, *Hard Right*, 126.

387 **Ronald Reagan complained** RRC, November 7, 1978.

387 **Echoed a conservative** David P. Vogel, *Fluctuating Fortunes: The Political Power of Business in America* (New York: Basic Books, 1989), 209.

387 **Sometime that summer** Paige, *The Right to Lifers*, 183.

387 **These Chamber and BIPAC** Ibid., 197; Thomas Edsall, *The New Politics of Inequality* (New York: W.W. Norton, 1985), 137; Vogel, *Fluctuating Fortunes*, 208.

388 **Prior to the fiscal year** John Judis, *The Paradox of American Democracy: Elites, Special Interests, and the Betrayal of Public Trust* (New York: Pantheon, 2000), 149.

388 **A subsequent analysis** Quoted in Richard Viguerie and David Franke, *Right Turn: How Conservatives Used New and Alternative Media to Take Over America* (Lanham, MD: Taylor Trade Publishing, 2004), 117.

388 **"rampant negativism"** "G.O.P. May Gain Nationally," NYT, November 6, 1978.

389 **drafted by William Gavin** Draft, Reagan annotations, and various versions in DH, Box 24, "R Reagan Speeches—9/78 and 10/78, master copy (2/3)."

390 **expanded advance manual** "Advance Procedures for Governor Reagan," September 1, 1978, DH, Box 84, "Advance Procedures" folder.

390 **holstered a memo** Hannaford to Reagan, cc MKD, LN, EM, MCA, Wirthlin, JS, RVA, Whalen, "Subject: Your Activities Since the Kansas City Convention," August 9, 1978.

391 **" 'saber rattler' "** Dick Allen, "Memorandum for Governor Reagan," August 25, 1978, DH, "Memorandum to Gov Reagan, Allen, Richard 1978-79" folder.

391 **"demean our nation"** *Des Moines Register*, September 15, 1978.

391 **"Somoza is the elected president"** RRC, October 1, 1978.

391 **"some other colonies"** RRC, October 30, 1978; CT, October 18, 1978, has photograph of Reagan and Smith.

391 **"Is it a third party"** Laura Kalman, *Right Star Rising: A New Politics, 1974–1980* (New York: Norton, 2010), 55.

391 **two nonpolitical stops** Schedule, October 6 and October 17, 1978, RRPL, Box 73; RRC, September 28, 1978.

391 **financier Maxwell Rabb** James Stockdale to Nofziger and Deaver, October 9, 1978, DH, Box 71 "Scheduling—New York Pending."

392 **"The whole thing is so familiar"** "For Reagan, 'The Speech' Says It All."

392 **passel of candidate ads** Jim Stockdale to Hannaford, October 2, 1978, RRPL, Box 17.

393 **"taken in moderation"** Rick Perlstein, *Invisible Bridge; The Fall of Nixon and the Rise of Reagan* (New York: Simon & Schuster, 2014), 546.

393 **fifteen points behind** ENIR, November 6, 1978; "Percy's Surprising Slide Linked to Voters' Revolt, Disenchantment," CT, November 2, 1978; Shapiro, *The Last Great Senate*, 212.

393 **"Washington go overboard"** View commercial at YouTube.com, accessed April 26, 2020.

393 **Percy people got wind** "Reagan Hits Trail for Old Foe Percy," CT, November 3,

1978; Peter Hannaford oral history, Miller Center, University of Virginia; ABC News, November 2, and NBC News, November 6, 1978, VTVNA.

393 **Wall Street was rocked** "Dollar Plunges to Record Lows Around the World," WP, October 31, 1978.

393 **two-for-one deal** Shilts, *The Mayor of Castro Street*, 238.

394 **"overwhelming majority"** RRC, October 27, 1978.

394 **Jerry Falwell** "Christianity Today," October 20, 1978; Michael Sean Winters, *God's Right Hand: How Jerry Falwell Made God a Republican and Baptized the American Right* (New York: HarperOne, 2012), 103.

394 **Senator Dick Clark** Clymer, *Drawing the Line at the Big Ditch*, 121.

394 **"will goof up"** ENIR, October 23, 1978.

394 **"THIS LITTLE GUY"** "Iowa Churchgoers Papered with Abortion-Issue Fliers," *Des Moines Register*, November 6, 1978.

394 **"no Yellow Pages listing"** Gorney, *Articles of Faith*, 333.

395 **call from his brother** Clymer, *Drawing the Line at the Big Ditch*, 122, who also reports on Hart's resurvey.

395 **"Best Man Lost"** *Des Moines Register*, November 9, 1978.

395 **Carolyn Gerster** William C. Inboden III, "Divine Elections: Abortion, Evangelicalism, and the New Right in American Politics, 1973–1980: The Politicization of Morality," Stanford University Department of History, honors thesis.

395 **Roger Mudd** Robert O. Self, *All in the Family: The Realignment of American Democracy Since the 1960s* (New York: Hill & Wang, 2012), 370.

395 **Terry Dolan devised** Clymer, *Drawing the Line at the Big Ditch*, 115.

396 **a colorful outsider** "Lee S. Dreyfus: 1926–2008," *Milwaukee Journal Sentinel*, March 25, 2008.

396 **with a "fanaticism"** Justin DeMello, "Contracted Politics: Media in the Gingrich Revolution and Political Polarization, 1978–1994," Vanderbilt University, Department of History, senior thesis.

396 **congressman David Broder** David Osborne, "The Swinging Days of Newt Gingrich," *Mother Jones*, November 1, 1984.

396 **A Gingrich flyer** "After Political Victory, A Personal Revolution," WP, December 19, 1994.

396 **"*Ilsa, She-Wolf of the SS*"** Ibid.

396 **Another addressed** Virginia Shapard oral history, Georgia State University, January 16, 1988.

396 **"North Atlanta bureaucrats"** *Atlanta World*, September 28, 1978.

396 **"Newt will take his family"** "After Political Victory, A Personal Revolution."

397 **"plain lying"** Ibid.

397 **"the GOP today is in a weaker"** Everett Carll Ladd, *Where Have All the Voters Gone? The Fracturing of America's Political Parties* (New York: Norton, 1978).

397 **aped George Wallace's** "Dukakis Upset, Brooke Leads in Mass.," WP, September 20, 1978.

397 **"listen very carefully"** Shapiro, *The Last Great Senate*, 225.

397 **In Delaware** Branko Marcetic, *Yesterday's Man: The Case Against Joe Biden* (New York: Verso, 2020), 27–42, 73.

398 **A colorful Republican** Mike Curb with Don Cusic, *Living the Business* (Los Angeles: Curb Recording Group, Inc., 2017), passim.

398 **visit to Sacramento** Shilts, *The Mayor of Castro Street*, 247.

398 **"victory over the despair"** Andrew E. Stoner, *The Journalist of Castro Street: The Life of Randy Shilts* (Champaign-Urbana: University of Illinois Press, 2019).

399 **smoking in public places** "Effort Apparently Douses Anti-Smoking Initiative," WP, October 26, 1978; UPI, September 21, 1978; "Proposition 5 Burning Issue for Californians," August 13, 1978.

399 **Tobacco Institute** *New York Times* Service, March 5, 1978; AP, August 3, 1978.

400 **"a piece of mischief"** Hannaford to Reagan, "SUBJECT: Proposition 5—Smoking Restrictions," August 2, 1978, DH, Box 2, Folder 7.

400 **"Shades of Newspeak"** RRC, October 27, 1978.

400 **"We just have never lost"** AP, August 3, 1978.

CHAPTER NINETEEN

401 **"little-noticed story"** UPI, June 15, 1978, *Santa Rosa Press Democrat.*

401 **Twelve days after** "In Response: Peoples Temple Disputes Guyana Article," *Santa Rosa Press Democrat,* June 27, 1978.

401 **In 1973, that newspaper** "Church Gives Grants to Media," *Santa Rose Press Democrat,* January 18, 1973. For Jonestown: Tim Reiterman with John Jacobs, *Raven: The Untold Story of the Rev. Jim Jones and His People* (New York: TarcherPerigree, 2008; Jonestown file, Protest Collection, Bancroft Library, University of California–Berkeley.

402 **That Monday** Index of ABC, NBC, and CBS newscasts, November 20, 1978, VTVNA.

402 **Ronald Reagan was asked** AP, November 30, 1978.

402 **"Weekend Update"** *Saturday Night Live* transcript, December 9, 1978, SNLTranscripts.jt.org, accessed April 26, 2020.

403 **Larry Berner** Jackie M. Blount, *Fit to Teach: Same-Sex Desire, Gender, and School Work in the Twentieth Century* (Albany: State University of New York Press, 2006), 154. Berner won a $10,000 defamation judgment against John Briggs.

403 **made-for-TV movie** AP, November 27, 1978.

403 **White changed his mind** Randy Shilts, *The Mayor of Castro Street: The Life and Times of Harvey Milk* (New York: St. Martin's Press, 1982), 250–54.

403 **Jerry Falwell** Michael Sean Winters, *God's Right Hand: How Jerry Falwell Made God a Republican and Baptized the American Right* (New York: HarperOne, 2012), 104.

403 **pollster Bob Teeter** "GOP May Gain Nationally," NYT, November 6, 1978.

404 **On front porches** UPI, November 19, 1978. The pamphlet is reproduced on page 188 of *FEMA Oversight: Will U.S. Nuclear Attack Evacuation Plans Work?*, Hearing Before a Subcommittee on Government Operations, House of Representatives, Ninety-Seventh Congress, Second Session, April 22, 1982.

404 **more immediate apocalypse** Love Canal background: Michael Stewart Foley, *Front Porch Politics: The Forgotten Heyday of American Activism in the 1970s and 1980s* (New York: Hill & Wang, 2013), 151–62; Knight-Ridder News Service, November 15, 1978.

404 **"Pollution Victims Told of Liver Disorders"** LAT, September 4, 1978.

404 **"Olfactory Niagara"** NYT, August 9, 1978.

404 **"Anything, Anywhere, Any Time"** Ibid.

404 **"set for a disaster movie"** Knight-Ridder News Service, November 15, 1978.

405 **Alfred Kahn** UPI, November 15, 1978.

405 **One Oregon newspaper** *Oregon Statesman/Capital Journal,* "Insight" section, November 26, 1978.

405 **"Winter of Discontent"** Christian Caryl, *Strange Rebels: 1979 and the Birth of the 21st Century* (New York: Basic Books, 2013), 52–54.

405 **four thousand Westerners** UPI, November 18, 1978.

405 **"very well-planned operation"** AP, December 24, 1978.

405 **"Dressed in a black turban"** "Exiled Holy Man Hints He'll Call for War in Iran," NYT, November 7, 1978.

406 **"full backing"** AP, December 13, 1978.

406 **Three weeks earlier** Paul Laxalt, *Paul Laxalt's Nevada: A Memoir* (Reno, NV: Jack Bacon & Co, 2000), 254.

406 **eccentric Southern Baptist** AP, November 23, 1978; *Washington Post* Service, September 29, 1978.

407 **Carter traveled to New York** "Remarks at a Fundraising Dinner for Former New York City Mayor Abraham Beame," December 5, 1978, APP.

407 **what had caused it** David Farber, *Taken Hostage: The Iran Hostage Crisis and America's First Encounter with Radical Islam* (Princeton: Princeton University Press, 2004), 20.

407 **Jamaica's bauxite** Judith Stein, *Pivotal Decade: How the United States Traded Factories for Finance in the 1970s* (New Haven: Yale University Press, 2010), 96–99.

408 **when he was a liberal** "Ronald Reagan Campaigns for Truman," YouTube.com, accessed April 6, 2020.

408 **radio commentary** RRB 76-05, track 04, "Inflation and the Property Tax I," recorded November 1976.

408 **"spendthrift Democratic-controlled"** Reagan NBC-TV speech, September 19, 1976, in *First Monday* magazine, November 1976.

408 **Jimmy Carter seemed to agree** "Message to Congress Transmitting the Fiscal Year 1980 Budget," January 22, 1979, APP.

408 **"For Democratic politicians"** RRC, November 14, 1978.

408 **Representative Tom Foley** "Tip O'Neill's Unpleasant Duty," WSJ, April 5, 1979.

409 **"wipe us out"** UPI, December 4, 1978.

409 **"unable to contain"** "Carter Warned by Blacks of Unrest If He Slights Programs for Cities," NYT, December 5, 1978.

409 **Alfred Kahn admitted** AP, January 11, 1979.

410 **"mini-convention"** Garry Wills, "Miniconvention '78," in *Lead Time: A Journalist's Education* (New York: Doubleday, 1983), 210; UPI, December 11, 1978; "Dems Give Carter Confidence Vote on Austerity Plan," *New York Daily News*, December 11, 1978.

410 **Ted Kennedy rose** "Democratic National Committee Workshop on Healthcare," December 9,1978, Edward M. Kennedy Institute website; view conclusion of speech on YouTube.com, accessed April 6, 2020.

413 **the young governor of Arkansas** Edward M. Kennedy, *True Compass: A Memoir* (New York: Simon & Schuster, 2009), 362.

413 **Cleveland ended 1978** Edward McClelland, *Nothin' But Blue Skies: The Heyday, Hard Times, and Hopes of America's Industrial Heartland* (New York: Bloomsbury Press, 2013), 44–53.

414 **OPEC oil ministers** AP, December 16, 1978; AP, December 18, 1979; UPI, December 18, 1979.

414 **John Wayne Gacy** *Chicago Tribune* Service, December 22, 1978; CT, December 23, 1978; Clifford L. Lindecker, *The Man Who Killed Boys: A True Story of Mass Murder in a Chicago Suburb* (New York: St. Martin's Press, 1980).

415 **"Christmas present"** *Nation,* January 6, 1979.

415   case of the hemorrhoids "Carter's 'Injury': Treating Those Hemorrhoids," *Time*, January 8, 1979.

415   "A Joyless Noel" NYT, December 27, 1978.

CHAPTER TWENTY

419   A historian Peter N. Carroll, *It Seemed Like Nothing Happened: America in the 1970s* (New Brunswick, NJ: Rutgers University Press, 1990).

419   "Hillside Strangler" "Police Intensify Hillside Strangler Probe," LAT, January 18, 1979.

419   snowed in Southern California "Southland Struck by Snow, Hail, and Cold Wins," LAT, January 29, 1979.

419   Fifty-two whales "52 Whales Beach Selves and Die in Baja California," LAT, January 7, 1979.

419   Skylab "NASA Ponders Safest Way to Allow Skylab to Die," LAT, January 14, 1979.

419   Nelson Rockefeller's publicist Richard Norton Smith, *On His Own Terms: A Life of Nelson Rockefeller* (New York: Random House, 2014), 708–14.

420   hijacked a 747 AP, January 29, 1979.

420   "I don't like Mondays" "Girl Sniper Kills 2, Wounds 9 at San Diego School," LAT, January 30 1979.

420   about vampires They are (films) *Dracula, Love At First Bite, Nocturna: Granddaughter of Dracula, Thirst, Nosferatu the Vampyre*; and (TV shows) *Vampire, Salem's Lot, Dracula, Play for Today: Vampires, Cliffhangers: The Curse of Dracula*.

421   16 percent Dominic Sandbrook, *Mad as Hell: The Crisis of the 1970s and the Rise of the Populist Right* (New York: Anchor Books, 2012), 234.

421   "Consumer revolving credit" Thomas A. Durkin, "Credit Cards: Use and Consumer Attitudes, 1970–2000," *Federal Reserve Bulletin*, September 2000.

421   "The brake is off" William Greider, *Secrets of the Temple: How the Federal Reserve Runs the Country* (New York: Simon & Schuster, 1989), 17.

421   pollster Daniel Yankelovich Charles S. Maier, Erez Manela, and Daniel J. Sargent, eds., *The Shock of the Global: The 1970s in Perspective* (Cambridge, MA: Harvard University Press, 2010), 27.

421   AFL-CIO's chief lobbyist "The Democrats: A President Confronts the Old Coalition," WP, January 15, 1979.

422   Stuart Eizenstat W. Carl Biven, *Jimmy Carter's Economy: Policy in an Age of Limits* (Chapel Hill: University of North Carolina Press, 2002), 261; Colman McCarthy column, January 15, 1979.

422   Governor Jerry Brown Patrick Buchanan column, January14, 1979.

422   even among conservative Russell L. Caplan, *Constitutional Brinksmanship: Amending the Constitution by National Convention* (New York: Oxford University Press, 1988), 80–81.

422   Brown's political success "Proposition 13, in 5 Months, Has Not Spurred Major Spending Cutbacks," NYT, November 7, 1978.

422   A new poll Richard Reeves column, *Esquire*, February 13, 1979.

422   Bill Winpisinger Jefferson Cowie, *Stayin' Alive: The 1970s and the Last Days of the Working Class* (New York: New Press, 2010), 261.

423 **prosecution memo** William Safire column, January 9, 1979.

423 **"a lot more Arabians"** "Libyan Visit to Miami Draws Jewish Protests," *Miami News*, January 12, 1979.

423 **"kiss my ass"** "Billy Carter Files as Foreign Agent," WP, July 15, 1980.

423 **"continued high inflation"** "President Warns of Fast Action If Teamsters Strike," WP, January 16, 1979.

423 **1979 spending proposal** "Message to Congress Transmitting the Fiscal Year 1980 Budget," January 22, 1979, APP.

423 **tasteless political cartoon** Bob Englehart cartoon, Copley Service, December 12, 1978.

423 **"like talking about a crash diet"** AP, January 22, 1979.

423 **pollster Peter Hart** "Democratic Party in Transition, But the Question Is, to What?" WP, January 14, 1979.

423 **On Tuesday evening** "State of the Union Address Delivered to a Joint Session of Congress," January 23, 1979.

423 **rattled the speechwriters** Robert Schlesinger, *White House Ghosts: Presidents and Their Speechwriters* (New York: Simon & Schuster, 2008), 293–96.

424 **"The Internationale"** Moynihan letter to the editor, WP, January 28, 1979.

424 **reviews from liberals** Meg Jacobs, *Panic at the Pump: The Energy Crisis and the Transformation of American Politics in the 1970s* (New York: Hill & Wang, 2016), 198.

424 **"I doubt it"** Schlesinger, *White House Ghosts*, 296.

424 **"a simple reality"** "Text of President's Statement on Ties with China," NYT, December 16, 1978.

424 **Barry Goldwater** Ian Shapiro, *The Last Great Senate: Courage and Statesmanship in Times of Crisis* (New York: Public Affairs Books, 2012), 234.

424 **Ronald Reagan** LeRoy Ashby and Rod Gramer, *Fighting the Odds: The Life of Frank Church* (Pullman: Washington State University Press, 1993), 568.

424 **wasn't just conservatives** Laura Kalman, *Right Star Rising: A New Politics, 1974–1980* (New York: Norton, 2010), 313.

425 **proved a tonic** Jimmy Carter, *White House Diary* (New York: Macmillan, 2010), 283–85.

425 **Deng was equally** Thomas Bortelsmann, *The 1970s: A New Global History from Civil Rights to Economic Inequality* (New York: Oxford University Press, 2011), 224; Christian Caryl, *Strange Rebels: 1979 and the Birth of the 21st Century* (New York: Basic Books, 2013), 170–75.

425 **Richard Nixon said** Shapiro, *Last Great Senate*, 68.

425 **nuclear "parity"** Francis J. Gavin, "Wrestling with Parity: The Nuclear Revolution Revisited," in Maier, Manela, and Sargent, eds., *The Shock of the Global*, 189.

426 **On the right** Steven F. Hayward, *The Age of Reagan: The Fall of the Old Liberal Order, 1964–1980* (New York: Three Rivers Press, 2001), 588.

426 **late in 1977** Walter LaFeber, *The American Age: United States Foreign Policy at Home and Abroad, Vol. 2: Since 1896* (New York: Norton, 1994), 648.

426 **human rights activists** *ABC World News Tonight*, July 10, 1978, YouTube, accessed April 7, 2020; CBS Radio News, July 25, 1978, and August 1, 1978, PastDaily.com, accessed April 7, 2020.

426 **to a mere "agreement"** Carter, *White House Diary*, 203.

426 **Coalition for Peace Through Strength** Sarah Diamond, *Roads to Dominion: Right-Wing Movements and Political Power in the United States* (New York: Guilford, 1995), 137.

426 *Soviet Might/American Myth* Ashby and Gramer, *Fighting the Odds*, 496; Thomas J. McIntyre, *The Fear Brokers* (Boston: Beacon Press, 1981), 132–33.

426 **"pro-SALT lobby"** NBC News, March 3, 1979, VTVNA.

426 **Eugene Rostow** "The Case Against SALT II," *Commentary*, February 1, 1979; "Slipping Toward Impotence Around the Globe," *Washington Star*, February 4, 1979.

427 **six straight radio commentaries** RRB 78-14, "Rostow I" through "Rostow VI," recorded October 10, 1978.

427 **"by 1985"** RBB 78-11, track A1, "SALT Talks II," recorded July 1978, in RRIHOH, 84.

427 **"as the dust settled"** Julian Zelizer, *Arsenal of Democracy: The Politics of National Security—from World War II to the War on Terrorism* (New York: Basic Books, 2009), 285.

427 **"a bit of Rafshoonery"** RRC, November 21, 1978.

428 **delegation of senators** J. Lee Annis, *Howard Baker: Conciliator in an Age of Crisis* (Knoxville, TN: Howard Baker Center, 2007), 151–52.

428 **Tidewater Inn** *New York Times* Service, February 4, 1979.

428 **"eerie parallel"** *New York Times* Service, March 2, 1979.

428 **agriculture depends** Catherine McNichol Stock, *Rural Radicals: Righteous Rage in the American Grain* (Ithaca, NY: Cornell University Press), 157–60; John Dinse and William P. Brown, "The Emergence of the American Agriculture Movement, 1977–79," *Great Plains Quarterly*, Fall 1985.

429 **"Tractorcade"** Sam Brasch, "When Tractors Invaded D.C.," *Modern Farmer*, February 2014; *In These Times*, February 21, 1979; "Farmers Occupy the Mall—Winter 1979," JoFreeman.com; AP, January 18, 1979; AP, January 20, 1979; "Plans of Farmers Stymied by Police," *Paris News*, February 6, 1979; "Missourian's Beef Lands Him in Jail," *St. Louis Post Dispatch*, February 6, 1979; AP, February 8, 1979; "Farm Protest Hogtied," *Ottawa Journal*, February 9, 1979; UPI, February 10, 1979; "How to Lose Friends," *Springfield Daily News*, February 10, 1979; "1979 Tractorcade to D.C.—Part 1" and "1979 Tractorcade Part 2," YouTube.com; "Tractorcade to Washington, D.C., Protest (Knoxville Story) 1/26/1979," YouTube.com; "Jack Wolfe Remembers 1979 Tractorcade to Washington, D.C.," YouTube.com; "Lester Derlsey Remembers 1979 Tractorcade to Washington, D.C.," YouTube.com; "Jerry Stapleton Remembers 1979 Tractorcade to Washington, D.C.," YouTube.com; "Marjory Scheufler Remembers 1979 Tractorcade to Washington, D.C.," YouTube.com. All clips accessed April 7, 2020.

431 **Alfred Kahn announced** AP, February 13, 1979.

431 **child froze to death** Meg Jacobs, *Panic at the Pump: The Energy Crisis and the Transformation of American Politics in the 1970s* (New York: Hill & Wang, 2016), 197.

431 **In Nicaragua** AP, February 9, 1979.

432 **"They found Iran"** *Doonesbury*, February 23, 1979.

432 **You might date** Iran background: Caryl, *Strange Rebels*, 41–50

433 **Oriana Fallaci** *Interviews with History and Conversations with Power* (New York: Rizzoli, 2011), 151–71.

434 **staggering celebration** Caryl, *Strange Rebels*, 49; David Farber, *Taken Hostage: The Iran Hostage Crisis and America's First Encounter with Radical Islam* (Princeton: Princeton University Press, 2004), 67; Vincent Franklin and Alex Johnson, *Menus That Made History: Over 2000 Years of Menus from Ancient Egyptian Food for the Afterlife to Elvis Presley's Wedding Breakfast* (London: Kyle Books, 2019),

84–88. For the price of Château Lafite Rothschild '45 in 1971 see "After Wine Bidding, Prices Flow," LAT, June 10, 1971.

436 **liberal Democratic senators** Shapiro, *The Last Great Senate,* 76–77.

436 **Nelson Rockefeller** Smith, *On His Own Terms,* 707.

437 **"island of stability"** "Tehran, Iran: Toasts of the President and the Shah at a State Dinner," December 31, 1977, APP.

437 **Brzezinski wanted** Shapiro, *Last Great Senate,* 217–18.

437 **shocking exposé** Gregory Rose, "The Shah's Secret Police Are Here," *New York,* September 18, 1978.

437 **"back him to the hilt"** Zbigniew Brzezinski, *Power and Principle: Memoirs of the National Security Adviser, 1977–1981* (New York: Farrar, Straus & Giroux), 365.

438 **"almost unrelieved ignorance"** Gary Sick, *All Fall Down: America's Fateful Encounter with Iran* (New York: Random House, 1985), 5, 122.

438 **"Thinking the Unthinkable"** "Vance Deflects a Call for Toughness," WP, October 28, 1980.

438 **"no identifiable leader"** "For Iran, No Clear Alternative to the Shah," NYT, November 6, 1978. The failure to grasp the emergence of revolutionary Islamism is a theme I take from Caryl's *Strange Rebels: 1979 and the Birth of the 21st Century.*

438 **On November 22** "Secretary Blumenthal's Meeting with Shah of Iran," November 22, 1978, Wikileaks Canonical ID 1978KUWAIT06258_d and 1978 STATE295264_d, Wikileaks.org.

439 **"on a vacation"** Translations of the Shah's statement differ. See AP, January 17, 1979.

439 **hushed awe** *Washington Post* Service, January 17, 1979; "Teary-Eyed Shah Flies Out of Iran and Millions Take to Streets in Joy," CT, January 17, 1979.

440 **"God is Great"** *Toronto Globe and Mail,* January 17, 1979.

440 **"a Gandhi-like role"** "Shah Said to Plan to Leave Iran Today for Egypt and U.S.," NYT, January 16, 1979.

440 **"receptive to friendship"** Carter, *White House Diary,* 271.

440 **"as you have in France"** Caryl, *Strange Rebels,* 142.

440 **Walter Annenberg's estate** UPI, January 18, 1979.

440 **Brzezinski still hoped** Arthur M. Schlesinger Jr., *Journals: 1952–2000* (New York: Penguin, 2007), 460.

440 **Stansfield Turner** Ibid.

440 **"a good PR man"** Carter, *White House Diary,* 261; Jean-Charles Brotons, *U.S. Officials and the Fall of the Shah* (Lanham, MD: Lexington Books), 69.

440 **Arba'een arrived** "A Million Marchers Rally for Khomeini in Teheran Streets," NYT, January 20, 1979.

440 **closed Tehran's airport** Reuters, January 24, 1979.

441 **"no-boat gunboat diplomacy"** William Safire column, January 4, 1979.

441 **"We have no intention"** "The President's News Conference," January 17, 1979, APP.

441 **barrels of fuel** "The President's News Conference," January 26, 1979.

441 **returned on February 1** UPI, February 1, 1979.

441 **"minimum of violence"** Carter, *White House Diary,* 287.

441 **on its roof** Caryl, *Strange Rebels,* 145.

441 **Andrew Young** UPI, February 9, 1979.

441 **Imperial Guard** Caryl, *Strange Rebels,* 149.

441 **Energy Secretary Schlesinger** AP, February 14, 1979.

441 **On February 14** Mark Bowden, *Guests of the Ayatollah: The First Battle in America's War with Militant Islam* (New York: Atlantic Monthly Press, 2006), 164.

442 **"the embassy's under siege"** Ibid., 167; "Feeling Helpless: Self-Inflicted Wound," *Newsweek*, February 26, 1979; UPI, February 15, 1979; "US Embassy Stormed by Tehran Mob," *Guardian*, February 15, 1979.

442 **banner headline** *Arizona Republic*, February 15, 1979.

442 **"U.S. Citizens Told: Flee Iran"** *State Journal*, February 15, 1979.

442 **goal of evacuating** "Another Airlift of Yanks from Iran Planned," CT, February 15, 1979.

442 **"except to hope for the cooperation"** ABC News, February 14, 1979, VTVNA.

442 **Kabul, Afghanistan** AP, February 15, 1979; Kalman, *Right Star Rising*, 314; "The Assassination of Ambassador Spike Dubs—Kabul, 1979," Association for Diplomatic Studies and Training, January 2013; Tim Weiner, *Legacy of Ashes: The History of the CIA* (New York: Doubleday, 2007), 422–23.

443 **"Carter, Vance, 'Mad' "** *Indianapolis Star*, February 15, 1979.

443 **third Valentine's Day humiliation** UPI, February 15, 1979; "Mexico City, Mexico: Toasts at the Luncheon Honoring President Carter," February 14, 1979, APP.

444 **Carter had tried to dissuade** Kalman, *Right Star Rising*, 316

444 **Jody Powell** AP, February 15, 1979.

444 **Lieutenant General Daniel Graham** Kalman, *Right Star Rising*, 315.

444 **"very likely" or "fairly likely"** George Gallup column, February 11, 1979.

445 **"rooftop evacuation"** Tom Wicker column, *New York Times* Service, February 19, 1979.

445 **ran side by side** See Broder and Wicker columns in *Tampa Bay Times*, February 18, 1979.

445 **"Feeling Helpless"** *Newsweek*, February 26, 1979.

445 **"Small-Stick Diplomacy"** *Newsweek*, March 5, 1979.

445 **Gerald Rafshoon** Kalman, *Right Star Rising*, 316.

CHAPTER TWENTY-ONE

446 **General Alexander Haig** "Citizens for Haig" brochure, RRPL, Box 85.

446 **George Bush** Doro Bush Koch, *My Father, My President: A Personal Account of the Life of George H. W. Bush* (New York: Grand Central, 2014), 148.

446 **Jerry Brown** "Brown Lashes Back at His Policy Critics," LAT, January 21, 1979.

446 **Ted Kennedy** Dominic Sandbrook, *Mad as Hell: The Crisis of the 1970s and the Rise of the Populist Right* (New York: Anchor Books, 2012), 236.

446 **Farrah Fawcett-Majors** William Graebner, *Patty's Got a Gun: Patricia Hearst in 1970s America* (Chicago: University of Chicago Press, 2008), 174.

447 *Superman* Personal correspondence with Eric Kleefeld; Eric Lundegaard, "Did Superman Resurrect Patriotism?: On Truth, Innocence, and the American Way," ErikLundegaard.com (the source of the quotations).

449 **"shorten my drawl"** Malcolm D. MacDougall, *We Almost Made It: President Ford's Adman Tells the Personal Story Behind One of the Most Surprising Campaigns in American Political History* (New York: Crown, 1977), 161.

449 **John Connally of Texas** Main source is the superlative biography by James Reston Jr., *Lone Star: The Life of John Connally* (New York: HarperCollins, 1989). See also Connally's memoir written with Mickey Herskowitz, *In History's Shadow: An American Odyssey* (New York: Hyperion, 1993), and Charles Ashman, *Connally: The Adventures of Big Bad John* (New York: Morrow, 1974).

456 **His Citizens Forum** Adam Clymer, *Drawing the Line at the Big Ditch: The Panama Canal Treaties and the Rise of the Right* (Lawrence: University Press of Kansas, 2008), 138.

456 **"only thing Connally didn't like"** David Nyan, "GOP Surveyed for Candidates to Oust Carter in 1980," BG, November 6, 1976.

456 **In the fall of 1978** "John B. Connally: *Strong* for 1980," *Saturday Evening Post*, November 1978.

456 **January 24, 1979** "Connally Takes the Big Plunge in '80 Campaign," WP, January 25, 1979; UPI, January 25, 1979; AP, January 25, 1979; Reston, *Lone Star*, 588.

457 **Arthur Schlesinger Jr.** Arthur M. Schlesinger Jr., *Journals: 1952–2000* (New York: Penguin, 2007), March 4, 1979.

457 **secretary of energy** Jimmy Carter, *White House Diary* (New York: Macmillan, 2010), 129.

457 **Richard Viguerie** HE, March 17, 1979.

457 **"It's really exciting"** "Younger Republicans Looking to '80, Conservatively," WP, March 1, 1979.

457 **"commie pinkos"** Geoffrey Kabaservice, *Rule and Ruin: The Downfall of Moderation and the Destruction of the Republican Party, from Eisenhower to the Tea Party* (New York: Oxford University Press, 2012), 356; author interview with Donald Barton Doyle.

457 **"Right-Wing Students Exert"** *Chronicle of Higher Education*, January 8, 1979.

457 **Leadership Institute** Richard Viguerie and David Franke, *Right Turn: How Conservatives Used New and Alternative Media to Take Over America* (Lanham, MD: Taylor Trade Publishing, 2004), 167.

457 **National Journalism Center** Reagan to Evans, June 23, 1978, and Evans to Reagan, August 18, 1978, DH, Box 4, folder 8 or 9.

457 **Institute for Educational Affairs** Sarah Diamond, *Roads to Dominion: Right-Wing Movements and Political Power in the United States* (New York: Guilford, 1995), 199–200; David P. Vogel, *Fluctuating Fortunes: The Political Power of Business in America* (New York: Basic Books, 1989), 222; *New Right Report*, March 15, 1979, in RRPL, Box 86.

458 **American Legislative Exchange Council** *New Right Report*, March 15, 1979.

458 **He had only lost** Ibid., January 28, 1979.

458 **Ted Stevens** Ian Shapiro, *The Last Great Senate: Courage and Statesmanship in Times of Crisis* (New York: Public Affairs Books, 2012), 224.

458 **Norm Ornstein and Thomas Mann** Jeffrey Crouch and Matthew N. Green, "New Gingrich: Strategic Political Entrepreneur," Paper Presented at 2017 Annual Meeting of the Midwest Political Science Association.

458 **Charles Diggs** "GOP Freshman After Diggs," *Detroit Free Press*, January 13, 1979; States News Service, January 19, 1979; Nick Thimmesch column, January 29, 1979; AP, February 3, 1979; Gingrich letter to the editor, *Carlisle Sentinel*, February 7, 1979; AP, February 24, 1979; AP, March 1, 1979.

459 **"Hitler or a Klansman"** AP, March 2, 1979.

459 **"My hat is off"** J. Brooks Flippen, *Speaker Jim Wright: Power, Scandal, and the Birth of Modern Politics* (Austin: University of Texas Press, 2018), 284.

459 **"three-dimensional chess"** "Gingrich Takes Presidents, Not Predecessors, as Model," NYT, April 11, 1979.

459 **Lyndon LaRouche** Diana McLellan column, *Washington Star* Service, February 14, 1979. Google "Debra Hananian-Freeman" and "1978," and one can

download several fantastical articles on the dispute from the LaRouche publication *Executive Intelligence Review*, and the file of her dismissed Federal Elections Commission case.

459 **local black newspaper** "We Must Help Send Gingrich to Congress," *Atlanta World*, November 5, 1978.

459 **"a national politician"** AP, February 11, 1979.

459 **Tidewater Inn** Tanya Melich, *The Republican War Against Women: An Insider's Report From Behind the Lines* (New York: Bantam, 1996), 103–94; George Will column, *Washington Post* Service, February 8, 1978.

459 **Irving Kristol's face** "The Reasonable Right," *Esquire*, February 13, 1979.

460 **used-car warranty rules** James J. Kilpatrick column, January 9, 1979.

460 **vocational schools** AP, December 13, 1978.

460 **message on cigarette packs** "Stiffer Cigarette Warning?" *Palm Beach Post*, January 18, 1979.

460 **door-to-door insurance** Michael Pertschuk, *Revolt Against Regulation* (Berkeley: University of California Press, 1983), 79–80.

461 **advertising by members** AP, December 3, 1978.

461 **energy efficiency** Scripps-Howard Service, June 29, 1979; UPI, August 23, 1979.

461 **holding celebrities liable** UPI, June 12, 1981.

461 **funeral homes** Pertschuk, *Revolt Against Regulation*, 60, 98; *Washington Post* Service, February 20, 1977; UPI, February 28, 1979; AP, March 23, 1979; James J. Kilpatrick column, November 28, 1978.

461 **feet of shelf space** "Thousands Protest Against Children's Advertising," *Longview News-Journal*, January 7, 1979.

461 **A war chest** "Foes of Child Ads Curbs Devised Strategy Here," *Washington Star*, March 7, 1979.

461 **opened in San Francisco** "Thousands Protest Against Children's Advertising"; AP, January 16, 1979; UPI, January 16, 1979; *Los Angeles Times* Service, January 16, 1979; "Saturday Morning Hard Sell: FTC Maintains TV Advertising Exploits Children," *Jackson Sun*, January 28, 1979. "Up to Their Teeth in Washington Over Children's Ads," *Broadcasting*, March 12, 1979.

461 **lavish press operation** "Cereal Ads on TV Grist for Hot Debate," LAT, January 28, 1979.

462 **"Consumer's Man at FTC"** *Newsday*, March 26, 1979.

462 **"FTC Is Becoming the Consumer's"** WP, January 2, 1979.

463 **Pertschuk should be recused** AP, March 15, 1979.

463 **His side hardly** "Up to Their Teeth in Washington Over Children's Ads," *Broadcasting*, March 12, 1979; AP, March 5, 1979; UPI, March 5, 1979.

463 **Kellogg's CEO** Gannett, March 8, 1979.

463 **A *Washington Star* investigation** "Foes of Child Ads Curbs Devised Strategy Here."

463 **testified before the House** *Departments of State, Justice, and Commerce, the Judiciary, and Related Agencies: Appropriations for 1980*, Hearings Before a Subcommittee of the Committee Appropriations, House of Representatives, Ninety-Sixth Congress, First Session: Part 1, The Judiciary. Pertschuk's testimony begins on page 690, the exchange with Early on 769.

465 **FTC staffers were baffled** Pertschuk, *Revolt Against Regulation*, 95.

465 **fat contributions** See 1980 Federal Elections Commission report for Joseph Early at FEC.gov.

465 **before Senate Appropriations** *Senate Hearings Before the Committee on Ap-*

propriations: State, Justice, and Commerce, the Judiciary, and Related Agencies Appropriations: Fiscal Year 1980, Ninety-Sixth Congress, First Session: Part 2, 2015.

CHAPTER TWENTY-TWO

466 **Christian Broadcasting Network** "Religious Networks Blossom," NYT, July 23, 1978.

466 **Heritage USA** "PTL Club: Jim Bakker's Gospel Talk Show Is $100-Million Success Story," *Tampa Bay Times*, March 11, 1978.

466 **radio stations** Jeremy Rifkin and Ted Howard, *The Emerging Order: God in the Age of Scarcity* (New York: G. P. Putnam's Sons, 1979), 99.

466 **pilgrimage to the Holy Land** "Israel Finding Born-Again Friends in U.S.," LAT, June 11, 1978.

467 **Falwell liked to tell** "The Next Billy Graham," *Esquire*, October 10, 1978.

468 **one 1958 sermon** "Segregation or Integration, Which?" *Word of Life* 1, No. 1 (October 1958). Thank you to Professor Jon Butler of Yale for sharing this document.

468 **327 television stations** Knight-Ridder Service, January 6, 1979.

468 **Lynchburg Catholic complained** "The Next Billy Graham."

468 **"Jerry will replace"** Ibid.

468 **"not to harangue"** Ibid.

469 **"subliminal sex"** Knight-Ridder Service, January 6, 1979.

470 **IBM mainframes** Daniel K. Williams, "Jerry Falwell's Sunbelt Politics: The Regional Origins of the Moral Majority," *Journal of Policy History* 11, No. 2 (2010).

470 **the modern shopping mall** Jerry Falwell and Elmer Towns, *Capturing a Town for Christ* (Grand Rapids, MI: Revell, 1973), 82.

470 **sermon published in 1979** Jerry Stroeber and Ruth Tomczak, *America Can Be Saved: Jerry Falwell Preaches on Revival* (Murfreesboro, TN: Sword of the Lord, 1979).

470 **"private school for white"** Randall Balmer, *Redeemer: The Life of Jimmy Carter* (New York: Basic Books, 2014), 106.

470 **famous 1965 sermon** Jerry Falwell, "Ministers and Marches," reprinted as Appendix B of Perry Deane Young, *God's Bullies, Native Reflections on Preachers and Politics* (New York: Holt, Rinehart and Winston, 1982).

470 **"group of nine idiots"** Daniel K. Williams, *God's Own Party: The Making of the Christian Right* (New York: Oxford University Press, 2012), 85.

470 **concert by Led Zeppelin** Gerald Strober and Ruth Tomczak, *Jerry Falwell: Aflame for God* (Nashville, TN: Thomas Nelson, 1979), 66.

470 **part of His plan** For Falwell's prophetic self-understanding see Susan Harding, *The Book of Jerry Falwell* (Princeton: Princeton University Press, 2000).

471 **In 1976, he avowed** J. Brooks Flippen, *Jimmy Carter, the Politics of Family, and the Rise of the Religious Right* (Athens, GA: University of Georgia Press, 2011), 110–11.

471 **"see a fight"** Jeffrey K. Hadden and Charles E. Swann, *Prime Time Preachers: The Rising Power of Televangelism* (New York: Addison-Wesley, 1981), 86.

471 **eagle-eyed Christian** Author interview with Peggy June Griffin; Martin P. Claussen and Evelyn Bills Claussen, eds., *The Voice of Christian and Jewish Dissenters in America: U.S. Internal Revenue Service Hearings on Proposed "Discrimination" Tax Controls over Christian, Jews, and Secular Private Schools, Dec. 5,6, 7,8, 1978* (Washington, D.C.: Piedmont Press, 1982), 274.

471 **gone out of its way** Ibid., 275.

472 **"surrender their children"** Michael J. McVicar, *Christian Reconstruction: R. J. Rushdoony and American Religious Conservatism* (Chapel Hill: University of North Carolina Press, 2015), 1.

472 **On August 15, 1978** Claussen and Claussen, *The Voice of Christian and Jewish Dissenters in America*, 161. All subsequent quotations from letters and hearing testimony come from this extraordinary volume, apparently privately published in 1982 in a numbered press run (the author possesses copy number 0909), designed as if a sacred text. On its cover, a Jewish star of David and "IHS" Christogram are arrayed next to the figure "IRS$USA" styled as if it were the symbol of a competing religion. A concordance of Biblical texts cited by witnesses is printed as an appendix; the back cover prints Biblical passages in Hebrew, English, and German, and quotations from *The Communist Manifesto*, *The Humanist Manifesto*, and the Constitution the Soviet Union; an old-fashioned extended subtitle begins, "comprising TEXTS OF ALL STATEMENTS OF WITNESSES *prepared and extemporaneous and supplemental presented by some 250 Christian and Jewish clergymen, teachers, and headmasters, lawyers and political leaders, and laymen of high and low estate, at this Chalcedon-like 'ecumenical council' council in Washington D.C. . . . .*" As best I can discern, no Jewish clergy members testified at the hearings.

474 **crowd rustled and rumbled** For atmospheric reconstruction of the hearings I rely, in addition to *The Voice of Christian and Jewish Dissenters in America*, on author interview with Peggy June Griffin; "Speakers Deplore IRS Proposal to Tax Schools Ruled Discriminatory," *Des Moines Register*, December 6, 1978; UPI, December 6, 1978; AP, December 6, 1978; UPI, December 7, 1978; "IRS May Reverse on Taxing Private Schools," *Montgomery Advertiser*, December 8, 1978; AP, December 10. 1978; "IRS Reconsiders Plan on School Taxing," LAT, December 16, 1978; and AB, CBS, and NBC News, December 5, 1978, VTVNA.

479 **hall-of-mirrors logic** On secular humanism as a religion see Martin E. Marty, "Secular Humanism, the Religion of," *University of Chicago Magazine*, Summer 1987; Carol Mason, *Reading Appalachia from Left to Right: Conservatives and the 1974 Kanawha County Textbook Controversy* (Ithaca, NY: Cornell University Press, 2009), 107–12.

480 **law review article** John W. Whitehead and John Conlan, "The Establishment of the Religion of Secular Humanism and Its First Amendment Implications," *Texas Tech Law Review* 10 (1978–1979).

480 **"newly established religion"** Patrick Buchanan column, October 9, 1978.

480 **to an Indiana newspaper** "Public Education," *Vidette Messenger of Porter County*, December 5, 1978.

480 **Ronald Reagan contributed** RRC, November 17, 1978; "Ronald Reagan Newspaper Columns, 11/1978–12/1978 (1/3), RRPL, Box 12.

482 **Randolph Thrower** "Randolph W. Thrower Dies at 100; Ran IRS Under Nixon," NYT, March 19, 2014.

483 **on February 9** "IRS Softens Proposal Aimed at 'Segregation Academies,' " WP, February 10, 1979.

483 **Editorials kept horsewhipping** "IRS and Private Schools," *San Bernardino County Sun*, December 7, 1978; "Let Us Put a Stop to This Outrage," *Tampa Times*, December 7, 1978; Paul Harvey column, December 7, 1978; "IRS No Social Agency," *Lincoln Star*, December 8, 1978.

483 **On February 18** UPI, February 21, 1979; Gannett Service, February 21, 1979; "IRS Chief Calls Tax Changes Vital in Fight Against Private School Bias," *Baltimore Sun*, February 21, 1979.

484 **Secret Service protection** Thomas Edsall and Jane Byrne Edsall, *Chain Reaction:*

The Impact of Race, Rights, and Taxes on American Politics (New York: W.W. Norton, 1991), 132.

484 **at least since 1962** Kim Phillips-Fein, *Invisible Hands: The Businessmen's Crusade Against the New Deal* (New York: Norton, 2009), 226.

484 **"The next real major"** Garry Wills, *Lead Time: A Journalist's Education* (New York: Doubleday, 1983), 284.

484 **"vote for Christianity"** Jewish Telegraphic Agency, October 21, 1976.

485 **the very next day** William Martin, *With God on Our Side: The Rise of the Religious Right in America* (New York: Broadway Books, 1996), 171.

485 **In another account** Dan Gilgoff, *The Jesus Machine: How James Dobson, Focus on the Family, and Evangelical America Are Winning the Culture War* (New York: St. Martin's Press, 2007), 80–81. In an interview with the author, Lance Tarrance could not recall when Weyrich introduced him to the preachers.

485 **actual, confirming document** Ballmer, *Redeemer*, 109.

485 **National Christian Action Coalition** Matthew C. Moen, *The Transformation of the Christian Right* (Tuscaloosa: University of Alabama Press, 1992), 17.

485 **Orange County** Darren Dochuk, *From Bible Belt to Sun Belt: Plain-Folk Religion, Grassroots Politics, and the Rise of Evangelical Conservatism* (New York: W. W. Norton, 2011), passim (quote on 243).

486 **Concerned Women for America** Susan Faludi, *Backlash: The Undeclared War Against American Women* (New York: Crown, 1991), 247; Dochuk, *From Bible Belt to Sun Belt*, 383.

486 **Christian Voice** Dochuk, *From Bible Belt to Sun Belt,*, 384.

486 **"WE WANT OUR COUNTRY BACK!"** Martin Durham, *The Christian Right: The Far Right and the Boundaries of American Conservatism* (Manchester, UK: Manchester University Press, 2000), 170.

486 **Gary Jarmin** Connie Paige, *The Right to Lifers: Who They Are, How They Operate, and Where They Get Their Money* (New York: Summit Books, 1983), 177; Knight News Service, May 8, 1980; "About Politics: Visit with an Election Year Lobbyist," March 31, 1980, NYT, March 31, 1980.

487 **"The beauty of it"** "Preachers in Politics," USNWR, September 24, 1979.

487 *Late, Great Planet Earth* Melani McAllister, *Epic Encounters: Cultural, Media, and U.S. Interests in the Middle East Since 1945* (Berkeley: University of California Press [Updated Edition], 2005), 165–78; Jesse Walker, "Orson Welles' Apocalyptic Trilogy," Reason.com, May 8, 2015; "Disastermania," *Time*, March 5, 1979; HBO advertisement, *Albuquerque Journal*, April 4, 1979; Laura Kalman, *Right Star Rising: A New Politics, 1974–1980* (New York: Norton, 2010), 313. The film can be viewed on YouTube.com, accessed April 9, 2020.

488 **the pastor's wife** Author correspondence with Duane Jackson.

489 **March for Life** AP, January 15, 1979; "Abortion Foes March in Capital on Anniversary of Legalization," NYT, January 23, 1979.

488 **Gray replied that sex education** Mary McGrory column, February 8, 1979.

488 **On Valentine's Day** UPI, February 15, 1979; UPI, February 16, 1979; Paige, *The Right to Lifers*, 106.

489 **"hottest single peacetime issue"** ABC News, January 5, 1979, VTVNA.

489 **crucial meeting in Lynchburg, Virginia** Ed McAteer's account of the Moral Majority founding meeting is in Paige, *The Right to Lifers*, 154.

490 **too busy** See Falwell's newspaper the *Journal-Champion*, November 10, 1978, downloaded at DigitalCommons.Liberty.edu. For Bicentennial Bibles see Frances FitzGerald, "A Disciplined, Charging Army," *New Yorker*, May 18, 1981.

490 **150 towns** Flippen, *Jimmy Carter*, 195.

491 **Although, in other accounts** The account where Weyrich speaks is Martin, *With God on Our Side*, 200. Falwell's claim is in his *Listen, America!* (New York: Doubleday, 1980), 343. David Snowball, *Continuity and Change in the Rhetoric of the Moral Majority* (New York: Praeger, 1991), 50–52, notes one account crediting Robert Bauman, and another the Conservative Caucus. Dinesh D'Souza, cited by Sara Diamond, *Spiritual Warfare: The Politics of the Christian Right* (Boston: South End Press, 199), 60, makes the claim about abortion. The version in which the name is brainstormed is in Michael Sean Winters, *God's Right Hand: How Jerry Falwell Made God a Republican and Baptized the American Right* (New York: HarperOne, 2012), 119.

491 **historical record** Falwell and Billings article in Jerry Falwell's newspaper the *Journal-Champion*, February 23, 1979, quoted in Phillips-Fein, *Invisible Hands*, 233.

492 **Viguerie's mailing lists** Richard Viguerie and David Franke, *Right Turn: How Conservatives Used New and Alternative Media to Take Over America* (Lanham, MD: Taylor Trade Publishing, 2004), 133.

492 **his own telling** "Political Gospel: Christian Soldiers Spread the 'Right' Word," *Minneapolis Star*, August 25, 1980.

492 **"crusade evangelists"** Martin, *With God on Our Side*, 198.

492 **oil magnate H. L. Hunt** Williams, *God's Own Party*, 182–83.

492 **The Sunday after Presidents' Day** "Robison Show Is Canceled by Channel 8," *Fort Worth Star-Telegram*, March 3, 1979; AP, March 4, 1979.

492 **Dallas Gay Political Caucus** AP, May 27, 1979.

493 **WFAA had suspended** Ibid.

493 **Falwell—who had run** "TV Time Is Offered by a Carter Critic," NYT, October 13, 1976; AP, October 15, 1976.

493 **Wallie Criswell** Flippen, *Jimmy Carter*, 209.

493 **Tim LaHaye pitched in** Phillips-Fein, *Invisible Hands*, 233.

493 **North Phoenix Baptist Church** "Evangelist Defends Right to Speak Out on Moral Issues," *Arizona Republic*, March 10, 1979.

493 **Michael Huckabee** Ariel Levy, "Prodigal Son: Is the Wayward Republican Mike Huckabee Now His Party's Best Hope?" *New Yorker*, June 21, 2010.

493 **news conference** AP, May 27, 1979.

493 **landed a feature** "Evangelist Fights Cancellation of TV Show," NYT, April 1, 1979.

493 **"Racehorse" Haynes** Ibid.

493 **TV special** See ad in *Philadelphia Enquirer*, April 1, 1979.

494 **Iowa Senate** "Tactics Against 'Creation Bill' Anger Author," *Sioux City Journal*, April 20, 1979.

494 **Bob Dylan** "Pop Scene," *Toledo Blade*, May 4, 1979; Michael D. Hammond, "Twice Born, Once Elected: The Making of the Religious Right During the Carter Administration," dissertation, University of Arkansas, 2009; "Born-Again Bob Dylan Sings the Gospel in His New LP," *People*, September 10. 1979.

494 **"I Love America" rally** AP, April 26, 1979; UPI, April 27. 1979; Flippen, *Jimmy Carter*, 208.

494 **Paul Weyrich wrote** Ballmer, *Redeemer*, 109.

494 **On May 4** Paige, *The Right to Lifers*, 199; "McCormack [*sic*] May Be Candidate for Presidency in 1980," *The Catholic Advance*, May 17, 1979.

495 **On May 11** Ballmer, *Redeemer*, 109.

495 **"Jesus '79"** "Rally for Jesus Attracts Cheering Throng of 35,000 to Shea," WP, June 3, 1979.

495 **Freedom Rally** "Robison Rally Draws 11,000," *Tampa Tribune*, June 9, 1979; Levy, "Prodigal Son"; Martin, *With God on Our Side*, 199.

496 **At a press conference** Scott Lamb, *Huckabee: The Authorized Biography* (Nashville, TN: Thomas Nelson, 2015), 137.

496 **board of directors** Diamond, *Spiritual Warfare*, 60.

496 **"floating crap game"** Martin, *With God on Our Side*, 175.

496 **John Connally called** ENIR, August 13, 1979; "Preachers in Politics," USNWR, September 24, 1979.

CHAPTER TWENTY-THREE

497 **columns, commentaries** RRC, November 17, 1978; RRB 78-16, track A1, "Private Schools," recorded November 28, 1978, in RIHOH, 354.

497 **Sears had managed** Sidney Blumenthal, *The Permanent Campaign: Inside the World of Elite Political Operatives* (Boston: Beacon Press, 1980), 198; Theodore White, *America In Search of Itself: The Making of the President, 1956–1980* (New York: Harper & Row, 1981), 248; Jules Witcover, *Marathon: Pursuit of the President, 1972–1976* (New York, Viking, 1977), 67.

498 **"John P. Satan"** "Reagan's Man Sears Ready to Roll," *Washington Star*, January 26, 1979.

498 **"Power of any kind"** Susan B. Trento, *The Power House: Robert Keith Gray and the Selling of Influence in Washington* (New York: St. Martin's Press, 1992), 84.

498 **"Politics is motion"** "Reagan Strategist Surveys Scene—and Picks a Winner," WSJ, August 30, 1979.

498 **lengthy benders** Author correspondence with David Keane; Bob Spitz, *Reagan: An American Journey* (New York: Penguin, 2018), 384, 433.

498 **Sears devised** Rick Perlstein, *Invisible Bridge; The Fall of Nixon and the Rise of Reagan* (New York: Simon & Schuster, 2014), 737.

498 **Nofziger tried to stab** Bob Colacello, *Ronnie and Nancy: Their Path to the White House—1911 to 1980* (New York: Grand Central Publishing, 2004), 474.

499 **"brain for hire"** Ibid., 475; also for Sears's persuasion of Nancy Reagan and Deaver, and Laxalt's objections.

499 **traveling party** Schedule Files, Box 59, RRPL; "Europe 1978," RVA, Folder 27, Box 21-22.

499 **"extremely concerned"** Reagan to Lorraine and Elwood Wagner, February 5, 1979, in RALIL, 785.

500 **from West Germany** RRC, December 14, 1978.

500 **From London** RRC, December 8, 1978. This column also reported from Paris.

500 **From Bavaria** RRC, December 12, 1978.

500 **West Berlin** RRC, December 8, 1978.

500 **Several times, he related** Ibid.; Reagan to Larry Beilensen, December 12, 1978, dictation file, RRPL, Box 1.

500 **Margaret Thatcher** Ronald Reagan, *An American Life: An Autobiography* (New York: Simon & Schuster, 1990), 204; November 27, 1978, schedule, Box 59, RRPL; Allen notes, "Mrs. Thatcher," RVA, Box 27, Folder 21.

500 **his former secretary** Reagan to Mrs. A. S. Betty Meyers, December 15, 1978, dictation file, RRPL, Box 1.

500 **Los Angeles World Affairs Council** "12/14/1978, World Affairs Council, Los Angeles, (1)-(2)" folders, RRPL, Box 24, including memos, flier, and speech.

502 **literally scripted answers** Hannaford to Deaver, December 12, 1978, and Hannaford to Reagan, cc MKD, December 12, 1978, RRPL, box 24.

502 **"Reagan Urges Debate"** LAT, December 15, 1978.

502 **"Reagan Challenges Carter"** *Louisville Courier-Journal*, December 15, 1978.

503 **"if this quote is correct"** Hannaford to Richard Allen, cc Martin Anderson, December 14, 1978, RRPL, Box 24

503 **His next column** CFTRN, January 4, 1979.

503 **following issue** CFTRN, January 18, 1979.

503 **next newspaper column** RRC, December 22, 1978.

503 **one after that** RRC, December 26, 1978.

503 **Witcover and Jack Germond reported** W&G, December 21, 1978.

504 **"gratuitous nonsense"** Hannaford to Richard Allen, December 29, 1978, RVA, Box 28, Folder 5.

504 **five weeks later** Ronald Reagan, "Decency for Taiwan," NYT, January 28, 1979.

504 **returned to the road** Schedule Files, Box 59, RRPL.

504 **"experts are telling us"** "Reagan: Soviet Ultimatum Near," *Palm Beach Post*, January 5, 1977.

504 **"People to Whom We Talk"** Hannaford to Molly Tuthill, DH, Box 12, Folder 3; mid-March 1979, six numbered copies, RRPL, Box 103.

505 **"Sign Personally"** "S P (signed personally?) letters, 1978–1979," DH, Box 4, Folders 8 and 9; RVA, Box 28, Folder 5.

506 **another** *Commentary* **article** Jeane Kirkpatrick, "Why the New Right Lost," *Commentary*, February 1, 1977.

507 **dictated personally** RRPL, Box 1, "Dictation" (by date).

507 **Kissingerian telegram** Reagan to Ohira, December 7, 1978, RVA, Box 27, Folder 27.

507 **"I realize there were some"** Reagan to to Ralph Tipton, December 11, 1978.

508 **"We want to shake"** W&G, January 3, 1979.

508 **addressed a luncheon** "1/21/79–1/25/1979—Washington D.C. Trip," Box 74, RRPL.

508 **"wouldn't recover politically"** Robert Novak, *The Prince of Darkness: 50 Years Reporting in Washington* (New York: Crown Forum, 2007), 334.

509 **Mafia-style ultimatum** W&G, January 4, 1979.

509 **Gallup asked Republicans** Gallup column, January 12, 1979.

509 **corporate lobbyists** Hannaford to Reagan, January 16, 1979, and speech text, "1/21/79–1/25/1979—Washington D.C. Trip," Box 74, RRPL; this folder also has information on CPD dinner.

510 **their next column** W&G, January 31, 1979.

510 **Godfrey Sperling** *Christian Science Monitor* Service, February 12, 1979.

510 **"Reagan–George Bush ticket"** "Washington Whispers," USNWR, February 26, 1979.

510 **headed east** Schedule file, February 18 to February 20, 1979, Box 75, RRPL.

510 **"Jewish community"** Loren Smith meeting, May 17, 1979, Box 103, RRPL.

510 **courting since autumn** James Stockdale to Nofziger and Deaver, October 9, 1978, "Pending, New York," Box 71, RRPL; Meese notes, "Finance," January 3, 1979, Box 103, RRPL, Box 75, "Rabb Luncheon," RRPL, which includes all the correspondence concerning the Rabb luncheon cited on page 511.

512 **"Power Struggle Grows"** *Rocky Mount* (North Carolina) *Telegram*, December 15, 1978.

512 **Sears had struck a deal** Author correspondence with David Keane.

513 "thinking man's candidate" *Time*, February 5, 1979.

513 piece on Keene's ENIR, February 27, 1979.

513 John Sears's cue "Elephant Master?" *Christian Science Monitor*, March 9. 1979.

514 activist from suburban Joseph M. Brudzinski to Paul Laxalt, February 22, 1979, RRPL, Box 4; author interview with Brudzinski.

514 "notches to the right" "Bush Acquires Top Conservative Operative," HE, March 3, 1979.

514 On March 6 Hannaford to Reagan, March 17, 1979, DH, Box 2, Folder 8.

514 the next morning "Many Former Ford Backers Join Reagan Funds Panel," *Washington Star*, March 7, 1979; AP, March 7, 1979; speech texts in "National Advisory Committee" folder, Box 86, RRPL; Reagan statement, DH, Box 9, Folder 9.

516 "the most impressive" UPI, March 8, 1979.

516 Laxalt responded "Backers of Reagan Open His Campaign," NYT, March 8, 1979.

517 William Loeb Kevin Cash, *Who the Hell Is William Loeb?* (Manchester, NH: Amoskeag Press, 1975).

517 Political experts estimated Thomas J. McIntyre, *The Fear Brokers* (Boston: Beacon Press, 1981), 201.

517 What positions For nuclear arsenal see Cash, *Who the Hell Is William Loeb?* For Joseph McCarthy and "Kissinger the Kike" see Myra McPherson, "Who Is William Loeb Is and Why He Says All Those Mean Things About . . . ," WP, February 24, 1980. For Shockley and South Africa quote see McIntyre, *The Fear Brokers*, xxii, 262–64, 272.

518 "The Two Faces of Congressman Crane" DH, Box 9, Folder 9; "The Early Bird," *Newsweek*, March 19, 1979; "Salvo from Editor Loeb Ignites a Crane-Reagan Fracas," WP, March 9, 1979; Gannett, March 9, 1979; UPI, March 9, 1979; documents in "Press Releases" files, DH, Box 9, Folder 9; "Black Files—Crane, Phillip," Box 85, RRPL; author interview with former congressman who wishes to remain anonymous; Jack Anderson column, February 12, 1980.

518 *New Right Report* March 15, 1979, RRPL, Box 86.

518 $1 million in debt Adam Clymer, *Drawing the Line at the Big Ditch: The Panama Canal Treaties and the Rise of the Right* (Lawrence: University Press of Kansas, 2008), 160.

519 Howard Baker UPI, March 10, 1979; Sidney Blumenthal, *The Permanent Campaign: Inside the World of Elite Political Operatives* (Boston: Beacon Press, 1980), 197; J. Lee Annis, *Howard Baker: Conciliator in an Age of Crisis* (Knoxville, TN: Howard Baker Center, 2007), 163–66; "GOP Raps Carter Defense Policy, "*Vidette-Messenger of Porter County*, March 12, 1979.

519 Bob Dole's turn HE, March 10, 1979; "Republican Hopefuls Tread the Path to Iowa," NYT, March 4, 1979; *Indianapolis News*, March 10, 1979.

520 George Herbert Walker Bush Kitty Kelley, *The Family: The Real Story of the Bush Dynasty* (New York: Doubleday, 2004), 362 (Christmas card list); "GOP Hopefuls: Analysis," *Vidette-Messenger of Porter County*, March 13, 1979; *Indianapolis News*, March 10, 1979.

520 shiny automobile Joe McGinnis, *The Selling of the President 1968* (New York: Trident Press, 1969), 43–44.

520 "Dear Mr. President" "George H. W. Bush: The Making of a President," BBC News, December 1, 2018.

521 "Listen, I believe in it" "To George Bush, Seeking Presidency Seems Almost a Duty," WSJ, July 6, 1979.

521 visit to China Doro Bush Koch, *My Father, My President: A Personal Account of the Life of George H. W. Bush* (New York: Grand Central, 20014), 144.

521 **"one with compassion"** *Time*, February 15, 1979.

521 **Safire pointed out** William Safire column, March 7, 1977.

521 **"bedwetting Trilateralist"** Craig Shirley, *Rendezvous with Destiny: Ronald Reagan and the Campaign That Changed America* (Wilmington, DE: Intercollegiate Studies Institute, 2009), 56.

522 **Big John stole the show** AP, March 12, 1979; ENIR, March 14, 1979; "Midwest Republicans See Candidates, Sow Early Preference for Connally," *Dayton Daily News*, March 11, 1979; UPI, March 12, 1979; *Indianapolis News*, March 10, 1979.

522 **"scheduling conflict"** UPI, March 10, 1979.

522 **in New York** Schedule Files, Box 59, RRPL.

522 **St. Patrick's Day Parade** Hannaford to Deaver, October 25, 1978, DH, Box 2, Folder 7.

522 **attendees filled out their ballots** "Connally Tabbed Top GOP Contender," *Vidette-Messenger of Porter County*, March 12, 1979.

523 **humorist Mark Russell** "Tony Knight: Good Evening," *Pensacola News*, March 14, 1979.

CHAPTER TWENTY-FOUR

524 **"CRISIS OF LEADERSHIP"** LAT, March 2, 1979; UPI, March 5, 1979.

524 **New York Times and CBS** CFTRN, March 16, 1979.

524 **memo laying out strategy** Hamilton Jordan, "EYES ONLY: The Myth of the Incumbent President," printed in WP, June 8 1980.

524 **"liberal cult"** *Doonesbury*, February 5, 1979; February 6, 1979; February 7, 1979; February 8, 1979; February 9, 1979; February 10, 1979; February 12, 1979.

524 **"the Army's still with us"** *Doonesbury*, February 22, 1979.

524 **Ted Kennedy repeated** Jules Witcover and Jack Germond, *Blue Smoke and Mirrors: How Reagan Won and Why Carter Lost the Election of 1980* (New York: Viking, 1981), 49.

524 **Scuttlebutt was** Ed Meese meeting notes, March 13, 1979, RRPL, Box 103; CFTRN, March 16, 1979.

524 **Arthur Schlesinger Jr.** Arthur M. Schlesinger Jr., *Journals: 1952–2000* (New York: Penguin, 2007), 461.

525 **special prosecutor** AP, March 20, 1979.

525 **"big enough for the job"** "Carter, at Midterm, Is Still 'Outsider' to Many in Congress," NYT, March 7, 1979.

525 **in the Middle East** Lawrence Wright, *Thirteen Days in September: Carter, Begin, and Sadat at Camp David* (New York: Knopf, 2014), 269–72; Jimmy Carter, *White House Diary* (New York: Macmillan, 2010), 300–304.

526 **On the front page** "Sadat and Begin Sign Treaty," WP, March 27, 1979.

526 **The pollster began** Theodore White, *America In Search of Itself: The Making of the President, 1956–1980* (New York: Harper & Row, 1981), 257.

526 **A new thriller** Garry Wills column, May 7, 1979.

527 **"Atoms for Peace"** "Address Before the General Assembly of the United Nations on Peaceful Uses of Atomic Energy," December 8, 1953, APP.

527 **"nuclear" was deliberate** Natasha Zaretsky, *Radiation Nation: Three Mile Island and the Political Transformation of the 1970s* (New York: Columbia University Press, 2018), 25.

527 **"the more abundant life"** Ibid., 20.

527   "Radioactivity. It's" *Life*, October 13, 1972, 75.

527   likelihood of a citizen dying Zaretsky, *Radiation Nation*, 61.

527   three General Electric nuclear engineers Ibid., 45.

527   "pseudo-environmentalists" RRC, October 13, 1976.

527   Jane Fonda had hoped Fonda interview, *Allentown Morning Call*, March 18, 1979.

528   discovered around Denver AP, March 10, 1979.

528   Silkwood family's lawsuit UPI, March 4, 1979.

528   five plants in the East shuttered AP, March 14, 1979.

528   "cancer clusters" For example AP, March 10, 1979, running in the *Arizona Republic* directly below story about Denver nuclear dumps.

528   For the producers See " 'The China Syndrome': More Than 'Just a Movie'?" LAT, March 25, 197.

528   "I saw a plume" Susan Stamberg, *Every Night at Five: Susan Stamberg's* All Things Considered *Book* (New York: Pantheon, 1982), 91.

528   A worker had mistakenly Ibid. and Zaretsky, *Radiation Nation*.

530   "can't tame it right" Alistair Cooke, *Alistair Cooke's America* (New York: Basic Books, 2009), 240.

530   "I am not a nuclear engineer" Zaretsky, *Radiation Nation*, 71.

530   "irresponsible scare tactics" Carter, *White House Diary*, 310.

530   With time to reflect *Meltdown at Three Mile Island*, PBS *American Experience* documentary, 1999.

530   blind men "Appendix II, Transcripts from NRC Meetings," *Washington Post* special report, 1979.

530   "We have more important things" Zaretsky, *Radiation Nation*, 69.

530   The mayor of Middleton AP, May 20, 1979.

530   "credibility meltdown" NYT, March 30, 1979. The editorial was widely reprinted.

530   Hill & Knowlton Susan B. Trento, *The Power House: Robert Keith Gray and the Selling of Influence in Washington* (New York: St. Martin's Press, 1992), 90.

531   Denton testified "Nuclear Inquiry Cites Absence of Cooling Water," WP, May 1, 1979.

531   major speech on energy "Energy Address to the Nation," April 5, 1979, APP.

532   excruciating decision Meg Jacobs, *Panic at the Pump: The Energy Crisis and the Transformation of American Politics in the 1970s* (New York: Hill & Wang, 2016), 199.

532   "spot market" had doubled David P. Vogel, *Fluctuating Fortunes: The Political Power of Business in America* (New York: Basic Books, 1989), 178.

532   as far away as El Paso *El Paso Times*, May 20, 1979.

532   "our door has a crack in it" Stamberg, *Every Night at Five*, 93–95; also pregnancy tests, T-shirts, "guinea pig."

533   "distinguish a cancer" AP, April 10, 1979.

533   "no flames" Zaretsky, *Radiation Nation*, 73.

533   "The Pepsi Syndrome" *Saturday Night Live*, April 7, 1979. See transcript and stills at "I remember TMI: Central PA Stories," PaPost.org.

534   By the time Jacobs, *Panic at the Pump*, 204; MFTVE, 7:26; "The Great Gas Crunch—Who Is to Blame?" LAT, May 20. 1979.

534   In Oregon *Eugene Register Guard*, March 31, 1979, 8A.

534   in Minneapolis *Minneapolis Star Tribune*, March 2, 1979.

534   "premature panic situation" AP, March 23, 1979.

534   On April 25 "Panel Rebuffs Carter, Rejects Gas Rationing," LAT, April 26, 1979; John A. Farrell, *Tip O'Neill and the Democratic Century* (New York: Little, Brown, 2001), 529.

534 **"transparent fig leaf"** Jules Witcover and Jack Germond, *Blue Smoke and Mirrors: How Reagan Won and Why Carter Lost the Election of 1980* (New York: Viking, 1981), 51; "The President's News Conference," April 30, 1979.

534 **the next day** "Gas Rationing Compromise," LAT, April 27, 1979.

535 **Only 25 percent** AP, March 23, 1979.

535 **Battle of Flowers parade** "April 27, 1979: Fiesta Sniper Kills 2, Injuries 51," MySanAntonio.com; "KSAT-TV News Coverage on Fiesta Sniper 1979," YouTube .com, accessed April 11, 2020.

535 **"*It finally happened*"** "The First Gasoline Panic," *Newsweek*, May 14, 1979.

535 **from all directions** For these scenes from California gasoline panic see Sandbrook, *Mad as Hell*, 296; MFTVE, 7:27; LAT, May 8, 1979, front page.

535 **"Most Major Oil Firms"** LAT, May 1, 1979.

536 **"sociology of unreason"** White, *America In Search of Itself*, 262.

536 **in Iowa** "Carter Supports Brown Odd-Even Gas Sales Plan," LAT, May 5, 1979.

536 **"youthful looking hairline"** "Reporter's Notebook: Suddenly a New Look for Carter," NYT, May 7, 1979.

537 **"In politics—or at least"** Robert Schlesinger, *White House Ghosts: Presidents and Their Speechwriters* (New York: Simon & Schuster, 2008), 299.

537 **Iowa press conference** "The President's News Conference," May 4, 1979, APP.

537 **fire trucks** "For Southland Drivers, Long Lines, Near-Dry Weekend," LAT, May 5, 1979.

537 **released a statement** "Gasoline Shortages in California: Statement by the President," May 5, 1979, APP.

538 **only one other utterance** "Gasoline Shortage to Worsen, Carter Says," LAT, May 6, 1979.

539 **Senator Long** Ian Shapiro, *The Last Great Senate: Courage and Statesmanship in Times of Crisis* (New York: Public Affairs Books, 2012), 243.

539 **Howard Baker** "Sen. Baker Hints at Oil Nationalization," WP, May 14, 1979.

539 **John Connally** "Md. GOP Hears Connally Voice Presidential Hopes," *Baltimore Sun*, May 12, 1979.

539 **Ronald Reagan** Reagan to A. M. "Turk" Swindle, May 2, 1979, RRPL, Box 1; RRB 79-07, tracks A2 and A3, "Three Mile Island I" (for quote) and "Three Mile Island II," recorded May 8, 1979, in RPV, 439, 440; RRB 79-09, track A4, "Nuclear Power," recorded June 29, 1979, in RPV, 454.

539 **Jerry Brown** "Odd-Even Gas Plan Reinstated by Governor," LAT, May 5, 1979

539 **antinuclear protest** "Biggest No-Nuke Rally Rocks Washington," *Circus Weekly*, June 12, 1979, reprinted at JoniMitchell.com; AP, May 8, 1979.

540 **"from necessity to albatross"** "L.A. Residents Shifting Down from Overdrive," LAT, May 8, 1979.

540 **rejected it overwhelmingly** "Carter Is Shocked by Ration Vote," CT, May 12, 1979.

540 **capital was atwitter** James Fallows, "The Passionless Presidency," *Atlantic Monthly*, May 1979; author correspondence with James Fallows.

541 **the White House tennis court** "The President's News Conference," April 30, 1979, APP.

541 **poll of New Hampshire Democrats** Meese notes, May 14, 1979, Reagan for President Committee executive council meeting, Box 103, RRPL.

541 **May 12 commencement address** "Carter's Oil Plan Is Burdening the Poor, Kennedy Says," WP, May 13, 1979.

541 **"angry jeremiad"** "Standby Gasoline Rationing Plan: Remarks on the House of Representatives Disapproval of the Plan," May 11, 1979, APP.

542   **In Illinois** "It's 55 m.p.h.—or Arrest," CT, May 17, 1979.

542   **In Ocean City** "All Gassed Up and Ready to Go," *Camden Courier-Post*, May 5, 1979; "Kelley Promises Tourists Gasoline," *Baltimore Sun*, May 10, 1979; "Resort Plan Is Secret," *Salisbury Daily Times*, May 11, 1979.

542   **newspaper in Allentown** "Resorts Court Fuel Minded; Shore Mayor Promises Gas," *Allentown Morning Call*, May 20, 1979.

542   **Oddball California** Governor Brown safari poll: Walter Mears, *Deadlines Past: Forty Years of Presidential Campaigning* (Kansas City, MO: Andrew McNeel Publishing, 2003), 165. Lieutenant governor: "Curb Cannot Call Election, Official Says," LAT, April 7, 1979. Tailgate parties: "All-Night Station Draws Crowd," LAT, May 13, 1979. Fitness instructor: "Exercises Help Lift Gas Line Ennui," LAT, May 20, 1979. Hot pants: "For Southland Drivers, Long Lines, Near-Dry Weekend," LAT, May 5, 1979. Lawnmower, horse riders: "L.A. Residents Shifting Down from Overdrive," LAT, May 8, 1979. Lew Wasserman: "People," *Santa Rosa Press Democrat*, May 9, 1979. Union 77 owner: " 'Sheik' Draws Shrieks from His Customers," LAT, May 9, 1979. Asking for "deposits": "Some Benefits Seen in Effects of Gas Crunch," LAT, May 9, 1979. Unmarked tanker truck: "1,000 Gallon Gang Gets the (Un)leaded Out," LAT, May 9, 1979.

543   **brandishing a pistol** White, *America In Search of Itself*, 262.

543   **Jody Powell mocked** USNWR, May 28, 1979.

543   **Senator Percy** "Californians: The Image Is Inaccurate," LAT, May 20, 1979.

543   **Tennessee Williams** "In His Beloved Key West, Tennessee Williams Is Center Stage in a Furor Over Gays," *People*, May 7, 1979.

544   **known as the Castro** My portrait of the Castro is indebted to Strange de Jim, *San Francisco's Castro* (Arcadia Publishing, 2003), and "The Castro," KQED San Francisco/PBS (1998), accessed at YouTube.com April 12, 2020.

544   **"Let's get the dykes!"** Randy Shilts, *The Mayor of Castro Street: The Life and Times of Harvey Milk* (New York: St. Martin's Press, 1982), 306.

544   **Ronald Reagan said** RBB 75-04, track 7, "The Work Ethic," recorded February 27, 1975.

545   **"social deviants"** Ibid., 162.

545   **"We've got to stand up"** Warren Hinckle, "Dan White's San Francisco," *Inquiry*, October 1979.

545   **During jury selection** My account of the Dan White trial derives from Ibid.; Shilts, *The Mayor of Castro Street*, 308–25; and the documents collected by Professor Douglas O. Lynder at https://famous-trials.com/danwhite, accessed April 12, 2020.

546   **seven-foot likeness** "It's John Wayne in That Rock," LAT, March 29, 1979.

546   **The president took time** Carter, *White House Diary*, May 5, 1979.

546   **At the Academy Awards** "The Duke's Last Hurrah," YouTube.com, accessed April 12, 2020; AP, April 10, 1979.

548   **legal observers** For suspicions the prosecution was throwing the case, and Undersheriff Jim Denman's presentation of the evidence, see Hinckle, "Dan White's San Francisco."

550   **Hinckle drafted** Shilts, *The Mayor of Castro Street*, 316.

551   **"A prolonged debate"** Hinckle, "Ten Days That Shook San Francisco," *San Francisco Examiner Magazine*, November 6, 1988.

551   **"We'll hire gays"** For abuse and threats against Chief Gain and Sheriff Hongisto see Shilts, *The Mayor of Castro Street*, 120–21, 165–67, 201–202, and Hinckle, "Dan White's San Francisco"; also for Milk recording and "What scares me."

552 **Dianne Feinstein** Shilts, *The Mayor of Castro Street*, 307; for "Gentle Dan," 209.

552 **It was** "Gas—Day No. 11: Fuel Situation About as Usual—Terrible," LAT, May 20. 1979.

552 **announced the verdict** Shilts, *The Mayor of Castro Street*, 336–37.

553 **As it happened** "Dan White Had Other Targets, Cop Says," *San Francisco Chronicle*, September 18, 1998.

553 **no one to stop a riot** Author interview with the late Maggie JoChild; "The Castro," KQED; "Rage in San Francisco," *Time*, June 4, 1979; de Jim, *San Francisco's Castro.*

553 **"outside agitators"** May 22, 1979, VTVNA.

554 **"Neighborhoods = good"** Deaver notes, June 12, 1978, RRPL, Box 103.

554 **"lame duck"** "GOP Leader Calls Carter a Lame Duck," LAT, May 20, 1979.

554 **"political hemophiliac"** UPI, May 28, 1979.

554 **Representative Toby Moffett** "Rep. Moffett Presses Energy Issue in Campaign Trip," NYT, May 21, 1979.

554 **two to one** "House Democrats Hand Carter Stinging Rebuff on Oil Decontrol," WP, May 23, 1979.

554 **called in his diary** Carter, *White House Diary*, 312.

554 **indicted Bert Lance** "Indict Lance for Fraud; 3 Associates Also Face Bank Charges," CT, May 24, 1979; "Carter: A Song of Woe" and "Carter: A Friend Is In Need," *Time*, June 4, 1979.

554 **"Lance Greased White House"** *Philadelphia Daily News*, April 10, 1979.

554 **exasperated D.C. commentariat** Loye Miller column, May 26, 1979.

554 **"American hopelessness"** "Democratic National Committee: Remarks and a Question-and-Answer Session at the Committee's Spring Meeting," May 25, 1979, APP.

555 **Etan Patz** The Patz case became a news story in New York within twenty-four hours (see *New York Daily News*, May 26, 1979) and nationally within a week (see *Lancaster Intelligencer Journal* and *Fort Worth Star Telegram*, May 31, 1979).

555 **at O'Hare International Airport** CT, May 26, May 27, May 28, May 29, May 30, May 31, June 5, June 6, and June 7, 1979.

556 **"We have no handle"** "Debacle of the DC-10," *Time*, June 18, 1979.

556 *more* **catastrophic crashes** AP, November 29, 1979.

556 **OPEC price hike** "More OPEC Hikes Called World Threat," CT, May 28, 1979, 3.

556 **"illegal transactions by oil companies"** "Charge U.S. Aides Cover UP Oil Ripoff," CT, May 31, 1979, 3.

556 **truckers to go on strike** "Truckers Threaten Strike," CT, May 30, 1979, 5.

556 **"Agent Orange"** "2, 4, 5-T: The Toxic Time Bomb" CT, May 27, 1979, 6.

556 **fiftieth press conference** "The President's News Conference," May 29, 1979, APP.

557 **explanatory article** "The Great Gas Crunch—Who Is to Blame?" LAT, May 20, 1979.

557 **closer to 20 percent** Jacobs, *Panic at the Pump*, 209.

CHAPTER TWENTY-FIVE

558 **Ocean City, Maryland** "Ocean City Mayor Victim of Own Hoopla," *Baltimore Sun*, June 14, 1979.

558 **key to the city** "Kelley's Gas Guarantee May Fail," *Baltimore Sun*, June 20, 1979.

558 **Carter called** "The Sky Is Falling on Washington!" *Time*, June 11, 1979.

558 **campaign chairman** Ibid.

558 **approved a resolution** *Los Angeles Times* Service, June 16, 1979.

558 **On May 31** "Bad Things Come in Threes," *Time*, June 11, 1979.

559 **In Texas** " 'Assault': A Federal Judge Is Shot," *Time*, June 11, 1979.

559 **In Sacramento** "Failing Pupils Try to Kill Teacher," CT, June 7, 1979.

559 **In Kansas City** "Prizewinning Arena Collapses," *Time*, June 18, 1979.

559 **"sometime between July 7"** AP, June 17, 1979.

559 **"space agency is moving"** UPI, June 14, 1979.

559 **Originally, nobody** "Skylab's Fiery Fall," *Time*, July 16, 1979.

560 **"Now it costs $140"** "Truckers, Motorists in Pa. Protest Gasoline Shortage," WP, June 25, 1979.

560 **On the first day** AP, June 7, 1979.

560 **On the third day** UPI, June 9, 1979.

560 **on the fifth** UPI, June 12, 1979.

560 **When the gunfire** UPI, June 9, 1979.

560 **"In another week"** AP, June 10, 1979.

560 **President Carter eulogized** "John Wayne: Statement on the Death of the Film Actor," June 12, 1979, APP.

560 **"just don't feel as safe"** "Eulogies for the Duke," *Time*, July 9, 1979; also for minister's letter.

560 **"white supremacy"** "John Wayne: The *Playboy* Interview," *Playboy*, May 1971.

560 **On June 12** "National Health Plan: Message to the Congress on Proposed Legislation," APP; *New York Times* Service, June 12, 1979.

561 **By Ted Kennedy's standards** "On Who Will Whip Whom," *Time*, June 25, 1979. See also Carter, *White House Diary*, 325.

561 **next morning's *Today* show** "Press: Whip His What?" *Time*, June 25, 1979.

561 **price of gas** "OPEC's Painful Squeeze," *Time*, July 9, 1979.

561 **Fifty-eight percent** James T. Patterson, *Restless Giant: The United States from Watergate to Bush v. Gore* (New York: Oxford University Press, 2007), 65.

561 **traveled to Vienna** Carter, *White House Diary*, 326.

562 ***The Effects of Nuclear War*** Susan Stamberg, *Every Night at Five: Susan Stamberg's All Things Considered Book* (New York: Pantheon, 1982), 103.

562 **one headline ran** "Grim N-War Study: Better to Be Dead," *Pittsburgh Press*, June 14, 1979.

562 **margin of two to one** Sean Wilentz, *The Age of Reagan: A History, 1974–2008* (New York: Harper, 2008), 108.

562 **Carter's speech** "The Energy Plague," *Newsweek*, July 2, 1979.

562 **phalanxes of Guardsmen** Ibid.

562 **roofing nails** AP, June 10, 1979.

562 **5.6 percent fuel surcharge** AP, June 16, 1979.

562 **Supermarket managers** AP, June 17, 1979.

562 **waterfront terminal** AP, June 19, 1979.

562 **"NUKE THEIR ASS"** Philip Jenkins, *Decade of Nightmares: The End of the Sixties and the Making of Eighties America* (New York: Oxford University Press, 2008), 155.

563 **first trucker to die** "The Energy Plague," *Newsweek*, July 2, 1979.

563 **"under the jailhouse"** AP, June 17, 1979.

563 **"Shoot somebody"** AP, June 22, 1979; "Truckers Strike Intensifies in Violence and Disruption," WP, January 22, 1979.

563 **eighty degrees for summer** "The Energy Plague," *Newsweek*, July 2, 1979.

563 **roof of the White House** "Carter Welcomes Solar Power," NYT, June 21, 1979; "Solar Energy: Remarks Announcing Administration Proposals," June 20, 1979, APP.

563 **options were "limited"** "Truckers' Strike Cuts Food Supply," *Philadelphia Inquirer*, June 21, 1979.

563 **Jody Powell** "The Great Energy Mess," *Time*, July 2, 1979.

563 **"a psychological problem"** Ibid.

563 **speech about trucking** "Trucking Industry Deregulation: Remarks Announcing Proposed Legislation," June 21, 1979, APP.

563 **two hours later** "Independent Truckers' Strikes: Remarks to Reporters on the Situation," June 21, 1979, APP.

564 **"this difficult time"** "The President's Trip to Japan and the Republic of Korea: Remarks on Departure from the White House," June 23, 1979, APP.

564 **suburb northeast of Philadelphia** "Levittown Is Burning! The 1979 Levittown, Pennsylvania Gas Riot and the Decline of the Blue-Collar American Dream," *Labor* 2, No. 3 (2005); "And the Gas Lines Grow," *Time*, July 9, 1979; "Rioting Follows Protests by Truckers in Levittown, Pa.," NYT, June 26, 1979. See also the recollections and photographs on the Levittown Comfort Facebook page.

563 **DJ in nearby Trenton** "Trenton DJ Makes a Hit Playin' the Gas-Line Blues," *Philadelphia Inquirer*, June 2, 1979.

566 **American Automobile Association** Dominic Sandbrook, *Mad as Hell: The Crisis of the 1970s and the Rise of the Populist Right* (New York: Anchor Books, 2012), 297.

566 **Carter was in Tokyo** UPI, June 25, 1979; "Thousands Guard Delegations to Summit in Japan," *St. Louis Post-Dispatch*, June 25, 1979; Carter, *White House Diary*, 334–40; "OPEC's Painful Squeeze," *Time*, July 9, 1979.

566 **"a colored girl"** "Shimoda, Japan: Remarks and a Question-and-Answer Session at a Town Meeting," June 27, 1979.

566 **General Alexander Haig** "General Haig Comes Home," *Time*, July 9, 1979.

567 **rotting crops** "What It Will Cost the U.S.," *Time*, July 9, 1979.

567 **"Like some Biblical plague"** "The Energy Plague," *Newsweek*, July 2, 1979.

567 **OPEC's oil ministers** Theodore White, *America In Search of Itself: The Making of the President, 1956–1980* (New York: Harper & Row, 1981), 264.

567 **up 1,000 percent** "OPEC's Painful Squeeze," *Time*, July 9, 1979. This article also describes different interests of consuming and producing nations.

568 **On PBS** *MacNeil-Lehrer News Hour* clip, YouTube.com, accessed April 13, 2020.

568 **"much more likely"** Laura Kalman, *Right Star Rising: A New Politics, 1974–1980* (New York: Norton, 2010), 324.

568 **yelped to a reporter** Ibid., 323.

568 **mini-panic on Wall Street** "What It Will Cost the U.S.," *Time*, July 9, 1979.

568 **"genuine political despair"** "Gas Crisis: Color the White House Blue," WP, July 1, 1979.

568 **"literally afraid"** Eizenstat to Carter, June 28, 1970; "Text of Eizenstat's Memorandum on Energy with Recommendations to Carter," NYT, July 8, 1979.

568 **"pulling guns"** Author interview with Hendrik Hertzberg.

569 **unflattering article** "Carter Was Speechless," *Time*, July 16, 1979.

569 **bashing out a draft** Robert Schlesinger, *White House Ghosts: Presidents and Their Speechwriters* (New York: Simon & Schuster, 2008), 300.

569 **"geothermally pressured"** "Carter Was Speechless."

569 **self-absorbed fool** Joe Klein, *Politics Lost: How American Democracy Was Trivialized by People Who Think You're Stupid* (New York: Doubleday, 2006), 60.

569 **"Pat Caddell, 27, Is the Whiz Kid"** *People*, November 21, 1977.

569 **"too powerful already"** Orrin Hatch column, Pacific News Service, June 15, 1978.

570 **most aggressive attempt** Meg Jacobs, *Panic at the Pump: The Energy Crisis and the Transformation of American Politics in the 1970s* (New York: Hill & Wang, 2016), 197.

570 **"splutter of words"** Klein, *Politics Lost*, 39.

570 **become besotted** Jordan Michael Smith, "The Man Who Predicted the Rise of Donald Trump—in 1976," *BuzzFeed*, February 7, 2017; "The Deluge of Disastermania," *Time*, March 5, 1979.

570 **breakfast with the first lady** White, *America in Search of Itself*, 258; Elizabeth Drew, "A Reporter At Large: Phrase: In Search of a Definition," *New Yorker*, August 27, 1979.

571 **Wayne Granquist** Hendrik Hertzberg, "A Very Merry Malaise," NewYorker.com, July 17, 2009; "A Malaise Footnote (Bonus: Carter Cusses)," NewYorker.com, July 21, 2009.

571 **"Apocalypse Now" memo** Patrick H. Caddell, "Of Crisis and Opportunity," April 23, 1979, Record of the White House Press Office; Series: Jody Powell's Memoranda Files; Memoranda: President Carter, 1/10/79–4/23/1979; Container 40, Jimmy Carter Presidential Library.

571 **curmudgeonly history professor** Natasha Zaretsky, *No Direction Home: The American Family and the Fear of National Decline, 1968–1980* (Chapel Hill: University of North Carolina Press, 2007), 206-208.

572 **a "masterpiece"** Leo P. Ribuffo, " 'Malaise' Revisited: Jimmy Carter and the Crisis of Confidence," in John Patrick Diggins, ed., *The Liberal Persuasion: Arthur Schlesinger Jr. and the Challenge of the American Past* (Princeton, NJ: Princeton University Press, 1997).

572 **labeled it "bullshit"** Ibid.

572 **Truman balcony** Elizabeth Drew, "A Reporter At Large."

572 **schedule a dinner** Carter, *White House Diary*, 322; Ribuffo, " 'Malaise' Revisited"; White, *America in Search of Itself*, 259; Eric Miller, *Hope in a Scattering Time: A Life of Christopher Lasch* (Grand Rapids, MI: Wm. B. Eerdmans Publishing, 2010), 240–43.

572 **"All I can say"** Zaretsky, *No Direction Home*, 219.

572 **Daniel Bell** Miller, *Hope in a Scattering Time*, 241.

572 **"unknown destination"** Kalman, *Right Star Rising*, 326.

573 **Vice President Mondale** Klein, *Politics Lost*, 71.

573 **CBS News** MFTVE, 8:09.

573 **John Denver** "Ecology-Minded Singer Fuels Gasoline Dispute," *Arizona Republic*, July 3, 1979.

573 **president did some fishing** William Safire column, NYT, July 9, 1979.

573 **read Caddell's** Carter, *White House Diary*, 340.

573 **"bullshit the American people"** Schlesinger, *White House Ghosts*, 300.

573 **dollar began collapsing** "Carter Was Speechless"; also for Treasury intervention and cruel jokes.

574 **Senator Abraham Ribicoff** White, *America In Search of Itself*, 265.

574 **"No one knows"** *Washington Star*, July 6, 1979.

574 **called to report ASAP** White, *America In Search of Itself*, 265, which also describes first Camp David meeting, Caddell memo, and Carter's walk with Mondale.

574 **"wise men and women"** Carter, *White House Diary*, 341.

575 **stewards feared** Ribuffo, " 'Malaise' Revisited."

575 **first platoon** Carter, *White House Diary*, 342.

575 **deliver to each assemblage** Rabbi Marc Tanenbaum to Bert Gold and Bob Jacobs, "Report on Camp David Meeting of President Carter with Religious Leaders," Jacob Rader Marcus Center of the American Jewish Archives, at DocPlayer.net.

575 **in news reports** For use of "malaise" see AP, July 9, 1979; "Carter Sees Need to Do Better Job, Counter 'Malaise,' " WP, July 10, 1979; "GOP Whip: Carter Headed for Breakdown?" *New York Daily News*, July 21, 1979. The word was already abroad in the land: see "July 4: An Unhappy Birthday for America," *Pittsburgh Press*, July 1, 1979; W&G, July 2, 1979; "Canceling Energy Speech Added to the Confusion" editorial, *Akron Beacon Journal*, July 6, 1979; and Richard Reeves column, July 9, 1979.

575 **then sat back down** Sandbrook, *Mad as Hell*, 302; Gordon Stewart, "Carter's Speech Therapy," NYT, July 14, 1979.

575 **from Clark Clifford** "Carter Sees Need to Do Better Job."

575 **The other** Knight-Ridder Service, July 10, 1979.

576 **The lead article** "Carter Was Speechless," *Time*, July 16, 1979.

576 **"reached the low point"** Tom Wicker column, New York Times Service, July 11, 1979.

576 **"I worked hard"** Carter, *White House Diary*, 342.

576 **A senator observed** Ribuffo, " 'Malaise' Revisited."

576 **"matter of conjecture"** AP, July 9, 1979.

576 **"remarkably compatible"** Carter, *White House Diary*, 342.

577 **group of religious leaders** Tanenbaum to Bert Gold and Bob Jacobs, "Report on Camp David Meeting of President Carter with Religious Leaders."

577 **Bellah argued** Robert Bellah, "Human Conditions for a Good Society," *St. Louis Post Dispatch*, March 25, 1979. My attention was drawn to Bellah's influence by Daniel Horowitz, *Jimmy Carter and the Energy Crisis of the 1970s: The "Crisis of Confidence" Speech of July 15, 1979* (New York: Bedford/St. Martin's, 2005).

578 **Rafshoon insisting** Horowitz, *Jimmy Carter and the Energy Crisis*, 100.

578 **Mondale imploring** White, *America In Search of Itself*, 267.

578 **Clinton of Arkansas** David Farber, *Taken Hostage: The Iran Hostage Crisis and America's First Encounter with Radical Islam* (Princeton, NJ: Princeton University Press, 2004), 32.

578 **Carter signed a declaration** "National Energy Supply Shortage: Message to the Congress on the Implementation of Energy Conservation Contingency Plan No. 2," July 10, 1979, APP.

578 **consulted with Speaker** Carter, *White House Diary*, July 11, 1979.

579 **Durant, Oklahoma** AP, July 9, 1979.

579 **In Miami** *Conversations with a Killer: The Ted Bundy Tapes* (Netflix, 2019). All quotations not from AP are from this documentary.

579 **"indescribably gruesome"** AP, July 12, 1979.

579 **"articulate, intelligent man"** AP, June 25, 1979.

579 **"personable"** AP, July 15, 1979.

579 **"quick, disarming smile"** AP, June 24, 1979.

579 **"Jail Hasn't Robbed Bundy"** *Fort Lauderdale News and Sun Sentinel*, March 5, 1978.

579 **"attractive, young, and single"** AP, July 25, 1979.

580 **"Disco Sucks"** Jefferson Cowie, *Stayin' Alive: The 1970s and the Last Days of the Working Class* (New York: New Press, 2010), 321.

580 **And at Comiskey Park** "The Night Disco Died," *Chicago Magazine*, July 2016; also for quote of *Rolling Stone* writer Dave Marsh.

580 **independent service stations** AP, July 10, 1979; "State's Gasoline Advice: Cool It!"

Pittsburgh Press, July 11, 1979; "Governor Consults Carter on Gas Strike," *Pittsburgh Post-Gazette*, July 12, 1979.

580   **"*People* magazine"** UPI, July 20, 1979, quoting Senator Ted Stevens.

580   **Mr. and Mrs. Bill Fisher** "Welcome to Carnegie, Mr. Carter," *Pittsburgh Press*, July 13, 1979; AP, July 13, 1979.

581   **Panhandle of West Virginia** AP, July 13, 1979.

581   **The *Pittsburgh Press*'s article** "Here's Partial List of Open Stations," "How Carter's Carnegie Visit Was Kept a Secret," "Violence Threatened If Fuel Redistributed," "Carter, Residents Hold Mini-Summit," all on page A-4, *Pittsburgh Press*, July 13, 1979.

581   **"They were pleased"** Carter, *White House Diary*, 343.

581   **"almost frightening"** Jack Germond, *Fat Man in the Middle Seat: Forty Years of Covering Politics* (New York: Random House, 1999), 136.

581   **Then came a final meeting** Gordon Stewart, "Carter's Speech Therapy," NYT, July 14, 1979; Schlesinger, *White House Ghosts*, 302.

582   **Camp David movie theater** Schlesinger, *White House Ghosts*, 303–4; Hendrik Hertzberg, "A Very Merry Malaise," NewYorker.com, July 17, 2009.

582   **"Inside ten minutes"** Jules Witcover and Jack Germond, *Blue Smoke and Mirrors: How Reagan Won and Why Carter Lost the Election of 1980* (New York: Viking, 1981), 30.

583   **Roger Mudd** MFTVE, 9:26.

583   **Jimmy Carter began** "Address to the Nation on Energy and National Goals," July 15, 1979, APP; YouTube.com, accessed April 13, 2020.

587   **Senator Metzenbaum** "Big Oil: A Struggle for Credibility" NYT, July 1, 1979.

587   **"*Funding for this program*"** MacNeil-Lehrer News Hour clip, accessed on You Tube.com, April 13, 2020. See also Exxon ad in *Time*, June 25, 1979.

587   **it *worked*** Sandbrook, *Mad as Hell*, 304; William Greider, *Secrets of the Temple: How the Federal Reserve Runs the Country* (New York: Simon & Schuster, 1989), 15.

588   **Tuesday after the speech** Witcover and Germond, *Blue Smoke and Mirrors*, 38.

588   **"Had a purge"** Editorial, *Nation*, July 28, 1979.

588   **Izvestia's Washington correspondent** Susan Stamberg, *Every Night at Five: Susan Stamberg's All Things Considered Book* (New York: Pantheon, 1982), 26.

588   **Gibson of ABC** WLS-TV, YouTube.com, accessed April 14, 2020.

588   **against the tobacco industry** See for instance Jules Witcover, *The Making of an Ink-Stained Wretch: Half a Century Pounding the Political Beat* (Baltimore: Johns Hopkins University Press, 2005), 229; "Winston-Salem, North Carolina: Informal Question-and-Answer Session with Reporters," March 17, 1978, APP; *New York Times* Service, May 5, 1979; AP, January 7, 1979; and James J. Kilpatrick column, March 27, 1979.

588   **Califano was summoned** Bob Woodward, *Shadow: Five Presidents and the Legacy of Watergate* (New York: Simon & Schuster, 1999), 87; UPI, July 20, 1979; "Adams, Schlesinger Last Out in Purge," WP, July 21, 1979.

589   **But the whispers** Greider, *Secrets of the Temple*, 20; Witcover and Germond, *Blue Smoke and Mirrors*, 39; AP, July 19, 1979.

589   **"Denver boot"** Witcover and Germond, *Blue Smoke and Mirrors*, 41.

589   **"keeping the monkeys"** "Notes on People," NYT, July 27, 1979.

589   **exchanging blue jeans** "Foley Wary of Carter Aide's Role," *Spokane Spokesman-Review*, August 8, 1979.

589   **apologizing to legislative leaders** John A. Farrell, *Tip O'Neill and the Democratic Century* (New York: Little, Brown, 2001), 530.

589   **"midsummer massacre"** Kalman, *Right Star Rising*, 330.

589   **"exercise in Rafshoonery"** Ribuffo, " 'Malaise' Revisited."

589   **A cartoonist** Ibid.

589   **"provoked new doubts"** "Carter's Great Purge," *Time*, July 30, 1979.

589   **"deep sadness"** "The Presidency: Trying to Show His Toughness," *Time*, July 30, 1979.

590   **unintended consequence** Witcover and Germond, *Blue Smoke and Mirrors*, 38.

590   **off-the-record briefing** Ibid., 42; "Changes in the Cabinet: Remarks to Reporters," July 20, 1979, APP.

590   **for hamburgers** Witcover and Germond, *Blue Smoke and Mirrors*, 44. The meeting was a rare presidential statement not to be included in the *Public Papers of the Presidents of the United States* compilation.

590   **"sugar to shit"** Kalman, *Right Star Rising*, 330.

590   **dipped to 23 percent** Sandbrook, *Mad as Hell*, 305.

590   **Eizenstat tried to comfort** Greider, *Secrets of the Temple*, 19.

590   **"Once a 'Barbarous Relic' "** NYT, July 22, 1979.

590   **He offered the job** Joel Rogers and Thomas Ferguson, *Right Turn: The Decline of the Democrats and the Future of American Politics* (New York: Macmillan, 1987), 11.

590   **Frederick Schultz** Greider, *Secrets of the Temple*, 21–22.

591   **Gold soared** The *New York Times* ran a daily update on precious metals trading on the financial page. On July 19, "Gold Surpasses $300 and Dollar Slumps on Fears about Oil" made the front page.

591   **In London** W. S. Ryrie to Chancellor of the Exchequer, "PERSONAL AND CONFIDENTIAL," July 25, 1979, Treasury Records, "PO-CH/Gh/0001, Part A, Miscellaneous Papers," pdf file downloaded April 14, 2020.

591   *Time* **headlined** "Volcker to the Rescue," *Time*, August 6, 1979. For Carter's thinking see *White House Diary*, 347; Stuart Eizenstat, *President Carter: The White House Years* (New York: St. Martin's Press, 2018), 334–449.

591   **"cowardly failure"** *New Republic*, August 8, 1979.

591   **"uniting his party"** Kalman, *Right Star Rising*, 331.

591   **Scoop Jackson** Ian Shapiro, *The Last Great Senate: Courage and Statesmanship in Times of Crisis* (New York: Public Affairs Books, 2012), 247.

591   **George McGovern** Ibid., 248.

591   **sailing around Cape Cod** Sidney Blumenthal, *The Permanent Campaign: Inside the World of Elite Political Operatives* (Boston: Beacon Press, 1980), 248.

591   **Evans and Novak hired** ENIR, July 25, 1979; Robert Novak, *The Prince of Darkness: 50 Years Reporting in Washington* (New York: Crown Forum, 2007), 339.

591   **Moynihan and Governor Carey** Shapiro, *Last Great Senate*, 248.

591   **Garry Trudeau** *Doonesbury*, July 11, July 12, July 16, July 20, and September 2, 1979; "Doonesbury Out for a Week," *Eugene Register-Guard*, July 16, 1979; UPI, July 17, 1979.

592   **Bardstown, Kentucky** "Bardstown, Kentucky: Remarks and a Question-and-Answer Session at a Town Meeting," July 31, 1979, APP.

592   **Andrew Young** Witcover and Germond, *Blue Smoke and Mirrors*, 45; Carter, *White House Diary*, 349–52; Steven F. Hayward, The Age of Reagan: The Fall of the Old Liberal Order, 1964–1980 (New York: Three Rivers Press, 2001), 544.

592   *Delta Queen* "Carter's River Trip Offers a Rare Peek into His Private Life," WP, August 21, 1979.

593   **Only 34 percent** "Reagan Leads Carter in Newest *Time* Poll," *Washington Star*, September 3, 1979.

593   **private prayers** Carter discusses this eloquently in his interview in the November 1976 *Playboy*.

593   **boasted in his diary** Carter, *White House Diary*, 153, 280, 215.

593   **jotted down his regret** Ibid., 348.

593   **"FBI Investigating"** WP, August 25, 1979; Woodward, *Shadow*, 68–83.

594   **hissing, frantic rabbit** Walter Mears, *Deadlines Past: Forty Years of Presidential Campaigning* (Kansas City, MO: Andrew McNeel Publishing, 2003), 167; "Bunny Goes Bugs," WP, August 30, 1979. The AP also released its own cartoon for member papers.

594   **Bob Dole** AP, August 31, 1979.

594   **Jerry Falwell** J. Brooks Flippen, *Jimmy Carter, the Politics of Family, and the Rise of the Religious Right* (Athens, GA: University of Georgia Press, 2011), 218.

594   **Ronald Reagan ahead** "Reagan Leads Carter in Newest *Time* Poll."

594   **Alan Greenspan and George Shultz** "Meeting on Public Policy Issues," September 8, 1979, RRPL Box 103.

594   **On September 13** White, *America In Search of Itself*, 270.

594   **"I've got to keep trying"** Sandbrook, *Mad as Hell*, 304; "Photos Through TIME: Week of Oct 1, 1979," Time.com.

CHAPTER TWENTY-SIX

595   **Viguerie's Virginia mansion** ABC News, *Battleground Washington: Armies of Influence*, August 19, 1979, VTVNA.

595   *Dear Friend* Alan Crawford, *Thunder on the Right: The "New Right" and the Politics of Resentment* (New York: Pantheon, 1981), 54.

595   **Neoconservatives held** Len Colodny and Tom Schachtman, *The Forty Years War: The Rise and Fall of the Neocons, from Nixon to Obama* (New York: Harper, 2009), 284.

595   *Soviet Might/American Myth* Congressional Quarterly Service, July 3, 1979.

596   **"window of vulnerability"** Frances Fitzgerald, *Way Out There in the Blue: Reagan, Star Wars, and the End of the Cold War* (New York: Simon & Schuster, 2000), 87, 94–97; Pavel Podvig, "The Window of Vulnerability That Wasn't: Soviet Military Buildup in the 1970s," *International Security* 33, No. 1 (Summer 2008).

596   **Minority Leader Baker declared** ENIR, June 6, 1979.

597   **"FRANK CHURCH"** LeRoy Ashby and Rod Gramer, *Fighting the Odds: The Life of Frank Church* (Pullman: Washington State University Press, 1993), 544.

597   **That spring** Ibid., 592.

597   **Soviet combat brigade** For the complete story of the "Soviet combat brigade in Cuba" see David D. Newsom, *The Soviet Brigade in Cuba: A Study in Political Diplomacy* (Bloomington: Indiana University Press, 1987).

597   **savage television commercial** Adam Clymer, *Drawing the Line at the Big Ditch: The Panama Canal Treaties and the Rise of the Right* (Lawrence: University Press of Kansas, 2008), 144.

597   **Nazi-style "big lie"** Ibid., 184; UPI, September 23, 1979.

597   **Dolan was unapologetic** *Wall Street Journal* Service, February 5, 1980.

597   **"Leave us alone"** "The New Right Brigade," WP, August 10, 1980.

598   **On August 16** UPI, August 16, 1979; AP, August 17, 1979; "Conservative Group Sets Its Sights on Five Senators," LAT, August 17, 1979; *New York Times* Service, August 21, 1979.

598 **"The beautiful thing"** Knight-Ridder Service, January 3, 1979.

598 **early fundraising appeal** Connie Paige, *The Right to Lifers: Who They Are, How They Operate, and Where They Get Their Money* (Summit Books, 1983), 203.

599 ***"McGovern sells out the U.S."*** David Broder column, July 8, 1979.

599 **"Well, SALT is dead"** Ashby and Gramer, *Fighting the Odds*, 594.

599 **a noncrisis** Newsom, *The Soviet Brigade in Cuba,* passim.

599 **walk the plank** Ashby and Gramer, *Fighting the Odds,* 594.

600 **Carter marched to the pressroom** "Soviet Combat Troops in Cubs: Remarks to Reporters," September 7, 1979, APP.

600 **"Operation Manhood"** *Doonesbury*, September 24, September 25, September 26, September 27, September 28, and September 29, 1979.

600 **In Los Angeles** "Miller Faces Uphill Fight Against Recall," LAT, March 25, 1979; editorial, "A Leader Who Has Led Well," LAT, March 22 and March 30, 1979, letters in response; Weintraub letter to editor ("social fabric"), LAT, May 18, 1979; "Recall Drive to End With Radio-TV Blitz," LAT, May 20, 1979; "School Board President Miller Ousted," LAT, May 30, 1979.

600 **United States Chamber of Commerce** Alyssa Katz, *The Influence Machine: The U.S. Chamber of Commerce and the Corporate Capture of American Life* (New York: Spiegel & Grau, 2015), 51; Jay Van Andel and W. Willard Marriot letter, January 1, 1979.

601 **public financing** ABC News, *Battleground Washington: Armies of Influence*, August 19, 1979, VTVNA.

601 **Walker reconstituted** Robert Kuttner, *Revolt of the Haves: Tax Rebellions and Hard Times* (New York: Simon & Schuster, 1980), 268.

601 **John Danforth of Missouri** "Consumer Group Aid Vs. Danforth's Ire," *St. Louis Post Dispatch*, May 24, 1979.

601 **By June** "Regulating the Regulators," NYT *Magazine*, June 30, 1979.

601 **By Labor Day** "Trying to Regulate Regulators," CT, August 26, 1979.

601 **Marty Russo** Michael Pertschuk, *Revolt Against Regulation* (Berkeley: University of California Press, 1983), 64.

602 **"like Sweden"** Ibid., 81.

602 **"No congressman needs** Ibid., 60.

602 **door-to-door insurance** "Senate Panel Votes Stiff Curbs on FTC Powers," WP, November 21, 1979.

602 **used car dealers** "Mike Pertschuk and the Federal Trade Commission: Sequel," Kennedy School of Government Case Program #C16–81–387.S (1981); also for Formica, Sunkist, generic drugs, Exxon-Mobile anti-trust, shared monopoly, and kidvid actions; Jane Bryant Quinn column, November 22, 1979; Pertschuk, *Revolt Against Regulation*, 105.

602 **Formica's CEO** Martha Angle and Robert Walters column, August 30, 1979.

602 **"moving in for the kill"** *Washington Post* Service, June 27, 1979.

602 **"The Bureaucrat Who Makes Business Turn Blue"** *People*, September 10, 1979.

602 **Ernest Pepples** "Brown & Williamson Ships Paper to FTC," *Louisville Courier-Journal*, June 30, 1979.

603 **Pepples demanded** Pertschuk, *Revolt Against Regulation*, 85; read testimony at *Oversight of the Federal Trade Commission*, Hearings Before the Subcommittee for Consumer of the Committee, Science, and Transportation, United States Senate, Ninety-Sixth Congress, First Session, September 18, 19, 27, 28; October 4, 5, and 10, 1979, 93. A longer quote from the memo on marketing tobacco to young people can be found in "Is the Industry Aiming Its Message at Teens?" *Louisville*

Courier-Journal, June 12, 1983. For Brown & William's letter to Joseph Califano see "Cigarette Maker Does Battle," *Detroit Free Press*, July 6, 1981.

604   **investigative articles** "Who's Protecting Whom?" *Philadelphia Inquirer*, November 23, 1979; "Behind FTC Foes in Congress Are Foes With Funds," *Philadelphia Inquirer*, December 23, 1979; "The Naderites of the Other Side," NYT, September 30, 1979.

604   *Calendar of Federal Regulations* "FTC Lauded for Plans, Analyses," WP, November 29, 1979.

604   *"STOP THE BABY KILLERS"* Paige, *The Right to Lifers*, 201.

605   **Postal Service** Knight-Ridder, August 22, 1979; Gannett Service, September 1, 1979.

605   **Southern Baptist Convention** "Ain't It the Gospel Truth?" *Texas Monthly*, August 1979; "Southern Baptists Call Off the Culture War," *Atlantic*, June 2018; *Exiled: Voices of the Southern Baptist Convention Holy War* (Knoxville: University of Tennessee Press, 2016); "No Errors?" *Time*, July 2, 1979; (for quotations from speeches) Walter B. Shurden and Randy Shepley, *Going for the Jugular: A Documentary History of the SBC Holy War* (Macon, GA: Mercer University Press 1996); J. Brooks Flippen, *Jimmy Carter, the Politics of Family, and the Rise of the Religious Right* (Athens, GA: University of Georgia Press, 2011), 218.

605   **Richard Viguerie solemnized** *Conservative Digest*, August 1979.

606   **In Richmond** "Politicizing the Word," *Time*, October 1, 1979.

606   **"Council of Fifty-Six"** Jeffrey K. Hadden and Charles E. Swann, *Prime Time Preachers: The Rising Power of Televangelism* (New York: Addison-Wesley, 1981), 137.

606   **Jesse Helms amendment** "Senate Exempts Private Schools from IRS Probes," *Des Moines Register*, September 5, 1979.

606   **"Biblical Scorecard"** "Preachers in Politics," USNWR, September 24, 1979.

606   **Dr. Francis Schaeffer** Frank Schaeffer, *Crazy for God: How I Grew Up as One of the Elect, Helped Found the Religious Right, and Lived to Take All (or Almost All) of It Back* (New York: De Capo Press, 2008), Chapter 44; "Theologian Francis Schaeffer to Hold Seminar, Film Series in Tampa," *Tampa Times*, July 28, 1979; James T. Patterson, *Restless Giant: The United States from Watergate to Bush v. Gore* (New York: Oxford University Press, 2007), 136–37. View the episodes on YouTube.com, accessed April 14, 2020.

607   **Reverend James D. Kennedy** John G. Turner, *Bill Bright and the Campus Crusade for Christ: The Renewal of Evangelism in Twentieth Century America* (Chapel Hill: University of North Carolina Press, 2009), 189–90.

607   **Bill Gavin** Gavin to Peter Hannaford and Martin Anderson, September 19, 1979, "Re: US News Article on 'Preachers in Politics,' September 24, 1979," DH, Box 3, Folder 5.

607   **Whittaker Chambers'** *Witness* Lou Cannon, *President Reagan: A Role of a Lifetime* (New York: Public Affairs, 2000), 252.

608   **Herbert Ellingwood** Darren Dochuk, *From Bible Belt to Sun Belt: Plain-Folk Religion, Grassroots Politics, and the Rise of Evangelical Conservatism* (New York: W. W. Norton, 2011), 370–71.

608   **state senate leader James Mills** David S. New, *Holy War: The Rise of Militant Christian, Jewish, and Islamic Fundamentalism* (Jefferson, NC: McFarland & Company, 2001), 70–71.

608   **Chuck Colson remembered** William Martin, *With God on Our Side: The Rise of the Religious Right in America* (New York: Broadway Books, 1996), 208.

608   **John Conlan** September 21 and 22, 1979, schedules, with briefing memo, RRPL, Box 77.

608 **"I wouldn't give"** Martin, *With God on Our Side*, 209.

608 **Sears reported gossip** Notes, May 14, 1978, 9 a.m., RRPL, Box 103.

609 **Gavin wondered** Gavin to Hannaford and Anderson, September 19, 1979, "Re: US News Article on 'Preachers in Politics,' Sept. 24, 1979" and Hannaford response, op cit.

609 **National Association of Arab Americans** Hannaford to Joanne McKenna, October 9, 1979, Ronald Reagan General File, Memoranda to Gov. Reagan, Allen, Richard, 1978–1979, DH, Box 3, Folder 3.

609 **"SUBJECT: 'gay issues' "** Hannaford to Meese, December 20, 1979, DH, Box 44.

CHAPTER TWENTY-SEVEN

610 **one week in July** TV listings researched at Newspapers.com.

610 **"felt this awful"** For filming dates see Internet Movie Database, *Airplane!* (1980). For gag see YouTube.com, accessed April 15, 2020.

610 **unexpectedly dropped out** Hannaford to Sears et al., August 2, 1979, RRPL, Box 103.

610 **"the polls are wrong"** James J. Kilpatrick column, October 8, 1979.

610 **"hanging around golf"** Richard Reeves column, August 10, 1979.

611 **National Federation of Independent Business's** ENIR, June 22, 1979.

611 **"Chautauqua circuit lecture"** *Wall Street Journal* Service, November 1, 1979.

611 **look greedy** "Reagan Tests Political Waters in a Shower of Fees," WP, August 15, 1979, reporting he charged $7,659 to speak at two Boy Scout dinners; NBC News, June 21, 1979, replayed on *Hardball with Chris Matthews*, YouTube.com, accessed April 15, 1979.

611 **jangling telephones** Ibid.

612 **"probably be Puerto Rican"** "TV's Newest Program: The 'Presidential Nominations Game,' " *Public Opinion*, May/June 1978.

612 **Ben Fernandez** Geraldo Cadava, *The Hispanic Republican: The Shaping of an American Political Identity, from Nixon to Trump* (New York: Ecco, 2020), 198.

612 **no one paid attention** Reagan to William Loeb, March 27, 1979 and Richard Womack, June 5, 1979, both in dictation file, RRPL, Box 1; NBC News, June 21, 1979; UPI, July 31, 1979.

612 **one Monday in May** Reagan May 21 schedule, RRPL, Box 76; "George Bush Tops Field in Republican Straw Poll," *Des Moines Register*, May 23, 1979.

612 **in Canada** May 22 and 23 schedule, RRPL, Box 76.

612 **breakfast honoring Gerald Ford** May 24 schedule, RRPL, Box 76.

612 **"Anyone who leaves"** AP, June 7, 1979. Brock also said Reagan was "slipping."

612 **operative on Capitol Hill** "Congressional Summary #4," May 14, 1979, RRPL, Box 84.

612 **meet-and-greet** See schedules, RRPL, Box 75: for example April 12, 1979, in Charleston ("VIP reception 30@$250").

612 **Self-respecting presidential campaigns** For trouble finding financial chairman see January 3, 1979, notes, and also February 1, 1979, "Finance Committee + Org" note with list of names apparently approached who refused, both RRPL, Box 103. On Nofziger as fundraiser: Helene von Damm, *At Reagan's Side: Twenty Years in the Political Mainstream* (New York: Doubleday, 1989), 81–83; Craig Shirley, *Rendezvous with Destiny: Ronald Reagan and the Campaign That Changed America*

(Wilmington, DE: Intercollegiate Studies Institute, 2009), 55; Meese meeting with Helene von Damm, May 17, 1979, RRPL, Box 103.

612 **Justin Dart** May 17 von Damm meeting; Bob Colacello, *Ronnie and Nancy: Their Path to the White House—1911 to 1980* (New York: Grand Central Publishing, 2004), 475. For meeting with garlic tycoon and failed Viguerie mailing see Bay Buchanan meeting, May 7, 1979, 2:15 p.m.; for Norman Rockwell T-shirt see Dave Fisher meeting, May 16, 1979, 2:35 p.m.; both RRPL, Box 103.

613 **$17 million** Shirley, *Rendezvous with Destiny*, 114. For campaign discussion on matching funds see July 9, 1979, meeting with Fred Russell, RRPL, Box 103.

613 **telex machines** Bay Buchanan meeting, May 7, 1979, 2:15 p.m., RRPL, Box 103.

613 **Houston banker** June 28, 1979, meeting, RRPL, Box 103.

613 **termination notices** Eriksen to Barbara, June 26, 1979, RRPL, Box 114.

613 **They had taken in** Meese notes "Per NBC," June 30, 1979, RRPL, Box 103.

613 **Rumor was** Loren Smith meeting, July 4, 11:45 a.m., RRPL, Box 103.

613 **"Connally's intentions"** Management meeting notes, June 28, 1979, noon, RRPL, Box 103.

613 **stature-enhancing junkets** Meeting agenda, March 12, 1979, "Possible Trips 1979," RRPL, Box 103.

613 *Dear Mr. President* RALIL, 732–33.

614 **Nancy Reagan's best** Eleanor Clift, "Nancy Reagan 90th Birthday: Changing Public Image for First Lady," *Daily Beast*, July 5, 2011, on Ruth Jones's annual birthday lunches for Nancy Reagan. See also Anna Chennault to Edward [*sic*] Meese, April 4, 1980, DH, Box 11, Folder 15, describing Thomas Jones as a "long-time friend of the Reagans."

614 **donated the maximum** See Jones's giving, 1979-1979 at FEC.gov.

614 **during Watergate** "Thomas V. Jones, Northrop CEO, Dies at 93," WP, January 9, 2014.

614 **chairman of Lockheed** "Big Money Is for Connally," *Philadelphia Inquirer*, September 16, 1979.

614 **Reagan had been invited** Robert N. Cleaves to Reagan, July 31, 1978, RVA, Box 28, Folder 4.

614 **in March 1979** Allen to Deaver, March 19, 1979, "SUBJECT: Conference of South African Investors"; Allen to Hannaford and Deaver, March 28, 1979; Allen to Hannaford and Deaver, March 29, 1979, "SUBJECT: My Memorandum for Mike Deaver of March 19"; all RVA, Box 28, Folder 6.

615 **metastasizing scandal** "Pretoria Puffery Is PR Firm's Plum," WP, March 25, 1979. For resignation see "Vorster, Accused of Role in Scandal, Quits as President," NYT, June 5, 1979.

615 **That did not** June 18 schedule, RRPL, Box 59.

615 **The next week** RRC, June 26, 1979. Thanks to Melanie Nathan and John Comaroff for help with South African "Information Scandal" and apartheid.

615 **Meese scrawled an arrow** March 12, 1979, agenda, RRPL, Box 103.

615 **every single member** Robin to Nofziger and related notes, March 27, 1979, RVA, Box 28, Folder 6.

615 **vast majority** See schedules for January 14, January 18, February 18, February 19, February 20, March 8, March 31, June 6, June 10, July 10, 1979, Boxes 74–76; Charlie Black to Hannaford et al., August 3, 1979, RVA, Box 44.

615 **"favorable to Israel"** Hannaford to Reagan, July 30, RVA, Box 27, Folder 27, documents the four-month process in drafts, memos, and notes. In RRPL, Box 10,

"Newspaper Columns—King Features Syndicate," find Hannaford to Allan Priaulx, August 29, 1979, explaining the project to him and why it was being pitched to a major newspaper and not written for the syndicate.

616 **"Recognizing the Israeli Asset"** WP, August 15, 1979.

616 **To staffers' delight** Allen to Reagan et al., August 24, 1979, RVA, Box 27.

616 **Another personnel crisis** Shirley, *Rendezvous with Destiny*, 54–55.

616 **"simply isn't true"** "Nofziger Resigns as Aide to Reagan in Reported Dispute Over His Role," NYT, August 29, 1979; also for Jim Lake quote.

616 **Nofziger refused to follow** "High-Ranking Aide in Reagan Campaign Quits," LAT, August 28, 1979.

616 **" 'East-West' tension"** "Long-Time Reagan Aide Resigns from Presidential Campaign Job," WS, August 28, 1979.

616 **Sears celebrated** "Reagan Strategist Surveys Scene—and Picks a Winner," WSJ, August 30, 1979.

617 **A Nofziger ally** Anonymous to "Dear Lyn," DH, Box 3, Folder 1.

617 **"as opposed as you"** Reagan to Lyman Rockey, June 1, 1979, dictation file, RRPL, Box 1.

617 **"once 'ultra-conservative' "** Reagan to William Loeb, April 25, 1979, dictation file, RRPL, Box 1, responding to Louis Rukeyser column, April 1, 1979.

617 **"DC-10s have replaced"** RRB 79-09, track A4, "Nuclear Power," recorded June 29, 1979, RPV, 454.

617 **wandering into staff meetings** See n.d. notes, early 9/79, page 8, "No nation can survive under fiat money"; "Meeting on Public Policy Issues," September 6, 1979; both RRPL, Box 103, "Meetings—9/1979" folder. See also PH, Box 11, Fred Iklé, for working drafts of fall 1979 policy position statements.

617 **Germond was skeptical** Jack Germond, *Fat Man in the Middle Seat: Forty Years of Covering Politics* (New York: Random House, 1999), 150–52.

618 **vituperation directed at Jackson** Ian Shapiro, *The Last Great Senate: Courage and Statesmanship in Times of Crisis* (New York: Public Affairs Books, 2012), 292.

618 **North American Aerospace Defense Command** July 30 and July 31, 1979, schedule, RRPL, Box 76; Frances FitzGerald, *Way Out There in the Blue: Reagan, Star Wars, and the End of the Cold War* (New York: Simon & Schuster, 2000), 20–21; Robert Scheer, *With Enough Shovels: Reagan, Bush, and Nuclear War* (New York: Random House, 1982), 104, 232.

618 **"All the way to Los Angeles"** Reagan to General James E. Hill, August 1979, in RALIL, 423; Martin Anderson, *Revolution: The Reagan Legacy* (Stanford, CA: Hoover Institution Press, 1990), 81.

618 **He wanted to mention** FitzGerald, *Way Out There in the Blue*, 100.

618 **"Inertia Projector"** Michael Paul Rogin, *Ronald Reagan, the Movie: And Other Episodes in Political Demonology* (Berkeley: University of California Press, 1988), Chapter One.

618 **Dick Allen hastened** Allen to executive committee, September 21, 1979, attached to September 17, 1979, Gavin memo, PH, Box 3, Folder 3.

618 **Allen scripted a response** Hannaford to Reagan, "SUBJECT: Your SALT speech insert," September 10, 1979, RRPL, Box 25.

618 **Godfrey Sperling** *Christian Science Monitor* Service, September 16, 1979.

618 **capitol in Sacramento** UPI, September 12, 1979.

619 **"really frightening"** "If Reagan Had His Way," *Philadelphia Inquirer*, September 13, 1979.

619 **delivered his speech** AP, September 15, 1979; speech, DH, Box 11, Folder 22.

619 **"Reagan Is Born Again"** *Time*, September 24, 1979.

619 **"moderately worded speech"** "Reagan Urges Senate to Arms Pact, But His Tone Is Softer," NYT, September 16, 1979.

619 **"*fact of the moderation*"** Gavin to Hannaford, Anderson, and Deaver, "RE: Moderation, RR, and Issues," September 17, 1979, DH, Box 3, Folder 5.

619 **"The Big Money's for Connally"** *Philadelphia Inquirer*, September 16, 1979.

619 **house in New Hampshire** "Congressional Summary #2," April 30, 1979, RRPL, Box 84.

619 **tour in March** W&G, March 23, 1979; James Reston Jr., *Lone Star: The Life of John Connally* (New York: HarperCollins, 1989), 563.

620 **"two-man race"** *Christian Science Monitor*, September 14, 1979.

620 **"This country is a hostage!"** "The Truth About John Connally," *Texas Monthly*, November 1979.

620 **"dock in Yokohama"** "Connally Wins Top Prize in GOP 'Cattle Show,' " CT, April 9, 1979; "Connally: Back Dreyfus, Expect Teddy," *Wisconsin State Journal*, April 11, 1979.

620 **stared down a Japanese** "Connally Warmly Received at Fundraiser," WP, April 18, 1979.

620 **"at his command"** *Springfield State Journal-Register*, May 11, 1979, clip in DH, Box 85.

620 **"ought to have been burned"** "Connally: Back Dreyfus, Expect Teddy." Also for "What more do you want?"

620 **"whooped for joy"** "Republican Hopefuls Unsure on Iowa," *Des Moines Register*, August 5, 1979. This article also quotes Connally's "wheeler-dealer" line.

620 **spend *more* money** UPI, July 29, 1979.

621 **"no question in my mind"** "Md. GOP Hears Connally Voice Presidential Hopes," *Baltimore Sun*, May 12, 1979.

621 **Bob Dole** "Republican Hopefuls Unsure on Iowa," *Des Moines Register*, August 5, 1979.

621 **Richard Wirthlin** Richard Wirthlin, "A National Survey of Voter Attitudes," April 1979, RRPL, Box 186.

621 **annoyed public opinion expert** Letter to the editor from Richard Scammon, *Newsweek*, August 13, 1979.

621 **Nowadays, Connally mocked** John Lofton column, February 15, 1979.

621 **"sleep in every bed"** ENIR, August 13, 1979.

621 **"immediately deregulate all oil"** Daniel Horowitz, *Jimmy Carter and the Energy Crisis of the 1970s: The "Crisis of Confidence" Speech of July 15, 1979* (New York: Bedford/St. Martin's, 2004), 127.

621 *Fortune* 500 **companies** *Philadelphia Inquirer*, September 16, 1979.

622 **Garry Trudeau** *Doonesbury*, January 3 through January 12, 1979.

622 **63.8 percent of ordinary voters** Wirthlin, "A National Survey of Voter Attitudes."

622 **"Connally's gamble"** "Two-Gun Connally Oil Blunder," *Business Week*, May 28. 1979.

622 **meeting in Arkansas** ENIR, June 15, 1979.

622 **"Killer Bees"** Reston, *Lone Star*, 564; "Flight of the 'Killer Bees,' " *Time*, June 4, 1979.

622 **"magnificently outfitted battleship"** Sidney Blumenthal, *The Permanent Campaign: Inside the World of Elite Political Operatives* (Boston: Beacon Press, 1980), 212.

622 **"SPECIAL MESSAGE"** September 3, 1979 *Time* regional edition. A version for Illinois ran in *Time*'s December 3, 1979, issue.

622 **The next week** "Hot on the Trail: G.O.P. Candidate John Connally," *Time*, September 10, 1979.

622 **forty of sixty** *Sarasota Tribune*, September 11, 1979.

622 **the "bold stroke"** Reston, *Lone Star*, 56–77; John Connally with Mickey Herskowitz, *In History's Shadow: An American Odyssey* (New York: Hyperion, 1993), 299. For bank he owned with Arab sheiks see Reston, *Lone Star*, 557.

624 **A *Times* editorial** "Merchants of Myth," NYT, October 21, 1979.

624 **Florida Republicans** Jon Meacham, *Destiny and Power: The American Odyssey of George Herbert Walker Bush* (New York: Random House, 2015), 219; Michael Kramer, "John Connally: Turning Them Off in the Heartland," *New York*, December 31, 1979; Reston, *Lone Star*, 583.

625 **those most disappointed** "Connally: Coming on Tough," NYT *Magazine*, November 18, 1979.

625 **remarkable event transpired** J. Brooks Flippen, *Jimmy Carter, the Politics of Family, and the Rise of the Religious Right* (Athens, GA: University of Georgia Press, 2011), 210; Martin, *With God on Our Side*, 205–6; author interview and correspondence with Lance Tarrance.

626 **public letter to Henry Hyde** Reagan to Hyde, July 27, 1979, RRPL, Box 114.

626 **TV preacher Jim Bakker** See clip at People for the American Way's *Right Wing Watch News*, January 17, 2017. See also "50 Christians Agree to Raise Reagan Funds," LAT, December 3, 1979.

CHAPTER TWENTY-EIGHT

628 **"be so crude"** Federal Reserve Open Market Committee meeting, October 6, 1979.

628 **sufficiently esoteric** UPI, October 7, 1979.

628 **"cruelest tax"** RBB 75-11, track 05, "Inflation as Tax," recorded June 1975.

628 **this is not so** Author correspondence with Professor Mark Blyth of Brown University.

629 **New York University economist** Edward Wolff, "The Distributional Effects of the 1969–1975 Inflation on Household Wealth Holdings in the United States," *Review of Income and Wealth*, Series 25, No. 2, June 1979.

629 **According to Arthur Burns** "The Anguish of Central Banking," 1979 Per Jacobson Lecture, September 30, 1979.

629 **blunt honesty** Buchanan and Friedman quotes: Mark Blyth, *Austerity: The History of a Dangerous Idea* (New York: Oxford University Press, 2015), 156. Hazlitt quote in Melinda Cooper, *Family Values: Between Neoliberalism and the New Social Conservatism* (New York: Zone Books, 2017), 31

630 **former Federal Reserve economist** Jefferson Cowie, *Stayin' Alive: The 1970s and the Last Days of the Working Class* (New York: New Press, 2010), 224.

630 **Manic financial speculation** William Greider, *Secrets of the Temple: How the Federal Reserve Runs the Country* (New York: Simon & Schuster, 1989), 83–86.

631 **"pact with the devil"** Ibid., 105.

632 **"What I hoped"** Ibid., 111.

632 **In Belgrade** Ibid., 118.

632 **against the Berlin Wall** Nicholas von Hoffman, "Can Volcker Stand Up to Inflation?" NYT *Magazine*, December 2, 1979.

632 **On October 4** Greider, *Secrets of the Temple*, 123–24.

633 **"pipe and cigar smoke"** von Hoffman, "Can Volcker Stand Up to Inflation?"

633 **In a dispatch** AP, October 7, 1979.

633 **"will not try to wring"** "Annual Message to the Congress; The Economic Report of the President," January 25, 1979, APP.

633 **Carter refused** Greider, *Secrets of the Temple*, 121.

633 **"what Mr. Stalin wants"** Matt Stoller, *Goliath: The 100 Year War Between Monopoly Power and Democracy* (New York: Simon & Schuster, 2019), 261.

634 **spokesman Jody Powell** AP, October 7, 1979.

634 **Milton Friedman's estimate** von Hoffman, "Can Volcker Stand Up to Inflation?"

634 **2.4 million manufacturing jobs** Michael A. McCarthy, "The Monetary Hawks," *Jacobin*, August 3, 2016.

634 **The immediate effects** Greider, *Secrets of the Temple*, 125; for "real economy," see 132.

634 **cover of *Time*** "The Squeeze of '79," *Time*, October 22, 1979.

635 **Friedrich Hayek** "Sifting for Lessons of the Crash," NYT, November 1, 1979.

635 **Paul Volcker offered similar** "Volcker Asserts U.S. Must Trim Living Standard," NYT, October 18, 1979.

635 **Two economists** "The Forgotten Dollar Stages a Comeback," *Business Week*, October 22, 1979.

635 **Robert Solow of MIT** "The Threatening Economy," NYT, December 30, 1979.

635 ***Newsweek* praised** "Shock Treatment for Inflation," *Newsweek*, October 22, 1979.

635 **Alan Greenspan enthused** Sidney Blumenthal, *The Rise of the Counter-Establishment: The Conservative Ascent to Political Power* (New York: Times Books, 2007), 108.

635 **Nicholas von Hoffman** von Hoffman, "Can Volcker Stand Up to Inflation?"

636 **mass in Chicago** *Chicago Days: 150 Defining Moments in the Life of a Great City* (New York: McGraw Hill, 1996); Cristian Caryl, *Strange Rebels: 1979 and the Birth of the 21st Century* (New York: Basic Books, 2013), 200–205.

636 **Meg Greenfield** "Leadership Chic," *Newsweek*, October 22,1979.

636 ***New York Times*/CBS poll** "Carter's Standing Drops to New Low in *Times*-CBS Poll," NYT, June 10, 1979.

636 **Victor Gold** "Gonna Tell You Once," *Washingtonian*, October 1979.

637 **"The Looming 1980s"** NYT *Magazine*, December 2, 1979.

637 **"interview this Khomeini"** Oriana Fallaci, *Interviews with History and Conversations with Power* (New York: Rizzoli, 2011), 172–261.

639 **undertook a purge** UPI, March 12, 1979; "11 Executed in Iran," *Sydney Morning Herald*, March 14, 1979.

639 **On April 1** "Iran timeline," AA, "Misc Issues" folder.

639 **The following week** "Khomeini Rule Stirs Unrest," LAT, April 17, 1979.

639 **A week later** "Attempt Made on Iran Leader's Life," LAT, April 24, 1979.

639 **his very own SAVAK** "Iran timeline," AA, "Misc Issues" folder.

639 **the Kurds** "Ayatollah Sadegh Khalkhali," *Telegraph*, November 28, 2003.

640 **high-class mendicant** "Iran timeline," AA, "Misc Issues" folder.

640 **"visit" to Morocco** David Farber, *Taken Hostage: The Iran Hostage Crisis and America's First Encounter with Radical Islam* (Princeton: Princeton University Press, 2004), 109, 120–21.

640 **Cuernavaca Racquet Club** "People," *Time*, June 25, 1979.

640 **four CIA agents** Timothy Weiner, *Legacy of Ashes: The History of the CIA* (New York: Doubleday, 2007), 429.

640 **beaten within an inch** Ibid., 427–28.

640 **Senator Jacob Javits** Farber, *Taken Hostage*, 126; "Iran Attacks Senate Executions Resolution," *Minneapolis Star*, May 21, 1979.

640 **In late February** Jimmy Carter, *White House Diary* (New York: Macmillan, 2010), 296.

640 **two emissaries** ABC News, "America Held Hostage: The Iran Crisis," YouTube .com, accessed April 17, 2020.

640 **"Don't worry"** Weiner, *Legacy of Ashes*, 429.

640 **Project Eagle** Farber, *Taken Hostage*, 122; "How a Chase Bank Chairman Helped the Deposed Shah of Iran Enter the U.S.," NYT, December 29, 2019.

640 **Nelson Rockefeller had first** Richard Norton Smith, *On His Own Terms: A Life of Nelson Rockefeller* (New York: Random House, 2014), 706–7.

641 **David Rockefeller's Chase Manhattan** Nomi Prins, *All the Presidents' Bankers: The Hidden Alliances That Drive American Power* (New York: Nation Books, 2014), 304.

641 **Howard Baker** Carter, *White House Diary*, 305.

641 **Gerald Ford** Ibid., 312.

641 **influenced, George Will** George Will column, April 19, 1979.

641 **John J. McCloy** Farber, *Taken Hostage*, 124.

641 **Richard Nixon** ABC News, "America Held Hostage."

641 **On April 19** "Iran timeline," AA, "Misc Issues" folder.

641 **Three weeks later** UPI, May 17, 1979; "People," *Time*, July 2, 1979

641 **doing it herself** "Empress Urged to Kill Shah," *The Age*, July 18, 1979.

641 **National Security Council** Blake Jones, *A Battle for Righteousness: Jimmy Carter and Religious Nationalism* (PhD dissertation, Department of History, Arizona State University, 2013), 113.

641 **at the State Department** Ibid., 106; ABC News, "America Held Hostage."

642 **kerosene and home heating oil** Carter, *White House Diary*, 334; "The Kerosene to Iran," WP, August 24, 1979.

642 **banned music** "Khomeini Bans Broadcast Music, Saying It Corrupts Iranian Youth," NYT, July 24, 1979.

642 **"insults, calumny, or falsehoods"** UPI, August 13, 1979.

642 **machine gun battle** "Iran timeline," AA, "Misc Issues" folder.

642 **worst riots** "Scores Injured in Tehran Rioting Over Press Curbs," LAT, August 13, 1979.

642 **Associated Press office** "Iran timeline," AA, "Misc Issues" folder.

642 **"his death provided"** Fallaci, *Interviews with History and Conversations with Power.*

642 **Ebrahim Yazdi** Farber, *Taken Hostage*, 119–20.

642 **"Whether the shah"** Laura Kalman, *Right Star Rising: A New Politics, 1974–1980* (New York: Norton, 2010), 337; also for Cy Vance reversal and Jordan comment.

643 **"*Fuck the Shah!*"** Farber, *Taken Hostage*, 125; Weiner, *Legacy of Ashes*, 430.

643 **"Does somebody here"** Steven F. Hayward, *The Age of Reagan: The Fall of the Old Liberal Order, 1964–1980* (New York: Three Rivers Press, 2001), 601.

643 **scrawled "OK"** Jimmy Carter, *Keeping Faith: Memoirs of a President* (Little Rock: University of Arkansas Press, 1995), 463.

643 **a CIA agent** Weiner, *Legacy of Ashes*, 429.

643 **"Pandora's box"** Ian Shapiro, *The Last Great Senate: Courage and Statesmanship in Times of Crisis* (New York: Public Affairs Books, 2012), 255.

643 **"The eagle has landed"** "How a Chase Bank Chairman Helped the Deposed Shah of Iran Enter the U.S.," NYT, December 29, 2019.

643 **On the 24th** Prins, *All the Presidents' Bankers*, 310.

643   meeting with Brzezinski Jones, *A Battle for Righteousness*, 107, 115–16.

643   *which* embassy to seize Mark Bowden, *Guests of the Ayatollah: The First Battle in America's War with Militant Islam* (New York: Atlantic Monthly Press, 2006), 10.

643   On Friday, November 2 Farber, *Taken Hostage*, 129.

644   National Student Day speech Ibid., 130.

644   The next morning My account of the embassy seizure comes from Bowden, *Guests of the Ayatollah*, 17–110.

646   "Good evening" MFTVE, 19:37.

647   all three network newscasts VTVNA.

647   "grisly cavalcade" "STARVATION: Deathwatch in Cambodia," *Time*, November 11, 1979.

647   USS *Pueblo* in 1968 Author canvassed newspaper indexes for volume of coverage of USS *Pueblo* and China's hostage-taking compared to Iran.

648   "US CAN NOT DO" This ubiquitous image was even turned into a postcard.

648   Roone Arledge Farber, *Taken Hostage*, 136, 153–55.

648   "*Police Story*" MFTVE, 20:00.

648   climbed by 3.8 "Bad News in Iran Has Been Good news for ABC," *Minneapolis Star*, November 30, 1979.

649   "ABC has finally" Melani McAllister, *Epic Encounters: Cultural, Media, and U.S. Interests in the Middle East Since 1945* (Berkeley: University of California Press [Updated Edition], 2005), 205.

649   "professional extras" Barbara Rosen and Barry Rosen with George Feiffer, *The Destined Hour: The Hostage Crisis and One Family's Ordeal* (New York: Doubleday, 1982).

649   portentous decision Farber, *Taken Hostage*, 147–48.

649   Ramsey Clark Ibid., 144; Jones, *A Battle for Righteousness*, 113.

649   Statue of Liberty UPI, November 5, 1979.

649   Immigration and Naturalization Service "Iranian Students in the United States Announcement on Actions to Be Taken by the Department of Justice," November 10, 1979, APP.

650   In a major speech "American Federation of Labor and Congress of Industrial Organization: Remarks at the 13th Constitutional Convention," November 15, 1979, APP.

650   National Cathedral Knight-Ridder Service, November 16, 1979.

650   "very visibly concerned" McAllister, *Epic Encounters*, 205.

650   Beverly Hills, California For Beverly Hills riot see "March by Iranians Banned," LAT, November 9. 1979; "Iranian Protest March Routed in Beverly Hills," LAT, November 10, 1979; and footage on all network news broadcasts, VTVNA. Muhammed Ali: AP, November 10, 1979.

CHAPTER TWENTY-NINE

653   TV debut of *Jaws* Jules Witcover and Jack Germond, *Blue Smoke and Mirrors: How Reagan Won and Why Carter Lost the Election of 1980* (New York: Viking, 1981), 75.

653   decision in his heart Ibid., 51; Edward M. Kennedy, *True Compass: A Memoir* (New York: Twelve, 2009), 209.

653   *New York Times/CBS poll New York Times* Service, July 13, 1979.

653 **"Kennedy could become president"** Tim Stanley, " 'Sailing Against the Wind': A Reappraisal of Edward Kennedy's Campaign for the 1980 Democratic Party Presidential Nomination," *Journal of American Studies* 32, 2 (August 2009).

653 **his wife, Joan** Theodore White, *America In Search of Itself: The Making of the President, 1956–1980* (New York: Harper & Row, 1981), 170; Arthur M. Schlesinger Jr., *Journals: 1952–2000* (New York: Penguin, 2007), May 25, 1979 and June 5, 1979; Witcover and Germond, *Blue Smoke and Mirrors*, 41.

653 **His figure** AP, November 3, 1979.

653 **The Army Signal Corps** Meg Jacobs, *Panic at the Pump: The Energy Crisis and the Transformation of American Politics in the 1970s* (New York: Hill & Wang, 2016), 218–19; "Kennedy's Coming Out Dispirits Some Carter Advisors," WP, September 16, 1979.

654 **by Labor Day weekend** White, *America In Search of Itself*, 271.

654 *Atlanta Constitution* Schlesinger, *Journals*, September 10, 1979.

654 **A political cartoon** Mike Peters cartoon, September 25, 1979.

654 **Rose Kennedy had told** Witcover and Germond, *Blue Smoke and Mirrors*, 54.

654 **"mean, cruel, brutal campaign"** AP, September 14, 1979.

654 **"not going to survive"** Schlesinger, *Journals*, September 10, 1979.

654 **grants to Dade County** Stanley, " 'Sailing Against the Wind.' "

654 **Chicago mayor Jane Byrne** White, *America In Search of Itself*, 295.

654 **dedication of the John F. Kennedy** Sidney Blumenthal, *The Permanent Campaign: Inside the World of Elite Political Operatives* (Boston: Beacon Press, 1980), 245; Robert Schlesinger, *White House Ghosts: Presidents and Their Speechwriters* (New York: Simon & Schuster, 2008), 306; Jimmy Carter, "Boston, Massachusetts Remarks at Dedication Ceremonies for the John F. Kennedy," APP, October 20, 1979. See Ted Kennedy speech at YouTube.com, accessed January 30, 2020.

654 **state dinner for Deng Xiaoping** Witcover and Germond, *Blue Smoke and Mirrors*, 50.

654 **Archibald Cox** Kennedy, *True Compass*, 365.

654 **political reporter wrote** Blumenthal, *The Permanent Campaign*, 264.

655 **A Harris poll** Louis Harris poll, October 11, 1979.

655 **"There are those voices!"** *CBS Reports: Teddy*, November 4, 1979, VTVNA.

655 *"It is a contest"* "Remarks of Senator John F. Kennedy at the University of Illinois, Urbana, Illinois," October 24, 1960, JFKLibrary.org, accessed January 30, 2020.

655 **"There are some who say"** Witcover and Germond, *Blue Smoke and Mirrors*, 55; *New York Times* Service, October 23, 1979.

655 **"all but official"** "Kennedy Presses Leadership Issue in Philadelphia," NYT, October 23, 1979.

655 **"Well, I, not, I have no, uh"** September 7, 1979, interview in MFTVE, 13:28.

655 **November 4 CBS special** VTVNA; Segments viewable in MFTVE, 16:27, and "The Interview That Blindsided Ted Kennedy," YouTube.com, accessed April 18. 2020.

658 **"If you can wind him up"** *St. Paul Dispatch*, November 7, 1979.

659 **"but the rest of us"** Tom Wicker column, *New York Times* Service, November 10, 1979.

659 **"hurled rotten egg"** CT, November 9, 1979.

659 **last Gallup sounding** Witcover and Germond, *Blue Smoke and Mirrors*, 55.

659 **after his candidacy announcement** Robert Novak, *The Prince of Darkness: 50 Years Reporting in Washington* (New York: Crown Forum, 2007), 341.

659 **ten points among independents** n.d., "Carter Mondale Quotes 8," Box 85, RRPL.

659 **straw poll** Witcover and Germond, *Blue Smoke and Mirrors*, 79.

659   **The family retainers** Ibid., 70–71.

659   **Ronald Reagan had no problem** Bill Moyers interview, RRPL, Box 59.

659   **particularly taken** Author interview and correspondence with Bill Moyers.

660   **maximum amount** Gannett, August 22, 1979, on June 4, 1979 FEC report.

660   **"Reagan's been my friend"** Tom Fox column, *Philadelphia Inquirer*, September 6, 1979.

660   **Helene von Damm** von Damm to Deaver, July 12, 1979, RRPL, Box 77; von Damm, *At Reagan's Side*, passim.

660   **estimated $400,000** "For Candidates, the Joyful Sound of Benefit Concerts," *Philadelphia Inquirer*, December 24, 1979.

660   **"strict limitation"** ca. November 15, 1979, Reagan to Mr. Dutton, RRPL, Box 1.

660   **A Mercedes pulled** "Ronald Reagan: Rugged Runner in Biggest Race," WP, November 13, 1979.

661   **ticket cost $500** For planning and execution of Reagan opening event see schedule materials in RRPL, Boxes 59 and 78; for briefings see Box 52; and for advertising see DH, Box 6, Folder 3. Also Peter Hannaford and Charles Wick oral histories, Miller Center, University of Virginia; Helene von Damm, *At Reagan's Side: Twenty Years in the Political Mainstream* (New York: Doubleday, 1988), 106–11; Bob Colacello, *Ronnie and Nancy: Their Path to the White House—1911 to 1980* (New York: Grand Central Publishing, 2004), 475–78.

661   **"I ♥ New York"** See commercial on YouTube.com, accessed February 1, 2020; Wikipedia entry, "I Love New York"; *ELSMERE MUSIC, INC., Plaintiff, against NATIONAL BROADCASTING COMPANY, INC., Defendant*, United States District Court, Southern District of New York, 482 F. Supp. 741, January 9, 1980.

661   **epidemic of bank robberies** WABC-TV newscast, August 23, 1979, viewable at YouTube.com, accessed February 1, 2020.

661   **poverty rate** Kim Phillips-Fein, *Fear City: New York's Fiscal Crisis and the Rise of Austerity Politics* (New York: Metropolitan Books, 2017), 295.

661   **second federal bailout** Ian Shapiro, *The Last Great Senate: Courage and Statesmanship in Times of Crisis* (New York: Public Affairs Books, 2012), 189–201.

661   **workforce cut back a fifth** Phillips-Fein, *Fear City*, 295.

661   **A band of** "In New York City: Down Under with the Red Berets," *Time*, May 7, 1979; Nicholas Pileggi, "The Guardian Angels: Help—or Hype," *New York*, November 24, 1980.

662   **"every time I cross the Mississippi"** Reagan interview with John Lofton, *Conservative Battle Line*, December 1979.

662   **Commodore Hotel** Phillips-Fein, *Fear City*, 75.

662   **The hungry young killer** "Donald Trump, Real Estate Promoter, Builds Image as He Buys Buildings," NYT, November 1, 1976. The *Times* fact-checked Trump's claims in their 1976 article in "Trump Engaged in Suspect Tax Schemes as He Reaped Riches from His Father," NYT, October 2, 2008.

663   **$160 million in the lurch** Jerome Tuccille, *Trump: The Saga of America's Most Powerful Real Estate Baron* (Beard Books, 1985), 107.

663   **generally accepted accounting principles** Graham Kates, "Inside a Donald Trump Audit: Missing Books and Unusual Accounting," CBS News, August 8, 2016.

663   **Harry Helmsley** Phillips-Fein, *Fear City*, 259.

663   **" 'dramatic *galleria*' "** "Where the Donald Trumps Rent," NYT, August 30, 1979.

663   **"best piece of property"** Ibid.; see also "60-Story Tower Sought for Bonwit-Teller Site," NYT, March 1, 1979, D1; "Plan for Bonwit Site: Gifts at What Price," NYT, March 15, 1979.

663 **The Staten Island Express** WABC-TV newscast, August 23, 1979, viewable here, accessed February 1, 2020.

664 **casino night for cerebral palsy** "Notes on People," NYT, November 8, 1979.

664 **"New *Your*"** "Reagan Decision to Be Aired Nationally," press release, November 6, 1979, RRPL, "Reagan for President News Releases, 11-6-79 to 6-12-80."

665 **syndication company** DH, Box 6, Folder 3, "Reagan, Entering Primary Race, Calls for North American 'Accord,' " NYT, November 14, 1979.

665 **survey from Dick Wirthlin** "A National Survey of Voter Attitudes," April 1979, RRPL, Boxes 186 and 188.

666 *Detroit News* "Reagan's Fit and Out Front, But He's No Kid," *Detroit News*, November 6, 1979.

666 *Washington Post's* "Ronald Reagan: Rugged Runner in Biggest Race," WP, November 13, 1979.

666 *Wall Street Journal* *Wall Street Journal* Service, November 1, 1979.

666 **"beautiful horse"** "Ronald Reagan: Rugged Runner in Biggest Race."

667 **"When you're a front-runner"** "California's Two Contenders," LAT, November 1, 1979.

667 **"returns your phone calls"** "Reagan's Fit and Out Front, but He's No Kid."

667 **"front-runner lets it"** "Reagan Strategist Surveys Scene—and Picks a Winner," WSJ, August 30, 1979.

667 **correspondent concerned** Reagan to Court McLeod, November 1979, in RALIL, 353.

667 **"Sagebrush Rebellion"** See Jefferson Decker, *The Other Rights Rebellion: Conservative Lawyers and the Remaking of American Government* (New York: Oxford University Press, 2016), 91.

667 **gold standard** Reagan to Mr. Kiesewetter, November 1979, dictation file, RRPL, Box 1.

667 **"drop quoting Marx"** Allen to Reagan, October 18, 1979, "SUBJECT: A Way to Handle the 'Return to the Cold War Question,' " DH, Box 3, Folder 3. See dossier of fall 1979 policy documents: "Norths American Union, "South African" "SALT and the Search for Peace," etc., DH, Box 11, Folder 13.

667 **Reagan's last stop** DH, Box 78, "Scheduling November 1979" file; "Ford, Reagan Say Carter Shares Iran Responsibility," LAT, November 7, 1979.

667 **On NBC's** *Today* Lou Cannon, *Governor Reagan: His Rise to Power* (New York: Public Affairs Books, 2003), 453; Mark Green, *Ronald Reagan's Reign of Error* (New York: Pantheon, 1987), 120.

668 **potential admen** Schedule, November 13, 1979, RRPL, Box 59; Hannaford to Ronald and Nancy Reagan, November 3, 1979, Ibid. See also Hannaford to Sears et al., August 2, "SUBJECT: Advertising," DH, Box 6; Wikipedia entry for Phil Dusenberry; "Philip B. Dusenberry, 71, Adman, Dies," NYT, December 31, 2007; Meese note, June 1979, "Advertising for Campaign (PDH)," RRPL, Box 103; "Kornhauser, N.Y. Adman, Dies at 73," *Adweek*, September 15, 2005.

668 **Secret Service** Schedule, November 13, 1979, RRPL, Box 59.

668 **call-in host Barry Gray** Cannon, *Governor Reagan*, 451.

668 **"Men can swear"** von Damm, *At Reagan's Side*, 109.

668 **"invited as special guests"** *Reagan Country* 1, No. 1, RRPL, Box 110.

668 **Soon 1,800** Charlie Zwick oral history interview, Miller Center.

668 **upon which Jimmy Stewart** "1980: Time for Reagan" script, "Advertising, Charlie Wick Film, 1979," DH, Box 6, which also includes script for Michael Landon.

669 *Tarzan Reagan* Shirley, *Rendezvous with Destiny*, 72.

669 **50 percent** Len Koch to Hannaford, October 19, 1979, DH, Box 6, Folder 3.

669 **The text bore the impress** View speech at YouTube.com, accessed April 25, 2020.

670 **a North American accord** For background see November 29, 1977, radio commentary "Apples"; Hannaford to Deaver, January 30, 1978, "SUBJECT: Foreign Travel, 1979" ("Combine Canada with Mexico in 'North American Alliance' strategy trip, July, 1979"); Reagan to Senator Charles Matthias and supporting draft, February 19, 1979, on Mathias op ed January 15, 1979, "Mending Fences with Mexico" (all DH, Box 4, Folder 8); "A National Survey on Attitudes Toward North American Accord, RRPL, Box 189; Reagan to Lennie Pickard, August 6, 1979, in RALIL, 332 ("I would like to see . . . an open border between ourselves and Mexico"). For the libertarian resonances of such a proposal see Quinn Slobodian, *Globalists: The End of Empire and the Birth of Neoliberalism* (Cambridge, MA: Harvard University Press, 2019).

671 **dictated a rare letter** Reagan to Richard Whalen, RRPL, Box 59.

671 **white paper** Whalen to Reagan, "Personal and Confidential: North American Free Trade Area," June 4, 1979, "Memoranda, Whalen, Richard, 1978–1979," DH, Box 3, Folder 9.

672 **"political packager"** "Ritual Reagan," WSJ, November 14, 1979.

672 **"Reagan Announces His Candidacy—Again"** *Rocky Mountain News*, November 14, 1979.

672 **"a muted restatement"** "Reagan Announces, Urges Strength at Home, Abroad," WP, November 14, 1979.

672 **The *Chicago Tribune* ran** "Reagan, in Race, Rips Carter Stance," CT, November 14, 1979.

672 **The *New York Times* front page** "Reagan, Entering Presidency Race, Calls for North America 'Accord,' " NYT, November 14, 1979, A1.

672 **"oldest and wisest"** Lou Cannon, *Governor Reagan: His Rise to Power* (New York: Public Affairs Books, 2003), 453.

672 **not having "encouraged the shah"** HE, November 24, 1979.

672 **"helped off the track"** Frank van der Linden, *The Real Reagan: What He Believes, What He Has Accomplished, What We Can Expect from Him* (New York: William & Morrow Co., 1981), 165.

672 **briefing on his first stop** Briefings for Campaign Appearances, Announcement Tour file, RRPL, Box 52; also Cicero, Milwaukee briefings, and Atlanta.

672 **Dapper O'Neil** "Dapper O'Neil Through the Years," Boston.com.

673 **Voting Rights Act** Lou Cannon, *President Reagan: A Role of a Lifetime* (New York: Public Affairs, 2000), 458.

673 **open housing law** Kurt Schuppara, *Triumph of the Right: The Rise of the California Conservative Movement, 1945–1966* (Armonk, NY: M. E. Sharpe, 1998), 104–5.

673 **Major League guidebook's** Jules Witcover, *Marathon: Pursuit of the President, 1972–1976* (New York, Viking, 1977), 95. Reagan repeated a version of the fiction as president. See "Question-and-Answer Session with Local Television Anchors on Domestic and Foreign Policy Issues," APP, February 7, 1983.

673 **William Franklin Burghardt** See RALIL, 16. The September 3, 1981, issue of *Jet* reported that after Reagan told a black reporter that his friend Burghardt had died, Burghardt himself received many confused phone calls, and realized Reagan had mistaken him for the other black player on the team, who had indeed just died.

673 **"onto a federal plantation"** "News Analysis: Reagan Stars in Screen Test," NYT, May 26, 1968.

674 **Dick Wirthlin's firm** Jack J. Honomichl, *Honomichl on Marketing Research* (Lincolnwood, IL: NTC Business Books, 1986), 29.

674 **amendments to the Civil Rights Act** Thomas Edsall and Jane Byrne Edsall, *Chain Reaction: The Impact of Race, Rights, and Taxes on American Politics* (New York: W. W. Norton, 1991), 124.

674 *Franks v. Bowman* Ibid.

674 **"a dirty little secret"** "The 'Secret' Key Issue," NYT, November 6, 1972.

674 **"welfare queens"** Josh Levin, *The Queen: The Forgotten Life Behind an American Myth* (New York: Little, Brown, 2019).

674 **National Election Studies poll** John Mueller, Richard Niemi, and Tom W. Smith, *Trends in Public Opinion: A Compendium of Survey Data* (Westport, CT: Greenwood: 1989), 33, 35, 76.

675 **a board game** "Game Satirizing Life on Welfare Draws Criticism, but Sells Well," NYT, November 30, 1980; game in possession of author.

675 **In Milwaukee** *Milwaukee Journal*, November 17, 1979, in DH, Box 1, Folder 11.

675 **50 percent support** Witcover and Germond, *Blue Smoke and Mirrors*, 110.

675 **Reagan watcher, Lou Cannon** "Reagan Displays Vitality but Bobbles a Few on Opening Tour," WP, November 19. 1979.

676 **"So far as I can tell"** Ronald Reagan, *An American Life: An Autobiography* (New York: Simon & Schuster, 1990), 220.

676 *Japan as Number One* "Old GI Buries War Grudges," WP Service, May 20, 1979; Garry Wills column, October 28, 1980.

676 **"Whirlpool Corporation"** *CBS Reports: Teddy*, November 4, 1979, VTVNA; Whirlpool ad at YouTube.com, accessed April 17, 2020.

676 **percentage of all manufactured** Stein, *Pivotal Decade*, 200.

677 **General Motors jingled** NBC News, July 17, 1980, VTVNA.

677 **only 8.3 million** Ibid., 252.

677 **sclerotic, stupid, and arrogant** David Halberstam, *The Reckoning* (New York: William Morrow & Co., 1986), passim.

677 **"lived in communes"** Ibid., 510.

677 **fuel tank on their Pinto** "Pinto Madness," *Mother Jones*, September 1977; AP, March 14, 1980.

677 **"sales bank"** Halberstam, *The Reckoning*, 247, 545–46.

678 **"lemons of the year"** Shapiro, *The Last Great Senate*, 270.

678 **"too risky to drive"** WP Service, June 15, 1978.

678 **called a "minivan"** Halberstam, *The Reckoning*, 562–63.

678 **lost $159 million in 1978** Shapiro, *The Last Great Senate*, 270–7, which also includes account of first attempt at aid package.

678 **Reagan replied haltingly** "Reagan Critical of Plan for U.S. Aid to Chrysler," NYT, November 17, 1979.

678 **did not "appear to have a clue"** "Reagan Displays Vitality but Bobbles a Few on Opening Tour."

679 **"baggage call"** Cannon, *Governor Reagan*, 455.

679 **"I envy you your visit to South Africa"** Reagan to Otis Carney, RALIL, 259.

679 **first political job** Michael Deaver and Mickey Herskowitz, *Behind the Scenes: In Which the Author Talks About Ronald and Nancy Reagan . . . and Himself* (New York: William Morrow & Co., 1988), 37–38.

679 **hadn't supported Ronald Reagan** Michael Deaver, *A Different Drummer: My Thirty Years with Ronald Reagan* (New York: Harper, 2000), 18–20.

679 **the two became close** Ibid., 26–30. Navy coffee: 42. French wine: 73. "Mental computer": 35. "Hurt people": 27.

680 **"He's too relaxed"** Hedrick Smith, *The Power Game: How Washington Works* (New York: Random House, 2012), 381–82, which also tells the South Africa story.

680 **The governor ushered** Deaver, *A Different Drummer*, 195; Von Damm, *At Reagan's Side*, 110–11, tells the story differently.

CHAPTER THIRTY

682 **Ayatollah Khomeini blamed** Laura Kalman, *Right Star Rising: A New Politics, 1974–1980* (New York: Norton, 2010), 338.

682 **"kill the American dogs"** KXAS Action News, Dallas-Fort Worth, November 21, 1979, YouTube.com, accessed April 17, 2020.

682 **In Houston** AP, November 9, 1979.

682 **Islamic Student Center** "Islamic Center at OU Target of Firebomber," *Daily Oklahoman*, November 23, 1979.

682 **new issues** *Time*, November 26, 1979; *Newsweek*, November 26, 1979.

683 **Elmo Zumwalt spoke** "The Marines Are Ruled Out," *Time*, November 19, 1979.

683 **speech in Des Moines** "Expert Warns of Nuclear Fight Over Iran," *Des Moines Register*, November 11, 1979.

683 **NBC News reported** KXAS Action News, Dallas–Ft. Worth, November 21, 1979.

683 **hostage Jerry Miele** Mark Bowden, *Guests of the Ayatollah: The First Battle in America's War with Militant Islam* (New York: Atlantic Monthly Press, 2006), 189–90.

683 **put the hostages on "trial"** Jules Witcover and Jack Germond, *Blue Smoke and Mirrors: How Reagan Won and Why Carter Lost the Election of 1980* (New York: Viking, 1981), 82.

683 **with whom to negotiate** Bowden, *Guests of the Ayatollah*, 249.

683 **signed a petition** David Farber, *Taken Hostage: The Iran Hostage Crisis and America's First Encounter with Radical Islam* (Princeton: Princeton University Press, 2004), 156.

683 **The Ayatollah announced** Ibid., 157. This is also the source for quotes from those released.

683 **By December** "Iran timeline," AA, "Misc Issues" folder.

684 **A man in the street** Bowden, *Guests of the Ayatollah*, 189.

684 **"Okay, why not"** *CBS Evening News*, November 16, 1979, on YouTube.com, accessed April 29, 2020.

684 **Marvin Kalb reported** Bowden, *Guests of the Ayatollah*, 189.

684 **Sacramento, California** *CBS Evening News*, November 16, 1979.

684 **President Carter appealed** AP, November 18, 1979.

684 **not to scapegoat** *CBS Evening News*, November 16, 1979.

684 **didn't reach Senator Robert Byrd** Ibid.

684 **"Nagasaki, Hiroshima"** AP, December 1, 1979. This article is also the source for Oxford, Ohio, event.

685 **"Message to Khomeini"** "The Greening of Patriotism in America," WP, December 8, 1979; YouTube.com, accessed April 17, 2020.

685 **U.S. Steel** AP, November 30, 1979.

685 **public schools closed** "Cincinnati, in Face of a Deficit, Closing School System," NYT, December 10, 1979.

685 the Who was playing "In The News," December 8, 1979, YouTube.com, accessed April 17, 2020.

685 college newspaper in Buffalo December 7, 1979, reprinted at the Mossadegh Project, accessed April 17, 2020.

685 "Iran Spurs Rebirth of Patriotism" *Akron Beacon Journal*, December 9, 1979. The headline in the *Washington Post* was "The Greening of Patriotism in America."

686 Reagan, flying from Minnesota AP, November 30, 1979.

686 Lackland Air Force Base ABC News, December 3, 1979, VTVNA.

687 in St. Paul UPI, November 11, 1979.

687 Ted Kennedy was asked CBS, ABC, and NBC newscasts, December 3, 1979, VTVNA; MFTVE, 25:12.

687 new ABC/Harris Poll Lou Harris column, November 15, 1979.

687 "deserve to be president" "Chappaquiddick Is a Bigger Negative for Kennedy Than Pollsters Expected," WSJ, December 3, 1979.

688 irascible Mike Royko Royko column, December 4, 1979.

688 Connally and Reagan had regularly AP, November 15, 1979.

688 Connally nonetheless "Kennedy Remark Shocks Leaders," *Palm Beach Post*, December 4, 1979. The remaining quotes are divided between the newscasts at VTVNA and this article.

688 "Throughout the day" NBC News, December 3, 1979, VTVNA.

689 "engraved invitation" "The Shah, Seven Presidents Later," WP, December 21, 1979.

688 "TEDDY IS THE TOAST" *New York Post*, December 9, 1979; MFTVE, 26:37; Patrick Brogan, "Citizen Murdoch: Can Yellow Journalism Cover the World," *New Republic*, October 10, 1982.

689 solemn event UPI, December 5, 1979; "1980 Democratic Presidential Nomination: Remarks Announcing Candidacy," December 4, 1979, APP.

689 pollsters at NBC AP, December 1, 1979.

689 much smaller survey ABC News, December 7, 1979, VTVNA.

689 "I'm sorry" Joe Klein, "Camelot Collapsing," NYT *Magazine*, December 24, 1979.

689 there were none Theodore White, *America In Search of Itself: The Making of the President, 1956–1980* (New York: Harper & Row, 1981), 276.

689 "tooling up time" W&G, October 13, 1979.

689 Charlie Guggenheim Kathleen Hall Jamieson, *Packaging the Presidency: A History and Criticism of Presidential Advertising* (New York: Oxford University Press, 1988), 382; Sidney Blumenthal, *The Permanent Campaign: Inside the World of Elite Political Operatives* (Boston: Beacon Press, 1980), 253, 260.

690 Herb Schmerz Ibid., 261.

690 a bemused witness Craig Shirley, *Rendezvous with Destiny* (Wilmington, DE: Intercollegiate Studies Institute, 2009), 61.

690 Rick Stearns White, *America In Search of Itself*, 276.

690 lobbyist for the Boston diocese Blumenthal, *The Permanent Campaign*, 272.

690 Kennedy traveled to Iowa Klein, "Camelot Collapsing."

690 "We pride ourselves" CBS News, December 9, 1979, VTVNA; also response in Iowa.

691 lost a dozen points MFTVE, 26:39.

691 persuaded Panama Bowden, *Guests of the Shah*, 250.

691 "All in all" Farber, *Taken Hostage*, 57.

691 Abolhassan Bani-Sadr Bowden, *Guests of the Ayatollah*, 249.

691 "filthy and satanic" Ibid., 250. Also for Khalkhali.

692 **head-scratching bafflement** On ABC's nightly "America Held Hostage" broadcast on November 22, 1979 (VTVNA), the correspondent notes the students told him they believed Americans could be convinced to support the revolution by television news like they had been convinced to oppose the Vietnam War.

692 **Thanksgiving-night newscast** ABC News, November 22, 1979, VTVNA.

692 **Ted Stevens had scourged** VTVNA, December 3, 1979.

693 **"without any reservation"** Zbigniew Brzezinski, *Power and Principle: Memoirs of the National Security Adviser, 1977–1981* (New York: Farrar, Straus & Giroux), 365.

693 **Lawrence, Massachusetts** Bowden, *Guests of the Ayatollah,* 24, which is also source for cabdrivers.

693 **Charleston, South Carolina** NBC News, December 2, 1979, VTVNA.

693 **Lincoln Memorial** ABC News, December 16, 1979, VTVNA.

694 **sister of Kathryn Koob** AP, December 17, 1979.

694 **"We will turn on"** "Christmas Pageant of Peace: Remarks on Lighting the National Community Christmas Tree," December 13, 1979, APP.

694 **local news brief** "NBC News Update," YouTube.com, accessed April 17, 2020.

694 **"National Unity Day"** ABC News, December 16, 1979, VTVNA.

694 **"six-week period of appeasement"** William Safire column, December 20, 1979.

694 **hostage wife** Barbara Rosen and Barry Rosen with George Feiffer, *The Destined Hour: The Hostage Crisis and One Family's Ordeal* (New York: Doubleday, 1982), passim.

695 **on December 12** "We'd Like to Bring Them Home to You . . . ," *New York Daily News,* December 12, 1979.

696 **Frank Reynolds of NBC** NBC News, December 24, 1979, VTVNA.

696 **recently viewed Afghanistan** My portrait of Afghanistan and its descent into war comes from Christian Caryl, *Strange Rebels: 1979 and the Birth of the 21st Century* (New York: Basic Books, 2013), passim; Jeremy Isaacs and Taylor Downing, *Cold War: An Illustrated History, 1945–1991* (New York: Little, Brown, 1998), 324–29; Tim Weiner, *Legacy of Ashes: The History of the CIA* (New York: Doubleday, 2007), 422; and minutes of Soviet Politburo meetings on March 17, April 12, December 27, and December 31, 1979, collected at DigitalArchive.WilsonCenter.org.

701 **"Every scrap"** "The Hardening Mood Toward Foreign Policy," *Public Opinion,* February/March 1980.

CHAPTER THIRTY-ONE

705 **"How can anyone"** *60 Minutes,* January 13, 1980, YouTube.com, accessed April 18, 2020.

705 **Back in 1978** "A Truly Unannounced Candidate," WP, September 15, 1978.

705 **Eight months later** "Into the Marathon with Earnest George Bush," WP, May 24, 1979.

705 **Jules Witcover joked** Jules Witcover and Jack Germond, *Blue Smoke and Mirrors: How Reagan Won and Why Carter Lost the Election of 1980* (New York: Viking, 1981), 119.

705 **Rich Bond** "Life and Career of Richard Bond," July 2, 1992, C-Span.org; "Candidates' 'Hired Guns' Stalking Iowa Caucuses," *Des Moines Register,* November 11, 1979.

705 **13.5 percentage point victory** "George Bush Tops Field in Republican Straw Poll," *Des Moines Register,* May 23, 1979.

706 **Amway-style pyramid** Craig Shirley, *Rendezvous with Destiny: Ronald Reagan and the Campaign that Changed America* (Wilmington, DE: Intercollegiate Studies Institute, 2009), 71.

706 **"I'm Rich Bond"** Jon Meacham, *Destiny and Power: The American Odyssey of George Herbert Walker Bush* (New York: Random House, 2015), 223; brick on 224.

706 **pushed by the political cult leader** Chip Berlet and Matthew N. Lyons, *Right-Wing Populism in America: Too Close for Comfort* (New York: Guilford, 2000), 273.

706 **"drop dead"** *Waterbury Republican*, December 23, 1979, clip in DH, Box 85.

706 **"I will always be"** "To George Bush, Seeking Presidency Seems Almost a Duty," WSJ, July 6, 1979.

706 **Keene, put it more bluntly** Shirley, *Rendezvous with Destiny*, 71.

706 **Possum Growers and Breeders** "Stumbles Aside, Bush Off on Right Foot," WP, May 6, 1979.

707 **Jerry Carmen** Theodore White, *America In Search of Itself: The Making of the President, 1956–1980* (New York: Harper & Row, 1981), 305.

707 **campaign committee** George Bush for President, "National Steering Committee Membership as of July 17, 1979," in RRPL, Box 84, "Bush (George)."

707 **"calls our candidate 'Poppy' "** "To George Bush, Seeking Presidency Seems Almost a Duty."

707 **"Now some of you know"** Joel Rogers and Thomas Ferguson, *The Hidden Election: Politics and Economics in the 1980 Presidential Campaign* (New York: Pantheon, 1981), 66.

707 **"Mummy and Daddy make certain"** Lisa Birnbach, *The Official Preppy Handbook* (New York: Workman Publishing, 1980), 17.

707 **youngest son, Marvin** Doro Bush Koch, *My Father, My President: A Personal Account of the Life of George H. W. Bush* (New York: Grand Central, 20014), 151.

707 **His son Neil** Meacham, *Destiny and Power*, 222; also for Jeb and Doro.

707 **"I don't question Reagan's"** Ibid., 215–16.

708 **"the crossover candidate"** Sidney Blumenthal, *The Permanent Campaign: Inside the World of Elite Political Operatives* (Boston: Beacon Press, 1980), 190.

708 **Maine cattle show** Witcover and Germond, *Blue Smoke and Mirrors*, 105.

708 **"honorable profession of politics"** Rogers and Ferguson, *The Hidden Election*, 67.

708 **"bulky Florida businessman"** Ibid., 69–70.

708 **William F. Buckley had** Rick Perlstein, "I Thought I Understood the Right. Donald Trump Proved Me Wrong," NYT *Magazine*, April 11, 2017.

708 **"As a civilized person"** White, *America In Search of Itself*, 303.

709 **"stylistic criteria"** Witcover and Germond, *Blue Smoke and Mirrors*, 117.

709 **New Hampshire, radio show** "Bush Buoyed by Success in Straw Polls," LAT, November 30, 1979.

709 **"I've *been there*"** "George Is Coming on Strong," *Time*, December 3, 1979.

709 **"Coffee with Connally"** James Reston Jr., *Lone Star: The Life of John Connally* (New York: HarperCollins, 1989), 566.

709 **Reagan's were weak** Author correspondence with Elliot Curson and Jeff Bell; Jeff Bell interview, DailyReckoning.com, June 6, 2016; "C. Terence Clyne, Ad Creator," NYT, December 4, 1981.

709 **Howard Baker's** Curson interview, *Fresh Air*, WHYY, 1980 (special thanks to Amy Salit); Witcover and Germond, *Blue Smoke and Mirrors*, 113; J. Lee Annis, *Howard Baker: Conciliator in an Age of Crisis* (Knoxville: Howard Baker Center, 2007), 168.

710 **"not a professional film"** Bush commercial, YouTube.com, accessed April 18, 2020.

710 **For another** *60 Minutes*, January 13, 1980, YouTube.com, accessed April 18, 2020.

710 **A third** Bush commercial, YouTube.com, accessed April 18, 2020.

710 **January 8 briefing** "Situation in Iran and Soviet Invasion of Afghanistan: Remarks at a White House Briefing for Members of Congress," *Weekly Compilation of Presidential Documents* 16, No. 1.

710 **disguised as a film crew** Tim Weiner, *Legacy of Ashes: The History of the CIA* (New York: Doubleday, 2007), 431.

711 **rumbled into Herat** *Issues and Answers*, December 30, 1979, transcript in RRPL, Box 51.

711 **tactical nuclear weapons** Mark Bowden, *Guests of the Ayatollah: The First Battle in America's War with Militant Islam* (New York: Atlantic Monthly Press, 2006), 287.

711 **pressed by Zbigniew Brzezinski** Interview with Brzezinski, *La Nouvel Observateur*, January 15–21, 1998. For CIA operations in Afghanistan prior to the Soviet invasion see David Zierler, ed, *Foreign Relations of the United States, 1977–1980, Volume XII, Afghanistan* (Washington, D.C.: United States State Department, 2018), 105–168, downloadable at History.State.gov.

711 **top-secret questionnaire** Jack Anderson column, December 13, 1979.

711 **"Vietnam complex"** Jimmy Carter, *White House Diary* (New York: Macmillan, 2010), 379.

711 **In April** For the events leading up to Carter's decision to prohibit assistance to Pakistan under the Symington Amendment, see the narrative and linked documents in "The United States and Pakistan's Quest for the Bomb," December 21, 2020, National Security Archive.

711 **"keeping with our constitutional"** *Issues and Answers*, December 30, 1979.

711 **authorized CIA operatives** Carter, *White House Diary*, 388.

711 **televised speech** "Address to the Nation on the Soviet Invasion of Afghanistan," January 4, 1980, APP.

712 **approaching 100 percent** Carter, *White House Diary*, 389.

712 **Kurt Waldheim** Bowden, *Guests of the Ayatollah*, 288–89.

712 **He reported back** Carter, *White House Diary*, 389.

712 **Foreign Minister Ghotbzadeh** For the emergence of these back-channel negotiations see Bowden, *Guests of the Ayatollah*, 287–88, 327–29.

713 **In Iowa** "Candidates As Thick as Corn as Caucuses Near," LAT, December 4, 1979.

713 **basketball gyms** "Hopefuls Attack Iowa as E-Day Nears," *New York Daily News*, January 19, 1980.

713 **cinema verité** Kathleen Hall Jamieson, *Packaging the Presidency: A History and Criticism of Presidential Advertising* (New York: Oxford University Press, 1988), 383.

713 **Sunday before the caucuses** " 'Meet the Press' Interview with Bill Monroe, Carl T. Rowan, David Broder, and Judy Woodruff," January 20, 1980, APP.

714 **Jerry Brown disagreed** AP, January 19, 1980.

714 **spent December accusing** Mary McGrory column, January 7, 1980; also for Mike Curb

714 **John Sears responded** "Hopefuls Attack Iowa as E-Day Nears," *New York Daily News*, January 19, 1980.

714 **equivalent conservatisms** Witcover and Germond, *Blue Smoke and Mirrors*, 113.

714 **"Weekend Update" gag** MFTVE, 38:31.

714 **Anderson gibed** Kim Phillips-Fein, *Invisible Hands: The Businessmen's Crusade Against the New Deal* (New York: Norton, 2009), 240–41; David Broder column, January 9, 1980.

714 **"a potential spoiler"** "The Worst Loneliness Facing Rep. John Anderson Is That of the Short-Distance Runner," *People*, February 4, 1980.

714 **The editors of** *Time* Jim Mason, *No Holding Back: The 1980 John B. Anderson Presidential Campaign* (Lanham, MD: University Press of America), 151.

715 **"Why Not the Best?"** NYT, January 13, 1980.

715 **Walter Cronkite** MFTVE, 38:22.

715 **producers of** *Saturday Night Live* Mason, *No Holding Back*, 129.

715 **"seven planes and helicopters"** AP, February 1, 1980.

715 **anything as foolish** "Faultfinder for Carter Starts Combing Reagan's Record," WP, May 16, 1980.

715 **"Chappaquiddick: The Still Unanswered Questions"** *Reader's Digest*, February 1980; see also "The Tide in Ted's Life," *Time*, January 28. 1980.

715 **Joan Kennedy was drafted** "Hopefuls Attack Iowa as E-Day Nears," *New York Daily News*, January 19, 1980.

715 **CBS News poll** MFTVE, 26:48.

715 **"The flame under the charisma"** Mary McGrory column, January 16, 1980.

715 **the Des Moines airport** Meacham, *Destiny and Power*, 222.

715 **"run out of underpants"** Kitty Kelley, *The Family: The Real Story of the Bush Dynasty* (New York: Doubleday, 2004), 363.

715 **On the big day** "Life and Career of Richard Bond," July 2, 1992, C-Span; "Candidates' 'Hired Guns' Stalking Iowa Caucuses," *Des Moines Register*, November 11, 1979.

716 **In January of 1976** ABC News, January 22, 1980, VTVNA.

716 **in Salem, Oregon** "They Shall Not Forget," *Oregon Statesman*, January 30, 1980.

716 **pen pals** Bowden, *Guests of the Ayatollah*, 353.

716 **yellow ribbon** Penne Laingen oral history interview, March 27, Association for Diplomatic Studies and Training Foreign Affairs, Oral History Program, Foreign Service Spouse Series; Melani McAllister, *Epic Encounters: Cultural, Media, and U.S. Interests in the Middle East Since 1945* (Berkeley: University of California Press [Updated Edition], 2005), 344; AP, December 28, 1979; "Kidnaped Envoy's Wife Bearing Up," LAT, January 11, 1980.

716 **"What does this mean?"** Laingen oral history.

CHAPTER THIRTY-TWO

717 **George Bush jumped** J. Lee Annis, *Howard Baker: Conciliator in an Age of Crisis* (Knoxville: Howard Baker Center, 2007), 170.

717 **"After First Blush"** WP, January 25, 1980.

717 **Bush profiles** "Bush Breaks Out of the Pack," *Newsweek*, February 4, 1980; Michael Kramer, "George Bush: A Republican for All Factions," *New York*, January 21, 1980.

717 **"man America turns to"** Annis, *Howard Baker*, 170.

717 **"*big mo*"** Michael Beschloss, "George Bush," *PBS News Hour*.

717 **Mike Royko** For instance March 7 and March 21, 1980, columns.

718 **"Join the Frontrunner"** *Newsday* Service, February 5, 1980.

718 **Hugh Gregg** "Bush Buoyed by Success in Straw Polls," LAT, November 30, 1979.

718 **State of the Union** "State of the Union Address Delivered Before a Joint Session of Congress," January 23, 1980, APP; video at C-SPan.org, accessed April 19, 2020.

719 **"in a power poker game"** "Reagan Attacks Carter as an Appeaser," WP, January 25, 1980; RVA, Box 33, "Reagan for President News Releases."

719 **appeared "tense"** "Reagan Meets to Review Strategy," NYT, January 24, 1980.

719 *60 Minutes* "Reagan Suggests Blockade of Cuba on Soviets' Move into Afghanistan," NYT, January 28, 1980.

720 **particularly unconvincing** "Eleanor" to "Ed," January 28, 1980, RRPL, Box 114.

720 **different newsworthy attack** RVA, Box 33.

720 **how eager** NBC News, January 22, VTVNA.

720 **On Monday** Gannett Service, February 6, 1980.

720 **"Some people ask"** "Reagan Likes Birthday, Considering Alternative," LAT, February 6, 1980; "Reagan Is Feted for His Birthday During N.H. Tour," WP, February 6, 1980. For origins of strategy see Lorelei Kinder to Charlie Black, October 4, 1979, and to Deaver, October 17, RRPL, Box 87.

720 **South Carolina** "Reagan Steps Up Attack on Carter's Foreign Policy," NYT, February 8, 1980.

721 *Boston Globe* **poll** "Bush Neck and Neck with Reagan in N.H. Poll," BG, February 3, 1980.

721 **National Right to Life Committee** Connie Paige, *The Right to Lifers: Who They Are, How They Operate, and Where They Get Their Money* (Summit Books, 1983), 24; AP, January 22, 1980.

721 **Judge John Dooling** "Abortion Ruling: An Order to Pay the Poor," *Time*, January 28. 1980.

721 **"voice breaks"** "Into the Marathon with Earnest George Bush," WP, May 24, 1979.

721 **nicknamed him "Rubbers"** Tanya Melich, *The Republican War Against Women: An Insider's Report From Behind the Lines* (New York: Bantam, 1996), 104.

721 **he had muttered** Robert Novak, *The Prince of Darkness: 50 Years Reporting in Washington* (New York: Crown Forum, 2007), 341.

722 **"What is the Moral Majority?"** David Snowball, *Continuity and Change in the Rhetoric of the Moral Majority* (New York: Praeger, 1991), 13.

722 **John Conlan** J. Brooks Flippen, *Jimmy Carter, the Politics of Family, and the Rise of the Religious Right* (Athens, GA: University of Georgia Press, 2011), 82.

722 **"visits to refugee camps"** *New York Times* Service, January 23, 1980.

722 **Trinity Christian Academy** "America, You're Too Young to Die," *Christian School Confidential*, January 12, 2012; author interview with Dwayne Walker.

722 **Charles Stanley's megachurch** Flippen, *Jimmy Carter*, 211; William Martin, *With God on Our Side: The Rise of the Religious Right in America* (New York: Broadway Books, 1996), 207.

772 **The first issue** Snowball, *Continuity and Change in the Rhetoric of the Moral Majority*, 69.

722 **Robert Maddox** Flippen, *Jimmy Carter*, passim, 245-48; "Carter Sways Some Evangelicals in 2-Day Blitz to Regain Support," NYT, January 28, 1980.

723 **"black iron gates"** John G. Turner, *Bill Bright and the Campus Crusade for Christ: The Renewal of Evangelism in Twentieth Century America* (Chapel Hill: University of North Carolina Press, 2009), 190–91.

723 **Bob Jones University** "Reagan to Debate His G.O.P. Rivals," NYT, January 31, 1980; AP, January 31, 1980; "In 1980, Ronald Reagan Received Warm Welcomes in Upstate," *Greenville News*, July 2, 2017.

723 **Falwell traveled to Alaska** Michael Sean Winters, *God's Right Hand: How Jerry Falwell Made God a Republican and Baptized the American Right* (New York: HarperOne, 2012), 129, 144; AP, August 7, 1980.

723 **field director, stunned** AP, February 22, 1980; Knight-Ridder Service, May 8, 1980.

724 **"Christians for Reagan"** William C. Inboden III, "Divine Elections: Abortion, Evangelicalism, and the New Right in American Politics, 1973–1980: The Politicization of Morality," Stanford University Department of History, honors thesis; Flippen, *Jimmy Carter*, 294. For pamphlet see "It Looks Like a Bill, But It's a Plug for Reagan," *Miami Herald*, September 21, 1980, which reports that the mailing was sufficiently deceptive that it drew contributions from Carter supporters. Identical language also appeared in letters to editors: to the *Lansing State Journal*, May 10, 1980; to the *Jasper* (Indiana) *Herald*, September 10, 1980.

724 **On February 7** RVA, Box 33, "Reagan for President News Releases"; same source for Tallahassee and Jacksonville.

724 **"another alternative"** "Reagan, After Iowa, Is Focusing on Foreign Policy," WP, February 9, 1980.

724 **"any of our business"** "Reagan Says America Should Not Bar Others from A-Bomb Output," NYT, February 2, 1980.

724 **not even speaking** " 'California Cronies' Have Reagan's Ears," LAT, June 26, 1980.

724 **"dusting off his references"** "The Granite State: Follies and Feuding in the GOP," WP, February 26, 1980.

724 **Trilateral Commission** "Reagan Steps Up Attack on Carter's Foreign Policy," NYT, February 8, 1980.

725 **three-point edge** Lou Harris column, February 12, 1980.

725 *Free to Choose* Milton Friedman and Rose Friedman, *Two Lucky People: Memoirs* (Chicago: University of Chicago, 1999), 471–96; Soren Brands, "The Market's People: The Media and the Making of Neoliberal Populism," draft shared with author; "Angus Burgen, "Age of Certainty: Galbraith, Friedman, and the Public Life of Economic Ideas," *History of Political Economy* 45, suppl. 1 (2013); *Free to Choose* episodes at YouTube.com, accessed April 19, 2020.

729 **fired its Madison Avenue** Author interview and correspondence with Elliott Curson; author correspondence with Jeff Bell; Jeff Bell interview, DailyReckoning.com, June 6, 2016; Kathleen Hall Jamieson, *Packaging the Presidency: A History and Criticism of Presidential Advertising* (New York: Oxford University Press, 1988), 393–95; Jude Wanniski, "A Reagan Landslide?", *Polynomics*, June, 1980; "Campaign '80: Reagan's Ad Man," *Detroit Free Press*, April 13, 1980; Sidney Blumenthal, *The Rise of the Counter-Establishment: The Conservative Ascent to Political Power* (New York: Times Books, 2007), 202; Curson interview, *Fresh Air*, WHYY, 1980.

729 **spending ceilings** Susan B. Trento, *The Power House: Robert Keith Gray and the Selling of Influence in Washington* (New York: St. Martin's Press, 1992), 118.

731 **frantic letter** Wanniski to Hannaford, March 5, 1980, DH, Box 11, Folder 8.

731 **Cockburn and James Ridgeway** Joel Rogers and Thomas Ferguson, *The Hidden Election: Politics and Economics in the 1980 Presidential Campaign* (New York: Pantheon, 1981), 82.

731 **focus groups** "TV Veteran Reagan Gets Good Reviews on Ad Performance," WP, March 25, 1980; Rowland Evans and Robert Novak, *The Reagan Revolution* (New York: Dutton, 1981), 60–62, 75, 78.

731 **Four years earlier** ABC News, February 14, 1976, at YouTube.com, accessed April 19, 2020.

731 *The Right Stuff* AP, January 2, 1980; "Astronauts Get the Wolfe Treatment," CT, September 15, 1979; "Tom Wolfe's Space Odyssey," CT, September 9, 1979; "Behind the Bestsellers," NYT *Book Review*, October 28, 1979; Bob Green column, September 25, 1979; "The Sky Is Our Domain," NYT *Book Review*, September 29,1979; Tom Wolfe, *The Right Stuff* (New York: Farrar, Straus & Giroux, 1979).

732 **Lake Placid** Travis Vogan, *ABC Sports: The Rise and Fall of Network Sports Television* (Berkeley: University of California Press, 2018), 156; Jules Witcover and Jack Germond, *Blue Smoke and Mirrors: How Reagan Won and Why Carter Lost the Election of 1980* (New York: Viking, 1981), 149; *Do You Believe in Miracles: The Story of the 1980 U.S. Hockey Team* (2001), on YouTube.com; also game against Soviet Union, YouTube.com, accessed April 19, 2020.

734 **"Statue of Liberty"** "Yes, America, Your Boys Did It," BG, February 25, 1980.

734 **Republican debate** "Bush Image Hurt by Big Debate," CT, February 28. 1980; WMUR-TV interview in 2015 with soundman Bob Molloy, YouTube.com, accessed April 20, 2020; New Hampshire Public Radio interview with Molloy, December 5, 2015, NHPR.org; Jeff Bell, "The Candidate and the Briefing Book," *Weekly Standard*, February 1, 2001; George Bush, *All the Best, George Bush: My Life in Letters and Other Writings* (New York: Simon & Schuster, 1999), 288–90; Theodore White, *America In Search of Itself: The Making of the President, 1956–1980* (New York: Harper & Row, 1981), 404; Witcover and Germond, *Blue Smoke and Mirrors*, 123–127; Robert Loerzel, Phillip Crane *Pioneer Press* profile from 1992, RobertLoerzel.com; MFTVE, 34:29. See also *State of the Union* (MGM, 1948).

739 **put out a statement** RVA, Box 33.

740 **"There was a feeling"** White, *America In Search of Itself*, 251.

740 **Once, shortly after** Garry Wills, *Reagan's America: Innocents at Home* (New York: Doubleday, 1986), 230.

740 **Sears got his revenge** "Ousted Reagan Aide Shuns Baker's Bid," NYT, February 29, 1980.

CHAPTER THIRTY-THREE

741 **let himself hope** Jimmy Carter, *White House Diary* (New York: Macmillan, 2010), 395.

741 **"my own terms"** Jules Witcover and Jack Germond, *Blue Smoke and Mirrors: How Reagan Won and Why Carter Lost the Election of 1980* (New York: Viking, 1981), 146.

741 **This speech** BG, January 28, 1980 (two articles); "Kennedy States His Case," BG, January 29, 1980; Kathleen Hall Jamieson, *Packaging the Presidency: A History and Criticism of Presidential Advertising* (New York: Oxford University Press, 1988), 384. Full text: "Sometimes a Party Must Sail Against the Wind," WP, January 29, 1980.

741 **"National Day of Prayer"** H.Con.Res.218, February 19, 1980. at Congress.gov.

742 **treasury bonds** My account of the February-March 1980 deficit panic, including media quotations (except those specifically cited), follows Aaron Wildavasky, *The Deficit and the Public Interest: The Search for Responsible Budgeting in the 1980s* (Berkeley: University of California Press 1989), 29–34.

742 **auto and steel** "1980 in Michigan," Wikipedia.org.

743 **64 percent** "Role of Issues Held Minor for '80 Race," NYT, June 11, 1979.

743 **"Milton" Feldstein** "Fed Advised to Tighten Credit Even Further," CT, February 27, 1980.

743 **went on TV** "Anti-Inflation Program: Remarks Introducing the Administration's Program," March 14, 1980, APP.

744 **"More Mush from the Wimp"** "Now It Can Be Told . . . the Story Behind Campaign '82's Favorite Insult," BG, November 6, 1982; "All Must Share the Burden," NYT, April 4, 1980.

745 **On March 18** WABC-TV News, Chicago, YouTube.com, accessed April 20, 2020.

745 *New York Daily News* **poll** Theodore White, *America In Search of Itself: The Making of the President, 1956–1980* (New York: Harper & Row, 1981), 298.

745 **"Not only to rescue"** "Effort Seen to Deprive Foes of a Political Issue," NYT, March 15, 1980.

745 **"Carter is forcing"** March 5, 1980, RVA, Box 33, "Reagan for President Press Releases."

745 **invited Adam Clymer** Jon Meacham, *Destiny and Power: The American Odyssey of George Herbert Walker Bush* (New York: Random House, 2015), 233.

745 **speech in Florida** Craig Shirley, *Rendezvous with Destiny: Ronald Reagan and the Campaign that Changed America* (Wilmington, DE: Intercollegiate Studies Institute, 2009), 195, which is also source for Teeter consultation with Ford.

745 **press conference** "Carter Is Confident as Bush Stages Final Florida Drive to Slow Reagan," NYT, March 11, 1980.

746 **"When I came"** Hobart Rowen, "Lesson: Carter's Mistakes," WP, March 6, 1980.

746 **ABC/Harris poll** AP, March 10, 1980.

746 **Cronkite exulted** MFTVE, 40:01.

746 **George Washington University** MFTVE, 39:10.

746 **"thinking man's candidate"** " 'Wow!' Said John Anderson After the Tuesday Count, But Can His Dark Horse Go the Distance?" WP, March 6, 1980.

746 **"Tweedledee and Tweedledum** "The Granite State Follies," WP, March 26, 1980.

746 **"something of a hair shirt"** John Anderson: The *Playboy* Interview, June 1980.

747 **"Mr. T. J. Hooton"** *Doonesbury*, April 20, 1980.

747 *SNL's* **producers** Jim Mason, *No Holding Back: The 1980 John B. Anderson Presidential Campaign* (Lanham, MD: University Press of America, 2011), 129.

747 **"right-wing exuberant"** Rick Perlstein, *Nixonland: The Rise of a President and the Fracturing of America* (New York: Scribner, 2008), 437.

747 **own PR firm** *Get Me Roger Stone* (2017, directed by Dylan Bank, Daniel DiMauro, and Morgan Perm).

748 **"Reporters ate it up"** Craig Unger, *Boss Rove: Inside Karl Rove's Secret Kingdom of Power* (New York: Scribner, 2012), 21.

748 **daughter in an integrated public school** Joseph Crespino, *Strom Thurmond's America* (New York: Hill & Wang, 2012), 280.

748 **Atwater explained** Rick Perlstein, "Exclusive: Lee Atwater's Infamous 1981 Interview on the Southern Strategy," TheNation.com, November 13, 2020.

748 **Strom Thurmond** For Atwater in South Carolina primary see Lee Brady, *Bad Boy: The Life and Politics of Lee Atwater* (New York: De Capo Press, 1997), 74–78.

749 **"most dangerous drug"** "Reagan Shows Conservative Stripes in GOP Debate," *Baltimore Sun*, February 29, 1980.

749 **Bush, incredulous** UPI, February 29, 1980.

749 **"When Chicago"** Mark Green, *Ronald Reagan's Reign of Error* (New York: Pantheon, 1987), 79–80.

749 **"totally unnecessary"** Ibid., 79–80.

749 **Robert Scheer** "Reagan Views Issues at Home, Abroad," LAT, March 6, 1980; MFTVE, 30:51, 1:04:06.

750 Saudi royal family "Winton M. Blount," Wikipedia.org.

750 "who has saved" "Carter Is Confident as Bush Stages Final Florida Drive."

750 "voluntary features" "A Time for Choosing," October 27, 1964, AmericanRhetoric.com.

750 Jimmy Stewart 1976 Social Security commercial, YouTube.com, accessed April 20, 2020.

751 "singled out" March 9, 1980, campaign statement, RVA, Box 33.

751 "attempt to harass" Green, *Reagan's Reign of Error*, 23.

751 One of the commercials Jeff Bell interview, DailyReckoning.com, June 6, 2016.

751 "no nation in history" "Economic Scene," NYT, March 14, 1980.

751 Ford signed a document "Member of John Kasich Team Worked to Block Reagan in 1980," Breitbart.com, April 2, 2016.

751 Two days later Witcover and Germond, *Blue Smoke and Mirrors*, 172.

751 On *Issues and Answers* Marianne Means column, March 26, 1980.

752 Reagan's supposed reduction WS, March 2, 1980.

752 "History shows no such thing" "Where Did He Get Those Figures?", *Time*, April 14, 1980.

752 Charls Walker Sidney Blumenthal, *The Rise of the Counter-Establishment: The Conservative Ascent to Political Power* (New York: Times Books, 2007), 73.

752 Donald Rumsfeld Wanniski to Meese, January 18, 1980, RRPL, Box 118.

752 Others, including Joel Rogers and Thomas Ferguson, *The Hidden Election: Politics and Economics in the 1980 Presidential Campaign* (New York: Pantheon, 1981), 49.

752 focus-group subject "TV Veteran Reagan Gets Good Reviews on Ad Performance," WP, March 25, 1980.

752 his friends at CBS MFTVE, 40:51.

752 debated on TV in Illinois MFTVE, 41:32; Green, *Reagan's Reign of Error*, 112;

753 Walter Cronkite MFTVE, 42:07.

753 "Learning to Live with Reagan" WSJ, March 13, 1980.

753 Bill Casey Tim Weiner, *Legacy of Ashes: The History of the CIA* (New York: Doubleday, 2007), 435; Rhoda Koenig, "Basket Casey," *New York*, October 15,1980.

753 "Len Hall's brains" F. Clifton White, *Politics as a Noble Calling: The Memoirs of F. Clifton White* (Ottawa, IL: Jameson Books, 1994), 4.

753 dabbled in economic development "Private Study on Cutting Costs of School, Govt.," *New York Daily News*, May 3, 1979; Casey to National Bank of North America executive, July 13, 1979; Casey to Poole, August 8, 1979, Casey papers, Hoover Institution, Box 204.

754 "Committee for Responsible" Casey to Thomas Murphy, August 20, 1979.

754 hedged his bets See William J. Casey 1980 contribution records at FEC.gov.

754 a "godsend" "The Men Around Reagan," BG, March 29, 1980.

754 like a chairman of the board ABC News, August 6, 1980, VTVNA.

754 lowered overhead Susan B. Trento, *The Power House: Robert Keith Gray and the Selling of Influence in Washington* (New York: St. Martin's Press, 1992), 118; "The Men Around Reagan."

754 old friend F. Clifton White, *Politics as a Noble Calling: The Memoirs of F. Clifton White* (Ottawa, IL: Jameson Books, 1994), 3.

754 establishment economists Business advisory panel press release, RVA, Box 33.

754 "young program-oriented aides" "Anticipating Carter, Reagan Adds Key Advisors," WP, March 23, 1980.

755 "deserved to die" " 'California Cronies' Have Reagan's Ears," LAT, June 26, 1980.

755 Allen wrote confidentially March 26, 1980, DH, Box 11, Folder 15.

755   **alternate budget** David Stockman, *The Triumph of Politics: Why the Reagan Revolution Failed* (New York: Harper & Row, 1986), 59–60.

755   **"unisex toilets"** Ibid., 53.

755   **"The neoconservative"** Irving Kristol, "The Battle for Reagan's Soul," WSJ, May 16, 1980.

755   **"The Battle for Ronald Reagan's Mind"** *Business Week*, April 7, 1980.

756   **New York Stock Exchange** Kim Phillips-Fein, *Invisible Hands: The Businessmen's Crusade Against the New Deal* (New York: Norton, 2009), 236.

756   **"U.S. Geological Survey"** Green, *Reagan's Reign of Error*, 106.

756   **credit controls** Stacey L. Schreft, "Credit Controls: 1980," *Economic Review*, November/December 1990.

756   **Rupert Murdoch** Jimmy Carter, *White House Diary*, 402; Patrick Brogan, "Citizen Murdoch: Can Yellow Journalism Cover the World," *New Republic*, October 10, 1982.

756   **United Nations ambassador** Witcover and Germond, *Blue Smoke Mirrors*, 152.

757   **"Friends, Herbert *Hoi*-ver"** Carroll O'Connor for Kennedy ad, YouTube.com, accessed April 20, 2020; Elliot Curson interview, *Fresh Air*, WHYY, 1980.

757   **New York City subway system** White, *America In Search of Itself*, 299.

757   **"My principles"** MFTVE, 27:49.

757   **Madison's Capitol grounds** Jesse Walker, "Friday A/V Club: Jerry Brown and Francis Ford Coppola's 'Transmission from Some Clandestine Place on Mars,' " Reason.com, June 6, 2014, including complete video; "Doug Moe: 35 Years On, Recalling 'Apocalypse Brown,'" Madison.com, March 27, 2015. Thanks to David Dayen for explaining the technical glitch.

759   **"The Hostage Prayer"** "People," *Indianapolis News*, April 24, 1980; YouTube.com, accessed April 20, 2020.

759   **"Bomb Iran"** "Bomb Iran," Wikpipedia.org. Vince and the Valiants 45 in possession of author.

759   **Villalon and Christian Bourget** Mark Bowden, *Guests of the Ayatollah: The First Battle in America's War with Militant Islam* (New York: Atlantic Monthly Press, 2006), 327–30, 360–68.

759   **dribble of news** Bani-Sadr interview, ABC News, February 2, 1980, VTVNA; AP, February 4, 1980; "Iran President: Militants Act Like 'Children,' " BG, February 7, 1980; "Hundredth Day: Iran Hints on Easing Shah's Return," *Des Moines Tribune*, February 11, 1980; "Iran Proposal to Free Hostages Is Reported," WP Service, February 12, 1980; "A New Chapter Opens in Epic of U.S. Hostages," WP, February 21, 1980.

759   **public statements cautiously** "Carter: Keep Hope on Iran," BG, February 25, 1980.

759   **surprise edict** UPI, February 24, 1980; Bowden, *Guests of the Ayatollah*, 365–66.

759   **UN commission** Ibid., 366–67.

760   **handwritten three-page letter** Ibid., 377–78, which is also source for Bush and Reagan statements.

760   **"empty bluff"** "Bush Assails Reagan Tax Cut Proposal," LAT, March 29, 1980.

760   **"I'm not going to"** "Carter Sees 'Positive' Signs on Hostages, Blasts Kennedy for His Remarks on Iran," BG, March 14, 1980.

760   **clamor inside** Bowden, *Guests of the Ayatollah*, 379.

760   **sunshine broke through** "Remarks to Reporters on American Hostages in Iran," April 1, 1980, APP.

CHAPTER THIRTY-FOUR

762 **"We are supporting"** Stacey L. Schreft, "Credit Controls: 1980," *Economic Review*, November/December 1990.

762 **talk of "pain"** Art Buchwald column, March 25, 1980.

762 **economy was grinding** Schreft, "Credit Controls: 1980"; Reagan-Bush press release, April 18, 1980, RVA, Box 33; "1980 in Michigan," Wikipedia.org; *Chicago Days: 150 Defining Moments in the Life of a Great City* (New York: McGraw Hill, 1996); Edward McClelland, *Nothin' But Blue Skies: The Heyday, Hard Times, and Hopes of America's Industrial Heartland* (New York: Bloomsbury Press, 2013), 97.

762 **"There had never"** "Headed for a Classic Bust?", *Newsweek*, April 14, 1980.

762 **banking deregulation** Nomi Prins, *All the Presidents' Bankers: The Hidden Alliances That Drive American Power* (New York: Nation Books, 2014), 303, 314; Matt Stoller, *Goliath: The 100 Year War Between Monopoly Power and Democracy* (New York: Simon & Schuster, 2019), 181, 268.

763 **Arthur Schlesinger** "The Carter Mystery—II," *Baltimore Sun*, April 8, 1980.

763 **Bani-Sadr** Mark Bowden, *Guests of the Ayatollah: The First Battle in America's War with Militant Islam* (New York: Atlantic Monthly Press, 2006), 400.

763 **The media questioned** MFTVE, 46:16.

763 **United Farm Workers** Tim Stanley, " 'Sailing Against the Wind': A Reappraisal of Edward Kennedy's Campaign for the 1980 Democratic Party Presidential Nomination," *Journal of American Studies* 32, Issue 2 (August 2009).

763 **"a little *cactus*"** WXIA-TV 11 p.m. News, April 13, 1980, YouTube.com, accessed April 21, 2020. This broadast is also the source for the Church quote.

764 **enhanced unemployment benefits** "131,000 Eligible for Import Aid," *Detroit Free Press*, April 27, 1980.

764 **awful TV commercial** Curson interview, *Fresh Air*, WHYY, 1980; Kathleen Hall Jamieson, *Packaging the Presidency: A History and Criticism of Presidential Advertising* (New York: Oxford University Press, 1988), 388.

764 **surprise Kennedy endorser** Ibid., 386.

764 **next-door Delaware** Branko Marcitec, *Yesterday's Man: The Case Against Joe Biden* (New York: Verso, 2020), 47; "Biden Heeds Carter Call to Go to Pennsylvania," *Wilmington News Journal*, April 20, 1980.

764 **Chrysler said** "1980 in Michigan," Wikipedia.org.

764 **Open Markets Committee** Schreft, "Credit Controls: 1980"; for April 22 minutes see Fraser.StLouisFed.org, ,April 24, 1980.

765 **The score stood** White, *America In Search of Itself*, 301.

765 **Democrat in West Allis** "Reagan's Crossovers," *Newsweek*, April 14, 1980.

765 **nearly half** Aaron Wildavasky, *The Deficit and the Public Interest: The Search for Responsible Budgeting in the 1980s* (Berkeley: University of California Press 1989), 78.

765 **"voodoo economics"** Kitty Kelley, *The Family: The Real Story of the Bush Dynasty* (New York: Doubleday, 2004), 368; "Underdog Bush Here, Slaps Reagan 'Voodoo,' " *Pittsburgh Press*, April 11, 1980; "Bush Accuses Reagan of 'Economic Madness,' " LAT, April 11, 1980.

765 **woke Hendrik Hertzberg** Author interview with Hertzberg.

766 **As best the first** "Jon Snow: first on scene at Iran hostage crisis crash," Channel 4 News, YouTube.com, accessed April 21, 2020.

766 **Operation Eagle Claw** Bowden, *Guests of the Ayatollah*, passim.

766 **Brzezinski had been** Blake Jones, *A Battle for Righteousness: Jimmy Carter and*

Religious Nationalism (PhD dissertation, Department of History, Arizona State University, 2013), 129.

766 **was *so* eager** Penne Laingen oral history interview, March 27, Association for Diplomatic Studies and Training Foreign Affairs, Oral History Program, Foreign Service Spouse Series.

767 **Walter Cronkite** MFTVE, 47:25.

767 **haunted and sallow** "Address to the Nation on the Rescue Attempt for American Hostages in Iran," April 25, 1980, APP; YouTube.com, courtesy of the Miller Center of the University of Virginia, accessed April 21, 2020.

767 **Barry Farber** UPI, April 25, 1980.

767 **CBS News reported** April 24, 1980, VTVNA.

767 **impressive 17 to 21 percent** "Carter's Reagan's Weakness Opens Door for John Anderson," *Owensboro* (Kentucky) *Messenger-Inquirer*, April 25, 1980.

767 **Morton Kondracke** "Anderson's Tall Order," *New Republic*, May 3, 1980; Mark Bisnow, *Diary of a Dark Horse: The 1980 Anderson Presidential Campaign* (Carbondale: Southern Illinois Press:), 271; Walter Cronkite, *A Reporter's Life* (New York: Random House, 1991), 210–11.

768 **special benefits** "131,000 Eligible for Import Aid," *Detroit Free Press*, April 27, 1980.

768 **"deliberate policy"** Reagan campaign statement from Philadelphia, April 26, 1980, RVA, Box 33.

768 **Nancy Reagan snapped** John Connally with Mickey Herskowitz, *In History's Shadow: An American Odyssey* (New York: Hyperion, 1993), 297.

768 **thousands of pilgrims** The author has reviewed CBN's entire live broadcast, provided courtesy of Kristina Lapinski from the archives of Liberty University. See also J. Brooks Flippen, *Jimmy Carter, the Politics of Family, and the Rise of the Religious Right* (Athens, GA: University of Georgia Press, 2011), 1–23; Darren Dochuk, *From Bible Belt to Sun Belt: Plain-Folk Religion, Grassroots Politics, and the Rise of Evangelical Conservatism* (New York: W.W. Norton, 2011); Sara Diamond, *Spiritual Warfare: The Politics of the Christian Right* (Boston: South End Press, 199), 61; Connie Paige, *The Right to Lifers: Who They Are, How They Operate, and Where They Get Their Money* (New York: Summit Books, 1983), 186; and John G. Turner, *Bill Bright and the Campus Crusade for Christ: The Renewal of Evangelism in Twentieth Century America* (Chapel Hill: University of North Carolina Press, 2009), 191–97.

772 **Jerry Falwell** "An Interview with Jerry Falwell," *Jewish Veteran*, January/February 1981.

772 **"incomplete success"** "The President's News Conference," April 29, 1980, APP; UPI, November 21, 1980.

772 **"pygmies in the White House"** "Why Vance Quit," WP, April 30, 1980.

773 **"manageable enough now"** "White House Briefing for Civic and Community Leaders: Remarks and a Question-and-Answer Session," April 30, 1980, APP.

773 **acid response** Gary Sick, *October Surprise: America's Hostages in Iran and the Election of Ronald Reagan* (New York: Crown, 1990), 192.

773 **"Death of Reason"** WSJ, March 27, 1980.

773 **forced to close** "Mike Pertschuk and the Federal Trade Commission: Sequel," Kennedy School of Government Case Program #C16–81–387.S (1981).

773 *Mandate for Leadership* Jason Stahl, *Right Moves: The Conservative Think Tank in American Politics and Culture Since 1945* (Chapel Hill: University of North Carolina Press, 2016), 109.

773 **section on the FTC** Charles L. Heatherly, ed., *Mandate for Leadership: Policy Management in a Conservative Administration* (Washington, D.C.: The Heritage Foundation, 1981), 759–66.

774 **weekly variety show** April 18, 1979, debut episode of *Real People* viewed by author at Amazon.com.

774 **"Coward of the County"** Jesse Walker, " 'Twenty Years of Crawling': Kenny Rogers' 'Coward of the County' and the Vietnam Syndrome," WeAretheMutants.com, March 31, 2020.

776 **Bush and Reagan** April 23, 1980, debate on YouTube.com, courtesy of Ronald Reagan Presidential Library.

777 **"freedom flotilla"** See, in general, Juan M. Clark, Jose I. Lasaga, and Rose S. Reque, "The 1980 Mariel Exodus: An Assessment and Prospect" (Miami: Council for Inter-American Security, 1981).

778 **On May 11** "Retarded People and Criminals Are Included in Cuban Exodus," NYT, May 11, 1980.

778 **Two days later** UPI, May 13, 1980.

778 **A plane soared** *Washington Star* Service, May 7, 1980.

778 **Marine ID** "Cubans Arriving at Fort Chaffee Shout 'Down With Castro,' " *Saturday Oklahoman and Times*, May 10, 1980.

778 **One fifty-six-year-old** Gannett Service, May 10, 1980.

778 **Colorado's Democratic governor** UPI, May 13, 1980.

779 **Liberty City** "The Day Miami Was Rocked by Riot after Cops Cleared in McDuffie Beating," *Miami Herald*, May 15, 2016.

779 **new memoir** *Will: The Autobiography of G. Gordon Liddy* (New York: St. Martin's Press, 1980).

779 **"man the USA needs"** "Book World," *Kosciusko* (Mississippi) *Star-Herald*, June 12, 1980.

779 **Love Canal** Michael Stewart Foley, *Front Porch Politics: The Forgotten Heyday of American Activism in the 1970s and 1980s* (New York: Hill & Wang, 2013), 161; AP, May 19, 1980; UPI, May 20, 1980; UPI, May 22, 1980; "The Century: America's Time: Starting Over (2 of 3)," YouTube.com, accessed April 21, 2020.

780 **fifteen-hour fire** "Chemical Control Fire Burned 15 Hours, Seared Memories for 35 Years," NJToday.net, April 20, 2016.

780 **advocacy for a "superfund"** "Jacksonville, Florida Remarks and a Question-and-Answer Session with Community and Civic Leaders," July 17, 1980, APP.

780 **Time/Yankelovich** "John Anderson: Candidate of the New Class," *Public Opinion*, June/July 1980.

780 **two of the three networks** Jon Meacham, *Destiny and Power: The American Odyssey of George Herbert Walker Bush* (New York: Random House, 2015), 236.

780 **Bush called key** Ibid, 237–39.

780 **day after Oregon** AP, May 22, 1980; "Last of Cuban Refugees Rounded Up Following 'Breakout,' " *Honolulu Star-Bulletin*, May 27, 1980.

780 **Fort McCoy** "Troops Ordered to Fort Chaffee," *Akron Beacon Journal*, June 3, 1980.

780 **six more days** "Cuban Refugees Riot at Fort Chafee," *Eau Claire Leader-Telegram*, June 2, 1980.

781 **Governor Clinton** Ibid.; "Arkansas Suffers, Too," *Tampa Tribune*, June 4, 1980.

781 **By this time** AP, June 2, 1980.

781 **relaxed credit controls** AP, June 6, 1980.

781 **first-quarter numbers** AP, May 20, 1980.

781   **Ted Kennedy's commercials** Jamieson, *Packaging the Presidency*, 386, 389.

781   **Eastern carpetbaggers** "McGovern a 'Target' Because of Campaign Cost Factors," *Sioux Falls Argus Leader*, April 13, 1979.

782   **"interested in ideology"** Richard Michael Marano, *Vote Your Conscience: The Last Campaign of George McGovern* (New York: Praeger, 2003), 25.

782   **"middle-of-the-road conservatives"** Paige, *The Right to Lifers*, 203.

782   **gambit faltered** "Jessup Says He Only Wanted to Help Unseat Bayh," *Richmond* (Indiana) *Palladium-Item*, August 26, 1979.

782   **Tom Harkin insisted** "Tax Warning by Harkin to 'New Right,' " *Des Moines Tribune*, September 27, 1980.

782   **In Indiana** "Anti-Bayh Drive Delayed," *Munster Times*, August 19, 1979.

782   **"nothing personal"** "Abortion Issue Can Shake Senate—Even in August," *Allentown Call-Chronicle*, August 26, 1979; "GOP Likes This Numbers Game," CT, October 7, 1979.

783   **"Verna Smith"** *Wall Street Journal* Service, February 2, 1980.

783   **citizen of Fort Worth** J. Brooks Flippen, *Speaker Jim Wright: Power, Scandal, and the Birth of Modern Politics* (Austin: University of Texas Press, 2018), 296–98, passim for Wright's ideological evolution.

783   **deceptions were systematic** "Contributions to Anti-Culver Unit Not Deductible: IRS Aide," *Des Moines Register*, September 3, 1979; AP, April 4, 1980.

784   **In Idaho** Adam Clymer, *Drawing the Line at the Big Ditch: The Panama Canal Treaties and the Rise of the Right* (Lawrence: University Press of Kansas, 2008), 185.

784   **Dan Quayle** "Rep. Quayle Wants Conservatives to Stop 'Disgusting' Anti-Bayh Ads," *Richmond Palladium-Item*, September 14, 1979.

784   **"lie through its teeth"** "The New Right Brigade," WP, August 10, 1980.

784   **"Mickelson is about 38"** Bob Moore to Senator Heinz, "RE: South Dakota Task Force," April 23, 1979, downloadable from Digital Collections, Carnegie Mellon University Library.

784   **blackjack in a bar** *Wall Street Journal* Service, February 5, 1980.

785   **"pick their nose"** "Nation: The New Right Takes Aim," *Time*, August 20, 1979.

785   **1979 state fair** Gannett Service, April 30, 1979; AP, May 1, 1980; "Conservative Poll: Abdnor over McGovern," *Sioux Falls Argus Leader*, December 9, 1979; Paige, *The Right to Lifers*, 208.

785   **Corn Palace** See ad in *Sioux Falls Argus Leader*, February 12, 1980; "It May Take 'a Political Miracle,' " *Sioux City Journal*, April 16, 1980; Marano, *Vote Your Conscience*, 23–25.

785   **Pro-lifers recruited** Ibid., 26–29.

786   **"I am a liberal Democrat"** *Los Angeles Times* Service, January 5, 1980.

786   **The *New Yorker*'s** Elizabeth Drew, *Senator* (New York: Simon & Schuster, 1979).

786   **trusted Iowans to tune out** AP, August 25, 1979; ENIR, August 31, 1979.

786   **restore school prayer** "With Reelection Endangered, Senator Church Shifts to Woo Rightists," *Baltimore Sun*, October 3, 1979.

786   **delegates from Virginia** "Va. Conference on Family Life Erupts in Emotion," WP, November 15, 1979; William Martin, *With God on Our Side: The Rise of the Religious Right in America* (New York: Broadway Books, 1996), 176–77.

787   **"awfully Abzugian"** "Lesbians Over 40, and Other Lovelies: Look Who Gov. Carey Is Sending to Washington for You," *New York Daily News*, January 30, 1980; "Feminists Gain Family Conference Posts," NYT, January 28, 1980.

787   **Paul Weyrich** *Conservative Digest*, January 1980.

787 **representing Washington, D.C.** WS, March 3, 1980; "Ex-Priest Pleads Guilty to Sodomy," WP, April 13, 1986; author correspondence with ABilly Jones-Hennin.

788 **hearings across the nation** Lewis Z. Koch, "Family Passages," *Washingtonian*, June 1980.

788 **They derided** Rosemary Thomson, *Withstanding Humanism's Challenge to Families: Anatomy of a White House Conference* (Morton, IL: Traditional Publications, 1981), passim.

788 **first lady of Alabama** Flippen, *Jimmy Carter*, 261.

788 **governor of Indiana** Koch, "Family Passages."

788 **a moving—to some—speech** "Baltimore Maryland: Remarks at the Opening Session of the White House Conference on Families," June 5, 1980, APP.

788 **Larry Pratt** Flippen, *Jimmy Carter*, 269.

788 **In Minneapolis** Ibid., 270; Thomson, *Withstanding Humanism's Challenge to Families*, 94–101; UPI, June 20, 1980; "Schlafly: White House Conference on Families Is a Farce," *Eau Claire Leader-Telegram*, June 21, 1980; AP, June 21, 1980; "Family Conference Meets in Minneapolis," *Tampa Tribune*, June 28, 1980; UPI, June 28, 1980.

789 **counter-conference** Flippen, *Jimmy Carter*, 271; "Left, Right Gird for Battle at Family Conference," *Baltimore Sun*, June 1, 1980; Religious News Service, June 26, 1980; Gannett News Service, July 2, 1980.

789 **letter went out to 160,000 ministers** Randall Balmer, *Redeemer: The Life of Jimmy Carter* (New York: Basic Books, 2014), 143.

789 **far more fulsome** Ibid.

789 **"do something!"** Ellen Goodman column, June 16, 1980.

790 **"where Boy Scouts"** "Merced, California: Remarks and a Question-and-Answer Session," July 4, 1980, APP; ABC News, July 4, 1980, VTVNA

790 **Prince of Peace Church** Ibid.; also source for Hermitage, Pennsylvania, and St. Louis.

790 **Wye, Maryland** Penne Laingen oral history; AP, July 6, 1980.

790 **Independence Hall** AP, July 5, 1980.

790 **"New Smash Single"** Kurt Loder, ". . . Notes," *Rolling Stone* Service, November 1, 1980; AP, July 24, 1980. See ad in July 28, 1980, *Austin American-Statesman*. Song on YouTube.com, accessed April 22, 2020.

791 **Clarksburg, Massachusetts** "Celebrations Honor Hostages," *Hartford Courant*, July 5, 1980; "Ayatollah to Burn in Effigy," *Cincinnati Enquirer*, July 3, 1980; AP, July 4, 1980.

791 **Family Protection Act** *Washington Post* Service, July 26, 1980.

791 **Rosemary Thomson attended** Thomson, *Withstanding Humanism's Challenge to Families*, 9.

CHAPTER THIRTY-FIVE

792 **63 percent African American** Theodore White, *America In Search of Itself: The Making of the President, 1956–1980* (New York: Harper & Row, 1981), 384.

792 **RNC's Bill Brock** CFTRN, February 15, 1979.

792 **"lift its skirts"** Tanya Melich, *The Republican War Against Women: An Insider's Report From Behind the Lines* (New York: Bantam, 1996), 100.

792 **Renaissance Center** Matthew Lewis and Aaron Mondry, "Lost in Hockeytown: The Joe Lewis Arena Story," *Radial Logic*, March 6, 2012.

792 **"A Spark of Spirit"** WP, July 16, 1976.

792 **A joke circulated** Jules Witcover and Jack Germond, *Blue Smoke and Mirrors: How Reagan Won and Why Carter Lost the Election of 1980* (New York: Viking, 1981), 248.

792 **One of the city's** For strikes, floods, traffic jam, and car theft: ABCIA, July 12, 1980. Charlie Diggs is July 14.

792 **Census Bureau** "Early Figures Bear Out Detroit Census Fears," *Detroit Free Press*, July 30, 1980; AP, September 11, 1980.

792 **Japan announced** AP, December 24, 1980.

792 **Prostitutes weren't** "Convention Diary: A Working Girl Awaits the Party," *Detroit Free Press*, June 22, 1980.

793 **party supplies** ABCIA, July 9, 1980.

793 **media personnel** ABCIA, July 13, 1980; MFTVE, 48:43; Travis Vogan, *ABC Sports: The Rise and Fall of Network Sports Television* (Berkeley: University of California Press, 2018), 26, 157.

793 **key player** Jon Meacham, *Destiny and Power: The American Odyssey of George Herbert Walker Bush* (New York: Random House, 2015), 239–40; Witcover and Germond, *Blue Smoke and Mirrors*, 167. The choice of running mate was discussed as early as May 21, 1979 (planning meeting agenda, RRPL, Box 103).

793 **Donald Rumsfeld** Michael Kramer, "Inside the Room with George Bush," *New York*, July 26, 1980, which also discusses the maneuvering of Luga and Kemp,.

793 **denied to a reporter** Kitty Kelley, *The Family: The Real Story of the Bush Dynasty* (New York: Doubleday, 2004), 368.

794 **elephant-head** "Unconventional Republicans," *In These Times*, July 30–August 12, 1980.

794 **Communists taking over** Ibid.

794 **"The message we want"** Meacham, *Destiny and Power*, 243.

794 **David Stockman** David Stockman, *The Triumph of Politics: Why the Reagan Revolution Failed* (New York: Harper & Row, 1986), 64–68. See "Republican Party Platform of 1980," July 15, 1980, APP.

795 **energy subcommittee** ABCIA, July 10, 1980.

795 **Cockburn and James Ridgeway** "Reagan in Detroit," in Alexander Cockburn, *Corruptions of Empire* (New York: Verso, 1988), 249.

795 **John Singlaub** Kyle Burke, *Revolutionaries for the Right: Anticommunist Internationalism and Paramilitary Warfare in the Cold War* (Charlotte: University of North Carolina Press, 2018), 20, 97, 99, 120, 129, 278; "L.A's Police Spy Probe Leads to Prominent Right-Wing Lawmaker," LAT, June 5, 1983.

795 **passion of General Graham's** Frances FitzGerald, *Way Out There in the Blue: Reagan, Star Wars, and the End of the Cold War* (New York: Simon & Schuster, 2000), 124–26.

795 **52 percent of Reagan** George Gallup column, September 12, 1980.

796 **"*Fascist baby-killer!*"** White, *America In Search of Itself*, 318.

796 **Mary Crisp** ABCIA, July 9, 1980.

796 **strengthened from a draft** ABCIA, July 10, 1980.

797 **Senator Lowell Weicker** WS, August 22, 1980.

797 **An "Anderson Republican"** "Unconventional Republicans," *In These Times*, July 30–August 12, 1980.

797 **Reagan arrived** ABCIA, July 14, 1980; White, *America In Search of Itself*, 393.

797 **automotive jobs** July 14, 1980, statement, RVA, Box 33.

797 **"*find out how loyal*"** ABCIA, July 9, 1980.

797 **In the news** ABCIA, July 14, 1980.

797 **"especially for the unborn"** "Reagan in Detroit."

797 **The opening gavel** ABCIA, July 14, 1980, which is also source for ERA march and Moyers.

797 **he surprised everyone** Witcover and Germond, *Blue Smoke and Mirrors*, 172.

798 **Then Ford reportedly** Ibid., 171.

798 **When Ronald Reagan gave** YouTube.com, courtesy of Ronald Reagan Presidential Library; for unuttered line see Rick Perlstein, *Invisible Bridge: The Fall of Nixon and the Rise of Reagan* (New York: Simon & Schuster, 2014), 802.

798 **talking points** "Talking Points for Monday 7/14 Delegate Reception," DH, Box 12, Folder 14.

798 **alternate set of remarks** "Mon. Reception, Remarks," DH, Box 12, Folder 14.

798 **judge from Cook County** ABCIA, July 14, 1980.

798 **attended a luncheon** ABCIA, July 16, 1980.

799 **Bush's radio ads** Kathleen Hall Jamieson, *Packaging the Presidency: A History and Criticism of Presidential Advertising* (New York: Oxford University Press, 1988), 384.

799 **campaign chroniclers** In turn, Steven F. Hayward, *The Age of Reagan: The Fall of the Old Liberal Order, 1964–1980* (New York: Three Rivers Press, 2001), 662; Kitty Kelley, *The Family: The Real Story of the Bush Dynasty* (New York: Doubleday, 2004), 372; Meacham, *Destiny and Power*, 233.

799 **"Why should I?"** Meacham, *Destiny and Power*, 243; Kelley, *The Family*, 370.

799 *New York* **magazine reporter** Kramer, "Inside the Room with George Bush."

800 **ABC News paid** ABCIA, July 15, 1980.

800 **"enthusiastic audiences"** ABCIA, July 16, 1980. Also for Guy Vander Jagt.

801 **"storm in the personal relations"** Ibid.

801 **Howard Phillips** " 'Christian 'New Right's' Rush to Power," NYT, July 18, 1980.

801 **Phyllis Schlafly** "Unconventional Republicans," *In These Times*, July 30– August 12, 1980.

801 **"had the devil on his ticket"** Cox News Service, September 1, 1980. Also "noisy Baptist."

801 **In Jesse Helms's suite** Meacham, *Destiny and Power*, 244.

801 **Boardroom Jacobins** Deaver to Stuart Spencer, June 13, 1980, DH; Kim Phillips-Fein, *Invisible Hands: The Businessmen's Crusade Against the New Deal* (New York: Norton, 2009), 248–49.

802 **Robert Mosbacher** William Kleinknecht, *The Man Who Sold the World: Ronald Reagan and the Betrayal of Main Street America* (New York: Nation Books, 2009), 60–61.

802 **dilemma of the sign-makers** ABCIA, July 16, 1980.

802 **"That's crazy"** Meacham, *Destiny and Power*, 248.

802 **Bush was up** Kramer, "Inside the Room with George Bush."

803 **"too simplistic"** ABCIA, July 15, 1980.

803 **Walter Cronkite** MFTVE, 51:40; White, *America In Search of Itself*, 323.

804 **gift-wrapped package** Witcover and Germond, *Blue Smoke and Mirrors,* 172; full account of the courtship is 166–76.

804 **after Reagan clinched** Richard V. Allen, "George Herbert Walker Bush: The Accidental Vice President," NYT *Magazine*, July 30, 2000.

804 **"With a Reagan"** Perlstein, *Invisible Bridge*, 182.

804 **"intellectual lightweight"** Fred Ikle to Richard V. Allen, January 10, 1980, RVA, Box 28, Folder 2.

804   **Reagan pledged** "Presidential Hopefuls," *Tampa Tribune*, February 23, 1980.

805   **"AVAILABLE"** Patrick Oliphant cartoon, July 17, 1980.

805   **"unemployed Metternich"** Mary McGrory column, July 17, 1980.

805   **white-hot center** For Ford-Reagan negotiations: Allen, "George Herbert Walker Bush"; Witcover and Germond, *Blue Smoke and Mirrors*, 176–88; White, *America In Search of Itself*, 321–25; Alan Greenspan, *The Age of Turbulence: Adventures in a New World* (New York: Penguin, 2008), 89–21.

805   **Unspecified "Reagan supporters"** "Tower Ticker," CT, July 18, 1980.

805   **teleprompter text** "Standby Remarks in Event of Ford Nomination," PH, Box 12, Folder 15.

805   **"Mr. Bush, really sorry"** Meacham, *Destiny and Power*, 248; for speech, 250.

806   **half a beer** Kramer, "Inside the Room with George Bush."

806   **"This is Susan King"** ABCIA, July 14, 1980.

806   **The signs waved** White, *America in Search of Itself*, 326.

806   **"$10 Million Delegate"** This popular piece of political folklore is belied by the fact that the official convention proceedings record no delegate vote for Connally.

806   **thirty minutes to midnight** MFTVE, 56:05.

807   **"grimaced"** Kelley, *The Family*, 372.

807   **Gerald Rafshoon** Meacham, *Destiny and Power*, 248.

807   **His whoops mixed** Kramer, "Inside the Room with George Bush."

807   **"losing *prime time*!"** Speech broadcast on YouTube.com, courtesy of Ronald Reagan Presidential Library, accessed April 23, 1980.

808   **had been drafted** Speech drafts and related correspondence, from which the following is constructed, in DH, Box 9, Folder 3; RVA Box 28, Folder 1.

808   **UAW's Douglas Fraser** ABCIA, July 11, 1980.

808   **socialist newspaper** Author correspondence with John Judis.

811   **Dick Wirthlin** Richard Wirthlin, Vincent Breglio, and Richard Seal, "Campaign Chronicle," *Public Opinion*, February/March 1981.

812   **The Harris Poll** White, *America In Search of Itself*, 328; LAT, July 24, 1980.

812   **Robert Teeter reported** UPI, July 8, 1980.

812   **Falwell said, sounding** "Minister Takes 'the People' Back to Moral Roots," *Minneapolis Star*, August 25, 1980.

812   **"have not been tried"** ABCIA, July 18, 1980.

812   **Six days later** ABCIA, July 24, 1980.

812   **22 percent approval** Tom Wicker column, August 8, 1980.

812   **for Senator Scoop Jackson** BCIA, July 27, July 29, August 5, 1980.

813   **Edmund Muskie** "Voters Saying Loud and Clear: Muskie over Carter According to Recent Harris Survey," *Polish American Journal*, July 12, 1980; ABCIA, July 28, 29, 30, August 12, 1980.

813   **Even Walter Mondale's** ABCIA, July 28, 1980.

813   **"phone has not stopped"** ABCIA, July 27, 1980.

813   **Both Governor Carey** ABCIA, July 29, 1980.

813   **Senate Majority Leader Byrd** ABCIA, August 4, 1980.

813   **"It's almost incomprehensible"** ABCIA, July 31, 1980.

813   **next press conference** "The President's News Conference," August 4, 1980, APP.

813   **Indiantown Gap** UPI, August 5, 1980; AP, August 7, 1980; *New York Times* Service, August 9, 1980; "Refugee Riots," *Danville* (Kentucky) *Advocate-Messenger*, August 12, 1980.

814   **Bill Clinton swore** Michael Takiff, *A Complicated Man: A Life of Bill Clinton as Told by Those Who Knew Him* (New Haven: Yale University Press, 2010), 191–93;

"Neighbors of Refugee Camps: We've Been Shafted," *Miami News*, August 12, 1980. The refugees remained in Arkansas until a month before Election Day; AP, October 4, 1980.

814 **Iranian students** ABCIA, July 27, August 3, August 4, August 7, August 8, 1980.

814 **"fugitive financier Robert Vesco"** ABCIA, July 23, July 27, July 28, August 12, 1980.

814 **"from Jimmy"** ABCIA, July 30, 1980.

814 **"Lisker is full of shit"** UPI, August 1, 1980.

814 **Abscam defendant** ABCIA, August 13, 1980.

814 **Jeff Carter** ABCIA, August 10, 1980.

815 **lined the highways** White, *America In Search of Itself*, 328.

815 **The social scene** Ibid., 340; AP, August 7, 1980; *New York Daily News* Service, August 15, 1980.

815 **Donald Trump** "Where the Donald Trumps Rent," NYT, August 3, 1979; *Trump: What's the Deal* (The Deadline Company, 1991), on YouTube.com, accessed April 24, 2020. Trump apparently timed a publicity blitz for the arrival of the out-of-town visitors; see "Playing the Trump Card," *New York Daily News*, August 3, 1980; UPI, August 16, 1980.

815 **"80 percent"** Angela Fox Dunn, "Ronald Reagan: 'I Never Saw Myself as the Little Guy,' " *Windsor Star*, July 12, 1980. Fox is the niece of 20th Century Fox founder William Fox, which may have loosened Reagan's tongue.

815 **friend Jeane Dixon** Martin Gardner, *The Night Is Large: Collected Essays, 1938–1995* (New York: St. Martin's Griffin, 1997), 136.

815 **Southern Californians** Richard Reeves, *President Reagan: The Triumph of the Imagination* (New York: Simon & Schuster, 2005), 456. Reeves received this information from an on-the-record interview with Ira Reiner, the former district attorney of Los Angeles County.

816 ***Chicago Tribune*'s seer** "Tower Ticker," CT, July 18, 1980; "Considering Horoscopes in a Reagan Presidency," CT, July 21, 1980 (for George Bush's chart); "Etcetera: Another Dawning of the Age of Aquarius," *Miami Herald*, September 8 1980 (for Nofziger denial and Jillson response).

816 **Carter's image-makers** White, *America In Search of Itself*, 337.

816 ***"Governor Clinton"*** ABCIA, August 13, 1980.

816 **Each side got** All speeches, platform language, and votes come from Dorothy Vredenburgh Bush, Sandra P. Perlmutter, and Elizabeth C Burke, eds., *Official Report of the Proceedings of the Democratic National Convention: Madison Square Garden, New York, August 11 Through August 14, 1980* (Washington, D.C.: Democratic National Committee, 1980).

817 ***"We Want Ted!"*** ABCIA, August 12, 1980; MFTVE, 1:01:00.

817 **printed for a fifth day** ABCIA, July 24, 1980.

817 **war footing** White, *America In Search of Itself*, 331, 339.

819 **Feminists had organized** "Feminist Bloc Wins Two Major Victories," *St. Louis Post-Dispatch*, August 13, 1980.

820 **Alabama's delegation** "James Proposes Ideas for Platform," *Montgomery Advertiser*, August 10, 1980.

820 **Missouri bloc** "Delegates from Area Force Roll Call Vote," *St. Louis Post-Dispatch*, August 13, 1980.

821 **tribal chief judge** Brianna Theobald, "A 1970 Law Led to the Mass Sterilization of Native American Women. That History Still Matters," *Time*, November 27, 2019.

821 **Virginia's law** *Washington Post* Service, February 23, 1980; UPI, February 24, 1980.

821 **Committee for Abortion Rights** Meredith Tax, "March to a Crossroads on Abortion," *Nation*, May 8, 1989. Thanks to Tax for teaching me about the issue.

821 **During this debate** " 'Spirited' Abortion Quarrel Sparks a Real Floor Fight," *St. Louis Post-Dispatch*, August 13, 1980.

822 **Kennedy approached** Speech on YouTube.com, accessed April 23, 2020; "Kennedy Wins Delegates' Hearts with Rousing, Emotional Speech," *St. Louis Post-Dispatch*, August 13, 1980.

824 **furious negotiations** UPI, August 13, 1980.

824 **city of Gdansk** UPI, August 14, 1980.

824 **Ron Dellums** AP, August 14, 1980. For walkout: ABCIA, August 12, August 14, 1980.

824 **"Carter walked out"** ABCIA, August 14, 1980.

824 **Miz Lillian** UPI, August 14, 1980.

824 **other Carter family news** *Washington Star* Service, August 14, 1980.

824 **Watts riot** ABCIA, August 12, 1980.

824 **And that John Anderson** ABCIA, August 13, 1980.

824 **was still mulling** "Carter-Kennedy Truce Appears in Doubt," *St. Louis Post-Dispatch*, August 13, 1980.

825 **no "rockets' red glare"** "National Anthem Willie Nelson-ized," *St. Louis Post-Dispatch*, August 14, 1980.

825 **increase in military spending** Joel Rogers and Thomas Ferguson, *The Hidden Election: Politics and Economics in the 1980 Presidential Campaign* (New York: Pantheon, 1981), 87.

825 **leaked top-secret** Fred Kaplan, "Going Native Without a Field Map: The Press Plunges into Limited Nuclear War," *Columbia Journalism Review*, January/February 1981.

825 **Henry Kissinger** ABCIA, August 12, 1980.

825 **Liberals hoisted signs** "President Gains Endorsement for MX Blockbuster Missile," WP, August 14, 1980, which also discusses briefings in Carter trailer and AFL-CIO message.

826 **poolside dinner buffet** Michael Novak, *Writing from Left to Right: My Journey from Liberal to Conservative* (New York: Random House, 2013), 187.

826 **joke at a luncheon** "New York, New York: Remarks at the Democratic Congressional Campaign Committee Victory Luncheon," August 14, 1980, APP.

827 **police clashed** AP, August 15, 1980; Shaun Asseal and Peter Keating, "The Massacre That Spawned the Alt-Right," *Politico*, November 3, 2019.

827 **biographical film** Jamieson, *Packaging the Presidency*, 413–14.

827 **suturing its mismatched** Hendrik Hertzberg, *Politics: Observations and Arguments, 1966–2004* (New York: Penguin, 2005), 138; author interview with Hertzberg, who is also the source for the teleprompter snafu.

827 **police closed the doors** AP, August 15, 1980.

827 **president took the podium** "Remarks Accepting the Presidential Nomination at the 1980 Democratic Convention in New York," August 14, 1980, APP; video at C-Span.org. For failed balloons and Kennedy handshake, MFTVE, 1:01:50

828 **Kennedy watched** ABCIA, August 14, August 15, 1980; MFTVE, 1:01:55.

828 **Walter Mondale subsequently** "Carter's Goal of Party Unity Remained Elusive," *St. Louis Post Dispatch*, August 15, 1980.

828 **post-convention Gallup** "Post-Convention Surge: Carter Closing In on Reagan in Polls," WP, August 20, 1980.

CHAPTER THIRTY-SIX

829 **"Black Book"** Jack J. Honomichl, *Honomichl on Marketing Research* (Lincolnwood, IL: NTC Business Books, 1986), 28–35; Richard Wirthlin, Vincent Breglio, and Richard Seal, "Campaign Chronicle," *Public Opinion*, February/March 1981; *Advertising Age*, December 1980. For an excellent summary of how Wirthlin's campaign plan and dynamic models worked in practice, see John H. Kessel, *Presidential Campaign Politics: Coalition Strategies and Citizen Response* (Dorsey, IL: Homewood Press, 1984), 200–202.

829 **"simulation modeling"** Richard Wirthlin, Vincent Breglio, and Richard Seal, "Campaign Chronicle," *Public Opinion*, February/March 1981.

829 **23,000-square-foot** "901 S. Highland St., Arlington: Reagan's Forgotten National Campaign Headquarters," ArlingtonVA.us, October 13, 2016.

829 **National Urban League** Marcus M. Witcher, "Carter and Reagan's Southern Strategy: The 1980 General Election in Mississippi," paper under review. Theodore White, in *America In Search of Itself: The Making of the President, 1956–1980* (New York: Harper & Row, 1981), 384, suggests the scheduling snafu excuse was sincere. But in "Reagan Campaigning from County Fair to Urban League," WP, August 4, 1980, a Reagan staffer is quoted as saying that the schedule switch was a deliberate strategic decision. See also discussion in Susan B. Trento, *The Power House: Robert Keith Gray and the Selling of Influence in Washington* (New York: St. Martin's Press, 1992), 119.

830 **"isn't any place"** YouTube.com, accessed January 25, 2020.

830 **Every July** *The Mississippi Encyclopedia*, "Neshoba County Fair," accessed January 25, 2020; NesobaCountyFair.org/history, accessed January 25, 2020; Kate Gregory, "The Neshoba County Fair," *The 'Sip* magazine; AP, August 2, 1992; also author correspondence with Joseph Crespino.

830 **"Alligators, Coons and Possums"** Michael Newton, *The Ku Klux Klan in Mississippi: A History* (Jefferson, NC: McFarland & Company, 2010), 134.

830 **small Klan unit** Greg Grandin, *The End of the Myth: From the Frontier to the Border Wall in the Mind of America* (New York: Macmillan, 2019), 224.

831 **In 1978** "He Would Say Yes to Anything—Even Confessing to Rape," CT, September 24, 1978; "One Major Klan Group Gains Members," NYT, March 25, 1979; AP, May 28, 1979.

831 **Greensboro, North Carolina** Shaun Asseal and Peter Keating, "The Massacre That Spawned the Alt-Right," *Politico*, November 3, 2019.

831 **widows of two** AP, August 15, 1980.

831 **Chattanooga's black neighborhood** "Klansman Convicted, 2 Freed in Wounding of Black Woman," WP, July 23, 1980.

831 **downtown Kokomo** UPI, August 27, 1980.

831 **avowed Nazi** AP, May 8, 1980.

831 **Mariel boatlift** *Washington Star* Service, May 7, 1980; AP, May 10, 1980; AP, May 12, 1980.

831 **A month later** "Calif. Klansman Nominated for Congress as Democrat," WP, June 8, 1980; "The Klan and the Campaign," *Christian Science Monitor*, August 26, 1980.

831 **Vernon Jordan** "John Paul Franklin," Wikipedia.org, accessed January 25, 2020.

831 **Klan membership** "The Klan and the Campaign."

831 **the *Spotlight*** Leonard Zeskind, *Blood and Politics: The History of the White Nationalist Movement from the Margin to the Mainstream* (New York: Farrar, Straus & Giroux, 2009), 51.

831 **Gallup found** George Gallup poll, November 11, 1979.

832 **in Winston-Salem, North Carolina** AP, February 24, 1979.

832 **part of a strategy** Witcher, "Carter and Reagan's Southern Strategy."

832 **target groups** Honomichl, *Honomichl on Marketing Research*, 29.

832 **Trent Lott** Witcher, "Carter and Reagan's Southern Strategy," citing Mississippi Republican chairman Mike Retzer.

833 **Jimmy Carter organized** Ibid.

833 **Andrew Young penned** "Chilling Words in Neshoba County," August 11, 1980.

833 **"written by a Klansman"** "The Klan and the Campaign."

833 **"specter of white sheets"** *Dallas Times Herald* Service, August 6, 1980; AP, August 6, 1980.

834 **Mississippi Reagan fan** Witcher, "Carter and Reagan's Southern Strategy."

834 **"permanent civil rights"** AP, August 6, 1980.

834 **just what Reagan** "Reagan Makes Appeal for Black Votes," WP, August 6, 1980.

834 **South Bronx** MFTVE, 1:04:58; Tom Wicker column, NYT, August 8, 1980. Ironically, the major component of federal disaster assistance is the same sort of interest-free loans Kemp's Enterprise Zones proposed.

834 **Gerald Carlson** "A GOP Embarrassment: Racist Nominee in Mich.," WP, August 18, 1980.

835 **A few weeks later** ABCIA, September 29, 1980.

835 **press conference** Transcript and talking points, RVA, Box 30, Folder 9.

835 **an economic advisor** Los Angeles Times Service, July 27, 1980.

835 **foreign policy experts** *Los Angeles Herald*, July 30, 1980.

835 **Norman Podhoretz** *The Present Danger: Do We Have the Will to Reverse the Decline of American Power?* (New York: Simon & Schuster, 1980).

835 **William van Cleave** Robert Sherman letter to the editor, July 31, 1980; van Cleave response, WP, August 17, 1980. See also cover of September 10, 1968, *National Review* illustrating van Cleave's article "Assertive Disarmament," here, accessed January 25, 2020.

836 **Reagan himself** Tim Naftali, "Ronald Reagan's Long-Hidden Racist Conversation with Richard Nixon," *Atlantic*, July 30, 2019.

836 **side deal** "Unconventional Republicans," *In These Times,* July 30–August 12, 1980.

837 **so muddled** Clips in RVA, Box 30, Folder 9.

837 **"brazen" and "irresponsible"** AP, August 22, 1980.

837 **"Governor Reagan hasn't proposed"** Mark Green, *Ronald Reagan's Reign of Error* (New York: Pantheon, 1987), 27.

837 **He arrived in Beijing** "Bush Reception in China Warms Up After a Cool Start," NYT, August 22, 1980.

837 **"remarks that have"** Ibid.; LAT, August 22, 1980.

837 **"very positive"** "Chinese Officials Scold Bush About Taiwan," *Baltimore Sun*, August 22, 1980.

837 **Xinhua, the official** AP, August 22, 1980.

837 **"I guess it's a yes"** AP, August 23, 1980.

837 **"Free Republic of China"** *New York Times* Service, August 24, 1980.

837 **"cancelled out"** AP, August 23, 1980.

838 **"I don't know that I said that"** Green, *Reign of Error*, 27.

838 **"He did not"** Ibid.

838 **"ideologue, living in a bygone past"** "Reagan's Chinese Checkers," *Christian Science Monitor*, August 27, 1980.

838 **"No more Taiwans!"** LAT, July 27, 1980.

838   **wheeled out John Sears** "News Analysis," NYT, August 27, 1980.

838   **Veterans of Foreign Wars** See large "VFW Speech" file in DH. Also, generally, "Reagan: 'Peace Through Strength,' " WP, August 19, 1980; MFTVE, 1:06:04.

838   **speech Richard Allen** See draft and final text in DH file. Also White, *America In Search of Itself*, 385; "Reagan, in Speech to Legion, Says Carter Has Falsified Military Statistics," NYT, August 20, 1980 (which includes extended excerpt).

839   **Joseph Kraft decried** Joseph Kraft column, August 21, 1980.

839   **"self-inflicted wound"** ENIR, August 23, 1980.

839   **"What, pray"** Mary McGrory column, August 22, 1980.

839   *Times* **news report** "Reagan, in Speech to Legion, Says Carter Has Falsified Military Statistics," NYT, August 20, 1980.

839   **Vietnam Veterans Memorial** "On Capitol Hill," WP, May 1, 1980; Elizabeth Wolfson, "The 'Black Gash of Shame'—Revisiting the Vietnam Veterans Memorial Controversy," *Art21*, March 15, 2017.

839   **Conservatives including** Guenther Lewy, *America in Vietnam* (New York: Oxford University Press, 1978); for Reagan's praise, see "Vietnam I" and "Vietnam II," radio commentaries recorded February 1978, reprinted in RPV, 390–93.

839   **Joan Baez** "Joan Baez Starts Protest on Repression by Hanoi," NYT, May 30, 1979; "Baez, Fonda Ignite Battle of the Left," LAT, July 1, 1979. See Reagan's reaction in RPV, 456–58.

840   *The Deer Hunter* Read Biskind's review here, accessed January 25, 2020.

840   **"The Gook Hunter"** John Pilger, NYT, April 26, 1979.

841   **inspired a veteran** Wolfson, "The 'Black Gash of Shame.' "

841   **"Reagan to Alter Style"** *Sumter Daily Item*, August 22, 1980.

841   **"I came to Dallas"** "Remarks at a Democratic National Committee Fundraiser," July 21, 1980, APP. For TV strike see ABCIA, July 21, July 24, August 1, 1980.

841   **"A DEMOCRAT SHOT J.R."** "TV's *Dallas*: Whodunit?" *Time*, August 11, 1980.

841   **T. Cullen Davis** "Is Priscilla Davis' Story True?" *D* magazine, March 1977; "The Conversion of Cullen," *D* magazine, December 1980.

842   **proud to welcome** Frances FitzGerald, "A Disciplined, Charging Army," *New Yorker*, May 18, 1981.

842   **father, H. L.** Jerome Tuccille, *Kingdom: The Story of the Hunt Family of Texas* (Ottawa, IL: Jameson Books, 1984), 282. For role of Helms, McDonald, and Symms, see "U.S. Plan to Sell Surplus Silver Foiled by Conservatives," *Chicago Sun-Times* Service, July 3, 1980.

842   **H.L.'s sons** Matt Stoller, *Goliath: The 100-Year War Between Monopoly Power and Democracy* (New York: Simon & Schuster, 2019), 366; Joel Rogers and Thomas Ferguson, *The Hidden Election: Politics and Economics in the 1980 Presidential Campaign* (New York: Pantheon, 1981), 3.

842   **rally in Harrisburg** Fitzgerald, "A Disciplined, Charging Army."

842   **his recent pamphlet** Jerry Falwell, *Armageddon and the Coming War with Russia* (1980), in possession of author; the pamphlet appears to have been available that August, as suggested by reference to Falwell promoting it on the air in "The Cross and the Tube," *New York Daily News*, September 7, 1980.

843   **Bailey Smith** Michael Sean Winters, *God's Right Hand: How Jerry Falwell Made God a Republican and Baptized the American Right* (New York: HarperOne, 2012), 145.

843   **Falwell apologized** "Anecdote Hurts Falwell Credibility," WS, August 23, 1980.

843   **opening address** Jeffrey K. Hadden and Charles E. Swann, *Prime Time Preachers: The Rising Power of Televangelism* (New York: Addison-Wesley, 1981), 125.

843 **black preacher** AP, August 22, 1980.

843 **Fob James of Alabama** "James' Official Refers to Burnett As 'New Rafshoon,' " *Anniston Star*, October 28, 1980.

843 **minister from Spartanburg** "Political Gospel: Christian Soldiers Spread the 'Right' Word," *Minneapolis Star*, August 25, 1980.

843 **Paul Weyrich** Ibid; see excerpt of Weyrich's address at YouTube.com, accessed January 26, 1980.

844 *Wake Up, America* "Few Ministers See 'Wake Up' Show," *Anniston Star*, July 26, 1980; "Documentary Airs with Local Affiliate," *Shreveport Times*, October 10, 1980; "Mountainview Offers Revival-Oriented Film," *Jackson Clarion-Ledger*, January 10, 1981; "Political Gospel."

844 **"time for Christians"** See Robison speech at AmericanRhetoric.com, accessed January 26, 2020.

845 **D. James Kennedy** For account of path to Reagan's introduction see "Political Gospel"; William C. Inboden III, "Divine Elections: Abortion, Evangelicalism, and the New Right in American Politics, 1973–1980: The Politicization of Morality," Stanford University Department of History, honors thesis.

845 **Organizers claimed** Rogers and Ferguson, *The Hidden Election*, 4.

845 **The text** Randall Balmer, *Redeemer: The Life of Jimmy Carter* (New York: Basic Books, 2014), 144; Gavin to Peter Hannaford and Martin Anderson, September 19, 1979, "Re: US News Article on 'Preachers in Politics,' Sept. 24, 1979," DH, Box 3, Folder 5.

845 **Reagan got the first of many** AmericanRhetoric.com, accessed January 26, 2020; pamphlet of transcript (not including "I endorse you") in RRPL, Box 227.

846 **Hannaford had inserted** Hannaford to Molly Tuthill, November 11, 1981, DH, Box 12, Folder 3.

847 **"I'm afraid"** Kim Phillips-Fein, *Invisible Hands: The Businessmen's Crusade Against the New Deal* (New York: Norton, 2009), 250; White, *America In Search of Itself*, 256.

847 **"If it weren't for"** Michael J. McVicar, *Christian Reconstruction: R. J. Rushdoony and American Religious Conservatism* (Chapel Hill: University of North Carolina Press, 2015), 144–45.

847 **major profile** "Rev. Falwell Inspires Evangelical Vote," NYT, August 20, 1980.

847 **most of the front page** *Minneapolis Star*, August 25, 1980.

847 **almost entirely missed** Joel Rogers and Thomas Ferguson, *The Hidden Election: Politics and Economics in the 1980 Presidential Campaign* (New York: Pantheon, 1981), 3.

847 **It wasn't until** David Rogers, "Oil's Role in Changing Country," BG, September 10, 1981.

848 **"questions about evolution"** MFTVE, 1:06:54; Winters, *God's Right Hand*, 143.

848 **"I think a lot"** "Political Gospel."

848 **"People want leadership"** Robert C. Liebman and Robert Wuthrow,, eds. *The New Christian Right: Mobilization and Legitimization* (New York: Adine Publishing Company, 1983), 37.

848 **Four days after** Alan Greenspan, *The Age of Turbulence: Adventures in a New World* (New York: Penguin, 2008), 88.

849 **added a refrain** August 26, 1980, AA, "News Releases" folder.

849 **New numbers showed** *Newsweek*, September 1, 1980.

849 **Stealth bomber** The entire story can be reviewed in *Leaks of Classified National Defense Information—Stealth Aircraft*, Hearings Before the Investigations Sub-

committee of the Committee on Armed Services, House of Representatives, Ninety-Sixth Congress, Second Session, August 27, September 4, 16, and October 1, 1980.

850 **"The way things"** "Reagan Seeks to Get Campaign on Track; Advisors Summoned to Va. for Meeting," WS, August 29, 1980. See also White, *America In Search of Itself*, 386.

850 **The only adjustment** "Shaky Start; Reagan Drive Wobbles as Nominee Misspeaks and His Advisors Feud," WSJ, September 4, 1980.

850 **Carter's Southern-states manager** Marcus M. Witcher, "Carter and Reagan's Southern Strategy: The 1980 General Election in Mississippi," paper under review in possession of author.

850 **On August 28** "Economic Renewal Program," APP, August 28, 1980; AA, "Carter Economic Program" file; Judith Stein, *Pivotal Decade: How the United States Traded Factories for Finance in the 1970s* (New Haven: Yale University Press, 2010), 249.

850 **Reagan issued a statement** AA, "Carter Economic Program" file.

850 **Carter spoke** "Tuscumbia, Alabama Remarks at a Campaign Rally at Spring Park," September 1, 1980, APP.

850 **in Jersey** See excerpt at YouTube.com, accessed April 26, 1980; "Remarks at Liberty State Park, Jersey City, New Jersey," September 1, 1980, APP.

851 **"gave birth to the Ku Klux Klan"** White, *America In Search of Itself*, 386.

852 **"if we had to fight"** Jules Witcover and Jack Germond, *Blue Smoke and Mirrors: How Reagan Won and Why Carter Lost the Election of 1980* (New York: Viking, 1981), 248.

852 **"presidential caliber"** "Faultfinder for Carter Starts Combing Reagan's Record," WP, May 16, 1980.

852 **DNC chairman John White** Witcher, "Carter and Reagan's Southern Strategy."

852 **Six Southern governors** AP, September 3, 1980.

852 **"an insult to Tuscumbia"** AP, September 3, 1980.

852 **"slurs and innuendo"** " 'Give-'em-hell' Jimmy Rips Ron," *New York Daily News*, September 3, 1980.

852 **"foot-in-mouth disease"** AP, September 3, 1980.

852 **"stay on the offensive"** "Shaky Start."

852 **It blamed** *Carter New York Times* Service, September 3, 1980.

853 **"groin kicking"** "Reagan Beats a Retreat on Klan Remark," WP, September 3, 1980.

853 **after much respectful throat clearing** James A. Baker III, *Work Hard, Study . . . and Keep Out of Politics: Adventures and Lessons from an Unexpected Public Life* (New York: Putnam, 2006), 110–11.

853 **Bush appeared on** *Meet the Press* AP, September 8, 1980.

853 **B'nai Brith** "Address By the Honorable Ronald Reagan, B'Nai B'rith Forum, Washington D.C., September 3, 1980," DH, Speech File, "Speeches, B'Nai Brith, 1980 Sept 3 Typescript" folder; also extensive drafts in RVA, "B'Nai Brith, September 3, 1980."

853 **standing ovation** Handwritten notes, "9/3/80 News 11:30," AA, "Bush Memos/ Assignments" folder.

853 **traveled to Jacksonville** AP, September 5, 1980.

853 **"never in my life"** Ibid.

853 **"I am sure that"** UPI, September 6, 1980.

853 **flew to Philadelphia** *Chicago Sun Times* Service, September 8, 1980.

853 **"self-inflicted blunders"** Richard Wirthlin, Vincent Breglio, and Richard Seal, "Campaign Chronicle," *Public Opinion*, February/March 1981.

853 **In Chicago** "Remarks at the International Business Council in Chicago," APP, September 9, 1980.

854 **Carter's budget director** Reuters, September 5, 1980.

854 **"emerged from Wonderland"** NYT, September 14, 1980.

854 **critic later pointed out** Aaron Wildavsky, *The Deficit and the Public Interest: The Search for Responsible Budgeting in the 1980s* (Berkeley: University of California Press 1989), 78.

854 **The League of Women Voters** "News Update," September 1, 1980, AA, "Bush Memos/Assignments" folder.

854 **One poll** "Carter, Reagan Now Running Exactly Even," WS, September 8, 1980; see also "Anderson Gains Relatively Little from Discontent," September 15, 1980.

855 **"Suppose the chair wins"** "Carter Winning Gamble on Debate," WP, September 18, 1980.

855 **Newt Gingrich** "Capitol Steps Theatrical," WP, September 10, 1980; Jeffrey Crouch and Matthew N. Green, "New Gingrich: Strategic Political Entrepreneur," Paper Presented at 2017 Annual Meeting of the Midwest Political Science Association.

855 **"Within a year"** Gannett, September 16, 1980.

855 **Tim Kraft** UPI, September 13, 1980; Bob Woodward, *Shadow: Five Presidents and the Legacy of Watergate* (New York: Simon & Schuster, 1999), 78.

856 **"most believe"** "Leader of Liberals Recalls Truman and 'Turnip Time,' " NYT, August 13, 1980. See also Nicholas Pileggi, "Reagan's Commandos in New York," *New York*, September 29, 1980.

856 **Roy Cohn** "Roger Stone, Political Animal," *Weekly Standard*, November 5, 2007.

856 **On Monday, September 15** AP, September 16, 1980; see also AP, September 16, 1980, datelined Atlanta; "Corpus Christi, Texas Remarks and a Question-and-Answer Session at a Townhall Meeting," APP, September 15, 1980; "Houston, Texas Remarks at a Democratic National Committee Fundraising Luncheon," September 15, 1980, APP.

856 **"shoebox war"** "The Shoebox War," editorial, WSJ, September 4, 1980.

857 **He couldn't believe** Author interview with Hendrik Hertzberg.

857 **serious staff scandal** Brian Tigue and Jeffrey Klein, *Mother Jones*, October-November, 1980; "Backstage," *Mother Jones*, February–March, 1982.

857 **over fifty *New York Times* articles** ProQuest Historical Newspapers, August 14 to September 14, 1980.

857 **"poor judgement"** ABCIA, September 30, 1980.

857 **"We assumed"** Author interview with Hendrik Hertzberg.

857 **Accuracy in Media** For Irvine to Sulzberger, July 10, 1980; Irvine to Gruson, August 12, 1980; Letter to Irvine cc A. O. Sulzberger, August 18, 1980; Frankel to Gruson, September 9, 1980; and "A Pre-Emptive Spike by the New York Times," in "Accuracy in Media" folder, *New York Times* Papers, New York Public Library.

858 **Ebenezer Baptist Church** MFTVE, 1:08:32; "Atlanta, Georgia Remarks at a Meeting with Southern Black Leaders," APP, September 16, 1980.

859 **only until four o'clock** n.d. note, 3 p.m. CDT, AA, "Annelise Carter race notes." ("Jody Powell—clarified—no implication RR a racist.")

859 **press conference** MFTVE, 1:08:01, accessed January 17, 2020; "The President's News Conference," September 18, 1980, APP.

859 **"President Carter must know"** James Reston, NYT, September 21, 1980.

859 **"the past few days"** Hugh Sidey, "The Presidency: More Than a Candidate," *Time*, September 29, 1980.

859 **Nancy Reagan** YouTube.com, accessed January 28, 2020.

860 **50 percent negative** Witcover and Germond, *Blue Smoke and Mirrors*, 243.

860 **In Knoxville** "Address By the Honorable Ronald Reagan, Knoxville, Tennessee, September 22, 1980," AA, "News Releases" folder.

860 **"Six weeks from now"** "Torrance, California Remarks at a Question-and-Answer Session at a Town Meeting," APP, September 22, 1980.

860 **"it's inconceivable"** ABCIA, September 23, 1980.

860 **"an overstatement"** Ibid.

861 **Carter, engineer-like** Witcover and Germond, *Blue Smoke and Mirrors*, 247.

861 **"Carter's biggest asset"** Ibid., 248.

861 **"We ain't got"** "Lyn Nofziger: Barometer In Reagan Strategy Shift," NYT, September 28, 1980.

861 **Harlington, Texas** *Calgary Herald*, September 18, 1980; "Tortilla Curtain Incident," *Texas History Online Handbook of Texas*, accessed January 13, 1980; "U.S. and Mexico Embroiled in Dispute over 'Tortilla Curtain,' " WP, December 28, 1978.

861 **Lincoln's tomb** Maureen Orth, "Sneer and Loathing on the Campaign Trail," *Village Voice*, October 29, 1980.

CHAPTER THIRTY-SEVEN

863 **"third world war"** Paul Laxalt, *Paul Laxalt's Nevada: A Memoir* (Reno, NV: Jack Bacon & Co, 2000), 254.

863 **In Torrance** APP, September 22, 1980.

863 **"shabby business"** "About Politics: Reagan's Quiet Campaign Chief," NYT, April 21, 1980.

864 **"Spooks for Bush"** Correspondence with Robert Perry.

864 **tail numbers** Jules Witcover and Jack Germond, *Blue Smoke and Mirrors: How Reagan Won and Why Carter Lost the Election of 1980* (New York: Viking, 1981), 8.

864 **"It never moved!"** Gary Sick, *October Surprise: America's Hostages in Iran and the Election of Ronald Reagan* (New York: Crown, 1990), 27.

864 **It was run** Sick, *October Surprise*; Susan B. Trento, *The Power House: Robert Keith Gray and the Selling of Influence in Washington* (New York: St. Martin's Press, 1992), 128–32.

864 **Jack Anderson published** Jack Anderson column, August 18, 1980. The column was frequently published, as here, alongside articles on the administration's strenuous denials. See also AP, August 19, 1980; Sick, *October Surprise*, 25.

864 **"tempted to take reckless"** AP, August 21, 1980.

864 **Bill Brock called a press conference** "Carter Accused of Abusing Power," WP, September 12, 1980.

865 **"minimize the ownership of private property"** William Kleinknecht, *The Man Who Sold the World: Ronald Reagan and the Betrayal of Main Street America* (New York: Nation Books, 2009), 108.

865 **"I bet everyone in this room"** Mark Green, *Ronald Reagan's Reign of Error* (New York: Pantheon, 1987), 75

865 **Laxalt released** "Senator Laxalt's Open Letter to Editorial Writers," August 29, 1980, AA, "News Releases" folder.

865 **Saudi newspaper** ABCIA, July 22, 1980.

866 **Mohammad Ali Rajai** Sick, *October Surprise*, 91.

866 **Majlis got its act together** "Network News Summaries," September 1, 1980, AA, "Bush Memos/Assignments" folder; "News 10:30 a.m.," Ibid.

866 **Anne Armstrong** *Christian Science Monitor*, September 5, 1980.

866 **active negotiations** "Iran timeline," AA, "Misc Issues" folder.

866 **"oft-predicted 'October Surprise'"** Patrick J. Buchanan column, September 25, 1980.

866 **The next day** ABCIA, September 26, 1980.

866 **"fucking buttercup"** Theodore White, *America In Search of Itself: The Making of the President, 1956–1980* (New York: Harper & Row, 1981), 393.

866 **armed with** n.d. notes for Pennsylvania trip, AA; Gannett, September 25, 1980.

867 **precinct lists** White, *America In Search of Itself*, 396.

867 **Frank Sinatra** Charlie Zwick oral history interview, Miller Center, University of Virginia. Speech excerpts in September 30, 1980, News Release, and "Prelude to Victory: A United Tribute to Ronald Reagan and George Bush" fact sheet, AA, "News Releases" folder.

867 **small business owners** Kim Phillips-Fein, *Invisible Hands: The Businessmen's Crusade Against the New Deal* (New York: Norton, 2009), 250; White, *America In Search of Itself*, 395.

867 **donned a hard hat** White, *America In Search of Itself*, 395 AA, News Summary, October 1, 1980, AA, "Notes/Clippings" folder ("told hard hats—changed mind on federal aid to NYC").

867 **"three 'bites'"** White, *America In Search of Itself*, 397.

867 **"wondered whether"** AP, October 1, 1980.

867 **his running mate** Sick, *October Surprise*, 127.

867 **Commerce Department reported** ABCIA, October 1, 1980.

867 **Arthur Burns** Handwritten note, October 3, 1980, AA, "Memorandums/Notes/Clippings" folder.

868 **Another statistic** MFTVE, 1:09:48.

868 **"WASHINGTON—A candidate seeking"** WSJ, October 1, 1980, A1.

868 **"lot of guts"** "In Flint, Carter's '76 Rhetoric Now Reagan's," BG, October 4, 1980.

868 **It was 25.9 percent** Ibid.

868 **lab coat** ABCIA, October 1, 1980.

868 **372,000 faulty Cadillacs** Ibid.

868 **unexpectedly stalled** David P. Vogel, *Fluctuating Fortunes: The Political Power of Business in America* (New York: Basic Books, 1989), 188; Gannett, October 2, 1980.

868 **Federal Election Commission** ABCIA, October 1 and October 2, 1980.

869 **accused the president** ABCIA, October 7, 1980; "News Summary," October 8, 1980, AA, "Notes/Clippings" folder.

869 **"A vote for Anderson"** ABCIA, October 1, 1980; "Why Is Anderson Staying in the Race?" WSJ, October 17, 1980.

869 **"near total failure"** Gannett, October 10, 1980; ABCIA, October 13, 1980.

870 **"It's gone on too long"** White, *America In Search of Itself*, 382.

870 **In Boston** Ad Hoc Committee in Defense of Life, *Lifeletter*, Issue 15, October 24, 1980, deposited in AA, "Women" folder.

870 **Jerry Falwell's face** *Newsweek*, September 15, 1980.

870 **"slow on the uptake"** Colonel Doner, *Christian Jihad: Neo-Fundamentalists and the Polarization of America* (Denver and Los Angeles: Samizdat, 2012), 55.

870 **Biblical Scorecards** Sara Diamond, *Spiritual Warfare: The Politics of the Christian Right* (Boston: South End Press, 199), 196.

870 **"Christian embassy"** *Jerusalem Post*, October 1, 1980.

870 **Jeremiah Denton** "Thunder from the Right," NYT *Magazine*, February 8, 1981.

871 **"beat my brains out with Christian love"** *Time*, October 13, 1980.

871　The *Los Angeles Times* gave "Enforcing God's Law in the Voting Booth," LAT, September 7, 1980. (See letters in response, September 14, 1980.)

871　*Listen, America!* (New York: Doubleday, 1980). Citations on 256 (South Africa), 80 (Milton Friedman), and 78 ("brown nuggets").

871　**Falwell toured** AP, September 15; AP, September 19; "Rally Hears Gospel of Christian Politics," *Green Bay Press-Gazette*, September 19, 1980.

871　*Moral Majority Report* Michael Sean Winters, *God's Right Hand: How Jerry Falwell Made God a Republican and Baptized the American Right* (New York: HarperOne, 2012), 149.

871　**ABC's cameras** ABCIA, September 24, 1980; also reviewed at VTVNA.

872　**On October 3, Reagan spoke** ABCIA, October 4, 1980; Winters, *God's Right Hand*, 144–46; J. Brooks Flippen, *Jimmy Carter, the Politics of Family, and the Rise of the Religious Right* (Athens, GA: University of Georgia Press, 2011), 302; "Reagan Stays Out of Religious Fray," BG, October 4, 1980.

872　**ACLU later discovered** Mike Royko column, CT, April 10, 1984.

873　**Rabbi Marc Tanenbaum** Frances FitzGerald, "A Disciplined, Charging Army," *New Yorker*, May 18, 1981.

873　**Robert Bauman** Connie Paige, *The Right to Lifers: Who They Are, How They Operate, and Where They Get Their Money* (New York: Summit Books, 1983), 215; ABCIA, October 3, 1980; Adam Clymer, *Drawing the Line at the Big Ditch: The Panama Canal Treaties and the Rise of the Right* (Lawrence: University Press of Kansas, 2008), 157. For Bauman generally see "Bob Bauman, Modern House Watchdog," WP, May 19, 1979, and Bauman, *The Gentleman from Maryland: The Conscience of a Gay Conservative* (Gettysburg, PA: Arbor House, 1986).

873　**Carter gave an interview** *Weekly Compilation of President Documents*, October 2, 1980.

873　**Egypt's Anwar Sadat** ABCIA, September 26, 1980.

874　**Strait of Hormuz** ABCIA, September 29 and October 1, 1980.

874　**friendship pact** ABCIA, September 26, 1980.

874　**end to the Mariel** Ibid; Juan M. Clark, Jose I. Lasaga, and Rose S. Reque, *The 1980 Mariel Exodus: An Assessment and Prospect* (Council for Inter-American Security, n.d.), in AA, "The 1980 Mariel Exodus" folders.

874　**At one, he sat at his desk** View ad at YouTube.com, accessed January 21, 2020.

874　**Practically the only TV commercial** View sixty-second version at LivingRoom Candidate.com, accessed January 21, 2020.

875　**The data points most crucial** Richard Wirthlin, Vincent Breglio, and Richard Seal, "Campaign Chronicle," *Public Opinion*, February/March 1981.

876　**demonstrated why** "Statistics Analyzed: Record Doesn't Always Support Reagan's Claims," LAT, April 12, 1980.

876　**going to throw up** Kathleen Hall Jamieson, *Packaging the Presidency: A History and Criticism of Presidential Advertising* (New York: Oxford University Press, 1988), 431.

876　**"monstrous, ill-conceived"** APP, September 29, 1980, before International Ladies Garment Workers Union.

876　**"against Medicaid"** APP, October 1, 1980, to Flint, Michigan, town hall.

876　**Mary McGrory asked** Mary McGrory column, September 28, 1980.

876　**political cartoonist** Pat Oliphant, *Los Angeles Herald Examiner*, September 30, 1980.

876　**standard stump speech** See late-September and early-October speech excerpts in AA, "News Releases" folder.

877 **"Why is it mean"** Mary McGrory column, September 28, 1980.

877 **"not a place for simplistic"** APP, October 6, 1980; ABCIA, October 7, 1980;.

877 **"jaws fell"** Witcover and Germond, *Blue Smoke and Mirrors*, 255

877 **Next Carter spoke** APP, October 6, 1980; Witcover and Germond, *Blue Smoke and Mirrors*, 257; also Reagan's response. Greg Schneider's is 259.

878 **Gerald Rafshoon** Jamieson, *Packaging the Presidency*, 411.

878 **Barbara Walters** ABCIA, October 8, 1980; MFTVE, 1:09:31, 1:10:00.

878 **Lacrosse, Wisconsin** October 8 speech excerpt in AA, "News Releases" folder.

878 **"Save Our Steel"** UPI, October 9, 1980.

879 **At Reagan headquarters** Richard Wirthlin, Vincent Breglio, and Ricard Seal, "Campaign Chronicle," *Public Opinion*, February/March 1981.

879 **John Anderson accused** Gannett, October 10, 1980.

879 **Jesse Jackson** News summary, October 7, 1980, AA, "Notes/Clippings" folder.

879 **"kind of dull"** Jamieson, *Packaging the Presidency*, 397.

879 **"stylized associations"** "Public Opinion Polling: Command and Control in Presidential Campaigns," in Alexander Heard and Michael Nelson, eds., *Presidential Selection* (Durham, NC: Duke University Press, 1987), 211.

879 **"champing at the bit"** Jack J. Honomichl, *Honomichl on Marketing Research* (Lincolnwood, IL: NTC Business Books, 1986), 35.

879 **sitting in a study** An example at YouTube.com, accessed January 21, 1980.

879 **"Have you thought"** AP, October 9, 1980.

879 **fighting between Iran** "Iran timeline," AA, "Misc Issues" folder.

880 **"dramatic actions"** "Reagan Aides Seek to Defeat Any 'Surprise,' " NYT, October 7, 1980.

880 **Carter replied** "Carter Says Reagan Can't Be Trusted with Presidency," WP, October 11, 1980.

880 **"oxides of nitrogen"** Green, *Ronald Reagan's Reign of Error*, 99; "Air Pollution," campaign statement, October 9, 1980.

880 **Claremont College** ABCIA, October 13, 1980; UPI, October 14, 1980.

880 **"He's talking, Lyn"** UPI, November 3, 1980.

880 **"Nofziger's Wall"** *San Francisco Chronicle*, October 13, 1980.

881 **"start a rumor"** "Campaign Watch: Powell Blasts Reagan Aide," *Atlanta Constitution*, September 10, 1980.

881 **Walter Mondale** Handwritten note, AA, October 11, 1980. ("Mondale—RR muzzled—reminds him of how he dealt w/ pet dog—let him go out to go to bathroom—comment?")

881 **George McGovern** ABCIA, September 26, 1980.

881 **Eastern reporter** "The Flint and Fire of Idaho's Sagebrush Rebellion," WP, October 12, 1980.

881 **Independent Petroleum Association** Thomas Edsall, *The New Politics of Inequality* (New York: W.W. Norton, 1985), 94.

881 **conservative junior senator** ABCIA, October 13, 1980.

882 **Scoop Jackson** Ibid.

882 **"The next administration"** UPI, October 15, 1980.

882 **"DEAR SENATOR JAVITS"** Alan Crawford, *Thunder on the Right: The "New Right" and the Politics of Resentment* (New York: Pantheon, 1981), 59.

882 **jockeying to replace** Joyce Purnick, "Senate 1980: See How They Run," *New York*, March 19, 1979.

882 **"completely irrelevant"** "Arthur Finkelstein, Influential Conservative Strategist, Dies at 72," NYT, August 19, 2007. Also for "Vote for my son."

882   *"in failing health"* "Arthur Finkelstein, Quietly Influential Campaign Mastermind, Dies at 72," WP, August 19, 2017.

882   **"Do you realize"** Myra MacPherson, WP, October 28, 1980.

883   **"running as a Liberal"** *Newsweek*, November 1, 1980.

883   **"old union man"** "Reagan's Gears Locked as President Pulls Even," WP, October 17, 1980.

883   **Morris Abrams** White, *America In Search of Itself*, 394.

883   **Edward Costikyan Ibid.**

883   **Franklin Delano Roosevelt's son** UPI, October 27, 1980.

883   **American Agriculture Movement** "State Capital Highlights," *Kerville* (Texas) *Mountain Sun*, September 24, 1980.

883   **Leon Jaworksi** ABCIA, September 29, 1980.

883   **Air Traffic Controllers** Richard Reeves, *President Reagan: The Triumph of the Imagination* (New York: Simon & Schuster, 2005), 63; Ray Abernathy, "The PATCO Conspiracy Revisited: From Carter to Reagan . . . to Obama," *In These Times*, August 17, 2009; correspondence with Professor Joseph McCartin.

884   **American Federation of Government Employees** "Federal Employees Union Official Endorses Reagan's Positions" October 27, 1980, AA, "News Releases" folder.

884   **Eleanor Smeal** "Women's Group Gets Appeal by Reagan," NYT, October 21, 1980.

884   **Dewey Burton** "One Man's Road to a Vote for Reagan," NYT, October 15, 1980; Jefferson Cowie, *Stayin' Alive: The 1970s and the Last Days of the Working Class* (New York: New Press, 2010), 1, 9, 13, 15, 353.

884   **Ralph Abernathy** "Pool Report, Detroit, Oct 16, Visit to St. John's Christian Methodist and Episcopal Church," AA; Adam Clymer, "Who Was Mitt Romney Talking To?" *Politico*, July 12, 2012.

885   **National Association of Police Associations** "Nation's Largest Police Organization Endorses Governor Ronald Reagan," October 16, 1980, AA, "News Releases" folder.

CHAPTER THIRTY-EIGHT

886   **new Gallup poll** *Minneapolis Star*, October 15, 1980.

886   **Mohammad Ali Rajai** See AA timeline, October 15, 1980; UPI, October 15, 1980.

886   **Barbara Walters** ABCIA, October 13, 1980.

886   **The previous night** AP, October 16, 1980; Susan B. Trento, *The Power House: Robert Keith Gray and the Selling of Influence in Washington* (New York: St. Martin's Press, 1992), 131 (Trento notes WLS was owned by the ABC network); Gary Sick, *October Surprise: America's Hostages in Iran and the Election of Ronald Reagan* (New York: Crown, 1990), 28, 139 (Sick notes that WLS-TV "seemed to be the favored Republican outlet for hostage information [or disinformation]").

886   *"Backlash"* News summary, October 31, 1980, AA, "Notes/Clippings" folder.

887   **League of Women Voters** WP, October 15, 1980; Jules Witcover and Jack Germond, *Blue Smoke and Mirrors: How Reagan Won and Why Carter Lost the Election of 1980* (New York: Viking, 1981), 267–68.

887   *"Some have criticized"* Richard Wirthlin and Richard S. Beal to RWR, Casey, and Baker, "First Debate—Integrating Memorandum," September 12, 1980, AA, Debates/Briefing Book folder.

887   **to the second** AA, "Press Releases" folder.

887 **TV studio** David Stockman, *The Triumph of Politics: Why the Reagan Revolution Failed* (New York: Harper & Row, 1986), 44; F. Clifton White, *Politics as a Noble Calling: The Memoirs of F. Clifton White* (Ottawa, IL: Jameson Books, 1994), 12.

888 **or not to debate** James A. Baker III, *Work Hard, Study . . . and Keep Out of Politics: Adventures and Lessons from an Unexpected Public Life* (New York: Putnam, 2006), 112–15; Jeff Bell, "The Candidate and the Briefing Book," *Weekly Standard*, February 5, 2001. See also ABCIA, October 15, 1980.

888 **"*Women voters* invited"** YouTube.com, accessed January 16, 2020.

888 **"CARTER IS SMARTER"** Kathleen Hall Jamieson, *Packaging the Presidency: A History and Criticism of Presidential Advertising* (New York: Oxford University Press, 1988), 401.

888 **umpteenth time** Theodore White, *America In Search of Itself: The Making of the President, 1956–1980* (New York: Harper & Row, 1981), 403.

888 **President Carter arrived** Baker, *Work Hard, Study . . . and Keep Out of Politics*, 116; Witcover and Germond, *Blue Smoke and Mirrors*, 269; APP, October 15, 1980.

889 **wanted extensive time** Author interview with Hendrik Hertzberg.

889 **remarkable ace** Trento, *The Power House*, 122–24; Baker, *Work Hard, Study . . . and Keep Out of Politics*, 118-19.

889 **It wasn't the first time** Trento, *The Power House*, 125. For the relevant materials see Subcommittee on Human Resources of the Committee on Post Office and Civil Service, House of Representatives, *Unauthorized Transfers of Nonpublic Information During the 1980 Presidential Election*, 2000–2008.

889 **"Jimmying" economic statistics** AA, August 22, 1980 fill-in-the-blank draft, "Bush memos/assignments" folder; "Reagan Blasts 'Jimmying' of New Statistics on Economy," WP, October 7, 1980; News Release, Richard V. Allen statement, October 10, 1980, AA, "Press Releases" folder.

890 **in Louisville** ABCIA, October 20, 1980; MFTVE, 1:17:44.

890 **National Conservative Political Action** Jamieson, *Packaging the Presidency*, 423.

890 **American Conservative Union's** Ibid., 425; YouTube.com, accessed January 17, 2020.

890 **Christians for Reagan** "Pro-Reagan TV Spots Depict President as a Gay Rights Advocate," WP, October 31, 1980; Colonel Doner, *Christian Jihad: Neo-Fundamentalists and the Polarization of America* (Denver and Los Angeles: Samizdat, 2012), 55–56; J. Brooks Flippen, *Jimmy Carter, the Politics of Family, and the Rise of the Religious Right* (Athens, GA: University of Georgia Press, 2011), 308.

891 **"Jimmy's anti-Christ"** Jamieson, *Packaging the Presidency*, 426.

891 **"It seems to be the popular"** APP, October 31, 1980.

892 **ACU had hoped** Jamieson, *Packaging the Presidency*, 425, 428.

892 **Common Cause** Ibid., 419–20. See *Common Cause v. Schmitt*, 512 F. Supp. 489 (D.C. 1980) 455 US 129.

893 **Independent groups spent** Jamieson, *Packaging the Presidency*, 419.

893 **"Killer trees!"** "James S. Brady, Reagan's Press Secretary and Survivor of 1981 Shooting, Dies at 73," WP, August 4, 2014.

893 **Team Reagan finally** "Public Opinion Polling: Command and Control in Presidential Campaigns," in Alexander Heard and Michael Nelson, eds., *Presidential Selection* (Durham, NC: Duke University Press, 1987), 211.

893 **featured a graph** Jamieson, *Packaging the Presidency*, 440.

893 **In another** YouTube.com, accessed January 20, 2020.

893 **Another reprised** YouTube.com, accessed January 17, 1980.

893 **The nastiest** YouTube.com, accessed January 17, 1980.

893   **"I was so amazed"** Jamieson, *Packaging the Presidency*, 442.

893   **"more negative"** Richard Wirthlin, Vincent Breglio, and Richard Seal, "Campaign Chronicle," *Public Opinion*, February/March 1981; also source for "more presidential" finding.

893   **in the final weeks** Jamieson, *Packaging the Presidency*, 409.

894   **"world heavyweight championship"** Sick, *October Surprise*, 170.

894   **Reagan's cornerman** ABCIA, October 27, 1980.

894   **president took a jog** Ibid.

894   **The Ayatollah had** ABCIA, October 27, 1980.

894   **"more clever stories"** Alan Greenspan, *The Age of Turbulence: Adventures in a New World* (New York: Penguin, 2008), 88.

894   **Back in 1976** CBS News interview, October 1, 1976, VTVNA.

894   **"a little shit"** Witcover and Germond, *Blue Smoke and Mirrors*, 275.

894   **ace up his sleeve** Eric Alterman, *Sound and Fury: The Making of the Punditocracy* (Ithaca, NY: Cornell University Press, 2000), 96; Trento, *Power House*, 122; UPI, June 30, 1983.

894   **George Will** MFTVE, 1:15:30.

895   **120 million viewers** ABCIA, October 29, 1980.

895   **ABC had organized** Ibid., October 27, 1980.

895   **pre-debate glass of wine** Michael Deaver, *A Different Drummer: My Thirty Years with Ronald Reagan* (New York: Harper, 2002), 73

895   **"I don't know what the differences"** Video at C-SPan.org, 2020; transcript, APP, October 28, 1980.

897   **the strangest thing** Interviews and correspondence with Carter staffers Hendrik Hertzberg, David Rubenstein, and Samuel Popkin, and Ronnie Dugger, the first to obtain transcripts and more widely publicize the extremist content of Reagan's radio commentaries. See *On Reagan: The Man and His Presidency* (New York: McGraw Hill, 1983).

897   **"oppo" was run by** "Faultfinder for Carter Starts Combing Reagan's Record," WP, May 16, 1980.

897   **"Nuclear 'Wastes' "** CFTRN, April 1, 1978.

897   **endorsement of Laetrile** CFTRN, July 17, 1978; Zach Dorfman, "The Congressman Who Created His Own Deep State," *Politico*, December 12, 2018.

898   **single football field** November 11, 1978, quoted in Mark Green, *Ronald Reagan's Reign of Error* (New York: Pantheon, 1987), 103–4.

898   **laid down by Hitler** "Teachers' Group Seeks National System Like Hitler's for U.S. Schools, Reagan Says," LAT, February 5, 1976.

898   **"Who the fuck"** Lou Cannon, *Governor Reagan: His Rise to Power* (New York: Public Affairs Books, 2003), 260.

898   **A former speaker** Email correspondence with Samuel Popkin, the young political science professor; interview with David Rubenstein, assistant to Stuart Eizenstat.

898   **Bill Gavin observed** Gavin to Hannaford, Anderson, and Deaver, "RE: Moderation, RR, and Issues," September 17, 1979, DH, Box 3, Folder 5.

899   **TV audience in 1964** Rick Perlstein, *Before the Storm: Barry Goldwater and the Unmaking of the American Consensus* (New York: Farrar, Straus & Giroux, 2001), 409–504. See Reagan speech for Goldwater at YouTube.com, accessed April 28, 2020, courtesy of Ronald Reagan Presidential Library; transcript at AMDOCS: Documents for the Study of American History, accessed April 28, 2020.

899   **This was exactly** Author interview with Hendrik Hertzberg.

899   **In 1961, Reagan** "Operation Coffee Cup" LP, accessed online on May 11, 2020.

For Reagan's firing from General Electric see Rick Perlstein, *Invisible Bridge: The Fall of Nixon and the Rise of Reagan* (New York: Simon & Schuster, 2014), 401–02.

900 **Backstage, Carter people** Hertzberg interview.

900 *our black neighbors* Jimmy Carter, *Why Not the Best?* (Nashville: Broadman Press, 1975), 33.

901 **she was interviewed** Witcover and Germond, *Blue Smoke and Mirrors*, 284.

901 **"REAGAN WINS TV POLL"** Todd Gitlin, "Media as Massage: Campaign '80," *Socialist Review*, March-April 1981.

901 **Carter campaign shrugged off** David Rubenstein interview

902 **traits of a "strong leader"** Jack J. Honomichl, *Honomichl on Marketing Research* (Lincolnwood, IL: NTC Business Books, 1986), 41.

902 **In Iran** Handwritten "10/28" note, AA, "Notes/Clippings" folder.

902 **Ayatollah Khalkhali** ABCIA, October 29, 1980.

902 **CBS reported** Handwritten news summary, "CBS News 10/31 1 pm EST," AA, "Notes/Clippings" folder.

902 **Senator John Tower** Reagan/Bush Committee news summary, October 31, 1980, AA, "Notes/Clippings" folder.

902 **Henry Kissinger** Handwritten news summary, "UPI 10/31," AA, "Notes/ Clippings" folder.

902 **Robert Teeter** "Analysis," *Minneapolis Tribune*, November 3, 1980.

902 **epic endorsements** "Campaign Report," NYT, October 30, 1980.

902 **a tantalizing** ABCIA, October 31, 1980.

903 **"year-long nightmare"** Stef Halper to George Bush, draft statement, "Hostages: If They Are Released," October 31, 1980, AA, "Notes/Clippings" folder.

903 **had an emergency** Jamieson, *Packaging the Presidency*, 439; YouTube.com, accessed January 18, 2020.

903 **minute by minute** AA, "News/Clippings" folder, Anderson notes; MFTVE, 1:18:03–1:20:02.

903 **Carter flew to Chicago** Witcover and Germond, *Blue Smoke and Mirrors*, 2, 288; MFTVE, 1:20:26.

904 **George Bush, on** *Face the Nation* Notes on Bush, Ford, and Muskie appearances can be found in AA, "Misc Issues" folder.

904 **broke into a football game** Witcover and Germond, *Blue Smoke and Mirrors*, 18; APP, November 2, 1980; MFTVE, 1:21:30.

904 **"Tie a Yellow Ribbon"** MFTVE, 1:23:18.

905 **Dick Wirthlin** Witcover and Germond, *Blue Smoke and Mirrors*, 291.

905 **Richard Allen** "Reagan Adviser Drops Out of Campaign Because of Reports on Business Activities," WSJ, October 27, 1980; ABCIA, October 27, 29, 30, and 31, 1980.

905 **Billy Carter** AP, October 31, 1980; "Billygate: Two Different Views," *Indianapolis News*, October 31, 1980; George C. Kohn, *The New Encyclopedia of American Scandal* (Facts on File, 1990), 70–72. ("There was no evidence of illegal government conduct but perhaps only some unprofessionalism by Brzezinski, Attorney General Benjamin Civiletti, and CIA Director Stansfield Turner in how they handled information available to them about the case.")

906 **swing through Texas** See October 29, 1980, Dallas rally, YouTube.com, accessed January 25, 2020.

907 **Carter swung** "Newark, New Jersey Remarks at the Essex County Democratic Committee Gala," October 29, 1980, APP.

908 **spent more** CBS News, November 8, 1980, VTVNA.

908 **weren't excited** AP, November 6, 1980; WS, November 8, 1980, Associated Press/ NBC poll. Cartoon reprinted in *Public Opinion*, December 1980/January 1981.

908 **A CBS/*New York Times* exit poll** Aaron Wildavasky, *The Deficit and the Public Interest: The Search for Responsible Budgeting in the 1980s* (Berkeley: University of California Press 1989), 68.

908 **"impossible to overestimate "** Bruce J. Schulman, *The Seventies: The Great Shift in American Culture, Society, and Politics* (New York: Simon & Schuster, 2001), 133. The finding that the public preferred protecting jobs even if inflation resulted was a a consistent one. A June *New York Times* poll, for example, found 71 percent preferred "protecting jobs at the cost of higher prices on foreign products," with only 19 percent preferring lower prices if unemployment resulted. Judith Stein, *Pivotal Decade: How the United States Traded Factories for Finance in the 1970s* (New Haven: Yale University Press, 2010), 252.

909 **"gender gap"** J. Zeitz, "Rejecting the Center: Radical Grassroots Politics in the 1970s," *Journal of Contemporary History* 43, 673–88.

909 **Reagan also ran** Thomas Edsall, *The New Politics of Inequality* (New York: W. W. Norton, 1985), 207.

910 **racial animus** Thomas Edsall and Jane Byrne Edsall, *Chain Reaction: The Impact of Race, Rights, and Taxes on American Politics* (New York: W. W. Norton, 1991), 150–52.

910 **"What's green and glows?"** Author interview with J. Lee Annis.

910 **In Dade County** Knight News Service, October 29, 1980; clip at YouTube.com, accessed April 27, 2020.

910 **David Koch** Daniel Schulman, *Sons of Wichita: How the Koch Brothers Became America's Most Powerful and Private Dynasty* (New York: Grand Central Publishing, 2014), 109–12.

911 **left-wing Citizens Party** "The Shocking Campaign Ad That Put a Third Party Candidate on the Political Map," *Time*, December 2, 2016; ABCIA, October 29, 1980; Lawrence Weschler, "Political Ad's Vulgarity Defines the Campaign," LAT, October 19, 1980.

911 **Lou Harris was** "Louis Harris: The Pollster Who Was Right . . . and Why," *Christian Science Monitor*, November 6. See also Sara Diamond, *Spiritual Warfare: The Politics of the Christian Right* (Boston: South End Press, 199), 63; Edsall and Edsall, *Chain Reaction*, 134.

911 **special edition of *Nightline*** I am grateful to the reader who provided me a DVD of the November 6, 1980, *Nightline*.

913 **independent oil** David Rogers, "Oil's Role in Changing Country," BG, September 10, 1981.

913 **neo-Nazi congressional nominee** "White Supremacist's Vote-Getting Talent Stuns His GOP Detractors," WP, November 15, 1980.

914 **day's wardrobe** "Reagan's Regalia: Nancy's $25,000 Inaugural Wardrobe," WP, January 19, 1981.

914 **coats so overloaded** "The Inaugural Weekend: The Furs! The Food! The Clout!" WP, January 19, 1981.

Index

Photo Credits

Alamy Stock Photo: 59, 61, 62

Alain MINGAM/Gamma-Rapho via Getty Images: 77

Arty Pomerantz/*New York Post* via Getty Images: 30

Associated Press: 7, 26, 28, 36, 53, 54, 64, 69, 78, 90

Author's personal collection: 5, 20, 21, 22, 23

Barry Thumma/AP: 68

Bettmann Archives/Getty Images: 14, 17, 33, 37, 72, 84

Bill Frakes/The LIFE Images Collection via Getty Images/Getty Images: 63

Bill Snead/*The Washington Post* via Getty Images: 42

Bill Varie/*Los Angeles Times*: 49

Bob Engelhart: 10

Bud Skinner/*Atlanta Journal-Constitution*/ AP: 38

Courtesy of CBS News: 75, 81

Corbis via Getty Images: 12, 32, 58, 65, 85

Diana Walker/The LIFE Images Collection via Getty Images: 91

David Hume Kennerly/Getty Images: 55

Ernie Leyba/*Denver Post* via Getty Images: 40

Esquire magazine, illustration by Nicholas Gaetano: 86

Everett Collection Historical/Alamy Stock Photo: 18

Flashbak.com: 13

Frank Johnston/*The Washington Post* via Getty Images: 67

Gary Bishop/*Texas Monthly*, 1975: 24

Gerald R. Ford Presidential Library and Museum: 3

Getty Images: 39, 88

Glasshouse Images/Alamy Stock Photo: 73

Henning Christoph/ullstein bild via Getty Images: 2

Hoover Institution: 82, 83

Jimmy Carter Presidential Library and Museum: 1, 71

John Dominis/The LIFE Picture Collection via Getty Images: 74

Keystone Press/Alamy Stock Photo: 8, 11

Keystone/Hulton Archive/Getty Images: 16

© Lennart Nilsson/TT: 56

Marion S. Trikosko/Library of Congress: 80

Michael Evans/ZUMAPRESS.com: 4

Mike Meadows/*Los Angeles Times*: 79

Ms. magazine: 44

New York Daily News via Getty Images: 87

Nick Ut/AP: 60

No credit (fair use): 29, 41, 89

Paul Szep: 9

Political Ad Archive: 57

Robert Clay/Alamy Stock Photo: 27

Robert R. McElroy/Getty Images: 76

Ronald Grant Archive/Alamy Stock Photo: 34

Ronald Reagan Presidential Library: 4, 6, 35

Salt Lake City Tribune: 15

Spencer Grant/Getty Images: 25

Steve Schapiro/Corbis via Getty Images: 31

Terry Schmitt/*SF Chronicle*/Polaris: 50

Tribune News Service via Getty Images: 66

Universal Images Group via Getty Images: 70

University of California Bancroft Library: 45, 46, 47, 48, 51, 52

U.S. National Archives and Records Administration: 19

White House via AP: 43